W9-BSM-098

MONTHLY INTEREST AMORTIZATION TABLES

Interest rates of 2% to 25.75%
Loan amounts of $50 to $300,000
Terms up to 40 years

CB
CONTEMPORARY
BOOKS
CHICAGO

Great care has been taken to ensure exact figures
in the production of these tables, but there is no
guarantee of accuracy assumed by the author or
publisher of this book.

Copyright © 1994 by Michael Sherman
All rights reserved
Published by Contemporary Books, Inc.
Two Prudential Plaza, Chicago, Illinois 60601-6790
Manufactured in the United States of America
International Standard Book Number: 0-8092-3564-1

CONTENTS

TABLE 1

MONTHLY PAYMENT REQUIRED TO AMORTIZE A LOAN

Use this Table to find the monthly payment amount required to completely pay off a loan amount over a given loan term at a fixed rate of interest.

2.00% MONTHLY AMORTIZING PAYMENTS

AMOUNT OF LOAN	NUMBER OF YEARS IN TERM											
	1	2	3	4	5	6	7	8	9	10	11	12
$ 50	4.22	2.13	1.44	1.09	0.88	0.74	0.64	0.57	0.51	0.47	0.43	0.40
100	8.43	4.26	2.87	2.17	1.76	1.48	1.28	1.13	1.02	0.93	0.85	0.79
200	16.85	8.51	5.73	4.34	3.51	2.96	2.56	2.26	2.03	1.85	1.69	1.57
300	25.28	12.77	8.60	6.51	5.26	4.43	3.84	3.39	3.04	2.77	2.54	2.35
400	33.70	17.02	11.46	8.68	7.02	5.91	5.11	4.52	4.06	3.69	3.38	3.13
500	42.12	21.28	14.33	10.85	8.77	7.38	6.39	5.65	5.07	4.61	4.23	3.91
600	50.55	25.53	17.19	13.02	10.52	8.86	7.67	6.77	6.08	5.53	5.07	4.70
700	58.97	29.78	20.05	15.19	12.27	10.33	8.94	7.90	7.09	6.45	5.92	5.48
800	67.40	34.04	22.92	17.36	14.03	11.81	10.22	9.03	8.11	7.37	6.76	6.26
900	75.82	38.29	25.78	19.53	15.78	13.28	11.50	10.16	9.12	8.29	7.61	7.04
1,000	84.24	42.55	28.65	21.70	17.53	14.76	12.77	11.29	10.13	9.21	8.45	7.82
2,000	168.48	85.09	57.29	43.40	35.06	29.51	25.54	22.57	20.26	18.41	16.90	15.64
3,000	252.72	127.63	85.93	65.09	52.59	44.26	38.31	33.85	30.38	27.61	25.34	23.46
4,000	336.96	170.17	114.58	86.79	70.12	59.01	51.07	45.13	40.51	36.81	33.79	31.27
5,000	421.20	212.71	143.22	108.48	87.64	73.76	63.84	56.41	50.63	46.01	42.23	39.09
6,000	505.44	255.25	171.86	130.18	105.17	88.51	76.61	67.69	60.76	55.21	50.68	46.91
7,000	589.68	297.79	200.50	151.87	122.70	103.26	89.38	78.97	70.88	64.41	59.13	54.72
8,000	673.92	340.33	229.15	173.57	140.23	118.01	102.14	90.25	81.01	73.62	67.57	62.54
9,000	758.15	382.87	257.79	195.26	157.75	132.76	114.91	101.53	91.13	82.82	76.02	70.36
10,000	842.39	425.41	286.43	216.96	175.28	147.51	127.68	112.81	101.26	92.02	84.46	78.17
15,000	1263.59	638.11	429.64	325.43	262.92	221.26	191.52	169.22	151.88	138.03	126.69	117.26
20,000	1684.78	850.81	572.86	433.91	350.56	295.01	255.35	225.62	202.51	184.03	168.92	156.34
25,000	2105.98	1063.51	716.07	542.38	438.20	368.77	319.19	282.03	253.14	230.04	211.15	195.43
30,000	2527.17	1276.21	859.28	650.86	525.84	442.52	383.03	338.43	303.76	276.05	253.38	234.51
35,000	2948.37	1488.91	1002.50	759.33	613.48	516.27	446.87	394.84	354.39	322.05	295.61	273.59
40,000	3369.56	1701.62	1145.71	867.81	701.12	590.02	510.70	451.24	405.02	368.06	337.84	312.68
45,000	3790.75	1914.32	1288.92	976.29	788.75	663.77	574.54	507.64	455.64	414.07	380.07	351.76
50,000	4211.95	2127.02	1432.13	1084.76	876.39	737.53	638.38	564.05	506.27	460.07	422.30	390.85
55,000	4633.14	2339.72	1575.35	1193.24	964.03	811.28	702.21	620.45	556.89	506.08	464.53	429.93
60,000	5054.34	2552.42	1718.56	1301.71	1051.67	885.03	766.05	676.86	607.52	552.09	506.76	469.02
65,000	5475.53	2765.12	1861.77	1410.19	1139.31	958.78	829.89	733.26	658.15	598.09	548.99	508.10
70,000	5896.73	2977.82	2004.99	1518.66	1226.95	1032.54	893.73	789.67	708.77	644.10	591.22	547.18
75,000	6317.92	3190.52	2148.20	1627.14	1314.59	1106.29	957.56	846.07	759.40	690.11	633.45	586.27
80,000	6739.11	3403.23	2291.41	1735.61	1402.23	1180.04	1021.40	902.47	810.03	736.11	675.68	625.35
85,000	7160.31	3615.93	2434.62	1844.09	1489.86	1253.79	1085.24	958.88	860.65	782.12	717.91	664.44
90,000	7581.50	3828.63	2577.84	1952.57	1577.50	1327.54	1149.07	1015.28	911.28	828.13	760.14	703.52
95,000	8002.70	4041.33	2721.05	2061.04	1665.14	1401.30	1212.91	1071.69	961.91	874.13	802.37	742.60
100,000	8423.89	4254.03	2864.26	2169.52	1752.78	1475.05	1276.75	1128.09	1012.53	920.14	844.60	781.69
105,000	8845.09	4466.73	3007.48	2277.99	1840.42	1548.80	1340.59	1184.50	1063.16	966.15	886.83	820.77
110,000	9266.28	4679.43	3150.69	2386.47	1928.06	1622.55	1404.42	1240.90	1113.78	1012.15	929.05	859.86
115,000	9687.47	4892.14	3293.90	2494.94	2015.70	1696.31	1468.26	1297.31	1164.41	1058.16	971.28	898.94
120,000	10108.67	5104.84	3437.11	2603.42	2103.34	1770.06	1532.10	1353.71	1215.04	1104.17	1013.51	938.03
125,000	10529.86	5317.54	3580.33	2711.90	2190.98	1843.81	1595.93	1410.11	1265.66	1150.17	1055.74	977.11
130,000	10951.06	5530.24	3723.54	2820.37	2278.61	1917.56	1659.77	1466.52	1316.29	1196.18	1097.97	1016.19
135,000	11372.25	5742.94	3866.75	2928.85	2366.25	1991.31	1723.61	1522.92	1366.92	1242.19	1140.20	1055.28
140,000	11793.45	5955.64	4009.97	3037.32	2453.89	2065.07	1787.45	1579.33	1417.54	1288.19	1182.43	1094.36
145,000	12214.64	6168.34	4153.18	3145.80	2541.53	2138.82	1851.28	1635.73	1468.17	1334.20	1224.66	1133.45
150,000	12635.84	6381.04	4296.39	3254.27	2629.17	2212.57	1915.12	1692.14	1518.80	1380.21	1266.89	1172.53
155,000	13057.03	6593.75	4439.60	3362.75	2716.81	2286.32	1978.96	1748.54	1569.42	1426.21	1309.12	1211.61
160,000	13478.22	6806.45	4582.82	3471.22	2804.45	2360.08	2042.79	1804.94	1620.05	1472.22	1351.35	1250.70
165,000	13899.42	7019.15	4726.03	3579.70	2892.09	2433.83	2106.63	1861.35	1670.67	1518.23	1393.58	1289.78
170,000	14320.61	7231.85	4869.24	3688.18	2979.72	2507.58	2170.47	1917.75	1721.30	1564.23	1435.81	1328.87
175,000	14741.81	7444.55	5012.46	3796.65	3067.36	2581.33	2234.31	1974.16	1771.93	1610.24	1478.04	1367.95
180,000	15163.00	7657.25	5155.67	3905.13	3155.00	2655.08	2298.14	2030.56	1822.55	1656.25	1520.27	1407.04
185,000	15584.20	7869.95	5298.88	4013.60	3242.64	2728.84	2361.98	2086.97	1873.18	1702.25	1562.50	1446.12
190,000	16005.39	8082.66	5442.09	4122.08	3330.28	2802.59	2425.82	2143.37	1923.81	1748.26	1604.73	1485.20
195,000	16426.58	8295.36	5585.31	4230.55	3417.92	2876.34	2489.65	2199.78	1974.43	1794.27	1646.96	1524.29
200,000	16847.78	8508.06	5728.52	4339.03	3505.56	2950.09	2553.49	2256.18	2025.06	1840.27	1689.19	1563.37
205,000	17268.97	8720.76	5871.73	4447.51	3593.20	3023.85	2617.33	2312.58	2075.69	1886.28	1731.42	1602.46
210,000	17690.17	8933.46	6014.95	4555.98	3680.83	3097.60	2681.17	2368.99	2126.31	1932.29	1773.65	1641.54
215,000	18111.36	9146.16	6158.16	4664.46	3768.47	3171.35	2745.00	2425.39	2176.94	1978.29	1815.88	1680.62
220,000	18532.56	9358.86	6301.37	4772.93	3856.11	3245.10	2808.84	2481.80	2227.56	2024.30	1858.10	1719.71
225,000	18953.75	9571.56	6444.59	4881.41	3943.75	3318.85	2872.68	2538.20	2278.19	2070.31	1900.33	1758.79
230,000	19374.94	9784.27	6587.80	4989.88	4031.39	3392.61	2936.52	2594.61	2328.82	2116.31	1942.56	1797.88
235,000	19796.14	9996.97	6731.01	5098.36	4119.03	3466.36	3000.35	2651.01	2379.44	2162.32	1984.79	1836.96
240,000	20217.33	10209.67	6874.22	5206.83	4206.67	3540.11	3064.19	2707.41	2430.07	2208.33	2027.02	1876.05
245,000	20638.53	10422.37	7017.44	5315.31	4294.31	3613.86	3128.03	2763.82	2480.70	2254.33	2069.25	1915.13
250,000	21059.72	10635.07	7160.65	5423.79	4381.95	3687.62	3191.86	2820.22	2531.32	2300.34	2111.48	1954.21
255,000	21480.92	10847.77	7303.86	5532.26	4469.58	3761.37	3255.70	2876.63	2581.95	2346.35	2153.71	1993.30
260,000	21902.11	11060.47	7447.08	5640.74	4557.22	3835.12	3319.54	2933.03	2632.58	2392.35	2195.94	2032.38
265,000	22323.30	11273.17	7590.29	5749.21	4644.86	3908.87	3383.38	2989.44	2683.20	2438.36	2238.17	2071.47
270,000	22744.50	11485.88	7733.50	5857.69	4732.50	3982.62	3447.21	3045.84	2733.83	2484.37	2280.40	2110.55
280,000	23586.89	11911.28	8019.93	6074.64	4907.78	4130.13	3574.89	3158.65	2835.08	2576.38	2364.86	2188.72
290,000	24429.28	12336.68	8306.35	6291.59	5083.06	4277.63	3702.56	3271.46	2936.33	2668.40	2449.32	2266.89
300,000	25271.67	12762.08	8592.78	6508.54	5258.33	4425.14	3830.24	3384.27	3037.59	2760.41	2533.78	2345.06

AMOUNT OF LOAN	NUMBER OF YEARS IN TERM											
	13	14	15	16	17	18	19	20	25	30	35	40
$ 50	0.37	0.35	0.33	0.31	0.29	0.28	0.27	0.26	0.22	0.19	0.17	0.16
100	0.73	0.69	0.65	0.61	0.58	0.56	0.53	0.51	0.43	0.37	0.34	0.31
200	1.46	1.37	1.29	1.22	1.16	1.11	1.06	1.02	0.85	0.74	0.67	0.61
300	2.19	2.05	1.94	1.83	1.74	1.66	1.59	1.52	1.28	1.11	1.00	0.91
400	2.92	2.74	2.58	2.44	2.32	2.21	2.12	2.03	1.70	1.48	1.33	1.22
500	3.65	3.42	3.22	3.05	2.90	2.76	2.64	2.53	2.12	1.85	1.66	1.52
600	4.38	4.10	3.87	3.66	3.48	3.32	3.17	3.04	2.55	2.22	1.99	1.82
700	5.10	4.79	4.51	4.27	4.06	3.87	3.70	3.55	2.97	2.59	2.32	2.12
800	5.83	5.47	5.15	4.88	4.63	4.42	4.23	4.05	3.40	2.96	2.66	2.43
900	6.56	6.15	5.80	5.49	5.21	4.97	4.75	4.56	3.82	3.33	2.99	2.73
1,000	7.29	6.83	6.44	6.10	5.79	5.52	5.28	5.06	4.24	3.70	3.32	3.03
2,000	14.57	13.66	12.88	12.19	11.58	11.04	10.56	10.12	8.48	7.40	6.63	6.06
3,000	21.86	20.49	19.31	18.28	17.36	16.56	15.83	15.18	12.72	11.09	9.94	9.09
4,000	29.14	27.32	25.75	24.37	23.15	22.07	21.11	20.24	16.96	14.79	13.26	12.12
5,000	36.43	34.15	32.18	30.46	28.94	27.59	26.38	25.30	21.20	18.49	16.57	15.15
6,000	43.71	40.98	38.62	36.55	34.72	33.11	31.66	30.36	25.44	22.18	19.88	18.17
7,000	51.00	47.81	45.05	42.64	40.51	38.62	36.93	35.42	29.67	25.88	23.19	21.20
8,000	58.28	54.64	51.49	48.73	46.30	44.14	42.21	40.48	33.91	29.57	26.51	24.23
9,000	65.57	61.47	57.92	54.82	52.08	49.66	47.49	45.53	38.15	33.27	29.82	27.26
10,000	72.85	68.30	64.36	60.91	57.87	55.17	52.76	50.59	42.39	36.97	33.13	30.29
15,000	109.28	102.45	96.53	91.36	86.80	82.76	79.14	75.89	63.58	55.45	49.69	45.43
20,000	145.70	136.59	128.71	121.81	115.73	110.34	105.52	101.18	84.78	73.93	66.26	60.57
25,000	182.13	170.74	160.88	152.26	144.67	137.92	131.89	126.48	105.97	92.41	82.82	75.71
30,000	218.55	204.89	193.06	182.72	173.60	165.51	158.27	151.77	127.16	110.89	99.38	90.85
35,000	254.98	239.04	225.23	213.17	202.53	193.09	184.65	177.06	148.35	129.37	115.95	105.99
40,000	291.40	273.18	257.41	243.62	231.46	220.67	211.03	202.36	169.55	147.85	132.51	121.14
45,000	327.83	307.33	289.58	274.07	260.40	248.26	237.41	227.65	190.74	166.33	149.07	136.28
50,000	364.25	341.48	321.76	304.52	289.33	275.84	263.78	252.95	211.93	184.81	165.64	151.42
55,000	400.68	375.63	353.93	334.97	318.26	303.42	290.16	278.24	233.12	203.30	182.20	166.56
60,000	437.10	409.77	386.11	365.43	347.19	331.01	316.54	303.54	254.32	221.78	198.76	181.70
65,000	473.53	443.92	418.29	395.88	376.13	358.59	342.92	328.83	275.51	240.26	215.33	196.84
70,000	509.95	478.07	450.46	426.33	405.06	386.17	369.29	354.12	296.70	258.74	231.89	211.98
75,000	546.38	512.22	482.64	456.78	433.99	413.76	395.67	379.42	317.90	277.22	248.45	227.12
80,000	582.80	546.36	514.81	487.23	462.92	441.34	422.05	404.71	339.09	295.70	265.02	242.27
85,000	619.23	580.51	546.99	517.68	491.85	468.92	448.43	430.01	360.28	314.18	281.58	257.41
90,000	655.65	614.66	579.16	548.14	520.79	496.51	474.81	455.30	381.47	332.66	298.14	272.55
95,000	692.08	648.81	611.34	578.59	549.72	524.09	501.18	480.59	402.67	351.14	314.70	287.69
100,000	728.50	682.95	643.51	609.04	578.65	551.67	527.56	505.89	423.86	369.62	331.27	302.83
105,000	764.93	717.10	675.69	639.49	607.58	579.26	553.94	531.18	445.05	388.11	347.83	317.97
110,000	801.35	751.25	707.86	669.94	636.52	606.84	580.32	556.48	466.24	406.59	364.39	333.11
115,000	837.78	785.40	740.04	700.39	665.45	634.42	606.69	581.77	487.44	425.07	380.96	348.25
120,000	874.20	810.54	772.22	730.85	694.38	662.01	633.07	607.07	508.63	443.55	397.52	363.40
125,000	910.63	853.69	804.39	761.30	723.31	689.59	659.45	632.36	529.82	462.03	414.08	378.54
130,000	947.05	887.84	836.57	791.75	752.25	717.17	685.83	657.65	551.02	480.51	430.65	393.68
135,000	983.48	921.98	868.74	822.20	781.18	744.76	712.21	682.95	572.21	498.99	447.21	408.82
140,000	1019.90	956.13	900.92	852.65	810.11	772.34	738.58	708.24	593.40	517.47	463.77	423.96
145,000	1056.33	990.28	933.09	883.10	839.04	799.92	764.96	733.54	614.59	535.95	480.34	439.10
150,000	1092.75	1024.43	965.27	913.56	867.98	827.51	791.34	758.83	635.79	554.43	496.90	454.24
155,000	1129.18	1058.57	997.44	944.01	896.91	855.09	817.72	784.12	656.98	572.92	513.46	469.38
160,000	1165.60	1092.72	1029.62	974.46	925.84	882.67	844.09	809.42	678.17	591.40	530.03	484.53
165,000	1202.03	1126.87	1061.79	1004.91	954.77	910.26	870.47	834.71	699.36	609.88	546.59	499.67
170,000	1238.45	1161.02	1093.97	1035.36	983.70	937.84	896.85	860.01	720.56	628.36	563.15	514.81
175,000	1274.87	1195.16	1126.15	1065.81	1012.64	965.42	923.23	885.30	741.75	646.84	579.71	529.95
180,000	1311.30	1229.31	1158.32	1096.27	1041.57	993.01	949.61	910.60	762.94	665.32	596.28	545.09
185,000	1347.72	1263.46	1190.50	1126.72	1070.50	1020.59	975.98	935.89	784.14	683.80	612.84	560.23
190,000	1384.15	1297.61	1222.67	1157.17	1099.43	1048.17	1002.36	961.18	805.33	702.28	629.40	575.37
195,000	1420.57	1331.75	1254.85	1187.62	1128.37	1075.76	1028.74	986.48	826.52	720.76	645.97	590.51
200,000	1457.00	1365.90	1287.02	1218.07	1157.30	1103.34	1055.12	1011.77	847.71	739.24	662.53	605.66
205,000	1493.42	1400.05	1319.20	1248.52	1186.23	1130.92	1081.49	1037.07	868.91	757.72	679.09	620.80
210,000	1529.85	1434.20	1351.37	1278.98	1215.16	1158.51	1107.87	1062.36	890.10	776.21	695.66	635.94
215,000	1566.27	1468.34	1383.55	1309.43	1244.10	1186.09	1134.25	1087.65	911.29	794.69	712.22	651.08
220,000	1602.70	1502.49	1415.72	1339.88	1273.03	1213.67	1160.63	1112.95	932.48	813.17	728.78	666.22
225,000	1639.12	1536.64	1447.90	1370.33	1301.96	1241.26	1187.01	1138.24	953.68	831.65	745.35	681.36
230,000	1675.55	1570.79	1480.08	1400.78	1330.89	1268.84	1213.38	1163.54	974.87	850.13	761.91	696.50
235,000	1711.97	1604.93	1512.25	1431.23	1359.83	1296.42	1239.76	1188.83	996.06	868.61	778.47	711.65
240,000	1748.40	1639.08	1544.43	1461.69	1388.76	1324.01	1266.14	1214.13	1017.26	887.09	795.04	726.79
245,000	1784.82	1673.23	1576.60	1492.14	1417.69	1351.59	1292.52	1239.42	1038.45	905.57	811.60	741.93
250,000	1821.25	1707.37	1608.78	1522.59	1446.62	1379.17	1318.89	1264.71	1059.64	924.05	828.16	757.07
255,000	1857.67	1741.52	1640.95	1553.04	1475.55	1406.76	1345.27	1290.01	1080.83	942.53	844.73	772.21
260,000	1894.10	1775.67	1673.13	1583.49	1504.49	1434.34	1371.65	1315.30	1102.03	961.02	861.29	787.35
265,000	1930.52	1809.82	1705.30	1613.94	1533.42	1461.92	1398.03	1340.60	1123.22	979.50	877.85	802.49
270,000	1966.95	1843.96	1737.48	1644.40	1562.35	1489.51	1424.41	1365.89	1144.41	997.98	894.41	817.63
280,000	2039.80	1912.26	1801.83	1705.30	1620.22	1544.67	1477.16	1416.48	1186.80	1034.94	927.54	847.92
290,000	2112.65	1980.55	1866.18	1766.20	1678.08	1599.84	1529.92	1467.07	1229.18	1071.90	960.67	878.20
300,000	2185.50	2048.85	1930.53	1827.11	1735.95	1655.01	1582.67	1517.66	1271.57	1108.86	993.79	908.48

3

AMOUNT OF LOAN	NUMBER OF YEARS IN TERM											
	1	2	3	4	5	6	7	8	9	10	11	12
$ 50	4.22	2.14	1.44	1.10	0.89	0.75	0.65	0.57	0.52	0.47	0.43	0.40
100	8.44	4.27	2.88	2.19	1.77	1.49	1.29	1.14	1.03	0.94	0.86	0.80
200	16.88	8.54	5.76	4.37	3.53	2.98	2.58	2.28	2.05	1.87	1.72	1.59
300	25.31	12.80	8.63	6.55	5.30	4.46	3.87	3.42	3.08	2.80	2.57	2.38
400	33.75	17.07	11.51	8.73	7.06	5.95	5.16	4.56	4.10	3.73	3.43	3.18
500	42.18	21.33	14.38	10.91	8.82	7.44	6.44	5.70	5.12	4.66	4.28	3.97
600	50.62	25.60	17.26	13.09	10.59	8.92	7.73	6.84	6.15	5.59	5.14	4.76
700	59.05	29.86	20.13	15.27	12.35	10.41	9.02	7.98	7.17	6.52	6.00	5.56
800	67.49	34.13	23.01	17.45	14.11	11.89	10.31	9.12	8.19	7.46	6.85	6.35
900	75.92	38.39	25.88	19.63	15.88	13.38	11.60	10.26	9.22	8.39	7.71	7.14
1,000	84.36	42.66	28.76	21.81	17.64	14.87	12.88	11.40	10.24	9.32	8.56	7.94
2,000	168.71	85.31	57.51	43.61	35.28	29.73	25.76	22.79	20.48	18.63	17.12	15.87
3,000	253.06	127.96	86.26	65.42	52.92	44.59	38.64	34.18	30.72	27.95	25.68	23.80
4,000	337.41	170.61	115.01	87.22	70.55	59.45	51.52	45.57	40.95	37.26	34.24	31.73
5,000	421.77	213.26	143.76	109.03	88.19	74.31	64.39	56.97	51.19	46.57	42.80	39.66
6,000	506.12	255.91	172.52	130.83	105.83	89.17	77.27	68.36	61.43	55.89	51.36	47.59
7,000	590.47	298.56	201.27	152.64	123.47	104.03	90.15	79.75	71.66	65.20	59.92	55.52
8,000	674.82	341.21	230.02	174.44	141.10	118.89	103.03	91.14	81.90	74.51	68.48	63.45
9,000	759.18	383.86	258.77	196.24	158.74	133.75	115.91	102.53	92.14	83.83	77.04	71.38
10,000	843.53	426.51	287.52	218.05	176.38	148.61	128.78	113.93	102.38	93.14	85.59	79.31
15,000	1265.29	639.76	431.28	327.07	264.57	222.91	193.17	170.89	153.56	139.71	128.39	118.96
20,000	1687.05	853.01	575.04	436.09	352.75	297.21	257.56	227.85	204.75	186.28	171.18	158.62
25,000	2108.82	1066.26	718.80	545.12	440.94	371.52	321.95	284.81	255.93	232.85	213.98	198.27
30,000	2530.58	1279.51	862.56	654.14	529.13	445.82	386.34	341.77	307.12	279.42	256.77	237.92
35,000	2952.34	1492.76	1006.32	763.16	617.31	520.12	450.73	398.73	358.30	325.99	299.57	277.57
40,000	3374.10	1706.01	1150.08	872.18	705.50	594.42	515.12	455.69	409.49	372.55	342.36	317.23
45,000	3795.87	1919.27	1293.84	981.20	793.69	668.73	579.51	512.65	460.67	419.12	385.16	356.88
50,000	4217.63	2132.52	1437.60	1090.23	881.87	743.03	643.90	569.61	511.86	465.69	427.95	396.53
55,000	4639.39	2345.77	1581.36	1199.25	970.06	817.33	708.29	626.57	563.04	512.26	470.75	436.19
60,000	5061.15	2559.02	1725.12	1308.27	1058.25	891.63	772.68	683.53	614.23	558.83	513.54	475.84
65,000	5482.91	2772.27	1868.88	1417.29	1146.43	965.94	837.07	740.49	665.41	605.40	556.34	515.49
70,000	5904.68	2985.52	2012.63	1526.31	1234.62	1040.24	901.46	797.45	716.60	651.97	599.13	555.14
75,000	6326.44	3198.77	2156.39	1635.34	1322.81	1114.54	965.85	854.41	767.78	698.54	641.93	594.80
80,000	6748.20	3412.02	2300.15	1744.36	1410.99	1188.84	1030.24	911.37	818.97	745.10	684.72	634.45
85,000	7169.96	3625.28	2443.91	1853.38	1499.18	1263.15	1094.63	968.33	870.15	791.67	727.52	674.10
90,000	7591.73	3838.53	2587.67	1962.40	1587.37	1337.45	1159.02	1025.29	921.34	838.24	770.31	713.75
95,000	8013.49	4051.78	2731.43	2071.42	1675.55	1411.75	1223.41	1082.25	972.52	884.81	813.11	753.41
100,000	8435.25	4265.03	2875.19	2180.45	1763.74	1486.05	1287.80	1139.21	1023.71	931.38	855.90	793.06
105,000	8857.01	4478.28	3018.95	2289.47	1851.93	1560.35	1352.19	1196.17	1074.89	977.95	898.70	832.71
110,000	9278.77	4691.53	3162.71	2398.49	1940.11	1634.66	1416.58	1253.13	1126.08	1024.52	941.49	872.37
115,000	9700.54	4904.78	3306.47	2507.51	2028.30	1708.96	1480.97	1310.09	1177.26	1071.08	984.28	912.02
120,000	10122.30	5118.03	3450.23	2616.53	2116.49	1783.26	1545.36	1367.05	1228.45	1117.65	1027.08	951.67
125,000	10544.06	5331.29	3593.99	2725.56	2204.67	1857.56	1609.75	1424.01	1279.63	1164.22	1069.87	991.32
130,000	10965.82	5544.54	3737.75	2834.58	2292.86	1931.87	1674.14	1480.97	1330.82	1210.79	1112.67	1030.98
135,000	11387.59	5757.79	3881.50	2943.60	2381.05	2006.17	1738.53	1537.93	1382.00	1257.36	1155.46	1070.63
140,000	11809.35	5971.04	4025.26	3052.62	2469.23	2080.47	1802.92	1594.89	1433.19	1303.93	1198.26	1110.28
145,000	12231.11	6184.29	4169.02	3161.64	2557.42	2154.77	1867.31	1651.85	1484.37	1350.50	1241.05	1149.93
150,000	12652.87	6397.54	4312.78	3270.67	2645.61	2229.08	1931.70	1708.81	1535.56	1397.07	1283.85	1189.59
155,000	13074.63	6610.79	4456.54	3379.69	2733.79	2303.38	1996.09	1765.77	1586.74	1443.63	1326.64	1229.24
160,000	13496.40	6824.04	4600.30	3488.71	2821.98	2377.68	2060.48	1822.73	1637.93	1490.20	1369.44	1268.89
165,000	13918.16	7037.29	4744.06	3597.73	2910.17	2451.98	2124.87	1879.69	1689.11	1536.77	1412.23	1308.55
170,000	14339.92	7250.55	4887.82	3706.75	2998.35	2526.29	2189.26	1936.65	1740.30	1583.34	1455.03	1348.20
175,000	14761.68	7463.80	5031.58	3815.78	3086.54	2600.59	2253.65	1993.61	1791.48	1629.91	1497.82	1387.85
180,000	15183.45	7677.05	5175.34	3924.80	3174.73	2674.89	2318.04	2050.57	1842.67	1676.48	1540.62	1427.50
185,000	15605.21	7890.30	5319.10	4033.82	3262.91	2749.19	2382.43	2107.53	1893.85	1723.05	1583.41	1467.16
190,000	16026.97	8103.55	5462.86	4142.84	3351.10	2823.49	2446.82	2164.49	1945.04	1769.62	1626.21	1506.81
195,000	16448.73	8316.80	5606.62	4251.86	3439.29	2897.80	2511.21	2221.45	1996.23	1816.18	1669.00	1546.46
200,000	16870.49	8530.05	5750.37	4360.89	3527.47	2972.10	2575.60	2278.41	2047.41	1862.75	1711.80	1586.11
205,000	17292.26	8743.30	5894.13	4469.91	3615.66	3046.40	2639.99	2335.37	2098.60	1909.32	1754.59	1625.77
210,000	17714.02	8956.56	6037.89	4578.93	3703.85	3120.70	2704.38	2392.33	2149.78	1955.89	1797.39	1665.42
215,000	18135.78	9169.81	6181.65	4687.95	3792.03	3195.01	2768.77	2449.29	2200.97	2002.46	1840.18	1705.07
220,000	18557.54	9383.06	6325.41	4796.97	3880.22	3269.31	2833.16	2506.25	2252.15	2049.03	1882.97	1744.73
225,000	18979.31	9596.31	6469.17	4906.00	3968.41	3343.61	2897.55	2563.21	2303.34	2095.60	1925.77	1784.38
230,000	19401.07	9809.56	6612.93	5015.02	4056.59	3417.91	2961.94	2620.17	2354.52	2142.16	1968.56	1824.03
235,000	19822.83	10022.81	6756.69	5124.04	4144.78	3492.22	3026.33	2677.13	2405.71	2188.73	2011.36	1863.68
240,000	20244.59	10236.06	6900.45	5233.06	4232.97	3566.52	3090.72	2734.09	2456.89	2235.30	2054.15	1903.34
245,000	20666.35	10449.31	7044.21	5342.08	4321.15	3640.82	3155.11	2791.05	2508.08	2281.87	2096.95	1942.99
250,000	21088.12	10662.57	7187.97	5451.11	4409.34	3715.12	3219.50	2848.01	2559.26	2328.44	2139.74	1982.64
255,000	21509.88	10875.82	7331.73	5560.13	4497.53	3789.43	3283.89	2904.97	2610.45	2375.01	2182.54	2022.30
260,000	21931.64	11089.07	7475.49	5669.15	4585.71	3863.73	3348.28	2961.93	2661.63	2421.58	2225.33	2061.95
265,000	22353.40	11302.32	7619.24	5778.17	4673.90	3938.03	3412.67	3018.89	2712.82	2468.15	2268.13	2101.60
270,000	22775.17	11515.57	7763.00	5887.19	4762.09	4012.33	3477.06	3075.85	2764.00	2514.71	2310.92	2141.25
280,000	23618.69	11942.07	8050.52	6105.24	4938.46	4160.94	3605.84	3189.77	2866.37	2607.85	2396.51	2220.56
290,000	24462.21	12368.58	8338.04	6323.28	5114.83	4309.54	3734.62	3303.69	2968.74	2700.99	2482.10	2299.86
300,000	25305.74	12795.08	8625.56	6541.33	5291.21	4458.15	3863.40	3417.61	3071.11	2794.13	2567.69	2379.17

AMOUNT OF LOAN	NUMBER OF YEARS IN TERM											
	13	14	15	16	17	18	19	20	25	30	35	40
$ 50	0.37	0.35	0.33	0.32	0.30	0.29	0.27	0.26	0.22	0.20	0.18	0.16
100	0.74	0.70	0.66	0.63	0.60	0.57	0.54	0.52	0.44	0.39	0.35	0.32
200	1.48	1.39	1.32	1.25	1.19	1.13	1.08	1.04	0.88	0.77	0.69	0.64
300	2.22	2.09	1.97	1.87	1.78	1.70	1.62	1.56	1.31	1.15	1.04	0.95
400	2.96	2.78	2.63	2.49	2.37	2.26	2.16	2.08	1.75	1.53	1.38	1.27
500	3.70	3.48	3.28	3.11	2.96	2.82	2.70	2.59	2.19	1.92	1.73	1.59
600	4.44	4.17	3.94	3.73	3.55	3.39	3.24	3.11	2.62	2.30	2.07	1.90
700	5.18	4.87	4.59	4.35	4.14	3.95	3.78	3.63	3.06	2.68	2.41	2.22
800	5.92	5.56	5.25	4.97	4.73	4.51	4.32	4.15	3.49	3.06	2.76	2.53
900	6.66	6.26	5.90	5.59	5.32	5.08	4.86	4.67	3.93	3.45	3.10	2.85
1,000	7.40	6.95	6.56	6.21	5.91	5.64	5.40	5.18	4.37	3.83	3.45	3.17
2,000	14.80	13.89	13.11	12.42	11.81	11.27	10.79	10.36	8.73	7.65	6.89	6.33
3,000	22.20	20.84	19.66	18.63	17.72	16.91	16.19	15.54	13.09	11.47	10.33	9.49
4,000	29.60	27.78	26.21	24.83	23.62	22.54	21.58	20.72	17.45	15.29	13.77	12.65
5,000	37.00	34.73	32.76	31.04	29.52	28.18	26.98	25.90	21.81	19.12	17.22	15.81
6,000	44.40	41.67	39.31	37.25	35.43	33.81	32.37	31.07	26.17	22.94	20.66	18.97
7,000	51.80	48.62	45.86	43.45	41.33	39.45	37.76	36.25	30.53	26.76	24.10	22.13
8,000	59.20	55.56	52.41	49.66	47.23	45.08	43.16	41.43	34.90	30.58	27.54	25.30
9,000	66.60	62.51	58.96	55.87	53.14	50.72	48.55	46.61	39.26	34.41	30.99	28.46
10,000	74.00	69.45	65.51	62.07	59.04	56.35	53.95	51.79	43.62	38.23	34.43	31.62
15,000	111.00	104.17	98.27	93.11	88.56	84.52	80.92	77.68	65.42	57.34	51.64	47.43
20,000	147.99	138.90	131.02	124.14	118.08	112.70	107.89	103.57	87.23	76.45	68.85	63.23
25,000	184.99	173.62	163.78	155.17	147.60	140.87	134.86	129.46	109.04	95.57	86.06	79.04
30,000	221.99	208.34	196.53	186.21	177.11	169.04	161.83	155.35	130.84	114.68	103.28	94.85
35,000	258.98	243.06	229.28	217.24	206.63	197.21	188.80	181.24	152.65	133.79	120.49	110.65
40,000	295.98	277.79	262.04	248.28	236.15	225.39	215.77	207.13	174.46	152.90	137.70	126.46
45,000	332.98	312.51	294.79	279.31	265.67	253.56	242.74	233.02	196.26	172.02	154.91	142.27
50,000	369.97	347.23	327.55	310.34	295.19	281.73	269.71	258.91	218.07	191.13	172.12	158.08
55,000	406.97	381.96	360.30	341.38	324.70	309.90	296.68	284.80	239.88	210.24	189.34	173.88
60,000	443.97	416.68	393.06	372.41	354.22	338.08	323.65	310.69	261.68	229.35	206.55	189.69
65,000	480.96	451.40	425.81	403.45	383.74	366.25	350.62	336.58	283.49	248.46	223.76	205.50
70,000	517.96	486.12	458.56	434.48	413.26	394.42	377.59	362.47	305.30	267.58	240.97	221.30
75,000	554.96	520.85	491.32	465.51	442.78	422.59	404.56	388.36	327.10	286.69	258.18	237.11
80,000	591.95	555.57	524.07	496.55	472.29	450.77	431.53	414.25	348.91	305.80	275.39	252.92
85,000	628.95	590.29	556.83	527.58	501.81	478.94	458.50	440.14	370.72	324.91	292.61	268.73
90,000	665.95	625.01	589.58	558.62	531.33	507.11	485.47	466.03	392.52	344.03	309.82	284.53
95,000	702.94	659.74	622.34	589.65	560.85	535.28	512.45	491.92	414.33	363.14	327.03	300.34
100,000	739.94	694.46	655.09	620.68	590.37	563.46	539.42	517.81	436.14	382.25	344.24	316.15
105,000	776.94	729.18	687.84	651.72	619.89	591.63	566.39	543.70	457.94	401.36	361.45	331.95
110,000	813.93	763.91	720.60	682.75	649.40	619.80	593.36	569.59	479.75	420.48	378.67	347.76
115,000	850.93	798.63	753.35	713.79	678.92	647.97	620.33	595.48	501.56	439.59	395.88	363.57
120,000	887.93	833.35	786.11	744.82	708.44	676.15	647.30	621.37	523.36	458.70	413.09	379.38
125,000	924.92	868.07	818.86	775.85	737.90	704.32	674.27	647.27	545.17	477.81	430.30	395.18
130,000	961.92	902.80	851.62	806.89	767.48	732.49	701.24	673.16	566.97	496.92	447.51	410.99
135,000	998.92	937.52	884.37	837.92	796.99	760.67	728.21	699.05	588.78	516.04	464.72	426.80
140,000	1035.92	972.24	917.12	868.96	826.51	788.84	755.18	724.94	610.59	535.15	481.94	442.60
145,000	1072.91	1006.96	949.88	899.99	856.03	817.01	782.15	750.83	632.39	554.26	499.15	458.41
150,000	1109.91	1041.69	982.63	931.02	885.55	845.18	809.12	776.72	654.20	573.37	516.36	474.22
155,000	1146.91	1076.41	1015.39	962.06	915.07	873.36	836.09	802.61	676.01	592.49	533.57	490.03
160,000	1183.90	1111.13	1048.14	993.09	944.58	901.53	863.06	828.50	697.81	611.60	550.78	505.83
165,000	1220.90	1145.86	1080.89	1024.13	974.10	929.70	890.03	854.39	719.62	630.71	568.00	521.64
170,000	1257.90	1180.58	1113.65	1055.16	1003.62	957.87	917.00	880.28	741.43	649.82	585.21	537.45
175,000	1294.89	1215.30	1146.40	1086.19	1033.14	986.05	943.97	906.17	763.23	668.94	602.42	553.25
180,000	1331.89	1250.02	1179.16	1117.23	1062.66	1014.22	970.94	932.06	785.04	688.05	619.63	569.06
185,000	1368.89	1284.75	1211.91	1148.26	1092.17	1042.39	997.91	957.95	806.85	707.16	636.84	584.87
190,000	1405.88	1319.47	1244.67	1179.30	1121.69	1070.56	1024.89	983.84	828.65	726.27	654.05	600.68
195,000	1442.88	1354.19	1277.42	1210.33	1151.21	1098.74	1051.86	1009.73	850.46	745.38	671.27	616.48
200,000	1479.88	1388.92	1310.17	1241.36	1180.73	1126.91	1078.83	1035.62	872.27	764.50	688.48	632.29
205,000	1516.87	1423.64	1342.93	1272.40	1210.25	1155.08	1105.80	1061.51	894.07	783.61	705.69	648.10
210,000	1553.87	1458.36	1375.68	1303.43	1239.77	1183.25	1132.77	1087.40	915.88	802.72	722.90	663.90
215,000	1590.87	1493.08	1408.44	1334.47	1269.28	1211.43	1159.74	1113.29	937.69	821.83	740.11	679.71
220,000	1627.86	1527.81	1441.19	1365.50	1298.80	1239.60	1186.71	1139.18	959.49	840.95	757.33	695.52
225,000	1664.86	1562.53	1473.95	1396.53	1328.32	1267.77	1213.68	1165.07	981.30	860.06	774.54	711.32
230,000	1701.86	1597.25	1506.70	1427.57	1357.84	1295.94	1240.65	1190.96	1003.11	879.17	791.75	727.13
235,000	1738.85	1631.97	1539.45	1458.60	1387.36	1324.12	1267.62	1216.85	1024.91	898.28	808.96	742.94
240,000	1775.85	1666.70	1572.21	1489.63	1416.87	1352.29	1294.59	1242.74	1046.72	917.40	826.17	758.75
245,000	1812.85	1701.42	1604.96	1520.67	1446.39	1380.46	1321.56	1268.64	1068.53	936.51	843.38	774.55
250,000	1849.84	1736.14	1637.72	1551.70	1475.91	1408.63	1348.53	1294.53	1090.33	955.62	860.60	790.36
255,000	1886.84	1770.87	1670.47	1582.74	1505.43	1436.81	1375.50	1320.42	1112.14	974.73	877.81	806.17
260,000	1923.84	1805.59	1703.23	1613.77	1534.95	1464.98	1402.47	1346.31	1133.94	993.84	895.02	821.97
265,000	1960.84	1840.31	1735.98	1644.80	1564.46	1493.15	1429.44	1372.20	1155.75	1012.96	912.23	837.78
270,000	1997.83	1875.03	1768.73	1675.84	1593.98	1521.33	1456.41	1398.09	1177.56	1032.07	929.44	853.59
280,000	2071.83	1944.48	1834.24	1737.91	1653.02	1577.67	1510.36	1449.87	1221.17	1070.29	963.87	885.20
290,000	2145.82	2013.92	1899.75	1799.97	1712.05	1634.02	1564.30	1501.65	1264.78	1108.52	998.29	916.82
300,000	2219.81	2083.37	1965.26	1862.04	1771.09	1690.36	1618.24	1553.43	1308.40	1146.74	1032.71	948.43

5

2.50%

AMOUNT OF LOAN	NUMBER OF YEARS IN TERM											
	1	2	3	4	5	6	7	8	9	10	11	12
$ 50	4.23	2.14	1.45	1.10	0.89	0.75	0.65	0.58	0.52	0.48	0.44	0.41
100	8.45	4.28	2.89	2.20	1.78	1.50	1.30	1.16	1.04	0.95	0.87	0.81
200	16.90	8.56	5.78	4.39	3.55	3.00	2.60	2.31	2.07	1.89	1.74	1.61
300	25.34	12.83	8.66	6.58	5.33	4.50	3.90	3.46	3.11	2.83	2.61	2.42
400	33.79	17.11	11.55	8.77	7.10	5.99	5.20	4.61	4.14	3.78	3.47	3.22
500	42.24	21.39	14.44	10.96	8.88	7.49	6.50	5.76	5.18	4.72	4.34	4.03
600	50.68	25.66	17.32	13.15	10.65	8.99	7.80	6.91	6.21	5.66	5.21	4.83
700	59.13	29.94	20.21	15.34	12.43	10.48	9.10	8.06	7.25	6.60	6.08	5.64
800	67.58	34.21	23.09	17.54	14.20	11.98	10.40	9.21	8.28	7.55	6.94	6.44
900	76.02	38.49	25.98	19.73	15.98	13.48	11.70	10.36	9.32	8.49	7.81	7.25
1,000	84.47	42.77	28.87	21.92	17.75	14.98	12.99	11.51	10.35	9.43	8.68	8.05
2,000	168.94	85.53	57.73	43.83	35.50	29.95	25.98	23.01	20.70	18.86	17.35	16.10
3,000	253.40	128.29	86.59	65.75	53.25	44.92	38.97	34.52	31.05	28.29	26.02	24.14
4,000	337.87	171.05	115.45	87.66	70.99	59.89	51.96	46.02	41.40	37.71	34.70	32.19
5,000	422.34	213.81	144.31	109.58	88.74	74.86	64.95	57.52	51.75	47.14	43.37	40.23
6,000	506.80	256.57	173.17	131.49	106.49	89.83	77.94	69.03	62.10	56.57	52.04	48.28
7,000	591.27	299.33	202.03	153.40	124.24	104.80	90.93	80.53	72.45	65.99	60.72	56.32
8,000	675.73	342.09	230.90	175.32	141.98	119.77	103.92	92.04	82.80	75.42	69.39	64.37
9,000	760.20	384.85	259.76	197.23	159.73	134.74	116.91	103.54	93.15	84.85	78.06	72.41
10,000	844.67	427.61	288.62	219.15	177.48	149.72	129.90	115.04	103.50	94.27	86.73	80.46
15,000	1267.00	641.41	432.93	328.72	266.22	224.57	194.84	172.56	155.25	141.41	130.10	120.68
20,000	1689.33	855.21	577.23	438.29	354.95	299.43	259.79	230.08	207.00	188.54	173.46	160.91
25,000	2111.66	1069.01	721.54	547.86	443.69	374.28	324.73	287.60	258.74	235.68	216.83	201.14
30,000	2533.99	1282.82	865.85	657.43	532.43	449.14	389.68	345.12	310.49	282.81	260.19	241.36
35,000	2956.32	1496.62	1010.15	767.00	621.16	523.99	454.63	402.64	362.24	329.95	303.56	281.59
40,000	3378.65	1710.42	1154.46	876.57	709.90	598.85	519.57	460.16	413.99	377.08	346.92	321.82
45,000	3800.98	1924.22	1298.77	986.14	798.64	673.70	584.52	517.68	465.74	424.22	390.29	362.04
50,000	4223.31	2138.02	1443.07	1095.71	887.37	748.56	649.46	575.20	517.48	471.35	433.65	402.27
55,000	4645.64	2351.83	1587.38	1205.28	976.11	823.41	714.41	632.72	569.23	518.49	477.02	442.50
60,000	5067.97	2565.63	1731.69	1314.85	1064.85	898.27	779.35	690.24	620.98	565.62	520.38	482.72
65,000	5490.30	2779.43	1875.99	1424.42	1153.58	973.12	844.30	747.75	672.73	612.76	563.75	522.95
70,000	5912.63	2993.23	2020.30	1533.99	1242.32	1047.98	909.25	805.27	724.47	659.89	607.11	563.18
75,000	6334.96	3207.03	2164.61	1643.56	1331.06	1122.83	974.19	862.79	776.22	707.03	650.48	603.40
80,000	6757.29	3420.84	2308.92	1753.13	1419.79	1197.69	1039.14	920.31	827.97	754.16	693.84	643.63
85,000	7179.62	3634.64	2453.22	1862.70	1508.53	1272.54	1104.08	977.83	879.72	801.30	737.21	683.85
90,000	7601.96	3848.44	2597.53	1972.27	1597.27	1347.40	1169.03	1035.35	931.47	848.43	780.57	724.08
95,000	8024.29	4062.24	2741.84	2081.84	1686.00	1422.25	1233.98	1092.87	983.21	895.57	823.93	764.31
100,000	8446.62	4276.04	2886.14	2191.41	1774.74	1497.11	1298.92	1150.39	1034.96	942.70	867.30	804.53
105,000	8868.95	4489.85	3030.45	2300.98	1863.48	1571.96	1363.87	1207.91	1086.71	989.84	910.66	844.76
110,000	9291.28	4703.65	3174.76	2410.55	1952.21	1646.82	1428.81	1265.43	1138.46	1036.97	954.03	884.99
115,000	9713.61	4917.45	3319.06	2520.12	2040.95	1721.67	1493.76	1322.95	1190.20	1084.11	997.39	925.21
120,000	10135.94	5131.25	3463.37	2629.69	2129.69	1796.53	1558.70	1380.47	1241.95	1131.24	1040.76	965.44
125,000	10558.27	5345.05	3607.68	2739.26	2218.43	1871.38	1623.65	1437.99	1293.70	1178.38	1084.12	1005.67
130,000	10980.60	5558.86	3751.98	2848.83	2307.16	1946.24	1688.60	1495.50	1345.45	1225.51	1127.49	1045.89
135,000	11402.93	5772.66	3896.29	2958.40	2395.90	2021.09	1753.54	1553.02	1397.20	1272.65	1170.85	1086.12
140,000	11825.26	5986.46	4040.60	3067.97	2484.64	2095.95	1818.49	1610.54	1448.94	1319.78	1214.22	1126.35
145,000	12247.59	6200.26	4184.90	3177.54	2573.37	2170.80	1883.43	1668.06	1500.69	1366.92	1257.58	1166.57
150,000	12669.92	6414.06	4329.21	3287.11	2662.11	2245.66	1948.38	1725.58	1552.44	1414.05	1300.95	1206.80
155,000	13092.25	6627.87	4473.52	3396.68	2750.85	2320.51	2013.32	1783.10	1604.19	1461.19	1344.31	1247.03
160,000	13514.58	6841.67	4617.82	3506.25	2839.58	2395.37	2078.27	1840.62	1655.93	1508.32	1387.68	1287.25
165,000	13936.91	7055.47	4762.13	3615.82	2928.32	2470.22	2143.22	1898.14	1707.68	1555.46	1431.04	1327.48
170,000	14359.24	7269.27	4906.44	3725.39	3017.06	2545.08	2208.16	1955.66	1759.43	1602.59	1474.41	1367.70
175,000	14781.57	7483.07	5050.75	3834.96	3105.79	2619.93	2273.11	2013.18	1811.18	1649.73	1517.77	1407.93
180,000	15203.91	7696.88	5195.05	3944.53	3194.53	2694.79	2338.05	2070.70	1862.93	1696.86	1561.14	1448.16
185,000	15626.24	7910.68	5339.36	4054.10	3283.27	2769.64	2403.00	2128.22	1914.67	1744.00	1604.50	1488.38
190,000	16048.57	8124.48	5483.67	4163.67	3372.00	2844.50	2467.95	2185.74	1966.42	1791.13	1647.86	1528.61
195,000	16470.90	8338.28	5627.97	4273.24	3460.74	2919.35	2532.89	2243.25	2018.17	1838.27	1691.23	1568.84
200,000	16893.23	8552.08	5772.28	4382.81	3549.48	2994.21	2597.84	2300.77	2069.92	1885.40	1734.59	1609.06
205,000	17315.56	8765.89	5916.59	4492.38	3638.21	3069.06	2662.78	2358.29	2121.66	1932.54	1777.96	1649.29
210,000	17737.89	8979.69	6060.89	4601.95	3726.95	3143.92	2727.73	2415.81	2173.41	1979.67	1821.32	1689.52
215,000	18160.22	9193.49	6205.20	4711.52	3815.69	3218.77	2792.67	2473.33	2225.16	2026.81	1864.69	1729.74
220,000	18582.55	9407.29	6349.51	4821.09	3904.42	3293.63	2857.62	2530.85	2276.91	2073.94	1908.05	1769.97
225,000	19004.88	9621.09	6493.81	4930.66	3993.16	3368.49	2922.57	2588.37	2328.66	2121.08	1951.42	1810.20
230,000	19427.21	9834.90	6638.12	5040.23	4081.90	3443.34	2987.51	2645.89	2380.40	2168.21	1994.78	1850.42
235,000	19849.54	10048.70	6782.43	5149.80	4170.63	3518.20	3052.46	2703.41	2432.15	2215.35	2038.15	1890.65
240,000	20271.87	10262.50	6926.74	5259.37	4259.37	3593.05	3117.40	2760.93	2483.90	2262.48	2081.51	1930.88
245,000	20694.20	10476.30	7071.04	5368.94	4348.11	3667.91	3182.35	2818.45	2535.65	2309.62	2124.88	1971.10
250,000	21116.53	10690.10	7215.35	5478.51	4436.85	3742.76	3247.29	2875.97	2587.39	2356.75	2168.24	2011.33
255,000	21538.86	10903.91	7359.66	5588.08	4525.58	3817.62	3312.24	2933.49	2639.14	2403.89	2211.61	2051.55
260,000	21961.19	11117.71	7503.96	5697.65	4614.32	3892.47	3377.19	2991.00	2690.89	2451.02	2254.97	2091.78
265,000	22383.52	11331.51	7648.27	5807.22	4703.06	3967.33	3442.13	3048.52	2742.64	2498.16	2298.34	2132.01
270,000	22805.86	11545.31	7792.58	5916.79	4791.79	4042.18	3507.08	3106.04	2794.39	2545.29	2341.70	2172.23
280,000	23650.52	11972.91	8081.19	6135.93	4969.27	4191.89	3636.97	3221.08	2897.88	2639.56	2428.43	2252.69
290,000	24495.18	12400.52	8369.80	6355.07	5146.74	4341.60	3766.86	3336.12	3001.38	2733.83	2515.16	2333.14
300,000	25339.84	12828.12	8658.42	6574.22	5324.21	4491.31	3896.75	3451.16	3104.87	2828.10	2601.89	2413.59

AMOUNT OF LOAN	NUMBER OF YEARS IN TERM											
	13	14	15	16	17	18	19	20	25	30	35	40
$ 50	0.38	0.36	0.34	0.32	0.31	0.29	0.28	0.27	0.23	0.20	0.18	0.17
100	0.76	0.71	0.67	0.64	0.61	0.58	0.56	0.53	0.45	0.40	0.36	0.33
200	1.51	1.42	1.34	1.27	1.21	1.16	1.11	1.06	0.90	0.80	0.72	0.66
300	2.26	2.12	2.01	1.90	1.81	1.73	1.66	1.59	1.35	1.19	1.08	0.99
400	3.01	2.83	2.67	2.53	2.41	2.31	2.21	2.12	1.80	1.59	1.43	1.32
500	3.76	3.54	3.34	3.17	3.02	2.88	2.76	2.65	2.25	1.98	1.79	1.65
600	4.51	4.24	4.01	3.80	3.62	3.46	3.31	3.18	2.70	2.38	2.15	1.98
700	5.27	4.95	4.67	4.43	4.22	4.03	3.86	3.71	3.15	2.77	2.51	2.31
800	6.02	5.65	5.34	5.06	4.82	4.61	4.42	4.24	3.59	3.17	2.86	2.64
900	6.77	6.36	6.01	5.70	5.42	5.18	4.97	4.77	4.04	3.56	3.22	2.97
1,000	7.52	7.07	6.67	6.33	6.03	5.76	5.52	5.30	4.49	3.96	3.58	3.30
2,000	15.03	14.13	13.34	12.65	12.05	11.51	11.03	10.60	8.98	7.91	7.15	6.60
3,000	22.55	21.19	20.01	18.98	18.07	17.27	16.55	15.90	13.46	11.86	10.73	9.90
4,000	30.06	28.25	26.68	25.30	24.09	23.02	22.06	21.20	17.95	15.81	14.30	13.20
5,000	37.58	35.31	33.34	31.63	30.12	28.77	27.58	26.50	22.44	19.76	17.88	16.49
6,000	45.09	42.37	40.01	37.95	36.14	34.53	33.09	31.80	26.92	23.71	21.45	19.79
7,000	52.61	49.43	46.68	44.28	42.16	40.28	38.60	37.10	31.41	27.66	25.03	23.09
8,000	60.12	56.49	53.35	50.60	48.18	46.04	44.12	42.40	35.89	31.61	28.60	26.39
9,000	67.64	63.55	60.02	56.93	54.20	51.79	49.63	47.70	40.38	35.57	32.18	29.69
10,000	75.15	70.61	66.68	63.25	60.23	57.54	55.15	53.00	44.87	39.52	35.75	32.98
15,000	112.73	105.92	100.02	94.87	90.34	86.31	82.72	79.49	67.30	59.27	53.63	49.47
20,000	150.30	141.22	133.36	126.50	120.45	115.08	110.29	105.99	89.73	79.03	71.50	65.96
25,000	187.88	176.53	166.70	158.12	150.56	143.85	137.86	132.48	112.16	98.79	89.38	82.45
30,000	225.45	211.83	200.04	189.74	180.67	172.62	165.43	158.98	134.59	118.54	107.25	98.94
35,000	263.03	247.13	233.38	221.37	210.78	201.39	193.00	185.47	157.02	138.30	125.13	115.43
40,000	300.60	282.44	266.72	252.99	240.89	230.16	220.58	211.97	179.45	158.05	143.00	131.92
45,000	338.17	317.74	300.06	284.61	271.00	258.93	248.15	238.46	201.88	177.01	160.88	148.41
50,000	375.75	353.05	333.40	316.24	301.12	287.70	275.72	264.96	224.31	197.57	178.75	164.89
55,000	413.32	388.35	366.74	347.86	331.23	316.47	303.29	291.45	246.74	217.32	196.63	181.38
60,000	450.90	423.65	400.08	379.48	361.34	345.24	330.86	317.95	269.18	237.08	214.50	197.87
65,000	488.47	458.96	433.42	411.10	391.45	374.01	358.43	344.44	291.61	256.83	232.38	214.36
70,000	526.05	494.26	466.76	442.73	421.56	402.78	386.00	370.94	314.04	276.59	250.25	230.85
75,000	563.62	529.57	500.10	474.35	451.67	431.55	413.58	397.43	336.47	296.35	268.13	247.34
80,000	601.19	564.87	533.44	505.97	481.78	460.32	441.15	423.93	358.90	316.10	286.00	263.83
85,000	638.77	600.17	566.78	537.60	511.89	489.09	468.72	450.42	381.33	335.86	303.88	280.32
90,000	676.34	635.48	600.12	569.22	542.00	517.86	496.29	476.92	403.76	355.61	321.75	296.81
95,000	713.92	670.78	633.45	600.84	572.12	546.63	523.86	503.41	426.19	375.37	339.63	313.29
100,000	751.49	706.09	666.79	632.47	602.23	575.39	551.43	529.91	448.62	395.13	357.50	329.78
105,000	789.07	741.39	700.13	664.09	632.34	604.16	579.00	556.40	471.05	414.88	375.37	346.27
110,000	826.64	776.70	733.47	695.71	662.45	632.93	606.57	582.90	493.48	434.64	393.25	362.76
115,000	864.21	812.00	766.81	727.34	692.56	661.70	634.15	609.39	515.91	454.39	411.12	379.25
120,000	901.79	847.30	800.15	758.96	722.67	690.47	661.72	635.80	538.36	474.16	429.00	395.74
125,000	939.36	882.61	833.49	790.58	752.78	719.24	689.29	662.38	560.78	493.91	446.87	412.23
130,000	976.94	917.91	866.83	822.20	782.89	748.01	716.86	688.88	583.21	513.66	464.75	428.72
135,000	1014.51	953.22	900.17	853.83	813.00	776.78	744.43	715.37	605.64	533.42	482.62	445.21
140,000	1052.09	988.52	933.51	885.45	843.12	805.55	772.00	741.87	628.07	553.17	500.50	461.69
145,000	1089.66	1023.82	966.85	917.07	873.23	834.32	799.57	768.36	650.50	572.93	518.37	478.18
150,000	1127.23	1059.13	1000.19	948.70	903.34	863.09	827.15	794.86	672.93	592.69	536.25	494.67
155,000	1164.81	1094.43	1033.53	980.32	933.45	891.86	854.72	821.35	695.36	612.44	554.12	511.16
160,000	1202.38	1129.74	1066.87	1011.94	963.56	920.63	882.29	847.85	717.79	632.20	572.00	527.65
165,000	1239.96	1165.04	1100.21	1043.57	993.67	949.40	909.86	874.34	740.22	651.95	589.87	544.14
170,000	1277.53	1200.34	1133.55	1075.19	1023.78	978.17	937.43	900.84	762.65	671.71	607.75	560.63
175,000	1315.11	1235.65	1166.89	1106.81	1053.89	1006.94	965.00	927.34	785.08	691.47	625.62	577.12
180,000	1352.68	1270.95	1200.23	1138.44	1084.00	1035.71	992.57	953.83	807.52	711.22	643.50	593.61
185,000	1390.25	1306.26	1233.57	1170.06	1114.12	1064.48	1020.15	980.33	829.95	730.98	661.37	610.09
190,000	1427.83	1341.56	1266.90	1201.68	1144.23	1093.25	1047.72	1006.82	852.38	750.73	679.25	626.58
195,000	1465.40	1376.87	1300.24	1233.30	1174.34	1122.02	1075.29	1033.32	874.81	770.49	697.12	643.07
200,000	1502.98	1412.17	1333.58	1264.93	1204.45	1150.78	1102.86	1059.81	897.24	790.25	715.00	659.56
205,000	1540.55	1447.47	1366.92	1296.55	1234.56	1179.55	1130.43	1086.31	919.67	810.00	732.87	676.05
210,000	1578.13	1482.78	1400.26	1328.17	1264.67	1208.32	1158.00	1112.80	942.10	829.76	750.74	692.54
215,000	1615.70	1518.08	1433.60	1359.80	1294.78	1237.09	1185.57	1139.30	964.53	849.51	768.62	709.03
220,000	1653.28	1553.39	1466.94	1391.42	1324.89	1265.86	1213.14	1165.79	986.96	869.27	786.49	725.52
225,000	1690.85	1588.69	1500.28	1423.04	1355.00	1294.63	1240.72	1192.29	1009.39	889.03	804.37	742.01
230,000	1728.42	1623.99	1533.62	1454.67	1385.12	1323.40	1268.29	1218.78	1031.82	908.78	822.24	758.49
235,000	1766.00	1659.30	1566.96	1486.29	1415.23	1352.17	1295.86	1245.28	1054.25	928.54	840.12	774.98
240,000	1803.57	1694.60	1600.30	1517.91	1445.34	1380.94	1323.43	1271.77	1076.69	948.30	857.99	791.47
245,000	1841.15	1729.91	1633.64	1549.53	1475.45	1409.71	1351.00	1298.27	1099.12	968.05	875.87	807.96
250,000	1878.72	1765.21	1666.98	1581.16	1505.56	1438.48	1378.57	1324.76	1121.55	987.81	893.74	824.45
255,000	1916.30	1800.51	1700.32	1612.78	1535.67	1467.25	1406.14	1351.26	1143.98	1007.56	911.62	840.94
260,000	1953.87	1835.82	1733.66	1644.40	1565.78	1496.02	1433.72	1377.75	1166.41	1027.32	929.49	857.43
265,000	1991.44	1871.12	1767.00	1676.03	1595.89	1524.79	1461.29	1404.25	1188.84	1047.08	947.37	873.92
270,000	2029.02	1906.43	1800.34	1707.65	1626.00	1553.56	1488.86	1430.74	1211.27	1066.83	965.24	890.41
280,000	2104.17	1977.04	1867.01	1770.90	1686.23	1611.10	1544.00	1483.73	1256.13	1106.34	1000.99	923.38
290,000	2179.32	2047.64	1933.69	1834.14	1746.45	1668.64	1599.14	1536.72	1300.99	1145.86	1036.74	956.36
300,000	2254.46	2118.25	2000.37	1897.39	1806.67	1726.17	1654.29	1589.71	1345.86	1185.37	1072.49	989.34

AMOUNT OF LOAN	NUMBER OF YEARS IN TERM											
	1	2	3	4	5	6	7	8	9	10	11	12
$ 50	4.23	2.15	1.45	1.11	0.90	0.76	0.66	0.59	0.53	0.48	0.44	0.41
100	8.46	4.29	2.90	2.21	1.79	1.51	1.32	1.17	1.05	0.96	0.88	0.82
200	16.92	8.58	5.80	4.41	3.58	3.02	2.63	2.33	2.10	1.91	1.76	1.64
300	25.38	12.87	8.70	6.61	5.36	4.53	3.94	3.49	3.14	2.87	2.64	2.45
400	33.84	17.15	11.59	8.81	7.15	6.04	5.25	4.65	4.19	3.82	3.52	3.27
500	42.29	21.44	14.49	11.02	8.93	7.55	6.56	5.81	5.24	4.78	4.40	4.09
600	50.75	25.73	17.39	13.22	10.72	9.05	7.87	6.97	6.28	5.73	5.28	4.90
700	59.21	30.01	20.28	15.42	12.51	10.56	9.18	8.14	7.33	6.68	6.16	5.72
800	67.67	34.30	23.18	17.62	14.29	12.07	10.49	9.30	8.38	7.64	7.04	6.53
900	76.13	38.59	26.08	19.83	16.08	13.58	11.80	10.46	9.42	8.59	7.91	7.35
1,000	84.58	42.88	28.98	22.03	17.86	15.09	13.11	11.62	10.47	9.55	8.79	8.17
2,000	169.16	85.75	57.95	44.05	35.72	30.17	26.21	23.24	20.93	19.09	17.58	16.33
3,000	253.74	128.62	86.92	66.08	53.58	45.25	39.31	34.85	31.39	28.63	26.37	24.49
4,000	338.32	171.49	115.89	88.10	71.44	60.33	52.41	46.47	41.86	38.17	35.16	32.65
5,000	422.90	214.36	144.86	110.13	89.29	75.42	65.51	58.09	52.32	47.71	43.94	40.81
6,000	507.48	257.23	173.83	132.15	107.15	90.50	78.61	69.70	62.78	57.25	52.73	48.97
7,000	592.06	300.10	202.80	154.17	125.01	105.58	91.71	81.32	73.25	66.79	61.52	57.13
8,000	676.64	342.97	231.77	176.20	142.87	120.66	104.81	92.94	83.71	76.33	70.31	65.29
9,000	761.22	385.84	260.75	198.22	160.73	135.74	117.91	104.55	94.17	85.87	79.10	73.45
10,000	845.80	428.71	289.72	220.25	178.58	150.83	131.01	116.17	104.63	95.42	87.88	81.62
15,000	1268.70	643.07	434.57	330.37	267.87	226.24	196.52	174.25	156.95	143.12	131.82	122.42
20,000	1691.60	857.42	579.43	440.49	357.16	301.65	262.02	232.33	209.26	190.83	175.76	163.23
25,000	2114.50	1071.77	724.28	550.61	446.45	377.06	327.53	290.41	261.58	238.53	219.70	204.03
30,000	2537.40	1286.13	869.14	660.73	535.74	452.47	393.03	348.50	313.89	286.24	263.64	244.84
35,000	2960.30	1500.48	1014.00	770.85	625.03	527.88	458.54	406.58	366.21	333.94	307.58	285.64
40,000	3383.20	1714.83	1158.85	880.97	714.32	603.29	524.04	464.66	418.52	381.65	351.52	326.45
45,000	3806.10	1929.19	1303.71	991.09	803.61	678.70	589.55	522.74	470.83	429.35	395.46	367.25
50,000	4229.00	2143.54	1448.56	1101.21	892.90	754.11	655.05	580.82	523.15	477.06	439.40	408.06
55,000	4651.90	2357.89	1593.42	1211.33	982.18	829.52	720.56	638.90	575.46	524.77	483.34	448.86
60,000	5074.80	2572.25	1738.27	1321.45	1071.47	904.93	786.06	696.99	627.78	572.47	527.28	489.67
65,000	5497.70	2786.60	1883.13	1431.57	1160.76	980.34	851.57	755.07	680.09	620.18	571.22	530.47
70,000	5920.60	3000.96	2027.99	1541.69	1250.05	1055.75	917.07	813.15	732.41	667.88	615.16	571.28
75,000	6343.49	3215.31	2172.84	1651.81	1339.34	1131.16	982.57	871.23	784.72	715.59	659.10	612.09
80,000	6766.39	3429.66	2317.70	1761.93	1428.63	1206.57	1048.08	929.31	837.03	763.29	703.04	652.89
85,000	7189.29	3644.02	2462.55	1872.05	1517.92	1281.98	1113.58	987.40	889.35	811.00	746.98	693.70
90,000	7612.19	3858.37	2607.41	1982.17	1607.21	1357.39	1179.09	1045.48	941.66	858.70	790.91	734.50
95,000	8035.09	4072.72	2752.27	2092.29	1696.50	1432.80	1244.59	1103.56	993.98	906.41	834.85	775.31
100,000	8457.99	4287.08	2897.12	2202.41	1785.79	1508.21	1310.10	1161.64	1046.29	954.12	878.79	816.11
105,000	8880.89	4501.43	3041.98	2312.53	1875.08	1583.62	1375.60	1219.72	1098.61	1001.82	922.73	856.92
110,000	9303.79	4715.78	3186.83	2422.65	1964.36	1659.03	1441.11	1277.80	1150.92	1049.53	966.67	897.72
115,000	9726.69	4930.14	3331.69	2532.77	2053.65	1734.45	1506.61	1335.89	1203.23	1097.23	1010.61	938.53
120,000	10149.59	5144.49	3476.54	2642.89	2142.94	1809.86	1572.12	1393.97	1255.55	1144.94	1054.55	979.33
125,000	10572.49	5358.84	3621.40	2753.01	2232.23	1885.27	1637.62	1452.05	1307.86	1192.64	1098.49	1020.14
130,000	10995.39	5573.20	3766.26	2863.13	2321.52	1960.68	1703.13	1510.13	1360.18	1240.35	1142.43	1060.94
135,000	11418.29	5787.55	3911.11	2973.25	2410.81	2036.09	1768.63	1568.21	1412.49	1288.05	1186.37	1101.75
140,000	11841.19	6001.91	4055.97	3083.37	2500.10	2111.50	1834.13	1626.30	1464.81	1335.76	1230.31	1142.55
145,000	12264.08	6216.26	4200.82	3193.49	2589.39	2186.91	1899.64	1684.38	1517.12	1383.46	1274.25	1183.36
150,000	12686.98	6430.61	4345.68	3303.61	2678.68	2262.32	1965.14	1742.46	1569.43	1431.17	1318.19	1224.17
155,000	13109.88	6644.97	4490.54	3413.73	2767.97	2337.73	2030.65	1800.54	1621.75	1478.88	1362.13	1264.97
160,000	13532.78	6859.32	4635.39	3523.85	2857.25	2413.14	2096.15	1858.62	1674.06	1526.58	1406.07	1305.78
165,000	13955.68	7073.67	4780.25	3633.97	2946.54	2488.55	2161.66	1916.70	1726.38	1574.29	1450.01	1346.58
170,000	14378.58	7288.03	4925.10	3744.09	3035.83	2563.96	2227.16	1974.79	1778.69	1621.99	1493.95	1387.39
175,000	14801.48	7502.38	5069.96	3854.21	3125.12	2639.37	2292.67	2032.87	1831.01	1669.70	1537.88	1428.19
180,000	15224.38	7716.73	5214.81	3964.33	3214.41	2714.78	2358.17	2090.95	1883.32	1717.40	1581.82	1469.00
185,000	15647.28	7931.09	5359.67	4074.45	3303.70	2790.19	2423.68	2149.03	1935.63	1765.11	1625.76	1509.80
190,000	16070.18	8145.44	5504.53	4184.57	3392.99	2865.60	2489.18	2207.11	1987.95	1812.81	1669.70	1550.61
195,000	16493.08	8359.79	5649.38	4294.69	3482.28	2941.01	2554.69	2265.20	2040.26	1860.52	1713.64	1591.41
200,000	16915.98	8574.15	5794.24	4404.81	3571.57	3016.42	2620.19	2323.28	2092.58	1908.23	1757.58	1632.22
205,000	17338.88	8788.50	5939.09	4514.93	3660.86	3091.83	2685.70	2381.36	2144.89	1955.93	1801.52	1673.02
210,000	17761.78	9002.86	6083.95	4625.05	3750.15	3167.24	2751.20	2439.44	2197.21	2003.64	1845.46	1713.83
215,000	18184.68	9217.21	6228.81	4735.17	3839.43	3242.65	2816.70	2497.52	2249.52	2051.34	1889.40	1754.63
220,000	18607.57	9431.56	6373.66	4845.29	3928.72	3318.06	2882.21	2555.60	2301.83	2099.05	1933.34	1795.44
225,000	19030.47	9645.92	6518.52	4955.41	4018.01	3393.48	2947.71	2613.69	2354.15	2146.75	1977.28	1836.25
230,000	19453.37	9860.27	6663.37	5065.53	4107.30	3468.89	3013.22	2671.77	2406.46	2194.46	2021.22	1877.05
235,000	19876.27	10074.62	6808.23	5175.65	4196.59	3544.30	3078.72	2729.85	2458.78	2242.16	2065.16	1917.86
240,000	20299.17	10288.98	6953.08	5285.77	4285.88	3619.71	3144.23	2787.93	2511.09	2289.87	2109.10	1958.66
245,000	20722.07	10503.33	7097.94	5395.89	4375.17	3695.12	3209.73	2846.01	2563.41	2337.58	2153.04	1999.47
250,000	21144.97	10717.68	7242.80	5506.01	4464.46	3770.53	3275.24	2904.10	2615.72	2385.28	2196.98	2040.27
255,000	21567.87	10932.04	7387.65	5616.13	4553.75	3845.94	3340.74	2962.18	2668.03	2432.99	2240.92	2081.08
260,000	21990.77	11146.39	7532.51	5726.25	4643.04	3921.35	3406.25	3020.26	2720.35	2480.69	2284.85	2121.88
265,000	22413.67	11360.74	7677.36	5836.37	4732.32	3996.76	3471.75	3078.34	2772.66	2528.40	2328.79	2162.69
270,000	22836.57	11575.10	7822.22	5946.49	4821.61	4072.17	3537.26	3136.42	2824.98	2576.10	2372.73	2203.49
280,000	23682.37	12003.81	8111.93	6166.73	5000.19	4222.99	3668.26	3252.59	2929.61	2671.51	2460.61	2285.10
290,000	24528.16	12432.51	8401.64	6386.97	5178.77	4373.81	3799.27	3368.75	3034.23	2766.92	2548.49	2366.71
300,000	25373.96	12861.22	8691.35	6607.21	5357.35	4524.63	3930.28	3484.91	3138.86	2862.34	2636.37	2448.33

AMOUNT OF LOAN	NUMBER OF YEARS IN TERM											
	13	14	15	16	17	18	19	20	25	30	35	40
$ 50	0.39	0.36	0.34	0.33	0.31	0.30	0.29	0.28	0.24	0.21	0.19	0.18
100	0.77	0.72	0.68	0.65	0.62	0.59	0.57	0.55	0.47	0.41	0.38	0.35
200	1.53	1.44	1.36	1.29	1.23	1.18	1.13	1.09	0.93	0.82	0.75	0.69
300	2.29	2.16	2.04	1.94	1.85	1.77	1.70	1.63	1.39	1.23	1.12	1.04
400	3.06	2.88	2.72	2.58	2.46	2.35	2.26	2.17	1.85	1.64	1.49	1.38
500	3.82	3.59	3.40	3.23	3.08	2.94	2.82	2.72	2.31	2.05	1.86	1.72
600	4.58	4.31	4.08	3.87	3.69	3.53	3.39	3.26	2.77	2.45	2.23	2.07
700	5.35	5.03	4.76	4.52	4.30	4.12	3.95	3.80	3.23	2.86	2.60	2.41
800	6.11	5.75	5.43	5.16	4.92	4.70	4.51	4.34	3.70	3.27	2.97	2.75
900	6.87	6.47	6.11	5.80	5.53	5.29	5.08	4.88	4.16	3.68	3.34	3.10
1,000	7.64	7.18	6.79	6.45	6.15	5.88	5.64	5.43	4.62	4.09	3.72	3.44
2,000	15.27	14.36	13.58	12.89	12.29	11.75	11.28	10.85	9.23	8.17	7.43	6.88
3,000	22.90	21.54	20.36	19.34	18.43	17.63	16.91	16.27	13.84	12.25	11.14	10.32
4,000	30.53	28.72	27.15	25.78	24.57	23.50	22.55	21.69	18.46	16.33	14.85	13.75
5,000	38.16	35.90	33.94	32.22	30.72	29.38	28.19	27.11	23.07	20.42	18.56	17.19
6,000	45.79	43.07	40.72	38.67	36.86	35.25	33.82	32.53	27.68	24.50	22.27	20.63
7,000	53.43	50.25	47.51	45.11	43.00	41.13	39.46	37.96	32.30	28.58	25.98	24.07
8,000	61.06	57.43	54.29	51.56	49.14	47.00	45.09	43.38	36.91	32.66	29.69	27.50
9,000	68.69	64.61	61.08	58.00	55.29	52.88	50.73	48.80	41.52	36.75	33.40	30.94
10,000	76.32	71.79	67.87	64.44	61.43	58.75	56.37	54.22	46.14	40.83	37.11	34.38
15,000	114.48	107.68	101.80	96.66	92.14	88.13	84.55	81.33	69.20	61.24	55.66	51.56
20,000	152.63	143.57	135.73	128.88	122.85	117.50	112.73	108.44	92.27	81.65	74.21	68.75
25,000	190.79	179.46	169.66	161.10	153.56	146.88	140.91	135.55	115.33	102.07	92.76	85.94
30,000	228.95	215.35	203.59	193.32	184.27	176.25	169.09	162.65	138.40	122.48	111.32	103.12
35,000	267.11	251.25	237.52	225.54	214.98	205.62	197.27	189.76	161.46	142.89	129.87	120.31
40,000	305.26	287.14	271.45	257.76	245.70	235.00	225.45	216.87	184.53	163.30	148.42	137.50
45,000	343.42	323.03	305.38	289.98	276.41	264.37	253.63	243.98	207.59	183.71	166.97	154.68
50,000	381.58	358.92	339.32	322.19	307.12	293.75	281.81	271.09	230.66	204.13	185.52	171.87
55,000	419.74	394.81	373.25	354.41	337.83	323.12	309.99	298.20	253.73	224.54	204.07	189.06
60,000	457.89	430.70	407.18	386.63	368.54	352.49	338.17	325.30	276.79	244.95	222.63	206.24
65,000	496.05	466.59	441.11	418.85	399.25	381.87	366.35	352.41	299.86	265.36	241.18	223.43
70,000	534.21	502.49	475.04	451.07	429.96	411.24	394.53	379.52	322.92	285.77	259.73	240.61
75,000	572.37	538.38	508.97	483.29	460.67	440.62	422.71	406.63	345.99	306.19	278.28	257.80
80,000	610.52	574.27	542.90	515.51	491.39	469.99	450.89	433.74	369.05	326.60	296.83	274.99
85,000	648.68	610.16	576.83	547.73	522.10	499.36	479.07	460.85	392.12	347.01	315.38	292.17
90,000	686.84	646.05	610.76	579.95	552.81	528.74	507.25	487.95	415.18	367.42	333.94	309.36
95,000	725.00	681.94	644.70	612.17	583.52	558.11	535.43	515.06	438.25	387.83	352.49	326.55
100,000	763.15	717.83	678.63	644.38	614.23	587.49	563.61	542.17	461.32	408.25	371.04	343.73
105,000	801.31	753.73	712.56	676.60	644.94	616.86	591.79	569.28	484.38	428.66	389.59	360.92
110,000	839.47	789.62	746.49	708.82	675.65	646.23	619.97	596.39	507.45	449.07	408.14	378.11
115,000	877.63	825.51	780.42	741.04	706.37	675.61	648.15	623.50	530.51	469.48	426.69	395.29
120,000	915.78	861.40	814.35	773.26	737.08	704.98	676.33	650.60	553.58	489.89	445.25	412.40
125,000	953.94	897.29	848.28	805.48	767.79	734.36	704.51	677.71	576.64	510.31	463.80	429.66
130,000	992.00	933.18	882.21	837.70	798.50	763.73	732.69	704.82	599.71	530.72	482.35	446.85
135,000	1030.26	969.07	916.14	869.92	829.21	793.10	760.87	731.93	622.77	551.13	500.90	464.04
140,000	1068.41	1004.97	950.08	902.14	859.92	822.48	789.05	759.04	645.84	571.54	519.45	481.22
145,000	1106.57	1040.86	984.01	934.36	890.63	851.85	817.23	786.15	668.91	591.95	538.01	498.41
150,000	1144.73	1076.75	1017.94	966.57	921.34	881.23	845.41	813.25	691.97	612.37	556.56	515.60
155,000	1182.88	1112.64	1051.87	998.79	952.06	910.60	873.59	840.36	715.04	632.78	575.11	532.78
160,000	1221.04	1148.53	1085.80	1031.01	982.77	939.97	901.77	867.47	738.10	653.19	593.66	549.97
165,000	1259.20	1184.42	1119.73	1063.23	1013.48	969.35	929.95	894.58	761.17	673.60	612.21	567.16
170,000	1297.36	1220.31	1153.66	1095.45	1044.19	998.72	958.13	921.69	784.23	694.02	630.76	584.34
175,000	1335.51	1256.21	1187.59	1127.67	1074.90	1028.10	986.31	948.80	807.30	714.43	649.32	601.53
180,000	1373.67	1292.10	1221.52	1159.89	1105.61	1057.47	1014.49	975.90	830.36	734.84	667.87	618.72
185,000	1411.83	1327.99	1255.46	1192.11	1136.32	1086.84	1042.67	1003.01	853.43	755.25	686.42	635.90
190,000	1449.99	1363.88	1289.39	1224.33	1167.04	1116.22	1070.85	1030.12	876.50	775.66	704.97	653.09
195,000	1488.14	1399.77	1323.32	1256.55	1197.75	1145.59	1099.03	1057.23	899.56	796.08	723.52	670.27
200,000	1526.30	1435.66	1357.25	1288.76	1228.46	1174.97	1127.21	1084.34	922.63	816.49	742.07	687.46
205,000	1564.46	1471.55	1391.18	1320.98	1259.17	1204.34	1155.39	1111.45	945.69	836.90	760.63	704.65
210,000	1602.62	1507.45	1425.11	1353.20	1289.88	1233.71	1183.57	1138.55	968.76	857.31	779.18	721.83
215,000	1640.77	1543.34	1459.04	1385.42	1320.59	1263.09	1211.75	1165.66	991.82	877.72	797.73	739.02
220,000	1678.93	1579.23	1492.97	1417.64	1351.30	1292.46	1239.93	1192.77	1014.89	898.14	816.28	756.21
225,000	1717.09	1615.12	1526.90	1449.86	1382.01	1321.84	1268.11	1219.88	1037.95	918.55	834.83	773.39
230,000	1755.25	1651.01	1560.83	1482.08	1412.73	1351.21	1296.29	1246.99	1061.02	938.96	853.38	790.58
235,000	1793.40	1686.90	1594.77	1514.30	1443.44	1380.58	1324.47	1274.10	1084.09	959.37	871.94	807.77
240,000	1831.56	1722.80	1628.70	1546.52	1474.15	1409.96	1352.65	1301.20	1107.15	979.78	890.49	824.95
245,000	1869.72	1758.69	1662.63	1578.73	1504.86	1439.33	1380.84	1328.31	1130.22	1000.20	909.04	842.14
250,000	1907.88	1794.58	1696.56	1610.95	1535.57	1468.71	1409.02	1355.42	1153.28	1020.61	927.59	859.32
255,000	1946.03	1830.47	1730.49	1643.17	1566.28	1498.08	1437.20	1382.53	1176.35	1041.02	946.14	876.51
260,000	1984.19	1866.36	1764.42	1675.39	1596.99	1527.45	1465.38	1409.64	1199.41	1061.43	964.70	893.70
265,000	2022.35	1902.25	1798.35	1707.61	1627.70	1556.83	1493.56	1436.75	1222.48	1081.84	983.25	910.88
270,000	2060.51	1938.14	1832.28	1739.83	1658.42	1586.20	1521.74	1463.85	1245.54	1102.26	1001.80	928.07
280,000	2136.82	2009.93	1900.15	1804.27	1719.84	1644.95	1578.10	1518.07	1291.68	1143.08	1038.90	962.44
290,000	2213.13	2081.71	1968.01	1868.71	1781.26	1703.70	1634.46	1572.29	1337.81	1183.90	1076.01	996.82
300,000	2289.45	2153.49	2035.87	1933.14	1842.68	1762.45	1690.82	1626.50	1383.94	1224.73	1113.11	1031.19

3.00%

MONTHLY AMORTIZING PAYMENTS

AMOUNT OF LOAN	1	2	3	4	5	6	7	8	9	10	11	12
$ 50	4.24	2.15	1.46	1.11	0.90	0.76	0.67	0.59	0.53	0.49	0.45	0.42
100	8.47	4.30	2.91	2.22	1.80	1.52	1.33	1.18	1.06	0.97	0.90	0.83
200	16.94	8.60	5.82	4.43	3.60	3.04	2.65	2.35	2.12	1.94	1.79	1.66
300	25.41	12.90	8.73	6.65	5.40	4.56	3.97	3.52	3.18	2.90	2.68	2.49
400	33.88	17.20	11.64	8.86	7.19	6.08	5.29	4.70	4.24	3.87	3.57	3.32
500	42.35	21.50	14.55	11.07	8.99	7.60	6.61	5.87	5.29	4.83	4.46	4.14
600	50.82	25.79	17.45	13.29	10.79	9.12	7.93	7.04	6.35	5.80	5.35	4.97
700	59.29	30.09	20.36	15.50	12.58	10.64	9.25	8.22	7.41	6.76	6.24	5.80
800	67.76	34.39	23.27	17.71	14.38	12.16	10.58	9.39	8.47	7.73	7.13	6.63
900	76.23	38.69	26.18	19.93	16.18	13.68	11.90	10.56	9.52	8.70	8.02	7.46
1,000	84.70	42.99	29.09	22.14	17.97	15.20	13.22	11.73	10.58	9.66	8.91	8.28
2,000	169.39	85.97	58.17	44.27	35.94	30.39	26.43	23.46	21.16	19.32	17.81	16.56
3,000	254.09	128.95	87.25	66.41	53.91	45.59	39.64	35.19	31.74	28.97	26.72	24.84
4,000	338.78	171.93	116.33	88.54	71.88	60.78	52.86	46.92	42.31	38.63	35.62	33.12
5,000	423.47	214.91	145.41	110.68	89.85	75.97	66.07	58.65	52.89	48.29	44.52	41.39
6,000	508.17	257.89	174.49	132.81	107.82	91.17	79.28	70.38	63.47	57.94	53.43	49.67
7,000	592.86	300.87	203.57	154.95	125.79	106.36	92.50	82.11	74.04	67.60	62.33	57.95
8,000	677.55	343.85	232.65	177.08	143.75	121.55	105.71	93.84	84.62	77.25	71.24	66.23
9,000	762.25	386.84	261.74	199.21	161.72	136.75	118.92	105.57	95.20	86.91	80.14	74.51
10,000	846.94	429.82	290.82	221.35	179.69	151.94	132.14	117.30	105.77	96.57	89.04	82.78
15,000	1270.41	644.72	436.22	332.02	269.54	227.91	198.20	175.95	158.66	144.85	133.56	124.17
20,000	1693.88	859.63	581.63	442.69	359.38	303.88	264.27	234.60	211.54	193.13	178.08	165.56
25,000	2117.35	1074.54	727.04	553.36	449.22	379.85	330.34	293.24	264.43	241.41	222.60	206.95
30,000	2540.82	1289.44	872.44	664.03	539.07	455.82	396.40	351.89	317.31	289.69	267.12	248.34
35,000	2964.28	1504.35	1017.85	774.71	628.91	531.78	462.47	410.54	370.20	337.97	311.64	289.73
40,000	3387.75	1719.25	1163.25	885.38	718.75	607.75	528.54	469.19	423.08	386.25	356.16	331.12
45,000	3811.22	1934.16	1308.66	996.05	808.60	683.72	594.60	527.84	475.97	434.53	400.67	372.51
50,000	4234.69	2149.07	1454.07	1106.72	898.44	759.69	660.67	586.48	528.85	482.81	445.19	413.90
55,000	4658.16	2363.97	1599.47	1217.39	988.28	835.66	726.74	645.13	581.74	531.09	489.71	455.29
60,000	5081.63	2578.88	1744.88	1328.06	1078.13	911.63	792.80	703.78	634.62	579.37	534.23	496.68
65,000	5505.10	2793.78	1890.28	1438.74	1167.97	987.59	858.87	762.43	687.51	627.65	578.75	538.07
70,000	5928.56	3008.69	2035.69	1549.41	1257.81	1063.56	924.94	821.08	740.39	675.93	623.27	579.46
75,000	6352.03	3223.60	2181.10	1660.08	1347.66	1139.53	991.00	879.72	793.28	724.21	667.79	620.85
80,000	6775.50	3438.50	2326.50	1770.75	1437.50	1215.50	1057.07	938.37	846.16	772.49	712.31	662.23
85,000	7198.97	3653.41	2471.91	1881.42	1527.34	1291.47	1123.14	997.02	899.04	820.77	756.82	703.62
90,000	7622.44	3868.31	2617.31	1992.09	1617.19	1367.44	1189.20	1055.67	951.93	869.05	801.34	745.01
95,000	8045.91	4083.22	2762.72	2102.77	1707.03	1443.40	1255.27	1114.31	1004.81	917.33	845.86	786.40
100,000	8469.37	4298.13	2908.13	2213.44	1796.87	1519.37	1321.34	1172.96	1057.70	965.61	890.38	827.79
105,000	8892.84	4513.03	3053.53	2324.11	1886.72	1595.34	1387.40	1231.61	1110.58	1013.89	934.90	869.18
110,000	9316.31	4727.94	3198.94	2434.78	1976.56	1671.31	1453.47	1290.26	1163.47	1062.17	979.42	910.57
115,000	9739.78	4942.84	3344.34	2545.45	2066.40	1747.28	1519.53	1348.91	1216.35	1110.45	1023.94	951.96
120,000	10163.25	5157.75	3489.75	2656.12	2156.25	1823.25	1585.60	1407.55	1269.24	1158.73	1068.46	993.35
125,000	10586.72	5372.66	3635.16	2766.80	2246.09	1899.21	1651.67	1466.20	1322.12	1207.01	1112.98	1034.74
130,000	11010.19	5587.56	3780.56	2877.47	2335.93	1975.18	1717.73	1524.85	1375.01	1255.29	1157.49	1076.13
135,000	11433.65	5802.47	3925.97	2988.14	2425.78	2051.15	1783.80	1583.50	1427.89	1303.58	1202.01	1117.52
140,000	11857.12	6017.37	4071.37	3098.81	2515.62	2127.12	1849.87	1642.15	1480.78	1351.86	1246.53	1158.91
145,000	12280.59	6232.28	4216.78	3209.48	2605.47	2203.09	1915.93	1700.79	1533.66	1400.14	1291.05	1200.30
150,000	12704.06	6447.19	4362.19	3320.15	2695.31	2279.06	1982.00	1759.44	1586.55	1448.42	1335.57	1241.69
155,000	13127.53	6662.09	4507.59	3430.83	2785.15	2355.02	2048.07	1818.09	1639.43	1496.70	1380.09	1283.07
160,000	13551.00	6877.00	4653.00	3541.50	2875.00	2430.99	2114.13	1876.74	1692.32	1544.98	1424.61	1324.46
165,000	13974.47	7091.90	4798.40	3652.17	2964.84	2506.96	2180.20	1935.38	1745.20	1593.26	1469.13	1365.85
170,000	14397.93	7306.81	4943.81	3762.84	3054.68	2582.93	2246.27	1994.03	1798.08	1641.54	1513.64	1407.24
175,000	14821.40	7521.72	5089.22	3873.51	3144.53	2658.90	2312.33	2052.68	1850.97	1689.82	1558.16	1448.63
180,000	15244.87	7736.62	5234.62	3984.18	3234.37	2734.87	2378.40	2111.33	1903.85	1738.10	1602.68	1490.02
185,000	15668.34	7951.53	5380.03	4094.86	3324.21	2810.84	2444.47	2169.98	1956.74	1786.38	1647.20	1531.41
190,000	16091.81	8166.44	5525.43	4205.53	3414.06	2886.80	2510.53	2228.62	2009.62	1834.66	1691.72	1572.80
195,000	16515.28	8381.34	5670.84	4316.20	3503.90	2962.77	2576.60	2287.27	2062.51	1882.94	1736.24	1614.19
200,000	16938.74	8596.25	5816.25	4426.87	3593.74	3038.74	2642.67	2345.92	2115.39	1931.22	1780.76	1655.58
205,000	17362.21	8811.15	5961.65	4537.54	3683.59	3114.71	2708.73	2404.57	2168.28	1979.50	1825.28	1696.97
210,000	17785.68	9026.06	6107.06	4648.21	3773.43	3190.68	2774.80	2463.22	2221.16	2027.78	1869.80	1738.36
215,000	18209.15	9240.97	6252.47	4758.89	3863.27	3266.65	2840.86	2521.86	2274.05	2076.06	1914.31	1779.75
220,000	18632.62	9455.87	6397.87	4869.56	3953.12	3342.61	2906.93	2580.51	2326.93	2124.34	1958.83	1821.14
225,000	19056.09	9670.78	6543.28	4980.23	4042.96	3418.58	2973.00	2639.16	2379.82	2172.62	2003.35	1862.53
230,000	19479.56	9885.68	6688.68	5090.90	4132.80	3494.55	3039.06	2697.81	2432.70	2220.90	2047.87	1903.91
235,000	19903.02	10100.59	6834.09	5201.57	4222.65	3570.52	3105.13	2756.45	2485.59	2269.18	2092.39	1945.30
240,000	20326.49	10315.50	6979.50	5312.24	4312.49	3646.49	3171.20	2815.10	2538.47	2317.46	2136.91	1986.69
245,000	20749.96	10530.40	7124.90	5422.92	4402.33	3722.46	3237.26	2873.75	2591.36	2365.74	2181.43	2028.08
250,000	21173.43	10745.31	7270.31	5533.59	4492.18	3798.42	3303.33	2932.40	2644.24	2414.02	2225.95	2069.47
255,000	21596.90	10960.21	7415.71	5644.26	4582.02	3874.39	3369.40	2991.05	2697.12	2462.30	2270.46	2110.86
260,000	22020.37	11175.12	7561.12	5754.93	4671.86	3950.36	3435.46	3049.69	2750.01	2510.58	2314.98	2152.25
265,000	22443.84	11390.03	7706.53	5865.60	4761.71	4026.33	3501.53	3108.34	2802.89	2558.86	2359.50	2193.64
270,000	22867.30	11604.93	7851.93	5976.27	4851.55	4102.30	3567.60	3166.99	2855.78	2607.15	2404.02	2235.03
280,000	23714.24	12034.74	8142.74	6197.62	5031.24	4254.23	3699.73	3284.29	2961.55	2703.71	2493.06	2317.81
290,000	24561.18	12464.56	8433.56	6418.96	5210.93	4406.17	3831.86	3401.58	3067.32	2800.27	2582.10	2400.59
300,000	25408.11	12894.37	8724.37	6640.30	5390.61	4558.11	3964.00	3518.88	3173.09	2896.83	2671.13	2483.37

10

AMOUNT OF LOAN	NUMBER OF YEARS IN TERM											
	13	14	15	16	17	18	19	20	25	30	35	40
$ 50	0.39	0.37	0.35	0.33	0.32	0.30	0.29	0.28	0.24	0.22	0.20	0.18
100	0.78	0.73	0.70	0.66	0.63	0.60	0.58	0.56	0.48	0.43	0.39	0.36
200	1.55	1.46	1.39	1.32	1.26	1.20	1.16	1.11	0.95	0.85	0.77	0.72
300	2.33	2.19	2.08	1.97	1.88	1.80	1.73	1.67	1.43	1.27	1.16	1.08
400	3.10	2.92	2.77	2.63	2.51	2.40	2.31	2.22	1.90	1.69	1.54	1.44
500	3.88	3.65	3.46	3.29	3.14	3.00	2.88	2.78	2.38	2.11	1.93	1.79
600	4.65	4.38	4.15	3.94	3.76	3.60	3.46	3.33	2.85	2.53	2.31	2.15
700	5.43	5.11	4.84	4.60	4.39	4.20	4.04	3.89	3.32	2.96	2.70	2.51
800	6.20	5.84	5.53	5.26	5.02	4.80	4.61	4.44	3.80	3.38	3.08	2.87
900	6.98	6.57	6.22	5.91	5.64	5.40	5.19	5.00	4.27	3.80	3.47	3.23
1,000	7.75	7.30	6.91	6.57	6.27	6.00	5.76	5.55	4.75	4.22	3.85	3.58
2,000	15.50	14.60	13.82	13.13	12.53	12.00	11.52	11.10	9.49	8.44	7.70	7.16
3,000	23.25	21.90	20.72	19.70	18.80	18.00	17.28	16.64	14.23	12.65	11.55	10.74
4,000	31.00	29.19	27.63	26.26	25.06	23.99	23.04	22.19	18.97	16.87	15.40	14.32
5,000	38.75	36.49	34.53	32.83	31.32	29.99	28.80	27.73	23.72	21.09	19.25	17.90
6,000	46.50	43.79	41.44	39.39	37.59	35.99	34.56	33.28	28.46	25.30	23.10	21.48
7,000	54.25	51.08	48.35	45.96	43.85	41.99	40.32	38.83	33.20	29.52	26.94	25.06
8,000	62.00	58.38	55.25	52.52	50.11	47.98	46.08	44.37	37.94	33.73	30.79	28.64
9,000	69.75	65.68	62.16	59.08	56.38	53.98	51.84	49.92	42.68	37.95	34.64	32.22
10,000	77.50	72.97	69.06	65.65	62.64	59.98	57.60	55.46	47.43	42.17	38.49	35.80
15,000	116.24	109.46	103.59	98.47	93.96	89.96	86.40	83.19	71.14	63.25	57.73	53.70
20,000	154.99	145.94	138.12	131.29	125.28	119.95	115.19	110.92	94.85	84.33	76.98	71.60
25,000	193.74	182.43	172.65	164.11	156.60	149.94	143.99	138.65	118.56	105.41	96.22	89.50
30,000	232.48	218.91	207.18	196.94	187.92	179.92	172.79	166.38	142.27	126.49	115.46	107.40
35,000	271.23	255.40	241.71	229.76	219.24	209.91	201.58	194.11	165.98	147.57	134.70	125.30
40,000	309.97	291.88	276.24	262.58	250.55	239.89	230.38	221.84	189.69	168.65	153.95	143.20
45,000	348.72	328.37	310.77	295.40	281.87	269.88	259.18	249.57	213.40	189.73	173.19	161.10
50,000	387.47	364.85	345.30	328.22	313.19	299.87	287.98	277.30	237.11	210.81	192.43	179.00
55,000	426.21	401.34	379.82	361.04	344.51	329.85	316.77	305.03	260.82	231.89	211.67	196.90
60,000	464.96	437.82	414.35	393.87	375.83	359.84	345.57	332.76	284.53	252.97	230.92	214.80
65,000	503.70	474.31	448.88	426.69	407.15	389.83	374.37	360.49	308.24	274.05	250.16	232.69
70,000	542.45	510.79	483.41	459.51	438.47	419.81	403.16	388.22	331.95	295.13	269.40	250.59
75,000	581.20	547.28	517.94	492.33	469.79	449.80	431.96	415.95	355.66	316.21	288.64	268.49
80,000	619.94	583.76	552.47	525.15	501.10	479.78	460.76	443.68	379.37	337.29	307.89	286.39
85,000	658.69	620.25	587.00	557.97	532.42	509.77	489.55	471.41	403.08	358.37	327.13	304.29
90,000	697.43	656.73	621.53	590.80	563.74	539.76	518.35	499.14	426.80	379.45	346.37	322.19
95,000	736.18	693.22	656.06	623.62	595.06	569.74	547.15	526.87	450.51	400.53	365.61	340.09
100,000	774.93	729.70	690.59	656.44	626.38	599.73	575.95	554.60	474.22	421.61	384.86	357.99
105,000	813.67	766.19	725.12	689.26	657.70	629.71	604.74	582.33	497.93	442.69	404.10	375.89
110,000	852.42	802.67	759.64	722.08	689.02	659.70	633.54	610.06	521.64	463.77	423.34	393.79
115,000	891.16	839.15	794.17	754.90	720.34	689.69	662.34	637.79	545.35	484.85	442.58	411.69
120,000	929.91	875.64	828.70	787.73	751.65	719.67	691.13	665.52	569.06	505.93	461.83	429.59
125,000	968.66	912.12	863.23	820.55	782.97	749.66	719.93	693.25	592.77	527.01	481.07	447.49
130,000	1007.40	948.61	897.76	853.37	814.29	779.65	748.73	720.98	616.48	548.09	500.31	465.38
135,000	1046.15	985.09	932.29	886.19	845.61	809.63	777.53	748.71	640.19	569.17	519.55	483.28
140,000	1084.89	1021.58	966.82	919.01	876.93	839.62	806.32	776.44	663.90	590.25	538.80	501.18
145,000	1123.64	1058.06	1001.35	951.83	908.25	869.60	835.12	804.17	687.61	611.33	558.04	519.08
150,000	1162.39	1094.55	1035.88	984.66	939.57	899.59	863.92	831.90	711.32	632.41	577.28	536.98
155,000	1201.13	1131.03	1070.41	1017.48	970.89	929.58	892.71	859.63	735.03	653.49	596.52	554.88
160,000	1239.88	1167.52	1104.94	1050.30	1002.20	959.56	921.51	887.36	758.74	674.57	615.77	572.78
165,000	1278.62	1204.00	1139.46	1083.12	1033.52	989.55	950.31	915.09	782.45	695.65	635.01	590.68
170,000	1317.37	1240.49	1173.99	1115.94	1064.84	1019.53	979.10	942.82	806.16	716.73	654.25	608.58
175,000	1356.12	1276.97	1208.52	1148.76	1096.16	1049.52	1007.90	970.55	829.87	737.81	673.49	626.48
180,000	1394.86	1313.46	1243.05	1181.59	1127.48	1079.51	1036.70	998.28	853.59	758.89	692.74	644.38
185,000	1433.61	1349.94	1277.58	1214.41	1158.80	1109.49	1065.50	1026.01	877.30	779.97	711.98	662.28
190,000	1472.35	1386.43	1312.11	1247.23	1190.12	1139.48	1094.29	1053.74	901.01	801.05	731.22	680.18
195,000	1511.10	1422.91	1346.64	1280.05	1221.44	1169.47	1123.09	1081.47	924.72	822.13	750.46	698.07
200,000	1549.85	1459.40	1381.17	1312.87	1252.75	1199.45	1151.89	1109.20	948.43	843.21	769.71	715.97
205,000	1588.59	1495.88	1415.70	1345.69	1284.07	1229.44	1180.68	1136.93	972.14	864.29	788.95	733.87
210,000	1627.34	1532.37	1450.23	1378.52	1315.39	1259.42	1209.48	1164.66	995.85	885.37	808.19	751.77
215,000	1666.09	1568.85	1484.76	1411.34	1346.71	1289.41	1238.28	1192.39	1019.56	906.45	827.43	769.67
220,000	1704.83	1605.33	1519.28	1444.16	1378.03	1319.40	1267.08	1220.12	1043.27	927.53	846.68	787.57
225,000	1743.58	1641.82	1553.81	1476.98	1409.35	1349.38	1295.87	1247.85	1066.98	948.61	865.92	805.47
230,000	1782.32	1678.30	1588.34	1509.80	1440.67	1379.37	1324.67	1275.58	1090.69	969.69	885.16	823.37
235,000	1821.07	1714.79	1622.87	1542.62	1471.99	1409.35	1353.47	1303.31	1114.40	990.77	904.40	841.27
240,000	1859.82	1751.27	1657.40	1575.45	1503.30	1439.34	1382.26	1331.04	1138.11	1011.85	923.65	859.17
245,000	1898.56	1787.76	1691.93	1608.27	1534.62	1469.33	1411.06	1358.77	1161.82	1032.93	942.89	877.07
250,000	1937.31	1824.24	1726.46	1641.09	1565.94	1499.31	1439.86	1386.50	1185.53	1054.02	962.13	894.97
255,000	1976.05	1860.73	1760.99	1673.91	1597.26	1529.30	1468.65	1414.23	1209.24	1075.10	981.37	912.87
260,000	2014.80	1897.21	1795.52	1706.73	1628.58	1559.29	1497.45	1441.96	1232.95	1096.18	1000.62	930.76
265,000	2053.55	1933.70	1830.05	1739.55	1659.90	1589.27	1526.25	1469.69	1256.66	1117.26	1019.86	948.66
270,000	2092.29	1970.18	1864.58	1772.38	1691.22	1619.26	1555.05	1497.42	1280.38	1138.34	1039.10	966.56
280,000	2169.78	2043.15	1933.63	1838.02	1753.85	1679.23	1612.64	1552.88	1327.80	1180.50	1077.59	1002.36
290,000	2247.28	2116.12	2002.69	1903.66	1816.49	1739.20	1670.23	1608.34	1375.22	1222.66	1116.07	1038.16
300,000	2324.77	2189.09	2071.75	1969.31	1879.13	1799.17	1727.83	1663.80	1422.64	1264.82	1154.56	1073.96

11

3.25% MONTHLY AMORTIZING PAYMENTS

AMOUNT OF LOAN	NUMBER OF YEARS IN TERM											
	1	2	3	4	5	6	7	8	9	10	11	12
$ 50	4.25	2.16	1.46	1.12	0.91	0.77	0.67	0.60	0.54	0.49	0.46	0.42
100	8.49	4.31	2.92	2.23	1.81	1.54	1.34	1.19	1.07	0.98	0.91	0.84
200	16.97	8.62	5.84	4.45	3.62	3.07	2.67	2.37	2.14	1.96	1.81	1.68
300	25.45	12.93	8.76	6.68	5.43	4.60	4.00	3.56	3.21	2.94	2.71	2.52
400	33.93	17.24	11.68	8.90	7.24	6.13	5.34	4.74	4.28	3.91	3.61	3.36
500	42.41	21.55	14.60	11.13	9.05	7.66	6.67	5.93	5.35	4.89	4.52	4.20
600	50.89	25.86	17.52	13.35	10.85	9.19	8.00	7.11	6.42	5.87	5.42	5.04
700	59.37	30.17	20.44	15.58	12.66	10.72	9.33	8.30	7.49	6.85	6.32	5.88
800	67.85	34.48	23.36	17.80	14.47	12.25	10.67	9.48	8.56	7.82	7.22	6.72
900	76.33	38.79	26.28	20.03	16.28	13.78	12.00	10.66	9.63	8.80	8.12	7.56
1,000	84.81	43.10	29.20	22.25	18.09	15.31	13.33	11.85	10.70	9.78	9.03	8.40
2,000	169.62	86.19	58.39	44.49	36.17	30.62	26.66	23.69	21.39	19.55	18.05	16.80
3,000	254.43	129.28	87.58	66.74	54.25	45.92	39.98	35.54	32.08	29.32	27.07	25.19
4,000	339.24	172.37	116.77	88.98	72.33	61.23	53.31	47.38	42.77	39.09	36.09	33.59
5,000	424.04	215.46	145.96	111.23	90.41	76.53	66.64	59.22	53.46	48.86	45.11	41.98
6,000	508.85	258.56	175.15	133.47	108.49	91.84	79.96	71.07	64.16	58.64	54.13	50.38
7,000	593.66	301.65	204.35	155.72	126.57	107.15	93.29	82.91	74.85	68.41	63.15	58.77
8,000	678.47	344.74	233.54	177.96	144.65	122.45	106.62	94.75	85.54	78.18	72.17	67.17
9,000	763.27	387.83	262.73	200.21	162.73	137.76	119.94	106.60	96.23	87.95	81.19	75.57
10,000	848.08	430.92	291.92	222.45	180.81	153.06	133.27	118.44	106.92	97.72	90.21	83.96
15,000	1272.12	646.38	437.88	333.68	271.21	229.59	199.90	177.66	160.38	146.58	135.31	125.94
20,000	1696.16	861.84	583.84	444.90	361.61	306.12	266.53	236.87	213.84	195.44	180.42	167.92
25,000	2120.20	1077.30	729.79	556.13	452.01	382.65	333.16	296.09	267.30	244.30	225.52	209.90
30,000	2544.23	1292.76	875.75	667.35	542.41	459.18	399.79	355.31	320.76	293.16	270.62	251.88
35,000	2968.27	1508.22	1021.71	778.58	632.81	535.71	466.42	414.53	374.22	342.02	315.73	293.85
40,000	3392.31	1723.68	1167.67	889.80	723.21	612.24	533.06	473.74	427.68	390.88	360.83	335.83
45,000	3816.35	1939.14	1313.62	1001.03	813.61	688.77	599.69	532.96	481.14	439.74	405.93	377.81
50,000	4240.39	2154.60	1459.58	1112.25	904.01	765.29	666.32	592.18	534.59	488.60	451.03	419.79
55,000	4664.42	2370.06	1605.54	1223.48	994.41	841.82	732.95	651.40	588.05	537.46	496.14	461.77
60,000	5088.46	2585.52	1751.50	1334.70	1084.81	918.35	799.58	710.61	641.51	586.32	541.24	503.75
65,000	5512.50	2800.98	1897.45	1445.93	1175.21	994.88	866.21	769.83	694.97	635.18	586.34	545.72
70,000	5936.54	3016.44	2043.41	1557.15	1265.61	1071.41	932.84	829.05	748.43	684.04	631.45	587.70
75,000	6360.58	3231.90	2189.37	1668.38	1356.01	1147.94	999.48	888.27	801.89	732.90	676.55	629.68
80,000	6784.61	3447.36	2335.33	1779.60	1446.41	1224.47	1066.11	947.48	855.35	781.76	721.65	671.66
85,000	7208.65	3662.81	2481.28	1890.83	1536.81	1301.00	1132.74	1006.70	908.81	830.62	766.75	713.64
90,000	7632.69	3878.27	2627.24	2002.05	1627.21	1377.53	1199.37	1065.92	962.27	879.48	811.86	755.62
95,000	8056.73	4093.73	2773.20	2113.28	1717.61	1454.05	1266.00	1125.13	1015.73	928.34	856.96	797.60
100,000	8480.77	4309.19	2919.16	2224.50	1808.01	1530.58	1332.63	1184.35	1069.18	977.20	902.06	839.57
105,000	8904.81	4524.65	3065.11	2335.73	1898.41	1607.11	1399.26	1243.57	1122.64	1026.05	947.17	881.55
110,000	9328.84	4740.11	3211.07	2446.95	1988.81	1683.64	1465.90	1302.79	1176.10	1074.91	992.27	923.53
115,000	9752.88	4955.57	3357.03	2558.18	2079.21	1760.17	1532.53	1362.00	1229.56	1123.77	1037.37	965.51
120,000	10176.92	5171.03	3502.99	2669.40	2169.61	1836.70	1599.16	1421.22	1283.02	1172.63	1082.48	1007.49
125,000	10600.96	5386.49	3648.94	2780.63	2260.01	1913.23	1665.79	1480.44	1336.48	1221.49	1127.58	1049.47
130,000	11025.00	5601.95	3794.90	2891.85	2350.41	1989.76	1732.42	1539.66	1389.94	1270.35	1172.68	1091.44
135,000	11449.03	5817.41	3940.86	3003.08	2440.81	2066.29	1799.05	1598.87	1443.40	1319.21	1217.78	1133.42
140,000	11873.07	6032.87	4086.82	3114.30	2531.21	2142.81	1865.68	1658.09	1496.86	1368.07	1262.89	1175.40
145,000	12297.11	6248.33	4232.77	3225.53	2621.61	2219.34	1932.31	1717.31	1550.31	1416.93	1307.99	1217.38
150,000	12721.15	6463.79	4378.73	3336.75	2712.01	2295.87	1998.95	1776.53	1603.77	1465.79	1353.09	1259.36
155,000	13145.19	6679.25	4524.69	3447.98	2802.41	2372.40	2065.58	1835.74	1657.23	1514.65	1398.20	1301.34
160,000	13569.22	6894.71	4670.65	3559.20	2892.81	2448.93	2132.21	1894.96	1710.69	1563.51	1443.30	1343.32
165,000	13993.26	7110.17	4816.61	3670.43	2983.21	2525.46	2198.84	1954.18	1764.15	1612.37	1488.40	1385.29
170,000	14417.30	7325.62	4962.56	3781.65	3073.61	2601.99	2265.47	2013.39	1817.61	1661.23	1533.50	1427.27
175,000	14841.34	7541.08	5108.52	3892.88	3164.01	2678.52	2332.10	2072.61	1871.07	1710.09	1578.61	1469.25
180,000	15265.38	7756.54	5254.48	4004.10	3254.41	2755.05	2398.73	2131.83	1924.53	1758.95	1623.71	1511.23
185,000	15689.41	7972.00	5400.44	4115.33	3344.81	2831.57	2465.37	2191.05	1977.99	1807.81	1668.81	1553.21
190,000	16113.45	8187.46	5546.39	4226.55	3435.21	2908.10	2532.00	2250.26	2031.45	1856.67	1713.92	1595.19
195,000	16537.49	8402.92	5692.35	4337.78	3525.61	2984.63	2598.63	2309.48	2084.90	1905.53	1759.02	1637.16
200,000	16961.53	8618.38	5838.31	4449.00	3616.01	3061.16	2665.26	2368.70	2138.36	1954.39	1804.12	1679.14
205,000	17385.57	8833.84	5984.27	4560.23	3706.41	3137.69	2731.89	2427.92	2191.82	2003.25	1849.22	1721.12
210,000	17809.61	9049.30	6130.22	4671.45	3796.81	3214.22	2798.52	2487.13	2245.28	2052.10	1894.33	1763.10
215,000	18233.64	9264.76	6276.18	4782.68	3887.21	3290.75	2865.15	2546.35	2298.74	2100.96	1939.43	1805.08
220,000	18657.68	9480.22	6422.14	4893.90	3977.61	3367.28	2931.79	2605.57	2352.20	2149.82	1984.53	1847.06
225,000	19081.72	9695.68	6568.10	5005.13	4068.01	3443.81	2998.42	2664.79	2405.66	2198.68	2029.64	1889.04
230,000	19505.76	9911.14	6714.05	5116.35	4158.41	3520.33	3065.05	2724.00	2459.12	2247.54	2074.74	1931.01
235,000	19929.80	10126.60	6860.01	5227.58	4248.81	3596.86	3131.68	2783.22	2512.58	2296.40	2119.84	1972.99
240,000	20353.83	10342.06	7005.97	5338.80	4339.21	3673.39	3198.31	2842.44	2566.04	2345.26	2164.95	2014.97
245,000	20777.87	10557.52	7151.93	5450.03	4429.61	3749.92	3264.94	2901.65	2619.49	2394.12	2210.05	2056.95
250,000	21201.91	10772.98	7297.88	5561.25	4520.01	3826.45	3331.57	2960.87	2672.95	2442.98	2255.15	2098.93
255,000	21625.95	10988.43	7443.84	5672.48	4610.41	3902.98	3398.20	3020.09	2726.41	2491.84	2300.25	2140.91
260,000	22049.99	11203.89	7589.80	5783.70	4700.81	3979.51	3464.84	3079.31	2779.87	2540.70	2345.36	2182.88
265,000	22474.02	11419.35	7735.76	5894.93	4791.21	4056.04	3531.47	3138.52	2833.33	2589.56	2390.46	2224.86
270,000	22898.06	11634.81	7881.71	6006.15	4881.61	4132.57	3598.10	3197.74	2886.79	2638.42	2435.56	2266.84
280,000	23746.14	12065.73	8173.63	6228.60	5062.41	4285.62	3731.36	3316.18	2993.71	2736.14	2525.77	2350.80
290,000	24594.22	12496.65	8465.54	6451.05	5243.21	4438.68	3864.62	3434.61	3100.62	2833.86	2615.97	2434.76
300,000	25442.29	12927.57	8757.46	6673.50	5424.01	4591.74	3997.89	3553.05	3207.54	2931.58	2706.18	2518.71

12

AMOUNT OF LOAN	NUMBER OF YEARS IN TERM											
	13	14	15	16	17	18	19	20	25	30	35	40
$ 50	0.40	0.38	0.36	0.34	0.32	0.31	0.30	0.29	0.25	0.22	0.20	0.19
100	0.79	0.75	0.71	0.67	0.64	0.62	0.59	0.57	0.49	0.44	0.40	0.38
200	1.58	1.49	1.41	1.34	1.28	1.23	1.18	1.14	0.98	0.88	0.80	0.75
300	2.37	2.23	2.11	2.01	1.92	1.84	1.77	1.71	1.47	1.31	1.20	1.12
400	3.15	2.97	2.82	2.68	2.56	2.45	2.36	2.27	1.95	1.75	1.60	1.50
500	3.94	3.71	3.52	3.35	3.20	3.07	2.95	2.84	2.44	2.18	2.00	1.87
600	4.73	4.46	4.22	4.02	3.84	3.68	3.54	3.41	2.93	2.62	2.40	2.24
700	5.51	5.20	4.92	4.69	4.48	4.29	4.12	3.98	3.42	3.05	2.80	2.61
800	6.30	5.94	5.63	5.35	5.11	4.90	4.71	4.54	3.90	3.49	3.20	2.99
900	7.09	6.68	6.33	6.02	5.75	5.51	5.30	5.11	4.39	3.92	3.60	3.36
1,000	7.87	7.42	7.03	6.69	6.39	6.13	5.89	5.68	4.88	4.36	3.99	3.73
2,000	15.74	14.84	14.06	13.38	12.78	12.25	11.77	11.35	9.75	8.71	7.98	7.46
3,000	23.61	22.26	21.09	20.06	19.16	18.37	17.66	17.02	14.62	13.06	11.97	11.18
4,000	31.48	29.67	28.11	26.75	25.55	24.49	23.54	22.69	19.50	17.41	15.96	14.91
5,000	39.35	37.09	35.14	33.44	31.94	30.61	29.43	28.36	24.37	21.77	19.95	18.63
6,000	47.21	44.51	42.17	40.12	38.32	36.73	35.31	34.04	29.24	26.12	23.94	22.36
7,000	55.08	51.92	49.19	46.81	44.71	42.85	41.20	39.71	34.12	30.47	27.93	26.08
8,000	62.95	59.34	56.22	53.49	51.10	48.97	47.08	45.38	38.99	34.82	31.92	29.81
9,000	70.82	66.76	63.25	60.18	57.48	55.10	52.96	51.05	43.86	39.17	35.91	33.53
10,000	78.69	74.17	70.27	66.87	63.87	61.22	58.85	56.72	48.74	43.53	39.90	37.26
15,000	118.03	111.26	105.41	100.30	95.80	91.82	88.27	85.08	73.10	65.29	59.85	55.89
20,000	157.37	148.34	140.54	133.73	127.74	122.43	117.69	113.44	97.47	87.05	79.79	74.51
25,000	196.71	185.43	175.67	167.16	159.67	153.03	147.11	141.80	121.83	108.81	99.74	93.14
30,000	236.05	222.51	210.81	200.59	191.60	183.64	176.54	170.16	146.20	130.57	119.69	111.77
35,000	275.39	259.59	245.94	234.02	223.54	214.25	205.96	198.52	170.57	152.33	139.63	130.39
40,000	314.73	296.68	281.07	267.45	255.47	244.85	235.38	226.88	194.93	174.09	159.58	149.02
45,000	354.07	333.76	316.21	300.89	287.40	275.46	264.80	255.24	219.30	195.85	179.53	167.65
50,000	393.41	370.85	351.34	334.32	319.34	306.06	294.22	283.60	243.66	217.61	199.47	186.28
55,000	432.75	407.93	386.47	367.75	351.27	336.67	323.65	311.96	268.03	239.37	219.42	204.90
60,000	472.09	445.01	421.61	401.18	383.20	367.28	353.07	340.32	292.39	261.13	239.37	223.53
65,000	511.43	482.10	456.74	434.61	415.14	397.88	382.49	368.68	316.76	282.89	259.31	242.16
70,000	550.77	519.18	491.87	468.04	447.07	428.49	411.91	397.04	341.13	304.65	279.26	260.78
75,000	590.11	556.27	527.01	501.47	479.00	459.09	441.33	425.40	365.49	326.41	299.21	279.41
80,000	629.45	593.35	562.14	534.90	510.94	489.70	470.75	453.76	389.86	348.17	319.15	298.04
85,000	668.79	630.43	597.27	568.33	542.87	520.30	500.18	482.12	414.22	369.93	339.10	316.67
90,000	708.13	667.52	632.41	601.77	574.80	550.91	529.60	510.48	438.59	391.69	359.05	335.29
95,000	747.47	704.60	667.54	635.20	606.74	581.52	559.02	538.84	462.96	413.45	379.00	353.92
100,000	786.81	741.69	702.67	668.63	638.67	612.12	588.44	567.20	487.32	435.21	398.94	372.55
105,000	826.15	778.77	737.81	702.06	670.60	642.73	617.86	595.56	511.69	456.97	418.89	391.17
110,000	865.40	815.85	772.94	735.49	702.54	673.33	647.29	623.92	536.05	478.73	438.84	409.80
115,000	904.83	852.94	808.07	768.92	734.47	703.94	676.71	652.28	560.42	500.49	458.78	428.43
120,000	944.17	890.02	843.21	802.35	766.40	734.55	706.13	680.64	584.78	522.25	478.73	447.05
125,000	983.51	927.11	878.34	835.78	798.34	765.15	735.55	709.00	609.15	544.01	498.68	465.68
130,000	1022.85	964.19	913.47	869.21	830.27	795.76	764.97	737.36	633.52	565.77	518.62	484.31
135,000	1062.19	1001.27	948.61	902.65	862.20	826.36	794.40	765.72	657.88	587.53	538.57	502.94
140,000	1101.53	1038.36	983.74	936.08	894.14	856.97	823.82	794.08	682.25	609.29	558.52	521.56
145,000	1140.87	1075.44	1018.87	969.51	926.07	887.57	853.24	822.44	706.61	631.05	578.46	540.19
150,000	1180.21	1112.53	1054.01	1002.94	958.00	918.18	882.66	850.80	730.98	652.81	598.41	558.82
155,000	1219.55	1149.61	1089.14	1036.37	989.94	948.79	912.08	879.16	755.35	674.57	618.36	577.44
160,000	1258.89	1186.69	1124.28	1069.80	1021.87	979.39	941.50	907.52	779.71	696.34	638.30	596.07
165,000	1298.23	1223.78	1159.41	1103.23	1053.80	1010.00	970.93	935.88	804.08	718.10	658.25	614.70
170,000	1337.57	1260.86	1194.54	1136.66	1085.74	1040.60	1000.35	964.24	828.44	739.86	678.20	633.33
175,000	1376.91	1297.95	1229.68	1170.10	1117.67	1071.21	1029.77	992.60	852.81	761.62	698.15	651.95
180,000	1416.25	1335.03	1264.81	1203.53	1149.60	1101.82	1059.19	1020.96	877.17	783.38	718.09	670.58
185,000	1455.59	1372.11	1299.94	1236.96	1181.54	1132.42	1088.61	1049.32	901.54	805.14	738.04	689.21
190,000	1494.93	1409.20	1335.08	1270.39	1213.47	1163.03	1118.04	1077.68	925.91	826.90	757.99	707.83
195,000	1534.27	1446.28	1370.21	1303.82	1245.40	1193.63	1147.46	1106.04	950.27	848.66	777.93	726.46
200,000	1573.61	1483.37	1405.34	1337.25	1277.34	1224.24	1176.88	1134.40	974.64	870.42	797.88	745.09
205,000	1612.95	1520.45	1440.48	1370.68	1309.27	1254.85	1206.30	1162.76	999.00	892.18	817.83	763.71
210,000	1652.29	1557.53	1475.61	1404.11	1341.20	1285.45	1235.72	1191.12	1023.37	913.94	837.77	782.34
215,000	1691.63	1594.62	1510.74	1437.54	1373.14	1316.06	1265.14	1219.48	1047.73	935.70	857.72	800.97
220,000	1730.97	1631.70	1545.88	1470.98	1405.07	1346.66	1294.57	1247.84	1072.10	957.46	877.67	819.60
225,000	1770.32	1668.79	1581.01	1504.41	1437.00	1377.27	1323.99	1276.20	1096.47	979.22	897.61	838.22
230,000	1809.66	1705.87	1616.14	1537.84	1468.94	1407.87	1353.41	1304.56	1120.83	1000.98	917.56	856.85
235,000	1849.00	1742.95	1651.28	1571.27	1500.87	1438.48	1382.83	1332.92	1145.20	1022.74	937.51	875.48
240,000	1888.34	1780.04	1686.41	1604.70	1532.80	1469.09	1412.25	1361.27	1169.56	1044.50	957.45	894.10
245,000	1927.68	1817.12	1721.54	1638.13	1564.74	1499.69	1441.68	1389.63	1193.93	1066.26	977.40	912.73
250,000	1967.02	1854.21	1756.68	1671.56	1596.67	1530.30	1471.10	1417.99	1218.30	1088.02	997.35	931.36
255,000	2006.36	1891.29	1791.81	1704.99	1628.60	1560.90	1500.52	1446.35	1242.66	1109.78	1017.29	949.99
260,000	2045.70	1928.37	1826.94	1738.42	1660.54	1591.51	1529.94	1474.71	1267.03	1131.54	1037.24	968.61
265,000	2085.04	1965.46	1862.08	1771.86	1692.47	1622.12	1559.36	1503.07	1291.39	1153.30	1057.19	987.24
270,000	2124.38	2002.54	1897.21	1805.29	1724.40	1652.72	1588.79	1531.43	1315.76	1175.06	1077.14	1005.87
280,000	2203.06	2076.71	1967.48	1872.15	1788.27	1713.93	1647.63	1588.15	1364.49	1218.58	1117.03	1043.12
290,000	2281.74	2150.88	2037.74	1939.01	1852.14	1775.14	1706.47	1644.87	1413.22	1262.10	1156.92	1080.37
300,000	2360.42	2225.05	2108.01	2005.87	1916.00	1836.36	1765.32	1701.59	1461.95	1305.62	1196.82	1117.63

3.50%   MONTHLY AMORTIZING PAYMENTS

AMOUNT OF LOAN	NUMBER OF YEARS IN TERM											
	1	2	3	4	5	6	7	8	9	10	11	12
$ 50	4.25	2.17	1.47	1.12	0.91	0.78	0.68	0.60	0.55	0.50	0.46	0.43
100	8.50	4.33	2.94	2.24	1.82	1.55	1.35	1.20	1.09	0.99	0.92	0.86
200	16.99	8.65	5.87	4.48	3.64	3.09	2.69	2.40	2.17	1.98	1.83	1.71
300	25.48	12.97	8.80	6.71	5.46	4.63	4.04	3.59	3.25	2.97	2.75	2.56
400	33.97	17.29	11.73	8.95	7.28	6.17	5.38	4.79	4.33	3.96	3.66	3.41
500	42.47	21.61	14.66	11.18	9.10	7.71	6.72	5.98	5.41	4.95	4.57	4.26
600	50.96	25.93	17.59	13.42	10.92	9.26	8.07	7.18	6.49	5.94	5.49	5.11
700	59.45	30.25	20.52	15.65	12.74	10.80	9.41	8.38	7.57	6.93	6.40	5.97
800	67.94	34.57	23.45	17.89	14.56	12.34	10.76	9.57	8.65	7.92	7.32	6.82
900	76.43	38.89	26.38	20.13	16.38	13.88	12.10	10.77	9.73	8.90	8.23	7.67
1,000	84.93	43.21	29.31	22.36	18.20	15.42	13.44	11.96	10.81	9.89	9.14	8.52
2,000	169.85	86.41	58.61	44.72	36.39	30.84	26.88	23.92	21.62	19.78	18.28	17.03
3,000	254.77	129.61	87.91	67.07	54.58	46.26	40.32	35.88	32.43	29.67	27.42	25.55
4,000	339.69	172.82	117.21	89.43	72.77	61.68	53.76	47.84	43.23	39.56	36.56	34.06
5,000	424.61	216.02	146.52	111.79	90.96	77.10	67.20	59.80	54.04	49.45	45.70	42.58
6,000	509.53	259.22	175.82	134.14	109.16	92.52	80.64	71.75	64.85	59.34	54.84	51.09
7,000	594.46	302.42	205.12	156.50	127.35	107.93	94.08	83.71	75.66	69.23	63.97	59.61
8,000	679.38	345.63	234.42	178.85	145.54	123.35	107.52	95.67	86.46	79.11	73.11	68.12
9,000	764.30	388.83	263.72	201.21	163.73	138.77	120.96	107.63	97.27	89.00	82.25	76.64
10,000	849.22	432.03	293.03	223.57	181.92	154.19	134.40	119.59	108.08	98.89	91.39	85.15
15,000	1273.83	648.05	439.54	335.35	272.88	231.28	201.60	179.38	162.12	148.33	137.08	127.72
20,000	1698.44	864.06	586.05	447.13	363.84	308.37	268.80	239.17	216.15	197.78	182.77	170.30
25,000	2123.05	1080.07	732.56	558.91	454.80	385.46	336.00	298.96	270.19	247.22	228.46	212.87
30,000	2547.65	1296.09	879.07	670.69	545.76	462.56	403.20	358.75	324.23	296.66	274.16	255.44
35,000	2972.26	1512.10	1025.58	782.47	636.72	539.65	470.40	418.54	378.26	346.11	319.85	298.01
40,000	3396.87	1728.11	1172.09	894.25	727.67	616.74	537.60	478.33	432.30	395.55	365.54	340.59
45,000	3821.48	1944.13	1318.60	1006.03	818.63	693.83	604.80	538.12	486.34	444.99	411.23	383.16
50,000	4246.09	2160.14	1465.11	1117.81	909.59	770.92	672.00	597.91	540.38	494.43	456.92	425.73
55,000	4670.69	2376.15	1611.62	1229.59	1000.55	848.02	739.20	657.70	594.41	543.88	502.61	468.30
60,000	5095.30	2592.17	1758.13	1341.37	1091.51	925.11	806.40	717.49	648.45	593.32	548.31	510.88
65,000	5519.91	2808.18	1904.64	1453.15	1182.47	1002.20	873.60	777.28	702.49	642.76	594.00	553.45
70,000	5944.52	3024.20	2051.15	1564.93	1273.43	1079.29	940.79	837.07	756.52	692.21	639.69	596.02
75,000	6369.13	3240.21	2197.66	1676.71	1364.39	1156.38	1007.99	896.86	810.56	741.65	685.38	638.60
80,000	6793.74	3456.22	2344.17	1788.49	1455.34	1233.48	1075.19	956.65	864.60	791.09	731.07	681.17
85,000	7218.34	3672.24	2490.68	1900.27	1546.30	1310.57	1142.39	1016.44	918.64	840.53	776.76	723.74
90,000	7642.95	3888.25	2637.19	2012.05	1637.26	1387.66	1209.59	1076.23	972.67	889.98	822.46	766.31
95,000	8067.56	4104.26	2783.70	2123.83	1728.22	1464.75	1276.79	1136.02	1026.71	939.42	868.15	808.89
100,000	8492.17	4320.28	2930.21	2235.61	1819.18	1541.84	1343.99	1195.81	1080.75	988.86	913.84	851.46
105,000	8916.78	4536.29	3076.72	2347.39	1910.14	1618.94	1411.19	1255.60	1134.78	1038.31	959.53	894.03
110,000	9341.38	4752.30	3223.23	2459.17	2001.10	1696.03	1478.39	1315.39	1188.82	1087.75	1005.22	936.60
115,000	9765.99	4968.32	3369.74	2570.95	2092.06	1773.12	1545.59	1375.18	1242.86	1137.19	1050.91	979.18
120,000	10190.60	5184.33	3516.25	2682.73	2183.01	1850.21	1612.79	1434.97	1296.89	1186.64	1096.61	1021.75
125,000	10615.21	5400.35	3662.76	2794.51	2273.97	1927.30	1679.99	1494.76	1350.93	1236.08	1142.30	1064.32
130,000	11039.82	5616.36	3809.28	2906.29	2364.93	2004.40	1747.19	1554.55	1404.97	1285.52	1187.99	1106.89
135,000	11464.43	5832.37	3955.79	3018.07	2455.89	2081.49	1814.38	1614.34	1459.01	1334.96	1233.68	1149.47
140,000	11889.03	6048.39	4102.30	3129.85	2546.85	2158.58	1881.58	1674.13	1513.04	1384.41	1279.37	1192.04
145,000	12313.64	6264.40	4248.81	3241.63	2637.81	2235.67	1948.78	1733.92	1567.08	1433.85	1325.06	1234.61
150,000	12738.25	6480.41	4395.32	3353.41	2728.77	2312.76	2015.98	1793.71	1621.12	1483.29	1370.76	1277.19
155,000	13162.86	6696.43	4541.83	3465.19	2819.73	2389.86	2083.18	1853.50	1675.15	1532.74	1416.45	1319.76
160,000	13587.47	6912.44	4688.34	3576.97	2910.68	2466.95	2150.38	1913.29	1729.19	1582.18	1462.14	1362.33
165,000	14012.07	7128.45	4834.85	3688.75	3001.64	2544.04	2217.58	1973.08	1783.23	1631.62	1507.83	1404.90
170,000	14436.68	7344.47	4981.36	3800.53	3092.60	2621.13	2284.78	2032.87	1837.27	1681.06	1553.52	1447.48
175,000	14861.29	7560.48	5127.87	3912.31	3183.56	2698.22	2351.98	2092.66	1891.30	1730.51	1599.22	1490.05
180,000	15285.90	7776.49	5274.38	4024.09	3274.52	2775.32	2419.18	2152.45	1945.34	1779.95	1644.91	1532.62
185,000	15710.51	7992.51	5420.89	4135.87	3365.48	2852.41	2486.38	2212.24	1999.38	1829.39	1690.60	1575.19
190,000	16135.11	8208.52	5567.40	4247.65	3456.44	2929.50	2553.58	2272.03	2053.41	1878.84	1736.29	1617.77
195,000	16559.72	8424.54	5713.91	4359.43	3547.40	3006.59	2620.78	2331.83	2107.45	1928.28	1781.98	1660.34
200,000	16984.33	8640.55	5860.42	4471.21	3638.35	3083.68	2687.98	2391.62	2161.49	1977.72	1827.67	1702.91
205,000	17408.94	8856.56	6006.93	4582.99	3729.31	3160.78	2755.17	2451.41	2215.52	2027.17	1873.37	1745.49
210,000	17833.55	9072.58	6153.44	4694.77	3820.27	3237.87	2822.37	2511.20	2269.56	2076.61	1919.06	1788.06
215,000	18258.16	9288.59	6299.95	4806.55	3911.23	3314.96	2889.57	2570.99	2323.60	2126.05	1964.75	1830.63
220,000	18682.76	9504.60	6446.46	4918.33	4002.19	3392.05	2956.77	2630.78	2377.64	2175.49	2010.44	1873.20
225,000	19107.37	9720.62	6592.97	5030.11	4093.15	3469.14	3023.97	2690.57	2431.67	2224.94	2056.13	1915.78
230,000	19531.98	9936.63	6739.48	5141.89	4184.11	3546.24	3091.17	2750.36	2485.71	2274.38	2101.82	1958.35
235,000	19956.59	10152.64	6885.99	5253.67	4275.07	3623.33	3158.37	2810.15	2539.75	2323.82	2147.52	2000.92
240,000	20381.20	10368.66	7032.50	5365.45	4366.02	3700.42	3225.57	2869.94	2593.78	2373.27	2193.21	2043.49
245,000	20805.80	10584.67	7179.01	5477.23	4456.98	3777.51	3292.77	2929.73	2647.82	2422.71	2238.90	2086.07
250,000	21230.41	10800.69	7325.52	5589.01	4547.94	3854.60	3359.97	2989.52	2701.86	2472.15	2284.59	2128.64
255,000	21655.02	11016.70	7472.04	5700.79	4638.90	3931.70	3427.17	3049.31	2755.90	2521.59	2330.28	2171.21
260,000	22079.63	11232.71	7618.55	5812.57	4729.86	4008.79	3494.37	3109.10	2809.93	2571.04	2375.97	2213.78
265,000	22504.24	11448.73	7765.06	5924.35	4820.82	4085.88	3561.57	3168.89	2863.97	2620.48	2421.67	2256.36
270,000	22928.85	11664.74	7911.57	6036.13	4911.78	4162.97	3628.76	3228.68	2918.01	2669.92	2467.36	2298.93
280,000	23778.06	12096.77	8204.59	6259.69	5093.69	4317.16	3763.16	3348.26	3026.08	2768.81	2558.74	2384.08
290,000	24627.28	12528.79	8497.61	6483.25	5275.61	4471.34	3897.56	3467.84	3134.16	2867.70	2650.12	2469.22
300,000	25476.49	12960.82	8790.63	6706.81	5457.53	4625.52	4031.96	3587.42	3242.23	2966.58	2741.51	2554.37

14

AMOUNT OF LOAN	NUMBER OF YEARS IN TERM											
	13	14	15	16	17	18	19	20	25	30	35	40
$ 50	0.40	0.38	0.36	0.35	0.33	0.32	0.31	0.29	0.26	0.23	0.21	0.20
100	0.80	0.76	0.72	0.69	0.66	0.63	0.61	0.58	0.51	0.45	0.42	0.39
200	1.60	1.51	1.43	1.37	1.31	1.25	1.21	1.16	1.01	0.90	0.83	0.78
300	2.40	2.27	2.15	2.05	1.96	1.88	1.81	1.74	1.51	1.35	1.24	1.17
400	3.20	3.02	2.86	2.73	2.61	2.50	2.41	2.32	2.01	1.80	1.66	1.55
500	4.00	3.77	3.58	3.41	3.26	3.13	3.01	2.90	2.51	2.25	2.07	1.94
600	4.80	4.53	4.29	4.09	3.91	3.75	3.61	3.48	3.01	2.70	2.48	2.33
700	5.60	5.28	5.01	4.77	4.56	4.38	4.21	4.06	3.51	3.15	2.90	2.72
800	6.40	6.04	5.72	5.45	5.21	5.00	4.81	4.64	4.01	3.60	3.31	3.10
900	7.19	6.79	6.44	6.13	5.86	5.63	5.41	5.22	4.51	4.05	3.72	3.49
1,000	7.99	7.54	7.15	6.81	6.52	6.25	6.02	5.80	5.01	4.50	4.14	3.88
2,000	15.98	15.08	14.30	13.62	13.03	12.50	12.03	11.60	10.02	8.99	8.27	7.75
3,000	23.97	22.62	21.45	20.43	19.54	18.74	18.04	17.40	15.02	13.48	12.40	11.63
4,000	31.96	30.16	28.60	27.24	26.05	24.99	24.05	23.20	20.03	17.97	16.54	15.50
5,000	39.94	37.69	35.75	34.05	32.56	31.24	30.06	29.00	25.04	22.46	20.67	19.37
6,000	47.93	45.23	42.90	40.86	39.07	37.48	36.07	34.80	30.04	26.95	24.80	23.25
7,000	55.92	52.77	50.05	47.67	45.58	43.73	42.08	40.60	35.05	31.44	28.94	27.12
8,000	63.91	60.31	57.20	54.48	52.09	49.98	48.09	46.40	40.05	35.93	33.07	31.00
9,000	71.90	67.85	64.34	61.29	58.60	56.22	54.10	52.20	45.06	40.42	37.20	34.87
10,000	79.88	75.38	71.49	68.10	65.12	62.47	60.11	58.00	50.07	44.91	41.33	38.74
15,000	119.82	113.07	107.24	102.15	97.67	93.70	90.17	87.00	75.10	67.36	62.00	58.11
20,000	159.76	150.76	142.98	136.19	130.23	124.94	120.22	116.00	100.13	89.81	82.66	77.48
25,000	199.70	188.45	178.73	170.24	162.78	156.17	150.28	144.99	125.16	112.27	103.33	96.85
30,000	239.64	226.14	214.47	204.29	195.34	187.40	180.33	173.99	150.19	134.72	123.99	116.22
35,000	279.58	263.83	250.21	238.34	227.89	218.64	210.39	202.99	175.22	157.17	144.66	135.59
40,000	319.52	301.52	285.96	272.38	260.45	249.87	240.44	231.99	200.25	179.62	165.32	154.96
45,000	359.46	339.21	321.70	306.43	293.00	281.10	270.50	260.99	225.29	202.08	185.99	174.33
50,000	399.40	376.90	357.45	340.48	325.56	312.34	300.55	289.98	250.32	224.53	206.65	193.70
55,000	439.34	414.59	393.19	374.53	358.11	343.57	330.61	318.98	275.35	246.98	227.31	213.07
60,000	479.28	452.28	428.93	408.57	390.67	374.80	360.66	347.98	300.38	269.43	247.98	232.44
65,000	519.22	489.96	464.68	442.62	423.22	406.03	390.71	376.98	325.41	291.88	268.64	251.81
70,000	559.16	527.65	500.42	476.67	455.78	437.27	420.77	405.98	350.44	314.34	289.31	271.18
75,000	599.10	565.34	536.17	510.72	488.33	468.50	450.82	434.97	375.47	336.79	309.97	290.55
80,000	639.04	603.03	571.91	544.76	520.89	499.73	480.88	463.97	400.50	359.24	330.64	309.92
85,000	678.98	640.72	607.66	578.81	553.44	530.97	510.93	492.97	425.54	381.69	351.30	329.29
90,000	718.92	678.41	643.40	612.86	586.00	562.20	540.99	521.97	450.57	404.15	371.97	348.66
95,000	758.86	716.10	679.14	646.90	618.55	593.43	571.04	550.97	475.60	426.60	392.63	368.03
100,000	798.80	753.79	714.89	680.95	651.11	624.67	601.10	579.96	500.63	449.05	413.30	387.40
105,000	838.74	791.48	750.63	715.00	683.66	655.90	631.15	608.96	525.66	471.50	433.96	406.77
110,000	878.68	829.17	786.38	749.05	716.22	687.13	661.21	637.96	550.69	493.95	454.62	426.14
115,000	918.62	866.86	822.12	783.09	748.77	718.37	691.26	666.96	575.72	516.41	475.29	445.50
120,000	958.56	904.55	857.86	817.14	781.33	749.60	721.91	695.90	600.75	538.86	495.95	464.87
125,000	998.50	942.24	893.61	851.19	813.88	780.83	751.37	724.95	625.78	561.31	516.62	484.24
130,000	1038.44	979.92	929.35	885.24	846.44	812.06	781.42	753.95	650.82	583.76	537.28	503.61
135,000	1078.38	1017.61	965.10	919.28	878.99	843.30	811.48	782.95	675.85	606.22	557.95	522.98
140,000	1118.32	1055.30	1000.84	953.33	911.55	874.53	841.53	811.95	700.88	628.67	578.61	542.35
145,000	1158.26	1092.99	1036.58	987.38	944.10	905.76	871.59	840.95	725.91	651.12	599.28	561.72
150,000	1198.20	1130.68	1072.33	1021.43	976.66	937.00	901.64	869.94	750.94	673.57	619.94	581.09
155,000	1238.14	1168.37	1108.07	1055.47	1009.21	968.23	931.70	898.94	775.97	696.02	640.61	600.46
160,000	1278.08	1206.06	1143.82	1089.52	1041.77	999.46	961.75	927.94	801.00	718.48	661.27	619.83
165,000	1318.02	1243.75	1179.56	1123.57	1074.32	1030.70	991.81	956.94	826.03	740.93	681.93	639.20
170,000	1357.96	1281.44	1215.31	1157.61	1106.88	1061.93	1021.86	985.94	851.07	763.38	702.60	658.57
175,000	1397.90	1319.13	1251.05	1191.66	1139.43	1093.16	1051.91	1014.93	876.10	785.83	723.26	677.94
180,000	1437.84	1356.82	1286.79	1225.71	1171.99	1124.40	1081.97	1043.93	901.13	808.29	743.93	697.31
185,000	1477.78	1394.51	1322.54	1259.76	1204.54	1155.63	1112.02	1072.93	926.16	830.74	764.59	716.68
190,000	1517.72	1432.20	1358.28	1293.80	1237.10	1186.86	1142.08	1101.93	951.19	853.19	785.26	736.05
195,000	1557.66	1469.88	1394.03	1327.85	1269.65	1218.09	1172.13	1130.93	976.22	875.64	805.92	755.42
200,000	1597.60	1507.57	1429.77	1361.90	1302.21	1249.33	1202.19	1159.92	1001.25	898.09	826.59	774.79
205,000	1637.54	1545.26	1465.51	1395.95	1334.76	1280.56	1232.24	1188.92	1026.28	920.55	847.25	794.16
210,000	1677.48	1582.95	1501.26	1429.99	1367.32	1311.79	1262.30	1217.92	1051.31	943.00	867.92	813.53
215,000	1717.42	1620.64	1537.00	1464.04	1399.87	1343.03	1292.35	1246.92	1076.35	965.45	888.58	832.90
220,000	1757.36	1658.33	1572.75	1498.09	1432.43	1374.26	1322.41	1275.92	1101.38	987.90	909.24	852.27
225,000	1797.30	1696.02	1608.49	1532.14	1464.98	1405.49	1352.46	1304.91	1126.41	1010.36	929.91	871.63
230,000	1837.24	1733.71	1644.23	1566.18	1497.54	1436.73	1382.52	1333.91	1151.44	1032.81	950.57	891.00
235,000	1877.18	1771.40	1679.98	1600.23	1530.09	1467.96	1412.57	1362.91	1176.47	1055.26	971.24	910.37
240,000	1917.12	1809.09	1715.72	1634.28	1562.65	1499.19	1442.62	1391.91	1201.50	1077.71	991.90	929.74
245,000	1957.06	1846.78	1751.47	1668.32	1595.20	1530.43	1472.68	1420.91	1226.53	1100.16	1012.57	949.11
250,000	1997.00	1884.47	1787.21	1702.37	1627.76	1561.66	1502.73	1449.90	1251.56	1122.62	1033.23	968.48
255,000	2036.94	1922.15	1822.96	1736.42	1660.31	1592.89	1532.79	1478.90	1276.60	1145.07	1053.90	987.85
260,000	2076.88	1959.84	1858.70	1770.47	1692.87	1624.12	1562.84	1507.90	1301.63	1167.52	1074.56	1007.22
265,000	2116.82	1997.53	1894.44	1804.51	1725.42	1655.36	1592.90	1536.90	1326.66	1189.97	1095.23	1026.59
270,000	2156.76	2035.22	1930.19	1838.56	1757.98	1686.59	1622.95	1565.90	1351.69	1212.43	1115.89	1045.96
280,000	2236.64	2110.60	2001.68	1906.66	1823.09	1749.06	1683.06	1623.89	1401.75	1257.33	1157.22	1084.70
290,000	2316.52	2185.98	2073.16	1974.75	1888.20	1811.52	1743.17	1681.89	1451.81	1302.23	1198.55	1123.44
300,000	2396.40	2261.36	2144.65	2042.85	1953.31	1873.99	1803.28	1739.88	1501.88	1347.14	1239.88	1162.18

15

3.75%

MONTHLY AMORTIZING PAYMENTS

AMOUNT OF LOAN	NUMBER OF YEARS IN TERM											
	1	2	3	4	5	6	7	8	9	10	11	12
$ 50	4.26	2.17	1.48	1.13	0.92	0.78	0.68	0.61	0.55	0.51	0.47	0.44
100	8.51	4.34	2.95	2.25	1.84	1.56	1.36	1.21	1.10	1.01	0.93	0.87
200	17.01	8.67	5.89	4.50	3.67	3.11	2.72	2.42	2.19	2.01	1.86	1.73
300	25.52	13.00	8.83	6.75	5.50	4.66	4.07	3.63	3.28	3.01	2.78	2.60
400	34.02	17.33	11.77	8.99	7.33	6.22	5.43	4.83	4.37	4.01	3.71	3.46
500	42.52	21.66	14.71	11.24	9.16	7.77	6.78	6.04	5.47	5.01	4.63	4.32
600	51.03	25.99	17.65	13.49	10.99	9.32	8.14	7.25	6.56	6.01	5.56	5.19
700	59.53	30.32	20.59	15.73	12.82	10.88	9.49	8.46	7.65	7.01	6.48	6.05
800	68.03	34.66	23.54	17.98	14.65	12.43	10.85	9.66	8.74	8.01	7.41	6.91
900	76.54	38.99	26.48	20.23	16.48	13.98	12.20	10.87	9.84	9.01	8.34	7.78
1,000	85.04	43.32	29.42	22.47	18.31	15.54	13.56	12.08	10.93	10.01	9.26	8.64
2,000	170.08	86.63	58.83	44.94	36.61	31.07	27.11	24.15	21.85	20.02	18.52	17.27
3,000	255.11	129.95	88.24	67.41	54.92	46.60	40.67	36.22	32.78	30.02	27.78	25.91
4,000	340.15	173.26	117.66	89.87	73.22	62.13	54.22	48.30	43.70	40.03	37.03	34.54
5,000	425.18	216.57	147.07	112.34	91.52	77.66	67.78	60.37	54.62	50.04	46.29	43.18
6,000	510.22	259.89	176.48	134.81	109.83	93.19	81.33	72.44	65.55	60.04	55.55	51.81
7,000	595.26	303.20	205.90	157.28	128.13	108.73	94.88	84.52	76.47	70.05	64.80	60.45
8,000	680.29	346.51	235.31	179.74	146.44	124.26	108.44	96.59	87.40	80.05	74.06	69.08
9,000	765.33	389.83	264.72	202.21	164.74	139.79	121.99	108.66	98.32	90.06	83.32	77.71
10,000	850.36	433.14	294.13	224.68	183.04	155.32	135.55	120.74	109.24	100.07	92.58	86.35
15,000	1275.54	649.71	441.20	337.02	274.56	232.98	203.32	181.10	163.86	150.10	138.86	129.52
20,000	1700.72	866.28	588.26	449.35	366.08	310.64	271.09	241.47	218.48	200.13	185.15	172.69
25,000	2125.90	1082.85	735.33	561.69	457.60	388.29	338.86	301.84	273.10	250.16	231.43	215.87
30,000	2551.08	1299.42	882.39	674.03	549.12	465.95	406.63	362.20	327.72	300.19	277.72	259.04
35,000	2976.26	1515.99	1029.46	786.36	640.64	543.61	474.40	422.57	382.34	350.22	324.00	302.21
40,000	3401.43	1732.55	1176.52	898.70	732.16	621.27	542.17	482.94	436.96	400.25	370.29	345.38
45,000	3826.61	1949.12	1323.59	1011.04	823.68	698.92	609.94	543.30	491.58	450.28	416.57	388.55
50,000	4251.79	2165.69	1470.65	1123.37	915.20	776.58	677.71	603.67	546.20	500.31	462.86	431.73
55,000	4676.97	2382.26	1617.71	1235.71	1006.72	854.24	745.48	664.04	600.81	550.34	509.14	474.90
60,000	5102.15	2598.83	1764.78	1348.05	1098.24	931.90	813.25	724.40	655.43	600.37	555.43	518.07
65,000	5527.33	2815.40	1911.84	1460.38	1189.76	1009.55	881.02	784.77	710.05	650.40	601.71	561.24
70,000	5952.51	3031.97	2058.91	1572.72	1281.28	1087.21	948.79	845.14	764.67	700.43	648.00	604.41
75,000	6377.68	3248.54	2205.97	1685.06	1372.80	1164.87	1016.56	905.50	819.29	750.46	694.28	647.59
80,000	6802.86	3465.10	2353.04	1797.39	1464.32	1242.53	1084.33	965.87	873.91	800.49	740.57	690.76
85,000	7228.04	3681.67	2500.10	1909.73	1555.84	1320.19	1152.10	1026.24	928.53	850.53	786.85	733.93
90,000	7653.22	3898.24	2647.17	2022.07	1647.36	1397.84	1219.87	1086.60	983.15	900.56	833.14	777.10
95,000	8078.40	4114.81	2794.23	2134.40	1738.88	1475.50	1287.64	1146.97	1037.77	950.59	879.42	820.27
100,000	8503.58	4331.38	2941.30	2246.74	1830.40	1553.16	1355.41	1207.34	1092.39	1000.62	925.71	863.45
105,000	8928.76	4547.95	3088.36	2359.08	1921.92	1630.82	1423.18	1267.70	1147.00	1050.65	971.99	906.62
110,000	9353.93	4764.52	3235.42	2471.41	2013.44	1708.47	1490.95	1328.07	1201.62	1100.68	1018.28	949.79
115,000	9779.11	4981.08	3382.49	2583.75	2104.96	1786.13	1558.72	1388.44	1256.24	1150.71	1064.56	992.96
120,000	10204.29	5197.65	3529.55	2696.09	2196.48	1863.79	1626.49	1448.80	1310.86	1200.74	1110.85	1036.13
125,000	10629.47	5414.22	3676.62	2808.42	2287.99	1941.45	1694.26	1509.17	1365.48	1250.77	1157.14	1079.31
130,000	11054.65	5630.79	3823.68	2920.76	2379.51	2019.10	1762.03	1569.54	1420.10	1300.80	1203.42	1122.48
135,000	11479.83	5847.36	3970.75	3033.10	2471.03	2096.76	1829.80	1629.90	1474.72	1350.83	1249.71	1165.65
140,000	11905.01	6063.93	4117.81	3145.43	2562.55	2174.42	1897.57	1690.27	1529.34	1400.86	1295.99	1208.82
145,000	12330.18	6280.50	4264.88	3257.77	2654.07	2252.08	1965.34	1750.64	1583.96	1450.89	1342.28	1251.99
150,000	12755.36	6497.07	4411.94	3370.11	2745.59	2329.73	2033.11	1811.00	1638.58	1500.92	1388.56	1295.17
155,000	13180.54	6713.63	4559.00	3482.45	2837.11	2407.39	2100.88	1871.37	1693.20	1550.95	1434.85	1338.34
160,000	13605.72	6930.20	4706.07	3594.78	2928.63	2485.05	2168.65	1931.74	1747.81	1600.98	1481.13	1381.51
165,000	14030.90	7146.77	4853.13	3707.12	3020.15	2562.71	2236.42	1992.10	1802.43	1651.02	1527.42	1424.68
170,000	14456.08	7363.34	5000.20	3819.46	3111.67	2640.37	2304.19	2052.47	1857.05	1701.05	1573.70	1467.85
175,000	14881.26	7579.91	5147.26	3931.79	3203.19	2718.02	2371.96	2112.84	1911.67	1751.08	1619.99	1511.03
180,000	15306.44	7796.48	5294.33	4044.13	3294.71	2795.68	2439.73	2173.20	1966.29	1801.11	1666.27	1554.20
185,000	15731.61	8013.05	5441.39	4156.47	3386.23	2873.34	2507.50	2233.57	2020.91	1851.14	1712.56	1597.37
190,000	16156.79	8229.61	5588.46	4268.80	3477.75	2951.00	2575.27	2293.94	2075.53	1901.17	1758.84	1640.54
195,000	16581.97	8446.18	5735.52	4381.14	3569.27	3028.65	2643.04	2354.30	2130.15	1951.20	1805.13	1683.71
200,000	17007.15	8662.75	5882.59	4493.48	3660.79	3106.31	2710.81	2414.67	2184.77	2001.23	1851.41	1726.89
205,000	17432.33	8879.32	6029.65	4605.81	3752.31	3183.97	2778.58	2475.04	2239.39	2051.26	1897.70	1770.06
210,000	17857.51	9095.89	6176.71	4718.15	3843.83	3261.63	2846.35	2535.40	2294.00	2101.29	1943.98	1813.23
215,000	18282.69	9312.46	6323.78	4830.49	3935.35	3339.28	2914.12	2595.77	2348.62	2151.32	1990.27	1856.40
220,000	18707.86	9529.03	6470.84	4942.82	4026.87	3416.94	2981.89	2656.14	2403.24	2201.35	2036.55	1899.57
225,000	19133.04	9745.60	6617.91	5055.16	4118.39	3494.60	3049.66	2716.50	2457.86	2251.38	2082.84	1942.75
230,000	19558.22	9962.16	6764.97	5167.50	4209.91	3572.26	3117.43	2776.87	2512.48	2301.41	2129.12	1985.92
235,000	19983.40	10178.73	6912.04	5279.83	4301.43	3649.92	3185.20	2837.24	2567.10	2351.44	2175.41	2029.09
240,000	20408.58	10395.30	7059.10	5392.17	4392.95	3727.57	3252.97	2897.60	2621.72	2401.47	2221.69	2072.26
245,000	20833.76	10611.87	7206.17	5504.51	4484.46	3805.23	3320.74	2957.97	2676.34	2451.51	2267.98	2115.43
250,000	21258.94	10828.44	7353.23	5616.84	4575.98	3882.89	3388.51	3018.34	2730.96	2501.54	2314.27	2158.61
255,000	21684.11	11045.01	7500.30	5729.18	4667.50	3960.55	3456.28	3078.70	2785.58	2551.57	2360.55	2201.78
260,000	22109.29	11261.58	7647.36	5841.52	4759.02	4038.20	3524.05	3139.07	2840.19	2601.60	2406.84	2244.95
265,000	22534.47	11478.15	7794.42	5953.85	4850.54	4115.86	3591.82	3199.44	2894.81	2651.63	2453.12	2288.12
270,000	22959.65	11694.71	7941.49	6066.19	4942.06	4193.52	3659.59	3259.80	2949.43	2701.66	2499.41	2331.29
280,000	23810.01	12127.85	8235.62	6290.86	5125.10	4348.83	3795.13	3380.53	3058.67	2801.72	2591.98	2417.64
290,000	24660.36	12560.99	8529.75	6515.54	5308.14	4504.15	3930.67	3501.27	3167.91	2901.78	2684.55	2503.98
300,000	25510.72	12994.13	8823.88	6740.21	5491.18	4659.46	4066.21	3622.00	3277.15	3001.84	2777.12	2590.33

16

3.75%

AMOUNT OF LOAN	NUMBER OF YEARS IN TERM											
	13	14	15	16	17	18	19	20	25	30	35	40
$ 50	0.41	0.39	0.37	0.35	0.34	0.32	0.31	0.30	0.26	0.24	0.22	0.21
100	0.82	0.77	0.73	0.70	0.67	0.64	0.62	0.60	0.52	0.47	0.43	0.41
200	1.63	1.54	1.46	1.39	1.33	1.28	1.23	1.19	1.03	0.93	0.86	0.81
300	2.44	2.30	2.19	2.09	2.00	1.92	1.85	1.78	1.55	1.39	1.29	1.21
400	3.25	3.07	2.91	2.78	2.66	2.55	2.46	2.38	2.06	1.86	1.72	1.62
500	4.06	3.84	3.64	3.47	3.32	3.19	3.07	2.97	2.58	2.32	2.14	2.02
600	4.87	4.60	4.37	4.17	3.99	3.83	3.69	3.56	3.09	2.78	2.57	2.42
700	5.68	5.37	5.10	4.86	4.65	4.47	4.30	4.16	3.60	3.25	3.00	2.82
800	6.49	6.13	5.82	5.55	5.31	5.10	4.92	4.75	4.12	3.71	3.43	3.23
900	7.30	6.90	6.55	6.25	5.98	5.74	5.53	5.34	4.63	4.17	3.86	3.63
1,000	8.11	7.67	7.28	6.94	6.64	6.38	6.14	5.93	5.15	4.64	4.28	4.03
2,000	16.22	15.33	14.55	13.87	13.28	12.75	12.28	11.86	10.29	9.27	8.56	8.06
3,000	24.33	22.99	21.82	20.81	19.92	19.13	18.42	17.79	15.43	13.90	12.84	12.08
4,000	32.44	30.65	29.09	27.74	26.55	25.50	24.56	23.72	20.57	18.53	17.12	16.11
5,000	40.55	38.31	36.37	34.68	33.19	31.87	30.70	29.65	25.71	23.16	21.40	20.13
6,000	48.66	45.97	43.64	41.61	39.83	38.25	36.84	35.58	30.85	27.79	25.68	24.16
7,000	56.77	53.63	50.91	48.54	46.46	44.62	42.98	41.51	35.99	32.42	29.96	28.18
8,000	64.88	61.29	58.18	55.48	53.10	50.99	49.12	47.44	41.14	37.05	34.24	32.21
9,000	72.99	68.95	65.46	62.41	59.74	57.37	55.26	53.36	46.28	41.69	38.52	36.23
10,000	81.10	76.61	72.73	69.35	66.37	63.74	61.40	59.29	51.42	46.32	42.80	40.26
15,000	121.64	114.91	109.09	104.02	99.56	95.61	92.09	88.94	77.12	69.47	64.19	60.38
20,000	162.19	153.21	145.45	138.69	132.74	127.48	122.79	118.58	102.83	92.63	85.59	80.51
25,000	202.73	191.51	181.81	173.36	165.92	159.34	153.48	148.23	128.54	115.78	106.98	100.64
30,000	243.28	229.81	218.17	208.03	199.11	191.21	184.18	177.87	154.24	138.94	128.38	120.76
35,000	283.82	268.11	254.53	242.70	232.29	223.08	214.87	207.52	179.95	162.10	149.77	140.89
40,000	324.37	306.41	290.89	277.37	265.48	254.95	245.57	237.16	205.66	185.25	171.17	161.02
45,000	364.91	344.71	327.26	312.04	298.66	286.81	276.26	266.80	231.36	208.41	192.56	181.14
50,000	405.46	383.01	363.62	346.71	331.84	318.68	306.96	296.45	257.07	231.56	213.96	201.27
55,000	446.00	421.31	399.98	381.38	365.03	350.55	337.65	326.09	282.78	254.72	235.35	221.39
60,000	486.55	459.61	436.34	416.05	398.21	382.42	368.35	355.74	308.48	277.87	256.75	241.52
65,000	527.09	497.91	472.70	450.72	431.39	414.29	399.04	385.38	334.19	301.03	278.14	261.65
70,000	567.64	536.21	509.06	485.39	464.58	446.15	429.74	415.03	359.90	324.19	299.54	281.77
75,000	608.18	574.51	545.42	520.06	497.76	478.02	460.43	444.67	385.60	347.34	320.93	301.90
80,000	648.73	612.81	581.78	554.73	530.95	509.89	491.13	474.32	411.31	370.50	342.33	322.03
85,000	689.27	651.11	618.14	589.40	564.13	541.76	521.82	503.96	437.02	393.65	363.72	342.15
90,000	729.82	689.41	654.51	624.07	597.31	573.62	552.52	533.60	462.72	416.81	385.12	362.28
95,000	770.36	727.71	690.87	658.74	630.50	605.49	583.21	563.25	488.43	439.96	406.51	382.40
100,000	810.91	766.01	727.23	693.41	663.68	637.36	613.91	592.89	514.14	463.12	427.91	402.53
105,000	851.45	804.31	763.59	728.08	696.87	669.23	644.60	622.54	539.84	486.28	449.31	422.66
110,000	892.00	842.61	799.95	762.75	730.05	701.10	675.30	652.18	565.55	509.43	470.70	442.78
115,000	932.54	880.91	836.31	797.42	763.23	732.96	705.99	681.83	591.26	532.59	492.10	462.91
120,000	973.09	919.21	872.67	832.09	796.42	764.83	736.69	711.47	616.96	555.74	513.49	483.04
125,000	1013.63	957.51	909.03	866.76	829.60	796.70	767.38	741.12	642.67	578.90	534.89	503.16
130,000	1054.18	995.81	945.39	901.43	862.78	828.57	798.08	770.76	668.38	602.06	556.28	523.29
135,000	1094.72	1034.11	981.76	936.10	895.97	860.43	828.77	800.40	694.08	625.21	577.68	543.42
140,000	1135.27	1072.41	1018.12	970.77	929.15	892.30	859.47	830.05	719.79	648.37	599.07	563.54
145,000	1175.81	1110.71	1054.48	1005.44	962.34	924.17	890.16	859.69	745.50	671.52	620.47	583.67
150,000	1216.36	1149.01	1090.84	1040.11	995.52	956.04	920.86	889.34	771.20	694.68	641.86	603.79
155,000	1256.90	1187.31	1127.20	1074.78	1028.70	987.91	951.55	918.98	796.91	717.83	663.26	623.92
160,000	1297.45	1225.61	1163.56	1109.45	1061.89	1019.77	982.25	948.63	822.61	740.99	684.65	644.05
165,000	1337.99	1263.92	1199.92	1144.12	1095.07	1051.64	1012.94	978.27	848.32	764.15	706.05	664.17
170,000	1378.54	1302.22	1236.28	1178.79	1128.25	1083.51	1043.64	1007.92	874.03	787.30	727.44	684.30
175,000	1419.08	1340.52	1272.64	1213.46	1161.44	1115.38	1074.33	1037.56	899.73	810.46	748.84	704.43
180,000	1459.63	1378.82	1309.01	1248.13	1194.62	1147.24	1105.03	1067.20	925.44	833.61	770.23	724.55
185,000	1500.17	1417.12	1345.37	1282.80	1227.81	1179.11	1135.73	1096.85	951.15	856.77	791.63	744.68
190,000	1540.72	1455.42	1381.73	1317.47	1260.99	1210.98	1166.42	1126.49	976.85	879.92	813.02	764.80
195,000	1581.26	1493.72	1418.09	1352.14	1294.17	1242.85	1197.12	1156.14	1002.56	903.08	834.42	784.93
200,000	1621.81	1532.02	1454.45	1386.81	1327.36	1274.72	1227.81	1185.78	1028.27	926.24	855.82	805.06
205,000	1662.36	1570.32	1490.81	1421.48	1360.54	1306.58	1258.51	1215.43	1053.97	949.39	877.21	825.18
210,000	1702.90	1608.62	1527.17	1456.16	1393.73	1338.45	1289.20	1245.07	1079.68	972.55	898.61	845.31
215,000	1743.45	1646.92	1563.53	1490.83	1426.91	1370.32	1319.90	1274.71	1105.39	995.70	920.00	865.44
220,000	1783.99	1685.22	1599.89	1525.50	1460.09	1402.19	1350.59	1304.36	1131.09	1018.86	941.40	885.56
225,000	1824.54	1723.52	1636.26	1560.17	1493.28	1434.05	1381.29	1334.00	1156.80	1042.02	962.79	905.69
230,000	1865.08	1761.82	1672.62	1594.84	1526.46	1465.92	1411.98	1363.65	1182.51	1065.17	984.19	925.81
235,000	1905.63	1800.12	1708.98	1629.51	1559.64	1497.79	1442.68	1393.29	1208.21	1088.33	1005.58	945.94
240,000	1946.17	1838.42	1745.34	1664.18	1592.83	1529.66	1473.37	1422.94	1233.92	1111.48	1026.98	966.07
245,000	1986.72	1876.72	1781.70	1698.85	1626.01	1561.53	1504.07	1452.58	1259.63	1134.64	1048.37	986.19
250,000	2027.26	1915.02	1818.06	1733.52	1659.20	1593.39	1534.76	1482.23	1285.33	1157.79	1069.77	1006.32
255,000	2067.81	1953.32	1854.42	1768.19	1692.38	1625.26	1565.46	1511.87	1311.04	1180.95	1091.16	1026.45
260,000	2108.35	1991.62	1890.78	1802.86	1725.56	1657.13	1596.15	1541.51	1336.75	1204.11	1112.56	1046.57
265,000	2148.90	2029.92	1927.14	1837.53	1758.75	1689.00	1626.85	1571.16	1362.45	1227.26	1133.95	1066.70
270,000	2189.44	2068.22	1963.51	1872.20	1791.93	1720.86	1657.54	1600.80	1388.16	1250.42	1155.35	1086.83
280,000	2270.53	2144.82	2036.23	1941.54	1858.30	1784.60	1718.93	1660.09	1439.57	1296.73	1198.14	1127.08
290,000	2351.62	2221.42	2108.95	2010.88	1924.67	1848.34	1780.32	1719.38	1490.99	1343.04	1240.93	1167.33
300,000	2432.71	2298.02	2181.67	2080.22	1991.03	1912.07	1841.71	1778.67	1542.40	1389.35	1283.72	1207.58

17

MONTHLY AMORTIZING PAYMENTS

AMOUNT OF LOAN	NUMBER OF YEARS IN TERM											
	1	2	3	4	5	6	7	8	9	10	11	12
$ 50	4.26	2.18	1.48	1.13	0.93	0.79	0.69	0.61	0.56	0.51	0.47	0.44
100	8.52	4.35	2.96	2.26	1.85	1.57	1.37	1.22	1.11	1.02	0.94	0.88
200	17.03	8.69	5.91	4.52	3.69	3.13	2.74	2.44	2.21	2.03	1.88	1.76
300	25.55	13.03	8.86	6.78	5.53	4.70	4.11	3.66	3.32	3.04	2.82	2.63
400	34.06	17.37	11.81	9.04	7.37	6.26	5.47	4.88	4.42	4.05	3.76	3.51
500	42.58	21.72	14.77	11.29	9.21	7.83	6.84	6.10	5.53	5.07	4.69	4.38
600	51.09	26.06	17.72	13.55	11.05	9.39	8.21	7.32	6.63	6.08	5.63	5.26
700	59.61	30.40	20.67	15.81	12.90	10.96	9.57	8.54	7.73	7.09	6.57	6.13
800	68.12	34.74	23.62	18.07	14.74	12.52	10.94	9.76	8.84	8.10	7.51	7.01
900	76.64	39.09	26.58	20.33	16.58	14.09	12.31	10.98	9.94	9.12	8.44	7.88
1,000	85.15	43.43	29.53	22.58	18.42	15.65	13.67	12.19	11.05	10.13	9.38	8.76
2,000	170.30	86.85	59.05	45.16	36.84	31.30	27.34	24.38	22.09	20.25	18.76	17.52
3,000	255.45	130.28	88.58	67.74	55.25	46.94	41.01	36.57	33.13	30.38	28.14	26.27
4,000	340.60	173.70	118.10	90.32	73.67	62.59	54.68	48.76	44.17	40.50	37.51	35.03
5,000	425.75	217.13	147.62	112.90	92.09	78.23	68.35	60.95	55.21	50.63	46.89	43.78
6,000	510.90	260.55	177.15	135.48	110.50	93.88	82.02	73.14	66.25	60.75	56.27	52.54
7,000	596.05	303.98	206.67	158.06	128.92	109.52	95.69	85.33	77.29	70.88	65.64	61.29
8,000	681.20	347.40	236.20	180.64	147.34	125.17	109.36	97.52	88.33	81.00	75.02	70.05
9,000	766.35	390.83	265.72	203.22	165.75	140.81	123.02	109.71	99.37	91.13	84.40	78.80
10,000	851.50	434.25	295.24	225.80	184.17	156.46	136.69	121.90	110.41	101.25	93.77	87.56
15,000	1277.25	651.38	442.86	338.69	276.25	234.68	205.04	182.84	165.62	151.87	140.66	131.33
20,000	1703.00	868.50	590.48	451.59	368.34	312.91	273.38	243.79	220.82	202.50	187.54	175.11
25,000	2128.75	1085.63	738.10	564.48	460.42	391.13	341.73	304.74	276.03	253.12	234.42	218.89
30,000	2554.50	1302.75	885.72	677.38	552.50	469.36	410.07	365.68	331.23	303.74	281.31	262.66
35,000	2980.25	1519.88	1033.34	790.27	644.58	547.59	478.41	426.63	386.44	354.36	328.19	306.44
40,000	3406.00	1737.00	1180.96	903.17	736.67	625.81	546.76	487.58	441.64	404.99	375.07	350.22
45,000	3831.75	1954.13	1328.58	1016.06	828.75	704.04	615.10	548.52	496.85	455.61	421.96	393.99
50,000	4257.50	2171.25	1476.20	1128.96	920.83	782.26	683.45	609.47	552.05	506.23	468.84	437.77
55,000	4683.25	2388.38	1623.82	1241.85	1012.91	860.49	751.79	670.42	607.26	556.85	515.72	481.55
60,000	5109.00	2605.50	1771.44	1354.75	1105.00	938.72	820.13	731.36	662.46	607.48	562.61	525.32
65,000	5534.75	2822.62	1919.06	1467.64	1197.08	1016.94	888.48	792.31	717.67	658.10	609.49	569.10
70,000	5960.50	3039.75	2066.68	1580.54	1289.16	1095.17	956.82	853.25	772.87	708.72	656.37	612.87
75,000	6386.25	3256.87	2214.30	1693.43	1381.24	1173.39	1025.17	914.20	828.08	759.34	703.26	656.65
80,000	6812.00	3474.00	2361.92	1806.33	1473.33	1251.62	1093.51	975.15	883.28	809.97	750.14	700.43
85,000	7237.75	3691.12	2509.54	1919.22	1565.41	1329.85	1161.85	1036.09	938.49	860.59	797.02	744.20
90,000	7663.50	3908.25	2657.16	2032.12	1657.49	1408.07	1230.20	1097.04	993.69	911.21	843.91	787.98
95,000	8089.25	4125.37	2804.78	2145.02	1749.57	1486.30	1298.54	1157.99	1048.90	961.83	890.79	831.76
100,000	8515.00	4342.50	2952.40	2257.91	1841.66	1564.52	1366.89	1218.93	1104.10	1012.46	937.67	875.53
105,000	8940.74	4559.62	3100.02	2370.81	1933.74	1642.75	1435.23	1279.88	1159.31	1063.08	984.56	919.31
110,000	9366.49	4776.75	3247.64	2483.70	2025.82	1720.98	1503.57	1340.83	1214.51	1113.70	1031.44	963.09
115,000	9792.24	4993.87	3395.26	2596.60	2117.91	1799.20	1571.92	1401.77	1269.72	1164.32	1078.32	1006.86
120,000	10217.99	5211.00	3542.88	2709.49	2209.99	1877.43	1640.26	1462.72	1324.92	1214.95	1125.21	1050.64
125,000	10643.74	5428.12	3690.50	2822.39	2302.07	1955.65	1708.61	1523.66	1380.13	1265.57	1172.09	1094.42
130,000	11069.49	5645.24	3838.12	2935.28	2394.15	2033.88	1776.95	1584.61	1435.33	1316.19	1218.97	1138.19
135,000	11495.24	5862.37	3985.74	3048.18	2486.24	2112.10	1845.29	1645.56	1490.54	1366.81	1265.86	1181.97
140,000	11920.99	6079.49	4133.36	3161.07	2578.32	2190.33	1913.64	1706.50	1545.74	1417.44	1312.74	1225.74
145,000	12346.74	6296.62	4280.98	3273.97	2670.40	2268.56	1981.98	1767.45	1600.95	1468.06	1359.62	1269.52
150,000	12772.49	6513.74	4428.60	3386.86	2762.48	2346.78	2050.33	1828.40	1656.15	1518.68	1406.51	1313.30
155,000	13198.24	6730.87	4576.22	3499.76	2854.57	2425.01	2118.67	1889.34	1711.36	1569.30	1453.39	1357.07
160,000	13623.99	6947.99	4723.84	3612.65	2946.65	2503.23	2187.01	1950.29	1766.56	1619.93	1500.27	1400.85
165,000	14049.74	7165.12	4871.46	3725.55	3038.73	2581.46	2255.36	2011.24	1821.76	1670.55	1547.16	1444.63
170,000	14475.49	7382.24	5019.08	3838.44	3130.81	2659.69	2323.70	2072.18	1876.97	1721.17	1594.04	1488.40
175,000	14901.24	7599.37	5166.70	3951.34	3222.90	2737.91	2392.05	2133.13	1932.17	1771.79	1640.92	1532.18
180,000	15326.99	7816.49	5314.32	4064.23	3314.98	2816.14	2460.39	2194.07	1987.38	1822.42	1687.81	1575.96
185,000	15752.74	8033.62	5461.94	4177.13	3407.06	2894.36	2528.73	2255.02	2042.58	1873.04	1734.69	1619.73
190,000	16178.49	8250.74	5609.56	4290.03	3499.14	2972.59	2597.08	2315.97	2097.79	1923.66	1781.57	1663.51
195,000	16604.24	8467.86	5757.18	4402.92	3591.23	3050.82	2665.42	2376.91	2152.99	1974.29	1828.46	1707.29
200,000	17029.99	8684.99	5904.80	4515.82	3683.31	3129.04	2733.77	2437.86	2208.20	2024.91	1875.34	1751.06
205,000	17455.74	8902.11	6052.42	4628.71	3775.39	3207.27	2802.11	2498.81	2263.40	2075.53	1922.22	1794.84
210,000	17881.48	9119.24	6200.04	4741.61	3867.47	3285.49	2870.45	2559.75	2318.61	2126.15	1969.11	1838.61
215,000	18307.23	9336.36	6347.66	4854.50	3959.56	3363.72	2938.80	2620.70	2373.81	2176.78	2015.99	1882.39
220,000	18732.98	9553.49	6495.28	4967.40	4051.64	3441.95	3007.14	2681.65	2429.02	2227.40	2062.87	1926.17
225,000	19158.73	9770.61	6642.90	5080.29	4143.72	3520.17	3075.49	2742.59	2484.22	2278.02	2109.76	1969.94
230,000	19584.48	9987.74	6790.52	5193.19	4235.81	3598.40	3143.83	2803.54	2539.43	2328.64	2156.64	2013.72
235,000	20010.23	10204.86	6938.14	5306.08	4327.89	3676.62	3212.17	2864.48	2594.63	2379.27	2203.52	2057.50
240,000	20435.98	10421.99	7085.76	5418.98	4419.97	3754.85	3280.52	2925.43	2649.84	2429.89	2250.41	2101.27
245,000	20861.73	10639.11	7233.38	5531.87	4512.05	3833.07	3348.86	2986.38	2705.04	2480.51	2297.29	2145.05
250,000	21287.48	10856.24	7381.00	5644.77	4604.14	3911.30	3417.21	3047.32	2760.25	2531.13	2344.17	2188.83
255,000	21713.23	11073.36	7528.62	5757.66	4696.22	3989.53	3485.55	3108.27	2815.45	2581.76	2391.06	2232.60
260,000	22138.98	11290.48	7676.24	5870.56	4788.30	4067.75	3553.89	3169.22	2870.66	2632.38	2437.94	2276.38
265,000	22564.73	11507.61	7823.86	5983.45	4880.38	4145.98	3622.24	3230.16	2925.86	2683.00	2484.82	2320.16
270,000	22990.48	11724.73	7971.48	6096.35	4972.47	4224.20	3690.58	3291.11	2981.07	2733.62	2531.71	2363.93
280,000	23841.98	12158.98	8266.72	6322.14	5156.63	4380.66	3827.27	3413.00	3091.48	2834.87	2625.47	2451.48
290,000	24693.48	12593.23	8561.96	6547.93	5340.80	4537.11	3963.96	3534.89	3201.89	2936.11	2719.24	2539.04
300,000	25544.98	13027.48	8857.20	6773.72	5524.96	4693.56	4100.65	3656.79	3312.30	3037.36	2813.01	2626.59

MONTHLY AMORTIZING PAYMENTS · 4.00%

AMOUNT OF LOAN	NUMBER OF YEARS IN TERM											
	13	14	15	16	17	18	19	20	25	30	35	40
$ 50	0.42	0.39	0.37	0.36	0.34	0.33	0.32	0.31	0.27	0.24	0.23	0.21
100	0.83	0.78	0.74	0.71	0.68	0.66	0.63	0.61	0.53	0.48	0.45	0.42
200	1.65	1.56	1.48	1.42	1.36	1.31	1.26	1.22	1.06	0.96	0.89	0.84
300	2.47	2.34	2.22	2.12	2.03	1.96	1.89	1.82	1.59	1.44	1.33	1.26
400	3.30	3.12	2.96	2.83	2.71	2.61	2.51	2.43	2.12	1.91	1.78	1.68
500	4.12	3.90	3.70	3.53	3.39	3.26	3.14	3.03	2.64	2.39	2.22	2.09
600	4.94	4.68	4.44	4.24	4.06	3.91	3.77	3.64	3.17	2.87	2.66	2.51
700	5.77	5.45	5.18	4.95	4.74	4.56	4.39	4.25	3.70	3.35	3.10	2.93
800	6.59	6.23	5.92	5.65	5.42	5.21	5.02	4.85	4.23	3.82	3.55	3.35
900	7.41	7.01	6.66	6.36	6.09	5.86	5.65	5.46	4.76	4.30	3.99	3.77
1,000	8.24	7.79	7.40	7.06	6.77	6.51	6.27	6.06	5.28	4.78	4.43	4.18
2,000	16.47	15.57	14.80	14.12	13.53	13.01	12.54	12.12	10.56	9.55	8.86	8.36
3,000	24.70	23.36	22.20	21.18	20.30	19.51	18.81	18.18	15.84	14.33	13.29	12.54
4,000	32.93	31.14	29.59	28.24	27.06	26.01	25.08	24.24	21.12	19.10	17.72	16.72
5,000	41.16	38.92	36.99	35.30	33.82	32.51	31.35	30.30	26.40	23.88	22.14	20.90
6,000	49.39	46.71	44.39	42.36	40.59	39.02	37.62	36.36	31.68	28.65	26.57	25.08
7,000	57.62	54.49	51.78	49.42	47.35	45.52	43.89	42.42	36.95	33.42	31.00	29.26
8,000	65.85	62.27	59.18	56.48	54.12	52.02	50.15	48.48	42.23	38.20	35.43	33.44
9,000	74.09	70.06	66.58	63.54	60.88	58.52	56.42	54.54	47.51	42.97	39.85	37.62
10,000	82.32	77.84	73.97	70.60	67.64	65.02	62.69	60.60	52.79	47.75	44.28	41.80
15,000	123.47	116.76	110.96	105.90	101.46	97.53	94.04	90.90	79.18	71.62	66.42	62.70
20,000	164.63	155.67	147.94	141.20	135.28	130.04	125.38	121.20	105.57	95.49	88.56	83.59
25,000	205.78	194.59	184.93	176.50	169.10	162.55	156.72	151.50	131.96	119.36	110.70	104.49
30,000	246.04	233.51	221.91	211.00	202.92	195.06	188.07	181.80	158.36	143.23	132.84	125.39
35,000	288.10	272.43	258.90	247.10	236.74	227.57	219.41	212.10	184.75	167.10	154.98	146.28
40,000	329.25	311.34	295.88	282.40	270.56	260.08	250.75	242.40	211.14	190.97	177.11	167.18
45,000	370.41	350.26	332.86	317.70	304.38	292.59	282.10	272.70	237.53	214.84	199.25	188.08
50,000	411.56	389.18	369.85	353.00	338.20	325.10	313.44	303.00	263.92	238.71	221.39	208.97
55,000	452.72	428.10	406.83	388.30	372.02	357.61	344.78	333.29	290.32	262.58	243.53	229.87
60,000	493.87	467.01	443.82	423.60	405.84	390.12	376.13	363.59	316.71	286.45	265.67	250.77
65,000	535.03	505.93	480.80	458.90	439.66	422.63	407.47	393.89	343.10	310.32	287.81	271.67
70,000	576.19	544.85	517.79	494.20	473.48	455.14	438.81	424.19	369.49	334.20	309.95	292.56
75,000	617.34	583.76	554.77	529.50	507.30	487.65	470.16	454.49	395.88	358.07	332.09	313.46
80,000	658.50	622.68	591.76	564.80	541.12	520.16	501.50	484.79	422.27	381.94	354.22	334.36
85,000	699.65	661.60	628.74	600.10	574.94	552.67	532.84	515.09	448.67	405.81	376.36	355.25
90,000	740.81	700.52	665.72	635.40	608.76	585.18	564.19	545.39	475.06	429.68	398.50	376.15
95,000	781.97	739.43	702.71	670.70	642.58	617.69	595.53	575.69	501.45	453.55	420.64	397.05
100,000	823.12	778.35	739.69	706.00	676.40	650.20	626.88	605.99	527.84	477.42	442.78	417.94
105,000	864.28	817.27	776.68	741.30	710.22	682.71	658.22	636.28	554.23	501.29	464.92	438.84
110,000	905.43	856.19	813.66	776.60	744.04	715.22	689.56	666.58	580.63	525.16	487.06	459.74
115,000	946.59	895.10	850.65	811.90	777.86	747.73	720.91	696.88	607.02	549.03	509.20	480.63
120,000	987.74	934.02	887.63	847.20	811.68	780.24	752.25	727.18	633.41	572.90	531.33	501.53
125,000	1028.90	972.94	924.61	882.50	845.50	812.75	783.59	757.48	659.80	596.77	553.47	522.43
130,000	1070.06	1011.85	961.60	917.80	879.32	845.26	814.94	787.78	686.19	620.64	575.61	543.33
135,000	1111.21	1050.77	998.58	953.10	913.14	877.77	846.28	818.08	712.58	644.52	597.75	564.22
140,000	1152.37	1089.69	1035.57	988.40	946.96	910.28	877.62	848.38	738.98	668.39	619.89	585.12
145,000	1193.52	1128.61	1072.55	1023.70	980.78	942.79	908.97	878.68	765.37	692.26	642.03	606.02
150,000	1234.68	1167.52	1109.54	1059.00	1014.60	975.30	940.31	908.98	791.76	716.13	664.17	626.91
155,000	1275.84	1206.44	1146.52	1094.30	1048.41	1007.81	971.65	939.27	818.15	740.00	686.31	647.81
160,000	1316.99	1245.36	1183.51	1129.60	1082.23	1040.32	1003.00	969.57	844.54	763.87	708.44	668.71
165,000	1358.15	1284.28	1220.49	1164.90	1116.05	1072.83	1034.34	999.87	870.94	787.74	730.58	689.60
170,000	1399.30	1323.19	1257.47	1200.20	1149.87	1105.34	1065.68	1030.17	897.33	811.61	752.72	710.50
175,000	1440.46	1362.11	1294.46	1235.50	1183.69	1137.85	1097.03	1060.47	923.72	835.48	774.86	731.40
180,000	1481.61	1401.03	1331.44	1270.80	1217.51	1170.36	1128.37	1090.77	950.11	859.35	797.00	752.29
185,000	1522.77	1439.94	1368.43	1306.10	1251.33	1202.87	1159.71	1121.07	976.50	883.22	819.14	773.19
190,000	1563.93	1478.86	1405.41	1341.40	1285.15	1235.38	1191.06	1151.37	1002.89	907.09	841.28	794.09
195,000	1605.08	1517.78	1442.40	1376.70	1318.97	1267.89	1222.40	1181.67	1029.29	930.96	863.42	814.99
200,000	1646.24	1556.70	1479.38	1412.00	1352.79	1300.40	1253.75	1211.97	1055.68	954.84	885.55	835.88
205,000	1687.39	1595.61	1516.37	1447.30	1386.61	1332.91	1285.09	1242.26	1082.07	978.71	907.69	856.78
210,000	1728.55	1634.53	1553.35	1482.60	1420.43	1365.42	1316.43	1272.56	1108.46	1002.58	929.83	877.68
215,000	1769.70	1673.45	1590.33	1517.90	1454.25	1397.93	1347.78	1302.86	1134.85	1026.45	951.97	898.57
220,000	1810.86	1712.37	1627.32	1553.20	1488.07	1430.44	1379.12	1333.16	1161.25	1050.32	974.11	919.47
225,000	1852.02	1751.28	1664.30	1588.50	1521.89	1462.95	1410.46	1363.46	1187.64	1074.19	996.25	940.37
230,000	1893.17	1790.20	1701.29	1623.80	1555.71	1495.46	1441.81	1393.76	1214.03	1098.06	1018.39	961.26
235,000	1934.33	1829.12	1738.27	1659.10	1589.53	1527.97	1473.15	1424.06	1240.42	1121.93	1040.53	982.16
240,000	1975.48	1868.03	1775.26	1694.40	1623.35	1560.48	1504.49	1454.36	1266.81	1145.80	1062.66	1003.06
245,000	2016.64	1906.95	1812.24	1729.70	1657.17	1592.99	1535.84	1484.66	1293.21	1169.67	1084.80	1023.95
250,000	2057.80	1945.87	1849.22	1765.00	1690.99	1625.50	1567.18	1514.96	1319.60	1193.54	1106.94	1044.85
255,000	2098.95	1984.79	1886.21	1800.30	1724.81	1658.01	1598.52	1545.25	1345.99	1217.41	1129.08	1065.75
260,000	2140.11	2023.70	1923.19	1835.60	1758.63	1690.52	1629.87	1575.55	1372.38	1241.28	1151.22	1086.65
265,000	2181.26	2062.62	1960.18	1870.89	1792.45	1723.03	1661.21	1605.85	1398.77	1265.16	1173.36	1107.54
270,000	2222.42	2101.54	1997.16	1906.19	1826.27	1755.54	1692.55	1636.15	1425.16	1289.03	1195.50	1128.44
280,000	2304.73	2179.37	2071.13	1976.79	1893.91	1820.56	1755.24	1696.75	1477.95	1336.77	1239.77	1170.23
290,000	2387.04	2257.21	2145.10	2047.39	1961.55	1885.58	1817.93	1757.35	1530.73	1384.51	1284.05	1212.03
300,000	2469.35	2335.04	2219.07	2117.99	2029.19	1950.60	1880.62	1817.95	1583.52	1432.25	1328.33	1253.82

19

AMOUNT OF LOAN	NUMBER OF YEARS IN TERM											
	1	2	3	4	5	6	7	8	9	10	11	12
$ 50	4.27	2.18	1.49	1.14	0.93	0.79	0.69	0.62	0.56	0.52	0.48	0.45
100	8.53	4.36	2.97	2.27	1.86	1.58	1.38	1.24	1.12	1.03	0.95	0.89
200	17.06	8.71	5.93	4.54	3.71	3.16	2.76	2.47	2.24	2.05	1.90	1.78
300	25.58	13.07	8.90	6.81	5.56	4.73	4.14	3.70	3.35	3.08	2.85	2.67
400	34.11	17.42	11.86	9.08	7.42	6.31	5.52	4.93	4.47	4.10	3.80	3.56
500	42.64	21.77	14.82	11.35	9.27	7.88	6.90	6.16	5.58	5.13	4.75	4.44
600	51.16	26.13	17.79	13.62	11.12	9.46	8.28	7.39	6.70	6.15	5.70	5.33
700	59.69	30.48	20.75	15.89	12.98	11.04	9.65	8.62	7.82	7.18	6.65	6.22
800	68.22	34.83	23.71	18.16	14.83	12.61	11.03	9.85	8.93	8.20	7.60	7.11
900	76.74	39.19	26.68	20.43	16.68	14.19	12.41	11.08	10.05	9.22	8.55	7.99
1,000	85.27	43.54	29.64	22.70	18.53	15.76	13.79	12.31	11.16	10.25	9.50	8.88
2,000	170.53	87.08	59.28	45.39	37.06	31.52	27.57	24.62	22.32	20.49	19.00	17.76
3,000	255.80	130.61	88.91	68.08	55.59	47.28	41.36	36.92	33.48	30.74	28.50	26.64
4,000	341.06	174.15	118.55	90.77	74.12	63.04	55.14	49.23	44.64	40.98	37.99	35.51
5,000	426.33	217.69	148.18	113.46	92.65	78.80	68.93	61.53	55.80	51.22	47.49	44.39
6,000	511.59	261.22	177.82	136.15	111.18	94.56	82.71	73.84	66.96	61.47	56.99	53.27
7,000	596.85	304.76	207.45	158.84	129.71	110.32	96.49	86.15	78.12	71.71	66.49	62.15
8,000	682.12	348.30	237.09	181.53	148.24	126.08	110.28	98.45	89.28	81.96	75.98	71.02
9,000	767.38	391.83	266.72	204.22	166.77	141.84	124.06	110.76	100.44	92.20	85.48	79.90
10,000	852.65	435.37	296.36	226.92	185.30	157.60	137.85	123.06	111.59	102.44	94.98	88.78
15,000	1278.97	653.05	444.53	340.37	277.95	236.40	206.77	184.59	167.39	153.66	142.46	133.16
20,000	1705.29	870.73	592.71	453.83	370.60	315.19	275.69	246.12	223.18	204.88	189.95	177.55
25,000	2131.61	1088.41	740.89	567.28	463.24	393.99	344.61	307.65	278.98	256.10	237.44	221.93
30,000	2557.93	1306.09	889.06	680.74	555.89	472.79	413.53	369.18	334.77	307.32	284.92	266.32
35,000	2984.25	1523.77	1037.24	794.19	648.54	551.58	482.45	430.71	390.57	358.54	332.41	310.71
40,000	3410.57	1741.46	1185.42	907.65	741.19	630.38	551.37	492.24	446.36	409.76	379.89	355.09
45,000	3836.89	1959.14	1333.59	1021.10	833.84	709.18	620.29	553.77	502.16	460.97	427.38	399.48
50,000	4263.21	2176.82	1481.77	1134.56	926.48	787.97	689.21	615.30	557.95	512.19	474.87	443.06
55,000	4689.53	2394.50	1629.95	1248.02	1019.13	866.77	758.14	676.83	613.74	563.41	522.35	488.25
60,000	5115.86	2612.18	1778.12	1361.47	1111.78	945.57	827.06	738.36	669.54	614.63	569.84	532.64
65,000	5542.18	2829.86	1926.30	1474.93	1204.43	1024.36	895.98	799.89	725.33	665.85	617.33	577.02
70,000	5968.50	3047.54	2074.48	1588.38	1297.07	1103.16	964.90	861.42	781.13	717.07	664.81	621.41
75,000	6394.82	3265.23	2222.65	1701.84	1389.72	1181.96	1033.82	922.95	836.92	768.29	712.30	665.79
80,000	6821.14	3482.91	2370.83	1815.29	1482.37	1260.75	1102.74	984.48	892.72	819.51	759.78	710.18
85,000	7247.46	3700.59	2519.01	1928.75	1575.02	1339.55	1171.66	1046.01	948.51	870.72	807.27	754.57
90,000	7673.78	3918.27	2667.18	2042.20	1667.67	1418.35	1240.58	1107.54	1004.31	921.94	854.76	798.95
95,000	8100.10	4135.95	2815.36	2155.66	1760.31	1497.14	1309.50	1169.07	1060.10	973.16	902.24	843.34
100,000	8526.42	4353.63	2963.54	2269.11	1852.96	1575.94	1378.42	1230.60	1115.89	1024.38	949.73	887.72
105,000	8952.74	4571.31	3111.71	2382.57	1945.61	1654.74	1447.34	1292.13	1171.69	1075.60	997.21	932.11
110,000	9379.06	4789.00	3259.89	2496.03	2038.26	1733.53	1516.27	1353.66	1227.48	1126.82	1044.70	976.49
115,000	9805.38	5006.68	3408.07	2609.48	2130.90	1812.33	1585.19	1415.19	1283.28	1178.04	1092.19	1020.88
120,000	10231.71	5224.36	3556.24	2722.94	2223.55	1891.13	1654.11	1476.71	1339.07	1229.26	1139.67	1065.27
125,000	10658.03	5442.04	3704.42	2836.39	2316.20	1969.92	1723.03	1538.24	1394.87	1280.47	1187.16	1109.65
130,000	11084.35	5659.72	3852.60	2949.85	2408.85	2048.72	1791.95	1599.77	1450.66	1331.69	1234.65	1154.04
135,000	11510.67	5877.40	4000.77	3063.30	2501.50	2127.52	1860.87	1661.30	1506.46	1382.91	1282.13	1198.42
140,000	11936.99	6095.08	4148.95	3176.76	2594.14	2206.31	1929.79	1722.83	1562.25	1434.13	1329.62	1242.81
145,000	12363.31	6312.77	4297.13	3290.21	2686.79	2285.11	1998.71	1784.36	1618.05	1485.35	1377.10	1287.20
150,000	12789.63	6530.45	4445.30	3403.67	2779.44	2363.91	2067.63	1845.89	1673.84	1536.57	1424.59	1331.58
155,000	13215.95	6748.13	4593.48	3517.13	2872.09	2442.70	2136.55	1907.42	1729.63	1587.79	1472.08	1375.97
160,000	13642.27	6965.81	4741.66	3630.58	2964.73	2521.50	2205.47	1968.95	1785.43	1639.01	1519.56	1420.35
165,000	14068.59	7183.49	4889.83	3744.04	3057.38	2600.30	2274.40	2030.48	1841.22	1690.22	1567.05	1464.74
170,000	14494.91	7401.17	5038.01	3857.49	3150.03	2679.09	2343.32	2092.01	1897.02	1741.44	1614.53	1509.13
175,000	14921.23	7618.85	5186.19	3970.95	3242.68	2757.89	2412.24	2153.54	1952.81	1792.66	1662.02	1553.51
180,000	15347.56	7836.54	5334.36	4084.40	3335.33	2836.69	2481.16	2215.07	2008.61	1843.88	1709.51	1597.90
185,000	15773.88	8054.22	5482.54	4197.86	3427.97	2915.48	2550.08	2276.60	2064.40	1895.10	1756.99	1642.28
190,000	16200.20	8271.90	5630.72	4311.31	3520.62	2994.28	2619.00	2338.13	2120.20	1946.32	1804.48	1686.67
195,000	16626.52	8489.58	5778.89	4424.77	3613.27	3073.08	2687.92	2399.66	2175.99	1997.54	1851.97	1731.05
200,000	17052.84	8707.26	5927.07	4538.22	3705.92	3151.87	2756.84	2461.19	2231.78	2048.76	1899.45	1775.44
205,000	17479.16	8924.94	6075.25	4651.68	3798.56	3230.67	2825.76	2522.72	2287.58	2099.97	1946.94	1819.83
210,000	17905.48	9142.62	6223.42	4765.14	3891.21	3309.47	2894.68	2584.25	2343.37	2151.19	1994.42	1864.21
215,000	18331.80	9360.31	6371.60	4878.59	3983.86	3388.27	2963.60	2645.78	2399.17	2202.41	2041.91	1908.60
220,000	18758.12	9577.99	6519.78	4992.05	4076.51	3467.06	3032.53	2707.31	2454.96	2253.63	2089.40	1952.98
225,000	19184.44	9795.67	6667.95	5105.50	4169.16	3545.86	3101.45	2768.84	2510.76	2304.85	2136.88	1997.37
230,000	19610.76	10013.35	6816.13	5218.96	4261.80	3624.66	3170.37	2830.37	2566.55	2356.07	2184.37	2041.76
235,000	20037.08	10231.03	6964.31	5332.41	4354.45	3703.45	3239.29	2891.89	2622.35	2407.29	2231.86	2086.14
240,000	20463.41	10448.71	7112.48	5445.87	4447.10	3782.25	3308.21	2953.42	2678.14	2458.51	2279.34	2130.53
245,000	20889.73	10666.39	7260.66	5559.32	4539.75	3861.05	3377.13	3014.95	2733.93	2509.72	2326.83	2174.91
250,000	21316.05	10884.08	7408.84	5672.78	4632.39	3939.84	3446.05	3076.48	2789.73	2560.94	2374.31	2219.30
255,000	21742.37	11101.76	7557.01	5786.24	4725.04	4018.64	3514.97	3138.01	2845.52	2612.16	2421.80	2263.69
260,000	22168.69	11319.44	7705.19	5899.69	4817.69	4097.44	3583.89	3199.54	2901.32	2663.38	2469.29	2308.07
265,000	22595.01	11537.12	7853.37	6013.15	4910.34	4176.23	3652.81	3261.07	2957.11	2714.60	2516.77	2352.46
270,000	23021.33	11754.80	8001.54	6126.60	5002.99	4255.03	3721.73	3322.60	3012.91	2765.82	2564.26	2396.84
280,000	23873.97	12190.16	8297.90	6353.51	5188.28	4412.62	3859.58	3445.66	3124.50	2868.26	2659.23	2485.61
290,000	24726.61	12625.53	8594.25	6580.42	5373.58	4570.22	3997.42	3568.72	3236.09	2970.69	2754.20	2574.39
300,000	25579.26	13060.89	8890.60	6807.33	5558.87	4727.81	4135.26	3691.78	3347.67	3073.13	2849.18	2663.16

AMOUNT OF LOAN	NUMBER OF YEARS IN TERM											
	13	14	15	16	17	18	19	20	25	30	35	40
$ 50	0.42	0.40	0.38	0.36	0.35	0.34	0.32	0.31	0.28	0.25	0.23	0.22
100	0.84	0.80	0.76	0.72	0.69	0.67	0.64	0.62	0.55	0.50	0.46	0.44
200	1.68	1.59	1.51	1.44	1.38	1.33	1.28	1.24	1.09	0.99	0.92	0.87
300	2.51	2.38	2.26	2.16	2.07	1.99	1.92	1.86	1.63	1.48	1.38	1.31
400	3.35	3.17	3.01	2.88	2.76	2.66	2.56	2.48	2.17	1.97	1.84	1.74
500	4.18	3.96	3.77	3.60	3.45	3.32	3.20	3.10	2.71	2.46	2.29	2.17
600	5.02	4.75	4.52	4.32	4.14	3.98	3.84	3.72	3.26	2.96	2.75	2.61
700	5.85	5.54	5.27	5.04	4.83	4.65	4.48	4.34	3.80	3.45	3.21	3.04
800	6.69	6.33	6.02	5.75	5.52	5.31	5.12	4.96	4.34	3.94	3.67	3.47
900	7.52	7.12	6.78	6.47	6.21	5.97	5.76	5.58	4.88	4.43	4.13	3.91
1,000	8.36	7.91	7.53	7.19	6.90	6.64	6.40	6.20	5.42	4.92	4.58	4.34
2,000	16.71	15.82	15.05	14.38	13.79	13.27	12.80	12.39	10.84	9.84	9.16	8.68
3,000	25.07	23.73	22.57	21.57	20.68	19.90	19.20	18.58	16.26	14.76	13.74	13.01
4,000	33.42	31.64	30.10	28.75	27.58	26.53	25.60	24.77	21.67	19.68	18.32	17.35
5,000	41.78	39.55	37.62	35.94	34.47	33.16	32.00	30.97	27.09	24.60	22.90	21.69
6,000	50.13	47.45	45.14	43.13	41.36	39.80	38.40	37.16	32.51	29.52	27.48	26.02
7,000	58.49	55.36	52.66	50.32	48.25	46.43	44.80	43.35	37.93	34.44	32.06	30.36
8,000	66.84	63.27	60.19	57.50	55.15	53.06	51.20	49.54	43.34	39.36	36.64	34.69
9,000	75.19	71.18	67.71	64.69	62.04	59.69	57.60	55.74	48.76	44.28	41.22	39.03
10,000	83.55	79.09	75.23	71.88	68.93	66.32	64.00	61.93	54.18	49.20	45.79	43.37
15,000	125.32	118.63	112.85	107.81	103.39	99.48	96.00	92.89	81.27	73.80	68.69	65.05
20,000	167.09	158.17	150.46	143.75	137.86	132.64	128.00	123.85	108.35	98.39	91.58	86.73
25,000	208.86	197.71	188.07	179.69	172.32	165.80	160.00	154.81	135.44	122.99	114.48	108.41
30,000	250.64	237.25	225.69	215.62	206.78	198.96	192.00	185.78	162.53	147.59	137.37	130.09
35,000	292.41	276.79	263.30	251.56	241.24	232.12	224.00	216.74	189.61	172.18	160.27	151.77
40,000	334.18	316.33	300.92	287.49	275.71	265.28	256.00	247.70	216.70	196.78	183.16	173.45
45,000	375.95	355.87	338.53	323.43	310.17	298.44	288.00	278.66	243.79	221.38	206.06	195.13
50,000	417.72	395.41	376.14	359.37	344.63	331.60	320.00	309.62	270.87	245.97	228.95	216.82
55,000	459.50	434.95	413.76	395.30	379.09	364.76	352.00	340.58	297.96	270.57	251.85	238.50
60,000	501.27	474.49	451.37	431.24	413.56	397.92	384.00	371.55	325.05	295.17	274.74	260.18
65,000	543.04	514.03	488.99	467.17	448.02	431.08	416.00	402.51	352.13	319.77	297.64	281.86
70,000	584.81	553.57	526.60	503.11	482.48	464.24	448.00	433.47	379.22	344.36	320.53	303.54
75,000	626.58	593.11	564.21	539.05	516.94	497.40	480.00	464.43	406.31	368.96	343.43	325.22
80,000	668.36	632.65	601.83	574.98	551.41	530.56	512.00	495.39	433.40	393.56	366.32	346.90
85,000	710.13	672.19	639.44	610.92	585.87	563.71	544.00	526.35	460.48	418.15	389.21	368.58
90,000	751.90	711.73	677.06	646.85	620.33	596.87	576.00	557.32	487.57	442.75	412.11	390.26
95,000	793.67	751.27	714.67	682.79	654.79	630.03	608.00	588.28	514.66	467.35	435.00	411.94
100,000	835.44	790.81	752.28	718.73	689.26	663.19	640.00	619.24	541.74	491.94	457.90	433.63
105,000	877.22	830.35	789.90	754.66	723.72	696.35	672.00	650.20	568.83	510.54	480.79	455.31
110,000	918.99	869.89	827.51	790.60	758.18	729.51	704.00	681.16	595.92	541.14	503.69	476.99
115,000	960.76	909.43	865.13	826.53	792.64	762.67	736.00	712.12	623.00	565.74	526.58	498.67
120,000	1002.53	948.97	902.74	862.47	827.11	795.83	768.00	743.09	650.09	590.33	549.48	520.35
125,000	1044.30	988.51	940.35	898.41	861.57	828.99	800.00	774.05	677.18	614.93	572.37	542.03
130,000	1086.08	1028.05	977.97	934.34	896.03	862.15	832.00	805.01	704.26	639.53	595.27	563.71
135,000	1127.85	1067.59	1015.58	970.28	930.49	895.31	864.00	835.97	731.35	664.12	618.16	585.39
140,000	1169.62	1107.13	1053.19	1006.21	964.96	928.47	895.99	866.93	758.44	688.72	641.06	607.07
145,000	1211.39	1146.67	1090.81	1042.15	999.42	961.63	927.99	897.89	785.53	713.32	663.95	628.75
150,000	1253.16	1186.21	1128.42	1078.09	1033.88	994.79	959.99	928.86	812.61	737.91	686.85	650.44
155,000	1294.94	1225.75	1166.04	1114.02	1068.34	1027.95	991.99	959.82	839.70	762.51	709.74	672.12
160,000	1336.71	1265.29	1203.65	1149.96	1102.81	1061.11	1023.99	990.78	866.79	787.11	732.64	693.80
165,000	1378.48	1304.83	1241.26	1185.89	1137.27	1094.26	1055.99	1021.74	893.87	811.71	755.53	715.48
170,000	1420.25	1344.37	1278.88	1221.83	1171.73	1127.42	1087.99	1052.70	920.96	836.30	778.42	737.16
175,000	1462.02	1383.91	1316.49	1257.77	1206.19	1160.58	1119.99	1083.67	948.05	860.90	801.32	758.84
180,000	1503.80	1423.45	1354.11	1293.70	1240.66	1193.74	1151.99	1114.63	975.13	885.50	824.21	780.52
185,000	1545.57	1462.99	1391.72	1329.64	1275.12	1226.90	1183.99	1145.59	1002.22	910.09	847.11	802.20
190,000	1587.34	1502.53	1429.33	1365.57	1309.58	1260.06	1215.99	1176.55	1029.31	934.69	870.00	823.88
195,000	1629.11	1542.07	1466.95	1401.51	1344.04	1293.22	1247.99	1207.51	1056.39	959.29	892.90	845.56
200,000	1670.88	1581.61	1504.56	1437.45	1378.51	1326.38	1279.99	1238.47	1083.48	983.88	915.79	867.25
205,000	1712.66	1621.15	1542.18	1473.38	1412.97	1359.54	1311.99	1269.44	1110.57	1008.48	938.69	888.93
210,000	1754.43	1660.69	1579.79	1509.32	1447.43	1392.70	1343.99	1300.40	1137.66	1033.08	961.58	910.61
215,000	1796.20	1700.23	1617.40	1545.25	1481.89	1425.86	1375.99	1331.36	1164.74	1057.68	984.48	932.29
220,000	1837.97	1739.77	1655.02	1581.19	1516.36	1459.02	1407.99	1362.32	1191.83	1082.27	1007.37	953.97
225,000	1879.74	1779.31	1692.63	1617.13	1550.82	1492.18	1439.99	1393.28	1218.92	1106.87	1030.27	975.65
230,000	1921.52	1818.85	1730.25	1653.06	1585.28	1525.34	1471.99	1424.24	1246.00	1131.47	1053.16	997.33
235,000	1963.29	1858.39	1767.86	1689.00	1619.74	1558.50	1503.99	1455.21	1273.09	1156.06	1076.06	1019.01
240,000	2005.06	1897.93	1805.47	1724.93	1654.21	1591.66	1535.99	1486.17	1300.18	1180.66	1098.95	1040.69
245,000	2046.83	1937.47	1843.09	1760.87	1688.67	1624.82	1567.99	1517.13	1327.26	1205.26	1121.85	1062.37
250,000	2088.60	1977.01	1880.70	1796.81	1723.13	1657.97	1599.99	1548.09	1354.35	1229.85	1144.74	1084.06
255,000	2130.37	2016.55	1918.31	1832.74	1757.59	1691.13	1631.99	1579.05	1381.44	1254.45	1167.63	1105.74
260,000	2172.15	2056.09	1955.93	1868.68	1792.06	1724.29	1663.99	1610.01	1408.52	1279.05	1190.53	1127.42
265,000	2213.92	2095.63	1993.54	1904.61	1826.52	1757.45	1695.99	1640.98	1435.61	1303.65	1213.42	1149.10
270,000	2255.69	2135.17	2031.16	1940.55	1860.98	1790.61	1727.99	1671.94	1462.70	1328.24	1236.32	1170.78
280,000	2339.23	2214.25	2106.38	2012.42	1929.91	1856.93	1791.98	1733.86	1516.87	1377.44	1282.11	1214.14
290,000	2422.78	2293.33	2181.61	2084.29	1998.83	1923.25	1855.98	1795.78	1571.05	1426.63	1327.90	1257.50
300,000	2506.32	2372.41	2256.84	2156.17	2067.76	1989.57	1919.98	1857.71	1625.22	1475.82	1373.69	1300.87

AMOUNT OF LOAN	NUMBER OF YEARS IN TERM											
	1	2	3	4	5	6	7	8	9	10	11	12
$ 50	4.27	2.19	1.49	1.15	0.94	0.80	0.70	0.63	0.57	0.52	0.49	0.46
100	8.54	4.37	2.98	2.29	1.87	1.59	1.40	1.25	1.13	1.04	0.97	0.91
200	17.08	8.73	5.95	4.57	3.73	3.18	2.79	2.49	2.26	2.08	1.93	1.81
300	25.62	13.10	8.93	6.85	5.60	4.77	4.18	3.73	3.39	3.11	2.89	2.71
400	34.16	17.46	11.90	9.13	7.46	6.35	5.57	4.97	4.52	4.15	3.85	3.61
500	42.69	21.83	14.88	11.41	9.33	7.94	6.96	6.22	5.64	5.19	4.81	4.51
600	51.23	26.19	17.85	13.69	11.19	9.53	8.35	7.46	6.77	6.22	5.78	5.41
700	59.77	30.56	20.83	15.97	13.06	11.12	9.74	8.70	7.90	7.26	6.74	6.31
800	68.31	34.92	23.80	18.25	14.92	12.70	11.13	9.94	9.03	8.30	7.70	7.21
900	76.85	39.29	26.78	20.53	16.78	14.29	12.52	11.19	10.15	9.33	8.66	8.11
1,000	85.38	43.65	29.75	22.81	18.65	15.88	13.91	12.43	11.28	10.37	9.62	9.01
2,000	170.76	87.30	59.50	45.61	37.29	31.75	27.81	24.85	22.56	20.73	19.24	18.01
3,000	256.14	130.95	89.25	68.42	55.93	47.63	41.71	37.27	33.84	31.10	28.86	27.01
4,000	341.52	174.60	118.99	91.22	74.58	63.50	55.61	49.70	45.12	41.46	38.48	36.01
5,000	426.90	218.24	148.74	114.02	93.22	79.38	69.51	62.12	56.39	51.82	48.10	45.01
6,000	512.28	261.89	178.49	136.83	111.86	95.25	83.41	74.54	67.67	62.19	57.72	54.01
7,000	597.65	305.54	208.23	159.63	130.51	111.12	97.31	86.97	78.95	72.55	67.34	63.01
8,000	683.03	349.19	237.98	182.43	149.15	127.00	111.21	99.39	90.23	82.92	76.95	72.01
9,000	768.41	392.84	267.73	205.24	167.79	142.87	125.11	111.81	101.50	93.28	86.57	81.01
10,000	853.79	436.48	297.47	228.04	186.44	158.75	139.01	124.24	112.78	103.64	96.19	90.01
15,000	1280.68	654.72	446.21	342.06	279.65	238.12	208.51	186.35	169.17	155.46	144.29	135.01
20,000	1707.58	872.96	594.94	456.07	372.87	317.49	278.01	248.47	225.56	207.28	192.38	180.01
25,000	2134.47	1091.20	743.68	570.09	466.08	396.86	347.51	310.59	281.94	259.10	240.47	225.01
30,000	2561.36	1309.44	892.41	684.11	559.30	476.23	417.01	372.70	338.33	310.92	288.57	270.01
35,000	2988.25	1527.68	1041.15	798.13	652.51	555.60	486.51	434.82	394.72	362.74	336.66	315.01
40,000	3415.15	1745.92	1189.88	912.14	745.73	634.97	556.01	496.93	451.11	414.56	384.75	360.01
45,000	3842.04	1964.16	1338.62	1026.16	838.94	714.34	625.51	559.05	507.50	466.38	432.85	405.01
50,000	4268.93	2182.40	1487.35	1140.18	932.16	793.71	695.01	621.17	563.88	518.20	480.94	450.01
55,000	4695.82	2400.63	1636.09	1254.20	1025.37	873.08	764.51	683.28	620.27	570.02	529.03	495.01
60,000	5122.72	2618.87	1784.82	1368.21	1118.59	952.45	834.01	745.40	676.66	621.84	577.13	540.01
65,000	5549.61	2837.11	1933.56	1482.23	1211.80	1031.82	903.52	807.52	733.05	673.65	625.22	585.01
70,000	5976.50	3055.35	2082.29	1596.25	1305.02	1111.19	973.02	869.63	789.44	725.47	673.32	630.01
75,000	6403.39	3273.59	2231.02	1710.27	1398.23	1190.56	1042.52	931.75	845.82	777.29	721.41	675.01
80,000	6830.29	3491.83	2379.76	1824.28	1491.45	1269.93	1112.02	993.86	902.21	829.11	769.50	720.01
85,000	7257.18	3710.07	2528.49	1938.30	1584.66	1349.30	1181.52	1055.98	958.60	880.93	817.60	765.01
90,000	7684.07	3928.31	2677.23	2052.32	1677.88	1428.67	1251.02	1118.10	1014.99	932.75	865.69	810.01
95,000	8110.96	4146.55	2825.96	2166.34	1771.09	1508.04	1320.52	1180.21	1071.38	984.57	913.78	855.01
100,000	8537.86	4364.79	2974.70	2280.35	1864.31	1587.41	1390.02	1242.33	1127.76	1036.39	961.88	900.01
105,000	8964.75	4583.03	3123.43	2394.37	1957.52	1666.78	1459.52	1304.44	1184.15	1088.21	1009.97	945.01
110,000	9391.64	4801.26	3272.17	2508.39	2050.74	1746.15	1529.02	1366.56	1240.54	1140.03	1058.06	990.01
115,000	9818.53	5019.50	3420.90	2622.41	2143.95	1825.52	1598.52	1428.68	1296.93	1191.85	1106.16	1035.01
120,000	10245.43	5237.74	3569.64	2736.42	2237.17	1904.89	1668.02	1490.79	1353.32	1243.67	1154.25	1080.02
125,000	10672.32	5455.98	3718.37	2850.44	2330.38	1984.26	1737.53	1552.91	1409.70	1295.49	1202.35	1125.02
130,000	11099.21	5674.22	3867.11	2964.46	2423.60	2063.63	1807.03	1615.03	1466.09	1347.30	1250.44	1170.02
135,000	11526.11	5892.46	4015.84	3078.48	2516.81	2143.00	1876.53	1677.14	1522.48	1399.12	1298.53	1215.02
140,000	11953.00	6110.70	4164.57	3192.49	2610.03	2222.37	1946.03	1739.26	1578.87	1450.94	1346.63	1260.02
145,000	12379.89	6328.94	4313.31	3306.51	2703.24	2301.74	2015.53	1801.37	1635.26	1502.76	1394.72	1305.02
150,000	12806.78	6547.18	4462.04	3420.53	2796.46	2381.11	2085.03	1863.49	1691.64	1554.58	1442.81	1350.02
155,000	13233.68	6765.42	4610.78	3534.55	2889.67	2460.48	2154.53	1925.61	1748.03	1606.40	1490.91	1395.02
160,000	13660.57	6983.65	4759.51	3648.56	2982.89	2539.85	2224.03	1987.72	1804.42	1658.22	1539.00	1440.02
165,000	14087.46	7201.89	4908.25	3762.58	3076.10	2619.22	2293.53	2049.84	1860.81	1710.04	1587.09	1485.02
170,000	14514.35	7420.13	5056.98	3876.60	3169.32	2698.59	2363.03	2111.95	1917.20	1761.86	1635.19	1530.02
175,000	14941.25	7638.37	5205.72	3990.62	3262.53	2777.96	2432.53	2174.07	1973.58	1813.68	1683.28	1575.02
180,000	15368.14	7856.61	5354.45	4104.63	3355.75	2857.33	2502.03	2236.19	2029.97	1865.50	1731.38	1620.02
185,000	15795.03	8074.85	5503.19	4218.65	3448.96	2936.70	2571.53	2298.30	2086.36	1917.32	1779.47	1665.02
190,000	16221.92	8293.09	5651.92	4332.67	3542.18	3016.07	2641.04	2360.42	2142.75	1969.13	1827.56	1710.02
195,000	16648.82	8511.33	5800.66	4446.68	3635.39	3095.44	2710.54	2422.54	2199.14	2020.95	1875.66	1755.02
200,000	17075.71	8729.57	5949.39	4560.70	3728.61	3174.81	2780.04	2484.65	2255.52	2072.77	1923.75	1800.02
205,000	17502.60	8947.81	6098.12	4674.72	3821.82	3254.18	2849.54	2546.77	2311.91	2124.59	1971.84	1845.02
210,000	17929.49	9166.05	6246.86	4788.74	3915.04	3333.55	2919.04	2608.88	2368.30	2176.41	2019.94	1890.02
215,000	18356.39	9384.28	6395.59	4902.75	4008.25	3412.92	2988.54	2671.00	2424.69	2228.23	2068.03	1935.02
220,000	18783.28	9602.52	6544.33	5016.77	4101.47	3492.29	3058.04	2733.12	2481.08	2280.05	2116.12	1980.02
225,000	19210.17	9820.76	6693.06	5130.79	4194.68	3571.66	3127.54	2795.23	2537.46	2331.87	2164.22	2025.02
230,000	19637.06	10039.00	6841.80	5244.81	4287.90	3651.03	3197.04	2857.35	2593.85	2383.69	2212.31	2070.02
235,000	20063.96	10257.24	6990.53	5358.82	4381.11	3730.40	3266.54	2919.47	2650.24	2435.51	2260.41	2115.02
240,000	20490.85	10475.48	7139.27	5472.84	4474.33	3809.77	3336.04	2981.58	2706.63	2487.33	2308.50	2160.02
245,000	20917.74	10693.72	7288.00	5586.86	4567.54	3889.14	3405.54	3043.70	2763.02	2539.15	2356.59	2205.02
250,000	21344.64	10911.96	7436.74	5700.88	4660.76	3968.51	3475.05	3105.81	2819.40	2590.97	2404.69	2250.03
255,000	21771.53	11130.20	7585.47	5814.89	4753.97	4047.88	3544.55	3167.93	2875.79	2642.78	2452.78	2295.03
260,000	22198.42	11348.44	7734.21	5928.91	4847.19	4127.25	3614.05	3230.05	2932.18	2694.60	2500.87	2340.03
265,000	22625.31	11566.68	7882.94	6042.93	4940.41	4206.62	3683.55	3292.16	2988.57	2746.42	2548.97	2385.03
270,000	23052.21	11784.91	8031.67	6156.95	5033.62	4285.99	3753.05	3354.28	3044.96	2798.24	2597.06	2430.03
280,000	23905.99	12221.39	8329.14	6384.98	5220.05	4444.73	3892.05	3478.51	3157.73	2901.88	2693.25	2520.03
290,000	24759.78	12657.87	8626.61	6613.02	5406.48	4603.47	4031.05	3602.74	3270.51	3005.52	2789.44	2610.03
300,000	25613.56	13094.35	8924.08	6841.05	5592.91	4762.21	4170.05	3726.98	3383.28	3109.16	2885.62	2700.03

AMOUNT OF LOAN	NUMBER OF YEARS IN TERM											
	13	14	15	16	17	18	19	20	25	30	35	40
$ 50	0.43	0.41	0.39	0.37	0.36	0.34	0.33	0.32	0.28	0.26	0.24	0.23
100	0.85	0.81	0.77	0.74	0.71	0.68	0.66	0.64	0.56	0.51	0.48	0.45
200	1.70	1.61	1.53	1.47	1.41	1.36	1.31	1.27	1.12	1.02	0.95	0.90
300	2.55	2.42	2.30	2.20	2.11	2.03	1.96	1.90	1.67	1.53	1.42	1.35
400	3.40	3.22	3.06	2.93	2.81	2.71	2.62	2.54	2.23	2.03	1.90	1.80
500	4.24	4.02	3.83	3.66	3.52	3.39	3.27	3.17	2.78	2.54	2.37	2.25
600	5.09	4.83	4.59	4.39	4.22	4.06	3.92	3.80	3.34	3.05	2.84	2.70
700	5.94	5.63	5.36	5.13	4.92	4.74	4.58	4.43	3.90	3.55	3.32	3.15
800	6.79	6.43	6.12	5.86	5.62	5.42	5.23	5.07	4.45	4.06	3.79	3.60
900	7.64	7.24	6.89	6.59	6.33	6.09	5.88	5.70	5.01	4.57	4.26	4.05
1,000	8.48	8.04	7.65	7.32	7.03	6.77	6.54	6.33	5.56	5.07	4.74	4.50
2,000	16.96	16.07	15.30	14.64	14.05	13.53	13.07	12.66	11.12	10.14	9.47	9.00
3,000	25.44	24.11	22.95	21.95	21.07	20.29	19.60	18.98	16.68	15.21	14.20	13.49
4,000	33.92	32.14	30.60	29.27	28.09	27.06	26.14	25.31	22.24	20.27	18.94	17.99
5,000	42.40	40.17	38.25	36.58	35.12	33.82	32.67	31.64	27.80	25.34	23.67	22.48
6,000	50.88	48.21	45.90	43.90	42.14	40.58	39.20	37.96	33.35	30.41	28.40	26.98
7,000	59.36	56.24	53.55	51.22	49.16	47.35	45.73	44.29	38.91	35.47	33.13	31.47
8,000	67.83	64.28	61.20	58.53	56.18	54.11	52.27	50.62	44.47	40.54	37.87	35.97
9,000	76.31	72.31	68.85	65.85	63.21	60.87	58.80	56.94	50.03	45.61	42.60	40.47
10,000	84.79	80.34	76.50	73.16	70.23	67.64	65.33	63.27	55.59	50.67	47.33	44.96
15,000	127.19	120.51	114.75	109.74	105.34	101.45	98.00	94.90	83.38	76.01	70.99	67.44
20,000	169.58	160.68	153.00	146.32	140.45	135.27	130.66	126.53	111.17	101.34	94.66	89.92
25,000	211.97	200.85	191.25	182.90	175.57	169.09	163.32	158.17	138.96	126.68	110.32	112.40
30,000	254.37	241.02	229.50	219.48	210.68	202.90	195.99	189.80	166.75	152.01	141.98	134.87
35,000	296.76	281.19	267.75	256.06	245.79	236.72	228.65	221.43	194.55	177.34	165.64	157.35
40,000	339.15	321.36	306.00	292.04	280.90	270.53	261.31	253.06	222.34	202.68	189.31	179.83
45,000	381.55	361.52	344.25	329.21	316.02	304.35	293.98	284.70	250.13	228.01	212.97	202.31
50,000	423.94	401.69	382.50	365.79	351.13	338.17	326.64	316.33	277.92	253.35	236.63	224.79
55,000	466.33	441.86	420.75	402.37	386.24	371.98	359.30	347.96	305.71	278.68	260.30	247.26
60,000	508.73	482.03	459.00	438.95	421.35	405.80	391.97	379.59	333.50	304.02	283.96	269.74
65,000	551.12	522.20	497.25	475.53	456.47	439.62	424.63	411.23	361.30	329.35	307.62	292.22
70,000	593.51	562.37	535.50	512.11	491.58	473.43	457.29	442.86	389.09	354.68	331.28	314.70
75,000	635.91	602.54	573.75	548.69	526.69	507.25	489.96	474.49	416.88	380.02	354.95	337.18
80,000	678.30	642.71	612.00	585.27	561.80	541.06	522.62	506.12	444.67	405.35	378.61	359.66
85,000	720.70	682.87	650.25	621.84	596.92	574.88	555.28	537.76	472.46	430.69	402.27	382.13
90,000	763.09	723.04	688.50	658.42	632.03	608.70	587.95	569.39	500.25	456.02	425.94	404.61
95,000	805.48	763.21	726.75	695.00	667.14	642.51	620.61	601.02	528.05	481.36	449.60	427.09
100,000	847.88	803.38	765.00	731.58	702.25	676.33	653.27	632.65	555.84	506.69	473.26	449.57
105,000	890.27	843.55	803.25	768.16	737.36	710.15	685.94	664.29	583.63	532.02	496.92	472.05
110,000	932.66	883.72	841.50	804.74	772.48	743.96	718.60	695.92	611.42	557.36	520.59	494.52
115,000	975.06	923.89	879.75	841.32	807.59	777.78	751.26	727.55	639.21	582.69	544.25	517.00
120,000	1017.45	964.06	918.00	877.90	842.70	811.60	783.93	759.19	667.00	608.03	567.91	539.48
125,000	1059.84	1004.22	956.25	914.48	877.81	845.41	816.59	790.82	694.80	633.36	591.58	561.96
130,000	1102.24	1044.39	994.50	951.05	912.93	879.23	849.25	822.45	722.59	658.70	615.24	584.44
135,000	1144.63	1084.56	1032.75	987.63	948.04	913.04	881.92	854.08	750.38	684.03	638.90	606.91
140,000	1187.02	1124.73	1071.00	1024.21	983.15	946.86	914.58	885.71	778.17	709.36	662.56	629.39
145,000	1229.42	1164.90	1109.25	1060.79	1018.26	980.68	947.24	917.35	805.96	734.70	686.23	651.87
150,000	1271.81	1205.07	1147.49	1097.37	1053.38	1014.49	979.91	948.98	833.75	760.03	709.89	674.35
155,000	1314.21	1245.24	1185.74	1133.95	1088.49	1048.31	1012.57	980.61	861.55	785.37	733.55	696.83
160,000	1356.60	1285.41	1223.99	1170.53	1123.60	1082.12	1045.24	1012.24	889.34	810.70	757.22	719.31
165,000	1398.99	1325.58	1262.24	1207.11	1158.71	1115.94	1077.90	1043.88	917.13	836.04	780.88	741.78
170,000	1441.39	1365.74	1300.49	1243.68	1193.83	1149.76	1110.56	1075.51	944.92	861.37	804.54	764.26
175,000	1483.78	1405.91	1338.74	1280.26	1228.94	1183.57	1143.23	1107.14	972.71	886.70	828.20	786.74
180,000	1526.17	1446.08	1376.99	1316.84	1264.05	1217.39	1175.89	1138.77	1000.50	912.04	851.87	809.22
185,000	1568.57	1486.25	1415.24	1353.42	1299.16	1251.21	1208.55	1170.41	1028.30	937.37	875.53	831.70
190,000	1610.96	1526.42	1453.49	1390.00	1334.28	1285.02	1241.22	1202.04	1056.09	962.71	899.19	854.17
195,000	1653.35	1566.59	1491.74	1426.58	1369.39	1318.84	1273.88	1233.67	1083.88	988.04	922.86	876.65
200,000	1695.75	1606.76	1529.99	1463.16	1404.50	1352.65	1306.54	1265.30	1111.67	1013.38	946.52	899.13
205,000	1738.14	1646.93	1568.24	1499.74	1439.61	1386.47	1339.21	1296.94	1139.46	1038.71	970.18	921.61
210,000	1780.53	1687.09	1606.49	1536.32	1474.72	1420.29	1371.87	1328.57	1167.25	1064.04	993.84	944.09
215,000	1822.93	1727.26	1644.74	1572.89	1509.84	1454.10	1404.53	1360.20	1195.04	1089.38	1017.51	966.57
220,000	1865.32	1767.43	1682.99	1609.47	1544.95	1487.92	1437.20	1391.83	1222.84	1114.71	1041.17	989.04
225,000	1907.71	1807.60	1721.24	1646.05	1580.06	1521.74	1469.86	1423.47	1250.63	1140.05	1064.83	1011.52
230,000	1950.11	1847.77	1759.49	1682.63	1615.17	1555.55	1502.52	1455.10	1278.42	1165.38	1088.50	1034.00
235,000	1992.50	1887.94	1797.74	1719.21	1650.29	1589.37	1535.19	1486.73	1306.21	1190.72	1112.16	1056.48
240,000	2034.90	1928.11	1835.99	1755.79	1685.40	1623.18	1567.85	1518.36	1334.00	1216.05	1135.82	1078.96
245,000	2077.29	1968.28	1874.24	1792.37	1720.51	1657.00	1600.51	1550.00	1361.79	1241.38	1159.48	1101.43
250,000	2119.68	2008.44	1912.49	1828.95	1755.62	1690.82	1633.18	1581.63	1389.59	1266.72	1183.15	1123.91
255,000	2162.08	2048.61	1950.74	1865.52	1790.74	1724.63	1665.84	1613.26	1417.38	1292.05	1206.81	1146.39
260,000	2204.47	2088.78	1988.99	1902.10	1825.85	1758.45	1698.50	1644.89	1445.17	1317.39	1230.47	1168.87
265,000	2246.86	2128.95	2027.24	1938.68	1860.96	1792.27	1731.17	1676.53	1472.96	1342.72	1254.14	1191.35
270,000	2289.26	2169.12	2065.49	1975.26	1896.07	1826.08	1763.83	1708.16	1500.75	1368.06	1277.80	1213.82
280,000	2374.04	2249.46	2141.99	2048.42	1966.30	1893.71	1829.16	1771.42	1556.34	1418.72	1325.12	1258.78
290,000	2458.83	2329.79	2218.49	2121.58	2036.52	1961.35	1894.48	1834.69	1611.92	1469.39	1372.45	1303.74
300,000	2543.62	2410.13	2294.98	2194.73	2106.75	2028.98	1959.81	1897.95	1667.50	1520.06	1419.78	1348.69

4.75% MONTHLY AMORTIZING PAYMENTS

AMOUNT OF LOAN	NUMBER OF YEARS IN TERM											
	1	2	3	4	5	6	7	8	9	10	11	12
$ 50	4.28	2.19	1.50	1.15	0.94	0.80	0.71	0.63	0.57	0.53	0.49	0.46
100	8.55	4.38	2.99	2.30	1.88	1.60	1.41	1.26	1.14	1.05	0.98	0.92
200	17.10	8.76	5.98	4.59	3.76	3.20	2.81	2.51	2.28	2.10	1.95	1.83
300	25.65	13.13	8.96	6.88	5.63	4.80	4.21	3.77	3.42	3.15	2.93	2.74
400	34.20	17.51	11.95	9.17	7.51	6.40	5.61	5.02	4.56	4.20	3.90	3.65
500	42.75	21.88	14.93	11.46	9.38	8.00	7.01	6.28	5.70	5.25	4.88	4.57
600	51.30	26.26	17.92	13.75	11.26	9.60	8.42	7.53	6.84	6.30	5.85	5.48
700	59.85	30.64	20.91	16.05	13.13	11.20	9.82	8.78	7.98	7.34	6.82	6.39
800	68.40	35.01	23.89	18.34	15.01	12.80	11.22	10.04	9.12	8.39	7.80	7.30
900	76.95	39.39	26.88	20.63	16.89	14.40	12.62	11.29	10.26	9.44	8.77	8.22
1,000	85.50	43.76	29.86	22.92	18.76	15.99	14.02	12.55	11.40	10.49	9.75	9.13
2,000	170.99	87.52	59.72	45.84	37.52	31.98	28.04	25.09	22.80	20.97	19.49	18.25
3,000	256.48	131.28	89.58	68.75	56.28	47.97	42.06	37.63	34.20	31.46	29.23	27.38
4,000	341.98	175.04	119.44	91.67	75.03	63.96	56.07	50.17	45.59	41.94	38.97	36.50
5,000	427.47	218.80	149.30	114.59	93.79	79.95	70.09	62.71	56.99	52.43	48.71	45.62
6,000	512.96	262.56	179.16	137.50	112.55	95.94	84.11	75.25	68.39	62.91	58.45	54.75
7,000	598.46	306.32	209.02	160.42	131.30	111.93	98.12	87.79	79.78	73.40	68.19	63.87
8,000	683.95	350.08	238.88	183.33	150.06	127.92	112.14	100.33	91.18	83.88	77.93	73.00
9,000	769.44	393.84	268.73	206.25	168.82	143.91	126.16	112.88	102.58	94.37	87.68	82.12
10,000	854.93	437.60	298.59	229.17	187.57	159.90	140.17	125.42	113.98	104.85	97.42	91.24
15,000	1282.40	656.40	447.89	343.75	281.36	239.84	210.26	188.12	170.96	157.28	146.12	136.86
20,000	1709.86	875.20	597.18	458.33	375.14	319.79	280.34	250.83	227.95	209.70	194.83	182.48
25,000	2137.33	1093.99	746.47	572.91	468.93	399.74	350.42	313.54	284.93	262.12	243.53	228.10
30,000	2564.79	1312.79	895.77	687.49	562.71	479.68	420.51	376.24	341.92	314.55	292.24	273.72
35,000	2992.26	1531.59	1045.06	802.07	656.50	559.63	490.59	438.95	398.90	366.97	340.95	319.34
40,000	3419.72	1750.39	1194.36	916.65	750.28	639.57	560.67	501.65	455.89	419.40	389.65	364.96
45,000	3847.19	1969.18	1343.65	1031.23	844.07	719.52	630.76	564.36	512.87	471.82	438.36	410.58
50,000	4274.65	2187.98	1492.94	1145.82	937.85	799.47	700.84	627.07	569.86	524.24	487.06	456.20
55,000	4702.12	2406.78	1642.24	1260.40	1031.64	879.41	770.93	689.77	626.84	576.67	535.77	501.82
60,000	5129.58	2625.58	1791.53	1374.98	1125.42	959.36	841.01	752.48	683.83	629.09	584.47	547.44
65,000	5557.05	2844.37	1940.83	1489.56	1219.20	1039.30	911.09	815.19	740.81	681.52	633.18	593.06
70,000	5984.51	3063.17	2090.12	1604.14	1312.99	1119.25	981.18	877.89	797.80	733.94	681.89	638.68
75,000	6411.98	3281.97	2239.41	1718.72	1406.77	1199.20	1051.26	940.60	854.78	786.36	730.59	684.30
80,000	6839.44	3500.77	2388.71	1833.30	1500.56	1279.14	1121.34	1003.30	911.77	838.79	779.30	729.92
85,000	7266.91	3719.56	2538.00	1947.88	1594.34	1359.09	1191.43	1066.01	968.75	891.21	828.00	775.54
90,000	7694.37	3938.36	2687.30	2062.46	1688.13	1439.04	1261.51	1128.72	1025.74	943.63	876.71	821.16
95,000	8121.84	4157.16	2836.59	2177.05	1781.91	1518.98	1331.59	1191.42	1082.72	996.06	925.41	866.78
100,000	8549.30	4375.96	2985.88	2291.63	1875.70	1598.93	1401.68	1254.13	1139.71	1048.48	974.12	912.40
105,000	8976.77	4594.75	3135.18	2406.21	1969.48	1678.87	1471.76	1316.83	1196.70	1100.91	1022.83	958.02
110,000	9404.23	4813.55	3284.47	2520.79	2063.27	1758.82	1541.85	1379.54	1253.68	1153.33	1071.53	1003.64
115,000	9831.70	5032.35	3433.76	2635.37	2157.05	1838.77	1611.93	1442.25	1310.67	1205.75	1120.24	1049.26
120,000	10259.16	5251.15	3583.06	2749.95	2250.83	1918.71	1682.01	1504.95	1367.65	1258.18	1168.94	1094.88
125,000	10686.62	5469.94	3732.35	2864.53	2344.62	1998.66	1752.10	1567.66	1424.64	1310.60	1217.65	1140.50
130,000	11114.09	5688.74	3881.65	2979.11	2438.40	2078.60	1822.18	1630.37	1481.62	1363.03	1266.35	1186.12
135,000	11541.55	5907.54	4030.94	3093.69	2532.19	2158.55	1892.26	1693.07	1538.61	1415.45	1315.06	1231.74
140,000	11969.02	6126.34	4180.23	3208.28	2625.97	2238.50	1962.35	1755.78	1595.59	1467.87	1363.77	1277.36
145,000	12396.48	6345.13	4329.53	3322.86	2719.76	2318.44	2032.43	1818.48	1652.58	1520.30	1412.47	1322.98
150,000	12823.95	6563.93	4478.82	3437.44	2813.54	2398.39	2102.52	1881.19	1709.56	1572.72	1461.18	1368.60
155,000	13251.41	6782.73	4628.12	3552.02	2907.33	2478.33	2172.60	1943.90	1766.55	1625.15	1509.88	1414.22
160,000	13678.88	7001.53	4777.41	3666.60	3001.11	2558.28	2242.68	2006.60	1823.53	1677.57	1558.59	1459.84
165,000	14106.34	7220.32	4926.70	3781.18	3094.90	2638.23	2312.77	2069.31	1880.52	1729.99	1607.29	1505.46
170,000	14533.81	7439.12	5076.00	3895.76	3188.68	2718.17	2382.85	2132.02	1937.50	1782.42	1656.00	1551.08
175,000	14961.27	7657.92	5225.29	4010.34	3282.46	2798.12	2452.93	2194.72	1994.49	1834.84	1704.71	1596.70
180,000	15388.74	7876.72	5374.59	4124.92	3376.25	2878.07	2523.02	2257.43	2051.47	1887.26	1753.41	1642.32
185,000	15816.20	8095.52	5523.88	4239.51	3470.03	2958.01	2593.10	2320.13	2108.46	1939.69	1802.12	1687.94
190,000	16243.67	8314.31	5673.17	4354.09	3563.82	3037.96	2663.18	2382.84	2165.44	1992.11	1850.82	1733.56
195,000	16671.13	8533.11	5822.47	4468.67	3657.60	3117.90	2733.27	2445.55	2222.43	2044.54	1899.53	1779.18
200,000	17098.60	8751.91	5971.76	4583.25	3751.39	3197.85	2803.35	2508.25	2279.42	2096.96	1948.23	1824.80
205,000	17526.06	8970.71	6121.06	4697.83	3845.17	3277.80	2873.44	2570.96	2336.40	2149.38	1996.94	1870.42
210,000	17953.53	9189.50	6270.35	4812.41	3938.96	3357.74	2943.52	2633.66	2393.39	2201.81	2045.65	1916.04
215,000	18380.99	9408.30	6419.64	4926.99	4032.74	3437.69	3013.60	2696.37	2450.37	2254.23	2094.35	1961.66
220,000	18808.46	9627.10	6568.94	5041.57	4126.53	3517.63	3083.69	2759.08	2507.36	2306.66	2143.06	2007.28
225,000	19235.92	9845.90	6718.23	5156.15	4220.31	3597.58	3153.77	2821.78	2564.34	2359.08	2191.76	2052.90
230,000	19663.39	10064.69	6867.52	5270.74	4314.09	3677.53	3223.85	2884.49	2621.33	2411.50	2240.47	2098.52
235,000	20090.85	10283.49	7016.82	5385.32	4407.88	3757.47	3293.94	2947.20	2678.31	2463.93	2289.17	2144.14
240,000	20518.32	10502.29	7166.11	5499.90	4501.66	3837.42	3364.02	3009.90	2735.30	2516.35	2337.88	2189.76
245,000	20945.78	10721.09	7315.41	5614.48	4595.45	3917.36	3434.11	3072.61	2792.28	2568.77	2386.59	2235.38
250,000	21373.24	10939.88	7464.70	5729.06	4689.23	3997.31	3504.19	3135.31	2849.27	2621.20	2435.29	2281.00
255,000	21800.71	11158.68	7613.99	5843.64	4783.02	4077.26	3574.27	3198.02	2906.25	2673.62	2484.00	2326.62
260,000	22228.17	11377.48	7763.29	5958.22	4876.80	4157.20	3644.36	3260.73	2963.24	2726.05	2532.70	2372.24
265,000	22655.64	11596.28	7912.58	6072.80	4970.59	4237.15	3714.44	3323.43	3020.22	2778.47	2581.41	2417.86
270,000	23083.10	11815.07	8061.88	6187.38	5064.37	4317.10	3784.52	3386.14	3077.21	2830.89	2630.11	2463.48
280,000	23938.03	12252.67	8360.46	6416.55	5251.94	4476.99	3924.69	3511.55	3191.18	2935.74	2727.53	2554.72
290,000	24792.96	12690.26	8659.05	6645.71	5439.51	4636.88	4064.86	3636.96	3305.15	3040.59	2824.94	2645.96
300,000	25647.89	13127.86	8957.64	6874.87	5627.08	4796.77	4205.03	3762.38	3419.12	3145.44	2922.35	2737.20

AMOUNT OF LOAN	NUMBER OF YEARS IN TERM											
	13	14	15	16	17	18	19	20	25	30	35	40
$ 50	0.44	0.41	0.39	0.38	0.36	0.35	0.34	0.33	0.29	0.27	0.25	0.24
100	0.87	0.82	0.78	0.75	0.72	0.69	0.67	0.65	0.58	0.53	0.49	0.47
200	1.73	1.64	1.56	1.49	1.44	1.38	1.34	1.30	1.15	1.05	0.98	0.94
300	2.59	2.45	2.34	2.24	2.15	2.07	2.01	1.94	1.72	1.57	1.47	1.40
400	3.45	3.27	3.12	2.98	2.87	2.76	2.67	2.59	2.29	2.09	1.96	1.87
500	4.31	4.09	3.89	3.73	3.58	3.45	3.34	3.24	2.86	2.61	2.45	2.33
600	5.17	4.90	4.67	4.47	4.30	4.14	4.01	3.88	3.43	3.13	2.94	2.80
700	6.03	5.72	5.45	5.22	5.01	4.83	4.67	4.53	4.00	3.66	3.43	3.27
800	6.89	6.53	6.23	5.96	5.73	5.52	5.34	5.17	4.57	4.18	3.92	3.73
900	7.75	7.35	7.01	6.71	6.44	6.21	6.01	5.82	5.14	4.70	4.40	4.20
1,000	8.61	8.17	7.78	7.45	7.16	6.90	6.67	6.47	5.71	5.22	4.89	4.66
2,000	17.21	16.33	15.56	14.90	14.31	13.80	13.34	12.93	11.41	10.44	9.78	9.32
3,000	25.82	24.49	23.34	22.34	21.47	20.69	20.01	19.39	17.11	15.65	14.67	13.98
4,000	34.42	32.65	31.12	29.79	28.62	27.59	26.67	25.85	22.81	20.87	19.56	18.64
5,000	43.03	40.81	38.90	37.23	35.77	34.49	33.34	32.32	28.51	26.09	24.45	23.29
6,000	51.63	48.97	46.67	44.68	42.93	41.38	40.01	38.78	34.21	31.30	29.34	27.95
7,000	60.23	57.13	54.45	52.12	50.08	48.28	46.67	45.24	39.91	36.52	34.22	32.61
8,000	68.84	65.29	62.23	59.57	57.24	55.17	53.34	51.70	45.61	41.74	39.11	37.27
9,000	77.44	73.45	70.01	67.02	64.39	62.07	60.01	58.17	51.32	46.95	44.00	41.92
10,000	86.05	81.61	77.79	74.46	71.54	68.97	66.67	64.63	57.02	52.17	48.89	46.58
15,000	129.07	122.41	116.68	111.69	107.31	103.45	100.01	96.94	85.52	78.25	73.33	69.87
20,000	172.09	163.22	155.57	148.92	143.08	137.93	133.34	129.25	114.03	104.33	97.78	93.16
25,000	215.11	204.02	194.46	186.15	178.85	172.41	166.68	161.56	142.53	130.42	122.22	116.44
30,000	258.13	244.82	233.35	223.37	214.62	206.89	200.01	193.87	171.04	156.50	146.66	139.73
35,000	301.15	285.63	272.25	260.60	250.39	241.37	233.35	226.18	199.55	182.58	171.10	163.02
40,000	344.17	326.43	311.14	297.83	286.16	275.85	266.68	258.49	228.05	208.66	195.55	186.31
45,000	387.19	367.23	350.03	335.06	321.93	310.33	300.02	290.81	256.56	234.75	219.99	209.60
50,000	430.21	408.04	388.92	372.29	357.70	344.81	333.35	323.12	285.06	260.83	244.43	232.88
55,000	473.23	448.84	427.81	409.51	393.47	379.29	366.69	355.43	313.57	286.91	268.88	256.17
60,000	516.25	489.64	466.70	446.74	429.23	413.77	400.02	387.74	342.08	312.99	293.32	279.46
65,000	559.27	530.45	505.60	483.97	465.00	448.25	433.36	420.05	370.58	339.08	317.76	302.75
70,000	602.29	571.25	544.49	521.20	500.77	482.73	466.69	452.36	399.09	365.16	342.20	326.04
75,000	645.31	612.05	583.38	558.43	536.54	517.21	500.03	484.67	427.59	391.24	366.65	349.32
80,000	688.33	652.86	622.27	595.66	572.31	551.69	533.36	516.98	456.10	417.32	391.09	372.61
85,000	731.35	693.66	661.16	632.88	608.08	586.17	566.70	549.30	484.60	443.41	415.53	395.90
90,000	774.38	734.46	700.05	670.11	643.85	620.65	600.03	581.61	513.11	469.49	439.98	419.19
95,000	817.40	775.27	738.95	707.34	679.62	655.13	633.37	613.92	541.62	495.57	464.42	442.47
100,000	860.42	816.07	777.84	744.57	715.39	689.61	666.70	646.23	570.12	521.65	488.86	465.76
105,000	903.44	856.87	816.73	781.80	751.16	724.09	700.04	678.54	598.63	547.73	513.30	489.05
110,000	946.46	897.68	855.62	819.02	786.93	758.57	733.37	710.85	627.13	573.82	537.75	512.34
115,000	989.48	938.48	894.51	856.25	822.70	793.05	766.71	743.16	655.64	599.90	562.19	535.63
120,000	1032.50	979.28	933.40	893.48	858.46	827.53	800.04	775.47	684.15	625.98	586.63	558.91
125,000	1075.52	1020.09	972.29	930.71	894.23	862.01	833.38	807.78	712.65	652.06	611.08	582.20
130,000	1118.54	1060.89	1011.19	967.94	930.00	896.49	866.71	840.10	741.16	678.15	635.52	605.49
135,000	1161.56	1101.69	1050.08	1005.17	965.77	930.97	900.05	872.41	769.66	704.23	659.96	628.78
140,000	1204.58	1142.50	1088.97	1042.39	1001.54	965.45	933.38	904.72	798.17	730.31	684.40	652.07
145,000	1247.60	1183.30	1127.86	1079.62	1037.31	999.94	966.72	937.03	826.68	756.39	708.85	675.35
150,000	1290.62	1224.10	1166.75	1116.85	1073.08	1034.42	1000.05	969.34	855.18	782.48	733.29	698.64
155,000	1333.64	1264.91	1205.64	1154.08	1108.85	1068.90	1033.39	1001.65	883.69	808.56	757.73	721.93
160,000	1376.66	1305.71	1244.54	1191.31	1144.62	1103.38	1066.72	1033.96	912.19	834.64	782.18	745.22
165,000	1419.68	1346.51	1283.43	1228.53	1180.39	1137.86	1100.06	1066.27	940.70	860.72	806.62	768.51
170,000	1462.70	1387.32	1322.32	1265.76	1216.16	1172.34	1133.39	1098.59	969.20	886.81	831.06	791.79
175,000	1505.72	1428.12	1361.21	1302.99	1251.92	1206.82	1166.73	1130.90	997.71	912.89	855.50	815.08
180,000	1548.75	1468.92	1400.10	1340.22	1287.69	1241.30	1200.06	1163.21	1026.22	938.97	879.95	838.37
185,000	1591.77	1509.73	1438.99	1377.45	1323.46	1275.78	1233.40	1195.52	1054.72	965.05	904.39	861.66
190,000	1634.79	1550.53	1477.89	1414.68	1359.23	1310.26	1266.73	1227.83	1083.23	991.13	928.83	884.94
195,000	1677.81	1591.33	1516.78	1451.90	1395.00	1344.74	1300.07	1260.14	1111.73	1017.22	953.28	908.23
200,000	1720.83	1632.14	1555.67	1489.13	1430.77	1379.22	1333.40	1292.45	1140.24	1043.30	977.72	931.52
205,000	1763.85	1672.94	1594.56	1526.36	1466.54	1413.70	1366.74	1324.76	1168.75	1069.38	1002.16	954.81
210,000	1806.87	1713.74	1633.45	1563.59	1502.31	1448.18	1400.07	1357.07	1197.25	1095.46	1026.60	978.10
215,000	1849.89	1754.55	1672.34	1600.82	1538.08	1482.66	1433.41	1389.39	1225.76	1121.55	1051.05	1001.38
220,000	1892.91	1795.35	1711.24	1638.04	1573.85	1517.14	1466.74	1421.70	1254.26	1147.63	1075.49	1024.67
225,000	1935.93	1836.15	1750.13	1675.27	1609.62	1551.62	1500.07	1454.01	1282.77	1173.71	1099.93	1047.96
230,000	1978.95	1876.96	1789.02	1712.50	1645.39	1586.10	1533.41	1486.32	1311.27	1199.79	1124.38	1071.25
235,000	2021.97	1917.76	1827.91	1749.73	1681.15	1620.58	1566.74	1518.63	1339.78	1225.88	1148.82	1094.54
240,000	2064.99	1958.56	1866.80	1786.96	1716.92	1655.06	1600.08	1550.94	1368.29	1251.96	1173.26	1117.82
245,000	2108.01	1999.37	1905.69	1824.19	1752.69	1689.54	1633.41	1583.25	1396.79	1278.04	1197.70	1141.11
250,000	2151.03	2040.17	1944.58	1861.41	1788.46	1724.02	1666.75	1615.56	1425.30	1304.12	1222.15	1164.40
255,000	2194.05	2080.97	1983.48	1898.64	1824.23	1758.50	1700.08	1647.88	1453.80	1330.21	1246.59	1187.69
260,000	2237.07	2121.78	2022.37	1935.87	1860.00	1792.98	1733.42	1680.19	1482.31	1356.29	1271.03	1210.98
265,000	2280.10	2162.58	2061.26	1973.10	1895.77	1827.46	1766.75	1712.50	1510.82	1382.37	1295.48	1234.26
270,000	2323.12	2203.38	2100.15	2010.33	1931.54	1861.94	1800.09	1744.81	1539.32	1408.45	1319.92	1257.55
280,000	2409.16	2284.99	2177.93	2084.78	2003.08	1930.90	1866.76	1809.43	1596.33	1460.62	1368.80	1304.13
290,000	2495.20	2366.59	2255.72	2159.24	2074.61	1999.87	1933.43	1874.05	1653.35	1512.78	1417.69	1350.70
300,000	2581.24	2448.20	2333.50	2233.70	2146.15	2068.83	2000.10	1938.68	1710.36	1564.95	1466.58	1397.28

5.00%

AMOUNT OF LOAN	NUMBER OF YEARS IN TERM											
	1	2	3	4	5	6	7	8	9	10	11	12
$ 50	4.29	2.20	1.50	1.16	0.95	0.81	0.71	0.64	0.58	0.54	0.50	0.47
100	8.57	4.39	3.00	2.31	1.89	1.62	1.42	1.27	1.16	1.07	0.99	0.93
200	17.13	8.78	6.00	4.61	3.78	3.23	2.83	2.54	2.31	2.13	1.98	1.85
300	25.69	13.17	9.00	6.91	5.67	4.84	4.25	3.80	3.46	3.19	2.96	2.78
400	34.25	17.55	11.99	9.22	7.55	6.45	5.66	5.07	4.61	4.25	3.95	3.70
500	42.81	21.94	14.99	11.52	9.44	8.06	7.07	6.33	5.76	5.31	4.94	4.63
600	51.37	26.33	17.99	13.82	11.33	9.67	8.49	7.60	6.92	6.37	5.92	5.55
700	59.93	30.71	20.98	16.13	13.21	11.28	9.90	8.87	8.07	7.43	6.91	6.48
800	68.49	35.10	23.98	18.43	15.10	12.89	11.31	10.13	9.22	8.49	7.90	7.40
900	77.05	39.49	26.98	20.73	16.99	14.50	12.73	11.40	10.37	9.55	8.88	8.33
1,000	85.61	43.88	29.98	23.03	18.88	16.11	14.14	12.66	11.52	10.61	9.87	9.25
2,000	171.22	87.75	59.95	46.06	37.75	32.21	28.27	25.32	23.04	21.22	19.73	18.50
3,000	256.83	131.62	89.92	69.09	56.62	48.32	42.41	37.98	34.56	31.82	29.60	27.75
4,000	342.43	175.49	119.89	92.12	75.49	64.42	56.54	50.64	46.07	42.43	39.46	37.00
5,000	428.04	219.36	149.86	115.15	94.36	80.53	70.67	63.30	57.59	53.04	49.33	46.25
6,000	513.65	263.23	179.83	138.18	113.23	96.63	84.81	75.96	69.11	63.64	59.19	55.50
7,000	599.26	307.10	209.80	161.21	132.10	112.74	98.94	88.62	80.63	74.25	69.06	64.75
8,000	684.86	350.98	239.77	184.24	150.97	128.84	113.08	101.28	92.14	84.86	78.92	74.00
9,000	770.47	394.85	269.74	207.27	169.85	144.95	127.21	113.94	103.66	95.46	88.79	83.25
10,000	856.08	438.72	299.71	230.30	188.72	161.05	141.34	126.60	115.18	106.07	98.65	92.49
15,000	1284.12	658.08	449.57	345.44	283.07	241.58	212.01	189.90	172.76	159.10	147.97	138.74
20,000	1712.15	877.43	599.42	460.59	377.43	322.10	282.68	253.20	230.35	212.14	197.29	184.98
25,000	2140.19	1096.79	749.28	575.74	471.79	402.63	353.35	316.50	287.94	265.17	246.62	231.23
30,000	2568.23	1316.15	899.13	690.88	566.14	483.15	424.02	379.80	345.52	318.20	295.94	277.47
35,000	2996.27	1535.50	1048.99	806.03	660.50	563.68	494.69	443.11	403.11	371.23	345.26	323.72
40,000	3424.30	1754.86	1198.84	921.18	754.85	644.20	565.36	506.40	460.70	424.27	394.58	369.96
45,000	3852.34	1974.22	1348.70	1036.32	849.21	724.73	636.03	569.70	518.28	477.30	443.91	416.21
50,000	4280.38	2193.57	1498.55	1151.47	943.57	805.25	706.70	633.00	575.87	530.33	493.23	462.45
55,000	4708.42	2412.93	1648.40	1266.62	1037.92	885.78	777.37	696.30	633.46	583.37	542.55	508.69
60,000	5136.45	2632.29	1798.26	1381.76	1132.28	966.30	848.04	759.60	691.04	636.40	591.87	554.94
65,000	5564.49	2851.65	1948.11	1496.91	1226.64	1046.83	918.71	822.90	748.63	689.43	641.20	601.18
70,000	5992.53	3071.00	2097.97	1612.06	1320.99	1127.35	989.38	886.20	806.21	742.46	690.52	647.43
75,000	6420.57	3290.36	2247.82	1727.20	1415.35	1207.87	1060.05	949.50	863.80	795.50	739.84	693.67
80,000	6848.60	3509.72	2397.68	1842.35	1509.70	1288.40	1130.72	1012.80	921.39	848.53	789.16	739.92
85,000	7276.64	3729.07	2547.53	1957.49	1604.06	1368.92	1201.39	1076.10	978.97	901.56	838.49	786.16
90,000	7704.68	3948.43	2697.39	2072.64	1698.42	1449.45	1272.06	1139.40	1036.56	954.59	887.81	832.41
95,000	8132.72	4167.79	2847.24	2187.79	1792.77	1529.97	1342.73	1202.70	1094.15	1007.63	937.13	878.65
100,000	8560.75	4387.14	2997.09	2302.93	1887.13	1610.50	1413.40	1266.00	1151.73	1060.66	986.45	924.90
105,000	8988.79	4606.50	3146.95	2418.08	1981.48	1691.02	1484.07	1329.30	1209.32	1113.69	1035.78	971.14
110,000	9416.83	4825.86	3296.80	2533.23	2075.84	1771.55	1554.73	1392.60	1266.91	1166.73	1085.10	1017.38
115,000	9844.87	5045.21	3446.66	2648.37	2170.20	1852.07	1625.40	1455.90	1324.49	1219.76	1134.42	1063.63
120,000	10272.90	5264.57	3596.51	2763.52	2264.55	1932.60	1696.07	1519.20	1382.08	1272.79	1183.74	1109.87
125,000	10700.94	5483.93	3746.37	2878.67	2358.91	2013.12	1766.74	1582.50	1439.66	1325.82	1233.07	1156.12
130,000	11128.98	5703.29	3896.22	2993.81	2453.27	2093.65	1837.41	1645.79	1497.25	1378.86	1282.39	1202.36
135,000	11557.02	5922.64	4046.08	3108.96	2547.62	2174.17	1908.08	1709.09	1554.84	1431.89	1331.71	1248.61
140,000	11985.05	6142.00	4195.93	3224.11	2641.98	2254.70	1978.75	1772.39	1612.42	1484.92	1381.03	1294.85
145,000	12413.09	6361.36	4345.79	3339.25	2736.33	2335.22	2049.42	1835.69	1670.01	1537.95	1430.36	1341.10
150,000	12841.13	6580.71	4495.64	3454.40	2830.69	2415.74	2120.09	1898.99	1727.60	1590.99	1479.68	1387.34
155,000	13269.16	6800.07	4645.49	3569.55	2925.05	2496.27	2190.76	1962.29	1785.18	1644.02	1529.00	1433.59
160,000	13697.20	7019.43	4795.35	3684.69	3019.40	2576.79	2261.43	2025.59	1842.77	1697.05	1578.32	1479.83
165,000	14125.24	7238.78	4945.20	3799.84	3113.76	2657.32	2332.10	2088.89	1900.36	1750.09	1627.65	1526.07
170,000	14553.28	7458.14	5095.06	3914.98	3208.11	2737.84	2402.77	2152.19	1957.94	1803.12	1676.97	1572.32
175,000	14981.31	7677.50	5244.91	4030.13	3302.47	2818.37	2473.44	2215.49	2015.53	1856.15	1726.29	1618.56
180,000	15409.35	7896.86	5394.77	4145.28	3396.83	2898.89	2544.11	2278.79	2073.11	1909.18	1775.61	1664.81
185,000	15837.39	8116.21	5544.62	4260.42	3491.18	2979.42	2614.78	2342.09	2130.70	1962.22	1824.94	1711.05
190,000	16265.43	8335.57	5694.48	4375.57	3585.54	3059.94	2685.45	2405.39	2188.29	2015.25	1874.26	1757.30
195,000	16693.46	8554.93	5844.33	4490.72	3679.90	3140.47	2756.12	2468.69	2245.87	2068.28	1923.58	1803.54
200,000	17121.50	8774.28	5994.18	4605.86	3774.25	3220.99	2826.79	2531.99	2303.46	2121.32	1972.90	1849.79
205,000	17549.54	8993.64	6144.04	4721.01	3868.61	3301.52	2897.46	2595.29	2361.05	2174.35	2022.23	1896.03
210,000	17977.58	9213.00	6293.89	4836.16	3962.96	3382.04	2968.13	2658.59	2418.63	2227.38	2071.55	1942.27
215,000	18405.61	9432.35	6443.75	4951.30	4057.32	3462.57	3038.80	2721.89	2476.22	2280.41	2120.87	1988.52
220,000	18833.65	9651.71	6593.60	5066.45	4151.68	3543.09	3109.46	2785.19	2533.81	2333.45	2170.19	2034.76
225,000	19261.69	9871.07	6743.46	5181.60	4246.03	3623.61	3180.13	2848.49	2591.39	2386.48	2219.51	2081.01
230,000	19689.73	10090.42	6893.31	5296.74	4340.39	3704.14	3250.80	2911.79	2648.98	2439.51	2268.84	2127.25
235,000	20117.76	10309.78	7043.17	5411.89	4434.74	3784.66	3321.47	2975.09	2706.56	2492.54	2318.16	2173.50
240,000	20545.80	10529.14	7193.02	5527.04	4529.10	3865.19	3392.14	3038.39	2764.15	2545.58	2367.48	2219.74
245,000	20973.84	10748.50	7342.87	5642.18	4623.46	3945.71	3462.81	3101.69	2821.74	2598.61	2416.80	2265.99
250,000	21401.88	10967.85	7492.73	5757.33	4717.81	4026.24	3533.48	3164.99	2879.32	2651.64	2466.13	2312.23
255,000	21829.91	11187.21	7642.58	5872.47	4812.17	4106.76	3604.15	3228.28	2936.91	2704.68	2515.45	2358.48
260,000	22257.95	11406.57	7792.44	5987.62	4906.53	4187.29	3674.82	3291.58	2994.50	2757.71	2564.77	2404.72
265,000	22685.99	11625.92	7942.29	6102.77	5000.88	4267.81	3745.49	3354.88	3052.08	2810.74	2614.09	2450.96
270,000	23114.03	11845.28	8092.15	6217.91	5095.24	4348.34	3816.16	3418.18	3109.67	2863.77	2663.42	2497.21
280,000	23970.10	12283.99	8391.86	6448.21	5283.95	4509.39	3957.50	3544.78	3224.84	2969.84	2762.06	2589.70
290,000	24826.17	12722.71	8691.57	6678.50	5472.66	4670.44	4098.84	3671.38	3340.01	3075.90	2860.71	2682.19
300,000	25682.25	13161.42	8991.27	6908.79	5661.38	4831.48	4240.18	3797.98	3455.19	3181.97	2959.35	2774.68

MONTHLY AMORTIZING PAYMENTS 5.00%

AMOUNT OF LOAN	NUMBER OF YEARS IN TERM											
	13	14	15	16	17	18	19	20	25	30	35	40
$ 50	0.44	0.42	0.40	0.38	0.37	0.36	0.35	0.33	0.30	0.27	0.26	0.25
100	0.88	0.83	0.80	0.76	0.73	0.71	0.69	0.66	0.59	0.54	0.51	0.49
200	1.75	1.66	1.59	1.52	1.46	1.41	1.37	1.32	1.17	1.08	1.01	0.97
300	2.62	2.49	2.38	2.28	2.19	2.11	2.05	1.98	1.76	1.62	1.52	1.45
400	3.50	3.32	3.17	3.04	2.92	2.82	2.73	2.64	2.34	2.15	2.02	1.93
500	4.37	4.15	3.96	3.79	3.65	3.52	3.41	3.30	2.93	2.69	2.53	2.42
600	5.24	4.98	4.75	4.55	4.38	4.22	4.09	3.96	3.51	3.23	3.03	2.90
700	6.12	5.81	5.54	5.31	5.11	4.93	4.77	4.62	4.10	3.76	3.54	3.38
800	6.99	6.64	6.33	6.07	5.83	5.63	5.45	5.28	4.68	4.30	4.04	3.86
900	7.86	7.46	7.12	6.82	6.56	6.33	6.13	5.94	5.27	4.84	4.55	4.34
1,000	8.74	8.29	7.91	7.58	7.29	7.04	6.81	6.60	5.85	5.37	5.05	4.83
2,000	17.47	16.58	15.82	15.16	14.58	14.07	13.61	13.20	11.70	10.74	10.10	9.65
3,000	26.20	24.87	23.73	22.74	21.86	21.10	20.41	19.80	17.54	16.11	15.15	14.47
4,000	34.93	33.16	31.64	30.31	29.15	28.13	27.22	26.40	23.39	21.48	20.19	19.29
5,000	43.66	41.45	39.54	37.89	36.44	35.16	34.02	33.00	29.23	26.85	25.24	24.11
6,000	52.39	49.74	47.45	45.47	43.72	42.19	40.82	39.60	35.08	32.21	30.29	28.94
7,000	61.12	58.03	55.36	53.04	51.01	49.22	47.62	46.20	40.93	37.58	35.33	33.76
8,000	69.85	66.31	63.27	60.62	58.30	56.25	54.43	52.80	46.77	42.95	40.38	38.58
9,000	78.58	74.60	71.18	68.20	65.58	63.28	61.23	59.40	52.62	48.32	45.43	43.40
10,000	87.31	82.89	79.08	75.77	72.87	70.31	68.03	66.00	58.46	53.69	50.47	48.22
15,000	130.96	124.34	118.62	113.66	109.30	105.46	102.05	99.00	87.69	80.53	75.71	72.33
20,000	174.62	165.78	158.16	151.54	145.74	140.61	136.06	132.00	116.92	107.37	100.94	96.44
25,000	218.27	207.22	197.70	189.43	182.17	175.76	170.07	164.99	146.15	134.21	126.18	120.55
30,000	261.92	248.67	237.24	227.31	218.60	210.92	204.09	197.99	175.38	161.05	151.41	144.66
35,000	305.58	290.11	276.78	265.19	255.03	246.07	238.10	230.99	204.61	187.89	176.65	168.77
40,000	349.23	331.55	316.32	303.08	291.47	281.22	272.12	263.99	233.84	214.73	201.88	192.88
45,000	392.88	373.00	355.86	340.96	327.00	316.37	306.13	296.99	263.07	241.57	227.11	216.99
50,000	436.53	414.44	395.40	378.85	364.33	351.52	340.14	329.98	292.30	268.42	252.35	241.10
55,000	480.19	455.88	434.94	416.73	400.77	386.67	374.16	362.98	321.53	295.26	277.58	265.21
60,000	523.84	497.33	474.48	454.61	437.20	421.83	408.17	395.98	350.76	322.10	302.82	289.32
65,000	567.49	538.77	514.02	492.50	473.63	456.98	442.19	428.98	379.99	348.94	328.05	313.43
70,000	611.15	580.21	553.56	530.38	510.06	492.13	476.20	461.97	409.22	375.78	353.29	337.54
75,000	654.80	621.66	593.10	568.27	546.50	527.28	510.21	494.97	438.45	402.62	378.52	361.65
80,000	698.45	663.10	632.64	606.15	582.93	562.43	544.23	527.97	467.68	429.46	403.76	385.76
85,000	742.11	704.55	672.18	644.03	619.36	597.58	578.24	560.97	496.91	456.30	428.99	409.87
90,000	785.76	745.99	711.72	681.92	655.79	632.74	612.25	593.97	526.14	483.14	454.22	433.98
95,000	829.41	787.43	751.26	719.80	692.23	667.89	646.27	626.96	555.37	509.99	479.46	458.09
100,000	873.06	828.88	790.80	757.69	728.66	703.04	680.28	659.96	584.60	536.83	504.69	482.20
105,000	916.72	870.32	830.34	795.57	765.09	738.19	714.30	692.96	613.82	563.67	529.93	506.31
110,000	960.37	911.76	869.88	833.45	801.53	773.34	748.31	725.96	643.05	590.51	555.16	530.42
115,000	1004.02	953.21	909.42	871.34	837.96	808.49	782.32	758.95	672.28	617.35	580.40	554.53
120,000	1047.68	994.65	948.96	909.22	874.30	843.65	816.34	791.95	701.51	644.19	605.63	578.64
125,000	1091.33	1036.09	988.50	947.11	910.82	878.80	850.35	824.95	730.74	671.03	630.86	602.75
130,000	1134.98	1077.54	1028.04	984.99	947.26	913.95	884.37	857.95	759.97	697.87	656.10	626.86
135,000	1178.64	1118.98	1067.58	1022.87	983.69	949.10	918.38	890.95	789.20	724.71	681.33	650.97
140,000	1222.29	1160.42	1107.12	1060.76	1020.12	984.25	952.39	923.94	818.43	751.56	706.57	675.08
145,000	1265.94	1201.87	1146.66	1098.64	1056.56	1019.40	986.41	956.94	847.66	778.40	731.80	699.19
150,000	1309.59	1243.31	1186.20	1136.53	1092.99	1054.56	1020.42	989.94	876.89	805.24	757.04	723.30
155,000	1353.25	1284.75	1225.74	1174.41	1129.42	1089.71	1054.44	1022.94	906.12	832.08	782.27	747.41
160,000	1396.90	1326.20	1265.27	1212.29	1165.85	1124.86	1088.45	1055.93	935.35	858.92	807.51	771.52
165,000	1440.55	1367.64	1304.81	1250.18	1202.29	1160.01	1122.46	1088.93	964.58	885.76	832.74	795.63
170,000	1484.21	1409.09	1344.35	1288.06	1238.72	1195.16	1156.48	1121.93	993.81	912.60	857.97	819.74
175,000	1527.86	1450.53	1383.89	1325.95	1275.15	1230.31	1190.49	1154.93	1023.04	939.44	883.21	843.85
180,000	1571.51	1491.97	1423.43	1363.83	1311.58	1265.47	1224.50	1187.93	1052.27	966.28	908.44	867.96
185,000	1615.17	1533.42	1462.97	1401.71	1348.02	1300.62	1258.52	1220.92	1081.50	993.13	933.68	892.07
190,000	1658.82	1574.86	1502.51	1439.60	1384.45	1335.77	1292.53	1253.92	1110.73	1019.97	958.91	916.18
195,000	1702.47	1616.30	1542.05	1477.48	1420.88	1370.92	1326.55	1286.92	1139.96	1046.81	984.15	940.29
200,000	1746.12	1657.75	1581.59	1515.37	1457.32	1406.07	1360.56	1319.92	1169.19	1073.65	1009.38	964.40
205,000	1789.78	1699.19	1621.13	1553.25	1493.75	1441.22	1394.57	1352.91	1198.41	1100.49	1034.61	988.51
210,000	1833.43	1740.63	1660.67	1591.14	1530.18	1476.38	1428.59	1385.91	1227.64	1127.33	1059.85	1012.62
215,000	1877.08	1782.08	1700.21	1629.02	1566.61	1511.53	1462.60	1418.91	1256.87	1154.17	1085.08	1036.73
220,000	1920.74	1823.52	1739.75	1666.90	1603.05	1546.68	1496.62	1451.91	1286.10	1181.01	1110.32	1060.84
225,000	1964.39	1864.96	1779.29	1704.79	1639.48	1581.83	1530.63	1484.91	1315.33	1207.85	1135.55	1084.95
230,000	2008.04	1906.41	1818.83	1742.67	1675.91	1616.98	1564.64	1517.90	1344.56	1234.69	1160.79	1109.06
235,000	2051.70	1947.85	1858.37	1780.56	1712.34	1652.13	1598.66	1550.90	1373.79	1261.54	1186.02	1133.17
240,000	2095.35	1989.29	1897.91	1818.44	1748.78	1687.29	1632.67	1583.90	1403.02	1288.38	1211.26	1157.28
245,000	2139.00	2030.74	1937.45	1856.32	1785.21	1722.44	1666.69	1616.90	1432.25	1315.22	1236.49	1181.39
250,000	2182.65	2072.18	1976.99	1894.21	1821.64	1757.59	1700.70	1649.89	1461.48	1342.06	1261.72	1205.50
255,000	2226.31	2113.63	2016.53	1932.09	1858.08	1792.74	1734.71	1682.89	1490.71	1368.90	1286.96	1229.61
260,000	2269.96	2155.07	2056.07	1969.98	1894.51	1827.89	1768.73	1715.89	1519.94	1395.74	1312.19	1253.72
265,000	2313.61	2196.51	2095.61	2007.86	1930.94	1863.04	1802.74	1748.89	1549.17	1422.58	1337.43	1277.83
270,000	2357.27	2237.96	2135.15	2045.74	1967.37	1898.20	1836.75	1781.89	1578.40	1449.42	1362.66	1301.94
280,000	2444.57	2320.84	2214.23	2121.51	2040.24	1968.50	1904.78	1847.88	1636.86	1503.11	1413.13	1350.16
290,000	2531.88	2403.73	2293.31	2197.28	2113.11	2038.80	1972.81	1913.88	1695.32	1556.79	1463.60	1398.38
300,000	2619.18	2486.62	2372.39	2273.05	2185.97	2109.11	2040.84	1979.87	1753.78	1610.47	1514.07	1446.59

27

AMOUNT OF LOAN	NUMBER OF YEARS IN TERM											
	1	2	3	4	5	6	7	8	9	10	11	12
$ 50	4.29	2.20	1.51	1.16	0.95	0.82	0.72	0.64	0.59	0.54	0.50	0.47
100	8.58	4.40	3.01	2.32	1.90	1.63	1.43	1.28	1.17	1.08	1.00	0.94
200	17.15	8.80	6.02	4.63	3.80	3.25	2.86	2.56	2.33	2.15	2.00	1.88
300	25.72	13.20	9.03	6.95	5.70	4.87	4.28	3.84	3.50	3.22	3.00	2.82
400	34.29	17.60	12.04	9.26	7.60	6.49	5.71	5.12	4.66	4.30	4.00	3.75
500	42.87	22.00	15.05	11.58	9.50	8.12	7.13	6.39	5.82	5.37	5.00	4.69
600	51.44	26.40	18.05	13.89	11.40	9.74	8.56	7.67	6.99	6.44	6.00	5.63
700	60.01	30.79	21.06	16.20	13.30	11.36	9.98	8.95	8.15	7.52	7.00	6.57
800	68.58	35.19	24.07	18.52	15.19	12.98	11.41	10.23	9.32	8.59	8.00	7.50
900	77.15	39.59	27.08	20.83	17.09	14.60	12.83	11.51	10.48	9.66	8.99	8.44
1,000	85.73	43.99	30.09	23.15	18.99	16.23	14.26	12.78	11.64	10.73	9.99	9.38
2,000	171.45	87.97	60.17	46.29	37.98	32.45	28.51	25.56	23.28	21.46	19.98	18.75
3,000	257.17	131.96	90.25	69.43	56.96	48.67	42.76	38.34	34.92	32.19	29.97	28.13
4,000	342.89	175.94	120.34	92.58	75.95	64.89	57.01	51.12	46.56	42.92	39.96	37.50
5,000	428.62	219.92	150.42	115.72	94.93	81.11	71.26	63.90	58.20	53.65	49.95	46.88
6,000	514.34	263.91	180.50	138.86	113.92	97.33	85.52	76.68	69.83	64.38	59.94	56.25
7,000	600.06	307.89	210.59	162.00	132.91	113.55	99.77	89.46	81.47	75.11	69.93	65.63
8,000	685.78	351.87	240.67	185.15	151.89	129.77	114.02	102.24	93.11	85.84	79.92	75.00
9,000	771.50	395.86	270.75	208.29	170.88	146.00	128.27	115.02	104.75	96.57	89.90	84.38
10,000	857.23	439.84	300.84	231.43	189.86	162.22	142.52	127.80	116.39	107.30	99.89	93.75
15,000	1285.84	659.76	451.25	347.15	284.79	243.32	213.78	191.69	174.58	160.94	149.84	140.63
20,000	1714.45	879.67	601.67	462.86	379.72	324.43	285.04	255.59	232.77	214.59	199.78	187.50
25,000	2143.06	1099.59	752.09	578.57	474.65	405.53	356.30	319.49	290.96	268.23	249.72	234.38
30,000	2571.67	1319.51	902.50	694.29	569.58	486.64	427.56	383.38	349.15	321.88	299.67	281.25
35,000	3000.28	1539.43	1052.92	810.00	664.51	567.75	498.81	447.28	407.34	375.53	349.61	328.12
40,000	3428.89	1759.34	1203.34	925.71	759.44	648.85	570.07	511.18	465.54	429.17	399.56	375.00
45,000	3857.50	1979.26	1353.75	1041.43	854.37	729.96	641.33	575.07	523.73	482.82	449.50	421.87
50,000	4286.11	2199.18	1504.17	1157.14	949.30	811.06	712.59	638.97	581.92	536.46	499.44	468.75
55,000	4714.72	2419.09	1654.58	1272.85	1044.23	892.17	783.85	702.87	640.11	590.11	549.39	515.62
60,000	5143.33	2639.01	1805.00	1388.57	1139.16	973.27	855.11	766.76	698.30	643.76	599.33	562.49
65,000	5571.94	2858.93	1955.42	1504.28	1234.09	1054.38	926.36	830.66	756.49	697.40	649.27	609.37
70,000	6000.55	3078.85	2105.83	1619.99	1329.02	1135.49	997.62	894.55	814.68	751.05	699.22	656.24
75,000	6429.16	3298.76	2256.25	1735.71	1423.95	1216.59	1068.88	958.45	872.87	804.69	749.16	703.12
80,000	6857.77	3518.68	2406.67	1851.42	1518.88	1297.70	1140.14	1022.35	931.07	858.34	799.11	749.99
85,000	7286.38	3738.60	2557.08	1967.14	1613.81	1378.80	1211.40	1086.24	989.26	911.98	849.05	796.86
90,000	7714.99	3958.51	2707.50	2082.85	1708.74	1459.91	1282.66	1150.14	1047.45	965.63	898.99	843.74
95,000	8143.60	4178.43	2857.92	2198.56	1803.67	1541.01	1353.91	1214.04	1105.64	1019.28	948.94	890.61
100,000	8572.21	4398.35	3008.33	2314.28	1898.60	1622.12	1425.17	1277.93	1163.83	1072.92	998.88	937.49
105,000	9000.82	4618.27	3158.75	2429.99	1993.53	1703.23	1496.43	1341.83	1222.02	1126.57	1048.82	984.36
110,000	9429.43	4838.18	3309.16	2545.70	2088.46	1784.33	1567.69	1405.73	1280.21	1180.21	1098.77	1031.23
115,000	9858.05	5058.10	3459.58	2661.42	2183.39	1865.44	1638.95	1469.62	1338.40	1233.86	1148.71	1078.11
120,000	10286.66	5278.02	3610.00	2777.13	2278.32	1946.54	1710.21	1533.52	1396.60	1287.51	1198.66	1124.98
125,000	10715.27	5497.93	3760.41	2892.84	2373.25	2027.65	1781.46	1597.42	1454.79	1341.15	1248.60	1171.86
130,000	11143.88	5717.85	3910.83	3008.56	2468.18	2108.75	1852.72	1661.31	1512.98	1394.80	1298.54	1218.73
135,000	11572.49	5937.77	4061.25	3124.27	2563.11	2189.86	1923.98	1725.21	1571.17	1448.44	1348.49	1265.61
140,000	12001.10	6157.69	4211.66	3239.98	2658.04	2270.97	1995.24	1789.10	1629.36	1502.09	1398.43	1312.48
145,000	12429.71	6377.60	4362.08	3355.70	2752.97	2352.07	2066.50	1853.00	1687.55	1555.73	1448.37	1359.35
150,000	12858.32	6597.52	4512.50	3471.41	2847.90	2433.18	2137.76	1916.90	1745.74	1609.38	1498.32	1406.23
155,000	13286.93	6817.44	4662.91	3587.13	2942.83	2514.28	2209.02	1980.79	1803.93	1663.03	1548.26	1453.10
160,000	13715.54	7037.35	4813.33	3702.84	3037.76	2595.39	2280.27	2044.69	1862.13	1716.67	1598.21	1499.98
165,000	14144.15	7257.27	4963.74	3818.55	3132.69	2676.50	2351.53	2108.59	1920.32	1770.32	1648.15	1546.85
170,000	14572.76	7477.19	5114.16	3934.27	3227.62	2757.60	2422.79	2172.48	1978.51	1823.96	1698.09	1593.72
175,000	15001.37	7697.11	5264.58	4049.98	3322.55	2838.71	2494.05	2236.38	2036.70	1877.61	1748.04	1640.60
180,000	15429.98	7917.02	5414.99	4165.69	3417.48	2919.81	2565.31	2300.28	2094.89	1931.26	1797.98	1687.47
185,000	15858.59	8136.94	5565.41	4281.41	3512.41	3000.92	2636.57	2364.17	2153.08	1984.90	1847.92	1734.35
190,000	16287.20	8356.86	5715.83	4397.12	3607.34	3082.02	2707.82	2428.07	2211.27	2038.55	1897.87	1781.22
195,000	16715.81	8576.78	5866.24	4512.83	3702.27	3163.13	2779.08	2491.97	2269.46	2092.19	1947.81	1828.09
200,000	17144.42	8796.69	6016.66	4628.55	3797.20	3244.24	2850.34	2555.86	2327.66	2145.84	1997.76	1874.97
205,000	17573.03	9016.61	6167.08	4744.26	3892.13	3325.34	2921.60	2619.76	2385.85	2199.48	2047.70	1921.84
210,000	18001.64	9236.53	6317.49	4859.97	3987.06	3406.45	2992.86	2683.65	2444.04	2253.13	2097.64	1968.72
215,000	18430.25	9456.44	6467.91	4975.69	4081.99	3487.55	3064.12	2747.55	2502.23	2306.78	2147.59	2015.59
220,000	18858.86	9676.36	6618.32	5091.40	4176.92	3568.66	3135.37	2811.45	2560.42	2360.42	2197.53	2062.46
225,000	19287.48	9896.28	6768.74	5207.12	4271.85	3649.76	3206.63	2875.34	2618.61	2414.07	2247.47	2109.34
230,000	19716.09	10116.20	6919.16	5322.83	4366.78	3730.87	3277.89	2939.24	2676.80	2467.71	2297.42	2156.21
235,000	20144.70	10336.11	7069.57	5438.54	4461.71	3811.98	3349.15	3003.14	2735.00	2521.36	2347.36	2203.09
240,000	20573.31	10556.03	7219.99	5554.26	4556.64	3893.08	3420.41	3067.03	2793.19	2575.01	2397.31	2249.96
245,000	21001.92	10775.95	7370.41	5669.97	4651.57	3974.19	3491.67	3130.93	2851.38	2628.65	2447.25	2296.83
250,000	21430.53	10995.86	7520.82	5785.68	4746.50	4055.29	3562.92	3194.83	2909.57	2682.30	2497.19	2343.71
255,000	21859.14	11215.78	7671.24	5901.40	4841.43	4136.40	3634.18	3258.72	2967.76	2735.94	2547.14	2390.58
260,000	22287.75	11435.70	7821.66	6017.11	4936.36	4217.50	3705.44	3322.62	3025.95	2789.59	2597.08	2437.46
265,000	22716.36	11655.62	7972.07	6132.82	5031.29	4298.61	3776.70	3386.51	3084.14	2843.24	2647.02	2484.33
270,000	23144.97	11875.53	8122.49	6248.54	5126.22	4379.72	3847.96	3450.41	3142.33	2896.88	2696.97	2531.21
280,000	24002.19	12315.37	8423.32	6479.96	5316.08	4541.93	3990.47	3578.20	3258.72	3004.17	2796.86	2624.95
290,000	24859.41	12755.20	8724.15	6711.39	5505.94	4704.14	4132.99	3706.00	3375.10	3111.46	2896.74	2718.70
300,000	25716.63	13195.04	9024.99	6942.82	5695.80	4866.35	4275.51	3833.79	3491.48	3218.76	2996.63	2812.45

AMOUNT OF LOAN	13	14	15	16	17	18	19	20	25	30	35	40
$ 50	0.45	0.43	0.41	0.39	0.38	0.36	0.35	0.34	0.30	0.28	0.27	0.25
100	0.89	0.85	0.81	0.78	0.75	0.72	0.70	0.68	0.60	0.56	0.53	0.50
200	1.78	1.69	1.61	1.55	1.49	1.44	1.39	1.35	1.20	1.11	1.05	1.00
300	2.66	2.53	2.42	2.32	2.23	2.15	2.09	2.03	1.80	1.66	1.57	1.50
400	3.55	3.37	3.22	3.09	2.97	2.87	2.78	2.70	2.40	2.21	2.09	2.00
500	4.43	4.21	4.02	3.86	3.72	3.59	3.48	3.37	3.00	2.77	2.61	2.50
600	5.32	5.06	4.83	4.63	4.46	4.30	4.17	4.05	3.60	3.32	3.13	3.00
700	6.21	5.90	5.63	5.40	5.20	5.02	4.86	4.72	4.20	3.87	3.65	3.50
800	7.09	6.74	6.44	6.17	5.94	5.74	5.56	5.40	4.80	4.42	4.17	4.00
900	7.98	7.58	7.24	6.94	6.68	6.45	6.25	6.07	5.40	4.97	4.69	4.49
1,000	8.86	8.42	8.04	7.71	7.43	7.17	6.95	6.74	6.00	5.53	5.21	4.99
2,000	17.72	16.84	16.08	15.42	14.85	14.34	13.89	13.48	11.99	11.05	10.42	9.98
3,000	26.58	25.26	24.12	23.13	22.27	21.50	20.83	20.22	17.98	16.57	15.63	14.97
4,000	35.44	33.68	32.16	30.84	29.69	28.67	27.77	26.96	23.97	22.09	20.83	19.96
5,000	44.30	42.09	40.20	38.55	37.11	35.84	34.71	33.70	29.97	27.62	26.04	24.95
6,000	53.15	50.51	48.24	46.26	44.53	43.00	41.65	40.44	35.96	33.14	31.25	29.94
7,000	62.01	58.93	56.28	53.97	51.95	50.17	48.59	47.17	41.95	38.66	36.46	34.93
8,000	70.87	67.35	64.32	61.68	59.37	57.33	55.53	53.91	47.94	44.18	41.66	39.91
9,000	79.73	75.77	72.35	69.39	66.79	64.50	62.47	60.65	53.94	49.70	46.87	44.90
10,000	88.59	84.18	80.39	77.10	74.21	71.67	69.41	67.39	59.93	55.23	52.08	49.89
15,000	132.88	126.27	120.59	115.64	111.31	107.50	104.11	101.08	89.89	82.84	78.12	74.84
20,000	177.17	168.36	160.78	154.19	148.42	143.33	138.81	134.77	119.85	110.45	104.15	99.78
25,000	221.46	210.45	200.97	192.74	185.52	179.16	173.51	168.47	149.82	138.06	130.19	124.72
30,000	265.75	252.54	241.17	231.28	222.62	214.99	208.21	202.16	179.78	165.67	156.23	149.67
35,000	310.04	294.63	281.36	269.83	259.73	250.82	242.91	235.85	209.74	193.28	182.27	174.61
40,000	354.33	336.72	321.56	308.38	296.83	286.65	277.61	269.54	239.70	220.89	208.30	199.55
45,000	398.62	378.81	361.75	346.92	333.93	322.48	312.31	303.23	269.67	248.50	234.34	224.50
50,000	442.91	420.90	401.94	385.47	371.04	358.31	347.01	336.93	299.63	276.11	260.38	249.44
55,000	487.20	462.99	442.14	424.02	408.14	394.14	381.71	370.62	329.59	303.72	286.41	274.38
60,000	531.49	505.08	482.33	462.56	445.24	429.97	416.41	404.31	359.55	331.33	312.45	299.33
65,000	575.79	547.17	522.53	501.11	482.35	465.80	451.11	438.00	389.52	358.94	338.49	324.27
70,000	620.08	589.26	562.72	539.65	519.45	501.63	485.81	471.70	419.48	386.55	364.53	349.21
75,000	664.37	631.35	602.91	578.20	556.55	537.46	520.51	505.39	449.44	414.16	390.56	374.16
80,000	708.66	673.44	643.11	616.75	593.66	573.29	555.21	539.08	479.40	441.77	416.60	399.10
85,000	752.95	715.53	683.30	655.29	630.76	609.12	589.91	572.77	509.37	469.38	442.64	424.04
90,000	797.24	757.62	723.49	693.84	667.86	644.95	624.61	606.46	539.33	496.99	468.67	448.99
95,000	841.53	799.71	763.69	732.39	704.97	680.78	659.31	640.16	569.29	524.60	494.71	473.93
100,000	885.82	841.80	803.88	770.93	742.07	716.61	694.01	673.85	599.25	552.21	520.75	498.88
105,000	930.11	883.89	844.08	809.48	779.17	752.44	728.71	707.54	629.22	579.82	546.79	523.82
110,000	974.40	925.98	884.27	848.03	816.28	788.27	763.41	741.23	659.18	607.43	572.82	548.76
115,000	1018.69	968.06	924.46	886.57	853.38	824.10	798.11	774.93	689.14	635.04	598.86	573.71
120,000	1062.98	1010.15	964.66	925.12	890.48	859.93	832.81	808.62	719.10	662.65	624.90	598.65
125,000	1107.27	1052.24	1004.05	963.67	927.59	895.76	867.51	842.31	749.06	690.26	650.94	623.60
130,000	1151.57	1094.33	1045.05	1002.21	964.69	931.59	902.22	876.00	779.03	717.87	676.97	648.54
135,000	1195.86	1136.42	1085.24	1040.76	1001.79	967.42	936.92	909.69	808.99	745.48	703.01	673.48
140,000	1240.15	1178.51	1125.43	1079.30	1038.90	1003.25	971.62	943.39	838.95	773.09	729.05	698.42
145,000	1284.44	1220.60	1165.63	1117.85	1076.00	1039.08	1006.32	977.08	868.91	800.70	755.08	723.37
150,000	1328.73	1262.69	1205.82	1156.40	1113.10	1074.91	1041.02	1010.77	898.88	828.31	781.12	748.31
155,000	1373.02	1304.78	1246.02	1194.94	1150.20	1110.74	1075.72	1044.46	928.84	855.92	807.16	773.25
160,000	1417.31	1346.87	1286.21	1233.49	1187.31	1146.57	1110.42	1078.16	958.80	883.53	833.19	798.20
165,000	1461.60	1388.96	1326.40	1272.04	1224.41	1182.40	1145.12	1111.85	988.76	911.14	859.23	823.14
170,000	1505.89	1431.05	1366.60	1310.58	1261.51	1218.23	1179.82	1145.54	1018.73	938.75	885.27	848.08
175,000	1550.18	1473.14	1406.79	1349.13	1298.62	1254.06	1214.52	1179.23	1048.69	966.36	911.31	873.03
180,000	1594.47	1515.23	1446.98	1387.68	1335.72	1289.89	1249.22	1212.92	1078.65	993.97	937.34	897.97
185,000	1638.76	1557.32	1487.18	1426.22	1372.82	1325.72	1283.92	1246.62	1108.61	1021.58	963.38	922.92
190,000	1683.05	1599.41	1527.37	1464.77	1409.93	1361.55	1318.62	1280.31	1138.58	1049.19	989.42	947.86
195,000	1727.35	1641.50	1567.57	1503.31	1447.03	1397.38	1353.32	1314.00	1168.54	1076.80	1015.45	972.80
200,000	1771.64	1683.59	1607.76	1541.86	1484.13	1433.21	1388.02	1347.69	1198.50	1104.41	1041.49	997.75
205,000	1815.93	1725.68	1647.95	1580.41	1521.24	1469.04	1422.72	1381.39	1228.46	1132.02	1067.53	1022.69
210,000	1860.22	1767.77	1688.15	1618.95	1558.34	1504.87	1457.42	1415.08	1258.43	1159.63	1093.57	1047.63
215,000	1904.51	1809.86	1728.34	1657.50	1595.44	1540.70	1492.12	1448.77	1288.39	1187.24	1119.60	1072.58
220,000	1948.80	1851.95	1768.54	1696.05	1632.55	1576.53	1526.82	1482.46	1318.35	1214.85	1145.64	1097.52
225,000	1993.09	1894.03	1808.73	1734.59	1669.65	1612.36	1561.52	1516.15	1348.31	1242.46	1171.68	1122.46
230,000	2037.38	1936.12	1848.92	1773.14	1706.75	1648.19	1596.22	1549.85	1378.27	1270.07	1197.71	1147.41
235,000	2081.67	1978.21	1889.12	1811.69	1743.86	1684.02	1630.92	1583.54	1408.24	1297.68	1223.75	1172.35
240,000	2125.96	2020.30	1929.31	1850.23	1780.96	1719.85	1665.62	1617.23	1438.20	1325.29	1249.79	1197.29
245,000	2170.25	2062.39	1969.51	1888.78	1818.06	1755.68	1700.32	1650.92	1468.16	1352.90	1275.83	1222.24
250,000	2214.54	2104.48	2009.70	1927.33	1855.17	1791.52	1735.02	1684.62	1498.12	1380.51	1301.86	1247.18
255,000	2258.83	2146.57	2049.89	1965.87	1892.27	1827.35	1769.72	1718.31	1528.09	1408.12	1327.90	1272.12
260,000	2303.13	2188.66	2090.09	2004.42	1929.37	1863.18	1804.43	1752.00	1558.05	1435.73	1353.94	1297.07
265,000	2347.42	2230.75	2130.28	2042.96	1966.48	1899.01	1839.13	1785.69	1588.01	1463.34	1379.97	1322.01
270,000	2391.71	2272.84	2170.47	2081.51	2003.58	1934.84	1873.83	1819.38	1617.97	1490.95	1406.01	1346.95
280,000	2480.29	2357.02	2250.86	2158.60	2077.79	2006.50	1943.23	1886.77	1677.90	1546.18	1458.09	1396.84
290,000	2568.87	2441.20	2331.25	2235.70	2151.99	2078.16	2012.63	1954.15	1737.82	1601.40	1510.16	1446.73
300,000	2657.45	2525.38	2411.64	2312.79	2226.20	2149.82	2082.03	2021.54	1797.75	1656.62	1562.23	1496.62

MONTHLY AMORTIZING PAYMENTS

AMOUNT OF LOAN	NUMBER OF YEARS IN TERM											
	1	2	3	4	5	6	7	8	9	10	11	12
$ 50	4.30	2.21	1.51	1.17	0.96	0.82	0.72	0.65	0.59	0.55	0.51	0.48
100	8.59	4.41	3.02	2.33	1.92	1.64	1.44	1.29	1.18	1.09	1.02	0.96
200	17.17	8.82	6.04	4.66	3.83	3.27	2.88	2.58	2.36	2.18	2.03	1.91
300	25.76	13.23	9.06	6.98	5.74	4.91	4.32	3.87	3.53	3.26	3.04	2.86
400	34.34	17.64	12.08	9.31	7.65	6.54	5.75	5.16	4.71	4.35	4.05	3.81
500	42.92	22.05	15.10	11.63	9.56	8.17	7.19	6.45	5.88	5.43	5.06	4.76
600	51.51	26.46	18.12	13.96	11.47	9.81	8.63	7.74	7.06	6.52	6.07	5.71
700	60.09	30.87	21.14	16.28	13.38	11.44	10.06	9.03	8.24	7.60	7.08	6.66
800	68.67	35.28	24.16	18.61	15.29	13.08	11.50	10.32	9.41	8.69	8.10	7.61
900	77.26	39.69	27.18	20.94	17.20	14.71	12.94	11.61	10.59	9.77	9.11	8.56
1,000	85.84	44.10	30.20	23.26	19.11	16.34	14.38	12.90	11.76	10.86	10.12	9.51
2,000	171.68	88.20	60.40	46.52	38.21	32.68	28.75	25.80	23.52	21.71	20.23	19.01
3,000	257.52	132.29	90.59	69.77	57.31	49.02	43.12	38.70	35.28	32.56	30.35	28.51
4,000	343.35	176.39	120.79	93.03	76.41	65.36	57.49	51.60	47.04	43.42	40.46	38.01
5,000	429.19	220.48	150.98	116.29	95.51	81.69	71.86	64.50	58.80	54.27	50.57	47.51
6,000	515.03	264.58	181.18	139.54	114.61	98.03	86.23	77.40	70.56	65.12	60.69	57.02
7,000	600.86	308.67	211.38	162.80	133.71	114.37	100.60	90.30	82.32	75.97	70.80	66.52
8,000	686.70	352.77	241.57	186.06	152.81	130.71	114.97	103.20	94.08	86.83	80.92	76.02
9,000	772.54	396.87	271.77	209.31	171.92	147.05	129.34	116.10	105.84	97.68	91.03	85.52
10,000	858.37	440.96	301.96	232.57	191.02	163.38	143.71	129.00	117.60	108.53	101.14	95.02
15,000	1287.56	661.44	452.94	348.85	286.52	245.07	215.56	193.49	176.40	162.79	151.71	142.53
20,000	1716.74	881.92	603.92	465.13	382.03	326.76	287.41	257.99	235.20	217.06	202.28	190.04
25,000	2145.92	1102.40	754.90	581.42	477.53	408.45	359.26	322.49	294.00	271.32	252.85	237.55
30,000	2575.11	1322.87	905.88	697.70	573.04	490.14	431.11	386.98	352.80	325.58	303.42	285.06
35,000	3004.29	1543.35	1056.86	813.98	668.55	571.83	502.96	451.48	411.60	379.85	353.99	332.57
40,000	3433.48	1763.83	1207.84	930.26	764.05	653.52	574.81	515.98	470.40	434.11	404.56	380.07
45,000	3862.66	1984.31	1358.82	1046.55	859.56	735.21	646.66	580.47	529.20	488.37	455.13	427.58
50,000	4291.84	2204.79	1509.80	1162.83	955.06	816.90	718.51	644.97	588.00	542.64	505.70	475.09
55,000	4721.03	2425.27	1660.78	1279.11	1050.57	898.59	790.36	709.47	646.80	596.90	556.27	522.60
60,000	5150.21	2645.74	1811.76	1395.39	1146.07	980.28	862.21	773.96	705.60	651.16	606.84	570.11
65,000	5579.40	2866.22	1962.74	1511.68	1241.58	1061.97	934.06	838.46	764.40	705.43	657.41	617.62
70,000	6008.58	3086.70	2113.72	1627.96	1337.09	1143.66	1005.91	902.96	823.20	759.69	707.98	665.13
75,000	6437.76	3307.18	2264.70	1744.24	1432.59	1225.35	1077.76	967.45	882.00	813.95	758.55	712.63
80,000	6866.95	3527.66	2415.68	1860.52	1528.10	1307.04	1149.61	1031.95	940.80	868.22	809.12	760.14
85,000	7296.13	3748.14	2566.66	1976.81	1623.60	1388.73	1221.46	1096.45	999.60	922.48	859.69	807.65
90,000	7725.32	3968.61	2717.64	2093.09	1719.11	1470.41	1293.31	1160.94	1058.40	976.74	910.26	855.16
95,000	8154.50	4189.09	2868.62	2209.37	1814.62	1552.10	1365.16	1225.44	1117.20	1031.00	960.83	902.67
100,000	8583.68	4409.57	3019.60	2325.65	1910.12	1633.79	1437.01	1289.94	1176.00	1085.27	1011.40	950.18
105,000	9012.87	4630.05	3170.57	2441.93	2005.63	1715.48	1508.86	1354.43	1234.80	1139.53	1061.97	997.69
110,000	9442.05	4850.53	3321.55	2558.22	2101.13	1797.17	1580.71	1418.93	1293.60	1193.79	1112.54	1045.19
115,000	9871.24	5071.01	3472.53	2674.50	2196.64	1878.86	1652.56	1483.43	1352.40	1248.06	1163.11	1092.70
120,000	10300.42	5291.48	3623.51	2790.78	2292.14	1960.55	1724.41	1547.92	1411.20	1302.32	1213.68	1140.21
125,000	10729.60	5511.96	3774.49	2907.06	2387.65	2042.24	1796.26	1612.42	1470.00	1356.58	1264.25	1187.72
130,000	11158.79	5732.44	3925.47	3023.35	2483.16	2123.93	1868.11	1676.92	1528.80	1410.85	1314.82	1235.23
135,000	11587.97	5952.92	4076.45	3139.63	2578.66	2205.62	1939.96	1741.41	1587.60	1465.11	1365.39	1282.74
140,000	12017.15	6173.40	4227.43	3255.91	2674.17	2287.31	2011.81	1805.91	1646.40	1519.37	1415.96	1330.25
145,000	12446.34	6393.88	4378.41	3372.19	2769.67	2369.00	2083.66	1870.41	1705.20	1573.64	1466.53	1377.75
150,000	12875.52	6614.35	4529.39	3488.48	2865.18	2450.69	2155.51	1934.90	1764.00	1627.90	1517.09	1425.26
155,000	13304.71	6834.83	4680.37	3604.76	2960.69	2532.38	2227.36	1999.40	1822.80	1682.16	1567.66	1472.77
160,000	13733.89	7055.31	4831.35	3721.04	3056.19	2614.07	2299.21	2063.90	1881.60	1736.43	1618.23	1520.28
165,000	14163.07	7275.79	4982.33	3837.32	3151.70	2695.76	2371.06	2128.39	1940.40	1790.69	1668.80	1567.79
170,000	14592.26	7496.27	5133.31	3953.61	3247.20	2777.45	2442.91	2192.89	1999.20	1844.95	1719.37	1615.30
175,000	15021.44	7716.74	5284.29	4069.89	3342.71	2859.14	2514.76	2257.39	2058.00	1899.21	1769.94	1662.81
180,000	15450.63	7937.22	5435.27	4186.17	3438.21	2940.82	2586.61	2321.88	2116.80	1953.48	1820.51	1710.31
185,000	15879.81	8157.70	5586.25	4302.45	3533.72	3022.51	2658.46	2386.38	2175.60	2007.74	1871.08	1757.82
190,000	16308.99	8378.18	5737.23	4418.74	3629.23	3104.20	2730.31	2450.88	2234.40	2062.00	1921.65	1805.33
195,000	16738.18	8598.66	5888.21	4535.02	3724.73	3185.89	2802.16	2515.37	2293.20	2116.27	1972.22	1852.84
200,000	17167.36	8819.14	6039.19	4651.30	3820.24	3267.58	2874.01	2579.87	2352.00	2170.53	2022.79	1900.35
205,000	17596.55	9039.61	6190.16	4767.58	3915.74	3349.27	2945.86	2644.37	2410.80	2224.79	2073.36	1947.86
210,000	18025.73	9260.09	6341.14	4883.86	4011.25	3430.96	3017.71	2708.86	2469.60	2279.06	2123.93	1995.37
215,000	18454.91	9480.57	6492.12	5000.15	4106.75	3512.65	3089.56	2773.36	2528.40	2333.32	2174.50	2042.88
220,000	18884.10	9701.05	6643.10	5116.43	4202.26	3594.34	3161.41	2837.86	2587.20	2387.58	2225.07	2090.38
225,000	19313.28	9921.53	6794.08	5232.71	4297.77	3676.03	3233.26	2902.35	2646.00	2441.85	2275.64	2137.89
230,000	19742.47	10142.01	6945.06	5348.99	4393.27	3757.72	3305.11	2966.85	2704.80	2496.11	2326.21	2185.40
235,000	20171.65	10362.48	7096.04	5465.28	4488.78	3839.41	3376.97	3031.35	2763.60	2550.37	2376.78	2232.91
240,000	20600.83	10582.96	7247.02	5581.56	4584.28	3921.10	3448.82	3095.84	2822.40	2604.64	2427.35	2280.42
245,000	21030.02	10803.44	7398.00	5697.84	4679.79	4002.79	3520.67	3160.34	2881.20	2658.90	2477.92	2327.93
250,000	21459.20	11023.92	7548.98	5814.12	4775.30	4084.48	3592.52	3224.84	2940.00	2713.16	2528.49	2375.44
255,000	21888.39	11244.40	7699.96	5930.41	4870.80	4166.17	3664.37	3289.33	2998.80	2767.43	2579.06	2422.94
260,000	22317.57	11464.88	7850.94	6046.69	4966.31	4247.86	3736.22	3353.83	3057.60	2821.69	2629.63	2470.45
265,000	22746.75	11685.35	8001.92	6162.97	5061.81	4329.55	3808.07	3418.33	3116.40	2875.95	2680.20	2517.96
270,000	23175.94	11905.83	8152.90	6279.25	5157.32	4411.23	3879.92	3482.82	3175.20	2930.21	2730.77	2565.47
280,000	24034.30	12346.79	8454.86	6511.82	5348.33	4574.61	4023.62	3611.82	3292.80	3038.74	2831.91	2660.49
290,000	24892.67	12787.75	8756.82	6744.38	5539.34	4737.99	4167.32	3740.81	3410.40	3147.27	2933.05	2755.50
300,000	25751.04	13228.70	9058.78	6976.95	5730.35	4901.37	4311.02	3869.80	3528.00	3255.79	3034.18	2850.52

AMOUNT OF LOAN	NUMBER OF YEARS IN TERM											
	13	14	15	16	17	18	19	20	25	30	35	40
$ 50	0.45	0.43	0.41	0.40	0.38	0.37	0.36	0.35	0.31	0.29	0.27	0.26
100	0.90	0.86	0.82	0.79	0.76	0.74	0.71	0.69	0.62	0.57	0.54	0.52
200	1.80	1.71	1.64	1.57	1.52	1.47	1.42	1.38	1.23	1.14	1.08	1.04
300	2.70	2.57	2.46	2.36	2.27	2.20	2.13	2.07	1.85	1.71	1.62	1.55
400	3.60	3.42	3.27	3.14	3.03	2.93	2.84	2.76	2.46	2.28	2.15	2.07
500	4.50	4.28	4.09	3.93	3.78	3.66	3.54	3.44	3.08	2.84	2.69	2.58
600	5.40	5.13	4.91	4.71	4.54	4.39	4.25	4.13	3.69	3.41	3.23	3.10
700	6.30	5.99	5.72	5.50	5.29	5.12	4.96	4.82	4.30	3.98	3.76	3.62
800	7.19	6.84	6.54	6.28	6.05	5.85	5.67	5.51	4.92	4.55	4.30	4.13
900	8.09	7.70	7.36	7.06	6.81	6.58	6.38	6.20	5.53	5.12	4.84	4.65
1,000	8.99	8.55	8.18	7.85	7.56	7.31	7.08	6.88	6.15	5.68	5.38	5.16
2,000	17.98	17.10	16.35	15.69	15.12	14.61	14.16	13.76	12.29	11.36	10.75	10.32
3,000	26.97	25.65	24.52	23.53	22.67	21.91	21.24	20.64	18.43	17.04	16.12	15.48
4,000	35.95	34.20	32.69	31.38	30.23	29.22	28.32	27.52	24.57	22.72	21.49	20.64
5,000	44.94	42.75	40.86	39.22	37.79	36.52	35.40	34.40	30.71	28.39	26.86	25.79
6,000	53.93	51.29	49.03	47.06	45.34	43.82	42.48	41.28	36.85	34.07	32.23	30.95
7,000	62.91	59.84	57.20	54.91	52.90	51.13	49.56	48.16	42.99	39.75	37.60	36.11
8,000	71.90	68.39	65.37	62.75	60.45	58.43	56.64	55.04	49.13	45.43	42.97	41.27
9,000	80.89	76.94	73.54	70.59	68.01	65.73	63.71	61.91	55.27	51.11	48.34	46.42
10,000	89.87	85.49	81.71	78.44	75.57	73.04	70.79	68.79	61.41	56.78	53.71	51.58
15,000	134.81	128.23	122.57	117.65	113.35	109.55	106.19	103.19	92.12	85.17	80.56	77.37
20,000	179.74	170.97	163.42	156.87	151.13	146.07	141.58	137.58	122.82	113.56	107.41	103.16
25,000	224.67	213.71	204.28	196.08	188.91	182.58	176.98	171.98	153.53	141.95	134.26	128.95
30,000	269.61	256.45	245.13	235.30	226.69	219.10	212.37	206.37	184.23	170.34	161.11	154.74
35,000	314.54	299.19	285.98	274.51	264.47	255.62	247.77	240.77	214.94	198.73	187.96	180.52
40,000	359.48	341.94	326.84	313.73	302.25	292.13	283.16	275.16	245.64	227.12	214.81	206.31
45,000	404.41	384.68	367.69	352.94	340.03	328.65	318.55	309.55	276.34	255.51	241.66	232.10
50,000	449.34	427.42	408.55	392.16	377.81	365.16	353.95	343.95	307.05	283.90	268.51	257.89
55,000	494.28	470.16	449.40	431.37	415.59	401.68	389.34	378.34	337.75	312.29	295.36	283.68
60,000	539.21	512.90	490.26	470.59	453.37	438.19	424.74	412.74	368.46	340.68	322.21	309.47
65,000	584.15	555.64	531.11	509.80	491.15	474.71	460.13	447.13	399.16	369.07	349.07	335.26
70,000	629.08	598.38	571.96	549.02	528.93	511.23	495.53	481.53	429.87	397.46	375.92	361.04
75,000	674.01	641.12	612.82	588.23	566.71	547.74	530.92	515.92	460.57	425.85	402.77	386.83
80,000	718.95	683.87	653.67	627.45	604.49	584.26	566.31	550.31	491.27	454.24	429.62	412.62
85,000	763.88	726.61	694.53	666.66	642.27	620.77	601.71	584.71	521.98	482.63	456.47	438.41
90,000	808.82	769.35	735.38	705.88	680.05	657.29	637.10	619.10	552.68	511.02	483.32	464.20
95,000	853.75	812.09	776.23	745.09	717.83	693.81	672.50	653.50	583.39	539.40	510.17	489.99
100,000	898.68	854.83	817.09	784.31	755.61	730.32	707.89	687.89	614.09	567.79	537.02	515.78
105,000	943.62	897.57	857.94	823.52	793.39	766.84	743.29	722.29	644.80	596.18	563.87	541.56
110,000	988.55	940.31	898.80	862.74	831.18	803.35	778.68	756.68	675.50	624.57	590.72	567.35
115,000	1033.49	983.05	939.65	901.95	868.96	839.87	814.07	791.08	706.21	652.96	617.57	593.14
120,000	1078.42	1025.80	980.51	941.17	906.74	876.38	849.47	826.47	736.91	681.35	644.42	618.93
125,000	1123.35	1068.54	1021.36	980.38	944.52	912.90	884.86	859.86	767.61	709.74	671.28	644.72
130,000	1168.29	1111.28	1062.21	1019.60	982.30	949.42	920.26	894.26	798.32	738.13	698.13	670.51
135,000	1213.22	1154.02	1103.07	1058.82	1020.08	985.93	955.65	928.65	829.02	766.52	724.98	696.29
140,000	1258.15	1196.76	1143.92	1098.03	1057.86	1022.45	991.05	963.05	859.73	794.91	751.83	722.08
145,000	1303.09	1239.50	1184.78	1137.25	1095.64	1058.96	1026.44	997.44	890.43	823.30	778.68	747.87
150,000	1348.02	1282.24	1225.63	1176.46	1133.42	1095.48	1061.83	1031.84	921.14	851.69	805.53	773.66
155,000	1392.96	1324.98	1266.48	1215.68	1171.20	1132.00	1097.23	1066.23	951.84	880.08	832.38	799.45
160,000	1437.89	1367.73	1307.34	1254.89	1208.98	1168.51	1132.62	1100.62	982.54	908.47	859.23	825.24
165,000	1482.82	1410.47	1348.19	1294.11	1246.76	1205.03	1168.02	1135.02	1013.25	936.86	886.08	851.03
170,000	1527.76	1453.21	1389.05	1333.32	1284.54	1241.54	1203.41	1169.41	1043.95	965.25	912.93	876.81
175,000	1572.69	1495.95	1429.90	1372.54	1322.32	1278.06	1238.81	1203.81	1074.66	993.64	939.78	902.60
180,000	1617.63	1538.69	1470.76	1411.75	1360.10	1314.57	1274.20	1238.20	1105.36	1022.03	966.63	928.39
185,000	1662.56	1581.43	1511.61	1450.97	1397.88	1351.09	1309.59	1272.60	1136.07	1050.41	993.49	954.18
190,000	1707.49	1624.17	1552.46	1490.18	1435.66	1387.61	1344.99	1306.99	1166.77	1078.80	1020.34	979.97
195,000	1752.43	1666.92	1593.32	1529.40	1473.44	1424.12	1380.38	1341.39	1197.48	1107.19	1047.19	1005.76
200,000	1797.36	1709.66	1634.17	1568.61	1511.22	1460.64	1415.78	1375.78	1228.18	1135.58	1074.04	1031.55
205,000	1842.30	1752.40	1675.03	1607.83	1549.00	1497.15	1451.17	1410.17	1258.88	1163.97	1100.89	1057.33
210,000	1887.23	1795.14	1715.88	1647.04	1586.78	1533.67	1486.57	1444.57	1289.59	1192.36	1127.74	1083.12
215,000	1932.16	1837.88	1756.73	1686.26	1624.56	1570.19	1521.96	1478.96	1320.29	1220.75	1154.59	1108.91
220,000	1977.10	1880.62	1797.59	1725.47	1662.35	1606.70	1557.35	1513.36	1351.00	1249.14	1181.44	1134.70
225,000	2022.03	1923.36	1838.44	1764.69	1700.13	1643.22	1592.75	1547.75	1381.70	1277.53	1208.29	1160.49
230,000	2066.97	1966.10	1879.30	1803.90	1737.91	1679.73	1628.14	1582.15	1412.41	1305.92	1235.14	1186.28
235,000	2111.90	2008.85	1920.15	1843.12	1775.69	1716.25	1663.54	1616.54	1443.11	1334.31	1261.99	1212.07
240,000	2156.83	2051.59	1961.01	1882.33	1813.47	1752.76	1698.93	1650.93	1473.81	1362.70	1288.84	1237.85
245,000	2201.77	2094.33	2001.86	1921.55	1851.25	1789.28	1734.33	1685.33	1504.52	1391.09	1315.69	1263.64
250,000	2246.70	2137.07	2042.71	1960.76	1889.03	1825.80	1769.72	1719.72	1535.22	1419.48	1342.55	1289.43
255,000	2291.64	2179.81	2083.57	1999.98	1926.81	1862.31	1805.11	1754.12	1565.93	1447.87	1369.40	1315.22
260,000	2336.57	2222.55	2124.42	2039.20	1964.59	1898.83	1840.51	1788.51	1596.63	1476.26	1396.25	1341.01
265,000	2381.50	2265.29	2165.28	2078.41	2002.37	1935.34	1875.90	1822.91	1627.34	1504.65	1423.10	1366.80
270,000	2426.44	2308.03	2206.13	2117.63	2040.15	1971.86	1911.30	1857.30	1658.04	1533.04	1449.95	1392.58
280,000	2516.30	2393.52	2287.84	2196.06	2115.71	2044.89	1982.09	1926.09	1719.45	1589.81	1503.65	1444.16
290,000	2606.17	2479.00	2369.55	2274.49	2191.27	2117.92	2052.88	1994.88	1780.86	1646.59	1557.35	1495.74
300,000	2696.04	2564.48	2451.26	2352.92	2266.83	2190.95	2123.66	2063.67	1842.27	1703.37	1611.05	1547.32

5.75%

AMOUNT OF LOAN	NUMBER OF YEARS IN TERM											
	1	2	3	4	5	6	7	8	9	10	11	12
$ 50	4.30	2.22	1.52	1.17	0.97	0.83	0.73	0.66	0.60	0.55	0.52	0.49
100	8.60	4.43	3.04	2.34	1.93	1.65	1.45	1.31	1.19	1.10	1.03	0.97
200	17.20	8.85	6.07	4.68	3.85	3.30	2.90	2.61	2.38	2.20	2.05	1.93
300	25.79	13.27	9.10	7.02	5.77	4.94	4.35	3.91	3.57	3.30	3.08	2.89
400	34.39	17.69	12.13	9.35	7.69	6.59	5.80	5.21	4.76	4.40	4.10	3.86
500	42.98	22.11	15.16	11.69	9.61	8.23	7.25	6.52	5.95	5.49	5.13	4.82
600	51.58	26.53	18.19	14.03	11.54	9.88	8.70	7.82	7.13	6.59	6.15	5.78
700	60.17	30.95	21.22	16.36	13.46	11.52	10.15	9.12	8.32	7.69	7.17	6.75
800	68.77	35.37	24.25	18.70	15.38	13.17	11.60	10.42	9.51	8.79	8.20	7.71
900	77.36	39.79	27.28	21.04	17.30	14.81	13.05	11.72	10.70	9.88	9.22	8.67
1,000	85.96	44.21	30.31	23.38	19.22	16.46	14.49	13.03	11.89	10.98	10.25	9.63
2,000	171.91	88.42	60.62	46.75	38.44	32.92	28.98	26.05	23.77	21.96	20.49	19.26
3,000	257.86	132.63	90.93	70.12	57.66	49.37	43.47	39.07	35.65	32.94	30.73	28.89
4,000	343.81	176.84	121.24	93.49	76.87	65.83	57.96	52.09	47.53	43.91	40.97	38.52
5,000	429.76	221.05	151.55	116.86	96.09	82.28	72.45	65.11	59.42	54.89	51.21	48.15
6,000	515.71	265.25	181.86	140.23	115.31	98.74	86.94	78.13	71.30	65.87	61.45	57.78
7,000	601.67	309.46	212.17	163.60	134.52	115.19	101.43	91.15	83.18	76.84	71.69	67.41
8,000	687.62	353.67	242.48	186.97	153.74	131.65	115.92	104.17	95.06	87.82	81.93	77.04
9,000	773.57	397.88	272.78	210.34	172.96	148.10	130.41	117.19	106.95	98.80	92.17	86.67
10,000	859.52	442.09	303.09	233.71	192.17	164.56	144.90	130.21	118.83	109.77	102.41	96.30
15,000	1289.28	663.13	454.64	350.56	288.26	246.83	217.34	195.31	178.24	164.66	153.61	144.45
20,000	1719.04	884.17	606.18	467.42	384.34	329.11	289.79	260.41	237.65	219.54	204.81	192.60
25,000	2148.79	1105.21	757.72	584.27	480.42	411.38	362.23	325.51	297.07	274.43	256.01	240.75
30,000	2578.55	1326.25	909.27	701.12	576.51	493.66	434.68	390.61	356.48	329.31	307.21	288.89
35,000	3008.31	1547.29	1060.81	817.98	672.59	575.93	507.12	455.71	415.89	384.20	358.41	337.04
40,000	3438.07	1768.33	1212.36	934.83	768.68	658.21	579.57	520.81	475.30	439.08	409.61	385.19
45,000	3867.83	1989.37	1363.90	1051.68	864.76	740.49	652.01	585.91	534.72	493.97	460.81	433.34
50,000	4297.58	2210.41	1515.44	1168.53	960.84	822.76	724.46	651.01	594.13	548.85	512.01	481.49
55,000	4727.34	2431.45	1666.99	1285.39	1056.93	905.04	796.90	716.11	653.54	603.74	563.21	529.63
60,000	5157.10	2652.49	1818.53	1402.24	1153.01	987.31	869.35	781.21	712.95	658.62	614.41	577.78
65,000	5586.86	2873.53	1970.08	1519.09	1249.09	1069.59	941.79	846.31	772.37	713.50	665.61	625.93
70,000	6016.61	3094.57	2121.62	1635.95	1345.18	1151.86	1014.24	911.41	831.78	768.39	716.81	674.08
75,000	6446.37	3315.61	2273.16	1752.80	1441.26	1234.14	1086.68	976.51	891.19	823.27	768.01	722.23
80,000	6876.13	3536.65	2424.71	1869.65	1537.35	1316.42	1159.13	1041.61	950.60	878.16	819.21	770.37
85,000	7305.89	3757.69	2576.25	1986.50	1633.43	1398.69	1231.57	1106.71	1010.02	933.04	870.41	818.52
90,000	7735.65	3978.73	2727.80	2103.36	1729.51	1480.97	1304.02	1171.81	1069.43	987.93	921.61	866.67
95,000	8165.40	4199.77	2879.34	2220.21	1825.60	1563.24	1376.46	1236.91	1128.84	1042.81	972.81	914.82
100,000	8595.16	4420.81	3030.88	2337.06	1921.68	1645.52	1448.91	1302.01	1188.25	1097.70	1024.01	962.97
105,000	9024.92	4641.85	3182.43	2453.92	2017.77	1727.79	1521.35	1367.11	1247.67	1152.58	1075.21	1011.11
110,000	9454.68	4862.89	3333.97	2570.77	2113.85	1810.07	1593.80	1432.21	1307.08	1207.47	1126.41	1059.26
115,000	9884.43	5083.93	3485.52	2687.62	2209.93	1892.35	1666.24	1497.31	1366.49	1262.35	1177.61	1107.41
120,000	10314.19	5304.97	3637.06	2804.47	2306.02	1974.62	1738.69	1562.41	1425.90	1317.24	1228.81	1155.56
125,000	10743.95	5526.01	3788.60	2921.33	2402.10	2056.90	1811.13	1627.51	1485.32	1372.12	1280.01	1203.71
130,000	11173.71	5747.05	3940.15	3038.18	2498.18	2139.17	1883.58	1692.61	1544.73	1427.00	1331.21	1251.86
135,000	11603.47	5968.09	4091.69	3155.03	2594.27	2221.45	1956.02	1757.71	1604.14	1481.89	1382.41	1300.00
140,000	12033.22	6189.13	4243.24	3271.89	2690.35	2303.72	2028.47	1822.81	1663.55	1536.77	1433.61	1348.15
145,000	12462.98	6410.17	4394.78	3388.74	2786.44	2386.00	2100.91	1887.91	1722.97	1591.66	1484.81	1396.30
150,000	12892.74	6631.21	4546.32	3505.59	2882.52	2468.27	2173.36	1953.01	1782.38	1646.54	1536.01	1444.45
155,000	13322.50	6852.25	4697.87	3622.45	2978.60	2550.55	2245.80	2018.11	1841.79	1701.43	1587.21	1492.60
160,000	13752.26	7073.29	4849.41	3739.30	3074.69	2632.83	2318.25	2083.21	1901.20	1756.31	1638.41	1540.74
165,000	14182.01	7294.33	5000.96	3856.15	3170.77	2715.10	2390.69	2148.31	1960.62	1811.20	1689.61	1588.89
170,000	14611.77	7515.37	5152.50	3973.00	3266.86	2797.38	2463.14	2213.41	2020.03	1866.08	1740.81	1637.04
175,000	15041.53	7736.41	5304.04	4089.86	3362.94	2879.65	2535.58	2278.51	2079.44	1920.97	1792.01	1685.19
180,000	15471.29	7957.45	5455.59	4206.71	3459.02	2961.93	2608.03	2343.61	2138.85	1975.85	1843.21	1733.34
185,000	15901.04	8178.49	5607.13	4323.56	3555.11	3044.20	2680.47	2408.71	2198.27	2030.74	1894.41	1781.48
190,000	16330.80	8399.53	5758.68	4440.42	3651.19	3126.48	2752.92	2473.81	2257.68	2085.62	1945.61	1829.63
195,000	16760.56	8620.57	5910.22	4557.27	3747.27	3208.76	2825.36	2538.91	2317.09	2140.50	1996.81	1877.78
200,000	17190.32	8841.61	6061.76	4674.12	3843.36	3291.03	2897.81	2604.01	2376.50	2195.39	2048.01	1925.93
205,000	17620.08	9062.65	6213.31	4790.97	3939.44	3373.31	2970.25	2669.11	2435.92	2250.27	2099.21	1974.08
210,000	18049.83	9283.69	6364.85	4907.83	4035.53	3455.58	3042.70	2734.21	2495.33	2305.16	2150.41	2022.22
215,000	18479.59	9504.74	6516.40	5024.68	4131.61	3537.86	3115.14	2799.31	2554.74	2360.04	2201.61	2070.37
220,000	18909.35	9725.78	6667.94	5141.53	4227.69	3620.13	3187.59	2864.41	2614.15	2414.93	2252.81	2118.52
225,000	19339.11	9946.82	6819.48	5258.39	4323.78	3702.41	3260.03	2929.51	2673.57	2469.81	2304.01	2166.67
230,000	19768.86	10167.86	6971.03	5375.24	4419.86	3784.69	3332.48	2994.61	2732.98	2524.70	2355.21	2214.82
235,000	20198.62	10388.90	7122.57	5492.09	4515.95	3866.96	3404.92	3059.71	2792.39	2579.58	2406.41	2262.97
240,000	20628.38	10609.94	7274.11	5608.94	4612.03	3949.24	3477.37	3124.81	2851.80	2634.47	2457.61	2311.11
245,000	21058.14	10830.98	7425.66	5725.80	4708.11	4031.51	3549.81	3189.91	2911.22	2689.35	2508.81	2359.26
250,000	21487.90	11052.02	7577.20	5842.65	4804.20	4113.79	3622.26	3255.01	2970.63	2744.24	2560.01	2407.41
255,000	21917.65	11273.06	7728.75	5959.50	4900.28	4196.06	3694.70	3320.11	3030.04	2799.12	2611.21	2455.56
260,000	22347.41	11494.10	7880.29	6076.36	4996.36	4278.34	3767.15	3385.22	3089.45	2854.00	2662.41	2503.71
265,000	22777.17	11715.14	8031.83	6193.21	5092.45	4360.61	3839.59	3450.32	3148.87	2908.89	2713.61	2551.85
270,000	23206.93	11936.18	8183.38	6310.06	5188.53	4442.89	3912.04	3515.42	3208.28	2963.77	2764.81	2600.00
280,000	24066.44	12378.26	8486.47	6543.77	5380.70	4607.44	4056.93	3645.62	3327.10	3073.54	2867.21	2696.30
290,000	24925.96	12820.34	8789.55	6777.47	5572.87	4771.99	4201.82	3775.82	3445.93	3183.31	2969.61	2792.59
300,000	25785.47	13262.42	9092.64	7011.18	5765.04	4936.54	4346.71	3906.02	3564.75	3293.08	3072.01	2888.89

AMOUNT OF LOAN	NUMBER OF YEARS IN TERM											
	13	14	15	16	17	18	19	20	25	30	35	40
$ 50	0.46	0.44	0.42	0.40	0.39	0.38	0.37	0.36	0.32	0.30	0.28	0.27
100	0.92	0.87	0.84	0.80	0.77	0.75	0.73	0.71	0.63	0.59	0.56	0.54
200	1.83	1.74	1.67	1.60	1.54	1.49	1.45	1.41	1.26	1.17	1.11	1.07
300	2.74	2.61	2.50	2.40	2.31	2.24	2.17	2.11	1.89	1.76	1.67	1.60
400	3.65	3.48	3.33	3.20	3.08	2.98	2.89	2.81	2.52	2.34	2.22	2.14
500	4.56	4.34	4.16	3.99	3.85	3.73	3.61	3.52	3.15	2.92	2.77	2.67
600	5.47	5.21	4.99	4.79	4.62	4.47	4.34	4.22	3.78	3.51	3.33	3.20
700	6.39	6.08	5.82	5.59	5.39	5.21	5.06	4.92	4.41	4.09	3.88	3.74
800	7.30	6.95	6.65	6.39	6.16	5.96	5.78	5.62	5.04	4.67	4.43	4.27
900	8.21	7.82	7.48	7.19	6.93	6.70	6.50	6.32	5.67	5.26	4.99	4.80
1,000	9.12	8.68	8.31	7.98	7.70	7.45	7.22	7.03	6.30	5.84	5.54	5.33
2,000	18.24	17.36	16.61	15.96	15.39	14.89	14.44	14.05	12.59	11.68	11.08	10.66
3,000	27.35	26.04	24.92	23.94	23.08	22.33	21.66	21.07	18.88	17.51	16.61	15.99
4,000	36.47	34.72	33.22	31.92	30.78	29.77	28.88	28.09	25.17	23.35	22.15	21.32
5,000	45.59	43.40	41.53	39.90	38.47	37.21	36.10	35.11	31.46	29.18	27.68	26.65
6,000	54.70	52.08	49.83	47.87	46.16	44.66	43.32	42.13	37.75	35.02	33.22	31.98
7,000	63.82	60.76	58.13	55.85	53.86	52.10	50.54	49.15	44.04	40.86	38.75	37.31
8,000	72.94	69.44	66.44	63.83	61.55	59.54	57.76	56.17	50.33	46.69	44.29	42.64
9,000	82.05	78.12	74.74	71.81	69.24	66.98	64.98	63.19	56.62	52.53	49.82	47.96
10,000	91.17	86.80	83.05	79.79	76.93	74.42	72.20	70.21	62.92	58.36	55.36	53.29
15,000	136.75	130.20	124.57	119.68	115.40	111.63	108.29	105.32	94.37	87.54	83.03	79.94
20,000	182.33	173.60	166.09	159.57	153.86	148.84	144.39	140.42	125.83	116.72	110.71	106.58
25,000	227.92	217.00	207.61	199.46	192.33	186.05	180.48	175.53	157.28	145.90	138.38	133.23
30,000	273.50	260.40	249.13	239.35	230.79	223.26	216.58	210.63	188.74	175.08	166.06	159.87
35,000	319.08	303.80	290.65	279.24	269.26	260.46	252.67	245.73	220.19	204.26	193.73	186.52
40,000	364.66	347.19	332.17	319.13	307.72	297.67	288.77	280.84	251.65	233.43	221.41	213.16
45,000	410.25	390.59	373.69	360.02	346.18	334.00	324.07	315.94	283.10	262.61	249.08	239.80
50,000	455.83	433.99	415.21	398.91	384.65	372.09	360.96	351.05	314.56	291.79	276.76	266.45
55,000	501.41	477.39	456.73	438.80	423.11	409.30	397.06	386.15	346.01	320.97	304.43	293.09
60,000	546.99	520.79	498.25	478.69	461.58	446.51	433.15	421.26	377.47	350.15	332.11	319.74
65,000	592.58	564.19	539.77	518.58	500.04	483.72	469.25	456.36	408.92	379.33	359.78	346.38
70,000	638.16	607.59	581.29	558.47	538.51	520.92	505.34	491.46	440.38	408.51	387.46	373.03
75,000	683.74	650.99	622.81	598.36	576.97	558.13	541.44	526.57	471.83	437.68	415.13	399.67
80,000	729.32	694.38	664.33	638.25	615.44	595.34	577.53	561.67	503.29	466.86	442.81	426.32
85,000	774.91	737.78	705.85	678.14	653.90	632.55	613.63	596.78	534.75	496.04	470.48	452.96
90,000	820.49	781.18	747.37	718.03	692.36	669.76	649.73	631.88	566.20	525.22	498.16	479.60
95,000	866.07	824.58	788.89	757.92	730.83	706.97	685.82	666.98	597.66	554.40	525.83	506.25
100,000	911.65	867.98	830.42	797.81	769.29	744.17	721.92	702.09	629.11	583.58	553.51	532.89
105,000	957.24	911.38	871.94	837.70	807.76	781.38	758.01	737.19	660.57	612.76	581.18	559.54
110,000	1002.82	954.78	913.46	877.59	846.22	818.59	794.11	772.30	692.02	641.94	608.86	586.18
115,000	1048.40	998.18	954.98	917.48	884.69	855.80	830.20	807.40	723.48	671.11	636.53	612.83
120,000	1093.98	1041.57	996.50	957.37	923.15	893.00	866.30	842.51	754.93	700.29	664.21	639.47
125,000	1139.56	1084.97	1038.02	997.26	961.62	930.22	902.39	877.61	786.39	729.47	691.88	666.11
130,000	1185.15	1128.37	1079.54	1037.15	1000.08	967.43	938.49	912.71	817.84	758.65	719.56	692.76
135,000	1230.73	1171.77	1121.06	1077.05	1038.54	1004.63	974.58	947.82	849.30	787.83	747.23	719.40
140,000	1276.31	1215.17	1162.58	1116.94	1077.01	1041.84	1010.68	982.92	880.75	817.01	774.91	746.05
145,000	1321.89	1258.57	1204.10	1156.83	1115.47	1079.05	1046.78	1018.03	912.21	846.19	802.58	772.69
150,000	1367.48	1301.97	1245.62	1196.72	1153.94	1116.26	1082.87	1053.13	943.66	875.36	830.26	799.34
155,000	1413.06	1345.37	1287.14	1236.61	1192.40	1153.47	1118.97	1088.23	975.12	904.54	857.93	825.98
160,000	1458.64	1388.76	1328.66	1276.50	1230.87	1190.68	1155.06	1123.34	1006.58	933.72	885.61	852.63
165,000	1504.22	1432.16	1370.18	1316.39	1269.33	1227.88	1191.16	1158.44	1038.03	962.90	913.28	879.27
170,000	1549.81	1475.56	1411.70	1356.28	1307.80	1265.09	1227.26	1193.55	1069.49	992.08	940.96	905.91
175,000	1595.39	1518.96	1453.22	1396.17	1346.26	1302.30	1263.35	1228.65	1100.94	1021.26	968.63	932.56
180,000	1640.97	1562.36	1494.74	1436.06	1384.72	1339.51	1299.45	1263.76	1132.40	1050.44	996.31	959.20
185,000	1686.55	1605.76	1536.26	1475.95	1423.19	1376.72	1335.54	1298.86	1163.85	1079.61	1023.98	985.85
190,000	1732.14	1649.16	1577.78	1515.84	1461.65	1413.93	1371.64	1333.96	1195.31	1108.79	1051.66	1012.49
195,000	1777.72	1692.55	1619.30	1555.73	1500.12	1451.14	1407.73	1369.07	1226.76	1137.97	1079.33	1039.14
200,000	1823.30	1735.95	1660.83	1595.62	1538.58	1488.34	1443.83	1404.17	1258.22	1167.15	1107.01	1065.78
205,000	1868.88	1779.35	1702.35	1635.51	1577.05	1525.55	1479.92	1439.28	1289.67	1196.33	1134.68	1092.42
210,000	1914.47	1822.75	1743.87	1675.40	1615.51	1562.76	1516.02	1474.38	1321.13	1225.51	1162.36	1119.07
215,000	1960.05	1866.15	1785.39	1715.29	1653.97	1599.97	1552.12	1509.48	1352.58	1254.69	1190.03	1145.71
220,000	2005.63	1909.55	1826.91	1755.18	1692.44	1637.18	1588.21	1544.59	1384.04	1283.87	1217.71	1172.36
225,000	2051.21	1952.95	1868.43	1795.07	1730.90	1674.39	1624.31	1579.69	1415.49	1313.04	1245.38	1199.00
230,000	2096.80	1996.35	1909.95	1834.96	1769.37	1711.59	1660.40	1614.80	1446.95	1342.22	1273.06	1225.65
235,000	2142.38	2039.74	1951.47	1874.85	1807.83	1748.80	1696.50	1649.90	1478.41	1371.40	1300.73	1252.29
240,000	2187.96	2083.14	1992.99	1914.74	1846.30	1786.01	1732.59	1685.01	1509.86	1400.58	1328.41	1278.94
245,000	2233.54	2126.54	2034.51	1954.63	1884.76	1823.22	1768.69	1720.11	1541.32	1429.76	1356.08	1305.58
250,000	2279.12	2169.94	2076.03	1994.52	1923.23	1860.43	1804.78	1755.21	1572.77	1458.94	1383.76	1332.22
255,000	2324.71	2213.34	2117.55	2034.41	1961.69	1897.64	1840.88	1790.32	1604.23	1488.12	1411.43	1358.87
260,000	2370.29	2256.74	2159.07	2074.30	2000.15	1934.85	1876.98	1825.42	1635.68	1517.29	1439.11	1385.51
265,000	2415.87	2300.14	2200.59	2114.19	2038.62	1972.05	1913.07	1860.53	1667.14	1546.47	1466.78	1412.16
270,000	2461.45	2343.54	2242.11	2154.09	2077.08	2009.26	1949.17	1895.63	1698.59	1575.65	1494.46	1438.80
280,000	2552.62	2430.33	2325.15	2233.87	2154.01	2083.68	2021.36	1965.84	1761.50	1634.01	1549.81	1492.09
290,000	2643.78	2517.13	2408.19	2313.65	2230.94	2158.10	2093.55	2036.05	1824.41	1692.37	1605.16	1545.38
300,000	2734.95	2603.93	2491.24	2393.43	2307.87	2232.51	2165.74	2106.26	1887.32	1750.72	1660.51	1598.67

6.00% MONTHLY AMORTIZING PAYMENTS

AMOUNT OF LOAN	NUMBER OF YEARS IN TERM											
	1	2	3	4	5	6	7	8	9	10	11	12
$ 50	4.31	2.22	1.53	1.18	0.97	0.83	0.74	0.66	0.61	0.56	0.52	0.49
100	8.61	4.44	3.05	2.35	1.94	1.66	1.47	1.32	1.21	1.12	1.04	0.98
200	17.22	8.87	6.09	4.70	3.87	3.32	2.93	2.63	2.41	2.23	2.08	1.96
300	25.82	13.30	9.13	7.05	5.80	4.98	4.39	3.95	3.61	3.34	3.12	2.93
400	34.43	17.73	12.17	9.40	7.74	6.63	5.85	5.26	4.81	4.45	4.15	3.91
500	43.04	22.17	15.22	11.75	9.67	8.29	7.31	6.58	6.01	5.56	5.19	4.88
600	51.64	26.60	18.26	14.10	11.60	9.95	8.77	7.89	7.21	6.67	6.23	5.86
700	60.25	31.03	21.30	16.44	13.54	11.61	10.23	9.20	8.41	7.78	7.26	6.84
800	68.86	35.46	24.34	18.79	15.47	13.26	11.69	10.52	9.61	8.89	8.30	7.81
900	77.46	39.89	27.38	21.14	17.40	14.92	13.15	11.83	10.81	10.00	9.34	8.79
1,000	86.07	44.33	30.43	23.49	19.34	16.58	14.61	13.15	12.01	11.11	10.37	9.76
2,000	172.14	88.65	60.85	46.98	38.67	33.15	29.22	26.29	24.02	22.21	20.74	19.52
3,000	258.20	132.97	91.27	70.46	58.00	49.72	43.83	39.43	36.02	33.31	31.11	29.28
4,000	344.27	177.29	121.69	93.95	77.34	66.30	58.44	52.57	48.03	44.41	41.47	39.04
5,000	430.34	221.61	152.11	117.43	96.67	82.87	73.05	65.71	60.03	55.52	51.84	48.80
6,000	516.40	265.93	182.54	140.92	116.00	99.44	87.66	78.85	72.04	66.62	62.21	58.56
7,000	602.47	310.25	212.96	164.40	135.33	116.02	102.26	92.00	84.05	77.72	72.57	68.31
8,000	688.54	354.57	243.38	187.89	154.67	132.59	116.87	105.14	96.05	88.82	82.94	78.07
9,000	774.60	398.89	273.80	211.37	174.00	149.16	131.48	118.28	108.06	99.92	93.31	87.83
10,000	860.67	443.21	304.22	234.86	193.33	165.73	146.09	131.42	120.06	111.03	103.68	97.59
15,000	1291.00	664.81	456.33	352.28	290.00	248.60	219.13	197.13	180.09	166.54	155.51	146.38
20,000	1721.33	886.42	608.44	469.71	386.66	331.46	292.18	262.83	240.12	222.05	207.35	195.18
25,000	2151.67	1108.02	760.55	587.13	483.33	414.33	365.22	328.54	300.15	277.56	259.18	243.97
30,000	2582.00	1329.62	912.66	704.56	579.99	497.19	438.26	394.25	360.18	333.07	311.02	292.76
35,000	3012.33	1551.23	1064.77	821.98	676.65	580.06	511.30	459.96	420.21	388.58	362.85	341.55
40,000	3442.66	1772.83	1216.88	939.41	773.32	662.92	584.35	525.66	480.23	444.09	414.69	390.35
45,000	3872.99	1994.43	1368.99	1056.03	869.98	745.78	657.39	591.37	540.26	499.60	466.52	439.14
50,000	4303.33	2216.04	1521.10	1174.26	966.65	828.65	730.43	657.08	600.29	555.11	518.36	487.93
55,000	4733.66	2437.64	1673.21	1291.68	1063.31	911.51	803.48	722.78	660.32	610.62	570.19	536.72
60,000	5163.99	2659.24	1825.32	1409.11	1159.97	994.38	876.52	788.49	720.35	666.13	622.03	585.52
65,000	5594.32	2880.84	1977.43	1526.53	1256.64	1077.24	949.56	854.20	780.38	721.64	673.86	634.31
70,000	6024.66	3102.45	2129.54	1643.96	1353.30	1160.11	1022.60	919.91	840.41	777.15	725.70	683.10
75,000	6454.99	3324.05	2281.65	1761.38	1449.97	1242.97	1095.65	985.61	900.44	832.66	777.53	731.89
80,000	6885.32	3545.65	2433.76	1878.81	1546.63	1325.84	1168.69	1051.32	960.46	888.17	829.37	780.69
85,000	7315.65	3767.26	2585.87	1996.23	1643.29	1408.70	1241.73	1117.03	1020.49	943.68	881.20	829.48
90,000	7745.98	3988.86	2737.98	2113.66	1739.96	1491.56	1314.77	1182.73	1080.52	999.19	933.04	878.27
95,000	8176.32	4210.46	2890.09	2231.08	1836.62	1574.43	1387.82	1248.44	1140.55	1054.70	984.87	927.06
100,000	8606.65	4432.07	3042.20	2348.51	1933.29	1657.29	1460.86	1314.15	1200.58	1110.21	1036.71	975.86
105,000	9036.98	4653.67	3194.31	2465.93	2029.95	1740.16	1533.90	1379.86	1260.61	1165.72	1088.54	1024.65
110,000	9467.31	4875.27	3346.42	2583.36	2126.61	1823.02	1606.95	1445.56	1320.64	1221.23	1140.38	1073.44
115,000	9897.64	5096.88	3498.53	2700.78	2223.28	1905.89	1679.99	1511.27	1380.67	1276.74	1192.21	1122.23
120,000	10327.98	5318.48	3650.64	2818.21	2319.94	1988.75	1753.03	1576.98	1440.69	1332.25	1244.05	1171.03
125,000	10758.31	5540.08	3802.75	2935.63	2416.61	2071.62	1826.07	1642.68	1500.72	1387.76	1295.88	1219.82
130,000	11188.64	5761.68	3954.86	3053.06	2513.27	2154.48	1899.12	1708.39	1560.75	1443.27	1347.72	1268.61
135,000	11618.97	5983.29	4106.97	3170.48	2609.93	2237.34	1972.16	1774.10	1620.78	1498.78	1399.55	1317.40
140,000	12049.31	6204.89	4259.08	3287.91	2706.60	2320.21	2045.20	1839.81	1680.81	1554.29	1451.39	1366.20
145,000	12479.64	6426.49	4411.19	3405.33	2803.26	2403.07	2118.25	1905.51	1740.84	1609.80	1503.23	1414.99
150,000	12909.97	6648.10	4563.30	3522.76	2899.93	2485.94	2191.29	1971.22	1800.87	1665.31	1555.06	1463.78
155,000	13340.30	6869.70	4715.41	3640.18	2996.59	2568.80	2264.33	2036.93	1860.90	1720.82	1606.90	1512.57
160,000	13770.63	7091.30	4867.51	3757.61	3093.25	2651.67	2337.37	2102.63	1920.92	1776.33	1658.73	1561.37
165,000	14200.97	7312.91	5019.62	3875.03	3189.92	2734.53	2410.42	2168.34	1980.95	1831.84	1710.57	1610.16
170,000	14631.30	7534.51	5171.73	3992.46	3286.58	2817.40	2483.46	2234.05	2040.98	1887.35	1762.40	1658.95
175,000	15061.63	7756.11	5323.84	4109.89	3383.25	2900.26	2556.50	2299.76	2101.01	1942.86	1814.24	1707.74
180,000	15491.96	7977.71	5475.95	4227.31	3479.91	2983.12	2629.54	2365.46	2161.04	1998.37	1866.07	1756.54
185,000	15922.29	8199.32	5628.06	4344.74	3576.57	3065.99	2702.59	2431.17	2221.07	2053.88	1917.91	1805.33
190,000	16352.63	8420.92	5780.17	4462.16	3673.24	3148.85	2775.63	2496.88	2281.10	2109.39	1969.74	1854.12
195,000	16782.96	8642.52	5932.28	4579.59	3769.90	3231.72	2848.67	2562.58	2341.13	2164.90	2021.58	1902.91
200,000	17213.29	8864.13	6084.39	4697.01	3866.57	3314.58	2921.72	2628.29	2401.15	2220.42	2073.41	1951.71
205,000	17643.62	9085.73	6236.50	4814.44	3963.23	3397.45	2994.76	2694.00	2461.18	2275.93	2125.25	2000.50
210,000	18073.96	9307.33	6388.61	4931.86	4059.89	3480.31	3067.80	2759.71	2521.21	2331.44	2177.08	2049.29
215,000	18504.29	9528.94	6540.72	5049.29	4156.56	3563.18	3140.84	2825.41	2581.24	2386.95	2228.92	2098.08
220,000	18934.62	9750.54	6692.83	5166.71	4253.22	3646.04	3213.89	2891.12	2641.27	2442.46	2280.75	2146.88
225,000	19364.95	9972.14	6844.94	5284.14	4349.89	3728.90	3286.93	2956.83	2701.30	2497.97	2332.59	2195.67
230,000	19795.28	10193.75	6997.05	5401.56	4446.55	3811.77	3359.97	3022.53	2761.33	2553.48	2384.42	2244.46
235,000	20225.62	10415.35	7149.16	5518.99	4543.21	3894.63	3433.02	3088.24	2821.36	2608.99	2436.26	2293.25
240,000	20655.95	10636.95	7301.27	5636.41	4639.88	3977.50	3506.06	3153.95	2881.38	2664.50	2488.09	2342.05
245,000	21086.28	10858.55	7453.38	5753.84	4736.54	4060.36	3579.10	3219.66	2941.41	2720.01	2539.93	2390.84
250,000	21516.61	11080.16	7605.49	5871.26	4833.21	4143.23	3652.14	3285.36	3001.44	2775.52	2591.76	2439.63
255,000	21946.94	11301.76	7757.60	5988.69	4929.87	4226.09	3725.19	3351.07	3061.47	2831.03	2643.60	2488.42
260,000	22377.28	11523.36	7909.71	6106.11	5026.53	4308.96	3798.23	3416.78	3121.50	2886.54	2695.43	2537.22
265,000	22807.61	11744.97	8061.82	6223.54	5123.20	4391.82	3871.27	3482.48	3181.53	2942.05	2747.27	2586.01
270,000	23237.94	11966.57	8213.93	6340.96	5219.86	4474.68	3944.31	3548.19	3241.56	2997.56	2799.10	2634.80
280,000	24098.61	12409.78	8518.15	6575.81	5413.19	4640.41	4090.40	3679.61	3361.61	3108.58	2902.77	2732.39
290,000	24959.27	12852.98	8822.37	6810.66	5606.52	4806.14	4236.49	3811.02	3481.67	3219.60	3006.45	2829.97
300,000	25819.93	13296.19	9126.59	7045.51	5799.85	4971.87	4382.57	3942.43	3601.73	3330.62	3110.12	2927.56

34

6.00%

AMOUNT OF LOAN	NUMBER OF YEARS IN TERM											
	13	14	15	16	17	18	19	20	25	30	35	40
$ 50	0.47	0.45	0.43	0.41	0.40	0.38	0.37	0.36	0.33	0.30	0.29	0.28
100	0.93	0.89	0.85	0.82	0.79	0.76	0.74	0.72	0.65	0.60	0.58	0.56
200	1.85	1.77	1.69	1.63	1.57	1.52	1.48	1.44	1.29	1.20	1.15	1.11
300	2.78	2.65	2.54	2.44	2.35	2.28	2.21	2.15	1.94	1.80	1.72	1.66
400	3.70	3.53	3.38	3.25	3.14	3.04	2.95	2.87	2.58	2.40	2.29	2.21
500	4.63	4.41	4.22	4.06	3.92	3.80	3.69	3.59	3.23	3.00	2.86	2.76
600	5.55	5.29	5.07	4.87	4.70	4.55	4.42	4.30	3.87	3.60	3.43	3.31
700	6.48	6.17	5.91	5.69	5.49	5.31	5.16	5.02	4.52	4.20	4.00	3.86
800	7.40	7.05	6.76	6.50	6.27	6.07	5.89	5.74	5.16	4.80	4.57	4.41
900	8.33	7.94	7.60	7.31	7.05	6.83	6.63	6.45	5.80	5.40	5.14	4.96
1,000	9.25	8.82	8.44	8.12	7.84	7.59	7.37	7.17	6.45	6.00	5.71	5.51
2,000	18.50	17.63	16.88	16.23	15.67	15.17	14.73	14.33	12.89	12.00	11.41	11.01
3,000	27.75	26.44	25.32	24.35	23.50	22.75	22.09	21.50	19.33	17.99	17.11	16.51
4,000	36.99	35.25	33.76	32.46	31.33	30.33	29.45	28.66	25.78	23.99	22.81	22.01
5,000	46.24	44.07	42.20	40.58	39.16	37.91	36.81	35.83	32.22	29.98	28.51	27.52
6,000	55.49	52.88	50.64	48.69	46.99	45.49	44.17	42.99	38.66	35.98	34.22	33.02
7,000	64.74	61.69	59.07	56.81	54.82	53.08	51.53	50.16	45.11	41.97	39.92	38.52
8,000	73.98	70.50	67.51	64.92	62.65	60.66	58.89	57.32	51.55	47.97	45.62	44.02
9,000	83.23	79.32	75.95	73.03	70.48	68.24	66.25	64.48	57.99	53.96	51.32	49.52
10,000	92.48	88.13	84.39	81.15	78.32	75.82	73.61	71.65	64.44	59.96	57.02	55.03
15,000	138.71	132.19	126.58	121.72	117.47	113.73	110.42	107.47	96.65	89.94	85.53	82.54
20,000	184.95	176.25	168.78	162.29	156.63	151.64	147.22	143.29	128.87	119.92	114.04	110.05
25,000	231.19	220.31	210.97	202.86	195.78	189.55	184.03	179.11	161.08	149.89	142.55	137.56
30,000	277.42	264.38	253.16	243.44	234.94	227.45	220.83	214.93	193.30	179.87	171.06	165.07
35,000	323.66	308.44	295.35	284.01	274.09	265.36	257.63	250.76	225.51	209.85	199.57	192.58
40,000	369.89	352.50	337.55	324.58	313.25	303.27	294.44	286.58	257.73	239.83	228.08	220.09
45,000	416.13	396.56	379.74	365.15	352.40	341.18	331.24	322.40	289.94	269.80	256.59	247.60
50,000	462.37	440.62	421.93	405.72	391.56	379.09	368.05	358.22	322.16	299.78	285.10	275.11
55,000	508.60	484.68	464.13	446.30	430.71	416.99	404.85	394.04	354.37	329.76	313.61	302.62
60,000	554.84	528.75	506.32	486.87	469.87	454.90	441.65	429.86	386.59	359.74	342.12	330.13
65,000	601.08	572.81	548.51	527.44	509.02	492.81	478.46	465.69	418.80	389.71	370.63	357.64
70,000	647.31	616.87	590.70	568.01	548.18	530.72	515.26	501.51	451.02	419.69	399.14	385.15
75,000	693.55	660.93	632.90	608.58	587.33	568.63	552.07	537.33	483.23	449.67	427.65	412.67
80,000	739.78	704.99	675.09	649.16	626.49	606.53	588.87	573.15	515.45	479.65	456.16	440.18
85,000	786.02	749.06	717.28	689.73	665.64	644.44	625.68	608.97	547.66	509.62	484.67	467.69
90,000	832.26	793.12	759.48	730.30	704.80	682.35	662.48	644.79	579.88	539.60	513.18	495.20
95,000	878.49	837.18	801.67	770.87	743.95	720.26	699.28	680.61	612.09	569.58	541.69	522.71
100,000	924.73	881.24	843.86	811.44	783.11	758.17	736.09	716.44	644.31	599.56	570.19	550.22
105,000	970.96	925.30	886.05	852.01	822.26	796.00	772.09	752.20	670.52	629.54	598.70	577.73
110,000	1017.20	969.36	928.25	892.59	861.42	833.98	809.70	788.08	708.74	659.51	627.21	605.24
115,000	1063.44	1013.43	970.44	933.16	900.57	871.89	846.50	823.90	740.95	689.49	655.72	632.75
120,000	1109.07	1057.49	1012.63	973.73	939.73	909.80	883.30	859.72	773.17	719.47	684.23	660.26
125,000	1155.91	1101.55	1054.83	1014.30	978.88	947.71	920.11	895.54	805.38	749.44	712.74	687.77
130,000	1202.15	1145.61	1097.02	1054.87	1018.04	985.62	956.91	931.37	837.60	779.42	741.25	715.28
135,000	1248.38	1189.67	1139.21	1095.45	1057.19	1023.52	993.72	967.19	869.81	809.40	769.76	742.79
140,000	1294.62	1233.74	1181.40	1136.02	1096.35	1061.43	1030.52	1003.01	902.03	839.38	798.27	770.30
145,000	1340.85	1277.80	1223.60	1176.59	1135.50	1099.34	1067.33	1038.83	934.24	869.35	826.78	797.81
150,000	1387.09	1321.86	1265.79	1217.16	1174.66	1137.25	1104.13	1074.65	966.46	899.33	855.29	825.33
155,000	1433.33	1365.92	1307.98	1257.73	1213.81	1175.16	1140.93	1110.47	998.67	929.31	883.80	852.84
160,000	1479.56	1409.98	1350.18	1298.31	1252.97	1213.06	1177.74	1146.29	1030.89	959.29	912.31	880.35
165,000	1525.80	1454.04	1392.37	1338.88	1292.12	1250.97	1214.54	1182.12	1063.10	989.26	940.82	907.86
170,000	1572.03	1498.11	1434.56	1379.45	1331.28	1288.88	1251.35	1217.94	1095.32	1019.24	969.33	935.37
175,000	1618.27	1542.17	1476.75	1420.02	1370.43	1326.79	1288.15	1253.76	1127.53	1049.22	997.84	962.88
180,000	1664.51	1586.23	1518.95	1460.59	1409.59	1364.70	1324.95	1289.58	1159.75	1079.20	1026.35	990.39
185,000	1710.74	1630.29	1561.14	1501.17	1448.74	1402.61	1361.76	1325.40	1191.96	1109.17	1054.86	1017.90
190,000	1756.98	1674.35	1603.33	1541.74	1487.90	1440.51	1398.56	1361.22	1224.18	1139.15	1083.37	1045.41
195,000	1803.22	1718.42	1645.53	1582.31	1527.05	1478.42	1435.37	1397.05	1256.39	1169.13	1111.87	1072.92
200,000	1849.45	1762.48	1687.72	1622.88	1566.21	1516.33	1472.17	1432.87	1288.61	1199.11	1140.38	1100.43
205,000	1895.69	1806.54	1729.91	1663.45	1605.36	1554.24	1508.98	1468.69	1320.82	1229.08	1168.89	1127.94
210,000	1941.92	1850.60	1772.10	1704.02	1644.52	1592.15	1545.78	1504.51	1353.04	1259.06	1197.40	1155.45
215,000	1988.16	1894.66	1814.30	1744.60	1683.67	1630.05	1582.58	1540.33	1385.25	1289.04	1225.91	1182.96
220,000	2034.40	1938.72	1856.49	1785.17	1722.83	1667.96	1619.39	1576.15	1417.47	1319.02	1254.42	1210.48
225,000	2080.63	1982.79	1898.68	1825.74	1761.98	1705.87	1656.19	1611.97	1449.68	1348.99	1282.93	1237.99
230,000	2126.87	2026.85	1940.88	1866.31	1801.14	1743.78	1693.00	1647.80	1481.90	1378.97	1311.44	1265.50
235,000	2173.11	2070.91	1983.07	1906.88	1840.29	1781.69	1729.80	1683.62	1514.11	1408.95	1339.95	1293.01
240,000	2219.34	2114.97	2025.26	1947.46	1879.45	1819.59	1766.60	1719.44	1546.33	1438.93	1368.46	1320.52
245,000	2265.58	2159.03	2067.45	1988.03	1918.60	1857.50	1803.41	1755.26	1578.54	1468.90	1396.97	1348.03
250,000	2311.81	2203.09	2109.65	2028.60	1957.76	1895.41	1840.21	1791.08	1610.76	1498.88	1425.48	1375.54
255,000	2358.05	2247.16	2151.84	2069.17	1996.91	1933.32	1877.02	1826.90	1642.97	1528.86	1453.99	1403.05
260,000	2404.29	2291.22	2194.03	2109.74	2036.07	1971.23	1913.82	1862.73	1675.19	1558.84	1482.50	1430.56
265,000	2450.52	2335.28	2236.23	2150.32	2075.22	2009.14	1950.62	1898.55	1707.40	1588.81	1511.01	1458.07
270,000	2496.76	2379.34	2278.42	2190.89	2114.38	2047.04	1987.43	1934.37	1739.62	1618.79	1539.52	1485.58
280,000	2589.23	2467.47	2362.80	2272.03	2192.69	2122.86	2061.04	2006.01	1804.05	1678.75	1596.54	1540.60
290,000	2681.70	2555.59	2447.19	2353.17	2271.00	2198.68	2134.65	2077.66	1868.48	1738.70	1653.56	1595.62
300,000	2774.18	2643.71	2531.58	2434.32	2349.31	2274.49	2208.25	2149.30	1932.91	1798.66	1710.57	1650.65

6.25%　MONTHLY AMORTIZING PAYMENTS

AMOUNT OF LOAN	NUMBER OF YEARS IN TERM											
	1	2	3	4	5	6	7	8	9	10	11	12
$ 50	4.31	2.23	1.53	1.18	0.98	0.84	0.74	0.67	0.61	0.57	0.53	0.50
100	8.62	4.45	3.06	2.36	1.95	1.67	1.48	1.33	1.22	1.13	1.05	0.99
200	17.24	8.89	6.11	4.72	3.89	3.34	2.95	2.66	2.43	2.25	2.10	1.98
300	25.86	13.34	9.17	7.08	5.84	5.01	4.42	3.98	3.64	3.37	3.15	2.97
400	34.48	17.78	12.22	9.44	7.78	6.68	5.90	5.31	4.86	4.50	4.20	3.96
500	43.10	22.22	15.27	11.80	9.73	8.35	7.37	6.64	6.07	5.62	5.25	4.95
600	51.71	26.67	18.33	14.16	11.67	10.02	8.84	7.96	7.28	6.74	6.30	5.94
700	60.33	31.11	21.38	16.52	13.62	11.69	10.32	9.29	8.50	7.86	7.35	6.93
800	68.95	35.55	24.43	18.88	15.56	13.36	11.79	10.62	9.71	8.99	8.40	7.92
900	77.57	40.00	27.49	21.24	17.51	15.03	13.26	11.94	10.92	10.11	9.45	8.90
1,000	86.19	44.44	30.54	23.60	19.45	16.70	14.73	13.27	12.13	11.23	10.50	9.89
2,000	172.37	88.87	61.08	47.20	38.90	33.39	29.46	26.53	24.26	22.46	20.99	19.78
3,000	258.55	133.31	91.61	70.80	58.35	50.08	44.19	39.80	36.39	33.69	31.49	29.67
4,000	344.73	177.74	122.15	94.40	77.80	66.77	58.92	53.06	48.52	44.92	41.98	39.56
5,000	430.91	222.17	152.68	118.00	97.25	83.46	73.65	66.32	60.65	56.15	52.48	49.45
6,000	517.09	266.61	183.22	141.60	116.70	100.15	88.38	79.59	72.78	67.37	62.97	59.34
7,000	603.27	311.04	213.75	165.20	136.15	116.84	103.11	92.85	84.91	78.60	73.47	69.22
8,000	689.46	355.47	244.29	188.80	155.60	133.53	117.83	106.11	97.04	89.83	83.96	79.11
9,000	775.64	399.91	274.82	212.40	175.05	150.23	132.56	119.38	109.17	101.06	94.46	89.00
10,000	861.82	444.34	305.36	236.00	194.50	166.92	147.29	132.64	121.30	112.29	104.95	98.89
15,000	1292.73	666.51	458.04	354.00	291.74	250.37	220.94	198.96	181.95	168.43	157.43	148.33
20,000	1723.63	888.67	610.71	472.00	388.99	333.83	294.58	265.27	242.60	224.57	209.90	197.77
25,000	2154.54	1110.84	763.39	590.00	486.24	417.28	368.22	331.59	303.25	280.71	262.38	247.21
30,000	2585.45	1333.01	916.07	708.00	583.48	500.74	441.87	397.91	363.90	336.85	314.85	296.66
35,000	3016.35	1555.17	1068.74	826.00	680.73	584.20	515.51	464.23	424.55	392.99	367.33	346.10
40,000	3447.26	1777.34	1221.42	944.00	777.98	667.65	589.15	530.54	485.20	449.13	419.80	395.54
45,000	3878.17	1999.51	1374.10	1062.00	875.22	751.11	662.80	596.86	545.84	505.27	472.28	444.98
50,000	4309.07	2221.67	1526.77	1180.00	972.47	834.56	736.44	663.18	606.49	561.41	524.75	494.42
55,000	4739.98	2443.84	1679.45	1298.00	1069.71	918.02	810.08	729.50	667.14	617.55	577.23	543.87
60,000	5170.89	2666.01	1832.13	1415.99	1166.96	1001.47	883.73	795.81	727.79	673.69	629.70	593.31
65,000	5601.79	2888.17	1984.80	1533.99	1264.21	1084.93	957.37	862.13	788.44	729.83	682.18	642.75
70,000	6032.70	3110.34	2137.48	1651.99	1361.45	1168.39	1031.01	928.45	849.09	785.97	734.65	692.19
75,000	6463.61	3332.51	2290.16	1769.99	1458.70	1251.84	1104.66	994.77	909.74	842.11	787.13	741.63
80,000	6894.52	3554.67	2442.83	1887.99	1555.95	1335.30	1178.30	1061.08	970.39	898.25	839.60	791.07
85,000	7325.42	3776.84	2595.51	2005.99	1653.19	1418.75	1251.94	1127.40	1031.03	954.39	892.08	840.52
90,000	7756.33	3999.01	2748.19	2123.99	1750.44	1502.21	1325.59	1193.72	1091.68	1010.53	944.55	889.96
95,000	8187.24	4221.17	2900.86	2241.99	1847.68	1585.66	1399.23	1260.04	1152.33	1066.67	997.03	939.40
100,000	8618.14	4443.34	3053.54	2359.99	1944.93	1669.12	1472.87	1326.35	1212.98	1122.81	1049.50	988.84
105,000	9049.05	4665.51	3206.22	2477.99	2042.18	1752.58	1546.52	1392.67	1273.63	1178.95	1101.97	1038.28
110,000	9479.96	4887.67	3358.89	2595.99	2139.42	1836.03	1620.16	1458.99	1334.28	1235.09	1154.45	1087.73
115,000	9910.86	5109.84	3511.57	2713.98	2236.67	1919.49	1693.81	1525.31	1394.93	1291.23	1206.92	1137.17
120,000	10341.77	5332.01	3664.25	2831.98	2333.92	2002.94	1767.45	1591.62	1455.58	1347.37	1259.40	1186.61
125,000	10772.68	5554.17	3816.92	2949.98	2431.16	2086.40	1841.09	1657.94	1516.22	1403.51	1311.87	1236.05
130,000	11203.58	5776.34	3969.60	3067.98	2528.41	2169.86	1914.74	1724.26	1576.87	1459.65	1364.35	1285.49
135,000	11634.49	5998.51	4122.28	3185.98	2625.66	2253.31	1988.38	1790.58	1637.52	1515.79	1416.82	1334.93
140,000	12065.40	6220.67	4274.95	3303.98	2722.90	2336.77	2062.02	1856.89	1698.17	1571.93	1469.30	1384.38
145,000	12496.31	6442.84	4427.63	3421.98	2820.15	2420.22	2135.67	1923.21	1758.82	1628.07	1521.77	1433.82
150,000	12927.21	6665.01	4580.31	3539.98	2917.39	2503.68	2209.31	1989.53	1819.47	1684.21	1574.25	1483.26
155,000	13358.12	6887.17	4732.98	3657.98	3014.64	2587.13	2282.95	2055.85	1880.12	1740.35	1626.72	1532.70
160,000	13789.03	7109.34	4885.66	3775.98	3111.89	2670.59	2356.60	2122.16	1940.77	1796.49	1679.20	1582.14
165,000	14219.93	7331.51	5038.34	3893.98	3209.13	2754.05	2430.24	2188.48	2001.41	1852.63	1731.67	1631.59
170,000	14650.84	7553.67	5191.01	4011.97	3306.38	2837.50	2503.88	2254.80	2062.06	1908.77	1784.15	1681.03
175,000	15081.75	7775.84	5343.69	4129.97	3403.63	2920.96	2577.53	2321.12	2122.71	1964.91	1836.62	1730.47
180,000	15512.65	7998.01	5496.37	4247.97	3500.87	3004.41	2651.17	2387.43	2183.36	2021.05	1889.10	1779.91
185,000	15943.56	8220.17	5649.04	4365.97	3598.12	3087.87	2724.81	2453.75	2244.01	2077.19	1941.57	1829.35
190,000	16374.47	8442.34	5801.72	4483.97	3695.36	3171.32	2798.46	2520.07	2304.66	2133.33	1994.05	1878.79
195,000	16805.37	8664.51	5954.40	4601.97	3792.61	3254.78	2872.10	2586.39	2365.31	2189.47	2046.52	1928.24
200,000	17236.28	8886.67	6107.07	4719.97	3889.86	3338.24	2945.74	2652.70	2425.96	2245.61	2098.99	1977.68
205,000	17667.19	9108.84	6259.75	4837.97	3987.10	3421.69	3019.39	2719.02	2486.61	2301.75	2151.47	2027.12
210,000	18098.09	9331.01	6412.43	4955.97	4084.35	3505.15	3093.03	2785.34	2547.25	2357.89	2203.94	2076.56
215,000	18529.00	9553.17	6565.10	5073.97	4181.60	3588.60	3166.68	2851.66	2607.90	2414.03	2256.42	2126.00
220,000	18959.91	9775.34	6717.78	5191.97	4278.84	3672.06	3240.32	2917.97	2668.55	2470.17	2308.89	2175.45
225,000	19390.82	9997.51	6870.46	5309.96	4376.09	3755.51	3313.96	2984.29	2729.20	2526.31	2361.37	2224.89
230,000	19821.72	10219.67	7023.13	5427.96	4473.34	3838.97	3387.61	3050.61	2789.85	2582.45	2413.84	2274.33
235,000	20252.63	10441.84	7175.81	5545.96	4570.58	3922.43	3461.25	3116.93	2850.50	2638.59	2466.32	2323.77
240,000	20683.54	10664.01	7328.49	5663.96	4667.83	4005.88	3534.89	3183.24	2911.15	2694.73	2518.79	2373.21
245,000	21114.44	10886.17	7481.16	5781.96	4765.07	4089.34	3608.54	3249.56	2971.80	2750.87	2571.27	2422.66
250,000	21545.35	11108.34	7633.84	5899.96	4862.32	4172.79	3682.18	3315.88	3032.44	2807.01	2623.74	2472.10
255,000	21976.26	11330.51	7786.52	6017.96	4959.57	4256.25	3755.82	3382.20	3093.09	2863.15	2676.22	2521.54
260,000	22407.16	11552.67	7939.19	6135.96	5056.81	4339.71	3829.47	3448.51	3153.74	2919.29	2728.69	2570.98
265,000	22838.07	11774.84	8091.87	6253.96	5154.06	4423.16	3903.11	3514.83	3214.39	2975.43	2781.17	2620.42
270,000	23268.98	11997.01	8244.55	6371.96	5251.31	4506.62	3976.75	3581.15	3275.04	3031.57	2833.64	2669.86
280,000	24130.79	12441.34	8549.90	6607.95	5445.80	4673.53	4124.04	3713.78	3396.34	3143.85	2938.59	2768.75
290,000	24992.61	12885.68	8855.25	6843.95	5640.29	4840.44	4271.33	3846.42	3517.63	3256.13	3043.54	2867.63
300,000	25854.42	13330.01	9160.61	7079.95	5834.78	5007.35	4418.61	3979.05	3638.93	3368.41	3148.49	2966.52

36

AMOUNT OF LOAN					NUMBER	OF YEARS	IN TERM					
	13	14	15	16	17	18	19	20	25	30	35	40
$ 50	0.47	0.45	0.43	0.42	0.40	0.39	0.38	0.37	0.33	0.31	0.30	0.29
100	0.94	0.90	0.86	0.83	0.80	0.78	0.76	0.74	0.66	0.62	0.59	0.57
200	1.88	1.79	1.72	1.66	1.60	1.55	1.51	1.47	1.32	1.24	1.18	1.14
300	2.82	2.69	2.58	2.48	2.40	2.32	2.26	2.20	1.98	1.85	1.77	1.71
400	3.76	3.58	3.43	3.31	3.19	3.09	3.01	2.93	2.64	2.47	2.35	2.28
500	4.69	4.48	4.29	4.13	3.99	3.87	3.76	3.66	3.30	3.08	2.94	2.84
600	5.63	5.37	5.15	4.96	4.79	4.64	4.51	4.39	3.96	3.70	3.53	3.41
700	6.57	6.27	6.01	5.78	5.58	5.41	5.26	5.12	4.62	4.32	4.11	3.98
800	7.51	7.16	6.86	6.61	6.38	6.18	6.01	5.85	5.28	4.93	4.70	4.55
900	8.45	8.06	7.72	7.43	7.18	6.96	6.76	6.58	5.94	5.55	5.29	5.11
1,000	9.38	8.95	8.58	8.26	7.98	7.73	7.51	7.31	6.60	6.16	5.88	5.68
2,000	18.76	17.90	17.15	16.51	15.95	15.45	15.01	14.62	13.20	12.32	11.75	11.36
3,000	28.14	26.84	25.73	24.76	23.92	23.17	22.52	21.93	19.80	18.48	17.62	17.04
4,000	37.52	35.79	34.30	33.01	31.89	30.90	30.02	29.24	26.39	24.63	23.49	22.71
5,000	46.90	44.74	42.88	41.26	39.86	38.62	37.52	36.55	32.99	30.79	29.36	28.39
6,000	56.28	53.68	51.45	49.52	47.83	46.34	45.03	43.86	39.59	36.95	35.23	34.07
7,000	65.66	62.63	60.02	57.77	55.80	54.07	52.53	51.17	46.18	43.11	41.10	39.75
8,000	75.04	71.57	68.60	66.02	63.77	61.79	60.04	58.48	52.78	49.26	46.97	45.42
9,000	84.42	80.52	77.17	74.27	71.74	69.51	67.54	65.79	59.38	55.42	52.84	51.10
10,000	93.80	89.47	85.75	82.52	79.71	77.23	75.04	73.10	65.97	61.58	58.71	56.78
15,000	140.69	134.20	128.62	123.78	119.56	115.85	112.56	109.64	98.96	92.36	88.07	85.17
20,000	187.59	178.93	171.49	165.04	159.41	154.46	150.08	146.19	131.94	123.15	117.42	113.55
25,000	234.48	223.66	214.36	206.30	199.27	193.08	187.60	182.74	164.92	153.93	146.77	141.94
30,000	281.38	268.30	257.23	247.56	239.12	231.69	225.12	219.28	197.91	184.72	176.13	170.33
35,000	328.27	313.12	300.10	288.82	278.97	270.31	262.64	255.83	230.89	215.51	205.48	198.71
40,000	375.17	357.85	342.97	330.08	318.82	308.92	300.16	292.38	263.87	246.29	234.84	227.10
45,000	422.06	402.58	385.85	371.34	358.68	347.54	337.68	328.92	296.86	277.08	264.19	255.49
50,000	468.96	447.31	428.72	412.60	398.53	386.15	375.20	365.47	329.84	307.86	293.54	283.87
55,000	515.85	492.04	471.59	453.86	438.38	424.77	412.72	402.02	362.82	338.65	322.90	312.26
60,000	562.75	536.77	514.46	495.12	478.23	463.38	450.24	438.56	395.81	369.44	352.25	340.65
65,000	609.64	581.50	557.33	536.38	518.08	502.00	487.76	475.11	428.79	400.22	381.60	369.04
70,000	656.54	626.23	600.20	577.64	557.94	540.61	525.28	511.65	461.77	431.01	410.96	397.42
75,000	703.43	670.96	643.07	618.90	597.79	579.23	562.80	548.20	494.76	461.79	440.31	425.81
80,000	750.33	715.69	685.94	660.16	637.64	617.84	600.32	584.75	527.74	492.58	469.67	454.20
85,000	797.22	760.42	728.81	701.42	677.49	656.45	637.84	621.29	560.72	523.36	499.02	482.58
90,000	844.12	805.15	771.69	742.68	717.35	695.07	675.36	657.84	593.71	554.15	528.37	510.97
95,000	891.01	849.88	814.56	783.94	757.20	733.68	712.88	694.39	626.69	584.94	557.73	539.36
100,000	937.91	894.62	857.43	825.20	797.05	772.30	750.40	730.93	659.67	615.72	587.08	567.74
105,000	984.80	939.35	900.30	866.46	836.90	810.91	787.92	767.48	692.66	646.51	616.44	596.13
110,000	1031.70	984.08	943.17	907.72	876.75	849.53	825.44	804.03	725.64	677.29	645.79	624.52
115,000	1078.60	1028.81	986.04	948.98	916.61	888.14	862.96	840.57	758.62	708.08	675.14	652.91
120,000	1125.49	1073.54	1028.91	990.24	956.46	926.76	900.48	877.12	791.61	738.87	704.50	681.29
125,000	1172.39	1118.27	1071.78	1031.50	996.31	965.37	938.00	913.67	824.59	769.65	733.85	709.68
130,000	1219.28	1163.00	1114.65	1072.76	1036.16	1003.99	975.52	950.21	857.58	800.44	763.20	738.07
135,000	1266.18	1207.73	1157.53	1114.02	1076.02	1042.60	1013.04	986.76	890.56	831.22	792.56	766.45
140,000	1313.07	1252.46	1200.40	1155.28	1115.87	1081.22	1050.56	1023.30	923.54	862.01	821.91	794.84
145,000	1359.97	1297.19	1243.27	1196.54	1155.72	1119.83	1088.08	1059.85	956.53	892.79	851.27	823.23
150,000	1406.86	1341.92	1286.14	1237.80	1195.57	1158.45	1125.60	1096.40	989.51	923.58	880.62	851.61
155,000	1453.76	1386.65	1329.01	1279.06	1235.43	1197.06	1163.12	1132.94	1022.49	954.37	909.97	880.00
160,000	1500.65	1431.38	1371.88	1320.32	1275.28	1235.67	1200.64	1169.49	1055.48	985.15	939.33	908.39
165,000	1547.55	1476.11	1414.75	1361.58	1315.13	1274.29	1238.16	1206.04	1088.46	1015.94	968.68	936.78
170,000	1594.44	1520.84	1457.62	1402.84	1354.98	1312.90	1275.68	1242.58	1121.44	1046.72	998.04	965.16
175,000	1641.34	1565.57	1500.50	1444.09	1394.83	1351.52	1313.20	1279.13	1154.43	1077.51	1027.39	993.55
180,000	1688.23	1610.30	1543.37	1485.35	1434.69	1390.13	1350.72	1315.68	1187.41	1108.30	1056.74	1021.94
185,000	1735.13	1655.03	1586.24	1526.61	1474.54	1428.75	1388.24	1352.22	1220.39	1139.08	1086.10	1050.32
190,000	1782.02	1699.76	1629.11	1567.87	1514.39	1467.36	1425.76	1388.77	1253.38	1169.87	1115.45	1078.71
195,000	1828.92	1744.49	1671.98	1609.13	1554.24	1505.98	1463.28	1425.31	1286.36	1200.65	1144.80	1107.10
200,000	1875.81	1789.23	1714.85	1650.39	1594.10	1544.59	1500.80	1461.86	1319.34	1231.44	1174.16	1135.48
205,000	1922.71	1833.96	1757.72	1691.65	1633.95	1583.21	1538.32	1498.41	1352.33	1262.23	1203.51	1163.87
210,000	1969.60	1878.69	1800.59	1732.91	1673.80	1621.82	1575.84	1534.95	1385.31	1293.01	1232.87	1192.26
215,000	2016.50	1923.42	1843.46	1774.17	1713.65	1660.44	1613.36	1571.50	1418.29	1323.80	1262.22	1220.65
220,000	2063.39	1968.15	1886.34	1815.43	1753.50	1699.05	1650.88	1608.05	1451.28	1354.58	1291.57	1249.03
225,000	2110.29	2012.88	1929.21	1856.69	1793.36	1737.67	1688.40	1644.59	1484.26	1385.37	1320.93	1277.42
230,000	2157.19	2057.61	1972.08	1897.95	1833.21	1776.28	1725.92	1681.14	1517.24	1416.15	1350.28	1305.81
235,000	2204.08	2102.34	2014.95	1939.21	1873.06	1814.89	1763.44	1717.69	1550.23	1446.94	1379.63	1334.19
240,000	2250.98	2147.07	2057.82	1980.47	1912.91	1853.51	1800.96	1754.23	1583.21	1477.73	1408.99	1362.58
245,000	2297.87	2191.80	2100.69	2021.73	1952.77	1892.12	1838.48	1790.78	1616.19	1508.51	1438.34	1390.97
250,000	2344.77	2236.53	2143.56	2062.99	1992.62	1930.74	1876.00	1827.33	1649.18	1539.30	1467.70	1419.35
255,000	2391.66	2281.26	2186.43	2104.25	2032.47	1969.35	1913.52	1863.87	1682.16	1570.08	1497.05	1447.74
260,000	2438.56	2325.99	2229.30	2145.51	2072.32	2007.97	1951.04	1900.42	1715.15	1600.87	1526.40	1476.13
265,000	2485.45	2370.72	2272.18	2186.77	2112.18	2046.58	1988.56	1936.96	1748.13	1631.66	1555.76	1504.51
270,000	2532.35	2415.45	2315.05	2228.03	2152.03	2085.20	2026.08	1973.51	1781.11	1662.44	1585.11	1532.90
280,000	2626.14	2504.91	2400.79	2310.55	2231.73	2162.43	2101.12	2046.60	1847.08	1724.01	1643.82	1589.68
290,000	2719.93	2594.37	2486.53	2393.07	2311.44	2239.66	2176.16	2119.70	1913.05	1785.58	1702.53	1646.45
300,000	2813.72	2683.84	2572.27	2475.59	2391.14	2316.89	2251.20	2192.79	1979.01	1847.16	1761.23	1703.22

6.50%

AMOUNT OF LOAN	NUMBER OF YEARS IN TERM											
	1	2	3	4	5	6	7	8	9	10	11	12
$ 50	4.32	2.23	1.54	1.19	0.98	0.85	0.75	0.67	0.62	0.57	0.54	0.51
100	8.63	4.46	3.07	2.38	1.96	1.69	1.49	1.34	1.23	1.14	1.07	1.01
200	17.26	8.91	6.13	4.75	3.92	3.37	2.97	2.68	2.46	2.28	2.13	2.01
300	25.89	13.37	9.20	7.12	5.87	5.05	4.46	4.02	3.68	3.41	3.19	3.01
400	34.52	17.82	12.26	9.49	7.83	6.73	5.94	5.36	4.91	4.55	4.25	4.01
500	43.15	22.28	15.33	11.86	9.79	8.41	7.43	6.70	6.13	5.68	5.32	5.01
600	51.78	26.73	18.39	14.23	11.74	10.09	8.91	8.04	7.36	6.82	6.38	6.02
700	60.41	31.19	21.46	16.61	13.70	11.77	10.40	9.38	8.58	7.95	7.44	7.02
800	69.04	35.64	24.52	18.98	15.66	13.45	11.88	10.71	9.81	9.09	8.50	8.02
900	77.67	40.10	27.59	21.35	17.61	15.13	13.37	12.05	11.03	10.22	9.57	9.02
1,000	86.30	44.55	30.65	23.72	19.57	16.81	14.85	13.39	12.26	11.36	10.63	10.02
2,000	172.60	89.10	61.30	47.43	39.14	33.62	29.70	26.78	24.51	22.71	21.25	20.04
3,000	258.89	133.64	91.95	71.15	58.70	50.43	44.55	40.16	36.77	34.07	31.88	30.06
4,000	345.19	178.19	122.60	94.86	78.27	67.24	59.40	53.55	49.02	45.42	42.50	40.08
5,000	431.49	222.74	153.25	118.58	97.84	84.05	74.25	66.94	61.28	56.78	53.12	50.10
6,000	517.78	267.28	183.90	142.29	117.40	100.86	89.10	80.32	73.53	68.13	63.75	60.12
7,000	604.08	311.83	214.55	166.01	136.97	117.67	103.95	93.71	85.79	79.49	74.37	70.14
8,000	690.38	356.38	245.20	189.72	156.53	134.48	118.80	107.09	98.04	90.84	85.00	80.16
9,000	776.67	400.92	275.85	213.44	176.10	151.29	133.65	120.48	110.30	102.20	95.62	90.18
10,000	862.97	445.47	306.50	237.15	195.67	168.10	148.50	133.87	122.55	113.55	106.24	100.20
15,000	1294.45	668.20	459.74	355.73	293.50	252.15	222.75	200.80	183.82	170.33	159.36	150.29
20,000	1725.93	890.93	612.99	474.30	391.33	336.20	296.99	267.73	245.10	227.10	212.48	200.39
25,000	2157.42	1113.66	766.23	592.88	489.16	420.25	371.24	334.66	306.37	283.87	265.60	250.49
30,000	2588.90	1336.39	919.48	711.45	586.99	504.30	445.49	401.59	367.64	340.65	318.72	300.58
35,000	3020.38	1559.12	1072.72	830.03	684.82	588.35	519.74	468.52	428.91	397.42	371.84	350.68
40,000	3451.86	1781.86	1225.97	948.60	782.65	672.40	593.98	535.45	490.19	454.20	424.96	400.77
45,000	3883.34	2004.59	1379.21	1067.18	880.48	756.45	668.23	602.39	551.46	510.97	478.07	450.87
50,000	4314.83	2227.32	1532.46	1185.75	978.31	840.50	742.48	669.32	612.73	567.74	531.19	500.97
55,000	4746.31	2450.05	1685.70	1304.33	1076.14	924.55	816.72	736.25	674.00	624.52	584.31	551.06
60,000	5177.79	2672.78	1838.95	1422.90	1173.97	1008.60	890.97	803.18	735.28	681.29	637.43	601.16
65,000	5609.27	2895.51	1992.19	1541.48	1271.80	1092.65	965.22	870.11	796.55	738.07	690.55	651.25
70,000	6040.75	3118.24	2145.44	1660.05	1369.64	1176.70	1039.47	937.04	857.82	794.84	743.67	701.35
75,000	6472.24	3340.97	2298.68	1778.63	1467.47	1260.75	1113.71	1003.97	919.09	851.61	796.79	751.45
80,000	6903.72	3563.71	2451.93	1897.20	1565.30	1344.80	1187.96	1070.90	980.37	908.39	849.91	801.54
85,000	7335.20	3786.44	2605.17	2015.78	1663.13	1428.85	1262.21	1137.83	1041.64	965.16	903.03	851.64
90,000	7766.68	4009.17	2758.42	2134.35	1760.96	1512.90	1336.45	1204.77	1102.91	1021.94	956.14	901.73
95,000	8198.16	4231.90	2911.66	2252.93	1858.79	1596.95	1410.70	1271.70	1164.18	1078.71	1009.26	951.83
100,000	8629.65	4454.63	3064.91	2371.50	1956.62	1681.00	1484.95	1338.63	1225.46	1135.48	1062.38	1001.93
105,000	9061.13	4677.36	3218.15	2490.08	2054.45	1765.05	1559.20	1405.56	1286.73	1192.26	1115.50	1052.02
110,000	9492.61	4900.09	3371.40	2608.65	2152.28	1849.10	1633.44	1472.49	1348.00	1249.03	1168.62	1102.12
115,000	9924.09	5122.82	3524.64	2727.22	2250.11	1933.15	1707.69	1539.42	1409.27	1305.81	1221.74	1152.21
120,000	10355.58	5345.56	3677.89	2845.80	2347.94	2017.20	1781.94	1606.35	1470.55	1362.58	1274.86	1202.31
125,000	10787.06	5568.29	3831.13	2964.37	2445.77	2101.25	1856.18	1673.28	1531.82	1419.35	1327.98	1252.41
130,000	11218.54	5791.02	3984.38	3082.95	2543.60	2185.30	1930.43	1740.22	1593.09	1476.13	1381.09	1302.50
135,000	11650.02	6013.75	4137.62	3201.52	2641.44	2269.35	2004.68	1807.15	1654.36	1532.90	1434.21	1352.60
140,000	12081.50	6236.48	4290.87	3320.10	2739.27	2353.40	2078.93	1874.08	1715.64	1589.68	1487.33	1402.69
145,000	12512.99	6459.21	4444.11	3438.67	2837.10	2437.44	2153.17	1941.01	1776.91	1646.45	1540.45	1452.79
150,000	12944.47	6681.94	4597.36	3557.25	2934.93	2521.49	2227.42	2007.94	1838.18	1703.22	1593.57	1502.89
155,000	13375.95	6904.67	4750.60	3675.82	3032.76	2605.54	2301.67	2074.87	1899.45	1760.00	1646.69	1552.98
160,000	13807.43	7127.41	4903.85	3794.40	3130.59	2689.59	2375.91	2141.80	1960.73	1816.77	1699.81	1603.08
165,000	14238.91	7350.14	5057.09	3912.97	3228.42	2773.64	2450.16	2208.73	2022.00	1873.55	1752.93	1653.17
170,000	14670.40	7572.87	5210.34	4031.55	3326.25	2857.69	2524.41	2275.66	2083.27	1930.32	1806.05	1703.27
175,000	15101.88	7795.60	5363.58	4150.12	3424.08	2941.74	2598.66	2342.60	2144.55	1987.09	1859.16	1753.37
180,000	15533.36	8018.33	5516.83	4268.70	3521.91	3025.79	2672.90	2409.53	2205.82	2043.87	1912.28	1803.46
185,000	15964.84	8241.06	5670.07	4387.27	3619.74	3109.84	2747.15	2476.46	2267.09	2100.64	1965.40	1853.56
190,000	16396.32	8463.79	5823.32	4505.85	3717.57	3193.89	2821.40	2543.39	2328.36	2157.42	2018.52	1903.66
195,000	16827.81	8686.52	5976.56	4624.42	3815.40	3277.94	2895.65	2610.32	2389.64	2214.19	2071.64	1953.75
200,000	17259.29	8909.26	6129.81	4743.00	3913.23	3361.99	2969.89	2677.25	2450.91	2270.96	2124.76	2003.85
205,000	17690.77	9131.99	6283.05	4861.57	4011.07	3446.04	3044.14	2744.18	2512.18	2327.74	2177.88	2053.94
210,000	18122.25	9354.72	6436.30	4980.15	4108.90	3530.09	3118.39	2811.11	2573.45	2384.51	2231.00	2104.04
215,000	18553.73	9577.45	6589.54	5098.72	4206.73	3614.14	3192.63	2878.05	2634.73	2441.29	2284.11	2154.14
220,000	18985.22	9800.18	6742.79	5217.29	4304.56	3698.19	3266.88	2944.98	2696.00	2498.06	2337.23	2204.23
225,000	19416.70	10022.91	6896.03	5335.87	4402.39	3782.24	3341.13	3011.91	2757.27	2554.83	2390.35	2254.33
230,000	19848.18	10245.64	7049.28	5454.44	4500.22	3866.29	3415.38	3078.84	2818.54	2611.61	2443.47	2304.42
235,000	20279.66	10468.37	7202.52	5573.02	4598.05	3950.34	3489.62	3145.77	2879.82	2668.38	2496.59	2354.52
240,000	20711.15	10691.11	7355.77	5691.59	4695.88	4034.39	3563.87	3212.70	2941.09	2725.16	2549.71	2404.62
245,000	21142.63	10913.84	7509.01	5810.17	4793.71	4118.44	3638.12	3279.63	3002.36	2781.93	2602.83	2454.71
250,000	21574.11	11136.57	7662.26	5928.74	4891.54	4202.49	3712.36	3346.56	3063.63	2838.70	2655.95	2504.81
255,000	22005.59	11359.30	7815.50	6047.32	4989.37	4286.54	3786.61	3413.49	3124.91	2895.48	2709.07	2554.90
260,000	22437.07	11582.03	7968.75	6165.89	5087.20	4370.59	3860.86	3480.43	3186.18	2952.25	2762.18	2605.00
265,000	22868.56	11804.76	8121.99	6284.47	5185.03	4454.64	3935.11	3547.36	3247.45	3009.03	2815.30	2655.10
270,000	23300.04	12027.49	8275.24	6403.04	5282.87	4538.69	4009.35	3614.29	3308.72	3065.80	2868.42	2705.19
280,000	24163.00	12472.96	8581.73	6640.19	5478.53	4706.79	4157.85	3748.15	3431.27	3179.35	2974.66	2805.38
290,000	25025.97	12918.42	8888.22	6877.34	5674.19	4874.88	4306.34	3882.01	3553.81	3292.90	3080.90	2905.58
300,000	25888.93	13363.88	9194.71	7114.49	5869.85	5042.98	4454.84	4015.87	3676.36	3406.44	3187.14	3005.77

AMOUNT OF LOAN	NUMBER OF YEARS IN TERM											
	13	14	15	16	17	18	19	20	25	30	35	40
$ 50	0.48	0.46	0.44	0.42	0.41	0.40	0.39	0.38	0.34	0.32	0.31	0.30
100	0.96	0.91	0.88	0.84	0.82	0.79	0.77	0.75	0.68	0.64	0.61	0.59
200	1.91	1.82	1.75	1.68	1.63	1.58	1.53	1.50	1.36	1.27	1.21	1.18
300	2.86	2.73	2.62	2.52	2.44	2.36	2.30	2.24	2.03	1.90	1.82	1.76
400	3.81	3.64	3.49	3.36	3.25	3.15	3.06	2.99	2.71	2.53	2.42	2.35
500	4.76	4.55	4.36	4.20	4.06	3.94	3.83	3.73	3.38	3.17	3.03	2.93
600	5.71	5.45	5.23	5.04	4.87	4.72	4.59	4.48	4.06	3.80	3.63	3.52
700	6.66	6.36	6.10	5.88	5.68	5.51	5.36	5.22	4.73	4.43	4.23	4.10
800	7.61	7.27	6.97	6.72	6.49	6.30	6.12	5.97	5.41	5.06	4.84	4.69
900	8.57	8.18	7.84	7.56	7.31	7.08	6.89	6.72	6.08	5.69	5.44	5.27
1,000	9.52	9.09	8.72	8.40	8.12	7.87	7.65	7.46	6.76	6.33	6.05	5.86
2,000	19.03	18.17	17.43	16.79	16.23	15.74	15.30	14.92	13.51	12.65	12.09	11.71
3,000	28.54	27.25	26.14	25.18	24.34	23.60	22.95	22.37	20.26	18.97	18.13	17.57
4,000	38.05	36.33	34.85	33.57	32.45	31.47	30.60	29.83	27.01	25.29	24.17	23.42
5,000	47.56	45.41	43.56	41.96	40.56	39.33	38.25	37.28	33.77	31.61	30.21	29.28
6,000	57.08	54.49	52.27	50.35	48.67	47.20	45.90	44.74	40.52	37.93	36.25	35.13
7,000	66.59	63.57	60.98	58.74	56.78	55.06	53.54	52.20	47.27	44.25	42.30	40.99
8,000	76.10	72.65	69.69	67.13	64.89	62.93	61.19	59.65	54.02	50.57	48.34	46.84
9,000	85.61	81.73	78.40	75.52	73.01	70.80	68.84	67.11	60.77	56.89	54.38	52.70
10,000	95.12	90.81	87.12	83.91	81.12	78.66	76.49	74.56	67.53	63.21	60.42	58.55
15,000	142.68	136.22	130.67	125.87	121.67	117.99	114.73	111.84	101.29	94.82	90.63	87.82
20,000	190.24	181.62	174.23	167.82	162.23	157.32	152.98	149.12	135.05	126.42	120.84	117.10
25,000	237.80	227.03	217.78	209.77	202.79	196.65	191.22	186.40	168.81	158.02	151.04	146.37
30,000	285.36	272.43	261.34	251.73	243.34	235.97	229.46	223.68	202.57	189.63	181.25	175.64
35,000	332.92	317.84	304.89	293.68	283.90	275.30	267.70	260.96	236.33	221.23	211.46	204.91
40,000	380.48	363.24	348.45	335.64	324.45	314.63	305.95	298.23	270.09	252.83	241.67	234.19
45,000	428.04	408.65	392.00	377.59	365.01	353.96	344.19	335.51	303.85	284.44	271.87	263.46
50,000	475.60	454.05	435.56	419.54	405.57	393.29	382.43	372.79	337.61	316.04	302.08	292.73
55,000	523.16	499.46	479.11	461.50	446.12	432.61	420.68	410.07	371.37	347.64	332.29	322.01
60,000	570.72	544.86	522.67	503.45	486.68	471.94	458.92	447.35	405.13	379.25	362.50	351.28
65,000	618.28	590.27	566.22	545.40	527.23	511.27	497.16	484.63	438.89	410.85	392.71	380.55
70,000	665.84	635.67	609.78	587.36	567.79	550.60	535.40	521.91	472.65	442.45	422.91	409.82
75,000	713.40	681.08	653.34	629.31	608.35	589.93	573.65	559.18	506.41	474.06	453.12	439.10
80,000	760.96	726.48	696.89	671.27	648.90	629.25	611.89	596.46	540.17	505.66	483.33	468.37
85,000	808.52	771.89	740.45	713.22	689.46	668.58	650.13	633.74	573.93	537.26	513.54	497.64
90,000	856.08	817.29	784.00	755.17	730.01	707.91	688.38	671.02	607.69	568.87	543.74	526.92
95,000	903.64	862.70	827.56	797.13	770.57	747.24	726.62	708.30	641.45	600.47	573.95	556.19
100,000	951.20	908.10	871.11	839.08	811.13	786.57	764.86	745.58	675.21	632.07	604.16	585.46
105,000	998.75	953.51	914.67	881.03	851.68	825.89	803.10	782.86	708.97	663.68	634.37	614.73
110,000	1046.31	998.91	958.22	922.99	892.24	865.22	841.35	820.14	742.73	695.28	664.57	644.01
115,000	1093.87	1044.32	1001.78	964.94	932.79	904.55	879.59	857.41	776.49	726.88	694.78	673.28
120,000	1141.43	1089.72	1045.33	1006.90	970.05	940.00	917.83	894.69	810.25	758.49	724.99	702.55
125,000	1188.99	1135.13	1088.89	1048.85	1013.91	983.21	956.07	931.97	844.01	790.09	755.20	731.83
130,000	1236.55	1180.53	1132.44	1090.80	1054.46	1022.53	994.32	969.25	877.77	821.69	785.41	761.10
135,000	1284.11	1225.93	1176.00	1132.76	1095.02	1061.86	1032.56	1006.53	911.53	853.30	815.61	790.37
140,000	1331.67	1271.34	1219.56	1174.71	1135.57	1101.19	1070.80	1043.81	945.30	884.90	845.82	819.64
145,000	1379.23	1316.74	1263.11	1216.66	1176.13	1140.52	1109.05	1081.09	979.06	916.50	876.03	848.92
150,000	1426.79	1362.15	1306.67	1258.62	1216.69	1179.85	1147.29	1118.36	1012.82	948.11	906.24	878.19
155,000	1474.35	1407.55	1350.22	1300.57	1257.24	1219.17	1185.53	1155.64	1046.58	979.71	936.44	907.46
160,000	1521.91	1452.96	1393.78	1342.53	1297.80	1258.50	1223.77	1192.92	1080.34	1011.31	966.65	936.74
165,000	1569.47	1498.36	1437.33	1384.48	1338.35	1297.83	1262.02	1230.20	1114.10	1042.92	996.86	966.01
170,000	1617.03	1543.77	1480.89	1426.43	1378.91	1337.16	1300.26	1267.48	1147.86	1074.52	1027.07	995.28
175,000	1664.59	1589.17	1524.44	1468.39	1419.47	1376.49	1338.50	1304.76	1181.62	1106.12	1057.28	1024.55
180,000	1712.15	1634.58	1568.00	1510.34	1460.02	1415.82	1376.75	1342.04	1215.38	1137.73	1087.48	1053.83
185,000	1759.71	1679.98	1611.55	1552.29	1500.58	1455.14	1414.99	1379.32	1249.14	1169.33	1117.69	1083.10
190,000	1807.27	1725.39	1655.11	1594.25	1541.14	1494.47	1453.23	1416.59	1282.90	1200.93	1147.90	1112.37
195,000	1854.83	1770.79	1698.66	1636.20	1581.69	1533.80	1491.47	1453.87	1316.66	1232.54	1178.11	1141.65
200,000	1902.39	1816.20	1742.22	1678.16	1622.25	1573.13	1529.72	1491.15	1350.42	1264.14	1208.31	1170.92
205,000	1949.94	1861.60	1785.78	1720.11	1662.80	1612.46	1567.96	1528.43	1384.18	1295.74	1238.52	1200.19
210,000	1997.50	1907.01	1829.33	1762.06	1703.36	1651.78	1606.20	1565.71	1417.94	1327.35	1268.73	1229.46
215,000	2045.06	1952.41	1872.89	1804.02	1743.92	1691.11	1644.45	1602.99	1451.70	1358.95	1298.94	1258.74
220,000	2092.62	1997.82	1916.44	1845.97	1784.47	1730.44	1682.69	1640.27	1485.46	1390.55	1329.14	1288.01
225,000	2140.18	2043.22	1960.00	1887.92	1825.03	1769.77	1720.93	1677.54	1519.22	1422.16	1359.35	1317.28
230,000	2187.74	2088.63	2003.55	1929.88	1865.58	1809.10	1759.17	1714.82	1552.98	1453.76	1389.56	1346.56
235,000	2235.30	2134.03	2047.11	1971.83	1906.14	1848.42	1797.42	1752.10	1586.74	1485.36	1419.77	1375.83
240,000	2282.86	2179.44	2090.66	2013.79	1946.70	1887.75	1835.66	1789.38	1620.50	1516.97	1449.98	1405.10
245,000	2330.42	2224.84	2134.22	2055.74	1987.25	1927.08	1873.90	1826.66	1654.26	1548.57	1480.18	1434.37
250,000	2377.98	2270.25	2177.77	2097.69	2027.81	1966.41	1912.14	1863.94	1688.02	1580.18	1510.39	1463.65
255,000	2425.54	2315.65	2221.33	2139.65	2068.36	2005.74	1950.39	1901.22	1721.78	1611.78	1540.60	1492.92
260,000	2473.10	2361.05	2264.88	2181.60	2108.92	2045.06	1988.63	1938.50	1755.54	1643.38	1570.81	1522.19
265,000	2520.66	2406.46	2308.44	2223.55	2149.48	2084.39	2026.87	1975.77	1789.30	1674.99	1601.01	1551.47
270,000	2568.22	2451.86	2351.99	2265.51	2190.03	2123.72	2065.12	2013.05	1823.06	1706.59	1631.22	1580.74
280,000	2663.34	2542.67	2439.11	2349.42	2271.14	2202.38	2141.60	2087.61	1890.59	1769.80	1691.64	1639.28
290,000	2758.46	2633.48	2526.22	2433.32	2352.26	2281.03	2218.09	2162.17	1958.11	1833.00	1752.05	1697.83
300,000	2853.58	2724.29	2613.33	2517.23	2433.37	2359.69	2294.57	2236.72	2025.63	1896.21	1812.47	1756.38

MONTHLY AMORTIZING PAYMENTS

AMOUNT OF LOAN	NUMBER OF YEARS IN TERM											
	1	2	3	4	5	6	7	8	9	10	11	12
$ 50	4.33	2.24	1.54	1.20	0.99	0.85	0.75	0.68	0.62	0.58	0.54	0.51
100	8.65	4.47	3.08	2.39	1.97	1.70	1.50	1.36	1.24	1.15	1.08	1.02
200	17.29	8.94	6.16	4.77	3.94	3.39	3.00	2.71	2.48	2.30	2.16	2.04
300	25.93	13.40	9.23	7.15	5.91	5.08	4.50	4.06	3.72	3.45	3.23	3.05
400	34.57	17.87	12.31	9.54	7.88	6.78	5.99	5.41	4.96	4.60	4.31	4.07
500	43.21	22.33	15.39	11.92	9.85	8.47	7.49	6.76	6.20	5.75	5.38	5.08
600	51.85	26.80	18.46	14.30	11.82	10.16	8.99	8.11	7.43	6.89	6.46	6.10
700	60.49	31.27	21.54	16.69	13.78	11.86	10.48	9.46	8.67	8.04	7.53	7.11
800	69.13	35.73	24.62	19.07	15.75	13.55	11.98	10.81	9.91	9.19	8.61	8.13
900	77.78	40.20	27.69	21.45	17.72	15.24	13.48	12.16	11.15	10.34	9.68	9.14
1,000	86.42	44.66	30.77	23.84	19.69	16.93	14.98	13.51	12.39	11.49	10.76	10.16
2,000	172.83	89.32	61.53	47.67	39.37	33.86	29.95	27.02	24.77	22.97	21.51	20.31
3,000	259.24	133.98	92.29	71.50	59.06	50.79	44.92	40.53	37.15	34.45	32.27	30.46
4,000	345.65	178.64	123.06	95.33	78.74	67.72	59.89	54.04	49.53	45.93	43.02	40.61
5,000	432.06	223.30	153.82	119.16	98.42	84.65	74.86	67.55	61.91	57.42	53.77	50.76
6,000	518.47	267.96	184.58	142.99	118.11	101.58	89.83	81.06	74.29	68.90	64.53	60.91
7,000	604.89	312.62	215.35	166.82	137.79	118.51	104.80	94.57	86.67	80.38	75.28	71.06
8,000	691.30	357.28	246.11	190.65	157.47	135.44	119.77	108.08	99.05	91.86	86.03	81.21
9,000	777.71	401.94	276.87	214.48	177.16	152.37	134.74	121.59	111.43	103.35	96.79	91.36
10,000	864.12	446.60	307.63	238.31	196.84	169.30	149.71	135.10	123.81	114.83	107.54	101.52
15,000	1296.18	669.89	461.45	357.46	295.26	253.94	224.57	202.65	185.71	172.24	161.31	152.27
20,000	1728.24	893.19	615.26	476.61	393.67	338.59	299.42	270.20	247.61	229.65	215.07	203.03
25,000	2160.29	1116.49	769.08	595.77	492.09	423.24	374.27	337.75	309.51	287.07	268.84	253.78
30,000	2592.35	1339.78	922.89	714.92	590.51	507.88	449.13	405.29	371.41	344.48	322.61	304.54
35,000	3024.41	1563.08	1076.71	834.07	688.93	592.53	523.98	472.84	433.31	401.89	376.38	355.29
40,000	3456.47	1786.38	1230.52	953.22	787.34	677.17	598.84	540.39	495.21	459.30	430.14	406.05
45,000	3888.52	2009.67	1384.34	1072.37	885.76	761.82	673.69	607.94	557.11	516.71	483.91	456.80
50,000	4320.58	2232.97	1538.15	1191.53	984.18	846.47	748.54	675.49	619.01	574.13	537.68	507.56
55,000	4752.64	2456.27	1691.97	1310.68	1082.60	931.11	823.40	743.04	680.91	631.54	591.45	558.31
60,000	5184.70	2679.56	1845.78	1429.83	1181.01	1015.76	898.25	810.58	742.81	688.95	645.21	609.07
65,000	5616.76	2902.86	1999.59	1548.98	1279.43	1100.40	973.10	878.13	804.71	746.36	698.98	659.82
70,000	6048.81	3126.16	2153.41	1668.13	1377.85	1185.05	1047.96	945.68	866.61	803.77	752.75	710.58
75,000	6480.87	3349.45	2307.22	1787.29	1476.26	1269.70	1122.81	1013.23	928.51	861.19	806.52	761.33
80,000	6912.93	3572.75	2461.04	1906.44	1574.68	1354.34	1197.67	1080.78	990.41	918.60	860.28	812.09
85,000	7344.99	3796.05	2614.85	2025.59	1673.10	1438.99	1272.52	1148.32	1052.31	976.01	914.05	862.84
90,000	7777.04	4019.34	2768.67	2144.74	1771.52	1523.63	1347.37	1215.87	1114.21	1033.42	967.82	913.60
95,000	8209.10	4242.64	2922.48	2263.90	1869.93	1608.28	1422.23	1283.42	1176.11	1090.83	1021.59	964.35
100,000	8641.16	4465.94	3076.30	2383.05	1968.35	1692.93	1497.08	1350.97	1238.01	1148.25	1075.35	1015.11
105,000	9073.22	4689.23	3230.11	2502.20	2066.77	1777.57	1571.94	1418.52	1299.91	1205.66	1129.12	1065.86
110,000	9505.27	4912.53	3383.93	2621.35	2165.19	1862.22	1646.79	1486.07	1361.81	1263.07	1182.89	1116.62
115,000	9937.33	5135.83	3537.74	2740.50	2263.60	1946.86	1721.64	1553.61	1423.71	1320.48	1236.66	1167.37
120,000	10369.39	5359.12	3691.56	2859.66	2362.02	2031.51	1796.50	1621.16	1485.61	1377.89	1290.42	1218.13
125,000	10801.45	5582.42	3845.37	2978.81	2460.44	2116.16	1871.35	1688.71	1547.51	1435.31	1344.19	1268.88
130,000	11233.51	5805.72	3999.18	3097.96	2558.85	2200.80	1946.20	1756.26	1609.41	1492.72	1397.96	1319.64
135,000	11665.56	6029.01	4153.00	3217.11	2657.27	2285.45	2021.06	1823.81	1671.31	1550.13	1451.73	1370.39
140,000	12097.62	6252.31	4306.81	3336.26	2755.69	2370.09	2095.91	1891.35	1733.21	1607.54	1505.49	1421.15
145,000	12529.68	6475.61	4460.63	3455.42	2854.11	2454.74	2170.77	1958.90	1795.11	1664.95	1559.26	1471.90
150,000	12961.74	6698.90	4614.44	3574.57	2952.52	2539.39	2245.62	2026.45	1857.01	1722.37	1613.03	1522.66
155,000	13393.79	6922.20	4768.26	3693.72	3050.94	2624.03	2320.47	2094.00	1918.91	1779.78	1666.80	1573.41
160,000	13825.85	7145.50	4922.07	3812.87	3149.36	2708.68	2395.33	2161.55	1980.81	1837.19	1720.56	1624.17
165,000	14257.91	7368.79	5075.89	3932.03	3247.78	2793.33	2470.18	2229.10	2042.71	1894.60	1774.33	1674.92
170,000	14689.97	7592.09	5229.70	4051.18	3346.19	2877.97	2545.03	2296.64	2104.61	1952.01	1828.10	1725.68
175,000	15122.02	7815.39	5383.52	4170.33	3444.61	2962.62	2619.89	2364.19	2166.51	2009.43	1881.87	1776.43
180,000	15554.08	8038.68	5537.33	4289.48	3543.03	3047.26	2694.74	2431.74	2228.41	2066.84	1935.63	1827.19
185,000	15986.14	8261.98	5691.15	4408.63	3641.45	3131.91	2769.60	2499.29	2290.31	2124.25	1989.40	1877.94
190,000	16418.20	8485.28	5844.96	4527.79	3739.86	3216.56	2844.45	2566.84	2352.21	2181.66	2043.17	1928.70
195,000	16850.26	8708.57	5998.77	4646.94	3838.28	3301.20	2919.30	2634.38	2414.11	2239.08	2096.93	1979.46
200,000	17282.31	8931.87	6152.59	4766.09	3936.70	3385.85	2994.16	2701.93	2476.01	2296.49	2150.70	2030.21
205,000	17714.37	9155.17	6306.40	4885.24	4035.11	3470.49	3069.01	2769.48	2537.91	2353.90	2204.47	2080.97
210,000	18146.43	9378.46	6460.22	5004.39	4133.53	3555.14	3143.87	2837.03	2599.81	2411.31	2258.24	2131.72
215,000	18578.49	9601.76	6614.03	5123.55	4231.95	3639.79	3218.72	2904.58	2661.71	2468.72	2312.00	2182.48
220,000	19010.54	9825.06	6767.85	5242.70	4330.37	3724.43	3293.57	2972.13	2723.61	2526.14	2365.77	2233.23
225,000	19442.60	10048.35	6921.66	5361.85	4428.78	3809.08	3368.43	3039.67	2785.51	2583.55	2419.54	2283.99
230,000	19874.66	10271.65	7075.48	5481.00	4527.20	3893.72	3443.28	3107.22	2847.41	2640.96	2473.31	2334.74
235,000	20306.72	10494.95	7229.29	5600.16	4625.62	3978.37	3518.13	3174.77	2909.31	2698.37	2527.07	2385.50
240,000	20738.77	10718.24	7383.11	5719.31	4724.04	4063.02	3592.99	3242.32	2971.21	2755.78	2580.84	2436.25
245,000	21170.83	10941.54	7536.92	5838.46	4822.45	4147.66	3667.84	3309.87	3033.11	2813.20	2634.61	2487.01
250,000	21602.89	11164.84	7690.74	5957.61	4920.87	4232.31	3742.70	3377.42	3095.01	2870.61	2688.38	2537.76
255,000	22034.95	11388.13	7844.55	6076.76	5019.29	4316.95	3817.55	3444.96	3156.91	2928.02	2742.14	2588.52
260,000	22467.01	11611.43	7998.36	6195.92	5117.70	4401.60	3892.40	3512.51	3218.81	2985.43	2795.91	2639.27
265,000	22899.06	11834.73	8152.18	6315.07	5216.12	4486.25	3967.26	3580.06	3280.71	3042.84	2849.68	2690.03
270,000	23331.12	12058.02	8305.99	6434.22	5314.54	4570.89	4042.11	3647.61	3342.61	3100.26	2903.45	2740.78
280,000	24195.24	12504.62	8613.62	6672.52	5511.37	4740.18	4191.82	3782.70	3466.41	3215.08	3010.98	2842.29
290,000	25059.35	12951.21	8921.25	6910.83	5708.21	4909.48	4341.53	3917.80	3590.21	3329.90	3118.52	2943.80
300,000	25923.47	13397.80	9228.88	7149.13	5905.04	5078.77	4491.23	4052.90	3714.01	3444.73	3226.05	3045.31

AMOUNT OF LOAN	NUMBER OF YEARS IN TERM											
	13	14	15	16	17	18	19	20	25	30	35	40
$ 50	0.49	0.47	0.45	0.43	0.42	0.41	0.39	0.39	0.35	0.33	0.32	0.31
100	0.97	0.93	0.89	0.86	0.83	0.81	0.78	0.77	0.70	0.65	0.63	0.61
200	1.93	1.85	1.77	1.71	1.66	1.61	1.56	1.53	1.39	1.30	1.25	1.21
300	2.90	2.77	2.66	2.56	2.48	2.41	2.34	2.29	2.08	1.95	1.87	1.82
400	3.86	3.69	3.54	3.42	3.31	3.21	3.12	3.05	2.77	2.60	2.49	2.42
500	4.83	4.61	4.43	4.27	4.13	4.01	3.90	3.81	3.46	3.25	3.11	3.02
600	5.79	5.54	5.31	5.12	4.96	4.81	4.68	4.57	4.15	3.90	3.73	3.63
700	6.76	6.46	6.20	5.98	5.78	5.61	5.46	5.33	4.84	4.55	4.35	4.23
800	7.72	7.38	7.08	6.83	6.61	6.41	6.24	6.09	5.53	5.19	4.98	4.83
900	8.69	8.30	7.97	7.68	7.43	7.21	7.02	6.85	6.22	5.84	5.60	5.44
1,000	9.65	9.22	8.85	8.54	8.26	8.01	7.80	7.61	6.91	6.49	6.22	6.04
2,000	19.30	18.44	17.70	17.07	16.51	16.02	15.59	15.21	13.82	12.98	12.43	12.07
3,000	28.94	27.66	26.55	25.60	24.76	24.03	23.39	22.82	20.73	19.46	18.65	18.11
4,000	38.59	36.87	35.40	34.13	33.02	32.04	31.18	30.42	27.64	25.95	24.86	24.14
5,000	48.23	46.09	44.25	42.66	41.27	40.05	38.98	38.02	34.55	32.43	31.08	30.17
6,000	57.88	55.31	53.10	51.19	49.52	48.06	46.77	45.63	41.46	38.92	37.29	36.21
7,000	67.53	64.52	61.95	59.72	57.78	56.07	54.57	53.23	48.37	45.41	43.50	42.24
8,000	77.17	73.74	70.80	68.25	66.03	64.08	62.36	60.83	55.28	51.89	49.72	48.27
9,000	86.82	82.96	79.65	76.78	74.28	72.09	70.16	68.44	62.19	58.38	55.93	54.31
10,000	96.46	92.17	88.50	85.31	82.54	80.10	77.95	76.04	69.10	64.86	62.15	60.34
15,000	144.69	138.26	132.74	127.97	123.80	120.15	116.92	114.06	103.64	97.29	93.22	90.51
20,000	192.92	184.34	176.99	170.62	165.07	160.20	155.90	152.08	138.19	129.72	124.29	120.68
25,000	241.15	230.43	221.23	213.28	206.34	200.25	194.87	190.10	172.73	162.15	155.36	150.84
30,000	289.38	276.51	265.48	255.93	247.60	240.20	233.84	228.11	207.28	194.58	186.43	181.01
35,000	337.61	322.60	309.72	290.58	288.07	280.34	272.81	266.13	241.82	227.01	217.50	211.18
40,000	385.84	368.68	353.97	341.24	330.14	320.39	311.79	304.15	276.37	259.44	248.57	241.35
45,000	434.07	414.77	398.21	383.89	371.40	360.44	350.76	342.17	310.92	291.87	279.64	271.52
50,000	482.30	460.85	442.46	426.55	412.67	400.49	389.73	380.19	345.46	324.30	310.71	301.68
55,000	530.52	506.94	486.71	469.20	453.93	440.54	428.71	418.21	380.01	356.73	341.78	331.85
60,000	578.75	553.02	530.95	511.85	495.20	480.58	467.68	456.22	414.55	389.16	372.85	362.02
65,000	626.98	599.11	575.20	554.51	536.47	520.63	506.65	494.24	449.10	421.59	403.93	392.19
70,000	675.21	645.19	619.44	597.16	577.73	560.68	545.62	532.26	483.64	454.02	435.00	422.35
75,000	723.44	691.27	663.69	639.82	619.00	600.73	584.60	570.28	518.19	486.45	466.07	452.52
80,000	771.67	737.36	707.93	682.47	660.27	640.78	623.57	608.30	552.73	518.88	497.14	482.69
85,000	819.90	783.44	752.18	725.12	701.53	680.82	662.54	646.31	587.28	551.31	528.21	512.86
90,000	868.13	829.53	796.42	767.78	742.80	720.87	701.51	684.33	621.83	583.74	559.28	543.03
95,000	916.36	875.61	840.67	810.43	784.07	760.92	740.49	722.35	656.37	616.17	590.35	573.19
100,000	964.59	921.70	884.91	853.09	825.33	800.97	779.46	760.37	690.92	648.60	621.42	603.36
105,000	1012.81	967.78	929.16	895.74	866.60	841.02	818.43	798.39	725.46	681.03	652.49	633.53
110,000	1001.04	1013.87	973.41	938.39	907.86	881.07	857.41	836.41	760.01	713.46	683.56	663.70
115,000	1109.27	1059.95	1017.65	981.05	949.13	921.11	896.38	874.42	794.55	745.89	714.63	693.87
120,000	1157.50	1106.04	1061.90	1023.70	990.40	961.16	935.35	912.44	829.10	778.32	745.70	724.03
125,000	1205.73	1152.12	1106.14	1066.36	1031.66	1001.21	974.32	950.46	863.64	810.75	776.78	754.20
130,000	1253.96	1198.21	1150.39	1109.01	1072.93	1041.26	1013.30	988.48	898.19	843.18	807.85	784.37
135,000	1302.19	1244.29	1194.63	1151.66	1114.20	1081.31	1052.27	1026.50	932.74	875.61	838.92	814.54
140,000	1350.42	1290.38	1238.88	1194.32	1155.46	1121.36	1091.24	1064.51	967.28	908.04	869.99	844.70
145,000	1398.65	1336.46	1283.12	1236.97	1196.73	1161.40	1130.21	1102.53	1001.83	940.47	901.06	874.87
150,000	1446.88	1382.54	1327.37	1279.63	1237.99	1201.45	1169.19	1140.55	1036.37	972.90	932.13	905.04
155,000	1495.10	1428.63	1371.61	1322.28	1279.26	1241.50	1208.16	1178.57	1070.92	1005.33	963.20	935.21
160,000	1543.33	1474.71	1415.86	1364.93	1320.53	1281.55	1247.13	1216.59	1105.46	1037.76	994.27	965.38
165,000	1591.56	1520.80	1460.11	1407.59	1361.79	1321.60	1286.11	1254.61	1140.01	1070.19	1025.34	995.54
170,000	1639.79	1566.88	1504.35	1450.24	1403.06	1361.64	1325.08	1292.62	1174.55	1102.62	1056.41	1025.71
175,000	1688.02	1612.97	1548.60	1492.90	1444.33	1401.69	1364.05	1330.64	1209.10	1135.05	1087.48	1055.88
180,000	1736.25	1659.05	1592.84	1535.55	1485.59	1441.74	1403.02	1368.66	1243.65	1167.48	1118.55	1086.05
185,000	1784.48	1705.14	1637.09	1578.20	1526.86	1481.79	1442.00	1406.68	1278.19	1199.91	1149.63	1116.22
190,000	1832.71	1751.22	1681.33	1620.86	1568.13	1521.84	1480.97	1444.70	1312.74	1232.34	1180.70	1146.38
195,000	1880.94	1797.31	1725.58	1663.51	1609.39	1561.89	1519.94	1482.71	1347.28	1264.77	1211.77	1176.55
200,000	1929.17	1843.39	1769.82	1706.17	1650.66	1601.93	1558.91	1520.73	1381.83	1297.20	1242.84	1206.72
205,000	1977.39	1889.48	1814.07	1748.82	1691.92	1641.98	1597.89	1558.75	1416.37	1329.63	1273.91	1236.89
210,000	2025.62	1935.56	1858.31	1791.47	1733.19	1682.03	1636.86	1596.77	1450.92	1362.06	1304.98	1267.05
215,000	2073.85	1981.65	1902.56	1834.13	1774.46	1722.08	1675.83	1634.79	1485.46	1394.49	1336.05	1297.22
220,000	2122.08	2027.73	1946.81	1876.78	1815.72	1762.13	1714.81	1672.81	1520.01	1426.92	1367.12	1327.39
225,000	2170.31	2073.81	1991.05	1919.44	1856.99	1802.18	1753.78	1710.82	1554.56	1459.35	1398.19	1357.56
230,000	2218.54	2119.90	2035.30	1962.09	1898.26	1842.22	1792.75	1748.84	1589.10	1491.78	1429.26	1387.73
235,000	2266.77	2165.98	2079.54	2004.74	1939.52	1882.27	1831.72	1786.86	1623.65	1524.21	1460.33	1417.89
240,000	2315.00	2212.07	2123.79	2047.40	1980.79	1922.32	1870.70	1824.88	1658.19	1556.64	1491.40	1448.06
245,000	2363.23	2258.15	2168.03	2090.05	2022.06	1962.37	1909.67	1862.90	1692.74	1589.07	1522.48	1478.23
250,000	2411.46	2304.24	2212.28	2132.71	2063.32	2002.42	1948.64	1900.92	1727.28	1621.50	1553.55	1508.40
255,000	2459.68	2350.32	2256.52	2175.36	2104.59	2042.46	1987.61	1938.93	1761.83	1653.93	1584.62	1538.56
260,000	2507.91	2396.41	2300.77	2218.01	2145.85	2082.51	2026.59	1976.95	1796.37	1686.36	1615.69	1568.73
265,000	2556.14	2442.49	2345.02	2260.67	2187.12	2122.56	2065.56	2014.97	1830.92	1718.79	1646.76	1598.90
270,000	2604.37	2488.58	2389.26	2303.32	2228.39	2162.61	2104.53	2052.99	1865.47	1751.22	1677.83	1629.07
280,000	2700.83	2580.75	2477.75	2388.63	2310.92	2242.71	2182.48	2129.02	1934.56	1816.08	1739.97	1689.40
290,000	2797.29	2672.92	2566.24	2473.94	2393.45	2322.80	2260.42	2205.06	2003.65	1880.94	1802.11	1749.74
300,000	2893.75	2765.08	2654.73	2559.25	2475.98	2402.90	2338.37	2281.10	2072.74	1945.80	1864.25	1810.08

7.00%
MONTHLY AMORTIZING PAYMENTS

AMOUNT OF LOAN	NUMBER OF YEARS IN TERM											
	1	2	3	4	5	6	7	8	9	10	11	12
$ 50	4.33	2.24	1.55	1.20	1.00	0.86	0.76	0.69	0.63	0.59	0.55	0.52
100	8.66	4.48	3.09	2.40	1.99	1.71	1.51	1.37	1.26	1.17	1.09	1.03
200	17.31	8.96	6.18	4.79	3.97	3.41	3.02	2.73	2.51	2.33	2.18	2.06
300	25.96	13.44	9.27	7.19	5.95	5.12	4.53	4.10	3.76	3.49	3.27	3.09
400	34.62	17.91	12.36	9.58	7.93	6.82	6.04	5.46	5.01	4.65	4.36	4.12
500	43.27	22.39	15.44	11.98	9.91	8.53	7.55	6.82	6.26	5.81	5.45	5.15
600	51.92	26.87	18.53	14.37	11.89	10.23	9.06	8.19	7.51	6.97	6.54	6.18
700	60.57	31.35	21.62	16.77	13.87	11.94	10.57	9.55	8.76	8.13	7.62	7.20
800	69.23	35.82	24.71	19.16	15.85	13.64	12.08	10.91	10.01	9.29	8.71	8.23
900	77.88	40.30	27.79	21.56	17.83	15.35	13.59	12.28	11.26	10.45	9.80	9.26
1,000	86.53	44.78	30.88	23.95	19.81	17.05	15.10	13.64	12.51	11.62	10.89	10.29
2,000	173.06	89.55	61.76	47.90	39.61	34.10	30.19	27.27	25.02	23.23	21.77	20.57
3,000	259.59	134.32	92.64	71.84	59.41	51.15	45.28	40.91	37.52	34.84	32.66	30.86
4,000	346.11	179.10	123.51	95.79	79.21	68.20	60.38	54.54	50.03	46.45	43.54	41.14
5,000	432.64	223.87	154.39	119.74	99.01	85.25	75.47	68.17	62.54	58.06	54.43	51.42
6,000	519.17	268.64	185.27	143.68	118.81	102.30	90.56	81.81	75.04	69.67	65.31	61.71
7,000	605.69	313.41	216.14	167.63	138.61	119.35	105.65	95.44	87.55	81.28	76.19	71.99
8,000	692.22	358.19	247.02	191.57	158.41	136.40	120.75	109.07	100.06	92.89	87.08	82.28
9,000	778.75	402.96	277.90	215.52	178.22	153.45	135.84	122.71	112.56	104.50	97.96	92.56
10,000	865.27	447.73	308.78	239.47	198.02	170.50	150.93	136.34	125.07	116.11	108.85	102.84
15,000	1297.91	671.59	463.16	359.20	297.02	255.74	226.40	204.51	187.60	174.17	163.27	154.26
20,000	1730.54	895.46	617.55	478.93	396.03	340.99	301.86	272.68	250.13	232.22	217.69	205.68
25,000	2163.17	1119.32	771.93	598.66	495.03	426.23	377.32	340.85	312.66	290.28	272.11	257.10
30,000	2595.81	1343.18	926.32	718.39	594.04	511.48	452.79	409.02	375.19	348.33	326.53	308.52
35,000	3028.44	1567.05	1080.70	838.12	693.05	596.72	528.25	477.19	437.72	406.38	380.95	359.94
40,000	3461.07	1790.91	1235.09	957.85	792.05	681.97	603.71	545.35	500.26	464.44	435.37	411.36
45,000	3893.71	2014.77	1389.47	1077.59	891.06	767.21	679.18	613.52	562.79	522.49	489.79	462.78
50,000	4326.34	2238.63	1543.86	1197.32	990.06	852.46	754.64	681.69	625.32	580.55	544.21	514.20
55,000	4758.98	2462.50	1698.25	1317.05	1089.07	937.70	830.10	749.86	687.85	638.60	598.63	565.61
60,000	5191.61	2686.36	1852.63	1436.78	1188.08	1022.95	905.57	818.03	750.38	696.66	653.05	617.03
65,000	5624.24	2910.22	2007.02	1556.51	1287.08	1108.19	981.03	886.20	812.91	754.71	707.47	668.45
70,000	6056.88	3134.09	2161.40	1676.24	1386.09	1193.44	1056.49	954.37	875.44	812.76	761.89	719.87
75,000	6489.51	3357.95	2315.79	1795.97	1485.09	1278.68	1131.96	1022.53	937.98	870.82	816.31	771.29
80,000	6922.14	3581.81	2470.17	1915.70	1584.10	1363.93	1207.42	1090.70	1000.51	928.87	870.73	822.71
85,000	7354.78	3805.67	2624.56	2035.44	1683.11	1449.17	1282.88	1158.87	1063.04	986.93	925.15	874.13
90,000	7787.41	4029.54	2778.94	2155.17	1782.11	1534.42	1358.35	1227.04	1125.57	1044.98	979.57	925.55
95,000	8220.05	4253.40	2933.33	2274.90	1881.12	1619.66	1433.81	1295.21	1188.10	1103.04	1033.99	976.97
100,000	8652.68	4477.26	3087.71	2394.63	1980.12	1704.91	1509.27	1363.38	1250.63	1161.09	1088.42	1028.39
105,000	9085.31	4701.13	3242.10	2514.36	2079.13	1790.15	1584.74	1431.55	1313.16	1219.14	1142.84	1079.81
110,000	9517.95	4924.99	3396.49	2634.09	2178.14	1875.40	1660.20	1499.71	1375.70	1277.20	1197.26	1131.22
115,000	9950.58	5148.85	3550.87	2753.82	2277.14	1960.64	1735.66	1567.88	1438.23	1335.25	1251.68	1182.64
120,000	10383.21	5372.71	3705.26	2873.55	2376.15	2045.89	1811.13	1636.05	1500.76	1393.31	1306.10	1234.06
125,000	10815.85	5596.58	3859.64	2993.29	2475.15	2131.13	1886.59	1704.22	1563.29	1451.36	1360.52	1285.48
130,000	11248.48	5820.44	4014.03	3113.02	2574.16	2216.38	1962.05	1772.39	1625.82	1509.42	1414.94	1336.90
135,000	11681.12	6044.30	4168.41	3232.75	2673.17	2301.62	2037.52	1840.56	1688.35	1567.47	1469.36	1388.32
140,000	12113.75	6268.17	4322.80	3352.48	2772.17	2386.87	2112.98	1908.73	1750.88	1625.52	1523.78	1439.74
145,000	12546.38	6492.03	4477.18	3472.21	2871.18	2472.11	2188.44	1976.89	1813.42	1683.58	1578.20	1491.16
150,000	12979.02	6715.89	4631.57	3591.94	2970.18	2557.36	2263.91	2045.06	1875.95	1741.63	1632.62	1542.58
155,000	13411.65	6939.75	4785.96	3711.67	3069.19	2642.60	2339.37	2113.23	1938.48	1799.69	1687.04	1594.00
160,000	13844.28	7163.62	4940.34	3831.40	3168.20	2727.85	2414.83	2181.40	2001.01	1857.74	1741.46	1645.41
165,000	14276.92	7387.48	5094.73	3951.14	3267.20	2813.09	2490.30	2249.57	2063.54	1915.79	1795.88	1696.83
170,000	14709.55	7611.34	5249.11	4070.87	3366.21	2898.34	2565.76	2317.74	2126.07	1973.85	1850.30	1748.25
175,000	15142.19	7835.21	5403.50	4190.60	3465.21	2983.58	2641.22	2385.91	2188.60	2031.90	1904.72	1799.67
180,000	15574.82	8059.07	5557.88	4310.33	3564.22	3068.83	2716.69	2454.07	2251.13	2089.96	1959.14	1851.09
185,000	16007.45	8282.93	5712.27	4430.06	3663.23	3154.07	2792.15	2522.24	2313.67	2148.01	2013.56	1902.51
190,000	16440.09	8506.80	5866.65	4549.79	3762.23	3239.32	2867.61	2590.41	2376.20	2206.07	2067.98	1953.93
195,000	16872.72	8730.66	6021.04	4669.52	3861.24	3324.56	2943.08	2658.58	2438.73	2264.12	2122.40	2005.35
200,000	17305.35	8954.52	6175.42	4789.25	3960.24	3409.81	3018.54	2726.75	2501.26	2322.17	2176.83	2056.77
205,000	17737.99	9178.38	6329.81	4908.99	4059.25	3495.05	3094.00	2794.92	2563.79	2380.23	2231.25	2108.19
210,000	18170.62	9402.25	6484.20	5028.72	4158.26	3580.30	3169.47	2863.09	2626.32	2438.28	2285.67	2159.60
215,000	18603.26	9626.11	6638.58	5148.45	4257.26	3665.54	3244.93	2931.25	2688.85	2496.34	2340.09	2211.02
220,000	19035.89	9849.97	6792.97	5268.18	4356.27	3750.79	3320.39	2999.42	2751.39	2554.39	2394.51	2262.44
225,000	19468.52	10073.84	6947.35	5387.91	4455.27	3836.03	3395.86	3067.59	2813.92	2612.45	2448.93	2313.86
230,000	19901.16	10297.70	7101.74	5507.64	4554.28	3921.28	3471.32	3135.76	2876.45	2670.50	2503.35	2365.28
235,000	20333.79	10521.56	7256.12	5627.37	4653.29	4006.52	3546.78	3203.93	2938.98	2728.55	2557.77	2416.70
240,000	20766.42	10745.42	7410.51	5747.10	4752.29	4091.77	3622.25	3272.10	3001.51	2786.61	2612.19	2468.12
245,000	21199.06	10969.29	7564.89	5866.83	4851.30	4177.01	3697.71	3340.27	3064.04	2844.66	2666.61	2519.54
250,000	21631.69	11193.15	7719.28	5986.57	4950.30	4262.26	3773.17	3408.43	3126.57	2902.72	2721.03	2570.96
255,000	22064.33	11417.01	7873.66	6106.30	5049.31	4347.50	3848.64	3476.60	3189.11	2960.77	2775.45	2622.38
260,000	22496.96	11640.88	8028.05	6226.03	5148.32	4432.75	3924.10	3544.77	3251.64	3018.83	2829.87	2673.80
265,000	22929.59	11864.74	8182.44	6345.76	5247.32	4517.99	3999.57	3612.94	3314.17	3076.88	2884.29	2725.21
270,000	23362.23	12088.60	8336.82	6465.49	5346.33	4603.24	4075.03	3681.11	3376.70	3134.93	2938.71	2776.63
280,000	24227.49	12536.33	8645.59	6704.95	5544.34	4773.73	4225.96	3817.45	3501.76	3251.04	3047.55	2879.47
290,000	25092.76	12984.05	8954.36	6944.42	5742.35	4944.22	4376.88	3953.78	3626.83	3367.15	3156.39	2982.31
300,000	25958.03	13431.78	9263.13	7183.88	5940.36	5114.71	4527.81	4090.12	3751.89	3483.26	3265.24	3085.15

42

MONTHLY AMORTIZING PAYMENTS — 7.00%

AMOUNT OF LOAN	13	14	15	16	17	18	19	20	25	30	35	40
$ 50	0.49	0.47	0.45	0.44	0.42	0.41	0.40	0.39	0.36	0.34	0.32	0.32
100	0.98	0.94	0.90	0.87	0.84	0.82	0.80	0.78	0.71	0.67	0.64	0.63
200	1.96	1.88	1.80	1.74	1.68	1.64	1.59	1.56	1.42	1.34	1.28	1.25
300	2.94	2.81	2.70	2.61	2.52	2.45	2.39	2.33	2.13	2.00	1.92	1.87
400	3.92	3.75	3.60	3.47	3.36	3.27	3.18	3.11	2.83	2.67	2.56	2.49
500	4.90	4.68	4.50	4.34	4.20	4.08	3.98	3.88	3.54	3.33	3.20	3.11
600	5.87	5.62	5.40	5.21	5.04	4.90	4.77	4.66	4.25	4.00	3.84	3.73
700	6.85	6.55	6.30	6.08	5.88	5.71	5.56	5.43	4.95	4.66	4.48	4.36
800	7.83	7.49	7.20	6.94	6.72	6.53	6.36	6.21	5.66	5.33	5.12	4.98
900	8.81	8.42	8.09	7.81	7.56	7.34	7.15	6.98	6.37	5.99	5.75	5.60
1,000	9.79	9.36	8.99	8.68	8.40	8.16	7.95	7.76	7.07	6.66	6.39	6.22
2,000	19.57	18.71	17.98	17.35	16.80	16.32	15.89	15.51	14.14	13.31	12.78	12.43
3,000	29.35	28.07	26.97	26.02	25.19	24.47	23.83	23.26	21.21	19.96	19.17	18.65
4,000	39.13	37.42	35.96	34.69	33.59	32.63	31.77	31.02	28.28	26.62	25.56	24.86
5,000	48.91	46.78	44.95	43.37	41.99	40.78	39.71	38.77	35.34	33.27	31.95	31.08
6,000	58.69	56.13	53.93	52.04	50.38	48.94	47.66	46.52	42.41	39.92	38.34	37.29
7,000	68.47	65.48	62.92	60.71	58.78	57.09	55.60	54.28	49.48	46.58	44.72	43.51
8,000	78.25	74.84	71.91	69.38	67.18	65.25	63.54	62.03	56.55	53.23	51.11	49.72
9,000	88.03	84.19	80.90	78.05	75.57	73.40	71.48	69.78	63.62	59.88	57.50	55.93
10,000	97.81	93.55	89.89	86.73	83.97	81.56	79.42	77.53	70.68	66.54	63.89	62.15
15,000	146.72	140.32	134.83	130.09	125.95	122.33	119.13	116.30	106.02	99.80	95.83	93.22
20,000	195.62	187.09	179.77	173.45	167.94	163.11	158.84	155.06	141.36	133.07	127.78	124.29
25,000	244.52	233.86	224.71	216.81	209.92	203.88	198.55	193.83	176.70	166.33	159.72	155.36
30,000	293.43	280.63	269.65	260.17	251.90	244.66	238.26	232.59	212.04	199.60	191.66	186.43
35,000	342.33	327.40	314.59	303.53	293.89	285.43	277.97	271.36	247.38	232.86	223.60	217.51
40,000	391.23	374.17	359.54	346.89	335.87	326.21	317.68	310.12	282.72	266.13	255.55	248.58
45,000	440.14	420.94	404.48	390.25	377.85	366.98	357.39	348.89	318.06	299.39	287.49	270.65
50,000	489.04	467.71	449.42	433.61	419.84	407.76	397.10	387.65	353.39	332.66	319.43	310.72
55,000	537.95	514.48	494.36	476.97	461.82	448.53	436.81	426.42	388.73	365.92	351.38	341.79
60,000	586.85	561.25	539.30	520.33	503.80	489.31	476.52	465.18	424.07	399.19	383.32	372.86
65,000	635.75	608.02	584.24	563.69	545.78	530.08	516.23	503.95	459.41	432.45	415.26	403.94
70,000	684.66	654.79	629.18	607.05	587.77	570.86	555.94	542.71	494.75	465.72	447.20	435.01
75,000	733.56	701.56	674.13	650.41	629.75	611.63	595.65	581.48	530.09	498.98	479.15	466.08
80,000	782.46	748.33	719.07	693.77	671.73	652.41	635.36	620.24	565.43	532.25	511.09	497.15
85,000	831.37	795.10	764.01	737.13	713.72	693.18	675.07	659.01	600.77	565.51	543.03	528.22
90,000	880.27	841.87	808.95	780.49	755.70	733.96	714.78	697.77	636.11	598.78	574.98	559.29
95,000	929.18	888.64	853.89	823.85	797.68	774.73	754.49	736.54	671.45	632.04	606.92	590.36
100,000	978.08	935.41	898.83	867.21	839.67	815.51	794.20	775.30	706.79	665.31	638.86	621.44
105,000	1026.98	982.18	943.77	910.57	881.65	856.28	833.91	814.07	742.12	698.57	670.80	652.51
110,000	1075.89	1028.95	988.72	953.93	923.63	897.06	873.62	852.83	777.46	731.84	702.75	683.58
115,000	1124.79	1075.72	1033.66	997.29	965.61	937.83	913.33	891.60	812.80	765.10	734.69	714.65
120,000	1173.69	1122.49	1078.60	1040.65	1007.60	978.61	953.04	930.36	848.14	798.37	766.63	745.72
125,000	1222.60	1160.26	1100.04	1004.02	1049.58	1019.38	992.75	969.13	883.48	831.63	798.58	776.79
130,000	1271.50	1216.03	1168.48	1127.38	1091.56	1060.16	1032.46	1007.89	918.82	864.90	830.52	807.87
135,000	1320.41	1262.80	1213.42	1170.74	1133.55	1100.93	1072.16	1046.66	954.16	898.16	862.46	838.94
140,000	1369.31	1309.57	1258.36	1214.10	1175.53	1141.71	1111.87	1085.42	989.50	931.43	894.40	870.01
145,000	1418.21	1356.34	1303.31	1257.46	1217.51	1182.48	1151.58	1124.19	1024.83	964.69	926.35	901.08
150,000	1467.12	1403.11	1348.25	1300.82	1259.50	1223.26	1191.29	1162.95	1060.17	997.96	958.29	932.15
155,000	1516.02	1449.88	1393.19	1344.18	1301.48	1264.03	1231.00	1201.72	1095.51	1031.22	990.23	963.22
160,000	1564.92	1496.65	1438.13	1387.54	1343.46	1304.81	1270.71	1240.48	1130.85	1064.49	1022.18	994.30
165,000	1613.83	1543.42	1483.07	1430.90	1385.45	1345.58	1310.42	1279.25	1166.19	1097.75	1054.12	1025.37
170,000	1662.73	1590.19	1528.01	1474.26	1427.43	1386.36	1350.13	1318.01	1201.53	1131.02	1086.06	1056.44
175,000	1711.63	1636.96	1572.95	1517.62	1469.41	1427.13	1389.84	1356.78	1236.87	1164.28	1118.00	1087.51
180,000	1760.54	1683.73	1617.90	1560.98	1511.39	1467.91	1429.55	1395.54	1272.21	1197.55	1149.95	1118.58
185,000	1809.44	1730.50	1662.84	1604.34	1553.38	1508.68	1469.26	1434.31	1307.55	1230.81	1181.89	1149.65
190,000	1858.35	1777.27	1707.78	1647.70	1595.36	1549.46	1508.97	1473.07	1342.89	1264.08	1213.83	1180.72
195,000	1907.25	1824.04	1752.72	1691.06	1637.34	1590.23	1548.68	1511.84	1378.22	1297.34	1245.77	1211.80
200,000	1956.15	1870.81	1797.66	1734.42	1679.33	1631.01	1588.39	1550.60	1413.56	1330.61	1277.72	1242.87
205,000	2005.06	1917.58	1842.60	1777.78	1721.31	1671.78	1628.10	1589.37	1448.90	1363.88	1309.66	1273.94
210,000	2053.96	1964.35	1887.54	1821.14	1763.29	1712.56	1667.81	1628.13	1484.24	1397.14	1341.60	1305.01
215,000	2102.86	2011.12	1932.49	1864.50	1805.28	1753.33	1707.52	1666.90	1519.58	1430.41	1373.55	1336.08
220,000	2151.77	2057.89	1977.43	1907.86	1847.26	1794.11	1747.23	1705.66	1554.92	1463.67	1405.49	1367.15
225,000	2200.67	2104.66	2022.37	1951.22	1889.24	1834.88	1786.94	1744.43	1590.26	1496.94	1437.43	1398.23
230,000	2249.58	2151.43	2067.31	1994.58	1931.22	1875.66	1826.65	1783.19	1625.60	1530.20	1469.37	1429.30
235,000	2298.48	2198.20	2112.25	2037.94	1973.21	1916.44	1866.36	1821.96	1660.94	1563.47	1501.32	1460.37
240,000	2347.38	2244.97	2157.19	2081.30	2015.19	1957.21	1906.07	1860.72	1696.28	1596.73	1533.26	1491.44
245,000	2396.29	2291.74	2202.13	2124.66	2057.17	1997.99	1945.78	1899.49	1731.61	1630.00	1565.20	1522.51
250,000	2445.19	2338.51	2247.08	2168.03	2099.16	2038.76	1985.49	1938.25	1766.95	1663.26	1597.15	1553.58
255,000	2494.09	2385.28	2292.02	2211.39	2141.14	2079.54	2025.20	1977.02	1802.29	1696.53	1629.09	1584.65
260,000	2543.00	2432.05	2336.96	2254.75	2183.12	2120.31	2064.91	2015.78	1837.63	1729.79	1661.03	1615.73
265,000	2591.90	2478.82	2381.90	2298.11	2225.11	2161.09	2104.61	2054.55	1872.97	1763.06	1692.97	1646.80
270,000	2640.81	2525.59	2426.84	2341.47	2267.09	2201.86	2144.32	2093.31	1908.31	1796.32	1724.92	1677.87
280,000	2738.61	2619.13	2516.72	2428.19	2351.05	2283.41	2223.74	2170.84	1978.99	1862.85	1788.80	1740.01
290,000	2836.42	2712.67	2606.61	2514.91	2435.02	2364.96	2303.16	2248.37	2049.66	1929.38	1852.69	1802.16
300,000	2934.23	2806.21	2696.49	2601.63	2518.99	2446.51	2382.58	2325.90	2120.34	1995.91	1916.57	1864.30

43

MONTHLY AMORTIZING PAYMENTS

AMOUNT OF LOAN	NUMBER OF YEARS IN TERM											
	1	2	3	4	5	6	7	8	9	10	11	12
$ 50	4.34	2.25	1.55	1.21	1.00	0.86	0.77	0.69	0.64	0.59	0.56	0.53
100	8.67	4.49	3.10	2.41	2.00	1.72	1.53	1.38	1.27	1.18	1.11	1.05
200	17.33	8.98	6.20	4.82	3.99	3.44	3.05	2.76	2.53	2.35	2.21	2.09
300	26.00	13.47	9.30	7.22	5.98	5.16	4.57	4.13	3.79	3.53	3.31	3.13
400	34.66	17.96	12.40	9.63	7.97	6.87	6.09	5.51	5.06	4.70	4.41	4.17
500	43.33	22.45	15.50	12.04	9.96	8.59	7.61	6.88	6.32	5.88	5.51	5.21
600	51.99	26.94	18.60	14.44	11.96	10.31	9.13	8.26	7.58	7.05	6.61	6.26
700	60.65	31.43	21.70	16.85	13.95	12.02	10.66	9.64	8.85	8.22	7.72	7.30
800	69.32	35.91	24.80	19.25	15.94	13.74	12.18	11.01	10.11	9.40	8.82	8.34
900	77.98	40.40	27.90	21.66	17.93	15.46	13.70	12.39	11.37	10.57	9.92	9.38
1,000	86.65	44.89	31.00	24.07	19.92	17.17	15.22	13.76	12.64	11.75	11.02	10.42
2,000	173.29	89.78	61.99	48.13	39.84	34.34	30.44	27.52	25.27	23.49	22.04	20.84
3,000	259.93	134.66	92.98	72.19	59.76	51.51	45.65	41.28	37.90	35.23	33.05	31.26
4,000	346.57	179.55	123.97	96.25	79.68	68.68	60.87	55.04	50.54	46.97	44.07	41.68
5,000	433.22	224.44	154.96	120.32	99.60	85.85	76.08	68.80	63.17	58.71	55.08	52.09
6,000	519.86	269.32	185.95	144.38	119.52	103.02	91.30	82.56	75.80	70.45	66.10	62.51
7,000	606.50	314.21	216.95	168.44	139.44	120.19	106.51	96.31	88.44	82.19	77.11	72.93
8,000	693.14	359.09	247.94	192.50	159.36	137.36	121.73	110.07	101.07	93.93	88.13	83.35
9,000	779.78	403.98	278.93	216.57	179.28	154.53	136.94	123.83	113.70	105.67	99.15	93.76
10,000	866.43	448.87	309.92	240.63	199.20	171.70	152.16	137.59	126.34	117.41	110.16	104.18
15,000	1299.64	673.30	464.88	360.94	298.80	257.54	228.23	206.38	189.50	176.11	165.24	156.27
20,000	1732.85	897.73	619.84	481.25	398.39	343.39	304.31	275.17	252.67	234.81	220.32	208.36
25,000	2166.06	1122.16	774.79	601.57	497.99	429.24	380.38	343.97	315.84	293.51	275.40	260.44
30,000	2599.27	1346.59	929.75	721.88	597.59	515.08	456.46	412.76	379.00	352.21	330.47	312.53
35,000	3032.48	1571.02	1084.71	842.19	697.18	600.93	532.54	481.55	442.17	410.91	385.55	364.62
40,000	3465.69	1795.45	1239.67	962.50	796.78	686.78	608.61	550.34	505.34	469.61	440.63	416.71
45,000	3898.90	2019.88	1394.62	1082.81	896.38	772.62	684.69	619.14	568.50	528.31	495.71	468.80
50,000	4332.11	2244.31	1549.58	1203.13	995.97	858.47	760.76	687.93	631.67	587.01	550.79	520.88
55,000	4765.32	2468.74	1704.54	1323.44	1095.57	944.32	836.84	756.72	694.84	645.71	605.86	572.97
60,000	5198.53	2693.17	1859.50	1443.75	1195.17	1030.16	912.92	825.51	758.00	704.41	660.94	625.06
65,000	5631.74	2917.60	2014.45	1564.06	1294.76	1116.01	988.99	894.30	821.17	763.11	716.02	677.15
70,000	6064.95	3142.03	2169.41	1684.37	1394.36	1201.86	1065.07	963.10	884.33	821.81	771.10	729.23
75,000	6498.16	3366.46	2324.37	1804.69	1493.96	1287.70	1141.14	1031.89	947.50	880.51	826.18	781.32
80,000	6931.37	3590.89	2479.33	1925.00	1593.55	1373.55	1217.22	1100.68	1010.67	939.21	881.25	833.41
85,000	7364.58	3815.32	2634.28	2045.31	1693.15	1459.40	1293.30	1169.47	1073.83	997.91	936.33	885.50
90,000	7797.79	4039.75	2789.24	2165.62	1792.75	1545.24	1369.37	1238.27	1137.00	1056.61	991.41	937.59
95,000	8231.00	4264.18	2944.20	2285.93	1892.34	1631.09	1445.45	1307.06	1200.17	1115.31	1046.49	989.67
100,000	8664.21	4488.61	3099.16	2406.25	1991.94	1716.94	1521.52	1375.85	1263.33	1174.02	1101.57	1041.76
105,000	9097.42	4713.04	3254.12	2526.56	2091.54	1802.78	1597.60	1444.64	1326.50	1232.72	1156.64	1093.85
110,000	9530.63	4937.42	3409.07	2646.87	2191.13	1888.63	1673.68	1513.44	1389.67	1291.42	1211.72	1145.94
115,000	9963.84	5161.90	3564.03	2767.18	2290.73	1974.48	1749.75	1582.23	1452.83	1350.12	1266.80	1198.02
120,000	10397.05	5386.33	3718.99	2887.49	2390.33	2060.32	1825.83	1651.02	1516.00	1408.82	1321.88	1250.11
125,000	10830.26	5610.76	3873.95	3007.81	2489.93	2146.17	1901.90	1719.81	1579.16	1467.52	1376.96	1302.20
130,000	11263.47	5835.19	4028.90	3128.12	2589.52	2232.01	1977.98	1788.60	1642.33	1526.22	1432.03	1354.29
135,000	11696.68	6059.62	4183.86	3248.43	2689.12	2317.86	2054.05	1857.40	1705.50	1584.92	1487.11	1406.38
140,000	12129.89	6284.05	4338.82	3368.74	2788.72	2403.71	2130.13	1926.19	1768.66	1643.62	1542.19	1458.46
145,000	12563.10	6508.48	4493.78	3489.05	2888.31	2489.55	2206.21	1994.98	1831.83	1702.32	1597.27	1510.55
150,000	12996.31	6732.91	4648.73	3609.37	2987.91	2575.40	2282.28	2063.77	1895.00	1761.02	1652.35	1562.64
155,000	13429.52	6957.34	4803.69	3729.68	3087.51	2661.25	2358.36	2132.57	1958.16	1819.72	1707.42	1614.73
160,000	13862.73	7181.77	4958.65	3849.99	3187.10	2747.09	2434.43	2201.36	2021.33	1878.42	1762.50	1666.81
165,000	14295.94	7406.20	5113.61	3970.30	3286.70	2832.94	2510.51	2270.15	2084.50	1937.12	1817.58	1718.90
170,000	14729.15	7630.63	5268.56	4090.61	3386.30	2918.79	2586.59	2338.94	2147.66	1995.82	1872.66	1770.99
175,000	15162.36	7855.06	5423.52	4210.93	3485.89	3004.63	2662.66	2407.74	2210.83	2054.52	1927.74	1823.08
180,000	15595.57	8079.49	5578.48	4331.24	3585.49	3090.48	2738.74	2476.53	2273.99	2113.22	1982.81	1875.17
185,000	16028.78	8303.92	5733.44	4451.55	3685.09	3176.33	2814.81	2545.32	2337.16	2171.92	2037.89	1927.25
190,000	16461.99	8528.35	5888.40	4571.86	3784.68	3262.17	2890.89	2614.11	2400.33	2230.62	2092.97	1979.34
195,000	16895.20	8752.78	6043.35	4692.17	3884.28	3348.02	2966.97	2682.90	2463.49	2289.33	2148.05	2031.43
200,000	17328.41	8977.21	6198.31	4812.49	3983.88	3433.87	3043.04	2751.70	2526.66	2348.03	2203.13	2083.52
205,000	17761.62	9201.64	6353.27	4932.80	4083.47	3519.71	3119.12	2820.49	2589.83	2406.73	2258.20	2135.60
210,000	18194.83	9426.07	6508.23	5053.11	4183.07	3605.56	3195.19	2889.28	2652.99	2465.43	2313.28	2187.69
215,000	18628.04	9650.50	6663.18	5173.42	4282.67	3691.41	3271.27	2958.07	2716.16	2524.13	2368.36	2239.78
220,000	19061.25	9874.93	6818.14	5293.73	4382.26	3777.25	3347.35	3026.87	2779.33	2582.83	2423.44	2291.87
225,000	19494.46	10099.36	6973.10	5414.05	4481.86	3863.10	3423.42	3095.66	2842.49	2641.53	2478.52	2343.96
230,000	19927.67	10323.79	7128.06	5534.36	4581.46	3948.95	3499.50	3164.45	2905.66	2700.23	2533.60	2396.04
235,000	20360.88	10548.22	7283.01	5654.67	4681.05	4034.79	3575.57	3233.24	2968.82	2758.93	2588.67	2448.13
240,000	20794.09	10772.65	7437.97	5774.98	4780.65	4120.64	3651.65	3302.04	3031.99	2817.63	2643.75	2500.22
245,000	21227.30	10997.08	7592.93	5895.29	4880.25	4206.49	3727.73	3370.83	3095.16	2876.33	2698.83	2552.31
250,000	21660.51	11221.51	7747.89	6015.61	4979.85	4292.33	3803.80	3439.62	3158.32	2935.03	2753.91	2604.39
255,000	22093.72	11445.94	7902.84	6135.92	5079.44	4378.18	3879.88	3508.41	3221.49	2993.73	2808.99	2656.48
260,000	22526.94	11670.37	8057.80	6256.23	5179.04	4464.02	3955.95	3577.20	3284.66	3052.43	2864.06	2708.57
265,000	22960.15	11894.80	8212.76	6376.54	5278.64	4549.87	4032.03	3646.00	3347.82	3111.13	2919.14	2760.66
270,000	23393.36	12119.23	8367.72	6496.85	5378.23	4635.72	4108.10	3714.79	3410.99	3169.83	2974.22	2812.75
280,000	24259.78	12568.09	8677.63	6737.48	5577.43	4807.41	4260.26	3852.37	3537.33	3287.23	3084.38	2916.92
290,000	25126.20	13016.95	8987.55	6978.10	5776.62	4979.10	4412.41	3989.96	3663.65	3404.64	3194.53	3021.10
300,000	25992.62	13465.81	9297.46	7218.73	5975.81	5150.80	4564.56	4127.54	3789.99	3522.04	3304.69	3125.27

MONTHLY AMORTIZING PAYMENTS 7.25%

AMOUNT OF LOAN	NUMBER OF YEARS IN TERM											
	13	14	15	16	17	18	19	20	25	30	35	40
$ 50	0.50	0.48	0.46	0.45	0.43	0.42	0.41	0.40	0.37	0.35	0.33	0.32
100	1.00	0.95	0.92	0.89	0.86	0.84	0.81	0.80	0.73	0.69	0.66	0.64
200	1.99	1.90	1.83	1.77	1.71	1.67	1.62	1.59	1.45	1.37	1.32	1.28
300	2.98	2.85	2.74	2.65	2.57	2.50	2.43	2.38	2.17	2.05	1.97	1.92
400	3.97	3.80	3.66	3.53	3.42	3.33	3.24	3.17	2.90	2.73	2.63	2.56
500	4.96	4.75	4.57	4.41	4.28	4.16	4.05	3.96	3.62	3.42	3.29	3.20
600	5.96	5.70	5.48	5.29	5.13	4.99	4.86	4.75	4.34	4.10	3.94	3.84
700	6.95	6.65	6.40	6.18	5.98	5.82	5.67	5.54	5.06	4.78	4.60	4.48
800	7.94	7.60	7.31	7.06	6.84	6.65	6.48	6.33	5.79	5.46	5.26	5.12
900	8.93	8.55	8.22	7.94	7.69	7.48	7.29	7.12	6.51	6.14	5.91	5.76
1,000	9.92	9.50	9.13	8.82	8.55	8.31	8.10	7.91	7.23	6.83	6.57	6.40
2,000	19.84	18.99	18.26	17.63	17.09	16.61	16.19	15.81	14.46	13.65	13.13	12.80
3,000	29.76	28.48	27.39	26.45	25.63	24.91	24.28	23.72	21.69	20.47	19.70	19.20
4,000	39.67	37.97	36.52	35.26	34.17	33.21	32.37	31.62	28.92	27.29	26.26	25.59
5,000	49.59	47.47	45.65	44.08	42.71	41.51	40.46	39.52	36.15	34.11	32.83	31.99
6,000	59.51	56.96	54.78	52.89	51.25	49.82	48.55	47.43	43.37	40.94	39.39	38.39
7,000	69.42	66.45	63.91	61.71	59.79	58.12	56.64	55.33	50.60	47.76	45.96	44.78
8,000	79.34	75.94	73.03	70.52	68.33	66.42	64.73	63.24	57.83	54.58	52.52	51.18
9,000	89.26	85.43	82.16	79.34	76.88	74.72	72.82	71.14	65.06	61.40	59.09	57.58
10,000	99.17	94.93	91.29	88.15	85.42	83.02	80.91	79.04	72.29	68.22	65.65	63.97
15,000	148.76	142.39	136.93	132.22	128.12	124.53	121.37	118.56	108.43	102.33	98.48	95.96
20,000	198.34	189.85	182.58	176.30	170.83	166.04	161.82	158.08	144.57	136.44	131.30	127.94
25,000	247.92	237.31	228.22	220.37	213.54	207.55	202.27	197.60	180.71	170.55	164.12	159.92
30,000	297.51	284.77	273.86	264.44	256.24	249.06	242.73	237.12	216.85	204.66	196.95	191.91
35,000	347.09	332.23	319.51	308.52	298.95	290.57	283.18	276.64	252.99	238.77	229.77	223.89
40,000	396.67	379.69	365.15	352.59	341.65	332.07	323.63	316.16	289.13	272.88	262.59	255.87
45,000	446.26	427.15	410.79	396.66	384.36	373.58	364.09	355.67	325.27	306.98	295.42	287.86
50,000	495.84	474.61	456.44	440.73	427.07	415.09	404.54	395.19	361.41	341.09	328.24	319.84
55,000	545.42	522.07	502.08	484.81	469.77	456.60	444.99	434.71	397.55	375.20	361.06	351.82
60,000	595.01	569.54	547.72	528.88	512.48	498.11	485.45	474.23	433.69	409.31	393.89	383.81
65,000	644.59	617.00	593.37	572.95	555.18	539.62	525.90	513.75	469.83	443.42	426.71	415.79
70,000	694.17	664.46	639.01	617.03	597.89	581.13	566.35	553.27	505.97	477.53	459.53	447.78
75,000	743.76	711.92	684.65	661.10	640.60	622.63	606.81	592.79	542.11	511.64	492.36	479.76
80,000	793.34	759.38	730.30	705.17	683.30	664.14	647.26	632.31	578.25	545.75	525.18	511.74
85,000	842.93	806.84	775.94	749.24	726.01	705.65	687.71	671.82	614.39	579.85	558.00	543.73
90,000	892.51	854.30	821.58	793.32	768.71	747.16	728.17	711.34	650.53	613.96	590.83	575.71
95,000	942.09	901.76	867.22	837.39	811.42	788.67	768.62	750.86	686.67	648.07	623.65	607.69
100,000	991.68	949.22	912.87	881.46	854.13	830.18	809.07	790.38	722.81	682.18	656.47	639.68
105,000	1041.26	996.68	958.51	925.54	896.83	871.69	849.53	829.90	758.95	716.29	689.30	671.66
110,000	1090.84	1044.14	1004.15	969.61	939.54	913.19	889.98	869.42	795.09	750.40	722.12	703.64
115,000	1140.43	1091.61	1049.80	1013.68	982.25	954.70	930.43	908.94	831.23	784.51	754.94	735.63
120,000	1190.01	1139.07	1095.44	1057.75	1024.95	996.21	970.89	948.46	867.37	818.62	787.77	767.61
125,000	1239.59	1186.53	1141.08	1101.83	1067.66	1037.72	1011.34	987.97	903.51	852.73	820.59	799.59
130,000	1289.18	1233.99	1186.73	1145.90	1110.36	1079.23	1051.79	1027.49	939.65	886.83	853.41	831.58
135,000	1338.76	1281.45	1232.37	1189.97	1153.07	1120.74	1092.25	1067.01	975.79	920.94	886.24	863.56
140,000	1388.34	1328.91	1278.01	1234.05	1195.78	1162.25	1132.70	1106.53	1011.93	955.05	919.06	895.55
145,000	1437.93	1376.37	1323.66	1278.12	1238.48	1203.75	1173.15	1146.05	1048.07	989.16	951.88	927.53
150,000	1487.51	1423.83	1369.30	1322.19	1281.19	1245.26	1213.61	1185.57	1084.22	1023.27	984.71	959.51
155,000	1537.10	1471.29	1414.94	1366.26	1323.89	1286.77	1254.06	1225.09	1120.36	1057.38	1017.53	991.50
160,000	1586.68	1518.75	1460.59	1410.34	1366.60	1328.28	1294.51	1264.61	1156.50	1091.49	1050.35	1023.48
165,000	1636.26	1566.21	1506.23	1454.41	1409.31	1369.79	1334.97	1304.13	1192.64	1125.60	1083.18	1055.46
170,000	1685.85	1613.67	1551.87	1498.48	1452.01	1411.30	1375.42	1343.64	1228.78	1159.70	1116.00	1087.45
175,000	1735.43	1661.14	1597.52	1542.56	1494.72	1452.81	1415.87	1383.16	1264.92	1193.81	1148.82	1119.43
180,000	1785.01	1708.60	1643.16	1586.63	1537.42	1494.31	1456.33	1422.68	1301.06	1227.92	1181.65	1151.41
185,000	1834.60	1756.06	1688.80	1630.70	1580.13	1535.82	1496.78	1462.20	1337.20	1262.03	1214.47	1183.40
190,000	1884.18	1803.52	1734.44	1674.77	1622.84	1577.33	1537.23	1501.72	1373.34	1296.14	1247.29	1215.38
195,000	1933.76	1850.98	1780.09	1718.85	1665.54	1618.84	1577.69	1541.24	1409.48	1330.25	1280.12	1247.37
200,000	1983.35	1898.44	1825.73	1762.92	1708.25	1660.35	1618.14	1580.76	1445.62	1364.36	1312.94	1279.35
205,000	2032.93	1945.90	1871.37	1806.99	1750.96	1701.86	1658.59	1620.28	1481.76	1398.47	1345.76	1311.33
210,000	2082.51	1993.36	1917.02	1851.07	1793.66	1743.37	1699.05	1659.79	1517.90	1432.58	1378.59	1343.32
215,000	2132.10	2040.82	1962.66	1895.14	1836.37	1784.88	1739.50	1699.31	1554.04	1466.68	1411.41	1375.30
220,000	2181.68	2088.28	2008.30	1939.21	1879.07	1826.38	1779.95	1738.83	1590.18	1500.79	1444.23	1407.28
225,000	2231.26	2135.74	2053.95	1983.28	1921.78	1867.89	1820.41	1778.35	1626.32	1534.90	1477.06	1439.27
230,000	2280.85	2183.21	2099.59	2027.36	1964.49	1909.40	1860.86	1817.87	1662.46	1569.01	1509.88	1471.25
235,000	2330.43	2230.67	2145.23	2071.43	2007.19	1950.91	1901.31	1857.39	1698.60	1603.12	1542.70	1503.23
240,000	2380.02	2278.13	2190.88	2115.50	2049.90	1992.42	1941.77	1896.91	1734.74	1637.23	1575.53	1535.22
245,000	2429.60	2325.59	2236.52	2159.58	2092.60	2033.93	1982.22	1936.43	1770.88	1671.34	1608.35	1567.20
250,000	2479.18	2373.05	2282.16	2203.65	2135.31	2075.44	2022.67	1975.94	1807.02	1705.45	1641.17	1599.18
255,000	2528.77	2420.51	2327.81	2247.72	2178.02	2116.94	2063.13	2015.46	1843.16	1739.55	1674.00	1631.17
260,000	2578.35	2467.97	2373.45	2291.79	2220.72	2158.45	2103.58	2054.98	1879.30	1773.66	1706.82	1663.15
265,000	2627.93	2515.43	2419.09	2335.87	2263.43	2199.96	2144.03	2094.50	1915.44	1807.77	1739.64	1695.14
270,000	2677.52	2562.89	2464.73	2379.94	2306.13	2241.47	2184.49	2134.02	1951.58	1841.88	1772.47	1727.12
280,000	2776.68	2657.81	2556.02	2468.09	2391.55	2324.49	2265.39	2213.06	2023.86	1910.10	1838.11	1791.09
290,000	2875.85	2752.74	2647.31	2556.23	2476.96	2407.50	2346.30	2292.10	2096.14	1978.32	1903.76	1855.05
300,000	2975.02	2847.66	2738.59	2644.38	2562.37	2490.52	2427.21	2371.13	2168.43	2046.53	1969.41	1919.02

45

7.50%　　MONTHLY AMORTIZING PAYMENTS

AMOUNT OF LOAN	NUMBER OF YEARS IN TERM											
	1	2	3	4	5	6	7	8	9	10	11	12
$ 50	4.34	2.25	1.56	1.21	1.01	0.87	0.77	0.70	0.64	0.60	0.56	0.53
100	8.68	4.50	3.12	2.42	2.01	1.73	1.54	1.39	1.28	1.19	1.12	1.06
200	17.36	9.00	6.23	4.84	4.01	3.46	3.07	2.78	2.56	2.38	2.23	2.12
300	26.03	13.50	9.34	7.26	6.02	5.19	4.61	4.17	3.83	3.57	3.35	3.17
400	34.71	18.00	12.45	9.68	8.02	6.92	6.14	5.56	5.11	4.75	4.46	4.23
500	43.38	22.50	15.56	12.09	10.02	8.65	7.67	6.95	6.39	5.94	5.58	5.28
600	52.06	27.00	18.67	14.51	12.03	10.38	9.21	8.34	7.66	7.13	6.69	6.34
700	60.74	31.50	21.78	16.93	14.03	12.11	10.74	9.72	8.94	8.31	7.81	7.39
800	69.41	36.00	24.89	19.35	16.04	13.84	12.28	11.11	10.21	9.50	8.92	8.45
900	78.09	40.50	28.00	21.77	18.04	15.57	13.81	12.50	11.49	10.69	10.04	9.50
1,000	86.76	45.00	31.11	24.18	20.04	17.30	15.34	13.89	12.77	11.88	11.15	10.56
2,000	173.52	90.00	62.22	48.36	40.08	34.59	30.68	27.77	25.53	23.75	22.30	21.11
3,000	260.28	135.00	93.32	72.54	60.12	51.88	46.02	41.66	38.29	35.62	33.45	31.66
4,000	347.03	180.00	124.43	96.72	80.16	69.17	61.36	55.54	51.05	47.49	44.60	42.21
5,000	433.79	225.00	155.54	120.90	100.19	86.46	76.70	69.42	63.81	59.36	55.75	52.77
6,000	520.55	270.00	186.64	145.08	120.23	103.75	92.03	83.31	76.57	71.23	66.89	63.32
7,000	607.31	315.00	217.75	169.26	140.27	121.04	107.37	97.19	89.33	83.10	78.04	73.87
8,000	694.06	360.00	248.85	193.44	160.31	138.33	122.71	111.08	102.09	94.97	89.19	84.42
9,000	780.82	405.00	279.96	217.62	180.35	155.62	138.05	124.96	114.85	106.84	100.34	94.98
10,000	867.58	450.00	311.07	241.79	200.38	172.91	153.39	138.84	127.62	118.71	111.49	105.53
15,000	1301.37	675.00	466.60	362.69	300.57	259.36	230.08	208.26	191.42	178.06	167.23	158.29
20,000	1735.15	900.00	622.13	483.58	400.76	345.81	306.77	277.68	255.23	237.41	222.97	211.05
25,000	2168.94	1124.99	777.66	604.48	500.95	432.26	383.46	347.10	319.03	296.76	278.71	263.81
30,000	2602.73	1349.99	933.19	725.37	601.14	518.71	460.15	416.52	382.84	356.11	334.45	316.57
35,000	3036.51	1574.99	1088.72	846.27	701.33	605.16	536.84	485.94	446.64	415.46	390.19	369.33
40,000	3470.30	1799.99	1244.25	967.16	801.52	691.61	613.54	555.36	510.45	474.81	445.93	422.10
45,000	3904.09	2024.99	1399.78	1088.06	901.71	778.06	690.23	624.78	574.25	534.16	501.67	474.86
50,000	4337.88	2249.98	1555.32	1208.95	1001.90	864.51	766.92	694.20	638.06	593.51	557.41	527.62
55,000	4771.66	2474.98	1710.85	1329.84	1102.09	950.96	843.61	763.62	701.86	652.86	613.15	580.38
60,000	5205.45	2699.98	1866.38	1450.74	1202.28	1037.41	920.30	833.04	765.67	712.22	668.89	633.14
65,000	5639.24	2924.98	2021.91	1571.63	1302.47	1123.86	996.99	902.46	829.47	771.57	724.63	685.90
70,000	6073.02	3149.98	2177.44	1692.53	1402.66	1210.31	1073.68	971.88	893.28	830.92	780.37	738.66
75,000	6506.81	3374.97	2332.97	1813.42	1502.85	1296.76	1150.38	1041.30	957.08	890.27	836.11	791.42
80,000	6940.60	3599.97	2488.50	1934.32	1603.04	1383.21	1227.07	1110.71	1020.89	949.62	891.85	844.19
85,000	7374.39	3824.97	2644.03	2055.21	1703.23	1469.66	1303.76	1180.13	1084.69	1008.97	947.59	896.95
90,000	7808.17	4049.97	2799.56	2176.11	1803.42	1556.12	1380.45	1249.55	1148.50	1068.32	1003.33	949.71
95,000	8241.96	4274.97	2955.10	2297.00	1903.61	1642.57	1457.14	1318.97	1212.30	1127.67	1059.07	1002.47
100,000	8675.75	4499.96	3110.63	2417.90	2003.80	1729.02	1533.83	1388.39	1276.11	1187.02	1114.81	1055.23
105,000	9109.53	4724.96	3266.16	2538.79	2103.99	1815.47	1610.52	1457.81	1339.91	1246.37	1170.55	1107.99
110,000	9543.32	4949.96	3421.69	2659.68	2204.18	1901.92	1687.22	1527.23	1403.72	1305.72	1226.29	1160.75
115,000	9977.11	5174.96	3577.22	2780.58	2304.37	1988.37	1763.91	1596.65	1467.52	1365.08	1282.03	1213.52
120,000	10410.90	5399.96	3732.75	2901.47	2404.56	2074.82	1840.60	1666.07	1531.33	1424.43	1337.77	1266.28
125,000	10844.68	5624.95	3888.28	3022.37	2504.75	2161.27	1917.29	1735.49	1595.13	1483.78	1393.51	1319.04
130,000	11278.47	5849.95	4043.81	3143.26	2604.94	2247.72	1993.98	1804.91	1658.94	1543.13	1449.25	1371.80
135,000	11712.26	6074.95	4199.34	3264.16	2705.13	2334.17	2070.67	1874.33	1722.74	1602.48	1504.99	1424.56
140,000	12146.04	6299.95	4354.88	3385.05	2805.32	2420.62	2147.36	1943.75	1786.55	1661.83	1560.73	1477.32
145,000	12579.83	6524.95	4510.41	3505.95	2905.51	2507.07	2224.05	2013.17	1850.35	1721.18	1616.47	1530.08
150,000	13013.62	6749.94	4665.94	3626.84	3005.70	2593.52	2300.75	2082.59	1914.16	1780.53	1672.21	1582.84
155,000	13447.40	6974.94	4821.47	3747.73	3105.89	2679.97	2377.44	2152.00	1977.96	1839.88	1727.95	1635.61
160,000	13881.19	7199.94	4977.00	3868.63	3206.08	2766.42	2454.13	2221.42	2041.77	1899.23	1783.69	1688.37
165,000	14314.98	7424.94	5132.53	3989.52	3306.27	2852.87	2530.82	2290.84	2105.57	1958.58	1839.43	1741.13
170,000	14748.77	7649.94	5288.06	4110.42	3406.46	2939.32	2607.51	2360.26	2169.38	2017.94	1895.17	1793.89
175,000	15182.55	7874.93	5443.59	4231.31	3506.65	3025.77	2684.20	2429.68	2233.18	2077.29	1950.91	1846.65
180,000	15616.34	8099.93	5599.12	4352.21	3606.84	3112.23	2760.89	2499.10	2296.99	2136.64	2006.65	1899.41
185,000	16050.13	8324.93	5754.66	4473.10	3707.03	3198.68	2837.59	2568.52	2360.79	2195.99	2062.39	1952.17
190,000	16483.91	8549.93	5910.19	4594.00	3807.22	3285.13	2914.28	2637.94	2424.60	2255.34	2118.13	2004.93
195,000	16917.70	8774.93	6065.72	4714.89	3907.40	3371.58	2990.97	2707.36	2488.40	2314.69	2173.87	2057.70
200,000	17351.49	8999.92	6221.25	4835.79	4007.59	3458.03	3067.66	2776.78	2552.21	2374.04	2229.61	2110.46
205,000	17785.28	9224.92	6376.78	4956.68	4107.78	3544.48	3144.35	2846.20	2616.01	2433.39	2285.35	2163.22
210,000	18219.06	9449.92	6532.31	5077.57	4207.97	3630.93	3221.04	2915.62	2679.82	2492.74	2341.09	2215.98
215,000	18652.85	9674.92	6687.84	5198.47	4308.16	3717.38	3297.73	2985.04	2743.62	2552.09	2396.83	2268.74
220,000	19086.64	9899.92	6843.37	5319.36	4408.35	3803.83	3374.43	3054.46	2807.43	2611.44	2452.57	2321.50
225,000	19520.42	10124.91	6998.90	5440.26	4508.54	3890.28	3451.12	3123.88	2871.23	2670.79	2508.31	2374.26
230,000	19954.21	10349.91	7154.44	5561.15	4608.73	3976.73	3527.81	3193.30	2935.04	2730.15	2564.05	2427.03
235,000	20388.00	10574.91	7309.97	5682.05	4708.92	4063.18	3604.50	3262.71	2998.84	2789.50	2619.79	2479.79
240,000	20821.79	10799.91	7465.50	5802.94	4809.11	4149.63	3681.19	3332.13	3062.65	2848.85	2675.53	2532.55
245,000	21255.57	11024.91	7621.03	5923.84	4909.30	4236.08	3757.88	3401.55	3126.45	2908.20	2731.27	2585.31
250,000	21689.36	11249.90	7776.56	6044.73	5009.49	4322.53	3834.57	3470.97	3190.26	2967.55	2787.01	2638.07
255,000	22123.15	11474.90	7932.09	6165.62	5109.68	4408.98	3911.27	3540.39	3254.06	3026.90	2842.75	2690.83
260,000	22556.93	11699.90	8087.62	6286.52	5209.87	4495.43	3987.96	3609.81	3317.87	3086.25	2898.49	2743.59
265,000	22990.72	11924.90	8243.15	6407.41	5310.06	4581.88	4064.65	3679.23	3381.67	3145.60	2954.23	2796.35
270,000	23424.51	12149.90	8398.68	6528.31	5410.25	4668.34	4141.34	3748.65	3445.48	3204.95	3009.97	2849.12
280,000	24292.08	12599.89	8709.75	6770.10	5610.63	4841.24	4294.72	3887.49	3573.09	3323.65	3121.45	2954.64
290,000	25159.66	13049.89	9020.81	7011.89	5811.01	5014.14	4448.10	4026.33	3700.70	3442.36	3232.93	3060.16
300,000	26027.23	13499.88	9331.87	7253.68	6011.39	5187.04	4601.49	4165.17	3828.31	3561.06	3344.41	3165.68

AMOUNT OF LOAN	NUMBER OF YEARS IN TERM											
	13	14	15	16	17	18	19	20	25	30	35	40
$ 50	0.51	0.49	0.47	0.45	0.44	0.43	0.42	0.41	0.37	0.35	0.34	0.33
100	1.01	0.97	0.93	0.90	0.87	0.85	0.83	0.81	0.74	0.70	0.68	0.66
200	2.02	1.93	1.86	1.80	1.74	1.69	1.65	1.62	1.48	1.40	1.35	1.32
300	3.02	2.89	2.79	2.69	2.61	2.54	2.48	2.42	2.22	2.10	2.03	1.98
400	4.03	3.86	3.71	3.59	3.48	3.38	3.30	3.23	2.96	2.80	2.70	2.64
500	5.03	4.82	4.64	4.48	4.35	4.23	4.13	4.03	3.70	3.50	3.38	3.30
600	6.04	5.78	5.57	5.38	5.22	5.07	4.95	4.84	4.44	4.20	4.05	3.95
700	7.04	6.75	6.49	6.28	6.09	5.92	5.77	5.64	5.18	4.90	4.72	4.61
800	8.05	7.71	7.42	7.17	6.95	6.76	6.60	6.45	5.92	5.60	5.40	5.27
900	9.05	8.67	8.35	8.07	7.82	7.61	7.42	7.26	6.66	6.30	6.07	5.93
1,000	10.06	9.64	9.28	8.96	8.69	8.45	8.25	8.06	7.39	7.00	6.75	6.59
2,000	20.11	19.27	18.55	17.92	17.38	16.90	16.49	16.12	14.78	13.99	13.49	13.17
3,000	30.17	28.90	27.82	26.88	26.07	25.35	24.73	24.17	22.17	20.98	20.23	19.75
4,000	40.22	38.53	37.09	35.84	34.75	33.80	32.97	32.23	29.56	27.97	26.97	26.33
5,000	50.27	48.16	46.36	44.80	43.44	42.25	41.21	40.28	36.95	34.97	33.72	32.91
6,000	60.33	57.79	55.63	53.75	52.13	50.70	49.45	48.34	44.34	41.96	40.46	39.49
7,000	70.38	67.43	64.90	62.71	60.81	59.15	57.69	56.40	51.73	48.95	47.20	46.07
8,000	80.43	77.06	74.17	71.67	69.50	67.60	65.93	64.45	59.12	55.94	53.94	52.65
9,000	90.49	86.69	83.44	80.63	78.19	76.05	74.17	72.51	66.51	62.93	60.69	59.23
10,000	100.54	96.32	92.71	89.59	86.88	84.50	82.41	80.56	73.90	69.93	67.43	65.81
15,000	150.81	144.48	139.06	134.38	130.31	126.75	123.62	120.84	110.85	104.89	101.14	98.72
20,000	201.08	192.63	185.41	179.17	173.75	169.00	164.82	161.12	147.80	139.85	134.85	131.62
25,000	251.35	240.79	231.76	223.96	217.18	211.25	206.02	201.40	184.75	174.81	168.57	164.52
30,000	301.62	288.95	278.11	268.75	260.62	253.50	247.23	241.68	221.70	209.77	202.28	197.43
35,000	351.88	337.11	324.46	313.54	304.05	295.75	288.43	281.96	258.65	244.73	235.99	230.33
40,000	402.15	385.26	370.81	358.34	347.49	337.99	329.64	322.24	295.60	279.69	269.70	263.23
45,000	452.42	433.42	417.16	403.13	390.92	380.24	370.84	362.52	332.55	314.65	303.41	296.14
50,000	502.69	481.58	463.51	447.92	434.36	422.49	412.04	402.80	369.50	349.61	337.13	329.04
55,000	552.96	529.73	509.86	492.71	477.80	464.74	453.25	443.08	406.45	384.57	370.84	361.94
60,000	603.23	577.89	556.21	537.50	521.23	506.99	494.45	483.36	443.40	419.53	404.55	394.85
65,000	653.50	626.05	602.56	582.29	564.67	549.24	535.66	523.64	480.35	454.49	438.26	427.75
70,000	703.76	674.21	648.91	627.08	608.10	591.49	576.86	563.92	517.30	489.46	471.97	460.65
75,000	754.03	722.36	695.26	671.88	651.54	633.73	618.06	604.20	554.25	524.42	505.69	493.56
80,000	804.30	770.52	741.61	716.67	694.97	675.98	659.27	644.48	591.20	559.38	539.40	526.46
85,000	854.57	818.68	787.97	761.46	738.41	718.23	700.47	684.76	628.15	591.34	573.11	559.37
90,000	904.84	866.83	834.32	806.25	781.84	760.48	741.68	725.04	665.10	629.30	606.82	592.27
95,000	955.11	914.99	880.67	851.04	825.28	802.73	782.88	765.32	702.05	664.26	640.54	625.17
100,000	1005.38	963.15	927.02	895.83	868.71	844.98	824.08	805.60	739.00	699.22	674.25	658.08
105,000	1055.64	1011.31	973.37	940.62	912.15	887.23	865.29	845.88	775.95	734.18	707.96	690.98
110,000	1105.91	1059.46	1019.72	985.42	955.59	929.48	906.49	886.16	812.90	769.14	741.67	723.88
115,000	1156.18	1107.62	1066.07	1030.21	999.02	971.72	947.70	926.44	849.84	804.10	775.38	756.79
120,000	1206.45	1155.78	1112.42	1075.00	1042.46	1013.97	988.90	966.72	886.79	839.06	809.10	789.69
125,000	1256.72	1203.93	1158.77	1119.79	1085.89	1056.22	1030.10	1007.00	923.74	874.02	842.81	822.59
130,000	1306.99	1252.09	1205.12	1164.58	1129.33	1098.47	1071.31	1047.28	960.69	908.98	876.52	855.50
135,000	1357.26	1300.25	1251.47	1209.37	1172.76	1140.72	1112.51	1087.56	997.64	943.94	910.23	888.40
140,000	1407.52	1348.41	1297.82	1254.16	1216.20	1182.97	1153.72	1127.84	1034.59	978.91	943.94	921.30
145,000	1457.79	1396.56	1344.17	1298.96	1259.63	1225.22	1194.92	1168.12	1071.54	1013.87	977.66	954.21
150,000	1508.06	1444.72	1390.52	1343.75	1303.07	1267.46	1236.12	1208.39	1108.49	1048.83	1011.37	987.11
155,000	1558.33	1492.88	1436.87	1388.54	1346.50	1309.71	1277.33	1248.67	1145.44	1083.79	1045.08	1020.01
160,000	1608.60	1541.03	1483.22	1433.33	1389.94	1351.96	1318.53	1288.95	1182.39	1118.75	1078.79	1052.92
165,000	1658.87	1589.19	1529.58	1478.12	1433.38	1394.21	1359.74	1329.23	1219.34	1153.71	1112.51	1085.82
170,000	1709.13	1637.35	1575.93	1522.91	1476.81	1436.46	1400.94	1369.51	1256.29	1188.67	1146.22	1118.73
175,000	1759.40	1685.51	1622.28	1567.70	1520.25	1478.71	1442.14	1409.79	1293.24	1223.63	1179.93	1151.63
180,000	1809.67	1733.66	1668.63	1612.49	1563.68	1520.96	1483.35	1450.07	1330.19	1258.59	1213.64	1184.53
185,000	1859.94	1781.82	1714.98	1657.29	1607.12	1563.21	1524.55	1490.35	1367.14	1293.55	1247.35	1217.44
190,000	1910.21	1829.98	1761.33	1702.08	1650.55	1605.45	1565.75	1530.63	1404.09	1328.51	1281.07	1250.34
195,000	1960.48	1878.13	1807.68	1746.87	1693.99	1647.70	1606.96	1570.91	1441.04	1363.47	1314.78	1283.24
200,000	2010.75	1926.29	1854.03	1791.66	1737.42	1689.95	1648.16	1611.19	1477.99	1398.43	1348.49	1316.15
205,000	2061.01	1974.45	1900.38	1836.45	1780.86	1732.20	1689.37	1651.47	1514.94	1433.39	1382.20	1349.05
210,000	2111.28	2022.61	1946.73	1881.24	1824.29	1774.45	1730.57	1691.75	1551.89	1468.36	1415.91	1381.95
215,000	2161.55	2070.76	1993.08	1926.03	1867.73	1816.70	1771.77	1732.03	1588.84	1503.32	1449.63	1414.86
220,000	2211.82	2118.92	2039.43	1970.83	1911.17	1858.95	1812.98	1772.31	1625.79	1538.28	1483.34	1447.76
225,000	2262.09	2167.08	2085.78	2015.62	1954.60	1901.19	1854.18	1812.59	1662.74	1573.24	1517.05	1480.66
230,000	2312.36	2215.23	2132.13	2060.41	1998.04	1943.44	1895.39	1852.87	1699.68	1608.20	1550.76	1513.57
235,000	2362.63	2263.39	2178.48	2105.20	2041.47	1985.69	1936.59	1893.15	1736.63	1643.16	1584.48	1546.47
240,000	2412.89	2311.55	2224.83	2149.99	2084.91	2027.94	1977.79	1933.43	1773.58	1678.12	1618.19	1579.37
245,000	2463.16	2359.71	2271.19	2194.78	2128.34	2070.19	2019.00	1973.71	1810.53	1713.08	1651.90	1612.28
250,000	2513.43	2407.86	2317.54	2239.57	2171.78	2112.44	2060.20	2013.99	1847.48	1748.04	1685.61	1645.18
255,000	2563.70	2456.02	2363.89	2284.37	2215.21	2154.69	2101.41	2054.27	1884.43	1783.00	1719.32	1678.09
260,000	2613.97	2504.18	2410.24	2329.16	2258.65	2196.94	2142.61	2094.55	1921.38	1817.96	1753.04	1710.99
265,000	2664.24	2552.33	2456.59	2373.95	2302.08	2239.18	2183.81	2134.83	1958.33	1852.92	1786.75	1743.89
270,000	2714.51	2600.49	2502.94	2418.74	2345.52	2281.43	2225.02	2175.11	1995.28	1887.88	1820.46	1776.80
280,000	2815.04	2696.81	2595.64	2508.32	2432.39	2365.93	2307.43	2255.67	2069.18	1957.81	1887.88	1842.60
290,000	2915.58	2793.12	2688.34	2597.91	2519.26	2450.43	2389.83	2336.23	2143.08	2027.73	1955.31	1908.41
300,000	3016.12	2889.44	2781.04	2687.49	2606.13	2534.92	2472.24	2416.78	2216.98	2097.65	2022.73	1974.22

7.75% MONTHLY AMORTIZING PAYMENTS

AMOUNT OF LOAN	NUMBER OF YEARS IN TERM											
	1	2	3	4	5	6	7	8	9	10	11	12
$ 50	4.35	2.26	1.57	1.22	1.01	0.88	0.78	0.71	0.65	0.61	0.57	0.54
100	8.69	4.52	3.13	2.43	2.02	1.75	1.55	1.41	1.29	1.21	1.13	1.07
200	17.38	9.03	6.25	4.86	4.04	3.49	3.10	2.81	2.58	2.41	2.26	2.14
300	26.07	13.54	9.37	7.29	6.05	5.23	4.64	4.21	3.87	3.61	3.39	3.21
400	34.75	18.05	12.49	9.72	8.07	6.97	6.19	5.61	5.16	4.81	4.52	4.28
500	43.44	22.56	15.62	12.15	10.08	8.71	7.74	7.01	6.45	6.01	5.65	5.35
600	52.13	27.07	18.74	14.58	12.10	10.45	9.28	8.41	7.74	7.21	6.77	6.42
700	60.82	31.58	21.86	17.01	14.11	12.19	10.83	9.81	9.03	8.41	7.90	7.49
800	69.50	36.10	24.98	19.44	16.13	13.93	12.37	11.21	10.32	9.61	9.03	8.56
900	78.19	40.61	28.10	21.87	18.15	15.68	13.92	12.61	11.61	10.81	10.16	9.62
1,000	86.88	45.12	31.23	24.30	20.16	17.42	15.47	14.01	12.89	12.01	11.29	10.69
2,000	173.75	90.23	62.45	48.60	40.32	34.83	30.93	28.02	25.78	24.01	22.57	21.38
3,000	260.62	135.35	93.67	72.89	60.48	52.24	46.39	42.03	38.67	36.01	33.85	32.07
4,000	347.50	180.46	124.89	97.19	80.63	69.65	61.85	56.04	51.56	48.01	45.13	42.76
5,000	434.37	225.57	156.11	121.48	100.79	87.06	77.31	70.05	64.45	60.01	56.41	53.44
6,000	521.24	270.69	187.33	145.78	120.95	104.47	92.78	84.06	77.34	72.01	67.69	64.13
7,000	608.12	315.80	218.55	170.08	141.10	121.88	108.24	98.07	90.23	84.01	78.97	74.82
8,000	694.99	360.91	249.77	194.37	161.26	139.30	123.70	112.08	103.12	96.01	90.26	85.51
9,000	781.86	406.03	281.00	218.67	181.42	156.71	139.16	126.09	116.01	108.01	101.54	96.20
10,000	868.73	451.14	312.22	242.96	201.57	174.12	154.62	140.10	128.90	120.02	112.82	106.88
15,000	1303.10	676.71	468.32	364.44	302.36	261.18	231.93	210.15	193.35	180.02	169.22	160.32
20,000	1737.46	902.27	624.43	485.92	403.14	348.23	309.24	280.20	257.79	240.03	225.63	213.76
25,000	2171.83	1127.84	780.53	607.40	503.93	435.29	386.55	350.25	322.24	300.03	282.04	267.20
30,000	2606.19	1353.41	936.64	728.88	604.71	522.35	463.86	420.30	386.69	360.04	338.44	320.64
35,000	3040.56	1578.97	1092.75	850.36	705.50	609.40	541.17	490.35	451.14	420.04	394.85	374.08
40,000	3474.92	1804.54	1248.85	971.83	806.28	696.46	618.48	560.40	515.58	480.05	451.26	427.52
45,000	3909.28	2030.11	1404.96	1093.31	907.07	783.52	695.79	630.45	580.03	540.05	507.66	480.96
50,000	4343.65	2255.67	1561.06	1214.79	1007.85	870.58	773.10	700.50	644.48	600.06	564.07	534.40
55,000	4778.01	2481.24	1717.17	1336.27	1108.64	957.63	850.41	770.55	708.93	660.06	620.48	587.84
60,000	5212.38	2706.81	1873.27	1457.75	1209.42	1044.69	927.72	840.60	773.37	720.07	676.88	641.28
65,000	5646.74	2932.37	2029.38	1579.23	1310.21	1131.75	1005.03	910.65	837.82	780.07	733.29	694.72
70,000	6081.11	3157.94	2185.49	1700.71	1410.99	1218.80	1082.34	980.70	902.27	840.08	789.70	748.16
75,000	6515.47	3383.51	2341.59	1822.19	1511.78	1305.86	1159.65	1050.75	966.72	900.08	846.10	801.60
80,000	6949.84	3609.07	2497.70	1943.66	1612.56	1392.92	1236.96	1120.80	1031.16	960.09	902.51	855.04
85,000	7384.20	3834.64	2653.80	2065.14	1713.35	1479.98	1314.27	1190.85	1095.61	1020.10	958.91	908.48
90,000	7818.56	4060.21	2809.91	2186.62	1814.13	1567.03	1391.58	1260.90	1160.06	1080.10	1015.32	961.92
95,000	8252.93	4285.77	2966.02	2308.10	1914.92	1654.09	1468.89	1330.95	1224.51	1140.11	1071.73	1015.36
100,000	8687.29	4511.34	3122.12	2429.58	2015.70	1741.15	1546.20	1401.00	1288.95	1200.11	1128.13	1068.80
105,000	9121.66	4736.91	3278.23	2551.06	2116.49	1828.20	1623.51	1471.05	1353.40	1260.12	1184.54	1122.24
110,000	9556.02	4962.47	3434.33	2672.54	2217.27	1915.26	1700.82	1541.10	1417.85	1320.12	1240.95	1175.68
115,000	9990.39	5188.04	3590.44	2794.02	2318.06	2002.32	1778.13	1611.15	1482.30	1380.13	1297.35	1229.12
120,000	10424.75	5413.61	3746.54	2915.49	2418.84	2089.38	1855.44	1681.20	1546.74	1440.13	1353.76	1282.56
125,000	10859.12	5639.17	3902.65	3036.97	2519.62	2176.43	1932.75	1751.25	1611.19	1500.14	1410.17	1336.00
130,000	11293.48	5864.74	4058.76	3158.45	2620.41	2263.49	2010.06	1821.30	1675.64	1560.14	1466.57	1389.43
135,000	11727.84	6090.31	4214.86	3279.93	2721.19	2350.55	2087.37	1891.35	1740.09	1620.15	1522.98	1442.87
140,000	12162.21	6315.87	4370.97	3401.41	2821.98	2437.60	2164.68	1961.40	1804.53	1680.15	1579.39	1496.31
145,000	12596.57	6541.44	4527.07	3522.89	2922.76	2524.66	2241.99	2031.45	1868.98	1740.16	1635.79	1549.75
150,000	13030.94	6767.01	4683.18	3644.37	3023.55	2611.72	2319.30	2101.50	1933.43	1800.16	1692.20	1603.19
155,000	13465.30	6992.58	4839.29	3765.84	3124.33	2698.78	2396.61	2171.55	1997.88	1860.17	1748.60	1656.63
160,000	13899.67	7218.14	4995.39	3887.32	3225.12	2785.83	2473.92	2241.60	2062.32	1920.18	1805.01	1710.07
165,000	14334.03	7443.71	5151.50	4008.80	3325.90	2872.89	2551.23	2311.65	2126.77	1980.18	1861.42	1763.51
170,000	14768.39	7669.28	5307.60	4130.28	3426.69	2959.95	2628.54	2381.70	2191.22	2040.19	1917.82	1816.95
175,000	15202.76	7894.84	5463.71	4251.76	3527.47	3047.00	2705.85	2451.75	2255.67	2100.19	1974.23	1870.39
180,000	15637.12	8120.41	5619.81	4373.24	3628.26	3134.06	2783.16	2521.79	2320.11	2160.20	2030.64	1923.83
185,000	16071.49	8345.98	5775.92	4494.72	3729.04	3221.12	2860.47	2591.84	2384.56	2220.20	2087.04	1977.27
190,000	16505.85	8571.54	5932.03	4616.20	3829.83	3308.18	2937.78	2661.89	2449.01	2280.21	2143.45	2030.71
195,000	16940.22	8797.11	6088.13	4737.67	3930.61	3395.23	3015.09	2731.94	2513.46	2340.21	2199.86	2084.15
200,000	17374.58	9022.68	6244.24	4859.15	4031.40	3482.29	3092.40	2801.99	2577.90	2400.22	2256.26	2137.59
205,000	17808.95	9248.24	6400.34	4980.63	4132.18	3569.35	3169.71	2872.04	2642.35	2460.22	2312.67	2191.03
210,000	18243.31	9473.81	6556.45	5102.11	4232.97	3656.40	3247.02	2942.09	2706.80	2520.23	2369.08	2244.47
215,000	18677.67	9699.38	6712.56	5223.59	4333.75	3743.46	3324.32	3012.14	2771.25	2580.23	2425.48	2297.91
220,000	19112.04	9924.94	6868.66	5345.07	4434.54	3830.52	3401.63	3082.19	2835.69	2640.24	2481.89	2351.35
225,000	19546.40	10150.51	7024.77	5466.55	4535.32	3917.58	3478.94	3152.24	2900.14	2700.24	2538.29	2404.79
230,000	19980.77	10376.08	7180.87	5588.03	4636.11	4004.63	3556.25	3222.29	2964.59	2760.25	2594.70	2458.23
235,000	20415.13	10601.64	7336.98	5709.50	4736.89	4091.69	3633.56	3292.34	3029.04	2820.25	2651.11	2511.67
240,000	20849.50	10827.21	7493.08	5830.98	4837.68	4178.75	3710.87	3362.39	3093.48	2880.26	2707.51	2565.11
245,000	21283.86	11052.78	7649.19	5952.46	4938.46	4265.80	3788.18	3432.44	3157.93	2940.27	2763.92	2618.55
250,000	21718.23	11278.34	7805.30	6073.94	5039.24	4352.86	3865.49	3502.49	3222.38	3000.27	2820.33	2671.99
255,000	22152.59	11503.91	7961.40	6195.42	5140.03	4439.92	3942.80	3572.54	3286.83	3060.28	2876.73	2725.42
260,000	22586.95	11729.48	8117.51	6316.90	5240.81	4526.98	4020.11	3642.59	3351.27	3120.28	2933.14	2778.86
265,000	23021.32	11955.04	8273.61	6438.38	5341.60	4614.03	4097.42	3712.64	3415.72	3180.29	2989.55	2832.30
270,000	23455.68	12180.61	8429.72	6559.86	5442.38	4701.09	4174.73	3782.69	3480.17	3240.29	3045.95	2885.74
280,000	24324.41	12631.74	8741.93	6802.81	5643.95	4875.20	4329.35	3922.79	3609.06	3360.30	3158.77	2992.62
290,000	25193.14	13082.88	9054.14	7045.77	5845.52	5049.32	4483.97	4062.89	3737.96	3480.31	3271.58	3099.50
300,000	26061.87	13534.01	9366.35	7288.73	6047.09	5223.43	4638.59	4202.99	3866.85	3600.32	3384.39	3206.38

48

AMOUNT OF LOAN	NUMBER OF YEARS IN TERM											
	13	14	15	16	17	18	19	20	25	30	35	40
$ 50	0.51	0.49	0.48	0.46	0.45	0.43	0.42	0.42	0.38	0.36	0.35	0.34
100	1.02	0.98	0.95	0.92	0.89	0.86	0.84	0.83	0.76	0.72	0.70	0.68
200	2.04	1.96	1.89	1.83	1.77	1.72	1.68	1.65	1.52	1.44	1.39	1.36
300	3.06	2.94	2.83	2.74	2.66	2.58	2.52	2.47	2.27	2.15	2.08	2.03
400	4.08	3.91	3.77	3.65	3.54	3.44	3.36	3.29	3.03	2.87	2.77	2.71
500	5.10	4.89	4.71	4.56	4.42	4.30	4.20	4.11	3.78	3.59	3.47	3.39
600	6.12	5.87	5.65	5.47	5.31	5.16	5.04	4.93	4.54	4.30	4.16	4.06
700	7.14	6.85	6.59	6.38	6.19	6.02	5.88	5.75	5.29	5.02	4.85	4.74
800	8.16	7.82	7.54	7.29	7.07	6.88	6.72	6.57	6.05	5.74	5.54	5.42
900	9.18	8.80	8.48	8.20	7.96	7.74	7.56	7.39	6.80	6.45	6.23	6.09
1,000	10.20	9.78	9.42	9.11	8.84	8.60	8.40	8.21	7.56	7.17	6.93	6.77
2,000	20.39	19.55	18.83	18.21	17.67	17.20	16.79	16.42	15.11	14.33	13.85	13.54
3,000	30.58	29.32	28.24	27.31	26.51	25.80	25.18	24.63	22.66	21.50	20.77	20.30
4,000	40.77	39.09	37.66	36.42	35.34	34.40	33.57	32.84	30.22	28.66	27.69	27.07
5,000	50.96	48.86	47.07	45.52	44.18	43.00	41.97	41.05	37.77	35.83	34.61	33.84
6,000	61.16	58.64	56.48	54.62	53.01	51.60	50.36	49.26	45.32	42.99	41.54	40.60
7,000	71.35	68.41	65.89	63.73	61.84	60.20	58.75	57.47	52.88	50.15	48.46	47.37
8,000	81.54	78.18	75.31	72.83	70.68	68.80	67.14	65.68	60.43	57.32	55.38	54.13
9,000	91.73	87.95	84.72	81.93	79.51	77.40	75.54	73.89	67.98	64.48	62.30	60.90
10,000	101.92	97.72	94.13	91.04	88.35	86.00	83.93	82.10	75.54	71.65	69.22	67.67
15,000	152.88	146.58	141.20	136.55	132.52	128.99	125.89	123.15	113.30	107.47	103.83	101.50
20,000	203.84	195.44	188.26	182.07	176.69	171.99	167.85	164.19	151.07	143.29	138.44	135.33
25,000	254.80	244.30	235.32	227.58	220.86	214.98	209.81	205.24	188.84	179.11	173.05	169.16
30,000	305.76	293.16	282.39	273.10	265.03	257.98	251.77	246.29	226.60	214.93	207.66	202.99
35,000	356.72	342.02	329.45	318.62	309.20	300.97	293.73	287.34	264.37	250.75	242.27	236.82
40,000	407.67	390.88	376.52	364.13	353.37	343.97	335.69	328.38	302.14	286.57	276.88	270.65
45,000	458.63	439.73	423.58	409.65	397.54	386.96	377.66	369.43	339.90	322.39	311.48	304.40
50,000	509.59	488.59	470.64	455.16	441.72	429.96	419.62	410.48	377.67	358.21	346.09	338.31
55,000	560.55	537.45	517.71	500.68	485.89	472.95	461.58	451.53	415.44	394.03	380.70	372.15
60,000	611.51	586.31	564.77	546.20	530.06	515.95	503.54	492.57	453.20	429.85	415.31	405.98
65,000	662.47	635.17	611.83	591.71	574.23	558.94	545.50	533.62	490.97	465.67	449.92	439.81
70,000	713.43	684.03	658.90	637.23	618.40	601.94	587.46	574.67	528.74	501.49	484.53	473.64
75,000	764.38	732.89	705.96	682.74	662.57	644.93	629.42	615.72	566.50	537.31	519.14	507.47
80,000	815.34	781.75	753.03	728.26	706.74	687.93	671.38	656.76	604.27	573.13	553.75	541.30
85,000	866.30	830.61	800.09	773.77	750.91	730.92	713.35	697.81	642.03	608.96	588.35	575.13
90,000	917.26	879.46	847.15	819.29	795.08	773.92	755.31	738.86	679.80	644.78	622.96	608.96
95,000	968.22	928.32	894.22	864.81	839.26	816.91	797.27	779.91	717.57	680.60	657.57	642.79
100,000	1019.18	977.18	941.28	910.32	883.43	859.91	839.23	820.95	755.33	716.42	692.18	676.62
105,000	1070.14	1026.04	988.34	955.84	927.60	902.90	881.19	862.00	793.10	752.24	726.79	710.46
110,000	1121.09	1074.90	1035.41	1001.35	971.77	945.90	923.15	903.05	830.87	788.06	761.40	744.29
115,000	1172.05	1123.76	1082.47	1046.87	1015.94	988.89	965.11	944.10	868.63	823.88	796.01	778.12
120,000	1223.01	1172.62	1129.54	1092.39	1060.11	1031.89	1007.07	985.14	906.40	859.70	830.62	811.95
125,000	1273.97	1221.40	1170.00	1137.90	1104.28	1074.88	1049.03	1026.19	944.17	895.52	865.22	845.78
130,000	1324.93	1270.34	1223.66	1183.42	1148.45	1117.88	1091.00	1067.24	981.93	931.34	899.83	879.61
135,000	1375.89	1319.19	1270.73	1228.93	1192.62	1160.88	1132.96	1108.29	1019.70	967.16	934.44	913.44
140,000	1426.85	1368.05	1317.79	1274.45	1236.80	1203.87	1174.92	1149.33	1057.47	1002.98	969.05	947.27
145,000	1477.80	1416.91	1364.85	1319.96	1280.97	1246.87	1216.88	1190.38	1095.23	1038.80	1003.66	981.10
150,000	1528.76	1465.77	1411.92	1365.48	1325.14	1289.86	1258.84	1231.43	1133.00	1074.62	1038.27	1014.93
155,000	1579.72	1514.63	1458.98	1411.00	1369.31	1332.86	1300.80	1272.48	1170.76	1110.44	1072.88	1048.77
160,000	1630.68	1563.49	1506.05	1456.51	1413.48	1375.85	1342.76	1313.52	1208.53	1146.26	1107.49	1082.60
165,000	1681.64	1612.35	1553.11	1502.03	1457.65	1418.85	1384.72	1354.57	1246.30	1182.09	1142.10	1116.43
170,000	1732.60	1661.21	1600.17	1547.54	1501.82	1461.84	1426.69	1395.62	1284.06	1217.91	1176.70	1150.26
175,000	1783.56	1710.07	1647.24	1593.06	1545.99	1504.84	1468.65	1436.66	1321.83	1253.73	1211.31	1184.09
180,000	1834.51	1758.92	1694.30	1638.58	1590.16	1547.83	1510.61	1477.71	1359.60	1289.55	1245.92	1217.92
185,000	1885.47	1807.78	1741.37	1684.09	1634.33	1590.83	1552.57	1518.76	1397.36	1325.37	1280.53	1251.75
190,000	1936.43	1856.64	1788.43	1729.61	1678.51	1633.82	1594.53	1559.81	1435.13	1361.19	1315.14	1285.58
195,000	1987.39	1905.50	1835.49	1775.12	1722.68	1676.82	1636.49	1600.85	1472.90	1397.01	1349.75	1319.41
200,000	2038.35	1954.36	1882.56	1820.64	1766.85	1719.81	1678.45	1641.90	1510.66	1432.83	1384.36	1353.24
205,000	2089.31	2003.22	1929.62	1866.16	1811.02	1762.81	1720.41	1682.95	1548.43	1468.65	1418.97	1387.08
210,000	2140.27	2052.08	1976.68	1911.67	1855.19	1805.80	1762.38	1724.00	1586.20	1504.47	1453.57	1420.91
215,000	2191.22	2100.94	2023.75	1957.19	1899.36	1848.80	1804.34	1765.04	1623.96	1540.29	1488.18	1454.74
220,000	2242.18	2149.79	2070.81	2002.70	1943.53	1891.79	1846.30	1806.09	1661.73	1576.11	1522.79	1488.57
225,000	2293.14	2198.65	2117.88	2048.22	1987.70	1934.79	1888.26	1847.14	1699.49	1611.93	1557.40	1522.40
230,000	2344.10	2247.51	2164.94	2093.73	2031.87	1977.78	1930.22	1888.19	1737.26	1647.75	1592.01	1556.23
235,000	2395.06	2296.37	2212.00	2139.25	2076.05	2020.78	1972.18	1929.23	1775.03	1683.57	1626.62	1590.06
240,000	2446.02	2345.23	2259.07	2184.77	2120.22	2063.77	2014.14	1970.28	1812.79	1719.39	1661.23	1623.89
245,000	2496.98	2394.09	2306.13	2230.28	2164.39	2106.77	2056.10	2011.33	1850.56	1755.22	1695.84	1657.72
250,000	2547.93	2442.95	2353.19	2275.80	2208.56	2149.76	2098.06	2052.38	1888.33	1791.04	1730.44	1691.55
255,000	2598.89	2491.81	2400.26	2321.31	2252.73	2192.76	2140.03	2093.42	1926.09	1826.86	1765.05	1725.39
260,000	2649.85	2540.67	2447.32	2366.83	2296.90	2235.76	2181.99	2134.47	1963.86	1862.68	1799.66	1759.22
265,000	2700.81	2589.52	2494.39	2412.35	2341.07	2278.75	2223.95	2175.52	2001.63	1898.50	1834.27	1793.05
270,000	2751.77	2638.38	2541.45	2457.86	2385.24	2321.75	2265.91	2216.57	2039.39	1934.32	1868.88	1826.88
280,000	2853.69	2736.10	2635.58	2548.89	2473.59	2407.74	2349.83	2298.66	2114.93	2005.96	1938.10	1894.54
290,000	2955.60	2833.82	2729.70	2639.92	2561.93	2493.73	2433.75	2380.76	2190.46	2077.60	2007.32	1962.20
300,000	3057.52	2931.54	2823.83	2730.96	2650.27	2579.72	2517.68	2462.85	2265.99	2149.24	2076.53	2029.86

8.00%

AMOUNT OF LOAN	NUMBER OF YEARS IN TERM											
	1	2	3	4	5	6	7	8	9	10	11	12
$ 50	4.35	2.27	1.57	1.23	1.02	0.88	0.78	0.71	0.66	0.61	0.58	0.55
100	8.70	4.53	3.14	2.45	2.03	1.76	1.56	1.42	1.31	1.22	1.15	1.09
200	17.40	9.05	6.27	4.89	4.06	3.51	3.12	2.83	2.61	2.43	2.29	2.17
300	26.10	13.57	9.41	7.33	6.09	5.26	4.68	4.25	3.91	3.64	3.43	3.25
400	34.80	18.10	12.54	9.77	8.12	7.02	6.24	5.66	5.21	4.86	4.57	4.33
500	43.50	22.62	15.67	12.21	10.14	8.77	7.80	7.07	6.51	6.07	5.71	5.42
600	52.20	27.14	18.81	14.65	12.17	10.52	9.36	8.49	7.82	7.28	6.85	6.50
700	60.90	31.66	21.94	17.09	14.20	12.28	10.92	9.90	9.12	8.50	8.00	7.58
800	69.60	36.19	25.07	19.54	16.23	14.03	12.47	11.31	10.42	9.71	9.14	8.66
900	78.29	40.71	28.21	21.98	18.25	15.78	14.03	12.73	11.72	10.92	10.28	9.75
1,000	86.99	45.23	31.34	24.42	20.28	17.54	15.59	14.14	13.02	12.14	11.42	10.83
2,000	173.98	90.46	62.68	48.83	40.56	35.07	31.18	28.28	26.04	24.27	22.84	21.65
3,000	260.97	135.69	94.01	73.24	60.83	52.60	46.76	42.42	39.06	36.40	34.25	32.48
4,000	347.96	180.91	125.35	97.66	81.11	70.14	62.35	56.55	52.08	48.54	45.67	43.30
5,000	434.95	226.14	156.69	122.07	101.39	87.67	77.94	70.69	65.10	60.67	57.08	54.13
6,000	521.94	271.37	188.02	146.48	121.66	105.20	93.52	84.83	78.12	72.80	68.50	64.95
7,000	608.92	316.60	219.36	170.90	141.94	122.74	109.11	98.96	91.14	84.93	79.91	75.78
8,000	695.91	361.82	250.70	195.31	162.22	140.27	124.69	113.10	104.15	97.07	91.33	86.60
9,000	782.90	407.05	282.03	219.72	182.49	157.80	140.28	127.24	117.17	109.20	102.74	97.43
10,000	869.89	452.28	313.37	244.13	202.77	175.34	155.87	141.37	130.19	121.33	114.16	108.25
15,000	1304.83	678.41	470.05	366.20	304.15	263.00	233.80	212.06	195.29	182.00	171.24	162.37
20,000	1739.77	904.55	626.73	488.26	405.53	350.67	311.73	282.74	260.38	242.66	228.31	216.50
25,000	2174.72	1130.69	783.41	610.33	506.91	438.34	389.66	353.42	325.47	303.32	285.39	270.62
30,000	2609.66	1356.82	940.10	732.39	608.30	526.00	467.59	424.11	390.57	363.99	342.47	324.74
35,000	3044.60	1582.96	1096.78	854.46	709.68	613.67	545.52	494.79	455.66	424.65	399.55	378.86
40,000	3479.54	1809.10	1253.46	976.52	811.06	701.33	623.45	565.47	520.75	485.32	456.62	432.99
45,000	3914.48	2035.23	1410.14	1098.59	912.44	789.00	701.38	636.16	585.85	545.98	513.70	487.11
50,000	4349.43	2261.37	1566.82	1220.65	1013.82	876.67	779.32	706.84	650.94	606.64	570.78	541.23
55,000	4784.37	2487.51	1723.51	1342.72	1115.21	964.33	857.25	777.52	716.03	667.31	627.85	595.35
60,000	5219.31	2713.64	1880.19	1464.78	1216.59	1052.00	935.18	848.21	781.13	727.97	684.93	649.48
65,000	5654.25	2939.78	2036.87	1586.84	1317.97	1139.67	1013.11	918.89	846.22	788.63	742.01	703.60
70,000	6089.20	3165.92	2193.55	1708.91	1419.35	1227.33	1091.04	989.57	911.32	849.30	799.09	757.72
75,000	6524.14	3392.05	2350.23	1830.97	1520.73	1315.00	1168.97	1060.26	976.41	909.96	856.16	811.84
80,000	6959.08	3618.19	2506.91	1953.04	1622.12	1402.66	1246.90	1130.94	1041.50	970.63	913.24	865.97
85,000	7394.02	3844.32	2663.60	2075.10	1723.50	1490.33	1324.83	1201.62	1106.60	1031.29	970.32	920.09
90,000	7828.96	4070.46	2820.28	2197.17	1824.88	1578.00	1402.76	1272.31	1171.69	1091.95	1027.40	974.21
95,000	8263.91	4296.60	2976.96	2319.23	1926.26	1665.66	1480.70	1342.99	1236.78	1152.62	1084.47	1028.33
100,000	8698.85	4522.73	3133.64	2441.30	2027.64	1753.33	1558.63	1413.67	1301.88	1213.28	1141.55	1082.46
105,000	9133.79	4748.87	3290.32	2563.36	2129.03	1841.00	1636.56	1484.36	1366.97	1273.94	1198.63	1136.58
110,000	9568.73	4975.01	3447.01	2685.43	2230.41	1928.66	1714.49	1555.04	1432.06	1334.61	1255.70	1190.70
115,000	10003.67	5201.14	3603.69	2807.49	2331.79	2016.33	1792.42	1625.72	1497.16	1395.27	1312.78	1244.83
120,000	10438.62	5427.28	3760.37	2929.56	2433.17	2103.99	1870.35	1696.41	1562.25	1455.94	1369.86	1298.95
125,000	10873.56	5653.42	3917.05	3051.62	2534.55	2191.66	1948.28	1767.09	1627.34	1516.60	1426.94	1353.07
130,000	11308.50	5879.55	4073.73	3173.68	2635.94	2279.33	2026.21	1837.77	1692.44	1577.26	1484.01	1407.19
135,000	11743.44	6105.69	4230.41	3295.75	2737.32	2366.99	2104.14	1908.46	1757.53	1637.93	1541.09	1461.32
140,000	12178.39	6331.83	4387.10	3417.81	2838.70	2454.66	2182.08	1979.14	1822.63	1698.59	1598.17	1515.44
145,000	12613.33	6557.96	4543.78	3539.88	2940.08	2542.32	2260.01	2049.82	1887.72	1759.26	1655.24	1569.56
150,000	13048.27	6784.10	4700.46	3661.94	3041.46	2629.99	2337.94	2120.51	1952.81	1819.92	1712.32	1623.68
155,000	13483.21	7010.24	4857.14	3784.01	3142.85	2717.66	2415.87	2191.19	2017.91	1880.58	1769.40	1677.81
160,000	13918.15	7236.37	5013.82	3906.07	3244.23	2805.32	2493.80	2261.87	2083.00	1941.25	1826.48	1731.93
165,000	14353.10	7462.51	5170.51	4028.14	3345.61	2892.99	2571.73	2332.56	2148.09	2001.91	1883.55	1786.05
170,000	14788.04	7688.64	5327.19	4150.20	3446.99	2980.66	2649.66	2403.24	2213.19	2062.57	1940.63	1840.17
175,000	15222.98	7914.78	5483.87	4272.27	3548.37	3068.32	2727.59	2473.92	2278.28	2123.24	1997.71	1894.30
180,000	15657.92	8140.92	5640.55	4394.33	3649.76	3155.99	2805.52	2544.61	2343.37	2183.90	2054.79	1948.42
185,000	16092.86	8367.05	5797.23	4516.40	3751.14	3243.65	2883.45	2615.29	2408.47	2244.57	2111.86	2002.54
190,000	16527.81	8593.19	5953.91	4638.46	3852.52	3331.32	2961.39	2685.97	2473.56	2305.23	2168.94	2056.66
195,000	16962.75	8819.33	6110.60	4760.52	3953.90	3418.99	3039.32	2756.66	2538.65	2365.89	2226.02	2110.79
200,000	17397.69	9045.46	6267.28	4882.59	4055.28	3506.65	3117.25	2827.34	2603.75	2426.56	2283.09	2164.91
205,000	17832.63	9271.60	6423.96	5004.65	4156.67	3594.32	3195.18	2898.02	2668.84	2487.22	2340.17	2219.03
210,000	18267.58	9497.74	6580.64	5126.72	4258.05	3681.99	3273.11	2968.71	2733.94	2547.88	2397.25	2273.16
215,000	18702.52	9723.87	6737.32	5248.78	4359.43	3769.65	3351.04	3039.39	2799.03	2608.55	2454.33	2327.28
220,000	19137.46	9950.01	6894.01	5370.85	4460.81	3857.32	3428.97	3110.07	2864.12	2669.21	2511.40	2381.40
225,000	19572.40	10176.15	7050.69	5492.91	4562.19	3944.98	3506.90	3180.76	2929.22	2729.88	2568.48	2435.52
230,000	20007.34	10402.28	7207.37	5614.98	4663.58	4032.65	3584.83	3251.44	2994.31	2790.54	2625.56	2489.65
235,000	20442.29	10628.42	7364.05	5737.04	4764.96	4120.32	3662.77	3322.12	3059.40	2851.20	2682.64	2543.77
240,000	20877.23	10854.55	7520.73	5859.11	4866.34	4207.98	3740.70	3392.81	3124.50	2911.87	2739.71	2597.89
245,000	21312.17	11080.69	7677.41	5981.17	4967.72	4295.65	3818.63	3463.49	3189.59	2972.53	2796.79	2652.01
250,000	21747.11	11306.83	7834.10	6103.24	5069.10	4383.32	3896.56	3534.17	3254.68	3033.19	2853.87	2706.14
255,000	22182.05	11532.96	7990.78	6225.30	5170.49	4470.98	3974.49	3604.86	3319.78	3093.86	2910.94	2760.26
260,000	22617.00	11759.10	8147.46	6347.36	5271.87	4558.65	4052.42	3675.54	3384.87	3154.52	2968.02	2814.38
265,000	23051.94	11985.24	8304.14	6469.43	5373.25	4646.31	4130.35	3746.23	3449.96	3215.19	3025.10	2868.50
270,000	23486.88	12211.37	8460.82	6591.49	5474.63	4733.98	4208.28	3816.91	3515.06	3275.85	3082.18	2922.63
280,000	24356.77	12663.65	8774.19	6835.62	5677.40	4909.31	4364.15	3958.28	3645.25	3397.18	3196.33	3030.87
290,000	25226.65	13115.92	9087.55	7079.75	5880.16	5084.64	4520.01	4099.64	3775.43	3518.51	3310.48	3139.12
300,000	26096.53	13568.19	9400.91	7323.88	6082.92	5259.98	4675.87	4241.01	3905.62	3639.83	3424.64	3247.36

AMOUNT OF LOAN	NUMBER OF YEARS IN TERM											
	13	14	15	16	17	18	19	20	25	30	35	40
$ 50	0.52	0.50	0.48	0.47	0.45	0.44	0.43	0.42	0.39	0.37	0.36	0.35
100	1.04	1.00	0.96	0.93	0.90	0.88	0.86	0.84	0.78	0.74	0.72	0.70
200	2.07	1.99	1.92	1.85	1.80	1.75	1.71	1.68	1.55	1.47	1.43	1.40
300	3.10	2.98	2.87	2.78	2.70	2.63	2.57	2.51	2.32	2.21	2.14	2.09
400	4.14	3.97	3.83	3.70	3.60	3.50	3.42	3.35	3.09	2.94	2.85	2.79
500	5.17	4.96	4.78	4.63	4.50	4.38	4.28	4.19	3.86	3.67	3.56	3.48
600	6.20	5.95	5.74	5.55	5.39	5.25	5.13	5.02	4.64	4.41	4.27	4.18
700	7.24	6.94	6.69	6.48	6.29	6.13	5.99	5.86	5.41	5.14	4.98	4.87
800	8.27	7.94	7.65	7.40	7.19	7.00	6.84	6.70	6.18	5.88	5.69	5.57
900	9.30	8.93	8.61	8.33	8.09	7.88	7.70	7.53	6.95	6.61	6.40	6.26
1,000	10.34	9.92	9.56	9.25	8.99	8.75	8.55	8.37	7.72	7.34	7.11	6.96
2,000	20.67	19.83	19.12	18.50	17.97	17.50	17.10	16.73	15.44	14.68	14.21	13.91
3,000	31.00	29.74	28.67	27.75	26.95	26.25	25.64	25.10	23.16	22.02	21.31	20.86
4,000	41.33	39.66	38.23	37.00	35.94	35.00	34.19	33.46	30.88	29.36	28.42	27.82
5,000	51.66	49.57	47.79	46.25	44.92	43.75	42.73	41.83	38.60	36.69	35.52	34.77
6,000	61.99	59.48	57.34	55.50	53.90	52.50	51.28	50.19	46.31	44.03	42.62	41.72
7,000	72.32	69.40	66.90	64.75	62.88	61.25	59.82	58.56	54.03	51.37	49.72	48.68
8,000	82.65	79.31	76.46	74.00	71.87	70.00	68.37	66.92	61.75	58.71	56.83	55.63
9,000	92.98	89.22	86.01	83.25	80.85	78.75	76.91	75.28	69.47	66.04	63.93	62.58
10,000	103.31	99.14	95.57	92.50	89.83	87.50	85.46	83.65	77.19	73.38	71.03	69.54
15,000	154.97	148.70	143.35	138.74	134.74	131.25	128.18	125.47	115.78	110.07	106.54	104.30
20,000	206.62	198.27	191.14	184.99	179.66	175.00	170.91	167.29	154.37	146.76	142.06	139.07
25,000	258.27	247.83	238.92	231.24	224.57	218.75	213.63	209.12	192.96	183.45	177.57	173.83
30,000	309.93	297.40	286.70	277.48	269.48	262.49	256.36	250.94	231.55	220.13	213.08	208.60
35,000	361.58	346.97	334.48	323.73	314.39	306.24	299.08	292.76	270.14	256.82	248.60	243.36
40,000	413.23	396.53	382.27	369.98	359.31	349.99	341.81	334.58	308.73	293.51	284.11	278.13
45,000	464.89	446.10	430.05	416.22	404.22	393.74	384.53	376.40	347.32	330.20	319.62	312.90
50,000	516.54	495.66	477.83	462.47	449.13	437.49	427.26	418.23	385.91	366.89	355.14	347.66
55,000	568.20	545.23	525.61	508.71	494.05	481.23	469.98	460.05	424.50	403.58	390.65	382.43
60,000	619.85	594.80	573.40	554.96	538.96	524.98	512.71	501.87	463.09	440.26	426.16	417.19
65,000	671.50	644.36	621.18	601.21	583.87	568.73	555.43	543.69	501.69	476.95	461.67	451.96
70,000	723.16	693.93	668.96	647.45	628.78	612.48	598.16	585.51	540.28	513.64	497.19	486.72
75,000	774.81	743.49	716.74	693.70	673.70	656.23	640.88	627.34	578.87	550.33	532.70	521.49
80,000	826.46	793.06	764.53	739.95	718.61	699.98	683.61	669.16	617.46	587.02	568.21	556.25
85,000	878.12	842.63	812.31	786.19	763.52	743.72	726.33	710.98	656.05	623.70	603.73	591.02
90,000	929.77	892.19	860.09	832.44	808.44	787.47	769.06	752.80	694.64	660.39	639.24	625.79
95,000	981.43	941.76	907.87	878.68	853.35	831.22	811.78	794.62	733.23	697.08	674.75	660.55
100,000	1033.08	991.32	955.66	924.93	898.26	874.97	854.51	836.45	771.82	733.77	710.27	695.32
105,000	1084.73	1040.89	1003.44	971.18	943.17	918.72	897.23	878.27	810.41	770.46	745.78	730.08
110,000	1136.39	1090.46	1051.22	1017.42	988.09	962.46	939.96	920.09	849.00	807.15	781.29	764.85
115,000	1188.04	1140.02	1099.00	1063.67	1033.00	1006.21	982.68	961.91	887.59	843.83	816.81	799.61
120,000	1239.69	1189.59	1146.79	1109.92	1077.91	1049.96	1025.41	1003.73	926.18	880.52	852.32	834.38
125,000	1291.35	1239.15	1194.57	1156.16	1122.83	1093.71	1068.13	1045.56	964.78	917.21	887.83	869.14
130,000	1343.00	1288.72	1242.35	1202.41	1167.74	1137.46	1110.86	1087.38	1003.37	953.90	923.34	903.91
135,000	1394.65	1338.28	1290.14	1248.65	1212.65	1181.20	1153.58	1129.20	1041.96	990.59	958.86	938.68
140,000	1446.31	1387.85	1337.92	1294.90	1257.56	1224.95	1196.31	1171.02	1080.55	1027.28	994.37	973.44
145,000	1497.96	1437.42	1385.70	1341.15	1302.48	1268.70	1239.03	1212.84	1119.14	1063.96	1029.88	1008.21
150,000	1549.62	1486.98	1433.48	1387.39	1347.39	1312.45	1281.76	1254.67	1157.73	1100.65	1065.40	1042.97
155,000	1601.27	1536.55	1481.27	1433.64	1392.30	1356.20	1324.48	1296.49	1196.32	1137.34	1100.91	1077.74
160,000	1652.92	1586.11	1529.05	1479.89	1437.22	1399.95	1367.21	1338.31	1234.91	1174.03	1136.42	1112.50
165,000	1704.58	1635.68	1576.83	1526.13	1482.13	1443.69	1409.93	1380.13	1273.50	1210.72	1171.94	1147.27
170,000	1756.23	1685.25	1624.61	1572.38	1527.04	1487.44	1452.66	1421.95	1312.09	1247.40	1207.45	1182.03
175,000	1807.88	1734.81	1672.40	1618.62	1571.95	1531.19	1495.38	1463.78	1350.68	1284.09	1242.96	1216.80
180,000	1859.54	1784.38	1720.18	1664.87	1616.87	1574.94	1538.11	1505.60	1389.27	1320.78	1278.47	1251.57
185,000	1911.19	1833.94	1767.96	1711.12	1661.78	1618.69	1580.83	1547.42	1427.87	1357.47	1313.99	1286.33
190,000	1962.85	1883.51	1815.74	1757.36	1706.69	1662.43	1623.56	1589.24	1466.46	1394.16	1349.50	1321.10
195,000	2014.50	1933.08	1863.53	1803.61	1751.61	1706.18	1666.28	1631.06	1505.05	1430.85	1385.01	1355.86
200,000	2066.15	1982.64	1911.31	1849.86	1796.52	1749.93	1709.01	1672.89	1543.64	1467.53	1420.53	1390.63
205,000	2117.81	2032.21	1959.09	1896.10	1841.43	1793.68	1751.73	1714.71	1582.23	1504.22	1456.04	1425.39
210,000	2169.46	2081.77	2006.87	1942.35	1886.34	1837.43	1794.46	1756.53	1620.82	1540.91	1491.55	1460.16
215,000	2221.11	2131.34	2054.66	1988.59	1931.26	1881.17	1837.18	1798.35	1659.41	1577.60	1527.07	1494.93
220,000	2272.77	2180.91	2102.44	2034.84	1976.17	1924.92	1879.91	1840.17	1698.00	1614.29	1562.58	1529.69
225,000	2324.42	2230.47	2150.22	2081.09	2021.08	1968.67	1922.63	1882.00	1736.59	1650.98	1598.09	1564.46
230,000	2376.07	2280.04	2198.00	2127.33	2066.00	2012.42	1965.36	1923.82	1775.18	1687.66	1633.61	1599.22
235,000	2427.73	2329.60	2245.79	2173.58	2110.91	2056.17	2008.08	1965.64	1813.77	1724.35	1669.12	1633.99
240,000	2479.38	2379.17	2293.57	2219.83	2155.82	2099.92	2050.81	2007.46	1852.36	1761.04	1704.63	1668.75
245,000	2531.04	2428.74	2341.35	2266.07	2200.73	2143.66	2093.53	2049.28	1890.95	1797.73	1740.14	1703.52
250,000	2582.69	2478.30	2389.14	2312.32	2245.65	2187.41	2136.26	2091.11	1929.55	1834.42	1775.66	1738.28
255,000	2634.34	2527.87	2436.92	2358.56	2290.56	2231.16	2178.98	2132.93	1968.14	1871.10	1811.17	1773.05
260,000	2686.00	2577.43	2484.70	2404.81	2335.47	2274.91	2221.71	2174.75	2006.73	1907.79	1846.68	1807.82
265,000	2737.65	2627.00	2532.48	2451.06	2380.39	2318.66	2264.43	2216.57	2045.32	1944.48	1882.20	1842.58
270,000	2789.30	2676.56	2580.27	2497.30	2425.30	2362.40	2307.16	2258.39	2083.91	1981.17	1917.71	1877.35
280,000	2892.61	2775.70	2675.83	2589.80	2515.12	2449.90	2392.61	2342.04	2161.09	2054.55	1988.74	1946.88
290,000	2995.92	2874.83	2771.40	2682.29	2604.95	2537.40	2478.06	2425.68	2238.27	2127.92	2059.76	2016.41
300,000	3099.23	2973.96	2866.96	2774.78	2694.78	2624.89	2563.51	2509.33	2315.45	2201.30	2130.79	2085.94

8.25%
MONTHLY AMORTIZING PAYMENTS

AMOUNT OF LOAN	NUMBER OF YEARS IN TERM											
	1	2	3	4	5	6	7	8	9	10	11	12
$ 50	4.36	2.27	1.58	1.23	1.02	0.89	0.79	0.72	0.66	0.62	0.58	0.55
100	8.72	4.54	3.15	2.46	2.04	1.77	1.58	1.43	1.32	1.23	1.16	1.10
200	17.43	9.07	6.30	4.91	4.08	3.54	3.15	2.86	2.63	2.46	2.32	2.20
300	26.14	13.61	9.44	7.36	6.12	5.30	4.72	4.28	3.95	3.68	3.47	3.29
400	34.85	18.14	12.59	9.82	8.16	7.07	6.29	5.71	5.26	4.91	4.63	4.39
500	43.56	22.68	15.73	12.27	10.20	8.83	7.86	7.14	6.58	6.14	5.78	5.49
600	52.27	27.21	18.88	14.72	12.24	10.60	9.43	8.56	7.89	7.36	6.94	6.58
700	60.98	31.74	22.02	17.18	14.28	12.36	11.00	9.99	9.21	8.59	8.09	7.68
800	69.69	36.28	25.17	19.63	16.32	14.13	12.57	11.42	10.52	9.82	9.25	8.77
900	78.40	40.81	28.31	22.08	18.36	15.90	14.14	12.84	11.84	11.04	10.40	9.87
1,000	87.11	45.35	31.46	24.54	20.40	17.66	15.72	14.27	13.15	12.27	11.56	10.97
2,000	174.21	90.69	62.91	49.07	40.80	35.32	31.43	28.53	26.30	24.54	23.11	21.93
3,000	261.32	136.03	94.36	73.60	61.19	52.97	47.14	42.80	39.45	36.80	34.66	32.89
4,000	348.42	181.37	125.81	98.13	81.59	70.63	62.85	57.06	52.60	49.07	46.21	43.85
5,000	435.53	226.71	157.26	122.66	101.99	88.28	78.56	71.33	65.75	61.33	57.76	54.82
6,000	522.63	272.05	188.72	147.19	122.38	105.94	94.27	85.59	78.90	73.60	69.31	65.78
7,000	609.73	317.39	220.17	171.72	142.78	123.59	109.98	99.85	92.05	85.86	80.86	76.74
8,000	696.84	362.74	251.62	196.25	163.18	141.25	125.69	114.12	105.19	98.13	92.41	87.70
9,000	783.94	408.08	283.07	220.78	183.57	158.91	141.40	128.38	118.34	110.39	103.96	98.66
10,000	871.05	453.42	314.52	245.31	203.97	176.56	157.12	142.65	131.49	122.66	115.51	109.63
15,000	1306.57	680.13	471.78	367.96	305.95	264.84	235.67	213.97	197.24	183.98	173.26	164.44
20,000	1742.09	906.83	629.04	490.61	407.93	353.12	314.23	285.29	262.98	245.31	231.01	219.25
25,000	2177.61	1133.54	786.30	613.27	509.91	441.39	392.78	356.61	328.72	306.64	288.77	274.06
30,000	2613.13	1360.25	943.56	735.92	611.89	529.67	471.34	427.93	394.47	367.96	346.52	328.87
35,000	3048.65	1586.95	1100.82	858.57	713.87	617.95	549.89	499.25	460.21	429.29	404.27	383.68
40,000	3484.17	1813.66	1258.08	981.22	815.86	706.23	628.45	570.57	525.95	490.62	462.02	438.49
45,000	3919.69	2040.37	1415.34	1103.87	917.84	794.51	707.00	641.89	591.70	551.94	519.78	493.30
50,000	4355.21	2267.07	1572.60	1226.53	1019.82	882.78	785.56	713.21	657.44	613.27	577.53	548.11
55,000	4790.73	2493.78	1729.86	1349.18	1121.80	971.06	864.11	784.53	723.18	674.59	635.28	602.92
60,000	5226.25	2720.49	1887.11	1471.83	1223.78	1059.34	942.67	855.85	788.93	735.92	693.03	657.73
65,000	5661.77	2947.20	2044.37	1594.48	1325.76	1147.62	1021.22	927.17	854.67	797.25	750.79	712.54
70,000	6097.29	3173.90	2201.63	1717.14	1427.74	1235.89	1099.78	998.49	920.41	858.57	808.54	767.35
75,000	6532.81	3400.61	2358.89	1839.79	1529.72	1324.17	1178.33	1069.81	986.16	919.90	866.29	822.16
80,000	6968.33	3627.32	2516.15	1962.44	1631.71	1412.45	1256.89	1141.13	1051.90	981.23	924.04	876.97
85,000	7403.85	3854.02	2673.41	2085.09	1733.69	1500.73	1335.45	1212.45	1117.64	1042.55	981.80	931.78
90,000	7839.37	4080.73	2830.67	2207.74	1835.67	1589.01	1414.00	1283.77	1183.39	1103.88	1039.55	986.59
95,000	8274.89	4307.44	2987.93	2330.40	1937.65	1677.28	1492.56	1355.09	1249.13	1165.20	1097.30	1041.40
100,000	8710.41	4534.14	3145.19	2453.05	2039.63	1765.56	1571.11	1426.41	1314.87	1226.53	1155.05	1096.21
105,000	9145.93	4760.85	3302.45	2575.70	2141.61	1853.84	1649.67	1497.73	1380.62	1287.86	1212.81	1151.02
110,000	9581.45	4987.56	3459.71	2698.35	2243.59	1942.12	1728.22	1569.05	1446.36	1349.18	1270.56	1205.83
115,000	10016.97	5214.27	3616.96	2821.01	2345.57	2030.39	1806.78	1640.37	1512.10	1410.51	1328.31	1260.64
120,000	10452.49	5440.97	3774.22	2943.66	2447.56	2118.67	1885.33	1711.69	1577.85	1471.84	1386.06	1315.45
125,000	10888.01	5667.68	3931.48	3066.31	2549.54	2206.95	1963.89	1783.01	1643.59	1533.16	1443.82	1370.26
130,000	11323.53	5894.39	4088.74	3188.96	2651.52	2295.23	2042.44	1854.33	1709.33	1594.49	1501.57	1425.07
135,000	11759.05	6121.09	4246.00	3311.61	2753.50	2383.51	2121.00	1925.66	1775.08	1655.82	1559.32	1479.88
140,000	12194.57	6347.80	4403.26	3434.27	2855.48	2471.78	2199.55	1996.98	1840.82	1717.14	1617.07	1534.70
145,000	12630.09	6574.51	4560.52	3556.92	2957.46	2560.06	2278.11	2068.30	1906.56	1778.47	1674.83	1589.51
150,000	13065.61	6801.21	4717.78	3679.57	3059.44	2648.34	2356.66	2139.62	1972.31	1839.79	1732.58	1644.32
155,000	13501.13	7027.92	4875.04	3802.22	3161.42	2736.62	2435.22	2210.94	2038.05	1901.12	1790.33	1699.13
160,000	13936.66	7254.63	5032.30	3924.88	3263.41	2824.89	2513.77	2282.26	2103.79	1962.45	1848.08	1753.94
165,000	14372.18	7481.34	5189.56	4047.53	3365.39	2913.17	2592.33	2353.58	2169.54	2023.77	1905.83	1808.75
170,000	14807.70	7708.04	5346.81	4170.18	3467.37	3001.45	2670.89	2424.90	2235.28	2085.10	1963.59	1863.56
175,000	15243.22	7934.75	5504.07	4292.83	3569.35	3089.73	2749.44	2496.22	2301.02	2146.43	2021.34	1918.37
180,000	15678.74	8161.46	5661.33	4415.48	3671.33	3178.01	2828.00	2567.54	2366.77	2207.75	2079.09	1973.18
185,000	16114.26	8388.16	5818.59	4538.14	3773.31	3266.28	2906.55	2638.86	2432.51	2269.08	2136.84	2027.99
190,000	16549.78	8614.87	5975.85	4660.79	3875.29	3354.56	2985.11	2710.18	2498.25	2330.40	2194.60	2082.80
195,000	16985.30	8841.58	6133.11	4783.44	3977.27	3442.84	3063.66	2781.50	2564.00	2391.73	2252.35	2137.61
200,000	17420.82	9068.28	6290.37	4906.09	4079.26	3531.12	3142.22	2852.82	2629.74	2453.06	2310.10	2192.42
205,000	17856.34	9294.99	6447.63	5028.75	4181.24	3619.40	3220.77	2924.14	2695.48	2514.38	2367.85	2247.23
210,000	18291.86	9521.70	6604.89	5151.40	4283.22	3707.67	3299.33	2995.46	2761.23	2575.71	2425.61	2302.04
215,000	18727.38	9748.41	6762.15	5274.05	4385.20	3795.95	3377.88	3066.78	2826.97	2637.04	2483.36	2356.85
220,000	19162.90	9975.11	6919.41	5396.70	4487.18	3884.23	3456.44	3138.10	2892.71	2698.36	2541.11	2411.66
225,000	19598.42	10201.82	7076.67	5519.35	4589.16	3972.51	3534.99	3209.42	2958.46	2759.69	2598.86	2466.47
230,000	20033.94	10428.53	7233.92	5642.01	4691.14	4060.78	3613.55	3280.74	3024.20	2821.02	2656.62	2521.28
235,000	20469.46	10655.23	7391.18	5764.66	4793.12	4149.06	3692.10	3352.06	3089.94	2882.34	2714.37	2576.09
240,000	20904.98	10881.94	7548.44	5887.31	4895.11	4237.34	3770.66	3423.38	3155.69	2943.67	2772.12	2630.90
245,000	21340.50	11108.65	7705.70	6009.96	4997.09	4325.62	3849.21	3494.70	3221.43	3004.99	2829.87	2685.71
250,000	21776.02	11335.35	7862.96	6132.62	5099.07	4413.90	3927.77	3566.02	3287.17	3066.32	2887.63	2740.52
255,000	22211.54	11562.06	8020.22	6255.27	5201.05	4502.17	4006.33	3637.34	3352.92	3127.65	2945.38	2795.33
260,000	22647.06	11788.77	8177.48	6377.92	5303.03	4590.45	4084.88	3708.66	3418.66	3188.97	3003.13	2850.14
265,000	23082.58	12015.48	8334.74	6500.57	5405.01	4678.73	4163.44	3779.98	3484.40	3250.30	3060.88	2904.95
270,000	23518.10	12242.18	8492.00	6623.22	5506.99	4767.01	4241.99	3851.31	3550.15	3311.63	3118.64	2959.76
280,000	24389.14	12695.60	8806.52	6868.53	5710.96	4943.56	4399.10	3993.95	3681.63	3434.28	3234.14	3069.39
290,000	25260.18	13149.01	9121.03	7113.83	5914.92	5120.12	4556.21	4136.59	3813.12	3556.93	3349.65	3179.01
300,000	26131.22	13602.42	9435.55	7359.14	6118.88	5296.67	4713.32	4279.23	3944.61	3679.58	3465.15	3288.63

AMOUNT OF LOAN	NUMBER OF YEARS IN TERM											
	13	14	15	16	17	18	19	20	25	30	35	40
$ 50	0.53	0.51	0.49	0.47	0.46	0.45	0.44	0.43	0.40	0.38	0.37	0.36
100	1.05	1.01	0.98	0.94	0.92	0.90	0.87	0.86	0.79	0.76	0.73	0.72
200	2.10	2.02	1.95	1.88	1.83	1.79	1.74	1.71	1.58	1.51	1.46	1.43
300	3.15	3.02	2.92	2.82	2.74	2.68	2.61	2.56	2.37	2.26	2.19	2.15
400	4.19	4.03	3.89	3.76	3.66	3.57	3.48	3.41	3.16	3.01	2.92	2.86
500	5.24	5.03	4.86	4.70	4.57	4.46	4.35	4.27	3.95	3.76	3.65	3.58
600	6.29	6.04	5.83	5.64	5.48	5.35	5.22	5.12	4.74	4.51	4.38	4.29
700	7.33	7.04	6.80	6.58	6.40	6.24	6.09	5.97	5.52	5.26	5.10	5.00
800	8.38	8.05	7.77	7.52	7.31	7.13	6.96	6.82	6.31	6.02	5.83	5.72
900	9.43	9.06	8.74	8.46	8.22	8.02	7.83	7.67	7.10	6.77	6.56	6.43
1,000	10.48	10.06	9.71	9.40	9.14	8.91	8.70	8.53	7.89	7.52	7.29	7.15
2,000	20.95	20.12	19.41	18.80	18.27	17.81	17.40	17.05	15.77	15.03	14.57	14.29
3,000	31.42	30.17	29.11	28.19	27.40	26.71	26.10	25.57	23.66	22.54	21.86	21.43
4,000	41.89	40.23	38.81	37.59	36.53	35.61	34.80	34.09	31.54	30.06	29.14	28.57
5,000	52.36	50.28	48.51	46.99	45.67	44.51	43.50	42.61	39.43	37.57	36.43	35.71
6,000	62.83	60.34	58.21	56.38	54.80	53.41	52.20	51.13	47.31	45.08	43.71	42.85
7,000	73.30	70.39	67.91	65.78	63.93	62.32	60.90	59.65	55.20	52.59	51.00	49.99
8,000	83.77	80.45	77.62	75.18	73.06	71.22	69.60	68.17	63.08	60.11	58.28	57.14
9,000	94.24	90.51	87.32	84.57	82.19	80.12	78.30	76.69	70.97	67.62	65.57	64.28
10,000	104.71	100.56	97.02	93.97	91.33	89.02	87.00	85.21	78.85	75.13	72.85	71.42
15,000	157.07	150.84	145.53	140.95	136.99	133.53	130.49	127.81	118.27	112.69	109.28	107.13
20,000	209.42	201.12	194.03	187.94	182.65	178.03	173.99	170.42	157.70	150.26	145.70	142.83
25,000	261.77	251.40	242.54	234.92	228.31	222.54	217.48	213.02	197.12	187.82	182.13	178.54
30,000	314.13	301.67	291.05	281.90	273.97	267.05	260.98	255.62	236.54	225.38	218.55	214.25
35,000	366.48	351.95	339.55	328.88	319.63	311.56	304.47	298.23	275.96	262.95	254.98	249.95
40,000	418.84	402.23	388.06	375.87	365.29	356.06	347.97	340.83	315.39	300.51	291.40	285.66
45,000	471.19	452.51	436.57	422.85	410.95	400.57	391.46	383.43	354.81	338.07	327.83	321.37
50,000	523.54	502.79	485.08	469.83	456.61	445.08	434.96	426.04	394.23	375.64	364.25	357.07
55,000	575.90	553.07	533.58	516.81	502.27	489.59	478.46	468.64	433.65	413.20	400.68	392.78
60,000	628.25	603.34	582.09	563.80	547.93	534.09	521.95	511.24	473.08	450.76	437.10	428.49
65,000	680.60	653.62	630.60	610.78	593.59	578.60	565.45	553.85	512.50	488.33	473.52	464.20
70,000	732.96	703.90	679.10	657.76	639.25	623.11	608.94	596.45	551.92	525.89	509.95	499.90
75,000	785.31	754.18	727.61	704.74	684.92	667.62	652.44	639.05	591.34	563.45	546.37	535.61
80,000	837.67	804.46	776.12	751.73	730.58	712.12	695.93	681.66	630.77	601.02	582.80	571.32
85,000	890.02	854.74	824.62	798.71	776.24	756.63	739.43	724.26	670.19	638.58	619.22	607.02
90,000	942.37	905.01	873.13	845.69	821.90	801.14	782.92	766.86	709.61	676.14	655.65	642.73
95,000	994.73	955.29	921.64	892.67	867.56	845.65	826.42	809.47	749.03	713.71	692.07	678.44
100,000	1047.08	1005.57	970.15	939.66	913.22	890.15	869.91	852.07	788.46	751.27	728.50	714.14
105,000	1099.44	1055.85	1018.65	986.64	958.88	934.66	913.41	894.67	827.88	788.83	764.92	749.85
110,000	1151.79	1106.13	1067.16	1033.62	1004.54	979.17	956.91	937.28	867.30	826.40	801.35	785.50
115,000	1204.14	1156.41	1115.67	1080.60	1050.20	1023.67	1000.40	979.88	906.72	863.96	837.77	821.26
120,000	1256.50	1206.68	1164.17	1127.59	1095.86	1068.18	1043.90	1022.48	946.15	901.52	874.19	856.97
125,000	1308.85	1256.96	1212.68	1174.57	1141.52	1112.69	1087.39	1065.09	985.57	939.09	910.62	902.69
130,000	1361.20	1307.24	1261.19	1221.55	1187.18	1157.20	1130.89	1107.69	1024.99	976.65	947.04	928.39
135,000	1413.56	1357.52	1309.69	1268.53	1232.84	1201.70	1174.38	1150.29	1064.41	1014.21	983.47	964.09
140,000	1465.91	1407.80	1358.20	1315.52	1278.50	1246.21	1217.88	1192.90	1103.84	1051.78	1019.89	999.80
145,000	1518.27	1458.08	1406.71	1362.50	1324.17	1290.72	1261.37	1235.50	1143.26	1089.34	1056.32	1035.51
150,000	1570.62	1508.35	1455.22	1409.48	1369.83	1335.23	1304.87	1278.10	1182.68	1126.90	1092.74	1071.21
155,000	1622.97	1558.63	1503.72	1456.46	1415.49	1379.73	1348.36	1320.71	1222.10	1164.47	1129.17	1106.92
160,000	1675.33	1608.91	1552.23	1503.45	1461.15	1424.24	1391.86	1363.31	1261.53	1202.03	1165.59	1142.63
165,000	1727.68	1659.19	1600.74	1550.43	1506.81	1468.75	1435.36	1405.91	1300.95	1239.59	1202.02	1178.33
170,000	1780.04	1709.47	1649.24	1597.41	1552.47	1513.26	1478.85	1448.52	1340.37	1277.16	1238.44	1214.04
175,000	1832.39	1759.74	1697.75	1644.39	1598.13	1557.76	1522.35	1491.12	1379.79	1314.72	1274.86	1249.75
180,000	1884.74	1810.02	1746.26	1691.38	1643.79	1602.27	1565.84	1533.72	1419.22	1352.28	1311.29	1285.45
185,000	1937.10	1860.30	1794.76	1738.36	1689.45	1646.78	1609.34	1576.33	1458.64	1389.85	1347.71	1321.16
190,000	1989.45	1910.58	1843.27	1785.34	1735.11	1691.29	1652.83	1618.93	1498.06	1427.41	1384.14	1356.87
195,000	2041.80	1960.86	1891.78	1832.32	1780.77	1735.79	1696.33	1661.53	1537.48	1464.97	1420.56	1392.58
200,000	2094.16	2011.14	1940.29	1879.31	1826.43	1780.30	1739.82	1704.14	1576.91	1502.54	1456.99	1428.28
205,000	2146.51	2061.41	1988.79	1926.29	1872.09	1824.81	1783.32	1746.74	1616.33	1540.10	1493.41	1463.99
210,000	2198.87	2111.69	2037.30	1973.27	1917.75	1869.32	1826.81	1789.34	1655.75	1577.66	1529.84	1499.70
215,000	2251.22	2161.97	2085.81	2020.25	1963.42	1913.82	1870.31	1831.95	1695.17	1615.23	1566.26	1535.40
220,000	2303.57	2212.25	2134.31	2067.24	2009.08	1958.33	1913.81	1874.55	1734.60	1652.79	1602.69	1571.11
225,000	2355.93	2262.53	2182.82	2114.22	2054.74	2002.84	1957.30	1917.15	1774.02	1690.35	1639.11	1606.82
230,000	2408.28	2312.81	2231.33	2161.20	2100.40	2047.34	2000.80	1959.76	1813.44	1727.92	1675.53	1642.52
235,000	2460.64	2363.08	2279.83	2208.18	2146.06	2091.85	2044.29	2002.36	1852.86	1765.48	1711.96	1678.23
240,000	2512.99	2413.36	2328.34	2255.17	2191.72	2136.36	2087.79	2044.96	1892.29	1803.04	1748.38	1713.94
245,000	2565.34	2463.64	2376.85	2302.15	2237.38	2180.87	2131.28	2087.57	1931.71	1840.61	1784.81	1749.65
250,000	2617.70	2513.92	2425.36	2349.13	2283.04	2225.37	2174.78	2130.17	1971.13	1878.17	1821.23	1785.35
255,000	2670.05	2564.20	2473.86	2396.11	2328.70	2269.88	2218.27	2172.77	2010.55	1915.73	1857.66	1821.06
260,000	2722.40	2614.48	2522.37	2443.10	2374.36	2314.39	2261.77	2215.38	2049.98	1953.30	1894.08	1856.77
265,000	2774.76	2664.75	2570.88	2490.08	2420.02	2358.90	2305.26	2257.98	2089.40	1990.86	1930.51	1892.47
270,000	2827.11	2715.03	2619.38	2537.06	2465.68	2403.40	2348.76	2300.58	2128.82	2028.42	1966.93	1928.18
280,000	2931.82	2815.59	2716.40	2631.03	2557.00	2492.42	2435.75	2385.79	2207.67	2103.55	2039.78	1999.59
290,000	3036.53	2916.15	2813.41	2724.99	2648.33	2581.43	2522.74	2471.00	2286.51	2178.68	2112.63	2071.01
300,000	3141.23	3016.70	2910.43	2818.96	2739.65	2670.45	2609.73	2556.20	2365.36	2253.80	2185.48	2142.42

8.50%

AMOUNT OF LOAN	NUMBER OF YEARS IN TERM											
	1	2	3	4	5	6	7	8	9	10	11	12
$ 50	4.37	2.28	1.58	1.24	1.03	0.89	0.80	0.72	0.67	0.62	0.59	0.56
100	8.73	4.55	3.16	2.47	2.06	1.78	1.59	1.44	1.33	1.24	1.17	1.12
200	17.45	9.10	6.32	4.93	4.11	3.56	3.17	2.88	2.66	2.48	2.34	2.23
300	26.17	13.64	9.48	7.40	6.16	5.34	4.76	4.32	3.99	3.72	3.51	3.34
400	34.89	18.19	12.63	9.86	8.21	7.12	6.34	5.76	5.32	4.96	4.68	4.45
500	43.61	22.73	15.79	12.33	10.26	8.89	7.92	7.20	6.64	6.20	5.85	5.56
600	52.34	27.28	18.95	14.79	12.31	10.67	9.51	8.64	7.97	7.44	7.02	6.67
700	61.06	31.82	22.10	17.26	14.37	12.45	11.09	10.08	9.30	8.68	8.19	7.78
800	69.78	36.37	25.26	19.72	16.42	14.23	12.67	11.52	10.63	9.92	9.35	8.89
900	78.50	40.92	28.42	22.19	18.47	16.01	14.26	12.96	11.96	11.16	10.52	10.00
1,000	87.22	45.46	31.57	24.65	20.52	17.78	15.84	14.40	13.28	12.40	11.69	11.11
2,000	174.44	90.92	63.14	49.30	41.04	35.56	31.68	28.79	26.56	24.80	23.38	22.21
3,000	261.66	136.37	94.71	73.95	61.55	53.34	47.51	43.18	39.84	37.20	35.06	33.31
4,000	348.88	181.83	126.28	98.60	82.07	71.12	63.35	57.57	53.12	49.60	46.75	44.41
5,000	436.10	227.28	157.84	123.25	102.59	88.90	79.19	71.97	66.40	62.00	58.44	55.51
6,000	523.32	272.74	189.41	147.89	123.10	106.68	95.02	86.36	79.68	74.40	70.12	66.61
7,000	610.54	318.19	220.98	172.54	143.62	124.45	110.86	100.75	92.96	86.79	81.81	77.71
8,000	697.76	363.65	252.55	197.19	164.14	142.23	126.70	115.14	106.24	99.19	93.50	88.81
9,000	784.98	409.11	284.11	221.84	184.65	160.01	142.53	129.53	119.52	111.59	105.18	99.91
10,000	872.20	454.56	315.68	246.49	205.17	177.79	158.37	143.93	132.80	123.99	116.87	111.01
15,000	1308.30	681.84	473.52	369.73	307.75	266.68	237.55	215.89	199.20	185.98	175.30	166.51
20,000	1744.40	909.12	631.36	492.97	410.34	355.57	316.73	287.85	265.59	247.98	233.73	222.02
25,000	2180.50	1136.40	789.19	616.21	512.92	444.46	395.92	359.81	331.99	309.97	292.16	277.52
30,000	2616.60	1363.68	947.03	739.45	615.50	533.36	475.10	431.77	398.39	371.96	350.60	333.02
35,000	3052.70	1590.95	1104.87	862.70	718.08	622.25	554.28	503.73	464.78	433.95	409.03	388.52
40,000	3488.80	1818.23	1262.71	985.94	820.67	711.14	633.46	575.69	531.18	495.95	467.46	444.03
45,000	3924.90	2045.51	1420.54	1109.18	923.25	800.03	712.65	647.65	597.58	557.94	525.89	499.53
50,000	4360.99	2272.79	1578.38	1232.42	1025.83	888.92	791.83	719.61	663.97	619.93	584.32	555.03
55,000	4797.09	2500.07	1736.22	1355.66	1128.41	977.82	871.01	791.57	730.37	681.93	642.76	610.54
60,000	5233.19	2727.35	1894.06	1478.90	1231.00	1066.71	950.19	863.53	796.77	743.92	701.19	666.04
65,000	5669.29	2954.62	2051.89	1602.14	1333.58	1155.60	1029.38	935.49	863.16	805.91	759.62	721.54
70,000	6105.39	3181.90	2209.73	1725.39	1436.16	1244.49	1108.56	1007.45	929.56	867.90	818.05	777.04
75,000	6541.49	3409.18	2367.57	1848.63	1538.74	1333.38	1187.74	1079.41	995.96	929.90	876.48	832.55
80,000	6977.59	3636.46	2525.41	1971.87	1641.33	1422.28	1266.92	1151.38	1062.35	991.89	934.92	888.05
85,000	7413.69	3863.74	2683.25	2095.11	1743.91	1511.17	1346.11	1223.34	1128.75	1053.88	993.35	943.55
90,000	7849.79	4091.02	2841.08	2218.35	1846.49	1600.06	1425.29	1295.30	1195.15	1115.88	1051.78	999.06
95,000	8285.88	4318.29	2998.92	2341.59	1949.08	1688.95	1504.47	1367.26	1261.54	1177.87	1110.21	1054.56
100,000	8721.98	4545.57	3156.76	2464.84	2051.66	1777.84	1583.65	1439.22	1327.94	1239.86	1168.64	1110.06
105,000	9158.08	4772.85	3314.60	2588.08	2154.24	1866.74	1662.84	1511.18	1394.34	1301.85	1227.08	1165.56
110,000	9594.18	5000.13	3472.43	2711.32	2256.82	1955.63	1742.02	1583.14	1460.73	1363.85	1285.51	1221.07
115,000	10030.28	5227.41	3630.27	2834.56	2359.41	2044.52	1821.20	1655.10	1527.13	1425.84	1343.94	1276.57
120,000	10466.38	5454.69	3788.11	2957.80	2461.99	2133.41	1900.38	1727.06	1593.53	1487.83	1402.37	1332.07
125,000	10902.48	5681.96	3945.95	3081.04	2564.57	2222.30	1979.57	1799.02	1659.92	1549.83	1460.80	1387.57
130,000	11338.58	5909.24	4103.78	3204.28	2667.15	2311.19	2058.75	1870.98	1726.32	1611.82	1519.24	1443.08
135,000	11774.68	6136.52	4261.62	3327.53	2769.74	2400.09	2137.93	1942.94	1792.72	1673.81	1577.67	1498.58
140,000	12210.77	6363.80	4419.46	3450.77	2872.32	2488.98	2217.11	2014.90	1859.11	1735.80	1636.10	1554.08
145,000	12646.87	6591.08	4577.30	3574.01	2974.90	2577.87	2296.30	2086.86	1925.51	1797.80	1694.53	1609.59
150,000	13082.97	6818.36	4735.14	3697.25	3077.48	2666.76	2375.48	2158.82	1991.91	1859.79	1752.96	1665.09
155,000	13519.07	7045.63	4892.97	3820.49	3180.07	2755.65	2454.66	2230.78	2058.30	1921.78	1811.40	1720.59
160,000	13955.17	7272.91	5050.81	3943.73	3282.65	2844.55	2533.84	2302.75	2124.70	1983.78	1869.83	1776.09
165,000	14391.27	7500.19	5208.65	4066.98	3385.23	2933.44	2613.03	2374.71	2191.10	2045.77	1928.26	1831.60
170,000	14827.37	7727.47	5366.49	4190.22	3487.82	3022.33	2692.21	2446.67	2257.49	2107.76	1986.69	1887.10
175,000	15263.47	7954.75	5524.32	4313.46	3590.40	3111.22	2771.39	2518.63	2323.89	2169.75	2045.12	1942.60
180,000	15699.57	8182.03	5682.16	4436.70	3692.98	3200.11	2850.57	2590.59	2390.29	2231.75	2103.56	1998.11
185,000	16135.66	8409.30	5840.00	4559.94	3795.56	3289.01	2929.75	2662.55	2456.69	2293.74	2161.99	2053.61
190,000	16571.76	8636.58	5997.84	4683.18	3898.15	3377.90	3008.94	2734.51	2523.08	2355.73	2220.42	2109.11
195,000	17007.86	8863.86	6155.67	4806.42	4000.73	3466.79	3088.12	2806.47	2589.48	2417.73	2278.85	2164.61
200,000	17443.96	9091.14	6313.51	4929.67	4103.31	3555.68	3167.30	2878.43	2655.88	2479.72	2337.28	2220.12
205,000	17880.06	9318.42	6471.35	5052.91	4205.89	3644.57	3246.48	2950.39	2722.27	2541.71	2395.72	2275.62
210,000	18316.16	9545.70	6629.19	5176.15	4308.48	3733.47	3325.67	3022.35	2788.67	2603.70	2454.15	2331.12
215,000	18752.26	9772.98	6787.03	5299.39	4411.06	3822.36	3404.85	3094.31	2855.07	2665.70	2512.58	2386.62
220,000	19188.36	10000.25	6944.86	5422.63	4513.64	3911.25	3484.03	3166.27	2921.46	2727.69	2571.01	2442.13
225,000	19624.46	10227.53	7102.70	5545.87	4616.22	4000.14	3563.21	3238.23	2987.86	2789.68	2629.44	2497.63
230,000	20060.55	10454.81	7260.54	5669.11	4718.81	4089.03	3642.40	3310.19	3054.26	2851.68	2687.88	2553.13
235,000	20496.65	10682.09	7418.38	5792.36	4821.39	4177.93	3721.58	3382.16	3120.65	2913.67	2746.31	2608.64
240,000	20932.75	10909.37	7576.21	5915.60	4923.97	4266.82	3800.76	3454.12	3187.05	2975.66	2804.74	2664.14
245,000	21368.85	11136.65	7734.05	6038.84	5026.56	4355.71	3879.94	3526.08	3253.45	3037.65	2863.17	2719.64
250,000	21804.95	11363.92	7891.89	6162.08	5129.14	4444.60	3959.13	3598.04	3319.84	3099.65	2921.60	2775.14
255,000	22241.05	11591.20	8049.73	6285.32	5231.72	4533.49	4038.31	3670.00	3386.24	3161.64	2980.03	2830.65
260,000	22677.15	11818.48	8207.56	6408.56	5334.30	4622.38	4117.49	3741.96	3452.64	3223.63	3038.47	2886.15
265,000	23113.25	12045.76	8365.40	6531.81	5436.89	4711.28	4196.67	3813.92	3519.03	3285.63	3096.90	2941.65
270,000	23549.35	12273.04	8523.24	6655.05	5539.47	4800.17	4275.86	3885.88	3585.43	3347.62	3155.33	2997.16
280,000	24421.54	12727.59	8838.92	6901.53	5744.63	4977.95	4434.22	4029.80	3718.22	3471.60	3272.19	3108.16
290,000	25293.74	13182.15	9154.59	7148.01	5949.80	5155.74	4592.59	4173.72	3851.02	3595.59	3389.06	3219.17
300,000	26165.94	13636.71	9470.27	7394.50	6154.96	5333.52	4750.95	4317.64	3983.81	3719.58	3505.92	3330.17

AMOUNT OF LOAN	NUMBER OF YEARS IN TERM											
	13	14	15	16	17	18	19	20	25	30	35	40
$ 50	0.54	0.51	0.50	0.48	0.47	0.46	0.45	0.44	0.41	0.39	0.38	0.37
100	1.07	1.02	0.99	0.96	0.93	0.91	0.89	0.87	0.81	0.77	0.75	0.74
200	2.13	2.04	1.97	1.91	1.86	1.82	1.78	1.74	1.62	1.54	1.50	1.47
300	3.19	3.06	2.96	2.87	2.79	2.72	2.66	2.61	2.42	2.31	2.25	2.20
400	4.25	4.08	3.94	3.82	3.72	3.63	3.55	3.48	3.23	3.08	2.99	2.94
500	5.31	5.10	4.93	4.78	4.65	4.53	4.43	4.34	4.03	3.85	3.74	3.67
600	6.37	6.12	5.91	5.73	5.57	5.44	5.32	5.21	4.84	4.62	4.49	4.40
700	7.43	7.14	6.90	6.69	6.50	6.34	6.20	6.08	5.64	5.39	5.23	5.14
800	8.49	8.16	7.88	7.64	7.43	7.25	7.09	6.95	6.45	6.16	5.98	5.87
900	9.56	9.18	8.87	8.60	8.36	8.15	7.97	7.82	7.25	6.93	6.73	6.60
1,000	10.62	10.20	9.85	9.55	9.29	9.06	8.86	8.68	8.06	7.69	7.47	7.34
2,000	21.23	20.40	19.70	19.09	18.57	18.11	17.71	17.36	16.11	15.38	14.94	14.67
3,000	31.84	30.60	29.55	28.64	27.85	27.17	26.57	26.04	24.16	23.07	22.41	22.00
4,000	42.45	40.80	39.39	38.18	37.14	36.22	35.42	34.72	32.21	30.76	29.88	29.33
5,000	53.06	51.00	49.24	47.73	46.42	45.28	44.28	43.40	40.27	38.45	37.35	36.66
6,000	63.68	61.20	59.09	57.27	55.70	54.33	53.13	52.07	48.32	46.14	44.82	43.99
7,000	74.29	71.40	68.94	66.82	64.99	63.39	61.99	60.75	56.37	53.83	52.29	51.32
8,000	84.90	81.60	78.78	76.36	74.27	72.44	70.84	69.43	64.42	61.52	59.75	58.65
9,000	95.51	91.80	88.63	85.91	83.55	81.50	79.70	78.11	72.48	69.21	67.22	65.98
10,000	106.12	102.00	98.48	95.45	92.83	90.55	88.55	86.79	80.53	76.90	74.69	73.31
15,000	159.18	152.99	147.72	143.18	139.25	135.82	132.82	130.18	120.79	115.34	112.03	109.97
20,000	212.24	203.99	196.95	190.90	185.66	181.10	177.09	173.57	161.05	153.79	149.38	146.62
25,000	265.30	254.98	246.19	238.63	232.08	226.37	221.37	216.96	201.31	192.23	186.72	183.28
30,000	318.36	305.98	295.43	286.35	278.49	271.64	265.64	260.35	241.57	230.68	224.00	219.93
35,000	371.42	356.98	344.66	334.08	324.91	316.92	309.91	303.74	281.83	269.12	261.41	256.59
40,000	424.48	407.97	393.90	381.80	371.32	362.19	354.18	347.13	322.10	307.57	298.75	293.24
45,000	477.54	458.97	443.14	429.53	417.74	407.46	398.46	390.53	362.36	346.02	336.09	329.90
50,000	530.59	509.96	492.37	477.25	464.15	452.73	442.73	433.92	402.62	384.46	373.43	366.55
55,000	583.65	560.96	541.61	524.98	510.57	498.01	487.00	477.31	442.88	422.91	410.78	403.21
60,000	636.71	611.96	590.85	572.70	556.98	543.28	531.27	520.70	483.14	461.35	448.12	439.86
65,000	689.77	662.95	640.08	620.42	603.39	588.55	575.54	564.09	523.40	499.80	485.46	476.52
70,000	742.83	713.95	689.32	668.15	649.81	633.83	619.82	607.48	563.66	538.24	522.81	513.17
75,000	795.89	764.94	738.56	715.87	696.22	679.10	664.09	650.87	603.93	576.69	560.15	549.83
80,000	848.95	815.94	787.80	763.60	742.64	724.37	708.36	694.26	644.19	615.14	597.49	586.48
85,000	902.01	866.94	837.03	811.32	789.05	769.64	752.63	737.65	684.45	653.58	634.84	623.13
90,000	955.07	917.93	886.27	859.05	835.47	814.92	796.91	781.05	724.71	692.03	672.18	659.79
95,000	1008.13	968.93	935.51	906.77	881.88	860.19	841.18	824.44	764.97	730.47	709.52	696.44
100,000	1061.18	1019.92	984.74	954.50	928.30	905.46	885.45	867.83	805.23	768.92	746.87	733.10
105,000	1114.24	1070.92	1033.98	1002.22	974.71	950.74	929.72	911.22	845.49	807.36	784.21	769.75
110,000	1167.30	1121.92	1083.22	1049.95	1021.13	996.01	974.00	954.61	885.75	845.81	821.55	806.41
115,000	1220.36	1172.91	1132.46	1097.67	1067.54	1041.28	1018.27	998.00	926.02	884.26	858.89	843.06
120,000	1273.42	1223.91	1181.69	1145.39	1113.96	1086.55	1062.54	1041.39	966.28	922.70	896.24	879.72
125,000	1326.48	1274.90	1230.93	1193.12	1160.37	1131.82	1106.81	1084.78	1006.54	961.15	933.58	916.37
130,000	1379.54	1325.90	1280.17	1240.84	1206.78	1177.10	1151.08	1128.18	1046.80	999.59	970.92	953.03
135,000	1432.60	1376.90	1329.40	1288.57	1253.20	1222.37	1195.36	1171.57	1087.06	1038.04	1008.27	989.68
140,000	1485.66	1427.89	1378.64	1336.29	1299.61	1267.65	1239.63	1214.96	1127.32	1076.48	1045.61	1026.34
145,000	1538.71	1478.89	1427.88	1384.02	1346.03	1312.92	1283.90	1258.35	1167.58	1114.93	1082.95	1062.99
150,000	1591.77	1529.88	1477.11	1431.74	1392.44	1358.19	1328.17	1301.74	1207.85	1153.38	1120.30	1099.65
155,000	1644.83	1580.88	1526.35	1479.47	1438.86	1403.46	1372.45	1345.13	1248.11	1191.82	1157.64	1136.30
160,000	1697.89	1631.87	1575.59	1527.19	1485.27	1448.74	1416.72	1388.52	1288.37	1230.27	1194.98	1172.96
165,000	1750.95	1682.87	1624.83	1574.92	1531.69	1494.01	1460.99	1431.91	1328.63	1268.71	1232.32	1209.61
170,000	1804.01	1733.87	1674.06	1622.64	1578.10	1539.28	1505.26	1475.30	1368.89	1307.16	1269.67	1246.26
175,000	1857.07	1784.86	1723.30	1670.36	1624.52	1584.56	1549.53	1518.70	1409.15	1345.60	1307.01	1282.92
180,000	1910.13	1835.86	1772.54	1718.09	1670.93	1629.83	1593.81	1562.09	1449.41	1384.05	1344.35	1319.57
185,000	1963.19	1886.85	1821.77	1765.81	1717.35	1675.10	1638.08	1605.48	1489.68	1422.49	1381.70	1356.23
190,000	2016.25	1937.85	1871.01	1813.54	1763.76	1720.37	1682.35	1648.87	1529.94	1460.94	1419.04	1392.88
195,000	2069.30	1988.85	1920.25	1861.26	1810.17	1765.65	1726.62	1692.26	1570.20	1499.39	1456.38	1429.54
200,000	2122.36	2039.84	1969.48	1908.99	1856.59	1810.92	1770.90	1735.65	1610.46	1537.83	1493.73	1466.19
205,000	2175.42	2090.84	2018.72	1956.71	1903.00	1856.19	1815.17	1779.04	1650.72	1576.28	1531.07	1502.85
210,000	2228.48	2141.83	2067.96	2004.44	1949.42	1901.47	1859.44	1822.43	1690.98	1614.72	1568.41	1539.50
215,000	2281.54	2192.83	2117.20	2052.16	1995.83	1946.74	1903.71	1865.82	1731.24	1653.17	1605.76	1576.16
220,000	2334.60	2243.83	2166.43	2099.89	2042.25	1992.01	1947.99	1909.22	1771.50	1691.61	1643.10	1612.81
225,000	2387.66	2294.82	2215.67	2147.61	2088.66	2037.28	1992.26	1952.61	1811.77	1730.06	1680.44	1649.47
230,000	2440.72	2345.82	2264.91	2195.33	2135.08	2082.56	2036.53	1996.00	1852.03	1768.51	1717.78	1686.12
235,000	2493.78	2396.81	2314.14	2243.06	2181.49	2127.83	2080.80	2039.39	1892.29	1806.95	1755.13	1722.78
240,000	2546.83	2447.81	2363.38	2290.78	2227.91	2173.10	2125.07	2082.78	1932.55	1845.40	1792.47	1759.43
245,000	2599.89	2498.81	2412.62	2338.51	2274.32	2218.38	2169.35	2126.17	1972.81	1883.84	1829.81	1796.09
250,000	2652.95	2549.80	2461.85	2386.23	2320.74	2263.65	2213.62	2169.56	2013.07	1922.29	1867.16	1832.74
255,000	2706.01	2600.80	2511.09	2433.96	2367.15	2308.92	2257.89	2212.95	2053.33	1960.73	1904.50	1869.39
260,000	2759.07	2651.79	2560.33	2481.68	2413.56	2354.19	2302.16	2256.35	2093.60	1999.18	1941.84	1906.05
265,000	2812.13	2702.79	2609.56	2529.41	2459.98	2399.47	2346.44	2299.74	2133.86	2037.63	1979.19	1942.70
270,000	2865.19	2753.79	2658.80	2577.13	2506.39	2444.74	2390.71	2343.13	2174.12	2076.07	2016.53	1979.36
280,000	2971.31	2855.78	2757.28	2672.58	2599.22	2535.29	2479.25	2429.91	2254.64	2152.96	2091.21	2052.67
290,000	3077.42	2957.77	2855.75	2768.03	2692.05	2625.83	2567.80	2516.69	2335.16	2229.85	2165.90	2125.98
300,000	3183.54	3059.76	2954.22	2863.48	2784.88	2716.38	2656.34	2603.47	2415.69	2306.75	2240.59	2199.29

8.75% MONTHLY AMORTIZING PAYMENTS

AMOUNT OF LOAN	NUMBER OF YEARS IN TERM											
	1	2	3	4	5	6	7	8	9	10	11	12
$ 50	4.37	2.28	1.59	1.24	1.04	0.90	0.80	0.73	0.68	0.63	0.60	0.57
100	8.74	4.56	3.17	2.48	2.07	1.80	1.60	1.46	1.35	1.26	1.19	1.13
200	17.47	9.12	6.34	4.96	4.13	3.59	3.20	2.91	2.69	2.51	2.37	2.25
300	26.21	13.68	9.51	7.43	6.20	5.38	4.79	4.36	4.03	3.76	3.55	3.38
400	34.94	18.23	12.68	9.91	8.26	7.17	6.39	5.81	5.37	5.02	4.73	4.50
500	43.67	22.79	15.85	12.39	10.32	8.96	7.99	7.27	6.71	6.27	5.92	5.62
600	52.41	27.35	19.02	14.86	12.39	10.75	9.58	8.72	8.05	7.52	7.10	6.75
700	61.14	31.90	22.18	17.34	14.45	12.54	11.18	10.17	9.39	8.78	8.28	7.87
800	69.87	36.46	25.35	19.82	16.51	14.33	12.77	11.62	10.73	10.03	9.46	9.00
900	78.61	41.02	28.52	22.29	18.58	16.12	14.37	13.07	12.07	11.28	10.65	10.12
1,000	87.34	45.58	31.69	24.77	20.64	17.91	15.97	14.53	13.42	12.54	11.83	11.24
2,000	174.68	91.15	63.37	49.54	41.28	35.81	31.93	29.05	26.83	25.07	23.65	22.48
3,000	262.01	136.72	95.06	74.30	61.92	53.71	47.89	43.57	40.24	37.60	35.47	33.72
4,000	349.35	182.29	126.74	99.07	82.55	71.61	63.85	58.09	53.65	50.14	47.30	44.96
5,000	436.68	227.86	158.42	123.84	103.19	89.51	79.82	72.61	67.06	62.67	59.12	56.20
6,000	524.02	273.43	190.11	148.60	123.83	107.42	95.78	87.13	80.47	75.20	70.94	67.44
7,000	611.35	319.00	221.79	173.37	144.47	125.32	111.74	101.65	93.88	87.73	82.77	78.68
8,000	698.69	364.57	253.47	198.14	165.10	143.22	127.70	116.17	107.29	100.27	94.59	89.92
9,000	786.03	410.14	285.16	222.90	185.74	161.12	143.67	130.69	120.70	112.80	106.41	101.16
10,000	873.36	455.71	316.84	247.67	206.38	179.02	159.63	145.21	134.11	125.33	118.24	112.40
15,000	1310.04	683.56	475.26	371.50	309.56	268.53	239.44	217.82	201.17	188.00	177.35	168.60
20,000	1746.72	911.41	633.68	495.34	412.75	358.04	319.25	290.42	268.22	250.66	236.47	224.80
25,000	2183.39	1139.26	792.09	619.17	515.94	447.55	399.07	363.03	335.27	313.32	295.58	281.00
30,000	2620.07	1367.11	950.51	743.00	619.12	537.06	478.88	435.63	402.33	375.99	354.70	337.20
35,000	3056.75	1594.96	1108.93	866.83	722.31	626.56	558.69	508.23	469.38	438.65	413.82	393.40
40,000	3493.43	1822.81	1267.35	990.67	825.49	716.07	638.50	580.84	536.44	501.31	472.93	449.60
45,000	3930.11	2050.66	1425.76	1114.50	928.68	805.58	718.32	653.44	603.49	563.98	532.05	505.80
50,000	4366.78	2278.51	1584.18	1238.33	1031.87	895.09	798.13	726.05	670.54	626.64	591.16	562.00
55,000	4803.46	2506.36	1742.60	1362.16	1135.05	984.60	877.94	798.65	737.60	689.30	650.28	618.20
60,000	5240.14	2734.21	1901.02	1486.00	1238.24	1074.11	957.75	871.26	804.65	751.97	709.40	674.40
65,000	5676.82	2962.06	2059.43	1609.83	1341.43	1163.62	1037.57	943.86	871.70	814.63	768.51	730.60
70,000	6113.50	3189.91	2217.85	1733.66	1444.61	1253.12	1117.38	1016.46	938.76	877.29	827.63	786.80
75,000	6550.17	3417.76	2376.27	1857.49	1547.80	1342.63	1197.19	1089.07	1005.81	939.96	886.74	843.00
80,000	6986.85	3645.61	2534.69	1981.33	1650.98	1432.14	1277.00	1161.67	1072.87	1002.62	945.86	899.20
85,000	7423.53	3873.47	2693.10	2105.16	1754.17	1521.65	1356.82	1234.28	1139.92	1065.28	1004.97	955.40
90,000	7860.21	4101.32	2851.52	2228.99	1857.36	1611.16	1436.63	1306.88	1206.97	1127.95	1064.09	1011.60
95,000	8296.89	4329.17	3009.94	2352.82	1960.54	1700.67	1516.44	1379.48	1274.03	1190.61	1123.21	1067.80
100,000	8733.56	4557.02	3168.36	2476.66	2063.73	1790.18	1596.25	1452.09	1341.08	1253.27	1182.32	1124.00
105,000	9170.24	4784.87	3326.77	2600.49	2166.91	1879.68	1676.07	1524.69	1408.14	1315.94	1241.44	1180.20
110,000	9606.92	5012.72	3485.19	2724.32	2270.10	1969.19	1755.88	1597.30	1475.19	1378.60	1300.55	1236.40
115,000	10043.60	5240.57	3643.61	2848.15	2373.29	2058.70	1835.69	1669.90	1542.24	1441.26	1359.67	1292.60
120,000	10480.28	5468.42	3802.03	2971.99	2476.47	2148.21	1915.50	1742.51	1609.30	1503.93	1418.79	1348.80
125,000	10916.95	5696.27	3960.44	3095.82	2579.66	2237.72	1995.32	1815.11	1676.35	1566.59	1477.90	1405.00
130,000	11353.63	5924.12	4118.86	3219.65	2682.85	2327.23	2075.13	1887.71	1743.40	1629.25	1537.02	1461.20
135,000	11790.31	6151.97	4277.28	3343.48	2786.03	2416.74	2154.94	1960.32	1810.46	1691.92	1596.13	1517.40
140,000	12226.99	6379.82	4435.70	3467.32	2889.22	2506.24	2234.75	2032.92	1877.51	1754.58	1655.25	1573.60
145,000	12663.67	6607.67	4594.11	3591.15	2992.40	2595.75	2314.57	2105.53	1944.57	1817.24	1714.36	1629.80
150,000	13100.34	6835.52	4752.53	3714.98	3095.59	2685.26	2394.38	2178.13	2011.62	1879.91	1773.48	1686.00
155,000	13537.02	7063.37	4910.95	3838.81	3198.78	2774.77	2474.19	2250.74	2078.67	1942.57	1832.60	1742.20
160,000	13973.70	7291.22	5069.37	3962.65	3301.96	2864.28	2554.00	2323.34	2145.73	2005.23	1891.71	1798.40
165,000	14410.38	7519.08	5227.78	4086.48	3405.15	2953.79	2633.82	2395.94	2212.78	2067.90	1950.83	1854.60
170,000	14847.05	7746.93	5386.20	4210.31	3508.33	3043.30	2713.63	2468.55	2279.84	2130.56	2009.94	1910.80
175,000	15283.73	7974.78	5544.62	4334.14	3611.52	3132.80	2793.44	2541.15	2346.89	2193.22	2069.06	1967.00
180,000	15720.41	8202.63	5703.04	4457.98	3714.71	3222.31	2873.25	2613.76	2413.94	2255.89	2128.18	2023.20
185,000	16157.09	8430.48	5861.45	4581.81	3817.89	3311.82	2953.07	2686.36	2481.00	2318.55	2187.29	2079.40
190,000	16593.77	8658.33	6019.87	4705.64	3921.08	3401.33	3032.88	2758.96	2548.05	2381.21	2246.41	2135.60
195,000	17030.44	8886.18	6178.29	4829.47	4024.27	3490.84	3112.69	2831.57	2615.10	2443.88	2305.52	2191.80
200,000	17467.12	9114.03	6336.71	4953.31	4127.45	3580.35	3192.50	2904.17	2682.16	2506.54	2364.64	2248.00
205,000	17903.80	9341.88	6495.12	5077.14	4230.64	3669.86	3272.32	2976.78	2749.21	2569.20	2423.75	2304.20
210,000	18340.48	9569.73	6653.54	5200.97	4333.82	3759.36	3352.13	3049.38	2816.27	2631.87	2482.87	2360.40
215,000	18777.16	9797.58	6811.96	5324.80	4437.01	3848.87	3431.94	3121.99	2883.32	2694.53	2541.99	2416.60
220,000	19213.83	10025.43	6970.38	5448.64	4540.20	3938.38	3511.75	3194.59	2950.37	2757.19	2601.10	2472.80
225,000	19650.51	10253.28	7128.79	5572.47	4643.38	4027.89	3591.57	3267.19	3017.43	2819.86	2660.22	2529.00
230,000	20087.19	10481.13	7287.21	5696.30	4746.57	4117.40	3671.38	3339.80	3084.48	2882.52	2719.33	2585.20
235,000	20523.87	10708.98	7445.63	5820.13	4849.75	4206.91	3751.19	3412.40	3151.54	2945.18	2778.45	2641.40
240,000	20960.55	10936.83	7604.05	5943.97	4952.94	4296.42	3831.00	3485.01	3218.59	3007.85	2837.57	2697.60
245,000	21397.22	11164.69	7762.46	6067.80	5056.13	4385.92	3910.82	3557.61	3285.64	3070.51	2896.68	2753.80
250,000	21833.90	11392.54	7920.88	6191.63	5159.31	4475.43	3990.63	3630.21	3352.70	3133.17	2955.80	2810.00
255,000	22270.58	11620.39	8079.30	6315.46	5262.50	4564.94	4070.44	3702.82	3419.75	3195.84	3014.91	2866.20
260,000	22707.26	11848.24	8237.72	6439.30	5365.69	4654.45	4150.25	3775.42	3486.80	3258.50	3074.03	2922.40
265,000	23143.94	12076.09	8396.13	6563.13	5468.87	4743.96	4230.07	3848.03	3553.86	3321.16	3133.14	2978.60
270,000	23580.61	12303.94	8554.55	6686.96	5572.06	4833.47	4309.88	3920.63	3620.91	3383.83	3192.26	3034.80
280,000	24453.97	12759.64	8871.39	6934.63	5778.43	5012.48	4469.50	4065.84	3755.02	3509.15	3310.49	3147.20
290,000	25327.33	13215.34	9188.22	7182.29	5984.80	5191.50	4629.13	4211.05	3889.13	3634.48	3428.72	3259.60
300,000	26200.68	13671.04	9505.06	7429.96	6191.17	5370.52	4788.75	4356.26	4023.24	3759.81	3546.96	3372.00

56

AMOUNT OF LOAN	NUMBER OF YEARS IN TERM											
	13	14	15	16	17	18	19	20	25	30	35	40
$ 50	0.54	0.52	0.50	0.49	0.48	0.47	0.46	0.45	0.42	0.40	0.39	0.38
100	1.08	1.04	1.00	0.97	0.95	0.93	0.91	0.89	0.83	0.79	0.77	0.76
200	2.16	2.07	2.00	1.94	1.89	1.85	1.81	1.77	1.65	1.58	1.54	1.51
300	3.23	3.11	3.00	2.91	2.84	2.77	2.71	2.66	2.47	2.37	2.30	2.26
400	4.31	4.14	4.00	3.88	3.78	3.69	3.61	3.54	3.29	3.15	3.07	3.01
500	5.38	5.18	5.00	4.85	4.72	4.61	4.51	4.42	4.12	3.94	3.83	3.77
600	6.46	6.21	6.00	5.82	5.67	5.53	5.41	5.31	4.94	4.73	4.60	4.52
700	7.53	7.25	7.00	6.79	6.61	6.45	6.31	6.19	5.76	5.51	5.36	5.27
800	8.61	8.28	8.00	7.76	7.55	7.37	7.21	7.07	6.58	6.30	6.13	6.02
900	9.68	9.31	9.00	8.73	8.50	8.29	8.11	7.96	7.40	7.09	6.89	6.77
1,000	10.76	10.35	10.00	9.70	9.44	9.21	9.02	8.84	8.23	7.87	7.66	7.53
2,000	21.51	20.69	19.99	19.39	18.87	18.42	18.03	17.68	16.45	15.74	15.31	15.05
3,000	32.27	31.04	29.99	29.09	28.31	27.63	27.04	26.52	24.67	23.61	22.97	22.57
4,000	43.02	41.38	39.98	38.78	37.74	36.84	36.05	35.35	32.89	31.47	30.62	30.09
5,000	53.77	51.72	49.98	48.48	47.18	46.05	45.06	44.19	41.11	39.34	38.27	37.61
6,000	64.53	62.07	59.97	58.17	56.61	55.26	54.07	53.03	49.33	47.21	45.93	45.14
7,000	75.28	72.41	69.97	67.87	66.05	64.47	63.08	61.86	57.56	55.07	53.58	52.66
8,000	86.04	82.76	79.96	77.56	75.48	73.68	72.09	70.70	65.78	62.94	61.23	60.18
9,000	96.79	93.10	89.96	87.26	84.92	82.89	81.10	79.54	74.00	70.81	68.89	67.70
10,000	107.54	103.44	99.95	96.95	94.35	92.09	90.12	88.38	82.22	78.68	76.54	75.22
15,000	161.31	155.16	149.92	145.42	141.53	138.14	135.17	132.56	123.33	118.01	114.81	112.83
20,000	215.08	206.88	199.89	193.89	188.70	184.18	180.23	176.75	164.43	157.35	153.08	150.44
25,000	268.85	258.60	249.87	242.37	235.88	230.23	225.28	220.93	205.54	196.68	191.35	188.05
30,000	322.62	310.32	299.84	290.84	283.05	276.27	270.34	265.12	246.65	236.02	229.61	225.66
35,000	376.39	362.04	349.81	339.31	330.23	322.32	315.39	309.30	287.76	275.35	267.88	263.26
40,000	430.16	413.76	399.78	387.78	377.40	368.36	360.45	353.49	328.86	314.69	306.15	300.87
45,000	483.93	465.47	449.76	436.26	424.58	414.41	405.50	397.67	369.97	354.02	344.42	338.48
50,000	537.70	517.19	499.73	484.73	471.75	460.45	450.56	441.86	411.08	393.36	382.69	376.09
55,000	591.46	568.91	549.70	533.20	518.92	506.49	495.61	486.05	452.18	432.69	420.95	413.70
60,000	645.23	620.63	599.67	581.67	566.10	552.54	540.67	530.23	493.29	472.03	459.22	451.31
65,000	699.00	672.35	649.65	630.15	613.27	598.58	585.73	574.42	534.40	511.36	497.49	488.92
70,000	752.77	724.07	699.62	678.62	660.45	644.63	630.78	618.60	575.51	550.70	535.76	526.52
75,000	806.54	775.79	749.59	727.09	707.62	690.67	675.84	662.79	616.61	590.03	574.03	564.13
80,000	860.31	827.51	799.56	775.56	754.80	736.72	720.89	706.97	657.72	629.37	612.30	601.74
85,000	914.08	879.22	849.54	824.03	801.97	782.76	765.95	751.16	698.83	668.70	650.56	639.35
90,000	967.85	930.94	899.51	872.51	849.15	828.81	811.00	795.34	739.93	708.04	688.83	676.96
95,000	1021.62	982.66	949.48	920.98	896.32	874.85	856.06	839.53	781.04	747.37	727.10	714.57
100,000	1075.39	1034.38	999.45	969.45	943.49	920.90	901.11	883.72	822.15	786.71	765.37	752.18
105,000	1129.15	1086.10	1049.43	1017.92	990.67	966.94	946.17	927.90	863.26	826.04	803.64	789.78
110,000	1182.92	1137.82	1099.40	1066.40	1037.84	1012.98	991.22	972.09	904.36	865.38	841.90	827.39
115,000	1236.69	1189.54	1149.37	1114.87	1085.02	1059.03	1036.28	1016.27	945.47	904.71	880.17	865.00
120,000	1290.40	1241.20	1199.34	1163.34	1132.19	1105.07	1081.34	1060.46	986.58	944.05	918.44	902.01
125,000	1344.23	1292.98	1249.32	1211.81	1179.37	1151.12	1126.39	1104.64	1027.68	983.38	956.71	940.22
130,000	1398.00	1344.69	1299.29	1260.29	1226.54	1197.16	1171.45	1148.83	1068.79	1022.72	994.98	977.83
135,000	1451.77	1396.41	1349.26	1308.76	1273.72	1243.21	1216.50	1193.01	1109.90	1062.05	1033.25	1015.44
140,000	1505.54	1448.13	1399.23	1357.23	1320.89	1289.25	1261.56	1237.20	1151.01	1101.39	1071.51	1053.04
145,000	1559.31	1499.85	1449.21	1405.70	1368.06	1335.30	1306.61	1281.39	1192.11	1140.72	1109.78	1090.65
150,000	1613.08	1551.57	1499.18	1454.18	1415.24	1381.34	1351.67	1325.57	1233.22	1180.06	1148.05	1128.26
155,000	1666.85	1603.29	1549.15	1502.65	1462.41	1427.39	1396.72	1369.76	1274.33	1219.39	1186.32	1165.87
160,000	1720.61	1655.01	1599.12	1551.12	1509.59	1473.43	1441.78	1413.94	1315.43	1258.73	1224.59	1203.48
165,000	1774.38	1706.73	1649.10	1599.59	1556.76	1519.47	1486.83	1458.13	1356.54	1298.06	1262.85	1241.09
170,000	1828.15	1758.44	1699.07	1648.06	1603.94	1565.52	1531.89	1502.31	1397.65	1337.40	1301.12	1278.69
175,000	1881.92	1810.16	1749.04	1696.54	1651.11	1611.56	1576.95	1546.50	1438.76	1376.73	1339.39	1316.30
180,000	1935.69	1861.88	1799.01	1745.01	1698.29	1657.61	1622.00	1590.68	1479.86	1416.07	1377.66	1353.91
185,000	1989.46	1913.60	1848.99	1793.48	1745.46	1703.65	1667.06	1634.87	1520.97	1455.40	1415.93	1391.52
190,000	2043.23	1965.32	1898.96	1841.95	1792.63	1749.70	1712.11	1679.06	1562.08	1494.74	1454.19	1429.13
195,000	2097.00	2017.04	1948.93	1890.43	1839.81	1795.74	1757.17	1723.24	1603.19	1534.07	1492.46	1466.74
200,000	2150.77	2068.76	1998.90	1938.90	1886.98	1841.79	1802.22	1767.43	1644.29	1573.41	1530.73	1504.35
205,000	2204.54	2120.48	2048.87	1987.37	1934.16	1887.83	1847.28	1811.61	1685.40	1612.74	1569.00	1541.95
210,000	2258.30	2172.19	2098.85	2035.84	1981.33	1933.87	1892.33	1855.80	1726.51	1652.08	1607.27	1579.56
215,000	2312.07	2223.91	2148.82	2084.32	2028.51	1979.92	1937.39	1899.98	1767.61	1691.41	1645.54	1617.17
220,000	2365.84	2275.63	2198.79	2132.79	2075.68	2025.96	1982.44	1944.17	1808.72	1730.75	1683.80	1654.78
225,000	2419.61	2327.35	2248.76	2181.26	2122.86	2072.01	2027.50	1988.35	1849.83	1770.08	1722.07	1692.39
230,000	2473.38	2379.07	2298.74	2229.73	2170.03	2118.05	2072.56	2032.54	1890.94	1809.42	1760.34	1730.00
235,000	2527.15	2430.79	2348.71	2278.20	2217.20	2164.10	2117.61	2076.73	1932.04	1848.75	1798.61	1767.61
240,000	2580.92	2482.51	2398.68	2326.68	2264.38	2210.14	2162.67	2120.91	1973.15	1888.09	1836.88	1805.21
245,000	2634.69	2534.23	2448.65	2375.15	2311.55	2256.19	2207.72	2165.10	2014.26	1927.42	1875.14	1842.82
250,000	2688.46	2585.95	2498.63	2423.62	2358.73	2302.23	2252.78	2209.28	2055.36	1966.76	1913.41	1880.43
255,000	2742.23	2637.66	2548.60	2472.09	2405.90	2348.28	2297.83	2253.47	2096.47	2006.09	1951.68	1918.04
260,000	2795.99	2689.38	2598.57	2520.57	2453.08	2394.32	2342.89	2297.65	2137.58	2045.43	1989.95	1955.65
265,000	2849.76	2741.10	2648.54	2569.04	2500.25	2440.36	2387.94	2341.84	2178.69	2084.76	2028.22	1993.26
270,000	2903.53	2792.82	2698.52	2617.51	2547.43	2486.41	2433.00	2386.02	2219.79	2124.10	2066.49	2030.87
280,000	3011.07	2896.26	2798.46	2714.46	2641.77	2578.50	2523.11	2474.39	2302.01	2202.77	2143.02	2106.08
290,000	3118.61	2999.70	2898.41	2811.40	2736.12	2670.59	2613.22	2562.77	2384.22	2281.44	2219.56	2181.30
300,000	3226.15	3103.13	2998.35	2908.35	2830.47	2762.68	2703.33	2651.14	2466.44	2360.11	2296.09	2256.52

MONTHLY AMORTIZING PAYMENTS

AMOUNT OF LOAN	NUMBER OF YEARS IN TERM											
	1	2	3	4	5	6	7	8	9	10	11	12
$ 50	4.38	2.29	1.59	1.25	1.04	0.91	0.81	0.74	0.68	0.64	0.60	0.57
100	8.75	4.57	3.18	2.49	2.08	1.81	1.61	1.47	1.36	1.27	1.20	1.14
200	17.50	9.14	6.36	4.98	4.16	3.61	3.22	2.94	2.71	2.54	2.40	2.28
300	26.24	13.71	9.54	7.47	6.23	5.41	4.83	4.40	4.07	3.81	3.59	3.42
400	34.99	18.28	12.72	9.96	8.31	7.22	6.44	5.87	5.42	5.07	4.79	4.56
500	43.73	22.85	15.90	12.45	10.38	9.02	8.05	7.33	6.78	6.34	5.99	5.70
600	52.48	27.42	19.08	14.94	12.46	10.82	9.66	8.80	8.13	7.61	7.18	6.83
700	61.22	31.98	22.26	17.42	14.54	12.62	11.27	10.26	9.49	8.87	8.38	7.97
800	69.97	36.55	25.44	19.91	16.61	14.43	12.88	11.73	10.84	10.14	9.57	9.11
900	78.71	41.12	28.62	22.40	18.69	16.23	14.49	13.19	12.19	11.41	10.77	10.25
1,000	87.46	45.69	31.80	24.89	20.76	18.03	16.09	14.66	13.55	12.67	11.97	11.39
2,000	174.91	91.37	63.60	49.78	41.52	36.06	32.18	29.31	27.09	25.34	23.93	22.77
3,000	262.36	137.06	95.40	74.66	62.28	54.08	48.27	43.96	40.63	38.01	35.89	34.15
4,000	349.81	182.74	127.20	99.55	83.04	72.11	64.36	58.61	54.18	50.68	47.85	45.53
5,000	437.26	228.43	159.00	124.43	103.80	90.13	80.45	73.26	67.72	63.34	59.81	56.91
6,000	524.71	274.11	190.80	149.32	124.56	108.16	96.54	87.91	81.26	76.01	71.77	68.29
7,000	612.17	319.80	222.60	174.20	145.31	126.18	112.63	102.56	94.81	88.68	83.73	79.67
8,000	699.62	365.48	254.40	199.09	166.07	144.21	128.72	117.21	108.35	101.35	95.69	91.05
9,000	787.07	411.17	286.20	223.97	186.83	162.23	144.81	131.86	121.89	114.01	107.65	102.43
10,000	874.52	456.85	318.00	248.86	207.59	180.26	160.90	146.51	135.43	126.68	119.61	113.81
15,000	1311.78	685.28	477.00	373.28	311.38	270.39	241.34	219.76	203.15	190.02	179.42	170.71
20,000	1749.03	913.70	636.00	497.71	415.17	360.52	321.79	293.01	270.86	253.36	239.22	227.61
25,000	2186.29	1142.12	795.00	622.13	518.96	450.64	402.23	366.26	338.58	316.69	299.03	284.51
30,000	2623.55	1370.55	954.00	746.56	622.76	540.77	482.68	439.51	406.29	380.03	358.83	341.41
35,000	3060.81	1598.97	1113.00	870.98	726.55	630.90	563.12	512.76	474.01	443.37	418.63	398.32
40,000	3498.06	1827.39	1271.99	995.41	830.34	721.03	643.57	586.01	541.72	506.71	478.44	455.22
45,000	3935.32	2055.82	1430.99	1119.83	934.13	811.15	724.01	659.26	609.44	570.05	538.24	512.12
50,000	4372.58	2284.24	1589.99	1244.26	1037.92	901.28	804.46	732.52	677.15	633.38	598.05	569.02
55,000	4809.84	2512.67	1748.99	1368.68	1141.71	991.41	884.90	805.77	744.86	696.72	657.85	625.92
60,000	5247.09	2741.09	1907.99	1493.11	1245.51	1081.54	965.35	879.02	812.58	760.06	717.65	682.82
65,000	5684.35	2969.51	2066.99	1617.53	1349.30	1171.66	1045.80	952.27	880.29	823.40	777.46	739.72
70,000	6121.61	3197.94	2225.99	1741.96	1453.09	1261.79	1126.24	1025.52	948.01	886.74	837.26	796.63
75,000	6558.87	3426.36	2384.98	1866.38	1556.88	1351.92	1206.69	1098.77	1015.72	950.07	897.07	853.53
80,000	6996.12	3654.78	2543.98	1990.81	1660.67	1442.05	1287.13	1172.02	1083.44	1013.41	956.87	910.43
85,000	7433.38	3883.21	2702.98	2115.23	1764.47	1532.18	1367.58	1245.27	1151.15	1076.75	1016.67	967.33
90,000	7870.64	4111.63	2861.98	2239.66	1868.26	1622.30	1448.02	1318.52	1218.87	1140.09	1076.48	1024.23
95,000	8307.90	4340.06	3020.98	2364.08	1972.05	1712.43	1528.47	1391.77	1286.58	1203.42	1136.28	1081.13
100,000	8745.15	4568.48	3179.98	2488.51	2075.84	1802.56	1608.91	1465.03	1354.30	1266.76	1196.09	1138.04
105,000	9182.41	4796.90	3338.98	2612.93	2179.63	1892.69	1689.36	1538.28	1422.01	1330.10	1255.89	1194.94
110,000	9619.67	5025.33	3497.98	2737.36	2283.42	1982.81	1769.80	1611.53	1489.72	1393.44	1315.69	1251.84
115,000	10056.92	5253.75	3656.97	2861.78	2387.22	2072.94	1850.25	1684.78	1557.44	1456.78	1375.50	1308.74
120,000	10494.18	5482.17	3815.97	2986.21	2491.01	2163.07	1930.69	1758.03	1625.15	1520.11	1435.30	1365.64
125,000	10931.44	5710.60	3974.97	3110.64	2594.80	2253.20	2011.14	1831.28	1692.87	1583.45	1495.11	1422.54
130,000	11368.70	5939.02	4133.97	3235.06	2698.59	2343.32	2091.59	1904.53	1760.58	1646.79	1554.91	1479.44
135,000	11805.95	6167.45	4292.97	3359.49	2802.38	2433.45	2172.03	1977.78	1828.30	1710.13	1614.71	1536.35
140,000	12243.21	6395.87	4451.97	3483.91	2906.17	2523.58	2252.48	2051.03	1896.01	1773.47	1674.52	1593.25
145,000	12680.47	6624.29	4610.97	3608.34	3009.97	2613.71	2332.92	2124.28	1963.73	1836.80	1734.32	1650.15
150,000	13117.73	6852.72	4769.96	3732.76	3113.76	2703.84	2413.37	2197.54	2031.44	1900.14	1794.13	1707.05
155,000	13554.98	7081.14	4928.96	3857.19	3217.55	2793.96	2493.81	2270.79	2099.16	1963.48	1853.93	1763.95
160,000	13992.24	7309.56	5087.96	3981.61	3321.34	2884.09	2574.26	2344.04	2166.87	2026.82	1913.73	1820.85
165,000	14429.50	7537.99	5246.96	4106.04	3425.13	2974.22	2654.70	2417.29	2234.58	2090.16	1973.54	1877.76
170,000	14866.76	7766.41	5405.96	4230.46	3528.93	3064.35	2735.15	2490.54	2302.30	2153.49	2033.34	1934.66
175,000	15304.01	7994.83	5564.96	4354.89	3632.72	3154.47	2815.59	2563.79	2370.01	2216.83	2093.15	1991.56
180,000	15741.27	8223.26	5723.96	4479.31	3736.51	3244.60	2896.04	2637.04	2437.73	2280.17	2152.95	2048.46
185,000	16178.53	8451.68	5882.96	4603.74	3840.30	3334.73	2976.48	2710.29	2505.44	2343.51	2212.75	2105.36
190,000	16615.79	8680.11	6041.95	4728.16	3944.09	3424.86	3056.93	2783.54	2573.16	2406.84	2272.56	2162.26
195,000	17053.04	8908.53	6200.95	4852.59	4047.88	3514.98	3137.38	2856.79	2640.87	2470.18	2332.36	2219.16
200,000	17490.30	9136.95	6359.95	4977.01	4151.68	3605.11	3217.82	2930.05	2708.59	2533.52	2392.17	2276.07
205,000	17927.56	9365.38	6518.95	5101.44	4255.47	3695.24	3298.27	3003.30	2776.30	2596.86	2451.97	2332.97
210,000	18364.82	9593.80	6677.95	5225.86	4359.26	3785.37	3378.71	3076.55	2844.02	2660.20	2511.77	2389.87
215,000	18802.07	9822.22	6836.95	5350.29	4463.05	3875.49	3459.16	3149.80	2911.73	2723.53	2571.58	2446.77
220,000	19239.33	10050.65	6995.95	5474.71	4566.84	3965.62	3539.60	3223.05	2979.44	2786.87	2631.38	2503.67
225,000	19676.59	10279.07	7154.94	5599.14	4670.63	4055.75	3620.05	3296.30	3047.16	2850.21	2691.19	2560.57
230,000	20113.84	10507.50	7313.94	5723.56	4774.43	4145.88	3700.49	3369.55	3114.87	2913.55	2750.99	2617.48
235,000	20551.10	10735.92	7472.94	5847.99	4878.22	4236.01	3780.94	3442.80	3182.59	2976.89	2810.79	2674.38
240,000	20988.36	10964.34	7631.94	5972.42	4982.01	4326.13	3861.38	3516.05	3250.30	3040.22	2870.60	2731.28
245,000	21425.62	11192.77	7790.94	6096.84	5085.80	4416.26	3941.83	3589.30	3318.02	3103.56	2930.40	2788.18
250,000	21862.87	11421.19	7949.94	6221.27	5189.59	4506.39	4022.27	3662.56	3385.73	3166.90	2990.21	2845.08
255,000	22300.13	11649.61	8108.94	6345.69	5293.39	4596.52	4102.72	3735.81	3453.45	3230.24	3050.01	2901.98
260,000	22737.39	11878.04	8267.94	6470.12	5397.18	4686.64	4183.17	3809.06	3521.16	3293.58	3109.81	2958.88
265,000	23174.65	12106.46	8426.93	6594.54	5500.97	4776.77	4263.61	3882.31	3588.88	3356.91	3169.62	3015.79
270,000	23611.90	12334.89	8585.93	6718.97	5604.76	4866.90	4344.06	3955.56	3656.59	3420.25	3229.42	3072.69
280,000	24486.42	12791.73	8903.93	6967.82	5812.34	5047.16	4504.95	4102.06	3792.02	3546.93	3349.03	3186.49
290,000	25360.93	13248.58	9221.93	7216.67	6019.93	5227.41	4665.84	4248.56	3927.45	3673.60	3468.64	3300.29
300,000	26235.45	13705.43	9539.92	7465.52	6227.51	5407.67	4826.73	4395.07	4062.88	3800.28	3588.25	3414.10

AMOUNT OF LOAN	NUMBER OF YEARS IN TERM											
	13	14	15	16	17	18	19	20	25	30	35	40
$ 50	0.55	0.53	0.51	0.50	0.48	0.47	0.46	0.45	0.42	0.41	0.40	0.39
100	1.09	1.05	1.02	0.99	0.96	0.94	0.92	0.90	0.84	0.81	0.79	0.78
200	2.18	2.10	2.03	1.97	1.92	1.88	1.84	1.80	1.68	1.61	1.57	1.55
300	3.27	3.15	3.05	2.96	2.88	2.81	2.76	2.70	2.52	2.42	2.36	2.32
400	4.36	4.20	4.06	3.94	3.84	3.75	3.67	3.60	3.36	3.22	3.14	3.09
500	5.45	5.25	5.08	4.93	4.80	4.69	4.59	4.50	4.20	4.03	3.92	3.86
600	6.54	6.30	6.09	5.91	5.76	5.62	5.51	5.40	5.04	4.83	4.71	4.63
700	7.63	7.35	7.10	6.90	6.72	6.56	6.42	6.30	5.88	5.64	5.49	5.40
800	8.72	8.40	8.12	7.88	7.68	7.50	7.34	7.20	6.72	6.44	6.28	6.18
900	9.81	9.45	9.13	8.87	8.63	8.43	8.26	8.10	7.56	7.25	7.06	6.95
1,000	10.90	10.49	10.15	9.85	9.59	9.37	9.17	9.00	8.40	8.05	7.84	7.72
2,000	21.80	20.98	20.29	19.70	19.18	18.73	18.34	18.00	16.79	16.10	15.68	15.43
3,000	32.70	31.47	30.43	29.54	28.77	28.10	27.51	27.00	25.18	24.14	23.52	23.15
4,000	43.59	41.96	40.58	39.39	38.36	37.46	36.68	35.99	33.57	32.19	31.36	30.86
5,000	54.49	52.45	50.72	49.23	47.95	46.83	45.85	44.99	41.96	40.24	39.20	38.57
6,000	65.39	62.94	60.86	59.08	57.53	56.19	55.02	53.99	50.36	48.28	47.04	46.29
7,000	76.28	73.43	71.00	68.92	67.12	65.56	64.19	62.99	58.75	56.33	54.88	54.00
8,000	87.18	83.92	81.15	78.77	76.71	74.92	73.36	71.98	67.14	64.37	62.72	61.71
9,000	98.08	94.41	91.29	88.61	86.30	84.29	82.53	80.98	75.53	72.42	70.56	69.43
10,000	108.97	104.90	101.43	98.46	95.89	93.65	91.69	89.98	83.92	80.47	78.40	77.14
15,000	163.46	157.35	152.14	147.68	143.83	140.47	137.54	134.96	125.88	120.70	117.60	115.71
20,000	217.94	209.79	202.86	196.91	191.77	187.29	183.38	179.95	167.84	160.93	156.80	154.28
25,000	272.43	262.24	253.57	246.13	239.71	234.12	229.23	224.94	209.80	201.16	190.00	192.05
30,000	326.91	314.69	304.28	295.36	287.65	280.94	275.07	269.92	251.76	241.39	235.20	231.41
35,000	381.39	367.13	355.00	344.59	335.59	327.76	320.92	314.91	293.72	281.62	274.40	269.98
40,000	435.88	419.58	405.71	393.81	383.53	374.58	366.76	359.90	335.68	321.85	313.60	308.55
45,000	490.36	472.03	456.42	443.04	431.47	421.41	412.61	404.88	377.64	362.09	352.80	347.12
50,000	544.85	524.47	507.14	492.26	479.41	468.23	458.45	449.87	419.60	402.32	392.00	385.69
55,000	599.33	576.92	557.85	541.49	527.35	515.05	504.30	494.85	461.56	442.55	431.20	424.25
60,000	653.81	629.37	608.56	590.71	575.29	561.87	550.14	539.84	503.52	482.78	470.40	462.82
65,000	708.30	681.81	659.28	639.94	623.23	608.69	595.99	584.83	545.48	523.01	509.60	501.39
70,000	762.78	734.26	709.99	689.17	671.17	655.52	641.83	629.81	587.44	563.24	548.80	539.96
75,000	817.27	786.71	760.70	738.39	719.11	702.34	687.68	674.80	629.40	603.47	588.00	578.53
80,000	871.75	839.16	811.42	787.62	767.05	749.16	733.52	719.79	671.36	643.70	627.20	617.09
85,000	926.23	891.60	862.13	836.84	814.99	795.98	779.37	764.77	713.32	683.93	666.40	655.66
90,000	980.72	944.05	912.84	886.07	862.93	842.81	825.21	809.76	755.28	724.17	705.60	694.23
95,000	1035.20	996.50	963.56	935.30	910.87	889.63	871.06	854.74	797.24	764.40	744.80	732.80
100,000	1089.69	1048.94	1014.27	984.52	958.81	936.45	916.90	899.73	839.20	804.63	784.00	771.37
105,000	1144.17	1101.39	1064.98	1033.75	1006.75	983.27	962.75	944.72	881.16	844.86	823.20	809.93
110,000	1198.65	1153.84	1115.70	1082.97	1054.69	1030.09	1008.59	989.70	923.12	885.09	862.40	848.50
115,000	1253.14	1206.28	1166.41	1132.20	1102.63	1076.92	1054.44	1034.69	965.08	925.32	901.60	887.07
120,000	1307.62	1258.73	1217.12	1181.42	1150.57	1120.74	1100.20	1079.00	1007.04	965.55	940.80	925.64
125,000	1362.11	1311.18	1267.84	1230.65	1198.51	1170.56	1146.13	1124.66	1049.00	1005.78	980.00	964.21
130,000	1416.59	1363.62	1318.55	1279.88	1246.45	1217.38	1191.97	1169.65	1090.96	1046.01	1019.20	1002.77
135,000	1471.07	1416.07	1369.26	1329.10	1294.39	1264.21	1237.82	1214.64	1132.92	1086.25	1058.40	1041.34
140,000	1525.56	1468.52	1419.98	1378.33	1342.33	1311.03	1283.66	1259.62	1174.88	1126.48	1097.60	1079.91
145,000	1580.04	1520.96	1470.69	1427.55	1390.27	1357.85	1329.51	1304.61	1216.84	1166.71	1136.79	1118.48
150,000	1634.53	1573.41	1521.40	1476.78	1438.21	1404.67	1375.35	1349.59	1258.80	1206.94	1175.99	1157.05
155,000	1689.01	1625.86	1572.12	1526.00	1486.15	1451.49	1421.20	1394.58	1300.76	1247.17	1215.19	1195.62
160,000	1743.49	1678.31	1622.83	1575.23	1534.09	1498.32	1467.04	1439.57	1342.72	1287.40	1254.39	1234.18
165,000	1797.98	1730.75	1673.54	1624.46	1582.03	1545.14	1512.88	1484.55	1384.68	1327.63	1293.59	1272.75
170,000	1852.46	1783.20	1724.26	1673.68	1629.97	1591.96	1558.73	1529.54	1426.64	1367.86	1332.79	1311.32
175,000	1906.95	1835.65	1774.97	1722.91	1677.91	1638.78	1604.57	1574.53	1468.60	1408.09	1371.99	1349.89
180,000	1961.43	1888.09	1825.68	1772.13	1725.85	1685.61	1650.42	1619.51	1510.56	1448.33	1411.19	1388.46
185,000	2015.91	1940.54	1876.40	1821.36	1773.79	1732.43	1696.26	1664.50	1552.52	1488.56	1450.39	1427.02
190,000	2070.40	1992.99	1927.11	1870.59	1821.73	1779.25	1742.11	1709.48	1594.48	1528.79	1489.59	1465.59
195,000	2124.88	2045.43	1977.82	1919.81	1869.67	1826.07	1787.95	1754.47	1636.44	1569.02	1528.79	1504.16
200,000	2179.37	2097.88	2028.54	1969.04	1917.61	1872.89	1833.80	1799.46	1678.40	1609.25	1567.99	1542.73
205,000	2233.85	2150.33	2079.25	2018.26	1965.55	1919.72	1879.64	1844.44	1720.36	1649.48	1607.19	1581.30
210,000	2288.33	2202.77	2129.96	2067.49	2013.49	1966.54	1925.49	1889.43	1762.32	1689.71	1646.39	1619.86
215,000	2342.82	2255.22	2180.68	2116.71	2061.43	2013.36	1971.33	1934.42	1804.28	1729.94	1685.59	1658.43
220,000	2397.30	2307.67	2231.39	2165.94	2109.37	2060.18	2017.18	1979.40	1846.24	1770.17	1724.79	1697.00
225,000	2451.79	2360.11	2282.10	2215.17	2157.31	2107.01	2063.02	2024.39	1888.20	1810.41	1763.99	1735.57
230,000	2506.27	2412.56	2332.82	2264.39	2205.25	2153.83	2108.87	2069.37	1930.16	1850.64	1803.19	1774.14
235,000	2560.75	2465.01	2383.53	2313.62	2253.19	2200.65	2154.71	2114.36	1972.12	1890.87	1842.39	1812.70
240,000	2615.24	2517.46	2434.24	2362.84	2301.13	2247.47	2200.56	2159.35	2014.08	1931.10	1881.59	1851.27
245,000	2669.72	2569.90	2484.96	2412.07	2349.07	2294.29	2246.40	2204.33	2056.04	1971.33	1920.79	1889.84
250,000	2724.21	2622.35	2535.67	2461.29	2397.01	2341.12	2292.25	2249.32	2098.00	2011.56	1959.99	1928.41
255,000	2778.69	2674.80	2586.38	2510.52	2444.95	2387.94	2338.09	2294.31	2139.96	2051.79	1999.19	1966.98
260,000	2833.17	2727.24	2637.10	2559.75	2492.90	2434.76	2383.94	2339.29	2181.92	2092.02	2038.39	2005.54
265,000	2887.66	2779.69	2687.81	2608.97	2540.84	2481.58	2429.78	2384.28	2223.88	2132.25	2077.59	2044.11
270,000	2942.14	2832.14	2738.52	2658.20	2588.78	2528.41	2475.63	2429.27	2265.84	2172.49	2116.79	2082.68
280,000	3051.11	2937.03	2839.95	2756.65	2684.66	2622.05	2567.32	2519.24	2349.76	2252.95	2195.19	2159.82
290,000	3160.08	3041.92	2941.38	2855.10	2780.54	2715.70	2659.01	2609.21	2433.67	2333.41	2273.58	2236.95
300,000	3269.05	3146.82	3042.80	2953.55	2876.42	2809.34	2750.70	2699.18	2517.59	2413.87	2351.98	2314.09

9.25%

AMOUNT OF LOAN	NUMBER OF YEARS IN TERM											
	1	2	3	4	5	6	7	8	9	10	11	12
$ 50	4.38	2.29	1.60	1.26	1.05	0.91	0.82	0.74	0.69	0.65	0.61	0.58
100	8.76	4.58	3.20	2.51	2.09	1.82	1.63	1.48	1.37	1.29	1.21	1.16
200	17.52	9.16	6.39	5.01	4.18	3.63	3.25	2.96	2.74	2.57	2.42	2.31
300	26.28	13.74	9.58	7.51	6.27	5.45	4.87	4.44	4.11	3.85	3.63	3.46
400	35.03	18.32	12.77	10.01	8.36	7.26	6.49	5.92	5.48	5.13	4.84	4.61
500	43.79	22.90	15.96	12.51	10.44	9.08	8.11	7.40	6.84	6.41	6.05	5.77
600	52.55	27.48	19.15	15.01	12.53	10.89	9.73	8.87	8.21	7.69	7.26	6.92
700	61.30	32.06	22.35	17.51	14.62	12.71	11.36	10.35	9.58	8.97	8.47	8.07
800	70.06	36.64	25.54	20.01	16.71	14.52	12.98	11.83	10.95	10.25	9.68	9.22
900	78.82	41.22	28.73	22.51	18.80	16.34	14.60	13.31	12.31	11.53	10.89	10.37
1,000	87.57	45.80	31.92	25.01	20.88	18.15	16.22	14.79	13.68	12.81	12.10	11.53
2,000	175.14	91.60	63.84	50.01	41.76	36.30	32.44	29.57	27.36	25.61	24.20	23.05
3,000	262.71	137.40	95.75	75.02	62.64	54.45	48.65	44.35	41.03	38.41	36.30	34.57
4,000	350.27	183.20	127.67	100.02	83.52	72.60	64.87	59.13	54.71	51.22	48.40	46.09
5,000	437.84	229.00	159.59	125.02	104.40	90.75	81.09	73.91	68.38	64.02	60.50	57.61
6,000	525.41	274.80	191.50	150.03	125.28	108.90	97.30	88.69	82.06	76.82	72.60	69.13
7,000	612.98	320.60	223.42	175.03	146.16	127.05	113.52	103.47	95.74	89.63	84.70	80.66
8,000	700.54	366.40	255.33	200.04	167.04	145.20	129.73	118.25	109.41	102.43	96.80	92.18
9,000	788.11	412.20	287.25	225.04	187.92	163.35	145.95	133.03	123.09	115.23	108.90	103.70
10,000	875.68	458.00	319.17	250.04	208.80	181.50	162.17	147.81	136.76	128.04	121.00	115.22
15,000	1313.52	687.00	478.75	375.06	313.20	272.25	243.25	221.71	205.14	192.05	181.49	172.83
20,000	1751.35	916.00	638.33	500.08	417.60	363.00	324.33	295.61	273.52	256.07	241.99	230.44
25,000	2189.19	1144.99	797.91	625.10	522.00	453.75	405.41	369.51	341.90	320.09	302.49	288.04
30,000	2627.03	1373.99	957.49	750.12	626.40	544.50	486.49	443.41	410.28	384.10	362.98	345.65
35,000	3064.87	1602.99	1117.07	875.14	730.80	635.25	567.57	517.31	478.66	448.12	423.48	403.26
40,000	3502.70	1831.99	1276.65	1000.16	835.20	726.00	648.65	591.21	547.04	512.14	483.98	460.87
45,000	3940.54	2060.98	1436.23	1125.18	939.60	816.75	729.74	665.11	615.41	576.15	544.47	518.48
50,000	4378.38	2289.98	1595.82	1250.20	1044.00	907.50	810.82	739.02	683.79	640.17	604.97	576.08
55,000	4816.21	2518.98	1755.40	1375.22	1148.40	998.25	891.90	812.92	752.17	704.18	665.47	633.69
60,000	5254.05	2747.98	1914.98	1500.24	1252.80	1089.00	972.98	886.82	820.55	768.20	725.96	691.30
65,000	5691.89	2976.97	2074.56	1625.26	1357.20	1179.75	1054.06	960.72	888.93	832.22	786.46	748.91
70,000	6129.73	3205.97	2234.14	1750.28	1461.60	1270.50	1135.14	1034.62	957.31	896.23	846.96	806.51
75,000	6567.56	3434.97	2393.72	1875.30	1566.00	1361.24	1216.22	1108.52	1025.69	960.25	907.45	864.12
80,000	7005.40	3663.97	2553.30	2000.32	1670.40	1451.99	1297.30	1182.42	1094.07	1024.27	967.95	921.73
85,000	7443.24	3892.97	2712.88	2125.34	1774.80	1542.74	1378.39	1256.32	1162.45	1088.28	1028.45	979.34
90,000	7881.08	4121.96	2872.46	2250.36	1879.20	1633.49	1459.47	1330.22	1230.82	1152.30	1088.94	1036.95
95,000	8318.91	4350.96	3032.05	2375.38	1983.60	1724.24	1540.55	1404.13	1299.20	1216.32	1149.44	1094.55
100,000	8756.75	4579.96	3191.63	2500.40	2087.99	1814.99	1621.63	1478.03	1367.58	1280.33	1209.93	1152.16
105,000	9194.59	4808.96	3351.21	2625.42	2192.39	1905.74	1702.71	1551.93	1435.96	1344.35	1270.43	1209.77
110,000	9632.42	5037.95	3510.79	2750.44	2296.79	1996.49	1783.79	1625.83	1504.34	1408.36	1330.93	1267.38
115,000	10070.26	5266.95	3670.37	2875.46	2401.19	2087.24	1864.87	1699.73	1572.72	1472.38	1391.42	1324.98
120,000	10508.10	5495.95	3829.95	3000.48	2505.59	2177.99	1945.95	1773.63	1641.10	1536.40	1451.92	1382.59
125,000	10945.94	5724.95	3989.53	3125.50	2609.99	2268.74	2027.04	1847.53	1709.48	1600.41	1512.42	1440.20
130,000	11383.77	5953.94	4149.11	3250.51	2714.39	2359.49	2108.12	1921.43	1777.86	1664.43	1572.91	1497.81
135,000	11821.61	6182.94	4308.69	3375.53	2818.79	2450.24	2189.20	1995.33	1846.23	1728.45	1633.41	1555.42
140,000	12259.45	6411.94	4468.27	3500.55	2923.19	2540.99	2270.28	2069.24	1914.61	1792.46	1693.91	1613.02
145,000	12697.29	6640.94	4627.86	3625.57	3027.59	2631.74	2351.36	2143.14	1982.99	1856.48	1754.40	1670.63
150,000	13135.12	6869.93	4787.44	3750.59	3131.99	2722.48	2432.44	2217.04	2051.37	1920.50	1814.90	1728.24
155,000	13572.96	7098.93	4947.02	3875.61	3236.39	2813.23	2513.52	2290.94	2119.75	1984.51	1875.40	1785.85
160,000	14010.80	7327.93	5106.60	4000.63	3340.79	2903.98	2594.60	2364.84	2188.13	2048.53	1935.89	1843.46
165,000	14448.63	7556.93	5266.18	4125.65	3445.19	2994.73	2675.68	2438.74	2256.51	2112.54	1996.39	1901.06
170,000	14886.47	7785.93	5425.76	4250.67	3549.59	3085.48	2756.77	2512.64	2324.89	2176.56	2056.89	1958.67
175,000	15324.31	8014.92	5585.34	4375.69	3653.99	3176.23	2837.85	2586.54	2393.27	2240.58	2117.38	2016.28
180,000	15762.15	8243.92	5744.92	4500.71	3758.39	3266.98	2918.93	2660.44	2461.64	2304.59	2177.88	2073.89
185,000	16199.98	8472.92	5904.50	4625.73	3862.79	3357.73	3000.01	2734.35	2530.02	2368.61	2238.38	2131.49
190,000	16637.82	8701.92	6064.09	4750.75	3967.19	3448.48	3081.09	2808.25	2598.40	2432.63	2298.87	2189.10
195,000	17075.66	8930.91	6223.67	4875.77	4071.59	3539.23	3162.17	2882.15	2666.78	2496.64	2359.37	2246.71
200,000	17513.50	9159.91	6383.25	5000.79	4175.98	3629.98	3243.25	2956.05	2735.16	2560.66	2419.86	2304.32
205,000	17951.33	9388.91	6542.83	5125.81	4280.38	3720.73	3324.33	3029.95	2803.54	2624.68	2480.36	2361.93
210,000	18389.17	9617.91	6702.41	5250.83	4384.78	3811.48	3405.42	3103.85	2871.92	2688.69	2540.86	2419.53
215,000	18827.01	9846.90	6861.99	5375.85	4489.18	3902.23	3486.50	3177.75	2940.30	2752.71	2601.35	2477.14
220,000	19264.84	10075.90	7021.57	5500.87	4593.58	3992.98	3567.58	3251.65	3008.68	2816.72	2661.85	2534.75
225,000	19702.68	10304.90	7181.15	5625.89	4697.98	4083.72	3648.66	3325.55	3077.05	2880.74	2722.35	2592.36
230,000	20140.52	10533.90	7340.73	5750.91	4802.38	4174.47	3729.74	3399.46	3145.43	2944.76	2782.84	2649.96
235,000	20578.36	10762.90	7500.32	5875.93	4906.78	4265.22	3810.82	3473.36	3213.81	3008.77	2843.34	2707.57
240,000	21016.19	10991.89	7659.90	6000.95	5011.18	4355.97	3891.90	3547.26	3282.19	3072.79	2903.84	2765.18
245,000	21454.03	11220.89	7819.48	6125.97	5115.58	4446.72	3972.98	3621.16	3350.57	3136.81	2964.33	2822.79
250,000	21891.87	11449.89	7979.06	6250.99	5219.98	4537.47	4054.07	3695.06	3418.95	3200.82	3024.83	2880.40
255,000	22329.71	11678.89	8138.64	6376.00	5324.38	4628.22	4135.15	3768.96	3487.33	3264.84	3085.33	2938.00
260,000	22767.54	11907.88	8298.22	6501.02	5428.78	4718.97	4216.23	3842.86	3555.71	3328.86	3145.82	2995.61
265,000	23205.38	12136.88	8457.80	6626.04	5533.18	4809.72	4297.31	3916.76	3624.09	3392.87	3206.32	3053.22
270,000	23643.22	12365.88	8617.38	6751.06	5637.58	4900.47	4378.39	3990.66	3692.46	3456.89	3266.82	3110.83
280,000	24518.89	12823.87	8936.54	7001.10	5846.38	5081.97	4540.55	4138.47	3829.22	3584.92	3387.81	3226.04
290,000	25394.57	13281.87	9255.71	7251.14	6055.18	5263.47	4702.72	4286.27	3965.98	3712.95	3508.80	3341.26
300,000	26270.24	13739.86	9574.87	7501.18	6263.97	5444.96	4864.88	4434.07	4102.74	3840.99	3629.79	3456.47

AMOUNT OF LOAN	NUMBER OF YEARS IN TERM											
	13	14	15	16	17	18	19	20	25	30	35	40
$ 50	0.56	0.54	0.52	0.50	0.49	0.48	0.47	0.46	0.43	0.42	0.41	0.40
100	1.11	1.07	1.03	1.00	0.98	0.96	0.94	0.92	0.86	0.83	0.81	0.80
200	2.21	2.13	2.06	2.00	1.95	1.91	1.87	1.84	1.72	1.65	1.61	1.59
300	3.32	3.20	3.09	3.00	2.93	2.86	2.80	2.75	2.57	2.47	2.41	2.38
400	4.42	4.26	4.12	4.00	3.90	3.81	3.74	3.67	3.43	3.30	3.22	3.17
500	5.53	5.32	5.15	5.00	4.88	4.77	4.67	4.58	4.29	4.12	4.02	3.96
600	6.63	6.39	6.18	6.00	5.85	5.72	5.60	5.50	5.14	4.94	4.82	4.75
700	7.73	7.45	7.21	7.00	6.82	6.67	6.53	6.42	6.00	5.76	5.62	5.54
800	8.84	8.51	8.24	8.00	7.80	7.62	7.47	7.33	6.86	6.59	6.43	6.33
900	9.94	9.58	9.27	9.00	8.77	8.57	8.40	8.25	7.71	7.41	7.23	7.12
1,000	11.05	10.64	10.30	10.00	9.75	9.53	9.33	9.16	8.57	8.23	8.03	7.91
2,000	22.09	21.28	20.59	20.00	19.49	19.05	18.66	18.32	17.13	16.46	16.06	15.82
3,000	33.13	31.91	30.88	30.00	29.23	28.57	27.99	27.48	25.70	24.69	24.09	23.72
4,000	44.17	42.55	41.17	39.99	38.97	38.09	37.32	36.64	34.26	32.91	32.11	31.63
5,000	55.21	53.19	51.46	49.99	48.72	47.61	46.65	45.80	42.82	41.14	40.14	39.54
6,000	66.25	63.82	61.76	59.99	58.46	57.13	55.97	54.96	51.39	49.37	48.17	47.44
7,000	77.29	74.46	72.05	69.98	68.20	66.65	65.30	64.12	59.95	57.59	56.20	55.35
8,000	88.33	85.09	82.34	79.98	77.94	76.17	74.63	73.27	68.52	65.82	64.22	63.26
9,000	99.37	95.73	92.63	89.98	87.69	85.70	83.96	82.43	77.08	74.05	72.25	71.16
10,000	110.41	106.37	102.92	99.97	97.43	95.22	93.29	91.59	85.64	82.27	80.28	79.07
15,000	165.62	159.55	154.38	149.96	146.14	142.82	139.93	137.39	128.46	123.41	120.42	118.60
20,000	220.82	212.73	205.84	199.94	194.85	190.43	186.57	183.18	171.28	164.54	160.55	158.14
25,000	276.02	265.91	257.30	249.93	243.56	238.03	233.21	228.97	214.10	205.67	200.69	197.67
30,000	331.23	319.09	308.76	299.91	292.28	285.64	279.85	274.77	256.92	246.81	240.83	237.20
35,000	386.43	372.27	360.22	349.90	340.99	333.25	326.49	320.56	299.74	287.94	280.97	276.74
40,000	441.64	425.45	411.68	399.88	389.70	380.85	373.13	366.35	342.56	329.08	321.10	316.27
45,000	496.84	478.63	463.14	440.87	430.41	420.46	419.77	412.15	385.38	370.21	361.24	355.80
50,000	552.04	531.81	514.60	499.85	487.12	476.06	466.41	457.94	428.20	411.34	401.38	395.34
55,000	607.25	584.99	566.06	549.84	535.83	523.67	513.05	503.73	471.02	452.48	441.51	434.87
60,000	662.45	638.17	617.52	599.82	584.55	571.28	559.69	549.53	513.83	493.61	481.65	474.40
65,000	717.66	691.35	668.98	649.81	633.26	618.88	606.33	595.32	556.65	534.74	521.79	513.93
70,000	772.86	744.53	720.44	699.79	681.97	666.49	652.97	641.11	599.47	575.88	561.93	553.47
75,000	828.06	797.71	771.90	749.78	730.68	714.09	699.61	686.91	642.29	617.01	602.06	593.00
80,000	883.27	850.89	823.36	799.76	779.39	761.70	746.25	732.70	685.11	658.15	642.20	632.53
85,000	938.47	904.07	874.82	849.75	828.10	809.31	792.89	778.49	727.93	699.28	682.34	672.07
90,000	993.68	957.25	926.28	899.73	876.82	856.91	839.53	824.29	770.75	740.41	722.47	711.60
95,000	1048.88	1010.43	977.74	949.72	925.53	904.52	886.17	870.08	813.57	781.55	762.61	751.13
100,000	1104.08	1063.61	1029.20	999.70	974.24	952.12	932.81	915.87	856.39	822.68	802.75	790.67
105,000	1159.29	1116.79	1080.66	1049.69	1022.95	999.73	979.45	961.67	899.21	863.81	842.89	830.20
110,000	1214.49	1169.97	1132.12	1099.67	1071.66	1047.34	1026.09	1007.46	942.03	904.95	883.02	869.73
115,000	1269.69	1223.15	1183.58	1149.66	1120.38	1094.94	1072.73	1053.25	984.84	946.08	923.16	909.26
120,000	1324.90	1276.33	1235.04	1199.64	1169.09	1142.55	1119.37	1099.05	1027.66	987.22	963.30	948.80
125,000	1380.10	1329.51	1286.50	1249.63	1217.80	1190.15	1166.01	1144.84	1070.48	1028.35	1003.44	988.33
130,000	1435.31	1382.69	1337.95	1299.61	1266.51	1237.76	1212.66	1190.63	1113.30	1069.48	1043.57	1027.86
135,000	1490.51	1435.87	1389.41	1349.60	1315.22	1285.37	1259.30	1236.43	1156.12	1110.62	1083.71	1067.40
140,000	1545.71	1489.05	1440.87	1399.58	1363.93	1332.97	1305.94	1282.22	1198.94	1151.75	1123.85	1106.93
145,000	1600.92	1542.23	1492.33	1449.57	1412.65	1380.58	1352.58	1328.01	1241.76	1192.88	1163.98	1146.46
150,000	1656.12	1595.41	1543.79	1499.55	1461.36	1428.18	1399.22	1373.81	1284.58	1234.02	1204.12	1186.00
155,000	1711.33	1648.59	1595.25	1549.54	1510.07	1475.79	1445.86	1419.60	1327.40	1275.15	1244.26	1225.53
160,000	1766.53	1701.77	1646.71	1599.52	1558.78	1523.40	1492.50	1465.39	1370.22	1316.29	1284.40	1265.06
165,000	1821.73	1754.95	1698.17	1649.51	1607.49	1571.00	1539.14	1511.19	1413.04	1357.42	1324.53	1304.59
170,000	1876.94	1808.13	1749.63	1699.49	1656.20	1618.61	1585.78	1556.98	1455.85	1398.55	1364.67	1344.13
175,000	1932.14	1861.31	1801.09	1749.48	1704.92	1666.21	1632.42	1602.77	1498.67	1439.69	1404.81	1383.66
180,000	1987.35	1914.49	1852.55	1799.46	1753.63	1713.82	1679.06	1648.57	1541.49	1480.82	1444.94	1423.19
185,000	2042.55	1967.67	1904.01	1849.44	1802.34	1761.43	1725.70	1694.36	1584.31	1521.95	1485.08	1462.73
190,000	2097.75	2020.85	1955.47	1899.43	1851.05	1809.03	1772.34	1740.15	1627.13	1563.09	1525.22	1502.26
195,000	2152.96	2074.03	2006.93	1949.41	1899.76	1856.64	1818.98	1785.95	1669.95	1604.22	1565.36	1541.79
200,000	2208.16	2127.21	2058.39	1999.40	1948.47	1904.24	1865.62	1831.74	1712.77	1645.36	1605.49	1581.33
205,000	2263.36	2180.39	2109.85	2049.38	1997.19	1951.85	1912.26	1877.53	1755.59	1686.49	1645.63	1620.86
210,000	2318.57	2233.57	2161.31	2099.37	2045.90	1999.46	1958.90	1923.33	1798.41	1727.62	1685.77	1660.39
215,000	2373.77	2286.75	2212.77	2149.35	2094.61	2047.06	2005.54	1969.12	1841.23	1768.76	1725.91	1699.93
220,000	2428.98	2339.93	2264.23	2199.34	2143.32	2094.67	2052.18	2014.91	1884.05	1809.89	1766.04	1739.46
225,000	2484.18	2393.11	2315.69	2249.32	2192.03	2142.27	2098.82	2060.71	1926.86	1851.02	1806.18	1778.99
230,000	2539.38	2446.29	2367.15	2299.31	2240.75	2189.88	2145.46	2106.50	1969.68	1892.16	1846.32	1818.53
235,000	2594.59	2499.47	2418.61	2349.29	2289.46	2237.48	2192.10	2152.29	2012.50	1933.29	1886.45	1858.06
240,000	2649.79	2552.65	2470.07	2399.28	2338.17	2285.09	2238.74	2198.09	2055.32	1974.43	1926.59	1897.59
245,000	2705.00	2605.83	2521.53	2449.26	2386.88	2332.70	2285.38	2243.88	2098.14	2015.56	1966.73	1937.12
250,000	2760.20	2659.01	2572.99	2499.25	2435.59	2380.30	2332.02	2289.67	2140.96	2056.69	2006.87	1976.66
255,000	2815.40	2712.19	2624.45	2549.23	2484.30	2427.91	2378.66	2335.47	2183.78	2097.83	2047.00	2016.19
260,000	2870.61	2765.37	2675.90	2599.22	2533.02	2475.51	2425.31	2381.26	2226.60	2138.96	2087.14	2055.72
265,000	2925.81	2818.55	2727.36	2649.20	2581.73	2523.12	2471.95	2427.05	2269.42	2180.09	2127.28	2095.26
270,000	2981.02	2871.73	2778.82	2699.19	2630.44	2570.73	2518.59	2472.85	2312.24	2221.23	2167.41	2134.79
280,000	3091.42	2978.09	2881.74	2799.16	2727.86	2665.94	2611.87	2564.43	2397.87	2303.50	2247.69	2213.85
290,000	3201.83	3084.45	2984.66	2899.13	2825.29	2761.15	2705.15	2656.02	2483.51	2385.76	2327.96	2292.92
300,000	3312.24	3190.81	3087.58	2999.10	2922.71	2856.36	2798.43	2747.61	2569.15	2468.03	2408.24	2371.99

61

9.50%

MONTHLY AMORTIZING PAYMENTS

AMOUNT OF LOAN	\multicolumn{12}{c}{NUMBER OF YEARS IN TERM}

AMOUNT OF LOAN	1	2	3	4	5	6	7	8	9	10	11	12
$ 50	4.39	2.30	1.61	1.26	1.06	0.92	0.82	0.75	0.70	0.65	0.62	0.59
100	8.77	4.60	3.21	2.52	2.11	1.83	1.64	1.50	1.39	1.30	1.23	1.17
200	17.54	9.19	6.41	5.03	4.21	3.66	3.27	2.99	2.77	2.59	2.45	2.34
300	26.31	13.78	9.61	7.54	6.31	5.49	4.91	4.48	4.15	3.89	3.68	3.50
400	35.08	18.37	12.82	10.05	8.41	7.31	6.54	5.97	5.53	5.18	4.90	4.67
500	43.85	22.96	16.02	12.57	10.51	9.14	8.18	7.46	6.91	6.47	6.12	5.84
600	52.62	27.55	19.22	15.08	12.61	10.97	9.81	8.95	8.29	7.77	7.35	7.00
700	61.38	32.15	22.43	17.59	14.71	12.80	11.45	10.44	9.67	9.06	8.57	8.17
800	70.15	36.74	25.63	20.10	16.81	14.62	13.08	11.93	11.05	10.36	9.80	9.34
900	78.92	41.33	28.83	22.62	18.91	16.45	14.71	13.42	12.43	11.65	11.02	10.50
1,000	87.69	45.92	32.04	25.13	21.01	18.28	16.35	14.92	13.81	12.94	12.24	11.67
2,000	175.37	91.83	64.07	50.25	42.01	36.55	32.69	29.83	27.62	25.88	24.48	23.33
3,000	263.06	137.75	96.10	75.37	63.01	54.83	49.04	44.74	41.43	38.82	36.72	35.00
4,000	350.74	183.66	128.14	100.50	84.01	73.10	65.38	59.65	55.24	51.76	48.96	46.66
5,000	438.42	229.58	160.17	125.62	105.01	91.38	81.72	74.56	69.05	64.70	61.20	58.32
6,000	526.11	275.49	192.20	150.74	126.02	109.65	98.07	89.47	82.86	77.64	73.44	69.99
7,000	613.79	321.41	224.24	175.87	147.02	127.93	114.41	104.38	96.67	90.58	85.68	81.65
8,000	701.47	367.32	256.27	200.99	168.02	146.20	130.76	119.29	110.48	103.52	97.91	93.31
9,000	789.16	413.24	288.30	226.11	189.02	164.48	147.10	134.20	124.29	116.46	110.15	104.98
10,000	876.84	459.15	320.33	251.24	210.02	182.75	163.44	149.11	138.10	129.40	122.39	116.64
15,000	1315.26	688.72	480.50	376.85	315.03	274.13	245.16	223.67	207.15	194.10	183.58	174.96
20,000	1753.68	918.29	640.66	502.47	420.04	365.50	326.88	298.22	276.19	258.80	244.78	233.28
25,000	2192.09	1147.87	800.83	628.08	525.05	456.87	408.60	372.78	345.24	323.50	305.97	291.60
30,000	2630.51	1377.44	960.99	753.70	630.06	548.25	490.32	447.33	414.29	388.20	367.16	349.92
35,000	3068.93	1607.01	1121.16	879.31	735.07	639.62	572.04	521.89	483.33	452.90	428.36	408.24
40,000	3507.35	1836.58	1281.32	1004.93	840.08	730.99	653.76	596.44	552.38	517.60	489.55	466.55
45,000	3945.76	2066.16	1441.49	1130.55	945.09	822.37	735.48	670.99	621.43	582.29	550.74	524.87
50,000	4384.18	2295.73	1601.65	1256.16	1050.10	913.74	817.20	745.55	690.47	646.99	611.94	583.19
55,000	4822.60	2525.30	1761.82	1381.78	1155.11	1005.11	898.92	820.10	759.52	711.69	673.13	641.51
60,000	5261.02	2754.87	1921.98	1507.39	1260.12	1096.49	980.64	894.66	828.57	776.39	734.32	699.83
65,000	5699.43	2984.45	2082.15	1633.01	1365.13	1187.86	1062.36	969.21	897.61	841.09	795.52	758.15
70,000	6137.85	3214.02	2242.31	1758.62	1470.14	1279.23	1144.08	1043.77	966.66	905.79	856.71	816.47
75,000	6576.27	3443.59	2402.48	1884.24	1575.14	1370.61	1225.80	1118.32	1035.71	970.49	917.90	874.78
80,000	7014.69	3673.16	2562.64	2009.86	1680.15	1461.98	1307.52	1192.88	1104.75	1035.19	979.10	933.10
85,000	7453.10	3902.74	2722.81	2135.47	1785.16	1553.35	1389.24	1267.43	1173.80	1099.88	1040.29	991.42
90,000	7891.52	4132.31	2882.97	2261.09	1890.17	1644.73	1470.96	1341.98	1242.85	1164.58	1101.48	1049.74
95,000	8329.94	4361.88	3043.14	2386.70	1995.18	1736.10	1552.68	1416.54	1311.89	1229.28	1162.68	1108.06
100,000	8768.36	4591.45	3203.30	2512.32	2100.19	1827.47	1634.40	1491.09	1380.94	1293.98	1223.87	1166.38
105,000	9206.77	4821.03	3363.46	2637.93	2205.20	1918.85	1716.12	1565.65	1449.99	1358.68	1285.06	1224.70
110,000	9645.19	5050.60	3523.63	2763.55	2310.21	2010.22	1797.84	1640.20	1519.03	1423.38	1346.26	1283.02
115,000	10083.61	5280.17	3683.79	2889.17	2415.22	2101.59	1879.56	1714.76	1588.08	1488.08	1407.45	1341.33
120,000	10522.03	5509.74	3843.96	3014.78	2520.23	2192.97	1961.28	1789.31	1657.13	1552.78	1468.64	1399.65
125,000	10960.44	5739.32	4004.12	3140.40	2625.24	2284.34	2043.00	1863.87	1726.18	1617.47	1529.84	1457.97
130,000	11398.86	5968.89	4164.29	3266.01	2730.25	2375.71	2124.72	1938.42	1795.22	1682.17	1591.03	1516.29
135,000	11837.28	6198.46	4324.45	3391.63	2835.26	2467.09	2206.44	2012.97	1864.27	1746.87	1652.22	1574.61
140,000	12275.70	6428.03	4484.62	3517.24	2940.27	2558.46	2288.16	2087.53	1933.32	1811.57	1713.42	1632.93
145,000	12714.11	6657.61	4644.78	3642.86	3045.27	2649.84	2369.88	2162.08	2002.36	1876.27	1774.61	1691.25
150,000	13152.53	6887.18	4804.95	3768.48	3150.28	2741.21	2451.60	2236.64	2071.41	1940.97	1835.80	1749.56
155,000	13590.95	7116.75	4965.11	3894.09	3255.29	2832.58	2533.32	2311.19	2140.46	2005.67	1897.00	1807.88
160,000	14029.37	7346.32	5125.28	4019.71	3360.30	2923.96	2615.04	2385.75	2209.50	2070.37	1958.19	1866.20
165,000	14467.78	7575.90	5285.44	4145.32	3465.31	3015.33	2696.76	2460.30	2278.55	2135.06	2019.38	1924.52
170,000	14906.20	7805.47	5445.61	4270.94	3570.32	3106.70	2778.48	2534.86	2347.60	2199.76	2080.57	1982.84
175,000	15344.62	8035.04	5605.77	4396.55	3675.33	3198.08	2860.20	2609.41	2416.64	2264.46	2141.77	2041.16
180,000	15783.04	8264.61	5765.94	4522.17	3780.34	3289.45	2941.92	2683.96	2485.69	2329.16	2202.96	2099.48
185,000	16221.45	8494.19	5926.10	4647.79	3885.35	3380.82	3023.64	2758.52	2554.74	2393.86	2264.15	2157.80
190,000	16659.87	8723.76	6086.27	4773.40	3990.36	3472.20	3105.36	2833.07	2623.78	2458.56	2325.35	2216.11
195,000	17098.29	8953.33	6246.43	4899.02	4095.37	3563.57	3187.08	2907.63	2692.83	2523.26	2386.54	2274.43
200,000	17536.71	9182.90	6406.59	5024.63	4200.38	3654.94	3268.80	2982.18	2761.88	2587.96	2447.73	2332.75
205,000	17975.12	9412.48	6566.76	5150.25	4305.39	3746.32	3350.52	3056.74	2830.92	2652.65	2508.93	2391.07
210,000	18413.54	9642.05	6726.92	5275.86	4410.40	3837.69	3432.24	3131.29	2899.97	2717.35	2570.12	2449.39
215,000	18851.96	9871.62	6887.09	5401.48	4515.41	3929.06	3513.96	3205.85	2969.02	2782.05	2631.31	2507.71
220,000	19290.38	10101.19	7047.25	5527.10	4620.41	4020.44	3595.68	3280.40	3038.06	2846.75	2692.51	2566.03
225,000	19728.80	10330.77	7207.42	5652.71	4725.42	4111.81	3677.40	3354.95	3107.11	2911.45	2753.70	2624.34
230,000	20167.21	10560.34	7367.58	5778.33	4830.43	4203.18	3759.12	3429.51	3176.16	2976.15	2814.89	2682.66
235,000	20605.63	10789.91	7527.75	5903.94	4935.44	4294.56	3840.84	3504.06	3245.20	3040.85	2876.09	2740.98
240,000	21044.05	11019.48	7687.91	6029.56	5040.45	4385.93	3922.56	3578.62	3314.25	3105.55	2937.28	2799.30
245,000	21482.47	11249.06	7848.08	6155.17	5145.46	4477.30	4004.28	3653.17	3383.30	3170.25	2998.47	2857.62
250,000	21920.88	11478.63	8008.24	6280.79	5250.47	4568.68	4086.00	3727.73	3452.35	3234.94	3059.67	2915.94
255,000	22359.30	11708.20	8168.41	6406.40	5355.48	4660.05	4167.72	3802.28	3521.39	3299.64	3120.86	2974.26
260,000	22797.72	11937.77	8328.57	6532.02	5460.49	4751.42	4249.44	3876.84	3590.44	3364.34	3182.05	3032.58
265,000	23236.14	12167.35	8488.74	6657.64	5565.50	4842.80	4331.16	3951.39	3659.49	3429.04	3243.25	3090.89
270,000	23674.55	12396.92	8648.90	6783.25	5670.51	4934.17	4412.88	4025.94	3728.53	3493.74	3304.44	3149.21
280,000	24551.39	12856.06	8969.23	7034.48	5880.53	5116.92	4576.32	4175.05	3866.63	3623.14	3426.83	3265.85
290,000	25428.22	13315.21	9289.56	7285.71	6090.54	5299.67	4739.76	4324.16	4004.72	3752.53	3549.21	3382.49
300,000	26305.06	13774.35	9609.89	7536.95	6300.56	5482.41	4903.20	4473.27	4142.81	3881.93	3671.60	3499.12

62

AMOUNT OF LOAN	NUMBER OF YEARS IN TERM											
	13	14	15	16	17	18	19	20	25	30	35	40
$ 50	0.56	0.54	0.53	0.51	0.50	0.49	0.48	0.47	0.44	0.43	0.42	0.41
100	1.12	1.08	1.05	1.02	0.99	0.97	0.95	0.94	0.88	0.85	0.83	0.82
200	2.24	2.16	2.09	2.03	1.98	1.94	1.90	1.87	1.75	1.69	1.65	1.63
300	3.36	3.24	3.14	3.05	2.97	2.91	2.85	2.80	2.63	2.53	2.47	2.44
400	4.48	4.32	4.18	4.06	3.96	3.88	3.80	3.73	3.50	3.37	3.29	3.25
500	5.60	5.40	5.23	5.08	4.95	4.84	4.75	4.67	4.37	4.21	4.11	4.06
600	6.72	6.48	6.27	6.09	5.94	5.81	5.70	5.60	5.25	5.05	4.93	4.87
700	7.84	7.55	7.31	7.11	6.93	6.78	6.65	6.53	6.12	5.89	5.76	5.68
800	8.95	8.63	8.36	8.12	7.92	7.75	7.60	7.46	6.99	6.73	6.58	6.49
900	10.07	9.71	9.40	9.14	8.91	8.72	8.54	8.39	7.87	7.57	7.40	7.30
1,000	11.19	10.79	10.45	10.15	9.90	9.68	9.49	9.33	8.74	8.41	8.22	8.11
2,000	22.38	21.57	20.89	20.30	19.80	19.36	18.98	18.65	17.48	16.82	16.44	16.21
3,000	33.56	32.36	31.33	30.45	29.70	29.04	28.47	27.97	26.22	25.23	24.65	24.31
4,000	44.75	43.14	41.77	40.60	39.60	38.72	37.96	37.29	34.95	33.64	32.87	32.41
5,000	55.93	53.92	52.22	50.75	49.49	48.40	47.45	46.61	43.69	42.05	41.09	40.51
6,000	67.12	64.71	62.66	60.90	59.39	58.08	56.94	55.93	52.43	50.46	49.30	48.61
7,000	78.31	75.49	73.10	71.05	69.29	67.76	66.42	65.25	61.16	58.86	57.52	56.71
8,000	89.49	86.27	83.54	81.20	79.19	77.44	75.91	74.58	69.90	67.27	65.73	64.81
9,000	100.68	97.06	93.99	91.35	89.09	87.12	85.40	83.90	78.64	75.68	73.95	72.91
10,000	111.86	107.84	104.43	101.50	98.98	96.80	94.89	93.22	87.37	84.09	82.17	81.01
15,000	167.79	161.76	156.64	152.25	148.47	145.19	142.33	139.82	131.06	126.13	123.25	121.51
20,000	223.72	215.68	208.85	203.00	197.96	193.59	189.77	186.43	174.74	168.18	164.33	162.02
25,000	279.65	269.60	261.06	253.75	247.45	241.98	237.21	233.04	218.43	210.22	205.41	202.52
30,000	335.58	323.52	313.27	304.50	296.94	290.38	284.66	279.64	262.11	252.26	246.49	243.02
35,000	391.51	377.43	365.48	355.25	346.43	338.77	332.10	326.25	305.80	294.30	287.57	283.53
40,000	447.43	431.35	417.69	406.00	395.92	387.17	379.54	372.86	349.48	336.35	328.65	324.03
45,000	503.36	485.27	469.91	456.75	445.41	435.57	426.98	419.46	393.17	378.39	369.73	364.53
50,000	559.29	539.19	522.12	507.50	494.90	483.96	474.42	466.07	436.85	420.43	410.81	405.04
55,000	615.22	593.11	574.33	558.25	544.38	532.36	521.87	512.68	480.54	462.47	451.89	445.54
60,000	671.15	647.03	626.54	609.00	593.87	580.75	569.31	559.28	524.22	504.52	492.97	486.04
65,000	727.08	700.94	678.75	659.75	643.36	629.15	616.75	605.89	567.91	546.56	534.05	526.55
70,000	783.01	754.86	730.96	710.50	692.85	677.54	664.19	652.50	611.59	588.60	575.13	567.05
75,000	838.93	808.78	783.17	761.25	742.34	725.94	711.63	699.10	655.28	630.65	616.21	607.55
80,000	894.86	862.70	835.38	812.00	791.83	774.33	759.08	745.71	698.96	672.69	657.29	648.05
85,000	950.79	916.62	887.60	862.75	841.32	822.73	806.52	792.32	742.65	714.73	698.37	688.56
90,000	1006.72	970.54	939.81	913.50	890.81	871.13	853.96	838.92	786.33	756.77	739.46	729.06
95,000	1062.65	1024.45	992.02	964.25	940.30	919.52	901.40	885.53	830.02	798.82	780.54	769.56
100,000	1118.58	1078.37	1044.23	1014.99	989.79	967.92	948.84	932.14	873.70	840.86	821.62	810.07
105,000	1174.51	1132.29	1096.44	1065.74	1039.27	1016.31	996.29	978.74	917.39	882.90	862.70	850.57
110,000	1230.43	1186.21	1148.65	1116.49	1088.76	1064.71	1043.73	1025.35	961.07	924.94	903.78	891.07
115,000	1286.36	1240.13	1200.86	1167.24	1138.25	1113.10	1091.17	1071.96	1004.76	966.99	944.86	931.58
120,000	1342.29	1294.05	1250.07	1217.99	1187.74	1161.50	1138.61	1118.56	1048.44	1009.03	985.94	972.08
125,000	1398.22	1347.97	1305.29	1268.74	1237.23	1209.89	1186.05	1165.17	1092.13	1051.07	1027.02	1012.58
130,000	1454.15	1401.88	1357.50	1319.49	1286.72	1258.29	1233.50	1211.78	1135.81	1093.12	1068.10	1053.09
135,000	1510.08	1455.80	1409.71	1370.24	1336.21	1306.69	1280.94	1258.38	1179.50	1135.16	1109.18	1093.59
140,000	1566.01	1509.72	1461.92	1420.99	1385.70	1355.08	1328.38	1304.99	1223.18	1177.20	1150.26	1134.09
145,000	1621.93	1563.64	1514.13	1471.74	1435.19	1403.48	1375.82	1351.60	1266.87	1219.24	1191.34	1174.59
150,000	1677.86	1617.56	1566.34	1522.49	1484.68	1451.87	1423.26	1398.20	1310.55	1261.29	1232.42	1215.10
155,000	1733.79	1671.48	1618.55	1573.24	1534.17	1500.27	1470.71	1444.81	1354.23	1303.33	1273.50	1255.60
160,000	1789.72	1725.39	1670.76	1623.99	1583.65	1548.66	1518.15	1491.41	1397.92	1345.37	1314.58	1296.10
165,000	1845.65	1779.31	1722.98	1674.74	1633.14	1597.06	1565.59	1538.02	1441.60	1387.41	1355.66	1336.61
170,000	1901.58	1833.23	1775.19	1725.49	1682.63	1645.45	1613.03	1584.63	1485.29	1429.46	1396.74	1377.11
175,000	1957.51	1887.15	1827.40	1776.24	1732.12	1693.85	1660.47	1631.23	1528.97	1471.50	1437.83	1417.61
180,000	2013.43	1941.07	1879.61	1826.99	1781.61	1742.25	1707.92	1677.84	1572.66	1513.54	1478.91	1458.12
185,000	2069.36	1994.99	1931.82	1877.74	1831.10	1790.64	1755.36	1724.45	1616.34	1555.59	1519.99	1498.62
190,000	2125.29	2048.90	1984.03	1928.49	1880.59	1839.04	1802.80	1771.05	1660.03	1597.63	1561.07	1539.12
195,000	2181.22	2102.82	2036.24	1979.23	1930.08	1887.43	1850.24	1817.66	1703.71	1639.67	1602.15	1579.63
200,000	2237.15	2156.74	2088.45	2029.98	1979.57	1935.83	1897.68	1864.27	1747.40	1681.71	1643.23	1620.13
205,000	2293.08	2210.66	2140.67	2080.73	2029.06	1984.22	1945.13	1910.87	1791.08	1723.76	1684.31	1660.63
210,000	2349.01	2264.58	2192.88	2131.48	2078.54	2032.62	1992.57	1957.48	1834.77	1765.80	1725.39	1701.13
215,000	2404.94	2318.50	2245.09	2182.23	2128.03	2081.01	2040.01	2004.09	1878.45	1807.84	1766.47	1741.64
220,000	2460.86	2372.41	2297.30	2232.98	2177.52	2129.41	2087.45	2050.69	1922.14	1849.88	1807.55	1782.14
225,000	2516.79	2426.33	2349.51	2283.73	2227.01	2177.81	2134.89	2097.30	1965.82	1891.93	1848.63	1822.64
230,000	2572.72	2480.25	2401.72	2334.48	2276.50	2226.20	2182.34	2143.91	2009.51	1933.97	1889.71	1863.15
235,000	2628.65	2534.17	2453.93	2385.23	2325.99	2274.60	2229.78	2190.51	2053.19	1976.01	1930.79	1903.65
240,000	2684.58	2588.09	2506.14	2435.98	2375.48	2322.99	2277.22	2237.12	2096.88	2018.06	1971.87	1944.15
245,000	2740.51	2642.01	2558.36	2486.73	2424.97	2371.39	2324.66	2283.73	2140.56	2060.10	2012.95	1984.66
250,000	2796.44	2695.93	2610.57	2537.48	2474.46	2419.78	2372.10	2330.33	2184.25	2102.14	2054.03	2025.16
255,000	2852.36	2749.84	2662.78	2588.23	2523.95	2468.18	2419.55	2376.94	2227.93	2144.18	2095.11	2065.66
260,000	2908.29	2803.76	2714.99	2638.98	2573.43	2516.57	2466.99	2423.55	2271.62	2186.23	2136.20	2106.17
265,000	2964.22	2857.68	2767.20	2689.73	2622.92	2564.97	2514.43	2470.15	2315.30	2228.27	2177.28	2146.67
270,000	3020.15	2911.60	2819.41	2740.48	2672.41	2613.37	2561.87	2516.76	2358.99	2270.31	2218.36	2187.17
280,000	3132.01	3019.44	2923.83	2841.98	2771.39	2710.16	2656.76	2609.97	2446.36	2354.40	2300.52	2268.18
290,000	3243.86	3127.27	3028.26	2943.47	2870.37	2806.95	2751.64	2703.19	2533.73	2438.48	2382.68	2349.18
300,000	3355.72	3235.11	3132.68	3044.97	2969.35	2903.74	2846.52	2796.40	2621.09	2522.57	2464.84	2430.19

MONTHLY AMORTIZING PAYMENTS

AMOUNT OF LOAN	NUMBER OF YEARS IN TERM											
	1	2	3	4	5	6	7	8	9	10	11	12
$ 50	4.39	2.31	1.61	1.27	1.06	0.93	0.83	0.76	0.70	0.66	0.62	0.60
100	8.78	4.61	3.22	2.53	2.12	1.85	1.65	1.51	1.40	1.31	1.24	1.19
200	17.56	9.21	6.43	5.05	4.23	3.69	3.30	3.01	2.79	2.62	2.48	2.37
300	26.34	13.81	9.65	7.58	6.34	5.53	4.95	4.52	4.19	3.93	3.72	3.55
400	35.12	18.42	12.86	10.10	8.45	7.37	6.59	6.02	5.58	5.24	4.96	4.73
500	43.90	23.02	16.08	12.63	10.57	9.21	8.24	7.53	6.98	6.54	6.19	5.91
600	52.68	27.62	19.29	15.15	12.68	11.05	9.89	9.03	8.37	7.85	7.43	7.09
700	61.46	32.23	22.51	17.67	14.79	12.89	11.54	10.53	9.77	9.16	8.67	8.27
800	70.24	36.83	25.72	20.20	16.90	14.73	13.18	12.04	11.16	10.47	9.91	9.45
900	79.02	41.43	28.94	22.72	19.02	16.57	14.83	13.54	12.55	11.77	11.15	10.63
1,000	87.80	46.03	32.15	25.25	21.13	18.41	16.48	15.05	13.95	13.08	12.38	11.81
2,000	175.60	92.06	64.30	50.49	42.25	36.81	32.95	30.09	27.89	26.16	24.76	23.62
3,000	263.40	138.09	96.45	75.73	63.38	55.21	49.42	45.13	41.84	39.24	37.14	35.43
4,000	351.20	184.12	128.60	100.98	84.50	73.61	65.89	60.17	55.78	52.31	49.52	47.23
5,000	439.00	230.15	160.75	126.22	105.63	92.01	82.37	75.22	69.72	65.39	61.90	59.04
6,000	526.80	276.18	192.90	151.46	126.75	110.41	98.84	90.26	83.67	78.47	74.28	70.85
7,000	614.60	322.21	225.05	176.70	147.87	128.81	115.31	105.30	97.61	91.54	86.66	82.65
8,000	702.40	368.24	257.20	201.95	169.00	147.21	131.78	120.34	111.55	104.62	99.04	94.46
9,000	790.20	414.27	289.35	227.19	190.12	165.61	148.26	135.38	125.50	117.70	111.41	106.27
10,000	878.00	460.30	321.50	252.43	211.25	184.01	164.73	150.43	139.44	130.78	123.79	118.07
15,000	1317.00	690.45	482.25	378.65	316.87	276.01	247.09	225.64	209.16	196.16	185.69	177.11
20,000	1756.00	920.60	643.00	504.86	422.49	368.01	329.45	300.85	278.88	261.55	247.58	236.14
25,000	2195.00	1150.75	803.75	631.07	528.11	460.01	411.81	376.06	348.60	326.93	309.48	295.18
30,000	2633.99	1380.89	964.50	757.29	633.73	552.01	494.17	451.27	418.31	392.32	371.37	354.21
35,000	3072.99	1611.04	1125.25	883.50	739.35	644.01	576.54	526.48	488.03	457.70	433.26	413.24
40,000	3511.99	1841.19	1286.00	1009.71	844.97	736.01	658.90	601.69	557.75	523.09	495.16	472.28
45,000	3950.99	2071.34	1446.75	1135.93	950.60	828.01	741.26	676.90	627.47	588.47	557.05	531.31
50,000	4389.99	2301.49	1607.50	1262.14	1056.22	920.01	823.62	752.12	697.19	653.86	618.95	590.35
55,000	4828.99	2531.63	1768.25	1388.35	1161.84	1012.01	905.98	827.33	766.91	719.24	680.84	649.38
60,000	5267.98	2761.78	1929.00	1514.57	1267.46	1104.01	988.34	902.54	836.62	784.63	742.74	708.41
65,000	5706.98	2991.93	2089.75	1640.78	1373.08	1196.01	1070.70	977.75	906.34	850.01	804.63	767.45
70,000	6145.98	3222.08	2250.50	1766.99	1478.70	1288.01	1153.07	1052.96	976.06	915.40	866.52	826.48
75,000	6584.98	3452.23	2411.25	1893.21	1584.32	1380.01	1235.43	1128.17	1045.78	980.78	928.42	885.52
80,000	7023.98	3682.37	2572.00	2019.42	1689.94	1472.01	1317.79	1203.38	1115.50	1046.17	990.31	944.55
85,000	7462.98	3912.52	2732.75	2145.63	1795.57	1564.01	1400.15	1278.59	1185.22	1111.55	1052.21	1003.58
90,000	7901.97	4142.67	2893.50	2271.85	1901.19	1656.01	1482.51	1353.80	1254.93	1176.94	1114.10	1062.62
95,000	8340.97	4372.82	3054.25	2398.06	2006.81	1748.01	1564.87	1429.01	1324.65	1242.32	1175.99	1121.65
100,000	8779.97	4602.97	3215.00	2524.27	2112.43	1840.01	1647.23	1504.23	1394.37	1307.71	1237.89	1180.69
105,000	9218.97	4833.12	3375.75	2650.49	2218.05	1932.01	1729.60	1579.44	1464.09	1373.09	1299.78	1239.72
110,000	9657.97	5063.26	3536.50	2776.70	2323.67	2024.01	1811.96	1654.65	1533.81	1438.48	1361.68	1298.75
115,000	10096.97	5293.41	3697.25	2902.91	2429.29	2116.01	1894.32	1729.86	1603.53	1503.86	1423.57	1357.79
120,000	10535.96	5523.56	3858.00	3029.13	2534.91	2208.01	1976.68	1805.07	1673.24	1569.25	1485.47	1416.82
125,000	10974.96	5753.71	4018.75	3155.34	2640.54	2300.01	2059.04	1880.28	1742.96	1634.63	1547.36	1475.86
130,000	11413.96	5983.86	4179.50	3281.55	2746.16	2392.01	2141.40	1955.49	1812.68	1700.02	1609.25	1534.89
135,000	11852.96	6214.00	4340.25	3407.77	2851.78	2484.01	2223.76	2030.70	1882.40	1765.40	1671.15	1593.92
140,000	12291.96	6444.15	4501.00	3533.98	2957.40	2576.01	2306.13	2105.91	1952.12	1830.79	1733.04	1652.96
145,000	12730.96	6674.30	4661.75	3660.20	3063.02	2668.01	2388.49	2181.12	2021.84	1896.17	1794.94	1711.99
150,000	13169.95	6904.45	4822.50	3786.41	3168.64	2760.01	2470.85	2256.34	2091.55	1961.56	1856.83	1771.03
155,000	13608.95	7134.60	4983.25	3912.62	3274.26	2852.01	2553.21	2331.55	2161.27	2026.94	1918.73	1830.06
160,000	14047.95	7364.74	5144.00	4038.84	3379.88	2944.01	2635.57	2406.76	2230.99	2092.33	1980.62	1889.09
165,000	14486.95	7594.89	5304.75	4165.05	3485.51	3036.01	2717.93	2481.97	2300.71	2157.71	2042.51	1948.13
170,000	14925.95	7825.04	5465.49	4291.26	3591.13	3128.01	2800.30	2557.18	2370.43	2223.10	2104.41	2007.16
175,000	15364.94	8055.19	5626.24	4417.48	3696.75	3220.01	2882.66	2632.39	2440.15	2288.48	2166.30	2066.20
180,000	15803.94	8285.34	5786.99	4543.69	3802.37	3312.01	2965.02	2707.60	2509.86	2353.87	2228.20	2125.23
185,000	16242.94	8515.49	5947.74	4669.90	3907.99	3404.01	3047.38	2782.81	2579.58	2419.25	2290.09	2184.26
190,000	16681.94	8745.63	6108.49	4796.12	4013.61	3496.01	3129.74	2858.02	2649.30	2484.64	2351.98	2243.30
195,000	17120.94	8975.78	6269.24	4922.33	4119.23	3588.01	3212.10	2933.23	2719.02	2550.02	2413.88	2302.33
200,000	17559.94	9205.93	6429.99	5048.54	4224.85	3680.01	3294.46	3008.45	2788.74	2615.41	2475.77	2361.37
205,000	17998.93	9436.08	6590.74	5174.76	4330.47	3772.01	3376.83	3083.66	2858.46	2680.79	2537.67	2420.40
210,000	18437.93	9666.23	6751.49	5300.97	4436.10	3864.01	3459.19	3158.87	2928.17	2746.18	2599.56	2479.43
215,000	18876.93	9896.37	6912.24	5427.18	4541.72	3956.01	3541.55	3234.08	2997.89	2811.57	2661.46	2538.47
220,000	19315.93	10126.52	7072.99	5553.40	4647.34	4048.01	3623.91	3309.29	3067.61	2876.95	2723.35	2597.50
225,000	19754.93	10356.67	7233.74	5679.61	4752.96	4140.01	3706.27	3384.50	3137.33	2942.34	2785.24	2656.54
230,000	20193.93	10586.82	7394.49	5805.82	4858.58	4232.01	3788.63	3459.71	3207.05	3007.72	2847.14	2715.57
235,000	20632.92	10816.97	7555.24	5932.04	4964.20	4324.01	3870.99	3534.92	3276.77	3073.11	2909.03	2774.60
240,000	21071.92	11047.11	7715.99	6058.25	5069.82	4416.01	3953.36	3610.13	3346.48	3138.49	2970.93	2833.64
245,000	21510.92	11277.26	7876.74	6184.46	5175.44	4508.01	4035.72	3685.34	3416.20	3203.88	3032.82	2892.67
250,000	21949.92	11507.41	8037.49	6310.68	5281.07	4600.01	4118.08	3760.56	3485.92	3269.26	3094.72	2951.71
255,000	22388.92	11737.56	8198.24	6436.89	5386.69	4692.01	4200.44	3835.77	3555.64	3334.65	3156.61	3010.74
260,000	22827.92	11967.71	8358.99	6563.10	5492.31	4784.01	4282.80	3910.98	3625.36	3400.03	3218.50	3069.77
265,000	23266.91	12197.86	8519.74	6689.32	5597.93	4876.01	4365.16	3986.19	3695.08	3465.42	3280.40	3128.81
270,000	23705.91	12428.00	8680.49	6815.53	5703.55	4968.01	4447.52	4061.40	3764.79	3530.80	3342.29	3187.84
280,000	24583.91	12888.30	9001.99	7067.96	5914.79	5152.01	4612.25	4211.82	3904.23	3661.57	3466.08	3305.91
290,000	25461.91	13348.60	9323.49	7320.39	6126.04	5336.01	4776.97	4362.24	4043.67	3792.34	3589.87	3423.98
300,000	26339.90	13808.89	9644.99	7572.81	6337.28	5520.01	4941.69	4512.67	4183.10	3923.11	3713.66	3542.05

AMOUNT OF LOAN	NUMBER OF YEARS IN TERM											
	13	14	15	16	17	18	19	20	25	30	35	40
$ 50	0.57	0.55	0.53	0.52	0.51	0.50	0.49	0.48	0.45	0.43	0.43	0.42
100	1.14	1.10	1.06	1.04	1.01	0.99	0.97	0.95	0.90	0.86	0.85	0.83
200	2.27	2.19	2.12	2.07	2.02	1.97	1.93	1.90	1.79	1.72	1.69	1.66
300	3.40	3.28	3.18	3.10	3.02	2.96	2.90	2.85	2.68	2.58	2.53	2.49
400	4.54	4.38	4.24	4.13	4.03	3.94	3.86	3.80	3.57	3.44	3.37	3.32
500	5.67	5.47	5.30	5.16	5.03	4.92	4.83	4.75	4.46	4.30	4.21	4.15
600	6.80	6.56	6.36	6.19	6.04	5.91	5.79	5.70	5.35	5.16	5.05	4.98
700	7.94	7.66	7.42	7.22	7.04	6.89	6.76	6.64	6.24	6.02	5.89	5.81
800	9.07	8.75	8.48	8.25	8.05	7.88	7.72	7.59	7.13	6.88	6.73	6.64
900	10.20	9.84	9.54	9.28	9.05	8.86	8.69	8.54	8.03	7.74	7.57	7.47
1,000	11.34	10.94	10.60	10.31	10.06	9.84	9.65	9.49	8.92	8.60	8.41	8.30
2,000	22.67	21.87	21.19	20.61	20.11	19.68	19.30	18.98	17.83	17.19	16.82	16.60
3,000	34.00	32.80	31.79	30.92	30.17	29.52	28.95	28.46	26.74	25.78	25.22	24.89
4,000	45.33	43.73	42.38	41.22	40.22	39.36	38.60	37.95	35.65	34.37	33.63	33.19
5,000	56.66	54.67	52.97	51.52	50.28	49.20	48.25	47.43	44.56	42.96	42.03	41.48
6,000	67.99	65.60	63.57	61.83	60.33	59.03	57.90	56.92	53.47	51.55	50.44	49.78
7,000	79.33	76.53	74.16	72.13	70.39	68.87	67.55	66.40	62.38	60.15	58.85	58.07
8,000	90.66	87.46	84.75	82.44	80.44	78.71	77.20	75.89	71.30	68.74	67.25	66.37
9,000	101.99	98.40	95.35	92.74	90.49	88.55	86.85	85.37	80.21	77.33	75.66	74.67
10,000	113.32	109.33	105.94	103.04	100.55	98.39	96.50	94.86	89.12	85.92	84.06	82.96
15,000	169.98	163.99	158.91	154.56	150.82	147.58	144.75	142.28	133.68	128.88	126.09	124.44
20,000	226.64	218.65	211.88	206.08	201.09	196.77	193.00	189.71	178.23	171.84	168.12	165.92
25,000	283.30	273.31	264.85	257.60	251.36	245.96	241.25	237.13	222.79	214.79	210.15	207.39
30,000	339.95	327.98	317.81	309.12	301.64	295.16	289.50	284.56	267.05	257.75	252.18	248.87
35,000	396.61	382.64	370.78	360.64	351.91	344.34	337.75	331.99	311.90	300.71	294.21	290.35
40,000	453.27	437.30	423.75	412.16	402.18	393.53	386.00	379.41	356.46	343.67	336.24	331.83
45,000	509.93	491.96	476.72	463.68	452.45	442.72	434.25	426.84	401.02	386.62	378.27	373.31
50,000	566.59	546.62	529.69	515.20	502.72	491.92	482.50	474.26	445.57	429.58	420.30	414.78
55,000	623.24	601.28	582.65	566.72	553.00	541.11	530.75	521.69	490.13	472.54	462.33	456.26
60,000	679.90	655.95	635.62	618.24	603.27	590.30	579.00	569.12	534.69	515.50	504.36	497.74
65,000	736.56	710.61	688.59	669.76	653.54	639.49	627.25	616.54	579.24	558.46	546.39	539.22
70,000	793.22	765.27	741.56	721.28	703.81	688.68	675.50	663.97	623.80	601.41	588.42	580.70
75,000	849.88	819.93	794.53	772.80	754.08	737.87	723.75	711.39	668.36	644.37	630.45	622.17
80,000	906.54	874.59	847.50	824.32	804.36	787.06	772.00	758.82	712.91	687.33	672.48	663.65
85,000	963.19	929.25	900.46	875.84	854.63	836.25	820.25	806.24	757.47	730.29	714.51	705.13
90,000	1019.85	983.92	953.43	927.36	904.90	885.44	868.50	853.67	802.03	773.24	756.54	746.61
95,000	1076.51	1038.58	1006.40	978.88	955.17	934.63	916.75	901.10	846.59	816.20	798.56	788.09
100,000	1133.17	1093.24	1059.37	1030.40	1005.44	983.83	965.00	948.52	891.14	859.16	840.59	829.56
105,000	1189.83	1147.90	1112.34	1081.92	1055.72	1033.02	1013.25	995.95	935.70	902.12	882.62	871.04
110,000	1246.48	1202.50	1165.30	1133.44	1105.99	1082.21	1061.49	1043.37	980.26	945.07	924.65	912.52
115,000	1303.14	1257.23	1218.27	1184.96	1156.26	1131.40	1109.74	1090.80	1024.81	988.03	966.68	954.00
120,000	1359.80	1311.89	1271.24	1236.47	1206.53	1180.59	1157.99	1138.23	1069.37	1030.99	1008.71	995.48
125,000	1416.46	1366.55	1324.21	1287.99	1256.80	1229.78	1206.24	1185.65	1113.93	1073.95	1050.74	1036.95
130,000	1473.12	1421.21	1377.18	1339.51	1307.08	1278.97	1254.49	1233.08	1158.48	1116.91	1092.77	1078.43
135,000	1529.77	1475.87	1430.14	1391.03	1357.35	1328.16	1302.74	1280.50	1203.04	1159.86	1134.80	1119.91
140,000	1586.43	1530.53	1483.11	1442.55	1407.62	1377.35	1350.99	1327.93	1247.60	1202.82	1176.83	1161.39
145,000	1643.09	1585.20	1536.08	1494.07	1457.89	1426.54	1399.24	1375.35	1292.15	1245.78	1218.86	1202.86
150,000	1699.75	1639.86	1589.05	1545.59	1508.16	1475.74	1447.49	1422.78	1336.71	1288.74	1260.89	1244.34
155,000	1756.41	1694.52	1642.02	1597.11	1558.44	1524.93	1495.74	1470.21	1381.27	1331.69	1302.92	1285.82
160,000	1813.07	1749.18	1694.99	1648.63	1608.71	1574.12	1543.99	1517.63	1425.82	1374.65	1344.95	1327.30
165,000	1869.72	1803.84	1747.95	1700.15	1658.98	1623.31	1592.24	1565.06	1470.38	1417.61	1386.98	1368.78
170,000	1926.38	1858.50	1800.92	1751.67	1709.25	1672.50	1640.49	1612.48	1514.94	1460.57	1429.01	1410.25
175,000	1983.04	1913.17	1853.89	1803.19	1759.52	1721.69	1688.74	1659.91	1559.50	1503.53	1471.04	1451.73
180,000	2039.70	1967.83	1906.86	1854.71	1809.80	1770.88	1736.99	1707.34	1604.05	1546.48	1513.07	1493.21
185,000	2096.36	2022.49	1959.83	1906.23	1860.07	1820.07	1785.24	1754.76	1648.61	1589.44	1555.10	1534.69
190,000	2153.01	2077.15	2012.79	1957.75	1910.34	1869.26	1833.49	1802.19	1693.17	1632.40	1597.12	1576.17
195,000	2209.67	2131.81	2065.76	2009.27	1960.61	1918.45	1881.74	1849.61	1737.72	1675.36	1639.15	1617.64
200,000	2266.33	2186.48	2118.73	2060.79	2010.88	1967.65	1929.99	1897.04	1782.28	1718.31	1681.18	1659.12
205,000	2322.99	2241.14	2171.70	2112.31	2061.16	2016.84	1978.24	1944.46	1826.84	1761.27	1723.21	1700.60
210,000	2379.65	2295.80	2224.67	2163.83	2111.43	2066.03	2026.49	1991.89	1871.39	1804.23	1765.24	1742.08
215,000	2436.30	2350.46	2277.63	2215.35	2161.70	2115.22	2074.74	2039.32	1915.95	1847.19	1807.27	1783.56
220,000	2492.96	2405.12	2330.60	2266.87	2211.97	2164.41	2122.98	2086.74	1960.51	1890.14	1849.30	1825.03
225,000	2549.62	2459.78	2383.57	2318.39	2262.24	2213.60	2171.23	2134.17	2005.06	1933.10	1891.33	1866.51
230,000	2606.28	2514.45	2436.54	2369.91	2312.52	2262.79	2219.48	2181.59	2049.62	1976.06	1933.36	1907.99
235,000	2662.94	2569.11	2489.51	2421.43	2362.79	2311.98	2267.73	2229.02	2094.18	2019.02	1975.39	1949.47
240,000	2719.60	2623.77	2542.48	2472.94	2413.06	2361.17	2315.98	2276.45	2138.73	2061.98	2017.42	1990.95
245,000	2776.25	2678.43	2595.44	2524.46	2463.33	2410.36	2364.23	2323.87	2183.29	2104.93	2059.45	2032.42
250,000	2832.91	2733.09	2648.41	2575.98	2513.60	2459.56	2412.48	2371.30	2227.85	2147.89	2101.48	2073.90
255,000	2889.57	2787.75	2701.38	2627.50	2563.88	2508.75	2460.73	2418.72	2272.41	2190.85	2143.51	2115.38
260,000	2946.23	2842.42	2754.35	2679.02	2614.15	2557.94	2508.98	2466.15	2316.96	2233.81	2185.54	2156.86
265,000	3002.89	2897.08	2807.32	2730.54	2664.42	2607.13	2557.23	2513.57	2361.52	2276.76	2227.57	2198.34
270,000	3059.54	2951.74	2860.28	2782.06	2714.69	2656.32	2605.48	2561.00	2406.08	2319.72	2269.60	2239.81
280,000	3172.86	3061.06	2966.22	2885.10	2815.24	2754.70	2701.98	2655.85	2495.19	2405.64	2353.66	2322.77
290,000	3286.18	3170.39	3072.16	2988.14	2915.78	2853.08	2798.48	2750.70	2584.30	2491.55	2437.71	2405.72
300,000	3399.49	3279.71	3178.09	3091.18	3016.32	2951.47	2894.98	2845.56	2673.42	2577.47	2521.77	2488.68

10.00%
MONTHLY AMORTIZING PAYMENTS

AMOUNT OF LOAN	NUMBER OF YEARS IN TERM											
	1	2	3	4	5	6	7	8	9	10	11	12
$ 50	4.40	2.31	1.62	1.27	1.07	0.93	0.84	0.76	0.71	0.67	0.63	0.60
100	8.80	4.62	3.23	2.54	2.13	1.86	1.67	1.52	1.41	1.33	1.26	1.20
200	17.59	9.23	6.46	5.08	4.25	3.71	3.33	3.04	2.82	2.65	2.51	2.40
300	26.38	13.85	9.69	7.61	6.38	5.56	4.99	4.56	4.23	3.97	3.76	3.59
400	35.17	18.46	12.91	10.15	8.50	7.42	6.65	6.07	5.64	5.29	5.01	4.79
500	43.96	23.08	16.14	12.69	10.63	9.27	8.31	7.59	7.04	6.61	6.26	5.98
600	52.75	27.69	19.37	15.22	12.75	11.12	9.97	9.11	8.45	7.93	7.52	7.18
700	61.55	32.31	22.59	17.76	14.88	12.97	11.63	10.63	9.86	9.26	8.77	8.37
800	70.34	36.92	25.82	20.30	17.00	14.83	13.29	12.14	11.27	10.58	10.02	9.57
900	79.13	41.54	29.05	22.83	19.13	16.68	14.95	13.66	12.68	11.90	11.27	10.76
1,000	87.92	46.15	32.27	25.37	21.25	18.53	16.61	15.18	14.08	13.22	12.52	11.96
2,000	175.84	92.29	64.54	50.73	42.50	37.06	33.21	30.35	28.16	26.44	25.04	23.91
3,000	263.75	138.44	96.81	76.09	63.75	55.58	49.81	45.53	42.24	39.65	37.56	35.86
4,000	351.67	184.58	129.07	101.46	84.99	74.11	66.41	60.70	56.32	52.87	50.08	47.81
5,000	439.58	230.73	161.34	126.82	106.24	92.63	83.01	75.88	70.40	66.08	62.60	59.76
6,000	527.50	276.87	193.61	152.18	127.49	111.16	99.61	91.05	84.48	79.30	75.12	71.71
7,000	615.42	323.02	225.88	177.54	148.73	129.69	116.21	106.22	98.56	92.51	87.64	83.66
8,000	703.33	369.16	258.14	202.91	169.98	148.21	132.81	121.40	112.63	105.73	100.16	95.61
9,000	791.25	415.31	290.41	228.27	191.23	166.74	149.42	136.57	126.71	118.94	112.68	107.56
10,000	879.16	461.45	322.68	253.63	212.48	185.26	166.02	151.75	140.79	132.16	125.20	119.51
15,000	1318.74	692.18	484.01	380.44	318.71	277.89	249.02	227.62	211.19	198.23	187.80	179.27
20,000	1758.32	922.90	645.35	507.26	424.95	370.52	332.03	303.49	281.58	264.31	250.40	239.02
25,000	2197.90	1153.63	806.68	634.07	531.18	463.15	415.03	379.36	351.97	330.38	313.00	298.77
30,000	2637.48	1384.35	968.02	760.88	637.42	555.78	498.04	455.23	422.37	396.46	375.60	358.53
35,000	3077.06	1615.08	1129.36	887.70	743.65	648.41	581.05	531.10	492.76	462.53	438.20	418.28
40,000	3516.64	1845.80	1290.69	1014.51	849.89	741.04	664.05	606.97	563.15	528.61	500.80	478.04
45,000	3956.22	2076.53	1452.03	1141.32	956.12	833.67	747.06	682.84	633.55	594.68	563.40	537.79
50,000	4395.80	2307.25	1613.36	1268.13	1062.36	926.30	830.06	758.71	703.94	660.76	626.00	597.54
55,000	4835.38	2537.98	1774.70	1394.95	1168.59	1018.93	913.07	834.58	774.33	726.83	688.60	657.30
60,000	5274.96	2768.70	1936.04	1521.76	1274.83	1111.56	996.08	910.45	844.73	792.91	751.20	717.05
65,000	5714.54	2999.43	2097.37	1648.57	1381.06	1204.18	1079.08	986.33	915.12	858.98	813.80	776.81
70,000	6154.12	3230.15	2258.71	1775.39	1487.30	1296.81	1162.09	1062.20	985.51	925.06	876.40	836.56
75,000	6593.70	3460.87	2420.04	1902.20	1593.53	1389.44	1245.09	1138.07	1055.91	991.14	939.00	896.31
80,000	7033.28	3691.60	2581.38	2029.01	1699.77	1482.07	1328.10	1213.94	1126.30	1057.21	1001.60	956.07
85,000	7472.86	3922.32	2742.72	2155.82	1806.00	1574.70	1411.11	1289.81	1196.69	1123.29	1064.19	1015.82
90,000	7912.43	4153.05	2904.05	2282.64	1912.24	1667.33	1494.11	1365.68	1267.09	1189.36	1126.79	1075.58
95,000	8352.01	4383.77	3065.39	2409.45	2018.47	1759.96	1577.12	1441.55	1337.48	1255.44	1189.39	1135.33
100,000	8791.59	4614.50	3226.72	2536.26	2124.71	1852.59	1660.12	1517.42	1407.87	1321.51	1251.99	1195.08
105,000	9231.17	4845.22	3388.06	2663.08	2230.94	1945.22	1743.13	1593.29	1478.27	1387.59	1314.59	1254.84
110,000	9670.75	5075.95	3549.40	2789.89	2337.18	2037.85	1826.14	1669.16	1548.66	1453.66	1377.19	1314.59
115,000	10110.33	5306.67	3710.73	2916.70	2443.42	2130.48	1909.14	1745.03	1619.05	1519.74	1439.79	1374.35
120,000	10549.91	5537.40	3872.07	3043.52	2549.65	2223.11	1992.15	1820.90	1689.45	1585.81	1502.39	1434.10
125,000	10989.49	5768.12	4033.40	3170.33	2655.89	2315.73	2075.15	1896.78	1759.84	1651.89	1564.99	1493.85
130,000	11429.07	5998.85	4194.74	3297.14	2762.12	2408.36	2158.16	1972.65	1830.23	1717.96	1627.59	1553.61
135,000	11868.65	6229.57	4356.08	3423.95	2868.36	2500.99	2241.16	2048.52	1900.63	1784.04	1690.19	1613.36
140,000	12308.23	6460.29	4517.41	3550.77	2974.59	2593.62	2324.17	2124.39	1971.02	1850.12	1752.79	1673.11
145,000	12747.81	6691.02	4678.75	3677.58	3080.83	2686.25	2407.18	2200.26	2041.41	1916.19	1815.39	1732.87
150,000	13187.39	6921.74	4840.08	3804.39	3187.06	2778.88	2490.18	2276.13	2111.81	1982.27	1877.99	1792.62
155,000	13626.97	7152.47	5001.42	3931.21	3293.30	2871.51	2573.19	2352.00	2182.20	2048.34	1940.59	1852.38
160,000	14066.55	7383.19	5162.75	4058.02	3399.53	2964.14	2656.19	2427.87	2252.59	2114.42	2003.19	1912.13
165,000	14506.13	7613.92	5324.09	4184.83	3505.77	3056.77	2739.20	2503.74	2322.99	2180.49	2065.78	1971.88
170,000	14945.71	7844.64	5485.43	4311.64	3612.00	3149.40	2822.21	2579.61	2393.38	2246.57	2128.38	2031.64
175,000	15385.29	8075.37	5646.76	4438.46	3718.24	3242.03	2905.21	2655.48	2463.78	2312.64	2190.98	2091.39
180,000	15824.86	8306.09	5808.10	4565.27	3824.47	3334.66	2988.22	2731.35	2534.17	2378.72	2253.58	2151.15
185,000	16264.44	8536.82	5969.43	4692.08	3930.71	3427.28	3071.22	2807.23	2604.56	2444.79	2316.18	2210.90
190,000	16704.02	8767.54	6130.77	4818.90	4036.94	3519.91	3154.23	2883.10	2674.96	2510.87	2378.78	2270.65
195,000	17143.60	8998.27	6292.11	4945.71	4143.18	3612.54	3237.24	2958.97	2745.35	2576.94	2441.38	2330.41
200,000	17583.18	9228.99	6453.44	5072.52	4249.41	3705.17	3320.24	3034.84	2815.74	2643.02	2503.98	2390.16
205,000	18022.76	9459.71	6614.78	5199.33	4355.65	3797.80	3403.25	3110.71	2886.14	2709.10	2566.58	2449.92
210,000	18462.34	9690.44	6776.11	5326.15	4461.88	3890.43	3486.25	3186.58	2956.53	2775.17	2629.18	2509.67
215,000	18901.92	9921.16	6937.45	5452.96	4568.12	3983.06	3569.26	3262.45	3026.92	2841.25	2691.78	2569.42
220,000	19341.50	10151.89	7098.79	5579.77	4674.35	4075.69	3652.27	3338.32	3097.32	2907.32	2754.38	2629.18
225,000	19781.08	10382.61	7260.12	5706.59	4780.59	4168.32	3735.27	3414.19	3167.71	2973.40	2816.98	2688.93
230,000	20220.66	10613.34	7421.46	5833.40	4886.83	4260.95	3818.28	3490.06	3238.10	3039.47	2879.58	2748.69
235,000	20660.24	10844.06	7582.79	5960.21	4993.06	4353.58	3901.28	3565.93	3308.50	3105.55	2942.18	2808.44
240,000	21099.82	11074.79	7744.13	6087.03	5099.30	4446.21	3984.29	3641.80	3378.89	3171.62	3004.78	2868.19
245,000	21539.40	11305.51	7905.47	6213.84	5205.53	4538.84	4067.30	3717.68	3449.28	3237.70	3067.37	2927.95
250,000	21978.98	11536.24	8066.80	6340.65	5311.77	4631.46	4150.30	3793.55	3519.68	3303.77	3129.97	2987.70
255,000	22418.56	11766.96	8228.14	6467.46	5418.00	4724.09	4233.31	3869.42	3590.07	3369.85	3192.57	3047.45
260,000	22858.14	11997.69	8389.47	6594.28	5524.24	4816.72	4316.31	3945.29	3660.46	3435.92	3255.17	3107.21
265,000	23297.72	12228.41	8550.81	6721.09	5630.47	4909.35	4399.32	4021.16	3730.86	3502.00	3317.77	3166.96
270,000	23737.29	12459.14	8712.15	6847.90	5736.71	5001.98	4482.32	4097.03	3801.25	3568.07	3380.37	3226.72
280,000	24616.45	12920.58	9034.82	7101.53	5949.18	5187.24	4648.34	4248.77	3942.04	3700.23	3505.57	3346.22
290,000	25495.61	13382.03	9357.49	7355.15	6161.65	5372.50	4814.35	4400.51	4082.82	3832.38	3630.77	3465.73
300,000	26374.77	13843.48	9680.16	7608.78	6374.12	5557.76	4980.36	4552.25	4223.61	3964.53	3755.97	3585.24

AMOUNT OF LOAN	NUMBER OF YEARS IN TERM											
	13	14	15	16	17	18	19	20	25	30	35	40
$ 50	0.58	0.56	0.54	0.53	0.52	0.50	0.50	0.49	0.46	0.44	0.43	0.43
100	1.15	1.11	1.08	1.05	1.03	1.00	0.99	0.97	0.91	0.88	0.86	0.85
200	2.30	2.22	2.15	2.10	2.05	2.00	1.97	1.94	1.82	1.76	1.72	1.70
300	3.45	3.33	3.23	3.14	3.07	3.00	2.95	2.90	2.73	2.64	2.58	2.55
400	4.60	4.44	4.30	4.19	4.09	4.00	3.93	3.87	3.64	3.52	3.44	3.40
500	5.74	5.55	5.38	5.23	5.11	5.00	4.91	4.83	4.55	4.39	4.30	4.25
600	6.89	6.65	6.45	6.28	6.13	6.00	5.89	5.80	5.46	5.27	5.16	5.10
700	8.04	7.76	7.53	7.33	7.15	7.00	6.87	6.76	6.37	6.15	6.02	5.95
800	9.19	8.87	8.60	8.37	8.17	8.00	7.86	7.73	7.27	7.03	6.88	6.80
900	10.34	9.98	9.68	9.42	9.20	9.00	8.84	8.69	8.18	7.90	7.74	7.65
1,000	11.48	11.09	10.75	10.46	10.22	10.00	9.82	9.66	9.09	8.78	8.60	8.50
2,000	22.96	22.17	21.50	20.92	20.43	20.00	19.63	19.31	18.18	17.56	17.20	16.99
3,000	34.44	33.25	32.24	31.38	30.64	30.00	29.44	28.96	27.27	26.33	25.80	25.48
4,000	45.92	44.33	42.99	41.84	40.85	40.00	39.26	38.61	36.35	35.11	34.39	33.97
5,000	57.40	55.42	53.74	52.30	51.07	50.00	49.07	48.26	45.44	43.88	42.99	42.46
6,000	68.88	66.50	64.48	62.76	61.28	60.00	58.88	57.91	54.53	52.66	51.59	50.95
7,000	80.35	77.58	75.23	73.22	71.49	69.99	68.69	67.56	63.61	61.44	60.18	59.45
8,000	91.83	88.66	85.97	83.68	81.70	79.99	78.51	77.21	72.70	70.21	68.78	67.94
9,000	103.31	99.74	96.72	94.14	91.91	89.99	88.32	86.86	81.79	78.99	77.38	76.43
10,000	114.79	110.83	107.47	104.60	102.13	99.99	98.13	96.51	90.88	87.76	85.97	84.92
15,000	172.18	166.24	161.20	156.89	153.19	149.98	147.19	144.76	136.31	131.64	128.96	127.38
20,000	229.57	221.65	214.93	209.19	204.25	199.97	196.26	193.01	181.75	175.52	171.94	169.83
25,000	286.97	277.06	268.66	261.48	255.31	249.97	245.32	241.26	227.18	219.40	214.92	212.29
30,000	344.36	332.47	322.39	313.78	306.37	299.96	294.38	289.51	272.62	263.28	257.91	254.75
35,000	401.75	387.88	376.12	366.07	357.43	349.95	343.45	337.76	318.05	307.16	300.89	297.21
40,000	459.14	443.29	429.85	418.37	408.49	399.94	392.51	386.01	363.49	351.03	343.87	339.66
45,000	516.54	498.70	483.58	470.66	459.55	449.93	441.57	434.26	408.92	394.91	386.86	382.12
50,000	573.93	554.11	537.31	522.96	510.61	499.93	490.63	482.52	454.36	438.79	429.84	424.58
55,000	631.32	609.52	591.04	575.25	561.67	549.92	539.70	530.77	499.79	482.67	472.82	467.04
60,000	688.71	664.93	644.77	627.55	612.73	599.91	588.76	579.02	545.23	526.55	515.81	509.49
65,000	746.11	720.34	698.50	679.84	663.79	649.90	637.82	627.27	590.66	570.43	558.79	551.95
70,000	803.50	775.75	752.23	732.14	714.85	699.90	686.89	675.52	636.10	614.31	601.78	594.41
75,000	860.89	831.16	805.96	784.43	765.91	749.89	735.95	723.77	681.53	658.18	644.76	636.86
80,000	918.28	886.57	859.69	836.73	816.97	799.88	785.01	772.02	726.97	702.06	687.74	679.32
85,000	975.68	941.98	913.42	889.02	868.03	849.87	834.08	820.27	772.40	745.94	730.73	721.78
90,000	1033.07	997.39	967.15	941.32	919.09	899.86	883.14	868.52	817.84	789.82	773.71	764.24
95,000	1090.46	1052.80	1020.88	993.61	970.15	949.86	932.20	916.78	863.27	833.70	816.69	806.69
100,000	1147.85	1108.21	1074.61	1045.91	1021.22	999.85	981.26	965.03	908.71	877.58	859.68	849.15
105,000	1205.25	1163.62	1128.34	1098.20	1072.28	1049.84	1030.33	1013.28	954.14	921.46	902.66	891.61
110,000	1262.64	1219.03	1182.07	1150.50	1123.34	1099.83	1079.39	1061.53	999.58	965.33	945.64	934.07
115,000	1320.03	1274.44	1235.80	1202.79	1174.40	1149.83	1128.45	1109.78	1045.01	1009.21	988.63	976.52
120,000	1377.42	1329.86	1289.53	1255.09	1225.46	1199.82	1177.52	1150.03	1090.45	1053.09	1031.61	1018.98
125,000	1434.82	1385.26	1343.26	1307.39	1276.53	1249.81	1226.58	1198.28	1135.89	1096.97	1074.60	1061.44
130,000	1492.21	1440.67	1396.99	1359.68	1327.58	1299.80	1275.64	1254.53	1181.32	1140.85	1117.58	1103.89
135,000	1549.60	1496.08	1450.72	1411.97	1378.64	1349.79	1324.70	1302.78	1226.75	1184.73	1160.56	1146.35
140,000	1606.99	1551.49	1504.45	1464.27	1429.70	1399.79	1373.77	1351.04	1272.19	1228.61	1203.55	1188.81
145,000	1664.38	1606.90	1558.18	1516.56	1480.76	1449.78	1422.83	1399.29	1317.62	1272.48	1246.53	1231.27
150,000	1721.78	1662.31	1611.91	1568.86	1531.82	1499.77	1471.89	1447.54	1363.06	1316.36	1289.51	1273.72
155,000	1779.17	1717.72	1665.64	1621.15	1582.88	1549.76	1520.96	1495.79	1408.49	1360.24	1332.50	1316.18
160,000	1836.56	1773.13	1719.37	1673.45	1633.94	1599.75	1570.02	1544.04	1453.93	1404.12	1375.48	1358.64
165,000	1893.95	1828.54	1773.10	1725.74	1685.00	1649.75	1619.08	1592.29	1499.36	1448.00	1418.46	1401.10
170,000	1951.35	1883.95	1826.83	1778.04	1736.06	1699.74	1668.15	1640.54	1544.80	1491.88	1461.45	1443.55
175,000	2008.74	1939.36	1880.56	1830.33	1787.12	1749.73	1717.21	1688.79	1590.23	1535.76	1504.43	1486.01
180,000	2066.13	1994.77	1934.29	1882.63	1838.18	1799.72	1766.27	1737.04	1635.67	1579.63	1547.42	1528.47
185,000	2123.52	2050.18	1988.02	1934.92	1889.24	1849.72	1815.33	1785.30	1681.10	1623.51	1590.40	1570.92
190,000	2180.92	2105.59	2041.75	1987.22	1940.30	1899.71	1864.40	1833.55	1726.54	1667.39	1633.38	1613.38
195,000	2238.31	2161.00	2095.48	2039.51	1991.37	1949.70	1913.46	1881.80	1771.97	1711.27	1676.37	1655.84
200,000	2295.70	2216.41	2149.22	2091.81	2042.43	1999.69	1962.52	1930.05	1817.41	1755.15	1719.35	1698.30
205,000	2353.09	2271.82	2202.95	2144.10	2093.49	2049.68	2011.59	1978.30	1862.84	1799.03	1762.33	1740.75
210,000	2410.49	2327.23	2256.68	2196.40	2144.55	2099.68	2060.65	2026.55	1908.28	1842.91	1805.32	1783.21
215,000	2467.88	2382.64	2310.41	2248.69	2195.61	2149.67	2109.71	2074.80	1953.71	1886.78	1848.30	1825.67
220,000	2525.27	2438.05	2364.14	2300.99	2246.67	2199.66	2158.77	2123.05	1999.15	1930.66	1891.28	1868.13
225,000	2582.66	2493.46	2417.87	2353.28	2297.73	2249.65	2207.84	2171.30	2044.58	1974.54	1934.27	1910.58
230,000	2640.06	2548.87	2471.60	2405.58	2348.79	2299.65	2256.90	2219.55	2090.02	2018.42	1977.25	1953.04
235,000	2697.45	2604.28	2525.33	2457.87	2399.85	2349.64	2305.96	2267.81	2135.45	2062.30	2020.24	1995.50
240,000	2754.84	2659.69	2579.06	2510.17	2450.91	2399.63	2355.03	2316.06	2180.89	2106.18	2063.22	2037.96
245,000	2812.23	2715.10	2632.79	2562.46	2501.97	2449.62	2404.09	2364.31	2226.32	2150.06	2106.20	2080.41
250,000	2869.63	2770.51	2686.52	2614.76	2553.03	2499.61	2453.15	2412.56	2271.76	2193.93	2149.19	2122.87
255,000	2927.02	2825.92	2740.25	2667.05	2604.09	2549.61	2502.22	2460.81	2317.19	2237.81	2192.17	2165.33
260,000	2984.41	2881.33	2793.98	2719.35	2655.15	2599.60	2551.28	2509.06	2362.63	2281.69	2235.15	2207.78
265,000	3041.80	2936.74	2847.71	2771.65	2706.21	2649.59	2600.34	2557.31	2408.06	2325.57	2278.14	2250.24
270,000	3099.19	2992.15	2901.44	2823.94	2757.27	2699.58	2649.40	2605.56	2453.50	2369.45	2321.12	2292.70
275,000	3213.98	3102.97	3008.90	2928.53	2859.39	2799.57	2747.53	2702.07	2544.37	2457.21	2407.09	2377.61
280,000	3213.98	3102.97	3008.90	2928.53	2859.39	2799.57	2747.53	2702.07	2544.37	2457.21	2407.09	2377.61
290,000	3328.76	3213.79	3116.36	3033.12	2961.52	2899.55	2845.66	2798.57	2635.24	2544.96	2493.06	2462.53
300,000	3443.55	3324.61	3223.82	3137.71	3063.64	2999.54	2943.78	2895.07	2726.11	2632.72	2579.02	2547.44

10.25%

AMOUNT OF LOAN	NUMBER OF YEARS IN TERM											
	1	2	3	4	5	6	7	8	9	10	11	12
$ 50	4.41	2.32	1.62	1.28	1.07	0.94	0.84	0.77	0.72	0.67	0.64	0.61
100	8.81	4.63	3.24	2.55	2.14	1.87	1.68	1.54	1.43	1.34	1.27	1.21
200	17.61	9.26	6.48	5.10	4.28	3.74	3.35	3.07	2.85	2.68	2.54	2.42
300	26.41	13.88	9.72	7.65	6.42	5.60	5.02	4.60	4.27	4.01	3.80	3.63
400	35.22	18.51	12.96	10.20	8.55	7.47	6.70	6.13	5.69	5.35	5.07	4.84
500	44.02	23.14	16.20	12.75	10.69	9.33	8.37	7.66	7.11	6.68	6.34	6.05
600	52.82	27.76	19.44	15.29	12.83	11.20	10.04	9.19	8.53	8.02	7.60	7.26
700	61.63	32.39	22.67	17.84	14.96	13.06	11.72	10.72	9.96	9.35	8.87	8.47
800	70.43	37.01	25.91	20.39	17.10	14.93	13.39	12.25	11.38	10.69	10.13	9.68
900	79.23	41.64	29.15	22.94	19.24	16.79	15.06	13.78	12.80	12.02	11.40	10.89
1,000	88.04	46.27	32.39	25.49	21.38	18.66	16.74	15.31	14.22	13.36	12.67	12.10
2,000	176.07	92.53	64.77	50.97	42.75	37.31	33.47	30.62	28.43	26.71	25.33	24.20
3,000	264.10	138.79	97.16	76.45	64.12	55.96	50.20	45.93	42.65	40.07	37.99	36.29
4,000	352.13	185.05	129.54	101.94	85.49	74.61	66.93	61.23	56.86	53.42	50.65	48.39
5,000	440.17	231.31	161.93	127.42	106.86	93.27	83.66	76.54	71.08	66.77	63.31	60.48
6,000	528.20	277.57	194.31	152.90	128.23	111.92	100.39	91.85	85.29	80.13	75.98	72.58
7,000	616.23	323.83	226.70	178.38	149.60	130.57	117.12	107.15	99.51	93.48	88.64	84.67
8,000	704.26	370.09	259.08	203.87	170.97	149.22	133.85	122.46	113.72	106.84	101.30	96.77
9,000	792.29	416.35	291.47	229.35	192.34	167.87	150.58	137.77	127.93	120.19	113.96	108.87
10,000	880.33	462.61	323.85	254.83	213.71	186.53	167.31	153.07	142.15	133.54	126.62	120.96
15,000	1320.49	693.91	485.78	382.25	320.56	279.79	250.96	229.61	213.22	200.31	189.93	181.44
20,000	1760.65	925.21	647.70	509.66	427.41	373.05	334.62	306.14	284.29	267.08	253.24	241.92
25,000	2200.81	1156.51	809.62	637.08	534.26	466.31	418.27	382.67	355.37	333.85	316.55	302.40
30,000	2640.97	1387.82	971.55	764.49	641.11	559.57	501.92	459.21	426.44	400.62	379.86	362.87
35,000	3081.13	1619.12	1133.47	891.90	747.96	652.83	585.58	535.74	497.51	467.39	443.17	423.35
40,000	3521.29	1850.42	1295.39	1019.32	854.82	746.09	669.23	612.28	568.58	534.16	506.48	483.83
45,000	3961.45	2081.72	1457.32	1146.73	961.67	839.35	752.88	688.81	639.65	600.93	569.78	544.31
50,000	4401.62	2313.02	1619.24	1274.15	1068.52	932.61	836.54	765.34	710.73	667.70	633.09	604.79
55,000	4841.78	2544.33	1781.16	1401.56	1175.37	1025.87	920.19	841.88	781.80	734.47	696.40	665.27
60,000	5281.94	2775.63	1943.09	1528.97	1282.22	1119.13	1003.84	918.41	852.87	801.24	759.71	725.74
65,000	5722.10	3006.93	2105.01	1656.39	1389.07	1212.40	1087.50	994.95	923.94	868.01	823.02	786.22
70,000	6162.26	3238.23	2266.93	1783.80	1495.92	1305.66	1171.15	1071.48	995.01	934.78	886.33	846.70
75,000	6602.42	3469.53	2428.86	1911.22	1602.77	1398.92	1254.80	1148.01	1066.09	1001.55	949.64	907.18
80,000	7042.58	3700.84	2590.78	2038.63	1709.63	1492.18	1338.46	1224.55	1137.16	1068.32	1012.95	967.66
85,000	7482.74	3932.14	2752.70	2166.04	1816.48	1585.44	1422.11	1301.08	1208.23	1135.09	1076.25	1028.14
90,000	7922.90	4163.44	2914.63	2293.46	1923.33	1678.70	1505.76	1377.61	1279.30	1201.86	1139.56	1088.61
95,000	8363.06	4394.74	3076.55	2420.87	2030.18	1771.96	1589.42	1454.15	1350.37	1268.63	1202.87	1149.09
100,000	8803.23	4626.04	3238.47	2548.29	2137.03	1865.22	1673.07	1530.68	1421.45	1335.40	1266.18	1209.57
105,000	9243.39	4857.35	3400.40	2675.70	2243.88	1958.48	1756.72	1607.22	1492.52	1402.16	1329.49	1270.05
110,000	9683.55	5088.65	3562.32	2803.11	2350.73	2051.74	1840.38	1683.75	1563.59	1468.93	1392.80	1330.53
115,000	10123.71	5319.95	3724.24	2930.53	2457.59	2145.00	1924.03	1760.28	1634.66	1535.70	1456.11	1391.00
120,000	10563.87	5551.25	3886.17	3057.94	2564.44	2238.26	2007.68	1836.82	1705.74	1602.47	1519.42	1451.48
125,000	11004.03	5782.55	4048.09	3185.36	2671.29	2331.52	2091.34	1913.35	1776.81	1669.24	1582.72	1511.96
130,000	11444.19	6013.86	4210.01	3312.77	2778.14	2424.79	2174.99	1989.89	1847.88	1736.01	1646.03	1572.44
135,000	11884.35	6245.16	4371.94	3440.18	2884.99	2518.05	2258.64	2066.42	1918.95	1802.78	1709.34	1632.92
140,000	12324.51	6476.46	4533.86	3567.60	2991.84	2611.31	2342.30	2142.95	1990.02	1869.55	1772.65	1693.40
145,000	12764.67	6707.76	4695.78	3695.01	3098.69	2704.57	2425.95	2219.49	2061.10	1936.32	1835.96	1753.87
150,000	13204.84	6939.06	4857.71	3822.43	3205.54	2797.83	2509.60	2296.02	2132.17	2003.09	1899.27	1814.35
155,000	13645.00	7170.37	5019.63	3949.84	3312.40	2891.09	2593.25	2372.55	2203.24	2069.86	1962.58	1874.83
160,000	14085.16	7401.67	5181.56	4077.26	3419.25	2984.35	2676.91	2449.09	2274.31	2136.63	2025.89	1935.31
165,000	14525.32	7632.97	5343.48	4204.67	3526.10	3077.61	2760.56	2525.62	2345.38	2203.40	2089.19	1995.79
170,000	14965.48	7864.27	5505.40	4332.08	3632.95	3170.87	2844.21	2602.16	2416.46	2270.17	2152.50	2056.27
175,000	15405.64	8095.57	5667.33	4459.50	3739.80	3264.13	2927.87	2678.69	2487.53	2336.94	2215.81	2116.74
180,000	15845.80	8326.88	5829.25	4586.91	3846.65	3357.39	3011.52	2755.22	2558.60	2403.71	2279.12	2177.22
185,000	16285.96	8558.18	5991.17	4714.33	3953.50	3450.65	3095.17	2831.76	2629.67	2470.48	2342.43	2237.70
190,000	16726.12	8789.48	6153.10	4841.74	4060.36	3543.91	3178.83	2908.29	2700.74	2537.25	2405.74	2298.18
195,000	17166.28	9020.78	6315.02	4969.15	4167.21	3637.18	3262.48	2984.83	2771.82	2604.02	2469.05	2358.66
200,000	17606.45	9252.08	6476.94	5096.57	4274.06	3730.44	3346.13	3061.36	2842.89	2670.79	2532.36	2419.14
205,000	18046.61	9483.39	6638.87	5223.98	4380.91	3823.70	3429.79	3137.89	2913.96	2737.55	2595.66	2479.61
210,000	18486.77	9714.69	6800.79	5351.40	4487.76	3916.96	3513.44	3214.43	2985.03	2804.32	2658.97	2540.09
215,000	18926.93	9945.99	6962.71	5478.81	4594.61	4010.22	3597.09	3290.96	3056.11	2871.09	2722.28	2600.57
220,000	19367.09	10177.29	7124.64	5606.22	4701.46	4103.48	3680.75	3367.49	3127.18	2937.86	2785.59	2661.05
225,000	19807.25	10408.59	7286.56	5733.64	4808.31	4196.74	3764.40	3444.03	3198.25	3004.63	2848.90	2721.53
230,000	20247.41	10639.90	7448.48	5861.05	4915.17	4290.00	3848.05	3520.56	3269.32	3071.40	2912.21	2782.00
235,000	20687.57	10871.20	7610.41	5988.47	5022.02	4383.26	3931.71	3597.10	3340.39	3138.17	2975.52	2842.48
240,000	21127.73	11102.50	7772.33	6115.88	5128.87	4476.52	4015.36	3673.63	3411.47	3204.94	3038.83	2902.96
245,000	21567.89	11333.80	7934.25	6243.29	5235.72	4569.78	4099.01	3750.16	3482.54	3271.71	3102.13	2963.44
250,000	22008.06	11565.10	8096.18	6370.71	5342.57	4663.04	4182.67	3826.70	3553.61	3338.48	3165.44	3023.92
255,000	22448.22	11796.41	8258.10	6498.12	5449.42	4756.30	4266.32	3903.23	3624.68	3405.25	3228.75	3084.40
260,000	22888.38	12027.71	8420.02	6625.54	5556.27	4849.57	4349.97	3979.77	3695.75	3472.02	3292.06	3144.87
265,000	23328.54	12259.01	8581.95	6752.95	5663.12	4942.83	4433.63	4056.30	3766.83	3538.79	3355.37	3205.35
270,000	23768.70	12490.31	8743.87	6880.36	5769.98	5036.09	4517.28	4132.83	3837.90	3605.56	3418.68	3265.83
280,000	24649.02	12952.92	9067.72	7135.19	5983.68	5222.61	4684.59	4285.90	3980.04	3739.10	3545.30	3386.79
290,000	25529.34	13415.52	9391.56	7390.02	6197.38	5409.13	4851.89	4438.97	4122.19	3872.64	3671.91	3507.74
300,000	26409.67	13878.12	9715.41	7644.85	6411.08	5595.65	5019.20	4592.04	4264.33	4006.18	3798.53	3628.70

MONTHLY AMORTIZING PAYMENTS 10.25%

| AMOUNT OF LOAN | \
NUMBER OF YEARS IN TERM											
	13	14	15	16	17	18	19	20	25	30	35	40
$ 50	0.59	0.57	0.55	0.54	0.52	0.51	0.50	0.50	0.47	0.45	0.44	0.44
100	1.17	1.13	1.09	1.07	1.04	1.02	1.00	0.99	0.93	0.90	0.88	0.87
200	2.33	2.25	2.18	2.13	2.08	2.04	2.00	1.97	1.86	1.80	1.76	1.74
300	3.49	3.37	3.27	3.19	3.12	3.05	3.00	2.95	2.78	2.69	2.64	2.61
400	4.66	4.50	4.36	4.25	4.15	4.07	4.00	3.93	3.71	3.59	3.52	3.48
500	5.82	5.62	5.45	5.31	5.19	5.08	4.99	4.91	4.64	4.49	4.40	4.35
600	6.98	6.74	6.54	6.37	6.23	6.10	5.99	5.89	5.56	5.38	5.28	5.22
700	8.14	7.87	7.63	7.44	7.26	7.12	6.99	6.88	6.49	6.28	6.16	6.09
800	9.31	8.99	8.72	8.50	8.30	8.13	7.99	7.86	7.42	7.17	7.04	6.96
900	10.47	10.11	9.81	9.56	9.34	9.15	8.98	8.84	8.34	8.07	7.91	7.82
1,000	11.63	11.24	10.90	10.62	10.38	10.16	9.98	9.82	9.27	8.97	8.79	8.69
2,000	23.26	22.47	21.80	21.24	20.75	20.32	19.96	19.64	18.53	17.93	17.58	17.38
3,000	34.88	33.70	32.70	31.85	31.12	30.48	29.93	29.45	27.80	26.89	26.37	26.07
4,000	46.51	44.94	43.60	42.47	41.49	40.64	39.91	39.27	37.06	35.85	35.16	34.76
5,000	58.14	56.17	54.50	53.08	51.86	50.80	49.89	49.09	46.32	44.81	43.95	43.45
6,000	69.76	67.40	65.40	63.70	62.23	60.96	59.86	58.90	55.59	53.77	52.74	52.13
7,000	81.39	78.63	76.30	74.31	72.60	71.12	69.84	68.72	64.85	62.73	61.52	60.82
8,000	93.02	89.87	87.20	84.93	82.97	81.28	79.82	78.54	74.12	71.69	70.31	69.51
9,000	104.64	101.10	98.10	95.54	93.34	91.44	89.79	88.35	83.38	80.65	79.10	78.20
10,000	116.27	112.33	109.00	106.16	103.71	101.60	99.77	98.17	92.64	89.62	87.89	86.89
15,000	174.40	168.50	163.50	159.23	155.57	152.40	149.65	147.25	138.96	134.42	131.83	130.33
20,000	232.53	224.66	218.00	212.31	207.42	203.20	199.53	196.33	185.28	179.23	175.78	173.77
25,000	290.66	280.82	272.49	265.38	259.28	254.00	249.42	245.42	231.60	224.03	219.72	217.21
30,000	348.79	336.99	326.99	318.46	311.13	304.80	299.30	294.50	277.92	268.84	263.66	260.65
35,000	406.92	393.15	381.49	371.54	362.99	355.60	349.18	343.58	324.24	313.64	307.60	304.09
40,000	465.06	449.31	435.99	424.61	414.84	406.40	399.06	392.66	370.56	358.45	351.55	347.53
45,000	523.19	505.48	490.48	477.69	466.70	457.20	448.94	441.74	416.88	403.25	395.49	390.97
50,000	581.32	561.64	544.98	530.76	518.55	508.00	498.83	490.83	463.20	448.06	439.43	434.41
55,000	639.45	617.80	599.48	583.84	570.41	558.79	548.71	539.91	509.52	492.86	483.38	477.86
60,000	697.58	673.97	653.98	636.92	622.26	609.59	598.59	588.99	555.83	537.67	527.32	521.30
65,000	755.71	730.13	708.47	689.99	674.11	660.39	648.47	638.07	602.15	582.47	571.26	564.74
70,000	813.84	786.29	762.97	743.07	725.97	711.19	698.35	687.16	648.47	627.28	615.20	608.18
75,000	871.98	842.46	817.47	796.14	777.82	761.99	748.24	736.24	694.79	672.08	659.15	651.62
80,000	930.11	898.62	871.97	849.22	829.68	812.79	798.12	785.32	741.11	716.89	703.09	695.06
85,000	988.24	954.78	926.46	902.30	881.53	863.59	848.00	834.40	787.43	761.69	747.03	738.50
90,000	1046.37	1010.95	980.96	955.37	933.39	914.39	897.88	883.48	833.75	806.50	790.98	781.94
95,000	1104.50	1067.11	1035.46	1008.45	985.24	965.19	947.77	932.57	880.07	851.30	834.92	825.38
100,000	1162.63	1123.27	1089.96	1061.52	1037.10	1015.99	997.65	981.65	926.39	896.11	878.86	868.82
105,000	1220.76	1179.44	1144.45	1114.60	1088.05	1066.70	1047.53	1030.73	972.71	940.91	922.80	912.26
110,000	1278.90	1235.60	1198.95	1167.68	1140.81	1117.58	1097.41	1079.81	1019.03	985.72	966.75	955.71
115,000	1337.03	1291.76	1253.45	1220.75	1192.66	1168.38	1147.29	1128.89	1065.35	1030.52	1010.69	999.15
120,000	1395.16	1347.93	1307.95	1273.83	1244.51	1219.18	1197.18	1177.98	1111.66	1075.33	1054.63	1042.60
125,000	1453.29	1404.09	1362.44	1326.90	1296.37	1269.98	1247.06	1227.06	1157.98	1120.13	1098.57	1086.03
130,000	1511.42	1460.26	1416.94	1379.98	1348.22	1320.78	1296.94	1276.14	1204.30	1164.94	1142.52	1129.47
135,000	1569.55	1516.42	1471.44	1433.06	1400.08	1371.58	1346.82	1325.22	1250.62	1209.74	1186.46	1172.91
140,000	1627.68	1572.58	1525.94	1486.13	1451.93	1422.38	1396.70	1374.31	1296.94	1254.55	1230.40	1216.35
145,000	1685.82	1628.75	1580.43	1539.21	1503.79	1473.18	1446.59	1423.39	1343.26	1299.35	1274.35	1259.79
150,000	1743.95	1684.91	1634.93	1592.28	1555.64	1523.98	1496.47	1472.47	1389.58	1344.16	1318.29	1303.23
155,000	1802.08	1741.07	1689.43	1645.36	1607.50	1574.77	1546.35	1521.55	1435.90	1388.96	1362.23	1346.67
160,000	1860.21	1797.24	1743.93	1698.44	1659.35	1625.57	1596.23	1570.63	1482.22	1433.77	1406.17	1390.11
165,000	1918.34	1853.40	1798.42	1751.51	1711.21	1676.37	1646.11	1619.72	1528.54	1478.57	1450.12	1433.56
170,000	1976.47	1909.56	1852.92	1804.59	1763.06	1727.17	1696.00	1668.80	1574.86	1523.38	1494.06	1477.00
175,000	2034.60	1965.73	1907.42	1857.66	1814.92	1777.97	1745.88	1717.88	1621.18	1568.18	1538.00	1520.44
180,000	2092.74	2021.89	1961.92	1910.74	1866.77	1828.77	1795.76	1766.96	1667.49	1612.99	1581.95	1563.88
185,000	2150.87	2078.05	2016.41	1963.82	1918.62	1879.57	1845.64	1816.05	1713.81	1657.79	1625.89	1607.32
190,000	2209.00	2134.22	2070.91	2016.89	1970.48	1930.37	1895.53	1865.13	1760.13	1702.60	1669.83	1650.76
195,000	2267.13	2190.38	2125.41	2069.97	2022.33	1981.17	1945.41	1914.21	1806.45	1747.40	1713.77	1694.20
200,000	2325.26	2246.54	2179.91	2123.04	2074.19	2031.97	1995.29	1963.29	1852.77	1792.21	1757.72	1737.64
205,000	2383.39	2302.71	2234.40	2176.12	2126.04	2082.76	2045.17	2012.37	1899.09	1837.01	1801.66	1781.08
210,000	2441.52	2358.87	2288.90	2229.20	2177.90	2133.56	2095.05	2061.46	1945.41	1881.82	1845.60	1824.52
215,000	2499.66	2415.03	2343.40	2282.27	2229.75	2184.36	2144.94	2110.54	1991.73	1926.62	1889.54	1867.96
220,000	2557.79	2471.20	2397.90	2335.35	2281.61	2235.16	2194.82	2159.62	2038.05	1971.43	1933.49	1911.41
225,000	2615.92	2527.36	2452.39	2388.42	2333.46	2285.96	2244.70	2208.70	2084.37	2016.23	1977.43	1954.85
230,000	2674.05	2583.52	2506.89	2441.50	2385.32	2336.76	2294.58	2257.78	2130.69	2061.04	2021.37	1998.29
235,000	2732.18	2639.69	2561.39	2494.58	2437.17	2387.56	2344.46	2306.87	2177.01	2105.84	2065.32	2041.73
240,000	2790.31	2695.85	2615.89	2547.65	2489.02	2438.36	2394.35	2355.95	2223.32	2150.65	2109.26	2085.17
245,000	2848.44	2752.01	2670.38	2600.73	2540.88	2489.16	2444.23	2405.03	2269.64	2195.45	2153.20	2128.61
250,000	2906.58	2808.18	2724.88	2653.80	2592.73	2539.96	2494.11	2454.11	2315.96	2240.26	2197.14	2172.05
255,000	2964.71	2864.34	2779.38	2706.88	2644.59	2590.75	2543.99	2503.20	2362.28	2285.06	2241.09	2215.49
260,000	3022.84	2920.51	2833.88	2759.96	2696.44	2641.55	2593.87	2552.28	2408.60	2329.87	2285.03	2258.93
265,000	3080.97	2976.67	2888.37	2813.03	2748.30	2692.35	2643.76	2601.36	2454.92	2374.67	2328.97	2302.37
270,000	3139.10	3032.83	2942.87	2866.11	2800.15	2743.15	2693.64	2650.44	2501.24	2419.48	2372.92	2345.81
280,000	3255.36	3145.16	3051.87	2972.26	2903.86	2844.75	2793.40	2748.61	2593.88	2509.09	2460.80	2432.70
290,000	3371.63	3257.49	3160.86	3078.41	3007.57	2946.35	2893.17	2846.77	2686.52	2598.70	2548.69	2519.58
300,000	3487.89	3369.81	3269.86	3184.56	3111.28	3047.95	2992.93	2944.94	2779.15	2688.31	2636.57	2606.46

69

10.50%

MONTHLY AMORTIZING PAYMENTS

AMOUNT OF LOAN	\multicolumn{12}{c}{NUMBER OF YEARS IN TERM}

AMOUNT OF LOAN	1	2	3	4	5	6	7	8	9	10	11	12
$ 50	4.41	2.32	1.63	1.29	1.08	0.94	0.85	0.78	0.72	0.68	0.65	0.62
100	8.82	4.64	3.26	2.57	2.15	1.88	1.69	1.55	1.44	1.35	1.29	1.23
200	17.63	9.28	6.51	5.13	4.30	3.76	3.38	3.09	2.88	2.70	2.57	2.45
300	26.45	13.92	9.76	7.69	6.45	5.64	5.06	4.64	4.31	4.05	3.85	3.68
400	35.26	18.56	13.01	10.25	8.60	7.52	6.75	6.18	5.75	5.40	5.13	4.90
500	44.08	23.19	16.26	12.81	10.75	9.39	8.44	7.73	7.18	6.75	6.41	6.13
600	52.89	27.83	19.51	15.37	12.90	11.27	10.12	9.27	8.62	8.10	7.69	7.35
700	61.71	32.47	22.76	17.93	15.05	13.15	11.81	10.81	10.05	9.45	8.97	8.57
800	70.52	37.11	26.01	20.49	17.20	15.03	13.49	12.36	11.49	10.80	10.25	9.80
900	79.34	41.74	29.26	23.05	19.35	16.91	15.18	13.90	12.92	12.15	11.53	11.02
1,000	88.15	46.38	32.51	25.61	21.50	18.78	16.87	15.45	14.36	13.50	12.81	12.25
2,000	176.30	92.76	65.01	51.21	42.99	37.56	33.73	30.89	28.71	26.99	25.61	24.49
3,000	264.45	139.13	97.51	76.82	64.49	56.34	50.59	46.33	43.06	40.49	38.42	36.73
4,000	352.60	185.51	130.01	102.42	85.98	75.12	67.45	61.77	57.41	53.98	51.22	48.97
5,000	440.75	231.89	162.52	128.02	107.47	93.90	84.31	77.21	71.76	67.47	64.03	61.21
6,000	528.90	278.26	195.02	153.63	128.97	112.68	101.17	92.65	86.11	80.97	76.83	73.45
7,000	617.05	324.64	227.52	179.23	150.46	131.46	118.03	108.09	100.46	94.46	89.64	85.69
8,000	705.19	371.01	260.02	204.83	171.96	150.24	134.89	123.53	114.81	107.95	102.44	97.94
9,000	793.34	417.39	292.53	230.44	193.45	169.02	151.75	138.97	129.16	121.45	115.25	110.18
10,000	881.49	463.77	325.03	256.04	214.94	187.79	168.61	154.41	143.51	134.94	128.05	122.42
15,000	1322.23	695.65	487.54	384.06	322.41	281.69	252.92	231.61	215.27	202.41	192.07	183.63
20,000	1762.98	927.53	650.05	512.07	429.88	375.58	337.22	308.81	287.02	269.87	256.09	244.83
25,000	2203.72	1159.41	812.57	640.09	537.35	469.48	421.52	386.01	358.78	337.34	320.12	306.04
30,000	2644.46	1391.29	975.08	768.11	644.82	563.37	505.83	463.21	430.53	404.81	384.14	367.25
35,000	3085.21	1623.17	1137.59	896.12	752.29	657.27	590.13	540.41	502.29	472.28	448.16	428.45
40,000	3525.95	1855.05	1300.10	1024.14	859.76	751.16	674.43	617.61	574.04	539.74	512.18	489.66
45,000	3966.69	2086.93	1462.61	1152.16	967.23	845.06	758.74	694.81	645.79	607.21	576.21	550.87
50,000	4407.44	2318.81	1625.13	1280.17	1074.70	938.95	843.04	772.01	717.55	674.68	640.23	612.08
55,000	4848.18	2550.69	1787.64	1408.19	1182.17	1032.85	927.34	849.21	789.30	742.15	704.25	673.28
60,000	5288.92	2782.57	1950.15	1536.21	1289.64	1126.74	1011.65	926.41	861.06	809.61	768.27	734.49
65,000	5729.66	3014.45	2112.66	1664.22	1397.11	1220.64	1095.95	1003.61	932.81	877.08	832.29	795.70
70,000	6170.41	3246.33	2275.18	1792.24	1504.58	1314.53	1180.25	1080.81	1004.57	944.55	896.32	856.90
75,000	6611.15	3478.21	2437.69	1920.26	1612.05	1408.43	1264.56	1158.01	1076.32	1012.02	960.34	918.11
80,000	7051.89	3710.09	2600.20	2048.28	1719.52	1502.32	1348.86	1235.21	1148.07	1079.48	1024.36	979.32
85,000	7492.64	3941.97	2762.71	2176.29	1826.99	1596.22	1433.16	1312.41	1219.83	1146.95	1088.38	1040.52
90,000	7933.38	4173.85	2925.22	2304.31	1934.46	1690.11	1517.47	1389.61	1291.58	1214.42	1152.41	1101.73
95,000	8374.12	4405.73	3087.74	2432.33	2041.93	1784.01	1601.77	1466.81	1363.34	1281.89	1216.43	1162.94
100,000	8814.87	4637.61	3250.25	2560.34	2149.40	1877.90	1686.07	1544.01	1435.09	1349.35	1280.45	1224.15
105,000	9255.61	4869.49	3412.76	2688.36	2256.86	1971.80	1770.38	1621.21	1506.85	1416.82	1344.47	1285.35
110,000	9696.35	5101.37	3575.27	2816.38	2364.33	2065.69	1854.68	1698.41	1578.60	1484.29	1408.50	1346.56
115,000	10137.09	5333.25	3737.79	2944.39	2471.80	2159.59	1938.98	1775.61	1650.35	1551.76	1472.52	1407.77
120,000	10577.84	5565.13	3900.30	3072.41	2579.27	2253.48	2023.29	1852.81	1722.11	1619.22	1536.54	1468.97
125,000	11018.58	5797.01	4062.81	3200.43	2686.74	2347.38	2107.59	1930.01	1793.86	1686.69	1600.56	1530.18
130,000	11459.32	6028.89	4225.32	3328.44	2794.21	2441.27	2191.89	2007.21	1865.62	1754.16	1664.58	1591.39
135,000	11900.07	6260.77	4387.83	3456.46	2901.68	2535.17	2276.20	2084.41	1937.37	1821.63	1728.61	1652.59
140,000	12340.81	6492.65	4550.35	3584.48	3009.15	2629.06	2360.50	2161.61	2009.13	1889.09	1792.63	1713.80
145,000	12781.55	6724.53	4712.86	3712.50	3116.62	2722.96	2444.80	2238.81	2080.88	1956.56	1856.65	1775.01
150,000	13222.30	6956.41	4875.37	3840.51	3224.09	2816.85	2529.11	2316.01	2152.63	2024.03	1920.67	1836.22
155,000	13663.04	7188.29	5037.88	3968.53	3331.56	2910.75	2613.41	2393.21	2224.39	2091.50	1984.70	1897.42
160,000	14103.78	7420.17	5200.40	4096.55	3439.03	3004.64	2697.71	2470.41	2296.14	2158.96	2048.72	1958.63
165,000	14544.52	7652.05	5362.91	4224.56	3546.50	3098.54	2782.02	2547.61	2367.90	2226.43	2112.74	2019.84
170,000	14985.27	7883.93	5525.42	4352.58	3653.97	3192.43	2866.32	2624.81	2439.65	2293.90	2176.76	2081.04
175,000	15426.01	8115.81	5687.93	4480.60	3761.44	3286.32	2950.62	2702.01	2511.41	2361.37	2240.79	2142.25
180,000	15866.75	8347.69	5850.44	4608.61	3868.91	3380.22	3034.93	2779.21	2583.16	2428.83	2304.81	2203.46
185,000	16307.50	8579.57	6012.96	4736.63	3976.38	3474.11	3119.23	2856.41	2654.91	2496.30	2368.83	2264.67
190,000	16748.24	8811.45	6175.47	4864.65	4083.85	3568.01	3203.53	2933.61	2726.67	2563.77	2432.85	2325.87
195,000	17188.98	9043.33	6337.98	4992.66	4191.32	3661.90	3287.84	3010.81	2798.42	2631.24	2496.87	2387.08
200,000	17629.73	9275.21	6500.49	5120.68	4298.79	3755.80	3372.14	3088.01	2870.18	2698.70	2560.90	2448.29
205,000	18070.47	9507.09	6663.01	5248.70	4406.25	3849.69	3456.44	3165.21	2941.93	2766.17	2624.92	2509.49
210,000	18511.21	9738.97	6825.52	5376.71	4513.72	3943.59	3540.75	3242.41	3013.69	2833.64	2688.94	2570.70
215,000	18951.95	9970.85	6988.03	5504.73	4621.19	4037.48	3625.05	3319.61	3085.44	2901.11	2752.96	2631.91
220,000	19392.70	10202.73	7150.54	5632.75	4728.66	4131.38	3709.35	3396.81	3157.19	2968.57	2816.99	2693.11
225,000	19833.44	10434.61	7313.05	5760.77	4836.13	4225.27	3793.66	3474.01	3228.95	3036.04	2881.01	2754.32
230,000	20274.18	10666.49	7475.57	5888.78	4943.60	4319.17	3877.96	3551.21	3300.70	3103.51	2945.03	2815.53
235,000	20714.93	10898.37	7638.08	6016.80	5051.07	4413.06	3962.26	3628.41	3372.46	3170.98	3009.05	2876.74
240,000	21155.67	11130.25	7800.59	6144.82	5158.54	4506.96	4046.57	3705.61	3444.21	3238.44	3073.08	2937.94
245,000	21596.41	11362.14	7963.10	6272.83	5266.01	4600.85	4130.87	3782.81	3515.97	3305.91	3137.10	2999.15
250,000	22037.16	11594.02	8125.62	6400.85	5373.48	4694.75	4215.17	3860.01	3587.72	3373.38	3201.12	3060.36
255,000	22477.90	11825.90	8288.13	6528.87	5480.95	4788.64	4299.48	3937.21	3659.47	3440.85	3265.14	3121.56
260,000	22918.64	12057.78	8450.64	6656.88	5588.42	4882.54	4383.78	4014.41	3731.23	3508.31	3329.16	3182.77
265,000	23359.38	12289.66	8613.15	6784.90	5695.89	4976.43	4468.08	4091.61	3802.98	3575.78	3393.19	3243.98
270,000	23800.13	12521.54	8775.66	6912.92	5803.36	5070.33	4552.39	4168.81	3874.74	3643.25	3457.21	3305.18
280,000	24681.61	12985.30	9100.69	7168.95	6018.30	5258.12	4720.99	4323.21	4018.25	3778.18	3585.25	3427.60
290,000	25563.10	13449.06	9425.71	7424.99	6233.24	5445.91	4889.60	4477.61	4161.75	3913.12	3713.30	3550.01
300,000	26444.59	13912.82	9750.74	7681.02	6448.18	5633.70	5058.21	4632.01	4305.26	4048.05	3841.34	3672.43

70

AMOUNT OF LOAN	13	14	15	16	17	18	19	20	25	30	35	40
					NUMBER OF YEARS IN TERM							
$ 50	0.59	0.57	0.56	0.54	0.53	0.52	0.51	0.50	0.48	0.46	0.45	0.45
100	1.18	1.14	1.11	1.08	1.06	1.04	1.02	1.00	0.95	0.92	0.90	0.89
200	2.36	2.28	2.22	2.16	2.11	2.07	2.03	2.00	1.89	1.83	1.80	1.78
300	3.54	3.42	3.32	3.24	3.16	3.10	3.05	3.00	2.84	2.75	2.70	2.67
400	4.72	4.56	4.43	4.31	4.22	4.13	4.06	4.00	3.78	3.66	3.60	3.56
500	5.89	5.70	5.53	5.39	5.27	5.17	5.08	5.00	4.73	4.58	4.50	4.45
600	7.07	6.84	6.64	6.47	6.32	6.20	6.09	6.00	5.67	5.49	5.39	5.34
700	8.25	7.97	7.74	7.55	7.38	7.23	7.10	6.99	6.61	6.41	6.29	6.22
800	9.43	9.11	8.85	8.62	8.43	8.26	8.12	7.99	7.56	7.32	7.19	7.11
900	10.60	10.25	9.95	9.70	9.48	9.30	9.13	8.99	8.50	8.24	8.09	8.00
1,000	11.78	11.39	11.06	10.78	10.54	10.33	10.15	9.99	9.45	9.15	8.99	8.89
2,000	23.56	22.77	22.11	21.55	21.07	20.65	20.29	19.97	18.89	18.30	17.97	17.78
3,000	35.33	34.16	33.17	32.32	31.60	30.97	30.43	29.96	28.33	27.45	26.95	26.66
4,000	47.11	45.54	44.22	43.09	42.13	41.29	40.57	39.94	37.77	36.59	35.93	35.55
5,000	58.88	56.93	55.27	53.87	52.66	51.62	50.71	49.92	47.21	45.74	44.91	44.43
6,000	70.66	68.31	66.33	64.64	63.19	61.94	60.85	59.91	56.66	54.89	53.89	53.32
7,000	82.43	79.70	77.38	75.41	73.72	72.26	70.99	69.89	66.10	64.04	62.87	62.20
8,000	94.21	91.08	88.44	86.18	84.25	82.58	81.14	79.88	75.54	73.18	71.86	71.09
9,000	105.98	102.46	99.49	96.96	94.78	92.91	91.28	89.86	84.98	82.33	80.84	79.98
10,000	117.76	113.85	110.54	107.73	105.31	103.23	101.42	99.84	94.42	91.48	89.82	88.86
15,000	176.63	170.77	165.81	161.59	157.97	154.84	152.13	149.76	141.63	137.22	134.73	133.29
20,000	235.51	227.69	221.08	215.45	210.62	206.45	202.83	199.68	188.84	182.95	179.63	177.72
25,000	294.38	284.61	276.35	269.32	263.28	258.06	253.54	249.60	236.05	228.69	224.54	222.15
30,000	353.26	341.54	331.62	323.18	315.93	309.67	304.25	299.52	283.26	274.43	269.45	266.58
35,000	412.13	398.46	386.89	377.04	368.58	361.28	354.95	349.44	330.47	320.16	314.35	311.00
40,000	471.01	455.38	442.16	430.90	421.24	412.90	405.66	399.36	377.68	365.90	359.26	355.43
45,000	529.88	512.30	497.43	484.76	473.89	464.51	456.37	449.28	424.89	411.64	404.17	399.86
50,000	588.76	569.22	552.70	538.63	526.55	516.12	507.07	499.19	472.10	457.37	449.07	444.29
55,000	647.63	626.14	607.97	592.49	579.20	567.73	557.78	549.11	519.30	503.11	493.98	488.72
60,000	706.51	683.07	663.24	646.35	631.85	619.34	608.49	599.03	566.51	548.85	538.89	533.15
65,000	765.38	739.99	718.51	700.21	684.51	670.95	659.20	648.95	613.72	594.59	583.79	577.58
70,000	824.26	796.91	773.78	754.07	737.16	722.56	709.90	698.87	660.93	640.32	628.70	622.00
75,000	883.13	853.83	829.05	807.94	789.82	774.18	760.61	748.79	708.14	686.06	673.61	666.43
80,000	942.01	910.75	884.32	861.80	842.47	825.79	811.32	798.71	755.35	731.80	718.51	710.86
85,000	1000.88	967.67	939.59	915.66	895.12	877.40	862.02	848.63	802.50	777.53	763.42	755.29
90,000	1059.76	1024.60	994.86	969.52	947.78	929.01	912.73	898.55	849.77	823.27	808.33	799.72
95,000	1118.63	1081.52	1050.13	1023.39	1000.43	980.62	963.44	948.47	896.98	869.01	853.23	844.15
100,000	1177.51	1138.44	1105.40	1077.25	1053.09	1032.23	1014.14	998.38	944.19	914.74	898.14	888.58
105,000	1236.38	1195.36	1160.67	1131.11	1105.74	1083.84	1064.85	1048.30	991.40	960.48	943.05	933.00
110,000	1295.26	1252.28	1215.94	1184.97	1158.39	1135.46	1115.56	1098.22	1038.60	1006.22	987.95	977.43
115,000	1354.13	1309.20	1271.21	1238.83	1211.05	1187.07	1166.26	1148.14	1085.81	1051.96	1032.86	1021.86
120,000	1413.01	1366.13	1326.48	1292.70	1263.70	1238.68	1216.97	1198.06	1133.02	1097.69	1077.77	1066.29
125,000	1471.88	1423.05	1381.75	1346.56	1316.36	1290.29	1267.68	1247.98	1180.23	1143.43	1122.67	1110.72
130,000	1530.76	1479.97	1437.02	1400.42	1369.01	1341.90	1318.39	1297.90	1227.44	1189.17	1167.58	1155.15
135,000	1589.63	1536.89	1492.29	1454.28	1421.66	1393.51	1369.09	1347.82	1274.65	1234.90	1212.49	1199.57
140,000	1648.51	1593.81	1547.56	1508.14	1474.32	1445.12	1419.80	1397.74	1321.86	1280.64	1257.39	1244.00
145,000	1707.38	1650.73	1602.83	1562.01	1526.97	1496.74	1470.51	1447.66	1369.07	1326.38	1302.30	1288.43
150,000	1766.26	1707.66	1658.10	1615.87	1579.63	1548.35	1521.21	1497.57	1416.28	1372.11	1347.21	1332.86
155,000	1825.13	1764.58	1713.37	1669.73	1632.28	1599.96	1571.92	1547.49	1463.49	1417.85	1392.11	1377.29
160,000	1884.01	1821.50	1768.64	1723.59	1684.93	1651.57	1622.63	1597.41	1510.70	1463.59	1437.02	1421.72
165,000	1942.88	1878.42	1823.91	1777.46	1737.59	1703.18	1673.33	1647.33	1557.90	1509.32	1481.93	1466.15
170,000	2001.76	1935.34	1879.18	1831.32	1790.24	1754.79	1724.04	1697.25	1605.11	1555.06	1526.83	1510.57
175,000	2060.63	1992.26	1934.45	1885.18	1842.90	1806.40	1774.75	1747.17	1652.32	1600.80	1571.74	1555.00
180,000	2119.51	2049.19	1989.72	1939.04	1895.55	1858.01	1825.46	1797.09	1699.53	1646.54	1616.65	1599.43
185,000	2178.38	2106.11	2044.99	1992.90	1948.21	1909.63	1876.16	1847.01	1746.74	1692.27	1661.55	1643.86
190,000	2237.26	2163.03	2100.26	2046.77	2000.86	1961.24	1926.87	1896.93	1793.95	1738.01	1706.46	1688.29
195,000	2296.13	2219.95	2155.53	2100.63	2053.51	2012.85	1977.58	1946.85	1841.16	1783.75	1751.37	1732.72
200,000	2355.01	2276.87	2210.80	2154.49	2106.17	2064.46	2028.28	1996.76	1888.37	1829.48	1796.27	1777.15
205,000	2413.88	2333.79	2266.07	2208.35	2158.82	2116.07	2078.99	2046.68	1935.58	1875.22	1841.18	1821.57
210,000	2472.76	2390.72	2321.34	2262.21	2211.48	2167.68	2129.70	2096.60	1982.79	1920.96	1886.09	1866.00
215,000	2531.63	2447.64	2376.61	2316.08	2264.13	2219.29	2180.40	2146.52	2030.00	1966.69	1930.99	1910.43
220,000	2590.51	2504.56	2431.88	2369.94	2316.78	2270.91	2231.11	2196.44	2077.20	2012.43	1975.90	1954.86
225,000	2649.38	2561.48	2487.15	2423.80	2369.44	2322.52	2281.82	2246.36	2124.41	2058.17	2020.81	1999.29
230,000	2708.26	2618.40	2542.42	2477.66	2422.09	2374.13	2332.52	2296.28	2171.62	2103.91	2065.71	2043.72
235,000	2767.13	2675.32	2597.69	2531.52	2474.75	2425.74	2383.23	2346.20	2218.83	2149.64	2110.62	2088.15
240,000	2826.01	2732.25	2652.96	2585.39	2527.40	2477.35	2433.94	2396.12	2266.04	2195.38	2155.53	2132.57
245,000	2884.88	2789.17	2708.23	2639.25	2580.05	2528.96	2484.65	2446.04	2313.25	2241.12	2200.43	2177.00
250,000	2943.76	2846.09	2763.50	2693.11	2632.71	2580.57	2535.35	2495.95	2360.46	2286.85	2245.34	2221.43
255,000	3002.63	2903.01	2818.77	2746.97	2685.36	2632.19	2586.06	2545.87	2407.67	2332.59	2290.25	2265.86
260,000	3061.51	2959.93	2874.04	2800.84	2738.02	2683.80	2636.77	2595.79	2454.88	2378.33	2335.15	2310.29
265,000	3120.39	3016.86	2929.31	2854.70	2790.67	2735.41	2687.47	2645.71	2502.09	2424.06	2380.06	2354.72
270,000	3179.26	3073.78	2984.58	2908.56	2843.32	2787.02	2738.18	2695.63	2549.30	2469.80	2424.97	2399.14
280,000	3297.01	3187.62	3095.12	3016.28	2948.63	2890.24	2839.59	2795.47	2643.71	2561.28	2514.78	2488.00
290,000	3414.76	3301.46	3205.66	3124.01	3053.94	2993.47	2941.01	2895.31	2738.13	2652.75	2604.59	2576.86
300,000	3532.51	3415.31	3316.20	3231.73	3159.25	3096.69	3042.42	2995.14	2832.55	2744.22	2694.41	2665.72

71

10.75%　　MONTHLY AMORTIZING PAYMENTS

AMOUNT OF LOAN	NUMBER OF YEARS IN TERM											
	1	2	3	4	5	6	7	8	9	10	11	12
$ 50	4.42	2.33	1.64	1.29	1.09	0.95	0.85	0.78	0.73	0.69	0.65	0.62
100	8.83	4.65	3.27	2.58	2.17	1.90	1.70	1.56	1.45	1.37	1.30	1.24
200	17.66	9.30	6.53	5.15	4.33	3.79	3.40	3.12	2.90	2.73	2.59	2.48
300	26.48	13.95	9.79	7.72	6.49	5.68	5.10	4.68	4.35	4.10	3.89	3.72
400	35.31	18.60	13.05	10.29	8.65	7.57	6.80	6.23	5.80	5.46	5.18	4.96
500	44.14	23.25	16.32	12.87	10.81	9.46	8.50	7.79	7.25	6.82	6.48	6.20
600	52.96	27.90	19.58	15.44	12.98	11.35	10.20	9.35	8.70	8.19	7.77	7.44
700	61.79	32.55	22.84	18.01	15.14	13.24	11.90	10.91	10.15	9.55	9.07	8.68
800	70.62	37.20	26.10	20.58	17.30	15.13	13.60	12.46	11.60	10.91	10.36	9.92
900	79.44	41.85	29.36	23.16	19.46	17.02	15.30	14.02	13.04	12.28	11.66	11.15
1,000	88.27	46.50	32.63	25.73	21.62	18.91	17.00	15.58	14.49	13.64	12.95	12.39
2,000	176.54	92.99	65.25	51.45	43.24	37.82	33.99	31.15	28.98	27.27	25.90	24.78
3,000	264.80	139.48	97.87	77.18	64.86	56.72	50.98	46.73	43.47	40.91	38.85	37.17
4,000	353.07	185.97	130.49	102.90	86.48	75.63	67.97	62.30	57.96	54.54	51.80	49.56
5,000	441.33	232.46	163.11	128.63	108.09	94.54	84.96	77.87	72.45	68.17	64.74	61.95
6,000	529.60	278.96	195.73	154.35	129.71	113.44	101.95	93.45	86.93	81.81	77.69	74.33
7,000	617.86	325.45	228.35	180.07	151.33	132.35	118.94	109.02	101.42	95.44	90.64	86.72
8,000	706.13	371.94	260.97	205.80	172.95	151.26	135.94	124.60	115.91	109.08	103.59	99.11
9,000	794.39	418.43	293.59	231.52	194.57	170.16	152.93	140.17	130.40	122.71	116.54	111.50
10,000	882.66	464.92	326.21	257.25	216.18	189.07	169.92	155.74	144.89	136.34	129.48	123.89
15,000	1323.98	697.38	489.31	385.87	324.27	283.60	254.87	233.61	217.33	204.51	194.22	185.83
20,000	1765.31	929.84	652.41	514.49	432.36	378.13	339.83	311.48	289.77	272.68	258.96	247.77
25,000	2206.63	1162.30	815.52	643.11	540.45	472.66	424.79	389.35	362.21	340.85	323.70	309.71
30,000	2647.96	1394.76	978.62	771.73	648.54	567.19	509.74	467.22	434.65	409.02	388.44	371.65
35,000	3089.28	1627.22	1141.72	900.35	756.63	661.72	594.70	545.09	507.09	477.19	453.18	433.59
40,000	3530.61	1859.68	1304.82	1028.98	864.72	756.26	679.66	622.96	579.53	545.36	517.92	495.53
45,000	3971.93	2092.14	1467.93	1157.60	972.81	850.79	764.61	700.83	651.97	613.53	582.66	557.47
50,000	4413.26	2324.60	1631.03	1286.22	1080.90	945.32	849.57	778.70	724.41	681.70	647.40	619.41
55,000	4854.58	2557.06	1794.13	1414.84	1188.99	1039.85	934.52	856.57	796.85	749.87	712.14	681.35
60,000	5295.91	2789.52	1957.23	1543.46	1297.08	1134.38	1019.48	934.44	869.29	818.04	776.88	743.29
65,000	5737.24	3021.98	2120.33	1672.08	1405.17	1228.91	1104.44	1012.31	941.73	886.21	841.62	805.23
70,000	6178.56	3254.43	2283.44	1800.70	1513.26	1323.44	1189.39	1090.18	1014.17	954.38	906.36	867.17
75,000	6619.89	3486.89	2446.54	1929.33	1621.35	1417.98	1274.35	1168.05	1086.61	1022.55	971.10	929.11
80,000	7061.21	3719.35	2609.64	2057.95	1729.44	1512.51	1359.31	1245.92	1159.05	1090.71	1035.84	991.05
85,000	7502.54	3951.81	2772.74	2186.57	1837.53	1607.04	1444.26	1323.79	1231.49	1158.88	1100.58	1052.99
90,000	7943.86	4184.27	2935.85	2315.19	1945.62	1701.57	1529.22	1401.66	1303.93	1227.05	1165.32	1114.93
95,000	8385.19	4416.73	3098.95	2443.81	2053.71	1796.10	1614.18	1479.53	1376.37	1295.22	1230.06	1176.87
100,000	8826.51	4649.19	3262.05	2572.43	2161.80	1890.63	1699.13	1557.40	1448.81	1363.39	1294.80	1238.81
105,000	9267.84	4881.65	3425.15	2701.05	2269.89	1985.16	1784.09	1635.26	1521.25	1431.56	1359.54	1300.75
110,000	9709.16	5114.11	3588.25	2829.68	2377.98	2079.70	1869.04	1713.13	1593.69	1499.73	1424.28	1362.69
115,000	10150.49	5346.57	3751.36	2958.30	2486.07	2174.23	1954.00	1791.00	1666.13	1567.90	1489.02	1424.63
120,000	10591.82	5579.03	3914.46	3086.92	2594.16	2268.76	2038.96	1868.87	1738.57	1636.07	1553.76	1486.57
125,000	11033.14	5811.49	4077.56	3215.54	2702.25	2363.29	2123.91	1946.74	1811.01	1704.24	1618.50	1548.51
130,000	11474.47	6043.95	4240.66	3344.16	2810.34	2457.82	2208.87	2024.61	1883.45	1772.41	1683.24	1610.45
135,000	11915.79	6276.41	4403.77	3472.78	2918.43	2552.35	2293.83	2102.48	1955.89	1840.58	1747.98	1672.39
140,000	12357.12	6508.86	4566.87	3601.40	3026.52	2646.88	2378.78	2180.35	2028.33	1908.75	1812.72	1734.33
145,000	12798.44	6741.32	4729.97	3730.03	3134.61	2741.42	2463.74	2258.22	2100.77	1976.92	1877.46	1796.27
150,000	13239.77	6973.78	4893.07	3858.65	3242.70	2835.95	2548.70	2336.09	2173.21	2045.09	1942.20	1858.21
155,000	13681.09	7206.24	5056.18	3987.27	3350.79	2930.48	2633.65	2413.96	2245.65	2113.25	2006.94	1920.15
160,000	14122.42	7438.70	5219.28	4115.89	3458.88	3025.01	2718.61	2491.83	2318.09	2181.42	2071.68	1982.09
165,000	14563.74	7671.16	5382.38	4244.51	3566.97	3119.54	2803.56	2569.70	2390.53	2249.59	2136.42	2044.03
170,000	15005.07	7903.62	5545.48	4373.13	3675.06	3214.07	2888.52	2647.57	2462.97	2317.76	2201.16	2105.97
175,000	15446.40	8136.08	5708.58	4501.75	3783.15	3308.60	2973.48	2725.44	2535.41	2385.93	2265.90	2167.91
180,000	15887.72	8368.54	5871.69	4630.38	3891.24	3403.14	3058.43	2803.31	2607.85	2454.10	2330.64	2229.85
185,000	16329.05	8601.00	6034.79	4759.00	3999.33	3497.67	3143.39	2881.18	2680.29	2522.27	2395.38	2291.79
190,000	16770.37	8833.46	6197.89	4887.62	4107.42	3592.20	3228.35	2959.05	2752.73	2590.44	2460.12	2353.73
195,000	17211.70	9065.92	6360.99	5016.24	4215.51	3686.73	3313.30	3036.92	2825.17	2658.61	2524.86	2415.67
200,000	17653.02	9298.38	6524.10	5144.86	4323.60	3781.26	3398.26	3114.79	2897.61	2726.78	2589.60	2477.61
205,000	18094.35	9530.84	6687.20	5273.48	4431.69	3875.79	3483.22	3192.65	2970.05	2794.95	2654.34	2539.55
210,000	18535.67	9763.29	6850.30	5402.10	4539.78	3970.32	3568.17	3270.52	3042.49	2863.12	2719.08	2601.49
215,000	18977.00	9995.75	7013.40	5530.73	4647.87	4064.85	3653.13	3348.39	3114.93	2931.29	2783.82	2663.43
220,000	19418.32	10228.21	7176.50	5659.35	4755.95	4159.39	3738.08	3426.26	3187.37	2999.46	2848.56	2725.37
225,000	19859.65	10460.67	7339.61	5787.97	4864.04	4253.92	3823.04	3504.13	3259.81	3067.63	2913.30	2787.31
230,000	20300.98	10693.13	7502.71	5916.59	4972.13	4348.45	3908.00	3582.00	3332.25	3135.79	2978.04	2849.25
235,000	20742.30	10925.59	7665.81	6045.21	5080.22	4442.98	3992.95	3659.87	3404.69	3203.96	3042.78	2911.20
240,000	21183.63	11158.05	7828.91	6173.83	5188.31	4537.51	4077.91	3737.74	3477.13	3272.13	3107.52	2973.14
245,000	21624.95	11390.51	7992.02	6302.45	5296.40	4632.04	4162.87	3815.61	3549.57	3340.30	3172.26	3035.08
250,000	22066.28	11622.97	8155.12	6431.08	5404.49	4726.57	4247.82	3893.48	3622.01	3408.47	3237.00	3097.02
255,000	22507.60	11855.43	8318.22	6559.70	5512.58	4821.11	4332.78	3971.35	3694.45	3476.64	3301.74	3158.96
260,000	22948.93	12087.89	8481.32	6688.32	5620.67	4915.64	4417.74	4049.22	3766.89	3544.81	3366.48	3220.90
265,000	23390.25	12320.35	8644.43	6816.94	5728.76	5010.17	4502.69	4127.09	3839.33	3612.98	3431.22	3282.84
270,000	23831.58	12552.81	8807.53	6945.56	5836.85	5104.70	4587.65	4204.96	3911.77	3681.15	3495.96	3344.78
280,000	24714.23	13017.72	9133.73	7202.80	6053.03	5293.76	4757.56	4360.70	4056.65	3817.49	3625.44	3468.66
290,000	25596.88	13482.64	9459.94	7460.05	6269.21	5482.83	4927.47	4516.44	4201.53	3953.83	3754.92	3592.54
300,000	26479.53	13947.56	9786.14	7717.29	6485.39	5671.89	5097.39	4672.18	4346.41	4090.17	3884.40	3716.42

72

AMOUNT OF LOAN	NUMBER OF YEARS IN TERM											
	13	14	15	16	17	18	19	20	25	30	35	40
$ 50	0.60	0.58	0.57	0.55	0.54	0.53	0.52	0.51	0.49	0.47	0.46	0.46
100	1.20	1.16	1.13	1.10	1.07	1.05	1.04	1.02	0.97	0.94	0.92	0.91
200	2.39	2.31	2.25	2.19	2.14	2.10	2.07	2.04	1.93	1.87	1.84	1.82
300	3.58	3.47	3.37	3.28	3.21	3.15	3.10	3.05	2.89	2.81	2.76	2.73
400	4.77	4.62	4.49	4.38	4.28	4.20	4.13	4.07	3.85	3.74	3.68	3.64
500	5.97	5.77	5.61	5.47	5.35	5.25	5.16	5.08	4.82	4.67	4.59	4.55
600	7.16	6.93	6.73	6.56	6.42	6.30	6.19	6.10	5.78	5.61	5.51	5.46
700	8.35	8.08	7.85	7.66	7.49	7.35	7.22	7.11	6.74	6.54	6.43	6.36
800	9.54	9.23	8.97	8.75	8.56	8.39	8.25	8.13	7.70	7.47	7.35	7.27
900	10.74	10.39	10.09	9.84	9.63	9.44	9.28	9.14	8.66	8.41	8.26	8.18
1,000	11.93	11.54	11.21	10.94	10.70	10.49	10.31	10.16	9.63	9.34	9.18	9.09
2,000	23.85	23.08	22.42	21.87	21.39	20.98	20.62	20.31	19.25	18.67	18.36	18.17
3,000	35.78	34.62	33.63	32.80	32.08	31.46	30.93	30.46	28.87	28.01	27.53	27.26
4,000	47.70	46.15	44.84	43.73	42.77	41.95	41.23	40.61	38.49	37.34	36.71	36.34
5,000	59.63	57.69	56.05	54.66	53.46	52.43	51.54	50.77	48.11	46.68	45.88	45.42
6,000	71.55	69.23	67.26	65.59	64.16	62.92	61.85	60.92	57.73	56.01	55.06	54.51
7,000	83.48	80.76	78.47	76.52	74.85	73.41	72.16	71.07	67.35	65.35	64.23	63.59
8,000	95.40	92.30	89.68	87.45	85.54	83.89	82.46	81.22	76.97	74.68	73.41	72.68
9,000	107.33	103.84	100.89	98.38	96.23	94.38	92.77	91.38	86.59	84.02	82.58	81.76
10,000	119.25	115.37	112.10	109.31	106.92	104.86	103.08	101.53	96.21	93.35	91.76	90.84
15,000	178.88	173.06	168.15	163.97	160.38	157.29	154.62	152.29	144.32	140.03	137.63	136.26
20,000	238.50	230.74	224.19	218.62	213.84	209.72	206.15	203.05	192.42	186.70	183.51	181.68
25,000	298.12	288.43	280.24	273.27	267.30	262.15	257.69	253.81	240.53	233.38	229.38	227.10
30,000	357.75	346.11	336.29	327.93	320.76	314.58	309.23	304.57	288.63	280.05	275.26	272.52
35,000	417.37	403.80	392.34	382.58	374.22	367.01	360.77	355.34	336.74	326.72	321.13	317.94
40,000	476.99	461.48	448.38	437.23	427.68	419.44	412.30	406.10	384.84	373.40	367.01	363.36
45,000	536.62	519.17	504.43	491.89	481.14	471.87	463.84	456.86	432.95	420.07	412.88	408.70
50,000	596.24	576.85	560.48	546.54	534.59	524.30	515.38	507.62	481.05	466.75	458.76	454.20
55,000	655.86	634.54	616.53	601.19	588.05	576.73	566.92	558.38	529.16	513.42	504.63	499.62
60,000	715.49	692.22	672.57	655.85	641.51	629.16	618.45	609.14	577.26	560.09	550.51	545.04
65,000	775.11	749.91	728.62	710.50	694.97	681.59	669.99	659.90	625.37	606.77	596.38	590.46
70,000	834.73	807.59	784.67	765.15	748.43	734.01	721.53	710.67	673.47	653.44	642.26	635.88
75,000	894.36	865.28	840.72	819.81	801.89	786.44	773.07	761.43	721.57	700.12	688.13	681.30
80,000	953.98	922.96	896.76	874.46	855.35	838.87	824.60	812.19	769.68	746.79	734.01	726.72
85,000	1013.60	980.65	952.81	929.11	908.81	891.30	876.14	862.95	817.78	793.46	779.88	772.14
90,000	1073.23	1038.33	1008.86	983.77	962.27	943.73	927.68	913.71	865.89	840.14	825.76	817.56
95,000	1132.85	1096.02	1064.91	1038.42	1015.72	996.16	979.21	964.47	913.99	886.81	871.63	862.98
100,000	1192.47	1153.70	1120.95	1093.07	1069.18	1048.59	1030.75	1015.23	962.10	933.49	917.51	908.40
105,000	1252.10	1211.39	1177.00	1147.73	1122.64	1101.02	1082.29	1066.00	1010.20	980.16	963.38	953.82
110,000	1311.72	1269.07	1233.05	1202.38	1176.10	1153.45	1133.83	1116.76	1058.31	1026.83	1009.26	999.24
115,000	1371.34	1326.76	1289.10	1257.04	1229.56	1205.88	1185.36	1167.52	1106.41	1073.51	1055.13	1044.66
120,000	1430.97	1384.44	1345.14	1311.69	1283.02	1258.31	1236.00	1218.28	1154.52	1120.18	1101.01	1090.08
125,000	1490.59	1442.12	1401.19	1366.34	1336.48	1310.74	1288.44	1269.04	1202.62	1166.86	1146.88	1135.50
130,000	1550.21	1499.81	1457.24	1421.00	1389.94	1363.17	1339.98	1319.80	1250.73	1213.53	1192.76	1180.92
135,000	1609.84	1557.49	1513.28	1475.65	1443.40	1415.59	1391.51	1370.56	1298.83	1260.20	1238.63	1226.34
140,000	1669.46	1615.18	1569.33	1530.30	1496.85	1468.02	1443.05	1421.33	1346.93	1306.88	1284.51	1271.76
145,000	1729.08	1672.86	1625.38	1584.96	1550.31	1520.45	1494.59	1472.09	1395.04	1353.55	1330.38	1317.18
150,000	1788.71	1730.55	1681.43	1639.61	1603.77	1572.88	1546.13	1522.85	1443.14	1400.23	1376.26	1362.60
155,000	1848.33	1788.23	1737.47	1694.26	1657.23	1625.31	1597.66	1573.61	1491.25	1446.90	1422.13	1408.02
160,000	1907.95	1845.92	1793.52	1748.92	1710.69	1677.74	1649.20	1624.37	1539.35	1493.58	1468.01	1453.44
165,000	1967.58	1903.60	1849.57	1803.57	1764.15	1730.17	1700.74	1675.13	1587.46	1540.25	1513.88	1498.86
170,000	2027.20	1961.29	1905.62	1858.22	1817.61	1782.60	1752.27	1725.89	1635.56	1586.92	1559.76	1544.28
175,000	2086.83	2018.97	1961.66	1912.88	1871.07	1835.03	1803.81	1776.66	1683.67	1633.60	1605.64	1589.70
180,000	2146.45	2076.66	2017.71	1967.53	1924.53	1887.46	1855.35	1827.42	1731.77	1680.27	1651.51	1635.12
185,000	2206.07	2134.34	2073.76	2022.18	1977.98	1939.89	1906.89	1878.18	1779.88	1726.95	1697.39	1680.54
190,000	2265.70	2192.03	2129.81	2076.84	2031.44	1992.32	1958.42	1928.94	1827.98	1773.62	1743.26	1725.96
195,000	2325.32	2249.71	2185.85	2131.49	2084.90	2044.75	2009.96	1979.70	1876.09	1820.29	1789.14	1771.38
200,000	2384.94	2307.40	2241.90	2186.14	2138.36	2097.17	2061.50	2030.46	1924.19	1866.97	1835.01	1816.80
205,000	2444.57	2365.08	2297.95	2240.80	2191.82	2149.60	2113.04	2081.22	1972.30	1913.64	1880.89	1862.22
210,000	2504.19	2422.77	2354.00	2295.45	2245.28	2202.03	2164.57	2131.99	2020.40	1960.32	1926.76	1907.64
215,000	2563.81	2480.45	2410.04	2350.11	2298.74	2254.46	2216.11	2182.75	2068.50	2006.99	1972.64	1953.06
220,000	2623.44	2538.14	2466.09	2404.76	2352.20	2306.89	2267.65	2233.51	2116.61	2053.66	2018.51	1998.48
225,000	2683.06	2595.82	2522.14	2459.41	2405.66	2359.32	2319.19	2284.27	2164.71	2100.34	2064.39	2043.90
230,000	2742.68	2653.51	2578.19	2514.07	2459.11	2411.75	2370.72	2335.03	2212.82	2147.01	2110.26	2089.32
235,000	2802.31	2711.19	2634.23	2568.72	2512.57	2464.18	2422.26	2385.79	2260.92	2193.69	2156.14	2134.74
240,000	2861.93	2768.88	2690.28	2623.37	2566.03	2516.61	2473.80	2436.55	2309.03	2240.36	2202.01	2180.16
245,000	2921.55	2826.56	2746.33	2678.03	2619.49	2569.04	2525.33	2487.32	2357.13	2287.03	2247.89	2225.58
250,000	2981.18	2884.24	2802.37	2732.68	2672.95	2621.47	2576.87	2538.08	2405.24	2333.71	2293.76	2271.00
255,000	3040.80	2941.93	2858.42	2787.33	2726.41	2673.90	2628.41	2588.84	2453.34	2380.38	2339.64	2316.42
260,000	3100.42	2999.61	2914.47	2841.99	2779.87	2726.33	2679.95	2639.60	2501.45	2427.06	2385.51	2361.84
265,000	3160.05	3057.30	2970.52	2896.64	2833.33	2778.75	2731.48	2690.36	2549.55	2473.73	2431.39	2407.26
270,000	3219.67	3114.98	3026.56	2951.29	2886.79	2831.18	2783.02	2741.12	2597.66	2520.40	2477.26	2452.68
280,000	3338.92	3230.35	3138.66	3060.60	2993.70	2936.04	2886.10	2842.65	2693.86	2613.75	2569.01	2543.52
290,000	3458.16	3345.72	3250.75	3169.91	3100.62	3040.90	2989.17	2944.17	2790.07	2707.10	2660.76	2634.36
300,000	3577.41	3461.09	3362.85	3279.21	3207.54	3145.76	3092.25	3045.69	2886.28	2800.45	2752.51	2725.20

11.00% MONTHLY AMORTIZING PAYMENTS

AMOUNT OF LOAN	NUMBER OF YEARS IN TERM											
	1	2	3	4	5	6	7	8	9	10	11	12
$ 50	4.42	2.34	1.64	1.30	1.09	0.96	0.86	0.79	0.74	0.69	0.66	0.63
100	8.84	4.67	3.28	2.59	2.18	1.91	1.72	1.58	1.47	1.38	1.31	1.26
200	17.68	9.33	6.55	5.17	4.35	3.81	3.43	3.15	2.93	2.76	2.62	2.51
300	26.52	13.99	9.83	7.76	6.53	5.72	5.14	4.72	4.39	4.14	3.93	3.77
400	35.36	18.65	13.10	10.34	8.70	7.62	6.85	6.29	5.86	5.52	5.24	5.02
500	44.20	23.31	16.37	12.93	10.88	9.52	8.57	7.86	7.32	6.89	6.55	6.27
600	53.03	27.97	19.65	15.51	13.05	11.43	10.28	9.43	8.78	8.27	7.86	7.53
700	61.87	32.63	22.92	18.10	15.22	13.33	11.99	11.00	10.24	9.65	9.17	8.78
800	70.71	37.29	26.20	20.68	17.40	15.23	13.70	12.57	11.71	11.03	10.48	10.03
900	79.55	41.95	29.47	23.27	19.57	17.14	15.42	14.14	13.17	12.40	11.79	11.29
1,000	88.39	46.61	32.74	25.85	21.75	19.04	17.13	15.71	14.63	13.78	13.10	12.54
2,000	176.77	93.22	65.48	51.70	43.49	38.07	34.25	31.42	29.26	27.56	26.19	25.08
3,000	265.15	139.83	98.22	77.54	65.23	57.11	51.37	47.13	43.88	41.33	39.28	37.61
4,000	353.53	186.44	130.96	103.39	86.97	76.14	68.49	62.84	58.51	55.11	52.37	50.15
5,000	441.91	233.04	163.70	129.23	108.72	95.18	85.62	78.55	73.13	68.88	65.47	62.68
6,000	530.29	279.65	196.44	155.08	130.46	114.21	102.74	94.26	87.76	82.66	78.56	75.22
7,000	618.68	326.26	229.18	180.92	152.20	133.24	119.86	109.96	102.39	96.43	91.65	87.75
8,000	707.06	372.87	261.91	206.77	173.94	152.28	136.98	125.67	117.01	110.21	104.74	100.29
9,000	795.44	419.48	294.65	232.61	195.69	171.31	154.11	141.38	131.64	123.98	117.84	112.82
10,000	883.82	466.08	327.39	258.46	217.43	190.35	171.23	157.09	146.26	137.76	130.93	125.36
15,000	1325.73	699.12	491.09	387.69	326.14	285.52	256.84	235.63	219.39	206.63	196.39	188.04
20,000	1767.64	932.16	654.78	516.92	434.85	380.69	342.45	314.17	292.52	275.51	261.85	250.72
25,000	2209.55	1165.20	818.47	646.14	543.57	475.86	428.07	392.72	365.65	344.38	327.31	313.39
30,000	2651.45	1398.24	982.17	775.37	652.28	571.03	513.68	471.26	438.78	413.26	392.78	376.07
35,000	3093.36	1631.28	1145.86	904.60	760.99	666.20	599.29	549.80	511.91	482.13	458.24	438.75
40,000	3535.27	1864.32	1309.55	1033.83	869.70	761.37	684.90	628.34	585.04	551.01	523.70	501.43
45,000	3977.18	2097.36	1473.25	1163.05	978.41	856.54	770.51	706.88	658.17	619.88	589.16	564.10
50,000	4419.09	2330.40	1636.94	1292.28	1087.13	951.71	856.13	785.43	731.30	688.76	654.62	626.78
55,000	4861.00	2563.44	1800.63	1421.51	1195.84	1046.88	941.74	863.97	804.43	757.63	720.08	689.46
60,000	5302.90	2796.48	1964.33	1550.74	1304.55	1142.05	1027.35	942.51	877.56	826.51	785.55	752.14
65,000	5744.81	3029.51	2128.02	1679.96	1413.26	1237.22	1112.96	1021.05	950.69	895.38	851.01	814.82
70,000	6186.72	3262.55	2291.72	1809.19	1521.97	1332.39	1198.58	1099.59	1023.82	964.26	916.47	877.49
75,000	6628.63	3495.59	2455.41	1938.42	1630.69	1427.56	1284.19	1178.14	1096.94	1033.13	981.93	940.17
80,000	7070.54	3728.63	2619.10	2067.65	1739.40	1522.73	1369.80	1256.68	1170.07	1102.01	1047.39	1002.85
85,000	7512.45	3961.67	2782.80	2196.87	1848.11	1617.90	1455.41	1335.22	1243.20	1170.88	1112.85	1065.53
90,000	7954.35	4194.71	2946.49	2326.10	1956.82	1713.07	1541.02	1413.76	1316.33	1239.76	1178.32	1128.20
95,000	8396.26	4427.75	3110.18	2455.33	2065.54	1808.24	1626.64	1492.31	1389.46	1308.63	1243.78	1190.88
100,000	8838.17	4660.79	3273.88	2584.56	2174.25	1903.41	1712.25	1570.85	1462.59	1377.51	1309.24	1253.56
105,000	9280.08	4893.83	3437.57	2713.78	2282.96	1998.58	1797.86	1649.39	1535.72	1446.38	1374.70	1316.24
110,000	9721.99	5126.87	3601.26	2843.01	2391.67	2093.75	1883.47	1727.93	1608.85	1515.26	1440.16	1378.92
115,000	10163.90	5359.91	3764.96	2972.24	2500.38	2188.92	1969.09	1806.47	1681.98	1584.13	1505.63	1441.59
120,000	10605.80	5592.95	3928.65	3101.47	2609.10	2284.09	2054.70	1885.02	1755.11	1653.01	1571.09	1504.27
125,000	11047.71	5825.98	4092.34	3230.70	2717.81	2379.26	2140.31	1963.56	1828.24	1721.88	1636.55	1566.95
130,000	11489.62	6059.02	4256.04	3359.92	2826.52	2474.44	2225.92	2042.10	1901.37	1790.76	1702.01	1629.63
135,000	11931.53	6292.06	4419.73	3489.15	2935.23	2569.61	2311.53	2120.64	1974.50	1859.63	1767.47	1692.30
140,000	12373.44	6525.10	4583.43	3618.38	3043.94	2664.78	2397.15	2199.18	2047.63	1928.51	1832.93	1754.98
145,000	12815.35	6758.14	4747.12	3747.61	3152.66	2759.95	2482.76	2277.73	2120.75	1997.38	1898.40	1817.66
150,000	13257.25	6991.18	4910.81	3876.83	3261.37	2855.12	2568.37	2356.27	2193.88	2066.26	1963.86	1880.34
155,000	13699.16	7224.22	5074.51	4006.06	3370.08	2950.29	2653.98	2434.81	2267.01	2135.13	2029.32	1943.02
160,000	14141.07	7457.26	5238.20	4135.29	3478.79	3045.46	2739.59	2513.35	2340.14	2204.01	2094.78	2005.69
165,000	14582.98	7690.30	5401.89	4264.52	3587.50	3140.63	2825.21	2591.90	2413.27	2272.88	2160.24	2068.37
170,000	15024.89	7923.34	5565.59	4393.74	3696.22	3235.80	2910.82	2670.44	2486.40	2341.76	2225.70	2131.05
175,000	15466.80	8156.38	5729.28	4522.97	3804.93	3330.97	2996.43	2748.98	2559.53	2410.63	2291.17	2193.73
180,000	15908.70	8389.42	5892.97	4652.20	3913.64	3426.14	3082.04	2827.52	2632.66	2479.51	2356.63	2256.40
185,000	16350.61	8622.46	6056.67	4781.43	4022.35	3521.31	3167.66	2906.06	2705.79	2548.38	2422.09	2319.08
190,000	16792.52	8855.49	6220.36	4910.65	4131.07	3616.48	3253.27	2984.61	2778.92	2617.26	2487.55	2381.76
195,000	17234.43	9088.53	6384.05	5039.88	4239.78	3711.65	3338.88	3063.15	2852.05	2686.13	2553.01	2444.44
200,000	17676.34	9321.57	6547.75	5169.11	4348.49	3806.82	3424.49	3141.69	2925.18	2755.01	2618.47	2507.12
205,000	18118.24	9554.61	6711.44	5298.34	4457.20	3901.99	3510.10	3220.23	2998.31	2823.88	2683.94	2569.79
210,000	18560.15	9787.65	6875.14	5427.56	4565.91	3997.16	3595.72	3298.77	3071.44	2892.76	2749.40	2632.47
215,000	19002.06	10020.69	7038.83	5556.79	4674.63	4092.33	3681.33	3377.32	3144.57	2961.63	2814.86	2695.15
220,000	19443.97	10253.73	7202.52	5686.02	4783.34	4187.50	3766.94	3455.86	3217.69	3030.51	2880.32	2757.83
225,000	19885.88	10486.77	7366.22	5815.25	4892.05	4282.67	3852.55	3534.40	3290.82	3099.38	2945.78	2820.50
230,000	20327.79	10719.81	7529.91	5944.48	5000.76	4377.84	3938.17	3612.94	3363.95	3168.26	3011.25	2883.18
235,000	20769.69	10952.85	7693.60	6073.70	5109.47	4473.01	4023.78	3691.49	3437.08	3237.13	3076.71	2945.86
240,000	21211.60	11185.89	7857.30	6202.93	5218.19	4568.18	4109.39	3770.03	3510.21	3306.01	3142.17	3008.54
245,000	21653.51	11418.93	8020.99	6332.16	5326.90	4663.35	4195.00	3848.57	3583.34	3374.88	3207.63	3071.22
250,000	22095.42	11651.96	8184.68	6461.39	5435.61	4758.52	4280.61	3927.11	3656.47	3443.76	3273.09	3133.89
255,000	22537.33	11885.00	8348.38	6590.61	5544.32	4853.70	4366.23	4005.65	3729.60	3512.63	3338.55	3196.57
260,000	22979.24	12118.04	8512.07	6719.84	5653.03	4948.87	4451.84	4084.20	3802.73	3581.51	3404.02	3259.25
265,000	23421.14	12351.08	8675.77	6849.07	5761.75	5044.04	4537.45	4162.74	3875.86	3650.38	3469.48	3321.93
270,000	23863.05	12584.12	8839.46	6978.30	5870.46	5139.21	4623.06	4241.28	3948.99	3719.26	3534.94	3384.60
280,000	24746.87	13050.20	9166.85	7236.75	6087.88	5329.55	4794.29	4398.36	4095.25	3857.01	3665.86	3509.96
290,000	25630.69	13516.28	9494.23	7495.21	6305.31	5519.89	4965.51	4555.45	4241.50	3994.76	3796.79	3635.32
300,000	26514.50	13982.36	9821.62	7753.66	6522.73	5710.23	5136.74	4712.53	4387.76	4132.51	3927.71	3760.67

AMOUNT OF LOAN	NUMBER OF YEARS IN TERM											
	13	14	15	16	17	18	19	20	25	30	35	40
$ 50	0.61	0.59	0.57	0.56	0.55	0.54	0.53	0.52	0.50	0.48	0.47	0.47
100	1.21	1.17	1.14	1.11	1.09	1.07	1.05	1.04	0.99	0.96	0.94	0.93
200	2.42	2.34	2.28	2.22	2.18	2.14	2.10	2.07	1.97	1.91	1.88	1.86
300	3.63	3.51	3.41	3.33	3.26	3.20	3.15	3.10	2.95	2.86	2.82	2.79
400	4.84	4.68	4.55	4.44	4.35	4.27	4.19	4.13	3.93	3.81	3.75	3.72
500	6.04	5.85	5.69	5.55	5.43	5.33	5.24	5.17	4.91	4.77	4.69	4.65
600	7.25	7.02	6.82	6.66	6.52	6.40	6.29	6.20	5.89	5.72	5.63	5.57
700	8.46	8.19	7.96	7.77	7.60	7.46	7.34	7.23	6.87	6.67	6.56	6.50
800	9.67	9.36	9.10	8.88	8.69	8.53	8.38	8.26	7.85	7.62	7.50	7.43
900	10.87	10.53	10.23	9.99	9.77	9.59	9.43	9.29	8.83	8.58	8.44	8.36
1,000	12.08	11.70	11.37	11.10	10.86	10.66	10.48	10.33	9.81	9.53	9.37	9.29
2,000	24.16	23.39	22.74	22.19	21.71	21.31	20.95	20.65	19.61	19.05	18.74	18.57
3,000	36.23	35.08	34.10	33.28	32.57	31.96	31.43	30.97	29.41	28.57	28.11	27.85
4,000	48.31	46.77	45.47	44.37	43.42	42.61	41.90	41.29	39.21	38.10	37.48	37.14
5,000	60.38	58.46	56.83	55.46	54.27	53.26	52.38	51.61	49.01	47.62	46.85	46.42
6,000	72.46	70.15	68.20	66.55	65.13	63.91	62.85	61.94	58.81	57.14	56.22	55.70
7,000	84.53	81.84	79.57	77.64	75.98	74.56	73.33	72.26	68.61	66.67	65.59	64.99
8,000	96.61	93.53	90.93	88.73	86.84	85.21	83.80	82.58	78.41	76.19	74.96	74.27
9,000	108.68	105.22	102.30	99.82	97.69	95.86	94.28	92.90	88.22	85.71	84.33	83.55
10,000	120.76	116.91	113.66	110.91	108.54	106.51	104.75	103.22	98.02	95.24	93.70	92.83
15,000	181.13	175.36	170.49	166.36	162.81	159.76	157.12	154.83	147.02	142.85	140.55	139.25
20,000	241.51	233.82	227.32	221.81	217.08	213.01	209.50	206.44	196.03	190.47	187.40	185.66
25,000	301.89	292.27	284.15	277.26	271.35	266.27	261.87	258.05	245.03	238.09	234.24	232.08
30,000	362.26	350.72	340.98	332.71	325.62	319.52	314.24	309.66	294.04	285.70	281.09	278.49
35,000	422.64	409.17	397.81	388.16	379.89	372.77	366.62	361.27	343.04	333.32	327.94	324.91
40,000	483.02	467.63	454.64	443.61	434.16	426.02	418.99	412.88	392.05	380.93	374.79	371.32
45,000	543.39	526.08	511.47	499.06	488.43	479.28	471.36	464.49	441.06	428.55	421.64	417.74
50,000	603.77	584.53	568.30	554.51	542.70	532.53	523.74	516.10	490.06	476.17	468.48	464.15
55,000	664.15	642.98	625.13	609.96	596.96	585.78	576.11	567.71	539.07	523.78	515.33	510.57
60,000	724.52	701.44	681.96	665.41	651.23	639.03	628.48	619.32	588.07	571.40	562.18	556.98
65,000	784.90	759.89	738.79	720.86	705.50	692.29	680.86	670.93	637.08	619.02	609.03	603.40
70,000	845.27	818.34	795.62	776.31	759.77	745.54	733.23	722.54	686.08	666.63	655.88	649.81
75,000	905.65	876.80	852.45	831.76	814.04	798.79	785.60	774.15	735.09	714.25	702.72	696.23
80,000	966.03	935.25	909.28	887.21	868.31	852.04	837.98	825.76	784.10	761.86	749.57	742.64
85,000	1026.40	993.70	966.11	942.66	922.58	905.30	890.35	877.37	833.10	809.48	796.42	789.06
90,000	1086.78	1052.15	1022.94	998.11	976.85	958.55	942.72	928.97	882.11	857.10	843.27	835.47
95,000	1147.16	1110.61	1079.77	1053.56	1031.12	1011.80	995.10	980.58	931.11	904.71	890.11	881.88
100,000	1207.53	1169.06	1136.60	1109.01	1085.39	1065.05	1047.47	1032.19	980.12	952.33	936.96	928.30
105,000	1267.91	1227.51	1193.43	1164.46	1139.65	1110.31	1099.84	1083.80	1029.12	999.94	983.81	974.71
110,000	1328.29	1285.96	1250.26	1219.91	1193.92	1171.56	1152.22	1135.41	1078.13	1047.56	1030.66	1021.13
115,000	1388.66	1344.42	1307.09	1275.36	1248.19	1224.81	1204.59	1187.02	1127.14	1095.18	1077.51	1067.54
120,000	1449.04	1402.87	1363.92	1330.81	1302.46	1278.06	1256.96	1238.63	1176.14	1142.79	1124.35	1110.06
125,000	1509.41	1461.32	1420.75	1386.26	1356.73	1331.32	1309.33	1290.24	1225.15	1190.41	1171.20	1160.37
130,000	1569.79	1519.78	1477.58	1441.71	1411.00	1384.57	1361.71	1341.85	1274.15	1238.03	1218.05	1206.79
135,000	1630.17	1578.23	1534.41	1497.16	1465.27	1437.82	1414.08	1393.46	1323.16	1285.64	1264.90	1253.20
140,000	1690.54	1636.68	1591.24	1552.61	1519.54	1491.07	1466.45	1445.07	1372.16	1333.26	1311.75	1299.62
145,000	1750.92	1695.13	1648.07	1608.06	1573.81	1544.33	1518.83	1496.68	1421.17	1380.87	1358.59	1346.03
150,000	1811.30	1753.59	1704.90	1663.51	1628.08	1597.58	1571.20	1548.29	1470.17	1428.49	1405.44	1392.45
155,000	1871.67	1812.04	1761.73	1718.96	1682.34	1650.83	1623.57	1599.90	1519.18	1476.11	1452.29	1438.86
160,000	1932.05	1870.49	1818.56	1774.41	1736.61	1704.08	1675.95	1651.51	1568.19	1523.72	1499.14	1485.28
165,000	1992.43	1928.94	1875.39	1829.86	1790.88	1757.34	1728.32	1703.12	1617.19	1571.34	1545.99	1531.69
170,000	2052.80	1987.40	1932.22	1885.31	1845.15	1810.59	1780.69	1754.73	1666.20	1618.95	1592.83	1578.11
175,000	2113.18	2045.85	1989.05	1940.76	1899.42	1863.84	1833.07	1806.33	1715.20	1666.57	1639.68	1624.52
180,000	2173.55	2104.30	2045.88	1996.21	1953.69	1917.09	1885.44	1857.94	1764.21	1714.19	1686.53	1670.93
185,000	2233.93	2162.76	2102.71	2051.66	2007.96	1970.35	1937.81	1909.55	1813.21	1761.80	1733.38	1717.35
190,000	2294.31	2221.21	2159.54	2107.11	2062.23	2023.60	1990.19	1961.16	1862.22	1809.42	1780.22	1763.76
195,000	2354.68	2279.66	2216.37	2162.56	2116.50	2076.85	2042.56	2012.77	1911.23	1857.04	1827.07	1810.18
200,000	2415.06	2338.11	2273.20	2218.01	2170.77	2130.10	2094.93	2064.38	1960.23	1904.65	1873.92	1856.59
205,000	2475.44	2396.57	2330.03	2273.46	2225.04	2183.36	2147.31	2115.99	2009.24	1952.27	1920.77	1903.01
210,000	2535.81	2455.02	2386.86	2328.91	2279.30	2236.61	2199.68	2167.60	2058.24	1999.88	1967.62	1949.42
215,000	2596.19	2513.47	2443.69	2384.36	2333.57	2289.86	2252.05	2219.21	2107.25	2047.50	2014.46	1995.84
220,000	2656.57	2571.92	2500.52	2439.81	2387.84	2343.11	2304.43	2270.82	2156.25	2095.12	2061.31	2042.25
225,000	2716.94	2630.38	2557.35	2495.26	2442.11	2396.37	2356.80	2322.43	2205.26	2142.73	2108.16	2088.67
230,000	2777.32	2688.83	2614.18	2550.71	2496.38	2449.62	2409.17	2374.04	2254.27	2190.35	2155.01	2135.08
235,000	2837.69	2747.28	2671.01	2606.16	2550.65	2502.87	2461.55	2425.65	2303.27	2237.96	2201.86	2181.50
240,000	2898.07	2805.74	2727.84	2661.61	2604.92	2556.12	2513.92	2477.26	2352.28	2285.58	2248.70	2227.91
245,000	2958.45	2864.19	2784.67	2717.06	2659.19	2609.38	2566.29	2528.87	2401.28	2333.20	2295.55	2274.33
250,000	3018.82	2922.64	2841.50	2772.51	2713.46	2662.63	2618.66	2580.48	2450.29	2380.81	2342.40	2320.74
255,000	3079.20	2981.09	2898.33	2827.96	2767.73	2715.88	2671.04	2632.09	2499.29	2428.43	2389.25	2367.16
260,000	3139.58	3039.55	2955.16	2883.41	2821.99	2769.13	2723.41	2683.69	2548.30	2476.05	2436.09	2413.57
265,000	3199.95	3098.00	3011.99	2938.86	2876.26	2822.39	2775.78	2735.30	2597.30	2523.66	2482.94	2459.99
270,000	3260.33	3156.45	3068.82	2994.31	2930.53	2875.64	2828.16	2786.91	2646.31	2571.28	2529.79	2506.40
280,000	3381.08	3273.36	3182.48	3105.21	3039.07	2982.14	2932.90	2890.13	2744.32	2666.51	2623.49	2599.23
290,000	3501.83	3390.26	3296.14	3216.11	3147.61	3088.65	3037.65	2993.35	2842.33	2761.74	2717.18	2692.06
300,000	3622.59	3507.17	3409.80	3327.01	3256.15	3195.15	3142.40	3096.57	2940.34	2856.98	2810.88	2784.89

11.25%
MONTHLY AMORTIZING PAYMENTS

AMOUNT OF LOAN	NUMBER OF YEARS IN TERM											
	1	2	3	4	5	6	7	8	9	10	11	12
$ 50	4.43	2.34	1.65	1.30	1.10	0.96	0.87	0.80	0.74	0.70	0.67	0.64
100	8.85	4.68	3.29	2.60	2.19	1.92	1.73	1.59	1.48	1.40	1.33	1.27
200	17.70	9.35	6.58	5.20	4.38	3.84	3.46	3.17	2.96	2.79	2.65	2.54
300	26.55	14.02	9.86	7.80	6.57	5.75	5.18	4.76	4.43	4.18	3.98	3.81
400	35.40	18.69	13.15	10.39	8.75	7.67	6.91	6.34	5.91	5.57	5.30	5.08
500	44.25	23.37	16.43	12.99	10.94	9.59	8.63	7.93	7.39	6.96	6.62	6.35
600	53.10	28.04	19.72	15.59	13.13	11.50	10.36	9.51	8.86	8.36	7.95	7.62
700	61.95	32.71	23.01	18.18	15.31	13.42	12.08	11.10	10.34	9.75	9.27	8.88
800	70.80	37.38	26.29	20.78	17.50	15.33	13.81	12.68	11.82	11.14	10.60	10.15
900	79.65	42.06	29.58	23.38	19.69	17.25	15.53	14.26	13.29	12.53	11.92	11.42
1,000	88.50	46.73	32.86	25.97	21.87	19.17	17.26	15.85	14.77	13.92	13.24	12.69
2,000	177.00	93.45	65.72	51.94	43.74	38.33	34.51	31.69	29.53	27.84	26.48	25.37
3,000	265.50	140.18	98.58	77.91	65.61	57.49	51.77	47.54	44.30	41.76	39.72	38.06
4,000	354.00	186.90	131.43	103.87	87.47	76.65	69.02	63.38	59.06	55.67	52.96	50.74
5,000	442.50	233.62	164.29	129.84	109.34	95.82	86.28	79.22	73.83	69.59	66.19	63.42
6,000	530.99	280.35	197.15	155.81	131.21	114.98	103.53	95.07	88.59	83.51	79.43	76.11
7,000	619.49	327.07	230.01	181.77	153.08	134.14	120.78	110.91	103.36	97.42	92.67	88.79
8,000	707.99	373.80	262.86	207.74	174.94	153.30	138.04	126.75	118.12	111.34	105.91	101.48
9,000	796.49	420.52	295.72	233.71	196.81	172.47	155.29	142.60	132.88	125.26	119.14	114.16
10,000	884.99	467.24	328.58	259.68	218.68	191.63	172.55	158.44	147.65	139.17	132.38	126.84
15,000	1327.48	700.86	492.86	389.51	328.01	287.44	258.82	237.66	221.47	208.76	198.57	190.26
20,000	1769.97	934.48	657.15	519.35	437.35	383.25	345.09	316.88	295.29	278.34	264.76	253.68
25,000	2212.46	1168.10	821.44	649.18	546.69	479.06	431.36	396.09	369.12	347.93	330.94	317.10
30,000	2654.95	1401.72	985.72	779.02	656.02	574.88	517.63	475.31	442.94	417.51	397.13	380.52
35,000	3097.45	1635.34	1150.01	908.85	765.36	670.69	603.90	554.53	516.76	487.10	463.32	443.94
40,000	3539.94	1868.96	1314.29	1038.69	874.70	766.50	690.17	633.75	590.58	556.68	529.51	507.36
45,000	3982.43	2102.58	1478.58	1168.52	984.03	862.31	776.44	712.97	664.40	626.27	595.69	570.78
50,000	4424.92	2336.20	1642.87	1298.36	1093.37	958.12	862.71	792.18	738.23	695.85	661.88	634.20
55,000	4867.41	2569.82	1807.15	1428.20	1202.71	1053.94	948.98	871.40	812.05	765.43	728.07	697.62
60,000	5309.90	2803.44	1971.44	1558.03	1312.04	1149.75	1035.26	950.62	885.87	835.02	794.26	761.04
65,000	5752.40	3037.06	2135.73	1687.87	1421.38	1245.56	1121.53	1029.84	959.69	904.60	860.44	824.46
70,000	6194.89	3270.68	2300.01	1817.70	1530.72	1341.37	1207.80	1109.06	1033.51	974.19	926.63	887.88
75,000	6637.38	3504.30	2464.30	1947.54	1640.05	1437.18	1294.07	1188.27	1107.34	1043.77	992.82	951.30
80,000	7079.87	3737.92	2628.58	2077.37	1749.39	1532.99	1380.34	1267.49	1181.16	1113.36	1059.01	1014.72
85,000	7522.36	3971.54	2792.87	2207.21	1858.73	1628.81	1466.61	1346.71	1254.98	1182.94	1125.19	1078.14
90,000	7964.85	4205.16	2957.16	2337.04	1968.06	1724.62	1552.88	1425.93	1328.80	1252.53	1191.38	1141.56
95,000	8407.34	4438.78	3121.44	2466.88	2077.40	1820.43	1639.15	1505.15	1402.62	1322.11	1257.57	1204.98
100,000	8849.84	4672.40	3285.73	2596.71	2186.74	1916.24	1725.42	1584.36	1476.45	1391.69	1323.76	1268.40
105,000	9292.33	4906.02	3450.01	2726.55	2296.07	2012.05	1811.69	1663.58	1550.27	1461.28	1389.94	1331.82
110,000	9734.82	5139.64	3614.30	2856.39	2405.41	2107.87	1897.96	1742.80	1624.09	1530.86	1456.13	1395.24
115,000	10177.31	5373.26	3778.59	2986.22	2514.75	2203.68	1984.23	1822.02	1697.91	1600.45	1522.32	1458.66
120,000	10619.80	5606.88	3942.87	3116.06	2624.08	2299.49	2070.51	1901.24	1771.73	1670.03	1588.51	1522.08
125,000	11062.29	5840.50	4107.16	3245.89	2733.42	2395.30	2156.78	1980.45	1845.56	1739.62	1654.70	1585.50
130,000	11504.79	6074.12	4271.45	3375.73	2842.76	2491.11	2243.05	2059.67	1919.38	1809.20	1720.88	1648.92
135,000	11947.28	6307.74	4435.73	3505.56	2952.09	2586.93	2329.32	2138.89	1993.20	1878.79	1787.07	1712.34
140,000	12389.77	6541.36	4600.02	3635.40	3061.43	2682.74	2415.59	2218.11	2067.02	1948.37	1853.26	1775.76
145,000	12832.26	6774.98	4764.30	3765.23	3170.76	2778.55	2501.86	2297.32	2140.84	2017.95	1919.45	1839.17
150,000	13274.75	7008.60	4928.59	3895.07	3280.10	2874.36	2588.13	2376.54	2214.67	2087.54	1985.63	1902.59
155,000	13717.24	7242.22	5092.88	4024.91	3389.44	2970.17	2674.40	2455.76	2288.49	2157.12	2051.82	1966.01
160,000	14159.74	7475.84	5257.16	4154.74	3498.77	3065.98	2760.67	2534.98	2362.31	2226.71	2118.01	2029.43
165,000	14602.23	7709.46	5421.45	4284.58	3608.11	3161.80	2846.94	2614.20	2436.13	2296.29	2184.20	2092.85
170,000	15044.72	7943.08	5585.73	4414.41	3717.45	3257.61	2933.21	2693.41	2509.96	2365.88	2250.38	2156.27
175,000	15487.21	8176.70	5750.02	4544.25	3826.78	3353.42	3019.48	2772.63	2583.78	2435.46	2316.57	2219.69
180,000	15929.70	8410.32	5914.31	4674.08	3936.12	3449.23	3105.76	2851.85	2657.60	2505.05	2382.76	2283.11
185,000	16372.19	8643.94	6078.59	4803.92	4045.46	3545.04	3192.03	2931.07	2731.42	2574.63	2448.95	2346.53
190,000	16814.68	8877.56	6242.88	4933.75	4154.79	3640.86	3278.30	3010.29	2805.24	2644.21	2515.13	2409.95
195,000	17257.18	9111.18	6407.17	5063.59	4264.13	3736.67	3364.57	3089.50	2879.07	2713.80	2581.32	2473.37
200,000	17699.67	9344.80	6571.45	5193.42	4373.47	3832.48	3450.84	3168.72	2952.89	2783.38	2647.51	2536.79
205,000	18142.16	9578.42	6735.74	5323.26	4482.80	3928.29	3537.11	3247.94	3026.71	2852.97	2713.70	2600.21
210,000	18584.65	9812.04	6900.02	5453.10	4592.14	4024.10	3623.38	3327.16	3100.53	2922.55	2779.88	2663.63
215,000	19027.14	10045.66	7064.31	5582.93	4701.48	4119.92	3709.65	3406.38	3174.35	2992.14	2846.07	2727.05
220,000	19469.63	10279.28	7228.60	5712.77	4810.81	4215.73	3795.92	3485.59	3248.18	3061.72	2912.26	2790.47
225,000	19912.13	10512.90	7392.88	5842.60	4920.15	4311.54	3882.19	3564.81	3322.00	3131.31	2978.45	2853.89
230,000	20354.62	10746.52	7557.17	5972.44	5029.49	4407.35	3968.46	3644.03	3395.82	3200.89	3044.63	2917.31
235,000	20797.11	10980.14	7721.46	6102.27	5138.82	4503.16	4054.73	3723.25	3469.64	3270.48	3110.82	2980.73
240,000	21239.60	11213.76	7885.74	6232.11	5248.16	4598.97	4141.01	3802.47	3543.46	3340.06	3177.01	3044.15
245,000	21682.09	11447.38	8050.03	6361.94	5357.50	4694.79	4227.28	3881.68	3617.29	3409.64	3243.20	3107.57
250,000	22124.58	11681.00	8214.31	6491.78	5466.83	4790.60	4313.55	3960.90	3691.11	3479.23	3309.39	3170.99
255,000	22567.08	11914.62	8378.60	6621.61	5576.17	4886.41	4399.82	4040.12	3764.93	3548.81	3375.57	3234.41
260,000	23009.57	12148.24	8542.89	6751.45	5685.51	4982.22	4486.09	4119.34	3838.75	3618.40	3441.76	3297.83
265,000	23452.06	12381.86	8707.17	6881.29	5794.84	5078.03	4572.36	4198.55	3912.57	3687.98	3507.95	3361.25
270,000	23894.55	12615.48	8871.46	7011.12	5904.18	5173.85	4658.63	4277.77	3986.40	3757.57	3574.14	3424.67
280,000	24779.53	13082.72	9200.03	7270.79	6122.85	5365.47	4831.17	4436.21	4134.04	3896.74	3706.51	3551.51
290,000	25664.52	13549.96	9528.60	7530.46	6341.52	5557.09	5003.71	4594.64	4281.68	4035.90	3838.89	3678.34
300,000	26549.50	14017.20	9857.18	7790.13	6560.20	5748.72	5176.26	4753.08	4429.33	4175.07	3971.26	3805.18

76

11.25%

AMOUNT OF LOAN	NUMBER OF YEARS IN TERM											
	13	14	15	16	17	18	19	20	25	30	35	40
$ 50	0.62	0.60	0.58	0.57	0.56	0.55	0.54	0.53	0.50	0.49	0.48	0.48
100	1.23	1.19	1.16	1.13	1.11	1.09	1.07	1.05	1.00	0.98	0.96	0.95
200	2.45	2.37	2.31	2.26	2.21	2.17	2.13	2.10	2.00	1.95	1.92	1.90
300	3.67	3.56	3.46	3.38	3.31	3.25	3.20	3.15	3.00	2.92	2.87	2.85
400	4.90	4.74	4.61	4.51	4.41	4.33	4.26	4.20	4.00	3.89	3.83	3.80
500	6.12	5.93	5.77	5.63	5.51	5.41	5.33	5.25	5.00	4.86	4.79	4.75
600	7.34	7.11	6.92	6.76	6.62	6.49	6.39	6.30	5.99	5.83	5.74	5.69
700	8.56	8.30	8.07	7.88	7.72	7.58	7.46	7.35	6.99	6.80	6.70	6.64
800	9.79	9.48	9.22	9.01	8.82	8.66	8.52	8.40	7.99	7.78	7.66	7.59
900	11.01	10.67	10.38	10.13	9.92	9.74	9.58	9.45	8.99	8.75	8.61	8.54
1,000	12.23	11.85	11.53	11.26	11.02	10.82	10.65	10.50	9.99	9.72	9.57	9.49
2,000	24.46	23.70	23.05	22.51	22.04	21.64	21.29	20.99	19.97	19.43	19.13	18.97
3,000	36.69	35.54	34.58	33.76	33.06	32.45	31.93	31.48	29.95	29.14	28.70	28.45
4,000	48.91	47.39	46.10	45.01	44.07	43.27	42.58	41.98	39.93	38.86	38.26	37.94
5,000	61.14	59.23	57.62	56.26	55.09	54.09	53.22	52.47	49.92	48.57	47.83	47.42
6,000	73.37	71.08	69.15	67.51	66.11	64.90	63.86	62.96	59.90	58.28	57.39	56.90
7,000	85.59	82.92	80.67	78.76	77.12	75.72	74.51	73.45	69.88	67.99	66.96	66.38
8,000	97.82	94.77	92.19	90.01	88.14	86.53	85.15	83.95	79.86	77.71	76.52	75.87
9,000	110.05	106.61	103.72	101.26	99.16	97.35	95.79	94.44	89.85	87.42	86.09	85.35
10,000	122.27	118.46	115.24	112.51	110.17	108.17	106.43	104.93	99.83	97.13	95.65	94.83
15,000	183.41	177.68	172.86	168.76	165.26	162.25	159.65	157.39	149.74	145.69	143.48	142.24
20,000	244.54	236.91	230.47	225.01	220.34	216.33	212.86	209.86	199.65	194.26	191.30	189.66
25,000	305.67	296.13	288.09	281.26	275.43	270.41	266.08	262.32	249.56	242.82	239.13	237.07
30,000	366.81	355.36	345.71	337.51	330.51	324.49	319.29	314.78	299.48	291.38	286.95	284.48
35,000	427.94	414.58	403.33	393.77	385.60	378.57	372.51	367.24	349.39	339.95	334.78	331.90
40,000	489.08	473.81	460.94	450.02	440.68	432.65	425.72	419.71	399.30	388.51	382.60	379.31
45,000	550.21	533.03	518.56	506.27	495.76	486.73	478.93	472.17	449.21	437.07	430.43	426.72
50,000	611.34	592.26	576.18	562.52	550.85	540.82	532.15	524.63	499.12	485.64	478.25	474.13
55,000	672.48	651.48	633.79	618.77	605.93	594.90	585.36	577.10	549.04	534.20	526.08	521.55
60,000	733.61	710.71	691.41	675.02	661.02	648.98	638.58	629.56	598.95	582.76	573.90	568.96
65,000	794.75	769.94	749.03	731.28	716.10	703.06	691.79	682.02	648.86	631.32	621.73	616.37
70,000	855.88	829.16	806.65	787.53	771.19	757.14	745.01	734.48	698.77	679.89	669.55	663.79
75,000	917.01	888.39	864.26	843.78	826.27	811.22	798.22	786.95	748.68	728.45	717.38	711.20
80,000	978.15	947.61	921.88	900.03	881.35	865.30	851.44	839.41	798.60	777.01	765.20	758.61
85,000	1039.28	1006.84	979.50	956.28	936.44	919.38	904.65	891.87	848.51	825.58	813.02	806.02
90,000	1100.41	1066.06	1037.12	1012.53	991.52	973.46	957.86	944.34	898.42	874.14	860.85	853.44
95,000	1161.55	1125.29	1094.73	1068.79	1046.61	1027.54	1011.08	996.80	948.33	922.70	908.67	900.85
100,000	1222.68	1184.51	1152.35	1125.04	1101.69	1081.63	1064.29	1049.26	998.24	971.27	956.50	948.26
105,000	1283.82	1243.74	1209.97	1181.29	1156.78	1135.71	1117.51	1101.72	1048.16	1019.83	1004.32	995.68
110,000	1344.95	1302.96	1267.58	1237.54	1211.86	1189.79	1170.72	1154.19	1098.07	1068.39	1052.15	1043.09
115,000	1406.08	1362.19	1325.20	1293.79	1266.95	1243.87	1223.94	1206.65	1147.98	1116.96	1099.97	1090.50
120,000	1467.22	1421.41	1382.82	1350.04	1322.03	1297.96	1277.15	1260.11	1197.89	1165.52	1147.80	1107.91
125,000	1528.35	1480.64	1440.44	1406.30	1377.11	1352.03	1330.37	1311.58	1247.80	1214.08	1195.62	1185.33
130,000	1589.49	1539.87	1498.05	1462.55	1432.20	1406.11	1383.58	1364.04	1297.72	1262.64	1243.45	1232.74
135,000	1650.62	1599.09	1555.67	1518.80	1487.28	1460.19	1436.79	1416.50	1347.63	1311.21	1291.27	1280.15
140,000	1711.75	1658.32	1613.29	1575.05	1542.37	1514.27	1490.01	1468.96	1397.54	1359.77	1339.10	1327.57
145,000	1772.89	1717.54	1670.90	1631.30	1597.45	1568.35	1543.22	1521.43	1447.45	1408.33	1386.92	1374.98
150,000	1834.02	1776.77	1728.52	1687.55	1652.54	1622.44	1596.44	1573.89	1497.36	1456.90	1434.75	1422.39
155,000	1895.15	1835.99	1786.14	1743.81	1707.62	1676.52	1649.65	1626.35	1547.28	1505.46	1482.57	1469.80
160,000	1956.29	1895.22	1843.76	1800.06	1762.70	1730.60	1702.87	1678.81	1597.19	1554.02	1530.40	1517.22
165,000	2017.42	1954.44	1901.37	1856.31	1817.79	1784.68	1756.08	1731.28	1647.10	1602.59	1578.22	1564.63
170,000	2078.56	2013.67	1958.99	1912.56	1872.87	1838.76	1809.30	1783.74	1697.01	1651.15	1626.04	1612.04
175,000	2139.69	2072.89	2016.61	1968.81	1927.96	1892.84	1862.51	1836.20	1746.92	1699.71	1673.87	1659.46
180,000	2200.82	2132.12	2074.23	2025.06	1983.04	1946.92	1915.72	1888.67	1796.84	1748.28	1721.69	1706.87
185,000	2261.96	2191.34	2131.84	2081.32	2038.13	2001.00	1968.94	1941.13	1846.75	1796.84	1769.52	1754.28
190,000	2323.09	2250.57	2189.46	2137.57	2093.21	2055.08	2022.15	1993.59	1896.66	1845.40	1817.34	1801.69
195,000	2384.23	2309.80	2247.08	2193.82	2148.30	2109.16	2075.37	2046.05	1946.57	1893.96	1865.17	1849.11
200,000	2445.36	2369.02	2304.69	2250.07	2203.38	2163.25	2128.58	2098.52	1996.48	1942.53	1912.99	1896.52
205,000	2506.49	2428.25	2362.31	2306.32	2258.46	2217.33	2181.80	2150.98	2046.40	1991.09	1960.82	1943.93
210,000	2567.63	2487.47	2419.93	2362.57	2313.55	2271.41	2235.01	2203.44	2096.31	2039.65	2008.64	1991.35
215,000	2628.76	2546.70	2477.55	2418.82	2368.63	2325.49	2288.22	2255.91	2146.22	2088.22	2056.47	2038.76
220,000	2689.90	2605.92	2535.16	2475.08	2423.72	2379.57	2341.44	2308.37	2196.13	2136.78	2104.29	2086.17
225,000	2751.03	2665.15	2592.78	2531.33	2478.80	2433.65	2394.65	2360.83	2246.04	2185.34	2152.12	2133.58
230,000	2812.16	2724.37	2650.40	2587.58	2533.89	2487.73	2447.87	2413.29	2295.96	2233.91	2199.94	2181.00
235,000	2873.30	2783.60	2708.01	2643.83	2588.97	2541.81	2501.08	2465.76	2345.87	2282.47	2247.77	2228.41
240,000	2934.43	2842.82	2765.63	2700.08	2644.05	2595.89	2554.30	2518.22	2395.78	2331.03	2295.59	2275.82
245,000	2995.56	2902.05	2823.25	2756.33	2699.14	2649.97	2607.51	2570.68	2445.69	2379.60	2343.42	2323.24
250,000	3056.70	2961.27	2880.87	2812.59	2754.22	2704.06	2660.73	2623.15	2495.60	2428.16	2391.24	2370.65
255,000	3117.83	3020.50	2938.48	2868.84	2809.31	2758.14	2713.94	2675.61	2545.52	2476.72	2439.06	2418.06
260,000	3178.97	3079.73	2996.10	2925.09	2864.39	2812.22	2767.15	2728.07	2595.43	2525.28	2486.89	2465.47
265,000	3240.10	3138.95	3053.72	2981.34	2919.48	2866.30	2820.37	2780.53	2645.34	2573.85	2534.71	2512.89
270,000	3301.23	3198.18	3111.34	3037.59	2974.56	2920.38	2873.58	2833.00	2695.25	2622.41	2582.54	2560.30
280,000	3423.50	3316.63	3226.57	3150.10	3084.73	3028.54	2980.01	2937.92	2795.08	2719.54	2678.19	2655.13
290,000	3545.77	3435.08	3341.80	3262.60	3194.90	3136.70	3086.44	3042.85	2894.90	2816.66	2773.84	2749.95
300,000	3668.04	3553.53	3457.04	3375.10	3305.07	3244.87	3192.87	3147.77	2994.72	2913.79	2869.49	2844.78

11.50%　　MONTHLY AMORTIZING PAYMENTS

AMOUNT OF LOAN	NUMBER OF YEARS IN TERM											
	1	2	3	4	5	6	7	8	9	10	11	12
$ 50	4.44	2.35	1.65	1.31	1.10	0.97	0.87	0.80	0.75	0.71	0.67	0.65
100	8.87	4.69	3.30	2.61	2.20	1.93	1.74	1.60	1.50	1.41	1.34	1.29
200	17.73	9.37	6.60	5.22	4.40	3.86	3.48	3.20	2.99	2.82	2.68	2.57
300	26.59	14.06	9.90	7.83	6.60	5.79	5.22	4.80	4.48	4.22	4.02	3.85
400	35.45	18.74	13.20	10.44	8.80	7.72	6.96	6.40	5.97	5.63	5.36	5.14
500	44.31	23.43	16.49	13.05	11.00	9.65	8.70	7.99	7.46	7.03	6.70	6.42
600	53.17	28.11	19.79	15.66	13.20	11.58	10.44	9.59	8.95	8.44	8.04	7.70
700	62.04	32.79	23.09	18.27	15.40	13.51	12.18	11.19	10.44	9.85	9.37	8.99
800	70.90	37.48	26.39	20.88	17.60	15.44	13.91	12.79	11.93	11.25	10.71	10.27
900	79.76	42.16	29.68	23.49	19.80	17.37	15.65	14.39	13.42	12.66	12.05	11.55
1,000	88.62	46.85	32.98	26.09	22.00	19.30	17.39	15.98	14.91	14.06	13.39	12.84
2,000	177.24	93.69	65.96	52.18	43.99	38.59	34.78	31.96	29.81	28.12	26.77	25.67
3,000	265.85	140.53	98.93	78.27	65.98	57.88	52.16	47.94	44.72	42.18	40.16	38.50
4,000	354.47	187.37	131.91	104.36	87.98	77.17	69.55	63.92	59.62	56.24	53.54	51.34
5,000	443.08	234.21	164.89	130.45	109.97	96.46	86.94	79.90	74.52	70.30	66.92	64.17
6,000	531.70	281.05	197.86	156.54	131.96	115.75	104.32	95.88	89.43	84.36	80.31	77.00
7,000	620.31	327.89	230.84	182.63	153.95	135.04	121.71	111.86	104.33	98.42	93.69	89.84
8,000	708.93	374.73	263.81	208.72	175.95	154.33	139.10	127.84	119.23	112.48	107.07	102.67
9,000	797.54	421.57	296.79	234.81	197.94	173.63	156.48	143.82	134.14	126.54	120.46	115.50
10,000	886.16	468.41	329.77	260.90	219.93	192.92	173.87	159.80	149.04	140.60	133.84	128.34
15,000	1329.23	702.61	494.65	391.34	329.89	289.37	260.80	239.70	223.56	210.90	200.76	192.50
20,000	1772.31	936.81	659.53	521.79	439.86	385.83	347.73	319.59	298.08	281.20	267.68	256.67
25,000	2215.38	1171.01	824.41	652.23	549.82	482.28	434.67	399.49	372.60	351.49	334.59	320.83
30,000	2658.46	1405.21	989.29	782.68	659.78	578.74	521.60	479.39	447.11	421.79	401.51	385.00
35,000	3101.53	1639.42	1154.17	913.12	769.75	675.20	608.53	559.28	521.63	492.09	468.43	449.17
40,000	3544.61	1873.62	1319.05	1043.57	879.71	771.65	695.46	639.18	596.15	562.39	535.35	513.33
45,000	3987.68	2107.82	1483.93	1174.01	989.67	868.11	782.40	719.08	670.67	632.68	602.26	577.50
50,000	4430.76	2342.02	1648.81	1304.46	1099.64	964.56	869.33	798.97	745.19	702.98	669.18	641.66
55,000	4873.83	2576.22	1813.69	1434.90	1209.60	1061.02	956.26	878.87	819.71	773.28	736.10	705.83
60,000	5316.91	2810.42	1978.57	1565.35	1319.56	1157.47	1043.19	958.77	894.22	843.58	803.02	769.99
65,000	5759.98	3044.63	2143.45	1695.79	1429.52	1253.93	1130.12	1038.66	968.74	913.88	869.93	834.16
70,000	6203.06	3278.83	2308.33	1826.24	1539.49	1350.39	1217.06	1118.56	1043.26	984.17	936.85	898.33
75,000	6646.13	3513.03	2473.21	1956.68	1649.45	1446.84	1303.99	1198.46	1117.78	1054.47	1003.77	962.49
80,000	7089.21	3747.23	2638.09	2087.13	1759.41	1543.30	1390.92	1278.35	1192.30	1124.77	1070.69	1026.66
85,000	7532.28	3981.43	2802.97	2217.57	1869.38	1639.75	1477.85	1358.25	1266.82	1195.07	1137.60	1090.82
90,000	7975.36	4215.63	2967.85	2348.02	1979.34	1736.21	1564.79	1438.15	1341.33	1265.36	1204.52	1154.99
95,000	8418.44	4449.83	3132.73	2478.46	2089.30	1832.66	1651.72	1518.05	1415.85	1335.66	1271.44	1219.16
100,000	8861.51	4684.04	3297.61	2608.91	2199.27	1929.12	1738.65	1597.94	1490.37	1405.96	1338.36	1283.32
105,000	9304.59	4918.24	3462.49	2739.35	2309.23	2025.58	1825.58	1677.84	1564.89	1476.26	1405.27	1347.49
110,000	9747.66	5152.44	3627.37	2869.80	2419.19	2122.03	1912.52	1757.74	1639.41	1546.55	1472.19	1411.65
115,000	10190.74	5386.64	3792.25	3000.24	2529.15	2218.49	1999.45	1837.63	1713.93	1616.85	1539.11	1475.82
120,000	10633.81	5620.84	3957.13	3130.69	2639.12	2314.94	2086.38	1917.53	1788.44	1687.15	1606.03	1539.98
125,000	11076.89	5855.04	4122.01	3261.13	2749.08	2411.40	2173.31	1997.43	1862.96	1757.45	1672.94	1604.15
130,000	11519.96	6089.25	4286.89	3391.58	2859.04	2507.86	2260.24	2077.32	1937.48	1827.75	1739.86	1668.32
135,000	11963.04	6323.45	4451.77	3522.02	2969.01	2604.31	2347.18	2157.22	2012.00	1898.04	1806.78	1732.48
140,000	12406.11	6557.65	4616.65	3652.47	3078.97	2700.77	2434.11	2237.12	2086.52	1968.34	1873.70	1796.65
145,000	12849.19	6791.85	4781.53	3782.91	3188.93	2797.22	2521.04	2317.01	2161.04	2038.64	1940.61	1860.81
150,000	13292.26	7026.05	4946.41	3913.36	3298.90	2893.68	2607.97	2396.91	2235.55	2108.94	2007.53	1924.98
155,000	13735.34	7260.25	5111.29	4043.80	3408.86	2990.13	2694.91	2476.81	2310.07	2179.23	2074.45	1989.15
160,000	14178.41	7494.46	5276.17	4174.25	3518.82	3086.59	2781.84	2556.70	2384.59	2249.53	2141.37	2053.31
165,000	14621.49	7728.66	5441.05	4304.69	3628.79	3183.05	2868.77	2636.60	2459.11	2319.83	2208.28	2117.48
170,000	15064.56	7962.86	5605.93	4435.14	3738.75	3279.50	2955.70	2716.50	2533.63	2390.13	2275.20	2181.64
175,000	15507.64	8197.06	5770.81	4565.58	3848.71	3375.96	3042.64	2796.40	2608.15	2460.43	2342.12	2245.81
180,000	15950.71	8431.26	5935.69	4696.03	3958.67	3472.41	3129.57	2876.29	2682.66	2530.72	2409.04	2309.97
185,000	16393.79	8665.46	6100.57	4826.47	4068.64	3568.87	3216.50	2956.19	2757.18	2601.02	2475.95	2374.14
190,000	16836.87	8899.66	6265.45	4956.92	4178.60	3665.32	3303.43	3036.09	2831.70	2671.32	2542.87	2438.31
195,000	17279.94	9133.87	6430.33	5087.36	4288.56	3761.78	3390.36	3115.98	2906.22	2741.62	2609.79	2502.47
200,000	17723.02	9368.07	6595.21	5217.81	4398.53	3858.24	3477.30	3195.88	2980.74	2811.91	2676.71	2566.64
205,000	18166.09	9602.27	6760.09	5348.25	4508.49	3954.69	3564.23	3275.78	3055.26	2882.21	2743.62	2630.80
210,000	18609.17	9836.47	6924.97	5478.70	4618.45	4051.15	3651.16	3355.67	3129.77	2952.51	2810.54	2694.97
215,000	19052.24	10070.67	7089.85	5609.14	4728.42	4147.60	3738.09	3435.57	3204.29	3022.81	2877.46	2759.14
220,000	19495.32	10304.87	7254.73	5739.59	4838.38	4244.06	3825.03	3515.47	3278.81	3093.10	2944.38	2823.30
225,000	19938.39	10539.08	7419.61	5870.03	4948.34	4340.52	3911.96	3595.36	3353.33	3163.40	3011.29	2887.47
230,000	20381.47	10773.28	7584.49	6000.48	5058.30	4436.97	3998.89	3675.26	3427.85	3233.70	3078.21	2951.63
235,000	20824.54	11007.48	7749.37	6130.92	5168.27	4533.43	4085.82	3755.16	3502.37	3304.00	3145.13	3015.80
240,000	21267.62	11241.68	7914.25	6261.37	5278.23	4629.88	4172.76	3835.05	3576.88	3374.30	3212.05	3079.96
245,000	21710.69	11475.88	8079.13	6391.81	5388.19	4726.34	4259.69	3914.95	3651.40	3444.59	3278.96	3144.13
250,000	22153.77	11710.08	8244.01	6522.26	5498.16	4822.79	4346.62	3994.85	3725.92	3514.89	3345.88	3208.30
255,000	22596.84	11944.29	8408.89	6652.70	5608.12	4919.25	4433.55	4074.75	3800.44	3585.19	3412.80	3272.46
260,000	23039.92	12178.49	8573.77	6783.15	5718.08	5015.71	4520.48	4154.64	3874.96	3655.49	3479.72	3336.63
265,000	23482.99	12412.69	8738.65	6913.59	5828.05	5112.16	4607.42	4234.54	3949.47	3725.78	3546.63	3400.79
270,000	23926.07	12646.89	8903.53	7044.04	5938.01	5208.62	4694.35	4314.44	4023.99	3796.08	3613.55	3464.96
280,000	24812.22	13115.29	9233.29	7304.93	6157.94	5401.53	4868.21	4474.23	4173.03	3936.68	3747.39	3593.29
290,000	25698.37	13583.70	9563.05	7565.82	6377.86	5594.44	5042.08	4634.02	4322.07	4077.27	3881.22	3721.62
300,000	26584.52	14052.10	9892.81	7826.71	6597.79	5787.35	5215.94	4793.82	4471.10	4217.87	4015.06	3849.95

78

AMOUNT OF LOAN	NUMBER OF YEARS IN TERM											
	13	14	15	16	17	18	19	20	25	30	35	40
$ 50	0.62	0.61	0.59	0.58	0.56	0.55	0.55	0.54	0.51	0.50	0.49	0.49
100	1.24	1.21	1.17	1.15	1.12	1.10	1.09	1.07	1.02	1.00	0.98	0.97
200	2.48	2.41	2.34	2.29	2.24	2.20	2.17	2.14	2.04	1.99	1.96	1.94
300	3.72	3.61	3.51	3.43	3.36	3.30	3.25	3.20	3.05	2.98	2.93	2.91
400	4.96	4.81	4.68	4.57	4.48	4.40	4.33	4.27	4.07	3.97	3.91	3.88
500	6.19	6.01	5.85	5.71	5.60	5.50	5.41	5.34	5.09	4.96	4.89	4.85
600	7.43	7.21	7.01	6.85	6.71	6.59	6.49	6.40	6.10	5.95	5.86	5.81
700	8.67	8.41	8.18	7.99	7.83	7.69	7.57	7.47	7.12	6.94	6.84	6.78
800	9.91	9.61	9.35	9.13	8.95	8.79	8.65	8.54	8.14	7.93	7.81	7.75
900	11.15	10.81	10.52	10.28	10.07	9.89	9.74	9.60	9.15	8.92	8.79	8.72
1,000	12.38	12.01	11.69	11.42	11.19	10.99	10.82	10.67	10.17	9.91	9.77	9.69
2,000	24.76	24.01	23.37	22.83	22.37	21.97	21.63	21.33	20.33	19.81	19.53	19.37
3,000	37.14	36.01	35.05	34.24	33.55	32.95	32.44	32.00	30.50	29.71	29.29	29.05
4,000	49.52	48.01	46.73	45.65	44.73	43.94	43.25	42.66	40.66	39.62	39.05	38.74
5,000	61.90	60.01	58.41	57.06	55.91	54.92	54.07	53.33	50.83	49.52	48.81	48.42
6,000	74.28	72.01	70.10	68.47	67.09	65.90	64.88	63.99	60.99	59.42	58.57	58.10
7,000	86.66	84.01	81.78	79.89	78.27	76.89	75.69	74.66	71.16	69.33	68.33	67.78
8,000	99.04	96.01	93.46	91.30	89.45	87.87	86.50	85.32	81.32	79.23	78.09	77.47
9,000	111.42	108.01	105.14	102.71	100.63	98.85	97.31	95.98	91.49	89.13	87.85	87.15
10,000	123.80	120.01	116.82	114.12	111.81	109.83	108.13	106.65	101.65	99.03	97.62	96.83
15,000	185.69	180.01	175.23	171.18	167.72	164.75	162.19	159.97	152.48	148.55	146.42	145.25
20,000	247.59	240.02	233.64	228.24	223.62	219.66	216.25	213.29	203.30	198.06	195.23	193.66
25,000	309.48	300.02	292.05	285.30	279.53	274.58	270.31	266.61	254.12	247.58	244.03	242.08
30,000	371.38	360.02	350.46	342.35	335.43	329.49	324.37	319.93	304.95	297.09	292.84	290.49
35,000	433.28	420.02	408.87	399.41	391.34	384.41	378.43	373.26	355.77	346.61	341.64	338.90
40,000	495.17	480.03	467.28	456.47	447.24	439.32	432.49	426.58	406.59	396.12	390.45	387.32
45,000	557.07	540.03	525.69	513.53	503.15	494.24	486.55	479.90	457.42	445.64	439.25	435.73
50,000	618.96	600.03	584.10	570.59	559.05	549.15	540.61	533.22	508.24	495.15	488.06	484.15
55,000	680.86	660.04	642.51	627.65	614.96	604.07	594.67	586.54	559.06	544.67	536.86	532.56
60,000	742.76	720.04	700.92	684.70	670.86	658.98	648.74	639.86	609.89	594.18	585.67	580.97
65,000	804.65	780.04	759.33	741.76	726.77	713.90	702.80	693.18	660.71	643.69	634.47	629.39
70,000	866.55	840.04	817.74	798.82	782.67	768.81	756.86	746.51	711.53	693.21	683.28	677.80
75,000	928.44	900.05	876.15	855.88	838.58	823.73	810.92	799.83	762.36	742.72	732.09	726.22
80,000	990.34	960.05	934.56	912.94	894.48	878.64	864.98	853.15	813.18	792.24	780.89	774.63
85,000	1052.24	1020.05	992.97	970.00	950.39	933.56	919.04	906.47	864.00	841.75	829.70	823.04
90,000	1114.13	1080.05	1051.38	1027.05	1006.29	988.47	973.10	959.79	914.83	891.27	878.50	871.46
95,000	1176.03	1140.06	1109.79	1084.11	1062.20	1043.39	1027.16	1013.11	965.65	940.78	927.31	919.87
100,000	1237.92	1200.06	1168.19	1141.17	1118.10	1098.30	1081.22	1066.43	1016.47	990.30	976.11	968.29
105,000	1299.82	1260.06	1226.60	1198.23	1174.01	1153.22	1135.28	1119.76	1067.30	1039.81	1024.92	1016.70
110,000	1361.71	1320.07	1285.01	1255.29	1229.91	1208.13	1189.34	1173.08	1118.12	1089.33	1073.72	1065.12
115,000	1423.61	1380.07	1343.42	1312.34	1285.82	1263.04	1243.41	1226.40	1168.94	1138.84	1122.53	1113.53
120,000	1485.51	1440.07	1401.83	1369.40	1341.72	1317.96	1297.47	1279.72	1219.77	1188.35	1171.33	1161.94
125,000	1547.40	1500.07	1460.24	1426.46	1397.63	1372.87	1351.53	1333.04	1270.59	1237.87	1220.14	1210.36
130,000	1609.30	1560.08	1518.65	1483.52	1453.53	1427.79	1405.59	1386.36	1321.41	1287.38	1268.94	1258.77
135,000	1671.19	1620.08	1577.06	1540.58	1509.43	1482.70	1459.65	1439.69	1372.24	1336.90	1317.75	1307.19
140,000	1733.09	1680.08	1635.47	1597.64	1565.34	1537.62	1513.71	1493.01	1423.06	1386.41	1366.56	1355.60
145,000	1794.99	1740.09	1693.88	1654.69	1621.24	1592.53	1567.77	1546.33	1473.88	1435.93	1415.36	1404.01
150,000	1856.88	1800.09	1752.29	1711.75	1677.15	1647.45	1621.83	1599.65	1524.71	1485.44	1464.17	1452.43
155,000	1918.78	1860.09	1810.70	1768.81	1733.05	1702.36	1675.89	1652.97	1575.53	1534.96	1512.97	1500.84
160,000	1980.67	1920.09	1869.11	1825.87	1788.96	1757.28	1729.95	1706.29	1626.36	1584.47	1561.78	1549.26
165,000	2042.57	1980.10	1927.52	1882.93	1844.86	1812.19	1784.01	1759.61	1677.18	1633.99	1610.58	1597.67
170,000	2104.47	2040.10	1985.93	1939.99	1900.77	1867.11	1838.08	1812.94	1728.00	1683.50	1659.39	1646.08
175,000	2166.36	2100.10	2044.34	1997.04	1956.67	1922.02	1892.14	1866.26	1778.83	1733.02	1708.19	1694.50
180,000	2228.26	2160.10	2102.75	2054.10	2012.58	1976.94	1946.20	1919.58	1829.65	1782.53	1757.00	1742.91
185,000	2290.15	2220.11	2161.16	2111.16	2068.48	2031.85	2000.26	1972.90	1880.47	1832.04	1805.80	1791.33
190,000	2352.05	2280.11	2219.57	2168.22	2124.39	2086.77	2054.32	2026.22	1931.30	1881.56	1854.61	1839.74
195,000	2413.94	2340.11	2277.98	2225.28	2180.29	2141.68	2108.38	2079.54	1982.12	1931.07	1903.41	1888.15
200,000	2475.84	2400.12	2336.38	2282.33	2236.20	2196.60	2162.44	2132.86	2032.94	1980.59	1952.22	1936.57
205,000	2537.74	2460.12	2394.79	2339.39	2292.10	2251.51	2216.50	2186.19	2083.77	2030.10	2001.03	1984.98
210,000	2599.63	2520.12	2453.20	2396.45	2348.01	2306.43	2270.56	2239.51	2134.59	2079.62	2049.83	2033.40
215,000	2661.53	2580.12	2511.61	2453.51	2403.91	2361.34	2324.62	2292.83	2185.41	2129.13	2098.64	2081.81
220,000	2723.42	2640.13	2570.02	2510.57	2459.82	2416.25	2378.68	2346.15	2236.24	2178.65	2147.44	2130.23
225,000	2785.32	2700.13	2628.43	2567.63	2515.72	2471.17	2432.75	2399.47	2287.06	2228.16	2196.25	2178.64
230,000	2847.22	2760.13	2686.84	2624.68	2571.63	2526.08	2486.81	2452.79	2337.88	2277.68	2245.05	2227.05
235,000	2909.11	2820.14	2745.25	2681.74	2627.53	2581.00	2540.87	2506.11	2388.71	2327.19	2293.86	2275.47
240,000	2971.01	2880.14	2803.66	2738.80	2683.44	2635.91	2594.93	2559.44	2439.53	2376.70	2342.66	2323.88
245,000	3032.90	2940.14	2862.07	2795.86	2739.34	2690.83	2648.99	2612.76	2490.35	2426.22	2391.47	2372.30
250,000	3094.80	3000.14	2920.48	2852.92	2795.25	2745.74	2703.05	2666.08	2541.18	2475.73	2440.27	2420.71
255,000	3156.70	3060.15	2978.89	2909.98	2851.15	2800.66	2757.11	2719.40	2592.00	2525.25	2489.08	2469.12
260,000	3218.59	3120.15	3037.30	2967.03	2907.06	2855.57	2811.17	2772.72	2642.82	2574.76	2537.88	2517.54
265,000	3280.49	3180.15	3095.71	3024.09	2962.96	2910.49	2865.23	2826.04	2693.65	2624.28	2586.69	2565.95
270,000	3342.38	3240.15	3154.12	3081.15	3018.86	2965.40	2919.29	2879.37	2744.47	2673.79	2635.49	2614.37
280,000	3466.17	3360.16	3270.94	3195.27	3130.67	3075.23	3027.42	2986.01	2846.12	2772.82	2733.11	2711.19
290,000	3589.97	3480.17	3387.76	3309.38	3242.48	3185.06	3135.54	3092.65	2947.76	2871.85	2830.72	2808.02
300,000	3713.76	3600.17	3504.57	3423.50	3354.29	3294.89	3243.66	3199.29	3049.41	2970.88	2928.33	2904.85

11.75%

AMOUNT OF LOAN	NUMBER OF YEARS IN TERM											
	1	2	3	4	5	6	7	8	9	10	11	12
$ 50	4.44	2.35	1.66	1.32	1.11	0.98	0.88	0.81	0.76	0.72	0.68	0.65
100	8.88	4.70	3.31	2.63	2.22	1.95	1.76	1.62	1.51	1.43	1.36	1.30
200	17.75	9.40	6.62	5.25	4.43	3.89	3.51	3.23	3.01	2.85	2.71	2.60
300	26.62	14.09	9.93	7.87	6.64	5.83	5.26	4.84	4.52	4.27	4.06	3.90
400	35.50	18.79	13.24	10.49	8.85	7.77	7.01	6.45	6.02	5.69	5.42	5.20
500	44.37	23.48	16.55	13.11	11.06	9.72	8.76	8.06	7.53	7.11	6.77	6.50
600	53.24	28.18	19.86	15.73	13.28	11.66	10.52	9.67	9.03	8.53	8.12	7.79
700	62.12	32.87	23.17	18.35	15.49	13.60	12.27	11.29	10.54	9.95	9.48	9.09
800	70.99	37.57	26.48	20.97	17.70	15.54	14.02	12.90	12.04	11.37	10.83	10.39
900	79.86	42.27	29.79	23.60	19.91	17.48	15.77	14.51	13.54	12.79	12.18	11.69
1,000	88.74	46.96	33.10	26.22	22.12	19.43	17.52	16.12	15.05	14.21	13.54	12.99
2,000	177.47	93.92	66.20	52.43	44.24	38.85	35.04	32.24	30.09	28.41	27.07	25.97
3,000	266.20	140.88	99.29	78.64	66.36	58.27	52.56	48.35	45.14	42.61	40.60	38.95
4,000	354.93	187.83	132.39	104.85	88.48	77.69	70.08	64.47	60.18	56.82	54.13	51.94
5,000	443.66	234.79	165.48	131.06	110.60	97.11	87.60	80.58	75.22	71.02	67.66	64.92
6,000	532.40	281.75	198.58	157.27	132.71	116.53	105.12	96.70	90.27	85.22	81.19	77.90
7,000	621.13	328.70	231.67	183.48	154.83	135.95	122.64	112.82	105.31	99.43	94.72	90.89
8,000	709.86	375.66	264.77	209.70	176.95	155.37	140.16	128.93	120.35	113.63	108.25	103.87
9,000	798.59	422.62	297.86	235.91	199.07	174.79	157.68	145.05	135.40	127.83	121.78	116.85
10,000	887.32	469.57	330.96	262.12	221.19	194.21	175.20	161.16	150.44	142.03	135.31	129.84
15,000	1330.98	704.36	496.43	393.17	331.78	291.31	262.79	241.74	225.66	213.05	202.96	194.75
20,000	1774.64	939.14	661.91	524.23	442.37	388.41	350.39	322.32	300.88	284.06	270.61	259.67
25,000	2218.30	1173.93	827.38	655.29	552.96	485.52	437.99	402.90	376.10	355.08	338.26	324.59
30,000	2661.96	1408.71	992.86	786.34	663.55	582.62	525.58	483.48	451.31	426.09	405.91	389.50
35,000	3105.62	1643.49	1158.33	917.40	774.15	679.72	613.18	564.06	526.53	497.11	473.57	454.42
40,000	3549.28	1878.28	1323.81	1048.46	884.74	776.82	700.78	644.64	601.75	568.12	541.22	519.34
45,000	3992.94	2113.06	1489.28	1179.51	995.33	873.92	788.37	725.22	676.97	639.14	608.87	584.25
50,000	4436.60	2347.85	1654.76	1310.57	1105.92	971.03	875.97	805.79	752.19	710.15	676.52	649.17
55,000	4880.26	2582.63	1820.23	1441.62	1216.51	1068.13	963.57	886.37	827.40	781.17	744.17	714.08
60,000	5323.92	2817.41	1985.71	1572.68	1327.10	1165.23	1051.16	966.95	902.62	852.18	811.82	779.00
65,000	5767.58	3052.20	2151.18	1703.74	1437.70	1262.33	1138.76	1047.53	977.84	923.20	879.47	843.92
70,000	6211.24	3286.98	2316.66	1834.79	1548.29	1359.44	1226.36	1128.11	1053.06	994.21	947.13	908.83
75,000	6654.90	3521.77	2482.13	1965.85	1658.88	1456.54	1313.95	1208.69	1128.28	1065.23	1014.78	973.75
80,000	7098.56	3756.55	2647.61	2096.91	1769.47	1553.64	1401.55	1289.27	1203.49	1136.24	1082.43	1038.67
85,000	7542.21	3991.33	2813.08	2227.96	1880.06	1650.74	1489.15	1369.85	1278.71	1207.26	1150.08	1103.58
90,000	7985.87	4226.12	2978.56	2359.02	1990.65	1747.84	1576.74	1450.43	1353.93	1278.27	1217.73	1168.50
95,000	8429.53	4460.90	3144.03	2490.07	2101.25	1844.95	1664.34	1531.01	1429.15	1349.28	1285.38	1233.41
100,000	8873.19	4695.69	3309.51	2621.13	2211.84	1942.05	1751.94	1611.58	1504.37	1420.30	1353.03	1298.33
105,000	9316.85	4930.47	3474.98	2752.19	2322.43	2039.15	1839.53	1692.16	1579.58	1491.31	1420.69	1363.25
110,000	9760.51	5165.25	3640.46	2883.24	2433.02	2136.25	1927.13	1772.74	1654.80	1562.33	1488.34	1428.16
115,000	10204.17	5400.04	3805.93	3014.30	2543.61	2233.35	2014.73	1853.32	1730.02	1633.34	1555.99	1493.08
120,000	10647.83	5634.82	3971.41	3145.36	2654.20	2330.46	2102.32	1933.90	1805.24	1704.36	1623.64	1558.00
125,000	11091.49	5869.61	4136.88	3276.41	2764.80	2427.56	2189.92	2014.48	1880.46	1775.37	1691.29	1622.91
130,000	11535.15	6104.39	4302.36	3407.47	2875.39	2524.66	2277.52	2095.06	1955.67	1846.39	1758.94	1687.83
135,000	11978.81	6339.17	4467.83	3538.52	2985.98	2621.76	2365.11	2175.64	2030.89	1917.40	1826.59	1752.74
140,000	12422.47	6573.96	4633.31	3669.58	3096.57	2718.87	2452.71	2256.22	2106.11	1988.42	1894.25	1817.66
145,000	12866.13	6808.74	4798.78	3800.64	3207.16	2815.97	2540.31	2336.80	2181.33	2059.43	1961.90	1882.58
150,000	13309.79	7043.53	4964.26	3931.69	3317.75	2913.07	2627.90	2417.37	2256.55	2130.45	2029.55	1947.49
155,000	13753.45	7278.31	5129.73	4062.75	3428.34	3010.17	2715.50	2497.95	2331.76	2201.46	2097.20	2012.41
160,000	14197.11	7513.09	5295.21	4193.81	3538.94	3107.27	2803.10	2578.53	2406.98	2272.48	2164.85	2077.33
165,000	14640.77	7747.88	5460.69	4324.86	3649.53	3204.38	2890.69	2659.11	2482.20	2343.49	2232.50	2142.24
170,000	15084.42	7982.66	5626.16	4455.92	3760.12	3301.48	2978.29	2739.69	2557.42	2414.51	2300.15	2207.16
175,000	15528.08	8217.45	5791.64	4586.97	3870.71	3398.58	3065.89	2820.27	2632.64	2485.52	2367.81	2272.07
180,000	15971.74	8452.23	5957.11	4718.03	3981.30	3495.68	3153.48	2900.85	2707.85	2556.54	2435.46	2336.99
185,000	16415.40	8687.01	6122.59	4849.09	4091.89	3592.78	3241.08	2981.43	2783.07	2627.55	2503.11	2401.91
190,000	16859.06	8921.80	6288.06	4980.14	4202.49	3689.89	3328.68	3062.01	2858.29	2698.56	2570.76	2466.82
195,000	17302.72	9156.58	6453.54	5111.20	4313.08	3786.99	3416.27	3142.58	2933.51	2769.58	2638.41	2531.74
200,000	17746.38	9391.37	6619.01	5242.26	4423.67	3884.09	3503.87	3223.16	3008.73	2840.59	2706.06	2596.66
205,000	18190.04	9626.15	6784.49	5373.31	4534.26	3981.19	3591.46	3303.74	3083.94	2911.61	2773.71	2661.57
210,000	18633.70	9860.93	6949.96	5504.37	4644.85	4078.30	3679.06	3384.32	3159.16	2982.62	2841.37	2726.49
215,000	19077.36	10095.72	7115.44	5635.42	4755.44	4175.40	3766.66	3464.90	3234.38	3053.64	2909.02	2791.40
220,000	19521.02	10330.50	7280.91	5766.48	4866.04	4272.50	3854.25	3545.48	3309.60	3124.65	2976.67	2856.32
225,000	19964.68	10565.29	7446.39	5897.54	4976.63	4369.60	3941.85	3626.06	3384.82	3195.67	3044.32	2921.24
230,000	20408.34	10800.07	7611.86	6028.59	5087.22	4466.70	4029.45	3706.64	3460.03	3266.68	3111.97	2986.15
235,000	20852.00	11034.86	7777.34	6159.65	5197.81	4563.81	4117.04	3787.22	3535.25	3337.70	3179.62	3051.07
240,000	21295.66	11269.64	7942.81	6290.71	5308.40	4660.91	4204.64	3867.80	3610.47	3408.71	3247.27	3115.99
245,000	21739.32	11504.42	8108.29	6421.76	5418.99	4758.01	4292.24	3948.37	3685.69	3479.73	3314.93	3180.90
250,000	22182.97	11739.21	8273.76	6552.82	5529.59	4855.11	4379.83	4028.95	3760.91	3550.74	3382.58	3245.82
255,000	22626.63	11973.99	8439.24	6683.87	5640.18	4952.21	4467.43	4109.53	3836.12	3621.76	3450.23	3310.74
260,000	23070.29	12208.78	8604.71	6814.93	5750.77	5049.32	4555.03	4190.11	3911.34	3692.77	3517.88	3375.65
265,000	23513.95	12443.56	8770.19	6945.99	5861.36	5146.42	4642.62	4270.69	3986.56	3763.79	3585.53	3440.57
270,000	23957.61	12678.34	8935.66	7077.04	5971.95	5243.52	4730.22	4351.27	4061.78	3834.80	3653.18	3505.48
280,000	24844.93	13147.91	9266.61	7339.16	6193.13	5437.73	4905.41	4512.43	4212.21	3976.83	3788.49	3635.32
290,000	25732.25	13617.48	9597.56	7601.27	6414.32	5631.93	5080.61	4673.59	4362.65	4118.86	3923.79	3765.15
300,000	26619.57	14087.05	9928.51	7863.38	6635.50	5826.13	5255.80	4834.74	4513.09	4260.89	4059.09	3894.98

AMOUNT OF LOAN	13	14	15	16	17	18	19	20	25	30	35	40
$ 50	0.63	0.61	0.60	0.58	0.57	0.56	0.55	0.55	0.52	0.51	0.50	0.50
100	1.26	1.22	1.19	1.16	1.14	1.12	1.10	1.09	1.04	1.01	1.00	0.99
200	2.51	2.44	2.37	2.32	2.27	2.24	2.20	2.17	2.07	2.02	2.00	1.98
300	3.76	3.65	3.56	3.48	3.41	3.35	3.30	3.26	3.11	3.03	2.99	2.97
400	5.02	4.87	4.74	4.63	4.54	4.47	4.40	4.34	4.14	4.04	3.99	3.96
500	6.27	6.08	5.93	5.79	5.68	5.58	5.50	5.42	5.18	5.05	4.98	4.95
600	7.52	7.30	7.11	6.95	6.81	6.70	6.59	6.51	6.21	6.06	5.98	5.94
700	8.78	8.51	8.29	8.11	7.95	7.81	7.69	7.59	7.25	7.07	6.98	6.92
800	10.03	9.73	9.48	9.26	9.08	8.93	8.79	8.67	8.28	8.08	7.97	7.91
900	11.28	10.95	10.66	10.42	10.22	10.04	9.89	9.76	9.32	9.09	8.97	8.90
1,000	12.54	12.16	11.85	11.58	11.35	11.16	10.99	10.84	10.35	10.10	9.96	9.89
2,000	25.07	24.32	23.69	23.15	22.70	22.31	21.97	21.68	20.70	20.19	19.92	19.77
3,000	37.60	36.48	35.53	34.73	34.04	33.46	32.95	32.52	31.05	30.29	29.88	29.66
4,000	50.13	48.63	47.37	46.30	45.39	44.61	43.94	43.35	41.40	40.38	39.84	39.54
5,000	62.67	60.79	59.21	57.87	56.74	55.76	54.92	54.19	51.74	50.48	49.79	49.42
6,000	75.20	72.95	71.05	69.45	68.08	66.91	65.90	65.03	62.09	60.57	59.75	59.31
7,000	87.73	85.10	82.89	81.02	79.43	78.06	76.88	75.86	72.44	70.66	69.71	69.19
8,000	100.26	97.26	94.74	92.60	90.77	89.21	87.87	86.70	82.79	80.76	79.67	79.07
9,000	112.80	109.42	106.58	104.17	102.12	100.36	98.85	97.54	93.14	90.85	89.63	88.96
10,000	125.33	121.57	118.42	115.74	113.47	111.51	109.83	108.38	103.48	100.95	99.58	98.84
15,000	187.99	182.36	177.62	173.61	170.20	167.27	164.74	162.56	155.22	151.42	149.37	148.26
20,000	250.65	243.14	236.83	231.48	226.93	223.02	219.66	216.75	206.96	201.89	199.16	197.68
25,000	313.32	303.93	296.04	289.35	283.66	278.77	274.57	270.93	258.70	252.36	248.95	247.10
30,000	375.98	364.71	355.24	347.22	340.39	334.53	329.48	325.12	310.44	302.83	298.74	296.51
35,000	438.64	425.50	414.45	405.09	397.12	390.28	384.39	379.30	362.18	353.30	348.53	345.93
40,000	501.30	486.28	473.66	462.96	453.85	446.03	439.31	433.49	413.92	403.77	398.32	395.35
45,000	563.97	547.07	532.86	520.83	510.58	501.79	494.22	487.07	465.66	454.24	448.11	444.77
50,000	626.63	607.85	592.07	578.70	567.31	557.54	549.13	541.06	517.40	504.71	497.90	494.19
55,000	689.29	668.64	651.28	636.57	624.04	613.29	604.04	596.04	569.14	555.18	547.69	543.61
60,000	751.95	729.42	710.48	694.44	680.77	669.05	658.96	650.23	620.88	605.65	597.48	593.02
65,000	814.62	790.21	769.69	752.31	737.50	724.80	713.87	704.41	672.62	656.12	647.27	642.44
70,000	877.28	850.99	828.90	810.18	794.23	780.56	768.78	758.60	724.36	706.59	697.06	691.86
75,000	939.94	911.78	888.10	868.05	850.96	836.31	823.69	812.79	776.10	757.06	746.85	741.28
80,000	1002.60	972.56	947.31	925.92	907.69	892.06	878.61	866.97	827.84	807.53	796.64	790.70
85,000	1065.27	1033.35	1006.52	983.79	964.42	947.82	933.52	921.16	879.58	858.00	846.43	840.11
90,000	1127.93	1094.13	1065.72	1041.66	1021.15	1003.57	988.43	975.34	931.32	908.47	896.22	889.53
95,000	1190.59	1154.92	1124.93	1099.53	1077.88	1059.32	1043.34	1029.53	983.06	958.94	946.01	938.95
100,000	1253.25	1215.70	1184.14	1157.40	1134.61	1115.08	1098.26	1083.71	1034.80	1009.41	995.80	988.37
105,000	1315.91	1276.49	1243.34	1215.27	1191.34	1170.83	1153.17	1137.90	1086.54	1059.89	1045.59	1037.79
110,000	1378.58	1337.27	1302.55	1273.14	1248.07	1226.58	1208.08	1192.08	1138.28	1110.36	1095.38	1087.21
115,000	1441.24	1398.06	1361.76	1331.01	1304.80	1282.34	1262.99	1246.27	1190.02	1160.83	1145.17	1136.62
120,000	1503.90	1458.84	1420.96	1388.88	1361.53	1338.09	1317.91	1300.45	1241.70	1211.30	1194.96	1186.04
125,000	1566.56	1519.63	1480.17	1446.75	1418.26	1393.85	1372.82	1354.64	1293.50	1261.77	1244.75	1235.46
130,000	1629.23	1580.41	1539.38	1504.62	1474.99	1449.60	1427.73	1408.82	1345.24	1312.24	1294.54	1284.88
135,000	1691.89	1641.20	1598.58	1562.49	1531.72	1505.35	1482.64	1463.01	1396.98	1362.71	1344.33	1334.30
140,000	1754.55	1701.98	1657.79	1620.36	1588.45	1561.11	1537.56	1517.19	1448.72	1413.18	1394.12	1383.71
145,000	1817.21	1762.76	1717.00	1678.23	1645.18	1616.86	1592.47	1571.38	1500.46	1463.65	1443.91	1433.13
150,000	1879.88	1823.55	1776.20	1736.10	1701.91	1672.61	1647.38	1625.57	1552.20	1514.12	1493.70	1482.55
155,000	1942.54	1884.33	1835.41	1793.97	1758.64	1728.37	1702.29	1679.75	1603.94	1564.59	1543.49	1531.97
160,000	2005.20	1945.12	1894.62	1851.84	1815.37	1784.12	1757.21	1733.94	1655.68	1615.06	1593.28	1581.39
165,000	2067.86	2005.90	1953.82	1909.71	1872.11	1839.87	1812.12	1788.12	1707.42	1665.53	1643.06	1630.81
170,000	2130.53	2066.69	2013.03	1967.58	1928.84	1895.63	1867.03	1842.31	1759.16	1716.00	1692.85	1680.22
175,000	2193.19	2127.47	2072.23	2025.45	1985.57	1951.38	1921.94	1896.49	1810.90	1766.47	1742.64	1729.64
180,000	2255.85	2188.26	2131.44	2083.32	2042.30	2007.14	1976.86	1950.68	1862.64	1816.94	1792.43	1779.06
185,000	2318.51	2249.04	2190.65	2141.19	2099.03	2062.89	2031.77	2004.86	1914.38	1867.41	1842.22	1828.48
190,000	2381.18	2309.83	2249.85	2199.06	2155.76	2118.64	2086.68	2059.05	1966.12	1917.88	1892.01	1877.90
195,000	2443.84	2370.61	2309.06	2256.93	2212.49	2174.40	2141.59	2113.23	2017.86	1968.35	1941.80	1927.31
200,000	2506.50	2431.40	2368.27	2314.80	2269.22	2230.15	2196.51	2167.42	2069.60	2018.82	1991.59	1976.73
205,000	2569.16	2492.18	2427.47	2372.67	2325.95	2285.90	2251.42	2221.60	2121.34	2069.29	2041.38	2026.15
210,000	2631.82	2552.97	2486.68	2430.54	2382.68	2341.66	2306.33	2275.79	2173.08	2119.77	2091.17	2075.57
215,000	2694.49	2613.75	2545.89	2488.41	2439.41	2397.41	2361.25	2329.98	2224.82	2170.24	2140.96	2124.99
220,000	2757.15	2674.54	2605.09	2546.28	2496.14	2453.16	2416.16	2384.16	2276.56	2220.71	2190.75	2174.41
225,000	2819.81	2735.32	2664.30	2604.15	2552.87	2508.92	2471.07	2438.35	2328.30	2271.18	2240.54	2223.82
230,000	2882.47	2796.11	2723.51	2662.02	2609.60	2564.67	2525.98	2492.53	2380.04	2321.65	2290.33	2273.24
235,000	2945.14	2856.89	2782.71	2719.89	2666.33	2620.43	2580.90	2546.72	2431.78	2372.12	2340.12	2322.66
240,000	3007.80	2917.68	2841.92	2777.76	2723.06	2676.18	2635.81	2600.90	2483.52	2422.59	2389.91	2372.08
245,000	3070.46	2978.46	2901.13	2835.63	2779.79	2731.93	2690.72	2655.09	2535.26	2473.06	2439.70	2421.50
250,000	3133.12	3039.25	2960.33	2893.50	2836.52	2787.69	2745.63	2709.27	2587.00	2523.53	2489.49	2470.91
255,000	3195.79	3100.03	3019.54	2951.37	2893.25	2843.44	2800.55	2763.46	2638.74	2574.00	2539.28	2520.33
260,000	3258.45	3160.82	3078.75	3009.24	2949.98	2899.19	2855.46	2817.64	2690.48	2624.47	2589.07	2569.75
265,000	3321.11	3221.60	3137.95	3067.11	3006.71	2954.95	2910.37	2871.83	2742.22	2674.94	2638.86	2619.17
270,000	3383.77	3282.39	3197.16	3124.97	3063.44	3010.70	2965.28	2926.01	2793.96	2725.41	2688.65	2668.59
280,000	3509.10	3403.95	3315.57	3240.71	3176.90	3122.21	3075.11	3034.38	2897.44	2826.35	2788.23	2767.42
290,000	3634.42	3525.52	3433.99	3356.45	3290.36	3233.72	3184.93	3142.76	3000.92	2927.29	2887.81	2866.26
300,000	3759.75	3647.09	3552.40	3472.19	3403.82	3345.22	3294.76	3251.13	3104.40	3028.23	2987.39	2965.10

12.00%

AMOUNT OF LOAN	NUMBER OF YEARS IN TERM											
	1	2	3	4	5	6	7	8	9	10	11	12
$ 50	4.45	2.36	1.67	1.32	1.12	0.98	0.89	0.82	0.76	0.72	0.69	0.66
100	8.89	4.71	3.33	2.64	2.23	1.96	1.77	1.63	1.52	1.44	1.37	1.32
200	17.77	9.42	6.65	5.27	4.45	3.92	3.54	3.26	3.04	2.87	2.74	2.63
300	26.66	14.13	9.97	7.91	6.68	5.87	5.30	4.88	4.56	4.31	4.11	3.95
400	35.54	18.83	13.29	10.54	8.90	7.83	7.07	6.51	6.08	5.74	5.48	5.26
500	44.43	23.54	16.61	13.17	11.13	9.78	8.83	8.13	7.60	7.18	6.84	6.57
600	53.31	28.25	19.93	15.81	13.35	11.74	10.60	9.76	9.12	8.61	8.21	7.89
700	62.20	32.96	23.26	18.44	15.58	13.69	12.36	11.38	10.63	10.05	9.58	9.20
800	71.08	37.66	26.58	21.07	17.80	15.65	14.13	13.01	12.15	11.48	10.95	10.51
900	79.97	42.37	29.90	23.71	20.03	17.60	15.89	14.63	13.67	12.92	12.32	11.83
1,000	88.85	47.08	33.22	26.34	22.25	19.56	17.66	16.26	15.19	14.35	13.68	13.14
2,000	177.70	94.15	66.43	52.67	44.49	39.11	35.31	32.51	30.37	28.70	27.36	26.27
3,000	266.55	141.23	99.65	79.01	66.74	58.66	52.96	48.76	45.56	43.05	41.04	39.41
4,000	355.40	188.30	132.86	105.34	88.98	78.21	70.62	65.02	60.74	57.39	54.72	52.54
5,000	444.25	235.37	166.08	131.67	111.23	97.76	88.27	81.27	75.93	71.74	68.39	65.68
6,000	533.10	282.45	199.29	158.01	133.47	117.31	105.92	97.52	91.11	86.09	82.07	78.81
7,000	621.95	329.52	232.51	184.34	155.72	136.86	123.57	113.77	106.29	100.43	95.75	91.94
8,000	710.80	376.59	265.72	210.68	177.96	156.41	141.23	130.03	121.48	114.78	109.43	105.08
9,000	799.64	423.67	298.93	237.01	200.21	175.96	158.88	146.28	136.66	129.13	123.11	118.21
10,000	888.49	470.74	332.15	263.34	222.45	195.51	176.53	162.53	151.85	143.48	136.78	131.35
15,000	1332.74	706.11	498.22	395.01	333.67	293.26	264.80	243.80	227.77	215.21	205.17	197.02
20,000	1776.98	941.47	664.29	526.68	444.89	391.01	353.06	325.06	303.69	286.95	273.56	262.69
25,000	2221.22	1176.84	830.36	658.35	556.12	488.76	441.32	406.33	379.61	358.68	341.95	328.36
30,000	2665.47	1412.21	996.43	790.02	667.34	586.51	529.59	487.59	455.53	430.42	410.34	394.03
35,000	3109.71	1647.58	1162.51	921.69	778.56	684.26	617.85	568.85	531.45	502.15	478.73	459.70
40,000	3553.96	1882.94	1328.58	1053.36	889.78	782.01	706.11	650.12	607.37	573.89	547.12	525.37
45,000	3998.20	2118.31	1494.65	1185.03	1001.01	879.76	794.38	731.38	683.30	645.62	615.51	591.04
50,000	4442.44	2353.68	1660.72	1316.70	1112.23	977.51	882.64	812.65	759.22	717.36	683.90	656.71
55,000	4886.69	2589.05	1826.79	1448.37	1223.45	1075.27	970.91	893.91	835.14	789.10	752.29	722.39
60,000	5330.93	2824.41	1992.86	1580.04	1334.67	1173.02	1059.17	975.18	911.06	860.83	820.68	788.06
65,000	5775.18	3059.78	2158.94	1711.70	1445.89	1270.77	1147.43	1056.44	986.98	932.57	889.07	853.73
70,000	6219.42	3295.15	2325.01	1843.37	1557.12	1368.52	1235.70	1137.70	1062.90	1004.30	957.46	919.40
75,000	6663.66	3530.52	2491.08	1975.04	1668.34	1466.27	1323.96	1218.97	1138.82	1076.04	1025.85	985.07
80,000	7107.91	3765.88	2657.15	2106.71	1779.56	1564.02	1412.22	1300.23	1214.74	1147.77	1094.24	1050.74
85,000	7552.15	4001.25	2823.22	2238.38	1890.78	1661.77	1500.49	1381.50	1290.66	1219.51	1162.62	1116.41
90,000	7996.40	4236.62	2989.29	2370.05	2002.01	1759.52	1588.75	1462.76	1366.59	1291.24	1231.01	1182.08
95,000	8440.64	4471.98	3155.36	2501.72	2113.23	1857.27	1677.01	1544.02	1442.51	1362.98	1299.40	1247.75
100,000	8884.88	4707.35	3321.44	2633.39	2224.45	1955.02	1765.28	1625.29	1518.43	1434.71	1367.79	1313.42
105,000	9329.13	4942.72	3487.51	2765.06	2335.67	2052.78	1853.54	1706.55	1594.35	1506.45	1436.18	1379.10
110,000	9773.37	5178.09	3653.58	2896.73	2446.89	2150.53	1941.81	1787.82	1670.27	1578.19	1504.57	1444.77
115,000	10217.62	5413.45	3819.65	3028.40	2558.12	2248.28	2030.07	1869.08	1746.19	1649.92	1572.96	1510.44
120,000	10661.86	5648.82	3985.72	3160.07	2669.34	2346.03	2118.33	1950.35	1822.11	1721.66	1641.35	1576.11
125,000	11106.10	5884.19	4151.79	3291.73	2780.56	2443.78	2206.60	2031.61	1898.03	1793.39	1709.74	1641.78
130,000	11550.35	6119.56	4317.87	3423.40	2891.78	2541.53	2294.86	2112.88	1973.96	1865.13	1778.13	1707.45
135,000	11994.59	6354.92	4483.94	3555.07	3003.01	2639.28	2383.12	2194.14	2049.88	1936.86	1846.52	1773.12
140,000	12438.84	6590.29	4650.01	3686.74	3114.23	2737.03	2471.39	2275.40	2125.80	2008.60	1914.91	1838.79
145,000	12883.08	6825.66	4816.08	3818.41	3225.45	2834.78	2559.65	2356.67	2201.72	2080.33	1983.30	1904.46
150,000	13327.32	7061.03	4982.15	3950.08	3336.67	2932.53	2647.91	2437.93	2277.64	2152.07	2051.69	1970.13
155,000	13771.57	7296.39	5148.22	4081.75	3447.89	3030.28	2736.18	2519.20	2353.56	2223.80	2120.08	2035.80
160,000	14215.81	7531.76	5314.29	4213.42	3559.12	3128.04	2824.44	2600.46	2429.48	2295.54	2188.47	2101.48
165,000	14660.06	7767.13	5480.37	4345.09	3670.34	3225.79	2912.71	2681.72	2505.40	2367.28	2256.85	2167.15
170,000	15104.30	8002.50	5646.44	4476.76	3781.56	3323.54	3000.97	2762.99	2581.32	2439.01	2325.24	2232.82
175,000	15548.54	8237.86	5812.51	4608.43	3892.78	3421.29	3089.23	2844.25	2657.25	2510.75	2393.63	2298.49
180,000	15992.79	8473.23	5978.58	4740.10	4004.01	3519.04	3177.50	2925.52	2733.17	2582.48	2462.02	2364.16
185,000	16437.03	8708.60	6144.65	4871.76	4115.23	3616.79	3265.76	3006.78	2809.09	2654.22	2530.41	2429.83
190,000	16881.27	8943.96	6310.72	5003.43	4226.45	3714.54	3354.02	3088.04	2885.01	2725.95	2598.80	2495.50
195,000	17325.52	9179.33	6476.80	5135.10	4337.67	3812.29	3442.29	3169.31	2960.93	2797.69	2667.19	2561.17
200,000	17769.76	9414.70	6642.87	5266.77	4448.89	3910.04	3530.55	3250.57	3036.85	2869.42	2735.58	2626.84
205,000	18214.01	9650.07	6808.94	5398.44	4560.12	4007.79	3618.82	3331.84	3112.77	2941.16	2803.97	2692.51
210,000	18658.25	9885.43	6975.01	5530.11	4671.34	4105.55	3707.08	3413.10	3188.69	3012.89	2872.36	2758.19
215,000	19102.49	10120.80	7141.08	5661.78	4782.56	4203.30	3795.34	3494.37	3264.62	3084.63	2940.75	2823.86
220,000	19546.74	10356.17	7307.15	5793.45	4893.78	4301.05	3883.61	3575.63	3340.54	3156.37	3009.14	2889.53
225,000	19990.98	10591.54	7473.22	5925.12	5005.01	4398.80	3971.87	3656.89	3416.46	3228.10	3077.53	2955.20
230,000	20435.23	10826.90	7639.30	6056.79	5116.23	4496.55	4060.13	3738.16	3492.38	3299.84	3145.92	3020.87
235,000	20879.47	11062.27	7805.37	6188.46	5227.45	4594.30	4148.40	3819.42	3568.30	3371.57	3214.31	3086.54
240,000	21323.71	11297.64	7971.44	6320.13	5338.67	4692.05	4236.66	3900.69	3644.22	3443.31	3282.70	3152.21
245,000	21767.96	11533.01	8137.51	6451.79	5449.89	4789.80	4324.92	3981.95	3720.14	3515.04	3351.09	3217.88
250,000	22212.20	11768.37	8303.58	6583.46	5561.12	4887.55	4413.19	4063.22	3796.06	3586.78	3419.47	3283.55
255,000	22656.45	12003.74	8469.65	6715.13	5672.34	4985.30	4501.45	4144.48	3871.98	3658.51	3487.86	3349.22
260,000	23100.69	12239.11	8635.73	6846.80	5783.56	5083.06	4589.72	4225.74	3947.91	3730.25	3556.25	3414.89
265,000	23544.93	12474.48	8801.80	6978.47	5894.78	5180.81	4677.98	4307.01	4023.83	3801.99	3624.64	3480.57
270,000	23989.18	12709.84	8967.87	7110.14	6006.01	5278.56	4766.24	4388.27	4099.75	3873.72	3693.03	3546.24
280,000	24877.67	13180.58	9300.01	7373.48	6228.45	5474.06	4942.77	4550.80	4251.59	4017.19	3829.81	3677.58
290,000	25766.15	13651.31	9632.15	7636.82	6450.89	5669.56	5119.30	4713.33	4403.43	4160.66	3966.59	3808.92
300,000	26654.64	14122.05	9964.30	7900.16	6673.34	5865.06	5295.82	4875.86	4555.27	4304.13	4103.37	3940.26

12.00%

AMOUNT OF LOAN	NUMBER OF YEARS IN TERM											
	13	14	15	16	17	18	19	20	25	30	35	40
$ 50	0.64	0.62	0.61	0.59	0.58	0.57	0.56	0.56	0.53	0.52	0.51	0.51
100	1.27	1.24	1.21	1.18	1.16	1.14	1.12	1.11	1.06	1.03	1.02	1.01
200	2.54	2.47	2.41	2.35	2.31	2.27	2.24	2.21	2.11	2.06	2.04	2.02
300	3.81	3.70	3.61	3.53	3.46	3.40	3.35	3.31	3.16	3.09	3.05	3.03
400	5.08	4.93	4.81	4.70	4.61	4.53	4.47	4.41	4.22	4.12	4.07	4.04
500	6.35	6.16	6.01	5.87	5.76	5.66	5.58	5.51	5.27	5.15	5.08	5.05
600	7.62	7.39	7.21	7.05	6.91	6.80	6.70	6.61	6.32	6.18	6.10	6.06
700	8.89	8.63	8.41	8.22	8.06	7.93	7.81	7.71	7.38	7.21	7.11	7.06
800	10.15	9.86	9.61	9.39	9.21	9.06	8.93	8.81	8.43	8.23	8.13	8.07
900	11.42	11.09	10.81	10.57	10.37	10.19	10.04	9.91	9.48	9.26	9.14	9.08
1,000	12.69	12.32	12.01	11.74	11.52	11.32	11.16	11.02	10.54	10.29	10.16	10.09
2,000	25.38	24.63	24.01	23.48	23.03	22.64	22.31	22.03	21.07	20.58	20.32	20.17
3,000	38.06	36.95	36.01	35.22	34.54	33.96	33.47	33.04	31.60	30.86	30.47	30.26
4,000	50.75	49.26	48.01	46.95	46.05	45.28	44.62	44.05	42.13	41.15	40.63	40.34
5,000	63.44	61.58	60.01	58.69	57.57	56.60	55.77	55.06	52.67	51.44	50.78	50.43
6,000	76.12	73.89	72.02	70.43	69.08	67.92	66.93	66.07	63.20	61.72	60.94	60.51
7,000	88.81	86.21	84.02	82.17	80.59	79.24	78.08	77.08	73.73	72.01	71.09	70.60
8,000	101.50	98.52	96.02	93.90	92.10	90.56	89.24	88.09	84.26	82.29	81.25	80.68
9,000	114.18	110.83	108.02	105.64	103.61	101.88	100.39	99.10	94.80	92.58	91.40	90.77
10,000	126.87	123.15	120.02	117.38	115.13	113.20	111.54	110.11	105.33	102.87	101.56	100.85
15,000	190.30	184.72	180.03	176.06	172.69	169.80	167.31	165.17	157.99	154.30	152.34	151.28
20,000	253.74	246.29	240.04	234.75	230.25	226.40	223.08	220.22	210.65	205.73	203.11	201.70
25,000	317.17	307.86	300.05	293.44	287.81	282.99	278.85	275.28	263.31	257.16	253.89	252.13
30,000	380.60	369.43	360.06	352.12	345.37	339.59	334.62	330.33	315.97	308.59	304.67	302.55
35,000	444.04	431.01	420.06	410.81	402.93	396.19	390.39	385.39	368.63	360.02	355.45	352.98
40,000	507.47	492.58	480.07	469.50	460.49	452.79	446.16	440.44	421.29	411.45	406.22	403.40
45,000	570.90	554.15	540.08	528.18	518.05	509.38	501.93	495.49	473.96	462.88	457.00	453.83
50,000	634.34	615.72	600.09	586.87	575.61	565.98	557.70	550.55	526.62	514.31	507.78	504.25
55,000	697.77	677.29	660.10	645.55	633.17	622.58	613.47	605.60	579.28	565.74	558.56	554.68
60,000	761.20	738.86	720.11	704.24	690.73	679.18	669.24	660.66	631.94	617.17	609.33	605.10
65,000	824.64	800.43	780.11	762.93	748.30	735.77	725.01	715.71	684.60	668.60	660.11	655.53
70,000	888.07	862.01	840.12	821.61	805.86	792.37	780.77	770.77	737.26	720.03	710.89	705.95
75,000	951.50	923.58	900.13	880.30	863.42	848.97	836.54	825.82	789.92	771.46	761.67	756.38
80,000	1014.94	985.15	960.14	938.99	920.98	905.57	892.31	880.87	842.58	822.90	812.44	806.80
85,000	1078.37	1046.72	1020.15	997.67	978.54	962.16	948.08	936.03	895.25	874.33	863.22	857.23
90,000	1141.80	1108.29	1080.16	1056.36	1036.10	1018.76	1003.85	990.98	947.91	925.76	914.00	907.65
95,000	1205.24	1169.86	1140.16	1115.04	1093.66	1075.36	1059.62	1046.04	1000.57	977.19	964.78	958.08
100,000	1268.67	1231.43	1200.17	1173.73	1151.22	1131.96	1115.39	1101.09	1053.23	1028.62	1015.55	1008.50
105,000	1332.10	1293.01	1260.18	1232.42	1208.78	1188.55	1171.16	1156.15	1105.89	1080.05	1066.33	1058.93
110,000	1395.54	1354.58	1320.19	1291.10	1266.34	1245.15	1226.93	1211.20	1158.55	1131.48	1117.11	1109.35
115,000	1458.97	1416.15	1380.20	1349.79	1323.90	1301.75	1282.70	1266.25	1211.21	1182.91	1167.89	1159.78
120,000	1522.40	1477.72	1440.21	1408.48	1381.46	1358.35	1338.47	1321.31	1263.88	1234.34	1218.66	1210.20
125,000	1585.84	1539.29	1500.22	1467.16	1439.02	1414.94	1394.24	1376.36	1316.54	1285.77	1269.44	1260.63
130,000	1649.27	1600.86	1560.22	1525.85	1496.59	1471.54	1450.01	1431.42	1369.20	1337.20	1320.22	1311.05
135,000	1712.70	1662.43	1620.23	1584.53	1554.15	1528.14	1505.78	1486.47	1421.86	1388.63	1371.00	1361.48
140,000	1776.14	1724.01	1680.24	1643.22	1611.71	1584.74	1561.54	1541.53	1474.52	1440.06	1421.77	1411.90
145,000	1839.57	1785.58	1740.25	1701.91	1669.27	1641.33	1617.31	1596.58	1527.18	1491.49	1472.55	1462.33
150,000	1903.00	1847.15	1800.26	1760.59	1726.83	1697.93	1673.08	1651.63	1579.84	1542.92	1523.33	1512.75
155,000	1966.44	1908.72	1860.27	1819.28	1784.39	1754.53	1728.85	1706.69	1632.50	1594.35	1574.11	1563.18
160,000	2029.87	1970.29	1920.27	1877.97	1841.95	1811.13	1784.62	1761.74	1685.16	1645.79	1624.88	1613.60
165,000	2093.30	2031.86	1980.28	1936.65	1899.51	1867.72	1840.39	1816.80	1737.82	1697.22	1675.66	1664.03
170,000	2156.74	2093.44	2040.29	1995.34	1957.07	1924.32	1896.16	1871.85	1790.49	1748.65	1726.44	1714.45
175,000	2220.17	2155.01	2100.30	2054.02	2014.63	1980.92	1951.93	1926.91	1843.15	1800.08	1777.22	1764.88
180,000	2283.60	2216.58	2160.31	2112.71	2072.19	2037.52	2007.70	1981.96	1895.81	1851.51	1827.99	1815.30
185,000	2347.04	2278.15	2220.32	2171.40	2129.75	2094.11	2063.47	2037.01	1948.47	1902.94	1878.77	1865.73
190,000	2410.47	2339.72	2280.32	2230.08	2187.31	2150.71	2119.24	2092.07	2001.13	1954.37	1929.55	1916.15
195,000	2473.90	2401.29	2340.33	2288.77	2244.88	2207.31	2175.01	2147.12	2053.79	2005.80	1980.33	1966.58
200,000	2537.34	2462.86	2400.34	2347.46	2302.44	2263.91	2230.78	2202.18	2106.45	2057.23	2031.10	2017.00
205,000	2600.77	2524.44	2460.35	2406.14	2360.00	2320.50	2286.55	2257.23	2159.11	2108.66	2081.88	2067.43
210,000	2664.20	2586.01	2520.36	2464.83	2417.56	2377.10	2342.31	2312.29	2211.78	2160.09	2132.66	2117.85
215,000	2727.64	2647.58	2580.37	2523.51	2475.12	2433.70	2398.08	2367.34	2264.44	2211.52	2183.44	2168.28
220,000	2791.07	2709.15	2640.37	2582.20	2532.68	2490.30	2453.85	2422.39	2317.10	2262.95	2234.21	2218.70
225,000	2854.50	2770.72	2700.38	2640.89	2590.24	2546.89	2509.62	2477.45	2369.76	2314.38	2284.99	2269.13
230,000	2917.94	2832.29	2760.39	2699.57	2647.80	2603.49	2565.39	2532.50	2422.42	2365.81	2335.77	2319.55
235,000	2981.37	2893.86	2820.40	2758.26	2705.36	2660.09	2621.16	2587.56	2475.08	2417.24	2386.55	2369.98
240,000	3044.80	2955.44	2880.41	2816.95	2762.92	2716.69	2676.93	2642.61	2527.74	2468.68	2437.32	2420.40
245,000	3108.24	3017.01	2940.42	2875.63	2820.48	2773.28	2732.70	2697.67	2580.40	2520.11	2488.10	2470.83
250,000	3171.67	3078.58	3000.43	2934.32	2878.04	2829.88	2788.47	2752.72	2633.07	2571.54	2538.88	2521.25
255,000	3235.10	3140.15	3060.43	2993.00	2935.60	2886.48	2844.24	2807.77	2685.73	2622.97	2589.66	2571.68
260,000	3298.54	3201.72	3120.44	3051.69	2993.17	2943.08	2900.01	2862.83	2738.39	2674.40	2640.43	2622.10
265,000	3361.97	3263.29	3180.45	3110.38	3050.73	2999.67	2955.78	2917.88	2791.05	2725.83	2691.21	2672.53
270,000	3425.40	3324.86	3240.46	3169.06	3108.29	3056.27	3011.55	2972.94	2843.71	2777.26	2741.99	2722.95
280,000	3552.27	3448.01	3360.48	3286.44	3223.41	3169.47	3123.08	3083.05	2949.03	2880.12	2843.54	2823.80
290,000	3679.14	3571.15	3480.49	3403.81	3338.53	3282.66	3234.62	3193.15	3054.36	2982.98	2945.10	2924.65
300,000	3806.00	3694.29	3600.51	3521.18	3453.65	3395.86	3346.16	3303.26	3159.68	3085.84	3046.65	3025.50

12.25% MONTHLY AMORTIZING PAYMENTS

AMOUNT OF LOAN	NUMBER OF YEARS IN TERM											
	1	2	3	4	5	6	7	8	9	10	11	12
$ 50	4.45	2.36	1.67	1.33	1.12	0.99	0.89	0.82	0.77	0.73	0.70	0.67
100	8.90	4.72	3.34	2.65	2.24	1.97	1.78	1.64	1.54	1.45	1.39	1.33
200	17.80	9.44	6.67	5.30	4.48	3.94	3.56	3.28	3.07	2.90	2.77	2.66
300	26.69	14.16	10.01	7.94	6.72	5.91	5.34	4.92	4.60	4.35	4.15	3.99
400	35.59	18.88	13.34	10.59	8.95	7.88	7.12	6.56	6.14	5.80	5.54	5.32
500	44.49	23.60	16.67	13.23	11.19	9.85	8.90	8.20	7.67	7.25	6.92	6.65
600	53.38	28.32	20.01	15.88	13.43	11.81	10.68	9.84	9.20	8.70	8.30	7.98
700	62.28	33.04	23.34	18.52	15.66	13.78	12.46	11.48	10.73	10.15	9.68	9.31
800	71.18	37.76	26.67	21.17	17.90	15.75	14.23	13.12	12.27	11.60	11.07	10.63
900	80.07	42.48	30.01	23.82	20.14	17.72	16.01	14.76	13.80	13.05	12.45	11.96
1,000	88.97	47.20	33.34	26.46	22.38	19.69	17.79	16.40	15.33	14.50	13.83	13.29
2,000	177.94	94.39	66.67	52.92	44.75	39.37	35.58	32.79	30.66	28.99	27.66	26.58
3,000	266.90	141.58	100.01	79.38	67.12	59.05	53.37	49.18	45.98	43.48	41.48	39.86
4,000	355.87	188.77	133.34	105.83	89.49	78.73	71.15	65.57	61.31	57.97	55.31	53.15
5,000	444.83	235.96	166.67	132.29	111.86	98.41	88.94	81.96	76.63	72.46	69.14	66.43
6,000	533.80	283.15	200.01	158.75	134.23	118.09	106.73	98.35	91.96	86.96	82.96	79.72
7,000	622.77	330.34	233.34	185.20	156.60	137.77	124.51	114.74	107.28	101.45	96.79	93.01
8,000	711.73	377.53	266.68	211.66	178.97	157.45	142.30	131.13	122.61	115.94	110.62	106.29
9,000	800.70	424.72	300.01	238.12	201.34	177.13	160.09	147.52	137.93	130.43	124.44	119.58
10,000	889.66	471.91	333.34	264.57	223.71	196.81	177.87	163.91	153.26	144.92	138.27	132.86
15,000	1334.49	707.86	500.01	396.86	335.57	295.21	266.81	245.86	229.89	217.38	207.40	199.29
20,000	1779.32	943.81	666.68	529.14	447.42	393.61	355.74	327.82	306.52	289.84	276.53	265.72
25,000	2224.15	1179.76	833.35	661.42	559.28	492.02	444.67	409.77	383.14	362.30	345.66	332.15
30,000	2668.98	1415.71	1000.02	793.71	671.13	590.42	533.61	491.72	459.77	434.76	414.79	398.58
35,000	3113.81	1651.67	1166.69	925.99	782.99	688.82	622.54	573.67	536.40	507.22	483.92	465.01
40,000	3558.64	1887.62	1333.36	1058.27	894.84	787.22	711.47	655.63	613.03	579.68	553.06	531.44
45,000	4003.47	2123.57	1500.03	1190.56	1006.70	885.62	800.41	737.58	689.65	652.14	622.19	597.87
50,000	4448.29	2359.52	1666.70	1322.84	1118.55	984.03	889.34	819.53	766.28	724.60	691.32	664.30
55,000	4893.12	2595.47	1833.37	1455.13	1230.41	1082.43	978.27	901.48	842.91	797.06	760.45	730.73
60,000	5337.95	2831.42	2000.04	1587.41	1342.26	1180.83	1067.21	983.44	919.54	869.52	829.58	797.16
65,000	5782.78	3067.37	2166.70	1719.69	1454.12	1279.23	1156.14	1065.39	996.17	941.98	898.71	863.59
70,000	6227.61	3303.33	2333.37	1851.98	1565.97	1377.64	1245.07	1147.34	1072.79	1014.44	967.84	930.02
75,000	6672.44	3539.28	2500.04	1984.26	1677.83	1476.04	1334.01	1229.29	1149.42	1086.90	1036.97	996.45
80,000	7117.27	3775.23	2666.71	2116.55	1789.68	1574.44	1422.94	1311.25	1226.05	1159.36	1106.11	1062.88
85,000	7562.10	4011.18	2833.38	2248.83	1901.54	1672.84	1511.88	1393.20	1302.68	1231.82	1175.24	1129.31
90,000	8006.93	4247.13	3000.05	2381.11	2013.39	1771.24	1600.81	1475.15	1379.30	1304.28	1244.37	1195.74
95,000	8451.75	4483.08	3166.72	2513.40	2125.25	1869.65	1689.74	1557.10	1455.93	1376.74	1313.50	1262.17
100,000	8896.58	4719.04	3333.39	2645.68	2237.10	1968.05	1778.68	1639.06	1532.56	1449.20	1382.63	1328.60
105,000	9341.41	4954.99	3500.06	2777.96	2348.96	2066.45	1867.61	1721.01	1609.19	1521.66	1451.76	1395.03
110,000	9786.24	5190.94	3666.73	2910.25	2460.81	2164.85	1956.54	1802.96	1685.82	1594.12	1520.89	1461.46
115,000	10231.07	5426.89	3833.40	3042.53	2572.67	2263.26	2045.48	1884.91	1762.44	1666.58	1590.02	1527.89
120,000	10675.90	5662.84	4000.07	3174.82	2684.52	2361.66	2134.41	1966.87	1839.07	1739.04	1659.16	1594.32
125,000	11120.73	5898.79	4166.74	3307.10	2796.38	2460.06	2223.34	2048.82	1915.70	1811.50	1728.29	1660.75
130,000	11565.56	6134.74	4333.40	3439.38	2908.23	2558.46	2312.28	2130.77	1992.33	1883.96	1797.42	1727.18
135,000	12010.39	6370.70	4500.07	3571.67	3020.09	2656.86	2401.21	2212.72	2068.95	1956.42	1866.55	1793.61
140,000	12455.21	6606.65	4666.74	3703.95	3131.94	2755.27	2490.14	2294.68	2145.58	2028.88	1935.68	1860.04
145,000	12900.04	6842.60	4833.41	3836.23	3243.80	2853.67	2579.08	2376.63	2222.21	2101.34	2004.81	1926.47
150,000	13344.87	7078.55	5000.08	3968.52	3355.65	2952.07	2668.01	2458.58	2298.84	2173.80	2073.94	1992.90
155,000	13789.70	7314.50	5166.75	4100.80	3467.51	3050.47	2756.94	2540.53	2375.47	2246.26	2143.08	2059.33
160,000	14234.53	7550.45	5333.42	4233.09	3579.36	3148.88	2845.88	2622.49	2452.09	2318.72	2212.21	2125.76
165,000	14679.36	7786.41	5500.09	4365.37	3691.22	3247.28	2934.81	2704.44	2528.72	2391.18	2281.34	2192.19
170,000	15124.19	8022.36	5666.76	4497.65	3803.07	3345.68	3023.75	2786.39	2605.35	2463.64	2350.47	2258.62
175,000	15569.02	8258.31	5833.43	4629.94	3914.93	3444.08	3112.68	2868.34	2681.98	2536.10	2419.60	2325.05
180,000	16013.85	8494.26	6000.10	4762.22	4026.78	3542.48	3201.61	2950.30	2758.60	2608.56	2488.73	2391.48
185,000	16458.67	8730.21	6166.77	4894.50	4138.64	3640.89	3290.55	3032.25	2835.23	2681.02	2557.86	2457.91
190,000	16903.50	8966.16	6333.43	5026.79	4250.49	3739.29	3379.48	3114.20	2911.86	2753.48	2626.99	2524.34
195,000	17348.33	9202.11	6500.10	5159.07	4362.35	3837.69	3468.41	3196.16	2988.49	2825.94	2696.13	2590.77
200,000	17793.16	9438.07	6666.77	5291.36	4474.20	3936.09	3557.35	3278.11	3065.12	2898.40	2765.26	2657.20
205,000	18237.99	9674.02	6833.44	5423.64	4586.06	4034.50	3646.28	3360.06	3141.74	2970.86	2834.39	2723.63
210,000	18682.82	9909.97	7000.11	5555.92	4697.91	4132.90	3735.21	3442.01	3218.37	3043.32	2903.52	2790.06
215,000	19127.65	10145.92	7166.78	5688.21	4809.77	4231.30	3824.15	3523.97	3295.00	3115.78	2972.65	2856.49
220,000	19572.48	10381.87	7333.45	5820.49	4921.62	4329.70	3913.08	3605.92	3371.63	3188.24	3041.78	2922.92
225,000	20017.31	10617.82	7500.12	5952.77	5033.48	4428.10	4002.01	3687.87	3448.25	3260.70	3110.91	2989.35
230,000	20462.14	10853.78	7666.79	6085.06	5145.33	4526.51	4090.95	3769.82	3524.88	3333.16	3180.04	3055.78
235,000	20906.96	11089.73	7833.46	6217.34	5257.19	4624.91	4179.88	3851.78	3601.51	3405.62	3249.18	3122.21
240,000	21351.79	11325.68	8000.13	6349.63	5369.04	4723.31	4268.81	3933.73	3678.14	3478.08	3318.31	3188.64
245,000	21796.62	11561.63	8166.80	6481.91	5480.90	4821.71	4357.75	4015.68	3754.76	3550.54	3387.44	3255.07
250,000	22241.45	11797.58	8333.47	6614.19	5592.75	4920.12	4446.68	4097.63	3831.39	3623.00	3456.57	3321.50
255,000	22686.28	12033.53	8500.13	6746.48	5704.61	5018.52	4535.62	4179.59	3908.02	3695.46	3525.70	3387.93
260,000	23131.11	12269.48	8666.80	6878.76	5816.46	5116.92	4624.55	4261.54	3984.65	3767.92	3594.83	3454.36
265,000	23575.94	12505.44	8833.47	7011.04	5928.32	5215.32	4713.48	4343.49	4061.28	3840.38	3663.96	3520.79
270,000	24020.77	12741.39	9000.14	7143.33	6040.17	5313.72	4802.42	4425.44	4137.90	3912.84	3733.10	3587.22
280,000	24910.42	13213.29	9333.48	7407.90	6263.88	5510.53	4980.28	4589.35	4291.16	4057.76	3871.36	3720.08
290,000	25800.08	13685.19	9666.82	7672.46	6487.59	5707.33	5158.15	4753.25	4444.41	4202.68	4009.62	3852.94
300,000	26689.74	14157.10	10000.16	7937.03	6711.30	5904.14	5336.02	4917.16	4597.67	4347.60	4147.88	3985.79

84

AMOUNT OF LOAN	NUMBER OF YEARS IN TERM											
	13	14	15	16	17	18	19	20	25	30	35	40
$ 50	0.65	0.63	0.61	0.60	0.59	0.58	0.57	0.56	0.54	0.53	0.52	0.52
100	1.29	1.25	1.22	1.20	1.17	1.15	1.14	1.12	1.08	1.05	1.04	1.03
200	2.57	2.50	2.44	2.39	2.34	2.30	2.27	2.24	2.15	2.10	2.08	2.06
300	3.86	3.75	3.65	3.58	3.51	3.45	3.40	3.36	3.22	3.15	3.11	3.09
400	5.14	4.99	4.87	4.77	4.68	4.60	4.54	4.48	4.29	4.20	4.15	4.12
500	6.43	6.24	6.09	5.96	5.84	5.75	5.67	5.60	5.36	5.24	5.18	5.15
600	7.71	7.49	7.30	7.15	7.01	6.90	6.80	6.72	6.44	6.29	6.22	6.18
700	8.99	8.74	8.52	8.34	8.18	8.05	7.93	7.83	7.51	7.34	7.25	7.21
800	10.28	9.98	9.74	9.53	9.35	9.20	9.07	8.95	8.58	8.39	8.29	8.23
900	11.56	11.23	10.95	10.72	10.52	10.35	10.20	10.07	9.65	9.44	9.32	9.26
1,000	12.85	12.48	12.17	11.91	11.68	11.49	11.33	11.19	10.72	10.48	10.36	10.29
2,000	25.69	24.95	24.33	23.81	23.36	22.98	22.66	22.38	21.44	20.96	20.71	20.58
3,000	38.53	37.42	36.49	35.71	35.04	34.47	33.98	33.56	32.16	31.44	31.07	30.87
4,000	51.37	49.90	48.66	47.61	46.72	45.96	45.31	44.75	42.87	41.92	41.42	41.15
5,000	64.21	62.37	60.82	59.51	58.40	57.45	56.64	55.93	53.59	52.40	51.77	51.44
6,000	77.06	74.84	72.98	71.41	70.08	68.94	67.96	67.12	64.31	62.88	62.13	61.73
7,000	89.90	87.31	85.15	83.32	81.76	80.43	79.29	78.30	75.03	73.36	72.48	72.01
8,000	102.74	99.79	97.31	95.22	93.44	91.92	90.61	89.49	85.74	83.84	82.83	82.30
9,000	115.58	112.26	109.47	107.12	105.12	103.41	101.94	100.68	96.46	94.32	93.19	92.59
10,000	128.42	124.73	121.63	119.02	116.80	114.90	113.27	111.86	107.18	104.79	103.54	102.87
15,000	192.63	187.09	182.45	178.53	175.19	172.34	169.90	167.79	160.77	157.19	155.31	154.31
20,000	256.84	249.46	243.26	238.04	233.59	229.79	226.53	223.72	214.35	209.58	207.08	205.74
25,000	321.05	311.82	304.08	297.54	291.99	287.24	283.16	279.65	267.94	261.98	258.85	257.18
30,000	385.26	374.10	364.89	357.05	350.38	344.68	339.79	335.57	321.53	314.37	310.62	308.61
35,000	449.47	436.54	425.71	416.56	408.78	402.13	396.42	391.50	375.12	366.77	362.38	360.05
40,000	513.67	498.91	486.52	476.07	467.17	459.58	453.05	447.43	428.70	419.16	414.15	411.48
45,000	577.88	561.27	547.34	535.57	525.57	517.02	509.68	503.36	482.29	471.56	465.92	462.91
50,000	642.09	623.63	608.15	595.08	583.97	574.47	566.31	559.29	535.88	523.95	517.69	514.35
55,000	706.30	685.99	668.97	654.59	642.36	631.91	622.95	615.22	589.46	576.35	569.46	565.78
60,000	770.51	748.36	729.78	714.10	700.76	689.36	679.58	671.14	643.05	628.74	621.23	617.22
65,000	834.72	810.72	790.60	773.60	759.15	746.81	736.21	727.07	696.64	681.14	673.00	668.65
70,000	898.93	873.08	851.41	833.11	817.55	804.25	792.84	783.00	750.23	733.53	724.76	720.09
75,000	963.13	935.45	912.23	892.62	875.95	861.70	849.47	838.93	803.81	785.93	776.53	771.52
80,000	1027.34	997.81	973.04	952.13	934.34	919.15	906.10	894.86	857.40	838.32	828.30	822.95
85,000	1091.55	1060.17	1033.86	1011.63	992.74	976.59	962.73	950.78	910.99	890.72	880.07	874.39
90,000	1155.76	1122.53	1094.67	1071.14	1051.14	1034.04	1019.36	1006.71	964.57	943.11	931.84	925.82
95,000	1219.97	1184.90	1155.49	1130.65	1109.53	1091.49	1075.99	1062.64	1018.16	995.51	983.61	977.26
100,000	1284.18	1247.26	1216.30	1190.16	1167.93	1148.93	1132.62	1118.57	1071.75	1047.90	1035.38	1028.69
105,000	1348.39	1309.62	1277.12	1249.66	1226.32	1206.38	1189.26	1174.50	1125.34	1100.30	1087.14	1080.13
110,000	1412.59	1371.98	1337.93	1309.17	1284.72	1263.82	1245.89	1230.43	1178.92	1152.69	1138.91	1131.56
115,000	1476.80	1434.35	1398.75	1368.68	1343.12	1321.27	1302.52	1286.35	1232.51	1205.09	1190.68	1182.99
120,000	1541.01	1496.71	1459.56	1428.19	1401.51	1378.72	1360.15	1342.28	1286.10	1257.40	1242.45	1234.43
125,000	1605.22	1559.07	1520.38	1487.69	1459.91	1436.16	1415.78	1398.21	1339.68	1309.88	1294.22	1285.86
130,000	1669.43	1621.44	1581.19	1547.20	1518.30	1493.61	1472.41	1454.14	1393.27	1362.27	1345.99	1337.30
135,000	1733.64	1683.80	1642.01	1606.71	1576.70	1551.06	1529.04	1510.07	1446.86	1414.67	1397.76	1388.73
140,000	1797.85	1746.16	1702.82	1666.22	1635.10	1608.50	1585.67	1566.00	1500.45	1467.06	1449.52	1440.17
145,000	1862.06	1808.52	1763.64	1725.72	1693.49	1665.95	1642.30	1621.92	1554.03	1519.45	1501.29	1491.60
150,000	1926.26	1870.89	1824.45	1785.23	1751.89	1723.40	1698.93	1677.85	1607.62	1571.85	1553.06	1543.03
155,000	1990.47	1933.25	1885.27	1844.74	1810.28	1780.84	1755.57	1733.78	1661.21	1624.24	1604.83	1594.47
160,000	2054.68	1995.61	1946.08	1904.25	1868.68	1838.29	1812.20	1789.71	1714.80	1676.64	1656.60	1645.90
165,000	2118.89	2057.97	2006.90	1963.75	1927.08	1895.73	1868.83	1845.64	1768.38	1729.03	1708.37	1697.34
170,000	2183.10	2120.34	2067.71	2023.26	1985.47	1953.18	1925.46	1901.56	1821.97	1781.43	1760.14	1748.77
175,000	2247.31	2182.70	2128.53	2082.77	2043.87	2010.63	1982.09	1957.49	1875.56	1833.82	1811.90	1800.21
180,000	2311.52	2245.06	2189.34	2142.28	2102.27	2068.07	2038.72	2013.42	1929.14	1886.22	1863.67	1851.64
185,000	2375.72	2307.42	2250.16	2201.78	2160.66	2125.52	2095.35	2069.35	1982.73	1938.61	1915.44	1903.07
190,000	2439.93	2369.79	2310.97	2261.29	2219.06	2182.97	2151.98	2125.28	2036.32	1991.01	1967.21	1954.51
195,000	2504.14	2432.15	2371.79	2320.80	2277.45	2240.41	2208.61	2181.21	2089.91	2043.40	2018.98	2005.94
200,000	2568.35	2494.51	2432.60	2380.31	2335.85	2297.86	2265.24	2237.13	2143.49	2095.80	2070.75	2057.38
205,000	2632.56	2556.88	2493.42	2439.81	2394.25	2355.31	2321.88	2293.06	2197.08	2148.19	2122.52	2108.81
210,000	2696.77	2619.24	2554.23	2499.32	2452.64	2412.75	2378.51	2348.99	2250.67	2200.59	2174.28	2160.25
215,000	2760.98	2681.60	2615.05	2558.83	2511.04	2470.20	2435.14	2404.92	2304.25	2252.98	2226.05	2211.68
220,000	2825.18	2743.96	2675.86	2618.34	2569.43	2527.64	2491.77	2460.85	2357.84	2305.38	2277.82	2263.11
225,000	2889.39	2806.33	2736.68	2677.84	2627.83	2585.09	2548.40	2516.78	2411.43	2357.77	2329.59	2314.55
230,000	2953.60	2868.69	2797.49	2737.35	2686.23	2642.54	2605.03	2572.70	2465.02	2410.17	2381.36	2365.98
235,000	3017.81	2931.05	2858.31	2796.86	2744.62	2699.98	2661.66	2628.63	2518.60	2462.56	2433.13	2417.42
240,000	3082.02	2993.41	2919.12	2856.37	2803.02	2757.43	2718.29	2684.56	2572.19	2514.96	2484.90	2468.85
245,000	3146.23	3055.78	2979.94	2915.87	2861.42	2814.88	2774.92	2740.49	2625.78	2567.35	2536.66	2520.29
250,000	3210.44	3118.14	3040.75	2975.38	2919.81	2872.32	2831.55	2796.42	2679.36	2619.75	2588.43	2571.72
255,000	3274.65	3180.50	3101.57	3034.89	2978.21	2929.77	2888.18	2852.34	2732.95	2672.14	2640.20	2623.15
260,000	3338.85	3242.87	3162.38	3094.40	3036.60	2987.22	2944.82	2908.27	2786.54	2724.54	2691.97	2674.59
265,000	3403.06	3305.23	3223.20	3153.90	3095.00	3044.66	3001.45	2964.20	2840.13	2776.93	2743.74	2726.02
270,000	3467.27	3367.59	3284.01	3213.41	3153.40	3102.11	3058.08	3020.13	2893.71	2829.33	2795.51	2777.46
280,000	3595.69	3492.32	3405.64	3332.43	3270.19	3217.00	3171.34	3131.99	3000.89	2934.12	2899.04	2880.33
290,000	3724.11	3617.04	3527.27	3451.44	3386.98	3331.89	3284.60	3243.84	3108.06	3038.90	3002.58	2983.19
300,000	3852.52	3741.77	3648.90	3570.46	3503.77	3446.79	3397.86	3355.70	3215.24	3143.69	3106.12	3086.06

12.50%

AMOUNT OF LOAN	NUMBER OF YEARS IN TERM											
	1	2	3	4	5	6	7	8	9	10	11	12
$ 50	4.46	2.37	1.68	1.33	1.13	1.00	0.90	0.83	0.78	0.74	0.70	0.68
100	8.91	4.74	3.35	2.66	2.25	1.99	1.80	1.66	1.55	1.47	1.40	1.35
200	17.82	9.47	6.70	5.32	4.50	3.97	3.59	3.31	3.10	2.93	2.80	2.69
300	26.73	14.20	10.04	7.98	6.75	5.95	5.38	4.96	4.65	4.40	4.20	4.04
400	35.64	18.93	13.39	10.64	9.00	7.93	7.17	6.62	6.19	5.86	5.60	5.38
500	44.55	23.66	16.73	13.29	11.25	9.91	8.97	8.27	7.74	7.32	6.99	6.72
600	53.45	28.39	20.08	15.95	13.50	11.89	10.76	9.92	9.29	8.79	8.39	8.07
700	62.36	33.12	23.42	18.61	15.75	13.87	12.55	11.58	10.83	10.25	9.79	9.41
800	71.27	37.85	26.77	21.27	18.00	15.85	14.34	13.23	12.38	11.72	11.19	10.76
900	80.18	42.58	30.11	23.93	20.25	17.84	16.13	14.88	13.93	13.18	12.58	12.10
1,000	89.09	47.31	33.46	26.58	22.50	19.82	17.93	16.53	15.47	14.64	13.98	13.44
2,000	178.17	94.62	66.91	53.16	45.00	39.63	35.85	33.06	30.94	29.28	27.96	26.88
3,000	267.25	141.93	100.37	79.74	67.50	59.44	53.77	49.59	46.41	43.92	41.93	40.32
4,000	356.34	189.23	133.82	106.32	90.00	79.25	71.69	66.12	61.88	58.56	55.91	53.76
5,000	445.42	236.54	167.27	132.90	112.49	99.06	89.61	82.65	77.34	73.19	69.88	67.20
6,000	534.50	283.85	200.73	159.48	134.99	118.87	107.53	99.18	92.81	87.83	83.86	80.64
7,000	623.59	331.16	234.18	186.06	157.49	138.68	125.45	115.71	108.28	102.47	97.83	94.08
8,000	712.67	378.46	267.63	212.64	179.99	158.49	143.37	132.24	123.75	117.11	111.81	107.51
9,000	801.75	425.77	301.09	239.22	202.49	178.31	161.30	148.76	139.21	131.74	125.78	120.95
10,000	890.83	473.08	334.54	265.80	224.98	198.12	179.22	165.29	154.68	146.38	139.76	134.39
15,000	1336.25	709.61	501.81	398.70	337.47	297.17	268.82	247.94	232.02	219.57	209.64	201.58
20,000	1781.66	946.15	669.08	531.60	449.96	396.23	358.43	330.58	309.36	292.76	279.51	268.78
25,000	2227.08	1182.69	836.35	664.50	562.45	495.28	448.04	413.23	386.69	365.95	349.39	335.97
30,000	2672.49	1419.22	1003.61	797.40	674.94	594.34	537.64	495.87	464.03	439.13	419.27	403.16
35,000	3117.91	1655.76	1170.88	930.30	787.43	693.40	627.25	578.51	541.37	512.32	489.15	470.36
40,000	3563.32	1892.30	1338.15	1063.20	899.92	792.45	716.85	661.16	618.71	585.51	559.02	537.55
45,000	4008.73	2128.83	1505.42	1196.10	1012.41	891.51	806.46	743.80	696.04	658.70	628.90	604.74
50,000	4454.15	2365.37	1672.69	1329.00	1124.90	990.56	896.07	826.45	773.38	731.89	698.78	671.93
55,000	4899.56	2601.91	1839.95	1461.90	1237.39	1089.62	985.67	909.09	850.72	805.07	768.65	739.13
60,000	5344.98	2838.44	2007.22	1594.80	1349.88	1188.68	1075.28	991.73	928.06	878.26	838.53	806.32
65,000	5790.39	3074.98	2174.49	1727.70	1462.37	1287.73	1164.89	1074.38	1005.40	951.45	908.41	873.51
70,000	6235.81	3311.52	2341.76	1860.60	1574.86	1386.79	1254.49	1157.02	1082.73	1024.64	978.29	940.71
75,000	6681.22	3548.05	2509.03	1993.50	1687.35	1485.84	1344.10	1239.67	1160.07	1097.83	1048.16	1007.90
80,000	7126.63	3784.59	2676.30	2126.40	1799.84	1584.90	1433.70	1322.31	1237.41	1171.01	1118.04	1075.09
85,000	7572.05	4021.13	2843.56	2259.30	1912.33	1683.96	1523.31	1404.95	1314.75	1244.20	1187.92	1142.28
90,000	8017.46	4257.66	3010.83	2392.20	2024.82	1783.01	1612.92	1487.60	1392.08	1317.39	1257.79	1209.48
95,000	8462.88	4494.20	3178.10	2525.10	2137.31	1882.07	1702.52	1570.24	1469.42	1390.58	1327.67	1276.67
100,000	8908.29	4730.74	3345.37	2658.00	2249.80	1981.12	1792.13	1652.89	1546.76	1463.77	1397.55	1343.86
105,000	9353.71	4967.27	3512.64	2790.90	2362.29	2080.18	1881.74	1735.53	1624.10	1536.95	1467.43	1411.06
110,000	9799.12	5203.81	3679.90	2923.80	2474.78	2179.23	1971.34	1818.17	1701.44	1610.14	1537.30	1478.25
115,000	10244.53	5440.35	3847.17	3056.70	2587.27	2278.29	2060.95	1900.82	1778.77	1683.33	1607.18	1545.44
120,000	10689.95	5676.88	4014.44	3189.60	2699.76	2377.35	2150.55	1983.46	1856.11	1756.52	1677.06	1612.63
125,000	11135.36	5913.42	4181.71	3322.50	2812.25	2476.40	2240.16	2066.11	1933.45	1829.71	1746.93	1679.83
130,000	11580.78	6149.96	4348.98	3455.40	2924.74	2575.46	2329.77	2148.75	2010.79	1902.90	1816.81	1747.02
135,000	12026.19	6386.49	4516.24	3588.30	3037.23	2674.51	2419.37	2231.39	2088.12	1976.08	1886.69	1814.21
140,000	12471.61	6623.03	4683.51	3721.20	3149.72	2773.57	2508.98	2314.04	2165.46	2049.27	1956.57	1881.41
145,000	12917.02	6859.56	4850.78	3854.10	3262.21	2872.63	2598.58	2396.68	2242.80	2122.46	2026.44	1948.60
150,000	13362.43	7096.10	5018.05	3987.00	3374.70	2971.68	2688.19	2479.33	2320.14	2195.65	2096.32	2015.79
155,000	13807.85	7332.64	5185.32	4119.90	3487.19	3070.74	2777.80	2561.97	2397.48	2268.84	2166.20	2082.98
160,000	14253.26	7569.17	5352.59	4252.80	3599.68	3169.79	2867.40	2644.61	2474.81	2342.02	2236.07	2150.18
165,000	14698.68	7805.71	5519.85	4385.70	3712.16	3268.85	2957.01	2727.26	2552.15	2415.21	2305.95	2217.37
170,000	15144.09	8042.25	5687.12	4518.60	3824.65	3367.91	3046.62	2809.90	2629.49	2488.40	2375.83	2284.56
175,000	15589.51	8278.78	5854.39	4651.50	3937.14	3466.96	3136.22	2892.55	2706.83	2561.59	2445.71	2351.76
180,000	16034.92	8515.32	6021.66	4784.40	4049.63	3566.02	3225.83	2975.19	2784.16	2634.78	2515.58	2418.95
185,000	16480.33	8751.86	6188.93	4917.30	4162.12	3665.07	3315.43	3057.83	2861.50	2707.96	2585.46	2486.14
190,000	16925.75	8988.39	6356.19	5050.20	4274.61	3764.13	3405.04	3140.48	2938.84	2781.15	2655.34	2553.33
195,000	17371.16	9224.93	6523.46	5183.10	4387.10	3863.18	3494.65	3223.12	3016.18	2854.34	2725.21	2620.53
200,000	17816.58	9461.47	6690.73	5316.00	4499.59	3962.24	3584.25	3305.77	3093.52	2927.53	2795.09	2687.72
205,000	18261.99	9698.00	6858.00	5448.90	4612.08	4061.30	3673.86	3388.41	3170.85	3000.72	2864.97	2754.91
210,000	18707.41	9934.54	7025.27	5581.80	4724.57	4160.35	3763.47	3471.05	3248.19	3073.90	2934.85	2822.11
215,000	19152.82	10171.08	7192.53	5714.70	4837.06	4259.41	3853.07	3553.70	3325.53	3147.09	3004.72	2889.30
220,000	19598.23	10407.61	7359.80	5847.60	4949.55	4358.46	3942.68	3636.34	3402.87	3220.28	3074.60	2956.49
225,000	20043.65	10644.15	7527.07	5980.50	5062.04	4457.52	4032.28	3718.99	3480.20	3293.47	3144.48	3023.68
230,000	20489.06	10880.69	7694.34	6113.40	5174.53	4556.58	4121.89	3801.63	3557.54	3366.66	3214.35	3090.88
235,000	20934.48	11117.22	7861.61	6246.30	5287.02	4655.63	4211.50	3884.28	3634.88	3439.84	3284.23	3158.07
240,000	21379.89	11353.76	8028.88	6379.20	5399.51	4754.69	4301.10	3966.92	3712.22	3513.03	3354.11	3225.26
245,000	21825.31	11590.29	8196.14	6512.10	5512.00	4853.74	4390.71	4049.56	3789.55	3586.22	3423.99	3292.46
250,000	22270.72	11826.83	8363.41	6645.00	5624.49	4952.80	4480.31	4132.21	3866.89	3659.41	3493.86	3359.65
255,000	22716.13	12063.37	8530.68	6777.90	5736.98	5051.86	4569.92	4214.85	3944.23	3732.60	3563.74	3426.84
260,000	23161.55	12299.91	8697.95	6910.80	5849.47	5150.91	4659.53	4297.50	4021.57	3805.79	3633.62	3494.03
265,000	23606.96	12536.44	8865.22	7043.70	5961.96	5249.97	4749.13	4380.14	4098.91	3878.97	3703.49	3561.23
270,000	24052.38	12772.98	9032.48	7176.60	6074.45	5349.02	4838.74	4462.78	4176.24	3952.16	3773.37	3628.42
280,000	24943.21	13246.05	9367.02	7442.40	6299.43	5547.14	5017.95	4628.07	4330.92	4098.54	3913.13	3762.81
290,000	25834.04	13719.12	9701.56	7708.20	6524.41	5745.25	5197.16	4793.36	4485.59	4244.91	4052.88	3897.19
300,000	26724.86	14192.20	10036.09	7974.00	6749.39	5943.36	5376.38	4958.65	4640.27	4391.29	4192.63	4031.58

MONTHLY AMORTIZING PAYMENTS 12.50%

AMOUNT OF LOAN	\multicolumn{12}{c}{NUMBER OF YEARS IN TERM}
	13	14	15	16	17	18	19	20	25	30	35	40
$ 50	0.65	0.64	0.62	0.61	0.60	0.59	0.58	0.57	0.55	0.54	0.53	0.53
100	1.30	1.27	1.24	1.21	1.19	1.17	1.15	1.14	1.10	1.07	1.06	1.05
200	2.60	2.53	2.47	2.42	2.37	2.34	2.30	2.28	2.19	2.14	2.12	2.10
300	3.90	3.79	3.70	3.63	3.56	3.50	3.45	3.41	3.28	3.21	3.17	3.15
400	5.20	5.06	4.94	4.83	4.74	4.67	4.60	4.55	4.37	4.27	4.23	4.20
500	6.50	6.32	6.17	6.04	5.93	5.84	5.75	5.69	5.46	5.34	5.28	5.25
600	7.80	7.58	7.40	7.25	7.11	7.00	6.90	6.82	6.55	6.41	6.34	6.30
700	9.10	8.85	8.63	8.45	8.30	8.17	8.05	7.96	7.64	7.48	7.39	7.35
800	10.40	10.11	9.87	9.66	9.48	9.33	9.20	9.09	8.73	8.54	8.45	8.40
900	11.70	11.37	11.10	10.87	10.67	10.50	10.35	10.23	9.82	9.61	9.50	9.45
1,000	13.00	12.64	12.33	12.07	11.85	11.67	11.50	11.37	10.91	10.68	10.56	10.49
2,000	26.00	25.27	24.66	24.14	23.70	23.33	23.00	22.73	21.81	21.35	21.11	20.98
3,000	39.00	37.90	36.98	36.21	35.55	34.99	34.50	34.09	32.72	32.02	31.66	31.47
4,000	52.00	50.53	49.31	48.27	47.39	46.65	46.00	45.45	43.62	42.70	42.22	41.96
5,000	64.99	63.16	61.63	60.34	59.24	58.31	57.50	56.81	54.52	53.37	52.77	52.45
6,000	77.99	75.80	73.96	72.41	71.09	69.97	69.00	68.17	65.43	64.04	63.32	62.94
7,000	90.99	88.43	86.28	84.47	82.94	81.63	80.50	79.53	76.33	74.71	73.87	73.43
8,000	103.99	101.06	98.61	96.54	94.78	93.29	92.00	90.90	87.23	85.39	84.43	83.92
9,000	116.98	113.69	110.93	108.61	106.63	104.95	103.50	102.26	98.14	96.06	94.98	94.41
10,000	129.98	126.32	123.26	120.67	118.48	116.61	115.00	113.62	109.04	106.73	105.53	104.90
15,000	194.97	189.48	184.88	181.01	177.71	174.91	172.50	170.43	163.56	160.09	158.29	157.34
20,000	259.96	252.64	246.51	241.34	236.95	233.21	230.00	227.23	218.08	213.46	211.06	209.79
25,000	324.95	315.80	308.14	301.67	296.19	291.51	287.49	284.04	272.59	266.82	263.82	262.23
30,000	389.93	378.96	369.76	362.01	355.42	349.81	344.99	340.85	327.11	320.18	316.58	314.68
35,000	454.92	442.11	431.39	422.34	414.66	408.11	402.49	397.65	381.63	373.55	369.34	367.13
40,000	519.91	505.27	493.01	482.67	473.90	466.41	459.99	454.46	436.15	426.91	422.11	419.57
45,000	584.90	568.43	554.64	543.01	533.13	524.71	517.48	511.27	490.66	480.27	474.87	472.02
50,000	649.89	631.59	616.27	603.34	592.37	583.01	574.98	568.08	545.18	533.63	527.63	524.46
55,000	714.88	694.75	677.89	663.67	651.60	641.31	632.48	624.88	599.70	587.00	580.39	576.91
60,000	779.86	757.91	739.52	724.01	710.84	699.61	689.98	681.69	654.22	640.36	633.16	629.36
65,000	844.85	821.06	801.14	784.34	770.08	757.91	747.47	738.50	708.74	693.72	685.92	681.80
70,000	909.84	884.22	862.77	844.67	829.31	816.21	804.97	795.30	763.25	747.09	738.68	734.25
75,000	974.83	947.38	924.40	905.01	888.55	874.51	862.47	852.11	817.77	800.45	791.45	786.69
80,000	1039.82	1010.54	986.02	965.34	947.79	932.81	919.97	908.92	872.29	853.81	844.21	839.14
85,000	1104.81	1073.70	1047.65	1025.67	1007.02	991.11	977.46	965.72	926.81	907.17	896.97	891.59
90,000	1169.79	1136.86	1109.27	1086.01	1066.26	1049.41	1034.96	1022.53	981.32	960.54	949.73	944.03
95,000	1234.78	1200.01	1170.90	1146.34	1125.49	1107.71	1092.46	1079.34	1035.84	1013.90	1002.50	996.48
100,000	1299.77	1263.17	1232.53	1206.67	1184.73	1166.01	1149.96	1136.15	1090.36	1067.26	1055.26	1048.92
105,000	1364.76	1326.33	1294.15	1267.01	1243.97	1224.31	1207.45	1192.95	1144.88	1120.63	1108.02	1101.37
110,000	1429.75	1389.49	1355.78	1327.34	1303.20	1282.61	1264.95	1249.76	1199.39	1173.99	1160.78	1153.82
115,000	1494.74	1452.65	1417.41	1387.68	1362.44	1340.91	1322.45	1306.57	1253.91	1227.35	1213.55	1206.26
120,000	1559.72	1515.81	1470.03	1448.01	1421.68	1399.21	1379.95	1363.37	1308.43	1280.71	1266.31	1258.71
125,000	1624.71	1578.97	1540.66	1508.34	1480.91	1457.51	1437.44	1420.18	1362.95	1334.08	1319.07	1311.15
130,000	1689.70	1642.12	1602.28	1568.68	1540.15	1515.81	1494.94	1476.99	1417.47	1387.44	1371.84	1363.60
135,000	1754.69	1705.28	1663.91	1629.01	1599.38	1574.11	1552.44	1533.79	1471.98	1440.80	1424.60	1416.05
140,000	1819.68	1768.44	1725.54	1689.34	1658.62	1632.41	1609.94	1590.60	1526.50	1494.17	1477.36	1468.49
145,000	1884.67	1831.60	1787.16	1749.68	1717.86	1690.71	1667.43	1647.41	1581.02	1547.53	1530.12	1520.94
150,000	1949.65	1894.76	1848.79	1810.01	1777.09	1749.01	1724.93	1704.22	1635.54	1600.89	1582.89	1573.38
155,000	2014.64	1957.92	1910.41	1870.34	1836.33	1807.31	1782.43	1761.02	1690.05	1654.25	1635.65	1625.83
160,000	2079.63	2021.07	1972.04	1930.68	1895.57	1865.61	1839.93	1817.83	1744.57	1707.62	1688.41	1678.28
165,000	2144.62	2084.23	2033.67	1991.01	1954.80	1923.91	1897.42	1874.64	1799.09	1760.98	1741.17	1730.72
170,000	2209.61	2147.39	2095.29	2051.34	2014.04	1982.21	1954.92	1931.44	1853.61	1814.34	1793.94	1783.17
175,000	2274.60	2210.55	2156.92	2111.68	2073.28	2040.51	2012.42	1988.25	1908.12	1867.71	1846.70	1835.61
180,000	2339.58	2273.71	2218.54	2172.01	2132.51	2098.81	2069.92	2045.06	1962.64	1921.07	1899.46	1888.06
185,000	2404.57	2336.87	2280.17	2232.34	2191.75	2157.11	2127.41	2101.87	2017.16	1974.43	1952.23	1940.51
190,000	2469.56	2400.02	2341.80	2292.68	2250.98	2215.41	2184.91	2158.67	2071.68	2027.79	2004.99	1992.95
195,000	2534.55	2463.18	2403.42	2353.01	2310.22	2273.71	2242.41	2215.48	2126.20	2081.16	2057.75	2045.40
200,000	2599.54	2526.34	2465.05	2413.34	2369.46	2332.01	2299.91	2272.29	2180.71	2134.52	2110.51	2097.84
205,000	2664.53	2589.50	2526.68	2473.68	2428.69	2390.31	2357.40	2329.09	2235.23	2187.88	2163.28	2150.29
210,000	2729.51	2652.66	2588.30	2534.01	2487.93	2448.61	2414.90	2385.90	2289.75	2241.25	2216.04	2202.74
215,000	2794.50	2715.82	2649.93	2594.35	2547.17	2506.91	2472.40	2442.71	2344.27	2294.61	2268.80	2255.18
220,000	2859.49	2778.98	2711.55	2654.68	2606.40	2565.21	2529.90	2499.51	2398.78	2347.97	2321.56	2307.63
225,000	2924.48	2842.13	2773.18	2715.01	2665.64	2623.51	2587.39	2556.32	2453.30	2401.33	2374.33	2360.07
230,000	2989.47	2905.29	2834.81	2775.35	2724.87	2681.81	2644.89	2613.13	2507.82	2454.70	2427.09	2412.52
235,000	3054.46	2968.45	2896.43	2835.68	2784.11	2740.11	2702.39	2669.94	2562.34	2508.06	2479.85	2464.97
240,000	3119.44	3031.61	2958.06	2896.01	2843.35	2798.41	2759.89	2726.74	2616.85	2561.42	2532.62	2517.41
245,000	3184.43	3094.77	3019.68	2956.35	2902.58	2856.71	2817.38	2783.55	2671.37	2614.79	2585.38	2569.86
250,000	3249.42	3157.93	3081.31	3016.68	2961.82	2915.01	2874.88	2840.36	2725.89	2668.15	2638.14	2622.30
255,000	3314.41	3221.08	3142.94	3077.01	3021.06	2973.31	2932.38	2897.16	2780.41	2721.51	2690.90	2674.75
260,000	3379.40	3284.24	3204.56	3137.35	3080.29	3031.61	2989.88	2953.97	2834.93	2774.88	2743.67	2727.20
265,000	3444.39	3347.40	3266.19	3197.68	3139.53	3089.91	3047.37	3010.78	2889.44	2828.24	2796.43	2779.64
270,000	3509.37	3410.56	3327.81	3258.01	3198.76	3148.21	3104.87	3067.58	2943.96	2881.60	2849.19	2832.09
280,000	3639.35	3536.88	3451.07	3378.68	3317.24	3264.81	3219.87	3181.20	3053.00	2988.33	2954.72	2936.98
290,000	3769.33	3663.19	3574.32	3499.35	3435.71	3381.41	3334.86	3294.81	3162.03	3095.05	3060.24	3041.87
300,000	3899.30	3789.51	3697.57	3620.01	3554.18	3498.01	3449.86	3408.43	3271.07	3201.78	3165.77	3146.76

87

12.75%　MONTHLY AMORTIZING PAYMENTS

AMOUNT OF LOAN	NUMBER OF YEARS IN TERM											
	1	2	3	4	5	6	7	8	9	10	11	12
$ 50	4.47	2.38	1.68	1.34	1.14	1.00	0.91	0.84	0.79	0.74	0.71	0.68
100	8.93	4.75	3.36	2.68	2.27	2.00	1.81	1.67	1.57	1.48	1.42	1.36
200	17.85	9.49	6.72	5.35	4.53	3.99	3.62	3.34	3.13	2.96	2.83	2.72
300	26.77	14.23	10.08	8.02	6.79	5.99	5.42	5.01	4.69	4.44	4.24	4.08
400	35.69	18.97	13.43	10.69	9.06	7.98	7.23	6.67	6.25	5.92	5.66	5.44
500	44.61	23.72	16.79	13.36	11.32	9.98	9.03	8.34	7.81	7.40	7.07	6.80
600	53.53	28.46	20.15	16.03	13.58	11.97	10.84	10.01	9.37	8.88	8.48	8.16
700	62.45	33.20	23.51	18.70	15.84	13.96	12.64	11.67	10.93	10.35	9.89	9.52
800	71.37	37.94	26.86	21.37	18.11	15.96	14.45	13.34	12.49	11.83	11.31	10.88
900	80.29	42.69	30.22	24.04	20.37	17.95	16.26	15.01	14.05	13.31	12.72	12.24
1,000	89.21	47.43	33.58	26.71	22.63	19.95	18.06	16.67	15.62	14.79	14.13	13.60
2,000	178.41	94.85	67.15	53.41	45.26	39.89	36.12	33.34	31.23	29.57	28.26	27.19
3,000	267.61	142.28	100.73	80.12	67.88	59.83	54.17	50.01	46.84	44.36	42.38	40.78
4,000	356.81	189.70	134.30	106.82	90.51	79.77	72.23	66.68	62.45	59.14	56.51	54.37
5,000	446.01	237.13	167.87	133.52	113.13	99.72	90.29	83.34	78.06	73.92	70.63	67.97
6,000	535.21	284.55	201.45	160.23	135.76	119.66	108.34	100.01	93.67	88.71	84.76	81.56
7,000	624.41	331.98	235.02	186.93	158.38	139.60	126.40	116.68	109.28	103.49	98.88	95.15
8,000	713.61	379.40	268.59	213.63	181.01	159.54	144.46	133.35	124.89	118.28	113.01	108.74
9,000	802.81	426.83	302.17	240.34	203.63	179.49	162.51	150.01	140.50	133.06	127.13	122.33
10,000	892.01	474.25	335.74	267.04	226.26	199.43	180.57	166.68	156.11	147.84	141.26	135.93
15,000	1338.01	711.37	503.61	400.56	339.38	299.14	270.85	250.02	234.16	221.76	211.89	203.89
20,000	1784.01	948.49	671.48	534.08	452.51	398.85	361.13	333.36	312.21	295.68	282.51	271.85
25,000	2230.01	1185.62	839.35	667.59	565.64	498.57	451.41	416.70	390.26	369.60	353.14	339.81
30,000	2676.01	1422.74	1007.21	801.11	678.76	598.28	541.69	500.04	468.31	443.52	423.77	407.77
35,000	3122.01	1659.86	1175.08	934.63	791.89	697.99	631.98	583.38	546.36	517.44	494.39	475.73
40,000	3568.01	1896.98	1342.95	1068.15	905.02	797.70	722.26	666.71	624.41	591.36	565.02	543.69
45,000	4014.01	2134.11	1510.82	1201.67	1018.14	897.41	812.54	750.05	702.47	665.28	635.65	611.65
50,000	4460.01	2371.23	1678.69	1335.18	1131.27	997.13	902.82	833.39	780.52	739.20	706.27	679.61
55,000	4906.01	2608.35	1846.56	1468.70	1244.40	1096.84	993.10	916.73	858.57	813.12	776.90	747.57
60,000	5352.01	2845.47	2014.42	1602.22	1357.52	1196.55	1083.38	1000.07	936.62	887.04	847.53	815.53
65,000	5798.01	3082.60	2182.29	1735.74	1470.65	1296.26	1173.67	1083.41	1014.67	960.96	918.15	883.49
70,000	6244.01	3319.72	2350.16	1869.26	1583.78	1395.97	1263.95	1166.75	1092.72	1034.88	988.78	951.45
75,000	6690.01	3556.84	2518.03	2002.77	1696.90	1495.69	1354.23	1250.08	1170.77	1108.80	1059.41	1019.41
80,000	7136.01	3793.96	2685.90	2136.29	1810.03	1595.40	1444.51	1333.42	1248.82	1182.72	1130.04	1087.37
85,000	7582.01	4031.09	2853.77	2269.81	1923.16	1695.11	1534.79	1416.76	1326.87	1256.64	1200.66	1155.33
90,000	8028.01	4268.21	3021.63	2403.33	2036.28	1794.82	1625.07	1500.10	1404.93	1330.56	1271.29	1223.29
95,000	8474.01	4505.33	3189.50	2536.85	2149.41	1894.53	1715.36	1583.44	1482.98	1404.48	1341.92	1291.25
100,000	8920.01	4742.45	3357.37	2670.36	2262.54	1994.25	1805.64	1666.78	1561.03	1478.40	1412.54	1359.21
105,000	9366.01	4979.58	3525.24	2803.88	2375.66	2093.96	1895.92	1750.12	1639.08	1552.32	1483.17	1427.17
110,000	9812.01	5216.70	3693.11	2937.40	2488.79	2193.67	1986.20	1833.45	1717.13	1626.24	1553.80	1495.13
115,000	10258.01	5453.82	3860.98	3070.92	2601.91	2293.38	2076.48	1916.79	1795.18	1700.16	1624.42	1563.09
120,000	10704.01	5690.94	4028.84	3204.43	2715.04	2393.09	2166.76	2000.13	1873.23	1774.08	1695.05	1631.05
125,000	11150.01	5928.07	4196.71	3337.95	2828.17	2492.81	2257.05	2083.47	1951.28	1848.00	1765.68	1699.01
130,000	11596.01	6165.19	4364.58	3471.47	2941.29	2592.52	2347.33	2166.81	2029.34	1921.92	1836.30	1766.97
135,000	12042.01	6402.31	4532.45	3604.99	3054.42	2692.23	2437.61	2250.15	2107.39	1995.84	1906.93	1834.93
140,000	12488.01	6639.43	4700.32	3738.51	3167.55	2791.94	2527.89	2333.49	2185.44	2069.76	1977.56	1902.89
145,000	12934.01	6876.55	4868.19	3872.02	3280.67	2891.65	2618.17	2416.82	2263.49	2143.68	2048.19	1970.85
150,000	13380.01	7113.68	5036.05	4005.54	3393.80	2991.37	2708.45	2500.16	2341.54	2217.60	2118.81	2038.81
155,000	13826.01	7350.80	5203.92	4139.06	3506.93	3091.08	2798.74	2583.50	2419.59	2291.52	2189.44	2106.77
160,000	14272.01	7587.92	5371.79	4272.58	3620.05	3190.79	2889.02	2666.84	2497.64	2365.44	2260.07	2174.73
165,000	14718.01	7825.04	5539.66	4406.10	3733.18	3290.50	2979.30	2750.18	2575.69	2439.36	2330.69	2242.69
170,000	15164.01	8062.17	5707.53	4539.61	3846.31	3390.21	3069.58	2833.52	2653.74	2513.28	2401.32	2310.65
175,000	15610.01	8299.29	5875.40	4673.13	3959.43	3489.93	3159.86	2916.86	2731.80	2587.20	2471.95	2378.61
180,000	16056.01	8536.41	6043.26	4806.65	4072.56	3589.64	3250.14	3000.20	2809.85	2661.12	2542.57	2446.57
185,000	16502.01	8773.53	6211.13	4940.17	4185.69	3689.35	3340.43	3083.53	2887.90	2735.04	2613.20	2514.53
190,000	16948.01	9010.66	6379.00	5073.69	4298.81	3789.06	3430.71	3166.87	2965.95	2808.96	2683.83	2582.49
195,000	17394.01	9247.78	6546.87	5207.20	4411.94	3888.77	3520.99	3250.21	3044.00	2882.88	2754.45	2650.45
200,000	17840.01	9484.90	6714.74	5340.72	4525.07	3988.49	3611.27	3333.55	3122.05	2956.80	2825.08	2718.41
205,000	18286.01	9722.02	6882.61	5474.24	4638.19	4088.20	3701.55	3416.89	3200.10	3030.72	2895.71	2786.37
210,000	18732.01	9959.15	7050.47	5607.76	4751.32	4187.91	3791.83	3500.23	3278.15	3104.64	2966.33	2854.33
215,000	19178.01	10196.27	7218.34	5741.27	4864.44	4287.62	3882.11	3583.57	3356.20	3178.56	3036.96	2922.29
220,000	19624.01	10433.39	7386.21	5874.79	4977.57	4387.33	3972.40	3666.90	3434.26	3252.48	3107.59	2990.25
225,000	20070.01	10670.51	7554.08	6008.31	5090.70	4487.05	4062.68	3750.24	3512.31	3326.40	3178.22	3058.21
230,000	20516.01	10907.64	7721.95	6141.83	5203.82	4586.76	4152.96	3833.58	3590.36	3400.32	3248.84	3126.17
235,000	20962.01	11144.76	7889.82	6275.35	5316.95	4686.47	4243.24	3916.92	3668.41	3474.24	3319.47	3194.13
240,000	21408.01	11381.88	8057.68	6408.86	5430.08	4786.18	4333.52	4000.26	3746.46	3548.16	3390.10	3262.09
245,000	21854.01	11619.00	8225.55	6542.38	5543.20	4885.89	4423.80	4083.60	3824.51	3622.08	3460.72	3330.05
250,000	22300.01	11856.13	8393.42	6675.90	5656.33	4985.61	4514.09	4166.94	3902.56	3696.00	3531.35	3398.01
255,000	22746.01	12093.25	8561.29	6809.42	5769.46	5085.32	4604.37	4250.27	3980.61	3769.92	3601.98	3465.97
260,000	23192.01	12330.37	8729.16	6942.94	5882.58	5185.03	4694.65	4333.61	4058.67	3843.84	3672.60	3533.93
265,000	23638.01	12567.49	8897.03	7076.45	5995.71	5284.74	4784.93	4416.95	4136.72	3917.76	3743.23	3601.89
270,000	24084.01	12804.61	9064.89	7209.97	6108.84	5384.45	4875.21	4500.29	4214.77	3991.68	3813.86	3669.85
280,000	24976.01	13278.86	9400.63	7477.01	6335.09	5583.88	5055.78	4666.97	4370.87	4139.52	3955.11	3805.77
290,000	25868.01	13753.10	9736.37	7744.04	6561.34	5783.30	5236.34	4833.64	4526.97	4287.36	4096.37	3941.69
300,000	26760.01	14227.35	10072.10	8011.08	6787.60	5982.73	5416.90	5000.32	4683.07	4435.20	4237.62	4077.61

88

AMOUNT OF LOAN	NUMBER OF YEARS IN TERM											
	13	14	15	16	17	18	19	20	25	30	35	40
$ 50	0.66	0.64	0.63	0.62	0.61	0.60	0.59	0.58	0.56	0.55	0.54	0.54
100	1.32	1.28	1.25	1.23	1.21	1.19	1.17	1.16	1.11	1.09	1.08	1.07
200	2.64	2.56	2.50	2.45	2.41	2.37	2.34	2.31	2.22	2.18	2.16	2.14
300	3.95	3.84	3.75	3.67	3.61	3.55	3.51	3.47	3.33	3.27	3.23	3.21
400	5.27	5.12	5.00	4.90	4.81	4.74	4.67	4.62	4.44	4.35	4.31	4.28
500	6.58	6.40	6.25	6.12	6.01	5.92	5.84	5.77	5.55	5.44	5.38	5.35
600	7.90	7.68	7.50	7.34	7.21	7.10	7.01	6.93	6.66	6.53	6.46	6.42
700	9.21	8.96	8.75	8.57	8.42	8.29	8.18	8.08	7.77	7.61	7.53	7.49
800	10.53	10.24	10.00	9.79	9.62	9.47	9.34	9.24	8.88	8.70	8.61	8.56
900	11.84	11.52	11.24	11.01	10.82	10.65	10.51	10.39	9.99	9.79	9.68	9.63
1,000	13.16	12.80	12.49	12.24	12.02	11.84	11.68	11.54	11.10	10.87	10.76	10.70
2,000	26.31	25.59	24.98	24.47	24.04	23.67	23.35	23.08	22.19	21.74	21.51	21.39
3,000	39.47	38.38	37.47	36.70	36.05	35.50	35.03	34.62	33.28	32.61	32.26	32.08
4,000	52.62	51.17	49.96	48.94	48.07	47.33	46.70	46.16	44.37	43.47	43.01	42.77
5,000	65.78	63.96	62.45	61.17	60.09	59.16	58.37	57.70	55.46	54.34	53.76	53.46
6,000	78.93	76.76	74.94	73.40	72.10	71.00	70.05	69.23	66.55	65.21	64.52	64.16
7,000	92.09	89.55	87.42	85.63	84.12	82.83	81.72	80.77	77.64	76.07	75.27	74.85
8,000	105.24	102.34	99.91	97.87	96.13	94.66	93.40	92.31	88.73	86.94	86.02	85.54
9,000	118.40	115.13	112.40	110.10	108.15	106.49	105.07	103.85	99.82	97.81	96.77	96.23
10,000	131.55	127.92	124.89	122.33	120.17	118.32	116.74	115.39	110.91	108.67	107.52	106.92
15,000	197.32	191.88	187.33	183.50	180.25	177.48	175.11	173.08	166.36	163.01	161.28	160.38
20,000	263.09	255.84	249.77	244.66	240.33	236.64	233.48	230.77	221.82	217.34	215.04	213.84
25,000	328.87	319.80	312.21	305.83	300.41	295.80	291.85	288.46	277.27	271.68	268.80	267.30
30,000	394.64	383.76	374.66	366.99	360.49	354.96	350.22	346.15	332.72	326.01	322.56	320.76
35,000	460.41	447.72	437.10	428.15	420.57	414.11	408.59	403.84	388.17	380.35	376.32	374.22
40,000	526.18	511.67	499.54	489.32	480.65	473.27	466.96	461.53	443.63	434.68	430.08	427.68
45,000	591.96	575.63	561.98	550.48	540.74	532.43	525.32	519.22	499.08	489.02	483.84	481.14
50,000	657.73	639.59	624.42	611.65	600.82	591.59	583.69	576.91	554.53	543.35	537.60	534.60
55,000	723.50	703.55	686.87	672.81	660.90	650.75	642.06	634.60	609.98	597.69	591.36	588.06
60,000	789.27	767.51	749.31	733.97	720.98	709.91	700.43	692.29	665.44	652.02	645.12	641.52
65,000	855.04	831.47	811.75	795.14	781.06	769.07	758.80	749.98	720.89	706.36	698.88	694.98
70,000	920.82	895.43	874.19	856.30	841.14	828.22	817.17	807.67	776.34	760.69	752.64	748.44
75,000	986.59	959.38	936.63	917.47	901.22	887.38	875.54	865.36	831.79	815.02	806.40	801.90
80,000	1052.36	1023.34	999.07	978.63	961.30	946.54	933.91	923.05	887.25	869.36	860.16	855.36
85,000	1118.13	1087.30	1061.52	1039.80	1021.39	1005.70	992.28	980.74	942.70	923.69	913.92	908.82
90,000	1183.91	1151.26	1123.96	1100.96	1081.47	1064.86	1050.64	1038.44	998.15	978.03	967.68	962.28
95,000	1249.68	1215.22	1186.40	1162.12	1141.55	1124.02	1109.01	1096.13	1053.60	1032.36	1021.44	1015.74
100,000	1315.45	1279.18	1248.84	1223.29	1201.63	1183.17	1167.38	1153.82	1109.06	1086.70	1075.20	1069.20
105,000	1381.22	1343.14	1311.28	1284.45	1261.71	1242.33	1225.75	1211.51	1164.51	1141.03	1128.96	1122.66
110,000	1447.00	1407.09	1373.73	1345.62	1321.79	1301.49	1284.12	1269.20	1219.96	1195.37	1182.72	1176.12
115,000	1512.77	1471.05	1436.17	1406.78	1381.87	1360.65	1342.49	1326.89	1275.42	1249.70	1236.48	1229.58
120,000	1578.54	1535.01	1498.61	1467.94	1441.95	1419.81	1400.86	1384.58	1330.87	1304.04	1290.24	1283.04
125,000	1644.31	1598.97	1561.05	1529.11	1502.03	1478.97	1459.23	1442.27	1386.32	1358.37	1344.00	1336.50
130,000	1710.08	1662.93	1623.49	1590.27	1562.12	1538.13	1517.60	1499.96	1441.77	1412.71	1397.76	1389.96
135,000	1775.86	1726.89	1685.93	1651.44	1622.20	1597.28	1575.96	1557.65	1497.23	1467.04	1451.52	1443.42
140,000	1841.63	1790.85	1748.38	1712.60	1682.28	1656.44	1634.33	1615.34	1552.68	1521.38	1505.28	1496.88
145,000	1907.40	1854.80	1810.82	1773.77	1742.36	1715.60	1692.70	1673.03	1608.13	1575.71	1559.04	1550.34
150,000	1973.17	1918.76	1873.26	1834.93	1802.44	1774.76	1751.07	1730.72	1663.58	1630.04	1612.80	1603.80
155,000	2038.95	1982.72	1935.70	1896.09	1862.52	1833.92	1809.44	1788.41	1719.04	1684.38	1666.56	1657.26
160,000	2104.72	2046.68	1998.14	1957.26	1922.60	1893.08	1867.81	1846.10	1774.49	1738.71	1720.32	1710.72
165,000	2170.49	2110.64	2060.59	2018.42	1982.68	1952.24	1926.18	1903.79	1829.94	1793.05	1774.08	1764.18
170,000	2236.26	2174.60	2123.03	2079.59	2042.77	2011.39	1984.55	1961.48	1885.39	1847.38	1827.84	1817.64
175,000	2302.03	2238.56	2185.47	2140.75	2102.85	2070.55	2042.92	2019.18	1940.85	1901.72	1881.60	1871.10
180,000	2367.81	2302.51	2247.91	2201.91	2162.93	2129.71	2101.28	2076.87	1996.30	1956.05	1935.36	1924.56
185,000	2433.58	2366.47	2310.35	2263.08	2223.01	2188.87	2159.65	2134.56	2051.75	2010.39	1989.12	1978.02
190,000	2499.35	2430.43	2372.80	2324.24	2283.09	2248.03	2218.02	2192.25	2107.20	2064.72	2042.88	2031.48
195,000	2565.12	2494.39	2435.24	2385.41	2343.17	2307.19	2276.39	2249.94	2162.66	2119.06	2096.64	2084.94
200,000	2630.90	2558.35	2497.68	2446.57	2403.25	2366.34	2334.76	2307.63	2218.11	2173.39	2150.40	2138.40
205,000	2696.67	2622.31	2560.12	2507.73	2463.33	2425.50	2393.13	2365.32	2273.56	2227.73	2204.16	2191.86
210,000	2762.44	2686.27	2622.56	2568.90	2523.41	2484.66	2451.50	2423.01	2329.01	2282.06	2257.92	2245.32
215,000	2828.21	2750.22	2685.00	2630.06	2583.50	2543.82	2509.87	2480.70	2384.47	2336.40	2311.68	2298.78
220,000	2893.99	2814.18	2747.45	2691.23	2643.58	2602.98	2568.24	2538.39	2439.92	2390.73	2365.44	2352.24
225,000	2959.76	2878.14	2809.89	2752.39	2703.66	2662.14	2626.60	2596.08	2495.37	2445.06	2419.20	2405.70
230,000	3025.53	2942.10	2872.33	2813.56	2763.74	2721.30	2684.97	2653.77	2550.83	2499.40	2472.96	2459.16
235,000	3091.30	3006.06	2934.77	2874.72	2823.82	2780.45	2743.34	2711.46	2606.28	2553.73	2526.72	2512.62
240,000	3157.07	3070.02	2997.21	2935.88	2883.90	2839.61	2801.71	2769.15	2661.73	2608.07	2580.48	2566.08
245,000	3222.85	3133.98	3059.66	2997.05	2943.98	2898.77	2860.08	2826.84	2717.18	2662.40	2634.24	2619.54
250,000	3288.62	3197.93	3122.10	3058.21	3004.06	2957.93	2918.45	2884.53	2772.64	2716.74	2688.00	2673.00
255,000	3354.39	3261.89	3184.54	3119.38	3064.15	3017.09	2976.82	2942.22	2828.09	2771.07	2741.76	2726.46
260,000	3420.16	3325.85	3246.98	3180.54	3124.23	3076.25	3035.19	2999.92	2883.54	2825.41	2795.51	2779.92
265,000	3485.94	3389.81	3309.42	3241.70	3184.31	3135.41	3093.56	3057.61	2938.99	2879.74	2849.27	2833.38
270,000	3551.71	3453.77	3371.86	3302.87	3244.39	3194.56	3151.92	3115.30	2994.45	2934.08	2903.03	2886.84
280,000	3683.25	3581.69	3496.75	3425.20	3364.55	3312.88	3268.66	3230.68	3105.35	3042.75	3010.55	2993.75
290,000	3814.80	3709.60	3621.63	3547.53	3484.71	3431.20	3385.40	3346.06	3216.26	3151.42	3118.07	3100.67
300,000	3946.34	3837.52	3746.52	3669.85	3604.88	3549.51	3502.14	3461.44	3327.16	3260.08	3225.59	3207.59

89

13.00% MONTHLY AMORTIZING PAYMENTS

AMOUNT OF LOAN	NUMBER OF YEARS IN TERM											
	1	2	3	4	5	6	7	8	9	10	11	12
$ 50	4.47	2.38	1.69	1.35	1.14	1.01	0.91	0.85	0.79	0.75	0.72	0.69
100	8.94	4.76	3.37	2.69	2.28	2.01	1.82	1.69	1.58	1.50	1.43	1.38
200	17.87	9.51	6.74	5.37	4.56	4.02	3.64	3.37	3.16	2.99	2.86	2.75
300	26.80	14.27	10.11	8.05	6.83	6.03	5.46	5.05	4.73	4.48	4.29	4.13
400	35.73	19.02	13.48	10.74	9.11	8.03	7.28	6.73	6.31	5.98	5.72	5.50
500	44.66	23.78	16.85	13.42	11.38	10.04	9.10	8.41	7.88	7.47	7.14	6.88
600	53.60	28.53	20.22	16.10	13.66	12.05	10.92	10.09	9.46	8.96	8.57	8.25
700	62.53	33.28	23.59	18.78	15.93	14.06	12.74	11.77	11.03	10.46	10.00	9.63
800	71.46	38.04	26.96	21.47	18.21	16.06	14.56	13.45	12.61	11.95	11.43	11.00
900	80.39	42.79	30.33	24.15	20.48	18.07	16.38	15.13	14.18	13.44	12.85	12.38
1,000	89.32	47.55	33.70	26.83	22.76	20.08	18.20	16.81	15.76	14.94	14.28	13.75
2,000	178.64	95.09	67.39	53.66	45.51	40.15	36.39	33.62	31.51	29.87	28.56	27.50
3,000	267.96	142.63	101.09	80.49	68.26	60.23	54.58	50.43	47.27	44.80	42.83	41.24
4,000	357.27	190.17	134.78	107.31	91.02	80.30	72.77	67.23	63.02	59.73	57.11	54.99
5,000	446.59	237.71	168.47	134.14	113.77	100.38	90.96	84.04	78.77	74.66	71.39	68.74
6,000	535.91	285.26	202.17	160.97	136.52	120.45	109.16	100.85	94.53	89.59	85.66	82.48
7,000	625.23	332.80	235.86	187.80	159.28	140.52	127.35	117.66	110.28	104.52	99.94	96.23
8,000	714.54	380.34	269.56	214.62	182.03	160.60	145.54	134.46	126.03	119.45	114.21	109.98
9,000	803.86	427.88	303.25	241.45	204.78	180.67	163.73	151.27	141.79	134.38	128.49	123.72
10,000	893.18	475.42	336.94	268.28	227.54	200.75	181.92	168.08	157.54	149.32	142.77	137.47
15,000	1339.76	713.13	505.41	402.42	341.30	301.12	272.88	252.11	236.31	223.97	214.15	206.20
20,000	1786.35	950.84	673.88	536.55	455.07	401.49	363.84	336.15	315.08	298.63	285.53	274.93
25,000	2232.94	1188.55	842.35	670.69	568.83	501.86	454.80	420.19	393.84	373.28	356.91	343.66
30,000	2679.52	1426.26	1010.82	804.83	682.60	602.23	545.76	504.22	472.61	447.94	428.29	412.39
35,000	3126.11	1663.97	1179.29	938.97	796.36	702.60	636.72	588.26	551.38	522.59	499.67	481.12
40,000	3572.70	1901.68	1347.76	1073.10	910.13	802.97	727.68	672.30	630.15	597.25	571.05	549.86
45,000	4019.28	2139.39	1516.23	1207.24	1023.89	903.34	818.64	756.33	708.92	671.90	642.43	618.59
50,000	4465.87	2377.10	1684.70	1341.38	1137.66	1003.71	909.60	840.37	787.68	746.56	713.81	687.32
55,000	4912.46	2614.81	1853.17	1475.52	1251.42	1104.08	1000.56	924.40	866.45	821.21	785.19	756.05
60,000	5359.04	2852.51	2021.64	1609.65	1365.19	1204.45	1091.52	1008.44	945.22	895.87	856.57	824.78
65,000	5805.63	3090.22	2190.11	1743.79	1478.95	1304.82	1182.48	1092.48	1023.99	970.52	927.95	893.51
70,000	6252.21	3327.93	2358.58	1877.93	1592.72	1405.19	1273.44	1176.51	1102.76	1045.18	999.33	962.24
75,000	6698.80	3565.64	2527.05	2012.07	1706.49	1505.56	1364.40	1260.55	1181.52	1119.84	1070.71	1030.97
80,000	7145.39	3803.35	2695.52	2146.20	1820.25	1605.93	1455.36	1344.59	1260.29	1194.49	1142.09	1099.71
85,000	7591.97	4041.06	2863.99	2280.34	1934.02	1706.30	1546.32	1428.62	1339.06	1269.15	1213.47	1168.44
90,000	8038.56	4278.77	3032.46	2414.48	2047.78	1806.67	1637.28	1512.66	1417.83	1343.80	1284.85	1237.17
95,000	8485.15	4516.48	3200.93	2548.62	2161.55	1907.04	1728.24	1596.69	1496.60	1418.46	1356.24	1305.90
100,000	8931.73	4754.19	3369.40	2682.75	2275.31	2007.42	1819.20	1680.73	1575.36	1493.11	1427.62	1374.63
105,000	9378.32	4991.90	3537.87	2816.89	2389.08	2107.79	1910.16	1764.77	1654.13	1567.77	1499.00	1443.36
110,000	9824.91	5229.61	3706.34	2951.03	2502.84	2208.16	2001.12	1848.80	1732.90	1642.42	1570.38	1512.09
115,000	10271.49	5467.31	3874.81	3085.17	2616.61	2308.53	2092.08	1932.84	1811.67	1717.08	1641.76	1580.82
120,000	10718.08	5705.02	4043.28	3219.30	2730.37	2408.90	2183.04	2016.88	1890.44	1791.73	1713.14	1649.56
125,000	11164.66	5942.73	4211.75	3353.44	2844.14	2509.27	2274.00	2100.91	1969.20	1866.39	1784.52	1718.29
130,000	11611.25	6180.44	4380.22	3487.58	2957.90	2609.64	2364.96	2184.95	2047.97	1941.04	1855.90	1787.02
135,000	12057.84	6418.15	4548.69	3621.72	3071.67	2710.01	2455.92	2268.98	2126.74	2015.70	1927.28	1855.75
140,000	12504.42	6655.86	4717.16	3755.85	3185.44	2810.38	2546.88	2353.02	2205.51	2090.36	1998.66	1924.48
145,000	12951.01	6893.57	4885.63	3889.99	3299.20	2910.75	2637.84	2437.06	2284.28	2165.01	2070.04	1993.21
150,000	13397.60	7131.28	5054.10	4024.13	3412.97	3011.12	2728.80	2521.09	2363.04	2239.67	2141.42	2061.94
155,000	13844.18	7368.99	5222.57	4158.27	3526.73	3111.49	2819.76	2605.13	2441.81	2314.32	2212.80	2130.67
160,000	14290.77	7606.70	5391.04	4292.40	3640.50	3211.86	2910.72	2689.17	2520.58	2388.98	2284.18	2199.41
165,000	14737.36	7844.41	5559.51	4426.54	3754.26	3312.23	3001.68	2773.20	2599.35	2463.63	2355.56	2268.14
170,000	15183.94	8082.11	5727.98	4560.68	3868.03	3412.60	3092.64	2857.24	2678.11	2538.29	2426.94	2336.87
175,000	15630.53	8319.82	5896.45	4694.82	3981.79	3512.97	3183.60	2941.27	2756.88	2612.94	2498.32	2405.60
180,000	16077.11	8557.53	6064.92	4828.95	4095.56	3613.34	3274.56	3025.31	2835.65	2687.60	2569.70	2474.33
185,000	16523.70	8795.24	6233.39	4963.09	4209.32	3713.71	3365.52	3109.35	2914.42	2762.25	2641.08	2543.06
190,000	16970.29	9032.95	6401.86	5097.23	4323.09	3814.08	3456.48	3193.38	2993.19	2836.91	2712.47	2611.79
195,000	17416.87	9270.66	6570.33	5231.37	4436.85	3914.46	3547.44	3277.42	3071.95	2911.56	2783.85	2680.52
200,000	17863.46	9508.37	6738.80	5365.50	4550.62	4014.83	3638.40	3361.46	3150.72	2986.22	2855.23	2749.26
205,000	18310.05	9746.08	6907.27	5499.64	4664.38	4115.20	3729.36	3445.49	3229.49	3060.88	2926.61	2817.99
210,000	18756.63	9983.79	7075.73	5633.78	4778.15	4215.57	3820.32	3529.53	3308.26	3135.53	2997.99	2886.72
215,000	19203.22	10221.50	7244.20	5767.92	4891.92	4315.94	3911.28	3613.56	3387.03	3210.19	3069.37	2955.45
220,000	19649.81	10459.21	7412.67	5902.05	5005.68	4416.31	4002.24	3697.60	3465.79	3284.84	3140.75	3024.18
225,000	20096.39	10696.92	7581.14	6036.19	5119.45	4516.68	4093.20	3781.64	3544.56	3359.50	3212.13	3092.91
230,000	20542.98	10934.62	7749.61	6170.33	5233.21	4617.05	4184.16	3865.67	3623.33	3434.15	3283.51	3161.64
235,000	20989.56	11172.33	7918.08	6304.47	5346.98	4717.42	4275.12	3949.71	3702.10	3508.81	3354.89	3230.37
240,000	21436.15	11410.04	8086.55	6438.60	5460.74	4817.79	4366.08	4033.75	3780.87	3583.46	3426.27	3299.11
245,000	21882.74	11647.75	8255.02	6572.74	5574.51	4918.16	4457.04	4117.78	3859.63	3658.12	3497.65	3367.84
250,000	22329.32	11885.46	8423.49	6706.88	5688.27	5018.53	4548.00	4201.82	3938.40	3732.77	3569.03	3436.57
255,000	22775.91	12123.17	8591.96	6841.02	5802.04	5118.90	4638.96	4285.86	4017.17	3807.43	3640.41	3505.30
260,000	23222.50	12360.88	8760.43	6975.15	5915.80	5219.27	4729.92	4369.89	4095.94	3882.08	3711.79	3574.03
265,000	23669.08	12598.59	8928.90	7109.29	6029.57	5319.64	4820.88	4453.93	4174.71	3956.74	3783.17	3642.76
270,000	24115.67	12836.30	9097.37	7243.43	6143.33	5420.01	4911.84	4537.96	4253.47	4031.39	3854.55	3711.49
280,000	25008.84	13311.72	9434.31	7511.70	6370.87	5620.75	5093.75	4706.04	4411.01	4180.71	3997.32	3848.96
290,000	25902.01	13787.13	9771.25	7779.98	6598.40	5821.50	5275.67	4874.11	4568.55	4330.02	4140.08	3986.42
300,000	26795.19	14262.55	10108.19	8048.25	6825.93	6022.24	5457.59	5042.18	4726.08	4479.33	4282.84	4123.88

90

AMOUNT OF LOAN	NUMBER OF YEARS IN TERM											
	13	14	15	16	17	18	19	20	25	30	35	40
$ 50	0.67	0.65	0.64	0.62	0.61	0.61	0.60	0.59	0.57	0.56	0.55	0.55
100	1.34	1.30	1.27	1.24	1.22	1.21	1.19	1.18	1.13	1.11	1.10	1.09
200	2.67	2.60	2.54	2.48	2.44	2.41	2.37	2.35	2.26	2.22	2.20	2.18
300	4.00	3.89	3.80	3.72	3.66	3.61	3.56	3.52	3.39	3.32	3.29	3.27
400	5.33	5.19	5.07	4.96	4.88	4.81	4.74	4.69	4.52	4.43	4.39	4.36
500	6.66	6.48	6.33	6.20	6.10	6.01	5.93	5.86	5.64	5.54	5.48	5.45
600	7.99	7.78	7.60	7.44	7.32	7.21	7.11	7.03	6.77	6.64	6.58	6.54
700	9.32	9.07	8.86	8.68	8.54	8.41	8.30	8.21	7.90	7.75	7.67	7.63
800	10.65	10.37	10.13	9.92	9.75	9.61	9.48	9.38	9.03	8.85	8.77	8.72
900	11.99	11.66	11.39	11.16	10.97	10.81	10.67	10.55	10.16	9.96	9.86	9.81
1,000	13.32	12.96	12.66	12.40	12.19	12.01	11.85	11.72	11.28	11.07	10.96	10.90
2,000	26.63	25.91	25.31	24.80	24.38	24.01	23.70	23.44	22.56	22.13	21.91	21.80
3,000	39.94	38.86	37.96	37.20	36.56	36.02	35.55	35.15	33.84	33.19	32.86	32.69
4,000	53.25	51.82	50.61	49.60	48.75	48.02	47.40	46.87	45.12	44.25	43.81	43.59
5,000	66.57	64.77	63.27	62.00	60.94	60.03	59.25	58.58	56.40	55.31	54.76	54.48
6,000	79.88	77.72	75.92	74.40	73.12	72.03	71.10	70.30	67.68	66.38	65.72	65.38
7,000	93.19	90.67	88.57	86.80	85.31	84.04	82.95	82.02	78.95	77.44	76.67	76.27
8,000	106.50	103.63	101.22	99.20	97.49	96.04	94.80	93.73	90.23	88.50	87.62	87.17
9,000	119.81	116.58	113.88	111.60	109.68	108.04	106.65	105.45	101.51	99.56	98.57	98.06
10,000	133.13	129.53	126.53	124.00	121.87	120.05	118.49	117.16	112.79	110.62	109.52	108.96
15,000	199.69	194.29	189.79	186.00	182.80	180.07	177.74	175.74	169.18	165.93	164.28	163.43
20,000	266.25	259.06	253.05	248.00	243.73	240.09	236.98	234.32	225.57	221.24	219.04	217.91
25,000	332.81	323.82	316.32	310.00	304.66	300.11	296.23	292.90	281.96	276.55	273.80	272.38
30,000	399.37	388.58	379.58	372.00	365.59	360.13	355.47	351.48	338.36	331.86	328.56	326.86
35,000	465.93	453.35	442.84	434.00	426.52	420.16	414.72	410.06	394.75	387.17	383.32	381.33
40,000	532.49	518.11	506.10	496.00	487.45	480.18	473.96	468.64	451.14	442.48	438.08	435.81
45,000	599.05	582.87	569.36	558.00	548.38	540.20	533.21	527.21	507.53	497.79	492.84	490.29
50,000	665.61	647.64	632.63	620.00	609.31	600.22	592.45	585.79	563.92	553.10	547.60	544.76
55,000	732.17	712.40	695.89	682.00	670.24	660.24	651.70	644.37	620.31	608.41	602.36	599.24
60,000	798.73	777.16	759.15	744.00	731.17	720.26	710.94	702.95	676.71	663.72	657.12	653.71
65,000	865.29	841.93	822.41	806.00	792.10	780.29	770.19	761.53	733.10	719.05	711.88	708.19
70,000	931.85	906.69	885.67	868.00	853.04	840.31	829.43	820.11	789.49	774.34	766.64	762.66
75,000	998.41	971.45	948.94	930.00	913.97	900.33	888.68	878.69	845.88	829.65	821.40	817.14
80,000	1064.97	1036.22	1012.20	992.00	974.90	960.35	947.92	937.27	902.27	884.96	876.16	871.62
85,000	1131.53	1100.98	1075.46	1053.99	1035.83	1020.37	1007.17	995.84	958.67	940.27	930.92	926.09
90,000	1198.09	1165.74	1138.72	1115.99	1096.76	1080.39	1066.41	1054.42	1015.06	995.58	985.68	980.57
95,000	1264.65	1230.51	1201.99	1177.99	1157.69	1140.42	1125.66	1113.00	1071.45	1050.89	1040.44	1035.04
100,000	1331.22	1295.27	1265.25	1239.99	1218.62	1200.44	1184.90	1171.58	1127.84	1106.20	1095.20	1089.52
105,000	1397.78	1360.03	1328.51	1301.99	1279.55	1260.46	1244.15	1230.16	1184.23	1161.51	1149.96	1143.99
110,000	1464.34	1424.79	1391.77	1363.99	1340.48	1320.48	1303.39	1288.74	1240.62	1216.82	1204.72	1198.47
115,000	1530.90	1489.56	1455.03	1425.99	1401.41	1380.50	1362.64	1347.32	1297.02	1272.13	1259.48	1252.95
120,000	1597.46	1554.32	1518.30	1487.99	1462.34	1440.52	1421.88	1405.90	1353.41	1327.44	1314.24	1307.42
125,000	1664.02	1619.08	1581.56	1549.99	1523.27	1500.55	1481.13	1464.47	1409.80	1382.75	1369.00	1361.90
130,000	1730.58	1683.85	1644.82	1611.99	1584.20	1560.57	1540.37	1523.05	1466.19	1438.06	1423.76	1416.37
135,000	1797.14	1748.61	1708.08	1673.99	1645.13	1620.59	1599.62	1581.63	1522.58	1493.37	1478.52	1470.85
140,000	1863.70	1813.37	1771.34	1735.99	1706.07	1680.61	1658.86	1640.21	1578.97	1548.68	1533.28	1525.32
145,000	1930.26	1878.14	1834.61	1797.99	1767.00	1740.63	1718.11	1698.79	1635.37	1603.99	1588.04	1579.80
150,000	1996.82	1942.90	1897.87	1859.99	1827.93	1800.65	1777.35	1757.37	1691.76	1659.30	1642.79	1634.28
155,000	2063.38	2007.66	1961.13	1921.99	1888.86	1860.68	1836.60	1815.95	1748.15	1714.61	1697.55	1688.75
160,000	2129.94	2072.43	2024.39	1983.99	1949.79	1920.70	1895.84	1874.53	1804.54	1769.92	1752.31	1743.23
165,000	2196.50	2137.19	2087.65	2045.98	2010.72	1980.72	1955.09	1933.10	1860.93	1825.23	1807.07	1797.70
170,000	2263.06	2201.95	2150.92	2107.98	2071.65	2040.74	2014.33	1991.68	1917.33	1880.54	1861.83	1852.18
175,000	2329.62	2266.72	2214.18	2169.98	2132.58	2100.76	2073.58	2050.26	1973.72	1935.85	1916.59	1906.65
180,000	2396.18	2331.48	2277.44	2231.98	2193.51	2160.78	2132.82	2108.84	2030.11	1991.16	1971.35	1961.13
185,000	2462.74	2396.24	2340.70	2293.98	2254.44	2220.81	2192.07	2167.42	2086.50	2046.47	2026.11	2015.61
190,000	2529.30	2461.01	2403.97	2355.98	2315.37	2280.83	2251.31	2226.00	2142.89	2101.78	2080.87	2070.08
195,000	2595.87	2525.77	2467.23	2417.98	2376.30	2340.85	2310.56	2284.58	2199.28	2157.09	2135.63	2124.56
200,000	2662.43	2590.53	2530.49	2479.98	2437.23	2400.87	2369.80	2343.16	2255.68	2212.40	2190.39	2179.03
205,000	2728.99	2655.30	2593.75	2541.98	2498.16	2460.89	2429.05	2401.74	2312.07	2267.71	2245.15	2233.51
210,000	2795.55	2720.06	2657.01	2603.98	2559.10	2520.91	2488.29	2460.31	2368.46	2323.02	2299.91	2287.98
215,000	2862.11	2784.82	2720.28	2665.98	2620.03	2580.93	2547.54	2518.89	2424.85	2378.33	2354.67	2342.46
220,000	2928.67	2849.58	2783.54	2727.98	2680.96	2640.96	2606.78	2577.47	2481.24	2433.64	2409.43	2396.94
225,000	2995.23	2914.35	2846.80	2789.98	2741.89	2700.98	2666.03	2636.05	2537.63	2488.95	2464.19	2451.41
230,000	3061.79	2979.11	2910.06	2851.98	2802.82	2761.00	2725.27	2694.63	2594.03	2544.26	2518.95	2505.89
235,000	3128.35	3043.87	2973.32	2913.98	2863.75	2821.02	2784.52	2753.21	2650.42	2599.57	2573.71	2560.36
240,000	3194.91	3108.64	3036.59	2975.98	2924.68	2881.04	2843.76	2811.79	2706.81	2654.88	2628.47	2614.84
245,000	3261.47	3173.40	3099.85	3037.98	2985.61	2941.06	2903.00	2870.37	2763.20	2710.19	2683.23	2669.31
250,000	3328.03	3238.16	3163.11	3099.97	3046.54	3001.09	2962.25	2928.94	2819.59	2765.50	2737.99	2723.79
255,000	3394.59	3302.93	3226.37	3161.97	3107.47	3061.11	3021.49	2987.52	2875.99	2820.81	2792.75	2778.27
260,000	3461.15	3367.69	3289.63	3223.97	3168.40	3121.13	3080.74	3046.10	2932.38	2876.12	2847.51	2832.74
265,000	3527.71	3432.45	3352.90	3285.97	3229.33	3181.15	3139.98	3104.68	2988.77	2931.43	2902.27	2887.22
270,000	3594.27	3497.22	3416.16	3347.97	3290.26	3241.17	3199.23	3163.26	3045.16	2986.74	2957.03	2941.69
280,000	3727.39	3626.74	3542.68	3471.97	3412.13	3361.22	3317.72	3280.42	3157.94	3097.36	3066.55	3050.64
290,000	3860.51	3756.27	3669.21	3595.97	3533.99	3481.26	3436.21	3397.57	3270.73	3207.98	3176.07	3159.60
300,000	3993.64	3885.80	3795.73	3719.97	3655.85	3601.30	3554.70	3514.73	3383.51	3318.60	3285.58	3268.55

13.25%

MONTHLY AMORTIZING PAYMENTS

AMOUNT OF LOAN	NUMBER OF YEARS IN TERM											
	1	2	3	4	5	6	7	8	9	10	11	12
$ 50	4.48	2.39	1.70	1.35	1.15	1.02	0.92	0.85	0.80	0.76	0.73	0.70
100	8.95	4.77	3.39	2.70	2.29	2.03	1.84	1.70	1.59	1.51	1.45	1.40
200	17.89	9.54	6.77	5.40	4.58	4.05	3.67	3.39	3.18	3.02	2.89	2.79
300	26.84	14.30	10.15	8.09	6.87	6.07	5.50	5.09	4.77	4.53	4.33	4.18
400	35.78	19.07	13.53	10.79	9.16	8.09	7.34	6.78	6.36	6.04	5.78	5.57
500	44.72	23.83	16.91	13.48	11.45	10.11	9.17	8.48	7.95	7.54	7.22	6.96
600	53.67	28.60	20.29	16.18	13.73	12.13	11.00	10.17	9.54	9.05	8.66	8.35
700	62.61	33.37	23.68	18.87	16.02	14.15	12.83	11.87	11.13	10.56	10.10	9.74
800	71.55	38.13	27.06	21.57	18.31	16.17	14.67	13.56	12.72	12.07	11.55	11.13
900	80.50	42.90	30.44	24.26	20.60	18.19	16.50	15.26	14.31	13.58	12.99	12.52
1,000	89.44	47.66	33.82	26.96	22.89	20.21	18.33	16.95	15.90	15.08	14.43	13.91
2,000	178.87	95.32	67.63	53.91	45.77	40.42	36.66	33.90	31.80	30.16	28.86	27.81
3,000	268.31	142.98	101.45	80.86	68.65	60.62	54.99	50.85	47.70	45.24	43.29	41.71
4,000	357.74	190.64	135.26	107.81	91.53	80.83	73.32	67.79	63.60	60.32	57.72	55.61
5,000	447.18	238.30	169.08	134.76	114.41	101.04	91.65	84.74	79.49	75.40	72.14	69.51
6,000	536.61	285.96	202.89	161.72	137.29	121.24	109.97	101.69	95.39	90.48	86.57	83.41
7,000	626.05	333.62	236.71	188.67	160.17	141.45	128.30	118.64	111.29	105.56	101.00	97.31
8,000	715.48	381.28	270.52	215.62	183.06	161.66	146.63	135.58	127.19	120.64	115.43	111.22
9,000	804.92	428.94	304.34	242.57	205.94	181.86	164.96	152.53	143.08	135.72	129.85	125.12
10,000	894.35	476.60	338.15	269.52	228.82	202.07	183.29	169.48	158.98	150.79	144.28	139.02
15,000	1341.52	714.90	507.22	404.28	343.22	303.10	274.93	254.22	238.47	226.19	216.42	208.52
20,000	1788.70	953.19	676.29	539.04	457.63	404.13	366.57	338.95	317.96	301.58	288.56	278.03
25,000	2235.87	1191.49	845.37	673.80	572.04	505.16	458.21	423.69	397.45	376.98	360.70	347.54
30,000	2683.04	1429.79	1014.44	808.56	686.44	606.19	549.85	508.43	476.93	452.37	432.83	417.04
35,000	3130.22	1668.08	1183.51	943.32	800.85	707.23	641.49	593.16	556.42	527.77	504.97	486.55
40,000	3577.39	1906.38	1352.58	1078.07	915.26	808.26	733.13	677.90	635.91	603.16	577.11	556.06
45,000	4024.56	2144.68	1521.66	1212.83	1029.66	909.29	824.77	762.64	715.40	678.56	649.25	625.56
50,000	4471.74	2382.97	1690.73	1347.59	1144.07	1010.32	916.41	847.38	794.89	753.95	721.39	695.07
55,000	4918.91	2621.27	1859.80	1482.35	1258.47	1111.35	1008.05	932.11	874.37	829.34	793.52	764.58
60,000	5366.08	2859.57	2028.87	1617.11	1372.88	1212.38	1099.69	1016.85	953.86	904.74	865.66	834.08
65,000	5813.25	3097.86	2197.95	1751.87	1487.29	1313.41	1191.33	1101.59	1033.35	980.13	937.80	903.59
70,000	6260.43	3336.16	2367.02	1886.63	1601.69	1414.45	1282.98	1186.32	1112.84	1055.53	1009.94	973.10
75,000	6707.60	3574.46	2536.09	2021.39	1716.10	1515.48	1374.62	1271.06	1192.33	1130.92	1082.08	1042.60
80,000	7154.77	3812.75	2705.16	2156.14	1830.51	1616.51	1466.26	1355.80	1271.81	1206.32	1154.21	1112.11
85,000	7601.95	4051.05	2874.24	2290.90	1944.91	1717.54	1557.90	1440.53	1351.30	1281.71	1226.35	1181.62
90,000	8049.12	4289.35	3043.31	2425.66	2059.32	1818.57	1649.54	1525.27	1430.79	1357.11	1298.49	1251.12
95,000	8496.29	4527.64	3212.38	2560.42	2173.72	1919.60	1741.18	1610.01	1510.28	1432.50	1370.63	1320.63
100,000	8943.47	4765.94	3381.45	2695.18	2288.13	2020.63	1832.82	1694.75	1589.77	1507.89	1442.77	1390.14
105,000	9390.64	5004.24	3550.53	2829.94	2402.54	2121.67	1924.46	1779.48	1669.25	1583.29	1514.90	1459.64
110,000	9837.81	5242.53	3719.60	2964.70	2516.94	2222.70	2016.10	1864.22	1748.74	1658.68	1587.04	1529.15
115,000	10284.99	5480.83	3888.67	3099.46	2631.35	2323.73	2107.74	1948.96	1828.23	1734.08	1659.18	1598.66
120,000	10732.16	5719.13	4057.74	3234.21	2745.76	2424.76	2199.38	2033.69	1907.72	1809.47	1731.32	1668.16
125,000	11179.33	5957.42	4226.82	3368.97	2860.16	2525.79	2291.02	2118.43	1987.21	1884.87	1803.46	1737.67
130,000	11626.50	6195.72	4395.89	3503.73	2974.57	2626.82	2382.66	2203.17	2066.70	1960.26	1875.59	1807.18
135,000	12073.68	6434.02	4564.96	3638.49	3088.97	2727.85	2474.31	2287.90	2146.18	2035.66	1947.73	1876.68
140,000	12520.85	6672.31	4734.03	3773.25	3203.38	2828.89	2565.95	2372.64	2225.67	2111.05	2019.87	1946.19
145,000	12968.02	6910.61	4903.11	3908.01	3317.79	2929.92	2657.59	2457.38	2305.16	2186.44	2092.01	2015.70
150,000	13415.20	7148.91	5072.18	4042.77	3432.19	3030.95	2749.23	2542.12	2384.65	2261.84	2164.15	2085.20
155,000	13862.37	7387.20	5241.25	4177.53	3546.60	3131.98	2840.87	2626.85	2464.14	2337.23	2236.28	2154.71
160,000	14309.54	7625.50	5410.32	4312.28	3661.01	3233.01	2932.51	2711.59	2543.62	2412.63	2308.42	2224.21
165,000	14756.72	7863.80	5579.40	4447.04	3775.41	3334.04	3024.15	2796.33	2623.11	2488.02	2380.56	2293.72
170,000	15203.89	8102.09	5748.47	4581.80	3889.82	3435.07	3115.79	2881.06	2702.60	2563.42	2452.70	2363.23
175,000	15651.06	8340.39	5917.54	4716.56	4004.22	3536.11	3207.43	2965.80	2782.09	2638.81	2524.84	2432.73
180,000	16098.23	8578.69	6086.61	4851.32	4118.63	3637.14	3299.07	3050.54	2861.58	2714.21	2596.97	2502.24
185,000	16545.41	8816.98	6255.69	4986.08	4233.04	3738.17	3390.71	3135.27	2941.06	2789.60	2669.11	2571.75
190,000	16992.58	9055.28	6424.76	5120.84	4347.44	3839.20	3482.35	3220.01	3020.55	2864.99	2741.25	2641.25
195,000	17439.75	9293.58	6593.83	5255.59	4461.85	3940.23	3573.99	3304.75	3100.04	2940.39	2813.39	2710.76
200,000	17886.93	9531.87	6762.90	5390.35	4576.26	4041.26	3665.64	3389.49	3179.53	3015.78	2885.53	2780.27
205,000	18334.10	9770.17	6931.98	5525.11	4690.66	4142.30	3757.28	3474.22	3259.02	3091.18	2957.66	2849.77
210,000	18781.27	10008.47	7101.05	5659.87	4805.07	4243.33	3848.92	3558.96	3338.50	3166.57	3029.80	2919.28
215,000	19228.45	10246.76	7270.12	5794.63	4919.47	4344.36	3940.56	3643.70	3417.99	3241.97	3101.94	2988.79
220,000	19675.62	10485.06	7439.19	5929.39	5033.88	4445.39	4032.20	3728.43	3497.48	3317.36	3174.08	3058.29
225,000	20122.79	10723.36	7608.27	6064.15	5148.29	4546.42	4123.84	3813.17	3576.97	3392.76	3246.22	3127.80
230,000	20569.97	10961.65	7777.34	6198.91	5262.69	4647.45	4215.48	3897.91	3656.46	3468.15	3318.35	3197.31
235,000	21017.14	11199.95	7946.41	6333.66	5377.10	4748.48	4307.12	3982.64	3735.94	3543.54	3390.49	3266.81
240,000	21464.31	11438.25	8115.48	6468.42	5491.51	4849.52	4398.76	4067.38	3815.43	3618.94	3462.63	3336.32
245,000	21911.48	11676.54	8284.56	6603.18	5605.91	4950.55	4490.40	4152.12	3894.92	3694.33	3534.77	3405.83
250,000	22358.66	11914.84	8453.63	6737.94	5720.32	5051.58	4582.04	4236.86	3974.41	3769.73	3606.91	3475.33
255,000	22805.83	12153.14	8622.70	6872.70	5834.73	5152.61	4673.68	4321.59	4053.90	3845.12	3679.04	3544.84
260,000	23253.00	12391.43	8791.77	7007.46	5949.13	5253.64	4765.32	4406.33	4133.39	3920.52	3751.18	3614.35
265,000	23700.18	12629.73	8960.85	7142.22	6063.54	5354.67	4856.97	4491.07	4212.87	3995.91	3823.32	3683.85
270,000	24147.35	12868.03	9129.92	7276.98	6177.94	5455.70	4948.61	4575.80	4292.36	4071.31	3895.46	3753.36
280,000	25041.70	13344.62	9468.06	7546.49	6406.76	5657.77	5131.89	4745.28	4451.34	4222.09	4039.73	3892.37
290,000	25936.04	13821.21	9806.21	7816.01	6635.57	5859.83	5315.17	4914.75	4610.31	4372.88	4184.01	4031.39
300,000	26830.39	14297.81	10144.35	8085.53	6864.38	6061.89	5498.45	5084.23	4769.29	4523.67	4328.29	4170.40

AMOUNT OF LOAN	NUMBER OF YEARS IN TERM											
	13	14	15	16	17	18	19	20	25	30	35	40
$ 50	0.68	0.66	0.65	0.63	0.62	0.61	0.61	0.60	0.58	0.57	0.56	0.56
100	1.35	1.32	1.29	1.26	1.24	1.22	1.21	1.19	1.15	1.13	1.12	1.11
200	2.70	2.63	2.57	2.52	2.48	2.44	2.41	2.38	2.30	2.26	2.24	2.22
300	4.05	3.94	3.85	3.78	3.71	3.66	3.61	3.57	3.45	3.38	3.35	3.33
400	5.39	5.25	5.13	5.03	4.95	4.88	4.82	4.76	4.59	4.51	4.47	4.44
500	6.74	6.56	6.41	6.29	6.18	6.09	6.02	5.95	5.74	5.63	5.58	5.55
600	8.09	7.87	7.70	7.55	7.42	7.31	7.22	7.14	6.89	6.76	6.70	6.66
700	9.43	9.19	8.98	8.80	8.65	8.53	8.42	8.33	8.03	7.89	7.81	7.77
800	10.78	10.50	10.26	10.06	9.89	9.75	9.63	9.52	9.18	9.01	8.93	8.88
900	12.13	11.81	11.54	11.32	11.13	10.97	10.83	10.71	10.33	10.14	10.04	9.99
1,000	13.48	13.12	12.82	12.57	12.36	12.18	12.03	11.90	11.47	11.26	11.16	11.10
2,000	26.95	26.23	25.64	25.14	24.72	24.36	24.06	23.79	22.94	22.52	22.31	22.20
3,000	40.42	39.35	38.46	37.71	37.08	36.54	36.08	35.69	34.41	33.78	33.46	33.30
4,000	53.89	52.46	51.27	50.28	49.43	48.72	48.11	47.58	45.87	45.04	44.61	44.40
5,000	67.36	65.58	64.09	62.84	61.79	60.89	60.13	59.48	57.34	56.29	55.77	55.50
6,000	80.83	78.69	76.91	75.41	74.15	73.07	72.16	71.37	68.81	67.55	66.92	66.60
7,000	94.30	91.81	89.73	87.98	86.50	85.25	84.18	83.27	80.27	78.81	78.07	77.70
8,000	107.77	104.92	102.54	100.55	98.86	97.43	96.21	95.16	91.74	90.07	89.22	88.79
9,000	121.24	118.03	115.36	113.12	111.22	109.61	108.23	107.05	103.21	101.32	100.38	99.89
10,000	134.71	131.15	128.18	125.68	123.57	121.78	120.26	118.95	114.68	112.58	111.53	110.99
15,000	202.06	196.72	192.27	188.52	185.36	182.67	180.38	178.42	172.01	168.87	167.29	166.49
20,000	269.42	262.29	256.35	251.36	247.14	243.56	240.51	237.89	229.35	225.16	223.05	221.98
25,000	336.77	327.87	320.44	314.20	308.93	304.45	300.63	297.36	286.68	281.45	278.82	277.47
30,000	404.12	393.44	384.53	377.04	370.71	365.34	360.76	356.83	344.02	337.74	334.58	332.97
35,000	471.48	459.01	448.61	439.88	432.50	426.23	420.88	416.31	401.35	394.03	390.34	388.46
40,000	538.83	524.58	512.70	502.72	494.28	487.12	481.01	475.78	458.69	450.31	446.10	443.95
45,000	606.18	590.15	576.79	565.56	556.07	548.01	541.13	535.25	516.02	506.60	501.86	499.45
50,000	673.53	655.73	640.87	628.40	617.85	608.90	601.26	594.72	573.36	562.89	557.63	554.94
55,000	740.89	721.30	704.96	691.24	679.64	669.79	661.39	654.19	630.69	619.18	613.39	610.43
60,000	808.24	786.87	769.05	754.08	741.42	730.68	721.51	713.66	688.03	675.47	669.15	665.93
65,000	875.59	852.44	833.13	816.91	803.21	791.57	781.64	773.13	745.36	731.76	724.91	721.42
70,000	942.95	918.01	897.22	879.75	864.99	852.46	841.76	832.61	802.70	788.05	780.67	776.91
75,000	1010.30	983.59	961.31	942.59	926.78	913.35	901.89	892.08	860.03	844.34	836.44	832.41
80,000	1077.65	1049.16	1025.39	1005.43	988.56	974.23	962.01	951.55	917.37	900.62	892.20	887.90
85,000	1145.01	1114.73	1089.48	1068.27	1050.35	1035.12	1022.14	1011.02	974.70	956.91	947.96	943.39
90,000	1212.36	1180.30	1153.57	1131.11	1112.13	1096.01	1082.26	1070.49	1032.04	1013.20	1003.72	998.89
95,000	1279.71	1245.88	1217.65	1193.95	1173.92	1156.90	1142.39	1129.96	1089.37	1069.49	1059.49	1054.38
100,000	1347.06	1311.45	1281.74	1256.79	1235.70	1217.79	1202.51	1189.44	1146.71	1125.78	1115.25	1109.87
105,000	1414.42	1377.02	1345.83	1319.63	1297.49	1278.68	1262.64	1240.91	1204.04	1182.07	1171.01	1165.37
110,000	1481.77	1442.59	1409.92	1382.47	1359.27	1339.57	1322.77	1308.38	1261.38	1238.36	1226.77	1220.86
115,000	1549.12	1508.16	1474.00	1445.31	1421.06	1400.46	1382.89	1367.85	1318.71	1294.64	1282.53	1276.36
120,000	1616.48	1573.74	1538.09	1508.15	1482.84	1461.35	1443.02	1427.32	1376.05	1350.93	1338.30	1331.85
125,000	1683.83	1639.31	1602.18	1570.98	1544.63	1522.24	1503.14	1486.79	1433.38	1407.22	1394.06	1387.34
130,000	1751.18	1704.88	1666.26	1633.82	1606.41	1583.13	1563.27	1546.26	1490.72	1463.51	1449.82	1442.84
135,000	1818.54	1770.45	1730.35	1696.66	1668.20	1644.02	1623.39	1605.74	1548.05	1519.80	1505.58	1498.33
140,000	1885.89	1836.02	1794.44	1759.50	1729.98	1704.91	1683.52	1665.21	1605.39	1576.09	1561.34	1553.82
145,000	1953.24	1901.60	1858.52	1822.34	1791.77	1765.80	1743.64	1724.68	1662.72	1632.38	1617.11	1609.32
150,000	2020.59	1967.17	1922.61	1885.18	1853.55	1826.69	1803.77	1784.15	1720.06	1688.67	1672.87	1664.81
155,000	2087.95	2032.74	1986.70	1948.02	1915.33	1887.57	1863.90	1843.62	1777.39	1744.95	1728.63	1720.30
160,000	2155.30	2098.31	2050.78	2010.86	1977.12	1948.46	1924.02	1903.09	1834.73	1801.24	1784.39	1775.80
165,000	2222.65	2163.88	2114.87	2073.70	2038.90	2009.35	1984.15	1962.57	1892.06	1857.53	1840.15	1831.29
170,000	2290.01	2229.46	2178.96	2136.54	2100.69	2070.24	2044.27	2022.04	1949.40	1913.82	1895.92	1886.78
175,000	2357.36	2295.03	2243.04	2199.38	2162.47	2131.13	2104.40	2081.51	2006.73	1970.11	1951.68	1942.28
180,000	2424.71	2360.60	2307.13	2262.22	2224.26	2192.02	2164.52	2140.98	2064.07	2026.40	2007.44	1997.77
185,000	2492.06	2426.17	2371.22	2325.05	2286.04	2252.91	2224.65	2200.45	2121.40	2082.69	2063.20	2053.26
190,000	2559.42	2491.75	2435.30	2387.89	2347.83	2313.80	2284.77	2259.92	2178.74	2138.97	2118.97	2108.76
195,000	2626.77	2557.32	2499.39	2450.73	2409.61	2374.69	2344.90	2319.39	2236.07	2195.26	2174.73	2164.25
200,000	2694.12	2622.89	2563.48	2513.57	2471.40	2435.58	2405.02	2378.87	2293.41	2251.55	2230.49	2219.74
205,000	2761.48	2688.46	2627.56	2576.41	2533.18	2496.47	2465.15	2438.34	2350.74	2307.84	2286.25	2275.24
210,000	2828.83	2754.03	2691.65	2639.25	2594.97	2557.36	2525.28	2497.81	2408.08	2364.13	2342.01	2330.73
215,000	2896.18	2819.61	2755.74	2702.09	2656.75	2618.25	2585.40	2557.28	2465.41	2420.42	2397.78	2386.23
220,000	2963.54	2885.18	2819.83	2764.93	2718.54	2679.14	2645.53	2616.75	2522.75	2476.71	2453.54	2441.72
225,000	3030.89	2950.75	2883.91	2827.77	2780.32	2740.03	2705.65	2676.22	2580.08	2533.00	2509.30	2497.21
230,000	3098.24	3016.32	2948.00	2890.61	2842.11	2800.91	2765.78	2735.70	2637.42	2589.28	2565.06	2552.71
235,000	3165.59	3081.89	3012.09	2953.45	2903.89	2861.80	2825.90	2795.17	2694.75	2645.57	2620.82	2608.20
240,000	3232.95	3147.47	3076.17	3016.29	2965.68	2922.69	2886.03	2854.64	2752.09	2701.86	2676.59	2663.69
245,000	3300.30	3213.04	3140.26	3079.12	3027.46	2983.58	2946.15	2914.11	2809.42	2758.15	2732.35	2719.19
250,000	3367.65	3278.61	3204.35	3141.96	3089.25	3044.47	3006.28	2973.58	2866.76	2814.44	2788.11	2774.68
255,000	3435.01	3344.18	3268.43	3204.80	3151.03	3105.36	3066.41	3033.05	2924.09	2870.73	2843.87	2830.17
260,000	3502.36	3409.75	3332.52	3267.64	3212.82	3166.25	3126.53	3092.52	2981.43	2927.02	2899.63	2885.67
265,000	3569.71	3475.33	3396.61	3330.48	3274.60	3227.14	3186.66	3152.00	3038.76	2983.30	2955.40	2941.16
270,000	3637.07	3540.90	3460.69	3393.32	3336.39	3288.03	3246.78	3211.47	3096.10	3039.59	3011.16	2996.65
280,000	3771.77	3672.04	3588.87	3519.00	3459.96	3409.81	3367.03	3330.41	3210.77	3152.17	3122.68	3107.64
290,000	3906.48	3803.19	3717.04	3644.68	3583.53	3531.59	3487.28	3449.35	3325.44	3264.75	3234.21	3218.63
300,000	4041.18	3934.33	3845.21	3770.36	3707.10	3653.37	3607.53	3568.30	3440.11	3377.33	3345.73	3329.61

93

13.50%

MONTHLY AMORTIZING PAYMENTS

AMOUNT OF LOAN	NUMBER OF YEARS IN TERM											
	1	2	3	4	5	6	7	8	9	10	11	12
$ 50	4.48	2.39	1.70	1.36	1.16	1.02	0.93	0.86	0.81	0.77	0.73	0.71
100	8.96	4.78	3.40	2.71	2.31	2.04	1.85	1.71	1.61	1.53	1.46	1.41
200	17.92	9.56	6.79	5.42	4.61	4.07	3.70	3.42	3.21	3.05	2.92	2.82
300	26.87	14.34	10.19	8.13	6.91	6.11	5.54	5.13	4.82	4.57	4.38	4.22
400	35.83	19.12	13.58	10.84	9.21	8.14	7.39	6.84	6.42	6.10	5.84	5.63
500	44.78	23.89	16.97	13.54	11.51	10.17	9.24	8.55	8.03	7.62	7.29	7.03
600	53.74	28.67	20.37	16.25	13.81	12.21	11.08	10.26	9.63	9.14	8.75	8.44
700	62.69	33.45	23.76	18.96	16.11	14.24	12.93	11.97	11.23	10.66	10.21	9.85
800	71.65	38.23	27.15	21.67	18.41	16.28	14.78	13.68	12.84	12.19	11.67	11.25
900	80.60	43.00	30.55	24.37	20.71	18.31	16.62	15.38	14.44	13.71	13.13	12.66
1,000	89.56	47.78	33.94	27.08	23.01	20.34	18.47	17.09	16.05	15.23	14.58	14.06
2,000	179.11	95.56	67.88	54.16	46.02	40.68	36.93	34.18	32.09	30.46	29.16	28.12
3,000	268.66	143.34	101.81	81.23	69.03	61.02	55.40	51.27	48.13	45.69	43.74	42.18
4,000	358.21	191.11	135.75	108.31	92.04	81.36	73.86	68.36	64.17	60.91	58.32	56.23
5,000	447.77	238.89	169.68	135.39	115.05	101.70	92.33	85.45	80.22	76.14	72.90	70.29
6,000	537.32	286.67	203.62	162.46	138.06	122.04	110.79	102.53	96.26	91.37	87.48	84.35
7,000	626.87	334.44	237.55	189.54	161.07	142.38	129.26	119.62	112.30	106.60	102.06	98.41
8,000	716.42	382.22	271.49	216.62	184.08	162.72	147.72	136.71	128.34	121.82	116.64	112.46
9,000	805.97	430.00	305.42	243.69	207.09	183.06	166.19	153.80	144.39	137.05	131.22	126.52
10,000	895.53	477.78	339.36	270.77	230.10	203.39	184.65	170.89	160.43	152.28	145.80	140.58
15,000	1343.29	716.66	509.03	406.15	345.15	305.09	276.98	256.33	240.64	228.42	218.70	210.86
20,000	1791.05	955.55	678.71	541.53	460.20	406.78	369.30	341.77	320.85	304.55	291.60	281.15
25,000	2238.81	1194.43	848.39	676.91	575.25	508.48	461.63	427.21	401.06	380.69	364.50	351.43
30,000	2686.57	1433.32	1018.06	812.29	690.30	610.17	553.95	512.65	481.27	456.83	437.40	421.72
35,000	3134.33	1672.20	1187.74	947.68	805.35	711.87	646.28	598.09	561.49	532.97	510.30	492.01
40,000	3582.09	1911.09	1357.42	1083.06	920.40	813.56	738.60	683.53	641.70	609.10	583.20	562.29
45,000	4029.85	2149.97	1527.09	1218.44	1035.45	915.26	830.93	768.97	721.91	685.24	656.10	632.58
50,000	4477.61	2388.86	1696.77	1353.82	1150.50	1016.95	923.25	854.41	802.12	761.38	729.00	702.86
55,000	4925.37	2627.74	1866.45	1489.20	1265.55	1118.65	1015.57	939.85	882.33	837.51	801.90	773.15
60,000	5373.13	2866.63	2036.12	1624.58	1380.60	1220.34	1107.90	1025.29	962.54	913.65	874.80	843.44
65,000	5820.89	3105.51	2205.80	1759.97	1495.64	1322.04	1200.22	1110.74	1042.76	989.79	947.70	913.72
70,000	6268.65	3344.40	2375.48	1895.35	1610.69	1423.73	1292.55	1196.18	1122.97	1065.93	1020.60	984.01
75,000	6716.41	3583.28	2545.15	2030.73	1725.74	1525.43	1384.87	1281.62	1203.18	1142.06	1093.50	1054.29
80,000	7164.17	3822.17	2714.83	2166.11	1840.79	1627.12	1477.20	1367.06	1283.39	1218.20	1166.39	1124.58
85,000	7611.93	4061.05	2884.50	2301.49	1955.84	1728.82	1569.52	1452.50	1363.60	1294.34	1239.29	1194.86
90,000	8059.69	4299.94	3054.18	2436.87	2070.89	1830.51	1661.85	1537.94	1443.81	1370.47	1312.19	1265.15
95,000	8507.45	4538.82	3223.86	2572.26	2185.94	1932.21	1754.17	1623.38	1524.02	1446.61	1385.09	1335.44
100,000	8955.21	4777.71	3393.53	2707.64	2300.99	2033.90	1846.49	1708.82	1604.24	1522.75	1457.99	1405.72
105,000	9402.97	5016.59	3563.21	2843.02	2416.04	2135.60	1938.82	1794.26	1684.45	1598.89	1530.89	1476.01
110,000	9850.73	5255.48	3732.89	2978.40	2531.09	2237.29	2031.14	1879.70	1764.66	1675.02	1603.79	1546.29
115,000	10298.49	5494.36	3902.56	3113.78	2646.14	2338.99	2123.47	1965.14	1844.87	1751.16	1676.69	1616.58
120,000	10746.25	5733.25	4072.24	3249.16	2761.19	2440.68	2215.79	2050.58	1925.08	1827.30	1749.59	1686.87
125,000	11194.01	5972.13	4241.92	3384.55	2876.24	2542.38	2308.12	2136.02	2005.29	1903.43	1822.49	1757.15
130,000	11641.77	6211.02	4411.59	3519.93	2991.28	2644.07	2400.44	2221.47	2085.51	1979.57	1895.39	1827.44
135,000	12089.53	6449.90	4581.27	3655.31	3106.33	2745.76	2492.77	2306.91	2165.72	2055.71	1968.29	1897.72
140,000	12537.29	6688.79	4750.95	3790.69	3221.38	2847.46	2585.09	2392.35	2245.93	2131.85	2041.19	1968.01
145,000	12985.05	6927.67	4920.62	3926.07	3336.43	2949.15	2677.41	2477.79	2326.14	2207.98	2114.09	2038.29
150,000	13432.81	7166.56	5090.30	4061.45	3451.48	3050.85	2769.74	2563.23	2406.35	2284.12	2186.99	2108.58
155,000	13880.57	7405.44	5259.97	4196.84	3566.53	3152.54	2862.06	2648.67	2486.56	2360.26	2259.88	2178.87
160,000	14328.33	7644.33	5429.65	4332.22	3681.58	3254.24	2954.39	2734.11	2566.78	2436.39	2332.78	2249.15
165,000	14776.09	7883.21	5599.33	4467.60	3796.63	3355.93	3046.71	2819.55	2646.99	2512.53	2405.68	2319.44
170,000	15223.85	8122.10	5769.00	4602.98	3911.68	3457.63	3139.04	2904.99	2727.20	2588.67	2478.58	2389.72
175,000	15671.61	8360.98	5938.68	4738.36	4026.73	3559.32	3231.36	2990.43	2807.41	2664.81	2551.48	2460.01
180,000	16119.37	8599.87	6108.36	4873.74	4141.78	3661.02	3323.69	3075.87	2887.62	2740.94	2624.38	2530.30
185,000	16567.13	8838.75	6278.03	5009.12	4256.83	3762.71	3416.01	3161.31	2967.83	2817.08	2697.28	2600.58
190,000	17014.89	9077.64	6447.71	5144.51	4371.88	3864.41	3508.33	3246.76	3048.04	2893.22	2770.18	2670.87
195,000	17462.65	9316.52	6617.39	5279.89	4486.92	3966.10	3600.66	3332.20	3128.26	2969.35	2843.08	2741.15
200,000	17910.41	9555.41	6787.06	5415.27	4601.97	4067.80	3692.98	3417.64	3208.47	3045.49	2915.98	2811.44
205,000	18358.17	9794.29	6956.74	5550.65	4717.02	4169.49	3785.31	3503.08	3288.68	3121.63	2988.88	2881.73
210,000	18805.93	10033.18	7126.42	5686.03	4832.07	4271.19	3877.63	3588.52	3368.89	3197.77	3061.78	2952.01
215,000	19253.69	10272.06	7296.09	5821.41	4947.12	4372.88	3969.96	3673.96	3449.10	3273.90	3134.68	3022.30
220,000	19701.45	10510.95	7465.77	5956.80	5062.17	4474.58	4062.28	3759.40	3529.31	3350.04	3207.58	3092.58
225,000	20149.21	10749.83	7635.44	6092.18	5177.22	4576.27	4154.61	3844.84	3609.53	3426.18	3280.48	3162.87
230,000	20596.97	10988.72	7805.12	6227.56	5292.27	4677.97	4246.93	3930.28	3689.74	3502.31	3353.37	3233.15
235,000	21044.73	11227.60	7974.80	6362.94	5407.32	4779.66	4339.25	4015.72	3769.95	3578.45	3426.27	3303.44
240,000	21492.49	11466.49	8144.47	6498.32	5522.37	4881.36	4431.58	4101.16	3850.16	3654.59	3499.17	3373.73
245,000	21940.25	11705.37	8314.15	6633.70	5637.42	4983.05	4523.90	4186.60	3930.37	3730.73	3572.07	3444.01
250,000	22388.01	11944.26	8483.83	6769.09	5752.47	5084.75	4616.23	4272.04	4010.58	3806.86	3644.97	3514.30
255,000	22835.77	12183.14	8653.50	6904.47	5867.52	5186.44	4708.55	4357.49	4090.80	3883.00	3717.87	3584.58
260,000	23283.53	12422.03	8823.18	7039.85	5982.56	5288.14	4800.88	4442.93	4171.01	3959.14	3790.77	3654.87
265,000	23731.29	12660.91	8992.86	7175.23	6097.61	5389.83	4893.20	4528.37	4251.22	4035.27	3863.67	3725.16
270,000	24179.05	12899.80	9162.53	7310.61	6212.66	5491.52	4985.53	4613.81	4331.43	4111.41	3936.57	3795.44
280,000	25074.57	13377.57	9501.89	7581.38	6442.76	5694.91	5170.17	4784.69	4491.85	4263.69	4082.37	3936.01
290,000	25970.09	13855.34	9841.24	7852.14	6672.86	5898.30	5354.82	4955.57	4652.28	4415.96	4228.17	4076.58
300,000	26865.61	14333.11	10180.59	8122.90	6902.96	6101.69	5539.47	5126.45	4812.70	4568.23	4373.97	4217.16

MONTHLY AMORTIZING PAYMENTS　　13.50%

AMOUNT OF LOAN	NUMBER OF YEARS IN TERM											
	13	14	15	16	17	18	19	20	25	30	35	40
$ 50	0.69	0.67	0.65	0.64	0.63	0.62	0.62	0.61	0.59	0.58	0.57	0.57
100	1.37	1.33	1.30	1.28	1.26	1.24	1.23	1.21	1.17	1.15	1.14	1.14
200	2.73	2.66	2.60	2.55	2.51	2.48	2.45	2.42	2.34	2.30	2.28	2.27
300	4.09	3.99	3.90	3.83	3.76	3.71	3.67	3.63	3.50	3.44	3.41	3.40
400	5.46	5.32	5.20	5.10	5.02	4.95	4.89	4.83	4.67	4.59	4.55	4.53
500	6.82	6.64	6.50	6.37	6.27	6.18	6.11	6.04	5.83	5.73	5.68	5.66
600	8.18	7.97	7.79	7.65	7.52	7.42	7.33	7.25	7.00	6.88	6.82	6.79
700	9.55	9.30	9.09	8.92	8.78	8.65	8.55	8.46	8.16	8.02	7.95	7.92
800	10.91	10.63	10.39	10.19	10.03	9.89	9.77	9.66	9.33	9.17	9.09	9.05
900	12.27	11.95	11.69	11.47	11.28	11.12	10.99	10.87	10.50	10.31	10.22	10.18
1,000	13.63	13.28	12.99	12.74	12.53	12.36	12.21	12.08	11.66	11.46	11.36	11.31
2,000	27.26	26.56	25.97	25.48	25.06	24.71	24.41	24.15	23.32	22.91	22.71	22.61
3,000	40.89	39.84	38.95	38.22	37.59	37.06	36.61	36.23	34.97	34.37	34.07	33.91
4,000	54.52	53.11	51.94	50.95	50.12	49.41	48.81	48.30	46.63	45.82	45.42	45.22
5,000	68.15	66.39	64.92	63.69	62.65	61.77	61.02	60.37	58.29	57.28	56.77	56.52
6,000	81.78	79.67	77.90	76.43	75.18	74.12	73.22	72.45	69.94	68.73	68.13	67.82
7,000	95.41	92.94	90.89	89.16	87.71	86.47	85.42	84.52	81.60	80.18	79.48	79.12
8,000	109.04	106.22	103.87	101.90	100.23	98.82	97.62	96.59	93.26	91.64	90.83	90.43
9,000	122.67	119.50	116.85	114.64	112.76	111.18	109.82	108.67	104.91	103.09	102.19	101.73
10,000	136.30	132.78	129.84	127.37	125.29	123.53	122.03	120.74	116.57	114.55	113.54	113.03
15,000	204.45	199.16	194.75	191.06	187.94	185.29	183.04	181.11	174.85	171.82	170.31	169.54
20,000	272.60	265.55	259.67	254.74	250.58	247.05	244.05	241.48	233.13	229.09	227.07	226.06
25,000	340.75	331.93	324.58	318.42	313.22	308.81	305.06	301.85	291.42	206.36	283.84	282.57
30,000	408.90	398.32	389.50	382.11	375.87	370.57	366.07	362.22	349.70	343.63	340.61	339.08
35,000	477.05	464.70	454.42	445.79	438.51	432.34	427.08	422.59	407.98	400.90	397.37	395.60
40,000	545.20	531.09	519.33	509.47	501.15	494.10	488.09	482.95	466.26	458.17	454.14	452.11
45,000	613.35	597.47	584.25	573.16	563.80	555.86	549.10	543.32	524.55	515.44	510.91	508.62
50,000	681.50	663.86	649.16	636.84	626.44	617.62	610.11	603.69	582.83	572.71	567.68	565.14
55,000	749.65	730.24	714.08	700.52	689.08	679.38	671.12	664.06	641.11	629.98	624.44	621.65
60,000	817.80	796.63	779.00	764.21	751.73	741.14	732.13	724.43	699.39	687.25	681.21	678.16
65,000	885.95	863.01	843.91	827.89	814.37	802.91	793.14	784.80	757.67	744.52	737.98	734.67
70,000	954.10	929.40	908.83	891.57	877.01	864.67	854.15	845.17	815.96	801.79	794.74	791.19
75,000	1022.25	995.79	973.74	955.26	939.66	926.43	915.16	905.54	874.24	859.06	851.51	847.70
80,000	1090.40	1062.17	1038.66	1018.94	1002.30	988.19	976.17	965.90	932.52	916.33	908.28	904.21
85,000	1158.55	1128.56	1103.58	1082.62	1064.94	1049.95	1037.18	1026.27	990.80	973.61	965.04	960.70
90,000	1226.70	1194.94	1168.49	1146.31	1127.59	1111.71	1098.20	1086.64	1049.09	1030.88	1021.81	1017.24
95,000	1294.85	1261.33	1233.41	1209.99	1190.23	1173.47	1159.21	1147.01	1107.37	1088.15	1078.58	1073.75
100,000	1363.00	1327.71	1298.32	1273.67	1252.87	1235.24	1220.22	1207.38	1165.65	1145.42	1135.35	1130.27
105,000	1431.15	1394.10	1363.24	1337.38	1315.52	1297.00	1281.23	1267.75	1223.93	1202.69	1192.11	1186.78
110,000	1499.30	1460.48	1428.16	1401.04	1378.16	1358.76	1342.24	1328.12	1282.21	1259.96	1248.88	1243.29
115,000	1567.45	1526.87	1493.07	1464.72	1440.80	1420.52	1403.25	1388.49	1340.50	1317.23	1305.65	1299.81
120,000	1635.60	1593.25	1557.99	1528.41	1503.45	1482.28	1464.26	1448.85	1398.78	1374.50	1362.41	1356.32
125,000	1703.74	1659.64	1622.90	1592.09	1566.09	1544.04	1525.27	1509.22	1457.06	1431.77	1419.18	1412.83
130,000	1771.89	1726.02	1687.82	1655.77	1628.73	1605.81	1586.28	1569.59	1515.34	1489.04	1475.95	1469.34
135,000	1840.04	1792.41	1752.74	1719.46	1691.38	1667.57	1647.29	1629.96	1573.63	1546.31	1532.71	1525.86
140,000	1908.19	1858.79	1817.65	1783.14	1754.02	1729.33	1708.30	1690.33	1631.91	1603.58	1589.48	1582.37
145,000	1976.34	1925.18	1882.57	1846.82	1816.66	1791.09	1769.31	1750.70	1690.19	1660.85	1646.25	1638.88
150,000	2044.49	1991.57	1947.48	1910.51	1879.31	1852.85	1830.32	1811.07	1748.47	1718.12	1703.02	1695.40
155,000	2112.64	2057.95	2012.40	1974.19	1941.95	1914.61	1891.33	1871.44	1806.75	1775.39	1759.78	1751.91
160,000	2180.79	2124.34	2077.31	2037.87	2004.60	1976.38	1952.34	1931.80	1865.04	1832.66	1816.55	1808.42
165,000	2248.94	2190.72	2142.23	2101.56	2067.24	2038.14	2013.35	1992.17	1923.32	1889.94	1873.32	1864.94
170,000	2317.09	2257.11	2207.15	2165.24	2129.88	2099.90	2074.36	2052.54	1981.60	1947.21	1930.08	1921.45
175,000	2385.24	2323.49	2272.06	2228.92	2192.53	2161.66	2135.38	2112.91	2039.88	2004.48	1986.85	1977.96
180,000	2453.39	2389.88	2336.98	2292.61	2255.17	2223.42	2196.39	2173.28	2098.17	2061.75	2043.62	2034.48
185,000	2521.54	2456.26	2401.89	2356.29	2317.81	2285.18	2257.40	2233.65	2156.45	2119.02	2100.38	2090.99
190,000	2589.69	2522.65	2466.81	2419.97	2380.46	2346.94	2318.41	2294.02	2214.73	2176.29	2157.15	2147.50
195,000	2657.84	2589.03	2531.73	2483.66	2443.10	2408.71	2379.42	2354.39	2273.01	2233.56	2213.92	2204.01
200,000	2725.99	2655.42	2596.64	2547.34	2505.74	2470.47	2440.43	2414.75	2331.29	2290.83	2270.69	2260.53
205,000	2794.14	2721.80	2661.56	2611.02	2568.39	2532.23	2501.44	2475.12	2389.58	2348.10	2327.45	2317.04
210,000	2862.29	2788.19	2726.47	2674.71	2631.03	2593.99	2562.45	2535.49	2447.86	2405.37	2384.22	2373.55
215,000	2930.44	2854.57	2791.39	2738.39	2693.67	2655.75	2623.46	2595.86	2506.14	2462.64	2440.99	2430.07
220,000	2998.59	2920.96	2856.31	2802.07	2756.32	2717.51	2684.47	2656.23	2564.42	2519.91	2497.75	2486.58
225,000	3066.74	2987.35	2921.22	2865.76	2818.96	2779.28	2745.48	2716.60	2622.71	2577.18	2554.52	2543.09
230,000	3134.89	3053.73	2986.14	2929.44	2881.60	2841.04	2806.49	2776.97	2680.99	2634.45	2611.29	2599.61
235,000	3203.04	3120.12	3051.05	2993.12	2944.25	2902.80	2867.50	2837.34	2739.27	2691.72	2668.06	2656.12
240,000	3271.19	3186.50	3115.97	3056.81	3006.89	2964.56	2928.51	2897.70	2797.55	2748.99	2724.82	2712.63
245,000	3339.33	3252.89	3180.89	3120.49	3069.53	3026.32	2989.52	2958.07	2855.83	2806.26	2781.59	2769.14
250,000	3407.48	3319.27	3245.80	3184.18	3132.18	3088.08	3050.53	3018.44	2914.12	2863.54	2838.36	2825.66
255,000	3475.63	3385.66	3310.72	3247.86	3194.82	3149.84	3111.54	3078.81	2972.40	2920.81	2895.12	2882.17
260,000	3543.78	3452.04	3375.63	3311.54	3257.46	3211.61	3172.55	3139.18	3030.68	2978.08	2951.89	2938.68
265,000	3611.93	3518.43	3440.55	3375.23	3320.11	3273.37	3233.57	3199.55	3088.96	3035.35	3008.66	2995.20
270,000	3680.08	3584.81	3505.47	3438.91	3382.75	3335.13	3294.58	3259.92	3147.25	3092.62	3065.42	3051.71
280,000	3816.38	3717.58	3635.30	3566.28	3508.04	3458.65	3416.60	3380.65	3263.81	3207.16	3178.96	3164.74
290,000	3952.68	3850.35	3765.13	3693.64	3633.32	3582.18	3538.62	3501.39	3380.38	3321.70	3292.49	3277.76
300,000	4088.98	3983.13	3894.96	3821.01	3758.61	3705.70	3660.64	3622.13	3496.94	3436.24	3406.03	3390.79

95

13.75% MONTHLY AMORTIZING PAYMENTS

AMOUNT OF LOAN	NUMBER OF YEARS IN TERM											
	1	2	3	4	5	6	7	8	9	10	11	12
$ 50	4.49	2.40	1.71	1.37	1.16	1.03	0.94	0.87	0.81	0.77	0.74	0.72
100	8.97	4.79	3.41	2.73	2.32	2.05	1.87	1.73	1.62	1.54	1.48	1.43
200	17.94	9.58	6.82	5.45	4.63	4.10	3.73	3.45	3.24	3.08	2.95	2.85
300	26.91	14.37	10.22	8.17	6.95	6.15	5.59	5.17	4.86	4.62	4.42	4.27
400	35.87	19.16	13.63	10.89	9.26	8.19	7.45	6.90	6.48	6.16	5.90	5.69
500	44.84	23.95	17.03	13.61	11.57	10.24	9.31	8.62	8.10	7.69	7.37	7.11
600	53.81	28.74	20.44	16.33	13.89	12.29	11.17	10.34	9.72	9.23	8.84	8.53
700	62.77	33.53	23.84	19.05	16.20	14.34	13.03	12.07	11.34	10.77	10.32	9.95
800	71.74	38.32	27.25	21.77	18.52	16.38	14.89	13.79	12.96	12.31	11.79	11.38
900	80.71	43.11	30.66	24.49	20.83	18.43	16.75	15.51	14.57	13.84	13.26	12.80
1,000	89.67	47.90	34.06	27.21	23.14	20.48	18.61	17.23	16.19	15.38	14.74	14.22
2,000	179.34	95.79	68.12	54.41	46.28	40.95	37.21	34.46	32.38	30.76	29.47	28.43
3,000	269.01	143.69	102.17	81.61	69.42	61.42	55.81	51.69	48.57	46.14	44.20	42.65
4,000	358.68	191.58	136.23	108.81	92.56	81.89	74.41	68.92	64.76	61.51	58.94	56.86
5,000	448.35	239.48	170.29	136.01	115.70	102.37	93.02	86.15	80.94	76.89	73.67	71.07
6,000	538.02	287.37	204.34	163.21	138.84	122.84	111.62	103.38	97.13	92.27	88.40	85.29
7,000	627.69	335.27	238.40	190.41	161.98	143.31	130.22	120.61	113.32	107.64	103.14	99.50
8,000	717.36	383.16	272.46	217.61	185.12	163.78	148.82	137.84	129.51	123.02	117.87	113.72
9,000	807.03	431.06	306.51	244.82	208.25	184.25	167.42	155.07	145.69	138.40	132.60	127.93
10,000	896.70	478.95	340.57	272.02	231.39	204.73	186.03	172.30	161.88	153.77	147.33	142.14
15,000	1345.05	718.43	510.85	408.02	347.09	307.09	279.04	258.45	242.82	230.66	221.00	213.21
20,000	1793.40	957.90	681.13	544.03	462.78	409.45	372.05	344.60	323.76	307.54	294.66	284.28
25,000	2241.74	1197.38	851.41	680.04	578.48	511.81	465.06	430.74	404.70	384.42	368.33	355.35
30,000	2690.09	1436.85	1021.69	816.04	694.17	614.17	558.07	516.89	485.64	461.31	441.99	426.42
35,000	3138.44	1676.33	1191.98	952.05	809.86	716.53	651.08	603.04	566.57	538.19	515.66	497.49
40,000	3586.79	1915.80	1362.26	1088.05	925.56	818.89	744.09	689.19	647.51	615.07	589.32	568.56
45,000	4035.13	2155.27	1532.54	1224.06	1041.25	921.25	837.10	775.33	728.45	691.96	662.98	639.63
50,000	4483.48	2394.75	1702.82	1360.07	1156.95	1023.61	930.11	861.48	809.39	768.84	736.65	710.70
55,000	4931.83	2634.22	1873.10	1496.07	1272.64	1125.97	1023.12	947.63	890.33	845.72	810.31	781.77
60,000	5380.18	2873.70	2043.38	1632.08	1388.34	1228.33	1116.14	1033.78	971.27	922.61	883.98	852.83
65,000	5828.52	3113.17	2213.67	1768.09	1504.03	1330.69	1209.15	1119.92	1052.20	999.49	957.64	923.90
70,000	6276.87	3352.65	2383.95	1904.09	1619.72	1433.05	1302.16	1206.07	1133.14	1076.37	1031.31	994.97
75,000	6725.22	3592.12	2554.23	2040.10	1735.42	1535.41	1395.17	1292.22	1214.08	1153.26	1104.97	1066.04
80,000	7173.57	3831.59	2724.51	2176.10	1851.11	1637.77	1488.18	1378.37	1295.02	1230.14	1178.64	1137.11
85,000	7621.92	4071.07	2894.79	2312.11	1966.81	1740.13	1581.19	1464.51	1375.96	1307.02	1252.30	1208.18
90,000	8070.26	4310.54	3065.07	2448.12	2082.50	1842.50	1674.20	1550.66	1456.90	1383.91	1325.96	1279.25
95,000	8518.61	4550.02	3235.36	2584.12	2198.20	1944.86	1767.21	1636.81	1537.83	1460.79	1399.63	1350.32
100,000	8966.96	4789.49	3405.64	2720.13	2313.89	2047.22	1860.22	1722.96	1618.77	1537.67	1473.29	1421.39
105,000	9415.31	5028.97	3575.92	2856.13	2429.58	2149.58	1953.23	1809.11	1699.71	1614.56	1546.96	1492.46
110,000	9863.65	5268.44	3746.20	2992.14	2545.28	2251.94	2046.24	1895.25	1780.65	1691.44	1620.62	1563.53
115,000	10312.00	5507.91	3916.48	3128.15	2660.97	2354.30	2139.26	1981.40	1861.59	1768.32	1694.29	1634.60
120,000	10760.35	5747.39	4086.76	3264.15	2776.67	2456.66	2232.27	2067.55	1942.53	1845.21	1767.95	1705.66
125,000	11208.70	5986.86	4257.05	3400.16	2892.36	2559.02	2325.28	2153.70	2023.46	1922.09	1841.62	1776.73
130,000	11657.04	6226.34	4427.33	3536.17	3008.05	2661.38	2418.29	2239.84	2104.40	1998.97	1915.28	1847.80
135,000	12105.39	6465.81	4597.61	3672.17	3123.75	2763.74	2511.30	2325.99	2185.34	2075.86	1988.94	1918.87
140,000	12553.74	6705.29	4767.89	3808.18	3239.44	2866.10	2604.31	2412.14	2266.28	2152.74	2062.61	1989.94
145,000	13002.09	6944.76	4938.17	3944.18	3355.14	2968.46	2697.32	2498.29	2347.22	2229.62	2136.27	2061.01
150,000	13450.43	7184.23	5108.45	4080.19	3470.83	3070.82	2790.33	2584.43	2428.16	2306.51	2209.94	2132.08
155,000	13898.78	7423.71	5278.74	4216.20	3586.53	3173.18	2883.34	2670.58	2509.09	2383.39	2283.60	2203.15
160,000	14347.13	7663.18	5449.02	4352.20	3702.22	3275.54	2976.35	2756.73	2590.03	2460.27	2357.27	2274.22
165,000	14795.48	7902.66	5619.30	4488.21	3817.91	3377.90	3069.36	2842.88	2670.97	2537.16	2430.93	2345.29
170,000	15243.83	8142.13	5789.58	4624.21	3933.61	3480.26	3162.38	2929.02	2751.91	2614.04	2504.60	2416.36
175,000	15692.17	8381.61	5959.86	4760.22	4049.30	3582.62	3255.39	3015.17	2832.85	2690.92	2578.26	2487.42
180,000	16140.52	8621.08	6130.14	4896.23	4165.00	3684.99	3348.40	3101.32	2913.79	2767.81	2651.92	2558.49
185,000	16588.87	8860.55	6300.43	5032.23	4280.69	3787.35	3441.41	3187.47	2994.73	2844.69	2725.59	2629.56
190,000	17037.22	9100.03	6470.71	5168.24	4396.39	3889.71	3534.42	3273.62	3075.66	2921.57	2799.25	2700.63
195,000	17485.56	9339.50	6640.99	5304.25	4512.08	3992.07	3627.43	3359.76	3156.60	2998.46	2872.92	2771.70
200,000	17933.91	9578.98	6811.27	5440.25	4627.77	4094.43	3720.44	3445.91	3237.54	3075.34	2946.58	2842.77
205,000	18382.26	9818.45	6981.55	5576.26	4743.47	4196.79	3813.45	3532.06	3318.48	3152.22	3020.25	2913.84
210,000	18830.61	10057.93	7151.83	5712.26	4859.16	4299.15	3906.46	3618.21	3399.42	3229.11	3093.91	2984.91
215,000	19278.95	10297.40	7322.12	5848.27	4974.86	4401.51	3999.47	3704.35	3480.36	3305.99	3167.58	3055.98
220,000	19727.30	10536.88	7492.40	5984.28	5090.55	4503.87	4092.48	3790.50	3561.29	3382.87	3241.24	3127.05
225,000	20175.65	10776.35	7662.68	6120.28	5206.25	4606.23	4185.50	3876.65	3642.23	3459.76	3314.90	3198.12
230,000	20624.00	11015.82	7832.96	6256.29	5321.94	4708.59	4278.51	3962.80	3723.17	3536.64	3388.57	3269.19
235,000	21072.34	11255.30	8003.24	6392.30	5437.63	4810.95	4371.52	4048.94	3804.11	3613.53	3462.23	3340.25
240,000	21520.69	11494.77	8173.52	6528.30	5553.33	4913.31	4464.53	4135.09	3885.05	3690.41	3535.90	3411.32
245,000	21969.04	11734.25	8343.81	6664.31	5669.02	5015.67	4557.54	4221.24	3965.99	3767.29	3609.56	3482.39
250,000	22417.39	11973.72	8514.09	6800.31	5784.72	5118.03	4650.55	4307.39	4046.92	3844.18	3683.23	3553.46
255,000	22865.74	12213.20	8684.37	6936.32	5900.41	5220.39	4743.56	4393.53	4127.86	3921.06	3756.89	3624.53
260,000	23314.08	12452.67	8854.65	7072.33	6016.10	5322.75	4836.57	4479.68	4208.80	3997.94	3830.56	3695.60
265,000	23762.43	12692.14	9024.93	7208.33	6131.80	5425.11	4929.58	4565.83	4289.74	4074.83	3904.22	3766.67
270,000	24210.78	12931.62	9195.21	7344.34	6247.49	5527.48	5022.59	4651.98	4370.68	4151.71	3977.88	3837.74
280,000	25107.47	13410.57	9535.78	7616.35	6478.88	5732.20	5208.62	4824.27	4532.55	4305.48	4125.21	3979.88
290,000	26004.17	13889.52	9876.34	7888.36	6710.27	5936.92	5394.64	4996.57	4694.43	4459.24	4272.54	4122.01
300,000	26900.86	14368.46	10216.90	8160.38	6941.66	6141.64	5580.66	5168.86	4856.31	4613.01	4419.87	4264.15

AMOUNT OF LOAN	NUMBER OF YEARS IN TERM											
	13	14	15	16	17	18	19	20	25	30	35	40
$ 50	0.69	0.68	0.66	0.65	0.64	0.63	0.62	0.62	0.60	0.59	0.58	0.58
100	1.38	1.35	1.32	1.30	1.28	1.26	1.24	1.23	1.19	1.17	1.16	1.16
200	2.76	2.69	2.63	2.59	2.55	2.51	2.48	2.46	2.37	2.34	2.32	2.31
300	4.14	4.04	3.95	3.88	3.82	3.76	3.72	3.68	3.56	3.50	3.47	3.46
400	5.52	5.38	5.26	5.17	5.09	5.02	4.96	4.91	4.74	4.67	4.63	4.61
500	6.90	6.73	6.58	6.46	6.36	6.27	6.20	6.13	5.93	5.83	5.78	5.76
600	8.28	8.07	7.89	7.75	7.63	7.52	7.43	7.36	7.11	7.00	6.94	6.91
700	9.66	9.41	9.21	9.04	8.90	8.77	8.67	8.58	8.30	8.16	8.09	8.06
800	11.04	10.76	10.52	10.33	10.17	10.03	9.91	9.81	9.48	9.33	9.25	9.21
900	12.42	12.10	11.84	11.62	11.44	11.28	11.15	11.03	10.67	10.49	10.40	10.36
1,000	13.80	13.45	13.15	12.91	12.71	12.53	12.39	12.26	11.85	11.66	11.56	11.51
2,000	27.59	26.89	26.30	25.82	25.41	25.06	24.77	24.51	23.70	23.31	23.11	23.02
3,000	41.38	40.33	39.45	38.72	38.11	37.59	37.15	36.77	35.54	34.96	34.67	34.53
4,000	55.17	53.77	52.60	51.63	50.81	50.12	49.53	49.02	47.39	46.61	46.22	46.03
5,000	68.96	67.21	65.75	64.54	63.51	62.64	61.91	61.28	59.24	58.26	57.78	57.54
6,000	82.75	80.65	78.90	77.44	76.21	75.17	74.29	73.53	71.08	69.91	69.33	69.05
7,000	96.54	94.09	92.05	90.35	88.91	87.70	86.67	85.78	82.93	81.56	80.89	80.55
8,000	110.33	107.53	105.20	103.26	101.62	100.23	99.05	98.04	94.78	93.21	92.44	92.06
9,000	124.12	120.97	118.35	116.16	114.32	112.75	111.43	110.29	106.62	104.87	104.00	103.57
10,000	137.91	134.41	131.50	129.07	127.02	125.28	123.81	122.55	118.47	116.52	115.55	115.07
15,000	206.86	201.61	197.25	193.60	190.52	187.92	185.71	183.82	177.70	174.77	173.33	172.61
20,000	275.81	268.82	263.00	258.13	254.03	250.56	247.61	245.09	236.94	233.03	231.10	230.14
25,000	344.76	336.02	328.75	322.67	317.54	313.20	309.51	306.36	296.17	291.28	288.88	287.68
30,000	413.71	403.22	394.50	387.20	381.04	375.83	371.41	367.63	355.40	349.54	346.65	345.21
35,000	482.66	470.42	460.25	451.73	444.55	438.47	433.31	428.90	414.64	407.79	404.42	402.74
40,000	551.61	537.63	526.00	516.26	508.06	501.11	495.21	490.17	473.87	466.05	462.20	460.28
45,000	620.56	604.83	591.76	580.79	571.56	563.75	557.11	551.44	533.10	524.31	519.97	517.81
50,000	689.51	672.03	657.50	645.33	635.07	626.39	619.01	612.71	592.34	582.56	577.75	575.35
55,000	758.46	739.24	723.25	709.86	698.58	689.03	680.91	673.98	651.57	640.82	635.52	632.88
60,000	827.41	806.44	789.00	774.39	762.08	751.66	742.81	735.25	710.80	699.07	693.30	690.42
65,000	896.36	873.64	854.75	838.92	825.59	814.30	804.71	796.52	770.04	757.33	751.07	747.95
70,000	965.31	940.84	920.50	903.45	889.10	876.94	866.61	857.79	829.27	815.58	808.84	805.48
75,000	1034.26	1008.05	986.25	967.99	952.60	939.58	928.51	919.06	888.50	873.84	866.62	863.02
80,000	1103.21	1075.25	1051.99	1032.52	1016.11	1002.22	990.41	980.33	947.74	932.10	924.39	920.55
85,000	1172.16	1142.45	1117.74	1097.05	1079.61	1064.85	1052.31	1041.60	1006.97	990.35	982.17	978.09
90,000	1241.11	1209.66	1183.49	1161.58	1143.12	1127.49	1114.21	1102.87	1066.20	1048.61	1039.94	1035.62
95,000	1310.06	1276.86	1249.24	1226.11	1206.63	1190.13	1176.11	1164.14	1125.44	1106.86	1097.72	1093.16
100,000	1379.01	1344.06	1314.99	1290.65	1270.13	1252.77	1230.01	1225.41	1184.67	1165.12	1155.49	1150.69
105,000	1447.96	1411.26	1380.74	1355.18	1333.64	1315.41	1299.91	1286.68	1243.90	1223.37	1213.26	1208.22
110,000	1516.91	1478.47	1446.49	1419.71	1397.15	1378.05	1361.81	1347.95	1303.14	1281.63	1271.04	1265.76
115,000	1585.86	1545.67	1512.24	1484.24	1460.65	1440.68	1423.71	1409.22	1362.37	1339.88	1328.81	1323.29
120,000	1654.81	1612.87	1577.99	1548.77	1524.16	1503.32	1485.61	1470.49	1421.60	1398.14	1386.59	1380.83
125,000	1723.76	1680.08	1643.74	1613.31	1587.67	1565.96	1547.51	1531.76	1480.84	1456.40	1444.36	1438.36
130,000	1792.71	1747.28	1709.49	1677.84	1651.17	1628.60	1609.41	1593.03	1540.07	1514.65	1502.14	1495.90
135,000	1861.66	1814.48	1775.24	1742.37	1714.68	1691.24	1671.31	1654.30	1599.30	1572.91	1559.91	1553.43
140,000	1930.61	1881.68	1840.99	1806.90	1778.19	1753.87	1733.21	1715.57	1658.54	1631.16	1617.68	1610.96
145,000	1999.56	1948.89	1906.74	1871.43	1841.69	1816.51	1795.11	1776.84	1717.77	1689.42	1675.46	1668.50
150,000	2068.51	2016.09	1972.49	1935.97	1905.20	1879.15	1857.01	1838.11	1777.00	1747.67	1733.23	1726.03
155,000	2137.47	2083.29	2038.24	2000.50	1968.71	1941.79	1918.91	1899.38	1836.24	1805.93	1791.01	1783.57
160,000	2206.42	2150.50	2103.98	2065.03	2032.21	2004.43	1980.81	1960.65	1895.47	1864.19	1848.78	1841.10
165,000	2275.37	2217.70	2169.73	2129.56	2095.72	2067.07	2042.71	2021.92	1954.70	1922.44	1906.56	1898.64
170,000	2344.32	2284.90	2235.48	2194.09	2159.22	2129.70	2104.61	2083.19	2013.94	1980.70	1964.33	1956.17
175,000	2413.27	2352.10	2301.23	2258.63	2222.73	2192.34	2166.51	2144.46	2073.17	2038.95	2022.10	2013.70
180,000	2482.22	2419.31	2366.98	2323.16	2286.24	2254.98	2228.41	2205.73	2132.40	2097.21	2079.88	2071.24
185,000	2551.17	2486.51	2432.73	2387.69	2349.74	2317.62	2290.31	2267.00	2191.64	2155.46	2137.65	2128.77
190,000	2620.12	2553.71	2498.48	2452.22	2413.25	2380.26	2352.21	2328.28	2250.87	2213.72	2195.43	2186.31
195,000	2689.07	2620.91	2564.23	2516.75	2476.76	2442.89	2414.11	2389.55	2310.10	2271.97	2253.20	2243.84
200,000	2758.02	2688.12	2629.98	2581.29	2540.26	2505.53	2476.01	2450.82	2369.34	2330.23	2310.98	2301.38
205,000	2826.97	2755.32	2695.73	2645.82	2603.77	2568.17	2537.91	2512.09	2428.57	2388.49	2368.75	2358.91
210,000	2895.92	2822.52	2761.48	2710.35	2667.28	2630.81	2599.81	2573.36	2487.80	2446.74	2426.52	2416.44
215,000	2964.87	2889.73	2827.23	2774.88	2730.78	2693.45	2661.71	2634.63	2547.04	2505.00	2484.30	2473.98
220,000	3033.82	2956.93	2892.98	2839.41	2794.29	2756.09	2723.61	2695.90	2606.27	2563.25	2542.07	2531.51
225,000	3102.77	3024.13	2958.73	2903.95	2857.80	2818.72	2785.51	2757.17	2665.50	2621.51	2599.85	2589.05
230,000	3171.72	3091.33	3024.48	2968.48	2921.30	2881.36	2847.41	2818.44	2724.74	2679.76	2657.62	2646.58
235,000	3240.67	3158.54	3090.23	3033.01	2984.81	2944.00	2909.31	2879.71	2783.97	2738.02	2715.39	2704.12
240,000	3309.62	3225.74	3155.97	3097.54	3048.31	3006.64	2971.21	2940.98	2843.20	2796.28	2773.17	2761.65
245,000	3378.57	3292.94	3221.72	3162.07	3111.82	3069.28	3033.11	3002.25	2902.44	2854.53	2830.94	2819.18
250,000	3447.52	3360.15	3287.47	3226.61	3175.33	3131.91	3095.01	3063.52	2961.67	2912.79	2888.72	2876.72
255,000	3516.47	3427.35	3353.22	3291.14	3238.83	3194.55	3156.91	3124.79	3020.90	2971.04	2946.49	2934.25
260,000	3585.42	3494.55	3418.97	3355.67	3302.34	3257.19	3218.81	3186.06	3080.14	3029.30	3004.27	2991.79
265,000	3654.37	3561.75	3484.72	3420.20	3365.85	3319.83	3280.71	3247.33	3139.37	3087.55	3062.04	3049.32
270,000	3723.32	3628.96	3550.47	3484.73	3429.35	3382.47	3342.61	3308.60	3198.60	3145.81	3119.81	3106.86
280,000	3861.22	3763.36	3681.97	3613.80	3556.37	3507.74	3466.41	3431.14	3317.07	3262.32	3235.36	3221.92
290,000	3999.12	3897.77	3813.47	3742.86	3683.38	3633.02	3590.21	3553.68	3435.54	3378.83	3350.91	3336.99
300,000	4137.02	4032.17	3944.97	3871.93	3810.39	3758.30	3714.01	3676.22	3554.00	3495.34	3466.46	3452.06

14.00%
MONTHLY AMORTIZING PAYMENTS

AMOUNT OF LOAN	NUMBER OF YEARS IN TERM											
	1	2	3	4	5	6	7	8	9	10	11	12
$ 50	4.49	2.41	1.71	1.37	1.17	1.04	0.94	0.87	0.82	0.78	0.75	0.72
100	8.98	4.81	3.42	2.74	2.33	2.07	1.88	1.74	1.64	1.56	1.49	1.44
200	17.96	9.61	6.84	5.47	4.66	4.13	3.75	3.48	3.27	3.11	2.98	2.88
300	26.94	14.41	10.26	8.20	6.99	6.19	5.63	5.22	4.91	4.66	4.47	4.32
400	35.92	19.21	13.68	10.94	9.31	8.25	7.50	6.95	6.54	6.22	5.96	5.75
500	44.90	24.01	17.09	13.67	11.64	10.31	9.38	8.69	8.17	7.77	7.45	7.19
600	53.88	28.81	20.51	16.40	13.97	12.37	11.25	10.43	9.81	9.32	8.94	8.63
700	62.86	33.61	23.93	19.13	16.29	14.43	13.12	12.17	11.44	10.87	10.43	10.06
800	71.83	38.42	27.35	21.87	18.62	16.49	15.00	13.90	13.07	12.43	11.91	11.50
900	80.81	43.22	30.76	24.60	20.95	18.55	16.87	15.64	14.71	13.98	13.40	12.94
1,000	89.79	48.02	34.18	27.33	23.27	20.61	18.75	17.38	16.34	15.53	14.89	14.38
2,000	179.58	96.03	68.36	54.66	46.54	41.22	37.49	34.75	32.67	31.06	29.78	28.75
3,000	269.37	144.04	102.54	81.98	69.81	61.82	56.23	52.12	49.01	46.58	44.66	43.12
4,000	359.15	192.06	136.72	109.31	93.08	82.43	74.97	69.49	65.34	62.11	59.55	57.49
5,000	448.94	240.07	170.89	136.64	116.35	103.03	93.71	86.86	81.67	77.64	74.44	71.86
6,000	538.73	288.08	205.07	163.96	139.61	123.64	112.45	104.23	98.01	93.16	89.32	86.23
7,000	628.51	336.10	239.25	191.29	162.88	144.25	131.19	121.61	114.34	108.69	104.21	100.60
8,000	718.30	384.11	273.43	218.62	186.15	164.85	149.93	138.98	130.67	124.22	119.10	114.98
9,000	808.09	432.12	307.60	245.94	209.42	185.46	168.67	156.35	147.01	139.74	133.98	129.35
10,000	897.88	480.13	341.78	273.27	232.69	206.06	187.41	173.72	163.34	155.27	148.87	143.72
15,000	1346.81	720.20	512.67	409.90	349.03	309.09	281.11	260.58	245.01	232.90	223.30	215.57
20,000	1795.75	960.26	683.56	546.53	465.37	412.12	374.81	347.44	326.68	310.54	297.74	287.43
25,000	2244.68	1200.33	854.45	683.17	581.71	515.15	468.51	434.29	408.35	388.17	372.17	359.29
30,000	2693.62	1440.39	1025.33	819.80	698.05	618.18	562.21	521.15	490.02	465.80	446.60	431.14
35,000	3142.55	1680.46	1196.22	956.43	814.39	721.21	655.91	608.01	571.68	543.44	521.04	503.00
40,000	3591.49	1920.52	1367.11	1093.06	930.74	824.23	749.61	694.87	653.35	621.07	595.47	574.86
45,000	4040.43	2160.58	1538.00	1229.70	1047.08	927.26	843.31	781.72	735.02	698.70	669.90	646.71
50,000	4489.36	2400.65	1708.89	1366.33	1163.42	1030.29	937.01	868.58	816.69	776.34	744.34	718.57
55,000	4938.30	2640.71	1879.77	1502.96	1279.76	1133.32	1030.71	955.44	898.36	853.97	818.77	790.42
60,000	5387.23	2880.78	2050.66	1639.59	1396.10	1236.35	1124.41	1042.30	980.03	931.60	893.20	862.28
65,000	5836.17	3120.84	2221.55	1776.23	1512.44	1339.38	1218.11	1129.15	1061.70	1009.24	967.64	934.14
70,000	6285.10	3360.91	2392.44	1912.86	1628.78	1442.41	1311.81	1216.01	1143.36	1086.87	1042.07	1005.99
75,000	6734.04	3600.97	2563.33	2049.49	1745.12	1545.44	1405.51	1302.87	1225.03	1164.50	1116.50	1077.85
80,000	7182.97	3841.04	2734.22	2186.12	1861.47	1648.46	1499.21	1389.73	1306.70	1242.14	1190.94	1149.71
85,000	7631.91	4081.10	2905.10	2322.76	1977.81	1751.49	1592.91	1476.58	1388.37	1319.77	1265.37	1221.56
90,000	8080.85	4321.16	3075.99	2459.39	2094.15	1854.52	1686.61	1563.44	1470.04	1397.40	1339.80	1293.42
95,000	8529.78	4561.23	3246.88	2596.02	2210.49	1957.55	1780.31	1650.30	1551.71	1475.04	1414.24	1365.28
100,000	8978.72	4801.29	3417.77	2732.65	2326.83	2060.58	1874.01	1737.16	1633.38	1552.67	1488.67	1437.13
105,000	9427.65	5041.36	3588.66	2869.29	2443.17	2163.61	1967.71	1824.01	1715.04	1630.30	1563.10	1508.99
110,000	9876.59	5281.42	3759.54	3005.92	2559.51	2266.64	2061.41	1910.87	1796.71	1707.94	1637.54	1580.84
115,000	10325.52	5521.49	3930.43	3142.55	2675.85	2369.67	2155.11	1997.73	1878.38	1785.57	1711.97	1652.70
120,000	10774.46	5761.55	4101.32	3279.18	2792.20	2472.69	2248.81	2084.59	1960.05	1863.20	1786.40	1724.56
125,000	11223.39	6001.62	4272.21	3415.81	2908.54	2575.72	2342.51	2171.44	2041.72	1940.84	1860.84	1796.41
130,000	11672.33	6241.68	4443.10	3552.45	3024.88	2678.75	2436.21	2258.30	2123.39	2018.47	1935.27	1868.27
135,000	12121.27	6481.74	4613.99	3689.08	3141.22	2781.78	2529.91	2345.16	2205.05	2096.10	2009.70	1940.13
140,000	12570.20	6721.81	4784.87	3825.71	3257.56	2884.81	2623.61	2432.02	2286.72	2173.74	2084.14	2011.98
145,000	13019.14	6961.87	4955.76	3962.34	3373.90	2987.84	2717.31	2518.87	2368.39	2251.37	2158.57	2083.84
150,000	13468.07	7201.94	5126.65	4098.98	3490.24	3090.87	2811.01	2605.73	2450.06	2329.00	2233.00	2155.70
155,000	13917.01	7442.00	5297.54	4235.61	3606.58	3193.89	2904.71	2692.59	2531.73	2406.63	2307.44	2227.55
160,000	14365.94	7682.07	5468.43	4372.24	3722.93	3296.92	2998.41	2779.45	2613.40	2484.27	2381.87	2299.41
165,000	14814.88	7922.13	5639.31	4508.87	3839.27	3399.95	3092.11	2866.30	2695.07	2561.90	2456.30	2371.26
170,000	15263.81	8162.20	5810.20	4645.51	3955.61	3502.98	3185.81	2953.16	2776.73	2639.53	2530.74	2443.12
175,000	15712.75	8402.26	5981.09	4782.14	4071.95	3606.01	3279.51	3040.02	2858.40	2717.17	2605.17	2514.98
180,000	16161.69	8642.32	6151.98	4918.77	4188.29	3709.04	3373.21	3126.88	2940.07	2794.80	2679.60	2586.83
185,000	16610.62	8882.39	6322.87	5055.40	4304.63	3812.07	3466.91	3213.73	3021.74	2872.43	2754.04	2658.69
190,000	17059.56	9122.45	6493.75	5192.04	4420.97	3915.10	3560.61	3300.59	3103.41	2950.07	2828.47	2730.55
195,000	17508.49	9362.52	6664.64	5328.67	4537.31	4018.12	3654.31	3387.45	3185.08	3027.70	2902.90	2802.40
200,000	17957.43	9602.58	6835.53	5465.30	4653.66	4121.15	3748.01	3474.31	3266.75	3105.33	2977.34	2874.26
205,000	18406.36	9842.65	7006.42	5601.93	4770.00	4224.18	3841.71	3561.16	3348.41	3182.97	3051.77	2946.12
210,000	18855.30	10082.71	7177.31	5738.57	4886.34	4327.21	3935.41	3648.02	3430.08	3260.60	3126.20	3017.97
215,000	19304.24	10322.77	7348.20	5875.20	5002.68	4430.24	4029.11	3734.88	3511.75	3338.23	3200.64	3089.83
220,000	19753.17	10562.84	7519.08	6011.83	5119.02	4533.27	4122.81	3821.74	3593.42	3415.87	3275.07	3161.68
225,000	20202.11	10802.90	7689.97	6148.46	5235.36	4636.30	4216.51	3908.59	3675.09	3493.50	3349.50	3233.54
230,000	20651.04	11042.97	7860.86	6285.09	5351.70	4739.33	4310.21	3995.45	3756.76	3571.13	3423.94	3305.40
235,000	21099.98	11283.03	8031.75	6421.73	5468.04	4842.35	4403.91	4082.31	3838.42	3648.77	3498.37	3377.25
240,000	21548.91	11523.10	8202.64	6558.36	5584.39	4945.38	4497.61	4169.17	3920.09	3726.40	3572.80	3449.11
245,000	21997.85	11763.16	8373.52	6694.99	5700.73	5048.41	4591.31	4256.02	4001.76	3804.03	3647.24	3520.97
250,000	22446.78	12003.23	8544.41	6831.62	5817.07	5151.44	4685.01	4342.88	4083.43	3881.67	3721.67	3592.82
255,000	22895.72	12243.29	8715.30	6968.26	5933.41	5254.47	4778.71	4429.74	4165.10	3959.30	3796.10	3664.68
260,000	23344.66	12483.35	8886.19	7104.89	6049.75	5357.50	4872.41	4516.60	4246.77	4036.93	3870.54	3736.54
265,000	23793.59	12723.42	9057.08	7241.52	6166.09	5460.53	4966.11	4603.45	4328.44	4114.57	3944.97	3808.39
270,000	24242.53	12963.48	9227.97	7378.15	6282.43	5563.55	5059.81	4690.31	4410.10	4192.20	4019.40	3880.25
280,000	25140.40	13443.61	9569.74	7651.42	6515.12	5769.61	5247.21	4864.03	4573.44	4347.47	4168.27	4023.96
290,000	26038.27	13923.74	9911.52	7924.68	6747.80	5975.67	5434.61	5037.74	4736.78	4502.73	4317.14	4167.67
300,000	26936.14	14403.87	10253.29	8197.95	6980.48	6181.73	5622.01	5211.46	4900.12	4658.00	4466.00	4311.39

AMOUNT OF LOAN	NUMBER OF YEARS IN TERM											
	13	14	15	16	17	18	19	20	25	30	35	40
$ 50	0.70	0.69	0.67	0.66	0.65	0.64	0.63	0.63	0.61	0.60	0.59	0.59
100	1.40	1.37	1.34	1.31	1.29	1.28	1.26	1.25	1.21	1.19	1.18	1.18
200	2.80	2.73	2.67	2.62	2.58	2.55	2.52	2.49	2.41	2.37	2.36	2.35
300	4.19	4.09	4.00	3.93	3.87	3.82	3.77	3.74	3.62	3.56	3.53	3.52
400	5.59	5.45	5.33	5.24	5.15	5.09	5.03	4.98	4.82	4.74	4.71	4.69
500	6.98	6.81	6.66	6.54	6.44	6.36	6.28	6.22	6.02	5.93	5.88	5.86
600	8.38	8.17	8.00	7.85	7.73	7.63	7.54	7.47	7.23	7.11	7.06	7.03
700	9.77	9.53	9.33	9.16	9.02	8.90	8.80	8.71	8.43	8.30	8.23	8.20
800	11.17	10.89	10.66	10.47	10.30	10.17	10.05	9.95	9.64	9.48	9.41	9.37
900	12.56	12.25	11.99	11.77	11.59	11.44	11.31	11.20	10.84	10.67	10.59	10.55
1,000	13.96	13.61	13.32	13.08	12.88	12.71	12.56	12.44	12.04	11.85	11.76	11.72
2,000	27.91	27.21	26.64	26.16	25.75	25.41	25.12	24.88	24.08	23.70	23.52	23.43
3,000	41.86	40.82	39.96	39.24	38.63	38.12	37.68	37.31	36.12	35.55	35.28	35.14
4,000	55.81	54.42	53.27	52.31	51.50	50.82	50.24	49.75	48.16	47.40	47.03	46.85
5,000	69.76	68.03	66.59	65.39	64.38	63.52	62.80	62.18	60.19	59.25	58.79	58.56
6,000	83.71	81.63	79.91	78.47	77.25	76.23	75.36	74.62	72.23	71.10	70.55	70.27
7,000	97.66	95.24	93.23	91.54	90.13	88.93	87.92	87.05	84.27	82.95	82.30	81.98
8,000	111.61	108.84	106.54	104.62	103.00	101.64	100.48	99.49	96.31	94.79	94.06	93.70
9,000	125.56	122.45	119.86	117.70	115.88	114.34	113.03	111.92	108.34	106.64	105.82	105.41
10,000	139.52	136.05	133.18	130.77	128.75	127.04	125.59	124.36	120.38	118.49	117.57	117.12
15,000	209.27	204.08	199.77	196.16	193.13	190.56	188.39	186.53	180.57	177.74	176.36	175.68
20,000	279.03	272.10	266.35	261.54	257.50	254.08	251.18	248.71	240.76	236.98	235.14	234.23
25,000	348.78	340.13	332.94	326.93	321.87	317.60	313.97	310.89	300.95	296.22	293.92	292.79
30,000	418.54	408.15	399.53	392.31	386.25	381.12	376.77	373.06	361.13	355.47	352.71	351.35
35,000	488.29	476.18	466.11	457.70	450.62	444.64	439.56	435.24	421.32	414.71	411.49	409.90
40,000	558.05	544.20	532.70	523.08	515.00	508.16	502.36	497.41	481.51	473.95	470.27	468.46
45,000	627.80	612.23	599.29	588.47	579.37	571.60	565.15	559.59	541.70	533.20	529.06	527.02
50,000	697.56	680.25	665.88	653.85	643.74	635.20	627.94	621.77	601.89	592.44	587.84	585.58
55,000	767.31	748.27	732.46	719.24	708.12	698.72	690.74	683.94	662.07	651.68	646.63	644.13
60,000	837.07	816.30	799.05	784.62	772.49	762.23	753.53	746.12	722.26	710.93	705.41	702.69
65,000	906.82	884.32	865.64	850.01	836.86	825.75	816.32	808.29	782.45	770.17	764.19	761.25
70,000	976.58	952.35	932.22	915.39	901.24	889.27	879.12	870.47	842.64	829.42	822.98	819.80
75,000	1046.33	1020.37	998.81	980.78	965.61	952.79	941.91	932.65	902.83	888.66	881.76	878.36
80,000	1116.09	1088.40	1065.40	1046.16	1029.99	1016.31	1004.71	994.82	963.01	947.90	940.54	936.92
85,000	1185.84	1156.42	1131.99	1111.55	1094.36	1079.83	1067.50	1057.00	1023.20	1007.15	999.33	995.47
90,000	1255.60	1224.45	1198.57	1176.93	1158.73	1143.35	1130.29	1119.17	1083.39	1066.39	1058.11	1054.03
95,000	1325.35	1292.47	1265.16	1242.32	1223.11	1206.87	1193.09	1181.35	1143.58	1125.63	1116.89	1112.59
100,000	1395.11	1360.49	1331.75	1307.70	1287.48	1270.39	1255.88	1243.53	1203.77	1184.88	1175.68	1171.15
105,000	1464.86	1428.52	1398.33	1373.09	1351.86	1333.91	1318.67	1305.70	1263.95	1244.12	1234.46	1229.70
110,000	1534.62	1496.54	1464.92	1438.47	1416.23	1397.43	1381.47	1367.88	1324.14	1303.36	1293.25	1288.26
115,000	1604.37	1564.57	1531.51	1503.86	1480.60	1460.95	1444.26	1430.05	1384.33	1362.61	1352.03	1346.82
120,000	1674.13	1632.59	1598.09	1569.24	1544.98	1524.46	1507.06	1492.23	1444.52	1421.85	1410.81	1405.37
125,000	1743.88	1700.62	1664.68	1634.63	1609.35	1587.98	1569.85	1554.41	1504.71	1481.09	1469.60	1463.93
130,000	1813.64	1768.64	1731.27	1700.01	1673.72	1651.50	1632.64	1616.58	1564.89	1540.34	1528.38	1522.49
135,000	1883.39	1836.67	1797.86	1765.40	1738.10	1715.02	1695.44	1678.76	1625.08	1599.58	1587.16	1581.04
140,000	1953.15	1904.69	1864.44	1830.78	1802.47	1778.54	1758.23	1740.93	1685.27	1658.83	1645.95	1639.60
145,000	2022.90	1972.71	1931.03	1896.17	1866.85	1842.06	1821.03	1803.11	1745.46	1718.07	1704.73	1698.16
150,000	2092.66	2040.74	1997.62	1961.55	1931.22	1905.58	1883.82	1865.29	1805.65	1777.31	1763.51	1756.72
155,000	2162.41	2108.76	2064.20	2026.94	1995.59	1969.10	1946.61	1927.46	1865.83	1836.56	1822.30	1815.27
160,000	2232.17	2176.79	2130.79	2092.32	2059.97	2032.62	2009.41	1989.64	1926.02	1895.80	1881.08	1873.83
165,000	2301.93	2244.81	2197.38	2157.71	2124.34	2096.14	2072.20	2051.81	1986.21	1955.04	1939.87	1932.39
170,000	2371.68	2312.84	2263.97	2223.09	2188.71	2159.66	2134.99	2113.99	2046.40	2014.29	1998.65	1990.94
175,000	2441.44	2380.86	2330.55	2288.48	2253.09	2223.18	2197.79	2176.17	2106.59	2073.53	2057.43	2049.50
180,000	2511.19	2448.89	2397.14	2353.86	2317.46	2286.69	2260.58	2238.34	2166.77	2132.77	2116.22	2108.06
185,000	2580.95	2516.91	2463.73	2419.25	2381.84	2350.21	2323.38	2300.52	2226.96	2192.02	2175.00	2166.61
190,000	2650.70	2584.94	2530.31	2484.63	2446.21	2413.73	2386.17	2362.69	2287.15	2251.26	2233.78	2225.17
195,000	2720.46	2652.96	2596.90	2550.02	2510.58	2477.25	2448.96	2424.87	2347.34	2310.50	2292.57	2283.73
200,000	2790.21	2720.98	2663.49	2615.40	2574.96	2540.77	2511.76	2487.05	2407.53	2369.75	2351.35	2342.29
205,000	2859.97	2789.01	2730.07	2680.79	2639.33	2604.29	2574.55	2549.22	2467.72	2428.99	2410.14	2400.84
210,000	2929.72	2857.03	2796.66	2746.17	2703.71	2667.81	2637.34	2611.40	2527.90	2488.24	2468.92	2459.40
215,000	2999.48	2925.06	2863.25	2811.56	2768.08	2731.33	2700.14	2673.57	2588.09	2547.48	2527.70	2517.96
220,000	3069.23	2993.08	2929.84	2876.94	2832.45	2794.85	2762.93	2735.75	2648.28	2606.72	2586.49	2576.51
225,000	3138.99	3061.11	2996.42	2942.33	2896.83	2858.37	2825.73	2797.93	2708.47	2665.97	2645.27	2635.07
230,000	3208.74	3129.13	3063.01	3007.71	2961.20	2921.89	2888.52	2860.10	2768.66	2725.21	2704.05	2693.63
235,000	3278.50	3197.16	3129.60	3073.10	3025.57	2985.41	2951.31	2922.28	2828.84	2784.45	2762.84	2752.18
240,000	3348.25	3265.18	3196.18	3138.48	3089.95	3048.92	3014.11	2984.45	2889.03	2843.70	2821.62	2810.74
245,000	3418.01	3333.20	3262.77	3203.87	3154.32	3112.44	3076.90	3046.63	2949.22	2902.94	2880.40	2869.30
250,000	3487.76	3401.23	3329.36	3269.25	3218.70	3175.96	3139.69	3108.81	3009.41	2962.18	2939.19	2927.86
255,000	3557.52	3469.25	3395.95	3334.64	3283.07	3239.48	3202.49	3170.98	3069.60	3021.43	2997.97	2986.41
260,000	3627.27	3537.28	3462.53	3400.02	3347.44	3303.00	3265.28	3233.16	3129.78	3080.67	3056.76	3044.97
265,000	3697.03	3605.30	3529.12	3465.41	3411.82	3366.52	3328.08	3295.34	3189.97	3139.92	3115.54	3103.53
270,000	3766.78	3673.33	3595.71	3530.79	3476.19	3430.04	3390.87	3357.51	3250.16	3199.16	3174.32	3162.08
280,000	3906.29	3809.38	3728.88	3661.56	3604.94	3557.08	3516.46	3481.86	3370.54	3317.65	3291.89	3279.20
290,000	4045.80	3945.42	3862.06	3792.33	3733.69	3684.12	3642.05	3606.22	3490.91	3436.13	3409.46	3396.31
300,000	4185.31	4081.47	3995.23	3923.10	3862.43	3811.15	3767.63	3730.57	3611.29	3554.62	3527.02	3513.43

MONTHLY AMORTIZING PAYMENTS

AMOUNT OF LOAN	NUMBER OF YEARS IN TERM											
	1	2	3	4	5	6	7	8	9	10	11	12
$ 50	4.50	2.41	1.72	1.38	1.17	1.04	0.95	0.88	0.83	0.79	0.76	0.73
100	9.00	4.82	3.43	2.75	2.34	2.08	1.89	1.76	1.65	1.57	1.51	1.46
200	17.99	9.63	6.86	5.50	4.68	4.15	3.78	3.51	3.30	3.14	3.01	2.91
300	26.98	14.44	10.29	8.24	7.02	6.23	5.67	5.26	4.95	4.71	4.52	4.36
400	35.97	19.26	13.72	10.99	9.36	8.30	7.56	7.01	6.60	6.28	6.02	5.82
500	44.96	24.07	17.15	13.73	11.70	10.37	9.44	8.76	8.25	7.84	7.53	7.27
600	53.95	28.88	20.58	16.48	14.04	12.45	11.33	10.51	9.89	9.41	9.03	8.72
700	62.94	33.70	24.01	19.22	16.38	14.52	13.22	12.26	11.54	10.98	10.53	10.18
800	71.93	38.51	27.44	21.97	18.72	16.60	15.11	14.02	13.19	12.55	12.04	11.63
900	80.92	43.32	30.87	24.71	21.06	18.67	17.00	15.77	14.84	14.11	13.54	13.08
1,000	89.91	48.14	34.30	27.46	23.40	20.74	18.88	17.52	16.49	15.68	15.05	14.53
2,000	179.81	96.27	68.60	54.91	46.80	41.48	37.76	35.03	32.97	31.36	30.09	29.06
3,000	269.72	144.40	102.90	82.36	70.20	62.22	56.64	52.55	49.45	47.04	45.13	43.59
4,000	359.62	192.53	137.20	109.81	93.60	82.96	75.52	70.06	65.93	62.71	60.17	58.12
5,000	449.53	240.66	171.50	137.27	117.00	103.70	94.40	87.58	82.41	78.39	75.21	72.65
6,000	539.43	288.79	205.80	164.72	140.39	124.44	113.28	105.09	98.89	94.07	90.25	87.18
7,000	629.34	336.92	240.10	192.17	163.79	145.18	132.15	122.60	115.37	109.75	105.29	101.71
8,000	719.24	385.05	274.40	219.62	187.19	165.92	151.03	140.12	131.85	125.42	120.33	116.24
9,000	809.15	433.18	308.70	247.07	210.59	186.66	169.91	157.63	148.33	141.10	135.38	130.77
10,000	899.05	481.32	343.00	274.53	233.99	207.40	188.79	175.15	164.81	156.78	150.42	145.30
15,000	1348.58	721.97	514.49	411.79	350.98	311.10	283.18	262.72	247.21	235.16	225.62	217.95
20,000	1798.10	962.63	685.99	549.05	467.97	414.80	377.57	350.29	329.61	313.55	300.83	290.59
25,000	2247.62	1203.28	857.48	686.31	584.96	518.50	471.96	437.86	412.01	391.94	376.03	363.24
30,000	2697.15	1443.94	1028.98	823.57	701.95	622.20	566.36	525.43	494.42	470.32	451.24	435.89
35,000	3146.67	1684.59	1200.48	960.83	818.94	725.90	660.75	613.00	576.82	548.71	526.45	508.54
40,000	3596.20	1925.25	1371.97	1098.09	935.93	829.60	755.14	700.57	659.22	627.10	601.65	581.18
45,000	4045.72	2165.90	1543.47	1235.35	1052.92	933.30	849.53	788.14	741.62	705.48	676.86	653.83
50,000	4495.24	2406.56	1714.96	1372.61	1169.91	1037.00	943.92	875.71	824.02	783.87	752.06	726.48
55,000	4944.77	2647.21	1886.46	1509.87	1286.90	1140.70	1038.32	963.28	906.43	862.26	827.27	799.13
60,000	5394.29	2887.87	2057.96	1647.13	1403.89	1244.40	1132.71	1050.85	988.83	940.64	902.48	871.77
65,000	5843.82	3128.52	2229.45	1784.39	1520.88	1348.09	1227.10	1138.42	1071.23	1019.03	977.68	944.42
70,000	6293.34	3369.18	2400.95	1921.65	1637.87	1451.79	1321.49	1225.99	1153.63	1097.42	1052.89	1017.07
75,000	6742.86	3609.84	2572.44	2058.91	1754.86	1555.49	1415.88	1313.56	1236.03	1175.80	1128.09	1089.72
80,000	7192.39	3850.49	2743.94	2196.17	1871.85	1659.19	1510.28	1401.13	1318.44	1254.19	1203.30	1162.36
85,000	7641.91	4091.15	2915.44	2333.43	1988.84	1762.89	1604.67	1488.70	1400.84	1332.58	1278.51	1235.01
90,000	8091.44	4331.80	3086.93	2470.69	2105.83	1866.59	1699.06	1576.27	1483.24	1410.96	1353.71	1307.66
95,000	8540.96	4572.46	3258.43	2607.95	2222.82	1970.29	1793.45	1663.84	1565.64	1489.35	1428.92	1380.31
100,000	8990.48	4813.11	3429.92	2745.21	2339.81	2073.99	1887.84	1751.41	1648.04	1567.74	1504.12	1452.95
105,000	9440.01	5053.77	3601.42	2882.47	2456.80	2177.69	1982.24	1838.98	1730.45	1646.12	1579.33	1525.60
110,000	9889.53	5294.42	3772.91	3019.73	2573.79	2281.39	2076.63	1926.55	1812.85	1724.51	1654.53	1598.25
115,000	10339.06	5535.08	3944.41	3156.99	2690.78	2385.09	2171.02	2014.12	1895.25	1802.90	1729.74	1670.90
120,000	10788.58	5775.73	4115.91	3294.25	2807.77	2488.79	2265.41	2101.69	1977.65	1881.28	1804.95	1743.54
125,000	11238.10	6016.39	4287.40	3431.51	2924.76	2592.49	2359.80	2189.26	2060.05	1959.67	1880.15	1816.19
130,000	11687.63	6257.04	4458.90	3568.77	3041.75	2696.18	2454.20	2276.84	2142.45	2038.06	1955.36	1888.84
135,000	12137.15	6497.70	4630.39	3706.03	3158.74	2799.88	2548.59	2364.41	2224.86	2116.44	2030.56	1961.49
140,000	12586.68	6738.35	4801.89	3843.29	3275.73	2903.58	2642.98	2451.98	2307.26	2194.83	2105.77	2034.13
145,000	13036.20	6979.01	4973.39	3980.55	3392.72	3007.28	2737.37	2539.55	2389.66	2273.22	2180.98	2106.78
150,000	13485.72	7219.67	5144.88	4117.81	3509.71	3110.98	2831.76	2627.12	2472.06	2351.60	2256.18	2179.43
155,000	13935.25	7460.32	5316.38	4255.07	3626.70	3214.68	2926.16	2714.69	2554.46	2429.99	2331.39	2252.08
160,000	14384.77	7700.98	5487.87	4392.33	3743.70	3318.38	3020.55	2802.26	2636.87	2508.37	2406.59	2324.72
165,000	14834.30	7941.63	5659.37	4529.59	3860.69	3422.08	3114.94	2889.83	2719.27	2586.76	2481.80	2397.37
170,000	15283.82	8182.29	5830.87	4666.85	3977.68	3525.78	3209.33	2977.40	2801.67	2665.15	2557.01	2470.02
175,000	15733.34	8422.94	6002.36	4804.11	4094.67	3629.48	3303.72	3064.97	2884.07	2743.53	2632.21	2542.67
180,000	16182.87	8663.60	6173.86	4941.37	4211.66	3733.18	3398.11	3152.54	2966.47	2821.92	2707.42	2615.31
185,000	16632.39	8904.25	6345.35	5078.63	4328.65	3836.88	3492.51	3240.11	3048.88	2900.31	2782.62	2687.96
190,000	17081.92	9144.91	6516.85	5215.89	4445.64	3940.58	3586.90	3327.68	3131.28	2978.69	2857.83	2760.61
195,000	17531.44	9385.56	6688.34	5353.15	4562.63	4044.27	3681.29	3415.25	3213.68	3057.08	2933.04	2833.26
200,000	17980.96	9626.22	6859.84	5490.41	4679.62	4147.97	3775.68	3502.82	3296.08	3135.47	3008.24	2905.90
205,000	18430.49	9866.87	7031.34	5627.68	4796.61	4251.67	3870.07	3590.39	3378.48	3213.85	3083.45	2978.55
210,000	18880.01	10107.53	7202.83	5764.94	4913.60	4355.37	3964.47	3677.96	3460.89	3292.24	3158.65	3051.20
215,000	19329.53	10348.19	7374.33	5902.20	5030.59	4459.07	4058.86	3765.53	3543.29	3370.63	3233.86	3123.85
220,000	19779.06	10588.84	7545.82	6039.46	5147.58	4562.77	4153.25	3853.10	3625.69	3449.01	3309.06	3196.49
225,000	20228.58	10829.50	7717.32	6176.72	5264.57	4666.47	4247.64	3940.67	3708.09	3527.40	3384.27	3269.14
230,000	20678.11	11070.15	7888.82	6313.98	5381.56	4770.17	4342.03	4028.24	3790.49	3605.79	3459.48	3341.79
235,000	21127.63	11310.81	8060.31	6451.24	5498.55	4873.87	4436.43	4115.81	3872.90	3684.17	3534.68	3414.44
240,000	21577.15	11551.46	8231.81	6588.50	5615.54	4977.57	4530.82	4203.38	3955.30	3762.56	3609.89	3487.08
245,000	22026.68	11792.12	8403.30	6725.76	5732.53	5081.27	4625.21	4290.95	4037.70	3840.95	3685.09	3559.73
250,000	22476.20	12032.77	8574.80	6863.02	5849.52	5184.97	4719.60	4378.52	4120.10	3919.33	3760.30	3632.38
255,000	22925.73	12273.43	8746.30	7000.28	5966.51	5288.67	4813.99	4466.10	4202.50	3997.72	3835.51	3705.03
260,000	23375.25	12514.08	8917.79	7137.54	6083.50	5392.36	4908.39	4553.67	4284.90	4076.11	3910.71	3777.67
265,000	23824.77	12754.74	9089.29	7274.80	6200.49	5496.06	5002.78	4641.24	4367.31	4154.49	3985.92	3850.32
270,000	24274.30	12995.39	9260.78	7412.06	6317.48	5599.76	5097.17	4728.81	4449.71	4232.88	4061.12	3922.97
280,000	25173.35	13476.70	9603.77	7686.58	6551.46	5807.16	5285.95	4903.95	4614.51	4389.65	4211.54	4068.26
290,000	26072.39	13958.02	9946.77	7961.10	6785.44	6014.56	5474.74	5079.09	4779.32	4546.43	4361.95	4213.56
300,000	26971.44	14439.33	10289.76	8235.62	7019.42	6221.96	5663.52	5254.23	4944.12	4703.20	4512.36	4358.85

AMOUNT OF LOAN	NUMBER OF YEARS IN TERM											
	13	14	15	16	17	18	19	20	25	30	35	40
$ 50	0.71	0.69	0.68	0.67	0.66	0.65	0.64	0.64	0.62	0.61	0.60	0.60
100	1.42	1.38	1.35	1.33	1.31	1.29	1.28	1.27	1.23	1.21	1.20	1.20
200	2.83	2.76	2.70	2.65	2.61	2.58	2.55	2.53	2.45	2.41	2.40	2.39
300	4.24	4.14	4.05	3.98	3.92	3.87	3.83	3.79	3.67	3.62	3.59	3.58
400	5.65	5.51	5.40	5.30	5.22	5.16	5.10	5.05	4.90	4.82	4.79	4.77
500	7.06	6.89	6.75	6.63	6.53	6.45	6.37	6.31	6.12	6.03	5.98	5.96
600	8.47	8.27	8.10	7.95	7.83	7.73	7.65	7.58	7.34	7.23	7.18	7.15
700	9.88	9.64	9.45	9.28	9.14	9.02	8.92	8.84	8.57	8.44	8.38	8.35
800	11.30	11.02	10.79	10.60	10.44	10.31	10.20	10.10	9.79	9.64	9.57	9.54
900	12.71	12.40	12.14	11.93	11.75	11.60	11.47	11.36	11.01	10.85	10.77	10.73
1,000	14.12	13.78	13.49	13.25	13.05	12.89	12.74	12.62	12.23	12.05	11.96	11.92
2,000	28.23	27.55	26.98	26.50	26.10	25.77	25.48	25.24	24.46	24.10	23.92	23.84
3,000	42.34	41.32	40.46	39.75	39.15	38.65	38.22	37.86	36.69	36.15	35.88	35.75
4,000	56.46	55.09	53.95	53.00	52.20	51.53	50.96	50.47	48.92	48.19	47.84	47.67
5,000	70.57	68.86	67.43	66.25	65.25	64.41	63.70	63.09	61.15	60.24	59.80	59.59
6,000	84.68	82.63	80.92	79.50	78.30	77.29	76.44	75.71	73.38	72.29	71.76	71.50
7,000	98.79	96.40	94.41	92.74	91.35	90.17	89.17	88.33	85.61	84.33	83.72	83.42
8,000	112.91	110.17	107.89	105.99	104.40	103.05	101.91	100.94	97.84	96.38	95.68	95.33
9,000	127.02	123.94	121.38	119.24	117.45	115.93	114.65	113.56	110.07	108.43	107.64	107.25
10,000	141.13	137.71	134.86	132.49	130.50	128.81	127.39	126.18	122.30	120.47	119.60	119.17
15,000	211.70	206.56	202.29	198.73	195.74	193.22	191.08	189.26	183.44	180.71	179.39	178.75
20,000	282.26	275.41	269.72	264.97	260.99	257.62	254.77	252.35	244.59	240.94	239.19	238.33
25,000	352.83	344.26	337.15	331.22	326.23	322.03	318.46	315.43	305.74	301.18	298.98	297.91
30,000	423.39	413.11	404.58	397.46	391.48	386.43	382.16	378.52	366.88	361.41	358.78	357.49
35,000	493.95	481.96	472.01	463.70	456.72	450.84	445.85	441.61	428.03	421.65	418.57	417.07
40,000	564.52	550.81	539.44	529.94	521.97	515.24	509.54	504.69	489.18	481.88	478.37	476.65
45,000	635.08	619.66	606.87	596.18	587.21	579.64	573.23	567.78	550.32	542.11	538.16	536.24
50,000	705.65	688.51	674.29	662.43	652.46	644.05	636.92	630.86	611.47	602.35	597.96	595.82
55,000	776.21	757.36	741.72	728.67	717.70	708.45	700.61	693.95	672.62	662.58	657.75	655.40
60,000	846.77	826.21	809.15	794.91	782.95	772.86	764.31	757.04	733.76	722.82	717.55	714.98
65,000	917.34	895.06	876.58	861.15	848.20	837.26	828.00	820.12	794.91	783.05	777.34	774.56
70,000	987.90	963.91	944.01	927.39	913.44	901.67	891.69	883.21	856.05	843.29	837.14	834.14
75,000	1058.47	1032.76	1011.44	993.64	978.69	966.07	955.38	946.29	917.20	903.52	896.93	893.72
80,000	1129.03	1101.61	1078.87	1059.88	1043.93	1030.47	1019.07	1009.38	978.35	963.75	956.73	953.30
85,000	1199.59	1170.46	1146.30	1126.12	1109.18	1094.88	1082.76	1072.47	1039.49	1023.99	1016.52	1012.88
90,000	1270.16	1239.31	1213.73	1192.36	1174.42	1159.28	1146.46	1135.55	1100.64	1084.22	1076.32	1072.47
95,000	1340.72	1308.16	1281.16	1258.61	1239.67	1223.69	1210.15	1198.64	1161.79	1144.46	1136.11	1132.05
100,000	1411.29	1377.01	1348.58	1324.85	1304.91	1288.09	1273.84	1261.72	1222.93	1204.69	1195.91	1191.63
105,000	1481.85	1445.86	1416.01	1391.09	1370.16	1352.50	1337.53	1324.81	1284.08	1264.93	1255.70	1251.21
110,000	1552.41	1514.71	1483.44	1457.33	1435.40	1416.90	1401.22	1387.90	1345.23	1325.16	1315.50	1310.79
115,000	1622.98	1583.56	1550.87	1523.57	1500.65	1481.31	1464.92	1450.98	1406.37	1385.40	1375.29	1370.37
120,000	1693.54	1652.41	1618.30	1589.82	1565.90	1545.71	1528.61	1514.07	1467.52	1445.63	1435.09	1429.95
125,000	1764.11	1721.26	1685.73	1656.06	1631.14	1610.11	1592.30	1577.15	1528.66	1505.86	1494.88	1489.53
130,000	1834.67	1790.11	1753.16	1722.30	1696.39	1674.52	1655.99	1640.24	1589.81	1566.10	1554.68	1549.12
135,000	1905.23	1858.96	1820.59	1788.54	1761.63	1738.92	1719.68	1703.33	1650.96	1626.33	1614.47	1608.70
140,000	1975.80	1927.81	1888.02	1854.78	1826.88	1803.33	1783.37	1766.41	1712.10	1686.57	1674.27	1668.28
145,000	2046.36	1996.66	1955.45	1921.03	1892.12	1867.73	1847.07	1829.50	1773.25	1746.80	1734.06	1727.86
150,000	2116.93	2065.51	2022.87	1987.27	1957.37	1932.14	1910.76	1892.58	1834.40	1807.04	1793.86	1787.44
155,000	2187.49	2134.36	2090.30	2053.51	2022.61	1996.54	1974.45	1955.67	1895.54	1867.27	1853.65	1847.02
160,000	2258.05	2203.21	2157.73	2119.75	2087.86	2060.94	2038.14	2018.76	1956.69	1927.50	1913.45	1906.60
165,000	2328.62	2272.06	2225.16	2186.00	2153.10	2125.35	2101.83	2081.84	2017.84	1987.74	1973.24	1966.18
170,000	2399.18	2340.91	2292.59	2252.24	2218.35	2189.75	2165.52	2144.93	2078.98	2047.97	2033.04	2025.76
175,000	2469.75	2409.76	2360.02	2318.48	2283.59	2254.16	2229.22	2208.01	2140.13	2108.21	2092.83	2085.35
180,000	2540.31	2478.62	2427.45	2384.72	2348.84	2318.56	2292.91	2271.10	2201.27	2168.44	2152.63	2144.93
185,000	2610.87	2547.47	2494.88	2450.96	2414.09	2382.97	2356.60	2334.19	2262.42	2228.68	2212.42	2204.51
190,000	2681.44	2616.32	2562.31	2517.21	2479.33	2447.37	2420.29	2397.27	2323.57	2288.91	2272.22	2264.09
195,000	2752.00	2685.17	2629.74	2583.45	2544.58	2511.77	2483.98	2460.36	2384.71	2349.14	2332.02	2323.67
200,000	2822.57	2754.02	2697.16	2649.69	2609.82	2576.18	2547.68	2523.44	2445.86	2409.38	2391.81	2383.25
205,000	2893.13	2822.87	2764.59	2715.93	2675.07	2640.58	2611.37	2586.53	2507.01	2469.61	2451.61	2442.83
210,000	2963.69	2891.72	2832.02	2782.17	2740.31	2704.99	2675.06	2649.61	2568.15	2529.85	2511.40	2502.41
215,000	3034.26	2960.57	2899.45	2848.42	2805.56	2769.39	2738.75	2712.70	2629.30	2590.08	2571.20	2562.00
220,000	3104.82	3029.42	2966.88	2914.66	2870.80	2833.80	2802.44	2775.79	2690.45	2650.32	2630.99	2621.58
225,000	3175.39	3098.27	3034.31	2980.90	2936.05	2898.20	2866.13	2838.87	2751.59	2710.55	2690.79	2681.16
230,000	3245.95	3167.12	3101.74	3047.14	3001.29	2962.61	2929.83	2901.96	2812.74	2770.79	2750.58	2740.74
235,000	3316.51	3235.97	3169.17	3113.39	3066.54	3027.01	2993.52	2965.04	2873.88	2831.02	2810.38	2800.32
240,000	3387.08	3304.82	3236.60	3179.63	3131.79	3091.41	3057.21	3028.13	2935.03	2891.25	2870.17	2859.90
245,000	3457.64	3373.67	3304.03	3245.87	3197.03	3155.82	3120.90	3091.22	2996.18	2951.49	2929.97	2919.48
250,000	3528.21	3442.52	3371.45	3312.11	3262.28	3220.22	3184.59	3154.30	3057.32	3011.72	2989.76	2979.06
255,000	3598.77	3511.37	3438.88	3378.35	3327.52	3284.63	3248.28	3217.39	3118.47	3071.96	3049.56	3038.64
260,000	3669.33	3580.22	3506.31	3444.60	3392.77	3349.03	3311.98	3280.47	3179.62	3132.19	3109.35	3098.23
265,000	3739.90	3649.07	3573.74	3510.84	3458.01	3413.44	3375.67	3343.56	3240.76	3192.43	3169.15	3157.81
270,000	3810.46	3717.92	3641.17	3577.08	3523.26	3477.84	3439.36	3406.65	3301.91	3252.66	3228.94	3217.39
280,000	3951.59	3855.62	3776.03	3709.57	3653.75	3606.65	3566.74	3532.82	3424.20	3373.13	3348.53	3336.55
290,000	4092.72	3993.32	3910.89	3842.05	3784.24	3735.46	3694.13	3658.99	3546.49	3493.60	3468.12	3455.71
300,000	4233.85	4131.02	4045.74	3974.53	3914.73	3864.27	3821.51	3785.16	3668.79	3614.07	3587.71	3574.87

14.50%

AMOUNT OF LOAN	NUMBER OF YEARS IN TERM											
	1	2	3	4	5	6	7	8	9	10	11	12
$ 50	4.51	2.42	1.73	1.38	1.18	1.05	0.96	0.89	0.84	0.80	0.76	0.74
100	9.01	4.83	3.45	2.76	2.36	2.09	1.91	1.77	1.67	1.59	1.52	1.47
200	18.01	9.65	6.89	5.52	4.71	4.18	3.81	3.54	3.33	3.17	3.04	2.94
300	27.01	14.48	10.33	8.28	7.06	6.27	5.71	5.30	4.99	4.75	4.56	4.41
400	36.01	19.30	13.77	11.04	9.42	8.35	7.61	7.07	6.66	6.34	6.08	5.88
500	45.02	24.13	17.22	13.79	11.77	10.44	9.51	8.83	8.32	7.92	7.60	7.35
600	54.02	28.95	20.66	16.55	14.12	12.53	11.42	10.60	9.98	9.50	9.12	8.82
700	63.02	33.78	24.10	19.31	16.47	14.62	13.32	12.37	11.64	11.09	10.64	10.29
800	72.02	38.60	27.54	22.07	18.83	16.70	15.22	14.13	13.31	12.67	12.16	11.76
900	81.03	43.43	30.98	24.83	21.18	18.79	17.12	15.90	14.97	14.25	13.68	13.22
1,000	90.03	48.25	34.43	27.58	23.53	20.88	19.02	17.66	16.63	15.83	15.20	14.69
2,000	180.05	96.50	68.85	55.16	47.06	41.75	38.04	35.32	33.26	31.66	30.40	29.38
3,000	270.07	144.75	103.27	82.74	70.59	62.63	57.06	52.98	49.89	47.49	45.59	44.07
4,000	360.10	193.00	137.69	110.32	94.12	83.50	76.07	70.63	66.52	63.32	60.79	58.76
5,000	450.12	241.25	172.11	137.89	117.65	104.38	95.09	88.29	83.14	79.15	75.99	73.45
6,000	540.14	289.50	206.53	165.47	141.17	125.25	114.11	105.95	99.77	94.98	91.18	88.14
7,000	630.16	337.75	240.95	193.05	164.70	146.13	133.13	123.61	116.40	110.81	106.38	102.82
8,000	720.19	386.00	275.37	220.63	188.23	167.00	152.14	141.26	133.03	126.63	121.58	117.51
9,000	810.21	434.25	309.79	248.21	211.76	187.87	171.16	158.92	149.65	142.46	136.77	132.20
10,000	900.23	482.50	344.21	275.78	235.29	208.75	190.18	176.58	166.28	158.29	151.97	146.89
15,000	1350.34	723.75	516.32	413.67	352.93	313.12	285.26	264.86	249.42	237.44	227.95	220.33
20,000	1800.46	964.99	688.42	551.56	470.57	417.49	380.35	353.15	332.56	316.58	303.93	293.77
25,000	2250.57	1206.24	860.53	689.45	588.21	521.87	475.44	441.44	415.70	395.72	379.92	367.22
30,000	2700.68	1447.49	1032.63	827.34	705.85	626.24	570.52	529.72	498.84	474.87	455.90	440.66
35,000	3150.79	1688.73	1204.74	965.23	823.49	730.61	665.61	618.01	581.98	554.01	531.88	514.10
40,000	3600.91	1929.98	1376.84	1103.12	941.14	834.98	760.70	706.30	665.11	633.15	607.86	587.54
45,000	4051.02	2171.23	1548.95	1241.01	1058.78	939.35	855.78	794.58	748.25	712.30	683.84	660.99
50,000	4501.13	2412.48	1721.05	1378.90	1176.42	1043.73	950.87	882.87	831.39	791.44	759.83	734.43
55,000	4951.25	2653.72	1893.16	1516.79	1294.06	1148.10	1045.96	971.15	914.53	870.58	835.81	807.87
60,000	5401.36	2894.97	2065.26	1654.68	1411.70	1252.47	1141.04	1059.44	997.67	949.73	911.79	881.31
65,000	5851.47	3136.22	2237.37	1792.57	1529.34	1356.84	1236.13	1147.73	1080.81	1028.87	987.77	954.76
70,000	6301.58	3377.46	2409.47	1930.46	1646.98	1461.21	1331.22	1236.01	1163.95	1108.01	1063.76	1028.20
75,000	6751.70	3618.71	2581.58	2068.35	1764.63	1565.59	1426.30	1324.30	1247.08	1187.16	1139.74	1101.64
80,000	7201.81	3859.96	2753.68	2206.24	1882.27	1669.96	1521.39	1412.59	1330.22	1266.30	1215.72	1175.08
85,000	7651.92	4101.21	2925.79	2344.13	1999.91	1774.33	1616.48	1500.87	1413.36	1345.44	1291.70	1248.53
90,000	8102.03	4342.45	3097.89	2482.02	2117.55	1878.70	1711.56	1589.16	1496.50	1424.59	1367.68	1321.97
95,000	8552.15	4583.70	3270.00	2619.91	2235.19	1983.08	1806.65	1677.44	1579.64	1503.73	1443.67	1395.41
100,000	9002.26	4824.95	3442.10	2757.80	2352.83	2087.45	1901.74	1765.73	1662.78	1582.87	1519.65	1468.85
105,000	9452.37	5066.19	3614.21	2895.69	2470.47	2191.82	1996.82	1854.02	1745.92	1662.02	1595.63	1542.30
110,000	9902.49	5307.44	3786.31	3033.58	2588.12	2296.19	2091.91	1942.30	1829.05	1741.16	1671.61	1615.74
115,000	10352.60	5548.69	3958.42	3171.47	2705.76	2400.56	2186.99	2030.59	1912.19	1820.30	1747.60	1689.18
120,000	10802.71	5789.94	4130.52	3309.36	2823.40	2504.94	2282.08	2118.88	1995.33	1899.45	1823.58	1762.62
125,000	11252.82	6031.18	4302.63	3447.25	2941.04	2609.31	2377.17	2207.16	2078.47	1978.59	1899.56	1836.07
130,000	11702.94	6272.43	4474.73	3585.14	3058.68	2713.68	2472.25	2295.45	2161.61	2057.73	1975.54	1909.51
135,000	12153.05	6513.68	4646.84	3723.03	3176.32	2818.05	2567.34	2383.73	2244.75	2136.88	2051.52	1982.95
140,000	12603.16	6754.92	4818.94	3860.92	3293.96	2922.42	2662.43	2472.02	2327.89	2216.02	2127.51	2056.39
145,000	13053.27	6996.17	4991.05	3998.81	3411.61	3026.80	2757.51	2560.31	2411.02	2295.16	2203.49	2129.84
150,000	13503.39	7237.42	5163.15	4136.70	3529.25	3131.17	2852.60	2648.59	2494.16	2374.31	2279.47	2203.28
155,000	13953.50	7478.67	5335.26	4274.59	3646.89	3235.54	2947.69	2736.88	2577.30	2453.45	2355.45	2276.72
160,000	14403.61	7719.91	5507.36	4412.48	3764.53	3339.91	3042.77	2825.17	2660.44	2532.59	2431.44	2350.16
165,000	14853.73	7961.16	5679.47	4550.37	3882.17	3444.29	3137.86	2913.45	2743.58	2611.74	2507.42	2423.61
170,000	15303.84	8202.41	5851.57	4688.26	3999.81	3548.66	3232.95	3001.74	2826.72	2690.88	2583.40	2497.05
175,000	15753.95	8443.65	6023.68	4826.15	4117.45	3653.03	3328.03	3090.02	2909.86	2770.02	2659.38	2570.49
180,000	16204.06	8684.90	6195.78	4964.04	4235.10	3757.40	3423.12	3178.31	2992.99	2849.17	2735.36	2643.93
185,000	16654.18	8926.15	6367.89	5101.93	4352.74	3861.77	3518.21	3266.60	3076.13	2928.31	2811.35	2717.38
190,000	17104.29	9167.40	6539.99	5239.82	4470.38	3966.15	3613.29	3354.88	3159.27	3007.45	2887.33	2790.82
195,000	17554.40	9408.64	6712.10	5377.71	4588.02	4070.52	3708.38	3443.17	3242.41	3086.60	2963.31	2864.26
200,000	18004.51	9649.89	6884.20	5515.60	4705.66	4174.89	3803.47	3531.46	3325.55	3165.74	3039.29	2937.70
205,000	18454.63	9891.14	7056.31	5653.49	4823.30	4279.26	3898.55	3619.74	3408.69	3244.88	3115.27	3011.15
210,000	18904.74	10132.38	7228.41	5791.38	4940.94	4383.63	3993.64	3708.03	3491.83	3324.03	3191.26	3084.59
215,000	19354.85	10373.63	7400.52	5929.26	5058.59	4488.01	4088.73	3796.32	3574.96	3403.17	3267.24	3158.03
220,000	19804.97	10614.88	7572.62	6067.15	5176.23	4592.38	4183.81	3884.60	3658.10	3482.31	3343.22	3231.47
225,000	20255.08	10856.13	7744.72	6205.04	5293.87	4696.75	4278.90	3972.89	3741.24	3561.46	3419.20	3304.92
230,000	20705.19	11097.37	7916.83	6342.93	5411.51	4801.12	4373.98	4061.17	3824.38	3640.60	3495.19	3378.36
235,000	21155.30	11338.62	8088.93	6480.82	5529.15	4905.50	4469.07	4149.46	3907.52	3719.74	3571.17	3451.80
240,000	21605.42	11579.87	8261.04	6618.71	5646.79	5009.87	4564.16	4237.75	3990.66	3798.89	3647.15	3525.24
245,000	22055.53	11821.11	8433.14	6756.60	5764.43	5114.24	4659.24	4326.03	4073.80	3878.03	3723.13	3598.69
250,000	22505.64	12062.36	8605.25	6894.49	5882.08	5218.61	4754.33	4414.32	4156.93	3957.17	3799.11	3672.13
255,000	22955.75	12303.61	8777.35	7032.38	5999.72	5322.98	4849.42	4502.61	4240.07	4036.32	3875.10	3745.57
260,000	23405.87	12544.86	8949.46	7170.27	6117.36	5427.36	4944.50	4590.89	4323.21	4115.46	3951.08	3819.01
265,000	23855.98	12786.10	9121.56	7308.16	6235.00	5531.73	5039.59	4679.18	4406.35	4194.60	4027.06	3892.45
270,000	24306.09	13027.35	9293.67	7446.05	6352.64	5636.10	5134.68	4767.46	4489.49	4273.75	4103.04	3965.90
280,000	25206.32	13509.84	9637.88	7721.83	6587.92	5844.84	5324.85	4944.04	4655.77	4432.04	4255.01	4112.78
290,000	26106.54	13992.34	9982.09	7997.61	6823.21	6053.59	5515.02	5120.61	4822.04	4590.32	4406.97	4259.67
300,000	27006.77	14474.83	10326.30	8273.39	7058.49	6262.33	5705.20	5297.18	4988.32	4748.61	4558.94	4406.55

14.50%

AMOUNT OF LOAN	NUMBER OF YEARS IN TERM											
	13	14	15	16	17	18	19	20	25	30	35	40
$ 50	0.72	0.70	0.69	0.68	0.67	0.66	0.65	0.64	0.63	0.62	0.61	0.61
100	1.43	1.40	1.37	1.35	1.33	1.31	1.30	1.28	1.25	1.23	1.22	1.22
200	2.86	2.79	2.74	2.69	2.65	2.62	2.59	2.56	2.49	2.45	2.44	2.43
300	4.29	4.19	4.10	4.03	3.97	3.92	3.88	3.84	3.73	3.68	3.65	3.64
400	5.72	5.58	5.47	5.37	5.29	5.23	5.17	5.12	4.97	4.90	4.87	4.85
500	7.14	6.97	6.83	6.72	6.62	6.53	6.46	6.40	6.22	6.13	6.09	6.07
600	8.57	8.37	8.20	8.06	7.94	7.84	7.76	7.68	7.46	7.35	7.30	7.28
700	10.00	9.76	9.56	9.40	9.26	9.15	9.05	8.96	8.70	8.58	8.52	8.49
800	11.43	11.15	10.93	10.74	10.58	10.45	10.34	10.24	9.94	9.80	9.73	9.70
900	12.85	12.55	12.29	12.08	11.91	11.76	11.63	11.52	11.18	11.03	10.95	10.91
1,000	14.28	13.94	13.66	13.43	13.23	13.06	12.92	12.80	12.43	12.25	12.17	12.13
2,000	28.56	27.88	27.32	26.85	26.45	26.12	25.84	25.60	24.85	24.50	24.33	24.25
3,000	42.83	41.81	40.97	40.27	39.68	39.18	38.76	38.40	37.27	36.74	36.49	36.37
4,000	57.11	55.75	54.63	53.69	52.90	52.24	51.68	51.20	49.69	48.99	48.65	48.49
5,000	71.38	69.69	68.28	67.11	66.13	65.30	64.60	64.00	62.11	61.23	60.81	60.61
6,000	85.66	83.62	81.94	80.53	79.35	78.36	77.52	76.80	74.53	73.48	72.98	72.73
7,000	99.93	97.56	95.59	93.95	92.57	91.42	90.44	89.60	86.96	85.72	85.14	84.85
8,000	114.21	111.49	109.25	107.37	105.80	104.47	103.36	102.40	99.38	97.97	97.30	96.98
9,000	128.48	125.43	122.90	120.79	119.02	117.53	116.27	115.20	111.80	110.22	109.46	109.10
10,000	142.76	139.37	136.56	134.21	132.25	130.59	129.19	128.00	124.22	122.46	121.62	121.22
15,000	214.14	209.05	204.83	201.32	198.37	195.89	193.79	192.00	186.33	183.69	182.43	181.82
20,000	285.51	278.73	273.11	268.42	264.49	261.18	258.38	256.00	248.44	244.92	243.24	242.43
25,000	356.89	348.41	341.38	335.52	330.61	326.47	322.97	320.00	310.55	306.14	304.05	303.04
30,000	420.27	418.09	409.66	402.63	396.73	391.77	387.57	384.00	372.65	367.37	364.86	363.64
35,000	499.64	487.77	477.93	469.73	462.85	457.06	452.16	448.00	434.76	428.60	425.66	424.25
40,000	571.02	557.45	546.21	536.83	528.97	522.35	516.76	512.00	496.87	489.83	486.47	484.86
45,000	642.40	627.13	614.48	603.94	595.10	587.65	581.36	576.00	558.98	551.06	547.28	545.40
50,000	713.77	696.81	682.76	671.04	661.22	652.94	645.94	640.00	621.09	612.28	608.09	606.07
55,000	785.15	766.49	751.03	738.14	727.34	718.24	710.54	704.00	683.19	673.51	668.90	666.68
60,000	856.53	836.17	819.31	805.25	793.46	783.53	775.13	768.00	745.30	734.74	729.71	727.28
65,000	927.90	905.85	887.58	872.35	859.58	848.82	839.72	832.00	807.41	795.97	790.52	787.89
70,000	999.28	975.53	955.86	939.45	925.70	914.12	904.32	896.00	869.52	857.19	851.32	848.50
75,000	1070.66	1045.21	1024.13	1006.56	991.82	979.41	968.91	960.00	931.63	918.42	912.13	909.10
80,000	1142.04	1114.89	1092.41	1073.66	1057.94	1044.70	1033.51	1024.00	993.74	979.65	972.94	969.71
85,000	1213.41	1184.57	1160.68	1140.76	1124.07	1110.00	1098.10	1088.00	1055.84	1040.88	1033.75	1030.32
90,000	1284.79	1254.25	1228.96	1207.87	1190.19	1175.29	1162.69	1152.00	1117.95	1102.11	1094.56	1090.92
95,000	1356.17	1323.93	1297.23	1274.97	1256.31	1240.59	1227.29	1216.00	1180.06	1163.33	1155.37	1151.53
100,000	1427.54	1393.61	1365.51	1342.08	1322.43	1305.88	1291.88	1280.00	1242.17	1224.56	1216.18	1212.14
105,000	1498.92	1463.29	1433.78	1409.18	1388.55	1371.17	1356.48	1344.00	1304.28	1285.79	1276.98	1272.74
110,000	1570.30	1532.97	1502.06	1476.28	1454.67	1436.47	1421.07	1408.00	1366.38	1347.02	1337.79	1333.35
115,000	1641.67	1602.05	1570.33	1543.39	1520.79	1501.76	1485.66	1472.00	1428.49	1408.24	1398.60	1393.96
120,000	1713.05	1672.33	1638.61	1610.49	1586.91	1567.06	1550.26	1536.00	1490.60	1469.47	1459.41	1454.50
125,000	1784.43	1742.01	1706.88	1677.59	1653.04	1632.35	1614.85	1600.00	1552.71	1530.70	1520.22	1515.17
130,000	1855.80	1811.69	1775.16	1744.70	1719.16	1697.64	1679.44	1664.00	1614.82	1591.93	1581.03	1575.78
135,000	1927.18	1881.37	1843.43	1811.80	1785.28	1762.94	1744.04	1728.00	1676.92	1653.16	1641.84	1636.38
140,000	1998.56	1951.05	1911.71	1878.90	1851.40	1828.23	1808.63	1792.00	1739.03	1714.38	1702.64	1696.99
145,000	2069.93	2020.73	1979.98	1946.01	1917.52	1893.52	1873.23	1856.00	1801.14	1775.61	1763.45	1757.60
150,000	2141.31	2090.41	2048.26	2013.11	1983.64	1958.82	1937.82	1920.00	1863.25	1836.84	1824.26	1818.20
155,000	2212.69	2160.09	2116.53	2080.21	2049.76	2024.11	2002.41	1984.00	1925.36	1898.07	1885.07	1878.81
160,000	2284.07	2229.77	2184.81	2147.32	2115.88	2089.40	2067.01	2048.00	1987.47	1959.29	1945.88	1939.42
165,000	2355.44	2299.45	2253.08	2214.42	2182.01	2154.70	2131.60	2112.00	2049.57	2020.52	2006.69	2000.02
170,000	2426.82	2369.13	2321.36	2281.52	2248.13	2219.99	2196.19	2176.00	2111.68	2081.75	2067.49	2060.63
175,000	2498.20	2438.81	2389.63	2348.63	2314.25	2285.28	2260.79	2240.00	2173.79	2142.98	2128.30	2121.24
180,000	2569.57	2508.49	2457.91	2415.73	2380.37	2350.58	2325.38	2304.00	2235.90	2204.21	2189.11	2181.84
185,000	2640.95	2578.17	2526.18	2482.83	2446.49	2415.87	2389.98	2368.00	2298.01	2265.43	2249.92	2242.45
190,000	2712.33	2647.85	2594.46	2549.94	2512.61	2481.17	2454.57	2432.00	2360.11	2326.66	2310.73	2303.06
195,000	2783.70	2717.53	2662.73	2617.04	2578.73	2546.46	2519.16	2496.00	2422.22	2387.89	2371.54	2363.66
200,000	2855.08	2787.21	2731.01	2684.15	2644.85	2611.75	2583.76	2560.00	2484.33	2449.12	2432.35	2424.27
205,000	2926.46	2856.89	2799.28	2751.25	2710.97	2677.05	2648.35	2624.00	2546.44	2510.34	2493.15	2484.88
210,000	2997.83	2926.57	2867.56	2818.35	2777.10	2742.34	2712.95	2688.00	2608.55	2571.57	2553.96	2545.48
215,000	3069.21	2996.25	2935.83	2885.46	2843.22	2807.63	2777.54	2752.00	2670.66	2632.80	2614.77	2606.09
220,000	3140.59	3065.93	3004.11	2952.56	2909.34	2872.93	2842.13	2816.00	2732.76	2694.03	2675.58	2666.70
225,000	3211.96	3135.61	3072.38	3019.66	2975.46	2938.22	2906.73	2880.00	2794.87	2755.26	2736.39	2727.30
230,000	3283.34	3205.29	3140.66	3086.77	3041.58	3003.52	2971.32	2944.00	2856.98	2816.48	2797.20	2787.91
235,000	3354.72	3274.97	3208.93	3153.87	3107.70	3068.81	3035.91	3008.00	2919.09	2877.71	2858.01	2848.52
240,000	3426.10	3344.65	3277.21	3220.97	3173.82	3134.10	3100.51	3072.00	2981.20	2938.94	2918.81	2909.12
245,000	3497.47	3414.33	3345.48	3288.08	3239.94	3199.40	3165.10	3136.00	3043.30	3000.17	2979.62	2969.73
250,000	3568.85	3484.01	3413.76	3355.18	3306.07	3264.69	3229.70	3200.00	3105.41	3061.39	3040.43	3030.34
255,000	3640.23	3553.69	3482.03	3422.28	3372.19	3329.98	3294.29	3264.00	3167.52	3122.62	3101.24	3090.94
260,000	3711.60	3623.37	3550.31	3489.39	3438.31	3395.28	3358.88	3328.00	3229.63	3183.85	3162.05	3151.55
265,000	3782.98	3693.05	3618.58	3556.49	3504.43	3460.57	3423.48	3392.00	3291.74	3245.08	3222.86	3212.16
270,000	3854.36	3762.73	3686.86	3623.59	3570.55	3525.87	3488.07	3456.00	3353.84	3306.31	3283.67	3272.76
280,000	3997.11	3902.09	3823.41	3757.80	3702.79	3656.45	3617.26	3584.00	3478.06	3428.76	3405.28	3393.98
290,000	4139.86	4041.45	3959.96	3892.01	3835.04	3787.04	3746.45	3712.00	3602.28	3551.22	3526.90	3515.19
300,000	4282.62	4180.82	4096.51	4026.22	3967.28	3917.63	3875.63	3840.00	3726.49	3673.67	3648.52	3636.40

14.75%

AMOUNT OF LOAN	NUMBER OF YEARS IN TERM											
	1	2	3	4	5	6	7	8	9	10	11	12
$ 50	4.51	2.42	1.73	1.39	1.19	1.06	0.96	0.90	0.84	0.80	0.77	0.75
100	9.02	4.84	3.46	2.78	2.37	2.11	1.92	1.79	1.68	1.60	1.54	1.49
200	18.03	9.68	6.91	5.55	4.74	4.21	3.84	3.57	3.36	3.20	3.08	2.97
300	27.05	14.52	10.37	8.32	7.10	6.31	5.75	5.35	5.04	4.80	4.61	4.46
400	36.06	19.35	13.82	11.09	9.47	8.41	7.67	7.13	6.72	6.40	6.15	5.94
500	45.08	24.19	17.28	13.86	11.83	10.51	9.58	8.91	8.39	8.00	7.68	7.43
600	54.09	29.03	20.73	16.63	14.20	12.61	11.50	10.69	10.07	9.59	9.22	8.91
700	63.10	33.86	24.19	19.40	16.57	14.71	13.41	12.47	11.75	11.19	10.75	10.40
800	72.12	38.70	27.64	22.17	18.93	16.81	15.33	14.25	13.43	12.79	12.29	11.88
900	81.13	43.54	31.09	24.94	21.30	18.91	17.25	16.03	15.10	14.39	13.82	13.37
1,000	90.15	48.37	34.55	27.71	23.66	21.01	19.16	17.81	16.78	15.99	15.36	14.85
2,000	180.29	96.74	69.09	55.41	47.32	42.02	38.32	35.61	33.56	31.97	30.71	29.70
3,000	270.43	145.11	103.63	83.12	70.98	63.03	57.48	53.41	50.33	47.95	46.06	44.55
4,000	360.57	193.48	138.18	110.82	94.64	84.04	76.63	71.21	67.11	63.93	61.41	59.40
5,000	450.71	241.84	172.72	138.53	118.30	105.05	95.79	89.01	83.88	79.91	76.77	74.25
6,000	540.85	290.21	207.26	166.23	141.96	126.06	114.95	106.81	100.66	95.89	92.12	89.09
7,000	630.99	338.58	241.81	193.93	165.62	147.07	134.10	124.61	117.43	111.87	107.47	103.94
8,000	721.13	386.95	276.35	221.64	189.28	168.08	153.26	142.41	134.21	127.85	122.82	118.79
9,000	811.27	435.32	310.89	249.34	212.94	189.09	172.42	160.21	150.99	143.83	138.18	133.64
10,000	901.41	483.68	345.44	277.05	236.59	210.10	191.57	178.02	167.76	159.81	153.53	148.49
15,000	1352.11	725.52	518.15	415.57	354.89	315.15	287.36	267.02	251.64	239.72	230.29	222.73
20,000	1802.81	967.36	690.87	554.09	473.18	420.19	383.14	356.03	335.52	319.62	307.05	296.97
25,000	2253.51	1209.20	863.58	692.61	591.48	525.24	478.92	445.03	419.40	399.52	383.82	371.21
30,000	2704.22	1451.04	1036.30	831.13	709.77	630.29	574.71	534.04	503.28	479.43	460.58	445.45
35,000	3154.92	1692.88	1209.01	969.65	828.07	735.34	670.49	623.04	587.15	559.33	537.34	519.69
40,000	3605.62	1934.72	1381.73	1108.17	946.36	840.38	766.28	712.05	671.03	639.23	614.10	593.94
45,000	4056.32	2176.56	1554.44	1246.69	1064.66	945.43	862.06	801.05	754.91	719.14	690.86	668.18
50,000	4507.02	2418.40	1727.16	1385.21	1182.95	1050.48	957.84	890.06	838.79	799.04	767.63	742.42
55,000	4957.73	2660.24	1899.87	1523.74	1301.24	1155.53	1053.63	979.06	922.67	878.95	844.39	816.66
60,000	5408.43	2902.08	2072.59	1662.26	1419.54	1260.57	1149.41	1068.07	1006.55	958.85	921.15	890.90
65,000	5859.13	3143.92	2245.30	1800.78	1537.83	1365.62	1245.19	1157.07	1090.43	1038.75	997.91	965.14
70,000	6309.83	3385.76	2418.02	1939.30	1656.13	1470.67	1340.98	1246.08	1174.30	1118.66	1074.68	1039.38
75,000	6760.53	3627.60	2590.73	2077.82	1774.42	1575.72	1436.76	1335.08	1258.18	1198.56	1151.44	1113.62
80,000	7211.24	3869.44	2763.45	2216.34	1892.72	1680.76	1532.55	1424.09	1342.06	1278.46	1228.20	1187.87
85,000	7661.94	4111.28	2936.16	2354.86	2011.01	1785.81	1628.33	1513.09	1425.94	1358.37	1304.96	1262.11
90,000	8112.64	4353.12	3108.88	2493.38	2129.31	1890.86	1724.11	1602.10	1509.82	1438.27	1381.72	1336.35
95,000	8563.34	4594.96	3281.59	2631.90	2247.60	1995.91	1819.90	1691.10	1593.70	1518.18	1458.49	1410.59
100,000	9014.04	4836.80	3454.31	2770.42	2365.90	2100.95	1915.68	1780.11	1677.58	1598.08	1535.25	1484.83
105,000	9464.75	5078.64	3627.02	2908.94	2484.19	2206.00	2011.46	1869.11	1761.45	1677.98	1612.01	1559.07
110,000	9915.45	5320.48	3799.74	3047.47	2602.48	2311.05	2107.25	1958.12	1845.33	1757.89	1688.77	1633.31
115,000	10366.15	5562.32	3972.45	3185.99	2720.78	2416.10	2203.03	2047.12	1929.21	1837.79	1765.53	1707.55
120,000	10816.85	5804.16	4145.17	3324.51	2839.07	2521.14	2298.82	2136.13	2013.09	1917.69	1842.30	1781.80
125,000	11267.55	6046.00	4317.88	3463.03	2957.37	2626.19	2394.60	2225.13	2096.97	1997.60	1919.06	1856.04
130,000	11718.26	6287.84	4490.60	3601.55	3075.66	2731.24	2490.39	2314.14	2180.85	2077.50	1995.82	1930.28
135,000	12168.96	6529.68	4663.31	3740.07	3193.96	2836.29	2586.17	2403.14	2264.73	2157.41	2072.58	2004.52
140,000	12619.66	6771.52	4836.03	3878.59	3312.25	2941.33	2681.95	2492.15	2348.60	2237.31	2149.35	2078.76
145,000	13070.36	7013.36	5008.74	4017.11	3430.55	3046.38	2777.74	2581.15	2432.48	2317.21	2226.11	2153.00
150,000	13521.06	7255.20	5181.46	4155.63	3548.84	3151.43	2873.52	2670.16	2516.36	2397.12	2302.87	2227.24
155,000	13971.76	7497.04	5354.17	4294.15	3667.14	3256.47	2969.30	2759.17	2600.24	2477.02	2379.63	2301.48
160,000	14422.47	7738.88	5526.89	4432.67	3785.43	3361.52	3065.09	2848.17	2684.12	2556.92	2456.39	2375.73
165,000	14873.17	7980.72	5699.60	4571.20	3903.72	3466.57	3160.87	2937.18	2768.00	2636.83	2533.16	2449.97
170,000	15323.87	8222.56	5872.32	4709.72	4022.02	3571.62	3256.65	3026.18	2851.87	2716.73	2609.92	2524.21
175,000	15774.57	8464.40	6045.03	4848.24	4140.31	3676.66	3352.44	3115.19	2935.75	2796.63	2686.68	2598.45
180,000	16225.27	8706.24	6217.75	4986.76	4258.61	3781.71	3448.22	3204.19	3019.63	2876.54	2763.44	2672.69
185,000	16675.98	8948.08	6390.47	5125.28	4376.90	3886.76	3544.01	3293.20	3103.51	2956.44	2840.20	2746.93
190,000	17126.68	9189.92	6563.18	5263.80	4495.20	3991.81	3639.79	3382.20	3187.39	3036.35	2916.97	2821.17
195,000	17577.38	9431.76	6735.90	5402.32	4613.49	4096.85	3735.57	3471.21	3271.27	3116.25	2993.73	2895.41
200,000	18028.08	9673.60	6908.61	5540.84	4731.79	4201.90	3831.36	3560.21	3355.15	3196.15	3070.49	2969.66
205,000	18478.78	9915.44	7081.33	5679.36	4850.08	4306.95	3927.14	3649.22	3439.02	3276.06	3147.25	3043.90
210,000	18929.49	10157.28	7254.04	5817.88	4968.37	4412.00	4022.92	3738.22	3522.90	3355.96	3224.02	3118.14
215,000	19380.19	10399.12	7426.76	5956.40	5086.67	4517.04	4118.71	3827.23	3606.78	3435.86	3300.78	3192.38
220,000	19830.89	10640.95	7599.47	6094.93	5204.96	4622.09	4214.49	3916.23	3690.66	3515.77	3377.54	3266.62
225,000	20281.59	10882.79	7772.19	6233.45	5323.26	4727.14	4310.28	4005.24	3774.54	3595.67	3454.30	3340.86
230,000	20732.29	11124.63	7944.90	6371.97	5441.55	4832.19	4406.06	4094.24	3858.42	3675.58	3531.06	3415.10
235,000	21183.00	11366.47	8117.62	6510.49	5559.85	4937.23	4501.84	4183.25	3942.30	3755.48	3607.83	3489.34
240,000	21633.70	11608.31	8290.33	6649.01	5678.14	5042.28	4597.63	4272.25	4026.17	3835.38	3684.59	3563.59
245,000	22084.40	11850.15	8463.05	6787.53	5796.44	5147.33	4693.41	4361.26	4110.05	3915.29	3761.35	3637.83
250,000	22535.10	12091.99	8635.76	6926.05	5914.73	5252.38	4789.20	4450.26	4193.93	3995.19	3838.11	3712.07
255,000	22985.80	12333.83	8808.48	7064.57	6033.03	5357.42	4884.98	4539.27	4277.81	4075.09	3914.87	3786.31
260,000	23436.51	12575.67	8981.19	7203.09	6151.32	5462.47	4980.76	4628.27	4361.69	4155.00	3991.64	3860.55
265,000	23887.21	12817.51	9153.91	7341.61	6269.61	5567.52	5076.55	4717.28	4445.57	4234.90	4068.40	3934.79
270,000	24337.91	13059.35	9326.62	7480.14	6387.91	5672.57	5172.33	4806.28	4529.45	4314.81	4145.16	4009.03
280,000	25239.31	13543.03	9672.05	7757.18	6624.50	5882.66	5363.90	4984.29	4697.20	4474.61	4298.69	4157.52
290,000	26140.72	14026.71	10017.48	8034.22	6861.09	6092.76	5555.47	5162.30	4864.96	4634.42	4452.21	4306.00
300,000	27042.12	14510.39	10362.91	8311.26	7097.68	6302.85	5747.03	5340.32	5032.72	4794.23	4605.73	4454.48

AMOUNT OF LOAN	NUMBER OF YEARS IN TERM											
	13	14	15	16	17	18	19	20	25	30	35	40
$ 50	0.73	0.71	0.70	0.68	0.68	0.67	0.66	0.65	0.64	0.63	0.62	0.62
100	1.45	1.42	1.39	1.36	1.35	1.33	1.31	1.30	1.27	1.25	1.24	1.24
200	2.89	2.83	2.77	2.72	2.69	2.65	2.62	2.60	2.53	2.49	2.48	2.47
300	4.34	4.24	4.15	4.08	4.03	3.98	3.93	3.90	3.79	3.74	3.71	3.70
400	5.78	5.65	5.54	5.44	5.37	5.30	5.24	5.20	5.05	4.98	4.95	4.94
500	7.22	7.06	6.92	6.80	6.71	6.62	6.55	6.50	6.31	6.23	6.19	6.17
600	8.67	8.47	8.30	8.16	8.05	7.95	7.86	7.80	7.57	7.47	7.42	7.40
700	10.11	9.88	9.68	9.52	9.39	9.27	9.17	9.09	8.84	8.72	8.66	8.63
800	11.56	11.29	11.07	10.88	10.73	10.59	10.48	10.39	10.10	9.96	9.90	9.87
900	13.00	12.70	12.45	12.24	12.07	11.92	11.79	11.69	11.36	11.21	11.13	11.10
1,000	14.44	14.11	13.83	13.60	13.41	13.24	13.10	12.99	12.62	12.45	12.37	12.33
2,000	28.88	28.21	27.66	27.19	26.81	26.48	26.20	25.97	25.23	24.89	24.73	24.66
3,000	43.32	42.31	41.48	40.79	40.21	39.72	39.30	38.96	37.85	37.34	37.10	36.99
4,000	57.76	56.42	55.31	54.38	53.61	52.95	52.40	51.94	50.46	49.78	49.46	49.31
5,000	72.20	70.52	69.13	67.97	67.01	66.19	65.50	64.92	63.08	62.23	61.83	61.64
6,000	86.64	84.62	82.96	81.57	80.41	79.43	78.60	77.91	75.69	74.67	74.19	73.97
7,000	101.08	98.72	96.78	95.16	93.81	92.67	91.70	90.89	88.31	87.12	86.56	86.29
8,000	115.51	112.83	110.61	108.76	107.21	105.90	104.80	103.87	100.92	99.56	98.92	98.62
9,000	129.95	126.93	124.43	122.35	120.61	119.14	117.90	116.86	113.54	112.01	111.29	110.95
10,000	144.39	141.03	138.26	135.94	134.01	132.38	131.00	129.84	126.15	124.45	123.65	123.27
15,000	216.59	211.55	207.38	203.91	201.01	198.57	196.50	194.76	189.22	186.68	185.48	184.91
20,000	288.78	282.06	276.51	271.88	268.01	264.75	262.00	259.68	252.30	248.90	247.30	246.54
25,000	360.97	352.58	345.63	339.85	335.01	330.94	327.50	324.59	315.37	311.12	309.12	308.17
30,000	433.17	423.09	414.76	407.82	402.01	397.13	393.00	389.51	378.44	373.35	370.95	369.81
35,000	505.36	493.60	483.88	475.79	469.01	463.31	458.50	454.43	441.52	435.57	432.77	431.44
40,000	577.55	564.12	553.01	543.76	536.01	529.50	524.00	519.35	504.59	497.80	494.59	493.07
45,000	649.75	634.63	622.13	611.73	603.01	595.69	589.50	584.26	567.66	560.02	556.42	554.71
50,000	721.94	705.15	691.26	679.69	670.02	661.88	655.00	649.18	630.74	622.24	618.24	616.34
55,000	794.14	775.66	760.38	747.66	737.02	728.06	720.50	714.10	693.81	684.47	680.07	677.97
60,000	866.33	846.17	829.51	815.63	804.02	794.25	786.00	779.02	756.88	746.69	741.89	739.61
65,000	938.52	916.69	898.63	883.60	871.02	860.44	851.50	843.94	819.96	808.91	803.71	801.24
70,000	1010.72	987.20	967.76	951.57	938.02	926.62	917.00	908.85	883.03	871.14	865.54	862.87
75,000	1082.91	1057.72	1036.88	1019.54	1005.02	992.81	982.50	973.77	946.10	933.36	927.36	924.51
80,000	1155.10	1128.23	1106.01	1087.51	1072.02	1059.00	1048.00	1038.69	1009.18	995.59	989.18	986.14
85,000	1227.30	1198.74	1175.13	1155.48	1139.02	1125.19	1113.50	1103.61	1072.25	1057.01	1051.01	1047.77
90,000	1299.49	1269.26	1244.26	1223.45	1206.02	1191.37	1179.00	1168.52	1135.32	1120.03	1112.83	1109.41
95,000	1371.68	1339.77	1313.38	1291.42	1273.03	1257.56	1244.50	1233.44	1198.40	1182.26	1174.66	1171.04
100,000	1443.88	1410.29	1382.51	1359.38	1340.03	1323.75	1310.00	1298.36	1261.47	1244.48	1236.48	1232.67
105,000	1516.07	1400.80	1451.63	1427.35	1407.03	1389.93	1375.50	1363.28	1324.54	1306.70	1298.30	1294.31
110,000	1588.27	1551.31	1520.76	1495.32	1474.03	1456.12	1441.00	1428.20	1387.62	1368.93	1360.13	1355.94
115,000	1660.46	1621.83	1589.88	1563.29	1541.03	1522.31	1506.50	1493.11	1450.69	1431.15	1421.95	1417.57
120,000	1732.65	1692.34	1659.01	1631.26	1608.03	1588.50	1572.00	1558.03	1513.76	1493.38	1483.77	1479.21
125,000	1804.85	1762.86	1728.13	1699.23	1675.03	1654.68	1637.50	1622.95	1576.84	1555.60	1545.60	1540.84
130,000	1877.04	1833.37	1797.26	1767.20	1742.03	1720.87	1703.00	1687.87	1639.91	1617.82	1607.42	1602.47
135,000	1949.23	1903.89	1866.39	1835.17	1809.03	1787.06	1768.50	1752.78	1702.98	1680.05	1669.25	1664.11
140,000	2021.43	1974.40	1935.51	1903.14	1876.04	1853.24	1834.00	1817.70	1766.06	1742.27	1731.07	1725.74
145,000	2093.62	2044.91	2004.64	1971.11	1943.04	1919.43	1899.50	1882.62	1829.13	1804.49	1792.89	1787.37
150,000	2165.82	2115.43	2073.76	2039.07	2010.04	1985.62	1965.00	1947.54	1892.20	1866.72	1854.72	1849.01
155,000	2238.01	2185.94	2142.89	2107.04	2077.04	2051.81	2030.50	2012.46	1955.28	1928.94	1916.54	1910.64
160,000	2310.20	2256.46	2212.01	2175.01	2144.04	2117.99	2096.00	2077.37	2018.35	1991.17	1978.36	1972.27
165,000	2382.40	2326.97	2281.14	2242.98	2211.04	2184.18	2161.50	2142.29	2081.42	2053.39	2040.19	2033.91
170,000	2454.59	2397.48	2350.26	2310.95	2278.04	2250.37	2227.00	2207.21	2144.50	2115.61	2102.01	2095.54
175,000	2526.78	2468.00	2419.39	2378.92	2345.04	2316.55	2292.50	2272.13	2207.57	2177.84	2163.84	2157.17
180,000	2598.98	2538.51	2488.51	2446.89	2412.04	2382.74	2358.00	2337.04	2270.64	2240.06	2225.66	2218.81
185,000	2671.17	2609.03	2557.64	2514.86	2479.05	2448.93	2423.50	2401.96	2333.71	2302.29	2287.48	2280.44
190,000	2743.36	2679.54	2626.76	2582.83	2546.05	2515.12	2489.00	2466.88	2396.79	2364.51	2349.31	2342.07
195,000	2815.56	2750.05	2695.89	2650.79	2613.05	2581.30	2554.50	2531.80	2459.86	2426.73	2411.13	2403.71
200,000	2887.75	2820.57	2765.01	2718.76	2680.05	2647.49	2620.00	2596.72	2522.93	2488.96	2472.95	2465.34
205,000	2959.95	2891.08	2834.14	2786.73	2747.05	2713.68	2685.50	2661.63	2586.01	2551.18	2534.78	2526.97
210,000	3032.14	2961.60	2903.26	2854.70	2814.05	2779.86	2751.00	2726.55	2649.08	2613.40	2596.60	2588.61
215,000	3104.33	3032.11	2972.39	2922.67	2881.05	2846.05	2816.50	2791.47	2712.15	2675.63	2658.43	2650.24
220,000	3176.53	3102.62	3041.51	2990.64	2948.05	2912.24	2882.00	2856.39	2775.23	2737.85	2720.25	2711.87
225,000	3248.72	3173.14	3110.64	3058.61	3015.05	2978.43	2947.50	2921.30	2838.30	2800.08	2782.07	2773.51
230,000	3320.91	3243.65	3179.76	3126.58	3082.06	3044.61	3013.00	2986.22	2901.37	2862.30	2843.90	2835.14
235,000	3393.11	3314.17	3248.89	3194.55	3149.06	3110.80	3078.50	3051.14	2964.45	2924.52	2905.72	2896.77
240,000	3465.30	3384.68	3318.01	3262.52	3216.06	3176.99	3144.00	3116.06	3027.52	2986.75	2967.54	2958.41
245,000	3537.50	3455.20	3387.14	3330.48	3283.06	3243.17	3209.50	3180.98	3090.59	3048.97	3029.37	3020.04
250,000	3609.69	3525.71	3456.26	3398.45	3350.06	3309.36	3275.00	3245.89	3153.67	3111.19	3091.19	3081.67
255,000	3681.88	3596.22	3525.39	3466.42	3417.06	3375.55	3340.50	3310.81	3216.74	3173.42	3153.02	3143.31
260,000	3754.08	3666.74	3594.51	3534.39	3484.06	3441.74	3406.00	3375.73	3279.81	3235.64	3214.84	3204.94
265,000	3826.27	3737.25	3663.64	3602.36	3551.06	3507.92	3471.50	3440.65	3342.89	3297.87	3276.66	3266.57
270,000	3898.46	3807.77	3732.77	3670.33	3618.06	3574.11	3537.00	3505.56	3405.96	3360.09	3338.49	3328.21
280,000	4042.85	3948.79	3871.02	3806.27	3752.07	3706.48	3668.00	3635.40	3532.11	3484.54	3462.13	3451.47
290,000	4187.24	4089.82	4009.27	3942.21	3886.07	3838.86	3799.00	3765.24	3658.25	3608.98	3585.78	3574.74
300,000	4331.63	4230.85	4147.52	4078.14	4020.07	3971.23	3930.00	3895.07	3784.40	3733.43	3709.43	3698.01

15.00%

AMOUNT OF LOAN	NUMBER OF YEARS IN TERM											
	1	2	3	4	5	6	7	8	9	10	11	12
$ 50	4.52	2.43	1.74	1.40	1.19	1.06	0.97	0.90	0.85	0.81	0.78	0.76
100	9.03	4.85	3.47	2.79	2.38	2.12	1.93	1.80	1.70	1.62	1.56	1.51
200	18.06	9.70	6.94	5.57	4.76	4.23	3.86	3.59	3.39	3.23	3.11	3.01
300	27.08	14.55	10.40	8.35	7.14	6.35	5.79	5.39	5.08	4.85	4.66	4.51
400	36.11	19.40	13.87	11.14	9.52	8.46	7.72	7.18	6.77	6.46	6.21	6.01
500	45.13	24.25	17.34	13.92	11.90	10.58	9.65	8.98	8.47	8.07	7.76	7.51
600	54.16	29.10	20.80	16.70	14.28	12.69	11.58	10.77	10.16	9.69	9.31	9.01
700	63.19	33.95	24.27	19.49	16.66	14.81	13.51	12.57	11.85	11.30	10.86	10.51
800	72.21	38.79	27.74	22.27	19.04	16.92	15.44	14.36	13.54	12.91	12.41	12.01
900	81.24	43.64	31.20	25.05	21.42	19.04	17.37	16.16	15.24	14.53	13.96	13.51
1,000	90.26	48.49	34.67	27.84	23.79	21.15	19.30	17.95	16.93	16.14	15.51	15.01
2,000	180.52	96.98	69.34	55.67	47.58	42.30	38.60	35.90	33.85	32.27	31.02	30.02
3,000	270.78	145.46	104.00	83.50	71.37	63.44	57.90	53.84	50.78	48.41	46.53	45.03
4,000	361.04	193.95	138.67	111.33	95.16	84.59	77.19	71.79	67.70	64.54	62.04	60.04
5,000	451.30	242.44	173.33	139.16	118.95	105.73	96.49	89.73	84.63	80.67	77.55	75.05
6,000	541.55	290.92	208.00	166.99	142.74	126.88	115.79	107.68	101.55	96.81	93.06	90.06
7,000	631.81	339.41	242.66	194.82	166.53	148.02	135.08	125.62	118.48	112.94	108.57	105.07
8,000	722.07	387.90	277.33	222.65	190.32	169.17	154.38	143.57	135.40	129.07	124.08	120.08
9,000	812.33	436.38	311.99	250.48	214.11	190.31	173.68	161.51	152.32	145.21	139.59	135.08
10,000	902.59	484.87	346.66	278.31	237.90	211.46	192.97	179.46	169.25	161.34	155.10	150.09
15,000	1353.88	727.30	519.98	417.47	356.85	317.18	289.46	269.19	253.87	242.01	232.64	225.14
20,000	1805.17	969.74	693.31	556.62	475.80	422.91	385.94	358.91	338.49	322.67	310.19	300.18
25,000	2256.46	1212.17	866.64	695.77	594.75	528.63	482.42	448.64	423.11	403.34	387.73	375.22
30,000	2707.75	1454.60	1039.96	834.93	713.70	634.36	578.91	538.37	507.74	484.01	465.28	450.27
35,000	3159.05	1697.04	1213.29	974.08	832.65	740.08	675.39	628.09	592.36	564.68	542.83	525.31
40,000	3610.34	1939.47	1386.62	1113.23	951.60	845.81	771.88	717.82	676.98	645.34	620.37	600.36
45,000	4061.63	2181.90	1559.94	1252.39	1070.55	951.53	868.36	807.55	761.60	726.01	697.92	675.40
50,000	4512.92	2424.34	1733.27	1391.54	1189.50	1057.26	964.84	897.28	846.22	806.68	775.46	750.44
55,000	4964.21	2666.77	1906.60	1530.70	1308.45	1162.98	1061.33	987.00	930.84	887.35	853.01	825.49
60,000	5415.50	2909.20	2079.92	1669.85	1427.40	1268.71	1157.81	1076.73	1015.47	968.01	930.55	900.53
65,000	5866.80	3151.64	2253.25	1809.00	1546.35	1374.43	1254.29	1166.46	1100.09	1048.68	1008.10	975.57
70,000	6318.09	3394.07	2426.58	1948.16	1665.30	1480.16	1350.78	1256.18	1184.71	1129.35	1085.65	1050.62
75,000	6769.38	3636.50	2599.90	2087.31	1784.25	1585.88	1447.26	1345.91	1269.33	1210.02	1163.19	1125.66
80,000	7220.67	3878.94	2773.23	2226.46	1903.20	1691.61	1543.75	1435.64	1353.95	1290.68	1240.74	1200.71
85,000	7671.96	4121.37	2946.56	2365.62	2022.15	1797.33	1640.23	1525.36	1438.57	1371.35	1318.28	1275.75
90,000	8123.25	4363.80	3119.88	2504.77	2141.10	1903.06	1736.71	1615.09	1523.20	1452.02	1395.83	1350.79
95,000	8574.54	4606.24	3293.21	2643.93	2260.05	2008.78	1833.20	1704.82	1607.82	1532.69	1473.37	1425.84
100,000	9025.84	4848.67	3466.54	2783.08	2379.00	2114.51	1929.68	1794.55	1692.44	1613.35	1550.92	1500.88
105,000	9477.13	5091.10	3639.86	2922.23	2497.95	2220.23	2026.16	1884.27	1777.06	1694.02	1628.47	1575.93
110,000	9928.42	5333.54	3813.19	3061.39	2616.90	2325.96	2122.65	1974.00	1861.68	1774.69	1706.01	1650.97
115,000	10379.71	5575.97	3986.52	3200.54	2735.85	2431.68	2219.13	2063.73	1946.30	1855.36	1783.56	1726.01
120,000	10831.00	5818.40	4159.84	3339.69	2854.80	2537.41	2315.62	2153.45	2030.93	1936.02	1861.10	1801.06
125,000	11282.29	6060.84	4333.17	3478.85	2973.75	2643.13	2412.10	2243.18	2115.55	2016.69	1938.65	1876.10
130,000	11733.59	6303.27	4506.50	3618.00	3092.70	2748.86	2508.58	2332.91	2200.17	2097.36	2016.19	1951.14
135,000	12184.88	6545.70	4679.82	3757.16	3211.65	2854.58	2605.07	2422.63	2284.79	2178.03	2093.74	2026.19
140,000	12636.17	6788.14	4853.15	3896.31	3330.60	2960.31	2701.55	2512.36	2369.41	2258.69	2171.29	2101.23
145,000	13087.46	7030.57	5026.48	4035.46	3449.54	3066.03	2798.03	2602.09	2454.03	2339.36	2248.83	2176.28
150,000	13538.75	7273.00	5199.80	4174.62	3568.49	3171.76	2894.52	2691.82	2538.66	2420.03	2326.38	2251.32
155,000	13990.04	7515.44	5373.13	4313.77	3687.44	3277.48	2991.00	2781.54	2623.28	2500.70	2403.92	2326.36
160,000	14441.33	7757.87	5546.46	4452.92	3806.39	3383.21	3087.49	2871.27	2707.90	2581.36	2481.47	2401.41
165,000	14892.63	8000.30	5719.78	4592.08	3925.34	3488.93	3183.97	2961.00	2792.52	2662.03	2559.01	2476.45
170,000	15343.92	8242.74	5893.11	4731.23	4044.29	3594.66	3280.45	3050.72	2877.14	2742.70	2636.56	2551.50
175,000	15795.21	8485.17	6066.44	4870.39	4163.24	3700.38	3376.94	3140.45	2961.76	2823.37	2714.11	2626.54
180,000	16246.50	8727.60	6239.76	5009.54	4282.19	3806.11	3473.42	3230.18	3046.39	2904.03	2791.65	2701.58
185,000	16697.79	8970.03	6413.09	5148.69	4401.14	3911.83	3569.90	3319.90	3131.01	2984.70	2869.20	2776.63
190,000	17149.08	9212.47	6586.42	5287.85	4520.09	4017.56	3666.39	3409.63	3215.63	3065.37	2946.74	2851.67
195,000	17600.38	9454.90	6759.74	5427.00	4639.04	4123.28	3762.87	3499.36	3300.25	3146.04	3024.29	2926.71
200,000	18051.67	9697.33	6933.07	5566.15	4757.99	4229.01	3859.36	3589.09	3384.87	3226.70	3101.83	3001.76
205,000	18502.96	9939.77	7106.40	5705.31	4876.94	4334.73	3955.84	3678.81	3469.49	3307.37	3179.38	3076.80
210,000	18954.25	10182.20	7279.72	5844.46	4995.89	4440.46	4052.32	3768.54	3554.12	3388.04	3256.93	3151.85
215,000	19405.54	10424.63	7453.05	5983.62	5114.84	4546.18	4148.81	3858.27	3638.74	3468.71	3334.47	3226.89
220,000	19856.83	10667.07	7626.38	6122.77	5233.79	4651.91	4245.29	3947.99	3723.36	3549.37	3412.02	3301.93
225,000	20308.13	10909.50	7799.70	6261.92	5352.74	4757.63	4341.77	4037.72	3807.98	3630.04	3489.56	3376.98
230,000	20759.42	11151.93	7973.03	6401.08	5471.69	4863.36	4438.26	4127.45	3892.60	3710.71	3567.11	3452.02
235,000	21210.71	11394.37	8146.36	6540.23	5590.64	4969.08	4534.74	4217.18	3977.22	3791.38	3644.66	3527.07
240,000	21662.00	11636.80	8319.68	6679.38	5709.59	5074.81	4631.23	4306.90	4061.85	3872.04	3722.20	3602.11
245,000	22113.29	11879.23	8493.01	6818.54	5828.54	5180.53	4727.71	4396.63	4146.47	3952.71	3799.75	3677.15
250,000	22564.58	12121.67	8666.34	6957.69	5947.49	5286.26	4824.19	4486.36	4231.09	4033.38	3877.29	3752.20
255,000	23015.87	12364.10	8839.66	7096.85	6066.44	5391.98	4920.68	4576.08	4315.71	4114.05	3954.84	3827.24
260,000	23467.17	12606.53	9012.99	7236.00	6185.39	5497.71	5017.16	4665.81	4400.33	4194.71	4032.38	3902.28
265,000	23918.46	12848.97	9186.32	7375.15	6304.34	5603.43	5113.65	4755.54	4484.95	4275.38	4109.93	3977.33
270,000	24369.75	13091.40	9359.64	7514.31	6423.29	5709.16	5210.13	4845.26	4569.58	4356.05	4187.48	4052.37
280,000	25272.33	13576.27	9706.30	7792.61	6661.19	5920.61	5403.10	5024.72	4738.82	4517.38	4342.57	4202.46
290,000	26174.92	14061.13	10052.95	8070.92	6899.08	6132.06	5596.06	5204.17	4908.06	4678.72	4497.66	4352.55
300,000	27077.50	14546.00	10399.60	8349.23	7136.98	6343.51	5789.03	5383.63	5077.31	4840.05	4652.75	4502.64

AMOUNT OF LOAN	NUMBER OF YEARS IN TERM											
	13	14	15	16	17	18	19	20	25	30	35	40
$ 50	0.74	0.72	0.70	0.69	0.68	0.68	0.67	0.66	0.65	0.64	0.63	0.63
100	1.47	1.43	1.40	1.38	1.36	1.35	1.33	1.32	1.29	1.27	1.26	1.26
200	2.93	2.86	2.80	2.76	2.72	2.69	2.66	2.64	2.57	2.53	2.52	2.51
300	4.39	4.29	4.20	4.14	4.08	4.03	3.99	3.96	3.85	3.80	3.78	3.76
400	5.85	5.71	5.60	5.51	5.44	5.37	5.32	5.27	5.13	5.06	5.03	5.02
500	7.31	7.14	7.00	6.89	6.79	6.71	6.65	6.59	6.41	6.33	6.29	6.27
600	8.77	8.57	8.40	8.27	8.15	8.06	7.97	7.91	7.69	7.59	7.55	7.52
700	10.23	9.99	9.80	9.64	9.51	9.40	9.30	9.22	8.97	8.86	8.80	8.78
800	11.69	11.42	11.20	11.02	10.87	10.74	10.63	10.54	10.25	10.12	10.06	10.03
900	13.15	12.85	12.60	12.40	12.22	12.08	11.96	11.86	11.53	11.38	11.32	11.28
1,000	14.61	14.28	14.00	13.77	13.58	13.42	13.29	13.17	12.81	12.65	12.57	12.54
2,000	29.21	28.55	28.00	27.54	27.16	26.84	26.57	26.34	25.62	25.29	25.14	25.07
3,000	43.81	42.82	41.99	41.31	40.74	40.26	39.85	39.51	38.43	37.94	37.71	37.60
4,000	58.42	57.09	55.99	55.08	54.31	53.67	53.13	52.68	51.24	50.58	50.28	50.13
5,000	73.02	71.36	69.98	68.84	67.89	67.09	66.41	65.84	64.05	63.23	62.85	62.67
6,000	87.62	85.63	83.98	82.61	81.47	80.51	79.70	79.01	76.85	75.87	75.41	75.20
7,000	102.23	99.90	97.98	96.38	95.04	93.92	92.98	92.18	89.66	88.52	87.98	87.73
8,000	116.83	114.17	111.97	110.15	108.62	107.34	106.26	105.35	102.47	101.16	100.55	100.26
9,000	131.43	128.44	125.97	123.91	122.20	120.76	119.54	118.52	115.28	113.80	113.12	112.80
10,000	146.03	142.71	139.96	137.68	135.78	134.17	132.82	131.68	128.09	126.45	125.69	125.33
15,000	219.05	214.06	209.94	206.52	203.66	201.26	199.23	197.52	192.13	189.67	188.53	187.99
20,000	292.06	285.41	279.92	275.36	271.55	268.34	265.64	263.36	256.17	252.89	251.37	250.65
25,000	365.00	356.76	349.90	344.20	339.43	335.43	332.05	329.20	320.21	316.12	314.21	313.31
30,000	438.09	428.12	419.88	413.04	407.32	402.51	398.46	395.04	384.25	379.34	377.05	375.97
35,000	511.11	499.47	489.86	481.87	475.20	469.60	464.87	460.88	448.30	442.56	439.89	438.63
40,000	584.12	570.82	559.84	550.71	543.09	536.68	531.28	526.72	512.34	505.78	502.73	501.29
45,000	657.13	642.17	629.82	619.55	610.97	603.77	597.69	592.56	576.38	569.00	565.57	563.96
50,000	730.15	713.52	699.80	688.39	678.85	670.85	664.10	658.40	640.42	632.23	628.41	626.62
55,000	803.16	784.88	769.78	757.23	746.74	737.93	730.51	724.24	704.46	695.45	691.25	689.28
60,000	876.18	856.23	839.76	826.07	814.63	805.02	796.92	790.08	768.50	758.67	754.09	751.94
65,000	949.19	927.58	909.74	894.91	882.51	872.10	863.33	855.92	832.54	821.89	816.93	814.60
70,000	1022.21	998.93	979.72	963.74	950.40	939.19	929.74	921.76	896.59	885.12	879.77	877.26
75,000	1095.22	1070.28	1049.70	1032.58	1018.28	1006.27	996.15	987.60	960.63	948.34	942.61	939.92
80,000	1168.23	1141.64	1119.67	1101.42	1086.17	1073.36	1062.56	1053.44	1024.67	1011.56	1005.46	1002.58
85,000	1241.25	1212.99	1189.65	1170.26	1154.05	1140.44	1128.97	1119.28	1088.71	1074.78	1068.30	1065.25
90,000	1314.26	1284.34	1259.63	1239.10	1221.94	1207.53	1195.38	1185.12	1152.75	1138.00	1131.14	1127.91
95,000	1387.28	1355.69	1329.61	1307.94	1289.82	1274.61	1261.79	1250.96	1216.79	1201.23	1193.98	1190.57
100,000	1460.29	1427.04	1399.59	1376.77	1357.71	1341.70	1328.20	1316.79	1280.84	1264.45	1256.82	1253.23
105,000	1533.31	1498.40	1469.57	1445.61	1425.59	1408.78	1394.61	1382.63	1344.88	1327.67	1319.66	1315.89
110,000	1606.32	1569.75	1539.55	1514.45	1493.48	1475.86	1461.02	1448.47	1408.92	1390.89	1382.50	1378.55
115,000	1679.34	1641.10	1609.53	1583.29	1561.36	1542.95	1527.43	1514.31	1472.96	1454.12	1445.34	1441.21
120,000	1752.35	1712.45	1679.51	1652.13	1629.25	1610.03	1593.84	1580.15	1537.00	1517.34	1508.18	1503.87
125,000	1825.36	1783.80	1749.49	1720.97	1697.13	1677.12	1660.25	1645.99	1601.04	1580.56	1571.02	1566.54
130,000	1898.38	1855.16	1819.47	1789.81	1765.02	1744.20	1726.66	1711.83	1665.08	1643.78	1633.86	1629.20
135,000	1971.39	1926.51	1889.45	1858.64	1832.90	1811.29	1793.07	1777.67	1729.13	1707.01	1696.70	1691.86
140,000	2044.41	1997.86	1959.43	1927.48	1900.79	1878.37	1859.48	1843.51	1793.17	1770.23	1759.54	1754.52
145,000	2117.42	2069.21	2029.41	1996.32	1968.67	1945.46	1925.89	1909.35	1857.21	1833.45	1822.38	1817.18
150,000	2190.44	2140.56	2099.39	2065.16	2036.56	2012.54	1992.30	1975.19	1921.25	1896.67	1885.22	1879.84
155,000	2263.45	2211.92	2169.37	2134.00	2104.44	2079.63	2058.71	2041.03	1985.29	1959.89	1948.07	1942.50
160,000	2336.46	2283.27	2239.34	2202.84	2172.33	2146.71	2125.12	2106.87	2049.33	2023.12	2010.91	2005.16
165,000	2409.48	2354.62	2309.32	2271.67	2240.21	2213.79	2191.53	2172.71	2113.38	2086.34	2073.75	2067.82
170,000	2482.49	2425.97	2379.30	2340.51	2308.10	2280.88	2257.94	2238.55	2177.42	2149.56	2136.59	2130.49
175,000	2555.51	2497.32	2449.28	2409.35	2375.98	2347.96	2324.35	2304.39	2241.46	2212.78	2199.43	2193.15
180,000	2628.52	2568.68	2519.26	2478.19	2443.87	2415.05	2390.76	2370.23	2305.50	2276.00	2262.27	2255.81
185,000	2701.54	2640.03	2589.24	2547.03	2511.75	2482.13	2457.17	2436.07	2369.54	2339.23	2325.11	2318.47
190,000	2774.55	2711.38	2659.22	2615.87	2579.64	2549.22	2523.58	2501.91	2433.58	2402.45	2387.95	2381.13
195,000	2847.57	2782.73	2729.20	2684.71	2647.52	2616.30	2589.99	2567.74	2497.62	2465.67	2450.79	2443.79
200,000	2920.58	2854.08	2799.18	2753.54	2715.41	2683.39	2656.40	2633.58	2561.67	2528.89	2513.63	2506.45
205,000	2993.59	2925.44	2869.16	2822.38	2783.29	2750.47	2722.81	2699.42	2625.71	2592.12	2576.47	2569.11
210,000	3066.61	2996.79	2939.14	2891.22	2851.18	2817.56	2789.22	2765.26	2689.75	2655.34	2639.31	2631.78
215,000	3139.62	3068.14	3009.12	2960.06	2919.06	2884.64	2855.63	2831.10	2753.79	2718.56	2702.15	2694.44
220,000	3212.64	3139.49	3079.10	3028.90	2986.95	2951.72	2922.04	2896.94	2817.83	2781.78	2764.99	2757.10
225,000	3285.65	3210.84	3149.08	3097.74	3054.83	3018.81	2988.45	2962.78	2881.87	2845.00	2827.83	2819.76
230,000	3358.67	3282.20	3219.06	3166.58	3122.72	3085.89	3054.86	3028.62	2945.92	2908.23	2890.68	2882.42
235,000	3431.68	3353.55	3289.03	3235.41	3190.60	3152.98	3121.27	3094.46	3009.96	2971.45	2953.52	2945.08
240,000	3504.69	3424.90	3359.01	3304.25	3258.49	3220.06	3187.68	3160.30	3074.00	3034.67	3016.36	3007.74
245,000	3577.71	3496.25	3428.99	3373.09	3326.37	3287.15	3254.09	3226.14	3138.04	3097.89	3079.20	3070.40
250,000	3650.72	3567.60	3498.97	3441.93	3394.26	3354.23	3320.50	3291.98	3202.08	3161.12	3142.04	3133.07
255,000	3723.74	3638.96	3568.95	3510.77	3462.14	3421.32	3386.91	3357.82	3266.12	3224.34	3204.88	3195.73
260,000	3796.75	3710.31	3638.93	3579.61	3530.03	3488.40	3453.32	3423.66	3330.16	3287.56	3267.72	3258.39
265,000	3869.77	3781.66	3708.91	3648.44	3597.91	3555.49	3519.73	3489.50	3394.21	3350.78	3330.56	3321.05
270,000	3942.78	3853.01	3778.89	3717.28	3665.80	3622.57	3586.14	3555.34	3458.25	3414.00	3393.40	3383.71
280,000	4088.81	3995.72	3918.85	3854.96	3801.57	3756.74	3718.96	3687.02	3586.33	3540.45	3519.08	3509.03
290,000	4234.84	4138.42	4058.81	3992.64	3937.34	3890.91	3851.78	3818.69	3714.41	3666.89	3644.76	3634.35
300,000	4380.87	4281.12	4198.77	4130.31	4073.11	4025.08	3984.60	3950.37	3842.50	3793.34	3770.44	3759.68

MONTHLY AMORTIZING PAYMENTS

AMOUNT OF LOAN	NUMBER OF YEARS IN TERM											
	1	2	3	4	5	6	7	8	9	10	11	12
$ 50	4.52	2.44	1.74	1.40	1.20	1.07	0.98	0.91	0.86	0.82	0.79	0.76
100	9.04	4.87	3.48	2.80	2.40	2.13	1.95	1.81	1.71	1.63	1.57	1.52
200	18.08	9.73	6.96	5.60	4.79	4.26	3.89	3.62	3.42	3.26	3.14	3.04
300	27.12	14.59	10.44	8.39	7.18	6.39	5.84	5.43	5.13	4.89	4.70	4.56
400	36.16	19.45	13.92	11.19	9.57	8.52	7.78	7.24	6.83	6.52	6.27	6.07
500	45.19	24.31	17.40	13.98	11.97	10.65	9.72	9.05	8.54	8.15	7.84	7.59
600	54.23	29.17	20.88	16.78	14.36	12.77	11.67	10.86	10.25	9.78	9.40	9.11
700	63.27	34.03	24.36	19.58	16.75	14.90	13.61	12.67	11.96	11.41	10.97	10.62
800	72.31	38.89	27.84	22.37	19.14	17.03	15.55	14.48	13.66	13.03	12.54	12.14
900	81.34	43.75	31.31	25.17	21.53	19.16	17.50	16.29	15.37	14.66	14.10	13.66
1,000	90.38	48.61	34.79	27.96	23.93	21.29	19.44	18.10	17.08	16.29	15.67	15.18
2,000	180.76	97.22	69.58	55.92	47.85	42.57	38.88	36.19	34.15	32.58	31.34	30.35
3,000	271.13	145.82	104.37	83.88	71.77	63.85	58.32	54.28	51.23	48.87	47.00	45.52
4,000	361.51	194.43	139.16	111.84	95.69	85.13	77.75	72.37	68.30	65.15	62.67	60.69
5,000	451.89	243.03	173.94	139.79	119.61	106.41	97.19	90.46	85.37	81.44	78.34	75.86
6,000	542.26	291.64	208.73	167.75	143.53	127.69	116.63	108.55	102.45	97.73	94.00	91.03
7,000	632.64	340.24	243.52	195.71	167.45	148.97	136.07	126.64	119.52	114.01	109.67	106.20
8,000	723.02	388.85	278.31	223.67	191.38	170.25	155.50	144.73	136.59	130.30	125.34	121.37
9,000	813.39	437.45	313.10	251.62	215.30	191.53	174.94	162.82	153.67	146.59	141.00	136.54
10,000	903.77	486.06	347.88	279.58	239.22	212.82	194.38	180.91	170.74	162.87	156.67	151.71
15,000	1355.65	729.09	521.82	419.37	358.83	319.22	291.56	271.36	256.11	244.31	235.00	227.56
20,000	1807.53	972.12	695.76	559.16	478.43	425.63	388.75	361.81	341.48	325.74	313.34	303.41
25,000	2259.41	1215.14	869.70	698.95	598.04	532.03	485.94	452.26	426.85	407.18	391.67	379.26
30,000	2711.29	1458.17	1043.64	838.73	717.65	638.44	583.12	542.72	512.21	488.61	470.00	455.11
35,000	3163.18	1701.20	1217.58	978.52	837.25	744.84	680.31	633.17	597.58	570.05	548.34	530.96
40,000	3615.06	1944.23	1391.52	1118.31	956.86	851.25	777.50	723.62	682.95	651.48	626.67	606.81
45,000	4066.94	2187.25	1565.46	1258.10	1076.47	957.65	874.68	814.07	768.32	732.92	705.00	682.66
50,000	4518.82	2430.28	1739.40	1397.89	1196.07	1064.06	971.87	904.52	853.69	814.35	783.33	758.51
55,000	4970.70	2673.31	1913.34	1537.68	1315.68	1170.46	1069.06	994.98	939.05	895.79	861.67	834.36
60,000	5422.58	2916.34	2087.28	1677.46	1435.29	1276.87	1166.24	1085.43	1024.42	977.22	940.00	910.21
65,000	5874.47	3159.36	2261.22	1817.25	1554.89	1383.27	1263.43	1175.88	1109.79	1058.66	1018.33	986.06
70,000	6326.35	3402.39	2435.16	1957.04	1674.50	1489.68	1360.61	1266.33	1195.16	1140.09	1096.67	1061.91
75,000	6778.23	3645.42	2609.10	2096.83	1794.11	1596.08	1457.80	1356.78	1280.53	1221.53	1175.00	1137.76
80,000	7230.11	3888.45	2783.04	2236.62	1913.71	1702.49	1554.99	1447.23	1365.89	1302.96	1253.33	1213.61
85,000	7681.99	4131.47	2956.97	2376.40	2033.32	1808.89	1652.17	1537.69	1451.26	1384.39	1331.67	1289.46
90,000	8133.87	4374.50	3130.91	2516.19	2152.93	1915.30	1749.36	1628.14	1536.63	1465.83	1410.00	1365.31
95,000	8585.76	4617.53	3304.85	2655.98	2272.53	2021.70	1846.55	1718.59	1622.00	1547.26	1488.33	1441.16
100,000	9037.64	4860.56	3478.79	2795.77	2392.14	2128.11	1943.73	1809.04	1707.37	1628.70	1566.66	1517.01
105,000	9489.52	5103.58	3652.73	2935.56	2511.75	2234.51	2040.92	1899.49	1792.73	1710.13	1645.00	1592.86
110,000	9941.40	5346.61	3826.67	3075.35	2631.35	2340.92	2138.11	1989.95	1878.10	1791.57	1723.33	1668.71
115,000	10393.28	5589.64	4000.61	3215.13	2750.96	2447.32	2235.29	2080.40	1963.47	1873.00	1801.66	1744.56
120,000	10845.16	5832.67	4174.55	3354.92	2870.57	2553.73	2332.48	2170.85	2048.84	1954.44	1880.00	1820.41
125,000	11297.05	6075.69	4348.49	3494.71	2990.17	2660.13	2429.67	2261.30	2134.21	2035.87	1958.33	1896.26
130,000	11748.93	6318.72	4522.43	3634.50	3109.78	2766.54	2526.85	2351.75	2219.57	2117.31	2036.66	1972.11
135,000	12200.81	6561.75	4696.37	3774.29	3229.39	2872.94	2624.04	2442.20	2304.94	2198.74	2114.99	2047.96
140,000	12652.69	6804.78	4870.31	3914.07	3349.00	2979.35	2721.22	2532.66	2390.31	2280.18	2193.33	2123.81
145,000	13104.57	7047.80	5044.25	4053.86	3468.60	3085.75	2818.41	2623.11	2475.68	2361.61	2271.66	2199.66
150,000	13556.45	7290.83	5218.19	4193.65	3588.21	3192.16	2915.60	2713.56	2561.05	2443.05	2349.99	2275.51
155,000	14008.33	7533.86	5392.13	4333.44	3707.82	3298.56	3012.78	2804.01	2646.41	2524.48	2428.33	2351.36
160,000	14460.22	7776.89	5566.07	4473.23	3827.42	3404.97	3109.97	2894.46	2731.78	2605.91	2506.66	2427.21
165,000	14912.10	8019.91	5740.01	4613.02	3947.03	3511.37	3207.16	2984.92	2817.15	2687.35	2584.99	2503.06
170,000	15363.98	8262.94	5913.94	4752.80	4066.64	3617.78	3304.34	3075.37	2902.52	2768.78	2663.33	2578.91
175,000	15815.86	8505.97	6087.88	4892.59	4186.24	3724.18	3401.53	3165.82	2987.89	2850.22	2741.66	2654.76
180,000	16267.74	8749.00	6261.82	5032.38	4305.85	3830.59	3498.72	3256.27	3073.26	2931.65	2819.99	2730.61
185,000	16719.62	8992.02	6435.76	5172.17	4425.46	3936.99	3595.90	3346.72	3158.62	3013.09	2898.32	2806.46
190,000	17171.51	9235.05	6609.70	5311.96	4545.06	4043.40	3693.09	3437.18	3243.99	3094.52	2976.66	2882.31
195,000	17623.39	9478.08	6783.64	5451.74	4664.67	4149.80	3790.28	3527.63	3329.36	3175.96	3054.99	2958.16
200,000	18075.27	9721.11	6957.58	5591.53	4784.28	4256.21	3887.46	3618.08	3414.73	3257.39	3133.32	3034.01
205,000	18527.15	9964.13	7131.52	5731.32	4903.88	4362.61	3984.65	3708.53	3500.10	3338.83	3211.66	3109.86
210,000	18979.03	10207.16	7305.46	5871.11	5023.49	4469.02	4081.83	3798.98	3585.46	3420.26	3289.99	3185.71
215,000	19430.91	10450.19	7479.40	6010.90	5143.10	4575.42	4179.02	3889.43	3670.83	3501.70	3368.32	3261.56
220,000	19882.80	10693.22	7653.34	6150.69	5262.70	4681.83	4276.21	3979.89	3756.20	3583.13	3446.65	3337.41
225,000	20334.68	10936.24	7827.28	6290.47	5382.31	4788.23	4373.39	4070.34	3841.57	3664.57	3524.99	3413.26
230,000	20786.56	11179.27	8001.22	6430.26	5501.92	4894.64	4470.58	4160.79	3926.94	3746.00	3603.32	3489.11
235,000	21238.44	11422.30	8175.16	6570.05	5621.52	5001.04	4567.77	4251.24	4012.30	3827.43	3681.65	3564.96
240,000	21690.32	11665.33	8349.10	6709.84	5741.13	5107.45	4664.95	4341.69	4097.67	3908.87	3759.99	3640.81
245,000	22142.20	11908.36	8523.04	6849.63	5860.74	5213.85	4762.14	4432.15	4183.04	3990.30	3838.32	3716.66
250,000	22594.09	12151.38	8696.97	6989.41	5980.34	5320.26	4859.33	4522.60	4268.41	4071.74	3916.65	3792.51
255,000	23045.97	12394.41	8870.91	7129.20	6099.95	5426.66	4956.51	4613.05	4353.78	4153.17	3994.99	3868.36
260,000	23497.85	12637.44	9044.85	7268.99	6219.56	5533.07	5053.70	4703.50	4439.14	4234.61	4073.32	3944.21
265,000	23949.73	12880.47	9218.79	7408.78	6339.17	5639.47	5150.89	4793.95	4524.51	4316.04	4151.65	4020.06
270,000	24401.61	13123.49	9392.73	7548.57	6458.77	5745.88	5248.07	4884.40	4609.88	4397.48	4229.98	4095.91
280,000	25305.38	13609.55	9740.61	7828.14	6697.99	5958.69	5442.44	5065.31	4780.62	4560.35	4386.65	4247.61
290,000	26209.14	14095.60	10088.49	8107.72	6937.20	6171.50	5636.82	5246.21	4951.35	4723.22	4543.32	4399.31
300,000	27112.90	14581.66	10436.37	8387.30	7176.41	6384.31	5831.19	5427.12	5122.09	4886.09	4699.98	4551.02

108

MONTHLY AMORTIZING PAYMENTS 15.25%

AMOUNT OF LOAN	NUMBER OF YEARS IN TERM											
	13	14	15	16	17	18	19	20	25	30	35	40
$ 50	0.74	0.73	0.71	0.70	0.69	0.68	0.68	0.67	0.66	0.65	0.64	0.64
100	1.48	1.45	1.42	1.40	1.38	1.36	1.35	1.34	1.31	1.29	1.28	1.28
200	2.96	2.89	2.84	2.79	2.76	2.72	2.70	2.68	2.61	2.57	2.56	2.55
300	4.44	4.34	4.26	4.19	4.13	4.08	4.04	4.01	3.91	3.86	3.84	3.83
400	5.91	5.78	5.67	5.58	5.51	5.44	5.39	5.35	5.21	5.14	5.11	5.10
500	7.39	7.22	7.09	6.98	6.88	6.80	6.74	6.68	6.51	6.43	6.39	6.37
600	8.87	8.67	8.51	8.37	8.26	8.16	8.08	8.02	7.81	7.71	7.67	7.65
700	10.34	10.11	9.92	9.76	9.63	9.52	9.43	9.35	9.11	9.00	8.95	8.92
800	11.82	11.56	11.34	11.16	11.01	10.88	10.78	10.69	10.41	10.28	10.22	10.20
900	13.30	13.00	12.76	12.55	12.38	12.24	12.12	12.02	11.71	11.57	11.50	11.47
1,000	14.77	14.44	14.17	13.95	13.76	13.60	13.47	13.36	13.01	12.85	12.78	12.74
2,000	29.54	28.88	28.34	27.89	27.51	27.20	26.93	26.71	26.01	25.69	25.55	25.48
3,000	44.31	43.32	42.51	41.83	41.27	40.80	40.40	40.06	39.01	38.54	38.32	38.22
4,000	59.08	57.76	56.67	55.77	55.02	54.39	53.86	53.42	52.02	51.38	51.09	50.96
5,000	73.84	72.20	70.84	69.72	68.78	67.99	67.33	66.77	65.02	64.23	63.86	63.70
6,000	88.61	86.64	85.01	83.66	82.53	81.59	80.79	80.12	78.02	77.07	76.64	76.43
7,000	103.38	101.08	99.18	97.60	96.29	95.19	94.26	93.48	91.02	89.92	89.41	89.17
8,000	118.15	115.52	113.34	111.54	110.04	108.78	107.72	106.83	104.03	102.76	102.18	101.91
9,000	132.92	129.95	127.51	125.49	123.80	122.38	121.19	120.18	117.03	115.61	114.95	114.65
10,000	147.68	144.39	141.68	139.43	137.55	135.98	134.65	133.53	130.03	128.45	127.72	127.39
15,000	221.52	216.59	212.52	209.14	206.32	203.96	201.98	200.30	195.04	192.67	191.58	191.08
20,000	295.36	288.78	283.35	278.85	275.10	271.95	269.30	267.06	260.06	256.90	255.44	254.77
25,000	369.20	360.97	354.19	348.56	343.87	339.93	336.62	333.83	325.07	321.12	319.30	318.46
30,000	443.04	433.17	425.03	418.28	412.64	407.92	403.95	400.59	390.08	385.34	383.16	382.15
35,000	516.88	505.36	495.87	487.99	481.42	475.91	471.27	467.36	455.10	449.57	447.02	445.84
40,000	590.72	577.56	566.70	557.70	550.19	543.89	538.59	534.12	520.11	513.79	510.88	509.53
45,000	004.50	649.75	637.54	627.41	618.96	611.88	605.92	600.89	585.12	578.01	574.74	573.22
50,000	738.39	721.94	708.38	697.12	687.73	679.86	673.24	667.65	650.13	642.23	638.60	636.91
55,000	812.23	794.14	779.22	766.84	756.51	747.85	740.57	734.42	715.15	706.46	702.46	700.60
60,000	886.07	866.33	850.05	836.55	825.28	815.84	807.89	801.18	780.16	770.68	766.32	764.29
65,000	959.91	938.52	920.89	906.26	894.05	883.82	875.21	867.95	845.17	834.90	830.17	827.98
70,000	1033.75	1010.72	991.73	975.97	962.83	951.81	942.54	934.71	910.19	899.13	894.03	891.67
75,000	1107.59	1082.91	1062.57	1045.68	1031.60	1019.79	1009.86	1001.48	975.20	963.35	957.89	955.36
80,000	1181.43	1155.11	1133.40	1115.40	1100.37	1087.78	1077.18	1068.24	1040.21	1027.57	1021.75	1019.05
85,000	1255.27	1227.30	1204.24	1185.11	1169.14	1155.76	1144.51	1135.01	1105.22	1091.79	1085.61	1082.74
90,000	1329.11	1299.49	1275.08	1254.82	1237.92	1223.75	1211.83	1201.77	1170.24	1156.02	1149.47	1146.43
95,000	1402.94	1371.69	1345.92	1324.53	1306.69	1291.74	1279.16	1268.54	1235.25	1220.24	1213.33	1210.12
100,000	1476.78	1443.88	1416.75	1394.24	1375.40	1359.72	1346.48	1335.30	1300.26	1284.46	1277.19	1273.81
105,000	1550.62	1516.07	1487.59	1463.96	1444.24	1427.71	1413.80	1402.07	1365.28	1348.69	1341.05	1337.50
110,000	1624.46	1588.27	1558.43	1533.67	1513.01	1495.69	1481.13	1468.83	1430.29	1412.91	1404.91	1401.19
115,000	1698.30	1660.46	1629.27	1603.38	1581.78	1563.68	1548.45	1535.60	1495.30	1477.13	1468.77	1464.88
120,000	1772.14	1732.00	1700.10	1673.09	1650.55	1631.67	1615.77	1602.36	1560.31	1541.36	1532.63	1528.57
125,000	1845.98	1804.85	1770.94	1742.80	1719.33	1699.65	1683.10	1669.13	1625.33	1605.58	1596.48	1592.26
130,000	1919.82	1877.04	1841.78	1812.52	1788.10	1767.64	1750.42	1735.89	1690.34	1669.80	1660.34	1655.95
135,000	1993.66	1949.24	1912.62	1882.23	1856.87	1835.62	1817.75	1802.66	1755.35	1734.02	1724.20	1719.64
140,000	2067.49	2021.43	1983.45	1951.94	1925.65	1903.61	1885.07	1869.42	1820.37	1798.25	1788.06	1783.33
145,000	2141.33	2093.63	2054.29	2021.65	1994.42	1971.59	1952.39	1936.19	1885.38	1862.47	1851.92	1847.02
150,000	2215.17	2165.82	2125.13	2091.36	2063.19	2039.58	2019.72	2002.95	1950.39	1926.69	1915.78	1910.71
155,000	2289.01	2238.01	2195.97	2161.08	2131.96	2107.57	2087.04	2069.72	2015.41	1990.92	1979.64	1974.40
160,000	2362.85	2310.21	2266.80	2230.79	2200.74	2175.55	2154.36	2136.48	2080.42	2055.14	2043.50	2038.09
165,000	2436.69	2382.40	2337.64	2300.50	2269.51	2243.54	2221.69	2203.25	2145.43	2119.36	2107.36	2101.78
170,000	2510.53	2454.59	2408.48	2370.21	2338.28	2311.52	2289.01	2270.01	2210.44	2183.58	2171.22	2165.47
175,000	2584.37	2526.79	2479.32	2439.92	2407.06	2379.51	2356.34	2336.78	2275.46	2247.81	2235.08	2229.16
180,000	2658.21	2598.98	2550.15	2509.64	2475.83	2447.50	2423.66	2403.54	2340.47	2312.03	2298.94	2292.85
185,000	2732.05	2671.18	2620.99	2579.35	2544.60	2515.48	2490.98	2470.31	2405.48	2376.25	2362.80	2356.54
190,000	2805.88	2743.37	2691.83	2649.06	2613.37	2583.47	2558.31	2537.07	2470.50	2440.48	2426.65	2420.23
195,000	2879.72	2815.56	2762.67	2718.77	2682.15	2651.45	2625.63	2603.84	2535.51	2504.70	2490.51	2483.92
200,000	2953.56	2887.76	2833.50	2788.48	2750.92	2719.44	2692.95	2670.60	2600.52	2568.92	2554.37	2547.61
205,000	3027.40	2959.95	2904.34	2858.20	2819.69	2787.42	2760.28	2737.37	2665.53	2633.14	2618.23	2611.30
210,000	3101.24	3032.14	2975.18	2927.91	2888.47	2855.41	2827.60	2804.13	2730.55	2697.37	2682.09	2674.99
215,000	3175.08	3104.34	3046.02	2997.62	2957.24	2923.40	2894.93	2870.90	2795.56	2761.59	2745.95	2738.68
220,000	3248.92	3176.53	3116.85	3067.33	3026.01	2991.38	2962.25	2937.66	2860.57	2825.81	2809.81	2802.37
225,000	3322.76	3248.73	3187.69	3137.04	3094.78	3059.37	3029.57	3004.43	2925.59	2890.04	2873.67	2866.06
230,000	3396.60	3320.92	3258.53	3206.76	3163.56	3127.35	3096.90	3071.19	2990.60	2954.26	2937.53	2929.75
235,000	3470.43	3393.11	3329.37	3276.47	3232.33	3195.34	3164.22	3137.96	3055.61	3018.48	3001.39	2993.44
240,000	3544.27	3465.31	3400.20	3346.18	3301.10	3263.33	3231.54	3204.72	3120.62	3082.71	3065.25	3057.13
245,000	3618.11	3537.50	3471.04	3415.89	3369.88	3331.31	3298.87	3271.49	3185.64	3146.93	3129.11	3120.82
250,000	3691.95	3609.70	3541.88	3485.60	3438.65	3399.30	3366.19	3338.25	3250.65	3211.15	3192.96	3184.51
255,000	3765.79	3681.89	3612.72	3555.31	3507.42	3467.28	3433.52	3405.02	3315.66	3275.37	3256.82	3248.20
260,000	3839.63	3754.08	3683.55	3625.03	3576.20	3535.27	3500.84	3471.78	3380.68	3339.60	3320.68	3311.89
265,000	3913.47	3826.28	3754.39	3694.74	3644.97	3603.25	3568.16	3538.55	3445.69	3403.82	3384.54	3375.58
270,000	3987.31	3898.47	3825.23	3764.45	3713.74	3671.24	3635.49	3605.31	3510.70	3468.04	3448.40	3439.27
280,000	4134.98	4042.86	3966.90	3903.87	3851.29	3807.21	3770.13	3738.84	3640.73	3596.49	3576.12	3566.65
290,000	4282.66	4187.25	4108.58	4043.30	3988.83	3943.18	3904.78	3872.37	3770.75	3724.93	3703.84	3694.03
300,000	4430.34	4331.63	4250.25	4182.72	4126.38	4079.16	4039.43	4005.90	3900.78	3853.38	3831.56	3821.41

109

15.50%

MONTHLY AMORTIZING PAYMENTS

AMOUNT OF LOAN	NUMBER OF YEARS IN TERM											
	1	2	3	4	5	6	7	8	9	10	11	12
$ 50	4.53	2.44	1.75	1.41	1.21	1.08	0.98	0.92	0.87	0.83	0.80	0.77
100	9.05	4.88	3.50	2.81	2.41	2.15	1.96	1.83	1.73	1.65	1.59	1.54
200	18.10	9.75	6.99	5.62	4.82	4.29	3.92	3.65	3.45	3.29	3.17	3.07
300	27.15	14.62	10.48	8.43	7.22	6.43	5.88	5.48	5.17	4.94	4.75	4.60
400	36.20	19.49	13.97	11.24	9.63	8.57	7.84	7.30	6.89	6.58	6.33	6.14
500	45.25	24.37	17.46	14.05	12.03	10.71	9.79	9.12	8.62	8.23	7.92	7.67
600	54.30	29.24	20.95	16.86	14.44	12.86	11.75	10.95	10.34	9.87	9.50	9.20
700	63.35	34.11	24.44	19.66	16.84	15.00	13.71	12.77	12.06	11.51	11.08	10.74
800	72.40	38.98	27.93	22.47	19.25	17.14	15.67	14.59	13.78	13.16	12.66	12.27
900	81.45	43.86	31.42	25.28	21.65	19.28	17.63	16.42	15.51	14.80	14.25	13.80
1,000	90.50	48.73	34.92	28.09	24.06	21.42	19.58	18.24	17.23	16.45	15.83	15.34
2,000	180.99	97.45	69.83	56.17	48.11	42.84	39.16	36.48	34.45	32.89	31.65	30.67
3,000	271.49	146.18	104.74	84.26	72.16	64.26	58.74	54.71	51.68	49.33	47.48	46.00
4,000	361.98	194.90	139.65	112.34	96.22	85.67	78.32	72.95	68.90	65.77	63.30	61.33
5,000	452.48	243.63	174.56	140.43	120.27	107.09	97.90	91.18	86.12	82.21	79.13	76.67
6,000	542.97	292.35	209.47	168.51	144.32	128.51	117.48	109.42	103.35	98.65	94.95	92.00
7,000	633.47	341.08	244.38	196.60	168.38	149.93	137.05	127.66	120.57	115.09	110.78	107.33
8,000	723.96	389.80	279.29	224.68	192.43	171.34	156.63	145.89	137.79	131.53	126.60	122.66
9,000	814.45	438.53	314.20	252.77	216.48	192.76	176.21	164.13	155.02	147.97	142.43	137.99
10,000	904.95	487.25	349.11	280.85	240.54	214.18	195.79	182.36	172.24	164.42	158.25	153.33
15,000	1357.42	730.87	523.67	421.28	360.80	321.27	293.68	273.54	258.36	246.62	237.38	229.99
20,000	1809.89	974.50	698.22	561.70	481.07	428.35	391.57	364.72	344.48	328.83	316.50	306.65
25,000	2262.37	1218.12	872.77	702.13	601.33	535.44	489.46	455.90	430.59	411.03	395.62	383.31
30,000	2714.84	1461.74	1047.33	842.55	721.60	642.53	587.36	547.08	516.71	493.24	474.75	459.97
35,000	3167.31	1705.36	1221.88	982.98	841.87	749.62	685.25	638.26	602.83	575.44	553.87	536.63
40,000	3619.78	1948.99	1396.43	1123.40	962.13	856.70	783.14	729.44	688.95	657.65	632.99	613.29
45,000	4072.25	2192.61	1570.99	1263.82	1082.40	963.79	881.03	820.62	775.06	739.85	712.12	689.95
50,000	4524.73	2436.23	1745.54	1404.25	1202.66	1070.88	978.92	911.80	861.18	822.06	791.24	766.61
55,000	4977.20	2679.85	1920.09	1544.67	1322.93	1177.97	1076.81	1002.98	947.30	904.26	870.37	843.27
60,000	5429.67	2923.48	2094.65	1685.10	1443.20	1285.05	1174.71	1094.16	1033.42	986.47	949.49	919.93
65,000	5882.14	3167.10	2269.20	1825.52	1563.46	1392.14	1272.60	1185.34	1119.53	1068.67	1028.61	996.59
70,000	6334.61	3410.72	2443.75	1965.95	1683.73	1499.23	1370.49	1276.52	1205.65	1150.88	1107.74	1073.25
75,000	6787.09	3654.35	2618.31	2106.37	1803.99	1606.32	1468.38	1367.70	1291.77	1233.08	1186.86	1149.91
80,000	7239.56	3897.97	2792.86	2246.79	1924.26	1713.40	1566.27	1458.88	1377.89	1315.29	1265.98	1226.57
85,000	7692.03	4141.59	2967.41	2387.22	2044.53	1820.49	1664.16	1550.06	1464.00	1397.49	1345.11	1303.23
90,000	8144.50	4385.21	3141.97	2527.64	2164.79	1927.58	1762.06	1641.24	1550.12	1479.70	1424.23	1379.89
95,000	8596.97	4628.84	3316.52	2668.07	2285.06	2034.67	1859.95	1732.42	1636.24	1561.91	1503.36	1456.55
100,000	9049.45	4872.46	3491.07	2808.49	2405.32	2141.75	1957.84	1823.60	1722.36	1644.11	1582.48	1533.21
105,000	9501.92	5116.08	3665.63	2948.92	2525.59	2248.84	2055.73	1914.78	1808.48	1726.32	1661.60	1609.87
110,000	9954.39	5359.70	3840.18	3089.34	2645.86	2355.93	2153.62	2005.96	1894.59	1808.52	1740.73	1686.53
115,000	10406.86	5603.33	4014.73	3229.76	2766.12	2463.02	2251.51	2097.14	1980.71	1890.73	1819.85	1763.19
120,000	10859.33	5846.95	4189.29	3370.19	2886.39	2570.10	2349.41	2188.32	2066.83	1972.93	1898.97	1839.85
125,000	11311.81	6090.57	4363.84	3510.61	3006.65	2677.19	2447.30	2279.50	2152.95	2055.14	1978.10	1916.51
130,000	11764.28	6334.20	4538.39	3651.04	3126.92	2784.28	2545.19	2370.67	2239.06	2137.34	2057.22	1993.17
135,000	12216.75	6577.82	4712.95	3791.46	3247.19	2891.37	2643.08	2461.85	2325.18	2219.55	2136.35	2069.83
140,000	12669.22	6821.44	4887.50	3931.89	3367.45	2998.45	2740.97	2553.03	2411.30	2301.75	2215.47	2146.49
145,000	13121.70	7065.06	5062.05	4072.31	3487.72	3105.54	2838.87	2644.21	2497.42	2383.96	2294.59	2223.15
150,000	13574.17	7308.69	5236.61	4212.73	3607.98	3212.63	2936.76	2735.39	2583.53	2466.16	2373.72	2299.81
155,000	14026.64	7552.31	5411.16	4353.16	3728.25	3319.72	3034.65	2826.57	2669.65	2548.37	2452.84	2376.47
160,000	14479.11	7795.93	5585.71	4493.58	3848.52	3426.80	3132.54	2917.75	2755.77	2630.57	2531.96	2453.13
165,000	14931.58	8039.55	5760.27	4634.01	3968.78	3533.89	3230.43	3008.93	2841.89	2712.78	2611.09	2529.79
170,000	15384.06	8283.18	5934.82	4774.43	4089.05	3640.98	3328.32	3100.11	2928.00	2794.98	2690.21	2606.45
175,000	15836.53	8526.80	6109.37	4914.86	4209.31	3748.07	3426.22	3191.29	3014.12	2877.19	2769.34	2683.11
180,000	16289.00	8770.42	6283.93	5055.28	4329.58	3855.15	3524.11	3282.47	3100.24	2959.39	2848.46	2759.77
185,000	16741.47	9014.05	6458.48	5195.70	4449.85	3962.24	3622.00	3373.65	3186.36	3041.60	2927.58	2836.43
190,000	17193.94	9257.67	6633.03	5336.13	4570.11	4069.33	3719.89	3464.83	3272.47	3123.81	3006.71	2913.09
195,000	17646.42	9501.29	6807.59	5476.55	4690.38	4176.42	3817.78	3556.01	3358.59	3206.01	3085.83	2989.75
200,000	18098.89	9744.91	6982.14	5616.98	4810.64	4283.50	3915.67	3647.19	3444.71	3288.22	3164.95	3066.41
205,000	18551.36	9988.54	7156.69	5757.40	4930.91	4390.59	4013.57	3738.37	3530.83	3370.42	3244.08	3143.07
210,000	19003.83	10232.16	7331.25	5897.83	5051.18	4497.68	4111.46	3829.55	3616.95	3452.63	3323.20	3219.73
215,000	19456.30	10475.78	7505.80	6038.25	5171.44	4604.76	4209.35	3920.73	3703.06	3534.83	3402.33	3296.39
220,000	19908.78	10719.40	7680.35	6178.67	5291.71	4711.85	4307.24	4011.91	3789.18	3617.04	3481.45	3373.05
225,000	20361.25	10963.03	7854.91	6319.10	5411.97	4818.94	4405.13	4103.09	3875.30	3699.24	3560.57	3449.71
230,000	20813.72	11206.65	8029.46	6459.52	5532.24	4926.03	4503.02	4194.27	3961.42	3781.45	3639.70	3526.37
235,000	21266.19	11450.27	8204.02	6599.95	5652.50	5033.11	4600.92	4285.45	4047.53	3863.65	3718.82	3603.04
240,000	21718.66	11693.90	8378.57	6740.37	5772.77	5140.20	4698.81	4376.63	4133.65	3945.86	3797.94	3679.70
245,000	22171.14	11937.52	8553.12	6880.80	5893.04	5247.29	4796.70	4467.81	4219.77	4028.06	3877.07	3756.36
250,000	22623.61	12181.14	8727.68	7021.22	6013.30	5354.38	4894.59	4558.99	4305.89	4110.27	3956.19	3833.02
255,000	23076.08	12424.76	8902.23	7161.64	6133.57	5461.46	4992.48	4650.17	4392.00	4192.47	4035.31	3909.68
260,000	23528.55	12668.39	9076.78	7302.07	6253.83	5568.55	5090.38	4741.34	4478.12	4274.68	4114.44	3986.34
265,000	23981.03	12912.01	9251.34	7442.49	6374.10	5675.64	5188.27	4832.52	4564.24	4356.88	4193.56	4063.00
270,000	24433.50	13155.63	9425.89	7582.92	6494.37	5782.73	5286.16	4923.70	4650.36	4439.09	4272.69	4139.66
280,000	25338.44	13642.88	9775.00	7863.77	6734.90	5996.90	5481.94	5106.06	4822.59	4603.50	4430.93	4292.98
290,000	26243.39	14130.12	10124.10	8144.61	6975.43	6211.08	5677.73	5288.42	4994.83	4767.91	4589.18	4446.30
300,000	27148.33	14617.37	10473.21	8425.46	7215.96	6425.25	5873.51	5470.78	5167.06	4932.32	4747.43	4599.62

AMOUNT OF LOAN	NUMBER OF YEARS IN TERM											
	13	14	15	16	17	18	19	20	25	30	35	40
$ 50	0.75	0.74	0.72	0.71	0.70	0.69	0.69	0.68	0.66	0.66	0.65	0.65
100	1.50	1.47	1.44	1.42	1.40	1.38	1.37	1.36	1.32	1.31	1.30	1.30
200	2.99	2.93	2.87	2.83	2.79	2.76	2.73	2.71	2.64	2.61	2.60	2.59
300	4.49	4.39	4.31	4.24	4.18	4.14	4.10	4.07	3.96	3.92	3.90	3.89
400	5.98	5.85	5.74	5.65	5.58	5.52	5.46	5.42	5.28	5.22	5.20	5.18
500	7.47	7.31	7.17	7.06	6.97	6.89	6.83	6.77	6.60	6.53	6.49	6.48
600	8.97	8.77	8.61	8.48	8.36	8.27	8.19	8.13	7.92	7.83	7.79	7.77
700	10.46	10.23	10.04	9.89	9.76	9.65	9.56	9.48	9.24	9.14	9.09	9.07
800	11.95	11.69	11.48	11.30	11.15	11.03	10.92	10.84	10.56	10.44	10.39	10.36
900	13.45	13.15	12.91	12.71	12.54	12.41	12.29	12.19	11.88	11.75	11.68	11.65
1,000	14.94	14.61	14.34	14.12	13.94	13.78	13.65	13.54	13.20	13.05	12.98	12.95
2,000	29.87	29.22	28.68	28.24	27.87	27.56	27.30	27.08	26.40	26.10	25.96	25.89
3,000	44.81	43.83	43.02	42.36	41.80	41.34	40.95	40.62	39.60	39.14	38.93	38.84
4,000	59.74	58.44	57.36	56.48	55.74	55.12	54.60	54.16	52.79	52.19	51.91	51.78
5,000	74.67	73.04	71.70	70.59	69.67	68.90	68.25	67.70	65.99	65.23	64.88	64.72
6,000	89.61	87.65	86.04	84.71	83.60	82.67	81.89	81.24	79.19	78.28	77.86	77.67
7,000	104.54	102.26	100.38	98.83	97.54	96.45	95.54	94.78	92.39	91.32	90.84	90.61
8,000	119.47	116.87	114.72	112.95	111.47	110.23	109.19	108.32	105.58	104.37	103.81	103.56
9,000	134.41	131.48	129.06	127.07	125.40	124.01	122.84	121.85	118.78	117.41	116.79	116.50
10,000	149.34	146.08	143.40	141.18	139.33	137.79	136.49	135.39	131.98	130.46	129.76	129.44
15,000	224.01	219.12	215.10	211.77	209.00	206.68	204.73	203.09	197.97	195.68	194.64	194.16
20,000	298.67	292.16	286.80	282.36	278.66	275.57	272.97	270.78	263.95	260.91	259.52	258.88
25,000	373.34	365.20	358.50	352.95	348.33	344.46	341.21	338.48	329.94	326.13	324.40	323.60
30,000	448.01	438.24	430.20	423.54	417.99	413.35	409.45	406.17	395.93	391.36	389.28	388.32
35,000	522.68	511.28	501.90	494.13	487.66	482.24	477.69	473.86	461.92	456.59	454.16	453.04
40,000	597.34	584.32	573.60	564.72	557.32	551.13	545.94	541.56	527.90	521.81	519.04	517.76
45,000	672.01	657.36	645.30	635.31	626.99	620.02	614.18	609.25	593.89	587.04	583.92	582.48
50,000	746.68	730.40	717.00	705.90	696.65	688.91	682.42	676.95	659.88	652.26	648.80	647.20
55,000	821.35	803.44	788.70	776.49	766.32	757.81	750.66	744.64	725.86	717.49	713.68	711.92
60,000	896.01	876.48	860.40	847.08	835.98	826.70	818.90	812.33	791.85	782.72	778.56	776.64
65,000	970.68	949.52	932.10	917.67	905.65	895.59	887.14	880.03	857.84	847.94	843.44	841.36
70,000	1045.35	1022.56	1003.80	988.26	975.31	964.48	955.38	947.72	923.83	913.17	908.31	906.08
75,000	1120.01	1095.60	1075.50	1058.85	1044.97	1033.37	1023.62	1015.42	989.81	978.39	973.19	970.80
80,000	1194.68	1168.64	1147.20	1129.43	1114.64	1102.26	1091.87	1083.11	1055.80	1043.62	1038.07	1035.52
85,000	1269.35	1241.68	1218.90	1200.02	1184.30	1171.15	1160.11	1150.80	1121.79	1108.84	1102.95	1100.24
90,000	1344.02	1314.72	1290.60	1270.61	1253.97	1240.04	1228.35	1218.50	1187.78	1174.07	1167.83	1164.96
95,000	1418.68	1387.76	1362.30	1341.20	1323.63	1308.93	1296.59	1286.19	1253.76	1239.30	1232.71	1229.68
100,000	1493.35	1460.79	1434.00	1411.79	1393.30	1377.82	1364.83	1353.89	1319.75	1304.52	1297.59	1294.40
105,000	1568.02	1533.83	1505.69	1482.38	1462.96	1446.72	1433.07	1421.58	1385.74	1369.75	1362.47	1359.12
110,000	1642.69	1606.87	1577.39	1552.97	1532.63	1515.61	1501.31	1489.27	1451.72	1434.97	1427.35	1423.84
115,000	1717.35	1679.91	1649.09	1623.56	1602.29	1584.50	1569.55	1556.97	1517.71	1500.20	1492.23	1488.56
120,000	1792.02	1752.95	1720.79	1694.15	1671.96	1653.39	1637.80	1624.66	1583.70	1565.43	1557.11	1553.28
125,000	1866.69	1825.99	1792.49	1764.74	1741.62	1722.28	1706.04	1692.36	1649.69	1630.65	1621.99	1618.00
130,000	1941.35	1899.03	1864.19	1835.33	1811.29	1791.17	1774.28	1760.05	1715.67	1695.88	1686.87	1682.72
135,000	2016.02	1972.07	1935.89	1905.92	1880.95	1860.06	1842.52	1827.74	1781.66	1761.10	1751.74	1747.44
140,000	2090.69	2045.11	2007.59	1976.51	1950.61	1928.95	1910.76	1895.44	1847.65	1826.33	1816.62	1812.16
145,000	2165.36	2118.15	2079.29	2047.10	2020.28	1997.84	1979.00	1963.13	1913.64	1891.55	1881.50	1876.88
150,000	2240.02	2191.19	2150.99	2117.69	2089.94	2066.73	2047.24	2030.83	1979.62	1956.78	1946.38	1941.60
155,000	2314.69	2264.23	2222.69	2188.27	2159.61	2135.63	2115.49	2098.52	2045.61	2022.01	2011.26	2006.32
160,000	2389.36	2337.27	2294.39	2258.86	2229.27	2204.52	2183.73	2166.21	2111.60	2087.23	2076.14	2071.04
165,000	2464.03	2410.31	2366.09	2329.45	2298.94	2273.41	2251.97	2233.91	2177.58	2152.46	2141.02	2135.76
170,000	2538.69	2483.35	2437.79	2400.04	2368.60	2342.30	2320.21	2301.60	2243.57	2217.68	2205.90	2200.48
175,000	2613.36	2556.39	2509.49	2470.63	2438.27	2411.19	2388.45	2369.30	2309.56	2282.91	2270.78	2265.20
180,000	2688.03	2629.43	2581.19	2541.22	2507.93	2480.08	2456.69	2436.99	2375.55	2348.14	2335.66	2329.92
185,000	2762.69	2702.47	2652.89	2611.81	2577.60	2548.97	2524.93	2504.68	2441.53	2413.36	2400.54	2394.64
190,000	2837.36	2775.51	2724.59	2682.40	2647.26	2617.86	2593.17	2572.38	2507.52	2478.59	2465.42	2459.36
195,000	2912.03	2848.55	2796.29	2752.99	2716.93	2686.75	2661.42	2640.07	2573.51	2543.81	2530.30	2524.08
200,000	2986.70	2921.58	2867.99	2823.58	2786.59	2755.64	2729.66	2707.77	2639.50	2609.04	2595.17	2588.80
205,000	3061.36	2994.62	2939.69	2894.17	2856.25	2824.53	2797.90	2775.46	2705.48	2674.26	2660.05	2653.52
210,000	3136.03	3067.66	3011.38	2964.76	2925.92	2893.43	2866.14	2843.15	2771.47	2739.49	2724.93	2718.24
215,000	3210.70	3140.70	3083.08	3035.35	2995.58	2962.32	2934.38	2910.85	2837.46	2804.72	2789.81	2782.96
220,000	3285.37	3213.74	3154.78	3105.94	3065.25	3031.21	3002.62	2978.54	2903.44	2869.94	2854.69	2847.68
225,000	3360.03	3286.78	3226.48	3176.53	3134.91	3100.10	3070.86	3046.24	2969.43	2935.17	2919.57	2912.40
230,000	3434.70	3359.82	3298.18	3247.11	3204.58	3168.99	3139.10	3113.93	3035.42	3000.39	2984.45	2977.12
235,000	3509.37	3432.86	3369.88	3317.70	3274.24	3237.88	3207.35	3181.62	3101.41	3065.62	3049.33	3041.84
240,000	3584.03	3505.90	3441.58	3388.29	3343.91	3306.77	3275.59	3249.32	3167.39	3130.85	3114.21	3106.56
245,000	3658.70	3578.94	3513.28	3458.88	3413.57	3375.66	3343.83	3317.01	3233.38	3196.07	3179.09	3171.28
250,000	3733.37	3651.98	3584.98	3529.47	3483.24	3444.55	3412.07	3384.71	3299.37	3261.30	3243.97	3236.00
255,000	3808.04	3725.02	3656.68	3600.06	3552.90	3513.44	3480.31	3452.40	3365.36	3326.52	3308.85	3300.72
260,000	3882.70	3798.06	3728.38	3670.65	3622.57	3582.34	3548.55	3520.09	3431.34	3391.75	3373.73	3365.44
265,000	3957.37	3871.10	3800.08	3741.24	3692.23	3651.23	3616.79	3587.79	3497.33	3456.97	3438.60	3430.16
270,000	4032.04	3944.14	3871.78	3811.83	3761.89	3720.12	3685.04	3655.48	3563.32	3522.20	3503.48	3494.88
280,000	4181.37	4090.22	4015.18	3953.01	3901.22	3857.90	3821.52	3790.87	3695.29	3652.65	3633.24	3624.32
290,000	4330.71	4236.30	4158.58	4094.19	4040.55	3995.68	3958.00	3926.26	3827.27	3783.10	3763.00	3753.76
300,000	4480.04	4382.37	4301.98	4235.37	4179.88	4133.46	4094.48	4061.65	3959.24	3913.56	3892.76	3883.20

15.75%

AMOUNT OF LOAN	NUMBER OF YEARS IN TERM											
	1	2	3	4	5	6	7	8	9	10	11	12
$ 50	4.54	2.45	1.76	1.42	1.21	1.08	0.99	0.92	0.87	0.83	0.80	0.78
100	9.07	4.89	3.51	2.83	2.42	2.16	1.98	1.84	1.74	1.66	1.60	1.55
200	18.13	9.77	7.01	5.65	4.84	4.32	3.95	3.68	3.48	3.32	3.20	3.10
300	27.19	14.66	10.52	8.47	7.26	6.47	5.92	5.52	5.22	4.98	4.80	4.65
400	36.25	19.54	14.02	11.29	9.68	8.63	7.89	7.36	6.95	6.64	6.40	6.20
500	45.31	24.43	17.52	14.11	12.10	10.78	9.86	9.20	8.69	8.30	8.00	7.75
600	54.37	29.31	21.03	16.93	14.52	12.94	11.84	11.03	10.43	9.96	9.60	9.30
700	63.43	34.20	24.53	19.75	16.93	15.09	13.81	12.87	12.17	11.62	11.19	10.85
800	72.50	39.08	28.03	22.57	19.35	17.25	15.78	14.71	13.90	13.28	12.79	12.40
900	81.56	43.96	31.54	25.40	21.77	19.40	17.75	16.55	15.64	14.94	14.39	13.95
1,000	90.62	48.85	35.04	28.22	24.19	21.56	19.72	18.39	17.38	16.60	15.99	15.50
2,000	181.23	97.69	70.07	56.43	48.38	43.11	39.44	36.77	34.75	33.20	31.97	30.99
3,000	271.84	146.54	105.11	84.64	72.56	64.67	59.16	55.15	52.13	49.79	47.96	46.49
4,000	362.46	195.38	140.14	112.85	96.75	86.22	78.88	73.53	69.50	66.39	63.94	61.98
5,000	453.07	244.22	175.17	141.07	120.93	107.78	98.60	91.92	86.88	82.98	79.92	77.48
6,000	543.68	293.07	210.21	169.28	145.12	129.33	118.32	110.30	104.25	99.58	95.91	92.97
7,000	634.29	341.91	245.24	197.49	169.30	150.89	138.04	128.68	121.62	116.18	111.89	108.47
8,000	724.91	390.75	280.27	225.70	193.49	172.44	157.76	147.06	139.00	132.77	127.87	123.96
9,000	815.52	439.60	315.31	253.92	217.67	193.99	177.48	165.44	156.37	149.37	143.86	139.46
10,000	906.13	488.44	350.34	282.13	241.86	215.55	197.20	183.83	173.75	165.96	159.84	154.95
15,000	1359.19	732.66	525.51	423.19	362.79	323.32	295.80	275.74	260.62	248.94	239.76	232.43
20,000	1812.26	976.88	700.68	564.25	483.71	431.09	394.40	367.65	347.49	331.92	319.68	309.90
25,000	2265.32	1221.10	875.85	705.32	604.64	538.87	493.00	459.56	434.36	414.90	399.60	387.37
30,000	2718.38	1465.32	1051.02	846.38	725.57	646.64	591.60	551.47	521.23	497.88	479.51	464.85
35,000	3171.45	1709.54	1226.19	987.44	846.49	754.41	690.20	643.38	608.10	580.86	559.43	542.32
40,000	3624.51	1953.75	1401.35	1128.50	967.42	862.18	788.80	735.29	694.97	663.84	639.35	619.80
45,000	4077.57	2197.97	1576.52	1269.56	1088.35	969.95	887.40	827.20	781.84	746.82	719.27	697.27
50,000	4530.63	2442.19	1751.69	1410.63	1209.28	1077.73	986.00	919.11	868.71	829.80	799.19	774.74
55,000	4983.70	2686.41	1926.86	1551.69	1330.20	1185.50	1084.60	1011.02	955.58	912.78	879.10	852.22
60,000	5436.76	2930.63	2102.03	1692.75	1451.13	1293.27	1183.20	1102.93	1042.45	995.76	959.02	929.69
65,000	5889.82	3174.85	2277.20	1833.81	1572.06	1401.04	1281.80	1194.84	1129.32	1078.74	1038.94	1007.17
70,000	6342.89	3419.07	2452.37	1974.87	1692.98	1508.82	1380.40	1286.75	1216.19	1161.71	1118.86	1084.64
75,000	6795.95	3663.29	2627.53	2115.94	1813.91	1616.59	1479.00	1378.66	1303.06	1244.69	1198.78	1162.11
80,000	7249.01	3907.50	2802.70	2257.00	1934.84	1724.36	1577.60	1470.57	1389.93	1327.67	1278.69	1239.59
85,000	7702.08	4151.72	2977.87	2398.06	2055.77	1832.13	1676.20	1562.48	1476.80	1410.65	1358.61	1317.06
90,000	8155.14	4395.94	3153.04	2539.12	2176.69	1939.90	1774.80	1654.39	1563.67	1493.63	1438.53	1394.54
95,000	8608.20	4640.16	3328.21	2680.18	2297.62	2047.68	1873.40	1746.30	1650.54	1576.61	1518.45	1472.01
100,000	9061.26	4884.38	3503.38	2821.25	2418.55	2155.45	1972.00	1838.21	1737.41	1659.59	1598.37	1549.48
105,000	9514.33	5128.60	3678.55	2962.31	2539.47	2263.22	2070.60	1930.12	1824.28	1742.57	1678.28	1626.96
110,000	9967.39	5372.82	3853.72	3103.37	2660.40	2370.99	2169.20	2022.03	1911.15	1825.55	1758.20	1704.43
115,000	10420.45	5617.04	4028.88	3244.43	2781.33	2478.76	2267.80	2113.94	1998.02	1908.53	1838.12	1781.91
120,000	10873.52	5861.25	4204.05	3385.49	2902.26	2586.54	2366.40	2205.85	2084.89	1991.51	1918.04	1859.38
125,000	11326.58	6105.47	4379.22	3526.56	3023.18	2694.31	2465.00	2297.76	2171.76	2074.49	1997.96	1936.85
130,000	11779.64	6349.69	4554.39	3667.62	3144.11	2802.08	2563.60	2389.67	2258.63	2157.47	2077.87	2014.33
135,000	12232.71	6593.91	4729.56	3808.68	3265.04	2909.85	2662.20	2481.58	2345.50	2240.44	2157.79	2091.80
140,000	12685.77	6838.13	4904.73	3949.74	3385.96	3017.63	2760.80	2573.49	2432.38	2323.42	2237.71	2169.27
145,000	13138.83	7082.35	5079.90	4090.80	3506.89	3125.40	2859.40	2665.40	2519.25	2406.40	2317.63	2246.75
150,000	13591.89	7326.57	5255.06	4231.87	3627.82	3233.17	2958.00	2757.31	2606.12	2489.38	2397.55	2324.22
155,000	14044.96	7570.79	5430.23	4372.93	3748.75	3340.94	3056.60	2849.22	2692.99	2572.36	2477.46	2401.70
160,000	14498.02	7815.00	5605.40	4513.99	3869.67	3448.71	3155.20	2941.14	2779.86	2655.34	2557.38	2479.17
165,000	14951.08	8059.22	5780.57	4655.05	3990.60	3556.49	3253.80	3033.05	2866.73	2738.32	2637.30	2556.64
170,000	15404.15	8303.44	5955.74	4796.11	4111.53	3664.26	3352.39	3124.96	2953.60	2821.30	2717.22	2634.12
175,000	15857.21	8547.66	6130.91	4937.18	4232.45	3772.03	3450.99	3216.87	3040.47	2904.28	2797.14	2711.59
180,000	16310.27	8791.88	6306.08	5078.24	4353.38	3879.80	3549.59	3308.78	3127.34	2987.26	2877.05	2789.07
185,000	16763.34	9036.10	6481.25	5219.30	4474.31	3987.57	3648.19	3400.69	3214.21	3070.24	2956.97	2866.54
190,000	17216.40	9280.32	6656.41	5360.36	4595.24	4095.35	3746.79	3492.60	3301.08	3153.22	3036.89	2944.01
195,000	17669.46	9524.53	6831.58	5501.42	4716.16	4203.12	3845.39	3584.51	3387.95	3236.20	3116.81	3021.49
200,000	18122.52	9768.75	7006.75	5642.49	4837.09	4310.89	3943.99	3676.42	3474.82	3319.17	3196.73	3098.96
205,000	18575.59	10012.97	7181.92	5783.55	4958.02	4418.66	4042.59	3768.33	3561.69	3402.15	3276.64	3176.44
210,000	19028.65	10257.19	7357.09	5924.61	5078.94	4526.44	4141.19	3860.24	3648.56	3485.13	3356.56	3253.91
215,000	19481.71	10501.41	7532.26	6065.67	5199.87	4634.21	4239.79	3952.15	3735.43	3568.11	3436.48	3331.38
220,000	19934.78	10745.63	7707.43	6206.73	5320.80	4741.98	4338.39	4044.06	3822.30	3651.09	3516.40	3408.86
225,000	20387.84	10989.85	7882.59	6347.80	5441.73	4849.75	4436.99	4135.97	3909.17	3734.07	3596.32	3486.33
230,000	20840.90	11234.07	8057.76	6488.86	5562.65	4957.52	4535.59	4227.88	3996.04	3817.05	3676.23	3563.81
235,000	21293.96	11478.28	8232.93	6629.92	5683.58	5065.30	4634.19	4319.79	4082.91	3900.03	3756.15	3641.28
240,000	21747.03	11722.50	8408.10	6770.98	5804.51	5173.07	4732.79	4411.70	4169.78	3983.01	3836.07	3718.75
245,000	22200.09	11966.72	8583.27	6912.04	5925.43	5280.84	4831.39	4503.61	4256.65	4065.99	3915.99	3796.23
250,000	22653.15	12210.94	8758.44	7053.11	6046.36	5388.61	4929.99	4595.52	4343.52	4148.97	3995.91	3873.70
255,000	23106.22	12455.16	8933.61	7194.17	6167.29	5496.38	5028.59	4687.43	4430.39	4231.95	4075.82	3951.18
260,000	23559.28	12699.38	9108.78	7335.23	6288.22	5604.16	5127.19	4779.34	4517.26	4314.93	4155.74	4028.65
265,000	24012.34	12943.60	9283.94	7476.29	6409.14	5711.93	5225.79	4871.25	4604.13	4397.90	4235.66	4106.12
270,000	24465.41	13187.82	9459.11	7617.35	6530.07	5819.70	5324.39	4963.16	4691.00	4480.88	4315.58	4183.60
280,000	25371.53	13676.25	9809.45	7899.48	6771.92	6035.25	5521.59	5146.98	4864.75	4646.84	4475.42	4338.54
290,000	26277.66	14164.69	10159.79	8181.60	7013.78	6250.79	5718.79	5330.80	5038.49	4812.80	4635.25	4493.49
300,000	27183.78	14653.13	10510.12	8463.73	7255.63	6466.33	5915.99	5514.62	5212.23	4978.76	4795.09	4648.44

112

AMOUNT OF LOAN	NUMBER OF YEARS IN TERM											
	13	14	15	16	17	18	19	20	25	30	35	40
$ 50	0.76	0.74	0.73	0.72	0.71	0.70	0.70	0.69	0.67	0.67	0.66	0.66
100	1.51	1.48	1.46	1.43	1.42	1.40	1.39	1.38	1.34	1.33	1.32	1.32
200	3.02	2.96	2.91	2.86	2.83	2.80	2.77	2.75	2.68	2.65	2.64	2.64
300	4.53	4.44	4.36	4.29	4.24	4.19	4.15	4.12	4.02	3.98	3.96	3.95
400	6.04	5.92	5.81	5.72	5.65	5.59	5.54	5.50	5.36	5.30	5.28	5.27
500	7.55	7.39	7.26	7.15	7.06	6.98	6.92	6.87	6.70	6.63	6.60	6.58
600	9.06	8.87	8.71	8.58	8.47	8.38	8.30	8.24	8.04	7.95	7.91	7.90
700	10.57	10.35	10.16	10.01	9.88	9.78	9.69	9.61	9.38	9.28	9.23	9.21
800	12.08	11.83	11.62	11.44	11.29	11.17	11.07	10.99	10.72	10.60	10.55	10.53
900	13.59	13.31	13.07	12.87	12.71	12.57	12.45	12.36	12.06	11.93	11.87	11.84
1,000	15.10	14.78	14.52	14.30	14.12	13.96	13.84	13.73	13.40	13.25	13.19	13.16
2,000	30.20	29.56	29.03	28.59	28.23	27.92	27.67	27.46	26.79	26.50	26.37	26.31
3,000	45.30	44.34	43.54	42.89	42.34	41.88	41.50	41.18	40.18	39.74	39.55	39.46
4,000	60.40	59.12	58.06	57.18	56.45	55.84	55.34	54.91	53.58	52.99	52.73	52.61
5,000	75.50	73.89	72.57	71.48	70.57	69.80	69.17	68.63	66.97	66.24	65.91	65.76
6,000	90.60	88.67	87.08	85.77	84.68	83.76	83.00	82.36	80.36	79.48	79.09	78.91
7,000	105.70	103.45	101.60	100.06	98.79	97.72	96.83	96.08	93.76	92.73	92.27	92.06
8,000	120.80	118.23	116.11	114.36	112.90	111.68	110.67	109.81	107.15	105.97	105.45	105.21
9,000	135.90	133.01	130.62	128.65	127.01	125.64	124.50	123.53	120.54	119.22	118.63	118.36
10,000	151.00	147.78	145.14	142.95	141.13	139.60	138.33	137.26	133.93	132.47	131.81	131.51
15,000	226.50	221.67	217.70	214.42	211.69	209.40	207.49	205.89	200.90	198.70	197.71	197.26
20,000	302.00	295.56	290.27	285.89	282.25	279.20	276.66	274.51	267.86	264.93	263.61	263.01
25,000	377.50	369.45	362.83	357.36	352.81	349.00	345.82	343.14	334.83	331.16	329.51	328.76
30,000	453.00	443.34	435.40	428.83	423.37	418.80	414.98	411.77	401.79	397.39	395.41	394.51
35,000	528.50	517.23	507.96	500.30	493.93	488.60	484.14	480.39	468.76	463.62	461.31	460.26
40,000	604.00	591.12	580.53	571.77	564.49	558.40	553.31	549.02	535.72	529.85	527.21	526.01
45,000	679.50	665.01	653.09	643.24	635.05	628.20	622.47	617.65	602.69	596.08	593.11	591.76
50,000	755.00	738.90	725.66	714.71	705.61	698.00	691.63	686.27	669.65	662.31	659.01	657.51
55,000	830.50	812.78	798.22	786.18	776.17	767.80	760.79	754.90	736.61	728.54	724.91	723.26
60,000	906.00	886.67	870.79	857.65	846.73	837.60	829.96	823.53	803.58	794.78	790.81	789.01
65,000	981.50	960.56	943.36	929.12	917.29	907.40	899.12	892.15	870.54	861.01	856.71	854.77
70,000	1057.00	1034.45	1015.92	1000.59	987.85	977.20	968.28	960.78	937.51	927.24	922.61	920.52
75,000	1132.50	1108.34	1088.49	1072.06	1058.41	1047.00	1037.44	1029.41	1004.47	993.47	988.52	986.27
80,000	1208.00	1182.23	1161.05	1143.53	1128.97	1116.80	1106.61	1098.03	1071.44	1059.70	1054.42	1052.02
85,000	1283.49	1256.12	1233.62	1215.00	1199.53	1186.60	1175.77	1166.66	1138.40	1125.93	1120.32	1117.77
90,000	1358.99	1330.01	1306.18	1286.47	1270.09	1256.40	1244.93	1235.29	1205.37	1192.16	1186.22	1183.52
95,000	1434.49	1403.90	1378.75	1357.95	1340.65	1326.20	1314.09	1303.91	1272.33	1258.39	1252.12	1249.27
100,000	1509.99	1477.79	1451.31	1429.42	1411.21	1396.00	1383.26	1372.54	1339.30	1324.62	1318.02	1315.02
105,000	1585.49	1551.67	1523.88	1500.89	1481.77	1465.80	1452.42	1441.17	1406.26	1390.85	1383.92	1380.77
110,000	1660.99	1625.56	1596.44	1572.36	1552.33	1535.60	1521.58	1509.79	1473.22	1457.08	1449.82	1446.52
115,000	1736.49	1699.45	1669.01	1643.83	1622.89	1605.40	1590.74	1578.42	1540.19	1523.31	1515.72	1512.27
120,000	1811.99	1773.34	1741.57	1715.30	1693.45	1675.20	1659.91	1647.05	1607.15	1589.55	1581.62	1578.02
125,000	1887.49	1847.23	1814.14	1786.77	1764.01	1745.00	1729.07	1715.67	1674.12	1655.78	1647.52	1643.77
130,000	1962.99	1921.12	1886.71	1858.24	1834.57	1814.80	1798.23	1784.30	1741.08	1722.01	1713.42	1709.53
135,000	2038.49	1995.01	1959.27	1929.71	1905.13	1884.60	1867.39	1852.93	1808.05	1788.24	1779.32	1775.28
140,000	2113.99	2068.90	2031.84	2001.18	1975.69	1954.40	1936.56	1921.55	1875.01	1854.47	1845.22	1841.03
145,000	2189.49	2142.79	2104.40	2072.65	2046.25	2024.20	2005.72	1990.18	1941.97	1920.70	1911.12	1906.78
150,000	2264.99	2216.68	2176.97	2144.12	2116.81	2094.00	2074.88	2058.81	2008.94	1986.93	1977.03	1972.53
155,000	2340.49	2290.56	2249.53	2215.59	2187.37	2163.80	2144.04	2127.43	2075.90	2053.16	2042.93	2038.28
160,000	2415.99	2364.45	2322.10	2287.06	2257.93	2233.60	2213.21	2196.06	2142.87	2119.39	2108.83	2104.03
165,000	2491.48	2438.34	2394.66	2358.53	2328.49	2303.40	2282.37	2264.69	2209.83	2185.62	2174.73	2169.78
170,000	2566.98	2512.23	2467.23	2430.00	2399.05	2373.20	2351.53	2333.31	2276.80	2251.85	2240.63	2235.53
175,000	2642.48	2586.12	2539.79	2501.47	2469.61	2443.00	2420.69	2401.94	2343.76	2318.08	2306.53	2301.28
180,000	2717.98	2660.01	2612.36	2572.94	2540.17	2512.80	2489.86	2470.57	2410.73	2384.32	2372.43	2367.03
185,000	2793.48	2733.90	2684.92	2644.42	2610.73	2582.60	2559.02	2539.19	2477.69	2450.55	2438.33	2432.78
190,000	2868.98	2807.79	2757.49	2715.89	2681.29	2652.40	2628.18	2607.82	2544.66	2516.78	2504.23	2498.54
195,000	2944.48	2881.68	2830.06	2787.36	2751.85	2722.20	2697.34	2676.45	2611.62	2583.01	2570.13	2564.29
200,000	3019.98	2955.57	2902.62	2858.83	2822.41	2792.00	2766.51	2745.07	2678.58	2649.24	2636.03	2630.04
205,000	3095.48	3029.45	2975.19	2930.30	2892.97	2861.80	2835.67	2813.70	2745.55	2715.47	2701.93	2695.79
210,000	3170.98	3103.34	3047.75	3001.77	2963.53	2931.60	2904.83	2882.33	2812.51	2781.70	2767.83	2761.54
215,000	3246.48	3177.23	3120.32	3073.24	3034.09	3001.40	2973.99	2950.95	2879.48	2847.93	2833.73	2827.29
220,000	3321.98	3251.12	3192.88	3144.71	3104.65	3071.20	3043.16	3019.58	2946.44	2914.16	2899.64	2893.04
225,000	3397.48	3325.01	3265.45	3216.18	3175.21	3141.00	3112.32	3088.21	3013.41	2980.39	2965.54	2958.79
230,000	3472.98	3398.90	3338.01	3287.65	3245.77	3210.80	3181.48	3156.83	3080.37	3046.62	3031.44	3024.54
235,000	3548.48	3472.79	3410.58	3359.12	3316.33	3280.60	3250.64	3225.46	3147.34	3112.86	3097.34	3090.29
240,000	3623.98	3546.68	3483.14	3430.59	3386.89	3350.40	3319.81	3294.09	3214.30	3179.09	3163.24	3156.04
245,000	3699.48	3620.57	3555.71	3502.06	3457.45	3420.20	3388.97	3362.71	3281.26	3245.32	3229.14	3221.79
250,000	3774.97	3694.46	3628.27	3573.53	3528.01	3490.00	3458.13	3431.34	3348.23	3311.55	3295.04	3287.54
255,000	3850.47	3768.34	3700.84	3645.00	3598.57	3559.80	3527.29	3499.97	3415.19	3377.78	3360.94	3353.30
260,000	3925.97	3842.23	3773.41	3716.47	3669.13	3629.60	3596.46	3568.59	3482.16	3444.01	3426.84	3419.05
265,000	4001.47	3916.12	3845.97	3787.94	3739.69	3699.40	3665.62	3637.22	3549.12	3510.24	3492.74	3484.80
270,000	4076.97	3990.01	3918.54	3859.41	3810.25	3769.20	3734.78	3705.85	3616.09	3576.47	3558.64	3550.55
280,000	4227.97	4137.79	4063.67	4002.36	3951.37	3908.80	3873.11	3843.10	3750.02	3708.93	3690.44	3682.05
290,000	4378.97	4285.57	4208.80	4145.30	4092.49	4048.40	4011.43	3980.35	3883.94	3841.39	3822.24	3813.55
300,000	4529.97	4433.35	4353.93	4288.24	4233.61	4188.00	4149.76	4117.61	4017.87	3973.86	3954.05	3945.05

16.00% MONTHLY AMORTIZING PAYMENTS

AMOUNT OF LOAN	NUMBER OF YEARS IN TERM											
	1	2	3	4	5	6	7	8	9	10	11	12
$ 50	4.54	2.45	1.76	1.42	1.22	1.09	1.00	0.93	0.88	0.84	0.81	0.79
100	9.08	4.90	3.52	2.84	2.44	2.17	1.99	1.86	1.76	1.68	1.62	1.57
200	18.15	9.80	7.04	5.67	4.87	4.34	3.98	3.71	3.51	3.36	3.23	3.14
300	27.22	14.69	10.55	8.51	7.30	6.51	5.96	5.56	5.26	5.03	4.85	4.70
400	36.30	19.59	14.07	11.34	9.73	8.68	7.95	7.42	7.02	6.71	6.46	6.27
500	45.37	24.49	17.58	14.18	12.16	10.85	9.94	9.27	8.77	8.38	8.08	7.83
600	54.44	29.38	21.10	17.01	14.60	13.02	11.92	11.12	10.52	10.06	9.69	9.40
700	63.52	34.28	24.61	19.84	17.03	15.19	13.91	12.98	12.27	11.73	11.31	10.97
800	72.59	39.18	28.13	22.68	19.46	17.36	15.89	14.83	14.03	13.41	12.92	12.53
900	81.66	44.07	31.65	25.51	21.89	19.53	17.88	16.68	15.78	15.08	14.53	14.10
1,000	90.74	48.97	35.16	28.35	24.32	21.70	19.87	18.53	17.53	16.76	16.15	15.66
2,000	181.47	97.93	70.32	56.69	48.64	43.39	39.73	37.06	35.06	33.51	32.29	31.32
3,000	272.20	146.89	105.48	85.03	72.96	65.08	59.59	55.59	52.58	50.26	48.43	46.98
4,000	362.93	195.86	140.63	113.37	97.28	86.77	79.45	74.12	70.11	67.01	64.58	62.64
5,000	453.66	244.82	175.79	141.71	121.60	108.46	99.32	92.65	87.63	83.76	80.72	78.30
6,000	544.39	293.78	210.95	170.05	145.91	130.16	119.18	111.18	105.16	100.51	96.86	93.95
7,000	635.12	342.75	246.10	198.39	170.23	151.85	139.04	129.71	122.68	117.26	113.01	109.61
8,000	725.85	391.71	281.26	226.73	194.55	173.54	158.90	148.24	140.21	134.02	129.15	125.27
9,000	816.58	440.67	316.42	255.07	218.87	195.23	178.76	166.76	157.73	150.77	145.29	140.93
10,000	907.31	489.64	351.58	283.41	243.19	216.92	198.63	185.29	175.26	167.52	161.44	156.59
15,000	1360.97	734.45	527.36	425.11	364.78	325.38	297.94	277.94	262.88	251.27	242.15	234.88
20,000	1814.62	979.27	703.15	566.81	486.37	433.84	397.25	370.58	350.51	335.03	322.87	313.17
25,000	2268.28	1224.08	878.93	708.51	607.96	542.30	496.56	463.22	438.14	418.79	403.58	391.46
30,000	2721.93	1468.90	1054.72	850.21	729.55	650.76	595.87	555.87	525.76	502.54	484.30	469.75
35,000	3175.59	1713.71	1230.50	991.91	851.14	759.22	695.18	648.51	613.39	586.30	565.02	548.04
40,000	3629.24	1958.53	1406.29	1133.62	972.73	867.68	794.49	741.16	701.02	670.06	645.73	626.34
45,000	4082.89	2203.34	1582.07	1275.32	1094.32	976.14	893.80	833.80	788.64	753.81	726.45	704.63
50,000	4536.55	2448.16	1757.86	1417.02	1215.91	1084.60	993.11	926.44	876.27	837.57	807.16	782.92
55,000	4990.20	2692.98	1933.64	1558.72	1337.50	1193.06	1092.42	1019.09	963.89	921.33	887.88	861.21
60,000	5443.86	2937.79	2109.43	1700.42	1459.09	1301.52	1191.73	1111.73	1051.52	1005.08	968.60	939.50
65,000	5897.51	3182.61	2285.21	1842.12	1580.68	1409.97	1291.04	1204.38	1139.15	1088.84	1049.31	1017.79
70,000	6351.17	3427.42	2461.00	1983.82	1702.27	1518.43	1390.35	1297.02	1226.77	1172.60	1130.03	1096.08
75,000	6804.82	3672.24	2636.78	2125.53	1823.86	1626.89	1489.66	1389.66	1314.40	1256.35	1210.74	1174.37
80,000	7258.47	3917.05	2812.57	2267.23	1945.45	1735.35	1588.97	1482.31	1402.03	1340.11	1291.46	1252.67
85,000	7712.13	4161.87	2988.35	2408.93	2067.04	1843.81	1688.28	1574.95	1489.65	1423.87	1372.17	1330.96
90,000	8165.78	4406.68	3164.14	2550.63	2188.63	1952.27	1787.59	1667.60	1577.28	1507.62	1452.89	1409.25
95,000	8619.44	4651.50	3339.92	2692.33	2310.22	2060.73	1886.90	1760.24	1664.90	1591.38	1533.61	1487.54
100,000	9073.09	4896.32	3515.71	2834.03	2431.81	2169.19	1986.21	1852.88	1752.53	1675.14	1614.32	1565.83
105,000	9526.75	5141.13	3691.49	2975.73	2553.40	2277.65	2085.52	1945.53	1840.16	1758.89	1695.04	1644.12
110,000	9980.40	5385.95	3867.28	3117.44	2674.99	2386.11	2184.83	2038.17	1927.78	1842.65	1775.75	1722.41
115,000	10434.05	5630.76	4043.06	3259.14	2796.58	2494.57	2284.14	2130.82	2015.41	1926.41	1856.47	1800.70
120,000	10887.71	5875.58	4218.85	3400.84	2918.17	2603.03	2383.45	2223.46	2103.04	2010.16	1937.19	1879.00
125,000	11341.36	6120.39	4394.63	3542.54	3039.76	2711.49	2482.76	2316.10	2190.66	2093.92	2017.90	1957.29
130,000	11795.02	6365.21	4570.42	3684.24	3161.35	2819.94	2582.07	2408.75	2278.29	2177.68	2098.62	2035.58
135,000	12248.67	6610.02	4746.20	3825.94	3282.94	2928.40	2681.38	2501.39	2365.91	2261.43	2179.33	2113.87
140,000	12702.33	6854.84	4921.99	3967.64	3404.53	3036.86	2780.69	2594.04	2453.54	2345.19	2260.05	2192.16
145,000	13155.98	7099.66	5097.77	4109.35	3526.12	3145.32	2880.00	2686.68	2541.17	2428.95	2340.77	2270.45
150,000	13609.63	7344.47	5273.56	4251.05	3647.71	3253.78	2979.31	2779.32	2628.79	2512.70	2421.48	2348.74
155,000	14063.29	7589.29	5449.35	4392.75	3769.30	3362.24	3078.62	2871.97	2716.42	2596.46	2502.20	2427.03
160,000	14516.94	7834.10	5625.13	4534.45	3890.89	3470.70	3177.94	2964.61	2804.05	2680.21	2582.91	2505.33
165,000	14970.60	8078.92	5800.92	4676.15	4012.48	3579.16	3277.25	3057.25	2891.67	2763.97	2663.63	2583.62
170,000	15424.25	8323.73	5976.70	4817.85	4134.07	3687.62	3376.56	3149.90	2979.30	2847.73	2744.34	2661.91
175,000	15877.91	8568.55	6152.49	4959.55	4255.66	3796.08	3475.87	3242.54	3066.92	2931.48	2825.06	2740.20
180,000	16331.56	8813.36	6328.27	5101.26	4377.26	3904.54	3575.18	3335.19	3154.55	3015.24	2905.78	2818.49
185,000	16785.21	9058.18	6504.06	5242.96	4498.85	4013.00	3674.49	3427.83	3242.18	3099.00	2986.49	2896.78
190,000	17238.87	9303.00	6679.84	5384.66	4620.44	4121.45	3773.80	3520.47	3329.80	3182.75	3067.21	2975.07
195,000	17692.52	9547.81	6855.63	5526.36	4742.03	4229.91	3873.11	3613.12	3417.43	3266.51	3147.92	3053.36
200,000	18146.18	9792.63	7031.41	5668.06	4863.62	4338.37	3972.42	3705.76	3505.06	3350.27	3228.64	3131.66
205,000	18599.83	10037.44	7207.20	5809.76	4985.21	4446.83	4071.73	3798.41	3592.68	3434.02	3309.36	3209.95
210,000	19053.49	10282.26	7382.98	5951.46	5106.80	4555.29	4171.04	3891.05	3680.31	3517.78	3390.07	3288.24
215,000	19507.14	10527.07	7558.77	6093.17	5228.39	4663.75	4270.35	3983.69	3767.93	3601.54	3470.79	3366.53
220,000	19960.79	10771.89	7734.55	6234.87	5349.98	4772.21	4369.66	4076.34	3855.56	3685.29	3551.50	3444.82
225,000	20414.45	11016.70	7910.34	6376.57	5471.57	4880.67	4468.97	4168.98	3943.19	3769.05	3632.22	3523.11
230,000	20868.10	11261.52	8086.12	6518.27	5593.16	4989.13	4568.28	4261.63	4030.81	3852.81	3712.93	3601.40
235,000	21321.76	11506.34	8261.91	6659.97	5714.75	5097.59	4667.59	4354.27	4118.44	3936.56	3793.65	3679.69
240,000	21775.41	11751.15	8437.69	6801.67	5836.34	5206.05	4766.90	4446.91	4206.07	4020.32	3874.37	3757.99
245,000	22229.07	11995.97	8613.48	6943.37	5957.93	5314.51	4866.21	4539.56	4293.69	4104.08	3955.08	3836.28
250,000	22682.72	12240.78	8789.26	7085.08	6079.52	5422.97	4965.52	4632.20	4381.32	4187.83	4035.80	3914.57
255,000	23136.37	12485.60	8965.05	7226.78	6201.11	5531.42	5064.83	4724.85	4468.94	4271.59	4116.51	3992.86
260,000	23590.03	12730.41	9140.83	7368.48	6322.70	5639.88	5164.14	4817.49	4556.57	4355.35	4197.23	4071.15
265,000	24043.68	12975.23	9316.62	7510.18	6444.29	5748.34	5263.45	4910.13	4644.20	4439.10	4277.95	4149.44
270,000	24497.34	13220.04	9492.40	7651.88	6565.88	5856.80	5362.76	5002.78	4731.82	4522.86	4358.66	4227.73
280,000	25404.65	13709.68	9843.97	7935.28	6809.06	6073.72	5561.38	5188.07	4907.08	4690.37	4520.09	4384.32
290,000	26311.95	14199.31	10195.54	8218.69	7052.24	6290.64	5760.00	5373.35	5082.33	4857.89	4681.53	4540.90
300,000	27219.26	14688.94	10547.11	8502.09	7295.42	6507.56	5958.62	5558.64	5257.58	5025.40	4842.96	4697.48

114

16.00%

AMOUNT OF LOAN	NUMBER OF YEARS IN TERM											
	13	14	15	16	17	18	19	20	25	30	35	40
$ 50	0.77	0.75	0.74	0.73	0.72	0.71	0.71	0.70	0.68	0.68	0.67	0.67
100	1.53	1.50	1.47	1.45	1.43	1.42	1.41	1.40	1.36	1.35	1.34	1.34
200	3.06	2.99	2.94	2.90	2.86	2.83	2.81	2.79	2.72	2.69	2.68	2.68
300	4.59	4.49	4.41	4.35	4.29	4.25	4.21	4.18	4.08	4.04	4.02	4.01
400	6.11	5.98	5.88	5.79	5.72	5.66	5.61	5.57	5.44	5.38	5.36	5.35
500	7.64	7.48	7.35	7.24	7.15	7.08	7.01	6.96	6.80	6.73	6.70	6.68
600	9.17	8.97	8.82	8.69	8.58	8.49	8.42	8.35	8.16	8.07	8.04	8.02
700	10.69	10.47	10.29	10.13	10.01	9.90	9.82	9.74	9.52	9.42	9.37	9.35
800	12.22	11.96	11.75	11.58	11.44	11.32	11.22	11.14	10.88	10.76	10.71	10.69
900	13.75	13.46	13.22	13.03	12.87	12.73	12.62	12.53	12.23	12.11	12.05	12.03
1,000	15.27	14.95	14.69	14.48	14.30	14.15	14.02	13.92	13.59	13.45	13.39	13.36
2,000	30.54	29.90	29.38	28.95	28.59	28.29	28.04	27.83	27.18	26.90	26.77	26.72
3,000	45.81	44.85	44.07	43.42	42.88	42.43	42.06	41.74	40.77	40.35	40.16	40.07
4,000	61.07	59.80	58.75	57.89	57.17	56.57	56.07	55.66	54.36	53.80	53.54	53.43
5,000	76.34	74.75	73.44	72.36	71.46	70.72	70.09	69.57	67.95	67.24	66.93	66.79
6,000	91.61	89.70	88.13	86.83	85.76	84.86	84.11	83.48	81.54	80.69	80.31	80.14
7,000	106.87	104.64	102.81	101.30	100.05	99.00	98.13	97.39	95.13	94.14	93.70	93.50
8,000	122.14	119.59	117.50	115.77	114.34	113.14	112.14	111.31	108.72	107.59	107.08	106.86
9,000	137.41	134.54	132.19	130.24	128.63	127.29	126.16	125.22	122.30	121.03	120.47	120.21
10,000	152.68	149.49	146.88	144.72	142.92	141.43	140.18	139.13	135.89	134.48	133.85	133.57
15,000	229.01	224.23	220.31	217.07	214.38	212.14	210.27	208.69	203.84	201.72	200.78	200.35
20,000	305.35	298.97	293.75	289.43	285.84	282.85	280.35	278.26	271.78	268.96	267.70	267.13
25,000	381.68	373.72	367.18	361.78	357.30	353.57	350.44	347.82	339.73	336.19	334.62	333.92
30,000	458.02	448.46	440.62	434.14	428.76	424.28	420.53	417.38	407.67	403.43	401.55	400.70
35,000	534.35	523.20	514.05	506.49	500.22	494.99	490.62	486.94	475.62	470.67	468.47	467.48
40,000	610.69	597.94	587.49	578.85	571.68	565.70	560.70	556.51	543.56	537.91	535.39	534.26
45,000	687.02	672.69	660.92	651.20	643.14	636.42	630.79	626.07	611.50	605.15	602.32	601.05
50,000	763.36	747.43	734.36	723.56	714.60	707.13	700.88	695.63	679.45	672.38	669.24	667.83
55,000	839.69	822.17	807.79	795.92	786.06	777.84	770.97	765.20	747.39	739.62	736.16	734.61
60,000	916.03	896.91	881.23	868.27	857.52	848.55	841.05	834.76	815.34	806.86	803.09	801.39
65,000	992.36	971.65	954.66	940.63	928.98	919.27	911.14	904.32	883.28	874.10	870.01	868.18
70,000	1068.70	1046.40	1028.10	1012.98	1000.44	989.98	981.23	973.88	951.23	941.33	936.93	934.96
75,000	1145.03	1121.14	1101.53	1085.34	1071.90	1060.69	1051.31	1043.45	1019.17	1008.57	1003.86	1001.74
80,000	1221.37	1195.88	1174.97	1157.69	1143.36	1131.40	1121.40	1113.01	1087.12	1075.81	1070.78	1068.52
85,000	1297.70	1270.62	1248.40	1230.05	1214.82	1202.12	1191.49	1182.57	1155.06	1143.05	1137.70	1135.31
90,000	1374.04	1345.37	1321.84	1302.40	1286.27	1272.83	1261.58	1252.14	1223.00	1210.29	1204.63	1202.09
95,000	1450.37	1420.11	1395.27	1374.76	1357.73	1343.54	1331.66	1321.70	1290.96	1277.52	1271.55	1268.87
100,000	1526.71	1494.85	1468.71	1447.12	1429.19	1414.25	1401.75	1391.26	1358.89	1344.76	1338.47	1335.65
105,000	1603.04	1569.59	1542.14	1519.47	1500.65	1404.96	1471.84	1460.82	1426.84	1412.00	1405.40	1402.44
110,000	1679.38	1644.33	1615.58	1591.83	1572.11	1555.68	1541.93	1530.39	1494.78	1479.24	1472.32	1460.22
115,000	1755.72	1719.08	1689.01	1664.18	1643.57	1626.39	1612.01	1599.95	1562.73	1546.48	1539.24	1536.00
120,000	1832.05	1793.82	1762.45	1736.54	1715.03	1697.10	1682.10	1669.51	1630.67	1613.71	1606.17	1602.78
125,000	1908.39	1868.56	1835.88	1808.89	1786.49	1767.81	1752.19	1739.07	1698.62	1680.95	1673.09	1669.57
130,000	1984.72	1943.30	1909.32	1881.25	1857.95	1838.53	1822.28	1808.64	1766.56	1748.19	1740.02	1736.35
135,000	2061.06	2018.05	1982.75	1953.60	1929.41	1909.24	1892.36	1878.20	1834.50	1815.43	1806.94	1803.13
140,000	2137.39	2092.79	2056.19	2025.96	2000.87	1979.95	1962.45	1947.76	1902.45	1882.66	1873.86	1869.91
145,000	2213.73	2167.53	2129.62	2098.31	2072.33	2050.66	2032.54	2017.33	1970.39	1949.90	1940.79	1936.70
150,000	2290.06	2242.27	2203.06	2170.67	2143.79	2121.38	2102.62	2086.89	2038.34	2017.14	2007.71	2003.48
155,000	2366.40	2317.02	2276.49	2243.03	2215.25	2192.09	2172.71	2156.45	2106.28	2084.38	2074.63	2070.26
160,000	2442.73	2391.76	2349.93	2315.38	2286.71	2262.80	2242.80	2226.01	2174.23	2151.62	2141.56	2137.04
165,000	2519.07	2466.50	2423.36	2387.74	2358.17	2333.51	2312.89	2295.58	2242.17	2218.85	2208.48	2203.82
170,000	2595.40	2541.24	2496.80	2460.09	2429.63	2404.23	2382.97	2365.14	2310.12	2286.09	2275.40	2270.61
175,000	2671.74	2615.98	2570.23	2532.45	2501.08	2474.94	2453.06	2434.70	2378.06	2353.33	2342.33	2337.39
180,000	2748.07	2690.73	2643.67	2604.80	2572.54	2545.65	2523.15	2504.27	2446.00	2420.57	2409.25	2404.17
185,000	2824.41	2765.47	2717.10	2677.16	2644.00	2616.36	2593.24	2573.83	2513.95	2487.81	2476.17	2470.95
190,000	2900.74	2840.21	2790.54	2749.51	2715.46	2687.07	2663.32	2643.39	2581.89	2555.04	2543.10	2537.74
195,000	2977.08	2914.95	2863.97	2821.87	2786.92	2757.79	2733.41	2712.95	2649.84	2622.28	2610.02	2604.52
200,000	3053.41	2989.70	2937.41	2894.23	2858.38	2828.50	2803.50	2782.52	2717.78	2689.52	2676.94	2671.30
205,000	3129.75	3064.44	3010.84	2966.58	2929.84	2899.21	2873.58	2852.08	2785.73	2756.76	2743.87	2738.08
210,000	3206.08	3139.18	3084.28	3038.94	3001.30	2969.92	2943.67	2921.64	2853.67	2823.99	2810.79	2804.87
215,000	3282.42	3213.92	3157.71	3111.29	3072.76	3040.64	3013.76	2991.21	2921.62	2891.23	2877.71	2871.65
220,000	3358.75	3288.66	3231.15	3183.65	3144.22	3111.35	3083.85	3060.77	2989.56	2958.47	2944.64	2938.43
225,000	3435.09	3363.41	3304.58	3256.00	3215.68	3182.06	3153.93	3130.33	3057.50	3025.71	3011.56	3005.21
230,000	3511.43	3438.15	3378.02	3328.36	3287.14	3252.77	3224.02	3199.89	3125.45	3092.95	3078.48	3072.00
235,000	3587.76	3512.89	3451.45	3400.71	3358.60	3323.49	3294.11	3269.46	3193.39	3160.18	3145.41	3138.78
240,000	3664.10	3587.63	3524.89	3473.07	3430.06	3394.20	3364.20	3339.02	3261.34	3227.42	3212.33	3205.56
245,000	3740.43	3662.38	3598.32	3545.43	3501.52	3464.91	3434.28	3408.58	3329.28	3294.66	3279.26	3272.34
250,000	3816.77	3737.12	3671.76	3617.78	3572.98	3535.62	3504.37	3478.14	3397.23	3361.90	3346.18	3339.13
255,000	3893.10	3811.86	3745.19	3690.14	3644.44	3606.34	3574.46	3547.71	3465.17	3429.14	3413.10	3405.91
260,000	3969.44	3886.60	3818.63	3762.49	3715.89	3677.05	3644.55	3617.27	3533.12	3496.37	3480.03	3472.69
265,000	4045.77	3961.35	3892.06	3834.85	3787.35	3747.76	3714.63	3686.83	3601.06	3563.61	3546.95	3539.47
270,000	4122.11	4036.09	3965.50	3907.20	3858.81	3818.47	3784.72	3756.40	3669.00	3630.85	3613.87	3606.26
280,000	4274.78	4185.57	4112.37	4051.91	4001.73	3959.90	3924.89	3895.52	3804.89	3765.32	3747.72	3739.82
290,000	4427.45	4335.06	4259.24	4196.62	4144.65	4101.32	4065.07	4034.65	3940.78	3899.80	3881.57	3873.39
300,000	4580.12	4484.54	4406.11	4341.34	4287.57	4242.75	4205.24	4173.77	4076.67	4034.28	4015.41	4006.95

16.25%

AMOUNT OF LOAN	NUMBER OF YEARS IN TERM											
	1	2	3	4	5	6	7	8	9	10	11	12
$ 50	4.55	2.46	1.77	1.43	1.23	1.10	1.01	0.94	0.89	0.85	0.82	0.80
100	9.09	4.91	3.53	2.85	2.45	2.19	2.01	1.87	1.77	1.70	1.64	1.59
200	18.17	9.82	7.06	5.70	4.90	4.37	4.01	3.74	3.54	3.39	3.27	3.17
300	27.26	14.73	10.59	8.55	7.34	6.55	6.01	5.61	5.31	5.08	4.90	4.75
400	36.34	19.64	14.12	11.39	9.79	8.74	8.01	7.48	7.08	6.77	6.53	6.33
500	45.43	24.55	17.65	14.24	12.23	10.92	10.01	9.34	8.84	8.46	8.16	7.92
600	54.51	29.45	21.17	17.09	14.68	13.10	12.01	11.21	10.61	10.15	9.79	9.50
700	63.60	34.36	24.70	19.93	17.12	15.29	14.01	13.08	12.38	11.84	11.42	11.08
800	72.68	39.27	28.23	22.78	19.57	17.47	16.01	14.95	14.15	13.53	13.05	12.66
900	81.77	44.18	31.76	25.63	22.01	19.65	18.01	16.81	15.91	15.22	14.68	14.25
1,000	90.85	49.09	35.29	28.47	24.46	21.83	20.01	18.68	17.68	16.91	16.31	15.83
2,000	181.70	98.17	70.57	56.94	48.91	43.66	40.01	37.36	35.36	33.82	32.61	31.65
3,000	272.55	147.25	105.85	85.41	73.36	65.49	60.02	56.03	53.04	50.73	48.92	47.47
4,000	363.40	196.34	141.13	113.88	97.81	87.32	80.02	74.71	70.71	67.63	65.22	63.29
5,000	454.25	245.42	176.41	142.35	122.26	109.15	100.03	93.39	88.39	84.54	81.52	79.12
6,000	545.10	294.50	211.69	170.82	146.71	130.98	120.03	112.06	106.07	101.45	97.83	94.94
7,000	635.95	343.58	246.97	199.28	171.16	152.81	140.04	130.74	123.74	118.36	114.13	110.76
8,000	726.80	392.67	282.25	227.75	195.61	174.64	160.04	149.41	141.42	135.26	130.43	126.58
9,000	817.65	441.75	317.53	256.22	220.06	196.47	180.05	168.09	159.10	152.17	146.74	142.41
10,000	908.50	490.83	352.81	284.69	244.52	218.30	200.05	186.77	176.78	169.08	163.04	158.23
15,000	1362.74	736.24	529.21	427.03	366.77	327.45	300.08	280.15	265.16	253.62	244.56	237.34
20,000	1816.99	981.66	705.62	569.37	489.03	436.60	400.10	373.53	353.55	338.15	326.07	316.45
25,000	2271.24	1227.07	882.02	711.72	611.28	545.75	500.12	466.91	441.93	422.69	407.59	395.57
30,000	2725.48	1472.48	1058.42	854.06	733.54	654.90	600.15	560.29	530.32	507.23	489.11	474.68
35,000	3179.73	1717.90	1234.83	996.40	855.79	764.05	700.17	653.67	618.70	591.77	570.63	553.79
40,000	3633.97	1963.31	1411.23	1138.74	978.05	873.19	800.19	747.05	707.09	676.30	652.14	632.90
45,000	4088.22	2208.72	1587.63	1281.09	1100.30	982.34	900.22	840.43	795.47	760.84	733.66	712.01
50,000	4542.47	2454.14	1764.03	1423.43	1222.56	1091.49	1000.24	933.81	883.86	845.38	815.18	791.13
55,000	4996.71	2699.55	1940.44	1565.77	1344.81	1200.64	1100.26	1027.19	972.24	929.91	896.69	870.24
60,000	5450.96	2944.96	2116.84	1708.11	1467.07	1309.79	1200.29	1120.57	1060.63	1014.45	978.21	949.35
65,000	5905.20	3190.38	2293.24	1850.46	1589.33	1418.94	1300.31	1213.95	1149.01	1098.99	1059.73	1028.46
70,000	6359.45	3435.79	2469.65	1992.80	1711.58	1528.09	1400.33	1307.33	1237.40	1183.53	1141.25	1107.58
75,000	6813.70	3681.20	2646.05	2135.14	1833.84	1637.23	1500.36	1400.71	1325.78	1268.06	1222.76	1186.69
80,000	7267.94	3926.62	2822.45	2277.48	1956.09	1746.38	1600.38	1494.09	1414.17	1352.60	1304.28	1265.80
85,000	7722.19	4172.03	2998.85	2419.83	2078.35	1855.53	1700.41	1587.47	1502.55	1437.14	1385.80	1344.91
90,000	8176.43	4417.44	3175.26	2562.17	2200.60	1964.68	1800.43	1680.85	1590.94	1521.67	1467.31	1424.02
95,000	8630.68	4662.86	3351.66	2704.51	2322.86	2073.83	1900.45	1774.23	1679.33	1606.21	1548.83	1503.14
100,000	9084.93	4908.27	3528.06	2846.85	2445.11	2182.98	2000.48	1867.61	1767.71	1690.75	1630.35	1582.25
105,000	9539.17	5153.68	3704.47	2989.20	2567.37	2292.13	2100.50	1960.99	1856.10	1775.29	1711.87	1661.36
110,000	9993.42	5399.10	3880.87	3131.54	2689.62	2401.27	2200.52	2054.37	1944.48	1859.82	1793.38	1740.47
115,000	10447.66	5644.51	4057.27	3273.88	2811.88	2510.42	2300.55	2147.76	2032.87	1944.36	1874.90	1819.59
120,000	10901.91	5889.92	4233.67	3416.22	2934.14	2619.57	2400.57	2241.14	2121.25	2028.90	1956.42	1898.70
125,000	11356.16	6135.34	4410.08	3558.57	3056.39	2728.72	2500.59	2334.52	2209.64	2113.44	2037.93	1977.81
130,000	11810.40	6380.75	4586.48	3700.91	3178.65	2837.87	2600.62	2427.90	2298.02	2197.97	2119.45	2056.92
135,000	12264.65	6626.16	4762.88	3843.25	3300.90	2947.02	2700.64	2521.28	2386.41	2282.51	2200.97	2136.03
140,000	12718.89	6871.58	4939.29	3985.59	3423.16	3056.17	2800.66	2614.66	2474.79	2367.05	2282.49	2215.15
145,000	13173.14	7116.99	5115.69	4127.93	3545.41	3165.31	2900.69	2708.04	2563.18	2451.58	2364.00	2294.26
150,000	13627.39	7362.40	5292.09	4270.28	3667.67	3274.46	3000.71	2801.42	2651.56	2536.12	2445.52	2373.37
155,000	14081.63	7607.82	5468.50	4412.62	3789.92	3383.61	3100.74	2894.80	2739.95	2620.66	2527.04	2452.48
160,000	14535.88	7853.23	5644.90	4554.96	3912.18	3492.76	3200.76	2988.18	2828.33	2705.20	2608.55	2531.60
165,000	14990.12	8098.64	5821.30	4697.30	4034.43	3601.91	3300.78	3081.56	2916.72	2789.73	2690.07	2610.71
170,000	15444.37	8344.05	5997.70	4839.65	4156.69	3711.06	3400.81	3174.94	3005.10	2874.27	2771.59	2689.82
175,000	15898.62	8589.47	6174.11	4981.99	4278.95	3820.21	3500.83	3268.32	3093.49	2958.81	2853.11	2768.93
180,000	16352.86	8834.88	6350.51	5124.33	4401.20	3929.35	3600.85	3361.70	3181.87	3043.34	2934.62	2848.04
185,000	16807.11	9080.29	6526.91	5266.67	4523.46	4038.50	3700.88	3455.08	3270.26	3127.88	3016.14	2927.16
190,000	17261.35	9325.71	6703.32	5409.02	4645.71	4147.65	3800.90	3548.46	3358.65	3212.42	3097.66	3006.27
195,000	17715.60	9571.12	6879.72	5551.36	4767.97	4256.80	3900.92	3641.84	3447.03	3296.96	3179.17	3085.38
200,000	18169.85	9816.53	7056.12	5693.70	4890.22	4365.95	4000.95	3735.22	3535.42	3381.49	3260.69	3164.49
205,000	18624.09	10061.95	7232.52	5836.04	5012.48	4475.10	4100.97	3828.60	3623.80	3466.03	3342.21	3243.61
210,000	19078.34	10307.36	7408.93	5978.39	5134.73	4584.25	4200.99	3921.98	3712.19	3550.57	3423.73	3322.72
215,000	19532.58	10552.77	7585.33	6120.73	5256.99	4693.39	4301.02	4015.36	3800.57	3635.10	3505.24	3401.83
220,000	19986.83	10798.19	7761.73	6263.07	5379.24	4802.54	4401.04	4108.74	3888.96	3719.64	3586.76	3480.94
225,000	20441.08	11043.60	7938.14	6405.41	5501.50	4911.69	4501.07	4202.13	3977.34	3804.18	3668.28	3560.05
230,000	20895.32	11289.01	8114.54	6547.76	5623.76	5020.84	4601.09	4295.51	4065.73	3888.72	3749.79	3639.17
235,000	21349.57	11534.43	8290.94	6690.10	5746.01	5129.99	4701.11	4388.89	4154.11	3973.25	3831.31	3718.28
240,000	21803.81	11779.84	8467.34	6832.44	5868.27	5239.14	4801.14	4482.27	4242.50	4057.79	3912.83	3797.39
245,000	22258.06	12025.25	8643.75	6974.78	5990.52	5348.29	4901.16	4575.65	4330.88	4142.33	3994.35	3876.50
250,000	22712.31	12270.67	8820.15	7117.13	6112.78	5457.43	5001.18	4669.03	4419.27	4226.87	4075.86	3955.61
255,000	23166.55	12516.08	8996.55	7259.47	6235.03	5566.58	5101.21	4762.41	4507.65	4311.40	4157.38	4034.73
260,000	23620.80	12761.49	9172.96	7401.81	6357.29	5675.73	5201.23	4855.79	4596.04	4395.94	4238.90	4113.84
265,000	24075.04	13006.91	9349.36	7544.15	6479.54	5784.88	5301.25	4949.17	4684.42	4480.48	4320.41	4192.95
270,000	24529.29	13252.32	9525.76	7686.50	6601.80	5894.03	5401.28	5042.55	4772.81	4565.01	4401.93	4272.06
280,000	25437.78	13743.15	9878.57	7971.18	6846.31	6112.33	5601.32	5229.31	4949.58	4734.09	4564.97	4430.29
290,000	26346.27	14233.97	10231.37	8255.86	7090.82	6330.62	5801.37	5416.07	5126.35	4903.16	4728.00	4588.51
300,000	27254.77	14724.80	10584.18	8540.55	7335.33	6548.92	6001.42	5602.83	5303.12	5072.24	4891.03	4746.74

AMOUNT OF LOAN	NUMBER OF YEARS IN TERM											
	13	14	15	16	17	18	19	20	25	30	35	40
$ 50	0.78	0.76	0.75	0.74	0.73	0.72	0.72	0.71	0.69	0.69	0.68	0.68
100	1.55	1.52	1.49	1.47	1.45	1.44	1.43	1.42	1.38	1.37	1.36	1.36
200	3.09	3.03	2.98	2.93	2.90	2.87	2.85	2.83	2.76	2.73	2.72	2.72
300	4.64	4.54	4.46	4.40	4.35	4.30	4.27	4.24	4.14	4.10	4.08	4.07
400	6.18	6.05	5.95	5.86	5.79	5.74	5.69	5.65	5.52	5.46	5.44	5.43
500	7.72	7.56	7.44	7.33	7.24	7.17	7.11	7.06	6.90	6.83	6.80	6.79
600	9.27	9.08	8.92	8.79	8.69	8.60	8.53	8.47	8.28	8.19	8.16	8.14
700	10.81	10.59	10.41	10.26	10.14	10.03	9.95	9.88	9.65	9.56	9.52	9.50
800	12.35	12.10	11.89	11.72	11.58	11.47	11.37	11.29	11.03	10.92	10.88	10.86
900	13.90	13.61	13.38	13.19	13.03	12.90	12.79	12.70	12.41	12.29	12.24	12.21
1,000	15.44	15.12	14.87	14.65	14.48	14.33	14.21	14.11	13.79	13.65	13.59	13.57
2,000	30.87	30.24	29.73	29.30	28.95	28.66	28.41	28.21	27.58	27.30	27.18	27.13
3,000	46.31	45.36	44.59	43.95	43.42	42.98	42.61	42.31	41.36	40.95	40.77	40.69
4,000	61.74	60.48	59.45	58.60	57.89	57.31	56.82	56.41	55.15	54.60	54.36	54.26
5,000	77.18	75.60	74.31	73.25	72.37	71.63	71.02	70.51	68.93	68.25	67.95	67.82
6,000	92.61	90.72	89.18	87.90	86.84	85.96	85.22	84.61	82.72	81.90	81.54	81.38
7,000	108.05	105.84	104.04	102.55	101.31	100.28	99.43	98.71	96.50	95.55	95.13	94.95
8,000	123.48	120.96	118.90	117.20	115.78	114.61	113.63	112.81	110.29	109.20	108.72	108.51
9,000	138.92	136.08	133.76	131.84	130.26	128.94	127.83	126.91	124.07	122.85	122.31	122.07
10,000	154.35	151.20	148.62	146.49	144.73	143.26	142.04	141.01	137.86	136.50	135.90	135.63
15,000	231.53	226.80	222.93	219.74	217.09	214.89	213.05	211.51	206.79	204.75	203.85	203.45
20,000	308.70	302.40	297.24	292.98	289.45	286.52	284.07	282.01	275.71	272.99	271.79	271.26
25,000	385.88	378.00	371.55	366.23	361.82	358.15	355.08	352.52	344.64	341.24	339.74	339.08
30,000	463.05	453.60	445.06	439.47	434.18	429.78	426.10	423.02	413.57	409.49	407.69	406.89
35,000	540.23	529.20	520.16	512.71	506.54	501.40	497.11	493.52	482.49	477.73	475.64	474.71
40,000	017.40	604.80	594.47	585.96	578.90	573.03	568.13	564.02	551.42	545.98	543.58	542.52
45,000	694.58	680.40	668.78	659.20	651.27	644.66	639.15	634.53	620.35	614.23	611.53	610.34
50,000	771.75	756.00	743.09	732.45	723.63	716.29	710.16	705.03	689.28	682.47	679.48	678.15
55,000	848.93	831.60	817.40	805.69	795.99	787.92	781.18	775.53	758.20	750.72	747.43	745.97
60,000	926.10	907.20	891.71	878.94	868.35	859.55	852.19	846.03	827.13	818.97	815.37	813.78
65,000	1003.28	982.80	966.01	952.18	940.72	931.17	923.21	916.53	896.06	887.21	883.32	881.60
70,000	1080.45	1058.39	1040.32	1025.42	1013.08	1002.80	994.22	987.04	964.98	955.46	951.27	949.41
75,000	1157.63	1133.99	1114.63	1098.67	1085.44	1074.43	1065.24	1057.54	1033.91	1023.71	1019.22	1017.23
80,000	1234.80	1209.59	1188.94	1171.91	1157.80	1146.06	1136.25	1128.04	1102.84	1091.95	1087.16	1085.04
85,000	1311.98	1285.19	1263.25	1245.16	1230.16	1217.69	1207.27	1198.54	1171.77	1160.20	1155.11	1152.06
90,000	1389.15	1360.79	1337.56	1318.40	1302.53	1289.32	1278.29	1269.05	1240.69	1228.45	1223.06	1220.67
95,000	1466.32	1436.39	1411.86	1391.64	1374.89	1360.95	1349.30	1339.55	1309.62	1296.69	1291.01	1288.49
100,000	1543.50	1511.99	1486.17	1464.89	1447.25	1432.57	1420.32	1410.05	1378.55	1364.94	1358.95	1356.30
105,000	1620.67	1587.59	1560.48	1538.13	1519.61	1504.20	1491.33	1480.55	1447.47	1433.19	1426.90	1424.12
110,000	1697.85	1663.19	1634.79	1611.38	1591.98	1575.83	1562.35	1551.06	1516.40	1501.43	1494.85	1491.93
115,000	1775.02	1738.79	1709.10	1684.62	1664.34	1647.46	1633.36	1621.56	1585.33	1569.68	1562.80	1559.75
120,000	1852.20	1814.39	1783.41	1757.87	1736.70	1719.09	1704.38	1692.06	1654.25	1637.93	1630.74	1627.56
125,000	1929.37	1889.99	1857.72	1831.11	1809.06	1790.72	1775.39	1762.56	1723.18	1706.17	1698.69	1695.38
130,000	2006.55	1965.59	1932.02	1904.35	1881.43	1862.34	1846.41	1833.06	1792.11	1774.42	1766.64	1763.19
135,000	2083.72	2041.18	2006.33	1977.60	1953.79	1933.97	1917.43	1903.57	1861.04	1842.67	1834.59	1831.01
140,000	2160.90	2116.78	2080.64	2050.84	2026.15	2005.60	1988.44	1974.07	1929.96	1910.91	1902.53	1898.82
145,000	2238.07	2192.38	2154.95	2124.09	2098.51	2077.23	2059.46	2044.57	1998.89	1979.16	1970.48	1966.64
150,000	2315.25	2267.98	2229.26	2197.33	2170.87	2148.86	2130.47	2115.07	2067.82	2047.41	2038.43	2034.45
155,000	2392.42	2343.58	2303.57	2270.57	2243.24	2220.49	2201.49	2185.58	2136.74	2115.65	2106.38	2102.26
160,000	2469.60	2419.18	2377.87	2343.82	2315.60	2292.12	2272.50	2256.08	2205.67	2183.90	2174.32	2170.08
165,000	2546.77	2494.78	2452.18	2417.06	2387.96	2363.74	2343.52	2326.58	2274.60	2252.15	2242.27	2237.89
170,000	2623.95	2570.38	2526.49	2490.31	2460.32	2435.37	2414.53	2397.08	2343.53	2320.39	2310.22	2305.71
175,000	2701.12	2645.98	2600.80	2563.55	2532.69	2507.00	2485.55	2467.58	2412.45	2388.64	2378.17	2373.52
180,000	2778.30	2721.58	2675.11	2636.80	2605.05	2578.63	2556.57	2538.09	2481.38	2456.89	2446.11	2441.34
185,000	2855.47	2797.18	2749.42	2710.04	2677.41	2650.26	2627.58	2608.59	2550.31	2525.13	2514.06	2509.15
190,000	2932.64	2872.78	2823.72	2783.28	2749.77	2721.89	2698.60	2679.09	2619.23	2593.38	2582.01	2576.97
195,000	3009.82	2948.38	2898.03	2856.53	2822.14	2793.51	2769.61	2749.59	2688.16	2661.63	2649.96	2644.78
200,000	3086.99	3023.98	2972.34	2929.77	2894.50	2865.14	2840.63	2820.10	2757.09	2729.87	2717.90	2712.60
205,000	3164.17	3099.58	3046.65	3003.02	2966.86	2936.77	2911.64	2890.60	2826.01	2798.12	2785.85	2780.41
210,000	3241.34	3175.17	3120.96	3076.26	3039.22	3008.40	2982.66	2961.10	2894.94	2866.37	2853.80	2848.23
215,000	3318.52	3250.77	3195.27	3149.51	3111.58	3080.03	3053.68	3031.60	2963.87	2934.61	2921.75	2916.04
220,000	3395.69	3326.37	3269.57	3222.75	3183.95	3151.66	3124.69	3102.11	3032.80	3002.86	2989.69	2983.86
225,000	3472.87	3401.97	3343.88	3295.99	3256.31	3223.28	3195.71	3172.61	3101.72	3071.11	3057.64	3051.67
230,000	3550.04	3477.57	3418.19	3369.24	3328.67	3294.91	3266.72	3243.11	3170.65	3139.35	3125.59	3119.49
235,000	3627.22	3553.17	3492.50	3442.48	3401.03	3366.54	3337.74	3313.61	3239.58	3207.60	3193.54	3187.30
240,000	3704.39	3628.77	3566.81	3515.73	3473.40	3438.17	3408.75	3384.11	3308.50	3275.85	3261.48	3255.12
245,000	3781.57	3704.37	3641.12	3588.97	3545.76	3509.80	3479.77	3454.62	3377.43	3344.09	3329.43	3322.93
250,000	3858.74	3779.97	3715.43	3662.21	3618.12	3581.43	3550.78	3525.12	3446.36	3412.34	3397.38	3390.75
255,000	3935.92	3855.57	3789.73	3735.46	3690.48	3653.06	3621.80	3595.62	3515.29	3480.59	3465.33	3458.56
260,000	4013.09	3931.17	3864.04	3808.70	3762.85	3724.68	3692.82	3666.12	3584.21	3548.84	3533.27	3526.38
265,000	4090.27	4006.77	3938.35	3881.95	3835.21	3796.31	3763.83	3736.63	3653.14	3617.08	3601.22	3594.19
270,000	4167.44	4082.36	4012.66	3955.19	3907.57	3867.94	3834.85	3807.13	3722.07	3685.33	3669.17	3662.01
280,000	4321.79	4233.56	4161.28	4101.68	4052.29	4011.20	3976.88	3948.13	3859.92	3821.82	3805.06	3797.64
290,000	4476.14	4384.76	4309.89	4248.17	4197.02	4154.45	4118.91	4089.14	3997.77	3958.32	3940.96	3933.27
300,000	4630.49	4535.96	4458.51	4394.66	4341.74	4297.71	4260.94	4230.14	4135.63	4094.81	4076.85	4068.90

16.50%

AMOUNT OF LOAN	NUMBER OF YEARS IN TERM											
	1	2	3	4	5	6	7	8	9	10	11	12
$ 50	4.55	2.47	1.78	1.43	1.23	1.10	1.01	0.95	0.90	0.86	0.83	0.80
100	9.10	4.93	3.55	2.86	2.46	2.20	2.02	1.89	1.79	1.71	1.65	1.60
200	18.20	9.85	7.09	5.72	4.92	4.40	4.03	3.77	3.57	3.42	3.30	3.20
300	27.30	14.77	10.63	8.58	7.38	6.60	6.05	5.65	5.35	5.12	4.94	4.80
400	36.39	19.69	14.17	11.44	9.84	8.79	8.06	7.53	7.14	6.83	6.59	6.40
500	45.49	24.61	17.71	14.30	12.30	10.99	10.08	9.42	8.92	8.54	8.24	8.00
600	54.59	29.53	21.25	17.16	14.76	13.19	12.09	11.30	10.70	10.24	9.88	9.60
700	63.68	34.45	24.79	20.02	17.21	15.38	14.11	13.18	12.49	11.95	11.53	11.20
800	72.78	39.37	28.33	22.88	19.67	17.58	16.12	15.06	14.27	13.66	13.18	12.79
900	81.88	44.29	31.87	25.74	22.13	19.78	18.14	16.95	16.05	15.36	14.82	14.39
1,000	90.97	49.21	35.41	28.60	24.59	21.97	20.15	18.83	17.83	17.07	16.47	15.99
2,000	181.94	98.41	70.81	57.20	49.17	43.94	40.30	37.65	35.66	34.13	32.93	31.98
3,000	272.91	147.61	106.22	85.80	73.76	65.91	60.45	56.48	53.49	51.20	49.40	47.97
4,000	363.88	196.81	141.62	114.39	98.34	87.88	80.60	75.30	71.32	68.26	65.86	63.95
5,000	454.84	246.02	177.03	142.99	122.93	109.85	100.74	94.12	89.15	85.33	82.33	79.94
6,000	545.81	295.22	212.43	171.59	147.51	131.81	120.89	112.95	106.98	102.39	98.79	95.93
7,000	636.78	344.42	247.84	200.18	172.10	153.78	141.04	131.77	124.81	119.45	115.26	111.92
8,000	727.75	393.62	283.24	228.78	196.68	175.75	161.19	150.60	142.64	136.52	131.72	127.90
9,000	818.71	442.83	318.64	257.38	221.27	197.72	181.34	169.42	160.47	153.58	148.18	143.89
10,000	909.68	492.03	354.05	285.98	245.85	219.69	201.48	188.24	178.30	170.65	164.65	159.88
15,000	1364.52	738.04	531.07	428.96	368.77	329.53	302.22	282.36	267.45	255.97	246.97	239.82
20,000	1819.36	984.05	708.09	571.95	491.70	439.37	402.96	376.48	356.59	341.29	329.29	319.75
25,000	2274.20	1230.06	885.11	714.93	614.62	549.21	503.70	470.60	445.74	426.61	411.61	399.69
30,000	2729.03	1476.08	1062.14	857.92	737.54	659.05	604.44	564.72	534.89	511.93	493.94	479.63
35,000	3183.87	1722.09	1239.16	1000.90	860.46	768.89	705.18	658.84	624.04	597.25	576.26	559.56
40,000	3638.71	1968.10	1416.18	1143.89	983.39	878.73	805.92	752.96	713.18	682.57	658.58	639.50
45,000	4093.55	2214.11	1593.20	1286.87	1106.31	988.57	906.66	847.08	802.33	767.90	740.90	719.44
50,000	4548.39	2460.12	1770.22	1429.86	1229.23	1098.41	1007.40	941.20	891.48	853.22	823.22	799.37
55,000	5003.23	2706.13	1947.25	1572.84	1352.15	1208.25	1108.14	1035.32	980.63	938.54	905.55	879.31
60,000	5458.06	2952.15	2124.27	1715.83	1475.08	1318.09	1208.88	1129.44	1069.77	1023.86	987.87	959.25
65,000	5912.90	3198.16	2301.29	1858.81	1598.00	1427.93	1309.62	1223.56	1158.92	1109.18	1070.19	1039.18
70,000	6367.74	3444.17	2478.31	2001.80	1720.92	1537.77	1410.36	1317.68	1248.07	1194.50	1152.51	1119.12
75,000	6822.58	3690.18	2655.33	2144.78	1843.84	1647.61	1511.10	1411.80	1337.22	1279.82	1234.83	1199.06
80,000	7277.42	3936.19	2832.36	2287.77	1966.77	1757.45	1611.84	1505.92	1426.36	1365.14	1317.16	1278.99
85,000	7732.25	4182.20	3009.38	2430.75	2089.69	1867.29	1712.58	1600.04	1515.51	1450.46	1399.48	1358.93
90,000	8187.09	4428.22	3186.40	2573.74	2212.61	1977.13	1813.32	1694.16	1604.66	1535.79	1481.80	1438.87
95,000	8641.93	4674.23	3363.42	2716.72	2335.53	2086.97	1914.05	1788.28	1693.81	1621.11	1564.12	1518.80
100,000	9096.77	4920.24	3540.44	2859.71	2458.46	2196.81	2014.79	1882.40	1782.95	1706.43	1646.44	1598.74
105,000	9551.61	5166.25	3717.47	3002.69	2581.38	2306.65	2115.53	1976.52	1872.10	1791.75	1728.77	1678.68
110,000	10006.45	5412.26	3894.49	3145.68	2704.30	2416.49	2216.27	2070.64	1961.25	1877.07	1811.09	1758.61
115,000	10461.28	5658.28	4071.51	3288.66	2827.22	2526.33	2317.01	2164.76	2050.40	1962.39	1893.41	1838.55
120,000	10916.12	5904.29	4248.53	3431.65	2950.15	2636.17	2417.75	2258.88	2139.54	2047.71	1975.73	1918.49
125,000	11370.96	6150.30	4425.55	3574.63	3073.07	2746.01	2518.49	2353.00	2228.69	2133.03	2058.05	1998.42
130,000	11825.80	6396.31	4602.57	3717.62	3195.99	2855.85	2619.23	2447.12	2317.84	2218.35	2140.37	2078.36
135,000	12280.64	6642.32	4779.60	3860.60	3318.92	2965.69	2719.97	2541.24	2406.99	2303.68	2222.70	2158.30
140,000	12735.47	6888.33	4956.62	4003.59	3441.84	3075.53	2820.71	2635.36	2496.13	2389.00	2305.02	2238.23
145,000	13190.31	7134.35	5133.64	4146.57	3564.76	3185.37	2921.45	2729.48	2585.28	2474.32	2387.34	2318.17
150,000	13645.15	7380.36	5310.66	4289.56	3687.68	3295.21	3022.19	2823.60	2674.43	2559.64	2469.66	2398.11
155,000	14099.99	7626.37	5487.68	4432.54	3810.61	3405.05	3122.93	2917.72	2763.57	2644.96	2551.98	2478.04
160,000	14554.83	7872.38	5664.71	4575.53	3933.53	3514.89	3223.67	3011.84	2852.72	2730.28	2634.31	2557.98
165,000	15009.67	8118.39	5841.73	4718.51	4056.45	3624.73	3324.41	3105.96	2941.87	2815.60	2716.63	2637.92
170,000	15464.50	8364.40	6018.75	4861.50	4179.37	3734.57	3425.15	3200.08	3031.02	2900.92	2798.95	2717.85
175,000	15919.34	8610.42	6195.77	5004.48	4302.30	3844.42	3525.89	3294.20	3120.16	2986.25	2881.27	2797.79
180,000	16374.18	8856.43	6372.79	5147.47	4425.22	3954.26	3626.63	3388.32	3209.31	3071.57	2963.59	2877.73
185,000	16829.02	9102.44	6549.82	5290.45	4548.14	4064.10	3727.36	3482.44	3298.46	3156.89	3045.92	2957.66
190,000	17283.86	9348.45	6726.84	5433.44	4671.06	4173.94	3828.10	3576.56	3387.61	3242.21	3128.24	3037.60
195,000	17738.69	9594.46	6903.86	5576.42	4793.99	4283.78	3928.84	3670.68	3476.75	3327.53	3210.56	3117.54
200,000	18193.53	9840.48	7080.88	5719.41	4916.91	4393.62	4029.58	3764.80	3565.90	3412.85	3292.88	3197.47
205,000	18648.37	10086.49	7257.90	5862.39	5039.83	4503.46	4130.32	3858.92	3655.05	3498.17	3375.20	3277.41
210,000	19103.21	10332.50	7434.93	6005.38	5162.75	4613.30	4231.06	3953.04	3744.20	3583.49	3457.53	3357.35
215,000	19558.05	10578.51	7611.95	6148.36	5285.68	4723.14	4331.80	4047.16	3833.34	3668.81	3539.85	3437.28
220,000	20012.89	10824.52	7788.97	6291.35	5408.60	4832.98	4432.54	4141.28	3922.49	3754.14	3622.17	3517.22
225,000	20467.72	11070.53	7965.99	6434.33	5531.52	4942.82	4533.28	4235.40	4011.64	3839.46	3704.49	3597.16
230,000	20922.56	11316.55	8143.01	6577.32	5654.44	5052.66	4634.02	4329.52	4100.79	3924.78	3786.81	3677.09
235,000	21377.40	11562.56	8320.03	6720.30	5777.37	5162.50	4734.76	4423.64	4189.93	4010.10	3869.13	3757.03
240,000	21832.24	11808.57	8497.06	6863.29	5900.29	5272.34	4835.50	4517.76	4279.08	4095.42	3951.46	3836.97
245,000	22287.08	12054.58	8674.08	7006.27	6023.21	5382.18	4936.24	4611.88	4368.23	4180.74	4033.78	3916.90
250,000	22741.91	12300.59	8851.10	7149.26	6146.14	5492.02	5036.98	4706.00	4457.38	4266.06	4116.10	3996.84
255,000	23196.75	12546.60	9028.12	7292.24	6269.06	5601.86	5137.72	4800.12	4546.52	4351.38	4198.42	4076.78
260,000	23651.59	12792.62	9205.14	7435.23	6391.98	5711.70	5238.46	4894.24	4635.67	4436.70	4280.74	4156.71
265,000	24106.43	13038.63	9382.17	7578.21	6514.90	5821.54	5339.20	4988.36	4724.82	4522.03	4363.07	4236.65
270,000	24561.27	13284.64	9559.19	7721.20	6637.83	5931.38	5439.94	5082.48	4813.97	4607.35	4445.39	4316.59
280,000	25470.94	13776.66	9913.23	8007.17	6883.67	6151.06	5641.41	5270.72	4992.26	4777.99	4610.03	4476.46
290,000	26380.62	14268.69	10267.28	8293.14	7129.52	6370.74	5842.89	5458.96	5170.55	4948.63	4774.68	4636.33
300,000	27290.30	14760.71	10621.32	8579.11	7375.36	6590.42	6044.37	5647.20	5348.85	5119.27	4939.32	4796.21

MONTHLY AMORTIZING PAYMENTS 16.50%

AMOUNT OF LOAN	NUMBER OF YEARS IN TERM											
	13	14	15	16	17	18	19	20	25	30	35	40
$ 50	0.79	0.77	0.76	0.75	0.74	0.73	0.72	0.72	0.70	0.70	0.69	0.69
100	1.57	1.53	1.51	1.49	1.47	1.46	1.44	1.43	1.40	1.39	1.38	1.38
200	3.13	3.06	3.01	2.97	2.94	2.91	2.88	2.86	2.80	2.78	2.76	2.76
300	4.69	4.59	4.52	4.45	4.40	4.36	4.32	4.29	4.20	4.16	4.14	4.14
400	6.25	6.12	6.02	5.94	5.87	5.81	5.76	5.72	5.60	5.55	5.52	5.51
500	7.81	7.65	7.52	7.42	7.33	7.26	7.20	7.15	7.00	6.93	6.90	6.89
600	9.37	9.18	9.03	8.90	8.80	8.71	8.64	8.58	8.39	8.32	8.28	8.27
700	10.93	10.71	10.53	10.38	10.26	10.16	10.08	10.01	9.79	9.70	9.66	9.64
800	12.49	12.24	12.03	11.87	11.73	11.61	11.52	11.44	11.19	11.09	11.04	11.02
900	14.05	13.77	13.54	13.35	13.19	13.06	12.96	12.87	12.59	12.47	12.42	12.40
1,000	15.61	15.30	15.04	14.83	14.66	14.51	14.39	14.29	13.99	13.86	13.80	13.77
2,000	31.21	30.59	30.08	29.66	29.31	29.02	28.78	28.58	27.97	27.71	27.59	27.54
3,000	46.82	45.88	45.12	44.49	43.97	43.53	43.17	42.87	41.95	41.56	41.39	41.31
4,000	62.42	61.17	60.15	59.31	58.62	58.04	57.56	57.16	55.93	55.41	55.18	55.08
5,000	78.02	76.46	75.19	74.14	73.27	72.55	71.95	71.45	69.92	69.26	68.98	68.85
6,000	93.63	91.76	90.23	88.97	87.93	87.06	86.34	85.74	83.90	83.11	82.77	82.62
7,000	109.23	107.05	105.26	103.80	102.58	101.57	100.73	100.03	97.88	96.97	96.57	96.39
8,000	124.83	122.34	120.30	118.62	117.24	116.08	115.12	114.32	111.86	110.82	110.36	110.16
9,000	140.44	137.63	135.34	133.45	131.89	130.59	129.51	128.61	125.85	124.67	124.16	123.93
10,000	156.04	152.92	150.38	148.28	146.54	145.10	143.90	142.90	139.83	138.52	137.95	137.70
15,000	234.06	229.38	225.56	222.41	219.81	217.65	215.85	214.34	209.74	207.78	206.92	206.55
20,000	312.08	305.84	300.75	296.55	293.08	290.20	287.79	285.79	279.65	277.03	275.90	275.40
25,000	390.09	382.30	375.93	370.69	366.35	362.75	359.74	357.23	349.57	346.29	344.87	344.24
30,000	468.11	458.76	451.12	444.82	439.62	435.29	431.69	428.68	419.48	415.55	413.84	413.09
35,000	546.13	535.22	526.30	518.96	512.89	507.84	503.64	500.12	489.39	484.81	482.81	481.94
40,000	024.15	611.68	601.49	593.10	586.16	580.39	575.58	571.57	559.30	554.06	551.79	550.79
45,000	702.17	688.14	676.67	667.23	659.42	652.94	647.53	643.01	629.22	623.32	620.76	619.64
50,000	780.18	764.60	751.86	741.37	732.69	725.49	719.48	714.46	699.13	692.58	689.73	688.48
55,000	858.20	841.06	827.04	815.51	805.96	798.03	791.42	785.90	769.04	761.84	758.70	757.33
60,000	936.22	917.52	902.23	889.64	879.23	870.58	863.37	857.35	838.95	831.09	827.68	826.18
65,000	1014.24	993.98	977.42	963.78	952.50	943.13	935.32	928.79	908.86	900.35	896.65	895.03
70,000	1092.25	1070.44	1052.60	1037.92	1025.77	1015.68	1007.27	1000.24	978.78	969.61	965.62	963.88
75,000	1170.27	1146.90	1127.79	1112.05	1099.04	1088.23	1079.21	1071.68	1048.69	1038.87	1034.60	1032.72
80,000	1248.29	1223.36	1202.97	1186.19	1172.31	1160.77	1151.16	1143.13	1118.60	1108.12	1103.57	1101.57
85,000	1326.31	1299.82	1278.16	1260.33	1245.57	1233.32	1223.11	1214.57	1188.51	1177.38	1172.54	1170.42
90,000	1404.33	1376.28	1353.34	1334.46	1318.84	1305.87	1295.06	1286.02	1258.43	1246.64	1241.51	1239.27
95,000	1482.34	1452.74	1428.53	1408.60	1392.11	1378.42	1367.00	1357.46	1328.34	1316.00	1310.40	1000.12
100,000	1560.36	1529.20	1503.71	1482.73	1465.38	1450.97	1438.95	1428.91	1398.25	1385.15	1379.46	1376.96
105,000	1638.38	1605.66	1578.90	1556.87	1538.65	1523.51	1510.90	1500.35	1468.16	1454.41	1448.43	1445.81
110,000	1716.40	1682.12	1654.08	1631.01	1611.92	1596.06	1582.84	1571.80	1538.07	1523.67	1517.40	1514.66
115,000	1794.42	1758.58	1729.27	1705.14	1685.19	1666.61	1654.79	1643.24	1607.99	1592.93	1586.38	1583.51
120,000	1872.43	1835.04	1804.46	1779.28	1758.46	1741.16	1726.74	1714.69	1677.90	1662.18	1655.35	1652.36
125,000	1950.45	1911.50	1879.64	1853.42	1831.72	1813.71	1798.69	1786.13	1747.81	1731.44	1724.32	1721.20
130,000	2028.47	1987.96	1954.83	1927.55	1904.99	1886.25	1870.63	1857.58	1817.72	1800.70	1793.30	1790.05
135,000	2106.49	2064.42	2030.01	2001.69	1978.26	1958.80	1942.58	1929.02	1887.64	1869.95	1862.27	1858.90
140,000	2184.50	2140.88	2105.20	2075.83	2051.53	2031.35	2014.53	2000.47	1957.55	1939.21	1931.24	1927.75
145,000	2262.52	2217.34	2180.38	2149.96	2124.80	2103.90	2086.48	2071.91	2027.46	2008.47	2000.21	1996.60
150,000	2340.54	2293.80	2255.57	2224.10	2198.07	2176.45	2158.42	2143.36	2097.37	2077.73	2069.19	2065.44
155,000	2418.56	2370.26	2330.75	2298.24	2271.34	2248.99	2230.37	2214.80	2167.28	2146.98	2138.16	2134.29
160,000	2496.58	2446.72	2405.94	2372.37	2344.61	2321.54	2302.32	2286.25	2237.20	2216.24	2207.13	2203.14
165,000	2574.59	2523.18	2481.12	2446.51	2417.88	2394.09	2374.26	2357.69	2307.11	2285.50	2276.10	2271.99
170,000	2652.61	2599.64	2556.31	2520.65	2491.14	2466.64	2446.21	2429.14	2377.02	2354.76	2345.08	2340.84
175,000	2730.63	2676.10	2631.50	2594.78	2564.41	2539.19	2518.16	2500.58	2446.93	2424.01	2414.05	2409.68
180,000	2808.65	2752.56	2706.68	2668.92	2637.68	2611.73	2590.11	2572.03	2516.85	2493.27	2483.02	2478.53
185,000	2886.67	2829.02	2781.87	2743.05	2710.95	2684.28	2662.05	2643.47	2586.76	2562.53	2551.99	2547.38
190,000	2964.68	2905.48	2857.05	2817.19	2784.22	2756.83	2734.00	2714.92	2656.67	2631.79	2620.97	2616.23
195,000	3042.70	2981.94	2932.24	2891.33	2857.49	2829.38	2805.95	2786.36	2726.58	2701.04	2689.94	2685.08
200,000	3120.72	3058.40	3007.42	2965.46	2930.76	2901.93	2877.89	2857.81	2796.49	2770.30	2758.91	2753.92
205,000	3198.74	3134.86	3082.61	3039.60	3004.03	2974.47	2949.84	2929.25	2866.41	2839.56	2827.89	2822.77
210,000	3276.75	3211.32	3157.79	3113.74	3077.29	3047.02	3021.79	3000.70	2936.32	2908.82	2896.86	2891.62
215,000	3354.77	3287.78	3232.98	3187.87	3150.56	3119.57	3093.74	3072.14	3006.23	2978.07	2965.83	2960.47
220,000	3432.79	3364.24	3308.16	3262.01	3223.83	3192.12	3165.68	3143.59	3076.14	3047.33	3034.80	3029.32
225,000	3510.81	3440.70	3383.35	3336.15	3297.10	3264.67	3237.63	3215.03	3146.06	3116.59	3103.78	3098.16
230,000	3588.83	3517.16	3458.53	3410.28	3370.37	3337.21	3309.58	3286.48	3215.97	3185.85	3172.75	3167.01
235,000	3666.84	3593.62	3533.72	3484.42	3443.64	3409.76	3381.53	3357.92	3285.88	3255.10	3241.72	3235.86
240,000	3744.86	3670.08	3608.91	3558.56	3516.91	3482.31	3453.47	3429.37	3355.79	3324.36	3310.69	3304.71
245,000	3822.88	3746.54	3684.09	3632.69	3590.18	3554.86	3525.42	3500.81	3425.70	3393.62	3379.67	3373.56
250,000	3900.90	3823.00	3759.28	3706.83	3663.44	3627.41	3597.37	3572.26	3495.62	3462.88	3448.64	3442.40
255,000	3978.91	3899.46	3834.46	3780.97	3736.71	3699.95	3669.31	3643.70	3565.53	3532.13	3517.61	3511.25
260,000	4056.93	3975.92	3909.65	3855.10	3809.98	3772.50	3741.26	3715.15	3635.44	3601.39	3586.59	3580.10
265,000	4134.95	4052.38	3984.83	3929.24	3883.25	3845.05	3813.21	3786.59	3705.35	3670.65	3655.56	3648.95
270,000	4212.97	4128.84	4060.02	4003.38	3956.52	3917.60	3885.16	3858.04	3775.27	3739.90	3724.53	3717.80
280,000	4369.00	4281.76	4210.39	4151.65	4103.06	4062.69	4029.05	4000.93	3915.09	3878.42	3862.48	3855.49
290,000	4525.04	4434.68	4360.76	4299.92	4249.59	4207.79	4172.95	4143.82	4054.91	4016.93	4000.42	3993.19
300,000	4681.08	4587.60	4511.13	4448.19	4396.13	4352.89	4316.84	4286.71	4194.74	4155.45	4138.37	4130.88

119

MONTHLY AMORTIZING PAYMENTS

AMOUNT OF LOAN	NUMBER OF YEARS IN TERM											
	1	2	3	4	5	6	7	8	9	10	11	12
$ 50	4.56	2.47	1.78	1.44	1.24	1.11	1.02	0.95	0.90	0.87	0.84	0.81
100	9.11	4.94	3.56	2.88	2.48	2.22	2.03	1.90	1.80	1.73	1.67	1.62
200	18.22	9.87	7.11	5.75	4.95	4.43	4.06	3.80	3.60	3.45	3.33	3.24
300	27.33	14.80	10.66	8.62	7.42	6.64	6.09	5.70	5.40	5.17	4.99	4.85
400	36.44	19.73	14.22	11.50	9.89	8.85	8.12	7.59	7.20	6.89	6.66	6.47
500	45.55	24.67	17.77	14.37	12.36	11.06	10.15	9.49	9.00	8.62	8.32	8.08
600	54.66	29.60	21.32	17.24	14.84	13.27	12.18	11.39	10.79	10.34	9.98	9.70
700	63.77	34.53	24.87	20.11	17.31	15.48	14.21	13.29	12.59	12.06	11.64	11.31
800	72.87	39.46	28.43	22.99	19.78	17.69	16.24	15.18	14.39	13.78	13.31	12.93
900	81.98	44.40	31.98	25.86	22.25	19.90	18.27	17.08	16.19	15.50	14.97	14.54
1,000	91.09	49.33	35.53	28.73	24.72	22.11	20.30	18.98	17.99	17.23	16.63	16.16
2,000	182.18	98.65	71.06	57.46	49.44	44.22	40.59	37.95	35.97	34.45	33.26	32.31
3,000	273.26	147.97	106.59	86.18	74.16	66.33	60.88	56.92	53.95	51.67	49.88	48.46
4,000	364.35	197.29	142.12	114.91	98.88	88.43	81.17	75.89	71.94	68.89	66.51	64.62
5,000	455.44	246.62	177.65	143.63	123.60	110.54	101.46	94.87	89.92	86.11	83.14	80.77
6,000	546.52	295.94	213.18	172.36	148.32	132.65	121.75	113.84	107.90	103.34	99.76	96.92
7,000	637.61	345.26	248.70	201.09	173.03	154.75	142.05	132.81	125.88	120.56	116.39	113.08
8,000	728.69	394.58	284.23	229.81	197.75	176.86	162.34	151.78	143.87	137.78	133.01	129.23
9,000	819.78	443.91	319.76	258.54	222.47	198.97	182.63	170.76	161.85	155.00	149.64	145.38
10,000	910.87	493.23	355.29	287.26	247.19	221.07	202.92	189.73	179.83	172.22	166.27	161.53
15,000	1366.30	739.84	532.93	430.89	370.78	331.61	304.38	284.59	269.74	258.33	249.40	242.30
20,000	1821.73	986.45	710.57	574.52	494.37	442.14	405.84	379.45	359.66	344.44	332.53	323.06
25,000	2277.16	1233.06	888.22	718.15	617.96	552.68	507.29	474.32	449.57	430.55	415.66	403.83
30,000	2732.59	1479.67	1065.86	861.78	741.56	663.21	608.75	569.18	539.48	516.66	498.79	484.59
35,000	3188.02	1726.28	1243.50	1005.41	865.15	773.75	710.21	664.04	629.39	602.76	581.92	565.36
40,000	3643.45	1972.89	1421.14	1149.04	988.74	884.28	811.67	758.90	719.31	688.87	665.05	646.12
45,000	4098.88	2219.51	1598.78	1292.67	1112.33	994.81	913.13	853.76	809.22	774.98	748.18	726.89
50,000	4554.31	2466.12	1776.43	1436.30	1235.92	1105.35	1014.58	948.63	899.13	861.09	831.31	807.65
55,000	5009.74	2712.73	1954.07	1579.93	1359.51	1215.88	1116.04	1043.49	989.04	947.20	914.44	888.42
60,000	5465.17	2959.34	2131.71	1723.56	1483.11	1326.42	1217.50	1138.35	1078.96	1033.31	997.57	969.18
65,000	5920.60	3205.95	2309.35	1867.19	1606.70	1436.95	1318.96	1233.21	1168.87	1119.41	1080.70	1049.95
70,000	6376.04	3452.56	2487.00	2010.82	1730.29	1547.49	1420.42	1328.07	1258.78	1205.52	1163.83	1130.71
75,000	6831.47	3699.17	2664.64	2154.44	1853.88	1658.02	1521.87	1422.94	1348.69	1291.63	1246.96	1211.48
80,000	7286.90	3945.78	2842.28	2298.07	1977.47	1768.55	1623.33	1517.80	1438.61	1377.74	1330.09	1292.24
85,000	7742.33	4192.39	3019.92	2441.70	2101.06	1879.09	1724.79	1612.66	1528.52	1463.85	1413.22	1373.00
90,000	8197.76	4439.01	3197.56	2585.33	2224.66	1989.62	1826.25	1707.52	1618.43	1549.96	1496.35	1453.77
95,000	8653.19	4685.62	3375.21	2728.96	2348.25	2100.16	1927.71	1802.39	1708.35	1636.06	1579.48	1534.53
100,000	9108.62	4932.23	3552.85	2872.59	2471.84	2210.69	2029.16	1897.25	1798.26	1722.17	1662.61	1615.30
105,000	9564.05	5178.84	3730.49	3016.22	2595.43	2321.23	2130.62	1992.11	1888.17	1808.28	1745.74	1696.06
110,000	10019.48	5425.45	3908.13	3159.85	2719.02	2431.76	2232.08	2086.97	1978.08	1894.39	1828.87	1776.83
115,000	10474.91	5672.06	4085.77	3303.48	2842.62	2542.29	2333.54	2181.83	2068.00	1980.50	1912.00	1857.59
120,000	10930.34	5918.67	4263.42	3447.11	2966.21	2652.83	2435.00	2276.70	2157.91	2066.61	1995.13	1938.36
125,000	11385.77	6165.28	4441.06	3590.74	3089.80	2763.36	2536.45	2371.56	2247.82	2152.71	2078.26	2019.12
130,000	11841.20	6411.89	4618.70	3734.37	3213.39	2873.90	2637.91	2466.42	2337.73	2238.82	2161.39	2099.89
135,000	12296.64	6658.51	4796.34	3878.00	3336.98	2984.43	2739.37	2561.28	2427.65	2324.93	2244.52	2180.65
140,000	12752.07	6905.12	4973.99	4021.63	3460.57	3094.97	2840.83	2656.14	2517.56	2411.04	2327.65	2261.42
145,000	13207.50	7151.73	5151.63	4165.26	3584.17	3205.50	2942.29	2751.01	2607.47	2497.15	2410.78	2342.18
150,000	13662.93	7398.34	5329.27	4308.88	3707.76	3316.03	3043.74	2845.87	2697.38	2583.26	2493.91	2422.95
155,000	14118.36	7644.95	5506.91	4452.51	3831.35	3426.57	3145.20	2940.73	2787.30	2669.36	2577.04	2503.71
160,000	14573.79	7891.56	5684.55	4596.14	3954.94	3537.10	3246.66	3035.59	2877.21	2755.47	2660.17	2584.47
165,000	15029.22	8138.17	5862.20	4739.77	4078.53	3647.64	3348.12	3130.46	2967.12	2841.58	2743.30	2665.24
170,000	15484.65	8384.78	6039.84	4883.40	4202.12	3758.17	3449.57	3225.32	3057.03	2927.69	2826.43	2746.00
175,000	15940.08	8631.39	6217.48	5027.03	4325.72	3868.71	3551.03	3320.18	3146.95	3013.80	2909.56	2826.77
180,000	16395.51	8878.01	6395.12	5170.66	4449.31	3979.24	3652.49	3415.04	3236.86	3099.91	2992.69	2907.53
185,000	16850.94	9124.62	6572.76	5314.29	4572.90	4089.77	3753.95	3509.90	3326.77	3186.01	3075.82	2988.30
190,000	17306.37	9371.23	6750.41	5457.92	4696.49	4200.31	3855.41	3604.77	3416.69	3272.12	3158.95	3069.06
195,000	17761.80	9617.84	6928.05	5601.55	4820.08	4310.84	3956.86	3699.63	3506.60	3358.23	3242.08	3149.83
200,000	18217.24	9864.45	7105.69	5745.18	4943.68	4421.38	4058.32	3794.49	3596.51	3444.34	3325.21	3230.59
205,000	18672.67	10111.06	7283.33	5888.81	5067.27	4531.91	4159.78	3889.35	3686.42	3530.45	3408.34	3311.36
210,000	19128.10	10357.67	7460.98	6032.44	5190.86	4642.45	4261.24	3984.21	3776.34	3616.56	3491.47	3392.12
215,000	19583.53	10604.28	7638.62	6176.07	5314.45	4752.98	4362.70	4079.08	3866.25	3702.66	3574.60	3472.89
220,000	20038.96	10850.89	7816.26	6319.69	5438.04	4863.52	4464.15	4173.94	3956.16	3788.77	3657.73	3553.65
225,000	20494.39	11097.51	7993.90	6463.32	5561.63	4974.05	4565.61	4268.80	4046.07	3874.88	3740.86	3634.42
230,000	20949.82	11344.12	8171.54	6606.95	5685.23	5084.58	4667.07	4363.66	4135.99	3960.99	3823.99	3715.18
235,000	21405.25	11590.73	8349.19	6750.58	5808.82	5195.12	4768.53	4458.53	4225.90	4047.10	3907.12	3795.94
240,000	21860.68	11837.34	8526.83	6894.21	5932.41	5305.65	4869.99	4553.39	4315.81	4133.21	3990.25	3876.71
245,000	22316.11	12083.95	8704.47	7037.84	6056.00	5416.19	4971.44	4648.25	4405.72	4219.31	4073.38	3957.47
250,000	22771.54	12330.56	8882.11	7181.47	6179.59	5526.72	5072.90	4743.11	4495.64	4305.42	4156.51	4038.24
255,000	23226.97	12577.17	9059.75	7325.10	6303.18	5637.26	5174.36	4837.97	4585.55	4391.53	4239.64	4119.00
260,000	23682.40	12823.78	9237.40	7468.73	6426.78	5747.79	5275.82	4932.84	4675.46	4477.64	4322.77	4199.77
265,000	24137.84	13070.39	9415.04	7612.36	6550.37	5858.32	5377.28	5027.70	4765.37	4563.75	4405.90	4280.53
270,000	24593.27	13317.01	9592.68	7755.99	6673.96	5968.86	5478.73	5122.56	4855.29	4649.86	4489.03	4361.30
280,000	25504.13	13810.23	9947.97	8043.25	6921.14	6189.93	5681.65	5312.28	5035.11	4822.07	4655.29	4522.83
290,000	26414.99	14303.45	10303.25	8330.51	7168.33	6411.00	5884.57	5502.01	5214.94	4994.29	4821.55	4684.36
300,000	27325.85	14796.67	10658.53	8617.76	7415.51	6632.06	6087.48	5691.73	5394.76	5166.51	4987.81	4845.89

AMOUNT OF LOAN	NUMBER OF YEARS IN TERM											
	13	14	15	16	17	18	19	20	25	30	35	40
$ 50	0.79	0.78	0.77	0.76	0.75	0.74	0.73	0.73	0.71	0.71	0.70	0.70
100	1.58	1.55	1.53	1.51	1.49	1.47	1.46	1.45	1.42	1.41	1.40	1.40
200	3.16	3.10	3.05	3.01	2.97	2.94	2.92	2.90	2.84	2.82	2.80	2.80
300	4.74	4.64	4.57	4.51	4.46	4.41	4.38	4.35	4.26	4.22	4.20	4.20
400	6.31	6.19	6.09	6.01	5.94	5.88	5.84	5.80	5.68	5.63	5.60	5.60
500	7.89	7.74	7.61	7.51	7.42	7.35	7.29	7.24	7.09	7.03	7.00	6.99
600	9.47	9.28	9.13	9.01	8.91	8.82	8.75	8.69	8.51	8.44	8.40	8.39
700	11.05	10.83	10.65	10.51	10.39	10.29	10.21	10.14	9.93	9.84	9.80	9.79
800	12.62	12.38	12.18	12.01	11.87	11.76	11.67	11.59	11.35	11.25	11.20	11.19
900	14.20	13.92	13.70	13.51	13.36	13.23	13.12	13.04	12.77	12.65	12.60	12.58
1,000	15.78	15.47	15.22	15.01	14.84	14.70	14.58	14.48	14.18	14.06	14.00	13.98
2,000	31.55	30.93	30.43	30.02	29.68	29.39	29.16	28.96	28.36	28.11	28.00	27.96
3,000	47.32	46.40	45.64	45.02	44.51	44.09	43.73	43.44	42.54	42.17	42.00	41.93
4,000	63.10	61.86	60.86	60.03	59.35	58.78	58.31	57.92	56.72	56.22	56.00	55.91
5,000	78.87	77.33	76.07	75.04	74.18	73.48	72.89	72.40	70.90	70.27	70.00	69.89
6,000	94.64	92.79	91.28	90.04	89.02	88.17	87.46	86.87	85.08	84.33	84.00	83.86
7,000	110.42	108.26	106.50	105.05	103.86	102.86	102.04	101.35	99.26	98.38	98.00	97.84
8,000	126.19	123.72	121.71	120.06	118.69	117.56	116.62	115.83	113.44	112.44	112.00	111.82
9,000	141.96	139.19	136.92	135.06	133.53	132.25	131.19	130.31	127.62	126.49	126.00	125.79
10,000	157.73	154.65	152.14	150.07	148.36	146.95	145.77	144.79	141.80	140.54	140.00	139.77
15,000	236.60	231.98	228.20	225.10	222.54	220.42	218.65	217.18	212.70	210.81	210.00	209.65
20,000	315.46	309.30	304.27	300.13	296.72	293.89	291.53	289.57	283.60	281.08	280.00	279.53
25,000	394.33	386.63	380.34	375.17	370.90	367.36	364.42	361.96	354.50	351.35	350.00	349.41
30,000	473.19	463.95	456.40	450.20	445.08	440.83	437.30	434.35	425.40	421.62	420.00	419.30
35,000	552.06	541.27	532.47	525.23	519.26	514.30	510.18	506.74	496.30	491.89	490.00	489.18
40,000	630.92	618.60	608.53	600.26	593.44	587.77	583.06	579.13	567.20	562.16	560.00	559.06
45,000	709.79	695.92	684.60	675.30	667.61	661.24	655.95	651.52	638.10	632.43	630.00	628.94
50,000	788.65	773.25	760.67	750.33	741.79	734.72	728.83	723.91	709.00	702.70	699.99	698.82
55,000	867.51	850.57	836.73	825.36	815.97	808.19	801.71	796.31	779.90	772.97	769.99	768.70
60,000	946.38	927.89	912.80	900.39	890.15	881.66	874.59	868.70	850.80	843.24	839.99	838.59
65,000	1025.24	1005.22	988.86	975.43	964.33	955.13	947.47	941.09	921.70	913.51	909.99	908.47
70,000	1104.11	1082.54	1064.93	1050.46	1038.51	1028.60	1020.36	1013.48	992.60	983.78	979.99	978.35
75,000	1182.97	1159.87	1141.00	1125.49	1112.69	1102.07	1093.24	1085.87	1063.50	1054.05	1049.99	1048.23
80,000	1261.84	1237.19	1217.06	1200.52	1186.87	1175.54	1166.12	1158.26	1134.40	1124.32	1119.99	1118.11
85,000	1340.70	1314.52	1293.13	1275.55	1261.04	1249.01	1239.00	1230.65	1205.30	1194.59	1189.99	1187.99
90,000	1419.57	1391.84	1369.19	1350.59	1335.22	1322.48	1311.89	1303.04	1276.20	1264.86	1259.99	1257.88
95,000	1498.43	1469.16	1445.26	1425.62	1409.40	1395.95	1384.77	1375.43	1347.10	1335.13	1329.99	1327.76
100,000	1577.30	1546.49	1521.33	1500.65	1483.58	1469.43	1457.65	1447.82	1418.00	1405.40	1399.98	1397.64
105,000	1656.16	1623.81	1597.39	1575.68	1557.76	1542.90	1530.53	1520.22	1488.90	1475.67	1469.98	1467.52
110,000	1735.02	1701.14	1673.46	1650.72	1631.94	1616.37	1603.41	1592.61	1559.80	1545.94	1539.98	1537.40
115,000	1813.89	1778.46	1749.52	1725.75	1706.12	1689.84	1676.30	1665.00	1630.70	1616.21	1609.98	1607.29
120,000	1892.75	1855.78	1825.60	1800.78	1780.30	1763.31	1749.18	1737.40	1701.60	1686.48	1679.98	1677.17
125,000	1971.62	1933.11	1901.66	1875.81	1854.47	1836.78	1822.06	1809.78	1772.50	1756.75	1749.98	1747.05
130,000	2050.48	2010.43	1977.72	1950.85	1928.65	1910.25	1894.94	1882.17	1843.40	1827.02	1819.98	1816.93
135,000	2129.35	2087.76	2053.79	2025.88	2002.83	1983.72	1967.83	1954.56	1914.30	1897.29	1889.98	1886.81
140,000	2208.21	2165.08	2129.85	2100.91	2077.01	2057.19	2040.71	2026.95	1985.20	1967.56	1959.98	1956.69
145,000	2287.08	2242.40	2205.92	2175.94	2151.19	2130.66	2113.59	2099.34	2056.10	2037.83	2029.98	2026.58
150,000	2365.94	2319.73	2281.99	2250.98	2225.37	2204.14	2186.47	2171.73	2127.00	2108.10	2099.97	2096.46
155,000	2444.81	2397.05	2358.05	2326.01	2299.55	2277.61	2259.35	2244.13	2197.90	2178.37	2169.97	2166.34
160,000	2523.67	2474.38	2434.12	2401.04	2373.73	2351.08	2332.24	2316.52	2268.80	2248.64	2239.97	2236.22
165,000	2602.53	2551.70	2510.18	2476.07	2447.90	2424.55	2405.12	2388.91	2339.70	2318.91	2309.97	2306.10
170,000	2681.40	2629.03	2586.25	2551.10	2522.08	2498.02	2478.00	2461.30	2410.60	2389.18	2379.97	2375.98
175,000	2760.26	2706.35	2662.32	2626.14	2596.26	2571.49	2550.88	2533.69	2481.50	2459.45	2449.97	2445.87
180,000	2839.13	2783.67	2738.38	2701.17	2670.44	2644.96	2623.77	2606.08	2552.40	2529.72	2519.97	2515.75
185,000	2917.99	2861.00	2814.45	2776.20	2744.62	2718.43	2696.65	2678.47	2623.30	2599.99	2589.97	2585.63
190,000	2996.86	2938.32	2890.52	2851.23	2818.80	2791.90	2769.53	2750.86	2694.20	2670.26	2659.97	2655.51
195,000	3075.72	3015.65	2966.58	2926.27	2892.98	2865.38	2842.41	2823.25	2765.10	2740.53	2729.97	2725.39
200,000	3154.59	3092.97	3042.65	3001.30	2967.16	2938.85	2915.29	2895.64	2836.00	2810.80	2799.96	2795.28
205,000	3233.45	3170.29	3118.71	3076.33	3041.33	3012.32	2988.18	2968.04	2906.90	2881.07	2869.96	2865.16
210,000	3312.32	3247.62	3194.78	3151.36	3115.51	3085.79	3061.06	3040.43	2977.80	2951.34	2939.96	2935.04
215,000	3391.18	3324.94	3270.85	3226.40	3189.69	3159.26	3133.94	3112.82	3048.70	3021.61	3009.96	3004.92
220,000	3470.04	3402.27	3346.91	3301.43	3263.87	3232.73	3206.82	3185.21	3119.60	3091.88	3079.96	3074.80
225,000	3548.91	3479.59	3422.98	3376.46	3338.05	3306.20	3279.71	3257.60	3190.50	3162.15	3149.96	3144.68
230,000	3627.77	3556.91	3499.04	3451.49	3412.23	3379.67	3352.59	3329.99	3261.40	3232.41	3219.96	3214.57
235,000	3706.64	3634.24	3575.11	3526.53	3486.41	3453.14	3425.47	3402.38	3332.30	3302.68	3289.96	3284.45
240,000	3785.50	3711.56	3651.18	3601.56	3560.59	3526.61	3498.35	3474.77	3403.20	3372.95	3359.96	3354.33
245,000	3864.37	3788.89	3727.24	3676.59	3634.76	3600.09	3571.23	3547.16	3474.10	3443.22	3429.96	3424.21
250,000	3943.23	3866.21	3803.31	3751.62	3708.94	3673.56	3644.12	3619.55	3545.00	3513.49	3499.95	3494.09
255,000	4022.10	3943.54	3879.37	3826.65	3783.12	3747.03	3717.00	3691.94	3615.90	3583.76	3569.95	3563.97
260,000	4100.96	4020.86	3955.44	3901.69	3857.30	3820.50	3789.88	3764.34	3686.80	3654.03	3639.95	3633.86
265,000	4179.83	4098.18	4031.51	3976.72	3931.48	3893.97	3862.76	3836.73	3757.70	3724.30	3709.95	3703.74
270,000	4258.69	4175.51	4107.57	4051.75	4005.66	3967.44	3935.65	3909.12	3828.60	3794.57	3779.95	3773.62
280,000	4416.42	4330.16	4259.70	4201.82	4154.02	4114.38	4081.41	4053.90	3970.40	3935.11	3919.95	3913.38
290,000	4574.15	4484.80	4411.84	4351.88	4302.37	4261.32	4227.17	4198.68	4112.20	4075.65	4059.95	4053.15
300,000	4731.88	4639.45	4563.97	4501.95	4450.73	4408.27	4372.94	4343.46	4254.00	4216.19	4199.94	4192.91

MONTHLY AMORTIZING PAYMENTS

AMOUNT OF LOAN	\multicolumn{12}{c}{NUMBER OF YEARS IN TERM}

AMOUNT OF LOAN	1	2	3	4	5	6	7	8	9	10	11	12
$ 50	4.57	2.48	1.79	1.45	1.25	1.12	1.03	0.96	0.91	0.87	0.84	0.82
100	9.13	4.95	3.57	2.89	2.49	2.23	2.05	1.92	1.82	1.74	1.68	1.64
200	18.25	9.89	7.14	5.78	4.98	4.45	4.09	3.83	3.63	3.48	3.36	3.27
300	27.37	14.84	10.70	8.66	7.46	6.68	6.14	5.74	5.45	5.22	5.04	4.90
400	36.49	19.78	14.27	11.55	9.95	8.90	8.18	7.65	7.26	6.96	6.72	6.53
500	45.61	24.73	17.83	14.43	12.43	11.13	10.22	9.57	9.07	8.69	8.40	8.16
600	54.73	29.67	21.40	17.32	14.92	13.35	12.27	11.48	10.89	10.43	10.08	9.80
700	63.85	34.61	24.96	20.20	17.40	15.58	14.31	13.39	12.70	12.17	11.76	11.43
800	72.97	39.56	28.53	23.09	19.89	17.80	16.35	15.30	14.51	13.91	13.44	13.06
900	82.09	44.50	32.09	25.97	22.37	20.03	18.40	17.21	16.33	15.65	15.11	14.69
1,000	91.21	49.45	35.66	28.86	24.86	22.25	20.44	19.13	18.14	17.38	16.79	16.32
2,000	182.41	98.89	71.31	57.72	49.71	44.50	40.88	38.25	36.28	34.76	33.58	32.64
3,000	273.62	148.33	106.96	86.57	74.56	66.74	61.31	57.37	54.41	52.14	50.37	48.96
4,000	364.82	197.77	142.62	115.43	99.42	88.99	81.75	76.49	72.55	69.52	67.16	65.28
5,000	456.03	247.22	178.27	144.28	124.27	111.24	102.18	95.61	90.69	86.90	83.95	81.60
6,000	547.23	296.66	213.92	173.14	149.12	133.48	122.62	114.73	108.82	104.28	100.73	97.92
7,000	638.44	346.10	249.57	201.99	173.97	155.73	143.06	133.86	126.96	121.66	117.52	114.24
8,000	729.64	395.54	285.23	230.85	198.83	177.97	163.49	152.98	145.09	139.04	134.31	130.56
9,000	820.85	444.99	320.88	259.70	223.68	200.22	183.93	172.10	163.23	156.42	151.10	146.88
10,000	912.05	494.43	356.53	288.56	248.53	222.47	204.36	191.22	181.37	173.80	167.89	163.20
15,000	1368.08	741.64	534.80	432.83	372.79	333.70	306.54	286.83	272.05	260.70	251.83	244.79
20,000	1824.10	988.85	713.06	577.11	497.06	444.93	408.72	382.43	362.73	347.60	335.77	326.39
25,000	2280.12	1236.06	891.32	721.38	621.32	556.16	510.90	478.04	453.41	434.50	419.71	407.99
30,000	2736.15	1483.27	1069.59	865.66	745.58	667.39	613.08	573.65	544.09	521.40	503.65	489.58
35,000	3192.17	1730.48	1247.85	1009.93	869.85	778.62	715.26	669.26	634.77	608.30	587.60	571.18
40,000	3648.20	1977.70	1426.11	1154.21	994.11	889.85	817.44	764.86	725.45	695.20	671.54	652.77
45,000	4104.22	2224.91	1604.38	1298.48	1118.37	1001.08	919.62	860.47	816.13	782.09	755.48	734.37
50,000	4560.24	2472.12	1782.64	1442.76	1242.63	1112.31	1021.80	956.08	906.81	868.99	839.42	815.97
55,000	5016.27	2719.33	1960.91	1587.03	1366.90	1223.54	1123.97	1051.68	997.50	955.89	923.36	897.56
60,000	5472.29	2966.54	2139.17	1731.31	1491.16	1334.77	1226.15	1147.29	1088.18	1042.79	1007.30	979.16
65,000	5928.31	3213.75	2317.43	1875.58	1615.42	1446.00	1328.33	1242.90	1178.86	1129.69	1091.25	1060.75
70,000	6384.34	3460.96	2495.70	2019.86	1739.69	1557.23	1430.51	1338.51	1269.54	1216.59	1175.19	1142.35
75,000	6840.36	3708.17	2673.96	2164.13	1863.95	1668.46	1532.69	1434.11	1360.22	1303.49	1259.13	1223.95
80,000	7296.39	3955.39	2852.22	2308.41	1988.21	1779.70	1634.87	1529.72	1450.90	1390.39	1343.07	1305.54
85,000	7752.41	4202.60	3030.49	2452.68	2112.47	1890.93	1737.05	1625.33	1541.58	1477.29	1427.01	1387.14
90,000	8208.43	4449.81	3208.75	2596.96	2236.74	2002.16	1839.23	1720.94	1632.26	1564.18	1510.95	1468.74
95,000	8664.46	4697.02	3387.01	2741.23	2361.00	2113.39	1941.41	1816.54	1722.94	1651.08	1594.90	1550.33
100,000	9120.48	4944.23	3565.28	2885.51	2485.26	2224.62	2043.59	1912.15	1813.62	1737.98	1678.84	1631.93
105,000	9576.50	5191.44	3743.54	3029.78	2609.53	2335.85	2145.76	2007.76	1904.30	1824.88	1762.78	1713.52
110,000	10032.53	5438.65	3921.81	3174.06	2733.79	2447.08	2247.94	2103.36	1994.99	1911.78	1846.72	1795.12
115,000	10488.55	5685.87	4100.07	3318.33	2858.05	2558.31	2350.12	2198.97	2085.67	1998.68	1930.66	1876.72
120,000	10944.58	5933.08	4278.33	3462.61	2982.31	2669.54	2452.30	2294.58	2176.35	2085.58	2014.60	1958.31
125,000	11400.60	6180.29	4456.60	3606.89	3106.58	2780.77	2554.48	2390.19	2267.03	2172.48	2098.55	2039.91
130,000	11856.62	6427.50	4634.86	3751.16	3230.84	2892.00	2656.66	2485.79	2357.71	2259.37	2182.49	2121.50
135,000	12312.65	6674.71	4813.12	3895.44	3355.10	3003.23	2758.84	2581.40	2448.39	2346.27	2266.43	2203.10
140,000	12768.67	6921.92	4991.39	4039.71	3479.37	3114.46	2861.02	2677.01	2539.07	2433.17	2350.37	2284.70
145,000	13224.69	7169.13	5169.65	4183.99	3603.63	3225.69	2963.20	2772.62	2629.75	2520.07	2434.31	2366.29
150,000	13680.72	7416.34	5347.91	4328.26	3727.89	3336.92	3065.38	2868.22	2720.43	2606.97	2518.25	2447.89
155,000	14136.74	7663.56	5526.18	4472.54	3852.15	3448.16	3167.55	2963.83	2811.11	2693.87	2602.19	2529.49
160,000	14592.77	7910.77	5704.44	4616.81	3976.42	3559.39	3269.73	3059.44	2901.80	2780.77	2686.14	2611.08
165,000	15048.79	8157.98	5882.71	4761.09	4100.68	3670.62	3371.91	3155.04	2992.48	2867.67	2770.08	2692.68
170,000	15504.81	8405.19	6060.97	4905.36	4224.94	3781.85	3474.09	3250.65	3083.16	2954.57	2854.02	2774.27
175,000	15960.84	8652.40	6239.23	5049.64	4349.21	3893.08	3576.27	3346.26	3173.84	3041.46	2937.96	2855.87
180,000	16416.86	8899.61	6417.50	5193.91	4473.47	4004.31	3678.45	3441.87	3264.52	3128.36	3021.90	2937.47
185,000	16872.88	9146.82	6595.76	5338.19	4597.73	4115.54	3780.63	3537.47	3355.20	3215.26	3105.84	3019.06
190,000	17328.91	9394.04	6774.02	5482.46	4721.99	4226.77	3882.81	3633.08	3445.88	3302.16	3189.79	3100.66
195,000	17784.93	9641.25	6952.29	5626.74	4846.26	4338.00	3984.99	3728.69	3536.56	3389.06	3273.73	3182.25
200,000	18240.96	9888.46	7130.55	5771.01	4970.52	4449.23	4087.17	3824.30	3627.24	3475.96	3357.67	3263.85
205,000	18696.98	10135.67	7308.81	5915.29	5094.78	4560.46	4189.34	3919.90	3717.92	3562.86	3441.61	3345.45
210,000	19153.00	10382.88	7487.08	6059.56	5219.05	4671.69	4291.52	4015.51	3808.60	3649.76	3525.55	3427.04
215,000	19609.03	10630.09	7665.34	6203.84	5343.31	4782.92	4393.70	4111.12	3899.29	3736.65	3609.49	3508.64
220,000	20065.05	10877.30	7843.61	6348.11	5467.57	4894.15	4495.88	4206.72	3989.97	3823.55	3693.44	3590.24
225,000	20521.07	11124.51	8021.87	6492.39	5591.83	5005.38	4598.06	4302.33	4080.65	3910.45	3777.38	3671.83
230,000	20977.10	11371.73	8200.13	6636.66	5716.10	5116.62	4700.24	4397.94	4171.33	3997.35	3861.32	3753.43
235,000	21433.12	11618.94	8378.40	6780.94	5840.36	5227.85	4802.42	4493.55	4262.01	4084.25	3945.26	3835.02
240,000	21889.15	11866.15	8556.66	6925.22	5964.62	5339.08	4904.60	4589.15	4352.69	4171.15	4029.20	3916.62
245,000	22345.17	12113.36	8734.92	7069.49	6088.89	5450.31	5006.78	4684.76	4443.37	4258.05	4113.14	3998.22
250,000	22801.19	12360.57	8913.19	7213.77	6213.15	5561.54	5108.96	4780.37	4534.05	4344.95	4197.09	4079.81
255,000	23257.22	12607.78	9091.45	7358.04	6337.41	5672.77	5211.14	4875.98	4624.73	4431.85	4281.03	4161.41
260,000	23713.24	12854.99	9269.71	7502.32	6461.67	5784.00	5313.31	4971.58	4715.41	4518.74	4364.97	4243.00
265,000	24169.26	13102.20	9447.98	7646.59	6585.94	5895.23	5415.49	5067.19	4806.09	4605.64	4448.91	4324.60
270,000	24625.29	13349.42	9626.24	7790.87	6710.20	6006.46	5517.67	5162.80	4896.78	4692.54	4532.85	4406.20
280,000	25537.34	13843.84	9982.77	8079.42	6958.73	6228.92	5722.03	5354.01	5078.14	4866.34	4700.73	4569.39
290,000	26449.38	14338.26	10339.30	8367.97	7207.25	6451.38	5926.39	5545.23	5259.50	5040.14	4868.62	4732.58
300,000	27361.43	14832.68	10695.82	8656.52	7455.78	6673.84	6130.75	5736.44	5440.86	5213.93	5036.50	4895.77

MONTHLY AMORTIZING PAYMENTS   **17.00%**

AMOUNT OF LOAN	NUMBER OF YEARS IN TERM											
	13	14	15	16	17	18	19	20	25	30	35	40
$ 50	0.80	0.79	0.77	0.76	0.76	0.75	0.74	0.74	0.72	0.72	0.72	0.71
100	1.60	1.57	1.54	1.52	1.51	1.49	1.48	1.47	1.44	1.43	1.43	1.42
200	3.19	3.13	3.08	3.04	3.01	2.98	2.96	2.94	2.88	2.86	2.85	2.84
300	4.79	4.70	4.62	4.56	4.51	4.47	4.43	4.41	4.32	4.28	4.27	4.26
400	6.38	6.26	6.16	6.08	6.01	5.96	5.91	5.87	5.76	5.71	5.69	5.68
500	7.98	7.82	7.70	7.60	7.51	7.44	7.39	7.34	7.19	7.13	7.11	7.10
600	9.57	9.39	9.24	9.12	9.02	8.93	8.86	8.81	8.63	8.56	8.53	8.51
700	11.17	10.95	10.78	10.64	10.52	10.42	10.34	10.27	10.07	9.98	9.95	9.93
800	12.76	12.52	12.32	12.15	12.02	11.91	11.82	11.74	11.51	11.41	11.37	11.35
900	14.35	14.08	13.86	13.67	13.52	13.40	13.29	13.21	12.95	12.84	12.79	12.77
1,000	15.95	15.64	15.40	15.19	15.02	14.88	14.77	14.67	14.38	14.26	14.21	14.19
2,000	31.89	31.28	30.79	30.38	30.04	29.76	29.53	29.34	28.76	28.52	28.42	28.37
3,000	47.83	46.92	46.18	45.56	45.06	44.64	44.30	44.01	43.14	42.78	42.62	42.55
4,000	63.78	62.56	61.57	60.75	60.08	59.52	59.06	58.68	57.52	57.03	56.83	56.74
5,000	79.72	78.20	76.96	75.94	75.10	74.40	73.83	73.35	71.89	71.29	71.03	70.92
6,000	95.66	93.84	92.35	91.12	90.12	89.28	88.59	88.01	86.27	85.55	85.24	85.10
7,000	111.61	109.47	107.74	106.31	105.13	104.16	103.35	102.68	100.65	99.80	99.44	99.29
8,000	127.55	125.11	123.13	121.50	120.15	119.04	118.12	117.35	115.03	114.06	113.65	113.47
9,000	143.49	140.75	138.52	136.68	135.17	133.92	132.88	132.02	129.41	128.32	127.85	127.65
10,000	159.43	156.39	153.91	151.87	150.19	148.80	147.65	146.69	143.78	142.57	142.06	141.84
15,000	239.15	234.58	230.86	227.80	225.28	223.20	221.47	220.03	215.07	213.86	213.08	212.75
20,000	318.86	312.77	307.81	303.73	300.37	297.59	295.29	293.37	287.56	285.14	284.11	283.67
25,000	398.58	390.96	384.76	379.66	375.47	371.99	369.11	366.71	359.45	356.42	355.14	354.59
30,000	478.29	469.16	461.71	455.60	450.56	446.39	442.93	440.05	431.34	427.71	426.16	425.50
35,000	558.01	547.35	538.66	531.53	525.65	520.79	516.75	513.39	503.23	498.99	497.19	496.42
40,000	637.72	625.54	615.61	607.46	600.74	595.18	590.57	586.73	575.12	570.28	568.22	567.33
45,000	717.44	703.73	692.56	683.39	675.83	669.58	664.39	660.07	647.01	641.56	639.24	638.25
50,000	797.15	781.92	769.51	759.32	750.93	743.98	738.21	733.41	718.90	712.84	710.27	709.17
55,000	876.87	860.12	846.46	835.25	826.02	818.38	812.03	806.75	790.79	784.13	781.29	780.08
60,000	956.58	938.31	923.41	911.19	901.11	892.77	885.85	880.09	862.68	855.41	852.32	851.00
65,000	1036.30	1016.50	1000.36	987.12	976.20	967.17	959.67	953.43	934.57	926.69	923.35	921.92
70,000	1116.01	1094.69	1077.31	1063.05	1051.30	1041.57	1033.49	1026.77	1006.46	997.98	994.37	992.83
75,000	1195.73	1172.88	1154.26	1138.98	1126.39	1115.97	1107.31	1100.11	1078.35	1069.26	1065.40	1063.75
80,000	1275.44	1251.08	1231.21	1214.91	1201.48	1190.36	1181.13	1173.45	1150.24	1140.55	1136.43	1134.66
85,000	1355.16	1329.27	1308.16	1290.84	1276.57	1264.76	1254.95	1246.79	1222.13	1211.83	1207.45	1205.58
90,000	1434.87	1407.46	1385.11	1366.78	1351.66	1339.16	1328.77	1320.13	1294.02	1283.11	1278.48	1276.50
95,000	1514.59	1485.65	1462.06	1442.71	1426.76	1413.55	1402.59	1393.47	1365.91	1354.40	1349.50	1347.41
100,000	1594.30	1563.84	1539.01	1518.64	1501.85	1487.95	1476.41	1466.81	1437.80	1425.68	1420.53	1418.33
105,000	1674.02	1642.04	1615.96	1594.57	1576.94	1562.35	1550.23	1540.15	1509.69	1496.96	1491.56	1489.24
110,000	1753.73	1720.23	1692.91	1670.50	1652.03	1636.75	1624.05	1613.49	1581.58	1568.25	1562.58	1560.16
115,000	1833.44	1798.42	1769.86	1746.43	1727.12	1711.14	1697.87	1686.83	1653.47	1639.53	1633.61	1631.08
120,000	1913.16	1876.61	1846.81	1822.37	1802.22	1785.54	1771.70	1760.17	1725.36	1710.82	1704.64	1701.99
125,000	1992.87	1954.80	1923.76	1898.30	1877.31	1859.94	1845.52	1833.51	1797.25	1782.10	1775.66	1772.91
130,000	2072.59	2032.99	2000.71	1974.23	1952.40	1934.34	1919.34	1906.85	1869.14	1853.38	1846.69	1843.83
135,000	2152.30	2111.19	2077.66	2050.16	2027.49	2008.73	1993.16	1980.19	1941.03	1924.67	1917.72	1914.74
140,000	2232.02	2189.38	2154.61	2126.09	2102.59	2083.13	2066.98	2053.53	2012.92	1995.95	1988.74	1985.66
145,000	2311.73	2267.57	2231.56	2202.02	2177.68	2157.53	2140.80	2126.87	2084.81	2067.23	2059.77	2056.57
150,000	2391.45	2345.76	2308.51	2277.96	2252.77	2231.93	2214.62	2200.21	2156.70	2138.52	2130.79	2127.49
155,000	2471.16	2423.95	2385.46	2353.89	2327.86	2306.32	2288.44	2273.55	2228.59	2209.80	2201.82	2198.41
160,000	2550.88	2502.15	2462.41	2429.82	2402.95	2380.72	2362.26	2346.89	2300.48	2281.09	2272.85	2269.32
165,000	2630.59	2580.34	2539.36	2505.75	2478.05	2455.12	2436.08	2420.23	2372.37	2352.37	2343.87	2340.24
170,000	2710.31	2658.53	2616.31	2581.68	2553.14	2529.52	2509.90	2493.57	2444.26	2423.65	2414.90	2411.16
175,000	2790.02	2736.72	2693.26	2657.61	2628.23	2603.91	2583.72	2566.91	2516.15	2494.94	2485.93	2482.07
180,000	2869.74	2814.91	2770.21	2733.55	2703.32	2678.31	2657.54	2640.25	2588.04	2566.22	2556.95	2552.99
185,000	2949.45	2893.11	2847.16	2809.48	2778.42	2752.71	2731.36	2713.59	2659.93	2637.50	2627.98	2623.90
190,000	3029.17	2971.30	2924.11	2885.41	2853.51	2827.10	2805.18	2786.93	2731.82	2708.79	2699.00	2694.82
195,000	3108.88	3049.49	3001.06	2961.34	2928.60	2901.50	2879.00	2860.27	2803.71	2780.07	2770.03	2765.74
200,000	3188.60	3127.68	3078.01	3037.27	3003.69	2975.90	2952.82	2933.61	2875.60	2851.36	2841.06	2836.65
205,000	3268.31	3205.87	3154.96	3113.20	3078.78	3050.30	3026.64	3006.95	2947.49	2922.64	2912.08	2907.57
210,000	3348.03	3284.07	3231.91	3189.14	3153.88	3124.69	3100.46	3080.29	3019.38	2993.92	2983.11	2978.48
215,000	3427.74	3362.26	3308.86	3265.07	3228.97	3199.09	3174.28	3153.63	3091.27	3065.21	3054.14	3049.40
220,000	3507.45	3440.45	3385.81	3341.00	3304.06	3273.49	3248.10	3226.97	3163.16	3136.49	3125.16	3120.32
225,000	3587.17	3518.64	3462.76	3416.93	3379.15	3347.89	3321.92	3300.31	3235.05	3207.77	3196.19	3191.23
230,000	3666.88	3596.83	3539.71	3492.86	3454.24	3422.28	3395.74	3373.65	3306.94	3279.06	3267.22	3262.15
235,000	3746.60	3675.02	3616.67	3568.80	3529.34	3496.68	3469.57	3446.99	3378.83	3350.34	3338.24	3333.07
240,000	3826.31	3753.22	3693.62	3644.73	3604.43	3571.08	3543.39	3520.33	3450.72	3421.63	3409.27	3403.98
245,000	3906.03	3831.41	3770.57	3720.66	3679.52	3645.48	3617.21	3593.67	3522.61	3492.91	3480.29	3474.90
250,000	3985.74	3909.60	3847.52	3796.59	3754.61	3719.87	3691.03	3667.01	3594.50	3564.19	3551.32	3545.81
255,000	4065.46	3987.79	3924.47	3872.53	3829.71	3794.27	3764.85	3740.35	3666.39	3635.48	3622.35	3616.73
260,000	4145.17	4065.98	4001.42	3948.45	3904.80	3868.67	3838.67	3813.69	3738.28	3706.76	3693.37	3687.65
265,000	4224.89	4144.18	4078.37	4024.39	3979.89	3943.07	3912.49	3887.03	3810.17	3778.04	3764.40	3758.56
270,000	4304.60	4222.37	4155.32	4100.32	4054.98	4017.46	3986.31	3960.37	3882.06	3849.33	3835.43	3829.48
280,000	4464.03	4378.75	4309.22	4252.18	4205.17	4166.26	4133.95	4107.05	4025.84	3991.90	3977.48	3971.31
290,000	4623.46	4535.14	4463.12	4404.04	4355.35	4315.05	4281.59	4253.73	4169.62	4134.46	4119.53	4113.14
300,000	4782.89	4691.52	4617.02	4555.91	4505.54	4463.85	4429.23	4400.41	4313.39	4277.03	4261.58	4254.98

123

MONTHLY AMORTIZING PAYMENTS

AMOUNT OF LOAN	NUMBER OF YEARS IN TERM											
	1	2	3	4	5	6	7	8	9	10	11	12
$ 50	4.57	2.48	1.79	1.45	1.25	1.12	1.03	0.97	0.92	0.88	0.85	0.83
100	9.14	4.96	3.58	2.90	2.50	2.24	2.06	1.93	1.83	1.76	1.70	1.65
200	18.27	9.92	7.16	5.80	5.00	4.48	4.12	3.86	3.66	3.51	3.40	3.30
300	27.40	14.87	10.74	8.70	7.50	6.72	6.18	5.79	5.49	5.27	5.09	4.95
400	36.53	19.83	14.32	11.60	10.00	8.96	8.24	7.71	7.32	7.02	6.79	6.60
500	45.67	24.79	17.89	14.50	12.50	11.20	10.30	9.64	9.15	8.77	8.48	8.25
600	54.80	29.74	21.47	17.40	15.00	13.44	12.35	11.57	10.98	10.53	10.18	9.90
700	63.93	34.70	25.05	20.29	17.50	15.68	14.41	13.49	12.81	12.28	11.87	11.55
800	73.06	39.65	28.63	23.19	19.99	17.91	16.47	15.42	14.64	14.04	13.57	13.19
900	82.20	44.61	32.20	26.09	22.49	20.15	18.53	17.35	16.47	15.79	15.26	14.84
1,000	91.33	49.57	35.78	28.99	24.99	22.39	20.59	19.28	18.30	17.54	16.96	16.49
2,000	182.65	99.13	71.56	57.97	49.98	44.78	41.17	38.55	36.59	35.08	33.91	32.98
3,000	273.98	148.69	107.34	86.96	74.97	67.16	61.75	57.82	54.88	52.62	50.86	49.46
4,000	365.30	198.25	143.11	115.94	99.95	89.55	82.33	77.09	73.17	70.16	67.81	65.95
5,000	456.62	247.82	178.89	144.93	124.94	111.93	102.91	96.36	91.46	87.70	84.76	82.44
6,000	547.95	297.38	214.67	173.91	149.93	134.32	123.49	115.63	109.75	105.24	101.71	98.92
7,000	639.27	346.94	250.45	202.90	174.92	156.71	144.07	134.90	128.04	122.77	118.66	115.41
8,000	730.59	396.50	286.22	231.88	199.90	179.09	164.65	154.17	146.33	140.31	135.62	131.89
9,000	821.92	446.07	322.00	260.87	224.89	201.48	185.23	173.44	164.62	157.85	152.57	148.38
10,000	913.24	495.63	357.78	289.85	249.88	223.86	205.81	192.72	182.91	175.39	169.52	164.87
15,000	1369.86	743.44	536.66	434.77	374.81	335.79	308.71	289.07	274.36	263.08	254.27	247.30
20,000	1826.47	991.25	715.55	579.70	499.75	447.72	411.62	385.43	365.81	350.78	339.03	329.73
25,000	2283.09	1239.07	894.44	724.62	624.68	559.65	514.52	481.78	457.27	438.47	423.79	412.16
30,000	2739.71	1486.88	1073.32	869.54	749.62	671.58	617.42	578.14	548.72	526.16	508.54	494.59
35,000	3196.33	1734.69	1252.21	1014.46	874.56	783.51	720.32	674.49	640.17	613.85	593.30	577.02
40,000	3652.94	1982.50	1431.10	1159.39	999.49	895.44	823.23	770.85	731.62	701.55	678.06	659.45
45,000	4109.56	2230.32	1609.98	1304.31	1124.43	1007.37	926.13	867.20	823.08	789.24	762.81	741.88
50,000	4566.18	2478.13	1788.87	1449.23	1249.36	1119.30	1029.03	963.56	914.53	876.93	847.57	824.32
55,000	5022.79	2725.94	1967.75	1594.16	1374.30	1231.23	1131.93	1059.91	1005.98	964.62	932.33	906.75
60,000	5479.41	2973.75	2146.64	1739.08	1499.24	1343.16	1234.84	1156.27	1097.43	1052.32	1017.08	989.18
65,000	5936.03	3221.57	2325.53	1884.00	1624.17	1455.09	1337.74	1252.62	1188.88	1140.01	1101.84	1071.61
70,000	6392.65	3469.38	2504.41	2028.92	1749.11	1567.02	1440.64	1348.98	1280.34	1227.70	1186.60	1154.04
75,000	6849.26	3717.19	2683.30	2173.85	1874.04	1678.94	1543.55	1445.33	1371.79	1315.39	1271.35	1236.47
80,000	7305.88	3965.00	2862.19	2318.77	1998.98	1790.87	1646.45	1541.69	1463.24	1403.09	1356.11	1318.90
85,000	7762.50	4212.82	3041.07	2463.69	2123.92	1902.80	1749.35	1638.04	1554.69	1490.78	1440.87	1401.33
90,000	8219.11	4460.63	3219.96	2608.61	2248.85	2014.73	1852.25	1734.40	1646.15	1578.47	1525.62	1483.76
95,000	8675.73	4708.44	3398.85	2753.54	2373.79	2126.66	1955.16	1830.75	1737.60	1666.16	1610.38	1566.19
100,000	9132.35	4956.25	3577.73	2898.46	2498.72	2238.59	2058.06	1927.11	1829.05	1753.86	1695.13	1648.63
105,000	9588.97	5204.06	3756.62	3043.38	2623.66	2350.52	2160.96	2023.47	1920.50	1841.55	1779.89	1731.06
110,000	10045.58	5451.88	3935.50	3188.31	2748.60	2462.45	2263.86	2119.82	2011.96	1929.24	1864.65	1813.49
115,000	10502.20	5699.69	4114.39	3333.23	2873.53	2574.38	2366.77	2216.18	2103.41	2016.93	1949.40	1895.92
120,000	10958.82	5947.50	4293.28	3478.15	2998.47	2686.31	2469.67	2312.53	2194.86	2104.63	2034.16	1978.35
125,000	11415.43	6195.31	4472.16	3623.07	3123.40	2798.24	2572.57	2408.89	2286.31	2192.32	2118.92	2060.78
130,000	11872.05	6443.13	4651.05	3768.00	3248.34	2910.17	2675.48	2505.24	2377.76	2280.01	2203.67	2143.21
135,000	12328.67	6690.94	4829.94	3912.92	3373.28	3022.10	2778.38	2601.60	2469.22	2367.70	2288.43	2225.64
140,000	12785.29	6938.75	5008.82	4057.84	3498.21	3134.03	2881.28	2697.95	2560.67	2455.40	2373.19	2308.07
145,000	13241.90	7186.56	5187.71	4202.76	3623.15	3245.95	2984.18	2794.31	2652.12	2543.09	2457.94	2390.51
150,000	13698.52	7434.38	5366.60	4347.69	3748.08	3357.88	3087.09	2890.66	2743.57	2630.78	2542.70	2472.94
155,000	14155.14	7682.19	5545.48	4492.61	3873.02	3469.81	3189.99	2987.02	2835.03	2718.47	2627.46	2555.37
160,000	14611.75	7930.00	5724.37	4637.53	3997.96	3581.74	3292.89	3083.37	2926.48	2806.17	2712.21	2637.80
165,000	15068.37	8177.81	5903.25	4782.46	4122.89	3693.67	3395.79	3179.73	3017.93	2893.86	2796.97	2720.23
170,000	15524.99	8425.63	6082.14	4927.38	4247.83	3805.60	3498.70	3276.08	3109.38	2981.55	2881.73	2802.66
175,000	15981.61	8673.44	6261.03	5072.30	4372.76	3917.53	3601.60	3372.44	3200.84	3069.24	2966.48	2885.09
180,000	16438.22	8921.25	6439.91	5217.22	4497.70	4029.46	3704.50	3468.79	3292.29	3156.94	3051.24	2967.52
185,000	16894.84	9169.06	6618.80	5362.15	4622.64	4141.39	3807.41	3565.15	3383.74	3244.63	3136.00	3049.95
190,000	17351.46	9416.87	6797.69	5507.07	4747.57	4253.32	3910.31	3661.50	3475.19	3332.32	3220.75	3132.38
195,000	17808.08	9664.69	6976.57	5651.99	4872.51	4365.25	4013.21	3757.86	3566.64	3420.01	3305.51	3214.82
200,000	18264.69	9912.50	7155.46	5796.91	4997.44	4477.18	4116.11	3854.21	3658.10	3507.71	3390.26	3297.25
205,000	18721.31	10160.31	7334.35	5941.84	5122.38	4589.11	4219.02	3950.57	3749.55	3595.40	3475.02	3379.68
210,000	19177.93	10408.12	7513.23	6086.76	5247.32	4701.04	4321.92	4046.93	3841.00	3683.09	3559.78	3462.11
215,000	19634.54	10655.94	7692.12	6231.68	5372.25	4812.96	4424.82	4143.28	3932.45	3770.78	3644.53	3544.54
220,000	20091.16	10903.75	7871.00	6376.61	5497.19	4924.89	4527.72	4239.64	4023.91	3858.48	3729.29	3626.97
225,000	20547.78	11151.56	8049.89	6521.53	5622.12	5036.82	4630.63	4335.99	4115.36	3946.17	3814.05	3709.40
230,000	21004.40	11399.37	8228.78	6666.45	5747.06	5148.75	4733.53	4432.35	4206.81	4033.86	3898.80	3791.83
235,000	21461.01	11647.19	8407.66	6811.37	5872.00	5260.68	4836.43	4528.70	4298.26	4121.55	3983.56	3874.26
240,000	21917.63	11895.00	8586.55	6956.30	5996.93	5372.61	4939.33	4625.06	4389.71	4209.25	4068.32	3956.70
245,000	22374.25	12142.81	8765.44	7101.22	6121.87	5484.54	5042.24	4721.41	4481.17	4296.94	4153.07	4039.13
250,000	22830.86	12390.62	8944.32	7246.14	6246.80	5596.47	5145.14	4817.77	4572.62	4384.63	4237.83	4121.56
255,000	23287.48	12638.44	9123.21	7391.06	6371.74	5708.40	5248.04	4914.12	4664.07	4472.32	4322.59	4203.99
260,000	23744.10	12886.25	9302.10	7535.99	6496.68	5820.33	5350.95	5010.48	4755.52	4560.02	4407.34	4286.42
265,000	24200.72	13134.06	9480.98	7680.91	6621.61	5932.26	5453.85	5106.83	4846.98	4647.71	4492.10	4368.85
270,000	24657.33	13381.87	9659.87	7825.83	6746.55	6044.19	5556.75	5203.19	4938.43	4735.40	4576.86	4451.28
280,000	25570.57	13877.50	10017.64	8115.68	6996.42	6268.05	5762.56	5395.90	5121.33	4910.79	4746.37	4616.14
290,000	26483.80	14373.12	10375.41	8405.52	7246.29	6491.90	5968.36	5588.61	5304.24	5086.17	4915.88	4781.01
300,000	27397.04	14868.75	10733.19	8695.37	7496.16	6715.76	6174.17	5781.32	5487.14	5261.56	5085.39	4945.87

AMOUNT OF LOAN	NUMBER OF YEARS IN TERM											
	13	14	15	16	17	18	19	20	25	30	35	40
$ 50	0.81	0.80	0.78	0.77	0.77	0.76	0.75	0.75	0.73	0.73	0.73	0.72
100	1.62	1.59	1.56	1.54	1.53	1.51	1.50	1.49	1.46	1.45	1.45	1.44
200	3.23	3.17	3.12	3.08	3.05	3.02	3.00	2.98	2.92	2.90	2.89	2.88
300	4.84	4.75	4.68	4.62	4.57	4.52	4.49	4.46	4.38	4.34	4.33	4.32
400	6.45	6.33	6.23	6.15	6.09	6.03	5.99	5.95	5.84	5.79	5.77	5.76
500	8.06	7.91	7.79	7.69	7.61	7.54	7.48	7.43	7.29	7.23	7.21	7.20
600	9.67	9.49	9.35	9.23	9.13	9.04	8.98	8.92	8.75	8.68	8.65	8.64
700	11.28	11.07	10.90	10.76	10.65	10.55	10.47	10.41	10.21	10.13	10.09	10.08
800	12.90	12.66	12.46	12.30	12.17	12.06	11.97	11.89	11.67	11.57	11.53	11.52
900	14.51	14.24	14.02	13.84	13.69	13.56	13.46	13.38	13.12	13.02	12.97	12.96
1,000	16.12	15.82	15.57	15.37	15.21	15.07	14.96	14.86	14.58	14.46	14.42	14.40
2,000	32.23	31.63	31.14	30.74	30.41	30.14	29.91	29.72	29.16	28.92	28.83	28.79
3,000	48.35	47.44	46.71	46.11	45.61	45.20	44.86	44.58	43.73	43.38	43.24	43.18
4,000	64.46	63.26	62.28	61.47	60.81	60.27	59.81	59.44	58.31	57.84	57.65	57.57
5,000	80.57	79.07	77.84	76.84	76.01	75.33	74.77	74.30	72.89	72.30	72.06	71.96
6,000	96.69	94.88	93.41	92.21	91.22	90.40	89.72	89.16	87.46	86.76	86.47	86.35
7,000	112.80	110.69	108.98	107.57	106.42	105.46	104.67	104.01	102.04	101.22	100.88	100.74
8,000	128.91	126.51	124.55	122.94	121.62	120.53	119.62	118.87	116.62	115.68	115.29	115.13
9,000	145.03	142.32	140.11	138.31	136.82	135.59	134.58	133.73	131.19	130.14	129.70	129.52
10,000	161.14	158.13	155.68	153.67	152.02	150.66	149.53	148.59	145.77	144.60	144.11	143.91
15,000	241.71	237.19	233.52	230.51	228.03	225.99	224.29	222.88	218.65	216.90	216.17	215.86
20,000	322.28	316.26	311.36	307.34	304.04	301.31	299.05	297.17	291.53	289.20	288.22	287.81
25,000	402.85	395.32	389.19	384.18	380.05	376.64	373.81	371.47	364.42	361.50	360.28	359.76
30,000	483.42	474.38	467.03	461.01	456.06	451.97	448.58	445.76	437.30	433.80	432.33	431.71
35,000	563.98	553.45	544.87	537.85	532.07	527.29	523.34	520.05	510.18	506.10	504.39	503.66
40,000	644.55	632.51	622.71	614.68	608.08	602.62	598.10	594.34	583.06	578.40	576.44	575.61
45,000	725.12	711.57	700.55	691.52	684.09	677.95	672.86	668.63	655.94	650.70	648.50	647.57
50,000	805.69	790.64	778.38	768.35	760.09	753.27	747.62	742.93	728.83	723.00	720.55	719.52
55,000	886.26	869.70	856.22	845.18	836.10	828.60	822.38	817.22	801.71	795.30	792.61	791.47
60,000	966.83	948.76	934.06	922.02	912.11	903.93	897.15	891.51	874.59	867.60	864.66	863.42
65,000	1047.40	1027.83	1011.90	998.85	988.12	979.26	971.91	965.80	947.47	939.90	936.71	935.37
70,000	1127.96	1106.89	1089.73	1075.69	1064.13	1054.58	1046.67	1040.09	1020.35	1012.20	1008.77	1007.32
75,000	1208.53	1185.95	1167.57	1152.52	1140.14	1129.91	1121.43	1114.39	1093.24	1084.49	1080.82	1079.27
80,000	1289.10	1265.02	1245.41	1229.36	1216.15	1205.24	1196.19	1188.68	1166.12	1156.79	1152.88	1151.22
85,000	1369.67	1344.08	1323.25	1306.19	1292.16	1280.56	1270.96	1262.97	1239.00	1229.09	1224.93	1223.17
90,000	1450.24	1423.14	1401.09	1383.03	1368.17	1355.89	1345.72	1337.26	1311.88	1301.39	1296.99	1295.13
95,000	1530.81	1502.21	1478.92	1459.86	1444.17	1431.22	1420.48	1411.55	1384.76	1373.69	1369.04	1367.08
100,000	1611.37	1581.27	1556.76	1536.69	1520.18	1506.54	1495.24	1485.85	1457.65	1445.99	1441.10	1439.03
105,000	1691.94	1660.33	1634.60	1613.53	1596.19	1581.87	1570.00	1560.14	1530.53	1518.29	1513.15	1510.98
110,000	1772.51	1739.40	1712.44	1690.36	1672.20	1657.20	1644.76	1634.43	1603.41	1590.59	1585.21	1582.93
115,000	1853.08	1818.46	1790.28	1767.20	1748.21	1732.53	1719.53	1708.72	1676.29	1662.89	1657.26	1654.88
120,000	1933.65	1897.52	1868.11	1844.03	1824.22	1807.85	1794.29	1783.02	1749.17	1735.19	1729.32	1726.83
125,000	2014.22	1976.58	1945.95	1920.87	1900.23	1883.18	1869.05	1857.31	1822.06	1807.49	1801.37	1798.78
130,000	2094.79	2055.65	2023.79	1997.70	1976.24	1958.51	1943.81	1931.60	1894.94	1879.79	1873.42	1870.74
135,000	2175.35	2134.71	2101.63	2074.54	2052.25	2033.83	2018.57	2005.89	1967.82	1952.09	1945.48	1942.69
140,000	2255.92	2213.77	2179.46	2151.37	2128.26	2109.16	2093.33	2080.18	2040.70	2024.39	2017.53	2014.64
145,000	2336.49	2292.84	2257.30	2228.21	2204.26	2184.49	2168.10	2154.48	2113.59	2096.68	2089.59	2086.59
150,000	2417.06	2371.90	2335.14	2305.04	2280.27	2259.81	2242.86	2228.77	2186.47	2168.98	2161.64	2158.54
155,000	2497.63	2450.96	2412.98	2381.87	2356.28	2335.14	2317.62	2303.06	2259.35	2241.28	2233.70	2230.49
160,000	2578.20	2530.03	2490.82	2458.71	2432.29	2410.47	2392.38	2377.35	2332.23	2313.58	2305.75	2302.44
165,000	2658.76	2609.09	2568.65	2535.54	2508.30	2485.79	2467.14	2451.64	2405.11	2385.88	2377.81	2374.39
170,000	2739.33	2688.15	2646.49	2612.38	2584.31	2561.12	2541.91	2525.94	2478.00	2458.18	2449.86	2446.34
175,000	2819.90	2767.22	2724.33	2689.21	2660.32	2636.45	2616.67	2600.23	2550.88	2530.48	2521.92	2518.30
180,000	2900.47	2846.28	2802.17	2766.05	2736.33	2711.78	2691.43	2674.52	2623.76	2602.78	2593.97	2590.25
185,000	2981.04	2925.34	2880.01	2842.88	2812.34	2787.10	2766.19	2748.81	2696.64	2675.08	2666.02	2662.20
190,000	3061.61	3004.41	2957.84	2919.72	2888.34	2862.43	2840.95	2823.10	2769.52	2747.38	2738.08	2734.15
195,000	3142.18	3083.47	3035.68	2996.55	2964.35	2937.76	2915.71	2897.40	2842.41	2819.68	2810.13	2806.10
200,000	3222.74	3162.53	3113.52	3073.38	3040.36	3013.08	2990.48	2971.69	2915.29	2891.98	2882.19	2878.05
205,000	3303.31	3241.60	3191.36	3150.22	3116.37	3088.41	3065.24	3045.98	2988.17	2964.28	2954.24	2950.00
210,000	3383.88	3320.66	3269.19	3227.05	3192.38	3163.74	3140.00	3120.27	3061.05	3036.58	3026.30	3021.95
215,000	3464.45	3399.72	3347.03	3303.89	3268.39	3239.06	3214.76	3194.57	3133.93	3108.87	3098.35	3093.90
220,000	3545.02	3478.79	3424.87	3380.72	3344.40	3314.39	3289.52	3268.86	3206.82	3181.17	3170.41	3165.86
225,000	3625.59	3557.85	3502.71	3457.56	3420.41	3389.72	3364.28	3343.15	3279.70	3253.47	3242.46	3237.81
230,000	3706.15	3636.91	3580.55	3534.39	3496.42	3465.05	3439.05	3417.44	3352.58	3325.77	3314.52	3309.76
235,000	3786.72	3715.98	3658.38	3611.23	3572.42	3540.37	3513.81	3491.73	3425.46	3398.07	3386.57	3381.71
240,000	3867.29	3795.04	3736.22	3688.06	3648.43	3615.70	3588.57	3566.03	3498.34	3470.37	3458.63	3453.66
245,000	3947.86	3874.10	3814.06	3764.90	3724.44	3691.03	3663.33	3640.32	3571.23	3542.67	3530.68	3525.61
250,000	4028.43	3953.16	3891.90	3841.73	3800.45	3766.35	3738.09	3714.61	3644.11	3614.97	3602.73	3597.56
255,000	4109.00	4032.23	3969.74	3918.56	3876.46	3841.68	3812.86	3788.90	3716.99	3687.27	3674.79	3669.51
260,000	4189.57	4111.29	4047.57	3995.40	3952.47	3917.01	3887.62	3863.19	3789.87	3759.57	3746.84	3741.47
265,000	4270.13	4190.35	4125.41	4072.23	4028.48	3992.33	3962.38	3937.49	3862.75	3831.87	3818.90	3813.42
270,000	4350.70	4269.42	4203.25	4149.07	4104.49	4067.66	4037.14	4011.78	3935.64	3904.17	3890.95	3885.37
280,000	4511.84	4427.54	4358.92	4302.74	4256.51	4218.32	4186.66	4160.36	4081.40	4048.77	4035.06	4029.27
290,000	4672.98	4585.67	4514.60	4456.41	4408.52	4368.97	4336.19	4308.95	4227.17	4193.36	4179.17	4173.17
300,000	4834.11	4743.80	4670.28	4610.07	4560.54	4519.62	4485.71	4457.53	4372.93	4337.96	4323.28	4317.07

MONTHLY AMORTIZING PAYMENTS

AMOUNT OF LOAN	NUMBER OF YEARS IN TERM											
	1	2	3	4	5	6	7	8	9	10	11	12
$ 50	4.58	2.49	1.80	1.46	1.26	1.13	1.04	0.98	0.93	0.89	0.86	0.84
100	9.15	4.97	3.60	2.92	2.52	2.26	2.08	1.95	1.85	1.77	1.72	1.67
200	18.29	9.94	7.19	5.83	5.03	4.51	4.15	3.89	3.69	3.54	3.43	3.34
300	27.44	14.91	10.78	8.74	7.54	6.76	6.22	5.83	5.54	5.31	5.14	5.00
400	36.58	19.88	14.37	11.65	10.05	9.02	8.30	7.77	7.38	7.08	6.85	6.67
500	45.73	24.85	17.96	14.56	12.57	11.27	10.37	9.72	9.23	8.85	8.56	8.33
600	54.87	29.81	21.55	17.47	15.08	13.52	12.44	11.66	11.07	10.62	10.27	10.00
700	64.01	34.78	25.14	20.39	17.59	15.77	14.51	13.60	12.92	12.39	11.99	11.66
800	73.16	39.75	28.73	23.30	20.10	18.03	16.59	15.54	14.76	14.16	13.70	13.33
900	82.30	44.72	32.32	26.21	22.61	20.28	18.66	17.48	16.61	15.93	15.41	14.99
1,000	91.45	49.69	35.91	29.12	25.13	22.53	20.73	19.43	18.45	17.70	17.12	16.66
2,000	182.89	99.37	71.81	58.23	50.25	45.06	41.46	38.85	36.90	35.40	34.23	33.31
3,000	274.33	149.05	107.71	87.35	75.37	67.58	62.18	58.27	55.34	53.10	51.35	49.97
4,000	365.77	198.74	143.61	116.46	100.49	90.11	82.91	77.69	73.79	70.80	68.46	66.62
5,000	457.22	248.42	179.52	145.58	125.62	112.64	103.63	97.11	92.23	88.49	85.58	83.27
6,000	548.66	298.10	215.42	174.69	150.74	135.16	124.36	116.53	110.68	106.19	102.69	99.93
7,000	640.10	347.78	251.32	203.81	175.86	157.69	145.09	135.95	129.12	123.89	119.81	116.58
8,000	731.54	397.47	287.22	232.92	200.98	180.21	165.81	155.37	147.57	141.59	136.92	133.24
9,000	822.98	447.15	323.12	262.03	226.10	202.74	186.54	174.80	166.01	159.29	154.04	149.89
10,000	914.43	496.83	359.03	291.15	251.23	225.27	207.26	194.22	184.46	176.98	171.15	166.54
15,000	1371.64	745.25	538.54	436.72	376.84	337.90	310.89	291.32	276.69	265.47	256.73	249.81
20,000	1828.85	993.66	718.05	582.29	502.45	450.53	414.52	388.43	368.91	353.96	342.30	333.08
25,000	2286.06	1242.08	897.56	727.86	628.06	563.16	518.15	485.54	461.14	442.45	427.88	416.35
30,000	2743.27	1490.49	1077.07	873.44	753.67	675.79	621.78	582.64	553.37	530.94	513.45	499.62
35,000	3200.48	1738.90	1256.58	1019.01	879.28	788.42	725.41	679.75	645.59	619.43	599.03	582.89
40,000	3657.69	1987.32	1436.09	1164.58	1004.89	901.05	829.04	776.85	737.82	707.92	684.60	666.16
45,000	4114.90	2235.73	1615.60	1310.15	1130.50	1013.68	932.67	873.96	830.05	796.41	770.18	749.43
50,000	4572.12	2484.15	1795.11	1455.72	1256.12	1126.31	1036.29	971.07	922.27	884.90	855.75	832.70
55,000	5029.33	2732.56	1974.62	1601.30	1381.73	1238.94	1139.92	1068.17	1014.50	973.39	941.33	915.97
60,000	5486.54	2980.98	2154.13	1746.87	1507.34	1351.57	1243.55	1165.28	1106.73	1061.88	1026.90	999.24
65,000	5943.75	3229.39	2333.64	1892.44	1632.95	1464.20	1347.18	1262.38	1198.95	1150.37	1112.48	1082.51
70,000	6400.96	3477.80	2513.15	2038.01	1758.56	1576.83	1450.81	1359.49	1291.18	1238.86	1198.05	1165.78
75,000	6858.17	3726.22	2692.66	2183.58	1884.17	1689.46	1554.44	1456.60	1383.41	1327.35	1283.63	1249.05
80,000	7315.38	3974.63	2872.17	2329.15	2009.78	1802.09	1658.07	1553.70	1475.63	1415.84	1369.20	1332.31
85,000	7772.59	4223.05	3051.68	2474.73	2135.39	1914.72	1761.70	1650.81	1567.86	1504.32	1454.77	1415.58
90,000	8229.80	4471.46	3231.19	2620.30	2261.00	2027.35	1865.33	1747.91	1660.09	1592.81	1540.35	1498.85
95,000	8687.01	4719.88	3410.70	2765.87	2386.62	2139.98	1968.96	1845.02	1752.31	1681.30	1625.92	1582.12
100,000	9144.23	4968.29	3590.21	2911.44	2512.23	2252.61	2072.58	1942.13	1844.54	1769.79	1711.50	1665.39
105,000	9601.44	5216.70	3769.72	3057.01	2637.84	2365.24	2176.21	2039.23	1936.77	1858.28	1797.07	1748.66
110,000	10058.65	5465.12	3949.23	3202.59	2763.45	2477.87	2279.84	2136.34	2028.99	1946.77	1882.65	1831.93
115,000	10515.86	5713.53	4128.74	3348.16	2889.06	2590.50	2383.47	2233.44	2121.22	2035.26	1968.22	1915.20
120,000	10973.07	5961.95	4308.25	3493.73	3014.67	2703.13	2487.10	2330.55	2213.45	2123.75	2053.80	1998.47
125,000	11430.28	6210.36	4487.76	3639.30	3140.28	2815.76	2590.73	2427.66	2305.67	2212.24	2139.37	2081.74
130,000	11887.49	6458.78	4667.27	3784.87	3265.89	2928.39	2694.36	2524.76	2397.90	2300.73	2224.95	2165.01
135,000	12344.70	6707.19	4846.78	3930.45	3391.50	3041.02	2797.99	2621.87	2490.13	2389.22	2310.52	2248.28
140,000	12801.91	6955.60	5026.29	4076.02	3517.11	3153.65	2901.62	2718.97	2582.35	2477.71	2396.10	2331.55
145,000	13259.12	7204.02	5205.80	4221.59	3642.73	3266.28	3005.25	2816.08	2674.58	2566.20	2481.67	2414.82
150,000	13716.34	7452.43	5385.31	4367.16	3768.34	3378.91	3108.87	2913.19	2766.81	2654.69	2567.25	2498.09
155,000	14173.55	7700.85	5564.83	4512.73	3893.95	3491.54	3212.50	3010.29	2859.03	2743.18	2652.82	2581.35
160,000	14630.76	7949.26	5744.34	4658.30	4019.56	3604.17	3316.13	3107.40	2951.26	2831.67	2738.39	2664.62
165,000	15087.97	8197.67	5923.85	4803.88	4145.17	3716.80	3419.76	3204.50	3043.49	2920.15	2823.97	2747.89
170,000	15545.18	8446.09	6103.36	4949.45	4270.78	3829.43	3523.39	3301.61	3135.71	3008.64	2909.54	2831.16
175,000	16002.39	8694.50	6282.87	5095.02	4396.39	3942.06	3627.02	3398.72	3227.94	3097.13	2995.12	2914.43
180,000	16459.60	8942.92	6462.38	5240.59	4522.00	4054.69	3730.65	3495.82	3320.17	3185.62	3080.69	2997.70
185,000	16916.81	9191.33	6641.89	5386.16	4647.61	4167.32	3834.28	3592.93	3412.39	3274.11	3166.27	3080.97
190,000	17374.02	9439.75	6821.40	5531.74	4773.23	4279.95	3937.91	3690.03	3504.62	3362.60	3251.84	3164.24
195,000	17831.23	9688.16	7000.91	5677.31	4898.84	4392.58	4041.53	3787.14	3596.85	3451.09	3337.42	3247.51
200,000	18288.45	9936.57	7180.42	5822.88	5024.45	4505.21	4145.16	3884.25	3689.07	3539.58	3422.99	3330.78
205,000	18745.66	10184.99	7359.93	5968.45	5150.06	4617.84	4248.79	3981.35	3781.30	3628.07	3508.57	3414.05
210,000	19202.87	10433.40	7539.44	6114.02	5275.67	4730.47	4352.42	4078.46	3873.53	3716.56	3594.14	3497.32
215,000	19660.08	10681.82	7718.95	6259.60	5401.28	4843.10	4456.05	4175.57	3965.75	3805.05	3679.72	3580.59
220,000	20117.29	10930.23	7898.46	6405.17	5526.89	4955.74	4559.68	4272.67	4057.98	3893.54	3765.29	3663.86
225,000	20574.50	11178.65	8077.97	6550.74	5652.50	5068.37	4663.31	4369.78	4150.21	3982.03	3850.87	3747.13
230,000	21031.71	11427.06	8257.48	6696.31	5778.11	5181.00	4766.94	4466.88	4242.43	4070.52	3936.44	3830.40
235,000	21488.92	11675.47	8436.99	6841.88	5903.73	5293.63	4870.57	4563.99	4334.66	4159.01	4022.02	3913.66
240,000	21946.13	11923.89	8616.50	6987.45	6029.34	5406.26	4974.20	4661.10	4426.89	4247.50	4107.59	3996.93
245,000	22403.35	12172.30	8796.01	7133.03	6154.95	5518.89	5077.82	4758.20	4519.11	4335.98	4193.16	4080.20
250,000	22860.56	12420.72	8975.52	7278.60	6280.56	5631.52	5181.45	4855.31	4611.34	4424.47	4278.74	4163.47
255,000	23317.77	12669.13	9155.03	7424.17	6406.17	5744.15	5285.08	4952.41	4703.57	4512.96	4364.31	4246.74
260,000	23774.98	12917.55	9334.54	7569.74	6531.78	5856.78	5388.71	5049.52	4795.79	4601.45	4449.89	4330.01
265,000	24232.19	13165.96	9514.05	7715.31	6657.39	5969.41	5492.34	5146.63	4888.02	4689.94	4535.46	4413.28
270,000	24689.40	13414.37	9693.56	7860.89	6783.00	6082.04	5595.97	5243.73	4980.25	4778.43	4621.04	4496.55
280,000	25603.82	13911.20	10052.58	8152.03	7034.22	6307.30	5803.23	5437.94	5164.70	4955.41	4792.19	4663.09
290,000	26518.24	14408.03	10411.60	8443.17	7285.45	6532.56	6010.49	5632.16	5349.15	5132.39	4963.34	4829.63
300,000	27432.67	14904.86	10770.62	8734.32	7536.67	6757.82	6217.74	5826.37	5533.61	5309.37	5134.49	4996.17

AMOUNT OF LOAN	NUMBER OF YEARS IN TERM											
	13	14	15	16	17	18	19	20	25	30	35	40
$ 50	0.82	0.80	0.79	0.78	0.77	0.77	0.76	0.76	0.74	0.74	0.74	0.73
100	1.63	1.60	1.58	1.56	1.54	1.53	1.52	1.51	1.48	1.47	1.47	1.46
200	3.26	3.20	3.15	3.11	3.08	3.06	3.03	3.01	2.96	2.94	2.93	2.92
300	4.89	4.80	4.73	4.67	4.62	4.58	4.55	4.52	4.44	4.40	4.39	4.38
400	6.52	6.40	6.30	6.22	6.16	6.11	6.06	6.02	5.92	5.87	5.85	5.84
500	8.15	8.00	7.88	7.78	7.70	7.63	7.58	7.53	7.39	7.34	7.31	7.30
600	9.78	9.60	9.45	9.33	9.24	9.16	9.09	9.03	8.87	8.80	8.78	8.76
700	11.40	11.20	11.03	10.89	10.78	10.68	10.60	10.54	10.35	10.27	10.24	10.22
800	13.03	12.80	12.60	12.44	12.31	12.21	12.12	12.04	11.83	11.74	11.70	11.68
900	14.66	14.39	14.18	14.00	13.85	13.73	13.63	13.55	13.30	13.20	13.16	13.14
1,000	16.29	15.99	15.75	15.55	15.39	15.26	15.15	15.05	14.78	14.67	14.62	14.60
2,000	32.58	31.98	31.50	31.10	30.78	30.51	30.29	30.10	29.56	29.33	29.24	29.20
3,000	48.86	47.97	47.24	46.65	46.16	45.76	45.43	45.15	44.33	43.99	43.86	43.80
4,000	65.15	63.96	62.99	62.20	61.55	61.01	60.57	60.20	59.11	58.66	58.47	58.39
5,000	81.43	79.94	78.73	77.75	76.93	76.26	75.71	75.25	73.88	73.32	73.09	72.99
6,000	97.72	95.93	94.48	93.29	92.32	91.52	90.85	90.30	88.66	87.98	87.71	87.59
7,000	114.00	111.92	110.23	108.84	107.71	106.77	105.99	105.35	103.43	102.65	102.32	102.19
8,000	130.29	127.91	125.97	124.39	123.09	122.02	121.13	120.40	118.21	117.31	116.94	116.78
9,000	146.57	143.89	141.72	139.94	138.48	137.27	136.28	135.45	132.98	131.97	131.56	131.38
10,000	162.86	159.88	157.46	155.49	153.86	152.52	151.42	150.50	147.76	146.64	146.17	145.98
15,000	244.28	239.82	236.19	233.23	230.79	228.78	227.12	225.75	221.63	219.95	219.26	218.97
20,000	325.71	319.76	314.92	310.97	307.72	305.04	302.83	300.99	295.51	293.27	292.34	291.95
25,000	407.13	399.69	393.65	388.71	384.65	381.30	378.54	376.24	369.39	366.59	365.42	364.94
30,000	488.56	479.63	472.38	466.45	461.58	457.56	454.24	451.49	443.26	439.90	438.51	437.93
35,000	569.98	559.57	551.11	544.19	538.51	533.82	529.95	526.73	517.14	513.22	511.59	510.91
40,000	651.41	639.51	629.84	621.93	615.44	610.08	605.65	601.98	591.02	586.54	584.68	583.90
45,000	732.84	719.45	708.57	699.67	692.37	686.34	681.36	677.23	664.89	659.85	657.76	656.89
50,000	814.26	799.38	787.29	777.41	769.29	762.60	757.07	752.48	738.77	733.17	730.84	729.87
55,000	895.69	879.32	866.02	855.15	846.22	838.86	832.77	827.72	812.65	806.48	803.93	802.86
60,000	977.11	959.26	944.75	932.89	923.15	915.12	908.48	902.97	886.52	879.80	877.01	875.85
65,000	1058.54	1039.20	1023.48	1010.63	1000.08	991.38	984.19	978.22	960.40	953.12	950.09	948.83
70,000	1139.96	1119.14	1102.21	1088.37	1077.01	1067.64	1059.89	1053.46	1034.28	1026.43	1023.18	1021.82
75,000	1221.39	1199.07	1180.94	1166.11	1153.94	1143.90	1135.60	1128.71	1108.15	1099.75	1096.26	1094.81
80,000	1302.81	1279.01	1259.67	1243.86	1230.87	1220.16	1211.30	1203.96	1182.03	1173.07	1169.35	1167.79
85,000	1384.24	1358.95	1338.40	1321.60	1307.80	1296.42	1287.01	1279.21	1255.91	1246.38	1242.43	1240.78
90,000	1465.67	1438.89	1417.13	1399.34	1384.73	1372.68	1362.72	1354.45	1329.78	1319.70	1315.51	1313.77
95,000	1547.09	1518.83	1495.85	1477.08	1461.66	1448.94	1438.42	1429.70	1403.66	1393.01	1388.60	1386.75
100,000	1628.52	1598.76	1574.58	1554.82	1538.58	1525.20	1514.13	1504.95	1477.53	1466.33	1461.68	1459.74
105,000	1709.94	1678.70	1653.31	1632.56	1615.51	1601.46	1589.84	1580.19	1551.41	1539.65	1534.76	1532.73
110,000	1791.37	1758.64	1732.04	1710.30	1692.44	1677.72	1665.54	1655.44	1625.28	1612.96	1607.85	1605.71
115,000	1872.79	1838.58	1810.77	1788.04	1769.37	1753.98	1741.25	1730.69	1699.16	1686.28	1680.93	1678.70
120,000	1954.22	1918.51	1889.50	1865.78	1846.30	1830.24	1816.96	1806.04	1773.04	1760.60	1754.02	1751.69
125,000	2035.65	1998.45	1968.23	1943.52	1923.23	1906.50	1892.66	1881.18	1846.92	1832.91	1827.10	1824.67
130,000	2117.07	2078.39	2046.96	2021.26	2000.16	1982.76	1968.37	1956.43	1920.79	1906.23	1900.18	1897.66
135,000	2198.50	2158.33	2125.69	2099.00	2077.09	2059.02	2044.07	2031.68	1994.67	1979.54	1973.27	1970.65
140,000	2279.92	2238.27	2204.41	2176.74	2154.02	2135.28	2119.78	2106.92	2068.55	2052.86	2046.35	2043.63
145,000	2361.35	2318.20	2283.14	2254.48	2230.95	2211.54	2195.48	2182.17	2142.42	2126.18	2119.43	2116.62
150,000	2442.77	2398.14	2361.87	2332.22	2307.87	2287.80	2271.19	2257.42	2216.30	2199.49	2192.52	2189.61
155,000	2524.20	2478.08	2440.60	2409.96	2384.80	2364.06	2346.90	2332.66	2290.18	2272.81	2265.60	2262.59
160,000	2605.62	2558.02	2519.33	2487.71	2461.73	2440.32	2422.60	2407.91	2364.05	2346.13	2338.69	2335.58
165,000	2687.05	2637.96	2598.06	2565.45	2538.66	2516.58	2498.31	2483.16	2437.93	2419.44	2411.77	2408.57
170,000	2768.48	2717.89	2676.79	2643.19	2615.59	2592.84	2574.02	2558.41	2511.81	2492.76	2484.85	2481.55
175,000	2849.90	2797.83	2755.52	2720.93	2692.52	2669.10	2649.72	2633.65	2585.68	2566.07	2557.94	2554.54
180,000	2931.33	2877.77	2834.25	2798.67	2769.45	2745.36	2725.43	2708.90	2659.56	2639.39	2631.02	2627.53
185,000	3012.75	2957.71	2912.97	2876.41	2846.38	2821.62	2801.13	2784.15	2733.43	2712.71	2704.10	2700.51
190,000	3094.18	3037.65	2991.70	2954.15	2923.31	2897.88	2876.84	2859.39	2807.31	2786.02	2777.19	2773.50
195,000	3175.60	3117.58	3070.43	3031.89	3000.24	2974.14	2952.55	2934.64	2881.19	2859.34	2850.27	2846.49
200,000	3257.03	3197.52	3149.16	3109.63	3077.16	3050.39	3028.25	3009.89	2955.06	2932.66	2923.36	2919.47
205,000	3338.46	3277.46	3227.89	3187.37	3154.09	3126.65	3103.96	3085.14	3028.94	3005.97	2996.44	2992.46
210,000	3419.88	3357.40	3306.62	3265.11	3231.02	3202.91	3179.67	3160.38	3102.82	3079.29	3069.52	3065.45
215,000	3501.31	3437.34	3385.35	3342.85	3307.95	3279.17	3255.37	3235.63	3176.69	3152.60	3142.61	3138.43
220,000	3582.73	3517.27	3464.08	3420.59	3384.88	3355.43	3331.08	3310.88	3250.57	3225.92	3215.69	3211.42
225,000	3664.16	3597.21	3542.81	3498.33	3461.81	3431.69	3406.78	3386.12	3324.45	3299.24	3288.77	3284.41
230,000	3745.58	3677.15	3621.53	3576.07	3538.74	3507.95	3482.49	3461.37	3398.32	3372.55	3361.86	3357.39
235,000	3827.01	3757.09	3700.26	3653.82	3615.67	3584.21	3558.20	3536.62	3472.20	3445.87	3434.94	3430.38
240,000	3908.43	3837.03	3778.99	3731.56	3692.60	3660.47	3633.90	3611.87	3546.08	3519.19	3508.03	3503.37
245,000	3989.86	3916.96	3857.72	3809.30	3769.52	3736.73	3709.61	3687.11	3619.95	3592.50	3581.11	3576.35
250,000	4071.29	3996.90	3936.45	3887.04	3846.45	3812.99	3785.31	3762.36	3693.83	3665.82	3654.19	3649.34
255,000	4152.71	4076.84	4015.18	3964.78	3923.38	3889.25	3861.02	3837.61	3767.71	3739.13	3727.28	3722.33
260,000	4234.14	4156.78	4093.91	4042.52	4000.31	3965.51	3936.73	3912.85	3841.58	3812.45	3800.36	3795.31
265,000	4315.56	4236.72	4172.64	4120.26	4077.24	4041.77	4012.43	3988.10	3915.46	3885.77	3873.44	3868.30
270,000	4396.99	4316.65	4251.37	4198.00	4154.17	4118.03	4088.14	4063.35	3989.34	3959.08	3946.53	3941.29
280,000	4559.84	4476.53	4408.82	4353.48	4308.03	4270.55	4239.55	4213.84	4137.09	4105.72	4092.70	4087.26
290,000	4722.69	4636.40	4566.28	4508.96	4461.89	4423.07	4390.96	4364.34	4284.84	4252.35	4238.86	4233.23
300,000	4885.54	4796.28	4723.74	4664.44	4615.74	4575.59	4542.38	4514.83	4432.59	4398.98	4385.03	4379.21

MONTHLY AMORTIZING PAYMENTS

AMOUNT OF LOAN	NUMBER OF YEARS IN TERM											
	1	2	3	4	5	6	7	8	9	10	11	12
$ 50	4.58	2.50	1.81	1.47	1.27	1.14	1.05	0.98	0.94	0.90	0.87	0.85
100	9.16	4.99	3.61	2.93	2.53	2.27	2.09	1.96	1.87	1.79	1.73	1.69
200	18.32	9.97	7.21	5.85	5.06	4.54	4.18	3.92	3.73	3.58	3.46	3.37
300	27.47	14.95	10.81	8.78	7.58	6.81	6.27	5.88	5.59	5.36	5.19	5.05
400	36.63	19.93	14.42	11.70	10.11	9.07	8.35	7.83	7.45	7.15	6.92	6.73
500	45.79	24.91	18.02	14.63	12.63	11.34	10.44	9.79	9.31	8.93	8.64	8.42
600	54.94	29.89	21.62	17.55	15.16	13.61	12.53	11.75	11.17	10.72	10.37	10.10
700	64.10	34.87	25.22	20.48	17.69	15.87	14.62	13.71	13.03	12.51	12.10	11.78
800	73.25	39.85	28.83	23.40	20.21	18.14	16.70	15.66	14.89	14.29	13.83	13.46
900	82.41	44.83	32.43	26.33	22.74	20.41	18.79	17.62	16.75	16.08	15.56	15.14
1,000	91.57	49.81	36.03	29.25	25.26	22.67	20.88	19.58	18.61	17.86	17.28	16.83
2,000	183.13	99.61	72.06	58.49	50.52	45.34	41.75	39.15	37.21	35.72	34.56	33.65
3,000	274.69	149.42	108.09	87.74	75.78	68.01	62.62	58.72	55.81	53.58	51.84	50.47
4,000	366.25	199.22	144.11	116.98	101.04	90.67	83.49	78.29	74.41	71.44	69.12	67.29
5,000	457.81	249.02	180.14	146.23	126.29	113.34	104.36	97.86	93.01	89.29	86.40	84.12
6,000	549.37	298.83	216.17	175.47	151.55	136.01	125.23	117.44	111.61	107.15	103.68	100.94
7,000	640.93	348.63	252.19	204.72	176.81	158.67	146.11	137.01	130.21	125.01	120.96	117.76
8,000	732.49	398.43	288.22	233.96	202.07	181.34	166.98	156.58	148.81	142.87	138.24	134.58
9,000	824.05	448.24	324.25	263.21	227.32	204.01	187.85	176.15	167.41	160.73	155.52	151.40
10,000	915.62	498.04	360.28	292.45	252.58	226.67	208.72	195.72	186.01	178.58	172.80	168.23
15,000	1373.42	747.06	540.41	438.67	378.87	340.01	313.08	293.58	279.02	267.87	259.19	252.34
20,000	1831.23	996.07	720.55	584.90	505.16	453.34	417.44	391.44	372.02	357.16	345.59	336.45
25,000	2289.03	1245.09	900.68	731.12	631.45	566.67	521.79	489.30	465.03	446.45	431.99	420.56
30,000	2746.84	1494.11	1080.82	877.34	757.73	680.01	626.15	587.16	558.03	535.74	518.38	504.67
35,000	3204.64	1743.12	1260.95	1023.56	884.02	793.34	730.51	685.02	651.03	625.03	604.78	588.78
40,000	3662.45	1992.14	1441.09	1169.79	1010.31	906.67	834.87	782.88	744.04	714.32	691.17	672.89
45,000	4120.25	2241.16	1621.22	1316.01	1136.60	1020.01	939.23	880.74	837.04	803.61	777.57	757.00
50,000	4578.06	2490.17	1801.36	1462.23	1262.89	1133.34	1043.58	978.60	930.05	892.90	863.97	841.12
55,000	5035.86	2739.19	1981.50	1608.45	1389.17	1246.67	1147.94	1076.46	1023.05	982.19	950.36	925.23
60,000	5493.67	2988.21	2161.63	1754.68	1515.46	1360.01	1252.30	1174.32	1116.05	1071.48	1036.76	1009.34
65,000	5951.47	3237.23	2341.77	1900.90	1641.75	1473.34	1356.66	1272.18	1209.06	1160.77	1123.16	1093.45
70,000	6409.28	3486.24	2521.90	2047.12	1768.04	1586.67	1461.01	1370.04	1302.06	1250.06	1209.55	1177.56
75,000	6867.08	3735.26	2702.04	2193.34	1894.33	1700.01	1565.37	1467.90	1395.07	1339.35	1295.95	1261.67
80,000	7324.89	3984.28	2882.17	2339.57	2020.61	1813.34	1669.73	1565.76	1488.07	1428.64	1382.34	1345.78
85,000	7782.69	4233.29	3062.31	2485.79	2146.90	1926.67	1774.09	1663.62	1581.07	1517.93	1468.74	1429.89
90,000	8240.50	4482.31	3242.44	2632.01	2273.19	2040.01	1878.45	1761.48	1674.08	1607.21	1555.14	1514.00
95,000	8698.31	4731.33	3422.58	2778.23	2399.48	2153.34	1982.80	1859.34	1767.08	1696.50	1641.53	1598.11
100,000	9156.11	4980.34	3602.72	2924.46	2525.77	2266.67	2087.16	1957.20	1860.09	1785.79	1727.93	1682.23
105,000	9613.92	5229.36	3782.85	3070.68	2652.06	2380.01	2191.52	2055.06	1953.09	1875.08	1814.32	1766.34
110,000	10071.72	5478.38	3962.99	3216.90	2778.34	2493.34	2295.88	2152.92	2046.09	1964.37	1900.72	1850.45
115,000	10529.53	5727.39	4143.12	3363.13	2904.63	2606.67	2400.23	2250.78	2139.10	2053.66	1987.12	1934.56
120,000	10987.33	5976.41	4323.26	3509.35	3030.92	2720.01	2504.59	2348.64	2232.10	2142.95	2073.51	2018.67
125,000	11445.14	6225.43	4503.39	3655.57	3157.21	2833.34	2608.95	2446.50	2325.11	2232.24	2159.91	2102.78
130,000	11902.94	6474.45	4683.53	3801.79	3283.50	2946.67	2713.31	2544.36	2418.11	2321.53	2246.31	2186.89
135,000	12360.75	6723.46	4863.66	3948.02	3409.78	3060.01	2817.67	2642.22	2511.11	2410.82	2332.70	2271.00
140,000	12818.55	6972.48	5043.80	4094.24	3536.07	3173.34	2922.02	2740.08	2604.12	2500.11	2419.10	2355.11
145,000	13276.36	7221.50	5223.94	4240.46	3662.36	3286.68	3026.38	2837.94	2697.12	2589.40	2505.49	2439.22
150,000	13734.16	7470.51	5404.07	4386.68	3788.65	3400.01	3130.74	2935.79	2790.13	2678.69	2591.89	2523.34
155,000	14191.97	7719.53	5584.21	4532.91	3914.94	3513.34	3235.10	3033.65	2883.13	2767.98	2678.29	2607.45
160,000	14649.77	7968.55	5764.34	4679.13	4041.22	3626.68	3339.45	3131.51	2976.13	2857.27	2764.68	2691.56
165,000	15107.58	8217.56	5944.48	4825.35	4167.51	3740.01	3443.81	3229.37	3069.14	2946.56	2851.08	2775.67
170,000	15565.38	8466.58	6124.61	4971.57	4293.80	3853.34	3548.17	3327.23	3162.14	3035.85	2937.47	2859.78
175,000	16023.19	8715.60	6304.75	5117.80	4420.09	3966.68	3652.53	3425.09	3255.15	3125.13	3023.87	2943.89
180,000	16481.00	8964.62	6484.88	5264.02	4546.38	4080.01	3756.89	3522.95	3348.15	3214.42	3110.27	3028.00
185,000	16938.80	9213.63	6665.02	5410.24	4672.67	4193.34	3861.24	3620.81	3441.16	3303.71	3196.66	3112.11
190,000	17396.61	9462.65	6845.16	5556.46	4798.95	4306.68	3965.60	3718.67	3534.16	3393.00	3283.06	3196.22
195,000	17854.41	9711.67	7025.29	5702.69	4925.24	4420.01	4069.96	3816.53	3627.16	3482.29	3369.46	3280.33
200,000	18312.22	9960.68	7205.43	5848.91	5051.53	4533.34	4174.32	3914.39	3720.17	3571.58	3455.85	3364.45
205,000	18770.02	10209.70	7385.56	5995.13	5177.82	4646.68	4278.67	4012.25	3813.17	3660.87	3542.25	3448.56
210,000	19227.83	10458.72	7565.70	6141.36	5304.11	4760.01	4383.03	4110.11	3906.18	3750.16	3628.64	3532.67
215,000	19685.63	10707.73	7745.83	6287.58	5430.39	4873.34	4487.39	4207.97	3999.18	3839.45	3715.04	3616.78
220,000	20143.44	10956.75	7925.97	6433.80	5556.68	4986.68	4591.75	4305.83	4092.18	3928.74	3801.44	3700.89
225,000	20601.24	11205.77	8106.10	6580.02	5682.97	5100.01	4696.11	4403.69	4185.19	4018.03	3887.83	3785.00
230,000	21059.05	11454.78	8286.24	6726.25	5809.26	5213.34	4800.46	4501.55	4278.19	4107.32	3974.23	3869.11
235,000	21516.85	11703.80	8466.38	6872.47	5935.55	5326.68	4904.82	4599.41	4371.20	4196.61	4060.62	3953.22
240,000	21974.66	11952.82	8646.51	7018.69	6061.83	5440.01	5009.18	4697.27	4464.20	4285.90	4147.02	4037.33
245,000	22432.46	12201.84	8826.65	7164.91	6188.12	5553.34	5113.54	4795.13	4557.20	4375.19	4233.42	4121.44
250,000	22890.27	12450.85	9006.78	7311.14	6314.41	5666.68	5217.90	4892.99	4650.21	4464.48	4319.81	4205.56
255,000	23348.07	12699.87	9186.92	7457.36	6440.70	5780.01	5322.25	4990.85	4743.21	4553.77	4406.21	4289.67
260,000	23805.88	12948.89	9367.05	7603.58	6566.99	5893.34	5426.61	5088.71	4836.22	4643.05	4492.61	4373.78
265,000	24263.68	13197.90	9547.19	7749.80	6693.28	6006.68	5530.97	5186.57	4929.22	4732.34	4579.00	4457.89
270,000	24721.49	13446.92	9727.32	7896.03	6819.56	6120.01	5635.33	5284.43	5022.22	4821.63	4665.40	4542.00
280,000	25637.10	13944.95	10087.59	8188.47	7072.14	6346.68	5844.04	5480.15	5208.23	5000.21	4838.19	4710.22
290,000	26552.71	14442.99	10447.87	8480.92	7324.72	6573.35	6052.76	5675.87	5394.24	5178.79	5010.98	4878.44
300,000	27468.32	14941.02	10808.14	8773.36	7577.29	6800.01	6261.47	5871.58	5580.25	5357.37	5183.77	5046.67

MONTHLY AMORTIZING PAYMENTS 17.75%

AMOUNT OF LOAN	NUMBER OF YEARS IN TERM											
	13	14	15	16	17	18	19	20	25	30	35	40
$ 50	0.83	0.81	0.80	0.79	0.78	0.78	0.77	0.77	0.75	0.75	0.75	0.75
100	1.65	1.62	1.60	1.58	1.56	1.55	1.54	1.53	1.50	1.49	1.49	1.49
200	3.30	3.24	3.19	3.15	3.12	3.09	3.07	3.05	3.00	2.98	2.97	2.97
300	4.94	4.85	4.78	4.72	4.68	4.64	4.60	4.58	4.50	4.47	4.45	4.45
400	6.59	6.47	6.37	6.30	6.23	6.18	6.14	6.10	5.99	5.95	5.93	5.93
500	8.23	8.09	7.97	7.87	7.79	7.72	7.67	7.63	7.49	7.44	7.42	7.41
600	9.88	9.70	9.56	9.44	9.35	9.27	9.20	9.15	8.99	8.93	8.90	8.89
700	11.53	11.32	11.15	11.02	10.90	10.81	10.74	10.67	10.49	10.41	10.38	10.37
800	13.17	12.94	12.74	12.59	12.46	12.36	12.27	12.20	11.98	11.90	11.86	11.85
900	14.82	14.55	14.34	14.16	14.02	13.90	13.80	13.72	13.48	13.39	13.35	13.33
1,000	16.46	16.17	15.93	15.74	15.58	15.44	15.34	15.25	14.98	14.87	14.83	14.81
2,000	32.92	32.33	31.85	31.47	31.15	30.88	30.67	30.49	29.95	29.74	29.65	29.61
3,000	49.38	48.49	47.78	47.20	46.72	46.32	46.00	45.73	44.93	44.61	44.47	44.42
4,000	65.83	64.66	63.70	62.93	62.29	61.76	61.33	60.97	59.90	59.47	59.30	59.22
5,000	82.29	80.82	79.63	78.66	77.86	77.20	76.66	76.21	74.88	74.34	74.12	74.03
6,000	98.75	96.98	95.55	94.39	93.43	92.64	91.99	91.45	89.85	89.21	88.94	88.83
7,000	115.21	113.15	111.48	110.12	109.00	108.08	107.32	106.69	104.83	104.07	103.76	103.64
8,000	131.66	129.31	127.40	125.85	124.57	123.52	122.65	121.93	119.80	118.94	118.59	118.44
9,000	148.12	145.47	143.33	141.58	140.14	138.96	137.98	137.17	134.78	133.81	133.41	133.25
10,000	164.58	161.64	159.25	157.31	155.71	154.40	153.31	152.41	149.75	148.67	148.23	148.05
15,000	246.86	242.45	238.87	235.96	233.56	231.59	229.97	228.62	224.62	223.01	222.35	222.07
20,000	329.15	323.27	318.50	314.61	311.41	308.79	306.62	304.82	299.50	297.34	296.46	296.10
25,000	411.44	404.09	398.12	393.26	389.27	385.98	383.27	381.03	374.37	371.68	370.57	370.12
30,000	493.72	484.90	477.74	471.91	467.12	463.18	459.93	457.23	449.24	446.01	444.69	444.14
35,000	576.01	565.72	557.37	550.56	544.97	540.37	536.58	533.44	524.12	520.35	518.80	518.16
40,000	658.29	646.53	636.99	629.21	622.82	617.57	613.23	609.64	598.99	594.68	592.92	592.19
45,000	740.58	727.35	716.61	707.86	700.68	694.77	689.89	685.85	673.86	669.02	667.03	666.21
50,000	822.87	808.17	796.24	786.51	778.53	771.96	766.54	762.05	748.73	743.35	741.14	740.23
55,000	905.15	888.98	875.86	865.16	856.38	849.16	843.19	838.26	823.61	817.69	815.26	814.25
60,000	987.44	969.80	955.48	943.81	934.23	926.35	919.85	914.46	898.48	892.02	889.37	888.28
65,000	1069.73	1050.61	1035.11	1022.46	1012.08	1003.55	996.50	990.67	973.35	966.35	963.48	962.30
70,000	1152.01	1131.43	1114.73	1101.11	1089.94	1080.74	1073.16	1066.87	1048.23	1040.69	1037.60	1036.32
75,000	1234.30	1212.25	1194.35	1179.76	1167.79	1157.94	1149.81	1143.08	1123.10	1115.02	1111.71	1110.35
80,000	1316.58	1293.06	1273.98	1258.41	1245.64	1235.14	1226.46	1219.28	1197.97	1189.36	1185.83	1184.37
85,000	1398.87	1373.88	1353.60	1337.06	1323.49	1312.33	1303.12	1295.49	1272.85	1263.69	1259.94	1258.39
90,000	1481.16	1454.69	1433.22	1415.71	1401.35	1389.53	1379.77	1371.69	1347.72	1338.03	1334.05	1332.41
95,000	1563.44	1535.51	1512.85	1494.36	1479.20	1466.72	1456.42	1447.90	1422.59	1412.36	1408.17	1406.44
100,000	1645.73	1616.33	1592.47	1573.01	1557.05	1543.92	1533.08	1524.10	1497.46	1486.70	1482.28	1480.46
105,000	1728.01	1697.14	1672.09	1651.66	1634.90	1621.11	1609.73	1600.31	1572.34	1561.03	1556.39	1554.48
110,000	1810.30	1777.96	1751.72	1730.31	1712.75	1698.31	1686.38	1676.51	1647.21	1635.37	1630.51	1628.50
115,000	1892.59	1858.77	1831.34	1808.96	1790.61	1775.50	1763.04	1752.72	1722.08	1709.70	1704.62	1702.53
120,000	1974.87	1939.59	1910.96	1887.61	1868.46	1852.70	1839.69	1828.92	1796.96	1784.04	1778.74	1776.55
125,000	2057.16	2020.41	1990.59	1966.26	1946.31	1929.90	1916.34	1905.13	1871.83	1858.37	1852.85	1850.57
130,000	2139.45	2101.22	2070.21	2044.91	2024.16	2007.09	1993.00	1981.33	1946.70	1932.70	1926.96	1924.59
135,000	2221.73	2182.04	2149.83	2123.56	2102.02	2084.29	2069.65	2057.54	2021.58	2007.04	2001.08	1998.62
140,000	2304.02	2262.85	2229.46	2202.21	2179.87	2161.48	2146.31	2133.74	2096.45	2081.37	2075.19	2072.64
145,000	2386.30	2343.67	2309.08	2280.86	2257.72	2238.68	2222.96	2209.95	2171.32	2155.71	2149.30	2146.66
150,000	2468.59	2424.49	2388.70	2359.51	2335.57	2315.87	2299.61	2286.15	2246.19	2230.04	2223.42	2220.69
155,000	2550.88	2505.30	2468.33	2438.16	2413.42	2393.07	2376.27	2362.36	2321.07	2304.38	2297.53	2294.71
160,000	2633.16	2586.12	2547.95	2516.81	2491.28	2470.27	2452.92	2438.56	2395.94	2378.71	2371.65	2368.73
165,000	2715.45	2666.93	2627.57	2595.46	2569.13	2547.46	2529.57	2514.77	2470.81	2453.05	2445.76	2442.75
170,000	2797.73	2747.75	2707.20	2674.11	2646.98	2624.66	2606.23	2590.97	2545.69	2527.38	2519.87	2516.78
175,000	2880.02	2828.57	2786.82	2752.76	2724.83	2701.85	2682.88	2667.18	2620.56	2601.72	2593.99	2590.80
180,000	2962.31	2909.38	2866.44	2831.41	2802.69	2779.05	2759.53	2743.38	2695.43	2676.05	2668.10	2664.82
185,000	3044.59	2990.20	2946.07	2910.06	2880.54	2856.24	2836.19	2819.59	2770.31	2750.39	2742.22	2738.84
190,000	3126.88	3071.02	3025.69	2988.71	2958.39	2933.44	2912.84	2895.79	2845.18	2824.72	2816.33	2812.87
195,000	3209.17	3151.83	3105.31	3067.36	3036.24	3010.64	2989.50	2972.00	2920.05	2899.05	2890.44	2886.89
200,000	3291.45	3232.65	3184.94	3146.01	3114.09	3087.83	3066.15	3048.20	2994.92	2973.39	2964.56	2960.91
205,000	3373.74	3313.46	3264.56	3224.66	3191.95	3165.03	3142.80	3124.41	3069.80	3047.72	3038.67	3034.93
210,000	3456.02	3394.28	3344.18	3303.31	3269.80	3242.22	3219.46	3200.61	3144.67	3122.06	3112.78	3108.96
215,000	3538.31	3475.10	3423.81	3381.96	3347.65	3319.42	3296.11	3276.82	3219.54	3196.39	3186.90	3182.98
220,000	3620.60	3555.91	3503.43	3460.61	3425.50	3396.61	3372.76	3353.02	3294.42	3270.73	3261.01	3257.00
225,000	3702.88	3636.73	3583.05	3539.26	3503.36	3473.81	3449.42	3429.23	3369.29	3345.06	3335.13	3331.03
230,000	3785.17	3717.54	3662.68	3617.91	3581.21	3551.00	3526.07	3505.43	3444.16	3419.40	3409.24	3405.05
235,000	3867.45	3798.36	3742.30	3696.56	3659.06	3628.20	3602.72	3581.64	3519.04	3493.73	3483.35	3479.07
240,000	3949.74	3879.18	3821.92	3775.21	3736.91	3705.40	3679.38	3657.84	3593.91	3568.07	3557.47	3553.09
245,000	4032.03	3959.99	3901.55	3853.86	3814.76	3782.59	3756.03	3734.05	3668.78	3642.40	3631.58	3627.12
250,000	4114.31	4040.81	3981.17	3932.51	3892.62	3859.79	3832.68	3810.25	3743.65	3716.74	3705.69	3701.14
255,000	4196.60	4121.62	4060.79	4011.16	3970.47	3936.98	3909.34	3886.46	3818.53	3791.07	3779.81	3775.16
260,000	4278.89	4202.44	4140.42	4089.81	4048.32	4014.18	3985.99	3962.66	3893.40	3865.40	3853.92	3849.18
265,000	4361.17	4283.26	4220.04	4168.46	4126.17	4091.37	4062.65	4038.87	3968.27	3939.74	3928.04	3923.21
270,000	4443.46	4364.07	4299.66	4247.11	4204.03	4168.57	4139.30	4115.07	4043.15	4014.07	4002.15	3997.23
280,000	4608.03	4525.70	4458.91	4404.41	4359.73	4322.96	4292.61	4267.48	4192.89	4162.74	4150.38	4145.27
290,000	4772.60	4687.34	4618.16	4561.71	4515.43	4477.35	4445.91	4419.89	4342.64	4311.41	4298.60	4293.32
300,000	4937.17	4848.97	4777.40	4719.01	4671.14	4631.74	4599.22	4572.30	4492.38	4460.08	4446.83	4441.37

18.00%

MONTHLY AMORTIZING PAYMENTS

AMOUNT OF LOAN	1	2	3	4	5	6	7	8	9	10	11	12
$ 50	4.59	2.50	1.81	1.47	1.27	1.15	1.06	0.99	0.94	0.91	0.88	0.85
100	9.17	5.00	3.62	2.94	2.54	2.29	2.11	1.98	1.88	1.81	1.75	1.70
200	18.34	9.99	7.24	5.88	5.08	4.57	4.21	3.95	3.76	3.61	3.49	3.40
300	27.51	14.98	10.85	8.82	7.62	6.85	6.31	5.92	5.63	5.41	5.24	5.10
400	36.68	19.97	14.47	11.75	10.16	9.13	8.41	7.89	7.51	7.21	6.98	6.80
500	45.84	24.97	18.08	14.69	12.70	11.41	10.51	9.87	9.38	9.01	8.73	8.50
600	55.01	29.96	21.70	17.63	15.24	13.69	12.62	11.84	11.26	10.82	10.47	10.20
700	64.18	34.95	25.31	20.57	17.78	15.97	14.72	13.81	13.13	12.62	12.22	11.90
800	73.35	39.94	28.93	23.50	20.32	18.25	16.82	15.78	15.01	14.42	13.96	13.60
900	82.52	44.94	32.54	26.44	22.86	20.53	18.92	17.76	16.89	16.22	15.70	15.30
1,000	91.68	49.93	36.16	29.38	25.40	22.81	21.02	19.73	18.76	18.02	17.45	17.00
2,000	183.36	99.85	72.31	58.75	50.79	45.62	42.04	39.45	37.52	36.04	34.89	33.99
3,000	275.04	149.78	108.46	88.13	76.19	68.43	63.06	59.17	56.28	54.06	52.34	50.98
4,000	366.72	199.70	144.61	117.50	101.58	91.24	84.08	78.90	75.03	72.08	69.78	67.97
5,000	458.40	249.63	180.77	146.88	126.97	114.04	105.09	98.62	93.79	90.10	87.23	84.96
6,000	550.08	299.55	216.92	176.25	152.37	136.85	126.11	118.34	112.55	108.12	104.67	101.95
7,000	641.76	349.47	253.07	205.63	177.76	159.66	147.13	138.07	131.30	126.13	122.11	118.94
8,000	733.44	399.40	289.22	235.00	203.15	182.47	168.15	157.79	150.06	144.15	139.56	135.93
9,000	825.12	449.32	325.38	264.38	228.55	205.28	189.17	177.51	168.82	162.17	157.00	152.93
10,000	916.80	499.25	361.53	293.75	253.94	228.08	210.18	197.24	187.57	180.19	174.45	169.92
15,000	1375.20	748.87	542.29	440.63	380.91	342.12	315.27	295.85	281.36	270.28	261.67	254.87
20,000	1833.60	998.49	723.05	587.50	507.87	456.16	420.36	394.47	375.14	360.38	348.89	339.83
25,000	2292.00	1248.11	903.81	734.38	634.84	570.20	525.45	493.09	468.93	450.47	436.11	424.78
30,000	2750.40	1497.73	1084.58	881.25	761.81	684.24	630.54	591.70	562.71	540.56	523.33	509.74
35,000	3208.80	1747.35	1265.34	1028.13	888.77	798.28	735.63	690.32	656.50	630.65	610.55	594.70
40,000	3667.20	1996.97	1446.10	1175.00	1015.74	912.32	840.72	788.93	750.28	720.75	697.77	679.65
45,000	4125.60	2246.59	1626.86	1321.88	1142.71	1026.36	945.81	887.55	844.06	810.84	784.99	764.61
50,000	4584.00	2496.21	1807.62	1468.75	1269.68	1140.39	1050.90	986.17	937.85	900.93	872.21	849.56
55,000	5042.40	2745.83	1988.39	1615.63	1396.64	1254.43	1155.99	1084.78	1031.63	991.02	959.43	934.52
60,000	5500.80	2995.45	2169.15	1762.50	1523.61	1368.47	1261.08	1183.40	1125.42	1081.12	1046.66	1019.48
65,000	5959.20	3245.07	2349.91	1909.38	1650.58	1482.51	1366.16	1282.01	1219.20	1171.21	1133.88	1104.43
70,000	6417.60	3494.69	2530.67	2056.25	1777.54	1596.55	1471.25	1380.63	1312.99	1261.30	1221.10	1189.39
75,000	6876.00	3744.31	2711.43	2203.13	1904.51	1710.59	1576.34	1479.25	1406.77	1351.39	1308.32	1274.34
80,000	7334.40	3993.93	2892.20	2350.00	2031.48	1824.63	1681.43	1577.86	1500.56	1441.49	1395.54	1359.30
85,000	7792.80	4243.55	3072.96	2496.88	2158.45	1938.67	1786.52	1676.48	1594.34	1531.58	1482.76	1444.26
90,000	8251.20	4493.17	3253.72	2643.75	2285.41	2052.71	1891.61	1775.09	1688.12	1621.67	1569.98	1529.21
95,000	8709.60	4742.79	3434.48	2790.63	2412.38	2166.75	1996.70	1873.71	1781.91	1711.76	1657.20	1614.17
100,000	9168.00	4992.42	3615.24	2937.50	2539.35	2280.78	2101.79	1972.33	1875.69	1801.86	1744.42	1699.12
105,000	9626.40	5242.04	3796.01	3084.38	2666.31	2394.82	2206.88	2070.94	1969.48	1891.95	1831.64	1784.08
110,000	10084.80	5491.66	3976.77	3231.25	2793.28	2508.86	2311.97	2169.56	2063.26	1982.04	1918.86	1869.04
115,000	10543.20	5741.28	4157.53	3378.13	2920.25	2622.90	2417.06	2268.17	2157.05	2072.13	2006.09	1953.99
120,000	11001.60	5990.90	4338.29	3525.00	3047.22	2736.94	2522.15	2366.79	2250.83	2162.23	2093.31	2038.95
125,000	11460.00	6240.52	4519.05	3671.88	3174.18	2850.98	2627.23	2465.41	2344.62	2252.32	2180.53	2123.90
130,000	11918.40	6490.14	4699.82	3818.75	3301.15	2965.02	2732.32	2564.02	2438.40	2342.41	2267.75	2208.86
135,000	12376.80	6739.76	4880.58	3965.63	3428.12	3079.06	2837.41	2662.64	2532.18	2432.51	2354.97	2293.82
140,000	12835.20	6989.38	5061.34	4112.50	3555.08	3193.10	2942.50	2761.25	2625.97	2522.60	2442.19	2378.77
145,000	13293.60	7239.00	5242.10	4259.38	3682.05	3307.13	3047.59	2859.87	2719.75	2612.69	2529.41	2463.73
150,000	13752.00	7488.62	5422.86	4406.25	3809.02	3421.17	3152.68	2958.49	2813.54	2702.78	2616.63	2548.68
155,000	14210.40	7738.24	5603.63	4553.13	3935.99	3535.21	3257.77	3057.10	2907.32	2792.88	2703.85	2633.64
160,000	14668.80	7987.86	5784.39	4700.00	4062.95	3649.25	3362.86	3155.72	3001.11	2882.97	2791.07	2718.60
165,000	15127.20	8237.48	5965.15	4846.88	4189.92	3763.29	3467.95	3254.34	3094.89	2973.06	2878.29	2803.55
170,000	15585.60	8487.10	6145.91	4993.75	4316.89	3877.33	3573.04	3352.95	3188.68	3063.15	2965.52	2888.51
175,000	16044.00	8736.72	6326.67	5140.63	4443.85	3991.37	3678.13	3451.57	3282.46	3153.25	3052.74	2973.46
180,000	16502.40	8986.34	6507.44	5287.50	4570.82	4105.41	3783.22	3550.18	3376.24	3243.34	3139.96	3058.42
185,000	16960.80	9235.96	6688.20	5434.38	4697.79	4219.45	3888.31	3648.80	3470.03	3333.43	3227.18	3143.38
190,000	17419.20	9485.58	6868.96	5581.25	4824.76	4333.49	3993.39	3747.42	3563.81	3423.52	3314.40	3228.33
195,000	17877.60	9735.20	7049.72	5728.13	4951.72	4447.52	4098.48	3846.03	3657.60	3513.62	3401.62	3313.29
200,000	18336.00	9984.83	7230.48	5875.00	5078.69	4561.56	4203.57	3944.65	3751.38	3603.71	3488.84	3398.24
205,000	18794.40	10234.45	7411.25	6021.88	5205.66	4675.60	4308.66	4043.26	3845.17	3693.80	3576.06	3483.20
210,000	19252.80	10484.07	7592.01	6168.75	5332.62	4789.64	4413.75	4141.88	3938.95	3783.89	3663.28	3568.16
215,000	19711.20	10733.69	7772.77	6315.63	5459.59	4903.68	4518.84	4240.50	4032.74	3873.99	3750.50	3653.11
220,000	20169.60	10983.31	7953.53	6462.50	5586.56	5017.72	4623.93	4339.11	4126.52	3964.08	3837.72	3738.07
225,000	20628.00	11232.93	8134.29	6609.38	5713.53	5131.76	4729.02	4437.73	4220.30	4054.17	3924.95	3823.02
230,000	21086.40	11482.55	8315.06	6756.25	5840.49	5245.80	4834.11	4536.34	4314.09	4144.26	4012.17	3907.98
235,000	21544.80	11732.17	8495.82	6903.13	5967.46	5359.84	4939.20	4634.96	4407.87	4234.36	4099.39	3992.94
240,000	22003.20	11981.79	8676.58	7050.00	6094.43	5473.87	5044.29	4733.58	4501.66	4324.45	4186.61	4077.89
245,000	22461.60	12231.41	8857.34	7196.88	6221.39	5587.91	5149.38	4832.19	4595.44	4414.54	4273.83	4162.85
250,000	22920.00	12481.03	9038.10	7343.75	6348.36	5701.95	5254.46	4930.81	4689.23	4504.63	4361.05	4247.80
255,000	23378.40	12730.65	9218.87	7490.63	6475.33	5815.99	5359.55	5029.42	4783.01	4594.73	4448.27	4332.76
260,000	23836.80	12980.27	9399.63	7637.50	6602.30	5930.03	5464.64	5128.04	4876.80	4684.82	4535.49	4417.72
265,000	24295.20	13229.89	9580.39	7784.38	6729.26	6044.07	5569.73	5226.66	4970.58	4774.91	4622.71	4502.67
270,000	24753.60	13479.51	9761.15	7931.25	6856.23	6158.11	5674.82	5325.27	5064.36	4865.01	4709.93	4587.63
280,000	25670.40	13978.75	10122.68	8225.00	7110.16	6386.19	5885.00	5522.50	5251.93	5045.19	4884.38	4757.54
290,000	26587.20	14477.99	10484.20	8518.75	7364.10	6614.26	6095.18	5719.74	5439.50	5225.38	5058.82	4927.45
300,000	27504.00	14977.24	10845.72	8812.50	7618.03	6842.34	6305.36	5916.97	5627.07	5405.56	5233.26	5097.36

130

AMOUNT OF LOAN	NUMBER OF YEARS IN TERM											
	13	14	15	16	17	18	19	20	25	30	35	40
$ 50	0.84	0.82	0.81	0.80	0.79	0.79	0.78	0.78	0.76	0.76	0.76	0.76
100	1.67	1.64	1.62	1.60	1.58	1.57	1.56	1.55	1.52	1.51	1.51	1.51
200	3.33	3.27	3.23	3.19	3.16	3.13	3.11	3.09	3.04	3.02	3.01	3.01
300	4.99	4.91	4.84	4.78	4.73	4.69	4.66	4.63	4.56	4.53	4.51	4.51
400	6.66	6.54	6.45	6.37	6.31	6.26	6.21	6.18	6.07	6.03	6.02	6.01
500	8.32	8.17	8.06	7.96	7.88	7.82	7.77	7.72	7.59	7.54	7.52	7.51
600	9.98	9.81	9.67	9.55	9.46	9.38	9.32	9.26	9.11	9.05	9.02	9.01
700	11.65	11.44	11.28	11.14	11.03	10.94	10.87	10.81	10.63	10.55	10.53	10.51
800	13.31	13.08	12.89	12.74	12.61	12.51	12.42	12.35	12.14	12.06	12.03	12.01
900	14.97	14.71	14.50	14.33	14.19	14.07	13.97	13.89	13.66	13.57	13.53	13.52
1,000	16.64	16.34	16.11	15.92	15.76	15.63	15.53	15.44	15.18	15.08	15.03	15.02
2,000	33.27	32.68	32.21	31.83	31.52	31.26	31.05	30.87	30.35	30.15	30.06	30.03
3,000	49.90	49.02	48.32	47.74	47.27	46.89	46.57	46.30	45.53	45.22	45.09	45.04
4,000	66.53	65.36	64.42	63.66	63.03	62.51	62.09	61.74	60.70	60.29	60.12	60.05
5,000	83.16	81.70	80.53	79.57	78.78	78.14	77.61	77.17	75.88	75.36	75.15	75.06
6,000	99.79	98.04	96.63	95.48	94.54	93.77	93.13	92.60	91.05	90.43	90.18	90.08
7,000	116.42	114.38	112.73	111.39	110.30	109.39	108.65	108.04	106.23	105.50	105.21	105.09
8,000	133.05	130.72	128.84	127.31	126.05	125.02	124.17	123.47	121.40	120.57	120.24	120.10
9,000	149.68	147.06	144.94	143.22	141.81	140.65	139.69	138.90	136.57	135.64	135.27	135.11
10,000	166.31	163.40	161.05	159.13	157.56	156.27	155.21	154.34	151.75	150.71	150.29	150.12
15,000	249.46	245.10	241.57	238.69	236.34	234.41	232.82	231.50	227.62	226.07	225.44	225.18
20,000	332.61	326.80	322.09	318.26	315.12	312.54	310.42	308.67	303.49	301.42	300.58	300.24
25,000	415.76	408.49	402.61	397.82	393.90	390.68	388.02	385.83	379.36	376.78	375.73	375.30
30,000	498.91	490.19	483.13	477.38	472.68	468.81	465.63	463.00	455.23	452.13	450.87	450.36
35,000	582.06	571.89	563.65	556.94	551.46	546.95	543.23	540.16	531.11	527.48	526.02	525.42
40,000	665.21	653.59	644.17	636.51	630.23	625.08	620.84	617.33	606.98	602.84	601.16	600.48
45,000	748.36	735.28	724.69	716.07	709.01	703.22	698.44	694.50	682.85	678.19	676.31	675.54
50,000	831.51	816.98	805.22	795.63	787.79	781.35	776.04	771.66	758.72	753.55	751.45	750.60
55,000	914.66	898.68	885.74	875.20	866.57	859.49	853.65	848.83	834.59	828.90	826.60	825.66
60,000	997.81	980.38	966.26	954.76	945.35	937.62	931.25	925.99	910.46	904.26	901.74	900.71
65,000	1080.96	1062.07	1046.78	1034.32	1024.13	1015.75	1008.86	1003.16	986.33	979.61	976.88	975.77
70,000	1164.11	1143.77	1127.30	1113.88	1102.91	1093.89	1086.46	1080.32	1062.21	1054.96	1052.03	1050.83
75,000	1247.26	1225.47	1207.82	1193.45	1181.68	1172.02	1164.06	1157.49	1138.08	1130.32	1127.17	1125.89
80,000	1330.41	1307.17	1288.34	1273.01	1260.46	1250.16	1241.67	1234.65	1213.95	1205.67	1202.32	1200.95
85,000	1413.56	1388.86	1368.86	1352.57	1339.24	1328.29	1319.27	1311.82	1289.82	1281.03	1277.46	1276.01
90,000	1496.71	1470.56	1449.38	1432.14	1418.02	1406.43	1396.88	1388.99	1365.69	1356.38	1352.61	1351.07
95,000	1579.86	1552.26	1529.90	1511.70	1496.80	1484.56	1474.48	1466.15	1441.56	1431.74	1427.75	1426.13
100,000	1663.01	1633.96	1610.43	1591.26	1575.58	1562.70	1552.08	1543.32	1517.43	1507.09	1502.90	1501.19
105,000	1746.16	1715.65	1690.95	1670.82	1654.36	1640.83	1629.69	1620.48	1593.31	1582.44	1578.04	1576.25
110,000	1829.31	1797.35	1771.47	1750.30	1733.14	1718.97	1707.29	1697.65	1669.18	1657.80	1653.19	1651.31
115,000	1912.46	1879.05	1851.99	1829.95	1811.91	1797.10	1784.89	1774.81	1745.05	1733.15	1728.33	1726.36
120,000	1995.61	1960.75	1932.51	1909.51	1890.69	1875.23	1862.50	1851.98	1820.92	1808.51	1803.48	1801.42
125,000	2078.76	2042.44	2013.03	1989.07	1969.47	1953.37	1940.10	1929.14	1896.79	1883.86	1878.62	1876.48
130,000	2161.91	2124.14	2093.55	2068.64	2048.25	2031.50	2017.71	2006.31	1972.66	1959.22	1953.76	1951.54
135,000	2245.06	2205.84	2174.07	2148.20	2127.03	2109.64	2095.31	2083.48	2048.54	2034.57	2028.91	2026.60
140,000	2328.21	2287.54	2254.59	2227.76	2205.81	2187.77	2172.91	2160.64	2124.41	2109.92	2104.05	2101.66
145,000	2411.36	2369.23	2335.12	2307.33	2284.59	2265.91	2250.52	2237.81	2200.28	2185.28	2179.20	2176.72
150,000	2494.51	2450.93	2415.64	2386.89	2363.36	2344.04	2328.12	2314.97	2276.15	2260.63	2254.34	2251.78
155,000	2577.66	2532.63	2496.16	2466.45	2442.14	2422.18	2405.73	2392.14	2352.02	2335.99	2329.49	2326.84
160,000	2660.81	2614.33	2576.68	2546.01	2520.92	2500.31	2483.33	2469.30	2427.89	2411.34	2404.63	2401.90
165,000	2743.96	2696.02	2657.20	2625.58	2599.70	2578.45	2560.93	2546.47	2503.76	2486.70	2479.78	2476.96
170,000	2827.11	2777.72	2737.72	2705.14	2678.48	2656.58	2638.54	2623.63	2579.64	2562.05	2554.92	2552.01
175,000	2910.26	2859.42	2818.24	2784.70	2757.26	2734.71	2716.14	2700.80	2655.51	2637.40	2630.07	2627.07
180,000	2993.41	2941.12	2898.76	2864.27	2836.04	2812.85	2793.75	2777.97	2731.38	2712.76	2705.21	2702.13
185,000	3076.56	3022.81	2979.28	2943.83	2914.81	2890.98	2871.35	2855.13	2807.25	2788.11	2780.36	2777.19
190,000	3159.71	3104.51	3059.80	3023.39	2993.59	2969.12	2948.95	2932.30	2883.12	2863.47	2855.50	2852.25
195,000	3242.86	3186.21	3140.33	3102.95	3072.37	3047.25	3026.56	3009.46	2958.99	2938.82	2930.64	2927.31
200,000	3326.01	3267.91	3220.85	3182.52	3151.15	3125.39	3104.16	3086.63	3034.86	3014.18	3005.79	3002.37
205,000	3409.16	3349.60	3301.37	3262.08	3229.93	3203.52	3181.77	3163.79	3110.74	3089.53	3080.93	3077.43
210,000	3492.31	3431.30	3381.89	3341.64	3308.71	3281.66	3259.37	3240.96	3186.61	3164.88	3156.08	3152.49
215,000	3575.46	3513.00	3462.41	3421.20	3387.49	3359.79	3336.97	3318.12	3262.48	3240.24	3231.22	3227.55
220,000	3658.61	3594.70	3542.93	3500.77	3466.27	3437.93	3414.58	3395.29	3338.35	3315.59	3306.37	3302.61
225,000	3741.76	3676.39	3623.45	3580.33	3545.04	3516.06	3492.18	3472.46	3414.22	3390.95	3381.51	3377.67
230,000	3824.91	3758.09	3703.97	3659.89	3623.82	3594.20	3569.78	3549.62	3490.09	3466.30	3456.66	3452.72
235,000	3908.06	3839.79	3784.49	3739.46	3702.60	3672.33	3647.39	3626.79	3565.97	3541.66	3531.80	3527.78
240,000	3991.21	3921.49	3865.02	3819.02	3781.38	3750.46	3724.99	3703.95	3641.84	3617.01	3606.95	3602.84
245,000	4074.36	4003.18	3945.54	3898.58	3860.16	3828.60	3802.60	3781.12	3717.71	3692.36	3682.09	3677.90
250,000	4157.51	4084.88	4026.06	3978.14	3938.94	3906.73	3880.20	3858.28	3793.58	3767.72	3757.23	3752.96
255,000	4240.66	4166.58	4106.58	4057.71	4017.72	3984.87	3957.80	3935.45	3869.45	3843.07	3832.38	3828.02
260,000	4323.81	4248.28	4187.10	4137.27	4096.49	4063.00	4035.41	4012.61	3945.32	3918.43	3907.52	3903.08
265,000	4406.96	4329.97	4267.62	4216.83	4175.27	4141.14	4113.01	4089.78	4021.19	3993.78	3982.67	3978.14
270,000	4490.11	4411.67	4348.14	4296.40	4254.05	4219.27	4190.62	4166.95	4097.07	4069.14	4057.81	4053.20
280,000	4656.41	4575.07	4509.18	4455.52	4411.61	4375.54	4345.82	4321.28	4248.81	4219.84	4208.10	4203.32
290,000	4822.71	4738.46	4670.23	4614.65	4569.17	4531.81	4501.03	4475.61	4400.55	4370.55	4358.39	4353.43
300,000	4989.01	4901.86	4831.27	4773.77	4726.72	4688.08	4656.24	4629.94	4552.29	4521.26	4508.68	4503.55

18.25% MONTHLY AMORTIZING PAYMENTS

AMOUNT OF LOAN	\multicolumn{12}{c}{NUMBER OF YEARS IN TERM}										
	1	2	3	4	5	6	7	8	9	10	11	12
$ 50	4.59	2.51	1.82	1.48	1.28	1.15	1.06	1.00	0.95	0.91	0.89	0.86
100	9.18	5.01	3.63	2.96	2.56	2.30	2.12	1.99	1.90	1.82	1.77	1.72
200	18.36	10.01	7.26	5.91	5.11	4.59	4.24	3.98	3.79	3.64	3.53	3.44
300	27.54	15.02	10.89	8.86	7.66	6.89	6.35	5.97	5.68	5.46	5.29	5.15
400	36.72	20.02	14.52	11.81	10.22	9.18	8.47	7.96	7.57	7.28	7.05	6.87
500	45.90	25.03	18.14	14.76	12.77	11.48	10.59	9.94	9.46	9.09	8.81	8.59
600	55.08	30.03	21.77	17.71	15.32	13.77	12.70	11.93	11.35	10.91	10.57	10.30
700	64.26	35.04	25.40	20.66	17.88	16.07	14.82	13.92	13.24	12.73	12.33	12.02
800	73.44	40.04	29.03	23.61	20.43	18.36	16.94	15.91	15.14	14.55	14.09	13.73
900	82.62	45.05	32.66	26.56	22.98	20.66	19.05	17.89	17.03	16.37	15.85	15.45
1,000	91.80	50.05	36.28	29.51	25.53	22.95	21.17	19.88	18.92	18.18	17.61	17.17
2,000	183.60	100.09	72.56	59.02	51.06	45.90	42.33	39.76	37.83	36.36	35.22	34.33
3,000	275.40	150.14	108.84	88.52	76.59	68.85	63.50	59.63	56.75	54.54	52.83	51.49
4,000	367.20	200.18	145.12	118.03	102.12	91.80	84.66	79.51	75.66	72.72	70.44	68.65
5,000	459.00	250.23	181.39	147.53	127.65	114.75	105.83	99.38	94.57	90.90	88.05	85.81
6,000	550.80	300.27	217.67	177.04	153.18	137.70	126.99	119.26	113.49	109.08	105.66	102.97
7,000	642.60	350.32	253.95	206.55	178.71	160.65	148.16	139.13	132.40	127.26	123.27	120.13
8,000	734.40	400.36	290.23	236.05	204.24	183.60	169.32	159.01	151.31	145.44	140.88	137.29
9,000	826.20	450.41	326.51	265.56	229.77	206.55	190.49	178.88	170.23	163.62	158.49	154.45
10,000	918.00	500.45	362.78	295.06	255.30	229.50	211.65	198.76	189.14	181.80	176.10	171.61
15,000	1376.99	750.68	544.17	442.59	382.95	344.25	317.47	298.13	283.71	272.70	264.15	257.42
20,000	1835.99	1000.90	725.56	590.12	510.60	458.99	423.30	397.51	378.28	363.60	352.20	343.22
25,000	2294.98	1251.13	906.95	737.65	638.25	573.74	529.12	496.88	472.84	454.50	440.25	429.03
30,000	2753.98	1501.35	1088.34	885.18	765.89	688.49	634.94	596.26	567.41	545.40	528.30	514.83
35,000	3212.97	1751.58	1269.73	1032.71	893.54	803.23	740.77	695.63	661.98	636.30	616.35	600.63
40,000	3671.97	2001.80	1451.12	1180.24	1021.19	917.98	846.59	795.01	756.55	727.20	704.40	686.44
45,000	4130.96	2252.03	1632.51	1327.77	1148.84	1032.73	952.41	894.38	851.12	818.10	792.44	772.24
50,000	4589.96	2502.25	1813.90	1475.29	1276.49	1147.47	1058.24	993.76	945.68	908.99	880.49	858.05
55,000	5048.95	2752.48	1995.29	1622.82	1404.13	1262.22	1164.06	1093.13	1040.25	999.89	968.54	943.85
60,000	5507.95	3002.70	2176.68	1770.35	1531.78	1376.97	1269.88	1192.51	1134.82	1090.79	1056.59	1029.66
65,000	5966.94	3252.93	2358.07	1917.88	1659.43	1491.71	1375.71	1291.88	1229.39	1181.69	1144.64	1115.46
70,000	6425.94	3503.15	2539.46	2065.41	1787.08	1606.46	1481.53	1391.26	1323.95	1272.59	1232.69	1201.26
75,000	6884.93	3753.38	2720.85	2212.94	1914.73	1721.21	1587.35	1490.63	1418.52	1363.49	1320.74	1287.07
80,000	7343.93	4003.60	2902.24	2360.47	2042.37	1835.95	1693.18	1590.01	1513.09	1454.39	1408.79	1372.87
85,000	7802.92	4253.83	3083.63	2508.00	2170.02	1950.70	1799.00	1689.38	1607.66	1545.29	1496.84	1458.68
90,000	8261.92	4504.05	3265.02	2655.53	2297.67	2065.45	1904.82	1788.76	1702.23	1636.19	1584.88	1544.48
95,000	8720.91	4754.28	3446.41	2803.06	2425.32	2180.19	2010.64	1888.13	1796.79	1727.08	1672.93	1630.29
100,000	9179.91	5004.50	3627.80	2950.58	2552.97	2294.94	2116.47	1987.51	1891.36	1817.98	1760.98	1716.09
105,000	9638.90	5254.73	3809.19	3098.11	2680.62	2409.69	2222.29	2086.89	1985.93	1908.88	1849.03	1801.89
110,000	10097.90	5504.95	3990.58	3245.64	2808.26	2524.43	2328.11	2186.26	2080.50	1999.78	1937.08	1887.70
115,000	10556.89	5755.18	4171.97	3393.17	2935.91	2639.18	2433.94	2285.64	2175.06	2090.68	2025.13	1973.50
120,000	11015.89	6005.40	4353.36	3540.70	3063.56	2753.93	2539.76	2385.01	2269.63	2181.58	2113.18	2059.31
125,000	11474.88	6255.63	4534.75	3688.23	3191.21	2868.67	2645.58	2484.39	2364.20	2272.48	2201.23	2145.11
130,000	11933.88	6505.85	4716.14	3835.76	3318.86	2983.42	2751.41	2583.76	2458.77	2363.38	2289.27	2230.91
135,000	12392.87	6756.08	4897.53	3983.29	3446.50	3098.17	2857.23	2683.14	2553.34	2454.28	2377.32	2316.72
140,000	12851.87	7006.30	5078.92	4130.82	3574.15	3212.91	2963.05	2782.51	2647.90	2545.17	2465.37	2402.52
145,000	13310.86	7256.53	5260.31	4278.35	3701.80	3327.66	3068.88	2881.89	2742.47	2636.07	2553.42	2488.33
150,000	13769.86	7506.75	5441.69	4425.87	3829.45	3442.41	3174.70	2981.26	2837.04	2726.97	2641.47	2574.13
155,000	14228.85	7756.98	5623.08	4573.40	3957.10	3557.15	3280.52	3080.64	2931.61	2817.87	2729.52	2659.94
160,000	14687.85	8007.20	5804.47	4720.93	4084.74	3671.90	3386.35	3180.01	3026.17	2908.77	2817.57	2745.74
165,000	15146.84	8257.43	5985.86	4868.46	4212.39	3786.65	3492.17	3279.39	3120.74	2999.67	2905.62	2831.54
170,000	15605.84	8507.65	6167.25	5015.99	4340.04	3901.39	3597.99	3378.76	3215.31	3090.57	2993.67	2917.35
175,000	16064.83	8757.88	6348.64	5163.52	4467.69	4016.14	3703.81	3478.14	3309.88	3181.47	3081.71	3003.15
180,000	16523.83	9008.10	6530.03	5311.05	4595.34	4130.89	3809.64	3577.51	3404.45	3272.37	3169.76	3088.96
185,000	16982.82	9258.33	6711.42	5458.58	4722.99	4245.63	3915.46	3676.89	3499.01	3363.26	3257.81	3174.76
190,000	17441.82	9508.55	6892.81	5606.11	4850.63	4360.38	4021.28	3776.26	3593.58	3454.16	3345.86	3260.57
195,000	17900.81	9758.78	7074.20	5753.64	4978.28	4475.13	4127.11	3875.64	3688.15	3545.06	3433.91	3346.37
200,000	18359.81	10009.00	7255.59	5901.16	5105.93	4589.87	4232.93	3975.02	3782.72	3635.96	3521.96	3432.17
205,000	18818.80	10259.23	7436.98	6048.69	5233.58	4704.62	4338.75	4074.39	3877.28	3726.86	3610.01	3517.98
210,000	19277.80	10509.45	7618.37	6196.22	5361.23	4819.37	4444.58	4173.77	3971.85	3817.76	3698.06	3603.78
215,000	19736.79	10759.68	7799.76	6343.75	5488.87	4934.11	4550.40	4273.14	4066.42	3908.66	3786.10	3689.59
220,000	20195.79	11009.90	7981.15	6491.28	5616.52	5048.86	4656.22	4372.52	4160.99	3999.56	3874.15	3775.39
225,000	20654.78	11260.13	8162.54	6638.81	5744.17	5163.61	4762.05	4471.89	4255.56	4090.46	3962.20	3861.20
230,000	21113.78	11510.35	8343.93	6786.34	5871.82	5278.35	4867.87	4571.27	4350.12	4181.35	4050.25	3947.00
235,000	21572.77	11760.58	8525.32	6933.87	5999.47	5393.10	4973.69	4670.64	4444.69	4272.25	4138.30	4032.80
240,000	22031.77	12010.80	8706.71	7081.40	6127.11	5507.85	5079.52	4770.02	4539.26	4363.15	4226.35	4118.61
245,000	22490.76	12261.03	8888.10	7228.93	6254.76	5622.59	5185.34	4869.39	4633.83	4454.05	4314.40	4204.41
250,000	22949.76	12511.25	9069.49	7376.45	6382.41	5737.34	5291.16	4968.77	4728.39	4544.95	4402.45	4290.22
255,000	23408.75	12761.47	9250.88	7523.98	6510.06	5852.09	5396.98	5068.14	4822.96	4635.85	4490.50	4376.02
260,000	23867.75	13011.70	9432.27	7671.51	6637.71	5966.84	5502.81	5167.52	4917.53	4726.75	4578.54	4461.82
265,000	24326.74	13261.92	9613.66	7819.04	6765.36	6081.58	5608.63	5266.89	5012.10	4817.65	4666.59	4547.63
270,000	24785.74	13512.15	9795.05	7966.57	6893.00	6196.33	5714.45	5366.27	5106.67	4908.55	4754.64	4633.43
280,000	25703.73	14012.60	10157.83	8261.63	7148.30	6425.82	5926.10	5565.02	5295.80	5090.34	4930.74	4805.04
290,000	26621.72	14513.05	10520.61	8556.69	7403.60	6655.32	6137.75	5763.77	5484.94	5272.14	5106.84	4976.65
300,000	27539.71	15013.50	10883.38	8851.74	7658.89	6884.81	6349.39	5962.52	5674.07	5453.94	5282.94	5148.26

132

AMOUNT OF LOAN	NUMBER OF YEARS IN TERM											
	13	14	15	16	17	18	19	20	25	30	35	40
$ 50	0.85	0.83	0.82	0.81	0.80	0.80	0.79	0.79	0.77	0.77	0.77	0.77
100	1.69	1.66	1.63	1.61	1.60	1.59	1.58	1.57	1.54	1.53	1.53	1.53
200	3.37	3.31	3.26	3.22	3.19	3.17	3.15	3.13	3.08	3.06	3.05	3.05
300	5.05	4.96	4.89	4.83	4.79	4.75	4.72	4.69	4.62	4.59	4.58	4.57
400	6.73	6.61	6.52	6.44	6.38	6.33	6.29	6.26	6.15	6.12	6.10	6.09
500	8.41	8.26	8.15	8.05	7.98	7.91	7.86	7.82	7.69	7.64	7.62	7.61
600	10.09	9.91	9.78	9.66	9.57	9.49	9.43	9.38	9.23	9.17	9.15	9.14
700	11.77	11.57	11.40	11.27	11.16	11.08	11.00	10.94	10.77	10.70	10.67	10.66
800	13.45	13.22	13.03	12.88	12.76	12.66	12.57	12.51	12.30	12.23	12.19	12.18
900	15.13	14.87	14.66	14.49	14.35	14.24	14.15	14.07	13.84	13.75	13.72	13.70
1,000	16.81	16.52	16.29	16.10	15.95	15.82	15.72	15.63	15.38	15.28	15.24	15.22
2,000	33.61	33.04	32.57	32.20	31.89	31.64	31.43	31.26	30.75	30.56	30.48	30.44
3,000	50.42	49.55	48.86	48.29	47.83	47.45	47.14	46.88	46.13	45.83	45.71	45.66
4,000	67.22	66.07	65.14	64.39	63.77	63.27	62.85	62.51	61.50	61.11	60.95	60.88
5,000	84.02	82.59	81.43	80.48	79.71	79.08	78.56	78.13	76.88	76.38	76.18	76.10
6,000	100.83	99.10	97.71	96.58	95.65	94.90	94.27	93.76	92.25	91.66	91.42	91.32
7,000	117.63	115.62	114.00	112.68	111.60	110.71	109.98	109.39	107.63	106.93	106.65	106.54
8,000	134.43	132.14	130.28	128.77	127.54	126.53	125.70	125.01	123.00	122.21	121.89	121.76
9,000	151.24	148.65	146.56	144.87	143.48	142.34	141.41	140.64	138.37	137.48	137.12	136.98
10,000	168.04	165.17	162.85	160.96	159.42	158.16	157.12	156.26	153.75	152.76	152.36	152.20
15,000	252.06	247.75	244.27	241.44	239.13	237.23	235.68	234.39	230.62	229.13	228.53	228.29
20,000	336.07	330.33	325.69	321.92	318.84	316.31	314.23	312.52	307.49	305.51	304.71	304.39
25,000	420.09	412.92	407.12	402.40	398.55	395.39	392.79	390.65	384.36	381.88	380.89	380.49
30,000	504.11	495.50	488.54	482.88	478.25	474.46	471.35	468.78	461.24	458.26	457.06	456.58
35,000	588.13	578.08	569.96	563.36	557.96	553.54	549.90	546.91	538.11	534.63	533.24	532.68
40,000	672.14	660.66	651.38	643.83	637.67	632.62	628.46	625.04	614.98	611.01	609.41	608.77
45,000	756.16	743.25	732.80	724.31	717.30	711.69	707.02	703.17	691.85	687.38	685.59	684.87
50,000	840.18	825.83	814.23	804.79	797.09	790.77	785.58	781.29	768.72	763.76	761.77	760.96
55,000	924.19	908.41	895.65	885.27	876.79	869.85	864.13	859.42	845.60	840.13	837.94	837.06
60,000	1008.21	990.99	977.07	965.75	956.50	948.92	942.69	937.55	922.47	916.51	914.12	913.16
65,000	1092.23	1073.57	1058.49	1046.23	1036.21	1028.00	1021.25	1015.68	999.34	992.88	990.29	989.25
70,000	1176.25	1156.16	1139.91	1126.71	1115.92	1107.08	1099.80	1093.81	1076.21	1069.26	1066.47	1065.35
75,000	1260.26	1238.74	1221.34	1207.18	1195.63	1186.15	1178.36	1171.94	1153.08	1145.63	1142.65	1141.44
80,000	1344.28	1321.32	1302.76	1287.66	1275.34	1265.23	1256.92	1250.07	1229.96	1222.01	1218.82	1217.54
85,000	1428.30	1403.90	1384.18	1368.14	1355.04	1344.30	1335.47	1328.20	1306.83	1298.38	1295.00	1293.64
90,000	1512.32	1486.49	1465.60	1448.62	1434.75	1423.38	1414.03	1406.33	1383.70	1374.76	1371.18	1369.73
95,000	1596.33	1569.07	1547.02	1529.10	1514.46	1502.46	1492.59	1484.45	1460.57	1451.13	1447.35	1445.83
100,000	1680.35	1651.65	1628.45	1609.58	1594.17	1581.53	1571.15	1562.58	1537.44	1527.51	1523.53	1521.92
105,000	1764.37	1734.23	1709.87	1690.06	1673.88	1660.61	1649.70	1640.71	1614.32	1603.88	1599.70	1598.02
110,000	1848.38	1816.81	1791.29	1770.54	1753.58	1739.69	1728.26	1718.84	1691.19	1680.26	1675.88	1674.12
115,000	1932.40	1899.40	1872.71	1851.01	1833.29	1818.76	1806.82	1796.97	1768.06	1756.63	1752.06	1750.21
120,000	2016.42	1981.98	1954.13	1931.49	1913.00	1897.84	1885.37	1875.10	1844.93	1833.01	1828.23	1826.31
125,000	2100.44	2064.56	2035.56	2011.97	1992.71	1976.92	1963.93	1953.23	1921.80	1909.38	1904.41	1902.40
130,000	2184.45	2147.14	2116.98	2092.45	2072.42	2055.99	2042.49	2031.36	1998.68	1985.76	1980.58	1978.50
135,000	2268.47	2229.73	2198.40	2172.93	2152.12	2135.07	2121.05	2109.49	2075.55	2062.13	2056.76	2054.60
140,000	2352.49	2312.31	2279.82	2253.41	2231.83	2214.15	2199.60	2187.61	2152.42	2138.51	2132.94	2130.69
145,000	2436.50	2394.89	2361.24	2333.89	2311.54	2293.22	2278.16	2265.74	2229.29	2214.88	2209.11	2206.79
150,000	2520.52	2477.47	2442.67	2414.36	2391.25	2372.30	2356.72	2343.87	2306.16	2291.26	2285.29	2282.88
155,000	2604.54	2560.06	2524.09	2494.84	2470.96	2451.38	2435.27	2422.00	2383.03	2367.64	2361.47	2358.98
160,000	2688.56	2642.64	2605.51	2575.32	2550.67	2530.45	2513.83	2500.13	2459.91	2444.01	2437.64	2435.08
165,000	2772.57	2725.22	2686.93	2655.80	2630.37	2609.53	2592.39	2578.26	2536.78	2520.39	2513.82	2511.17
170,000	2856.59	2807.80	2768.35	2736.28	2710.08	2688.60	2670.94	2656.39	2613.65	2596.76	2589.99	2587.27
175,000	2940.61	2890.38	2849.78	2816.76	2789.79	2767.68	2749.50	2734.52	2690.52	2673.14	2666.17	2663.36
180,000	3024.63	2972.97	2931.20	2897.24	2869.50	2846.76	2828.06	2812.65	2767.39	2749.51	2742.35	2739.46
185,000	3108.64	3055.55	3012.62	2977.71	2949.21	2925.83	2906.62	2890.77	2844.27	2825.89	2818.52	2815.56
190,000	3192.66	3138.13	3094.04	3058.19	3028.91	3004.91	2985.17	2968.90	2921.14	2902.26	2894.70	2891.65
195,000	3276.68	3220.71	3175.46	3138.67	3108.62	3083.99	3063.73	3047.03	2998.01	2978.64	2970.87	2967.75
200,000	3360.69	3303.30	3256.89	3219.15	3188.33	3163.06	3142.29	3125.16	3074.88	3055.01	3047.05	3043.84
205,000	3444.71	3385.88	3338.31	3299.63	3268.04	3242.14	3220.84	3203.29	3151.75	3131.39	3123.23	3119.94
210,000	3528.73	3468.46	3419.73	3380.11	3347.75	3321.22	3299.40	3281.42	3228.63	3207.76	3199.40	3196.04
215,000	3612.75	3551.04	3501.15	3460.59	3427.45	3400.29	3377.96	3359.55	3305.50	3284.14	3275.58	3272.13
220,000	3696.76	3633.62	3582.57	3541.07	3507.16	3479.37	3456.52	3437.68	3382.37	3360.51	3351.76	3348.23
225,000	3780.78	3716.21	3664.00	3621.54	3586.87	3558.45	3535.07	3515.81	3459.24	3436.89	3427.93	3424.32
230,000	3864.80	3798.79	3745.42	3702.02	3666.58	3637.52	3613.63	3593.93	3536.11	3513.26	3504.11	3500.42
235,000	3948.81	3881.37	3826.84	3782.50	3746.29	3716.60	3692.19	3672.06	3612.99	3589.64	3580.28	3576.52
240,000	4032.83	3963.95	3908.26	3862.98	3826.00	3795.68	3770.74	3750.19	3689.86	3666.01	3656.46	3652.61
245,000	4116.85	4046.54	3989.68	3943.46	3905.70	3874.75	3849.30	3828.32	3766.73	3742.39	3732.64	3728.71
250,000	4200.87	4129.12	4071.11	4023.94	3985.41	3953.83	3927.86	3906.45	3843.60	3818.76	3808.81	3804.80
255,000	4284.88	4211.70	4152.53	4104.42	4065.12	4032.90	4006.41	3984.58	3920.47	3895.14	3884.99	3880.90
260,000	4368.90	4294.28	4233.95	4184.89	4144.83	4111.98	4084.97	4062.71	3997.35	3971.51	3961.16	3957.00
265,000	4452.92	4376.87	4315.37	4265.37	4224.54	4191.06	4163.53	4140.84	4074.22	4047.89	4037.34	4033.09
270,000	4536.94	4459.45	4396.79	4345.85	4304.24	4270.13	4242.09	4218.97	4151.09	4124.26	4113.52	4109.19
280,000	4704.97	4624.61	4559.64	4506.81	4463.66	4428.29	4399.20	4375.22	4304.83	4277.01	4265.87	4261.38
290,000	4873.00	4789.78	4722.48	4667.77	4623.08	4586.44	4556.31	4531.48	4458.58	4429.76	4418.22	4413.57
300,000	5041.04	4954.94	4885.33	4828.72	4782.49	4744.59	4713.43	4687.74	4612.32	4582.51	4570.57	4565.76

18.50%　MONTHLY AMORTIZING PAYMENTS

AMOUNT OF LOAN	NUMBER OF YEARS IN TERM											
	1	2	3	4	5	6	7	8	9	10	11	12
$ 50	4.60	2.51	1.83	1.49	1.29	1.16	1.07	1.01	0.96	0.92	0.89	0.87
100	9.20	5.02	3.65	2.97	2.57	2.31	2.14	2.01	1.91	1.84	1.78	1.74
200	18.39	10.04	7.29	5.93	5.14	4.62	4.27	4.01	3.82	3.67	3.56	3.47
300	27.58	15.05	10.93	8.90	7.70	6.93	6.40	6.01	5.73	5.51	5.34	5.20
400	36.77	20.07	14.57	11.86	10.27	9.24	8.53	8.02	7.63	7.34	7.12	6.94
500	45.96	25.09	18.21	14.82	12.84	11.55	10.66	10.02	9.54	9.18	8.89	8.67
600	55.16	30.10	21.85	17.79	15.40	13.86	12.79	12.02	11.45	11.01	10.67	10.40
700	64.35	35.12	25.49	20.75	17.97	16.17	14.92	14.02	13.35	12.84	12.45	12.14
800	73.54	40.14	29.13	23.71	20.54	18.48	17.05	16.03	15.26	14.68	14.23	13.87
900	82.73	45.15	32.77	26.68	23.10	20.79	19.19	18.03	17.17	16.51	16.00	15.60
1,000	91.92	50.17	36.41	29.64	25.67	23.10	21.32	20.03	19.08	18.35	17.78	17.34
2,000	183.84	100.34	72.81	59.28	51.34	46.19	42.63	40.06	38.15	36.69	35.56	34.67
3,000	275.76	150.50	109.22	88.92	77.00	69.28	63.94	60.09	57.22	55.03	53.33	52.00
4,000	367.68	200.67	145.62	118.55	102.67	92.37	85.25	80.11	76.29	73.37	71.11	69.33
5,000	459.60	250.84	182.02	148.19	128.34	115.46	106.56	100.14	95.36	91.71	88.88	86.66
6,000	551.51	301.00	218.43	177.83	154.00	138.55	127.88	120.17	114.43	110.05	106.66	103.99
7,000	643.43	351.17	254.83	207.46	179.67	161.64	149.19	140.20	133.50	128.40	124.44	121.32
8,000	735.35	401.33	291.23	237.10	205.33	184.74	170.50	160.22	152.57	146.74	142.21	138.65
9,000	827.27	451.50	327.64	266.74	231.00	207.83	191.81	180.25	171.64	165.08	159.99	155.99
10,000	919.19	501.67	364.04	296.37	256.67	230.92	213.12	200.28	190.71	183.42	177.76	173.32
15,000	1378.78	752.50	546.06	444.56	385.00	346.38	319.68	300.42	286.07	275.13	266.64	259.97
20,000	1838.37	1003.33	728.08	592.74	513.33	461.83	426.24	400.55	381.42	366.84	355.52	346.63
25,000	2297.96	1254.16	910.10	740.93	641.66	577.29	532.80	500.69	476.78	458.55	444.40	433.28
30,000	2757.55	1504.99	1092.12	889.11	769.99	692.75	639.36	600.83	572.13	550.25	533.28	519.94
35,000	3217.14	1755.82	1274.14	1037.30	898.32	808.20	745.92	700.97	667.48	641.96	622.16	606.59
40,000	3676.73	2006.65	1456.15	1185.48	1026.65	923.66	852.48	801.10	762.84	733.67	711.04	693.25
45,000	4136.32	2257.48	1638.17	1333.67	1154.98	1039.12	959.04	901.24	858.19	825.38	799.92	779.91
50,000	4595.91	2508.31	1820.19	1481.85	1283.32	1154.57	1065.60	1001.38	953.55	917.09	888.80	866.56
55,000	5055.50	2759.14	2002.21	1630.04	1411.65	1270.03	1172.16	1101.51	1048.90	1008.80	977.68	953.22
60,000	5515.09	3009.97	2184.23	1778.22	1539.98	1385.49	1278.72	1201.65	1144.25	1100.50	1066.56	1039.87
65,000	5974.68	3260.80	2366.25	1926.40	1668.31	1500.94	1385.28	1301.79	1239.61	1192.21	1155.44	1126.53
70,000	6434.27	3511.63	2548.27	2074.59	1796.64	1616.40	1491.84	1401.93	1334.96	1283.92	1244.32	1213.18
75,000	6893.86	3762.46	2730.28	2222.77	1924.97	1731.86	1598.40	1502.06	1430.32	1375.63	1333.20	1299.84
80,000	7353.45	4013.29	2912.30	2370.96	2053.30	1847.31	1704.96	1602.20	1525.67	1467.34	1422.08	1386.50
85,000	7813.04	4264.12	3094.32	2519.14	2181.63	1962.77	1811.52	1702.34	1621.02	1559.05	1510.96	1473.15
90,000	8272.64	4514.95	3276.34	2667.33	2309.96	2078.23	1918.08	1802.47	1716.38	1650.75	1599.84	1559.81
95,000	8732.23	4765.78	3458.36	2815.51	2438.29	2193.68	2024.64	1902.61	1811.73	1742.46	1688.72	1646.46
100,000	9191.82	5016.61	3640.38	2963.70	2566.63	2309.14	2131.20	2002.75	1907.09	1834.17	1777.60	1733.12
105,000	9651.41	5267.44	3822.40	3111.88	2694.96	2424.60	2237.76	2102.89	2002.44	1925.88	1866.48	1819.77
110,000	10111.00	5518.27	4004.41	3260.07	2823.29	2540.05	2344.32	2203.02	2097.79	2017.59	1955.36	1906.43
115,000	10570.59	5769.10	4186.43	3408.25	2951.62	2655.51	2450.88	2303.16	2193.15	2109.30	2044.24	1993.09
120,000	11030.18	6019.93	4368.45	3556.43	3079.95	2770.97	2557.44	2403.30	2288.50	2201.00	2133.12	2079.74
125,000	11489.77	6270.76	4550.47	3704.62	3208.28	2886.42	2663.99	2503.44	2383.86	2292.71	2222.00	2166.40
130,000	11949.36	6521.59	4732.49	3852.80	3336.61	3001.88	2770.55	2603.57	2479.21	2384.42	2310.88	2253.05
135,000	12408.95	6772.42	4914.51	4000.99	3464.94	3117.34	2877.11	2703.71	2574.57	2476.13	2399.76	2339.71
140,000	12868.54	7023.25	5096.53	4149.17	3593.27	3232.79	2983.67	2803.85	2669.92	2567.84	2488.64	2426.36
145,000	13328.13	7274.08	5278.54	4297.36	3721.61	3348.25	3090.23	2903.98	2765.27	2659.54	2577.52	2513.02
150,000	13787.72	7524.91	5460.56	4445.54	3849.94	3463.71	3196.79	3004.12	2860.63	2751.25	2666.40	2599.68
155,000	14247.31	7775.74	5642.58	4593.73	3978.27	3579.16	3303.35	3104.26	2955.98	2842.96	2755.28	2686.33
160,000	14706.90	8026.57	5824.60	4741.91	4106.60	3694.62	3409.91	3204.40	3051.34	2934.67	2844.16	2772.99
165,000	15166.49	8277.40	6006.62	4890.10	4234.93	3810.08	3516.47	3304.53	3146.69	3026.38	2933.04	2859.64
170,000	15626.08	8528.23	6188.64	5038.28	4363.26	3925.54	3623.03	3404.67	3242.04	3118.09	3021.92	2946.30
175,000	16085.68	8779.06	6370.66	5186.47	4491.59	4040.99	3729.59	3504.81	3337.40	3209.79	3110.80	3032.95
180,000	16545.27	9029.89	6552.67	5334.65	4619.92	4156.45	3836.15	3604.94	3432.75	3301.50	3199.68	3119.61
185,000	17004.86	9280.72	6734.69	5482.83	4748.25	4271.91	3942.71	3705.08	3528.11	3393.21	3288.56	3206.27
190,000	17464.45	9531.55	6916.71	5631.02	4876.58	4387.36	4049.27	3805.22	3623.46	3484.92	3377.44	3292.92
195,000	17924.04	9782.38	7098.73	5779.20	5004.92	4502.82	4155.83	3905.36	3718.81	3576.63	3466.32	3379.58
200,000	18383.63	10033.21	7280.75	5927.39	5133.25	4618.28	4262.39	4005.49	3814.17	3668.34	3555.20	3466.23
205,000	18843.22	10284.04	7462.77	6075.57	5261.58	4733.73	4368.95	4105.63	3909.52	3760.04	3644.08	3552.89
210,000	19302.81	10534.87	7644.79	6223.76	5389.91	4849.19	4475.51	4205.77	4004.88	3851.75	3732.96	3639.54
215,000	19762.40	10785.70	7826.80	6371.94	5518.24	4964.65	4582.07	4305.90	4100.23	3943.46	3821.84	3726.20
220,000	20221.99	11036.53	8008.82	6520.13	5646.57	5080.10	4688.63	4406.04	4195.58	4035.17	3910.72	3812.86
225,000	20681.58	11287.36	8190.84	6668.31	5774.90	5195.56	4795.19	4506.18	4290.94	4126.88	3999.60	3899.51
230,000	21141.17	11538.19	8372.86	6816.50	5903.23	5311.02	4901.75	4606.32	4386.29	4218.59	4088.48	3986.17
235,000	21600.76	11789.02	8554.88	6964.68	6031.56	5426.47	5008.31	4706.45	4481.65	4310.29	4177.36	4072.82
240,000	22060.35	12039.85	8736.90	7112.86	6159.90	5541.93	5114.87	4806.59	4577.00	4402.00	4266.24	4159.48
245,000	22519.94	12290.68	8918.92	7261.05	6288.23	5657.39	5221.43	4906.73	4672.35	4493.71	4355.12	4246.13
250,000	22979.53	12541.51	9100.93	7409.23	6416.56	5772.84	5327.98	5006.87	4767.71	4585.42	4444.00	4332.79
255,000	23439.12	12792.34	9282.95	7557.42	6544.89	5888.30	5434.54	5107.00	4863.06	4677.13	4532.88	4419.45
260,000	23898.72	13043.17	9464.97	7705.60	6673.22	6003.76	5541.10	5207.14	4958.42	4768.84	4621.76	4506.10
265,000	24358.31	13294.00	9646.99	7853.79	6801.55	6119.21	5647.66	5307.28	5053.77	4860.54	4710.64	4592.76
270,000	24817.90	13544.83	9829.01	8001.97	6929.88	6234.67	5754.22	5407.41	5149.13	4952.25	4799.52	4679.41
280,000	25737.08	14046.49	10193.05	8298.34	7186.54	6465.58	5967.34	5607.69	5339.83	5135.67	4977.28	4852.72
290,000	26656.26	14548.15	10557.08	8594.71	7443.21	6696.50	6180.46	5807.96	5530.54	5319.08	5155.04	5026.04
300,000	27575.44	15049.81	10921.12	8891.08	7699.87	6927.41	6393.58	6008.24	5721.25	5502.50	5332.80	5199.35

134

AMOUNT OF LOAN	NUMBER OF YEARS IN TERM											
	13	14	15	16	17	18	19	20	25	30	35	40
$ 50	0.85	0.84	0.83	0.82	0.81	0.81	0.80	0.80	0.78	0.78	0.78	0.78
100	1.70	1.67	1.65	1.63	1.62	1.61	1.60	1.59	1.56	1.55	1.55	1.55
200	3.40	3.34	3.30	3.26	3.23	3.21	3.19	3.17	3.12	3.10	3.09	3.09
300	5.10	5.01	4.94	4.89	4.84	4.81	4.78	4.75	4.68	4.65	4.64	4.63
400	6.80	6.68	6.59	6.52	6.46	6.41	6.37	6.33	6.23	6.20	6.18	6.18
500	8.49	8.35	8.24	8.14	8.07	8.01	7.96	7.91	7.79	7.74	7.73	7.72
600	10.19	10.02	9.88	9.77	9.68	9.61	9.55	9.50	9.35	9.29	9.27	9.26
700	11.89	11.69	11.53	11.40	11.29	11.21	11.14	11.08	10.91	10.84	10.81	10.80
800	13.59	13.36	13.18	13.03	12.91	12.81	12.73	12.66	12.46	12.39	12.36	12.35
900	15.28	15.03	14.82	14.66	14.52	14.41	14.32	14.24	14.02	13.94	13.90	13.89
1,000	16.98	16.70	16.47	16.28	16.13	16.01	15.91	15.82	15.58	15.48	15.45	15.43
2,000	33.96	33.39	32.94	32.56	32.26	32.01	31.81	31.64	31.15	30.96	30.89	30.86
3,000	50.94	50.09	49.40	48.84	48.39	48.02	47.71	47.46	46.73	46.44	46.33	46.28
4,000	67.92	66.78	65.87	65.12	64.52	64.02	63.62	63.28	62.30	61.92	61.77	61.71
5,000	84.89	83.48	82.33	81.40	80.65	80.03	79.52	79.10	77.88	77.40	77.21	77.14
6,000	101.87	100.17	98.80	97.68	96.77	96.03	95.42	94.92	93.45	92.88	92.66	92.56
7,000	118.85	116.86	115.26	113.96	112.90	112.03	111.32	110.74	109.03	108.36	108.10	107.99
8,000	135.83	133.56	131.73	130.24	129.03	128.04	127.23	126.56	124.60	123.84	123.54	123.42
9,000	152.80	150.25	148.19	146.52	145.16	144.04	143.13	142.38	140.18	139.32	138.98	138.84
10,000	169.78	166.95	164.66	162.80	161.29	160.05	159.03	158.19	155.75	154.80	154.42	154.27
15,000	254.67	250.42	246.98	244.20	241.93	240.07	238.54	237.29	233.63	232.20	231.63	231.40
20,000	339.56	333.89	329.31	325.60	322.57	320.09	318.06	316.38	311.50	309.59	308.84	308.54
25,000	424.44	417.36	411.64	406.99	403.21	400.11	397.57	395.48	389.38	386.99	386.05	385.67
30,000	509.33	500.83	493.96	488.39	483.85	480.13	477.08	474.57	467.25	464.39	463.26	462.80
35,000	594.22	584.30	576.29	569.79	564.49	560.15	556.60	553.67	545.12	541.79	540.46	539.94
40,000	679.11	667.77	658.61	651.19	645.13	640.17	636.11	632.76	623.00	619.18	617.67	617.07
45,000	763.99	751.24	740.94	732.58	725.77	720.20	715.62	711.86	700.87	696.58	694.88	694.20
50,000	848.88	834.71	823.27	813.98	806.41	800.22	795.13	790.95	778.75	773.98	772.09	771.34
55,000	933.77	918.18	905.59	895.38	887.05	880.24	874.65	870.05	856.62	851.37	849.30	848.47
60,000	1018.66	1001.65	987.92	976.78	967.69	960.26	954.16	949.14	934.50	928.77	926.51	925.60
65,000	1103.54	1085.12	1070.25	1058.17	1048.33	1040.28	1033.67	1028.24	1012.37	1006.17	1003.71	1002.74
70,000	1188.43	1168.59	1152.57	1139.57	1128.97	1120.30	1113.19	1107.33	1090.24	1083.57	1080.92	1079.87
75,000	1273.32	1252.06	1234.90	1220.97	1209.61	1200.32	1192.70	1186.43	1168.12	1160.96	1158.13	1157.00
80,000	1358.21	1335.53	1317.22	1302.37	1290.25	1280.34	1272.21	1265.52	1245.99	1238.36	1235.34	1234.14
85,000	1443.10	1419.00	1399.55	1383.76	1370.90	1360.37	1351.73	1344.62	1323.87	1315.76	1312.55	1311.27
90,000	1527.98	1502.47	1481.88	1465.16	1451.54	1440.39	1431.24	1423.71	1401.74	1393.16	1389.76	1388.40
95,000	1612.87	1585.94	1564.20	1546.56	1532.18	1520.41	1510.75	1502.81	1479.61	1470.55	1466.96	1465.54
100,000	1697.76	1669.41	1646.53	1627.96	1612.82	1600.43	1590.26	1581.90	1557.49	1547.95	1544.17	1542.67
105,000	1782.65	1752.88	1728.85	1709.35	1693.46	1680.45	1669.78	1661.00	1635.36	1625.35	1621.38	1619.80
110,000	1867.53	1836.35	1811.18	1790.75	1774.10	1760.47	1749.29	1740.09	1713.24	1702.74	1698.59	1696.94
115,000	1952.42	1919.82	1893.51	1872.15	1854.74	1840.49	1828.80	1819.19	1791.11	1780.14	1775.80	1774.07
120,000	2037.31	2003.29	1975.83	1953.55	1935.38	1920.51	1908.32	1898.28	1868.99	1857.54	1853.01	1851.20
125,000	2122.20	2086.76	2058.16	2034.95	2016.02	2000.54	1987.83	1977.38	1946.86	1934.94	1930.21	1928.34
130,000	2207.08	2170.23	2140.49	2116.34	2096.66	2080.56	2067.34	2056.47	2024.73	2012.33	2007.42	2005.47
135,000	2291.97	2253.70	2222.81	2197.74	2177.30	2160.58	2146.86	2135.57	2102.61	2089.73	2084.63	2082.60
140,000	2376.86	2337.17	2305.14	2279.14	2257.94	2240.60	2226.37	2214.66	2180.48	2167.13	2161.84	2159.74
145,000	2461.75	2420.64	2387.46	2360.54	2338.58	2320.62	2305.88	2293.76	2258.36	2244.52	2239.05	2236.87
150,000	2546.63	2504.11	2469.79	2441.93	2419.22	2400.64	2385.39	2372.85	2336.23	2321.92	2316.26	2314.00
155,000	2631.52	2587.58	2552.12	2523.33	2499.86	2480.66	2464.91	2451.94	2414.11	2399.32	2393.46	2391.13
160,000	2716.41	2671.05	2634.44	2604.73	2580.50	2560.68	2544.42	2531.04	2491.98	2476.72	2470.67	2468.27
165,000	2801.30	2754.52	2716.77	2686.13	2661.15	2640.71	2623.93	2610.13	2569.85	2554.11	2547.88	2545.40
170,000	2886.19	2837.99	2799.09	2767.52	2741.79	2720.73	2703.45	2689.23	2647.73	2631.51	2625.09	2622.53
175,000	2971.07	2921.46	2881.42	2848.92	2822.43	2800.75	2782.96	2768.32	2725.60	2708.91	2702.30	2699.67
180,000	3055.96	3004.93	2963.75	2930.32	2903.07	2880.77	2862.47	2847.42	2803.48	2786.31	2779.51	2776.80
185,000	3140.85	3088.40	3046.07	3011.72	2983.71	2960.79	2941.98	2926.51	2881.35	2863.70	2856.71	2853.93
190,000	3225.74	3171.87	3128.40	3093.11	3064.35	3040.81	3021.50	3005.61	2959.22	2941.10	2933.92	2931.07
195,000	3310.62	3255.34	3210.73	3174.51	3144.99	3120.83	3101.01	3084.70	3037.10	3018.50	3011.13	3008.20
200,000	3395.51	3338.82	3293.05	3255.91	3225.63	3200.85	3180.52	3163.80	3114.97	3095.89	3088.34	3085.33
205,000	3480.40	3422.29	3375.38	3337.31	3306.27	3280.88	3260.04	3242.89	3192.85	3173.29	3165.55	3162.47
210,000	3565.29	3505.76	3457.70	3418.70	3386.91	3360.90	3339.55	3321.99	3270.72	3250.69	3242.76	3239.60
215,000	3650.17	3589.23	3540.03	3500.10	3467.55	3440.92	3419.06	3401.08	3348.60	3328.09	3319.97	3316.73
220,000	3735.06	3672.70	3622.36	3581.50	3548.19	3520.94	3498.58	3480.18	3426.47	3405.48	3397.17	3393.87
225,000	3819.95	3756.17	3704.68	3662.90	3628.83	3600.96	3578.09	3559.27	3504.34	3482.88	3474.38	3471.00
230,000	3904.84	3839.64	3787.01	3744.30	3709.47	3680.98	3657.60	3638.37	3582.22	3560.28	3551.59	3548.13
235,000	3989.73	3923.11	3869.33	3825.69	3790.11	3761.00	3737.11	3717.46	3660.09	3637.67	3628.80	3625.27
240,000	4074.61	4006.58	3951.66	3907.09	3870.75	3841.02	3816.63	3796.56	3737.97	3715.07	3706.01	3702.40
245,000	4159.50	4090.05	4033.99	3988.49	3951.40	3921.05	3896.14	3875.65	3815.84	3792.47	3783.22	3779.53
250,000	4244.39	4173.52	4116.31	4069.89	4032.04	4001.07	3975.65	3954.75	3893.72	3869.87	3860.42	3856.67
255,000	4329.28	4256.99	4198.64	4151.28	4112.68	4081.09	4055.17	4033.84	3971.59	3947.26	3937.63	3933.80
260,000	4414.16	4340.46	4280.97	4232.68	4193.32	4161.11	4134.68	4112.94	4049.46	4024.66	4014.84	4010.93
265,000	4499.05	4423.93	4363.29	4314.08	4273.96	4241.13	4214.19	4192.03	4127.34	4102.06	4092.05	4088.07
270,000	4583.94	4507.40	4445.62	4395.48	4354.60	4321.15	4293.71	4271.13	4205.21	4179.46	4169.26	4165.20
280,000	4753.71	4674.34	4610.27	4558.27	4515.88	4481.19	4452.73	4429.32	4360.96	4334.25	4323.67	4319.47
290,000	4923.49	4841.28	4774.92	4721.07	4677.16	4641.24	4611.76	4587.51	4516.71	4489.04	4478.09	4473.73
300,000	5093.26	5008.22	4939.58	4883.86	4838.44	4801.28	4770.78	4745.69	4672.46	4643.84	4632.51	4628.00

18.75%

AMOUNT OF LOAN	NUMBER OF YEARS IN TERM											
	1	2	3	4	5	6	7	8	9	10	11	12
$ 50	4.61	2.52	1.83	1.49	1.30	1.17	1.08	1.01	0.97	0.93	0.90	0.88
100	9.21	5.03	3.66	2.98	2.59	2.33	2.15	2.02	1.93	1.86	1.80	1.76
200	18.41	10.06	7.31	5.96	5.17	4.65	4.30	4.04	3.85	3.71	3.59	3.51
300	27.62	15.09	10.96	8.94	7.75	6.98	6.44	6.06	5.77	5.56	5.39	5.26
400	36.82	20.12	14.62	11.91	10.33	9.30	8.59	8.08	7.70	7.41	7.18	7.01
500	46.02	25.15	18.27	14.89	12.91	11.62	10.73	10.10	9.62	9.26	8.98	8.76
600	55.23	30.18	21.92	17.87	15.49	13.95	12.88	12.11	11.54	11.11	10.77	10.51
700	64.43	35.21	25.58	20.84	18.07	16.27	15.03	14.13	13.47	12.96	12.56	12.26
800	73.63	40.23	29.23	23.82	20.65	18.59	17.17	16.15	15.39	14.81	14.36	14.01
900	82.84	45.26	32.88	26.80	23.23	20.92	19.32	18.17	17.31	16.66	16.15	15.76
1,000	92.04	50.29	36.53	29.77	25.81	23.24	21.46	20.19	19.23	18.51	17.95	17.51
2,000	184.08	100.58	73.06	59.54	51.61	46.47	42.92	40.37	38.46	37.01	35.89	35.01
3,000	276.12	150.87	109.59	89.31	77.41	69.71	64.38	60.55	57.69	55.52	53.83	52.51
4,000	368.15	201.15	146.12	119.08	103.22	92.94	85.84	80.73	76.92	74.02	71.78	70.01
5,000	460.19	251.44	182.65	148.85	129.02	116.17	107.30	100.91	96.15	92.53	89.72	87.52
6,000	552.23	301.73	219.18	178.62	154.82	139.41	128.76	121.09	115.38	111.03	107.66	105.02
7,000	644.27	352.02	255.71	208.38	180.63	162.64	150.22	141.27	134.61	129.53	125.60	122.52
8,000	736.30	402.30	292.24	238.15	206.43	185.88	171.68	161.45	153.83	148.04	143.55	140.02
9,000	828.34	452.59	328.77	267.92	232.23	209.11	193.14	181.63	173.06	166.54	161.49	157.52
10,000	920.38	502.88	365.30	297.69	258.04	232.34	214.60	201.81	192.29	185.05	179.43	175.03
15,000	1380.56	754.31	547.95	446.53	387.05	348.51	321.90	302.71	288.43	277.57	269.15	262.54
20,000	1840.75	1005.75	730.60	595.37	516.07	464.68	429.20	403.61	384.58	370.09	358.86	350.05
25,000	2300.94	1257.19	913.25	744.21	645.08	580.85	536.50	504.51	480.72	462.61	448.58	437.56
30,000	2761.12	1508.62	1095.90	893.06	774.10	697.02	643.80	605.42	576.86	555.13	538.29	525.07
35,000	3221.31	1760.06	1278.55	1041.90	903.12	813.19	751.10	706.32	673.01	647.65	628.00	612.58
40,000	3681.50	2011.49	1461.19	1190.74	1032.13	929.36	858.39	807.22	769.15	740.17	717.72	700.09
45,000	4141.68	2262.93	1643.84	1339.58	1161.15	1045.53	965.69	908.12	865.29	832.69	807.43	787.60
50,000	4601.87	2514.37	1826.49	1488.42	1290.16	1161.70	1072.99	1009.02	961.44	925.21	897.15	875.11
55,000	5062.06	2765.80	2009.14	1637.26	1419.18	1277.86	1180.29	1109.93	1057.58	1017.73	986.86	962.62
60,000	5522.24	3017.24	2191.79	1786.11	1548.20	1394.03	1287.59	1210.83	1153.72	1110.25	1076.58	1050.13
65,000	5982.43	3268.68	2374.44	1934.95	1677.21	1510.20	1394.89	1311.73	1249.87	1202.77	1166.29	1137.64
70,000	6442.62	3520.11	2557.09	2083.79	1806.23	1626.37	1502.19	1412.63	1346.01	1295.29	1256.00	1225.15
75,000	6902.80	3771.55	2739.74	2232.63	1935.24	1742.54	1609.48	1513.53	1442.15	1387.82	1345.72	1312.66
80,000	7362.99	4022.98	2922.38	2381.47	2064.26	1858.71	1716.78	1614.44	1538.30	1480.34	1435.43	1400.17
85,000	7823.18	4274.42	3105.03	2530.32	2193.28	1974.88	1824.08	1715.34	1634.44	1572.86	1525.15	1487.68
90,000	8283.36	4525.86	3287.68	2679.16	2322.29	2091.05	1931.38	1816.24	1730.58	1665.38	1614.86	1575.19
95,000	8743.55	4777.29	3470.33	2828.00	2451.31	2207.22	2038.68	1917.14	1826.73	1757.90	1704.58	1662.70
100,000	9203.74	5028.73	3652.98	2976.84	2580.32	2323.39	2145.98	2018.04	1922.87	1850.42	1794.29	1750.21
105,000	9663.92	5280.16	3835.63	3125.68	2709.34	2439.56	2253.28	2118.94	2019.01	1942.94	1884.00	1837.72
110,000	10124.11	5531.60	4018.28	3274.52	2838.36	2555.72	2360.57	2219.85	2115.16	2035.46	1973.72	1925.23
115,000	10584.30	5783.04	4200.93	3423.37	2967.37	2671.89	2467.87	2320.75	2211.30	2127.98	2063.43	2012.74
120,000	11044.48	6034.47	4383.57	3572.21	3096.39	2788.06	2575.17	2421.65	2307.44	2220.50	2153.15	2100.25
125,000	11504.67	6285.91	4566.22	3721.05	3225.40	2904.23	2682.47	2522.55	2403.59	2313.02	2242.86	2187.76
130,000	11964.85	6537.35	4748.87	3869.89	3354.42	3020.40	2789.77	2623.45	2499.73	2405.54	2332.58	2275.28
135,000	12425.04	6788.78	4931.52	4018.73	3483.44	3136.57	2897.07	2724.36	2595.87	2498.06	2422.29	2362.79
140,000	12885.23	7040.22	5114.17	4167.57	3612.45	3252.74	3004.37	2825.26	2692.02	2590.58	2512.00	2450.30
145,000	13345.41	7291.65	5296.82	4316.42	3741.47	3368.91	3111.66	2926.16	2788.16	2683.11	2601.72	2537.81
150,000	13805.60	7543.09	5479.47	4465.26	3870.48	3485.08	3218.96	3027.06	2884.30	2775.63	2691.43	2625.32
155,000	14265.79	7794.53	5662.12	4614.10	3999.50	3601.25	3326.26	3127.96	2980.45	2868.15	2781.15	2712.83
160,000	14725.97	8045.96	5844.76	4762.94	4128.51	3717.42	3433.56	3228.87	3076.59	2960.67	2870.86	2800.34
165,000	15186.16	8297.40	6027.41	4911.78	4257.53	3833.58	3540.86	3329.77	3172.73	3053.19	2960.57	2887.85
170,000	15646.35	8548.84	6210.06	5060.63	4386.55	3949.75	3648.16	3430.67	3268.88	3145.71	3050.29	2975.36
175,000	16106.53	8800.27	6392.71	5209.47	4515.56	4065.92	3755.46	3531.57	3365.02	3238.23	3140.00	3062.87
180,000	16566.72	9051.71	6575.36	5358.31	4644.58	4182.09	3862.75	3632.47	3461.16	3330.75	3229.72	3150.38
185,000	17026.91	9303.14	6758.01	5507.15	4773.59	4298.26	3970.05	3733.38	3557.31	3423.27	3319.43	3237.89
190,000	17487.09	9554.58	6940.66	5655.99	4902.61	4414.43	4077.35	3834.28	3653.45	3515.79	3409.15	3325.40
195,000	17947.28	9806.02	7123.31	5804.83	5031.63	4530.60	4184.65	3935.18	3749.59	3608.31	3498.86	3412.91
200,000	18407.47	10057.45	7305.95	5953.68	5160.64	4646.77	4291.95	4036.08	3845.74	3700.83	3588.57	3500.42
205,000	18867.65	10308.89	7488.60	6102.52	5289.66	4762.94	4399.25	4136.98	3941.88	3793.35	3678.29	3587.93
210,000	19327.84	10560.32	7671.25	6251.36	5418.67	4879.11	4506.55	4237.88	4038.02	3885.87	3768.00	3675.44
215,000	19788.03	10811.76	7853.90	6400.20	5547.69	4995.27	4613.84	4338.79	4134.17	3978.40	3857.72	3762.95
220,000	20248.21	11063.20	8036.55	6549.04	5676.71	5111.44	4721.14	4439.69	4230.31	4070.92	3947.43	3850.46
225,000	20708.40	11314.63	8219.20	6697.89	5805.72	5227.61	4828.44	4540.59	4326.45	4163.44	4037.15	3937.97
230,000	21168.59	11566.07	8401.85	6846.73	5934.74	5343.78	4935.74	4641.49	4422.60	4255.96	4126.86	4025.48
235,000	21628.77	11817.51	8584.49	6995.57	6063.75	5459.95	5043.04	4742.39	4518.74	4348.48	4216.57	4112.99
240,000	22088.96	12068.94	8767.14	7144.41	6192.77	5576.12	5150.34	4843.30	4614.88	4441.00	4306.29	4200.50
245,000	22549.14	12320.38	8949.79	7293.25	6321.79	5692.29	5257.64	4944.20	4711.03	4533.52	4396.00	4288.01
250,000	23009.33	12571.81	9132.44	7442.09	6450.80	5808.46	5364.93	5045.10	4807.17	4626.04	4485.72	4375.52
255,000	23469.52	12823.25	9315.09	7590.94	6579.82	5924.63	5472.23	5146.00	4903.31	4718.56	4575.43	4463.04
260,000	23929.70	13074.69	9497.74	7739.78	6708.83	6040.80	5579.53	5246.90	4999.46	4811.08	4665.15	4550.55
265,000	24389.89	13326.12	9680.39	7888.62	6837.85	6156.97	5686.83	5347.81	5095.60	4903.60	4754.86	4638.06
270,000	24850.08	13577.56	9863.04	8037.46	6966.87	6273.13	5794.13	5448.71	5191.74	4996.12	4844.57	4725.57
280,000	25770.45	14080.43	10228.33	8335.14	7224.90	6505.47	6008.73	5650.51	5384.03	5181.16	5024.00	4900.59
290,000	26690.82	14583.30	10593.63	8632.83	7482.93	6737.81	6223.32	5852.32	5576.32	5366.21	5203.43	5075.61
300,000	27611.20	15086.18	10958.93	8930.51	7740.96	6970.15	6437.92	6054.12	5768.60	5551.25	5382.86	5250.63

AMOUNT OF LOAN	\$	NUMBER OF YEARS IN TERM										
		13	14	15	16	17	18	19	20	25	30	35	40
$ 50	0.86	0.85	0.84	0.83	0.82	0.81	0.81	0.81	0.79	0.79	0.79	0.79
100	1.72	1.69	1.67	1.65	1.64	1.62	1.61	1.61	1.58	1.57	1.57	1.57
200	3.44	3.38	3.33	3.30	3.27	3.24	3.22	3.21	3.16	3.14	3.13	3.13
300	5.15	5.07	5.00	4.94	4.90	4.86	4.83	4.81	4.74	4.71	4.70	4.70
400	6.87	6.75	6.66	6.59	6.53	6.48	6.44	6.41	6.32	6.28	6.26	6.26
500	8.58	8.44	8.33	8.24	8.16	8.10	8.05	8.01	7.89	7.85	7.83	7.82
600	10.30	10.13	9.99	9.88	9.79	9.72	9.66	9.61	9.47	9.42	9.39	9.39
700	12.01	11.82	11.66	11.53	11.43	11.34	11.27	11.21	11.05	10.98	10.96	10.95
800	13.73	13.50	13.32	13.18	13.06	12.96	12.88	12.82	12.63	12.55	12.52	12.51
900	15.44	15.19	14.99	14.82	14.69	14.58	14.49	14.42	14.20	14.12	14.09	14.08
1,000	17.16	16.88	16.65	16.47	16.32	16.20	16.10	16.02	15.78	15.69	15.65	15.64
2,000	34.31	33.75	33.30	32.93	32.64	32.39	32.19	32.03	31.56	31.37	31.30	31.27
3,000	51.46	50.62	49.95	49.40	48.95	48.59	48.29	48.04	47.33	47.06	46.95	46.91
4,000	68.61	67.49	66.59	65.86	65.27	64.78	64.38	64.06	63.11	62.74	62.60	62.54
5,000	85.77	84.37	83.24	82.32	81.58	80.97	80.48	80.07	78.88	78.43	78.25	78.18
6,000	102.92	101.24	99.89	98.79	97.90	97.17	96.57	96.08	94.66	94.11	93.89	93.81
7,000	120.07	118.11	116.53	115.25	114.21	113.36	112.67	112.09	110.43	109.79	109.54	109.44
8,000	137.22	134.98	133.18	131.72	130.53	129.56	128.76	128.11	126.21	125.48	125.19	125.08
9,000	154.38	151.86	149.83	148.18	146.84	145.75	144.85	144.12	141.99	141.16	140.84	140.71
10,000	171.53	168.73	166.47	164.64	163.16	161.94	160.95	160.13	157.76	156.85	156.49	156.35
15,000	257.29	253.09	249.71	246.96	244.73	242.91	241.42	240.19	236.64	235.27	234.73	234.52
20,000	343.05	337.45	332.94	329.28	326.31	323.88	321.89	320.26	315.52	313.69	312.97	312.69
25,000	428.81	421.81	416.17	411.60	407.89	404.85	402.36	400.32	394.40	392.11	391.21	390.86
30,000	514.57	506.17	499.41	493.92	489.46	485.82	482.83	480.38	473.27	470.53	469.45	469.03
35,000	600.33	590.53	582.64	576.24	571.04	566.79	563.31	560.45	552.15	548.95	547.69	547.20
40,000	686.10	674.90	665.87	658.56	652.61	647.76	643.78	640.51	631.03	627.37	625.94	625.37
45,000	771.86	759.26	749.11	740.88	734.19	720.72	724.25	720.57	709.91	705.79	704.10	703.54
50,000	857.62	843.62	832.34	823.20	815.77	809.69	804.72	800.64	788.79	784.21	782.42	781.71
55,000	943.38	927.98	915.57	905.52	897.34	890.66	885.19	880.70	867.67	862.63	860.66	859.88
60,000	1029.14	1012.34	998.81	987.84	978.92	971.63	965.66	960.76	946.54	941.05	938.90	938.05
65,000	1114.90	1096.70	1082.04	1070.16	1060.49	1052.60	1046.14	1040.83	1025.42	1019.47	1017.14	1016.23
70,000	1200.66	1181.06	1165.27	1152.48	1142.07	1133.57	1126.61	1120.89	1104.30	1097.89	1095.38	1094.40
75,000	1286.42	1265.43	1248.51	1234.80	1223.65	1214.54	1207.08	1200.95	1183.18	1176.31	1173.62	1172.57
80,000	1372.19	1349.79	1331.74	1317.12	1305.22	1295.51	1287.55	1281.02	1262.06	1254.73	1251.87	1250.74
85,000	1457.95	1434.15	1414.97	1399.44	1386.80	1376.48	1368.02	1361.08	1340.94	1333.15	1330.11	1328.91
90,000	1543.71	1518.51	1498.21	1481.76	1468.37	1457.44	1448.49	1441.14	1419.81	1411.57	1408.35	1407.08
95,000	1629.47	1602.87	1581.44	1564.08	1549.95	1538.41	1528.96	1521.21	1498.69	1489.99	1486.59	1485.25
100,000	1715.23	1687.23	1664.67	1646.40	1631.53	1619.38	1609.44	1601.27	1577.57	1568.41	1564.83	1563.42
105,000	1800.99	1771.59	1747.91	1728.72	1713.10	1700.35	1689.91	1681.33	1656.45	1646.83	1643.07	1641.59
110,000	1886.75	1855.96	1831.14	1811.04	1794.68	1781.32	1770.38	1761.40	1735.33	1725.25	1721.31	1719.76
115,000	1972.52	1940.32	1914.37	1893.36	1876.25	1862.29	1850.85	1841.46	1814.20	1803.67	1799.55	1797.93
120,000	2058.28	2024.68	1997.61	1975.68	1957.83	1943.26	1931.32	1921.52	1893.08	1882.09	1877.79	1876.10
125,000	2144.04	2109.04	2080.84	2058.00	2039.41	2024.23	2011.79	2001.59	1971.96	1960.52	1956.04	1954.28
130,000	2229.80	2193.40	2164.07	2140.32	2120.98	2105.20	2092.27	2081.65	2050.84	2038.94	2034.28	2032.45
135,000	2315.56	2277.76	2247.31	2222.64	2202.56	2186.16	2172.74	2161.71	2129.72	2117.36	2112.52	2110.62
140,000	2401.32	2362.12	2330.54	2304.95	2284.13	2267.13	2253.21	2241.78	2208.60	2195.78	2190.76	2188.79
145,000	2487.08	2446.49	2413.78	2387.27	2365.71	2348.10	2333.68	2321.84	2287.47	2274.20	2269.00	2266.96
150,000	2572.84	2530.85	2497.01	2469.59	2447.29	2429.07	2414.15	2401.90	2366.35	2352.62	2347.24	2345.13
155,000	2658.61	2615.21	2580.24	2551.91	2528.86	2510.04	2494.62	2481.97	2445.23	2431.04	2425.48	2423.30
160,000	2744.37	2699.57	2663.48	2634.23	2610.44	2591.01	2575.09	2562.03	2524.11	2509.46	2503.73	2501.47
165,000	2830.13	2783.93	2746.71	2716.55	2692.02	2671.98	2655.57	2642.09	2602.99	2587.88	2581.97	2579.64
170,000	2915.89	2868.29	2829.94	2798.87	2773.59	2752.95	2736.04	2722.16	2681.87	2666.30	2660.21	2657.81
175,000	3001.65	2952.65	2913.18	2881.19	2855.17	2833.91	2816.51	2802.22	2760.74	2744.72	2738.45	2735.98
180,000	3087.41	3037.02	2996.41	2963.51	2936.74	2914.88	2896.98	2882.28	2839.62	2823.14	2816.69	2814.15
185,000	3173.17	3121.38	3079.64	3045.83	3018.32	2995.85	2977.45	2962.35	2918.50	2901.56	2894.93	2892.33
190,000	3258.93	3205.74	3162.88	3128.15	3099.90	3076.82	3057.92	3042.41	2997.38	2979.98	2973.17	2970.50
195,000	3344.70	3290.10	3246.11	3210.47	3181.47	3157.79	3138.40	3122.47	3076.26	3058.40	3051.41	3048.67
200,000	3430.46	3374.46	3329.34	3292.79	3263.05	3238.76	3218.87	3202.54	3155.14	3136.82	3129.66	3126.84
205,000	3516.22	3458.82	3412.58	3375.11	3344.62	3319.73	3299.34	3282.60	3234.01	3215.24	3207.90	3205.01
210,000	3601.98	3543.18	3495.81	3457.43	3426.20	3400.70	3379.81	3362.66	3312.89	3293.66	3286.14	3283.18
215,000	3687.74	3627.55	3579.04	3539.75	3507.78	3481.67	3460.28	3442.73	3391.77	3372.08	3364.38	3361.35
220,000	3773.50	3711.91	3662.28	3622.07	3589.35	3562.63	3540.75	3522.79	3470.65	3450.50	3442.62	3439.52
225,000	3859.26	3796.27	3745.51	3704.39	3670.93	3643.60	3621.23	3602.85	3549.53	3528.92	3520.86	3517.69
230,000	3945.03	3880.63	3828.74	3786.71	3752.50	3724.57	3701.70	3682.92	3628.40	3607.34	3599.10	3595.86
235,000	4030.79	3964.99	3911.98	3869.03	3834.08	3805.54	3782.17	3762.98	3707.28	3685.76	3677.34	3674.03
240,000	4116.55	4049.35	3995.21	3951.35	3915.66	3886.51	3862.64	3843.04	3786.16	3764.18	3755.59	3752.20
245,000	4202.31	4133.71	4078.44	4033.67	3997.23	3967.48	3943.11	3923.11	3865.04	3842.60	3833.83	3830.38
250,000	4288.07	4218.08	4161.68	4115.99	4078.81	4048.45	4023.58	4003.17	3943.92	3921.03	3912.07	3908.55
255,000	4373.83	4302.44	4244.91	4198.31	4160.38	4129.42	4104.05	4083.23	4022.80	3999.45	3990.31	3986.72
260,000	4459.59	4386.80	4328.14	4280.63	4241.96	4210.39	4184.53	4163.30	4101.67	4077.87	4068.55	4064.89
265,000	4545.35	4471.16	4411.38	4362.95	4323.54	4291.35	4265.00	4243.36	4180.55	4156.29	4146.79	4143.06
270,000	4631.12	4555.52	4494.61	4445.27	4405.11	4372.32	4345.47	4323.42	4259.43	4234.71	4225.03	4221.23
280,000	4802.64	4724.24	4661.08	4609.90	4568.26	4534.26	4506.41	4483.55	4417.19	4391.55	4381.52	4377.57
290,000	4974.16	4892.97	4827.55	4774.54	4731.42	4696.20	4667.36	4643.68	4574.94	4548.39	4538.00	4533.91
300,000	5145.68	5061.69	4994.01	4939.18	4894.57	4858.14	4828.30	4803.80	4732.70	4705.23	4694.48	4690.25

137

19.00%

MONTHLY AMORTIZING PAYMENTS

AMOUNT OF LOAN	NUMBER OF YEARS IN TERM											
	1	2	3	4	5	6	7	8	9	10	11	12
$ 50	4.61	2.53	1.84	1.50	1.30	1.17	1.09	1.02	0.97	0.94	0.91	0.89
100	9.22	5.05	3.67	3.00	2.60	2.34	2.17	2.04	1.94	1.87	1.82	1.77
200	18.44	10.09	7.34	5.99	5.19	4.68	4.33	4.07	3.88	3.74	3.63	3.54
300	27.65	15.13	11.00	8.98	7.79	7.02	6.49	6.11	5.82	5.61	5.44	5.31
400	36.87	20.17	14.67	11.97	10.38	9.36	8.65	8.14	7.76	7.47	7.25	7.07
500	46.08	25.21	18.33	14.96	12.98	11.69	10.81	10.17	9.70	9.34	9.06	8.84
600	55.30	30.25	22.00	17.95	15.57	14.03	12.97	12.21	11.64	11.21	10.87	10.61
700	64.51	35.29	25.66	20.94	18.16	16.37	15.13	14.24	13.58	13.07	12.68	12.38
800	73.73	40.33	29.33	23.93	20.76	18.71	17.29	16.27	15.51	14.94	14.49	14.14
900	82.95	45.37	33.00	26.92	23.35	21.04	19.45	18.31	17.45	16.81	16.30	15.91
1,000	92.16	50.41	36.66	29.91	25.95	23.38	21.61	20.34	19.39	18.67	18.12	17.68
2,000	184.32	100.82	73.32	59.81	51.89	46.76	43.22	40.67	38.78	37.34	36.23	35.35
3,000	276.47	151.23	109.97	89.71	77.83	70.14	64.83	61.01	58.17	56.01	54.34	53.03
4,000	368.63	201.64	146.63	119.61	103.77	93.51	86.44	81.34	77.55	74.67	72.45	70.70
5,000	460.79	252.05	183.29	149.51	129.71	116.89	108.05	101.67	96.94	93.34	90.56	88.37
6,000	552.94	302.46	219.94	179.41	155.65	140.27	129.65	122.01	116.33	112.01	108.67	106.05
7,000	645.10	352.87	256.60	209.31	181.59	163.64	151.26	142.34	135.71	130.68	126.78	123.72
8,000	737.26	403.27	293.25	239.21	207.53	187.02	172.87	162.68	155.10	149.34	144.89	141.39
9,000	829.41	453.68	329.91	269.11	233.47	210.40	194.48	183.01	174.49	168.01	163.00	159.07
10,000	921.57	504.09	366.57	299.01	259.41	233.77	216.09	203.34	193.88	186.68	181.11	176.74
15,000	1382.35	756.13	549.85	448.51	389.11	350.66	324.13	305.01	290.81	280.01	271.66	265.11
20,000	1843.14	1008.18	733.13	598.01	518.82	467.54	432.17	406.68	387.75	373.35	362.21	353.48
25,000	2303.92	1260.22	916.41	747.51	648.52	584.42	540.21	508.35	484.68	466.69	452.76	441.85
30,000	2764.70	1512.26	1099.69	897.01	778.22	701.31	648.25	610.02	581.62	560.02	543.31	530.21
35,000	3225.49	1764.31	1282.97	1046.51	907.92	818.19	756.29	711.69	678.55	653.36	633.87	618.58
40,000	3686.27	2016.35	1466.25	1196.01	1037.63	935.07	864.33	813.36	775.49	746.69	724.42	706.95
45,000	4147.05	2268.39	1649.53	1345.51	1167.33	1051.96	972.37	915.03	872.42	840.03	814.97	795.32
50,000	4607.83	2520.44	1832.81	1495.01	1297.03	1168.84	1080.41	1016.70	969.36	933.37	905.52	883.69
55,000	5068.62	2772.48	2016.09	1644.51	1426.74	1285.72	1188.45	1118.37	1066.29	1026.70	996.07	972.06
60,000	5529.40	3024.52	2199.37	1794.01	1556.44	1402.61	1296.49	1220.04	1163.23	1120.04	1086.62	1060.42
65,000	5990.18	3276.57	2382.65	1943.51	1686.14	1519.49	1404.53	1321.71	1260.17	1213.38	1177.18	1148.79
70,000	6450.97	3528.61	2565.93	2093.01	1815.84	1636.38	1512.57	1423.38	1357.10	1306.71	1267.73	1237.16
75,000	6911.75	3780.65	2749.21	2242.51	1945.55	1753.26	1620.61	1525.04	1454.04	1400.05	1358.28	1325.53
80,000	7372.53	4032.69	2932.49	2392.01	2075.25	1870.14	1728.65	1626.71	1550.97	1493.38	1448.83	1413.90
85,000	7833.31	4284.74	3115.77	2541.52	2204.95	1987.03	1836.69	1728.38	1647.91	1586.72	1539.38	1502.27
90,000	8294.10	4536.78	3299.05	2691.02	2334.65	2103.91	1944.73	1830.05	1744.84	1680.06	1629.93	1590.63
95,000	8754.88	4788.82	3482.33	2840.52	2464.36	2220.79	2052.77	1931.72	1841.78	1773.39	1720.49	1679.00
100,000	9215.66	5040.87	3665.61	2990.02	2594.06	2337.68	2160.81	2033.39	1938.71	1866.73	1811.04	1767.37
105,000	9676.45	5292.91	3848.89	3139.52	2723.76	2454.56	2268.85	2135.06	2035.65	1960.06	1901.59	1855.74
110,000	10137.23	5544.95	4032.17	3289.02	2853.47	2571.44	2376.89	2236.73	2132.58	2053.40	1992.14	1944.11
115,000	10598.01	5797.00	4215.45	3438.52	2983.17	2688.33	2484.93	2338.40	2229.52	2146.74	2082.69	2032.47
120,000	11058.79	6049.04	4398.73	3588.02	3112.87	2805.21	2592.97	2440.07	2326.45	2240.07	2173.24	2120.84
125,000	11519.58	6301.08	4582.01	3737.52	3242.57	2922.10	2701.01	2541.74	2423.39	2333.41	2263.80	2209.21
130,000	11980.36	6553.13	4765.29	3887.02	3372.28	3038.98	2809.05	2643.41	2520.33	2426.75	2354.35	2297.58
135,000	12441.14	6805.17	4948.57	4036.52	3501.98	3155.86	2917.09	2745.08	2617.26	2520.08	2444.90	2385.95
140,000	12901.93	7057.21	5131.85	4186.02	3631.68	3272.75	3025.13	2846.75	2714.20	2613.42	2535.45	2474.32
145,000	13362.71	7309.25	5315.13	4335.52	3761.38	3389.63	3133.17	2948.42	2811.13	2706.75	2626.00	2562.68
150,000	13823.49	7561.30	5498.41	4485.02	3891.09	3506.51	3241.21	3050.08	2908.07	2800.09	2716.55	2651.05
155,000	14284.27	7813.34	5681.69	4634.52	4020.79	3623.40	3349.25	3151.75	3005.00	2893.43	2807.11	2739.42
160,000	14745.06	8065.38	5864.97	4784.02	4150.49	3740.28	3457.29	3253.42	3101.94	2986.76	2897.66	2827.79
165,000	15205.84	8317.43	6048.25	4933.52	4280.20	3857.16	3565.33	3355.09	3198.87	3080.10	2988.21	2916.16
170,000	15666.62	8569.47	6231.53	5083.03	4409.90	3974.05	3673.37	3456.76	3295.81	3173.44	3078.76	3004.53
175,000	16127.41	8821.51	6414.81	5232.53	4539.60	4090.93	3781.41	3558.43	3392.74	3266.77	3169.31	3092.89
180,000	16588.19	9073.56	6598.09	5382.03	4669.30	4207.82	3889.45	3660.10	3489.68	3360.11	3259.86	3181.26
185,000	17048.97	9325.60	6781.37	5531.53	4799.01	4324.70	3997.49	3761.77	3586.62	3453.44	3350.42	3269.63
190,000	17509.75	9577.64	6964.65	5681.03	4928.71	4441.58	4105.53	3863.44	3683.55	3546.78	3440.97	3358.00
195,000	17970.54	9829.69	7147.93	5830.53	5058.41	4558.47	4213.57	3965.11	3780.49	3640.12	3531.52	3446.37
200,000	18431.32	10081.73	7331.21	5980.03	5188.12	4675.35	4321.61	4066.78	3877.42	3733.45	3622.07	3534.73
205,000	18892.10	10333.77	7514.49	6129.53	5317.82	4792.23	4429.65	4168.45	3974.36	3826.79	3712.62	3623.10
210,000	19352.89	10585.81	7697.77	6279.03	5447.52	4909.12	4537.69	4270.12	4071.29	3920.12	3803.17	3711.47
215,000	19813.67	10837.86	7881.05	6428.53	5577.22	5026.00	4645.73	4371.79	4168.23	4013.46	3893.73	3799.84
220,000	20274.45	11089.90	8064.33	6578.03	5706.93	5142.88	4753.77	4473.46	4265.16	4106.80	3984.28	3888.21
225,000	20735.24	11341.94	8247.61	6727.53	5836.63	5259.77	4861.81	4575.12	4362.10	4200.13	4074.83	3976.58
230,000	21196.02	11593.99	8430.89	6877.03	5966.33	5376.65	4969.85	4676.79	4459.03	4293.47	4165.38	4064.94
235,000	21656.80	11846.03	8614.17	7026.53	6096.03	5493.53	5077.89	4778.46	4555.97	4386.81	4255.93	4153.31
240,000	22117.58	12098.07	8797.45	7176.03	6225.74	5610.42	5185.93	4880.13	4652.90	4480.14	4346.48	4241.68
245,000	22578.37	12350.12	8980.73	7325.53	6355.44	5727.30	5293.97	4981.80	4749.84	4573.48	4437.03	4330.05
250,000	23039.15	12602.16	9164.01	7475.03	6485.14	5844.19	5402.01	5083.47	4846.78	4666.81	4527.59	4418.42
255,000	23499.93	12854.20	9347.29	7624.54	6614.85	5961.07	5510.05	5185.14	4943.71	4760.15	4618.14	4506.79
260,000	23960.72	13106.25	9530.57	7774.04	6744.55	6077.95	5618.09	5286.81	5040.65	4853.49	4708.69	4595.15
265,000	24421.50	13358.29	9713.85	7923.54	6874.25	6194.84	5726.13	5388.48	5137.58	4946.82	4799.24	4683.52
270,000	24882.28	13610.33	9897.13	8073.04	7003.95	6311.72	5834.17	5490.15	5234.52	5040.16	4889.79	4771.89
280,000	25803.85	14114.42	10263.69	8372.04	7263.36	6545.49	6050.25	5693.49	5428.39	5226.83	5070.90	4948.63
290,000	26725.41	14618.50	10630.25	8671.04	7522.76	6779.25	6266.33	5896.83	5622.26	5413.50	5252.00	5125.36
300,000	27646.98	15122.59	10996.81	8970.04	7782.17	7013.02	6482.41	6100.16	5816.13	5600.18	5433.10	5302.10

138

AMOUNT OF LOAN	\multicolumn{11}{c}{NUMBER OF YEARS IN TERM}										
	13	14	15	16	17	18	19	20	25	30	35	40
$ 50	0.87	0.86	0.85	0.84	0.83	0.82	0.82	0.82	0.80	0.80	0.80	0.80
100	1.74	1.71	1.69	1.67	1.66	1.64	1.63	1.63	1.60	1.59	1.59	1.59
200	3.47	3.42	3.37	3.33	3.31	3.28	3.26	3.25	3.20	3.18	3.18	3.17
300	5.20	5.12	5.05	5.00	4.96	4.92	4.89	4.87	4.80	4.77	4.76	4.76
400	6.94	6.83	6.74	6.66	6.61	6.56	6.52	6.49	6.40	6.36	6.35	6.34
500	8.67	8.53	8.42	8.33	8.26	8.20	8.15	8.11	7.99	7.95	7.93	7.93
600	10.40	10.24	10.10	9.99	9.91	9.84	9.78	9.73	9.59	9.54	9.52	9.51
700	12.13	11.94	11.79	11.66	11.56	11.47	11.41	11.35	11.19	11.13	11.10	11.09
800	13.87	13.65	13.47	13.32	13.21	13.11	13.03	12.97	12.79	12.72	12.69	12.68
900	15.60	15.35	15.15	14.99	14.86	14.75	14.66	14.59	14.38	14.31	14.27	14.26
1,000	17.33	17.06	16.83	16.65	16.51	16.39	16.29	16.21	15.98	15.89	15.86	15.85
2,000	34.66	34.11	33.66	33.30	33.01	32.77	32.58	32.42	31.96	31.78	31.71	31.69
3,000	51.99	51.16	50.49	49.95	49.51	49.16	48.86	48.63	47.94	47.67	47.57	47.53
4,000	69.32	68.21	67.32	66.60	66.02	65.54	65.15	64.83	63.91	63.56	63.42	63.37
5,000	86.64	85.26	84.15	83.25	82.52	81.92	81.44	81.04	79.89	79.45	79.28	79.21
6,000	103.97	102.31	100.98	99.90	99.02	98.31	97.72	97.25	95.87	95.34	95.13	95.06
7,000	121.30	119.36	117.81	116.55	115.53	114.69	114.01	113.45	111.84	111.23	110.99	110.90
8,000	138.63	136.41	134.64	133.20	132.03	131.08	130.30	129.66	127.82	127.12	126.84	126.74
9,000	155.95	153.47	151.46	149.85	148.53	147.46	146.58	145.87	143.80	143.01	142.70	142.58
10,000	173.28	170.52	168.29	166.49	165.03	163.84	162.87	162.07	159.77	158.89	158.55	158.42
15,000	259.92	255.77	252.44	249.74	247.55	245.76	244.30	243.11	239.66	238.34	237.83	237.63
20,000	346.56	341.03	336.58	332.98	330.06	327.68	325.74	324.14	319.54	317.78	317.10	316.84
25,000	433.20	426.28	420.72	416.23	412.58	409.60	407.17	405.18	399.43	397.23	396.38	396.05
30,000	519.83	511.54	504.87	499.47	495.09	491.52	488.60	486.21	479.31	476.67	475.65	475.26
35,000	606.47	596.80	589.01	582.72	577.61	573.44	570.03	567.24	559.19	556.12	554.93	554.47
40,000	693.11	682.05	673.16	665.96	660.12	655.36	651.47	648.28	639.08	635.56	634.20	633.67
45,000	770.75	767.31	757.30	749.21	742.63	737.28	732.90	729.31	718.96	715.01	713.48	712.88
50,000	866.39	852.56	841.44	832.45	825.15	819.20	814.33	810.35	798.85	794.45	792.75	792.09
55,000	953.02	937.82	925.59	915.70	907.66	901.12	895.77	891.38	878.73	873.90	872.03	871.30
60,000	1039.66	1023.07	1009.73	998.94	990.18	983.04	977.20	972.42	958.61	953.34	951.30	950.51
65,000	1126.30	1108.33	1093.87	1082.19	1072.69	1064.95	1058.63	1053.45	1038.50	1032.79	1030.58	1029.72
70,000	1212.94	1193.59	1178.02	1165.43	1155.21	1146.87	1140.06	1134.48	1118.38	1112.23	1109.85	1108.93
75,000	1299.58	1278.84	1262.16	1248.67	1237.72	1228.79	1221.50	1215.52	1198.27	1191.67	1189.13	1188.14
80,000	1386.21	1364.10	1346.31	1331.92	1320.24	1310.71	1302.93	1296.55	1278.15	1271.12	1268.40	1267.34
85,000	1472.85	1449.35	1430.45	1415.16	1402.75	1392.63	1384.36	1377.59	1358.03	1350.56	1347.68	1346.55
90,000	1559.49	1534.61	1514.59	1498.41	1485.26	1474.55	1465.79	1458.62	1437.92	1430.01	1426.95	1425.76
95,000	1646.13	1619.86	1598.74	1581.65	1567.78	1556.47	1547.23	1539.66	1517.80	1509.45	1506.22	1504.97
100,000	1732.77	1705.12	1682.88	1664.90	1650.29	1638.39	1628.66	1620.69	1597.69	1588.90	1585.50	1584.18
105,000	1819.41	1790.38	1767.02	1748.14	1732.81	1720.31	1710.09	1701.72	1677.57	1668.34	1664.77	1663.39
110,000	1906.04	1875.63	1851.17	1831.39	1815.32	1802.23	1791.53	1782.76	1757.45	1747.79	1744.05	1742.60
115,000	1992.68	1960.89	1935.31	1914.63	1897.84	1884.15	1872.96	1863.79	1837.34	1827.23	1823.32	1821.81
120,000	2079.32	2046.14	2019.46	1997.87	1980.35	1966.07	1954.39	1944.83	1917.22	1906.68	1902.60	1901.01
125,000	2165.96	2131.40	2103.60	2081.12	2062.86	2047.99	2035.82	2025.86	1997.11	1986.12	1981.87	1980.22
130,000	2252.60	2216.65	2187.74	2164.37	2145.38	2129.90	2117.26	2106.90	2076.99	2065.57	2061.15	2059.43
135,000	2339.23	2301.91	2271.89	2247.61	2227.89	2211.82	2198.69	2187.93	2156.87	2145.01	2140.42	2138.64
140,000	2425.87	2387.17	2356.03	2330.85	2310.41	2293.74	2280.12	2268.96	2236.76	2224.45	2219.70	2217.85
145,000	2512.51	2472.42	2440.18	2414.10	2392.92	2375.66	2361.56	2350.00	2316.64	2303.90	2298.97	2297.06
150,000	2599.15	2557.68	2524.32	2497.34	2475.44	2457.58	2442.99	2431.03	2396.53	2383.34	2378.25	2376.27
155,000	2685.79	2642.93	2608.46	2580.59	2557.95	2539.50	2524.42	2512.07	2476.41	2462.79	2457.52	2455.48
160,000	2772.42	2728.19	2692.61	2663.83	2640.47	2621.42	2605.85	2593.10	2556.29	2542.23	2536.80	2534.68
165,000	2859.06	2813.44	2776.75	2747.08	2722.98	2703.34	2687.29	2674.14	2636.18	2621.68	2616.07	2613.89
170,000	2945.70	2898.70	2860.89	2830.32	2805.49	2785.26	2768.72	2755.17	2716.06	2701.12	2695.35	2693.10
175,000	3032.34	2983.96	2945.04	2913.57	2888.01	2867.18	2850.15	2836.20	2795.95	2780.57	2774.62	2772.31
180,000	3118.98	3069.21	3029.18	2996.81	2970.52	2949.10	2931.58	2917.24	2875.83	2860.01	2853.90	2851.52
185,000	3205.62	3154.47	3113.33	3080.06	3053.04	3031.02	3013.02	2998.27	2955.71	2939.46	2933.17	2930.73
190,000	3292.25	3239.72	3197.47	3163.30	3135.55	3112.94	3094.45	3079.31	3035.60	3018.90	3012.44	3009.94
195,000	3378.89	3324.98	3281.61	3246.55	3218.07	3194.85	3175.88	3160.34	3115.48	3098.35	3091.72	3089.15
200,000	3465.53	3410.23	3365.76	3329.79	3300.58	3276.77	3257.32	3241.37	3195.37	3177.79	3170.99	3168.35
205,000	3552.17	3495.49	3449.90	3413.04	3383.09	3358.69	3338.75	3322.41	3275.25	3257.23	3250.27	3247.56
210,000	3638.81	3580.75	3534.04	3496.28	3465.61	3440.61	3420.18	3403.44	3355.13	3336.68	3329.54	3326.77
215,000	3725.44	3666.00	3618.19	3579.52	3548.12	3522.53	3501.61	3484.48	3435.02	3416.12	3408.82	3405.98
220,000	3812.08	3751.26	3702.33	3662.77	3630.64	3604.45	3583.05	3565.51	3514.90	3495.57	3488.09	3485.19
225,000	3898.72	3836.51	3786.48	3746.01	3713.15	3686.37	3664.48	3646.55	3594.79	3575.01	3567.37	3564.40
230,000	3985.36	3921.77	3870.62	3829.26	3795.67	3768.29	3745.91	3727.58	3674.67	3654.46	3646.64	3643.61
235,000	4072.00	4007.02	3954.76	3912.50	3878.18	3850.21	3827.34	3808.61	3754.55	3733.90	3725.92	3722.82
240,000	4158.63	4092.28	4038.91	3995.75	3960.70	3932.13	3908.78	3889.65	3834.44	3813.35	3805.19	3802.02
245,000	4245.27	4177.54	4123.05	4078.99	4043.21	4014.05	3990.21	3970.68	3914.32	3892.79	3884.47	3881.23
250,000	4331.91	4262.79	4207.20	4162.24	4125.72	4095.97	4071.64	4051.72	3994.21	3972.24	3963.74	3960.44
255,000	4418.55	4348.05	4291.34	4245.48	4208.24	4177.88	4153.08	4132.75	4074.09	4051.68	4043.02	4039.65
260,000	4505.19	4433.30	4375.48	4328.73	4290.75	4259.80	4234.51	4213.79	4153.97	4131.13	4122.29	4118.86
265,000	4591.83	4518.56	4459.63	4411.97	4373.27	4341.72	4315.94	4294.82	4233.86	4210.57	4201.57	4198.07
270,000	4678.46	4603.81	4543.77	4495.22	4455.78	4423.64	4397.37	4375.85	4313.74	4290.01	4280.84	4277.28
280,000	4851.74	4774.33	4712.06	4661.70	4620.81	4587.48	4560.24	4537.92	4473.51	4448.90	4439.39	4435.69
290,000	5025.02	4944.84	4880.35	4828.19	4785.84	4751.32	4723.11	4699.99	4633.28	4607.79	4597.94	4594.11
300,000	5198.29	5115.35	5048.63	4994.68	4950.87	4915.16	4885.97	4862.06	4793.05	4766.68	4756.49	4752.53

19.25%

MONTHLY AMORTIZING PAYMENTS

AMOUNT OF LOAN	NUMBER OF YEARS IN TERM											
	1	2	3	4	5	6	7	8	9	10	11	12
$ 50	4.62	2.53	1.84	1.51	1.31	1.18	1.09	1.03	0.98	0.95	0.92	0.90
100	9.23	5.06	3.68	3.01	2.61	2.36	2.18	2.05	1.96	1.89	1.83	1.79
200	18.46	10.11	7.36	6.01	5.22	4.71	4.36	4.10	3.91	3.77	3.66	3.57
300	27.69	15.16	11.04	9.01	7.83	7.06	6.53	6.15	5.87	5.65	5.49	5.36
400	36.92	20.22	14.72	12.02	10.44	9.41	8.71	8.20	7.82	7.54	7.32	7.14
500	46.14	25.27	18.40	15.02	13.04	11.77	10.88	10.25	9.78	9.42	9.14	8.93
600	55.37	30.32	22.07	18.02	15.65	14.12	13.06	12.30	11.73	11.30	10.97	10.71
700	64.60	35.38	25.75	21.03	18.26	16.47	15.23	14.35	13.69	13.19	12.80	12.50
800	73.83	40.43	29.43	24.03	20.87	18.82	17.41	16.40	15.64	15.07	14.63	14.28
900	83.05	45.48	33.11	27.03	23.48	21.17	19.59	18.44	17.60	16.95	16.46	16.07
1,000	92.28	50.54	36.79	30.04	26.08	23.53	21.76	20.49	19.55	18.84	18.28	17.85
2,000	184.56	101.07	73.57	60.07	52.16	47.05	43.52	40.98	39.10	37.67	36.56	35.70
3,000	276.83	151.60	110.35	90.10	78.24	70.57	65.28	61.47	58.64	56.50	54.84	53.54
4,000	369.11	202.13	147.14	120.13	104.32	94.09	87.03	81.96	78.19	75.33	73.12	71.39
5,000	461.38	252.66	183.92	150.17	130.40	117.61	108.79	102.44	97.74	94.16	91.40	89.23
6,000	553.66	303.19	220.70	180.20	156.47	141.13	130.55	122.93	117.28	112.99	109.68	107.08
7,000	645.94	353.72	257.48	210.23	182.55	164.65	152.30	143.42	136.83	131.82	127.95	124.93
8,000	738.21	404.25	294.27	240.26	208.63	188.17	174.06	163.91	156.37	150.65	146.23	142.77
9,000	830.49	454.78	331.05	270.29	234.71	211.69	195.82	184.40	175.92	169.48	164.51	160.62
10,000	922.76	505.31	367.83	300.33	260.79	235.21	217.57	204.88	195.47	188.31	182.79	178.46
15,000	1384.14	757.96	551.74	450.49	391.18	352.81	326.36	307.32	293.20	282.47	274.18	267.69
20,000	1845.52	1010.61	735.66	600.65	521.57	470.41	435.14	409.76	390.93	376.62	365.57	356.92
25,000	2306.90	1263.26	919.57	750.81	651.96	588.01	543.93	512.20	488.66	470.78	456.97	446.15
30,000	2768.28	1515.91	1103.48	900.97	782.35	705.61	652.71	614.64	586.39	564.93	548.36	535.38
35,000	3229.66	1768.56	1287.39	1051.13	912.75	823.21	761.49	717.08	684.12	659.09	639.75	624.61
40,000	3691.04	2021.21	1471.31	1201.29	1043.14	940.81	870.28	819.52	781.85	753.24	731.14	713.84
45,000	4152.42	2273.86	1655.22	1351.45	1173.53	1058.41	979.06	921.96	879.58	847.40	822.53	803.07
50,000	4613.80	2526.51	1839.13	1501.62	1303.92	1176.01	1087.85	1024.40	977.31	941.55	913.93	892.30
55,000	5075.18	2779.16	2023.04	1651.78	1434.31	1293.61	1196.63	1126.84	1075.04	1035.71	1005.32	981.53
60,000	5536.56	3031.81	2206.96	1801.94	1564.70	1411.21	1305.41	1229.28	1172.77	1129.86	1096.71	1070.76
65,000	5997.94	3284.47	2390.87	1952.10	1695.09	1528.81	1414.20	1331.72	1270.50	1224.02	1188.10	1159.98
70,000	6459.32	3537.12	2574.78	2102.26	1825.49	1646.41	1522.98	1434.16	1368.23	1318.17	1279.49	1249.21
75,000	6920.70	3789.77	2758.70	2252.42	1955.88	1764.01	1631.77	1536.60	1465.96	1412.32	1370.89	1338.44
80,000	7382.08	4042.42	2942.61	2402.58	2086.27	1881.61	1740.55	1639.04	1563.69	1506.48	1462.28	1427.67
85,000	7843.46	4295.07	3126.52	2552.74	2216.66	1999.21	1849.33	1741.48	1661.42	1600.63	1553.67	1516.90
90,000	8304.84	4547.72	3310.43	2702.90	2347.05	2116.81	1958.12	1843.92	1759.15	1694.79	1645.06	1606.13
95,000	8766.22	4800.37	3494.35	2853.06	2477.44	2234.41	2066.90	1946.35	1856.88	1788.94	1736.45	1695.36
100,000	9227.60	5053.02	3678.26	3003.23	2607.84	2352.01	2175.69	2048.79	1954.61	1883.10	1827.85	1784.59
105,000	9688.98	5305.67	3862.17	3153.39	2738.23	2469.61	2284.47	2151.23	2052.34	1977.25	1919.24	1873.82
110,000	10150.36	5558.32	4046.08	3303.55	2868.62	2587.21	2393.26	2253.67	2150.07	2071.41	2010.63	1963.05
115,000	10611.74	5810.97	4230.00	3453.71	2999.01	2704.81	2502.04	2356.11	2247.80	2165.56	2102.02	2052.28
120,000	11073.12	6063.62	4413.91	3603.87	3129.40	2822.41	2610.82	2458.55	2345.54	2259.72	2193.42	2141.51
125,000	11534.50	6316.28	4597.82	3754.03	3259.79	2940.02	2719.61	2560.99	2443.27	2353.87	2284.81	2230.74
130,000	11995.88	6568.93	4781.74	3904.19	3390.18	3057.62	2828.39	2663.43	2541.00	2448.03	2376.20	2319.96
135,000	12457.26	6821.58	4965.65	4054.35	3520.58	3175.22	2937.18	2765.87	2638.73	2542.18	2467.59	2409.19
140,000	12918.64	7074.23	5149.56	4204.51	3650.97	3292.82	3045.96	2868.31	2736.46	2636.34	2558.98	2498.42
145,000	13380.02	7326.88	5333.47	4354.67	3781.36	3410.42	3154.74	2970.75	2834.19	2730.49	2650.38	2587.65
150,000	13841.40	7579.53	5517.39	4504.84	3911.75	3528.02	3263.53	3073.19	2931.92	2824.64	2741.77	2676.88
155,000	14302.77	7832.18	5701.30	4655.00	4042.14	3645.62	3372.31	3175.63	3029.65	2918.80	2833.16	2766.11
160,000	14764.15	8084.83	5885.21	4805.16	4172.53	3763.22	3481.10	3278.07	3127.38	3012.95	2924.55	2855.34
165,000	15225.53	8337.48	6069.12	4955.32	4302.93	3880.82	3589.88	3380.51	3225.11	3107.11	3015.94	2944.57
170,000	15686.91	8590.13	6253.04	5105.48	4433.32	3998.42	3698.66	3482.95	3322.84	3201.26	3107.34	3033.80
175,000	16148.29	8842.78	6436.95	5255.64	4563.71	4116.02	3807.45	3585.39	3420.57	3295.42	3198.73	3123.03
180,000	16609.67	9095.43	6620.86	5405.80	4694.10	4233.62	3916.23	3687.83	3518.30	3389.57	3290.12	3212.26
185,000	17071.05	9348.09	6804.78	5555.96	4824.49	4351.22	4025.02	3790.27	3616.03	3483.73	3381.51	3301.49
190,000	17532.43	9600.74	6988.69	5706.12	4954.88	4468.82	4133.80	3892.70	3713.76	3577.88	3472.90	3390.71
195,000	17993.81	9853.39	7172.60	5856.28	5085.27	4586.42	4242.58	3995.14	3811.49	3672.04	3564.30	3479.94
200,000	18455.19	10106.04	7356.51	6006.45	5215.67	4704.02	4351.37	4097.58	3909.22	3766.19	3655.69	3569.17
205,000	18916.57	10358.69	7540.43	6156.61	5346.06	4821.62	4460.15	4200.02	4006.95	3860.35	3747.08	3658.40
210,000	19377.95	10611.34	7724.34	6306.77	5476.45	4939.22	4568.94	4302.46	4104.68	3954.50	3838.47	3747.63
215,000	19839.33	10863.99	7908.25	6456.93	5606.84	5056.82	4677.72	4404.90	4202.41	4048.66	3929.87	3836.86
220,000	20300.71	11116.64	8092.16	6607.09	5737.23	5174.42	4786.51	4507.34	4300.14	4142.81	4021.26	3926.09
225,000	20762.09	11369.29	8276.08	6757.25	5867.62	5292.02	4895.29	4609.78	4397.87	4236.96	4112.65	4015.32
230,000	21223.47	11621.94	8459.99	6907.41	5998.02	5409.62	5004.07	4712.22	4495.60	4331.12	4204.04	4104.55
235,000	21684.85	11874.59	8643.90	7057.57	6128.41	5527.22	5112.86	4814.66	4593.33	4425.27	4295.43	4193.78
240,000	22146.23	12127.24	8827.82	7207.73	6258.80	5644.82	5221.64	4917.10	4691.07	4519.43	4386.83	4283.01
245,000	22607.61	12379.90	9011.73	7357.89	6389.19	5762.42	5330.43	5019.54	4788.80	4613.58	4478.22	4372.24
250,000	23068.99	12632.55	9195.64	7508.06	6519.58	5880.03	5439.21	5121.98	4886.53	4707.74	4569.61	4461.47
255,000	23530.37	12885.20	9379.55	7658.22	6649.97	5997.63	5547.99	5224.42	4984.26	4801.89	4661.00	4550.69
260,000	23991.75	13137.85	9563.47	7808.38	6780.36	6115.23	5656.78	5326.86	5081.99	4896.05	4752.39	4639.92
265,000	24453.13	13390.50	9747.38	7958.54	6910.76	6232.83	5765.56	5429.30	5179.72	4990.20	4843.79	4729.15
270,000	24914.51	13643.15	9931.29	8108.70	7041.15	6350.43	5874.35	5531.74	5277.45	5084.36	4935.18	4818.38
280,000	25837.27	14148.45	10299.12	8409.02	7301.93	6585.63	6091.91	5736.61	5472.91	5272.67	5117.96	4996.84
290,000	26760.03	14653.75	10666.94	8709.34	7562.71	6820.83	6309.48	5941.49	5668.37	5460.97	5300.75	5175.30
300,000	27682.79	15159.05	11034.77	9009.67	7823.50	7056.03	6527.05	6146.37	5863.83	5649.28	5483.53	5353.76

AMOUNT OF LOAN	NUMBER OF YEARS IN TERM											
	13	14	15	16	17	18	19	20	25	30	35	40
$ 50	0.88	0.87	0.86	0.85	0.84	0.83	0.83	0.83	0.81	0.81	0.81	0.81
100	1.76	1.73	1.71	1.69	1.67	1.66	1.65	1.65	1.62	1.61	1.61	1.61
200	3.51	3.45	3.41	3.37	3.34	3.32	3.30	3.29	3.24	3.22	3.22	3.21
300	5.26	5.17	5.11	5.06	5.01	4.98	4.95	4.93	4.86	4.83	4.82	4.82
400	7.01	6.90	6.81	6.74	6.68	6.63	6.60	6.57	6.48	6.44	6.43	6.42
500	8.76	8.62	8.51	8.42	8.35	8.29	8.24	8.21	8.09	8.05	8.04	8.03
600	10.51	10.34	10.21	10.11	10.02	9.95	9.89	9.85	9.71	9.66	9.64	9.63
700	12.26	12.07	11.91	11.79	11.69	11.61	11.54	11.49	11.33	11.27	11.25	11.24
800	14.01	13.79	13.61	13.47	13.36	13.26	13.19	13.13	12.95	12.88	12.85	12.84
900	15.76	15.51	15.32	15.16	15.03	14.92	14.84	14.77	14.57	14.49	14.46	14.45
1,000	17.51	17.24	17.02	16.84	16.70	16.58	16.48	16.41	16.18	16.10	16.07	16.05
2,000	35.01	34.47	34.03	33.67	33.39	33.15	32.96	32.81	32.36	32.19	32.13	32.10
3,000	52.52	51.70	51.04	50.51	50.08	49.73	49.44	49.21	48.54	48.29	48.19	48.15
4,000	70.02	68.93	68.05	67.34	66.77	66.30	65.92	65.61	64.72	64.38	64.25	64.20
5,000	87.52	86.16	85.06	84.18	83.46	82.88	82.40	82.01	80.90	80.47	80.31	80.25
6,000	105.03	103.39	102.07	101.01	100.15	99.45	98.88	98.41	97.07	96.57	96.38	96.30
7,000	122.53	120.62	119.09	117.85	116.84	116.03	115.36	114.82	113.25	112.66	112.44	112.35
8,000	140.03	137.85	136.10	134.68	133.53	132.60	131.84	131.22	129.43	128.76	128.50	128.40
9,000	157.54	155.08	153.11	151.52	150.22	149.18	148.32	147.62	145.61	144.85	144.56	144.45
10,000	175.04	172.31	170.12	168.35	166.92	165.75	164.80	164.02	161.79	160.94	160.62	160.50
15,000	262.56	258.46	255.18	252.52	250.37	248.62	247.19	246.03	242.68	241.41	240.93	240.75
20,000	350.08	344.62	340.23	336.70	333.83	331.49	329.59	328.04	323.57	321.88	321.24	320.99
25,000	437.60	430.77	425.29	420.87	417.28	414.37	411.99	410.04	404.46	402.35	401.55	401.24
30,000	525.11	516.92	510.35	505.04	500.74	497.24	494.38	492.05	485.35	482.82	481.86	481.49
35,000	612.63	603.08	595.41	589.21	584.19	580.11	576.78	574.06	566.24	563.29	562.17	561.73
40,000	700.15	689.23	680.46	673.39	667.65	662.98	659.18	656.07	647.14	643.76	642.48	641.98
45,000	787.67	775.38	765.52	757.56	751.10	746.86	741.57	738.07	728.03	724.23	722.70	722.23
50,000	875.19	861.54	850.58	841.73	834.56	828.73	823.97	820.08	808.92	804.70	803.09	802.47
55,000	962.70	947.69	935.63	925.90	918.02	911.60	906.37	902.09	889.81	885.17	883.40	882.72
60,000	1050.22	1033.84	1020.69	1010.08	1001.47	994.47	988.76	984.10	970.70	965.64	963.71	962.97
65,000	1137.74	1120.00	1105.75	1094.25	1084.93	1077.34	1071.16	1066.10	1051.59	1046.11	1044.02	1043.22
70,000	1225.26	1206.15	1190.81	1178.42	1168.38	1160.22	1153.56	1148.11	1132.48	1126.58	1124.33	1123.46
75,000	1312.78	1292.30	1275.86	1262.59	1251.84	1243.09	1235.95	1230.12	1213.38	1207.05	1204.64	1203.71
80,000	1400.29	1378.45	1360.92	1346.77	1335.29	1325.96	1318.35	1312.13	1294.27	1287.52	1284.95	1283.96
85,000	1487.81	1464.61	1445.98	1430.94	1418.75	1408.83	1400.75	1394.13	1375.16	1367.99	1365.25	1364.20
90,000	1575.33	1550.76	1531.03	1515.11	1502.20	1491.71	1483.14	1476.14	1456.05	1448.46	1445.56	1444.45
95,000	1662.85	1636.91	1616.09	1599.28	1585.66	1574.58	1565.54	1558.15	1536.94	1528.93	1525.87	1524.70
100,000	1750.37	1723.07	1701.15	1683.46	1669.12	1657.45	1647.94	1640.16	1617.83	1609.40	1606.18	1604.94
105,000	1837.88	1809.22	1786.21	1767.63	1752.57	1740.32	1730.33	1722.16	1698.72	1689.87	1686.49	1685.19
110,000	1925.40	1895.37	1871.26	1851.80	1836.03	1823.19	1812.73	1804.17	1779.62	1770.34	1766.80	1765.44
115,000	2012.92	1981.53	1956.32	1935.97	1919.48	1906.07	1895.12	1886.18	1860.51	1850.81	1847.11	1845.69
120,000	2100.44	2067.68	2041.38	2020.15	2002.94	1988.94	1977.52	1968.18	1941.40	1931.28	1927.42	1925.93
125,000	2187.96	2153.83	2126.43	2104.32	2086.39	2071.81	2059.92	2050.19	2022.29	2011.75	2007.72	2006.18
130,000	2275.47	2239.99	2211.49	2188.49	2169.85	2154.68	2142.31	2132.20	2103.18	2092.22	2088.03	2086.43
135,000	2362.99	2326.14	2296.55	2272.66	2253.30	2237.56	2224.71	2214.21	2184.07	2172.69	2168.34	2166.67
140,000	2450.51	2412.29	2381.61	2356.84	2336.76	2320.43	2307.11	2296.22	2264.96	2253.16	2248.65	2246.92
145,000	2538.03	2498.45	2466.66	2441.01	2420.21	2403.30	2389.50	2378.22	2345.85	2333.63	2328.96	2327.17
150,000	2625.55	2584.60	2551.72	2525.18	2503.67	2486.17	2471.90	2460.23	2426.75	2414.10	2409.27	2407.41
155,000	2713.06	2670.75	2636.78	2609.35	2587.13	2569.04	2554.30	2542.24	2507.64	2494.57	2489.58	2487.66
160,000	2800.58	2756.90	2721.83	2693.53	2670.58	2651.92	2636.69	2624.25	2588.53	2575.04	2569.89	2567.91
165,000	2888.10	2843.06	2806.89	2777.70	2754.04	2734.79	2719.09	2706.25	2669.42	2655.51	2650.19	2648.15
170,000	2975.62	2929.21	2891.95	2861.87	2837.49	2817.66	2801.49	2788.26	2750.31	2735.98	2730.50	2728.40
175,000	3063.14	3015.36	2977.01	2946.04	2920.95	2900.53	2883.88	2870.27	2831.20	2816.45	2810.81	2808.65
180,000	3150.65	3101.52	3062.06	3030.22	3004.40	2983.41	2966.28	2952.28	2912.09	2896.92	2891.12	2888.90
185,000	3238.17	3187.67	3147.12	3114.39	3087.86	3066.28	3048.68	3034.29	2992.99	2977.39	2971.43	2969.14
190,000	3325.69	3273.82	3232.18	3198.56	3171.31	3149.15	3131.07	3116.29	3073.88	3057.86	3051.74	3049.39
195,000	3413.21	3359.98	3317.23	3282.74	3254.77	3232.02	3213.47	3198.30	3154.77	3138.33	3132.05	3129.64
200,000	3500.73	3446.13	3402.29	3366.91	3338.23	3314.90	3295.87	3280.31	3235.66	3218.80	3212.36	3209.88
205,000	3588.25	3532.28	3487.35	3451.08	3421.68	3397.77	3378.26	3362.32	3316.55	3299.27	3292.66	3290.13
210,000	3675.76	3618.44	3572.41	3535.25	3505.14	3480.64	3460.66	3444.32	3397.44	3379.74	3372.97	3370.38
215,000	3763.28	3704.59	3657.46	3619.43	3588.59	3563.51	3543.05	3526.33	3478.33	3460.21	3453.28	3450.62
220,000	3850.80	3790.74	3742.52	3703.60	3672.05	3646.38	3625.45	3608.34	3559.23	3540.68	3533.59	3530.87
225,000	3938.32	3876.90	3827.58	3787.77	3755.50	3729.26	3707.85	3690.35	3640.12	3621.15	3613.90	3611.12
230,000	4025.84	3963.05	3912.63	3871.94	3838.96	3812.13	3790.24	3772.35	3721.01	3701.62	3694.21	3691.37
235,000	4113.35	4049.20	3997.69	3956.12	3922.41	3895.00	3872.64	3854.36	3801.90	3782.09	3774.52	3771.61
240,000	4200.87	4135.35	4082.75	4040.29	4005.87	3977.87	3955.04	3936.37	3882.79	3862.56	3854.83	3851.86
245,000	4288.39	4221.51	4167.81	4124.46	4089.32	4060.75	4037.43	4018.38	3963.68	3943.03	3935.14	3932.11
250,000	4375.91	4307.66	4252.86	4208.63	4172.78	4143.62	4119.83	4100.38	4044.57	4023.50	4015.44	4012.35
255,000	4463.43	4393.81	4337.92	4292.81	4256.24	4226.49	4202.23	4182.39	4125.47	4103.97	4095.75	4092.60
260,000	4550.94	4479.97	4422.98	4376.98	4339.69	4309.36	4284.62	4264.40	4206.36	4184.44	4176.06	4172.85
265,000	4638.46	4566.12	4508.04	4461.15	4423.15	4392.23	4367.02	4346.41	4287.25	4264.91	4256.37	4253.09
270,000	4725.98	4652.27	4593.09	4545.32	4506.60	4475.11	4449.42	4428.41	4368.14	4345.38	4336.68	4333.34
280,000	4901.02	4824.58	4763.21	4713.67	4673.51	4640.85	4614.21	4592.43	4529.92	4506.32	4497.30	4493.83
290,000	5076.05	4996.89	4933.32	4882.01	4840.42	4806.60	4779.00	4756.44	4691.70	4667.26	4657.91	4654.33
300,000	5251.09	5169.19	5103.44	5050.36	5007.34	4972.34	4943.80	4920.46	4853.49	4828.20	4818.53	4814.82

19.50%　MONTHLY AMORTIZING PAYMENTS

AMOUNT OF LOAN	1	2	3	4	5	6	7	8	9	10	11	12
$ 50	4.62	2.54	1.85	1.51	1.32	1.19	1.10	1.04	0.99	0.95	0.93	0.91
100	9.24	5.07	3.70	3.02	2.63	2.37	2.20	2.07	1.98	1.90	1.85	1.81
200	18.48	10.14	7.39	6.04	5.25	4.74	4.39	4.13	3.95	3.80	3.69	3.61
300	27.72	15.20	11.08	9.05	7.87	7.10	6.58	6.20	5.92	5.70	5.54	5.41
400	36.96	20.27	14.77	12.07	10.49	9.47	8.77	8.26	7.89	7.60	7.38	7.21
500	46.20	25.33	18.46	15.09	13.11	11.84	10.96	10.33	9.86	9.50	9.23	9.01
600	55.44	30.40	22.15	18.10	15.73	14.20	13.15	12.39	11.83	11.40	11.07	10.82
700	64.68	35.46	25.84	21.12	18.36	16.57	15.34	14.45	13.80	13.30	12.92	12.62
800	73.92	40.53	29.53	24.14	20.98	18.94	17.53	16.52	15.77	15.20	14.76	14.42
900	83.16	45.59	33.22	27.15	23.60	21.30	19.72	18.58	17.74	17.10	16.61	16.22
1,000	92.40	50.66	36.91	30.17	26.22	23.67	21.91	20.65	19.71	19.00	18.45	18.02
2,000	184.80	101.31	73.82	60.33	52.44	47.33	43.82	41.29	39.42	38.00	36.90	36.04
3,000	277.19	151.96	110.73	90.50	78.65	71.00	65.72	61.93	59.12	56.99	55.35	54.06
4,000	369.59	202.61	147.64	120.66	104.87	94.66	87.63	82.57	78.83	75.99	73.79	72.08
5,000	461.98	253.26	184.55	150.83	131.09	118.32	109.54	103.22	98.53	94.98	92.24	90.10
6,000	554.38	303.92	221.46	180.99	157.30	141.99	131.44	123.86	118.24	113.98	110.69	108.12
7,000	646.77	354.57	258.37	211.16	183.52	165.65	153.35	144.50	137.94	132.97	129.13	126.14
8,000	739.17	405.22	295.28	241.32	209.74	189.32	175.25	165.14	157.65	151.97	147.58	144.15
9,000	831.56	455.87	332.19	271.49	235.95	212.98	197.16	185.79	177.36	170.96	166.03	162.17
10,000	923.96	506.52	369.10	301.65	262.17	236.64	219.07	206.43	197.06	189.96	184.48	180.19
15,000	1385.94	759.78	553.64	452.47	393.25	354.96	328.60	309.64	295.59	284.93	276.71	270.28
20,000	1847.91	1013.04	738.19	603.30	524.33	473.28	438.13	412.85	394.12	379.91	368.95	360.38
25,000	2309.89	1266.30	922.74	754.12	655.42	591.60	547.66	516.07	492.65	474.89	461.18	450.47
30,000	2771.87	1519.56	1107.28	904.94	786.50	709.92	657.19	619.28	591.17	569.86	553.42	540.56
35,000	3233.84	1772.82	1291.83	1055.77	917.58	828.24	766.72	722.49	689.70	664.84	645.65	630.66
40,000	3695.82	2026.08	1476.38	1206.59	1048.66	946.56	876.25	825.70	788.23	759.81	737.89	720.75
45,000	4157.80	2279.34	1660.92	1357.41	1179.75	1064.88	985.78	928.92	886.76	854.79	830.13	810.84
50,000	4619.77	2532.60	1845.47	1508.24	1310.83	1183.20	1095.31	1032.13	985.29	949.77	922.36	900.94
55,000	5081.75	2785.86	2030.02	1659.06	1441.91	1301.52	1204.84	1135.34	1083.82	1044.74	1014.60	991.03
60,000	5543.73	3039.12	2214.56	1809.88	1572.99	1419.84	1314.37	1238.55	1182.34	1139.72	1106.83	1081.12
65,000	6005.70	3292.38	2399.11	1960.70	1704.07	1538.16	1423.90	1341.76	1280.87	1234.69	1199.07	1171.22
70,000	6467.68	3545.64	2583.66	2111.53	1835.16	1656.48	1533.43	1444.98	1379.40	1329.67	1293.30	1261.31
75,000	6929.66	3798.90	2768.20	2262.35	1966.24	1774.80	1642.96	1548.19	1477.93	1424.65	1383.54	1351.40
80,000	7391.63	4052.16	2952.75	2413.17	2097.32	1893.12	1752.49	1651.40	1576.46	1519.62	1475.78	1441.50
85,000	7853.61	4305.41	3137.30	2564.00	2228.40	2011.44	1862.03	1754.61	1674.99	1614.60	1568.01	1531.59
90,000	8315.59	4558.67	3321.84	2714.82	2359.49	2129.75	1971.56	1857.83	1773.51	1709.57	1660.25	1621.68
95,000	8777.57	4811.93	3506.39	2865.64	2490.57	2248.07	2081.09	1961.04	1872.04	1804.55	1752.48	1711.78
100,000	9239.54	5065.19	3690.94	3016.47	2621.65	2366.39	2190.62	2064.25	1970.57	1899.53	1844.72	1801.87
105,000	9701.52	5318.45	3875.48	3167.29	2752.73	2484.71	2300.15	2167.46	2069.10	1994.50	1936.95	1891.96
110,000	10163.50	5571.71	4060.03	3318.11	2883.81	2603.03	2409.68	2270.68	2167.63	2089.48	2029.19	1982.06
115,000	10625.47	5824.97	4244.58	3468.93	3014.90	2721.35	2519.21	2373.89	2266.16	2184.46	2121.42	2072.15
120,000	11087.45	6078.23	4429.12	3619.76	3145.98	2839.67	2628.74	2477.10	2364.68	2279.43	2213.66	2162.24
125,000	11549.43	6331.49	4613.67	3770.58	3277.06	2957.99	2738.27	2580.31	2463.21	2374.41	2305.90	2252.34
130,000	12011.40	6584.75	4798.22	3921.40	3408.14	3076.31	2847.80	2683.52	2561.74	2469.38	2398.13	2342.43
135,000	12473.38	6838.01	4982.76	4072.23	3539.23	3194.63	2957.33	2786.74	2660.27	2564.36	2490.37	2432.52
140,000	12935.36	7091.27	5167.31	4223.05	3670.31	3312.95	3066.86	2889.95	2758.80	2659.34	2582.60	2522.62
145,000	13397.33	7344.53	5351.86	4373.87	3801.39	3431.27	3176.39	2993.16	2857.33	2754.31	2674.84	2612.71
150,000	13859.31	7597.79	5536.40	4524.70	3932.47	3549.59	3285.92	3096.37	2955.85	2849.29	2767.07	2702.80
155,000	14321.29	7851.05	5720.95	4675.52	4063.55	3667.91	3395.45	3199.59	3054.38	2944.26	2859.31	2792.90
160,000	14783.26	8104.31	5905.49	4826.34	4194.64	3786.23	3504.98	3302.80	3152.91	3039.24	2951.55	2882.99
165,000	15245.24	8357.56	6090.04	4977.16	4325.72	3904.55	3614.51	3406.01	3251.44	3134.22	3043.78	2973.08
170,000	15707.22	8610.82	6274.59	5127.99	4456.80	4022.87	3724.05	3509.22	3349.97	3229.19	3136.02	3063.18
175,000	16169.20	8864.08	6459.13	5278.81	4587.88	4141.18	3833.58	3612.44	3448.49	3324.17	3228.25	3153.27
180,000	16631.17	9117.34	6643.68	5429.63	4718.97	4259.50	3943.11	3715.65	3547.02	3419.14	3320.49	3243.36
185,000	17093.15	9370.60	6828.23	5580.46	4850.05	4377.82	4052.64	3818.86	3645.55	3514.12	3412.72	3333.46
190,000	17555.13	9623.86	7012.77	5731.28	4981.13	4496.14	4162.17	3922.07	3744.08	3609.10	3504.96	3423.55
195,000	18017.10	9877.12	7197.32	5882.10	5112.21	4614.46	4271.70	4025.28	3842.61	3704.07	3597.19	3513.64
200,000	18479.08	10130.38	7381.87	6032.93	5243.29	4732.78	4381.23	4128.50	3941.14	3799.05	3689.43	3603.73
205,000	18941.06	10383.64	7566.41	6183.75	5374.38	4851.10	4490.76	4231.71	4039.66	3894.03	3781.67	3693.83
210,000	19403.03	10636.90	7750.96	6334.57	5505.46	4969.42	4600.29	4334.92	4138.19	3989.00	3873.90	3783.92
215,000	19865.01	10890.16	7935.51	6485.39	5636.54	5087.74	4709.82	4438.13	4236.72	4083.98	3966.14	3874.01
220,000	20326.99	11143.42	8120.05	6636.22	5767.62	5206.06	4819.35	4541.35	4335.25	4178.95	4058.37	3964.11
225,000	20788.96	11396.68	8304.60	6787.04	5898.71	5324.38	4928.88	4644.56	4433.78	4273.93	4150.61	4054.20
230,000	21250.94	11649.94	8489.15	6937.86	6029.79	5442.70	5038.41	4747.77	4532.31	4368.91	4242.84	4144.29
235,000	21712.92	11903.20	8673.69	7088.69	6160.87	5561.02	5147.94	4850.98	4630.83	4463.88	4335.08	4234.39
240,000	22174.89	12156.46	8858.24	7239.51	6291.95	5679.34	5257.47	4954.20	4729.36	4558.86	4427.32	4324.48
245,000	22636.87	12409.71	9042.79	7390.33	6423.03	5797.66	5367.00	5057.41	4827.89	4653.83	4519.55	4414.57
250,000	23098.85	12662.97	9227.33	7541.16	6554.12	5915.98	5476.53	5160.62	4926.42	4748.81	4611.79	4504.67
255,000	23560.83	12916.23	9411.88	7691.98	6685.20	6034.30	5586.07	5263.83	5024.95	4843.79	4704.02	4594.76
260,000	24022.80	13169.49	9596.43	7842.80	6816.28	6152.61	5695.60	5367.04	5123.48	4938.76	4796.26	4684.85
265,000	24484.78	13422.75	9780.97	7993.62	6947.36	6270.93	5805.13	5470.26	5222.00	5033.74	4888.49	4774.95
270,000	24946.76	13676.01	9965.52	8144.45	7078.45	6389.25	5914.66	5573.47	5320.53	5128.71	4980.73	4865.04
280,000	25870.71	14182.53	10334.61	8446.09	7340.61	6625.89	6133.72	5779.89	5517.59	5318.67	5165.20	5045.23
290,000	26794.66	14689.05	10703.71	8747.74	7602.77	6862.53	6352.78	5986.32	5714.65	5508.62	5349.67	5225.41
300,000	27718.62	15195.57	11072.80	9049.39	7864.94	7099.17	6571.84	6192.74	5911.70	5698.57	5534.14	5405.60

AMOUNT OF LOAN	NUMBER OF YEARS IN TERM											
	13	14	15	16	17	18	19	20	25	30	35	40
$ 50	0.89	0.88	0.86	0.86	0.85	0.84	0.84	0.83	0.82	0.82	0.82	0.82
100	1.77	1.75	1.72	1.71	1.69	1.68	1.67	1.66	1.64	1.63	1.63	1.63
200	3.54	3.49	3.44	3.41	3.38	3.36	3.34	3.32	3.28	3.26	3.26	3.26
300	5.31	5.23	5.16	5.11	5.07	5.03	5.01	4.98	4.92	4.89	4.89	4.88
400	7.08	6.97	6.88	6.81	6.76	6.71	6.67	6.64	6.56	6.52	6.51	6.51
500	8.85	8.71	8.60	8.52	8.44	8.39	8.34	8.30	8.20	8.15	8.14	8.13
600	10.61	10.45	10.32	10.22	10.13	10.06	10.01	9.96	9.83	9.78	9.77	9.76
700	12.38	12.19	12.04	11.92	11.82	11.74	11.68	11.62	11.47	11.41	11.39	11.38
800	14.15	13.93	13.76	13.62	13.51	13.42	13.34	13.28	13.11	13.04	13.02	13.01
900	15.92	15.67	15.48	15.32	15.20	15.09	15.01	14.94	14.75	14.67	14.65	14.64
1,000	17.69	17.42	17.20	17.03	16.88	16.77	16.68	16.60	16.39	16.30	16.27	16.26
2,000	35.37	34.83	34.39	34.05	33.76	33.54	33.35	33.20	32.77	32.60	32.54	32.52
3,000	53.05	52.24	51.59	51.07	50.64	50.30	50.02	49.79	49.15	48.90	48.81	48.78
4,000	70.73	69.65	68.78	68.09	67.52	67.07	66.70	66.39	65.53	65.20	65.08	65.03
5,000	88.41	87.06	85.98	85.11	84.40	83.83	83.37	82.99	81.91	81.50	81.35	81.29
6,000	106.09	104.47	103.17	102.13	101.28	100.60	100.04	99.58	98.29	97.80	97.62	97.55
7,000	123.77	121.88	120.37	119.15	118.16	117.36	116.71	116.18	114.67	114.10	113.89	113.80
8,000	141.45	139.29	137.56	136.17	135.04	134.13	133.39	132.78	131.05	130.40	130.15	130.06
9,000	159.13	156.70	154.76	153.19	151.92	150.90	150.06	149.37	147.43	146.70	146.42	146.32
10,000	176.81	174.11	171.95	170.21	168.80	167.66	166.73	165.97	163.81	163.00	162.69	162.58
15,000	265.21	261.17	257.93	255.32	253.20	251.49	250.09	248.95	245.71	244.49	244.04	243.86
20,000	353.61	348.22	343.90	340.42	337.60	335.32	333.46	331.94	327.61	325.99	325.38	325.15
25,000	442.01	435.27	429.87	425.52	422.00	419.14	416.82	414.92	409.51	407.49	406.72	406.43
30,000	530.41	522.33	515.85	510.63	506.40	502.97	500.18	497.90	491.41	488.98	488.07	487.72
35,000	618.81	609.38	601.82	595.73	590.80	586.80	583.54	580.89	573.31	570.48	569.41	569.00
40,000	707.21	696.43	687.79	680.83	675.20	670.63	666.91	663.87	655.21	651.97	650.75	650.29
45,000	795.61	783.49	773.77	765.94	759.60	754.46	750.27	746.85	737.11	733.47	732.10	731.57
50,000	884.02	870.54	859.74	851.04	844.00	838.28	833.63	829.84	819.01	814.97	813.44	812.86
55,000	972.42	957.59	945.71	936.14	928.40	922.11	917.00	912.82	900.91	896.46	894.78	894.15
60,000	1060.82	1044.65	1031.69	1021.25	1012.80	1005.94	1000.36	995.80	982.81	977.96	976.13	975.43
65,000	1149.22	1131.70	1117.66	1106.35	1097.20	1089.77	1083.72	1078.79	1064.71	1059.45	1057.47	1056.72
70,000	1237.62	1218.75	1203.63	1191.45	1181.60	1173.60	1167.08	1161.77	1146.61	1140.95	1138.81	1138.00
75,000	1326.02	1305.81	1289.61	1276.56	1266.00	1257.42	1250.45	1244.75	1228.51	1222.45	1220.16	1219.29
80,000	1414.42	1392.86	1375.58	1361.66	1350.40	1341.25	1333.81	1327.74	1310.41	1303.94	1301.50	1300.57
85,000	1502.82	1479.92	1461.55	1446.76	1434.79	1425.08	1417.17	1410.72	1392.31	1385.44	1382.84	1381.86
90,000	1591.22	1566.97	1547.53	1531.87	1519.19	1508.91	1500.53	1493.70	1474.21	1466.93	1464.19	1463.14
95,000	1679.63	1654.02	1633.50	1616.97	1603.59	1592.74	1583.90	1576.69	1556.11	1548.43	1545.53	1544.43
100,000	1768.03	1741.08	1719.48	1702.07	1687.99	1676.56	1667.26	1659.67	1638.01	1629.93	1626.87	1625.71
105,000	1866.43	1828.13	1805.45	1787.18	1772.39	1760.39	1750.62	1742.65	1719.91	1711.42	1708.22	1707.00
110,000	1944.83	1915.18	1891.42	1872.28	1856.79	1844.22	1833.99	1825.64	1801.81	1792.92	1789.56	1788.29
115,000	2033.23	2002.24	1977.40	1957.38	1941.19	1928.05	1917.35	1908.62	1883.71	1874.41	1870.90	1869.57
120,000	2121.03	2089.29	2063.37	2042.49	2025.59	2011.87	2000.71	1991.60	1965.61	1955.91	1952.25	1950.86
125,000	2210.03	2176.34	2149.34	2127.59	2109.99	2095.70	2084.07	2074.59	2047.51	2037.41	2033.59	2032.14
130,000	2298.43	2263.40	2235.32	2212.69	2194.39	2179.53	2167.44	2157.57	2129.41	2118.90	2114.93	2113.43
135,000	2386.83	2350.45	2321.29	2297.80	2278.79	2263.36	2250.80	2240.55	2211.31	2200.40	2196.28	2194.71
140,000	2475.23	2437.50	2407.26	2382.90	2363.19	2347.19	2334.16	2323.54	2293.21	2281.89	2277.62	2276.00
145,000	2563.64	2524.56	2493.24	2468.00	2447.59	2431.01	2417.52	2406.52	2375.11	2363.39	2358.96	2357.28
150,000	2652.04	2611.61	2579.21	2553.11	2531.99	2514.84	2500.89	2489.50	2457.01	2444.89	2440.31	2438.57
155,000	2740.44	2698.66	2665.18	2638.21	2616.39	2598.67	2584.25	2572.49	2538.91	2526.38	2521.65	2519.85
160,000	2828.84	2785.72	2751.16	2723.31	2700.79	2682.50	2667.61	2655.47	2620.81	2607.88	2602.99	2601.14
165,000	2917.24	2872.77	2837.13	2808.42	2785.18	2766.33	2750.98	2738.45	2702.72	2689.37	2684.34	2682.43
170,000	3005.64	2959.83	2923.10	2893.52	2869.58	2850.15	2834.34	2821.43	2784.62	2770.87	2765.68	2763.71
175,000	3094.04	3046.88	3009.08	2978.62	2953.98	2933.98	2917.70	2904.42	2866.52	2852.37	2847.02	2845.00
180,000	3182.44	3133.93	3095.05	3063.73	3038.38	3017.81	3001.06	2987.40	2948.42	2933.86	2928.37	2926.28
185,000	3270.84	3220.99	3181.02	3148.83	3122.78	3101.64	3084.43	3070.38	3030.32	3015.36	3009.71	3007.57
190,000	3359.25	3308.04	3267.00	3233.93	3207.18	3185.47	3167.79	3153.37	3112.22	3096.85	3091.05	3088.85
195,000	3447.65	3395.09	3352.97	3319.04	3291.58	3269.29	3251.15	3236.35	3194.12	3178.35	3172.40	3170.14
200,000	3536.05	3482.15	3438.95	3404.14	3375.98	3353.12	3334.51	3319.33	3276.02	3259.85	3253.74	3251.42
205,000	3624.45	3569.20	3524.92	3489.24	3460.38	3436.95	3417.88	3402.32	3357.92	3341.34	3335.08	3332.71
210,000	3712.85	3656.25	3610.89	3574.35	3544.78	3520.78	3501.24	3485.30	3439.82	3422.84	3416.43	3413.99
215,000	3801.25	3743.31	3696.87	3659.45	3629.18	3604.61	3584.60	3568.28	3521.72	3504.33	3497.77	3495.28
220,000	3889.65	3830.36	3782.84	3744.55	3713.58	3688.43	3667.97	3651.27	3603.62	3585.83	3579.11	3576.57
225,000	3978.05	3917.41	3868.81	3829.66	3797.98	3772.26	3751.33	3734.25	3685.52	3667.33	3660.46	3657.85
230,000	4066.45	4004.47	3954.79	3914.76	3882.38	3856.09	3834.69	3817.23	3767.42	3748.82	3741.80	3739.14
235,000	4154.85	4091.52	4040.76	3999.86	3966.78	3939.92	3918.05	3900.22	3849.32	3830.32	3823.14	3820.42
240,000	4243.26	4178.57	4126.73	4084.97	4051.18	4023.74	4001.42	3983.20	3931.22	3911.81	3904.49	3901.71
245,000	4331.66	4265.63	4212.71	4170.07	4135.57	4107.57	4084.78	4066.18	4013.12	3993.31	3985.83	3982.99
250,000	4420.06	4352.68	4298.68	4255.17	4219.97	4191.40	4168.14	4149.17	4095.02	4074.81	4067.17	4064.28
255,000	4508.46	4439.74	4384.65	4340.28	4304.37	4275.23	4251.50	4232.15	4176.92	4156.30	4148.52	4145.56
260,000	4596.86	4526.79	4470.63	4425.38	4388.77	4359.06	4334.87	4315.13	4258.82	4237.80	4229.86	4226.85
265,000	4685.26	4613.84	4556.60	4510.48	4473.17	4442.88	4418.23	4398.12	4340.72	4319.29	4311.20	4308.13
270,000	4773.66	4700.90	4642.57	4595.59	4557.57	4526.71	4501.59	4481.10	4422.62	4400.79	4392.55	4389.42
280,000	4950.46	4875.00	4814.52	4765.79	4726.37	4694.37	4668.32	4647.07	4586.42	4563.78	4555.23	4551.99
290,000	5127.27	5049.11	4986.47	4936.00	4895.17	4862.02	4835.04	4813.03	4750.22	4726.77	4717.92	4714.56
300,000	5304.07	5223.22	5158.42	5106.21	5063.97	5029.68	5001.77	4979.00	4914.02	4889.77	4880.61	4877.13

MONTHLY AMORTIZING PAYMENTS

AMOUNT OF LOAN	NUMBER OF YEARS IN TERM											
	1	2	3	4	5	6	7	8	9	10	11	12
$ 50	4.63	2.54	1.86	1.52	1.32	1.20	1.11	1.04	1.00	0.96	0.94	0.91
100	9.26	5.08	3.71	3.03	2.64	2.39	2.21	2.08	1.99	1.92	1.87	1.82
200	18.51	10.16	7.41	6.06	5.28	4.77	4.42	4.16	3.98	3.84	3.73	3.64
300	27.76	15.24	11.12	9.09	7.91	7.15	6.62	6.24	5.96	5.75	5.59	5.46
400	37.01	20.31	14.82	12.12	10.55	9.53	8.83	8.32	7.95	7.67	7.45	7.28
500	46.26	25.39	18.52	15.15	13.18	11.91	11.03	10.40	9.94	9.59	9.31	9.10
600	55.51	30.47	22.23	18.18	15.82	14.29	13.24	12.48	11.92	11.50	11.17	10.92
700	64.77	35.55	25.93	21.21	18.45	16.67	15.44	14.56	13.91	13.42	13.04	12.74
800	74.02	40.62	29.63	24.24	21.09	19.05	17.65	16.64	15.90	15.33	14.90	14.56
900	83.27	45.70	33.34	27.27	23.72	21.43	19.86	18.72	17.88	17.25	16.76	16.38
1,000	92.52	50.78	37.04	30.30	26.36	23.81	22.06	20.80	19.87	19.17	18.62	18.20
2,000	185.03	101.55	74.08	60.60	52.71	47.62	44.12	41.60	39.74	38.33	37.24	36.39
3,000	277.55	152.33	111.11	90.90	79.07	71.43	66.17	62.40	59.60	57.49	55.85	54.58
4,000	370.06	203.10	148.15	121.19	105.42	95.24	88.23	83.20	79.47	76.65	74.47	72.77
5,000	462.58	253.87	185.19	151.49	131.78	119.05	110.28	103.99	99.33	95.81	93.09	90.97
6,000	555.09	304.65	222.22	181.79	158.13	142.85	132.34	124.79	119.20	114.97	111.70	109.16
7,000	647.61	355.42	259.26	212.09	184.49	166.66	154.40	145.59	139.07	134.13	130.32	127.35
8,000	740.12	406.20	296.30	242.38	210.84	190.47	176.45	166.39	158.93	153.29	148.94	145.54
9,000	832.64	456.97	333.33	272.68	237.20	214.28	198.51	187.18	178.80	172.45	167.55	163.73
10,000	925.15	507.74	370.37	302.98	263.55	238.09	220.56	207.98	198.66	191.61	186.17	181.93
15,000	1387.73	761.61	555.55	454.46	395.33	357.13	330.84	311.97	297.99	287.41	279.25	272.89
20,000	1850.30	1015.48	740.73	605.95	527.10	476.17	441.12	415.96	397.32	383.21	372.33	363.85
25,000	2312.88	1269.35	925.91	757.44	658.88	595.21	551.40	519.94	496.65	479.01	465.42	454.81
30,000	2775.45	1523.22	1111.09	908.92	790.65	714.25	661.68	623.93	595.98	574.81	558.50	545.77
35,000	3238.03	1777.09	1296.28	1060.41	922.43	833.29	771.96	727.92	695.31	670.61	651.58	636.73
40,000	3700.60	2030.96	1481.46	1211.90	1054.20	952.33	882.24	831.91	794.64	766.41	744.66	727.69
45,000	4163.18	2284.82	1666.64	1363.38	1185.98	1071.37	992.52	935.90	893.97	862.21	837.74	818.65
50,000	4625.75	2538.69	1851.82	1514.87	1317.75	1190.41	1102.80	1039.88	993.29	958.01	930.83	909.61
55,000	5088.32	2792.56	2037.00	1666.36	1449.53	1309.45	1213.08	1143.87	1092.62	1053.81	1023.91	1000.57
60,000	5550.90	3046.43	2222.18	1817.84	1581.30	1428.49	1323.36	1247.86	1191.95	1149.61	1116.99	1091.53
65,000	6013.47	3300.30	2407.37	1969.33	1713.08	1547.53	1433.64	1351.85	1291.28	1245.41	1210.07	1182.49
70,000	6476.05	3554.17	2592.55	2120.82	1844.85	1666.57	1543.92	1455.83	1390.61	1341.21	1303.16	1273.45
75,000	6938.62	3808.04	2777.73	2272.30	1976.63	1785.62	1654.20	1559.82	1489.94	1437.01	1396.24	1364.41
80,000	7401.20	4061.91	2962.91	2423.79	2108.40	1904.66	1764.48	1663.81	1589.27	1532.81	1489.32	1455.37
85,000	7863.77	4315.77	3148.09	2575.28	2240.18	2023.70	1874.76	1767.80	1688.60	1628.61	1582.40	1546.33
90,000	8326.35	4569.64	3333.27	2726.76	2371.95	2142.74	1985.04	1871.79	1787.93	1724.41	1675.48	1637.29
95,000	8788.92	4823.51	3518.46	2878.25	2503.73	2261.78	2095.32	1975.77	1887.26	1820.21	1768.57	1728.25
100,000	9251.49	5077.38	3703.64	3029.74	2635.50	2380.82	2205.60	2079.76	1986.58	1916.02	1861.65	1819.21
105,000	9714.07	5331.25	3888.82	3181.22	2767.28	2499.86	2315.88	2183.75	2085.91	2011.82	1954.73	1910.17
110,000	10176.64	5585.12	4074.00	3332.71	2899.05	2618.90	2426.16	2287.74	2185.24	2107.62	2047.81	2001.13
115,000	10639.22	5838.99	4259.18	3484.20	3030.83	2737.94	2536.43	2391.72	2284.57	2203.42	2140.89	2092.09
120,000	11101.79	6092.86	4444.36	3635.68	3162.60	2856.98	2646.71	2495.71	2383.90	2299.22	2233.98	2183.05
125,000	11564.37	6346.72	4629.55	3787.17	3294.38	2976.02	2756.99	2599.70	2483.23	2395.02	2327.06	2274.01
130,000	12026.94	6600.59	4814.73	3938.66	3426.15	3095.06	2867.27	2703.69	2582.56	2490.82	2420.14	2364.97
135,000	12489.52	6854.46	4999.91	4090.14	3557.93	3214.10	2977.55	2807.68	2681.89	2586.62	2513.22	2455.93
140,000	12952.09	7108.33	5185.09	4241.63	3689.70	3333.14	3087.83	2911.66	2781.22	2682.42	2606.31	2546.89
145,000	13414.67	7362.20	5370.27	4393.12	3821.48	3452.18	3198.11	3015.65	2880.55	2778.22	2699.39	2637.85
150,000	13877.24	7616.07	5555.45	4544.60	3953.25	3571.23	3308.39	3119.64	2979.87	2874.02	2792.47	2728.82
155,000	14339.81	7869.94	5740.64	4696.09	4085.03	3690.27	3418.67	3223.63	3079.20	2969.82	2885.55	2819.78
160,000	14802.39	8123.81	5925.82	4847.58	4216.80	3809.31	3528.95	3327.62	3178.53	3065.62	2978.63	2910.74
165,000	15264.96	8377.67	6111.00	4999.06	4348.58	3928.35	3639.23	3431.60	3277.86	3161.42	3071.72	3001.70
170,000	15727.54	8631.54	6296.18	5150.55	4480.35	4047.39	3749.51	3535.59	3377.19	3257.22	3164.80	3092.66
175,000	16190.11	8885.41	6481.36	5302.04	4612.13	4166.43	3859.79	3639.58	3476.52	3353.02	3257.88	3183.62
180,000	16652.69	9139.28	6666.54	5453.52	4743.90	4285.47	3970.07	3743.57	3575.85	3448.82	3350.96	3274.58
185,000	17115.26	9393.15	6851.72	5605.01	4875.67	4404.51	4080.35	3847.55	3675.18	3544.62	3444.05	3365.54
190,000	17577.84	9647.02	7036.91	5756.50	5007.45	4523.55	4190.63	3951.54	3774.51	3640.42	3537.13	3456.50
195,000	18040.41	9900.89	7222.09	5907.98	5139.22	4642.59	4300.91	4055.53	3873.84	3736.22	3630.21	3547.46
200,000	18502.98	10154.76	7407.27	6059.47	5271.00	4761.63	4411.19	4159.52	3973.16	3832.03	3723.29	3638.42
205,000	18965.56	10408.63	7592.45	6210.96	5402.77	4880.67	4521.47	4263.51	4072.49	3927.83	3816.37	3729.38
210,000	19428.13	10662.49	7777.63	6362.44	5534.55	4999.71	4631.75	4367.49	4171.82	4023.63	3909.46	3820.34
215,000	19890.71	10916.36	7962.81	6513.93	5666.32	5118.75	4742.03	4471.48	4271.15	4119.43	4002.54	3911.30
220,000	20353.28	11170.23	8148.00	6665.42	5798.10	5237.79	4852.31	4575.47	4370.48	4215.23	4095.62	4002.26
225,000	20815.86	11424.10	8333.18	6816.90	5929.87	5356.84	4962.59	4679.46	4469.81	4311.03	4188.70	4093.22
230,000	21278.43	11677.97	8518.36	6968.39	6061.65	5475.88	5072.86	4783.44	4569.14	4406.83	4281.78	4184.18
235,000	21741.01	11931.84	8703.54	7119.88	6193.42	5594.92	5183.14	4887.43	4668.47	4502.63	4374.87	4275.14
240,000	22203.58	12185.71	8888.72	7271.36	6325.20	5713.96	5293.42	4991.42	4767.80	4598.43	4467.95	4366.10
245,000	22666.16	12439.58	9073.90	7422.85	6456.97	5833.00	5403.70	5095.41	4867.13	4694.23	4561.03	4457.06
250,000	23128.73	12693.44	9259.09	7574.34	6588.75	5952.04	5513.98	5199.40	4966.45	4790.03	4654.11	4548.02
255,000	23591.30	12947.31	9444.27	7725.82	6720.52	6071.08	5624.26	5303.38	5065.78	4885.83	4747.20	4638.98
260,000	24053.88	13201.18	9629.45	7877.31	6852.30	6190.12	5734.54	5407.37	5165.11	4981.63	4840.28	4729.94
265,000	24516.45	13455.05	9814.63	8028.80	6984.07	6309.16	5844.82	5511.36	5264.44	5077.43	4933.36	4820.90
270,000	24979.03	13708.92	9999.81	8180.28	7115.85	6428.20	5955.10	5615.35	5363.77	5173.23	5026.44	4911.86
280,000	25904.18	14216.66	10370.18	8483.26	7379.40	6666.28	6175.66	5823.32	5562.43	5364.83	5212.61	5093.78
290,000	26829.33	14724.39	10740.54	8786.23	7642.95	6904.36	6396.22	6031.30	5761.09	5556.43	5398.77	5275.70
300,000	27754.47	15232.13	11110.90	9089.20	7906.50	7142.45	6616.78	6239.27	5959.74	5748.04	5584.94	5457.63

AMOUNT OF LOAN	13	14	15	16	17	18	19	20	25	30	35	40
$ 50	0.90	0.88	0.87	0.87	0.86	0.85	0.85	0.84	0.83	0.83	0.83	0.83
100	1.79	1.76	1.74	1.73	1.71	1.70	1.69	1.68	1.66	1.66	1.65	1.65
200	3.58	3.52	3.48	3.45	3.42	3.40	3.38	3.36	3.32	3.31	3.30	3.30
300	5.36	5.28	5.22	5.17	5.13	5.09	5.06	5.04	4.98	4.96	4.95	4.94
400	7.15	7.04	6.96	6.89	6.83	6.79	6.75	6.72	6.64	6.61	6.60	6.59
500	8.93	8.80	8.69	8.61	8.54	8.48	8.44	8.40	8.30	8.26	8.24	8.24
600	10.72	10.56	10.43	10.33	10.25	10.18	10.12	10.08	9.95	9.91	9.89	9.88
700	12.51	12.32	12.17	12.05	11.95	11.88	11.81	11.76	11.61	11.56	11.54	11.53
800	14.29	14.08	13.91	13.77	13.66	13.57	13.50	13.44	13.27	13.21	13.19	13.18
900	16.08	15.84	15.65	15.49	15.37	15.27	15.18	15.12	14.93	14.86	14.83	14.82
1,000	17.86	17.60	17.38	17.21	17.07	16.96	16.87	16.80	16.59	16.51	16.48	16.47
2,000	35.72	35.19	34.76	34.42	34.14	33.92	33.74	33.59	33.17	33.01	32.96	32.93
3,000	53.58	52.78	52.14	51.63	51.21	50.88	50.60	50.38	49.75	49.52	49.43	49.40
4,000	71.43	70.37	69.52	68.83	68.28	67.83	67.47	67.17	66.33	66.02	65.91	65.86
5,000	89.29	87.96	86.90	86.04	85.35	84.79	84.34	83.97	82.92	82.53	82.38	82.33
6,000	107.15	105.55	104.28	103.25	102.42	101.75	101.20	100.76	99.50	99.03	98.86	98.79
7,000	125.01	123.14	121.65	120.46	119.49	118.71	118.07	117.55	116.08	115.54	115.33	115.26
8,000	142.86	140.74	139.03	137.66	136.56	135.66	134.94	134.34	132.66	132.04	131.81	131.72
9,000	160.72	158.33	156.41	154.87	153.63	152.62	151.80	151.14	149.24	148.55	148.29	148.19
10,000	178.58	175.92	173.79	172.08	170.70	169.58	168.67	167.93	165.83	165.05	164.76	164.65
15,000	267.87	263.88	260.68	258.12	256.04	254.36	253.00	251.89	248.74	247.57	247.14	246.98
20,000	357.15	351.83	347.58	344.15	341.39	339.15	337.33	335.85	331.65	330.10	329.52	329.30
25,000	446.44	439.79	434.47	430.19	426.73	423.94	421.66	419.81	414.56	412.62	411.90	411.63
30,000	535.73	527.75	521.36	516.23	512.08	508.72	505.99	503.77	497.47	495.14	494.28	493.95
35,000	625.01	615.70	608.25	602.26	597.43	593.51	590.32	587.73	580.38	577.67	576.65	576.27
40,000	714.30	703.66	695.15	688.30	682.77	678.29	674.66	671.69	663.29	660.19	659.03	658.60
45,000	803.59	791.62	782.04	774.34	768.12	763.08	758.99	755.66	746.20	742.71	741.41	740.92
50,000	892.88	879.57	868.93	860.37	853.46	847.87	843.32	839.62	829.11	825.24	823.79	823.25
55,000	982.16	967.53	955.83	946.41	938.81	932.65	927.65	923.58	912.02	907.76	906.17	905.57
60,000	1071.45	1055.49	1042.72	1032.45	1024.16	1017.44	1011.98	1007.54	994.93	990.28	988.55	987.90
65,000	1160.74	1143.45	1129.61	1118.49	1109.50	1102.22	1096.31	1091.50	1077.84	1072.80	1070.92	1070.22
70,000	1250.02	1231.40	1216.50	1204.52	1194.85	1187.01	1180.64	1175.46	1160.76	1155.33	1153.30	1152.54
75,000	1339.31	1319.36	1303.40	1290.56	1280.19	1271.80	1264.98	1259.42	1243.67	1237.85	1235.68	1234.87
80,000	1428.60	1407.32	1390.29	1376.60	1365.54	1356.58	1349.31	1343.38	1326.58	1320.37	1318.06	1317.19
85,000	1517.89	1495.27	1477.18	1462.63	1450.89	1441.37	1433.64	1427.34	1409.49	1402.90	1400.44	1399.52
90,000	1607.17	1583.23	1564.07	1548.67	1536.23	1526.16	1517.97	1511.31	1492.40	1485.42	1482.82	1481.84
95,000	1696.46	1671.19	1650.97	1634.71	1621.58	1610.94	1602.30	1595.27	1575.31	1567.94	1565.19	1564.17
100,000	1785.75	1759.14	1737.86	1720.74	1706.92	1695.73	1686.63	1679.23	1658.22	1650.47	1647.57	1646.49
105,000	1875.03	1847.10	1824.75	1806.78	1792.27	1780.51	1770.96	1763.19	1741.13	1732.99	1729.95	1728.81
110,000	1964.32	1935.06	1911.65	1892.82	1877.62	1865.30	1855.29	1847.15	1824.04	1815.51	1812.33	1811.14
115,000	2053.61	2023.01	1998.54	1978.86	1962.96	1950.09	1939.63	1931.11	1906.95	1898.04	1894.71	1893.46
120,000	2142.90	2110.97	2085.43	2064.89	2048.31	2034.87	2023.96	2015.07	1989.86	1980.56	1977.09	1975.79
125,000	2232.18	2198.93	2172.32	2150.93	2133.65	2119.66	2108.29	2099.03	2072.77	2063.08	2059.47	2058.11
130,000	2321.47	2286.89	2259.22	2236.97	2219.00	2204.44	2192.62	2182.99	2155.68	2145.60	2141.84	2140.43
135,000	2410.76	2374.84	2346.11	2323.00	2304.35	2289.23	2276.95	2266.96	2238.59	2228.13	2224.22	2222.76
140,000	2500.04	2462.80	2433.00	2409.04	2389.69	2374.02	2361.28	2350.92	2321.51	2310.65	2306.60	2305.08
145,000	2589.33	2550.76	2519.89	2495.08	2475.04	2458.80	2445.61	2434.88	2404.42	2393.17	2388.98	2387.41
150,000	2678.62	2638.71	2606.79	2581.11	2560.38	2543.59	2529.95	2518.84	2487.33	2475.70	2471.36	2469.73
155,000	2767.90	2726.67	2693.68	2667.15	2645.73	2628.37	2614.28	2602.80	2570.24	2558.22	2553.74	2552.06
160,000	2857.19	2814.63	2780.57	2753.19	2731.08	2713.16	2698.61	2686.76	2653.15	2640.74	2636.11	2634.38
165,000	2946.48	2902.58	2867.47	2839.22	2816.42	2797.95	2782.94	2770.72	2736.06	2723.27	2718.49	2716.70
170,000	3035.77	2990.54	2954.36	2925.26	2901.77	2882.73	2867.27	2854.68	2818.97	2805.79	2800.87	2799.03
175,000	3125.05	3078.50	3041.25	3011.30	2987.11	2967.52	2951.60	2938.64	2901.88	2888.31	2883.25	2881.35
180,000	3214.34	3166.45	3128.14	3097.34	3072.46	3052.31	3035.93	3022.61	2984.79	2970.83	2965.63	2963.68
185,000	3303.63	3254.41	3215.04	3183.37	3157.80	3137.09	3120.27	3106.57	3067.70	3053.36	3048.01	3046.00
190,000	3392.91	3342.37	3301.93	3269.41	3243.15	3221.88	3204.60	3190.53	3150.61	3135.88	3130.38	3128.33
195,000	3482.20	3430.33	3388.82	3355.45	3328.50	3306.66	3288.93	3274.49	3233.52	3218.40	3212.76	3210.65
200,000	3571.49	3518.28	3475.71	3441.48	3413.84	3391.45	3373.26	3358.45	3316.43	3300.93	3295.14	3292.97
205,000	3660.78	3606.24	3562.61	3527.52	3499.19	3476.24	3457.59	3442.41	3399.35	3383.45	3377.52	3375.30
210,000	3750.06	3694.20	3649.50	3613.56	3584.53	3561.02	3541.92	3526.37	3482.26	3465.97	3459.90	3457.62
215,000	3839.35	3782.15	3736.39	3699.59	3669.88	3645.81	3626.25	3610.33	3565.17	3548.50	3542.28	3539.95
220,000	3928.64	3870.11	3823.29	3785.63	3755.23	3730.59	3710.58	3694.30	3648.08	3631.02	3624.65	3622.27
225,000	4017.92	3958.07	3910.18	3871.67	3840.57	3815.38	3794.92	3778.26	3730.99	3713.54	3707.03	3704.59
230,000	4107.21	4046.02	3997.07	3957.71	3925.92	3900.17	3879.25	3862.22	3813.90	3796.07	3789.41	3786.92
235,000	4196.50	4133.98	4083.96	4043.74	4011.26	3984.95	3963.58	3946.18	3896.81	3878.59	3871.79	3869.24
240,000	4285.79	4221.94	4170.86	4129.78	4096.61	4069.74	4047.91	4030.14	3979.72	3961.11	3954.17	3951.57
245,000	4375.07	4309.89	4257.75	4215.82	4181.96	4154.52	4132.24	4114.10	4062.63	4043.63	4036.55	4033.89
250,000	4464.36	4397.85	4344.64	4301.85	4267.30	4239.31	4216.57	4198.06	4145.54	4126.16	4118.93	4116.22
255,000	4553.65	4485.81	4431.53	4387.89	4352.65	4324.10	4300.90	4282.02	4228.45	4208.68	4201.30	4198.54
260,000	4642.93	4573.77	4518.43	4473.93	4437.99	4408.88	4385.24	4365.98	4311.36	4291.20	4283.68	4280.86
265,000	4732.22	4661.72	4605.32	4559.96	4523.34	4493.67	4469.57	4449.95	4394.27	4373.73	4366.06	4363.19
270,000	4821.51	4749.68	4692.21	4646.00	4608.69	4578.46	4553.90	4533.91	4477.18	4456.25	4448.44	4445.51
280,000	5000.08	4925.59	4866.00	4818.07	4779.38	4748.03	4722.56	4701.83	4643.01	4621.30	4613.20	4610.16
290,000	5178.66	5101.51	5039.78	4990.15	4950.07	4917.60	4891.22	4869.75	4808.83	4786.34	4777.95	4774.81
300,000	5357.23	5277.42	5213.57	5162.22	5120.76	5087.17	5059.89	5037.67	4974.65	4951.39	4942.71	4939.46

20.00%

MONTHLY AMORTIZING PAYMENTS

AMOUNT OF LOAN	NUMBER OF YEARS IN TERM											
	1	2	3	4	5	6	7	8	9	10	11	12
$ 50	4.64	2.55	1.86	1.53	1.33	1.20	1.12	1.05	1.01	0.97	0.94	0.92
100	9.27	5.09	3.72	3.05	2.65	2.40	2.23	2.10	2.01	1.94	1.88	1.84
200	18.53	10.18	7.44	6.09	5.30	4.80	4.45	4.20	4.01	3.87	3.76	3.68
300	27.80	15.27	11.15	9.13	7.95	7.19	6.67	6.29	6.01	5.80	5.64	5.51
400	37.06	20.36	14.87	12.18	10.60	9.59	8.89	8.39	8.02	7.74	7.52	7.35
500	46.32	25.45	18.59	15.22	13.25	11.98	11.11	10.48	10.02	9.67	9.40	9.19
600	55.59	30.54	22.30	18.26	15.90	14.38	13.33	12.58	12.02	11.60	11.28	11.02
700	64.85	35.63	26.02	21.31	18.55	16.77	15.55	14.67	14.02	13.53	13.16	12.86
800	74.11	40.72	29.74	24.35	21.20	19.17	17.77	16.77	16.03	15.47	15.03	14.70
900	83.38	45.81	33.45	27.39	23.85	21.56	19.99	18.86	18.03	17.40	16.91	16.53
1,000	92.64	50.90	37.17	30.44	26.50	23.96	22.21	20.96	20.03	19.33	18.79	18.37
2,000	185.27	101.80	74.33	60.87	52.99	47.91	44.42	41.91	40.06	38.66	37.58	36.74
3,000	277.91	152.69	111.50	91.30	79.49	71.86	66.62	62.86	60.08	57.98	56.36	55.10
4,000	370.54	203.59	148.66	121.73	105.98	95.82	88.83	83.82	80.11	77.31	75.15	73.47
5,000	463.18	254.48	185.82	152.16	132.47	119.77	111.04	104.77	100.14	96.63	93.94	91.84
6,000	555.81	305.38	222.99	182.59	158.97	143.72	133.24	125.72	120.16	115.96	112.72	110.20
7,000	648.45	356.28	260.15	213.02	185.46	167.67	155.45	146.68	140.19	135.28	131.51	128.57
8,000	741.08	407.17	297.31	243.45	211.96	191.63	177.65	167.63	160.22	154.61	150.30	146.93
9,000	833.72	458.07	334.48	273.88	238.45	215.58	199.86	188.58	180.24	173.94	169.08	165.30
10,000	926.35	508.96	371.64	304.31	264.94	239.53	222.07	209.54	200.27	193.26	187.87	183.67
15,000	1389.52	763.44	557.46	456.46	397.41	359.30	333.10	314.30	300.40	289.89	281.80	275.50
20,000	1852.70	1017.92	743.28	608.61	529.88	479.06	444.13	419.07	400.54	386.52	375.73	367.33
25,000	2315.87	1272.40	929.09	760.76	662.35	598.83	555.16	523.84	500.67	483.14	469.66	459.16
30,000	2779.04	1526.88	1114.91	912.92	794.82	718.59	666.19	628.60	600.80	579.77	563.60	550.99
35,000	3242.21	1781.36	1300.73	1065.07	927.29	838.35	777.22	733.37	700.93	676.40	657.53	642.82
40,000	3705.39	2035.84	1486.55	1217.22	1059.76	958.12	888.25	838.13	801.07	773.03	751.46	734.65
45,000	4168.56	2290.32	1672.37	1369.37	1192.23	1077.88	999.28	942.90	901.20	869.66	845.39	826.48
50,000	4631.73	2544.80	1858.18	1521.52	1324.70	1197.65	1110.31	1047.67	1001.33	966.28	939.32	918.31
55,000	5094.90	2799.27	2044.00	1673.67	1457.17	1317.41	1221.35	1152.43	1101.46	1062.91	1033.25	1010.14
60,000	5558.08	3053.75	2229.82	1825.83	1589.64	1437.17	1332.38	1257.20	1201.60	1159.54	1127.19	1101.97
65,000	6021.25	3308.23	2415.64	1977.98	1722.11	1556.94	1443.41	1361.96	1301.73	1256.17	1221.12	1193.80
70,000	6484.42	3562.71	2601.46	2130.13	1854.58	1676.70	1554.44	1466.73	1401.86	1352.79	1315.05	1285.63
75,000	6947.59	3817.19	2787.27	2282.28	1987.05	1796.47	1665.47	1571.50	1501.99	1449.42	1408.98	1377.46
80,000	7410.77	4071.67	2973.09	2434.43	2119.52	1916.23	1776.50	1676.26	1602.13	1546.05	1502.91	1469.29
85,000	7873.94	4326.15	3158.91	2586.59	2251.99	2036.00	1887.53	1781.03	1702.26	1642.68	1596.84	1561.12
90,000	8337.11	4580.63	3344.73	2738.74	2384.45	2155.76	1998.56	1885.79	1802.39	1739.31	1690.78	1652.95
95,000	8800.28	4835.11	3530.55	2890.89	2516.92	2275.52	2109.59	1990.56	1902.52	1835.93	1784.71	1744.78
100,000	9263.46	5089.59	3716.36	3043.04	2649.39	2395.29	2220.62	2095.33	2002.66	1932.56	1878.64	1836.61
105,000	9726.63	5344.06	3902.18	3195.19	2781.86	2515.05	2331.66	2200.09	2102.79	2029.19	1972.57	1928.44
110,000	10189.80	5598.54	4088.00	3347.34	2914.33	2634.82	2442.69	2304.86	2202.92	2125.82	2066.50	2020.27
115,000	10652.97	5853.02	4273.82	3499.50	3046.80	2754.58	2553.72	2409.62	2303.05	2222.45	2160.43	2112.10
120,000	11116.15	6107.50	4459.64	3651.65	3179.27	2874.34	2664.75	2514.39	2403.19	2319.07	2254.37	2203.94
125,000	11579.32	6361.98	4645.45	3803.80	3311.74	2994.11	2775.78	2619.16	2503.32	2415.70	2348.30	2295.77
130,000	12042.49	6616.46	4831.27	3955.95	3444.21	3113.87	2886.81	2723.92	2603.45	2512.33	2442.23	2387.60
135,000	12505.66	6870.94	5017.09	4108.10	3576.68	3233.64	2997.84	2828.69	2703.58	2608.96	2536.16	2479.43
140,000	12968.84	7125.42	5202.91	4260.26	3709.15	3353.40	3108.87	2933.45	2803.72	2705.58	2630.09	2571.26
145,000	13432.01	7379.90	5388.72	4412.41	3841.62	3473.16	3219.90	3038.22	2903.85	2802.21	2724.02	2663.09
150,000	13895.18	7634.38	5574.54	4564.56	3974.09	3592.93	3330.93	3142.99	3003.98	2898.84	2817.96	2754.92
155,000	14358.35	7888.85	5760.36	4716.71	4106.56	3712.69	3441.97	3247.75	3104.11	2995.47	2911.89	2846.75
160,000	14821.53	8143.33	5946.18	4868.86	4239.03	3832.46	3553.00	3352.52	3204.25	3092.10	3005.82	2938.58
165,000	15284.70	8397.81	6132.00	5021.01	4371.50	3952.22	3664.03	3457.28	3304.38	3188.72	3099.75	3030.41
170,000	15747.87	8652.29	6317.81	5173.17	4503.97	4071.99	3775.06	3562.05	3404.51	3285.35	3193.68	3122.24
175,000	16211.04	8906.77	6503.63	5325.32	4636.43	4191.75	3886.09	3666.82	3504.64	3381.98	3287.61	3214.07
180,000	16674.22	9161.25	6689.45	5477.47	4768.90	4311.51	3997.12	3771.58	3604.78	3478.61	3381.55	3305.90
185,000	17137.39	9415.73	6875.27	5629.62	4901.37	4431.28	4108.15	3876.35	3704.91	3575.23	3475.48	3397.73
190,000	17600.56	9670.21	7061.09	5781.77	5033.84	4551.04	4219.18	3981.11	3805.04	3671.86	3569.41	3489.56
195,000	18063.73	9924.69	7246.90	5933.93	5166.31	4670.81	4330.21	4085.88	3905.17	3768.49	3663.34	3581.39
200,000	18526.91	10179.17	7432.72	6086.08	5298.78	4790.57	4441.24	4190.65	4005.31	3865.12	3757.27	3673.22
205,000	18990.08	10433.64	7618.54	6238.23	5431.25	4910.33	4552.28	4295.41	4105.44	3961.75	3851.20	3765.05
210,000	19453.25	10688.12	7804.36	6390.38	5563.72	5030.10	4663.31	4400.18	4205.57	4058.37	3945.14	3856.88
215,000	19916.42	10942.60	7990.18	6542.53	5696.19	5149.86	4774.34	4504.94	4305.70	4155.00	4039.07	3948.71
220,000	20379.60	11197.08	8175.99	6694.68	5828.66	5269.63	4885.37	4609.71	4405.84	4251.63	4133.00	4040.54
225,000	20842.77	11451.56	8361.81	6846.84	5961.13	5389.39	4996.40	4714.48	4505.97	4348.26	4226.93	4132.37
230,000	21305.94	11706.04	8547.63	6998.99	6093.60	5509.15	5107.43	4819.24	4606.10	4444.89	4320.86	4224.20
235,000	21769.11	11960.52	8733.45	7151.14	6226.07	5628.92	5218.46	4924.01	4706.23	4541.51	4414.79	4316.04
240,000	22232.29	12215.00	8919.27	7303.29	6358.54	5748.68	5329.49	5028.77	4806.37	4638.14	4508.73	4407.87
245,000	22695.46	12469.48	9105.08	7455.44	6491.01	5868.45	5440.52	5133.54	4906.50	4734.77	4602.66	4499.70
250,000	23158.63	12723.96	9290.90	7607.60	6623.48	5988.21	5551.55	5238.31	5006.63	4831.40	4696.59	4591.53
255,000	23621.80	12978.43	9476.72	7759.75	6755.95	6107.98	5662.59	5343.07	5106.76	4928.02	4790.52	4683.36
260,000	24084.98	13232.91	9662.54	7911.90	6888.41	6227.74	5773.62	5447.84	5206.90	5024.65	4884.45	4775.19
265,000	24548.15	13487.39	9848.35	8064.05	7020.88	6347.50	5884.65	5552.60	5307.03	5121.28	4978.39	4867.02
270,000	25011.32	13741.87	10034.17	8216.20	7153.35	6467.27	5995.68	5657.37	5407.16	5217.91	5072.32	4958.85
280,000	25937.67	14250.83	10405.81	8520.51	7418.29	6706.80	6217.74	5866.90	5607.43	5411.16	5260.18	5142.51
290,000	26864.01	14759.79	10777.44	8824.81	7683.23	6946.32	6439.80	6076.43	5807.69	5604.42	5448.04	5326.17
300,000	27790.36	15268.75	11149.08	9129.11	7948.17	7185.85	6661.86	6285.97	6007.96	5797.68	5635.91	5509.83

146

AMOUNT OF LOAN	NUMBER OF YEARS IN TERM											
	13	14	15	16	17	18	19	20	25	30	35	40
$ 50	0.91	0.89	0.88	0.87	0.87	0.86	0.86	0.85	0.84	0.84	0.84	0.84
100	1.81	1.78	1.76	1.74	1.73	1.72	1.71	1.70	1.68	1.68	1.67	1.67
200	3.61	3.56	3.52	3.48	3.46	3.43	3.42	3.40	3.36	3.35	3.34	3.34
300	5.42	5.34	5.27	5.22	5.18	5.15	5.12	5.10	5.04	5.02	5.01	5.01
400	7.22	7.11	7.03	6.96	6.91	6.86	6.83	6.80	6.72	6.69	6.68	6.67
500	9.02	8.89	8.79	8.70	8.63	8.58	8.54	8.50	8.40	8.36	8.35	8.34
600	10.83	10.67	10.54	10.44	10.36	10.29	10.24	10.20	10.08	10.03	10.01	10.01
700	12.63	12.45	12.30	12.18	12.09	12.01	11.95	11.90	11.75	11.70	11.68	11.68
800	14.43	14.22	14.06	13.92	13.81	13.72	13.65	13.60	13.43	13.37	13.35	13.34
900	16.24	16.00	15.81	15.66	15.54	15.44	15.36	15.29	15.11	15.04	15.02	15.01
1,000	18.04	17.78	17.57	17.40	17.26	17.15	17.07	16.99	16.79	16.72	16.69	16.68
2,000	36.08	35.55	35.13	34.79	34.52	34.30	34.13	33.98	33.57	33.43	33.37	33.35
3,000	54.11	53.32	52.69	52.19	51.78	51.45	51.19	50.97	50.36	50.14	50.05	50.02
4,000	72.15	71.10	70.26	69.58	69.04	68.60	68.25	67.96	67.14	66.85	66.74	66.70
5,000	90.18	88.87	87.82	86.98	86.30	85.75	85.31	84.95	83.93	83.56	83.42	83.37
6,000	108.22	106.64	105.38	104.37	103.56	102.90	102.37	101.93	100.71	100.27	100.10	100.04
7,000	126.25	124.41	122.95	121.77	120.82	120.05	119.43	118.92	117.50	116.98	116.78	116.71
8,000	144.29	142.19	140.51	139.16	138.08	137.20	136.49	135.91	134.28	133.69	133.47	133.39
9,000	162.32	159.96	158.07	156.56	155.34	154.35	153.55	152.90	151.07	150.40	150.15	150.06
10,000	180.36	177.73	175.63	173.95	172.60	171.50	170.61	169.89	167.85	167.11	166.83	166.73
15,000	270.53	266.59	263.45	260.92	258.89	257.25	255.91	254.83	251.77	250.66	250.25	250.09
20,000	360.71	355.46	351.26	347.90	345.19	342.99	341.21	339.77	335.70	334.21	333.66	333.46
25,000	450.89	444.32	439.08	434.87	431.48	428.74	426.52	424.71	419.62	417.76	417.07	416.82
30,000	541.06	533.18	526.89	521.84	517.78	514.49	511.82	509.65	503.54	501.31	500.49	500.18
35,000	631.24	622.05	614.71	608.82	604.07	600.23	597.12	594.59	587.46	584.86	583.90	583.55
40,000	721.41	710.91	702.52	695.79	690.37	685.98	682.42	679.53	671.39	668.41	667.32	666.91
45,000	811.59	799.77	790.34	782.76	776.66	771.73	767.73	764.40	755.31	751.96	750.73	750.27
50,000	901.77	888.64	878.15	869.74	862.96	857.47	853.03	849.42	839.23	835.51	834.14	833.64
55,000	991.94	977.50	965.97	956.71	949.25	943.22	938.33	934.36	923.15	919.07	917.56	917.00
60,000	1082.12	1066.36	1053.78	1043.68	1035.55	1028.97	1023.63	1019.30	1007.08	1002.62	1000.97	1000.36
65,000	1172.29	1155.23	1141.60	1130.66	1121.84	1114.71	1108.94	1104.24	1091.00	1086.17	1084.39	1083.73
70,000	1262.47	1244.09	1229.41	1217.63	1208.14	1200.46	1194.24	1189.18	1174.92	1169.72	1167.80	1167.09
75,000	1352.65	1332.95	1317.23	1304.60	1294.43	1286.21	1279.54	1274.12	1258.84	1253.27	1251.21	1250.45
80,000	1442.82	1421.82	1405.04	1391.58	1380.73	1371.95	1364.84	1359.06	1342.77	1336.82	1334.63	1333.82
85,000	1533.00	1510.68	1492.86	1478.55	1467.02	1457.70	1450.14	1444.01	1426.69	1420.37	1418.04	1417.18
90,000	1623.17	1599.54	1580.67	1565.52	1553.32	1543.45	1535.45	1528.95	1510.61	1503.92	1501.46	1500.54
95,000	1713.35	1688.41	1668.49	1652.50	1639.61	1629.19	1620.75	1613.89	1594.53	1587.47	1584.87	1583.91
100,000	1803.53	1777.27	1756.30	1739.47	1725.91	1714.94	1706.05	1698.83	1678.46	1671.02	1668.29	1667.27
105,000	1893.70	1866.13	1844.12	1826.44	1812.20	1800.69	1791.35	1783.77	1762.38	1754.57	1751.70	1760.63
110,000	1983.88	1955.00	1931.93	1913.42	1898.50	1886.43	1876.66	1868.71	1846.30	1838.13	1835.11	1834.00
115,000	2074.06	2043.86	2019.75	2000.39	1984.79	1972.18	1961.96	1953.65	1930.22	1921.68	1918.53	1917.36
120,000	2164.23	2132.72	2107.56	2007.06	2071.09	2057.90	2047.26	2000.59	2014.15	2005.23	2001.94	2000.72
125,000	2254.41	2221.59	2195.38	2174.34	2157.38	2143.68	2132.56	2123.54	2098.07	2088.78	2085.35	2084.09
130,000	2344.58	2310.45	2283.19	2261.31	2243.68	2229.42	2217.87	2208.48	2181.99	2172.33	2168.77	2167.45
135,000	2434.76	2399.31	2371.01	2348.28	2329.97	2315.17	2303.17	2293.42	2265.91	2255.88	2252.18	2250.81
140,000	2524.94	2488.18	2458.82	2435.26	2416.27	2400.92	2388.47	2378.36	2349.84	2339.43	2335.59	2334.17
145,000	2615.11	2577.04	2546.63	2522.23	2502.56	2486.66	2473.77	2463.30	2433.76	2422.98	2419.01	2417.54
150,000	2705.29	2665.90	2634.45	2609.20	2588.86	2572.41	2559.07	2548.24	2517.68	2506.53	2502.42	2500.90
155,000	2795.46	2754.77	2722.26	2696.18	2675.15	2658.16	2644.38	2633.18	2601.61	2590.08	2585.84	2584.26
160,000	2885.64	2843.63	2810.08	2783.15	2761.45	2743.90	2729.68	2718.12	2685.53	2673.63	2669.25	2667.63
165,000	2975.82	2932.49	2897.89	2870.12	2847.74	2829.65	2814.98	2803.07	2769.45	2757.19	2752.66	2750.99
170,000	3065.99	3021.36	2985.71	2957.10	2934.04	2915.40	2900.28	2888.01	2853.37	2840.74	2836.08	2834.35
175,000	3156.17	3110.22	3073.52	3044.07	3020.33	3001.14	2985.59	2972.95	2937.30	2924.29	2919.49	2917.72
180,000	3246.34	3199.08	3161.34	3131.04	3106.63	3086.89	3070.89	3057.89	3021.22	3007.84	3002.91	3001.08
185,000	3336.52	3287.95	3249.15	3218.02	3192.92	3172.64	3156.19	3142.83	3105.14	3091.39	3086.32	3084.44
190,000	3426.70	3376.81	3336.97	3304.99	3279.22	3258.38	3241.49	3227.77	3189.06	3174.94	3169.73	3167.81
195,000	3516.87	3465.67	3424.78	3391.96	3365.52	3344.13	3326.80	3312.71	3272.99	3258.49	3253.15	3251.17
200,000	3607.05	3554.54	3512.60	3478.94	3451.81	3429.88	3412.10	3397.65	3356.91	3342.04	3336.56	3334.53
205,000	3697.23	3643.40	3600.41	3565.91	3538.11	3515.62	3497.40	3482.60	3440.83	3425.59	3419.98	3417.90
210,000	3787.40	3732.26	3688.23	3652.88	3624.40	3601.37	3582.70	3567.54	3524.75	3509.14	3503.39	3501.26
215,000	3877.58	3821.13	3776.04	3739.86	3710.70	3687.12	3668.00	3652.48	3608.68	3592.70	3586.80	3584.62
220,000	3967.75	3909.99	3863.86	3826.83	3796.99	3772.86	3753.31	3737.42	3692.60	3676.25	3670.22	3667.99
225,000	4057.93	3998.85	3951.67	3913.80	3883.29	3858.61	3838.61	3822.36	3776.52	3759.80	3753.63	3751.35
230,000	4148.11	4087.72	4039.49	4000.78	3969.58	3944.36	3923.91	3907.30	3860.44	3843.35	3837.05	3834.71
235,000	4238.28	4176.58	4127.30	4087.75	4055.88	4030.11	4009.21	3992.24	3944.37	3926.90	3920.46	3918.08
240,000	4328.46	4265.44	4215.12	4174.72	4142.17	4115.85	4094.52	4077.18	4028.29	4010.45	4003.87	4001.44
245,000	4418.63	4354.31	4302.93	4261.70	4228.47	4201.60	4179.82	4162.13	4112.21	4094.00	4087.29	4084.80
250,000	4508.81	4443.17	4390.75	4348.67	4314.76	4287.35	4265.12	4247.07	4196.13	4177.55	4170.70	4168.17
255,000	4598.99	4532.03	4478.56	4435.64	4401.06	4373.09	4350.42	4332.01	4280.06	4261.10	4254.11	4251.53
260,000	4689.16	4620.89	4566.38	4522.62	4487.35	4458.84	4435.73	4416.95	4363.98	4344.65	4337.53	4334.89
265,000	4779.34	4709.76	4654.19	4609.59	4573.65	4544.59	4521.03	4501.89	4447.90	4428.20	4420.94	4418.25
270,000	4869.51	4798.62	4742.01	4696.56	4659.94	4630.33	4606.33	4586.83	4531.82	4511.76	4504.36	4501.62
280,000	5049.87	4976.35	4917.64	4870.51	4832.53	4801.83	4776.94	4756.71	4699.67	4678.86	4671.18	4668.34
290,000	5230.22	5154.07	5093.26	5044.46	5005.12	4973.32	4947.54	4926.60	4867.52	4845.96	4838.01	4835.07
300,000	5410.57	5331.80	5268.89	5218.40	5177.71	5144.81	5118.14	5096.48	5035.36	5013.06	5004.84	5001.80

20.25%　　MONTHLY AMORTIZING PAYMENTS

AMOUNT OF LOAN	NUMBER OF YEARS IN TERM											
	1	2	3	4	5	6	7	8	9	10	11	12
$ 50	4.64	2.56	1.87	1.53	1.34	1.21	1.12	1.06	1.01	0.98	0.95	0.93
100	9.28	5.11	3.73	3.06	2.67	2.41	2.24	2.12	2.02	1.95	1.90	1.86
200	18.56	10.21	7.46	6.12	5.33	4.82	4.48	4.23	4.04	3.90	3.80	3.71
300	27.83	15.31	11.19	9.17	7.99	7.23	6.71	6.34	6.06	5.85	5.69	5.57
400	37.11	20.41	14.92	12.23	10.66	9.64	8.95	8.45	8.08	7.80	7.59	7.42
500	46.38	25.51	18.65	15.29	13.32	12.05	11.18	10.56	10.10	9.75	9.48	9.28
600	55.66	30.62	22.38	18.34	15.98	14.46	13.42	12.67	12.12	11.70	11.38	11.13
700	64.93	35.72	26.11	21.40	18.65	16.87	15.65	14.78	14.14	13.65	13.27	12.98
800	74.21	40.82	29.84	24.46	21.31	19.28	17.89	16.89	16.16	15.60	15.17	14.84
900	83.48	45.92	33.57	27.51	23.97	21.69	20.13	19.00	18.17	17.55	17.07	16.69
1,000	92.76	51.02	37.30	30.57	26.64	24.10	22.36	21.11	20.19	19.50	18.96	18.55
2,000	185.51	102.04	74.59	61.13	53.27	48.20	44.72	42.22	40.38	38.99	37.92	37.09
3,000	278.27	153.06	111.88	91.70	79.90	72.30	67.08	63.33	60.57	58.48	56.88	55.63
4,000	371.02	204.08	149.17	122.26	106.54	96.40	89.43	84.44	80.76	77.97	75.83	74.17
5,000	463.78	255.10	186.46	152.82	133.17	120.49	111.79	105.55	100.94	97.46	94.79	92.71
6,000	556.53	306.11	223.75	183.39	159.80	144.59	134.15	126.66	121.13	116.95	113.75	111.25
7,000	649.28	357.13	261.04	213.95	186.44	168.69	156.50	147.77	141.32	136.45	132.70	129.79
8,000	742.04	408.15	298.33	244.51	213.07	192.79	178.86	168.88	161.51	155.94	151.66	148.33
9,000	834.79	459.17	335.62	275.08	239.70	216.89	201.22	189.99	181.69	175.43	170.62	166.87
10,000	927.55	510.19	372.92	305.64	266.34	240.98	223.57	211.10	201.88	194.92	189.57	185.41
15,000	1391.32	765.28	559.37	458.46	399.50	361.47	335.36	316.65	302.82	292.38	284.36	278.12
20,000	1855.09	1020.37	745.83	611.28	532.67	481.96	447.14	422.19	403.76	389.84	379.14	370.82
25,000	2318.86	1275.46	932.28	764.10	665.83	602.45	558.93	527.74	504.70	487.30	473.93	463.52
30,000	2782.63	1530.55	1118.74	916.92	799.00	722.94	670.71	633.29	605.64	584.75	568.71	556.23
35,000	3246.40	1785.64	1305.19	1069.74	932.17	843.43	782.50	738.83	706.58	682.21	663.49	648.93
40,000	3710.17	2040.73	1491.65	1222.55	1065.33	963.92	894.28	844.38	807.52	779.67	758.28	741.63
45,000	4173.94	2295.82	1678.10	1375.37	1198.50	1084.41	1006.07	949.93	908.45	877.13	853.06	834.34
50,000	4637.71	2550.91	1864.56	1528.19	1331.66	1204.90	1117.85	1055.47	1009.39	974.59	947.85	927.04
55,000	5101.49	2806.00	2051.01	1681.01	1464.83	1325.39	1229.64	1161.02	1110.33	1072.04	1042.63	1019.74
60,000	5565.26	3061.09	2237.47	1833.83	1598.00	1445.88	1341.42	1266.57	1211.27	1169.50	1137.42	1112.45
65,000	6029.03	3316.18	2423.93	1986.65	1731.16	1566.37	1453.21	1372.11	1312.21	1266.96	1232.20	1205.15
70,000	6492.80	3571.27	2610.38	2139.47	1864.33	1686.86	1564.99	1477.66	1413.15	1364.42	1326.98	1297.85
75,000	6956.57	3826.36	2796.84	2292.28	1997.49	1807.35	1676.78	1583.21	1514.09	1461.88	1421.77	1390.56
80,000	7420.34	4081.45	2983.29	2445.10	2130.66	1927.84	1788.56	1688.75	1615.03	1559.33	1516.55	1483.26
85,000	7884.11	4336.54	3169.75	2597.92	2263.83	2048.33	1900.35	1794.30	1715.97	1656.79	1611.34	1575.96
90,000	8347.88	4591.63	3356.20	2750.74	2396.99	2168.82	2012.13	1899.85	1816.90	1754.25	1706.12	1668.67
95,000	8811.65	4846.72	3542.66	2903.56	2530.16	2289.31	2123.92	2005.39	1917.84	1851.71	1800.90	1761.37
100,000	9275.42	5101.81	3729.11	3056.38	2663.32	2409.80	2235.70	2110.94	2018.78	1949.17	1895.69	1854.07
105,000	9739.20	5356.90	3915.57	3209.20	2796.49	2530.29	2347.49	2216.49	2119.72	2046.62	1990.47	1946.78
110,000	10202.97	5611.99	4102.02	3362.01	2929.65	2650.78	2459.27	2322.04	2220.66	2144.08	2085.26	2039.48
115,000	10666.74	5867.08	4288.48	3514.83	3062.82	2771.27	2571.06	2427.58	2321.60	2241.54	2180.04	2132.19
120,000	11130.51	6122.17	4474.94	3667.65	3195.99	2891.76	2682.84	2533.13	2422.54	2339.00	2274.83	2224.89
125,000	11594.28	6377.26	4661.39	3820.47	3329.15	3012.25	2794.63	2638.68	2523.48	2436.46	2369.61	2317.59
130,000	12058.05	6632.35	4847.85	3973.29	3462.32	3132.74	2906.41	2744.22	2624.41	2533.91	2464.39	2410.30
135,000	12521.82	6887.44	5034.30	4126.11	3595.48	3253.23	3018.20	2849.77	2725.35	2631.37	2559.18	2503.00
140,000	12985.59	7142.53	5220.76	4278.93	3728.65	3373.72	3129.98	2955.32	2826.29	2728.83	2653.96	2595.70
145,000	13449.36	7397.62	5407.21	4431.74	3861.82	3494.21	3241.77	3060.86	2927.23	2826.29	2748.75	2688.41
150,000	13913.13	7652.71	5593.67	4584.56	3994.98	3614.70	3353.55	3166.41	3028.17	2923.75	2843.53	2781.11
155,000	14376.91	7907.80	5780.12	4737.38	4128.15	3735.19	3465.34	3271.96	3129.11	3021.20	2938.31	2873.81
160,000	14840.68	8162.89	5966.58	4890.20	4261.31	3855.68	3577.12	3377.50	3230.05	3118.66	3033.10	2966.52
165,000	15304.45	8417.98	6153.03	5043.02	4394.48	3976.17	3688.91	3483.05	3330.99	3216.12	3127.88	3059.22
170,000	15768.22	8673.07	6339.49	5195.84	4527.65	4096.66	3800.69	3588.60	3431.93	3313.58	3222.67	3151.92
175,000	16231.99	8928.16	6525.95	5348.66	4660.81	4217.15	3912.48	3694.14	3532.86	3411.04	3317.45	3244.63
180,000	16695.76	9183.25	6712.40	5501.47	4793.98	4337.64	4024.26	3799.69	3633.80	3508.50	3412.24	3337.33
185,000	17159.53	9438.34	6898.86	5654.29	4927.14	4458.13	4136.05	3905.24	3734.74	3605.95	3507.02	3430.03
190,000	17623.30	9693.43	7085.31	5807.11	5060.31	4578.62	4247.83	4010.78	3835.68	3703.41	3601.80	3522.74
195,000	18087.07	9948.52	7271.77	5959.93	5193.47	4699.11	4359.62	4116.33	3936.62	3800.87	3696.59	3615.44
200,000	18550.84	10203.61	7458.22	6112.75	5326.64	4819.60	4471.40	4221.88	4037.56	3898.33	3791.37	3708.14
205,000	19014.62	10458.70	7644.68	6265.57	5459.81	4940.09	4583.19	4327.43	4138.50	3995.79	3886.16	3800.85
210,000	19478.39	10713.79	7831.13	6418.39	5592.97	5060.58	4694.97	4432.97	4239.44	4093.24	3980.94	3893.55
215,000	19942.16	10968.88	8017.59	6571.20	5726.14	5181.07	4806.75	4538.52	4340.37	4190.70	4075.72	3986.25
220,000	20405.93	11223.97	8204.04	6724.02	5859.30	5301.56	4918.54	4644.07	4441.31	4288.16	4170.51	4078.96
225,000	20869.70	11479.06	8390.50	6876.84	5992.47	5422.05	5030.32	4749.61	4542.25	4385.62	4265.29	4171.66
230,000	21333.47	11734.15	8576.96	7029.66	6125.64	5542.54	5142.11	4855.16	4643.19	4483.08	4360.08	4264.37
235,000	21797.24	11989.24	8763.41	7182.48	6258.80	5663.03	5253.89	4960.71	4744.13	4580.53	4454.86	4357.07
240,000	22261.01	12244.33	8949.87	7335.30	6391.97	5783.52	5365.68	5066.25	4845.07	4677.99	4549.65	4449.77
245,000	22724.78	12499.42	9136.32	7488.12	6525.13	5904.01	5477.46	5171.80	4946.01	4775.45	4644.43	4542.48
250,000	23188.55	12754.51	9322.78	7640.93	6658.30	6024.50	5589.25	5277.35	5046.95	4872.91	4739.21	4635.18
255,000	23652.33	13009.60	9509.23	7793.75	6791.47	6144.98	5701.03	5382.89	5147.89	4970.37	4834.00	4727.88
260,000	24116.10	13264.69	9695.69	7946.57	6924.63	6265.47	5812.82	5488.44	5248.82	5067.82	4928.78	4820.59
265,000	24579.87	13519.78	9882.14	8099.39	7057.80	6385.96	5924.60	5593.99	5349.76	5165.20	5023.57	4913.29
270,000	25043.64	13774.87	10068.60	8252.21	7190.96	6506.45	6036.39	5699.53	5450.70	5262.74	5118.35	5005.99
280,000	25971.18	14285.05	10441.51	8557.85	7457.30	6747.43	6259.96	5910.63	5652.58	5457.66	5307.92	5191.40
290,000	26898.72	14795.23	10814.42	8863.48	7723.63	6988.41	6483.53	6121.72	5854.46	5652.57	5497.49	5376.81
300,000	27826.26	15305.41	11187.33	9169.12	7989.96	7229.39	6707.10	6332.81	6056.33	5847.49	5687.06	5562.21

AMOUNT OF LOAN	\multicolumn{12}{NUMBER OF YEARS IN TERM}

AMOUNT OF LOAN	13	14	15	16	17	18	19	20	25	30	35	40
$ 50	0.92	0.90	0.89	0.88	0.88	0.87	0.87	0.86	0.85	0.85	0.85	0.85
100	1.83	1.80	1.78	1.76	1.75	1.74	1.73	1.72	1.70	1.70	1.69	1.69
200	3.65	3.60	3.55	3.52	3.49	3.47	3.46	3.44	3.40	3.39	3.38	3.38
300	5.47	5.39	5.33	5.28	5.24	5.21	5.18	5.16	5.10	5.08	5.07	5.07
400	7.29	7.19	7.10	7.04	6.98	6.94	6.91	6.88	6.80	6.77	6.76	6.76
500	9.11	8.98	8.88	8.80	8.73	8.68	8.63	8.60	8.50	8.46	8.45	8.45
600	10.93	10.78	10.65	10.55	10.47	10.41	10.36	10.32	10.20	10.15	10.14	10.13
700	12.75	12.57	12.43	12.31	12.22	12.14	12.08	12.03	11.90	11.85	11.83	11.82
800	14.58	14.37	14.20	14.07	13.96	13.88	13.81	13.75	13.59	13.54	13.52	13.51
900	16.40	16.16	15.98	15.83	15.71	15.61	15.53	15.47	15.29	15.23	15.21	15.20
1,000	18.22	17.96	17.75	17.59	17.45	17.35	17.26	17.19	16.99	16.92	16.89	16.89
2,000	36.43	35.91	35.50	35.17	34.90	34.69	34.52	34.37	33.98	33.84	33.78	33.77
3,000	54.65	53.87	53.25	52.75	52.35	52.03	51.77	51.56	50.97	50.75	50.67	50.65
4,000	72.86	71.82	71.00	70.33	69.80	69.37	69.03	68.74	67.95	67.67	67.56	67.53
5,000	91.07	89.78	88.74	87.92	87.25	86.71	86.28	85.93	84.94	84.58	84.45	84.41
6,000	109.29	107.73	106.49	105.50	104.70	104.06	103.54	103.11	101.93	101.50	101.34	101.29
7,000	127.50	125.69	124.24	123.08	122.15	121.40	120.79	120.30	118.92	118.42	118.23	118.17
8,000	145.71	143.64	141.99	140.66	139.60	138.74	138.05	137.48	135.90	135.33	135.12	135.05
9,000	163.93	161.60	159.74	158.25	157.05	156.08	155.30	154.67	152.89	152.25	152.01	151.93
10,000	182.14	179.55	177.48	175.83	174.50	173.42	172.56	171.85	169.88	169.16	168.90	168.81
15,000	273.21	269.32	266.22	263.74	261.75	260.13	258.83	257.78	254.81	253.74	253.35	253.21
20,000	364.28	359.09	354.96	351.65	348.99	346.84	345.11	343.70	339.75	338.32	337.80	337.61
25,000	455.35	448.87	443.70	439.57	436.24	433.55	431.38	429.62	424.68	422.90	422.25	422.02
30,000	546.41	538.64	532.44	527.48	523.49	520.26	517.66	515.55	509.62	507.48	506.70	506.42
35,000	637.48	628.41	621.18	615.39	610.73	606.97	603.93	601.47	594.56	592.06	591.15	590.82
40,000	728.55	718.18	709.92	703.30	697.98	693.68	690.21	687.39	679.49	676.64	675.60	675.22
45,000	819.62	807.96	798.66	791.22	785.23	780.39	776.49	773.32	764.43	761.22	760.05	759.63
50,000	910.69	897.73	887.40	879.13	872.47	867.10	862.76	859.24	849.36	845.80	844.50	844.03
55,000	1001.75	987.50	976.14	967.04	959.72	953.81	949.04	945.16	934.30	930.38	928.95	928.43
60,000	1092.82	1077.27	1064.88	1054.95	1046.97	1040.52	1035.31	1031.09	1019.23	1014.96	1013.40	1012.83
65,000	1183.89	1167.05	1153.62	1142.87	1134.21	1127.23	1121.59	1117.01	1104.17	1099.54	1097.85	1097.24
70,000	1274.96	1256.82	1242.36	1230.78	1221.46	1213.94	1207.86	1202.93	1189.11	1184.12	1182.30	1181.64
75,000	1366.03	1346.59	1331.10	1318.69	1308.71	1300.65	1294.14	1288.86	1274.04	1268.70	1266.75	1266.04
80,000	1457.09	1436.36	1419.84	1406.60	1395.96	1387.36	1380.41	1374.78	1358.98	1353.28	1351.20	1350.44
85,000	1548.16	1526.14	1508.58	1494.51	1483.20	1474.07	1466.69	1460.70	1443.91	1437.86	1435.65	1434.85
90,000	1639.23	1615.91	1597.32	1582.43	1570.45	1560.78	1552.97	1546.63	1528.85	1522.44	1520.10	1519.25
95,000	1730.30	1705.68	1686.06	1670.34	1657.70	1647.49	1639.24	1632.55	1613.79	1607.02	1604.55	1603.65
100,000	1821.37	1795.45	1774.80	1758.25	1744.94	1734.20	1725.52	1718.47	1698.72	1691.60	1689.00	1688.05
105,000	1912.43	1885.23	1863.54	1846.16	1832.19	1820.91	1811.79	1804.40	1783.66	1776.18	1773.45	1772.46
110,000	2003.50	1975.00	1952.28	1934.08	1919.44	1907.62	1898.07	1890.32	1868.59	1860.76	1857.90	1856.86
115,000	2094.57	2064.77	2041.02	2021.99	2006.68	1994.33	1984.34	1976.24	1953.53	1945.34	1942.35	1941.26
120,000	2185.64	2154.54	2129.76	2109.90	2093.93	2081.04	2070.62	2062.17	2038.46	2029.92	2026.80	2025.66
125,000	2276.71	2244.32	2218.50	2197.81	2181.18	2167.75	2156.89	2148.09	2123.40	2114.50	2111.25	2110.07
130,000	2367.77	2334.09	2307.24	2285.73	2268.42	2254.46	2243.17	2234.01	2208.34	2199.08	2195.70	2194.47
135,000	2458.84	2423.86	2395.98	2373.64	2355.67	2341.17	2329.45	2319.94	2293.27	2283.65	2280.15	2278.87
140,000	2549.91	2513.63	2484.72	2461.55	2442.92	2427.88	2415.72	2405.86	2378.21	2368.23	2364.60	2363.27
145,000	2640.98	2603.41	2573.46	2549.46	2530.16	2514.59	2502.00	2491.78	2463.14	2452.81	2449.05	2447.67
150,000	2732.05	2693.18	2662.20	2637.38	2617.41	2601.30	2588.27	2577.71	2548.08	2537.39	2533.50	2532.08
155,000	2823.12	2782.95	2750.94	2725.29	2704.66	2688.01	2674.55	2663.63	2633.02	2621.97	2617.95	2616.48
160,000	2914.18	2872.72	2839.68	2813.20	2791.91	2774.72	2760.82	2749.56	2717.95	2706.55	2702.40	2700.88
165,000	3005.25	2962.50	2928.42	2901.11	2879.15	2861.43	2847.10	2835.48	2802.89	2791.13	2786.85	2785.28
170,000	3096.32	3052.27	3017.16	2989.02	2966.40	2948.14	2933.37	2921.40	2887.82	2875.71	2871.30	2869.69
175,000	3187.39	3142.04	3105.89	3076.94	3053.65	3034.85	3019.65	3007.33	2972.76	2960.29	2955.75	2954.09
180,000	3278.46	3231.81	3194.63	3164.85	3140.89	3121.56	3105.93	3093.25	3057.69	3044.87	3040.20	3038.49
185,000	3369.52	3321.59	3283.37	3252.76	3228.14	3208.27	3192.20	3179.17	3142.63	3129.45	3124.65	3122.89
190,000	3460.59	3411.36	3372.11	3340.67	3315.39	3294.98	3278.48	3265.10	3227.57	3214.03	3209.10	3207.30
195,000	3551.66	3501.13	3460.85	3428.59	3402.63	3381.69	3364.75	3351.02	3312.50	3298.61	3293.55	3291.70
200,000	3642.73	3590.90	3549.59	3516.50	3489.88	3468.40	3451.03	3436.94	3397.44	3383.19	3378.00	3376.10
205,000	3733.80	3680.68	3638.33	3604.41	3577.13	3555.11	3537.30	3522.87	3482.37	3467.77	3462.45	3460.50
210,000	3824.86	3770.45	3727.07	3692.32	3664.37	3641.82	3623.58	3608.79	3567.31	3552.35	3546.90	3544.91
215,000	3915.93	3860.22	3815.81	3780.24	3751.62	3728.53	3709.85	3694.71	3652.25	3636.93	3631.35	3629.31
220,000	4007.00	3949.99	3904.55	3868.15	3838.87	3815.24	3796.13	3780.64	3737.18	3721.51	3715.80	3713.71
225,000	4098.07	4039.77	3993.29	3956.06	3926.11	3901.95	3882.41	3866.56	3822.12	3806.09	3800.25	3798.11
230,000	4189.14	4129.54	4082.03	4043.97	4013.36	3988.66	3968.68	3952.48	3907.05	3890.67	3884.70	3882.52
235,000	4280.20	4219.31	4170.77	4131.88	4100.61	4075.37	4054.96	4038.41	3991.99	3975.25	3969.15	3966.92
240,000	4371.27	4309.08	4259.51	4219.80	4187.86	4162.08	4141.23	4124.33	4076.92	4059.83	4053.60	4051.32
245,000	4462.34	4398.86	4348.25	4307.71	4275.10	4248.79	4227.51	4210.25	4161.86	4144.41	4138.05	4135.72
250,000	4553.41	4488.63	4436.99	4395.62	4362.35	4335.50	4313.78	4296.18	4246.80	4228.99	4222.50	4220.13
255,000	4644.48	4578.40	4525.73	4483.53	4449.60	4422.21	4400.06	4382.10	4331.73	4313.57	4306.95	4304.53
260,000	4735.54	4668.17	4614.47	4571.45	4536.84	4508.92	4486.33	4468.02	4416.67	4398.15	4391.40	4388.93
265,000	4826.61	4757.95	4703.21	4659.36	4624.09	4595.63	4572.61	4553.95	4501.60	4482.72	4475.85	4473.33
270,000	4917.68	4847.72	4791.95	4747.27	4711.34	4682.34	4658.89	4639.87	4586.54	4567.30	4560.30	4557.74
280,000	5099.82	5027.26	4969.43	4923.10	4885.83	4855.76	4831.44	4811.72	4756.41	4736.46	4729.20	4726.54
290,000	5281.95	5206.81	5146.91	5098.92	5060.32	5029.18	5003.99	4983.56	4926.28	4905.62	4898.10	4895.34
300,000	5464.09	5386.35	5324.39	5274.75	5234.82	5202.60	5176.54	5155.41	5096.15	5074.78	5067.00	5064.15

20.50%　MONTHLY AMORTIZING PAYMENTS

AMOUNT OF LOAN	NUMBER OF YEARS IN TERM											
	1	2	3	4	5	6	7	8	9	10	11	12
$ 50	4.65	2.56	1.88	1.54	1.34	1.22	1.13	1.07	1.02	0.99	0.96	0.94
100	9.29	5.12	3.75	3.07	2.68	2.43	2.26	2.13	2.04	1.97	1.92	1.88
200	18.58	10.23	7.49	6.14	5.36	4.85	4.51	4.26	4.07	3.94	3.83	3.75
300	27.87	15.35	11.23	9.21	8.04	7.28	6.76	6.38	6.11	5.90	5.74	5.62
400	37.15	20.46	14.97	12.28	10.71	9.70	9.01	8.51	8.14	7.87	7.66	7.49
500	46.44	25.58	18.71	15.35	13.39	12.13	11.26	10.64	10.18	9.83	9.57	9.36
600	55.73	30.69	22.46	18.42	16.07	14.55	13.51	12.76	12.21	11.80	11.48	11.23
700	65.02	35.80	26.20	21.49	18.75	16.98	15.76	14.89	14.25	13.77	13.39	13.11
800	74.30	40.92	29.94	24.56	21.42	19.40	18.01	17.02	16.28	15.73	15.31	14.98
900	83.59	46.03	33.68	27.63	24.10	21.82	20.26	19.14	18.32	17.70	17.22	16.85
1,000	92.88	51.15	37.42	30.70	26.78	24.25	22.51	21.27	20.35	19.66	19.13	18.72
2,000	185.75	102.29	74.84	61.40	53.55	48.49	45.02	42.54	40.70	39.32	38.26	37.44
3,000	278.63	153.43	112.26	92.10	80.32	72.74	67.53	63.80	61.05	58.98	57.39	56.15
4,000	371.50	204.57	149.68	122.79	107.10	96.98	90.04	85.07	81.40	78.64	76.52	74.87
5,000	464.37	255.71	187.10	153.49	133.87	121.22	112.55	106.34	101.75	98.30	95.64	93.58
6,000	557.25	306.85	224.52	184.19	160.64	145.47	135.05	127.60	122.10	117.95	114.77	112.30
7,000	650.12	357.99	261.94	214.89	187.42	169.71	157.56	148.87	142.45	137.61	133.90	131.02
8,000	743.00	409.13	299.36	245.58	214.19	193.95	180.07	170.13	162.80	157.27	153.03	149.73
9,000	835.87	460.27	336.77	276.28	240.96	218.20	202.58	191.40	183.15	176.93	172.16	168.45
10,000	928.74	511.41	374.19	306.98	267.73	242.44	225.09	212.67	203.50	196.59	191.28	187.16
15,000	1393.11	767.11	561.29	460.47	401.60	363.66	337.63	319.00	305.25	294.88	286.92	280.74
20,000	1857.48	1022.81	748.38	613.95	535.46	484.88	450.17	425.33	407.00	393.17	382.56	374.32
25,000	2321.85	1278.51	935.48	767.44	669.33	606.09	562.71	531.66	508.74	491.46	478.20	467.90
30,000	2786.22	1534.22	1122.57	920.93	803.19	727.31	675.25	637.99	610.49	589.75	573.84	561.48
35,000	3250.59	1789.92	1309.66	1074.41	937.06	848.53	787.79	744.32	712.24	688.04	669.48	655.06
40,000	3714.96	2045.62	1496.76	1227.90	1070.92	969.75	900.33	850.65	813.99	786.33	765.12	748.64
45,000	4179.33	2301.32	1683.85	1381.39	1204.78	1090.96	1012.88	956.98	915.74	884.63	860.76	842.22
50,000	4643.70	2557.02	1870.95	1534.87	1338.65	1212.18	1125.42	1063.31	1017.48	982.92	956.40	935.80
55,000	5108.07	2812.73	2058.04	1688.36	1472.51	1333.40	1237.96	1169.64	1119.23	1081.21	1052.04	1029.38
60,000	5572.44	3068.43	2245.14	1841.85	1606.38	1454.62	1350.50	1275.97	1220.98	1179.50	1147.68	1122.96
65,000	6036.81	3324.13	2432.23	1995.34	1740.24	1575.83	1463.04	1382.30	1322.73	1277.79	1243.32	1216.54
70,000	6501.18	3579.83	2619.32	2148.82	1874.11	1697.05	1575.58	1488.63	1424.48	1376.08	1338.96	1310.12
75,000	6965.55	3835.53	2806.42	2302.31	2007.97	1818.27	1688.12	1594.96	1526.22	1474.37	1434.60	1403.70
80,000	7429.92	4091.24	2993.51	2455.80	2141.83	1939.49	1800.66	1701.29	1627.97	1572.66	1530.24	1497.28
85,000	7894.29	4346.94	3180.61	2609.28	2275.70	2060.71	1913.21	1807.62	1729.72	1670.95	1625.88	1590.86
90,000	8358.66	4602.64	3367.70	2762.77	2409.56	2181.92	2025.75	1913.95	1831.47	1769.25	1721.52	1684.44
95,000	8823.03	4858.34	3554.79	2916.26	2543.43	2303.14	2138.29	2020.28	1933.22	1867.54	1817.16	1778.01
100,000	9287.40	5114.04	3741.89	3069.74	2677.29	2424.36	2250.83	2126.61	2034.96	1965.83	1912.80	1871.59
105,000	9751.77	5369.75	3928.98	3223.23	2811.16	2545.58	2363.37	2232.94	2136.71	2064.12	2008.44	1965.17
110,000	10216.14	5625.45	4116.08	3376.72	2945.02	2666.79	2475.91	2339.27	2238.46	2162.41	2104.08	2058.75
115,000	10680.51	5881.15	4303.17	3530.21	3078.88	2788.01	2588.45	2445.60	2340.21	2260.70	2199.72	2152.33
120,000	11144.88	6136.85	4490.27	3683.69	3212.75	2909.23	2700.99	2551.93	2441.96	2358.99	2295.35	2245.91
125,000	11609.25	6392.55	4677.36	3837.18	3346.61	3030.45	2813.54	2658.26	2543.70	2457.28	2390.99	2339.49
130,000	12073.62	6648.26	4864.45	3990.67	3480.48	3151.66	2926.08	2764.59	2645.45	2555.57	2486.63	2433.07
135,000	12537.99	6903.96	5051.55	4144.15	3614.34	3272.88	3038.62	2870.92	2747.20	2653.87	2582.27	2526.65
140,000	13002.36	7159.66	5238.64	4297.64	3748.21	3394.10	3151.16	2977.25	2848.95	2752.16	2677.91	2620.23
145,000	13466.73	7415.36	5425.74	4451.13	3882.07	3515.32	3263.70	3083.58	2950.69	2850.45	2773.55	2713.81
150,000	13931.10	7671.06	5612.83	4604.61	4015.93	3636.54	3376.24	3189.91	3052.44	2948.74	2869.19	2807.39
155,000	14395.47	7926.77	5799.92	4758.10	4149.80	3757.75	3488.78	3296.24	3154.19	3047.03	2964.83	2900.97
160,000	14859.84	8182.47	5987.02	4911.59	4283.66	3878.97	3601.32	3402.57	3255.94	3145.32	3060.47	2994.55
165,000	15324.21	8438.17	6174.11	5065.08	4417.53	4000.19	3713.86	3508.90	3357.69	3243.61	3156.11	3088.13
170,000	15788.58	8693.87	6361.21	5218.56	4551.39	4121.41	3826.41	3615.24	3459.43	3341.90	3251.75	3181.71
175,000	16252.95	8949.57	6548.30	5372.05	4685.26	4242.62	3938.95	3721.57	3561.18	3440.20	3347.39	3275.29
180,000	16717.32	9205.28	6735.40	5525.54	4819.12	4363.84	4051.49	3827.90	3662.93	3538.49	3443.03	3368.87
185,000	17181.69	9460.98	6922.49	5679.02	4952.98	4485.06	4164.03	3934.23	3764.68	3636.78	3538.67	3462.45
190,000	17646.06	9716.68	7109.58	5832.51	5086.85	4606.28	4276.57	4040.56	3866.43	3735.07	3634.31	3556.02
195,000	18110.43	9972.38	7296.68	5986.00	5220.71	4727.49	4389.11	4146.89	3968.17	3833.36	3729.95	3649.60
200,000	18574.80	10228.08	7483.77	6139.48	5354.58	4848.71	4501.65	4253.22	4069.92	3931.65	3825.59	3743.18
205,000	19039.17	10483.79	7670.87	6292.97	5488.44	4969.93	4614.19	4359.55	4171.67	4029.94	3921.23	3836.76
210,000	19503.54	10739.49	7857.96	6446.46	5622.31	5091.15	4726.74	4465.88	4273.42	4128.23	4016.87	3930.34
215,000	19967.91	10995.19	8045.05	6599.94	5756.17	5212.36	4839.28	4572.21	4375.17	4226.52	4112.51	4023.92
220,000	20432.28	11250.89	8232.15	6753.43	5890.03	5333.58	4951.82	4678.54	4476.91	4324.82	4208.15	4117.50
225,000	20896.65	11506.59	8419.24	6906.92	6023.90	5454.80	5064.36	4784.87	4578.66	4423.11	4303.79	4211.08
230,000	21361.02	11762.30	8606.34	7060.41	6157.76	5576.02	5176.90	4891.20	4680.41	4521.40	4399.43	4304.66
235,000	21825.39	12018.00	8793.43	7213.89	6291.63	5697.24	5289.44	4997.53	4782.16	4619.69	4495.07	4398.24
240,000	22289.76	12273.70	8980.53	7367.38	6425.49	5818.45	5401.98	5103.86	4883.91	4717.98	4590.70	4491.82
245,000	22754.13	12529.40	9167.62	7520.87	6559.36	5939.67	5514.52	5210.19	4985.65	4816.27	4686.34	4585.40
250,000	23218.50	12785.10	9354.71	7674.35	6693.22	6060.89	5627.07	5316.52	5087.40	4914.56	4781.98	4678.98
255,000	23682.87	13040.81	9541.81	7827.84	6827.08	6182.11	5739.61	5422.85	5189.15	5012.85	4877.62	4772.56
260,000	24147.24	13296.51	9728.90	7981.33	6960.95	6303.32	5852.15	5529.18	5290.90	5111.14	4973.26	4866.14
265,000	24611.61	13552.21	9916.00	8134.81	7094.81	6424.54	5964.69	5635.51	5392.64	5209.44	5068.90	4959.72
270,000	25075.98	13807.91	10103.09	8288.30	7228.68	6545.76	6077.23	5741.84	5494.39	5307.73	5164.54	5053.30
280,000	26004.72	14319.32	10477.28	8595.28	7496.41	6788.19	6302.31	5954.50	5697.89	5504.31	5355.82	5240.46
290,000	26933.46	14830.72	10851.47	8902.25	7764.13	7030.63	6527.40	6167.16	5901.38	5700.89	5547.10	5427.61
300,000	27862.20	15342.12	11225.66	9209.22	8031.86	7273.07	6752.48	6379.82	6104.88	5897.47	5738.38	5614.77

150

AMOUNT OF LOAN	NUMBER OF YEARS IN TERM											
	13	14	15	16	17	18	19	20	25	30	35	40
$ 50	0.92	0.91	0.90	0.89	0.89	0.88	0.88	0.87	0.86	0.86	0.86	0.86
100	1.84	1.82	1.80	1.78	1.77	1.76	1.75	1.74	1.72	1.72	1.71	1.71
200	3.68	3.63	3.59	3.56	3.53	3.51	3.50	3.48	3.44	3.43	3.42	3.42
300	5.52	5.45	5.39	5.34	5.30	5.27	5.24	5.22	5.16	5.14	5.13	5.13
400	7.36	7.26	7.18	7.11	7.06	7.02	6.99	6.96	6.88	6.85	6.84	6.84
500	9.20	9.07	8.97	8.89	8.83	8.77	8.73	8.70	8.60	8.57	8.55	8.55
600	11.04	10.89	10.77	10.67	10.59	10.53	10.48	10.43	10.32	10.28	10.26	10.26
700	12.88	12.70	12.56	12.44	12.35	12.28	12.22	12.17	12.04	11.99	11.97	11.97
800	14.72	14.51	14.35	14.22	14.12	14.03	13.97	13.91	13.76	13.70	13.68	13.68
900	16.56	16.33	16.15	16.00	15.88	15.79	15.71	15.65	15.48	15.41	15.39	15.38
1,000	18.40	18.14	17.94	17.78	17.65	17.54	17.46	17.39	17.20	17.13	17.10	17.09
2,000	36.79	36.28	35.87	35.55	35.29	35.08	34.91	34.77	34.39	34.25	34.20	34.18
3,000	55.18	54.42	53.81	53.32	52.93	52.61	52.36	52.15	51.58	51.37	51.30	51.27
4,000	73.58	72.55	71.74	71.09	70.57	70.15	69.81	69.53	68.77	68.49	68.39	68.36
5,000	91.97	90.69	89.67	88.86	88.21	87.68	87.26	86.91	85.96	85.61	85.49	85.45
6,000	110.36	108.83	107.61	106.63	105.85	105.22	104.71	104.29	103.15	102.74	102.59	102.54
7,000	128.75	126.96	125.54	124.40	123.49	122.75	122.16	121.68	120.34	119.86	119.69	119.62
8,000	147.15	145.10	143.47	142.17	141.13	140.29	139.61	139.06	137.53	136.98	136.78	136.71
9,000	165.54	163.24	161.41	159.94	158.77	157.82	157.06	156.44	154.72	154.10	153.88	153.80
10,000	183.93	181.37	179.34	177.71	176.41	175.36	174.51	173.82	171.91	171.22	170.98	170.89
15,000	275.89	272.06	269.01	266.57	264.61	263.03	261.76	260.73	257.86	256.83	256.46	256.33
20,000	367.86	362.74	358.67	355.42	352.81	350.71	349.01	347.64	343.81	342.44	341.95	341.77
25,000	459.82	453.43	448.34	444.28	441.01	438.38	436.26	434.54	429.76	428.05	427.44	427.21
30,000	551.78	544.11	538.01	533.13	529.21	526.06	523.51	521.45	515.71	513.66	512.92	512.66
35,000	643.75	634.80	627.68	621.90	617.41	613.73	610.76	608.36	601.66	599.27	598.41	598.10
40,000	735.71	725.48	717.34	710.84	705.61	701.41	698.01	695.27	687.61	684.88	683.89	683.54
45,000	827.67	816.17	807.01	799.69	793.82	789.08	785.26	782.17	773.56	770.49	769.38	768.98
50,000	919.63	906.85	896.68	888.55	882.02	876.76	872.52	869.08	859.51	856.10	854.87	854.42
55,000	1011.60	997.53	986.35	977.40	970.22	964.43	959.77	955.99	945.46	941.70	940.35	939.86
60,000	1103.56	1088.22	1076.01	1066.25	1058.42	1052.11	1047.02	1042.90	1031.41	1027.31	1025.84	1025.31
65,000	1195.52	1178.90	1165.68	1155.11	1146.62	1139.79	1134.27	1129.81	1117.36	1112.92	1111.33	1110.75
70,000	1287.49	1269.59	1255.35	1243.96	1234.82	1227.46	1221.52	1216.71	1203.31	1198.53	1196.81	1196.19
75,000	1379.45	1360.27	1345.02	1332.82	1323.02	1315.14	1308.77	1303.62	1289.26	1284.14	1282.30	1281.63
80,000	1471.41	1450.96	1434.68	1421.67	1411.22	1402.81	1396.02	1390.53	1375.21	1369.75	1367.78	1367.07
85,000	1563.37	1541.64	1524.35	1510.52	1499.42	1490.49	1483.27	1477.44	1461.16	1455.36	1453.27	1452.52
90,000	1655.34	1632.33	1614.02	1599.38	1587.63	1578.16	1570.52	1564.34	1547.11	1540.97	1538.76	1537.96
95,000	1747.30	1723.01	1703.68	1688.23	1675.83	1665.84	1657.77	1651.25	1633.06	1626.58	1624.24	1623.40
100,000	1839.26	1813.70	1793.35	1777.09	1764.03	1753.51	1745.03	1738.16	1719.01	1712.19	1709.73	1708.84
105,000	1931.23	1904.38	1883.02	1865.94	1852.23	1841.19	1832.28	1825.07	1804.96	1797.80	1795.22	1794.28
110,000	2023.19	1995.06	1972.69	1954.79	1940.43	1928.86	1919.53	1911.97	1890.91	1883.40	1880.70	1879.72
115,000	2115.15	2085.75	2062.35	2043.65	2028.63	2016.54	2006.78	1998.88	1976.86	1969.01	1966.19	1965.17
120,000	2207.12	2176.43	2152.02	2132.50	2116.83	2104.21	2094.03	2085.79	2062.81	2054.62	2051.67	2050.61
125,000	2299.08	2267.12	2241.69	2221.36	2205.03	2191.89	2181.28	2172.70	2148.76	2140.23	2137.16	2136.05
130,000	2391.04	2357.80	2331.36	2310.21	2293.23	2279.57	2268.53	2259.61	2234.71	2225.84	2222.65	2221.49
135,000	2483.00	2448.49	2421.02	2399.06	2381.44	2367.24	2355.78	2346.51	2320.66	2311.45	2308.13	2306.93
140,000	2574.97	2539.17	2510.69	2487.92	2469.64	2454.92	2443.03	2433.42	2406.61	2397.06	2393.62	2392.38
145,000	2666.93	2629.86	2600.36	2576.77	2557.84	2542.59	2530.28	2520.33	2492.57	2482.67	2479.10	2477.82
150,000	2758.89	2720.54	2690.03	2665.63	2646.04	2630.27	2617.54	2607.24	2578.52	2568.28	2564.59	2563.26
155,000	2850.86	2811.23	2779.69	2754.48	2734.24	2717.94	2704.79	2694.14	2664.47	2653.89	2650.08	2648.70
160,000	2942.82	2901.91	2869.36	2843.33	2822.44	2805.62	2792.04	2781.05	2750.42	2739.49	2735.56	2734.14
165,000	3034.78	2992.59	2959.03	2932.19	2910.64	2893.29	2879.29	2867.96	2836.37	2825.10	2821.05	2819.58
170,000	3126.74	3083.28	3048.69	3021.04	2998.84	2980.97	2966.54	2954.87	2922.32	2910.71	2906.54	2905.03
175,000	3218.71	3173.96	3138.36	3109.90	3087.04	3068.64	3053.79	3041.77	3008.27	2996.32	2992.02	2990.47
180,000	3310.67	3264.65	3228.03	3198.75	3175.25	3156.32	3141.04	3128.68	3094.22	3081.93	3077.51	3075.91
185,000	3402.63	3355.33	3317.70	3287.60	3263.45	3243.99	3228.29	3215.59	3180.17	3167.54	3162.99	3161.35
190,000	3494.60	3446.02	3407.36	3376.46	3351.65	3331.67	3315.54	3302.50	3266.12	3253.15	3248.48	3246.79
195,000	3586.56	3536.70	3497.03	3465.31	3439.85	3419.35	3402.79	3389.41	3352.07	3338.76	3333.97	3332.24
200,000	3678.52	3627.39	3586.70	3554.17	3528.05	3507.02	3490.05	3476.31	3438.02	3424.37	3419.45	3417.68
205,000	3770.48	3718.07	3676.37	3643.02	3616.25	3594.70	3577.30	3563.22	3523.97	3509.98	3504.94	3503.12
210,000	3862.45	3808.76	3766.03	3731.87	3704.45	3682.37	3664.55	3650.13	3609.92	3595.59	3590.43	3588.56
215,000	3954.41	3899.44	3855.70	3820.73	3792.65	3770.05	3751.80	3737.04	3695.87	3681.19	3675.91	3674.00
220,000	4046.37	3990.12	3945.37	3909.58	3880.85	3857.72	3839.05	3823.94	3781.82	3766.80	3761.40	3759.44
225,000	4138.34	4080.81	4035.04	3998.44	3969.06	3945.40	3926.30	3910.85	3867.77	3852.41	3846.88	3844.89
230,000	4230.30	4171.49	4124.70	4087.29	4057.26	4033.07	4013.55	3997.76	3953.72	3938.02	3932.37	3930.33
235,000	4322.26	4262.18	4214.37	4176.14	4145.46	4120.75	4100.80	4084.67	4039.67	4023.63	4017.86	4015.77
240,000	4414.23	4352.86	4304.04	4265.00	4233.66	4208.42	4188.05	4171.57	4125.62	4109.24	4103.34	4101.21
245,000	4506.19	4443.55	4393.70	4353.85	4321.86	4296.10	4275.30	4258.48	4211.57	4194.85	4188.83	4186.65
250,000	4598.15	4534.23	4483.37	4442.71	4410.06	4383.78	4362.56	4345.39	4297.52	4280.46	4274.31	4272.10
255,000	4690.11	4624.92	4573.04	4531.56	4498.26	4471.45	4449.81	4432.30	4383.47	4366.07	4359.80	4357.54
260,000	4782.08	4715.60	4662.71	4620.41	4586.46	4559.13	4537.06	4519.21	4469.42	4451.68	4445.29	4442.98
265,000	4874.04	4806.29	4752.37	4709.27	4674.66	4646.80	4624.31	4606.11	4555.37	4537.28	4530.77	4528.42
270,000	4966.00	4896.97	4842.04	4798.12	4762.87	4734.48	4711.56	4693.02	4641.32	4622.89	4616.26	4613.86
280,000	5149.93	5078.34	5021.38	4975.83	4939.27	4909.83	4886.06	4866.84	4813.22	4794.11	4787.23	4784.75
290,000	5333.85	5259.71	5200.71	5153.54	5115.67	5085.18	5060.56	5040.65	4985.13	4965.33	4958.20	4955.63
300,000	5517.78	5441.08	5380.05	5331.25	5292.07	5260.53	5235.07	5214.47	5157.03	5136.55	5129.18	5126.51

20.75%

AMOUNT OF LOAN	NUMBER OF YEARS IN TERM											
	1	2	3	4	5	6	7	8	9	10	11	12
$ 50	4.65	2.57	1.88	1.55	1.35	1.22	1.14	1.08	1.03	1.00	0.97	0.95
100	9.30	5.13	3.76	3.09	2.70	2.44	2.27	2.15	2.06	1.99	1.93	1.89
200	18.60	10.26	7.51	6.17	5.39	4.88	4.54	4.29	4.11	3.97	3.86	3.78
300	27.90	15.38	11.27	9.25	8.08	7.32	6.80	6.43	6.16	5.95	5.79	5.67
400	37.20	20.51	15.02	12.34	10.77	9.76	9.07	8.57	8.21	7.94	7.72	7.56
500	46.50	25.64	18.78	15.42	13.46	12.20	11.33	10.72	10.26	9.92	9.65	9.45
600	55.80	30.76	22.53	18.50	16.15	14.64	13.60	12.86	12.31	11.90	11.58	11.34
700	65.10	35.89	26.29	21.59	18.84	17.08	15.87	15.00	14.36	13.88	13.51	13.23
800	74.40	41.02	30.04	24.67	21.54	19.52	18.13	17.14	16.41	15.87	15.44	15.12
900	83.70	46.14	33.80	27.75	24.23	21.96	20.40	19.29	18.47	17.85	17.37	17.01
1,000	93.00	51.27	37.55	30.84	26.92	24.39	22.66	21.43	20.52	19.83	19.30	18.90
2,000	185.99	102.53	75.10	61.67	53.83	48.78	45.32	42.85	41.03	39.66	38.60	37.79
3,000	278.99	153.79	112.65	92.50	80.74	73.17	67.98	64.27	61.54	59.48	57.90	56.68
4,000	371.98	205.06	150.19	123.33	107.66	97.56	90.64	85.70	82.05	79.31	77.20	75.57
5,000	464.97	256.32	187.74	154.16	134.57	121.95	113.30	107.12	102.56	99.13	96.50	94.46
6,000	557.97	307.58	225.29	184.99	161.48	146.34	135.96	128.54	123.08	118.96	115.80	113.36
7,000	650.96	358.85	262.83	215.82	188.40	170.73	158.62	149.97	143.59	138.78	135.10	132.25
8,000	743.96	410.11	300.38	246.66	215.31	195.12	181.28	171.39	164.10	158.61	154.40	151.14
9,000	836.95	461.37	337.93	277.49	242.22	219.51	203.94	192.81	184.61	178.43	173.70	170.03
10,000	929.94	512.63	375.47	308.32	269.13	243.90	226.60	214.24	205.12	198.26	193.00	188.92
15,000	1394.91	768.95	563.21	462.48	403.70	365.85	339.90	321.35	307.68	297.39	289.50	283.38
20,000	1859.88	1025.26	750.94	616.63	538.26	487.80	453.20	428.47	410.24	396.51	386.00	377.84
25,000	2324.85	1281.58	938.68	770.79	672.83	609.74	566.50	535.59	512.80	495.64	482.49	472.30
30,000	2789.82	1537.89	1126.41	924.95	807.39	731.69	679.80	642.70	615.36	594.77	578.99	566.76
35,000	3254.79	1794.21	1314.14	1079.10	941.96	853.64	793.10	749.82	717.92	693.89	675.49	661.21
40,000	3719.76	2050.52	1501.88	1233.26	1076.52	975.59	906.40	856.94	820.48	793.02	771.99	755.67
45,000	4184.73	2306.84	1689.61	1387.42	1211.09	1097.53	1019.70	964.05	923.04	892.15	868.49	850.13
50,000	4649.70	2563.15	1877.35	1541.57	1345.65	1219.48	1133.00	1071.17	1025.60	991.28	964.98	944.59
55,000	5114.67	2819.47	2065.08	1695.73	1480.22	1341.43	1246.30	1178.29	1128.16	1090.40	1061.48	1039.05
60,000	5579.63	3075.78	2252.81	1849.89	1614.78	1463.38	1359.60	1285.40	1230.72	1189.53	1157.98	1133.51
65,000	6044.60	3332.10	2440.55	2004.05	1749.34	1585.33	1472.90	1392.52	1333.28	1288.66	1254.48	1227.96
70,000	6509.57	3588.41	2628.28	2158.20	1883.91	1707.27	1586.20	1499.63	1435.84	1387.78	1350.98	1322.42
75,000	6974.54	3844.73	2816.02	2312.36	2018.47	1829.22	1699.50	1606.75	1538.40	1486.91	1447.47	1416.88
80,000	7439.51	4101.04	3003.75	2466.52	2153.04	1951.17	1812.80	1713.87	1640.96	1586.04	1543.97	1511.34
85,000	7904.48	4357.35	3191.49	2620.67	2287.60	2073.12	1926.10	1820.98	1743.52	1685.17	1640.47	1605.80
90,000	8369.45	4613.67	3379.22	2774.83	2422.17	2195.06	2039.40	1928.10	1846.08	1784.29	1736.97	1700.26
95,000	8834.42	4869.98	3566.95	2928.99	2556.73	2317.01	2152.70	2035.22	1948.64	1883.42	1833.46	1794.71
100,000	9299.39	5126.30	3754.69	3083.14	2691.30	2438.96	2266.00	2142.33	2051.20	1982.55	1929.96	1889.17
105,000	9764.36	5382.61	3942.42	3237.30	2825.86	2560.91	2379.30	2249.45	2153.76	2081.67	2026.46	1983.63
110,000	10229.33	5638.93	4130.16	3391.46	2960.43	2682.86	2492.60	2356.57	2256.32	2180.80	2122.96	2078.09
115,000	10694.30	5895.24	4317.89	3545.61	3094.99	2804.80	2605.90	2463.68	2358.88	2279.93	2219.46	2172.55
120,000	11159.26	6151.56	4505.62	3699.77	3229.56	2926.75	2719.20	2570.80	2461.44	2379.06	2315.95	2267.01
125,000	11624.23	6407.87	4693.36	3853.93	3364.12	3048.70	2832.50	2677.91	2564.00	2478.18	2412.45	2361.46
130,000	12089.20	6664.19	4881.09	4008.09	3498.68	3170.65	2945.80	2785.03	2666.56	2577.31	2508.95	2455.92
135,000	12554.17	6920.50	5068.83	4162.24	3633.25	3292.59	3059.10	2892.15	2769.12	2676.44	2605.45	2550.38
140,000	13019.14	7176.82	5256.56	4316.40	3767.81	3414.54	3172.40	2999.26	2871.68	2775.56	2701.95	2644.84
145,000	13484.11	7433.13	5444.30	4470.56	3902.38	3536.49	3285.70	3106.38	2974.24	2874.69	2798.44	2739.30
150,000	13949.08	7689.45	5632.03	4624.71	4036.94	3658.44	3399.00	3213.50	3076.80	2973.82	2894.94	2833.76
155,000	14414.05	7945.76	5819.76	4778.87	4171.51	3780.38	3512.30	3320.61	3179.36	3072.94	2991.44	2928.21
160,000	14879.02	8202.08	6007.50	4933.03	4306.07	3902.33	3625.60	3427.73	3281.92	3172.07	3087.94	3022.67
165,000	15343.99	8458.39	6195.23	5087.18	4440.64	4024.28	3738.90	3534.85	3384.48	3271.20	3184.43	3117.13
170,000	15808.96	8714.70	6382.97	5241.34	4575.20	4146.23	3852.20	3641.96	3487.04	3370.33	3280.93	3211.59
175,000	16273.93	8971.02	6570.70	5395.50	4709.77	4268.18	3965.50	3749.08	3589.60	3469.45	3377.43	3306.05
180,000	16738.89	9227.33	6758.43	5549.65	4844.33	4390.12	4078.80	3856.19	3692.16	3568.58	3473.93	3400.51
185,000	17203.86	9483.65	6946.17	5703.81	4978.89	4512.07	4192.10	3963.31	3794.72	3667.71	3570.43	3494.96
190,000	17668.83	9739.96	7133.90	5857.97	5113.46	4634.02	4305.40	4070.43	3897.28	3766.83	3666.92	3589.42
195,000	18133.80	9996.28	7321.64	6012.13	5248.02	4755.97	4418.70	4177.54	3999.84	3865.96	3763.42	3683.88
200,000	18598.77	10252.59	7509.37	6166.28	5382.59	4877.91	4532.00	4284.66	4102.40	3965.09	3859.92	3778.34
205,000	19063.74	10508.91	7697.11	6320.44	5517.15	4999.86	4645.30	4391.78	4204.96	4064.22	3956.42	3872.80
210,000	19528.71	10765.22	7884.84	6474.60	5651.72	5121.81	4758.60	4498.89	4307.52	4163.34	4052.92	3967.26
215,000	19993.68	11021.54	8072.57	6628.75	5786.28	5243.76	4871.90	4606.01	4410.07	4262.47	4149.41	4061.71
220,000	20458.65	11277.85	8260.31	6782.91	5920.85	5365.71	4985.20	4713.13	4512.63	4361.60	4245.91	4156.17
225,000	20923.62	11534.17	8448.04	6937.07	6055.41	5487.65	5098.50	4820.24	4615.19	4460.72	4342.41	4250.63
230,000	21388.59	11790.48	8635.78	7091.22	6189.98	5609.60	5211.80	4927.36	4717.75	4559.85	4438.91	4345.09
235,000	21853.56	12046.80	8823.51	7245.38	6324.54	5731.55	5325.10	5034.47	4820.31	4658.98	4535.40	4439.55
240,000	22318.52	12303.11	9011.24	7399.54	6459.11	5853.50	5438.40	5141.59	4922.87	4758.11	4631.90	4534.01
245,000	22783.49	12559.43	9198.98	7553.69	6593.67	5975.44	5551.70	5248.71	5025.43	4857.23	4728.40	4628.46
250,000	23248.46	12815.74	9386.71	7707.85	6728.23	6097.39	5665.00	5355.82	5127.99	4956.36	4824.90	4722.92
255,000	23713.43	13072.05	9574.45	7862.01	6862.80	6219.34	5778.30	5462.94	5230.55	5055.49	4921.40	4817.38
260,000	24178.40	13328.37	9762.18	8016.17	6997.36	6341.29	5891.60	5570.06	5333.11	5154.61	5017.89	4911.84
265,000	24643.37	13584.68	9949.91	8170.32	7131.93	6463.23	6004.90	5677.17	5435.67	5253.74	5114.39	5006.30
270,000	25108.34	13841.00	10137.65	8324.48	7266.49	6585.18	6118.20	5784.29	5538.23	5352.87	5210.89	5100.76
280,000	26038.28	14353.63	10513.12	8632.79	7535.62	6829.08	6344.80	5998.52	5743.35	5551.12	5403.89	5289.67
290,000	26968.22	14866.26	10888.59	8941.11	7804.75	7072.97	6571.40	6212.75	5948.47	5749.38	5596.88	5478.59
300,000	27898.15	15378.89	11264.05	9249.42	8073.88	7316.87	6798.00	6426.99	6153.59	5947.63	5789.88	5667.51

AMOUNT OF LOAN	NUMBER OF YEARS IN TERM										
	13	14	15	16	17	18	19	20	25	30	35	40
$ 50	0.93	0.92	0.91	0.90	0.90	0.89	0.89	0.88	0.87	0.87	0.87	0.87
100	1.86	1.84	1.82	1.80	1.79	1.78	1.77	1.76	1.74	1.74	1.74	1.73
200	3.72	3.67	3.63	3.60	3.57	3.55	3.53	3.52	3.48	3.47	3.47	3.46
300	5.58	5.50	5.44	5.39	5.35	5.32	5.30	5.28	5.22	5.20	5.20	5.19
400	7.43	7.33	7.25	7.19	7.14	7.10	7.06	7.04	6.96	6.94	6.93	6.92
500	9.29	9.16	9.06	8.98	8.92	8.87	8.83	8.79	8.70	8.67	8.66	8.65
600	11.15	11.00	10.88	10.78	10.70	10.64	10.59	10.55	10.44	10.40	10.39	10.38
700	13.01	12.83	12.69	12.58	12.49	12.42	12.36	12.31	12.18	12.13	12.12	12.11
800	14.86	14.66	14.50	14.37	14.27	14.19	14.12	14.07	13.92	13.87	13.85	13.84
900	16.72	16.49	16.31	16.17	16.05	15.96	15.89	15.83	15.66	15.60	15.58	15.57
1,000	18.58	18.32	18.12	17.96	17.84	17.73	17.65	17.58	17.40	17.33	17.31	17.30
2,000	37.15	36.64	36.24	35.92	35.67	35.46	35.30	35.16	34.79	34.66	34.61	34.60
3,000	55.72	54.96	54.36	53.88	53.50	53.19	52.94	52.74	52.18	51.99	51.92	51.89
4,000	74.29	73.28	72.48	71.84	71.33	70.92	70.59	70.32	69.58	69.32	69.22	69.19
5,000	92.87	91.60	90.60	89.80	89.16	88.65	88.23	87.90	86.97	86.64	86.53	86.49
6,000	111.44	109.92	108.72	107.76	106.99	106.38	105.88	105.48	104.36	103.97	103.83	103.78
7,000	130.01	128.24	126.84	125.72	124.83	124.11	123.53	123.06	121.76	121.30	121.14	121.08
8,000	148.58	146.56	144.96	143.68	142.66	141.83	141.17	140.64	139.15	138.63	138.44	138.38
9,000	167.15	164.88	163.08	161.64	160.49	159.56	158.82	158.21	156.54	155.96	155.75	155.67
10,000	185.73	183.20	181.20	179.60	178.32	177.29	176.46	175.79	173.94	173.28	173.05	172.97
15,000	278.59	274.80	271.80	269.40	267.48	265.93	264.69	263.69	260.90	259.92	259.57	259.45
20,000	371.45	366.40	362.40	359.20	356.64	354.58	352.92	351.58	347.87	346.56	346.10	345.93
25,000	464.31	458.00	452.99	449.00	445.79	443.22	441.15	439.47	434.84	433.20	432.62	432.41
30,000	557.17	549.60	543.59	538.79	534.95	531.86	529.38	527.37	521.80	519.84	519.14	518.89
35,000	650.03	641.20	634.19	628.59	624.11	620.51	617.61	615.26	608.77	606.48	605.67	605.37
40,000	742.89	732.80	724.79	718.39	713.27	709.15	705.83	703.16	695.73	693.12	692.19	691.86
45,000	835.75	824.40	815.38	808.19	802.43	797.79	794.06	791.05	782.70	779.76	778.71	778.34
50,000	928.61	916.00	905.98	897.99	891.58	886.44	882.29	878.94	869.67	866.40	865.23	864.82
55,000	1021.47	1007.60	996.58	987.79	980.74	975.08	970.52	966.84	956.63	953.04	951.76	951.30
60,000	1114.33	1099.20	1087.18	1077.58	1069.90	1063.72	1058.75	1054.73	1043.60	1039.68	1038.28	1037.78
65,000	1207.19	1190.80	1177.77	1167.38	1159.06	1152.37	1146.98	1142.63	1130.56	1126.31	1124.80	1124.26
70,000	1300.05	1282.40	1268.37	1257.18	1248.21	1241.01	1235.21	1230.52	1217.53	1212.95	1211.33	1210.74
75,000	1392.91	1374.00	1358.97	1346.98	1337.37	1329.65	1323.43	1318.41	1304.50	1299.59	1297.85	1297.23
80,000	1485.78	1465.59	1449.57	1436.78	1426.53	1418.30	1411.66	1406.31	1391.46	1386.23	1384.37	1383.71
85,000	1578.64	1557.19	1540.17	1526.58	1515.69	1506.94	1499.89	1494.20	1478.43	1472.87	1470.89	1470.19
90,000	1671.50	1648.79	1630.76	1616.37	1604.85	1595.58	1588.12	1582.10	1565.40	1559.51	1557.42	1556.67
95,000	1764.36	1740.39	1721.36	1706.17	1694.00	1684.23	1676.35	1669.99	1652.36	1646.15	1643.94	1643.15
100,000	1857.22	1831.99	1811.96	1795.97	1783.16	1772.87	1764.58	1757.88	1739.33	1732.79	1730.46	1729.63
105,000	1950.08	1923.59	1902.56	1885.77	1872.32	1861.51	1852.81	1845.78	1826.29	1819.43	1816.99	1816.11
110,000	2042.94	2015.19	1993.15	1975.57	1961.48	1950.15	1941.03	1933.67	1913.26	1906.07	1903.51	1902.60
115,000	2135.80	2106.79	2083.75	2065.36	2050.63	2038.80	2029.26	2021.57	2000.23	1992.71	1990.03	1989.08
120,000	2228.66	2190.39	2174.35	2155.10	2139.79	2127.44	2117.49	2109.46	2087.19	2079.35	2076.55	2075.56
125,000	2321.52	2289.99	2264.95	2244.96	2228.95	2216.08	2205.72	2197.35	2174.16	2165.98	2163.08	2162.04
130,000	2414.38	2381.59	2355.54	2334.76	2318.11	2304.73	2293.95	2285.25	2261.12	2252.62	2249.60	2248.52
135,000	2507.24	2473.19	2446.14	2424.56	2407.27	2393.37	2382.18	2373.14	2348.09	2339.26	2336.12	2335.00
140,000	2600.10	2564.79	2536.74	2514.36	2496.42	2482.01	2470.41	2461.04	2435.06	2425.90	2422.65	2421.48
145,000	2692.96	2656.39	2627.34	2604.15	2585.58	2570.66	2558.63	2548.93	2522.02	2512.54	2509.17	2507.97
150,000	2785.82	2747.99	2717.93	2693.95	2674.74	2659.30	2646.86	2636.82	2608.99	2599.18	2595.69	2594.45
155,000	2878.68	2839.59	2808.53	2783.75	2763.90	2747.94	2735.09	2724.72	2695.96	2685.82	2682.21	2680.93
160,000	2971.55	2931.18	2899.13	2873.55	2853.06	2836.59	2823.32	2812.61	2782.92	2772.46	2768.74	2767.41
165,000	3064.41	3022.78	2989.73	2963.35	2942.21	2925.23	2911.55	2900.51	2869.89	2859.10	2855.26	2853.89
170,000	3157.27	3114.38	3080.33	3053.15	3031.37	3013.87	2999.78	2988.40	2956.85	2945.74	2941.78	2940.37
175,000	3250.13	3205.98	3170.92	3142.94	3120.53	3102.52	3088.01	3076.29	3043.82	3032.38	3028.31	3026.85
180,000	3342.99	3297.58	3261.52	3232.74	3209.69	3191.16	3176.23	3164.19	3130.79	3119.02	3114.83	3113.34
185,000	3435.85	3389.18	3352.12	3322.54	3298.84	3279.80	3264.46	3252.08	3217.75	3205.66	3201.35	3199.82
190,000	3528.71	3480.78	3442.72	3412.34	3388.00	3368.45	3352.69	3339.98	3304.72	3292.29	3287.88	3286.30
195,000	3621.57	3572.38	3533.31	3502.14	3477.16	3457.09	3440.92	3427.87	3391.68	3378.93	3374.40	3372.78
200,000	3714.43	3663.98	3623.91	3591.93	3566.32	3545.73	3529.15	3515.76	3478.65	3465.57	3460.92	3459.26
205,000	3807.29	3755.58	3714.51	3681.73	3655.48	3634.38	3617.38	3603.66	3565.62	3552.21	3547.44	3545.74
210,000	3900.15	3847.18	3805.11	3771.53	3744.63	3723.02	3705.61	3691.55	3652.58	3638.85	3633.97	3632.22
215,000	3993.01	3938.78	3895.70	3861.33	3833.79	3811.66	3793.83	3779.45	3739.55	3725.49	3720.49	3718.71
220,000	4085.87	4030.38	3986.30	3951.13	3922.95	3900.30	3882.06	3867.34	3826.52	3812.13	3807.01	3805.19
225,000	4178.73	4121.98	4076.90	4040.93	4012.11	3988.95	3970.29	3955.23	3913.48	3898.77	3893.54	3891.67
230,000	4271.59	4213.58	4167.50	4130.72	4101.26	4077.59	4058.52	4043.13	4000.45	3985.41	3980.06	3978.15
235,000	4364.45	4305.18	4258.09	4220.52	4190.42	4166.23	4146.75	4131.02	4087.41	4072.05	4066.58	4064.63
240,000	4457.32	4396.77	4348.69	4310.32	4279.58	4254.88	4234.98	4218.92	4174.38	4158.69	4153.10	4151.11
245,000	4550.18	4488.37	4439.29	4400.12	4368.74	4343.52	4323.21	4306.81	4261.35	4245.33	4239.63	4237.59
250,000	4643.04	4579.97	4529.89	4489.92	4457.90	4432.16	4411.43	4394.70	4348.31	4331.96	4326.15	4324.08
255,000	4735.90	4671.57	4620.49	4579.72	4547.05	4520.81	4499.66	4482.60	4435.28	4418.60	4412.67	4410.56
260,000	4828.76	4763.17	4711.08	4669.51	4636.21	4609.45	4587.89	4570.49	4522.24	4505.24	4499.20	4497.04
265,000	4921.62	4854.77	4801.68	4759.31	4725.37	4698.09	4676.12	4658.38	4609.21	4591.88	4585.72	4583.52
270,000	5014.48	4946.37	4892.28	4849.11	4814.53	4786.74	4764.35	4746.28	4696.18	4678.52	4672.24	4670.00
280,000	5200.20	5129.57	5073.47	5028.71	4992.84	4964.02	4940.81	4922.07	4870.11	4851.80	4845.29	4842.96
290,000	5385.92	5312.77	5254.67	5208.30	5171.16	5141.31	5117.26	5097.85	5044.04	5025.08	5018.33	5015.93
300,000	5571.64	5495.97	5435.86	5387.90	5349.47	5318.60	5293.72	5273.64	5217.97	5198.36	5191.38	5188.89

21.00% MONTHLY AMORTIZING PAYMENTS

AMOUNT OF LOAN	NUMBER OF YEARS IN TERM											
	1	2	3	4	5	6	7	8	9	10	11	12
$ 50	4.66	2.57	1.89	1.55	1.36	1.23	1.15	1.08	1.04	1.00	0.98	0.96
100	9.32	5.14	3.77	3.10	2.71	2.46	2.29	2.16	2.07	2.00	1.95	1.91
200	18.63	10.28	7.54	6.20	5.42	4.91	4.57	4.32	4.14	4.00	3.90	3.82
300	27.94	15.42	11.31	9.29	8.12	7.37	6.85	6.48	6.21	6.00	5.85	5.73
400	37.25	20.56	15.08	12.39	10.83	9.82	9.13	8.64	8.27	8.00	7.79	7.63
500	46.56	25.70	18.84	15.49	13.53	12.27	11.41	10.80	10.34	10.00	9.74	9.54
600	55.87	30.84	22.61	18.58	16.24	14.73	13.69	12.95	12.41	12.00	11.69	11.45
700	65.18	35.97	26.38	21.68	18.94	17.18	15.97	15.11	14.48	14.00	13.64	13.35
800	74.50	41.11	30.15	24.78	21.65	19.63	18.25	17.27	16.54	16.00	15.58	15.26
900	83.81	46.25	33.91	27.87	24.35	22.09	20.54	19.43	18.61	18.00	17.53	17.17
1,000	93.12	51.39	37.68	30.97	27.06	24.54	22.82	21.59	20.68	20.00	19.48	19.07
2,000	186.23	102.78	75.36	61.94	54.11	49.08	45.63	43.17	41.35	39.99	38.95	38.14
3,000	279.35	154.16	113.03	92.90	81.17	73.61	68.44	64.75	62.03	59.98	58.42	57.21
4,000	372.46	205.55	150.71	123.87	108.22	98.15	91.25	86.33	82.70	79.98	77.89	76.28
5,000	465.57	256.93	188.38	154.83	135.27	122.68	114.07	107.91	103.38	99.97	97.36	95.35
6,000	558.69	308.32	226.06	185.80	162.33	147.22	136.88	129.49	124.05	119.96	116.84	114.41
7,000	651.80	359.70	263.73	216.76	189.38	171.76	159.69	151.07	144.73	139.96	136.31	133.48
8,000	744.92	411.09	301.41	247.73	216.43	196.29	182.50	172.65	165.40	159.95	155.78	152.55
9,000	838.03	462.48	339.08	278.70	243.49	220.83	205.32	194.23	186.08	179.94	175.25	171.62
10,000	931.14	513.86	376.76	309.66	270.54	245.36	228.13	215.82	206.75	199.94	194.72	190.69
15,000	1396.71	770.79	565.13	464.49	405.81	368.04	342.19	323.72	310.13	299.90	292.08	286.03
20,000	1862.28	1027.72	753.51	619.32	541.07	490.72	456.25	431.63	413.50	399.87	389.44	381.37
25,000	2327.85	1284.65	941.88	774.15	676.34	613.40	570.31	539.53	516.88	499.83	486.80	476.71
30,000	2793.42	1541.57	1130.26	928.98	811.61	736.08	684.37	647.44	620.25	599.80	584.16	572.05
35,000	3258.99	1798.50	1318.63	1083.80	946.87	858.76	798.43	755.34	723.63	699.77	681.52	667.39
40,000	3724.56	2055.43	1507.01	1238.63	1082.14	981.44	912.49	863.25	827.00	799.73	778.88	762.73
45,000	4190.12	2312.36	1695.38	1393.46	1217.41	1104.12	1026.56	971.15	930.37	899.70	876.24	858.07
50,000	4655.69	2569.29	1883.76	1548.29	1352.67	1226.80	1140.62	1079.06	1033.75	999.66	973.60	953.41
55,000	5121.26	2826.22	2072.13	1703.12	1487.94	1349.48	1254.68	1186.96	1137.12	1099.63	1070.95	1048.75
60,000	5586.83	3083.14	2260.51	1857.95	1623.21	1472.16	1368.74	1294.87	1240.50	1199.60	1168.31	1144.09
65,000	6052.40	3340.07	2448.88	2012.78	1758.47	1594.84	1482.80	1402.77	1343.87	1299.56	1265.67	1239.43
70,000	6517.97	3597.00	2637.26	2167.60	1893.74	1717.52	1596.86	1510.68	1447.25	1399.53	1363.03	1334.77
75,000	6983.54	3853.93	2825.64	2322.43	2029.01	1840.20	1710.92	1618.58	1550.62	1499.49	1460.39	1430.11
80,000	7449.11	4110.86	3014.01	2477.26	2164.27	1962.88	1824.98	1726.49	1653.99	1599.46	1557.75	1525.45
85,000	7914.68	4367.79	3202.39	2632.09	2299.54	2085.56	1939.04	1834.39	1757.37	1699.42	1655.11	1620.79
90,000	8380.24	4624.71	3390.76	2786.92	2434.81	2208.24	2053.11	1942.30	1860.74	1799.39	1752.47	1716.13
95,000	8845.81	4881.64	3579.14	2941.75	2570.07	2330.92	2167.17	2050.20	1964.12	1899.36	1849.83	1811.47
100,000	9311.38	5138.57	3767.51	3096.57	2705.34	2453.60	2281.23	2158.11	2067.49	1999.32	1947.19	1906.81
105,000	9776.95	5395.50	3955.89	3251.40	2840.61	2576.28	2395.29	2266.01	2170.87	2099.29	2044.54	2002.15
110,000	10242.52	5652.43	4144.26	3406.23	2975.87	2698.96	2509.35	2373.92	2274.24	2199.25	2141.90	2097.49
115,000	10708.09	5909.35	4332.64	3561.06	3111.14	2821.64	2623.41	2481.82	2377.61	2299.22	2239.26	2192.83
120,000	11173.66	6166.28	4521.01	3715.89	3246.41	2944.32	2737.47	2589.73	2480.99	2399.19	2336.62	2288.17
125,000	11639.23	6423.21	4709.39	3870.72	3381.67	3067.00	2851.53	2697.63	2584.36	2499.15	2433.98	2383.51
130,000	12104.80	6680.14	4897.76	4025.55	3516.94	3189.68	2965.59	2805.54	2687.74	2599.12	2531.34	2478.85
135,000	12570.36	6937.07	5086.14	4180.37	3652.21	3312.36	3079.66	2913.44	2791.11	2699.08	2628.70	2574.19
140,000	13035.93	7194.00	5274.51	4335.20	3787.48	3435.04	3193.72	3021.35	2894.49	2799.05	2726.06	2669.53
145,000	13501.50	7450.92	5462.89	4490.03	3922.74	3557.72	3307.78	3129.25	2997.86	2899.01	2823.42	2764.87
150,000	13967.07	7707.85	5651.27	4644.86	4058.01	3680.40	3421.84	3237.16	3101.24	2998.98	2920.78	2860.21
155,000	14432.64	7964.78	5839.64	4799.69	4193.28	3803.08	3535.90	3345.06	3204.61	3098.95	3018.13	2955.55
160,000	14898.21	8221.71	6028.02	4954.52	4328.54	3925.76	3649.96	3452.97	3307.98	3198.91	3115.49	3050.89
165,000	15363.78	8478.64	6216.39	5109.34	4463.81	4048.44	3764.02	3560.87	3411.36	3298.88	3212.85	3146.23
170,000	15829.35	8735.57	6404.77	5264.17	4599.08	4171.12	3878.08	3668.78	3514.73	3398.84	3310.21	3241.57
175,000	16294.92	8992.49	6593.14	5419.00	4734.34	4293.80	3992.14	3776.68	3618.11	3498.81	3407.57	3336.91
180,000	16760.48	9249.42	6781.52	5573.83	4869.61	4416.48	4106.21	3884.59	3721.48	3598.78	3504.93	3432.25
185,000	17226.05	9506.35	6969.89	5728.66	5004.88	4539.16	4220.27	3992.49	3824.86	3698.74	3602.29	3527.59
190,000	17691.62	9763.28	7158.27	5883.49	5140.14	4661.84	4334.33	4100.40	3928.23	3798.71	3699.65	3622.93
195,000	18157.19	10020.21	7346.64	6038.32	5275.41	4784.52	4448.39	4208.30	4031.60	3898.67	3797.01	3718.27
200,000	18622.76	10277.14	7535.02	6193.14	5410.68	4907.20	4562.45	4316.21	4134.98	3998.64	3894.37	3813.61
205,000	19088.33	10534.06	7723.39	6347.97	5545.94	5029.88	4676.51	4424.11	4238.35	4098.60	3991.72	3908.95
210,000	19553.90	10790.99	7911.77	6502.80	5681.21	5152.56	4790.57	4532.02	4341.73	4198.57	4089.08	4004.29
215,000	20019.47	11047.92	8100.14	6657.63	5816.48	5275.24	4904.63	4639.92	4445.10	4298.54	4186.44	4099.63
220,000	20485.04	11304.85	8288.52	6812.46	5951.74	5397.92	5018.69	4747.83	4548.48	4398.50	4283.80	4194.97
225,000	20950.60	11561.78	8476.90	6967.29	6087.01	5520.60	5132.76	4855.73	4651.85	4498.47	4381.16	4290.31
230,000	21416.17	11818.70	8665.27	7122.11	6222.28	5643.28	5246.82	4963.64	4755.22	4598.43	4478.52	4385.65
235,000	21881.74	12075.63	8853.65	7276.94	6357.54	5765.96	5360.88	5071.54	4858.60	4698.40	4575.88	4480.99
240,000	22347.31	12332.56	9042.02	7431.77	6492.81	5888.64	5474.94	5179.45	4961.97	4798.37	4673.24	4576.33
245,000	22812.88	12589.49	9230.40	7586.60	6628.08	6011.32	5589.00	5287.35	5065.35	4898.33	4770.60	4671.67
250,000	23278.45	12846.42	9418.77	7741.43	6763.34	6134.00	5703.06	5395.26	5168.72	4998.30	4867.96	4767.01
255,000	23744.02	13103.35	9607.15	7896.26	6898.61	6256.68	5817.12	5503.16	5272.10	5098.26	4965.31	4862.35
260,000	24209.59	13360.27	9795.52	8051.09	7033.88	6379.36	5931.18	5611.07	5375.47	5198.23	5062.67	4957.69
265,000	24675.16	13617.20	9983.90	8205.91	7169.15	6502.04	6045.24	5718.97	5478.84	5298.19	5160.03	5053.03
270,000	25140.72	13874.13	10172.27	8360.74	7304.41	6624.72	6159.31	5826.88	5582.22	5398.16	5257.39	5148.37
280,000	26071.86	14387.99	10549.02	8670.40	7574.95	6870.08	6387.43	6042.69	5788.97	5598.09	5452.11	5339.05
290,000	27003.00	14901.84	10925.77	8980.06	7845.48	7115.44	6615.55	6258.50	5995.72	5798.02	5646.83	5529.73
300,000	27934.14	15415.70	11302.53	9289.71	8116.01	7360.80	6843.67	6474.31	6202.47	5997.96	5841.55	5720.41

AMOUNT OF LOAN	NUMBER OF YEARS IN TERM											
	13	14	15	16	17	18	19	20	25	30	35	40
$ 50	0.94	0.93	0.92	0.91	0.91	0.90	0.90	0.89	0.88	0.88	0.88	0.88
100	1.88	1.86	1.84	1.82	1.81	1.80	1.79	1.78	1.76	1.76	1.76	1.76
200	3.76	3.71	3.67	3.63	3.61	3.59	3.57	3.56	3.52	3.51	3.51	3.51
300	5.63	5.56	5.50	5.45	5.41	5.38	5.36	5.34	5.28	5.27	5.26	5.26
400	7.51	7.41	7.33	7.26	7.21	7.17	7.14	7.12	7.04	7.02	7.01	7.01
500	9.38	9.26	9.16	9.08	9.02	8.97	8.93	8.89	8.80	8.77	8.76	8.76
600	11.26	11.11	10.99	10.89	10.82	10.76	10.71	10.67	10.56	10.53	10.51	10.51
700	13.13	12.96	12.82	12.71	12.62	12.55	12.49	12.45	12.32	12.28	12.26	12.26
800	15.01	14.81	14.65	14.52	14.42	14.34	14.28	14.23	14.08	14.03	14.01	14.01
900	16.88	16.66	16.48	16.34	16.23	16.14	16.06	16.00	15.84	15.79	15.77	15.76
1,000	18.76	18.51	18.31	18.15	18.03	17.93	17.85	17.78	17.60	17.54	17.52	17.51
2,000	37.51	37.01	36.62	36.30	36.05	35.85	35.69	35.56	35.20	35.07	35.03	35.01
3,000	56.26	55.52	54.92	54.45	54.08	53.77	53.53	53.33	52.79	52.61	52.54	52.52
4,000	75.01	74.02	73.23	72.60	72.10	71.70	71.37	71.11	70.39	70.14	70.05	70.02
5,000	93.77	92.52	91.54	90.75	90.12	89.62	89.21	88.89	87.99	87.68	87.56	87.53
6,000	112.52	111.03	109.84	108.90	108.15	107.54	107.05	106.66	105.58	105.21	105.08	105.03
7,000	131.27	129.53	128.15	127.05	126.17	125.46	124.90	124.44	123.18	122.74	122.59	122.53
8,000	150.02	148.03	146.45	145.20	144.19	143.39	142.74	142.22	140.78	140.28	140.10	140.04
9,000	168.78	166.54	164.76	163.35	162.22	161.31	160.58	159.99	158.37	157.81	157.61	157.54
10,000	187.53	185.04	183.07	181.49	180.24	179.23	178.42	177.77	175.97	175.35	175.12	175.05
15,000	281.29	277.56	274.60	272.24	270.36	268.84	267.63	266.65	263.95	263.02	262.68	262.57
20,000	375.05	370.07	366.13	362.98	360.47	358.46	356.84	355.53	351.94	350.69	350.24	350.09
25,000	468.81	462.59	457.66	453.73	450.59	448.07	446.05	444.42	439.92	438.36	437.80	437.61
30,000	562.57	555.11	549.19	544.47	540.71	537.68	535.25	533.30	527.90	526.03	525.36	525.13
35,000	656.33	647.62	640.72	635.22	630.82	627.30	624.46	622.18	615.89	613.70	612.92	612.65
40,000	750.09	740.14	732.25	725.96	720.94	716.91	713.67	711.06	703.87	701.37	700.48	700.17
45,000	843.86	832.66	823.78	816.71	811.06	806.52	802.89	799.94	791.85	789.04	788.04	787.70
50,000	937.62	925.17	915.31	907.45	901.17	896.14	892.09	888.83	879.84	876.71	875.60	875.22
55,000	1031.38	1017.69	1006.84	998.20	991.29	985.75	981.30	977.71	967.82	964.38	963.16	962.74
60,000	1125.14	1110.21	1098.37	1088.94	1081.41	1075.36	1070.50	1066.59	1055.80	1052.05	1050.72	1050.26
65,000	1218.90	1202.73	1189.90	1179.69	1171.52	1164.98	1159.71	1155.47	1143.79	1139.72	1138.28	1137.78
70,000	1312.66	1295.24	1281.43	1270.43	1261.64	1254.59	1248.92	1244.36	1231.77	1227.39	1225.84	1225.30
75,000	1406.42	1387.76	1372.96	1361.18	1351.76	1344.20	1338.13	1333.24	1319.75	1315.06	1313.40	1312.82
80,000	1500.18	1480.28	1464.49	1451.92	1441.88	1433.82	1427.34	1422.12	1407.74	1402.73	1400.96	1400.34
85,000	1593.94	1572.79	1556.03	1542.67	1531.99	1523.43	1516.55	1511.00	1495.72	1490.40	1488.52	1487.86
90,000	1687.71	1665.31	1647.56	1633.41	1622.11	1613.04	1605.75	1599.88	1583.70	1578.07	1576.08	1575.39
95,000	1781.47	1757.83	1739.09	1724.16	1712.23	1702.66	1694.96	1688.77	1671.68	1665.74	1663.64	1662.91
100,000	1875.23	1850.34	1830.62	1814.90	1802.34	1792.27	1784.17	1777.65	1759.67	1753.41	1751.20	1750.43
105,000	1968.99	1942.86	1922.15	1905.65	1892.46	1881.88	1873.38	1866.53	1847.65	1841.08	1838.76	1837.95
110,000	2062.75	2035.38	2013.68	1996.39	1982.58	1971.50	1962.59	1955.41	1935.63	1928.75	1926.32	1925.47
115,000	2156.51	2127.89	2105.21	2087.14	2072.69	2061.11	2051.80	2044.29	2023.62	2016.42	2013.88	2012.99
120,000	2250.27	2220.41	2196.74	2177.88	2162.81	2150.72	2141.00	2133.18	2111.60	2104.09	2101.44	2100.51
125,000	2344.03	2312.93	2288.27	2268.63	2252.93	2240.33	2230.21	2222.06	2199.58	2191.76	2189.00	2188.03
130,000	2437.79	2405.45	2379.80	2359.37	2343.04	2329.95	2319.42	2310.94	2287.57	2279.43	2276.56	2275.55
135,000	2531.56	2497.96	2471.33	2450.12	2433.16	2419.56	2408.63	2399.82	2375.55	2367.10	2364.12	2363.08
140,000	2625.32	2590.48	2562.86	2540.86	2523.28	2509.17	2497.84	2488.71	2463.53	2454.77	2451.68	2450.60
145,000	2719.08	2683.00	2654.39	2631.61	2613.39	2598.79	2587.04	2577.59	2551.52	2542.44	2539.24	2538.12
150,000	2812.84	2775.51	2745.92	2722.35	2703.51	2688.40	2676.25	2666.47	2639.50	2630.11	2626.80	2625.64
155,000	2906.60	2868.03	2837.45	2813.10	2793.63	2778.01	2765.46	2755.35	2727.48	2717.78	2714.36	2713.16
160,000	3000.36	2960.55	2928.98	2903.84	2883.75	2867.63	2854.67	2844.23	2815.47	2805.45	2801.92	2800.68
165,000	3094.12	3053.06	3020.52	2994.59	2973.86	2957.24	2943.88	2933.12	2903.45	2893.12	2889.48	2888.20
170,000	3187.88	3145.58	3112.05	3085.33	3063.98	3046.85	3033.09	3022.00	2991.43	2980.79	2977.04	2975.72
175,000	3281.65	3238.10	3203.58	3176.08	3154.10	3136.47	3122.29	3110.88	3079.41	3068.46	3064.60	3063.25
180,000	3375.41	3330.61	3295.11	3266.82	3244.21	3226.08	3211.50	3199.76	3167.40	3156.13	3152.16	3150.77
185,000	3469.17	3423.13	3386.64	3357.57	3334.33	3315.69	3300.71	3288.64	3255.38	3243.80	3239.72	3238.29
190,000	3562.93	3515.65	3478.17	3448.31	3424.45	3405.31	3389.92	3377.53	3343.36	3331.47	3327.28	3325.81
195,000	3656.69	3608.17	3569.70	3539.06	3514.56	3494.92	3479.13	3466.41	3431.35	3419.14	3414.84	3413.33
200,000	3750.45	3700.68	3661.23	3629.80	3604.68	3584.53	3568.34	3555.29	3519.33	3506.81	3502.40	3500.85
205,000	3844.21	3793.20	3752.76	3720.55	3694.80	3674.15	3657.54	3644.17	3607.31	3594.48	3589.96	3588.37
210,000	3937.97	3885.72	3844.29	3811.29	3784.91	3763.76	3746.75	3733.06	3695.30	3682.15	3677.52	3675.89
215,000	4031.73	3978.23	3935.82	3902.04	3875.03	3853.37	3835.96	3821.94	3783.28	3769.82	3765.08	3763.42
220,000	4125.50	4070.75	4027.35	3992.78	3965.15	3942.99	3925.17	3910.82	3871.26	3857.49	3852.64	3850.94
225,000	4219.26	4163.27	4118.88	4083.53	4055.26	4032.60	4014.38	3999.70	3959.25	3945.16	3940.20	3938.46
230,000	4313.02	4255.78	4210.41	4174.27	4145.38	4122.21	4103.59	4088.58	4047.23	4032.83	4027.76	4025.98
235,000	4406.78	4348.30	4301.94	4265.02	4235.50	4211.82	4192.79	4177.47	4135.21	4120.50	4115.32	4113.50
240,000	4500.54	4440.82	4393.47	4355.76	4325.62	4301.44	4282.00	4266.35	4223.20	4208.17	4202.88	4201.02
245,000	4594.30	4533.34	4485.01	4446.51	4415.73	4391.05	4371.21	4355.23	4311.18	4295.84	4290.44	4288.54
250,000	4688.06	4625.85	4576.54	4537.25	4505.85	4480.66	4460.42	4444.11	4399.16	4383.51	4378.00	4376.06
255,000	4781.82	4718.37	4668.07	4628.00	4595.97	4570.28	4549.63	4532.99	4487.15	4471.18	4465.56	4463.58
260,000	4875.58	4810.89	4759.60	4718.74	4686.08	4659.89	4638.84	4621.88	4575.13	4558.85	4553.12	4551.11
265,000	4969.35	4903.40	4851.13	4809.49	4776.20	4749.50	4728.04	4710.76	4663.11	4646.52	4640.68	4638.63
270,000	5063.11	4995.92	4942.66	4900.23	4866.32	4839.12	4817.25	4799.64	4751.09	4734.19	4728.24	4726.15
280,000	5250.63	5180.95	5125.72	5081.72	5046.55	5018.34	4995.67	4977.41	4927.06	4909.53	4903.36	4901.19
290,000	5438.15	5365.99	5308.78	5263.21	5226.78	5197.57	5174.08	5155.17	5103.03	5084.87	5078.48	5076.23
300,000	5625.67	5551.02	5491.84	5444.70	5407.02	5376.80	5352.50	5332.93	5278.99	5260.21	5253.60	5251.27

MONTHLY AMORTIZING PAYMENTS

AMOUNT OF LOAN	NUMBER OF YEARS IN TERM											
	1	2	3	4	5	6	7	8	9	10	11	12
$ 50	4.67	2.58	1.90	1.56	1.36	1.24	1.15	1.09	1.05	1.01	0.99	0.97
100	9.33	5.16	3.79	3.12	2.72	2.47	2.30	2.18	2.09	2.02	1.97	1.93
200	18.65	10.31	7.57	6.23	5.44	4.94	4.60	4.35	4.17	4.04	3.93	3.85
300	27.98	15.46	11.35	9.34	8.16	7.41	6.89	6.53	6.26	6.05	5.90	5.78
400	37.30	20.61	15.13	12.45	10.88	9.88	9.19	8.70	8.34	8.07	7.86	7.70
500	46.62	25.76	18.91	15.56	13.60	12.35	11.49	10.87	10.42	10.09	9.83	9.63
600	55.95	30.91	22.69	18.67	16.32	14.81	13.78	13.05	12.51	12.10	11.79	11.55
700	65.27	36.06	26.47	21.78	19.04	17.28	16.08	15.22	14.59	14.12	13.76	13.48
800	74.59	41.21	30.25	24.89	21.76	19.75	18.38	17.40	16.68	16.13	15.72	15.40
900	83.92	46.36	34.03	28.00	24.48	22.22	20.67	19.57	18.76	18.15	17.69	17.33
1,000	93.24	51.51	37.81	31.11	27.20	24.69	22.97	21.74	20.84	20.17	19.65	19.25
2,000	186.47	103.02	75.61	62.21	54.39	49.37	45.93	43.48	41.68	40.33	39.29	38.49
3,000	279.71	154.53	113.42	93.31	81.59	74.05	68.90	65.22	62.52	60.49	58.94	57.74
4,000	372.94	206.04	151.22	124.41	108.78	98.74	91.86	86.96	83.36	80.65	78.58	76.98
5,000	466.17	257.55	189.02	155.51	135.98	123.42	114.83	108.70	104.20	100.81	98.23	96.23
6,000	559.41	309.06	226.83	186.61	163.17	148.10	137.79	130.44	125.03	120.97	117.87	115.47
7,000	652.64	360.56	264.63	217.71	190.36	172.79	160.76	152.18	145.87	141.14	137.52	134.72
8,000	745.88	412.07	302.43	248.81	217.56	197.47	183.72	173.92	166.71	161.30	157.16	153.96
9,000	839.11	463.58	340.24	279.91	244.75	222.15	206.69	195.66	187.55	181.46	176.81	173.21
10,000	932.34	515.09	378.04	311.01	271.95	246.83	229.65	217.40	208.39	201.62	196.45	192.45
15,000	1398.51	772.63	567.06	466.51	407.92	370.25	344.48	326.09	312.58	302.43	294.67	288.68
20,000	1864.68	1030.18	756.08	622.01	543.89	493.66	459.30	434.79	416.77	403.23	392.90	384.90
25,000	2330.85	1287.72	945.09	777.51	679.86	617.08	574.13	543.49	520.96	504.04	491.12	481.13
30,000	2797.02	1545.26	1134.11	933.01	815.83	740.49	688.95	652.18	625.15	604.85	589.34	577.35
35,000	3263.19	1802.80	1323.13	1088.52	951.80	863.91	803.78	760.88	729.35	705.66	687.57	673.58
40,000	3729.36	2060.35	1512.15	1244.02	1087.77	987.32	918.60	869.58	833.54	806.46	785.79	769.80
45,000	4195.53	2317.89	1701.16	1399.52	1223.74	1110.73	1033.43	978.27	937.73	907.27	884.01	866.03
50,000	4661.69	2575.43	1890.18	1555.02	1359.71	1234.15	1148.25	1086.97	1041.92	1008.08	982.23	962.25
55,000	5127.86	2832.97	2079.20	1710.52	1495.68	1357.56	1263.08	1195.66	1146.11	1108.89	1080.46	1058.48
60,000	5594.03	3090.52	2268.22	1866.02	1631.66	1480.98	1377.90	1304.36	1250.30	1209.69	1178.68	1154.70
65,000	6060.20	3348.06	2457.24	2021.53	1767.63	1604.39	1492.73	1413.06	1354.50	1310.50	1276.90	1250.92
70,000	6526.37	3605.60	2646.25	2177.03	1903.60	1727.81	1607.55	1521.75	1458.69	1411.31	1375.13	1347.15
75,000	6992.54	3863.14	2835.27	2332.53	2039.57	1851.22	1722.38	1630.45	1562.88	1512.12	1473.35	1443.37
80,000	7458.71	4120.69	3024.29	2488.03	2175.54	1974.64	1837.20	1739.15	1667.07	1612.92	1571.57	1539.60
85,000	7924.88	4378.23	3213.31	2643.53	2311.51	2098.05	1952.02	1847.84	1771.26	1713.73	1669.80	1635.82
90,000	8391.05	4635.77	3402.32	2799.03	2447.48	2221.46	2066.85	1956.54	1875.45	1814.54	1768.02	1732.05
95,000	8857.22	4893.32	3591.34	2954.54	2583.45	2344.88	2181.67	2065.23	1979.65	1915.35	1866.24	1828.27
100,000	9323.38	5150.86	3780.36	3110.04	2719.42	2468.29	2296.50	2173.93	2083.84	2016.15	1964.46	1924.50
105,000	9789.55	5408.40	3969.38	3265.54	2855.39	2591.71	2411.32	2282.63	2188.03	2116.96	2062.69	2020.72
110,000	10255.72	5665.94	4158.40	3421.04	2991.36	2715.12	2526.15	2391.32	2292.22	2217.77	2160.91	2116.95
115,000	10721.89	5923.49	4347.41	3576.54	3127.34	2838.54	2640.97	2500.02	2396.41	2318.57	2259.13	2213.17
120,000	11188.06	6181.03	4536.43	3732.04	3263.31	2961.95	2755.80	2608.72	2500.60	2419.38	2357.36	2309.40
125,000	11654.23	6438.57	4725.45	3887.54	3399.28	3085.37	2870.62	2717.41	2604.80	2520.19	2455.58	2405.62
130,000	12120.40	6696.11	4914.47	4043.05	3535.25	3208.78	2985.45	2826.11	2708.99	2621.00	2553.80	2501.84
135,000	12586.57	6953.66	5103.48	4198.55	3671.22	3332.19	3100.27	2934.81	2813.18	2721.80	2652.02	2598.07
140,000	13052.74	7211.20	5292.50	4354.05	3807.19	3455.61	3215.10	3043.50	2917.37	2822.61	2750.25	2694.29
145,000	13518.91	7468.74	5481.52	4509.55	3943.16	3579.02	3329.92	3152.20	3021.56	2923.42	2848.47	2790.52
150,000	13985.07	7726.28	5670.54	4665.05	4079.13	3702.44	3444.75	3260.89	3125.75	3024.23	2946.69	2886.74
155,000	14451.24	7983.83	5859.56	4820.55	4215.10	3825.85	3559.57	3369.59	3229.95	3125.03	3044.92	2982.97
160,000	14917.41	8241.37	6048.57	4976.06	4351.07	3949.27	3674.40	3478.29	3334.14	3225.84	3143.14	3079.19
165,000	15383.58	8498.91	6237.59	5131.56	4487.04	4072.68	3789.22	3586.98	3438.33	3326.65	3241.36	3175.42
170,000	15849.75	8756.45	6426.61	5287.06	4623.02	4196.09	3904.04	3695.68	3542.52	3427.46	3339.59	3271.64
175,000	16315.92	9014.00	6615.63	5442.56	4758.99	4319.51	4018.87	3804.38	3646.71	3528.26	3437.81	3367.87
180,000	16782.09	9271.54	6804.64	5598.06	4894.96	4442.92	4133.69	3913.07	3750.90	3629.07	3536.03	3464.09
185,000	17248.26	9529.08	6993.66	5753.56	5030.93	4566.34	4248.52	4021.77	3855.09	3729.88	3634.25	3560.31
190,000	17714.43	9786.63	7182.68	5909.07	5166.90	4689.75	4363.34	4130.46	3959.29	3830.69	3732.48	3656.54
195,000	18180.60	10044.17	7371.70	6064.57	5302.87	4813.17	4478.17	4239.16	4063.48	3931.49	3830.70	3752.76
200,000	18646.76	10301.71	7560.71	6220.07	5438.84	4936.58	4592.99	4347.86	4167.67	4032.30	3928.92	3848.99
205,000	19112.93	10559.25	7749.73	6375.57	5574.81	5060.00	4707.82	4456.55	4271.86	4133.11	4027.15	3945.21
210,000	19579.10	10816.80	7938.75	6531.07	5710.78	5183.41	4822.64	4565.25	4376.05	4233.91	4125.37	4041.44
215,000	20045.27	11074.34	8127.77	6686.57	5846.75	5306.82	4937.47	4673.95	4480.24	4334.72	4223.59	4137.66
220,000	20511.44	11331.88	8316.79	6842.08	5982.72	5430.24	5052.29	4782.64	4584.44	4435.53	4321.82	4233.89
225,000	20977.61	11589.42	8505.80	6997.58	6118.70	5553.65	5167.12	4891.34	4688.63	4536.34	4420.04	4330.11
230,000	21443.78	11846.97	8694.82	7153.08	6254.67	5677.07	5281.94	5000.04	4792.82	4637.14	4518.26	4426.34
235,000	21909.95	12104.51	8883.84	7308.58	6390.64	5800.48	5396.77	5108.73	4897.01	4737.95	4616.48	4522.56
240,000	22376.12	12362.05	9072.86	7464.08	6526.61	5923.90	5511.59	5217.43	5001.20	4838.76	4714.71	4618.79
245,000	22842.29	12619.59	9261.87	7619.58	6662.58	6047.31	5626.42	5326.12	5105.39	4939.57	4812.93	4715.01
250,000	23308.45	12877.14	9450.89	7775.08	6798.55	6170.73	5741.24	5434.82	5209.59	5040.37	4911.15	4811.23
255,000	23774.62	13134.68	9639.91	7930.59	6934.52	6294.14	5856.06	5543.52	5313.78	5141.18	5009.38	4907.46
260,000	24240.79	13392.22	9828.93	8086.09	7070.49	6417.55	5970.89	5652.21	5417.97	5241.99	5107.60	5003.68
265,000	24706.96	13649.76	10017.95	8241.59	7206.46	6540.97	6085.71	5760.91	5522.16	5342.80	5205.82	5099.91
270,000	25173.13	13907.31	10206.96	8397.09	7342.43	6664.38	6200.54	5869.61	5626.35	5443.60	5304.04	5196.13
280,000	26105.47	14422.39	10585.00	8708.09	7614.38	6911.21	6430.19	6087.00	5834.74	5645.22	5500.49	5388.58
290,000	27037.81	14937.48	10963.03	9019.10	7886.32	7158.04	6659.84	6304.39	6043.12	5846.83	5696.94	5581.03
300,000	27970.14	15452.56	11341.07	9330.10	8158.26	7404.87	6889.49	6521.78	6251.50	6048.45	5893.38	5773.48

AMOUNT OF LOAN	NUMBER OF YEARS IN TERM											
	13	14	15	16	17	18	19	20	25	30	35	40
$ 50	0.95	0.94	0.93	0.92	0.92	0.91	0.91	0.90	0.90	0.89	0.89	0.89
100	1.90	1.87	1.85	1.84	1.83	1.82	1.81	1.80	1.79	1.78	1.78	1.78
200	3.79	3.74	3.70	3.67	3.65	3.63	3.61	3.60	3.57	3.55	3.55	3.55
300	5.68	5.61	5.55	5.51	5.47	5.44	5.42	5.40	5.35	5.33	5.32	5.32
400	7.58	7.48	7.40	7.34	7.29	7.25	7.22	7.19	7.13	7.10	7.09	7.09
500	9.47	9.35	9.25	9.17	9.11	9.06	9.02	8.99	8.91	8.88	8.86	8.86
600	11.36	11.22	11.10	11.01	10.93	10.88	10.83	10.79	10.69	10.65	10.64	10.63
700	13.26	13.09	12.95	12.84	12.76	12.69	12.63	12.59	12.47	12.42	12.41	12.40
800	15.15	14.95	14.80	14.68	14.58	14.50	14.44	14.38	14.25	14.20	14.18	14.17
900	17.04	16.82	16.65	16.51	16.40	16.31	16.24	16.18	16.03	15.97	15.95	15.95
1,000	18.94	18.69	18.50	18.34	18.22	18.12	18.04	17.98	17.81	17.75	17.72	17.72
2,000	37.87	37.38	36.99	36.68	36.44	36.24	36.08	35.95	35.61	35.49	35.44	35.43
3,000	56.80	56.07	55.48	55.02	54.65	54.36	54.12	53.93	53.41	53.23	53.16	53.14
4,000	75.74	74.75	73.98	73.36	72.87	72.47	72.16	71.90	71.21	70.97	70.88	70.85
5,000	94.67	93.44	92.47	91.70	91.08	90.59	90.19	89.88	89.01	88.71	88.60	88.57
6,000	113.60	112.13	110.96	110.04	109.30	108.71	108.23	107.85	106.81	106.45	106.32	106.28
7,000	132.54	130.82	129.46	128.38	127.51	126.82	126.27	125.83	124.61	124.19	124.04	123.99
8,000	151.47	149.50	147.95	146.72	145.73	144.94	144.31	143.80	142.41	141.93	141.76	141.70
9,000	170.40	168.19	166.44	165.05	163.95	163.06	162.35	161.77	160.21	159.67	159.48	159.41
10,000	189.33	186.88	184.94	183.39	182.16	181.18	180.38	179.75	178.01	177.41	177.20	177.13
15,000	284.00	280.32	277.40	275.09	273.24	271.76	270.57	269.62	267.01	266.11	265.80	265.69
20,000	378.66	373.75	369.87	366.78	364.32	362.35	360.76	359.49	356.01	354.81	354.39	354.25
25,000	473.33	467.19	462.34	458.48	455.40	452.93	450.95	449.37	445.01	443.51	442.99	442.81
30,000	567.99	560.63	554.80	550.17	546.47	543.52	541.14	539.24	534.01	532.21	531.59	531.37
35,000	662.66	654.07	647.27	641.86	637.55	634.10	631.33	629.11	623.01	620.92	620.19	619.93
40,000	757.32	747.50	739.73	733.56	728.63	724.69	721.52	718.98	712.02	709.62	708.78	708.49
45,000	851.98	840.94	832.20	825.25	819.71	815.27	811.71	808.85	801.02	798.32	797.38	797.05
50,000	946.65	934.38	924.67	916.95	910.79	905.86	901.90	898.73	890.02	887.02	885.98	885.62
55,000	1041.31	1027.81	1017.13	1008.64	1001.87	996.44	992.09	988.60	979.02	975.72	974.58	974.18
60,000	1135.98	1121.25	1109.60	1100.34	1092.94	1087.03	1082.28	1078.47	1068.02	1064.42	1063.17	1062.74
65,000	1230.64	1214.69	1202.07	1192.03	1184.02	1177.61	1172.47	1168.34	1157.02	1153.12	1151.77	1151.30
70,000	1325.31	1308.13	1294.53	1283.72	1275.10	1268.20	1262.66	1258.22	1246.02	1241.83	1240.37	1239.86
75,000	1419.97	1401.56	1387.00	1375.42	1366.18	1358.79	1352.85	1348.09	1335.02	1330.53	1328.97	1328.42
80,000	1514.64	1495.00	1479.46	1467.11	1457.26	1449.37	1443.04	1437.96	1424.03	1419.23	1417.56	1416.98
85,000	1609.30	1588.44	1571.93	1558.81	1548.34	1539.96	1533.23	1527.83	1513.03	1507.93	1506.16	1505.54
90,000	1703.96	1681.87	1664.40	1650.50	1639.41	1630.54	1623.42	1617.70	1602.03	1596.63	1594.76	1594.10
95,000	1798.63	1775.31	1756.86	1742.20	1730.49	1721.13	1713.61	1707.58	1691.03	1685.33	1683.35	1682.67
100,000	1893.29	1868.75	1849.33	1833.89	1821.57	1811.71	1803.80	1797.45	1780.03	1774.03	1771.95	1771.23
105,000	1987.96	1962.19	1941.79	1925.58	1912.65	1902.30	1893.99	1887.32	1869.03	1862.74	1860.55	1859.79
110,000	2082.62	2055.62	2034.26	2017.28	2003.73	1992.88	1984.18	1977.19	1958.03	1951.44	1949.15	1948.35
115,000	2177.29	2149.06	2126.73	2108.97	2094.81	2083.47	2074.37	2067.07	2047.03	2040.14	2037.74	2036.91
120,000	2271.95	2242.50	2219.19	2200.07	2185.88	2174.05	2164.56	2156.94	2136.04	2128.84	2126.34	2125.47
125,000	2366.62	2335.94	2311.66	2292.36	2276.96	2264.64	2254.75	2246.81	2225.04	2217.54	2214.94	2214.03
130,000	2461.28	2429.37	2404.13	2384.05	2368.04	2355.22	2344.94	2336.68	2314.04	2306.24	2303.54	2302.59
135,000	2555.94	2522.81	2496.59	2475.75	2459.12	2445.81	2435.13	2426.55	2403.04	2394.94	2392.13	2391.15
140,000	2650.61	2616.25	2589.06	2567.44	2550.20	2536.40	2525.32	2516.43	2492.04	2483.65	2480.73	2479.72
145,000	2745.27	2709.68	2681.52	2659.14	2641.28	2626.98	2615.51	2606.30	2581.04	2572.35	2569.33	2568.28
150,000	2839.94	2803.12	2773.99	2750.83	2732.35	2717.57	2705.70	2696.17	2670.04	2661.05	2657.93	2656.84
155,000	2934.60	2896.56	2866.46	2842.53	2823.43	2808.15	2795.89	2786.04	2759.04	2749.75	2746.52	2745.40
160,000	3029.27	2990.00	2958.92	2934.22	2914.51	2898.74	2886.08	2875.92	2848.05	2838.45	2835.12	2833.96
165,000	3123.93	3083.43	3051.39	3025.91	3005.59	2989.32	2976.27	2965.79	2937.05	2927.15	2923.72	2922.52
170,000	3218.60	3176.87	3143.85	3117.61	3096.67	3079.91	3066.46	3055.66	3026.05	3015.85	3012.31	3011.08
175,000	3313.26	3270.31	3236.32	3209.30	3187.75	3170.49	3156.65	3145.53	3115.05	3104.56	3100.91	3099.64
180,000	3407.92	3363.74	3328.79	3301.00	3278.82	3261.08	3246.84	3235.40	3204.05	3193.26	3189.51	3188.20
185,000	3502.59	3457.18	3421.25	3392.69	3369.90	3351.66	3337.03	3325.28	3293.05	3281.96	3278.11	3276.76
190,000	3597.25	3550.62	3513.72	3484.39	3460.98	3442.25	3427.22	3415.15	3382.05	3370.66	3366.70	3365.33
195,000	3691.92	3644.06	3606.19	3576.08	3552.06	3532.83	3517.41	3505.02	3471.06	3459.36	3455.30	3453.89
200,000	3786.58	3737.49	3698.65	3667.77	3643.14	3623.42	3607.60	3594.89	3560.06	3548.06	3543.90	3542.45
205,000	3881.25	3830.93	3791.12	3759.47	3734.21	3714.01	3697.79	3684.77	3649.06	3636.76	3632.50	3631.01
210,000	3975.91	3924.37	3883.58	3851.16	3825.29	3804.59	3787.98	3774.64	3738.06	3725.47	3721.09	3719.57
215,000	4070.58	4017.80	3976.05	3942.86	3916.37	3895.18	3878.17	3864.51	3827.06	3814.17	3809.69	3808.13
220,000	4165.24	4111.24	4068.52	4034.55	4007.45	3985.76	3968.36	3954.38	3916.06	3902.87	3898.29	3896.69
225,000	4259.90	4204.68	4160.98	4126.24	4098.53	4076.35	4058.55	4044.25	4005.06	3991.57	3986.89	3985.25
230,000	4354.57	4298.12	4253.45	4217.94	4189.61	4166.93	4148.74	4134.13	4094.06	4080.27	4075.48	4073.81
235,000	4449.23	4391.55	4345.91	4309.63	4280.68	4257.52	4238.93	4224.00	4183.07	4168.97	4164.08	4162.38
240,000	4543.90	4484.99	4438.38	4401.33	4371.76	4348.10	4329.12	4313.87	4272.07	4257.67	4252.68	4250.94
245,000	4638.56	4578.43	4530.85	4493.02	4462.84	4438.69	4419.31	4403.74	4361.07	4346.38	4341.27	4339.50
250,000	4733.23	4671.87	4623.31	4584.72	4553.92	4529.27	4509.50	4493.62	4450.07	4435.08	4429.87	4428.06
255,000	4827.89	4765.30	4715.78	4676.41	4645.00	4619.86	4599.69	4583.49	4539.07	4523.78	4518.47	4516.62
260,000	4922.56	4858.74	4808.25	4768.10	4736.08	4710.44	4689.88	4673.36	4628.07	4612.48	4607.07	4605.18
265,000	5017.22	4952.18	4900.71	4859.80	4827.15	4801.03	4780.07	4763.23	4717.07	4701.18	4695.66	4693.74
270,000	5111.88	5045.61	4993.18	4951.49	4918.23	4891.62	4870.26	4853.10	4806.07	4789.88	4784.26	4782.30
280,000	5301.21	5232.49	5178.11	5134.88	5100.39	5072.79	5050.64	5032.85	4984.08	4967.29	4961.46	4959.43
290,000	5490.54	5419.36	5363.04	5318.27	5282.55	5253.96	5231.02	5212.59	5162.08	5144.69	5138.65	5136.55
300,000	5679.87	5606.24	5547.97	5501.66	5464.70	5435.13	5411.40	5392.34	5340.08	5322.09	5315.85	5313.67

21.50%　MONTHLY AMORTIZING PAYMENTS

AMOUNT OF LOAN	NUMBER OF YEARS IN TERM											
	1	2	3	4	5	6	7	8	9	10	11	12
$ 50	4.67	2.59	1.90	1.57	1.37	1.25	1.16	1.10	1.06	1.02	1.00	0.98
100	9.34	5.17	3.80	3.13	2.74	2.49	2.32	2.19	2.11	2.04	1.99	1.95
200	18.68	10.33	7.59	6.25	5.47	4.97	4.63	4.38	4.21	4.07	3.97	3.89
300	28.01	15.49	11.38	9.38	8.21	7.45	6.94	6.57	6.31	6.10	5.95	5.83
400	37.35	20.66	15.18	12.50	10.94	9.94	9.25	8.76	8.41	8.14	7.93	7.77
500	46.68	25.82	18.97	15.62	13.67	12.42	11.56	10.95	10.51	10.17	9.91	9.72
600	56.02	30.98	22.76	18.75	16.41	14.90	13.88	13.14	12.61	12.20	11.90	11.66
700	65.35	36.15	26.56	21.87	19.14	17.39	16.19	15.33	14.71	14.24	13.88	13.60
800	74.69	41.31	30.35	24.99	21.87	19.87	18.50	17.52	16.81	16.27	15.86	15.54
900	84.02	46.47	34.14	28.12	24.61	22.35	20.81	19.71	18.91	18.30	17.84	17.49
1,000	93.36	51.64	37.94	31.24	27.34	24.84	23.12	21.90	21.01	20.34	19.82	19.43
2,000	186.71	103.27	75.87	62.48	54.68	49.67	46.24	43.80	42.01	40.67	39.64	38.85
3,000	280.07	154.90	113.80	93.71	82.01	74.50	69.36	65.70	63.01	61.00	59.46	58.27
4,000	373.42	206.53	151.73	124.95	109.35	99.33	92.48	87.60	84.01	81.33	79.28	77.69
5,000	466.77	258.16	189.67	156.18	136.68	124.16	115.60	109.50	105.02	101.66	99.09	97.12
6,000	560.13	309.79	227.60	187.42	164.02	148.99	138.71	131.39	126.02	121.99	118.91	116.54
7,000	653.48	361.43	265.53	218.65	191.35	173.82	161.83	153.29	147.02	142.32	138.73	135.96
8,000	746.84	413.06	303.46	249.89	218.69	198.65	184.95	175.19	168.02	162.65	158.55	155.38
9,000	840.19	464.69	341.40	281.12	246.02	223.48	208.07	197.09	189.03	182.98	178.37	174.81
10,000	933.54	516.32	379.33	312.36	273.36	248.31	231.19	218.99	210.03	203.31	198.18	194.23
15,000	1400.31	774.48	568.99	468.53	410.04	372.46	346.78	328.48	315.04	304.96	297.27	291.34
20,000	1867.08	1032.64	758.65	624.71	546.71	496.61	462.37	437.97	420.05	406.61	396.36	388.45
25,000	2333.85	1290.79	948.31	780.89	683.39	620.76	577.96	547.46	525.06	508.26	495.45	485.56
30,000	2800.62	1548.95	1137.97	937.06	820.07	744.91	693.55	656.95	630.07	609.92	594.54	582.68
35,000	3267.39	1807.11	1327.63	1093.24	956.74	869.06	809.14	766.44	735.09	711.57	693.63	679.79
40,000	3734.16	2065.27	1517.30	1249.42	1093.42	993.21	924.73	875.93	840.10	813.22	792.72	776.90
45,000	4200.93	2323.43	1706.96	1405.59	1230.10	1117.36	1040.32	985.42	945.11	914.87	891.81	874.01
50,000	4667.70	2581.58	1896.62	1561.77	1366.77	1241.51	1155.91	1094.91	1050.12	1016.52	990.90	971.12
55,000	5134.47	2839.74	2086.28	1717.94	1503.45	1365.67	1271.50	1204.40	1155.13	1118.17	1089.99	1068.24
60,000	5601.24	3097.90	2275.94	1874.12	1640.13	1489.82	1387.09	1313.89	1260.14	1219.83	1189.08	1165.35
65,000	6068.01	3356.06	2465.60	2030.30	1776.80	1613.97	1502.68	1423.38	1365.16	1321.48	1288.17	1262.46
70,000	6534.78	3614.21	2655.26	2186.47	1913.48	1738.12	1618.27	1532.87	1470.17	1423.13	1387.26	1359.57
75,000	7001.55	3872.37	2844.93	2342.65	2050.16	1862.27	1733.87	1642.36	1575.18	1524.78	1486.35	1456.68
80,000	7468.32	4130.53	3034.59	2498.83	2186.84	1986.42	1849.46	1751.85	1680.19	1626.43	1585.44	1553.80
85,000	7935.09	4388.69	3224.25	2655.00	2323.51	2110.57	1965.05	1861.34	1785.20	1728.08	1684.53	1650.91
90,000	8401.86	4646.85	3413.91	2811.18	2460.19	2234.72	2080.64	1970.83	1890.21	1829.74	1783.62	1748.02
95,000	8868.63	4905.00	3603.57	2967.35	2596.87	2358.87	2196.23	2080.32	1995.23	1931.39	1882.71	1845.13
100,000	9335.40	5163.16	3793.23	3123.53	2733.54	2483.02	2311.82	2189.81	2100.24	2033.04	1981.80	1942.24
105,000	9802.17	5421.32	3982.89	3279.71	2870.22	2607.18	2427.41	2299.30	2205.25	2134.69	2080.89	2039.35
110,000	10268.94	5679.48	4172.56	3435.88	3006.90	2731.33	2543.00	2408.79	2310.26	2236.34	2179.98	2136.47
115,000	10735.70	5937.64	4362.22	3592.06	3143.57	2855.48	2658.59	2518.28	2415.27	2337.99	2279.07	2233.58
120,000	11202.47	6195.79	4551.88	3748.24	3280.25	2979.63	2774.18	2627.77	2520.28	2439.65	2378.16	2330.69
125,000	11669.24	6453.95	4741.54	3904.41	3416.93	3103.78	2889.77	2737.26	2625.29	2541.30	2477.25	2427.80
130,000	12136.01	6712.11	4931.20	4060.59	3553.60	3227.93	3005.36	2846.75	2730.31	2642.95	2576.34	2524.91
135,000	12602.78	6970.27	5120.86	4216.76	3690.28	3352.08	3120.95	2956.24	2835.32	2744.60	2675.43	2622.03
140,000	13069.55	7228.42	5310.52	4372.94	3826.96	3476.23	3236.54	3065.73	2940.33	2846.25	2774.52	2719.14
145,000	13536.32	7486.58	5500.18	4529.12	3963.64	3600.38	3352.13	3175.22	3045.34	2947.90	2873.61	2816.25
150,000	14003.09	7744.74	5689.85	4685.29	4100.31	3724.53	3467.72	3284.71	3150.35	3049.56	2972.70	2913.36
155,000	14469.86	8002.90	5879.51	4841.47	4236.99	3848.69	3583.32	3394.20	3255.36	3151.21	3071.79	3010.47
160,000	14936.63	8261.06	6069.17	4997.65	4373.67	3972.84	3698.91	3503.69	3360.38	3252.86	3170.88	3107.59
165,000	15403.40	8519.21	6258.83	5153.82	4510.34	4096.99	3814.50	3613.18	3465.39	3354.51	3269.97	3204.70
170,000	15870.17	8777.37	6448.49	5310.00	4647.02	4221.14	3930.09	3722.67	3570.40	3456.16	3369.05	3301.81
175,000	16336.94	9035.53	6638.15	5466.18	4783.70	4345.29	4045.68	3832.16	3675.41	3557.81	3468.14	3398.92
180,000	16803.71	9293.69	6827.81	5622.35	4920.37	4469.44	4161.27	3941.65	3780.42	3659.47	3567.23	3496.03
185,000	17270.48	9551.85	7017.48	5778.53	5057.05	4593.59	4276.86	4051.14	3885.43	3761.12	3666.32	3593.15
190,000	17737.25	9810.00	7207.14	5934.70	5193.73	4717.74	4392.45	4160.63	3990.45	3862.77	3765.41	3690.26
195,000	18204.02	10068.16	7396.80	6090.88	5330.40	4841.89	4508.04	4270.12	4095.46	3964.42	3864.50	3787.37
200,000	18670.79	10326.32	7586.46	6247.06	5467.08	4966.04	4623.63	4379.61	4200.47	4066.07	3963.59	3884.48
205,000	19137.56	10584.48	7776.12	6403.23	5603.76	5090.20	4739.22	4489.10	4305.48	4167.72	4062.68	3981.59
210,000	19604.33	10842.63	7965.78	6559.41	5740.43	5214.35	4854.81	4598.59	4410.49	4269.38	4161.77	4078.70
215,000	20071.10	11100.79	8155.44	6715.59	5877.11	5338.50	4970.40	4708.08	4515.50	4371.03	4260.86	4175.82
220,000	20537.87	11358.95	8345.11	6871.76	6013.79	5462.65	5085.99	4817.57	4620.52	4472.68	4359.95	4272.93
225,000	21004.63	11617.11	8534.77	7027.94	6150.47	5586.80	5201.59	4927.06	4725.53	4574.33	4459.04	4370.04
230,000	21471.40	11875.27	8724.43	7184.11	6287.14	5710.95	5317.18	5036.55	4830.54	4675.98	4558.13	4467.15
235,000	21938.17	12133.42	8914.09	7340.29	6423.82	5835.10	5432.77	5146.04	4935.55	4777.63	4657.22	4564.26
240,000	22404.94	12391.58	9103.75	7496.47	6560.50	5959.25	5548.36	5255.53	5040.56	4879.29	4756.31	4661.38
245,000	22871.71	12649.74	9293.41	7652.64	6697.17	6083.40	5663.95	5365.02	5145.57	4980.94	4855.40	4758.49
250,000	23338.48	12907.90	9483.07	7808.82	6833.85	6207.55	5779.54	5474.51	5250.58	5082.59	4954.49	4855.60
255,000	23805.25	13166.06	9672.73	7965.00	6970.53	6331.71	5895.13	5584.00	5355.60	5184.24	5053.58	4952.71
260,000	24272.02	13424.21	9862.40	8121.17	7107.20	6455.86	6010.72	5693.49	5460.61	5285.89	5152.67	5049.82
265,000	24738.79	13682.37	10052.06	8277.35	7243.88	6580.01	6126.31	5802.98	5565.62	5387.54	5251.76	5146.94
270,000	25205.56	13940.53	10241.72	8433.52	7380.56	6704.16	6241.90	5912.47	5670.63	5489.20	5350.85	5244.05
280,000	26139.10	14456.84	10621.04	8745.88	7653.91	6952.46	6473.08	6131.45	5880.65	5692.50	5549.03	5438.27
290,000	27072.64	14973.16	11000.36	9058.23	7927.27	7200.76	6704.26	6350.43	6090.68	5895.80	5747.21	5632.49
300,000	28006.18	15489.48	11379.69	9370.58	8200.62	7449.06	6935.45	6569.41	6300.70	6099.11	5945.39	5826.72

AMOUNT OF LOAN	NUMBER OF YEARS IN TERM											
	13	14	15	16	17	18	19	20	25	30	35	40
$ 50	0.96	0.95	0.94	0.93	0.93	0.92	0.92	0.91	0.91	0.90	0.90	0.90
100	1.92	1.89	1.87	1.86	1.85	1.84	1.83	1.82	1.81	1.80	1.80	1.80
200	3.83	3.78	3.74	3.71	3.69	3.67	3.65	3.64	3.61	3.59	3.59	3.59
300	5.74	5.67	5.61	5.56	5.53	5.50	5.48	5.46	5.41	5.39	5.38	5.38
400	7.65	7.55	7.48	7.42	7.37	7.33	7.30	7.27	7.21	7.18	7.18	7.17
500	9.56	9.44	9.35	9.27	9.21	9.16	9.12	9.09	9.01	8.98	8.97	8.97
600	11.47	11.33	11.21	11.12	11.05	10.99	10.95	10.91	10.81	10.77	10.76	10.76
700	13.38	13.22	13.08	12.98	12.89	12.82	12.77	12.73	12.61	12.57	12.55	12.55
800	15.30	15.10	14.95	14.83	14.73	14.65	14.59	14.54	14.41	14.36	14.35	14.34
900	17.21	16.99	16.82	16.68	16.57	16.49	16.42	16.36	16.21	16.16	16.14	16.13
1,000	19.12	18.88	18.69	18.53	18.41	18.32	18.24	18.18	18.01	17.95	17.93	17.93
2,000	38.23	37.75	37.37	37.06	36.82	36.63	36.47	36.35	36.01	35.90	35.86	35.85
3,000	57.35	56.62	56.05	55.59	55.23	54.94	54.71	54.52	54.02	53.85	53.79	53.77
4,000	76.46	75.49	74.73	74.12	73.64	73.25	72.94	72.70	72.02	71.79	71.71	71.69
5,000	95.58	94.37	93.41	92.65	92.05	91.56	91.18	90.87	90.03	89.74	89.64	89.61
6,000	114.69	113.24	112.09	111.18	110.46	109.88	109.41	109.04	108.03	107.69	107.57	107.53
7,000	133.80	132.11	130.77	129.71	128.86	128.19	127.65	127.21	126.03	125.63	125.49	125.45
8,000	152.92	150.98	149.45	148.24	147.27	146.50	145.88	145.39	144.04	143.58	143.42	143.37
9,000	172.03	169.85	168.13	166.77	165.68	164.81	164.12	163.56	162.04	161.53	161.35	161.29
10,000	191.15	188.73	186.81	185.30	184.09	183.12	182.35	181.73	180.05	179.47	179.28	179.21
15,000	286.72	283.09	280.22	277.94	276.13	274.68	273.53	272.60	270.07	269.21	268.91	268.81
20,000	382.29	377.45	373.62	370.59	368.17	366.24	364.70	363.46	360.09	358.94	358.55	358.41
25,000	477.86	471.81	467.03	463.23	460.21	457.80	455.87	454.33	450.11	448.67	448.18	448.01
30,000	573.43	566.17	560.43	555.88	552.26	549.36	547.05	545.19	540.13	538.41	537.82	537.61
35,000	669.00	660.53	653.83	648.53	644.30	640.92	638.22	636.05	630.15	628.14	627.45	627.21
40,000	764.57	754.89	747.24	741.17	736.34	732.48	729.39	726.92	720.17	717.87	717.09	716.81
45,000	860.14	849.25	840.64	833.82	828.38	824.04	820.57	817.78	810.19	807.61	806.72	806.42
50,000	955.71	943.61	934.05	926.46	920.42	915.60	911.74	908.65	900.21	897.34	896.36	896.02
55,000	1051.28	1037.97	1027.45	1019.11	1012.47	1007.16	1002.92	999.51	990.23	987.07	985.99	985.62
60,000	1146.85	1132.33	1120.86	1111.76	1104.51	1098.72	1094.09	1090.37	1080.25	1076.81	1075.63	1075.22
65,000	1242.42	1226.69	1214.26	1204.40	1196.55	1190.28	1185.26	1181.24	1170.27	1166.54	1165.26	1164.82
70,000	1337.99	1321.05	1307.66	1297.05	1288.59	1281.84	1276.44	1272.10	1260.29	1256.27	1254.90	1254.42
75,000	1433.56	1415.41	1401.07	1389.69	1380.63	1373.40	1367.61	1362.97	1350.31	1346.01	1344.53	1344.02
80,000	1529.13	1509.77	1494.47	1482.34	1472.68	1464.96	1458.78	1453.83	1440.33	1435.74	1434.17	1433.62
85,000	1624.70	1604.13	1587.88	1574.98	1564.72	1556.52	1549.96	1544.69	1530.35	1525.47	1523.80	1523.22
90,000	1720.27	1698.49	1681.28	1667.63	1656.76	1648.08	1641.13	1635.56	1620.37	1615.21	1613.44	1612.83
95,000	1815.84	1792.85	1774.69	1760.28	1748.80	1739.64	1732.30	1726.42	1710.40	1704.94	1703.07	1702.43
100,000	1911.41	1887.21	1868.09	1852.92	1840.84	1831.20	1823.48	1817.29	1800.42	1794.67	1792.71	1792.03
105,000	2006.98	1981.57	1961.49	1945.57	1932.89	1922.76	1914.65	1908.15	1890.44	1884.41	1882.34	1881.63
110,000	2102.55	2075.93	2054.90	2038.21	2024.93	2014.32	2005.83	1999.01	1980.46	1974.14	1971.98	1971.23
115,000	2198.12	2170.29	2148.30	2130.86	2116.97	2105.88	2097.00	2089.88	2070.48	2063.88	2061.61	2060.83
120,000	2293.70	2264.65	2241.71	2223.51	2209.01	2197.44	2188.17	2180.74	2160.50	2153.61	2151.25	2150.43
125,000	2389.27	2359.01	2335.11	2316.15	2301.05	2289.00	2279.35	2271.61	2250.52	2243.34	2240.88	2240.03
130,000	2484.84	2453.37	2428.52	2408.80	2393.10	2380.56	2370.52	2362.47	2340.54	2333.08	2330.52	2329.63
135,000	2580.41	2547.73	2521.92	2501.44	2485.14	2472.12	2461.69	2453.33	2430.56	2422.81	2420.15	2419.24
140,000	2675.98	2642.09	2615.32	2594.09	2577.18	2563.68	2552.87	2544.20	2520.58	2512.54	2509.79	2508.84
145,000	2771.55	2736.45	2708.73	2686.73	2669.22	2655.24	2644.04	2635.06	2610.60	2602.28	2599.42	2598.44
150,000	2867.12	2830.81	2802.13	2779.38	2761.26	2746.80	2735.21	2725.93	2700.62	2692.01	2689.06	2688.04
155,000	2962.69	2925.17	2895.54	2872.03	2853.31	2838.36	2826.39	2816.79	2790.64	2781.74	2778.69	2777.64
160,000	3058.26	3019.53	2988.94	2964.67	2945.35	2929.91	2917.56	2907.66	2880.66	2871.48	2868.33	2867.24
165,000	3153.83	3113.89	3082.34	3057.32	3037.39	3021.47	3008.74	2998.52	2970.68	2961.21	2957.96	2956.84
170,000	3249.40	3208.25	3175.75	3149.96	3129.43	3113.03	3099.91	3089.38	3060.70	3050.94	3047.60	3046.44
175,000	3344.97	3302.61	3269.15	3242.61	3221.47	3204.59	3191.08	3180.25	3150.72	3140.68	3137.23	3136.04
180,000	3440.54	3396.97	3362.56	3335.26	3313.52	3296.15	3282.26	3271.11	3240.74	3230.41	3226.87	3225.65
185,000	3536.11	3491.33	3455.96	3427.90	3405.56	3387.71	3373.43	3361.98	3330.76	3320.14	3316.50	3315.25
190,000	3631.68	3585.69	3549.37	3520.55	3497.60	3479.27	3464.60	3452.84	3420.79	3409.88	3406.14	3404.85
195,000	3727.25	3680.05	3642.77	3613.19	3589.64	3570.83	3555.78	3543.70	3510.81	3499.61	3495.77	3494.45
200,000	3822.82	3774.41	3736.17	3705.84	3681.68	3662.39	3646.95	3634.57	3600.83	3589.34	3585.41	3584.05
205,000	3918.39	3868.77	3829.58	3798.48	3773.73	3753.95	3738.12	3725.43	3690.85	3679.08	3675.04	3673.65
210,000	4013.96	3963.13	3922.98	3891.13	3865.77	3845.51	3829.30	3816.30	3780.87	3768.81	3764.68	3763.25
215,000	4109.53	4057.49	4016.39	3983.78	3957.81	3937.07	3920.47	3907.16	3870.89	3858.55	3854.31	3852.85
220,000	4205.10	4151.85	4109.79	4076.42	4049.85	4028.63	4011.65	3998.02	3960.91	3948.28	3943.95	3942.45
225,000	4300.67	4246.21	4203.20	4169.07	4141.89	4120.19	4102.82	4088.89	4050.93	4038.01	4033.58	4032.06
230,000	4396.24	4340.57	4296.60	4261.71	4233.93	4211.75	4193.99	4179.75	4140.95	4127.75	4123.22	4121.66
235,000	4491.82	4434.93	4390.00	4354.36	4325.98	4303.31	4285.17	4270.62	4230.97	4217.48	4212.85	4211.26
240,000	4587.39	4529.29	4483.41	4447.01	4418.02	4394.87	4376.34	4361.48	4320.99	4307.21	4302.49	4300.86
245,000	4682.96	4623.65	4576.81	4539.65	4510.06	4486.43	4467.51	4452.34	4411.01	4396.95	4392.12	4390.46
250,000	4778.53	4718.01	4670.22	4632.30	4602.10	4577.99	4558.69	4543.21	4501.03	4486.68	4481.76	4480.06
255,000	4874.10	4812.37	4763.62	4724.94	4694.14	4669.55	4649.86	4634.07	4591.05	4576.41	4571.39	4569.66
260,000	4969.67	4906.73	4857.03	4817.59	4786.19	4761.11	4741.03	4724.94	4681.07	4666.15	4661.03	4659.26
265,000	5065.24	5001.09	4950.43	4910.24	4878.23	4852.67	4832.21	4815.80	4771.09	4755.88	4750.66	4748.87
270,000	5160.81	5095.45	5043.83	5002.88	4970.27	4944.23	4923.38	4906.66	4861.11	4845.61	4840.30	4838.47
280,000	5351.95	5284.17	5230.64	5188.17	5154.35	5127.35	5105.73	5088.39	5041.15	5025.08	5019.57	5017.67
290,000	5543.09	5472.89	5417.45	5373.46	5338.44	5310.47	5288.08	5270.12	5221.20	5204.55	5198.84	5196.87
300,000	5734.23	5661.61	5604.26	5558.76	5522.52	5493.59	5470.42	5451.85	5401.24	5384.01	5378.11	5376.07

21.75%

AMOUNT OF LOAN	NUMBER OF YEARS IN TERM											
	1	2	3	4	5	6	7	8	9	10	11	12
$ 50	4.68	2.59	1.91	1.57	1.38	1.25	1.17	1.11	1.06	1.03	1.00	0.99
100	9.35	5.18	3.81	3.14	2.75	2.50	2.33	2.21	2.12	2.05	2.00	1.97
200	18.70	10.36	7.62	6.28	5.50	5.00	4.66	4.42	4.24	4.10	4.00	3.93
300	28.05	15.53	11.42	9.42	8.25	7.50	6.99	6.62	6.36	6.15	6.00	5.89
400	37.39	20.71	15.23	12.55	11.00	10.00	9.31	8.83	8.47	8.20	8.00	7.85
500	46.74	25.88	19.04	15.69	13.74	12.49	11.64	11.03	10.59	10.25	10.00	9.81
600	56.09	31.06	22.84	18.83	16.49	14.99	13.97	13.24	12.71	12.30	12.00	11.77
700	65.44	36.23	26.65	21.96	19.24	17.49	16.30	15.45	14.82	14.35	14.00	13.73
800	74.78	41.41	30.45	25.10	21.99	19.99	18.62	17.65	16.94	16.40	16.00	15.69
900	84.13	46.58	34.26	28.24	24.73	22.49	20.95	19.86	19.06	18.45	18.00	17.65
1,000	93.48	51.76	38.07	31.38	27.48	24.98	23.28	22.06	21.17	20.50	20.00	19.61
2,000	186.95	103.51	76.13	62.75	54.96	49.96	46.55	44.12	42.34	41.00	39.99	39.21
3,000	280.43	155.27	114.19	94.12	82.44	74.94	69.82	66.18	63.51	61.50	59.98	58.81
4,000	373.90	207.02	152.25	125.49	109.91	99.92	93.09	88.23	84.67	82.00	79.97	78.41
5,000	467.38	258.78	190.31	156.86	137.39	124.89	116.36	110.29	105.84	102.50	99.96	98.01
6,000	560.85	310.53	228.37	188.23	164.87	149.87	139.64	132.35	127.01	123.00	119.96	117.61
7,000	654.32	362.29	266.43	219.60	192.34	174.85	162.91	154.41	148.17	143.50	139.95	137.21
8,000	747.80	414.04	304.49	250.97	219.82	199.83	186.18	176.46	169.34	164.00	159.94	156.81
9,000	841.27	465.80	342.56	282.34	247.30	224.81	209.45	198.52	190.51	184.50	179.93	176.41
10,000	934.75	517.55	380.62	313.71	274.77	249.78	232.72	220.58	211.67	205.00	199.92	196.01
15,000	1402.12	776.33	570.92	470.56	412.16	374.67	349.08	330.86	317.51	307.50	299.88	294.01
20,000	1869.49	1035.10	761.23	627.42	549.54	499.56	465.44	441.15	423.34	410.00	399.84	392.01
25,000	2336.86	1293.87	951.54	784.27	686.93	624.45	581.80	551.44	529.18	512.50	499.80	490.01
30,000	2804.23	1552.65	1141.84	941.12	824.31	749.34	698.16	661.72	635.01	615.00	599.76	588.02
35,000	3271.60	1811.42	1332.15	1097.97	961.70	874.23	814.52	772.01	740.84	717.50	699.72	686.02
40,000	3738.97	2070.20	1522.45	1254.83	1099.08	999.12	930.88	882.30	846.68	819.99	799.68	784.02
45,000	4206.34	2328.97	1712.76	1411.68	1236.47	1124.01	1047.24	992.58	952.51	922.49	899.64	882.02
50,000	4673.71	2587.74	1903.07	1568.53	1373.85	1248.90	1163.60	1102.87	1058.35	1024.99	999.60	980.02
55,000	5141.08	2846.52	2093.37	1725.38	1511.24	1373.79	1279.95	1213.16	1164.18	1127.49	1099.56	1078.03
60,000	5608.45	3105.29	2283.68	1882.24	1648.62	1498.68	1396.31	1323.44	1270.02	1229.99	1199.52	1176.03
65,000	6075.82	3364.07	2473.99	2039.09	1786.01	1623.57	1512.67	1433.73	1375.85	1332.49	1299.47	1274.03
70,000	6543.19	3622.84	2664.29	2195.94	1923.39	1748.46	1629.03	1544.02	1481.68	1434.99	1399.43	1372.03
75,000	7010.56	3881.61	2854.60	2352.79	2060.78	1873.35	1745.39	1654.30	1587.52	1537.49	1499.39	1470.03
80,000	7477.93	4140.39	3044.90	2509.65	2198.16	1998.24	1861.75	1764.59	1693.35	1639.98	1599.35	1568.04
85,000	7945.30	4399.16	3235.21	2666.50	2335.55	2123.13	1978.11	1874.88	1799.19	1742.48	1699.31	1666.04
90,000	8412.67	4657.94	3425.52	2823.35	2472.93	2248.02	2094.47	1985.16	1905.02	1844.98	1799.27	1764.04
95,000	8880.04	4916.71	3615.82	2980.20	2610.32	2372.91	2210.83	2095.45	2010.86	1947.48	1899.23	1862.04
100,000	9347.42	5175.48	3806.13	3137.06	2747.70	2497.80	2327.19	2205.73	2116.69	2049.98	1999.19	1960.04
105,000	9814.79	5434.26	3996.44	3293.91	2885.09	2622.69	2443.54	2316.02	2222.52	2152.48	2099.15	2058.05
110,000	10282.16	5693.03	4186.74	3450.76	3022.47	2747.58	2559.90	2426.31	2328.36	2254.98	2199.11	2156.05
115,000	10749.53	5951.80	4377.05	3607.61	3159.86	2872.47	2676.26	2536.59	2434.19	2357.48	2299.07	2254.05
120,000	11216.90	6210.58	4567.35	3764.47	3297.24	2997.36	2792.62	2646.88	2540.03	2459.97	2399.03	2352.05
125,000	11684.27	6469.35	4757.66	3921.32	3434.62	3122.25	2908.98	2757.17	2645.86	2562.47	2498.99	2450.05
130,000	12151.64	6728.13	4947.97	4078.17	3572.01	3247.14	3025.34	2867.45	2751.69	2664.97	2598.94	2548.06
135,000	12619.01	6986.90	5138.27	4235.02	3709.39	3372.03	3141.70	2977.74	2857.53	2767.47	2698.90	2646.06
140,000	13086.38	7245.67	5328.58	4391.88	3846.78	3496.92	3258.06	3088.03	2963.36	2869.97	2798.86	2744.06
145,000	13553.75	7504.45	5518.89	4548.73	3984.16	3621.81	3374.42	3198.31	3069.20	2972.47	2898.82	2842.06
150,000	14021.12	7763.22	5709.19	4705.58	4121.55	3746.70	3490.78	3308.60	3175.03	3074.97	2998.78	2940.06
155,000	14488.49	8022.00	5899.50	4862.43	4258.93	3871.59	3607.13	3418.89	3280.87	3177.46	3098.74	3038.07
160,000	14955.86	8280.77	6089.80	5019.29	4396.32	3996.48	3723.49	3529.17	3386.70	3279.96	3198.70	3136.07
165,000	15423.23	8539.54	6280.11	5176.14	4533.70	4121.37	3839.85	3639.46	3492.53	3382.46	3298.66	3234.07
170,000	15890.60	8798.32	6470.42	5332.99	4671.09	4246.26	3956.21	3749.75	3598.37	3484.96	3398.62	3332.07
175,000	16357.97	9057.09	6660.72	5489.84	4808.47	4371.15	4072.57	3860.03	3704.20	3587.46	3498.58	3430.07
180,000	16825.34	9315.87	6851.03	5646.70	4945.86	4496.04	4188.93	3970.32	3810.04	3689.96	3598.54	3528.07
185,000	17292.71	9574.64	7041.33	5803.55	5083.24	4620.93	4305.29	4080.61	3915.87	3792.46	3698.50	3626.08
190,000	17760.08	9833.41	7231.64	5960.40	5220.63	4745.82	4421.65	4190.89	4021.71	3894.96	3798.45	3724.08
195,000	18227.46	10092.19	7421.95	6117.25	5358.01	4870.70	4538.01	4301.18	4127.54	3997.45	3898.41	3822.08
200,000	18694.83	10350.96	7612.25	6274.11	5495.40	4995.59	4654.37	4411.46	4233.37	4099.95	3998.37	3920.08
205,000	19162.20	10609.73	7802.56	6430.96	5632.78	5120.48	4770.72	4521.75	4339.21	4202.45	4098.33	4018.08
210,000	19629.57	10868.51	7992.87	6587.81	5770.17	5245.37	4887.08	4632.04	4445.04	4304.95	4198.29	4116.09
215,000	20096.94	11127.28	8183.17	6744.66	5907.55	5370.26	5003.44	4742.32	4550.88	4407.45	4298.25	4214.09
220,000	20564.31	11386.06	8373.48	6901.52	6044.94	5495.15	5119.80	4852.61	4656.71	4509.95	4398.21	4312.09
225,000	21031.68	11644.83	8563.78	7058.37	6182.32	5620.04	5236.16	4962.90	4762.55	4612.45	4498.17	4410.09
230,000	21499.05	11903.60	8754.09	7215.22	6319.71	5744.93	5352.52	5073.18	4868.38	4714.95	4598.13	4508.09
235,000	21966.42	12162.38	8944.40	7372.08	6457.09	5869.82	5468.88	5183.47	4974.21	4817.44	4698.09	4606.10
240,000	22433.79	12421.15	9134.70	7528.93	6594.47	5994.71	5585.24	5293.76	5080.05	4919.94	4798.05	4704.10
245,000	22901.16	12679.93	9325.01	7685.78	6731.86	6119.60	5701.60	5404.04	5185.88	5022.44	4898.01	4802.10
250,000	23368.53	12938.70	9515.32	7842.63	6869.24	6244.49	5817.96	5514.33	5291.72	5124.94	4997.97	4900.10
255,000	23835.90	13197.47	9705.62	7999.49	7006.63	6369.38	5934.31	5624.62	5397.55	5227.44	5097.92	4998.10
260,000	24303.27	13456.25	9895.93	8156.34	7144.01	6494.27	6050.67	5734.90	5503.38	5329.94	5197.88	5096.11
265,000	24770.64	13715.02	10086.23	8313.19	7281.40	6619.16	6167.03	5845.19	5609.22	5432.44	5297.84	5194.11
270,000	25238.01	13973.80	10276.54	8470.04	7418.78	6744.05	6283.39	5955.48	5715.05	5534.93	5397.80	5292.11
280,000	26172.75	14491.34	10657.15	8783.75	7693.55	6993.83	6516.11	6176.05	5926.72	5739.93	5597.72	5488.11
290,000	27107.49	15008.89	11037.77	9097.45	7968.32	7243.61	6748.83	6396.62	6138.39	5944.93	5797.64	5684.12
300,000	28042.24	15526.44	11418.38	9411.16	8243.09	7493.39	6981.55	6617.19	6350.06	6149.93	5997.56	5880.12

AMOUNT OF LOAN	NUMBER OF YEARS IN TERM											
	13	14	15	16	17	18	19	20	25	30	35	40
$ 50	0.97	0.96	0.95	0.94	0.94	0.93	0.93	0.92	0.92	0.91	0.91	0.91
100	1.93	1.91	1.89	1.88	1.87	1.86	1.85	1.84	1.83	1.82	1.82	1.82
200	3.86	3.82	3.78	3.75	3.73	3.71	3.69	3.68	3.65	3.64	3.63	3.63
300	5.79	5.72	5.67	5.62	5.59	5.56	5.53	5.52	5.47	5.45	5.45	5.44
400	7.72	7.63	7.55	7.49	7.45	7.41	7.38	7.35	7.29	7.27	7.26	7.26
500	9.65	9.53	9.44	9.36	9.31	9.26	9.22	9.19	9.11	9.08	9.07	9.07
600	11.58	11.44	11.33	11.24	11.17	11.11	11.06	11.03	10.93	10.90	10.88	10.88
700	13.51	13.34	13.21	13.11	13.03	12.96	12.91	12.87	12.75	12.71	12.70	12.69
800	15.44	15.25	15.10	14.98	14.89	14.81	14.75	14.70	14.57	14.53	14.51	14.51
900	17.37	17.16	16.99	16.85	16.75	16.66	16.59	16.54	16.39	16.34	16.33	16.32
1,000	19.30	19.06	18.87	18.72	18.61	18.51	18.44	18.38	18.21	18.16	18.14	18.13
2,000	38.60	38.12	37.74	37.44	37.21	37.02	36.87	36.75	36.42	36.31	36.27	36.26
3,000	57.89	57.18	56.61	56.16	55.81	55.53	55.30	55.12	54.63	54.46	54.41	54.39
4,000	77.19	76.23	75.48	74.88	74.41	74.03	73.73	73.49	72.84	72.62	72.54	72.52
5,000	96.48	95.29	94.35	93.60	93.01	92.54	92.16	91.86	91.05	90.77	90.68	90.65
6,000	115.78	114.35	113.22	112.32	111.61	111.05	110.60	110.23	109.25	108.92	108.81	108.77
7,000	135.08	133.40	132.09	131.04	130.22	129.56	129.03	128.61	127.46	127.08	126.95	126.90
8,000	154.37	152.46	150.96	149.76	148.82	148.06	147.46	146.98	145.67	145.23	145.08	145.03
9,000	173.67	171.52	169.83	168.48	167.42	166.57	165.89	165.35	163.88	163.38	163.22	163.16
10,000	192.96	190.58	188.69	187.20	186.02	185.08	184.32	183.72	182.09	181.54	181.35	181.29
15,000	289.44	285.86	283.04	280.80	279.03	277.61	276.48	275.58	273.13	272.30	272.02	271.93
20,000	385.92	381.15	377.38	374.40	372.04	370.15	368.64	367.44	364.17	363.07	362.70	362.57
25,000	482.40	476.43	471.73	468.00	465.04	462.69	460.80	459.29	455.21	453.84	453.37	453.21
30,000	578.88	571.72	566.07	561.60	558.05	555.22	552.96	551.15	546.25	544.60	544.04	543.85
35,000	675.36	667.00	660.42	655.20	651.06	647.76	645.12	643.01	637.29	635.37	634.72	634.49
40,000	771.84	762.29	754.76	748.80	744.07	740.29	737.28	734.87	728.33	726.13	725.39	725.14
45,000	868.32	857.58	849.11	842.40	837.08	832.83	829.44	826.72	819.37	816.00	816.06	815.78
50,000	964.80	952.86	943.45	936.00	930.08	925.37	921.60	918.58	910.41	907.67	906.73	906.42
55,000	1061.28	1048.15	1037.80	1029.60	1023.09	1017.90	1013.76	1010.44	1001.45	998.43	997.41	997.06
60,000	1157.75	1143.43	1132.14	1123.20	1116.10	1110.44	1105.92	1102.30	1092.49	1089.20	1088.08	1087.70
65,000	1254.23	1238.72	1226.49	1216.80	1209.11	1202.97	1198.07	1194.15	1183.54	1179.96	1178.75	1178.34
70,000	1350.71	1334.00	1320.83	1310.40	1302.11	1295.51	1290.23	1286.01	1274.58	1270.73	1269.43	1268.98
75,000	1447.19	1429.29	1415.18	1404.00	1395.12	1388.05	1382.39	1377.87	1365.62	1361.50	1360.10	1359.62
80,000	1543.67	1524.57	1509.52	1497.60	1488.13	1480.58	1474.55	1469.73	1456.66	1452.26	1450.77	1450.27
85,000	1640.15	1619.86	1603.87	1591.20	1581.14	1573.12	1566.71	1561.59	1547.70	1543.03	1541.45	1540.91
90,000	1736.63	1715.15	1698.21	1684.80	1674.15	1665.65	1658.87	1653.44	1638.74	1633.79	1632.12	1631.55
95,000	1833.11	1810.43	1792.56	1778.40	1767.15	1758.19	1751.03	1745.30	1729.78	1724.56	1722.79	1722.19
100,000	1929.59	1905.72	1886.90	1872.00	1860.16	1850.73	1843.19	1837.16	1820.82	1815.33	1813.46	1812.83
105,000	2026.07	2001.00	1981.25	1965.60	1953.17	1943.26	1935.35	1929.02	1911.86	1906.09	1904.14	1903.47
110,000	2122.55	2096.29	2075.59	2059.20	2046.18	2035.80	2027.51	2020.87	2002.90	1996.86	1994.81	1994.11
115,000	2219.02	2191.57	2169.94	2152.80	2139.19	2128.33	2119.67	2112.73	2093.94	2087.63	2085.48	2084.76
120,000	2315.50	2286.86	2264.28	2246.40	2232.19	2220.87	2211.83	2204.59	2184.98	2178.39	2176.16	2175.40
125,000	2411.98	2382.15	2358.63	2340.00	2325.20	2313.41	2303.99	2296.45	2276.03	2269.16	2266.83	2266.04
130,000	2508.46	2477.43	2452.97	2433.60	2418.21	2405.94	2396.14	2388.30	2367.07	2359.92	2357.50	2356.68
135,000	2604.94	2572.72	2547.31	2527.20	2511.22	2498.48	2488.30	2480.16	2458.11	2450.69	2448.18	2447.32
140,000	2701.42	2668.00	2641.66	2620.80	2604.22	2591.01	2580.46	2572.02	2549.15	2541.46	2538.85	2537.96
145,000	2797.90	2763.29	2736.00	2714.40	2697.23	2683.55	2672.62	2663.88	2640.19	2632.22	2629.52	2628.60
150,000	2894.38	2858.57	2830.35	2808.00	2790.24	2776.09	2764.78	2755.74	2731.23	2722.99	2720.19	2719.24
155,000	2990.86	2953.86	2924.69	2901.60	2883.25	2868.62	2856.94	2847.59	2822.27	2813.75	2810.87	2809.89
160,000	3087.34	3049.14	3019.04	2995.20	2976.26	2961.16	2949.10	2939.45	2913.31	2904.52	2901.54	2900.53
165,000	3183.82	3144.43	3113.38	3088.80	3069.26	3053.69	3041.26	3031.31	3004.35	2995.29	2992.21	2991.17
170,000	3280.30	3239.72	3207.73	3182.40	3162.27	3146.23	3133.42	3123.17	3095.39	3086.05	3082.89	3081.81
175,000	3376.77	3335.00	3302.07	3276.00	3255.28	3238.77	3225.58	3215.02	3186.43	3176.82	3173.56	3172.45
180,000	3473.25	3430.29	3396.42	3369.60	3348.29	3331.30	3317.74	3306.88	3277.47	3267.58	3264.23	3263.09
185,000	3569.73	3525.57	3490.76	3463.20	3441.30	3423.84	3409.90	3398.74	3368.52	3358.35	3354.91	3353.73
190,000	3666.21	3620.86	3585.11	3556.80	3534.30	3516.38	3502.06	3490.60	3459.56	3449.12	3445.58	3444.38
195,000	3762.69	3716.14	3679.45	3650.40	3627.31	3608.91	3594.21	3582.45	3550.60	3539.88	3536.25	3535.02
200,000	3859.17	3811.43	3773.80	3744.00	3720.32	3701.45	3686.37	3674.31	3641.64	3630.65	3626.92	3625.66
205,000	3955.65	3906.71	3868.14	3837.60	3813.33	3793.98	3778.53	3766.17	3732.68	3721.42	3717.60	3716.30
210,000	4052.13	4002.00	3962.49	3931.20	3906.33	3886.52	3870.69	3858.03	3823.72	3812.18	3808.27	3806.94
215,000	4148.61	4097.29	4056.83	4024.80	3999.34	3979.06	3962.85	3949.89	3914.76	3902.95	3898.94	3897.58
220,000	4245.09	4192.57	4151.18	4118.40	4092.35	4071.59	4055.01	4041.74	4005.80	3993.71	3989.62	3988.22
225,000	4341.57	4287.86	4245.52	4212.00	4185.36	4164.13	4147.17	4133.60	4096.84	4084.48	4080.29	4078.86
230,000	4438.04	4383.14	4339.87	4305.60	4278.37	4256.66	4239.33	4225.46	4187.88	4175.25	4170.96	4169.51
235,000	4534.52	4478.43	4434.21	4399.20	4371.37	4349.20	4331.49	4317.32	4278.92	4266.01	4261.63	4260.15
240,000	4631.00	4573.71	4528.56	4492.80	4464.38	4441.74	4423.65	4409.17	4369.96	4356.78	4352.31	4350.79
245,000	4727.48	4669.00	4622.90	4586.40	4557.39	4534.27	4515.81	4501.03	4461.01	4447.54	4442.98	4441.43
250,000	4823.96	4764.29	4717.25	4680.00	4650.40	4626.81	4607.97	4592.89	4552.05	4538.31	4533.65	4532.07
255,000	4920.44	4859.57	4811.59	4773.60	4743.40	4719.34	4700.13	4684.75	4643.09	4629.08	4624.33	4622.71
260,000	5016.92	4954.86	4905.93	4867.20	4836.41	4811.88	4792.28	4776.60	4734.13	4719.84	4715.00	4713.35
265,000	5113.40	5050.14	5000.28	4960.80	4929.42	4904.42	4884.44	4868.46	4825.17	4810.61	4805.67	4804.00
270,000	5209.88	5145.43	5094.62	5054.40	5022.43	4996.95	4976.60	4960.32	4916.21	4901.37	4896.35	4894.64
280,000	5402.84	5336.00	5283.31	5241.60	5208.44	5182.02	5160.92	5144.04	5098.29	5082.91	5077.69	5075.92
290,000	5595.79	5526.57	5472.00	5428.80	5394.46	5367.10	5345.24	5327.75	5280.37	5264.44	5259.04	5257.20
300,000	5788.75	5717.14	5660.69	5616.00	5580.48	5552.17	5529.56	5511.47	5462.45	5445.97	5440.38	5438.48

22.00% MONTHLY AMORTIZING PAYMENTS

AMOUNT OF LOAN	NUMBER OF YEARS IN TERM											
	1	2	3	4	5	6	7	8	9	10	11	12
$ 50	4.68	2.60	1.91	1.58	1.39	1.26	1.18	1.12	1.07	1.04	1.01	0.99
100	9.36	5.19	3.82	3.16	2.77	2.52	2.35	2.23	2.14	2.07	2.02	1.98
200	18.72	10.38	7.64	6.31	5.53	5.03	4.69	4.45	4.27	4.14	4.04	3.96
300	28.08	15.57	11.46	9.46	8.29	7.54	7.03	6.67	6.40	6.21	6.05	5.94
400	37.44	20.76	15.28	12.61	11.05	10.06	9.38	8.89	8.54	8.27	8.07	7.92
500	46.80	25.94	19.10	15.76	13.81	12.57	11.72	11.11	10.67	10.34	10.09	9.89
600	56.16	31.13	22.92	18.91	16.58	15.08	14.06	13.34	12.80	12.41	12.10	11.87
700	65.52	36.32	26.74	22.06	19.34	17.59	16.40	15.56	14.94	14.47	14.12	13.85
800	74.88	41.51	30.56	25.21	22.10	20.11	18.75	17.78	17.07	16.54	16.14	15.83
900	84.24	46.70	34.38	28.36	24.86	22.62	21.09	20.00	19.20	18.61	18.15	17.81
1,000	93.60	51.88	38.20	31.51	27.62	25.13	23.43	22.22	21.34	20.67	20.17	19.78
2,000	187.19	103.76	76.39	63.02	55.24	50.26	46.86	44.44	42.67	41.34	40.34	39.56
3,000	280.79	155.64	114.58	94.52	82.86	75.38	70.28	66.66	64.00	62.01	60.50	59.34
4,000	374.38	207.52	152.77	126.03	110.48	100.51	93.71	88.87	85.33	82.68	80.67	79.12
5,000	467.98	259.40	190.96	157.54	138.10	125.64	117.13	111.09	106.66	103.35	100.84	98.90
6,000	561.57	311.27	229.15	189.04	165.72	150.76	140.56	133.31	128.00	124.02	121.00	118.68
7,000	655.17	363.15	267.34	220.55	193.34	175.89	163.99	155.52	149.33	144.69	141.17	138.46
8,000	748.76	415.03	305.53	252.05	220.96	201.01	187.41	177.74	170.66	165.36	161.34	158.24
9,000	842.35	466.91	343.72	283.56	248.58	226.14	210.84	199.96	191.99	186.03	181.50	178.02
10,000	935.95	518.79	381.91	315.07	276.19	251.27	234.26	222.18	213.32	206.70	201.67	197.79
15,000	1403.92	778.18	572.86	472.60	414.29	376.90	351.39	333.26	319.98	310.05	302.50	296.69
20,000	1871.89	1037.57	763.81	630.13	552.38	502.53	468.52	444.35	426.64	413.40	403.33	395.58
25,000	2339.86	1296.96	954.77	787.66	690.48	628.16	585.65	555.43	533.30	516.75	504.16	494.48
30,000	2807.84	1556.35	1145.72	945.19	828.57	753.79	702.78	666.52	639.96	620.10	604.99	593.37
35,000	3275.81	1815.74	1336.67	1102.72	966.67	879.42	819.91	777.60	746.62	723.44	705.83	692.27
40,000	3743.78	2075.13	1527.62	1260.25	1104.76	1005.05	937.04	888.69	853.28	826.79	806.66	791.16
45,000	4211.75	2334.52	1718.58	1417.78	1242.86	1130.68	1054.17	999.77	959.94	930.14	907.49	890.06
50,000	4679.72	2593.91	1909.53	1575.31	1380.95	1256.31	1171.30	1110.86	1066.60	1033.49	1008.32	988.95
55,000	5147.70	2853.30	2100.48	1732.84	1519.05	1381.94	1288.43	1221.94	1173.26	1136.84	1109.15	1087.85
60,000	5615.67	3112.69	2291.43	1890.37	1657.14	1507.57	1405.56	1333.03	1279.92	1240.19	1209.98	1186.74
65,000	6083.64	3372.09	2482.38	2047.90	1795.23	1633.20	1522.69	1444.12	1386.58	1343.53	1310.81	1285.64
70,000	6551.61	3631.48	2673.34	2205.43	1933.33	1758.83	1639.82	1555.20	1493.24	1446.88	1411.65	1384.53
75,000	7019.58	3890.87	2864.29	2362.96	2071.42	1884.46	1756.95	1666.29	1599.90	1550.23	1512.48	1483.43
80,000	7487.56	4150.26	3055.24	2520.49	2209.52	2010.10	1874.08	1777.37	1706.56	1653.58	1613.31	1582.32
85,000	7955.53	4409.65	3246.19	2678.02	2347.61	2135.73	1991.21	1888.46	1813.22	1756.93	1714.14	1681.21
90,000	8423.50	4669.04	3437.15	2835.55	2485.71	2261.36	2108.34	1999.54	1919.88	1860.28	1814.97	1780.11
95,000	8891.47	4928.43	3628.10	2993.08	2623.80	2386.99	2225.47	2110.63	2026.54	1963.63	1915.80	1879.00
100,000	9359.44	5187.82	3819.05	3150.61	2761.90	2512.62	2342.60	2221.71	2133.20	2066.97	2016.63	1977.90
105,000	9827.41	5447.21	4010.00	3308.14	2899.99	2638.25	2459.73	2332.80	2239.85	2170.32	2117.47	2076.79
110,000	10295.39	5706.60	4200.95	3465.67	3038.09	2763.88	2576.86	2443.88	2346.51	2273.67	2218.30	2175.69
115,000	10763.36	5965.99	4391.91	3623.20	3176.18	2889.51	2693.99	2554.97	2453.17	2377.02	2319.13	2274.58
120,000	11231.33	6225.38	4582.86	3780.73	3314.27	3015.14	2811.12	2666.05	2559.83	2480.37	2419.96	2373.48
125,000	11699.30	6484.77	4773.81	3938.26	3452.37	3140.77	2928.25	2777.14	2666.49	2583.72	2520.79	2472.37
130,000	12167.27	6744.17	4964.76	4095.80	3590.46	3266.40	3045.38	2888.23	2773.15	2687.06	2621.62	2571.27
135,000	12635.25	7003.56	5155.72	4253.33	3728.56	3392.03	3162.51	2999.31	2879.81	2790.41	2722.45	2670.16
140,000	13103.22	7262.95	5346.67	4410.86	3866.65	3517.66	3279.64	3110.40	2986.47	2893.76	2823.29	2769.06
145,000	13571.19	7522.34	5537.62	4568.39	4004.75	3643.29	3396.77	3221.48	3093.13	2997.11	2924.12	2867.95
150,000	14039.16	7781.73	5728.57	4725.92	4142.84	3768.92	3513.90	3332.57	3199.79	3100.46	3024.95	2966.85
155,000	14507.13	8041.12	5919.53	4883.45	4280.94	3894.55	3631.03	3443.65	3306.45	3203.81	3125.78	3065.74
160,000	14975.11	8300.51	6110.48	5040.98	4419.03	4020.19	3748.16	3554.74	3413.11	3307.16	3226.61	3164.63
165,000	15443.08	8559.90	6301.43	5198.51	4557.13	4145.82	3865.29	3665.82	3519.77	3410.50	3327.44	3263.53
170,000	15911.05	8819.29	6492.38	5356.04	4695.22	4271.45	3982.42	3776.91	3626.43	3513.85	3428.27	3362.42
175,000	16379.02	9078.68	6683.33	5513.57	4833.31	4397.08	4099.55	3887.99	3733.09	3617.20	3529.11	3461.32
180,000	16846.99	9338.07	6874.29	5671.10	4971.41	4522.71	4216.67	3999.08	3839.75	3720.55	3629.94	3560.21
185,000	17314.97	9597.46	7065.24	5828.63	5109.50	4648.34	4333.80	4110.16	3946.41	3823.90	3730.77	3659.11
190,000	17782.94	9856.85	7256.19	5986.16	5247.60	4773.97	4450.93	4221.25	4053.07	3927.25	3831.60	3758.00
195,000	18250.91	10116.25	7447.14	6143.69	5385.69	4899.60	4568.06	4332.34	4159.73	4030.59	3932.43	3856.90
200,000	18718.88	10375.64	7638.10	6301.22	5523.79	5025.23	4685.19	4443.42	4266.39	4133.94	4033.26	3955.79
205,000	19186.85	10635.03	7829.05	6458.75	5661.88	5150.86	4802.32	4554.51	4373.04	4237.29	4134.09	4054.69
210,000	19654.82	10894.42	8020.00	6616.28	5799.98	5276.49	4919.45	4665.59	4479.70	4340.64	4234.93	4153.58
215,000	20122.80	11153.81	8210.95	6773.81	5938.07	5402.12	5036.58	4776.68	4586.36	4443.99	4335.76	4252.48
220,000	20590.77	11413.20	8401.90	6931.34	6076.17	5527.75	5153.71	4887.76	4693.02	4547.34	4436.59	4351.37
225,000	21058.74	11672.59	8592.86	7088.87	6214.26	5653.38	5270.84	4998.85	4799.68	4650.68	4537.42	4450.27
230,000	21526.71	11931.98	8783.81	7246.40	6352.35	5779.01	5387.97	5109.93	4906.34	4754.03	4638.25	4549.16
235,000	21994.68	12191.37	8974.76	7403.93	6490.45	5904.64	5505.10	5221.02	5013.00	4857.38	4739.08	4648.05
240,000	22462.66	12450.76	9165.71	7561.46	6628.54	6030.28	5622.23	5332.10	5119.66	4960.73	4839.91	4746.95
245,000	22930.63	12710.15	9356.67	7718.99	6766.64	6155.91	5739.36	5443.19	5226.32	5064.08	4940.75	4845.84
250,000	23398.60	12969.54	9547.62	7876.52	6904.73	6281.54	5856.49	5554.27	5332.98	5167.43	5041.58	4944.74
255,000	23866.57	13228.93	9738.57	8034.05	7042.83	6407.17	5973.62	5665.36	5439.64	5270.78	5142.41	5043.63
260,000	24334.54	13488.33	9929.52	8191.59	7180.92	6532.80	6090.75	5776.45	5546.30	5374.12	5243.24	5142.53
265,000	24802.52	13747.72	10120.48	8349.12	7319.02	6658.43	6207.88	5887.53	5652.96	5477.47	5344.07	5241.42
270,000	25270.49	14007.11	10311.43	8506.65	7457.11	6784.06	6325.01	5998.62	5759.62	5580.82	5444.90	5340.32
280,000	26206.43	14525.89	10693.33	8821.71	7733.30	7035.32	6559.27	6220.79	5972.94	5787.52	5646.57	5538.11
290,000	27142.38	15044.67	11075.24	9136.77	8009.49	7286.58	6793.53	6442.96	6186.26	5994.21	5848.23	5735.90
300,000	28078.32	15563.45	11457.14	9451.83	8285.68	7537.84	7027.79	6665.13	6399.58	6200.91	6049.89	5933.69

162

AMOUNT OF LOAN	NUMBER OF YEARS IN TERM											
	13	14	15	16	17	18	19	20	25	30	35	40
$ 50	0.98	0.97	0.96	0.95	0.94	0.94	0.94	0.93	0.93	0.92	0.92	0.92
100	1.95	1.93	1.91	1.90	1.88	1.88	1.87	1.86	1.85	1.84	1.84	1.84
200	3.90	3.85	3.82	3.79	3.76	3.75	3.73	3.72	3.69	3.68	3.67	3.67
300	5.85	5.78	5.72	5.68	5.64	5.62	5.59	5.58	5.53	5.51	5.51	5.51
400	7.80	7.70	7.63	7.57	7.52	7.49	7.46	7.43	7.37	7.35	7.34	7.34
500	9.74	9.63	9.53	9.46	9.40	9.36	9.32	9.29	9.21	9.18	9.18	9.17
600	11.69	11.55	11.44	11.35	11.28	11.23	11.18	11.15	11.05	11.02	11.01	11.01
700	13.64	13.47	13.35	13.24	13.16	13.10	13.05	13.00	12.89	12.86	12.84	12.84
800	15.59	15.40	15.25	15.13	15.04	14.97	14.91	14.86	14.73	14.69	14.68	14.67
900	17.54	17.32	17.16	17.03	16.92	16.84	16.77	16.72	16.58	16.53	16.51	16.51
1,000	19.48	19.25	19.06	18.92	18.80	18.71	18.63	18.58	18.42	18.36	18.35	18.34
2,000	38.96	38.49	38.12	37.83	37.60	37.41	37.26	37.15	36.83	36.72	36.69	36.68
3,000	58.44	57.73	57.18	56.74	56.39	56.11	55.89	55.72	55.24	55.08	55.03	55.01
4,000	77.92	76.98	76.24	75.65	75.19	74.82	74.52	74.29	73.65	73.44	73.37	73.35
5,000	97.40	96.22	95.29	94.56	93.98	93.52	93.15	92.86	92.07	91.80	91.72	91.69
6,000	116.87	115.46	114.35	113.47	112.78	112.22	111.78	111.43	110.48	110.16	110.06	110.02
7,000	136.35	134.70	133.41	132.38	131.57	130.93	130.41	130.00	128.89	128.52	128.40	128.36
8,000	155.83	153.95	152.47	151.29	150.37	149.63	149.04	148.57	147.30	146.88	146.74	146.70
9,000	175.31	173.19	171.52	170.21	169.16	168.33	167.67	167.14	165.72	165.24	165.09	165.03
10,000	194.79	192.43	190.58	189.12	187.96	187.03	186.30	185.71	184.13	183.60	183.43	183.37
15,000	292.18	288.65	285.87	283.67	281.93	280.55	279.44	278.56	276.19	275.40	275.14	275.05
20,000	389.57	384.86	381.16	378.23	375.91	374.06	372.59	371.42	368.25	367.20	366.85	366.73
25,000	486.96	481.07	476.44	472.79	469.88	467.58	465.74	464.27	460.32	459.00	458.56	458.41
30,000	584.35	577.29	571.73	567.34	563.86	561.09	558.88	557.12	552.38	550.80	550.27	550.09
35,000	681.74	673.50	667.02	661.90	657.84	654.61	652.03	649.98	644.44	642.60	641.98	641.78
40,000	779.13	769.71	762.31	756.45	751.81	748.12	745.18	742.83	736.50	734.40	733.69	733.46
45,000	876.52	865.93	857.60	851.01	846.70	841.63	838.32	835.68	828.56	826.20	825.41	825.14
50,000	973.91	962.14	952.88	945.57	939.76	935.15	931.47	928.53	920.63	918.00	917.12	916.82
55,000	1071.30	1058.36	1048.17	1040.12	1033.74	1028.66	1024.62	1021.39	1012.69	1009.80	1008.83	1008.50
60,000	1168.69	1154.57	1143.46	1134.68	1127.72	1122.18	1117.76	1114.24	1104.75	1101.60	1100.54	1100.18
65,000	1266.08	1250.78	1238.75	1229.23	1221.69	1215.69	1210.91	1207.09	1196.81	1193.40	1192.25	1191.87
70,000	1363.47	1347.00	1334.03	1323.79	1315.67	1309.21	1304.06	1299.95	1288.87	1285.19	1283.96	1283.55
75,000	1460.86	1443.21	1429.32	1418.35	1409.64	1402.72	1397.20	1392.80	1380.94	1376.99	1375.67	1375.23
80,000	1558.25	1539.42	1524.61	1512.90	1503.62	1496.24	1490.35	1485.65	1473.00	1468.79	1467.38	1466.91
85,000	1655.64	1635.64	1619.90	1607.46	1597.60	1589.75	1583.50	1578.51	1565.06	1560.59	1559.10	1558.59
90,000	1753.03	1731.85	1715.19	1702.02	1691.57	1683.26	1676.64	1671.36	1657.12	1652.39	1650.81	1650.27
95,000	1850.42	1828.06	1810.47	1796.57	1785.55	1776.78	1769.79	1764.21	1749.19	1744.19	1742.52	1741.96
100,000	1947.81	1924.28	1905.76	1891.13	1879.52	1870.29	1862.94	1857.06	1841.25	1835.99	1834.23	1833.64
105,000	2045.20	2020.49	2001.05	1985.68	1973.50	1963.81	1956.08	1949.92	1933.31	1927.79	1925.94	1925.32
110,000	2142.59	2116.71	2096.34	2080.24	2067.47	2057.32	2049.23	2042.77	2025.37	2019.59	2017.65	2017.00
115,000	2239.99	2212.92	2191.62	2174.80	2161.45	2150.84	2142.38	2135.62	2117.43	2111.39	2109.36	2108.68
120,000	2337.38	2309.13	2286.91	2269.35	2255.43	2244.35	2235.52	2228.48	2209.50	2203.19	2201.07	2200.36
125,000	2434.77	2405.35	2382.20	2363.91	2349.40	2337.87	2328.67	2321.33	2301.56	2294.99	2292.78	2292.05
130,000	2532.16	2501.56	2477.49	2458.46	2443.38	2431.38	2421.82	2414.18	2393.62	2386.79	2384.50	2383.73
135,000	2629.55	2597.77	2572.78	2553.02	2537.35	2524.89	2514.96	2507.04	2485.68	2478.58	2476.21	2475.41
140,000	2726.94	2693.99	2668.06	2647.58	2631.33	2618.41	2608.11	2599.89	2577.74	2570.38	2567.92	2567.09
145,000	2824.33	2790.20	2763.35	2742.13	2725.31	2711.92	2701.26	2692.74	2669.81	2662.18	2659.63	2658.77
150,000	2921.72	2886.41	2858.64	2836.69	2819.28	2805.44	2794.40	2785.59	2761.87	2753.98	2751.34	2750.45
155,000	3019.11	2982.63	2953.93	2931.25	2913.26	2898.95	2887.55	2878.45	2853.93	2845.78	2843.05	2842.14
160,000	3116.50	3078.84	3049.21	3025.80	3007.23	2992.47	2980.70	2971.30	2945.99	2937.58	2934.76	2933.82
165,000	3213.89	3175.06	3144.50	3120.36	3101.21	3085.98	3073.84	3064.15	3038.05	3029.38	3026.47	3025.50
170,000	3311.28	3271.27	3239.79	3214.91	3195.19	3179.50	3166.99	3157.01	3130.12	3121.18	3118.19	3117.18
175,000	3408.67	3367.48	3335.08	3309.47	3289.16	3273.01	3260.14	3249.86	3222.18	3212.98	3209.90	3208.86
180,000	3506.06	3463.70	3430.37	3404.03	3383.14	3366.52	3353.28	3342.71	3314.24	3304.78	3301.61	3300.54
185,000	3603.45	3559.91	3525.65	3498.58	3477.11	3460.04	3446.43	3435.57	3406.30	3396.58	3393.32	3392.23
190,000	3700.84	3656.12	3620.94	3593.14	3571.09	3553.55	3539.58	3528.42	3498.37	3488.38	3485.03	3483.91
195,000	3798.23	3752.34	3716.23	3687.69	3665.06	3647.07	3632.72	3621.27	3590.43	3580.18	3576.74	3575.59
200,000	3895.62	3848.55	3811.52	3782.25	3759.04	3740.58	3725.87	3714.12	3682.49	3671.97	3668.45	3667.27
205,000	3993.01	3944.76	3906.80	3876.81	3853.02	3834.10	3819.02	3806.98	3774.55	3763.77	3760.16	3758.95
210,000	4090.40	4040.98	4002.09	3971.36	3946.99	3927.61	3912.16	3899.83	3866.61	3855.57	3851.88	3850.63
215,000	4187.79	4137.19	4097.38	4065.92	4040.97	4021.13	4005.31	3992.68	3958.68	3947.37	3943.59	3942.32
220,000	4285.18	4233.41	4192.67	4160.47	4134.94	4114.64	4098.46	4085.54	4050.74	4039.17	4035.30	4034.00
225,000	4382.57	4329.62	4287.96	4255.03	4228.92	4208.15	4191.60	4178.39	4142.80	4130.97	4127.01	4125.68
230,000	4479.97	4425.83	4383.24	4349.59	4322.90	4301.67	4284.75	4271.24	4234.86	4222.77	4218.72	4217.36
235,000	4577.36	4522.05	4478.53	4444.14	4416.87	4395.18	4377.90	4364.10	4326.92	4314.57	4310.43	4309.04
240,000	4674.75	4618.26	4573.82	4538.70	4510.85	4488.70	4471.04	4456.95	4418.99	4406.37	4402.14	4400.72
245,000	4772.14	4714.47	4669.11	4633.26	4604.82	4582.21	4564.19	4549.80	4511.05	4498.17	4493.85	4492.40
250,000	4869.53	4810.69	4764.40	4727.81	4698.80	4675.73	4657.34	4642.65	4603.11	4589.97	4585.56	4584.09
255,000	4966.92	4906.90	4859.68	4822.37	4792.78	4769.24	4750.48	4735.51	4695.17	4681.77	4677.28	4675.77
260,000	5064.31	5003.11	4954.97	4916.92	4886.75	4862.76	4843.63	4828.36	4787.24	4773.57	4768.99	4767.45
265,000	5161.70	5099.33	5050.26	5011.48	4980.73	4956.27	4936.78	4921.21	4879.30	4865.36	4860.70	4859.13
270,000	5259.09	5195.54	5145.55	5106.04	5074.70	5049.78	5029.92	5014.07	4971.36	4957.16	4952.41	4950.81
280,000	5453.87	5387.97	5336.12	5295.15	5262.65	5236.81	5216.22	5199.77	5155.48	5140.76	5135.83	5134.18
290,000	5648.65	5580.40	5526.70	5484.26	5450.61	5423.84	5402.51	5385.48	5339.61	5324.36	5319.25	5317.54
300,000	5843.43	5772.82	5717.27	5673.37	5638.56	5610.87	5588.80	5571.18	5523.73	5507.96	5502.68	5500.90

163

22.25%

AMOUNT OF LOAN	NUMBER OF YEARS IN TERM											
	1	2	3	4	5	6	7	8	9	10	11	12
$ 50	4.69	2.61	1.92	1.59	1.39	1.27	1.18	1.12	1.08	1.05	1.02	1.00
100	9.38	5.21	3.84	3.17	2.78	2.53	2.36	2.24	2.15	2.09	2.04	2.00
200	18.75	10.41	7.67	6.33	5.56	5.06	4.72	4.48	4.30	4.17	4.07	4.00
300	28.12	15.61	11.50	9.50	8.33	7.59	7.08	6.72	6.45	6.26	6.11	5.99
400	37.49	20.81	15.33	12.66	11.11	10.11	9.44	8.96	8.60	8.34	8.14	7.99
500	46.86	26.01	19.16	15.83	13.89	12.64	11.80	11.19	10.75	10.43	10.18	9.98
600	56.23	31.21	23.00	18.99	16.66	15.17	14.15	13.43	12.90	12.51	12.21	11.98
700	65.61	36.41	26.83	22.15	19.44	17.70	16.51	15.67	15.05	14.59	14.24	13.98
800	74.98	41.61	30.66	25.32	22.21	20.22	18.87	17.91	17.20	16.68	16.28	15.97
900	84.35	46.81	34.49	28.48	24.99	22.75	21.23	20.14	19.35	18.76	18.31	17.97
1,000	93.72	52.01	38.32	31.65	27.77	25.28	23.59	22.38	21.50	20.85	20.35	19.96
2,000	187.43	104.01	76.64	63.29	55.53	50.55	47.17	44.76	43.00	41.69	40.69	39.92
3,000	281.15	156.01	114.96	94.93	83.29	75.83	70.75	67.14	64.50	62.53	61.03	59.88
4,000	374.86	208.01	153.28	126.57	111.05	101.10	94.33	89.51	85.99	83.37	81.37	79.84
5,000	468.58	260.01	191.60	158.21	138.81	126.38	117.91	111.89	107.49	104.21	101.71	99.80
6,000	562.29	312.02	229.92	189.86	166.57	151.65	141.49	134.27	128.99	125.05	122.05	119.75
7,000	656.01	364.02	268.24	221.50	194.33	176.93	165.07	156.65	150.49	145.89	142.39	139.71
8,000	749.72	416.02	306.56	253.14	222.09	202.20	188.65	179.02	171.98	166.73	162.74	159.67
9,000	843.44	468.02	344.88	284.78	249.86	227.48	212.23	201.40	193.48	187.57	183.08	179.63
10,000	937.15	520.02	383.20	316.42	277.62	252.75	235.81	223.78	214.98	208.41	203.42	199.59
15,000	1405.73	780.03	574.80	474.63	416.42	379.13	353.71	335.67	322.47	312.61	305.12	299.38
20,000	1874.30	1040.04	766.40	632.84	555.23	505.50	471.62	447.55	429.95	416.81	406.83	399.17
25,000	2342.87	1300.05	958.00	791.05	694.04	631.87	589.52	559.44	537.44	521.01	508.54	498.96
30,000	2811.45	1560.06	1149.60	949.26	832.84	758.25	707.42	671.33	644.93	625.21	610.24	598.75
35,000	3280.02	1820.06	1341.20	1107.47	971.65	884.62	825.32	783.21	752.42	729.41	711.95	698.54
40,000	3748.59	2080.07	1532.80	1265.68	1110.45	1010.99	943.23	895.10	859.90	833.61	813.66	798.33
45,000	4217.17	2340.08	1724.40	1423.89	1249.26	1137.37	1061.13	1006.99	967.39	937.81	915.36	898.12
50,000	4685.74	2600.09	1916.00	1582.10	1388.07	1263.74	1179.03	1118.87	1074.88	1042.01	1017.07	997.91
55,000	5154.32	2860.10	2107.60	1740.31	1526.87	1390.12	1296.94	1230.76	1182.37	1146.21	1118.77	1097.70
60,000	5622.89	3120.11	2299.20	1898.52	1665.68	1516.49	1414.84	1342.65	1289.85	1250.42	1220.48	1197.49
65,000	6091.46	3380.12	2490.80	2056.73	1804.49	1642.86	1532.74	1454.53	1397.34	1354.62	1322.19	1297.28
70,000	6560.04	3640.12	2682.40	2214.94	1943.29	1769.24	1650.64	1566.42	1504.83	1458.82	1423.89	1397.07
75,000	7028.61	3900.13	2874.00	2373.15	2082.10	1895.61	1768.55	1678.31	1612.32	1563.02	1525.60	1496.86
80,000	7497.18	4160.14	3065.60	2531.36	2220.90	2021.98	1886.45	1790.19	1719.80	1667.22	1627.31	1596.65
85,000	7965.76	4420.15	3257.20	2689.57	2359.71	2148.36	2004.35	1902.08	1827.29	1771.42	1729.01	1696.44
90,000	8434.33	4680.16	3448.80	2847.78	2498.52	2274.73	2122.26	2013.97	1934.78	1875.62	1830.72	1796.23
95,000	8902.91	4940.17	3640.40	3005.99	2637.32	2401.10	2240.16	2125.85	2042.27	1979.82	1932.43	1896.02
100,000	9371.48	5200.17	3832.00	3164.20	2776.13	2527.48	2358.06	2237.74	2149.75	2084.02	2034.13	1995.81
105,000	9840.05	5460.18	4023.60	3322.41	2914.94	2653.85	2475.96	2349.63	2257.24	2188.22	2135.84	2095.60
110,000	10308.63	5720.19	4215.19	3480.62	3053.74	2780.23	2593.87	2461.51	2364.73	2292.42	2237.54	2195.39
115,000	10777.20	5980.20	4406.79	3638.83	3192.55	2906.60	2711.77	2573.40	2472.22	2396.62	2339.25	2295.18
120,000	11245.77	6240.21	4598.39	3797.04	3331.35	3032.97	2829.67	2685.29	2579.70	2500.83	2440.96	2394.97
125,000	11714.35	6500.22	4789.99	3955.25	3470.16	3159.35	2947.57	2797.18	2687.19	2605.03	2542.66	2494.76
130,000	12182.92	6760.23	4981.59	4113.46	3608.97	3285.72	3065.48	2909.06	2794.68	2709.23	2644.37	2594.55
135,000	12651.49	7020.23	5173.19	4271.67	3747.77	3412.09	3183.38	3020.95	2902.16	2813.43	2746.08	2694.34
140,000	13120.07	7280.24	5364.79	4429.88	3886.58	3538.47	3301.28	3132.84	3009.65	2917.63	2847.78	2794.13
145,000	13588.64	7540.25	5556.39	4588.09	4025.39	3664.84	3419.19	3244.72	3117.14	3021.83	2949.49	2893.92
150,000	14057.22	7800.26	5747.99	4746.30	4164.19	3791.22	3537.09	3356.61	3224.63	3126.03	3051.20	2993.71
155,000	14525.79	8060.27	5939.59	4904.51	4303.00	3917.59	3654.99	3468.50	3332.11	3230.23	3152.90	3093.50
160,000	14994.36	8320.28	6131.19	5062.72	4441.80	4043.96	3772.89	3580.38	3439.60	3334.43	3254.61	3193.29
165,000	15462.94	8580.28	6322.79	5220.93	4580.61	4170.34	3890.80	3692.27	3547.09	3438.63	3356.31	3293.08
170,000	15931.51	8840.29	6514.39	5379.14	4719.42	4296.71	4008.70	3804.16	3654.58	3542.83	3458.02	3392.87
175,000	16400.08	9100.30	6705.99	5537.35	4858.22	4423.08	4126.60	3916.04	3762.06	3647.03	3559.73	3492.66
180,000	16868.66	9360.31	6897.59	5695.56	4997.03	4549.46	4244.51	4027.93	3869.55	3751.24	3661.43	3592.45
185,000	17337.23	9620.32	7089.19	5853.77	5135.83	4675.83	4362.41	4139.82	3977.04	3855.44	3763.14	3692.24
190,000	17805.81	9880.33	7280.79	6011.98	5274.64	4802.20	4480.31	4251.70	4084.53	3959.64	3864.85	3792.03
195,000	18274.38	10140.34	7472.39	6170.19	5413.45	4928.58	4598.21	4363.59	4192.01	4063.84	3966.55	3891.82
200,000	18742.95	10400.34	7663.99	6328.40	5552.25	5054.95	4716.12	4475.48	4299.50	4168.04	4068.26	3991.61
205,000	19211.53	10660.35	7855.59	6486.61	5691.06	5181.33	4834.02	4587.36	4406.99	4272.24	4169.97	4091.40
210,000	19680.10	10920.36	8047.19	6644.82	5829.87	5307.70	4951.92	4699.25	4514.48	4376.44	4271.67	4191.19
215,000	20148.67	11180.37	8238.79	6803.03	5968.67	5434.07	5069.82	4811.14	4621.96	4480.64	4373.38	4290.98
220,000	20617.25	11440.38	8430.38	6961.24	6107.48	5560.45	5187.73	4923.02	4729.45	4584.84	4475.08	4390.77
225,000	21085.82	11700.39	8621.98	7119.45	6246.28	5686.82	5305.63	5034.91	4836.94	4689.04	4576.79	4490.56
230,000	21554.40	11960.39	8813.58	7277.66	6385.09	5813.19	5423.53	5146.80	4944.43	4793.24	4678.50	4590.35
235,000	22022.97	12220.40	9005.18	7435.87	6523.90	5939.57	5541.44	5258.69	5051.91	4897.45	4780.20	4690.14
240,000	22491.54	12480.41	9196.78	7594.07	6662.70	6065.94	5659.34	5370.57	5159.40	5001.65	4881.91	4789.93
245,000	22960.12	12740.42	9388.38	7752.28	6801.51	6192.32	5777.24	5482.46	5266.89	5105.85	4983.62	4889.72
250,000	23428.69	13000.43	9579.98	7910.49	6940.32	6318.69	5895.14	5594.35	5374.38	5210.05	5085.32	4989.51
255,000	23897.26	13260.44	9771.58	8068.70	7079.12	6445.06	6013.05	5706.23	5481.86	5314.25	5187.03	5089.30
260,000	24365.84	13520.45	9963.18	8226.91	7217.93	6571.44	6130.95	5818.12	5589.35	5418.45	5288.73	5189.09
265,000	24834.41	13780.45	10154.78	8385.12	7356.73	6697.81	6248.85	5930.01	5696.84	5522.65	5390.44	5288.88
270,000	25302.98	14040.46	10346.38	8543.33	7495.54	6824.18	6366.76	6041.89	5804.32	5626.85	5492.15	5388.67
280,000	26240.13	14560.48	10729.58	8859.75	7773.15	7076.93	6602.56	6265.67	6019.30	5835.25	5695.56	5588.25
290,000	27177.28	15080.50	11112.78	9176.17	8050.77	7329.68	6838.37	6489.44	6234.27	6043.65	5898.97	5787.83
300,000	28114.43	15600.51	11495.98	9492.59	8328.38	7582.43	7074.17	6713.21	6449.25	6252.06	6102.39	5987.41

AMOUNT OF LOAN	NUMBER OF YEARS IN TERM											
	13	14	15	16	17	18	19	20	25	30	35	40
$ 50	0.99	0.98	0.97	0.96	0.95	0.95	0.95	0.94	0.94	0.93	0.93	0.93
100	1.97	1.95	1.93	1.92	1.90	1.89	1.89	1.88	1.87	1.86	1.86	1.86
200	3.94	3.89	3.85	3.83	3.80	3.78	3.77	3.76	3.73	3.72	3.71	3.71
300	5.90	5.83	5.78	5.74	5.70	5.67	5.65	5.64	5.59	5.57	5.57	5.57
400	7.87	7.78	7.70	7.65	7.60	7.56	7.54	7.51	7.45	7.43	7.42	7.42
500	9.84	9.72	9.63	9.56	9.50	9.45	9.42	9.39	9.31	9.29	9.28	9.28
600	11.80	11.66	11.55	11.47	11.40	11.34	11.30	11.27	11.18	11.14	11.13	11.13
700	13.77	13.61	13.48	13.38	13.30	13.23	13.18	13.14	13.04	13.00	12.99	12.99
800	15.73	15.55	15.40	15.29	15.20	15.12	15.07	15.02	14.90	14.86	14.84	14.84
900	17.70	17.49	17.33	17.20	17.10	17.01	16.95	16.90	16.76	16.71	16.70	16.69
1,000	19.67	19.43	19.25	19.11	18.99	18.90	18.83	18.77	18.62	18.57	18.55	18.55
2,000	39.33	38.86	38.50	38.21	37.98	37.80	37.66	37.54	37.24	37.14	37.10	37.09
3,000	58.99	58.29	57.74	57.31	56.97	56.70	56.49	56.31	55.86	55.70	55.65	55.64
4,000	78.65	77.72	76.99	76.42	75.96	75.60	75.31	75.08	74.47	74.27	74.20	74.18
5,000	98.31	97.15	96.24	95.52	94.95	94.50	94.14	93.85	93.09	92.84	92.75	92.73
6,000	117.97	116.58	115.48	114.62	113.94	113.40	112.97	112.62	111.71	111.40	111.30	111.27
7,000	137.63	136.01	134.73	133.73	132.93	132.30	131.80	131.39	130.32	129.97	129.85	129.82
8,000	157.29	155.44	153.98	152.83	151.92	151.20	150.62	150.16	148.94	148.54	148.40	148.36
9,000	176.95	174.86	173.22	171.93	170.91	170.10	169.45	168.93	167.56	167.10	166.95	166.90
10,000	196.61	194.29	192.47	191.03	189.90	188.99	188.28	187.70	186.17	185.67	185.50	185.45
15,000	294.92	291.44	288.70	286.55	284.84	283.49	282.41	281.55	279.26	278.50	278.25	278.17
20,000	393.22	388.58	384.94	382.06	379.79	377.98	376.55	375.40	372.34	371.34	371.00	370.89
25,000	491.53	485.73	481.17	477.58	474.74	472.48	470.68	469.25	465.43	464.17	463.75	463.62
30,000	589.83	582.87	577.40	573.09	569.68	566.97	564.82	563.10	558.51	557.00	556.50	556.34
35,000	688.14	680.01	673.64	668.61	664.63	661.47	658.96	656.95	651.60	649.84	649.25	649.06
40,000	786.44	777.16	769.87	764.12	759.57	755.96	753.09	750.80	744.68	742 67	742.00	741.78
45,000	884.74	874.30	866.10	859.64	854.52	850.46	847.23	844.65	837.76	835.50	834.75	834.50
50,000	983.05	971.45	962.34	955.15	949.47	944.95	941.36	938.50	930.85	928.33	927.50	927.23
55,000	1081.35	1068.59	1058.57	1050.67	1044.41	1039.45	1035.50	1032.35	1023.93	1021.17	1020.25	1019.95
60,000	1179.66	1165.74	1154.80	1146.18	1139.36	1133.94	1129.64	1126.20	1117.02	1114.00	1113.00	1112.67
65,000	1277.96	1262.88	1251.04	1241.70	1234.30	1228.44	1223.77	1220.05	1210.10	1206.83	1205.75	1205.39
70,000	1376.27	1360.02	1347.27	1337.21	1329.25	1322.93	1317.91	1313.90	1303.19	1299.67	1298.50	1298.11
75,000	1474.57	1457.17	1443.50	1432.73	1424.20	1417.43	1412.04	1407.75	1396.27	1392.50	1391.25	1390.84
80,000	1572.87	1554.31	1539.74	1528.24	1519.14	1511.92	1506.18	1501.60	1489.36	1485.33	1484.00	1483.56
85,000	1671.18	1651.46	1635.97	1623.75	1614.09	1606.42	1600.31	1595.45	1582.44	1578.16	1576.75	1576.28
90,000	1769.48	1748.60	1732.20	1719.27	1709.03	1700.91	1694.45	1689.30	1675.52	1671.00	1669.50	1669.00
95,000	1867.79	1845.74	1828.44	1814.78	1803.98	1795.41	1788.59	1783.15	1768.61	1763.83	1762.25	1761.72
100,000	1966.09	1942.89	1924.67	1910.30	1898.93	1889.90	1882.72	1877.00	1861.69	1856.66	1855.00	1854.45
105,000	2064.40	2040.03	2020.90	2005.81	1993.87	1984.40	1976.86	1970.85	1954.78	1949.50	1947.75	1947.17
110,000	2162.70	2137.18	2117.14	2101.33	2088.82	2078.89	2070.99	2064.70	2047.86	2042.33	2040.50	2039.89
115,000	2261.01	2234.32	2213.37	2196.84	2183.76	2173.38	2165.13	2158.55	2140.95	2135.16	2133.25	2132.61
120,000	2359.31	2331.47	2309.60	2292.36	2278.71	2267.88	2259.27	2252.40	2234.03	2227.99	2226.00	2225.33
125,000	2457.61	2428.61	2405.83	2387.87	2373.66	2362.37	2353.40	2346.25	2327.11	2320.83	2318.75	2318.06
130,000	2555.92	2525.75	2502.07	2483.39	2468.60	2456.87	2447.54	2440.10	2420.20	2413.66	2411.50	2410.78
135,000	2654.22	2622.90	2598.30	2578.90	2563.55	2551.36	2541.67	2533.95	2513.28	2506.49	2504.25	2503.50
140,000	2752.53	2720.04	2694.53	2674.42	2658.49	2645.86	2635.81	2627.80	2606.37	2599.33	2597.00	2596.22
145,000	2850.83	2817.19	2790.77	2769.93	2753.44	2740.35	2729.95	2721.65	2699.45	2692.16	2689.75	2688.94
150,000	2949.14	2914.33	2887.00	2865.45	2848.39	2834.85	2824.08	2815.50	2792.54	2784.99	2782.49	2781.67
155,000	3047.44	3011.48	2983.23	2960.96	2943.33	2929.34	2918.22	2909.35	2885.62	2877.82	2875.24	2874.39
160,000	3145.74	3108.62	3079.47	3056.47	3038.28	3023.84	3012.35	3003.20	2978.71	2970.66	2967.99	2967.11
165,000	3244.05	3205.76	3175.70	3151.99	3133.22	3118.33	3106.49	3097.05	3071.79	3063.49	3060.74	3059.83
170,000	3342.35	3302.91	3271.93	3247.50	3228.17	3212.83	3200.62	3190.90	3164.87	3156.32	3153.49	3152.55
175,000	3440.66	3400.05	3368.17	3343.02	3323.12	3307.32	3294.76	3284.75	3257.96	3249.16	3246.24	3245.28
180,000	3538.96	3497.20	3464.40	3438.53	3418.06	3401.82	3388.90	3378.60	3351.04	3341.99	3338.99	3338.00
185,000	3637.27	3594.34	3560.63	3534.05	3513.01	3496.31	3483.03	3472.45	3444.13	3434.82	3431.74	3430.72
190,000	3735.57	3691.48	3656.87	3629.56	3607.95	3590.81	3577.17	3566.30	3537.21	3527.65	3524.49	3523.44
195,000	3833.88	3788.63	3753.10	3725.08	3702.90	3685.30	3671.30	3660.15	3630.30	3620.49	3617.24	3616.17
200,000	3932.18	3885.77	3849.33	3820.59	3797.85	3779.80	3765.44	3754.00	3723.38	3713.32	3709.99	3708.89
205,000	4030.48	3982.92	3945.57	3916.11	3892.79	3874.29	3859.58	3847.85	3816.46	3806.15	3802.74	3801.61
210,000	4128.79	4080.06	4041.80	4011.62	3987.74	3968.79	3953.71	3941.70	3909.55	3898.99	3895.49	3894.33
215,000	4227.09	4177.21	4138.03	4107.14	4082.68	4063.28	4047.85	4035.55	4002.63	3991.82	3988.24	3987.05
220,000	4325.40	4274.35	4234.27	4202.65	4177.63	4157.77	4141.98	4129.40	4095.72	4084.65	4080.99	4079.78
225,000	4423.70	4371.49	4330.50	4298.17	4272.58	4252.27	4236.12	4223.25	4188.80	4177.48	4173.74	4172.50
230,000	4522.01	4468.64	4426.73	4393.68	4367.52	4346.76	4330.26	4317.10	4281.89	4270.32	4266.49	4265.22
235,000	4620.31	4565.78	4522.96	4489.19	4462.47	4441.26	4424.39	4410.95	4374.97	4363.15	4359.24	4357.94
240,000	4718.61	4662.93	4619.20	4584.71	4557.41	4535.75	4518.53	4504.80	4468.06	4455.98	4451.99	4450.66
245,000	4816.92	4760.07	4715.43	4680.22	4652.36	4630.25	4612.66	4598.65	4561.14	4548.82	4544.74	4543.39
250,000	4915.22	4857.22	4811.66	4775.74	4747.31	4724.74	4706.80	4692.50	4654.22	4641.65	4637.49	4636.11
255,000	5013.53	4954.36	4907.90	4871.25	4842.25	4819.24	4800.93	4786.35	4747.31	4734.48	4730.24	4728.83
260,000	5111.83	5051.50	5004.13	4966.77	4937.20	4913.73	4895.07	4880.20	4840.39	4827.31	4822.99	4821.55
265,000	5210.14	5148.65	5100.36	5062.28	5032.14	5008.23	4989.21	4974.05	4933.48	4920.15	4915.74	4914.27
270,000	5308.44	5245.79	5196.60	5157.80	5127.09	5102.72	5083.34	5067.90	5026.56	5012.98	5008.49	5007.00
280,000	5505.05	5440.08	5389.06	5348.83	5316.98	5291.71	5271.61	5255.60	5212.73	5198.65	5193.99	5192.44
290,000	5701.66	5634.37	5581.53	5539.86	5506.87	5480.70	5459.89	5443.30	5398.90	5384.31	5379.49	5377.88
300,000	5898.27	5828.66	5774.00	5730.89	5696.77	5669.69	5648.16	5631.00	5585.07	5569.98	5564.98	5563.33

MONTHLY AMORTIZING PAYMENTS

AMOUNT OF LOAN	NUMBER OF YEARS IN TERM											
	1	2	3	4	5	6	7	8	9	10	11	12
$ 50	4.70	2.61	1.93	1.59	1.40	1.28	1.19	1.13	1.09	1.06	1.03	1.01
100	9.39	5.22	3.85	3.18	2.80	2.55	2.38	2.26	2.17	2.11	2.06	2.02
200	18.77	10.43	7.69	6.36	5.59	5.09	4.75	4.51	4.34	4.21	4.11	4.03
300	28.16	15.64	11.54	9.54	8.38	7.63	7.13	6.77	6.50	6.31	6.16	6.05
400	37.54	20.86	15.38	12.72	11.17	10.17	9.50	9.02	8.67	8.41	8.21	8.06
500	46.92	26.07	19.23	15.89	13.96	12.72	11.87	11.27	10.84	10.51	10.26	10.07
600	56.31	31.28	23.07	19.07	16.75	15.26	14.25	13.53	13.00	12.61	12.32	12.09
700	65.69	36.49	26.92	22.25	19.54	17.80	16.62	15.78	15.17	14.71	14.37	14.10
800	75.07	41.71	30.76	25.43	22.33	20.34	18.99	18.04	17.34	16.81	16.42	16.12
900	84.46	46.92	34.61	28.61	25.12	22.89	21.37	20.29	19.50	18.92	18.47	18.13
1,000	93.84	52.13	38.45	31.78	27.91	25.43	23.74	22.54	21.67	21.02	20.52	20.14
2,000	187.68	104.26	76.90	63.56	55.81	50.85	47.48	45.08	43.33	42.03	41.04	40.28
3,000	281.51	156.38	115.35	95.34	83.72	76.28	71.21	67.62	65.00	63.04	61.56	60.42
4,000	375.35	208.51	153.80	127.12	111.62	101.70	94.95	90.16	86.66	84.05	82.07	80.56
5,000	469.18	260.63	192.25	158.90	139.52	127.12	118.68	112.70	108.32	105.06	102.59	100.69
6,000	563.02	312.76	230.70	190.67	167.43	152.55	142.42	135.23	129.99	126.07	123.11	120.83
7,000	656.85	364.88	269.15	222.45	195.33	177.97	166.15	157.77	151.65	147.08	143.62	140.97
8,000	750.69	417.01	307.60	254.23	223.24	203.40	189.89	180.31	173.31	168.09	164.14	161.11
9,000	844.52	469.13	346.05	286.01	251.14	228.82	213.63	202.85	194.98	189.11	184.66	181.24
10,000	938.36	521.26	384.50	317.79	279.04	254.24	237.36	225.39	216.64	210.12	205.17	201.38
15,000	1407.53	781.89	576.75	476.68	418.56	381.36	356.04	338.08	324.96	315.17	307.76	302.07
20,000	1876.71	1042.51	769.00	635.57	558.08	508.48	474.72	450.77	433.28	420.23	410.34	402.76
25,000	2345.88	1303.14	961.25	794.46	697.60	635.60	593.40	563.46	541.59	525.28	512.92	503.45
30,000	2815.06	1563.77	1153.49	953.35	837.12	762.72	712.07	676.15	649.91	630.34	615.51	604.13
35,000	3284.24	1824.39	1345.74	1112.24	976.64	889.84	830.75	788.84	758.23	735.40	718.09	704.82
40,000	3753.41	2085.02	1537.99	1271.13	1116.16	1016.96	949.43	901.53	866.55	840.45	820.68	805.51
45,000	4222.59	2345.65	1730.24	1430.02	1255.68	1144.07	1068.11	1014.22	974.87	945.51	923.26	906.20
50,000	4691.76	2606.27	1922.49	1588.91	1395.20	1271.19	1186.79	1126.91	1083.18	1050.56	1025.84	1006.89
55,000	5160.94	2866.90	2114.73	1747.80	1534.72	1398.31	1305.47	1239.60	1191.50	1155.62	1128.43	1107.57
60,000	5630.12	3127.53	2306.98	1906.69	1674.24	1525.43	1424.14	1352.29	1299.82	1260.68	1231.01	1208.26
65,000	6099.29	3388.16	2499.23	2065.58	1813.76	1652.55	1542.82	1464.98	1408.14	1365.73	1333.60	1308.95
70,000	6568.47	3648.78	2691.48	2224.48	1953.28	1779.67	1661.50	1577.68	1516.46	1470.79	1436.18	1409.64
75,000	7037.64	3909.41	2883.73	2383.37	2092.80	1906.79	1780.18	1690.37	1624.77	1575.84	1538.76	1510.33
80,000	7506.82	4170.04	3075.97	2542.26	2232.32	2033.91	1898.86	1803.06	1733.09	1680.90	1641.35	1611.01
85,000	7976.00	4430.66	3268.22	2701.15	2371.84	2161.03	2017.53	1915.75	1841.41	1785.96	1743.93	1711.70
90,000	8445.17	4691.29	3460.47	2860.04	2511.36	2288.14	2136.21	2028.44	1949.73	1891.01	1846.52	1812.39
95,000	8914.35	4951.92	3652.72	3018.93	2650.88	2415.26	2254.89	2141.13	2058.05	1996.07	1949.10	1913.08
100,000	9383.52	5212.54	3844.97	3177.82	2790.40	2542.38	2373.57	2253.82	2166.36	2101.12	2051.68	2013.77
105,000	9852.70	5473.17	4037.21	3336.71	2929.92	2669.50	2492.25	2366.51	2274.68	2206.18	2154.27	2114.46
110,000	10321.88	5733.80	4229.46	3495.60	3069.44	2796.62	2610.93	2479.20	2383.00	2311.24	2256.85	2215.14
115,000	10791.05	5994.43	4421.71	3654.49	3208.96	2923.74	2729.60	2591.89	2491.32	2416.29	2359.44	2315.83
120,000	11260.23	6255.05	4613.96	3813.38	3348.48	3050.86	2848.28	2704.58	2599.63	2521.35	2462.02	2416.52
125,000	11729.40	6515.68	4806.21	3972.27	3488.00	3177.98	2966.96	2817.27	2707.95	2626.40	2564.60	2517.21
130,000	12198.58	6776.31	4998.45	4131.16	3627.52	3305.09	3085.64	2929.96	2816.27	2731.46	2667.19	2617.90
135,000	12667.75	7036.93	5190.70	4290.06	3767.04	3432.21	3204.32	3042.65	2924.59	2836.51	2769.77	2718.58
140,000	13136.93	7297.56	5382.95	4448.95	3906.56	3559.33	3322.99	3155.35	3032.91	2941.57	2872.35	2819.27
145,000	13606.11	7558.19	5575.20	4607.84	4046.08	3686.45	3441.67	3268.04	3141.22	3046.63	2974.94	2919.96
150,000	14075.28	7818.81	5767.45	4766.73	4185.60	3813.57	3560.35	3380.73	3249.54	3151.68	3077.52	3020.65
155,000	14544.46	8079.44	5959.69	4925.62	4325.12	3940.69	3679.03	3493.42	3357.86	3256.74	3180.11	3121.34
160,000	15013.63	8340.07	6151.94	5084.51	4464.64	4067.81	3797.71	3606.11	3466.18	3361.79	3282.69	3222.02
165,000	15482.81	8600.70	6344.19	5243.40	4604.16	4194.93	3916.39	3718.80	3574.50	3466.85	3385.27	3322.71
170,000	15951.99	8861.32	6536.44	5402.29	4743.68	4322.05	4035.06	3831.49	3682.81	3571.91	3487.86	3423.40
175,000	16421.16	9121.95	6728.69	5561.18	4883.20	4449.16	4153.74	3944.18	3791.13	3676.96	3590.44	3524.09
180,000	16890.34	9382.58	6920.93	5720.07	5022.72	4576.28	4272.42	4056.87	3899.45	3782.02	3693.03	3624.78
185,000	17359.51	9643.20	7113.18	5878.96	5162.23	4703.40	4391.10	4169.56	4007.77	3887.07	3795.61	3725.46
190,000	17828.69	9903.83	7305.43	6037.85	5301.75	4830.52	4509.78	4282.25	4116.09	3992.13	3898.19	3826.15
195,000	18297.87	10164.46	7497.68	6196.74	5441.27	4957.64	4628.45	4394.94	4224.40	4097.19	4000.78	3926.84
200,000	18767.04	10425.08	7689.93	6355.64	5580.79	5084.76	4747.13	4507.63	4332.72	4202.24	4103.36	4027.53
205,000	19236.22	10685.71	7882.17	6514.53	5720.31	5211.88	4865.81	4620.32	4441.04	4307.30	4205.95	4128.22
210,000	19705.39	10946.34	8074.42	6673.42	5859.83	5339.00	4984.49	4733.02	4549.36	4412.35	4308.53	4228.91
215,000	20174.57	11206.97	8266.67	6832.31	5999.35	5466.12	5103.17	4845.71	4657.67	4517.41	4411.11	4329.59
220,000	20643.75	11467.59	8458.92	6991.20	6138.87	5593.23	5221.85	4958.40	4765.99	4622.47	4513.70	4430.28
225,000	21112.92	11728.22	8651.17	7150.09	6278.39	5720.35	5340.52	5071.09	4874.31	4727.52	4616.28	4530.97
230,000	21582.10	11988.85	8843.41	7308.98	6417.91	5847.47	5459.20	5183.78	4982.63	4832.58	4718.87	4631.66
235,000	22051.27	12249.47	9035.66	7467.87	6557.43	5974.59	5577.88	5296.47	5090.95	4937.63	4821.45	4732.35
240,000	22520.45	12510.10	9227.91	7626.76	6696.95	6101.71	5696.56	5409.16	5199.26	5042.69	4924.03	4833.03
245,000	22989.62	12770.73	9420.16	7785.65	6836.47	6228.83	5815.24	5521.85	5307.58	5147.75	5026.62	4933.72
250,000	23458.80	13031.35	9612.41	7944.54	6975.99	6355.95	5933.91	5634.54	5415.90	5252.80	5129.20	5034.41
255,000	23927.98	13291.98	9804.65	8103.43	7115.51	6483.07	6052.59	5747.23	5524.22	5357.86	5231.79	5135.10
260,000	24397.15	13552.61	9996.90	8262.32	7255.03	6610.18	6171.27	5859.92	5632.54	5462.91	5334.37	5235.79
265,000	24866.33	13813.24	10189.15	8421.21	7394.55	6737.30	6289.95	5972.61	5740.85	5567.97	5436.95	5336.47
270,000	25335.50	14073.86	10381.40	8580.11	7534.07	6864.42	6408.63	6085.30	5849.17	5673.02	5539.54	5437.16
280,000	26273.86	14595.12	10765.89	8897.89	7813.11	7118.66	6645.98	6310.69	6065.81	5883.14	5744.70	5638.54
290,000	27212.21	15116.37	11150.39	9215.67	8092.15	7372.90	6883.34	6536.07	6282.44	6093.25	5949.87	5839.91
300,000	28150.56	15637.62	11534.89	9533.45	8371.19	7627.14	7120.70	6761.45	6499.08	6303.36	6155.04	6041.29

AMOUNT OF LOAN	NUMBER OF YEARS IN TERM											
	13	14	15	16	17	18	19	20	25	30	35	40
$ 50	1.00	0.99	0.98	0.97	0.96	0.96	0.96	0.95	0.95	0.94	0.94	0.94
100	1.99	1.97	1.95	1.93	1.92	1.91	1.91	1.90	1.89	1.88	1.88	1.88
200	3.97	3.93	3.89	3.86	3.84	3.82	3.81	3.80	3.77	3.76	3.76	3.76
300	5.96	5.89	5.84	5.79	5.76	5.73	5.71	5.70	5.65	5.64	5.63	5.63
400	7.94	7.85	7.78	7.72	7.68	7.64	7.62	7.59	7.53	7.51	7.51	7.51
500	9.93	9.81	9.72	9.65	9.60	9.55	9.52	9.49	9.42	9.39	9.38	9.38
600	11.91	11.77	11.67	11.58	11.52	11.46	11.42	11.39	11.30	11.27	11.26	11.26
700	13.90	13.74	13.61	13.51	13.43	13.37	13.32	13.28	13.18	13.15	13.14	13.13
800	15.88	15.70	15.55	15.44	15.35	15.28	15.23	15.18	15.06	15.02	15.01	15.01
900	17.86	17.66	17.50	17.37	17.27	17.19	17.13	17.08	16.94	16.90	16.89	16.88
1,000	19.85	19.62	19.44	19.30	19.19	19.10	19.03	18.97	18.83	18.78	18.76	18.76
2,000	39.69	39.24	38.88	38.60	38.37	38.20	38.06	37.94	37.65	37.55	37.52	37.51
3,000	59.54	58.85	58.31	57.89	57.56	57.29	57.08	56.91	56.47	56.33	56.28	56.26
4,000	79.38	78.47	77.75	77.19	76.74	76.39	76.11	75.88	75.29	75.10	75.04	75.02
5,000	99.23	98.08	97.19	96.48	95.92	95.48	95.13	94.85	94.11	93.87	93.79	93.77
6,000	119.07	117.70	116.62	115.78	115.11	114.58	114.16	113.82	112.93	112.65	112.55	112.52
7,000	138.91	137.31	136.06	135.07	134.29	133.67	133.18	132.79	131.76	131.42	131.31	131.27
8,000	158.76	156.93	155.49	154.37	153.47	152.77	152.21	151.76	150.58	150.19	150.07	150.03
9,000	178.60	176.54	174.93	173.66	172.66	171.86	171.23	170.73	169.40	168.97	168.82	168.78
10,000	198.45	196.16	194.37	192.96	191.84	190.96	190.26	189.70	188.22	187.74	187.58	187.53
15,000	297.67	294.24	291.55	289.43	287.76	286.44	285.39	284.55	282.33	281.61	281.37	281.29
20,000	396.89	392.31	388.73	385.91	383.68	381.91	380.51	379.40	376.44	375.47	375.16	375.06
25,000	496.11	490.39	485.91	482.38	479.60	477.39	475.64	474.25	470.54	469.34	468.95	468.82
30,000	595.33	588.47	583.09	578.86	575.51	572.87	570.77	569.10	564.65	563.21	562.74	562.58
35,000	694.55	686.55	680.27	675.33	671.43	668.34	665.89	663.94	658.76	657.07	656.52	656.34
40,000	793.77	784.62	777.45	771.81	767.35	763.82	761.02	758.79	752.87	750.94	750.31	750.11
45,000	892.99	882.70	874.63	868.28	863.27	859.30	856.15	853.64	846.97	844.81	844.10	843.87
50,000	992.21	980.78	971.81	964.76	959.19	954.78	951.27	948.49	941.08	938.67	937.89	937.63
55,000	1091.43	1078.85	1068.99	1061.23	1055.11	1050.25	1046.40	1043.34	1035.19	1032.54	1031.68	1031.39
60,000	1190.66	1176.93	1166.18	1157.71	1151.02	1145.73	1141.53	1138.19	1129.30	1126.41	1125.47	1125.16
65,000	1289.88	1275.01	1263.36	1254.19	1246.94	1241.21	1236.65	1233.04	1223.40	1220.28	1219.25	1218.92
70,000	1389.10	1373.09	1360.54	1350.66	1342.86	1336.68	1331.78	1327.88	1317.51	1314.14	1313.04	1312.68
75,000	1488.32	1471.16	1457.72	1447.14	1438.78	1432.16	1426.91	1422.73	1411.62	1408.01	1406.83	1406.44
80,000	1587.54	1569.24	1554.90	1543.61	1534.70	1527.64	1522.03	1517.58	1505.73	1501.88	1500.62	1500.21
85,000	1686.76	1667.32	1652.08	1640.09	1630.61	1623.11	1617.16	1612.43	1599.83	1595.74	1594.41	1593.97
90,000	1785.98	1765.39	1749.26	1736.56	1726.53	1718.59	1712.29	1707.28	1693.94	1689.61	1688.20	1687.73
95,000	1885.20	1863.47	1846.44	1833.04	1822.45	1814.07	1807.42	1802.13	1788.05	1783.48	1781.98	1781.49
100,000	1984.42	1961.55	1943.62	1929.51	1918.37	1909.55	1902.54	1896.98	1882.16	1877.34	1875.77	1875.26
105,000	2083.64	2059.63	2040.80	2025.99	2014.29	2005.02	1997.67	1991.82	1976.26	1971.21	1969.56	1969.02
110,000	2182.86	2157.70	2137.98	2122.46	2110.21	2100.50	2092.80	2086.67	2070.37	2065.08	2063.35	2062.78
115,000	2282.08	2255.78	2235.17	2218.94	2206.12	2195.98	2187.92	2181.52	2164.40	2158.95	2157.14	2156.54
120,000	2381.31	2353.86	2332.35	2315.42	2302.04	2291.45	2283.05	2276.37	2258.59	2252.81	2250.93	2250.31
125,000	2480.53	2451.94	2429.53	2411.89	2397.96	2386.93	2378.18	2371.22	2352.69	2346.68	2344.71	2344.07
130,000	2579.75	2550.01	2526.71	2508.37	2493.88	2482.41	2473.30	2466.07	2446.80	2440.55	2438.50	2437.83
135,000	2678.97	2648.09	2623.89	2604.84	2589.80	2577.88	2568.43	2560.91	2540.91	2534.41	2532.29	2531.59
140,000	2778.19	2746.17	2721.07	2701.32	2685.72	2673.36	2663.56	2655.76	2635.02	2628.28	2626.08	2625.36
145,000	2877.41	2844.24	2818.25	2797.79	2781.63	2768.84	2758.68	2750.61	2729.12	2722.15	2719.87	2719.12
150,000	2976.63	2942.32	2915.43	2894.27	2877.55	2864.32	2853.81	2845.46	2823.23	2816.01	2813.66	2812.88
155,000	3075.85	3040.40	3012.61	2990.74	2973.47	2959.79	2948.94	2940.31	2917.34	2909.88	2907.44	2906.64
160,000	3175.07	3138.48	3109.79	3087.22	3069.39	3055.27	3044.06	3035.16	3011.45	3003.75	3001.23	3000.41
165,000	3274.29	3236.55	3206.97	3183.69	3165.31	3150.75	3139.19	3130.01	3105.55	3097.62	3095.02	3094.17
170,000	3373.51	3334.63	3304.16	3280.17	3261.22	3246.22	3234.32	3224.85	3199.66	3191.48	3188.81	3187.93
175,000	3472.73	3432.71	3401.34	3376.64	3357.14	3341.70	3329.44	3319.70	3293.77	3285.35	3282.60	3281.70
180,000	3571.96	3530.78	3498.52	3473.12	3453.06	3437.18	3424.57	3414.55	3387.88	3379.22	3376.39	3375.46
185,000	3671.18	3628.86	3595.70	3569.60	3548.98	3532.65	3519.70	3509.40	3481.98	3473.08	3470.17	3469.22
190,000	3770.40	3726.94	3692.88	3666.07	3644.90	3628.13	3614.83	3604.25	3576.09	3566.95	3563.96	3562.98
195,000	3869.62	3825.02	3790.06	3762.55	3740.82	3723.61	3709.95	3699.10	3670.20	3660.82	3657.75	3656.75
200,000	3968.84	3923.09	3887.24	3859.02	3836.73	3819.09	3805.08	3793.95	3764.31	3754.68	3751.54	3750.51
205,000	4068.06	4021.17	3984.42	3955.50	3932.65	3914.56	3900.21	3888.79	3858.41	3848.55	3845.33	3844.27
210,000	4167.28	4119.25	4081.60	4051.97	4028.57	4010.04	3995.33	3983.64	3952.52	3942.42	3939.12	3938.03
215,000	4266.50	4217.32	4178.78	4148.45	4124.49	4105.52	4090.46	4078.49	4046.63	4036.29	4032.90	4031.80
220,000	4365.72	4315.40	4275.96	4244.92	4220.41	4200.99	4185.59	4173.34	4140.74	4130.15	4126.69	4125.56
225,000	4464.94	4413.47	4373.15	4341.40	4316.33	4296.47	4280.71	4268.19	4234.84	4224.02	4220.48	4219.32
230,000	4564.16	4511.56	4470.33	4437.87	4412.24	4391.95	4375.84	4363.04	4328.95	4317.89	4314.27	4313.08
235,000	4663.38	4609.63	4567.51	4534.35	4508.16	4487.42	4470.97	4457.88	4423.06	4411.75	4408.06	4406.85
240,000	4762.61	4707.71	4664.69	4630.83	4604.08	4582.90	4566.09	4552.73	4517.17	4505.62	4501.85	4500.61
245,000	4861.83	4805.79	4761.87	4727.30	4700.00	4678.38	4661.22	4647.58	4611.27	4599.49	4595.63	4594.37
250,000	4961.05	4903.87	4859.05	4823.78	4795.92	4773.86	4756.35	4742.43	4705.38	4693.35	4689.42	4688.13
255,000	5060.27	5001.94	4956.23	4920.25	4891.83	4869.33	4851.47	4837.28	4799.49	4787.22	4783.21	4781.90
260,000	5159.49	5100.02	5053.41	5016.73	4987.75	4964.81	4946.60	4932.13	4893.60	4881.09	4877.00	4875.66
265,000	5258.71	5198.10	5150.59	5113.20	5083.67	5060.29	5041.73	5026.98	4987.71	4974.96	4970.79	4969.42
270,000	5357.93	5296.17	5247.77	5209.68	5179.59	5155.76	5136.85	5121.82	5081.81	5068.82	5064.58	5063.18
280,000	5556.37	5492.33	5442.14	5402.63	5371.43	5346.72	5327.11	5311.52	5270.03	5256.56	5252.15	5250.71
290,000	5754.81	5688.48	5636.50	5595.58	5563.26	5537.67	5517.36	5501.22	5458.24	5444.29	5439.73	5438.23
300,000	5953.26	5884.64	5830.86	5788.53	5755.10	5728.63	5707.62	5690.92	5646.46	5632.02	5627.31	5625.76

22.75%　　MONTHLY AMORTIZING PAYMENTS

AMOUNT OF LOAN	NUMBER OF YEARS IN TERM											
	1	2	3	4	5	6	7	8	9	10	11	12
$ 50	4.70	2.62	1.93	1.60	1.41	1.28	1.20	1.14	1.10	1.06	1.04	1.02
100	9.40	5.23	3.86	3.20	2.81	2.56	2.39	2.27	2.19	2.12	2.07	2.04
200	18.80	10.45	7.72	6.39	5.61	5.12	4.78	4.54	4.37	4.24	4.14	4.07
300	28.19	15.68	11.58	9.58	8.42	7.68	7.17	6.81	6.55	6.36	6.21	6.10
400	37.59	20.90	15.44	12.77	11.22	10.23	9.56	9.08	8.74	8.48	8.28	8.13
500	46.98	26.13	19.29	15.96	14.03	12.79	11.95	11.35	10.92	10.60	10.35	10.16
600	56.38	31.35	23.15	19.15	16.83	15.35	14.34	13.62	13.10	12.71	12.42	12.20
700	65.77	36.58	27.01	22.35	19.64	17.91	16.73	15.89	15.29	14.83	14.49	14.23
800	75.17	41.80	30.87	25.54	22.44	20.46	19.12	18.16	17.47	16.95	16.56	16.26
900	84.57	47.03	34.73	28.73	25.25	23.02	21.51	20.43	19.65	19.07	18.63	18.29
1,000	93.96	52.25	38.58	31.92	28.05	25.58	23.90	22.70	21.84	21.19	20.70	20.32
2,000	187.92	104.50	77.16	63.83	56.10	51.15	47.79	45.40	43.67	42.37	41.39	40.64
3,000	281.87	156.75	115.74	95.75	84.15	76.72	71.68	68.10	65.50	63.55	62.08	60.96
4,000	375.83	209.00	154.32	127.66	112.19	102.30	95.57	90.80	87.33	84.74	82.78	81.28
5,000	469.78	261.25	192.90	159.58	140.24	127.87	119.46	113.50	109.16	105.92	103.47	101.59
6,000	563.74	313.50	231.48	191.49	168.29	153.44	143.35	136.20	130.99	127.10	124.16	121.91
7,000	657.69	365.75	270.06	223.41	196.33	179.02	167.24	158.90	152.82	148.28	144.85	142.23
8,000	751.65	418.00	308.64	255.32	224.38	204.59	191.13	181.60	174.65	169.47	165.55	162.55
9,000	845.61	470.25	347.22	287.24	252.43	230.16	215.03	204.30	196.48	190.65	186.24	182.86
10,000	939.56	522.50	385.80	319.15	280.48	255.74	238.92	227.00	218.31	211.83	206.93	203.18
15,000	1409.34	783.74	578.70	478.72	420.71	383.60	358.37	340.50	327.46	317.75	310.40	304.77
20,000	1879.12	1044.99	771.60	638.30	560.95	511.47	477.83	453.99	436.61	423.66	413.86	406.36
25,000	2348.90	1306.24	964.49	797.87	701.18	639.34	597.28	567.49	545.76	529.57	517.33	507.95
30,000	2818.68	1567.48	1157.39	957.44	841.42	767.20	716.74	680.99	654.91	635.49	620.79	609.54
35,000	3288.45	1828.73	1350.29	1117.02	981.65	895.07	836.20	794.48	764.06	741.40	724.25	711.13
40,000	3758.23	2089.98	1543.19	1276.59	1121.89	1022.93	955.65	907.98	873.21	847.31	827.72	812.71
45,000	4228.01	2351.22	1736.08	1436.16	1262.12	1150.80	1075.11	1021.48	982.36	953.23	931.18	914.30
50,000	4697.79	2612.47	1928.98	1595.74	1402.36	1278.67	1194.56	1134.98	1091.51	1059.14	1034.65	1015.89
55,000	5167.57	2873.71	2121.88	1755.31	1542.59	1406.53	1314.02	1248.47	1200.67	1165.05	1138.11	1117.48
60,000	5637.35	3134.96	2314.78	1914.88	1682.83	1534.40	1433.48	1361.97	1309.82	1270.97	1241.57	1219.07
65,000	6107.13	3396.21	2507.68	2074.46	1823.06	1662.26	1552.93	1475.47	1418.97	1376.88	1345.04	1320.66
70,000	6576.90	3657.45	2700.57	2234.03	1963.30	1790.13	1672.39	1588.96	1528.12	1482.80	1448.50	1422.25
75,000	7046.68	3918.70	2893.47	2393.60	2103.53	1918.00	1791.84	1702.46	1637.27	1588.71	1551.97	1523.84
80,000	7516.46	4179.95	3086.37	2553.18	2243.77	2045.86	1911.30	1815.96	1746.42	1694.62	1655.43	1625.42
85,000	7986.24	4441.19	3279.27	2712.75	2384.00	2173.73	2030.76	1929.46	1855.57	1800.54	1758.89	1727.01
90,000	8456.02	4702.44	3472.16	2872.32	2524.24	2301.60	2150.21	2042.95	1964.72	1906.45	1862.36	1828.60
95,000	8925.80	4963.69	3665.06	3031.90	2664.47	2429.46	2269.67	2156.45	2073.87	2012.36	1965.82	1930.19
100,000	9395.58	5224.93	3857.96	3191.47	2804.71	2557.33	2389.12	2269.95	2183.02	2118.28	2069.29	2031.78
105,000	9865.35	5486.18	4050.86	3351.04	2944.94	2685.19	2508.58	2383.44	2292.18	2224.19	2172.75	2133.37
110,000	10335.13	5747.42	4243.75	3510.62	3085.18	2813.06	2628.04	2496.94	2401.33	2330.10	2276.22	2234.96
115,000	10804.91	6008.67	4436.65	3670.19	3225.41	2940.93	2747.49	2610.44	2510.48	2436.02	2379.68	2336.55
120,000	11274.69	6269.92	4629.55	3829.76	3365.65	3068.79	2866.95	2723.94	2619.63	2541.93	2483.14	2438.13
125,000	11744.47	6531.16	4822.45	3989.34	3505.88	3196.66	2986.40	2837.43	2728.78	2647.85	2586.61	2539.72
130,000	12214.25	6792.41	5015.35	4148.91	3646.12	3324.52	3105.86	2950.93	2837.93	2753.76	2690.07	2641.31
135,000	12684.03	7053.66	5208.24	4308.48	3786.35	3452.39	3225.31	3064.43	2947.08	2859.67	2793.54	2742.90
140,000	13153.80	7314.90	5401.14	4468.06	3926.59	3580.26	3344.77	3177.92	3056.23	2965.59	2897.00	2844.49
145,000	13623.58	7576.15	5594.04	4627.63	4066.82	3708.12	3464.23	3291.42	3165.38	3071.50	3000.46	2946.08
150,000	14093.36	7837.40	5786.94	4787.20	4207.06	3835.99	3583.68	3404.92	3274.53	3177.41	3103.93	3047.67
155,000	14563.14	8098.64	5979.83	4946.78	4347.29	3963.86	3703.14	3518.42	3383.69	3283.33	3207.39	3149.26
160,000	15032.92	8359.89	6172.73	5106.35	4487.53	4091.72	3822.59	3631.91	3492.84	3389.24	3310.86	3250.84
165,000	15502.70	8621.13	6365.63	5265.92	4627.76	4219.59	3942.05	3745.41	3601.99	3495.15	3414.32	3352.43
170,000	15972.48	8882.38	6558.53	5425.50	4768.00	4347.45	4061.51	3858.91	3711.14	3601.07	3517.78	3454.02
175,000	16442.25	9143.63	6751.42	5585.07	4908.23	4475.32	4180.96	3972.40	3820.29	3706.98	3621.25	3555.61
180,000	16912.03	9404.87	6944.32	5744.64	5048.47	4603.19	4300.42	4085.90	3929.44	3812.90	3724.71	3657.20
185,000	17381.81	9666.12	7137.22	5904.22	5188.70	4731.05	4419.87	4199.40	4038.59	3918.81	3828.18	3758.79
190,000	17851.59	9927.37	7330.12	6063.79	5328.94	4858.92	4539.33	4312.90	4147.74	4024.72	3931.64	3860.38
195,000	18321.37	10188.61	7523.02	6223.36	5469.17	4986.78	4658.79	4426.39	4256.89	4130.64	4035.11	3961.96
200,000	18791.15	10449.86	7715.91	6382.94	5609.41	5114.65	4778.24	4539.89	4366.04	4236.55	4138.57	4063.55
205,000	19260.93	10711.11	7908.81	6542.51	5749.64	5242.52	4897.70	4653.39	4475.20	4342.46	4242.03	4165.14
210,000	19730.70	10972.35	8101.71	6702.08	5889.88	5370.38	5017.15	4766.88	4584.35	4448.38	4345.50	4266.73
215,000	20200.48	11233.60	8294.61	6861.66	6030.11	5498.25	5136.61	4880.38	4693.50	4554.29	4448.96	4368.32
220,000	20670.26	11494.84	8487.50	7021.23	6170.35	5626.12	5256.07	4993.88	4802.65	4660.20	4552.43	4469.91
225,000	21140.04	11756.09	8680.40	7180.80	6310.58	5753.98	5375.52	5107.37	4911.80	4766.12	4655.89	4571.50
230,000	21609.82	12017.34	8873.30	7340.38	6450.82	5881.85	5494.98	5220.87	5020.95	4872.03	4759.35	4673.09
235,000	22079.60	12278.58	9066.20	7499.95	6591.06	6009.71	5614.43	5334.37	5130.10	4977.94	4862.82	4774.67
240,000	22549.38	12539.83	9259.09	7659.52	6731.29	6137.58	5733.89	5447.87	5239.25	5083.86	4966.28	4876.26
245,000	23019.15	12801.08	9451.99	7819.10	6871.53	6265.45	5853.34	5561.36	5348.40	5189.77	5069.75	4977.85
250,000	23488.93	13062.32	9644.89	7978.67	7011.76	6393.31	5972.80	5674.86	5457.55	5295.69	5173.21	5079.44
255,000	23958.71	13323.57	9837.79	8138.24	7152.00	6521.18	6092.26	5788.36	5566.71	5401.60	5276.67	5181.03
260,000	24428.49	13584.82	10030.69	8297.82	7292.23	6649.04	6211.71	5901.85	5675.86	5507.51	5380.14	5282.62
265,000	24898.27	13846.06	10223.58	8457.39	7432.47	6776.91	6331.17	6015.35	5785.01	5613.43	5483.60	5384.21
270,000	25368.05	14107.31	10416.48	8616.96	7572.70	6904.78	6450.62	6128.85	5894.16	5719.34	5587.07	5485.80
280,000	26307.60	14629.80	10802.28	8936.11	7853.17	7160.51	6689.54	6355.84	6112.46	5931.17	5794.00	5688.97
290,000	27247.16	15152.29	11188.07	9255.26	8133.64	7416.24	6928.45	6582.84	6330.76	6142.99	6000.92	5892.15
300,000	28186.72	15674.79	11573.87	9574.40	8414.11	7671.97	7167.36	6809.83	6549.06	6354.82	6207.85	6095.33

168

AMOUNT OF LOAN	NUMBER OF YEARS IN TERM											
	13	14	15	16	17	18	19	20	25	30	35	40
$ 50	1.01	1.00	0.99	0.98	0.97	0.97	0.97	0.96	0.96	0.95	0.95	0.95
100	2.01	1.99	1.97	1.95	1.94	1.93	1.93	1.92	1.91	1.90	1.90	1.90
200	4.01	3.97	3.93	3.90	3.88	3.86	3.85	3.84	3.81	3.80	3.80	3.80
300	6.01	5.95	5.89	5.85	5.82	5.79	5.77	5.76	5.71	5.70	5.69	5.69
400	8.02	7.93	7.86	7.80	7.76	7.72	7.69	7.67	7.62	7.60	7.59	7.59
500	10.02	9.91	9.82	9.75	9.69	9.65	9.62	9.59	9.52	9.50	9.49	9.49
600	12.02	11.89	11.78	11.70	11.63	11.58	11.54	11.51	11.42	11.39	11.38	11.38
700	14.02	13.87	13.74	13.65	13.57	13.51	13.46	13.42	13.32	13.29	13.28	13.28
800	16.03	15.85	15.71	15.60	15.51	15.44	15.38	15.34	15.23	15.19	15.18	15.17
900	18.03	17.83	17.67	17.54	17.45	17.37	17.31	17.26	17.13	17.09	17.07	17.07
1,000	20.03	19.81	19.63	19.49	19.38	19.30	19.23	19.17	19.03	18.99	18.97	18.97
2,000	40.06	39.61	39.26	38.98	38.76	38.59	38.45	38.34	38.06	37.97	37.94	37.93
3,000	60.09	59.41	58.88	58.47	58.14	57.88	57.68	57.51	57.08	56.95	56.90	56.89
4,000	80.12	79.22	78.51	77.96	77.52	77.17	76.90	76.68	76.11	75.93	75.87	75.85
5,000	100.14	99.02	98.14	97.44	96.90	96.47	96.12	95.85	95.14	94.91	94.83	94.81
6,000	120.17	118.82	117.76	116.93	116.28	115.76	115.35	115.02	114.16	113.89	113.80	113.77
7,000	140.20	138.62	137.39	136.42	135.65	135.05	134.57	134.19	133.19	132.87	132.76	132.73
8,000	160.23	158.43	157.01	155.91	155.03	154.34	153.80	153.36	152.22	151.85	151.73	151.69
9,000	180.26	178.23	176.64	175.39	174.41	173.63	173.02	172.53	171.24	170.83	170.69	170.65
10,000	200.28	198.03	196.27	194.88	193.79	192.93	192.24	191.70	190.27	189.81	189.66	189.61
15,000	300.42	297.04	294.40	292.32	290.68	289.39	288.36	287.55	285.40	284.71	284.49	284.41
20,000	400.56	396.06	392.53	389.76	387.57	385.85	384.48	383.40	380.53	379.61	379.31	379.22
25,000	500.70	495.07	490.66	487.20	484.47	482.31	480.60	479.25	475.66	474.51	474.14	474.02
30,000	600.84	594.08	588.79	584.63	581.36	578.77	576.72	575.10	570.79	569.41	568.97	568.82
35,000	700.98	693.09	686.92	682.07	678.25	675.23	672.84	670.95	665.93	664.32	663.80	663.63
40,000	801.12	792.11	785.05	779.51	775.14	771.69	768.96	766.79	761.06	759.22	758.62	758.43
45,000	901.26	891.12	883.18	876.95	872.04	868.15	865.08	862.64	856.19	854.12	853.45	853.23
50,000	1001.40	990.13	981.31	974.39	968.93	964.62	961.20	958.49	951.32	949.02	948.28	948.04
55,000	1101.54	1089.14	1079.45	1071.83	1065.82	1061.08	1057.32	1054.34	1046.45	1043.92	1043.10	1042.84
60,000	1201.68	1188.16	1177.58	1169.26	1162.71	1157.54	1153.44	1150.19	1141.58	1138.82	1137.93	1137.64
65,000	1301.82	1287.17	1275.71	1266.70	1259.61	1254.00	1249.56	1246.04	1236.72	1233.73	1232.76	1232.45
70,000	1401.96	1386.18	1373.84	1364.14	1356.50	1350.46	1345.68	1341.89	1331.85	1328.63	1327.59	1327.25
75,000	1502.10	1485.19	1471.97	1461.58	1453.39	1446.92	1441.80	1437.73	1426.98	1423.53	1422.41	1422.05
80,000	1602.24	1584.21	1570.10	1559.02	1550.28	1543.38	1537.92	1533.58	1522.11	1518.43	1517.24	1516.86
85,000	1702.38	1683.22	1668.23	1656.46	1647.18	1639.84	1634.04	1629.43	1617.24	1613.33	1612.07	1611.66
90,000	1802.52	1782.23	1766.36	1753.89	1744.07	1736.30	1730.16	1725.28	1712.37	1708.23	1706.90	1706.46
95,000	1902.66	1881.24	1864.49	1851.33	1840.96	1832.77	1826.28	1821.13	1807.51	1803.13	1801.72	1801.27
100,000	2002.80	1980.26	1962.62	1948.77	1937.85	1929.23	1922.40	1916.98	1902.64	1898.04	1896.55	1896.07
105,000	2102.94	2079.27	2060.75	2046.21	2034.75	2025.69	2018.51	2012.83	1997.77	1992.94	1991.38	1990.87
110,000	2203.08	2178.28	2158.89	2143.65	2131.64	2122.15	2114.63	2108.67	2092.90	2087.84	2086.20	2085.68
115,000	2303.22	2277.30	2257.02	2241.09	2228.53	2218.61	2210.75	2204.52	2188.03	2182.74	2181.03	2180.48
120,000	2403.36	2376.31	2355.15	2338.52	2325.42	2315.07	2306.87	2300.37	2283.16	2277.64	2275.86	2275.28
125,000	2503.50	2475.32	2453.28	2435.96	2422.32	2411.53	2402.99	2396.22	2378.30	2372.54	2370.69	2370.08
130,000	2603.64	2574.33	2551.41	2533.40	2519.21	2507.99	2499.11	2492.07	2473.43	2467.45	2465.51	2464.89
135,000	2703.78	2673.35	2649.54	2630.84	2616.10	2604.45	2595.23	2587.92	2568.56	2562.35	2560.34	2559.69
140,000	2803.92	2772.36	2747.67	2728.28	2712.99	2700.92	2691.35	2683.77	2663.69	2657.25	2655.17	2654.49
145,000	2904.06	2871.37	2845.80	2825.72	2809.89	2797.38	2787.47	2779.61	2758.82	2752.15	2750.00	2749.30
150,000	3004.20	2970.38	2943.93	2923.15	2906.78	2893.84	2883.59	2875.46	2853.95	2847.05	2844.82	2844.10
155,000	3104.34	3069.40	3042.06	3020.59	3003.67	2990.30	2979.71	2971.31	2949.08	2941.95	2939.65	2938.90
160,000	3204.48	3168.41	3140.19	3118.03	3100.56	3086.76	3075.83	3067.16	3044.22	3036.85	3034.48	3033.71
165,000	3304.62	3267.42	3238.33	3215.47	3197.46	3183.22	3171.95	3163.01	3139.35	3131.76	3129.30	3128.51
170,000	3404.76	3366.43	3336.46	3312.91	3294.35	3279.68	3268.07	3258.86	3234.48	3226.66	3224.13	3223.31
175,000	3504.90	3465.45	3434.59	3410.35	3391.24	3376.14	3364.19	3354.71	3329.61	3321.56	3318.96	3318.12
180,000	3605.04	3564.46	3532.72	3507.78	3488.13	3472.60	3460.31	3450.55	3424.74	3416.46	3413.79	3412.92
185,000	3705.18	3663.47	3630.85	3605.22	3585.03	3569.07	3556.43	3546.40	3519.87	3511.36	3508.61	3507.72
190,000	3805.32	3762.48	3728.98	3702.66	3681.92	3665.53	3652.55	3642.25	3615.01	3606.26	3603.44	3602.53
195,000	3905.46	3861.50	3827.11	3800.10	3778.81	3761.99	3748.67	3738.10	3710.14	3701.17	3698.27	3697.33
200,000	4005.60	3960.51	3925.24	3897.54	3875.70	3858.45	3844.79	3833.95	3805.27	3796.07	3793.09	3792.13
205,000	4105.74	4059.52	4023.37	3994.98	3972.60	3954.91	3940.90	3929.80	3900.40	3890.97	3887.92	3886.94
210,000	4205.88	4158.54	4121.50	4092.41	4069.49	4051.37	4037.02	4025.65	3995.53	3985.87	3982.75	3981.74
215,000	4306.02	4257.55	4219.63	4189.85	4166.38	4147.83	4133.14	4121.49	4090.66	4080.77	4077.58	4076.54
220,000	4406.16	4356.56	4317.77	4287.29	4263.27	4244.29	4229.26	4217.34	4185.80	4175.67	4172.40	4171.35
225,000	4506.30	4455.57	4415.90	4384.73	4360.16	4340.75	4325.38	4313.19	4280.93	4270.58	4267.23	4266.15
230,000	4606.44	4554.59	4514.03	4482.17	4457.06	4437.21	4421.50	4409.04	4376.06	4365.48	4362.06	4360.95
235,000	4706.58	4653.60	4612.16	4579.61	4553.95	4533.68	4517.62	4504.89	4471.19	4460.38	4456.89	4455.76
240,000	4806.72	4752.61	4710.29	4677.04	4650.84	4630.14	4613.74	4600.74	4566.32	4555.28	4551.71	4550.56
245,000	4906.86	4851.62	4808.42	4774.48	4747.73	4726.60	4709.86	4696.59	4661.45	4650.18	4646.54	4645.36
250,000	5007.00	4950.64	4906.55	4871.92	4844.63	4823.06	4805.98	4792.43	4756.59	4745.08	4741.37	4740.16
255,000	5107.14	5049.65	5004.68	4969.36	4941.52	4919.52	4902.10	4888.28	4851.72	4839.98	4836.19	4834.97
260,000	5207.28	5148.66	5102.81	5066.80	5038.41	5015.98	4998.22	4984.13	4946.85	4934.89	4931.02	4929.77
265,000	5307.42	5247.67	5200.94	5164.24	5135.30	5112.44	5094.34	5079.98	5041.98	5029.79	5025.85	5024.57
270,000	5407.56	5346.69	5299.07	5261.67	5232.20	5208.90	5190.46	5175.83	5137.11	5124.69	5120.68	5119.38
280,000	5607.84	5544.71	5495.34	5456.55	5425.98	5401.83	5382.70	5367.53	5327.37	5314.49	5310.33	5308.98
290,000	5808.12	5742.74	5691.60	5651.43	5619.77	5594.75	5574.94	5559.22	5517.64	5504.30	5499.99	5498.59
300,000	6008.39	5940.76	5887.86	5846.30	5813.55	5787.67	5767.18	5750.92	5707.90	5694.10	5689.64	5688.20

169

MONTHLY AMORTIZING PAYMENTS

AMOUNT OF LOAN	NUMBER OF YEARS IN TERM											
	1	2	3	4	5	6	7	8	9	10	11	12
$ 50	4.71	2.62	1.94	1.61	1.41	1.29	1.21	1.15	1.10	1.07	1.05	1.03
100	9.41	5.24	3.88	3.21	2.82	2.58	2.41	2.29	2.20	2.14	2.09	2.05
200	18.82	10.48	7.75	6.42	5.64	5.15	4.81	4.58	4.40	4.28	4.18	4.10
300	28.23	15.72	11.62	9.62	8.46	7.72	7.22	6.86	6.60	6.41	6.27	6.15
400	37.64	20.95	15.49	12.83	11.28	10.29	9.62	9.15	8.80	8.55	8.35	8.20
500	47.04	26.19	19.36	16.03	14.10	12.87	12.03	11.44	11.00	10.68	10.44	10.25
600	56.45	31.43	23.23	19.24	16.92	15.44	14.43	13.72	13.20	12.82	12.53	12.30
700	65.86	36.67	27.10	22.44	19.74	18.01	16.84	16.01	15.40	14.95	14.61	14.35
800	75.27	41.90	30.97	25.65	22.56	20.58	19.24	18.29	17.60	17.09	16.70	16.40
900	84.67	47.14	34.84	28.85	25.38	23.16	21.65	20.58	19.80	19.22	18.79	18.45
1,000	94.08	52.38	38.71	32.06	28.20	25.73	24.05	22.87	22.00	21.36	20.87	20.50
2,000	188.16	104.75	77.42	64.11	56.39	51.45	48.10	45.73	44.00	42.71	41.74	41.00
3,000	282.23	157.12	116.13	96.16	84.58	77.17	72.15	68.59	66.00	64.07	62.61	61.50
4,000	376.31	209.50	154.84	128.21	112.77	102.90	96.19	91.45	87.99	85.42	83.48	82.00
5,000	470.39	261.87	193.55	160.26	140.96	128.62	120.24	114.31	109.99	106.78	104.35	102.50
6,000	564.46	314.24	232.26	192.31	169.15	154.34	144.29	137.17	131.99	128.13	125.22	123.00
7,000	658.54	366.62	270.97	224.37	197.34	180.07	168.34	160.03	153.99	149.49	146.09	143.49
8,000	752.62	418.99	309.68	256.42	225.53	205.79	192.38	182.89	175.98	170.84	166.96	163.99
9,000	846.69	471.36	348.39	288.47	253.72	231.51	216.43	205.76	197.98	192.20	187.83	184.49
10,000	940.77	523.74	387.10	320.52	281.91	257.24	240.48	228.62	219.98	213.55	208.70	204.99
15,000	1411.15	785.60	580.65	480.78	422.86	385.85	360.71	342.92	329.96	320.33	313.05	307.48
20,000	1881.53	1047.47	774.20	641.03	563.81	514.47	480.95	457.23	439.95	427.10	417.39	409.97
25,000	2351.91	1309.34	967.75	801.29	704.77	643.08	601.18	571.53	549.94	533.87	521.74	512.46
30,000	2822.29	1571.20	1161.30	961.55	845.72	771.70	721.42	685.84	659.92	640.65	626.09	614.96
35,000	3292.68	1833.07	1354.85	1121.81	986.67	900.31	841.66	800.15	769.91	747.42	730.43	717.45
40,000	3763.06	2094.94	1548.39	1282.06	1127.62	1028.93	961.89	914.45	879.90	854.20	834.78	819.94
45,000	4233.44	2356.80	1741.94	1442.32	1268.58	1157.54	1082.13	1028.76	989.88	960.97	939.13	922.43
50,000	4703.82	2618.67	1935.49	1602.58	1409.53	1286.16	1202.36	1143.06	1099.87	1067.74	1043.47	1024.92
55,000	5174.20	2880.54	2129.04	1762.84	1550.48	1414.78	1322.60	1257.37	1209.86	1174.52	1147.82	1127.42
60,000	5644.58	3142.40	2322.59	1923.09	1691.43	1543.39	1442.84	1371.68	1319.84	1281.29	1252.17	1229.91
65,000	6114.97	3404.27	2516.14	2083.35	1832.39	1672.01	1563.07	1485.98	1429.83	1388.07	1356.51	1332.40
70,000	6585.35	3666.14	2709.69	2243.61	1973.34	1800.62	1683.31	1600.29	1539.82	1494.84	1460.86	1434.89
75,000	7055.73	3928.00	2903.23	2403.87	2114.29	1929.24	1803.54	1714.59	1649.80	1601.61	1565.21	1537.38
80,000	7526.11	4189.87	3096.78	2564.12	2255.24	2057.85	1923.78	1828.90	1759.79	1708.39	1669.56	1639.87
85,000	7996.49	4451.74	3290.33	2724.38	2396.20	2186.47	2044.02	1943.21	1869.78	1815.16	1773.90	1742.37
90,000	8466.87	4713.60	3483.88	2884.64	2537.15	2315.08	2164.25	2057.51	1979.76	1921.94	1878.25	1844.86
95,000	8937.26	4975.47	3677.43	3044.89	2678.10	2443.70	2284.49	2171.82	2089.75	2028.71	1982.60	1947.35
100,000	9407.64	5237.34	3870.98	3205.15	2819.05	2572.32	2404.72	2286.12	2199.74	2135.48	2086.94	2049.84
105,000	9878.02	5499.20	4064.53	3365.41	2960.00	2700.93	2524.96	2400.43	2309.72	2242.26	2191.29	2152.33
110,000	10348.40	5761.07	4258.07	3525.67	3100.96	2829.55	2645.20	2514.74	2419.71	2349.03	2295.64	2254.83
115,000	10818.78	6022.94	4451.62	3685.92	3241.91	2958.16	2765.43	2629.04	2529.71	2455.80	2399.98	2357.32
120,000	11289.16	6284.80	4645.17	3846.18	3382.86	3086.78	2885.67	2743.35	2639.68	2562.58	2504.33	2459.81
125,000	11759.55	6546.67	4838.72	4006.44	3523.81	3215.39	3005.90	2857.65	2749.67	2669.35	2608.68	2562.30
130,000	12229.93	6808.53	5032.27	4166.70	3664.77	3344.01	3126.14	2971.96	2859.66	2776.13	2713.02	2664.79
135,000	12700.31	7070.40	5225.82	4326.95	3805.72	3472.62	3246.38	3086.27	2969.64	2882.90	2817.37	2767.29
140,000	13170.69	7332.27	5419.37	4487.21	3946.67	3601.24	3366.61	3200.57	3079.63	2989.67	2921.72	2869.78
145,000	13641.07	7594.13	5612.91	4647.47	4087.62	3729.86	3486.85	3314.88	3189.62	3096.45	3026.07	2972.27
150,000	14111.45	7856.00	5806.46	4807.73	4228.58	3858.47	3607.08	3429.18	3299.60	3203.22	3130.41	3074.76
155,000	14581.83	8117.87	6000.01	4967.98	4369.53	3987.09	3727.32	3543.49	3409.59	3310.00	3234.76	3177.25
160,000	15052.22	8379.73	6193.56	5128.24	4510.48	4115.70	3847.56	3657.80	3519.58	3416.77	3339.11	3279.74
165,000	15522.60	8641.60	6387.11	5288.50	4651.43	4244.32	3967.79	3772.10	3629.56	3523.54	3443.45	3382.24
170,000	15992.98	8903.47	6580.66	5448.76	4792.39	4372.93	4088.03	3886.41	3739.55	3630.32	3547.80	3484.73
175,000	16463.36	9165.33	6774.21	5609.01	4933.34	4501.55	4208.26	4000.71	3849.54	3737.09	3652.15	3587.22
180,000	16933.74	9427.20	6967.75	5769.27	5074.29	4630.16	4328.50	4115.02	3959.52	3843.87	3756.49	3689.71
185,000	17404.12	9689.07	7161.30	5929.53	5215.24	4758.78	4448.74	4229.33	4069.51	3950.64	3860.84	3792.20
190,000	17874.51	9950.93	7354.85	6089.78	5356.19	4887.40	4568.97	4343.63	4179.50	4057.41	3965.19	3894.70
195,000	18344.89	10212.80	7548.40	6250.04	5497.15	5016.01	4689.21	4457.94	4289.48	4164.19	4069.53	3997.19
200,000	18815.27	10474.67	7741.95	6410.30	5638.10	5144.63	4809.44	4572.24	4399.47	4270.96	4173.88	4099.68
205,000	19285.65	10736.53	7935.50	6570.56	5779.05	5273.24	4929.68	4686.55	4509.46	4377.73	4278.23	4202.17
210,000	19756.03	10998.40	8129.05	6730.81	5920.00	5401.86	5049.92	4800.86	4619.44	4484.51	4382.57	4304.66
215,000	20226.41	11260.27	8322.60	6891.07	6060.96	5530.47	5170.15	4915.16	4729.43	4591.28	4486.92	4407.16
220,000	20696.80	11522.13	8516.14	7051.33	6201.91	5659.09	5290.39	5029.47	4839.42	4698.06	4591.27	4509.65
225,000	21167.18	11784.00	8709.69	7211.59	6342.86	5787.70	5410.62	5143.77	4949.40	4804.83	4695.62	4612.14
230,000	21637.56	12045.87	8903.24	7371.84	6483.81	5916.32	5530.86	5258.08	5059.39	4911.60	4799.96	4714.63
235,000	22107.94	12307.73	9096.79	7532.10	6624.77	6044.94	5651.10	5372.39	5169.38	5018.38	4904.31	4817.12
240,000	22578.32	12569.60	9290.34	7692.36	6765.72	6173.55	5771.33	5486.69	5279.36	5125.15	5008.66	4919.61
245,000	23048.70	12831.46	9483.89	7852.62	6906.67	6302.17	5891.57	5601.00	5389.35	5231.93	5113.00	5022.11
250,000	23519.09	13093.33	9677.44	8012.87	7047.62	6430.78	6011.80	5715.30	5499.34	5338.70	5217.35	5124.60
255,000	23989.47	13355.20	9870.98	8173.13	7188.58	6559.40	6132.04	5829.61	5609.32	5445.47	5321.70	5227.09
260,000	24459.85	13617.06	10064.53	8333.39	7329.53	6688.01	6252.28	5943.91	5719.31	5552.25	5426.04	5329.58
265,000	24930.23	13878.93	10258.08	8493.64	7470.48	6816.63	6372.51	6058.22	5829.30	5659.02	5530.39	5432.07
270,000	25400.61	14140.80	10451.63	8653.90	7611.43	6945.24	6492.75	6172.53	5939.28	5765.80	5634.74	5534.57
280,000	26341.37	14664.53	10838.73	8974.42	7893.34	7202.48	6733.22	6401.14	6159.26	5979.34	5843.43	5739.55
290,000	27282.14	15188.26	11225.82	9294.93	8175.24	7459.71	6973.69	6629.75	6379.23	6192.89	6052.13	5944.53
300,000	28222.90	15712.00	11612.92	9615.45	8457.15	7716.94	7214.16	6858.36	6599.20	6406.44	6260.82	6149.52

AMOUNT OF LOAN	NUMBER OF YEARS IN TERM											
	13	14	15	16	17	18	19	20	25	30	35	40
$ 50	1.02	1.00	1.00	0.99	0.98	0.98	0.98	0.97	0.97	0.96	0.96	0.96
100	2.03	2.00	1.99	1.97	1.96	1.95	1.95	1.94	1.93	1.92	1.92	1.92
200	4.05	4.00	3.97	3.94	3.92	3.90	3.89	3.88	3.85	3.84	3.84	3.84
300	6.07	6.00	5.95	5.91	5.88	5.85	5.83	5.82	5.77	5.76	5.76	5.76
400	8.09	8.00	7.93	7.88	7.83	7.80	7.77	7.75	7.70	7.68	7.67	7.67
500	10.11	10.00	9.91	9.85	9.79	9.75	9.72	9.69	9.62	9.60	9.59	9.59
600	12.13	12.00	11.89	11.81	11.75	11.70	11.66	11.63	11.54	11.52	11.51	11.51
700	14.15	14.00	13.88	13.78	13.71	13.65	13.60	13.56	13.47	13.44	13.43	13.42
800	16.17	16.00	15.86	15.75	15.66	15.60	15.54	15.50	15.39	15.35	15.34	15.34
900	18.20	18.00	17.84	17.72	17.62	17.55	17.49	17.44	17.31	17.27	17.26	17.26
1,000	20.22	20.00	19.82	19.69	19.58	19.49	19.43	19.38	19.24	19.19	19.18	19.17
2,000	40.43	39.99	39.64	39.37	39.15	38.98	38.85	38.75	38.47	38.38	38.35	38.34
3,000	60.64	59.98	59.45	59.05	58.73	58.47	58.27	58.12	57.70	57.57	57.52	57.51
4,000	80.85	79.97	79.27	78.73	78.30	77.96	77.70	77.49	76.93	76.75	76.70	76.68
5,000	101.07	99.96	99.09	98.41	97.87	97.45	97.12	96.86	96.16	95.94	95.87	95.85
6,000	121.28	119.95	118.90	118.09	117.45	116.94	116.54	116.23	115.39	115.13	115.04	115.02
7,000	141.49	139.94	138.72	137.77	137.02	136.43	135.96	135.60	134.62	134.32	134.22	134.19
8,000	161.70	159.93	158.54	157.45	156.59	155.92	155.39	154.97	153.86	153.50	153.39	153.36
9,000	181.92	179.92	178.35	177.13	176.17	175.41	174.81	174.34	173.09	172.69	172.56	172.52
10,000	202.13	199.91	198.17	196.81	195.74	194.90	194.23	193.71	192.32	191.88	191.74	191.69
15,000	303.19	299.86	297.25	295.21	293.61	292.35	291.35	290.56	288.47	287.81	287.60	287.54
20,000	404.25	399.81	396.34	393.62	391.48	389.79	388.46	387.41	384.63	383.75	383.47	383.38
25,000	505.31	499.76	495.42	492.02	489.35	487.24	485.57	484.26	480.79	479.69	479.34	479.22
30,000	606.37	599.71	594.50	590.42	587.22	584.69	582.69	581.11	576.94	575.62	575.20	575.07
35,000	707.43	699.66	693.59	688.83	685.09	682.13	679.80	677.96	673.10	671.56	671.07	670.91
40,000	808.50	799.61	792.67	787.23	782.95	779.58	776.92	774.81	769.26	767.50	766.94	766.76
45,000	909.56	899.56	891.75	885.63	880.82	877.03	874.03	871.66	865.41	863.43	862.80	862.60
50,000	1010.62	999.51	990.84	984.04	978.69	974.47	971.14	968.51	961.57	959.37	958.67	958.44
55,000	1111.68	1099.46	1089.92	1082.44	1076.56	1071.92	1068.26	1065.36	1057.73	1055.31	1054.53	1054.29
60,000	1212.74	1199.41	1189.00	1180.84	1174.43	1169.37	1165.37	1162.21	1153.88	1151.24	1150.40	1150.13
65,000	1313.80	1299.36	1288.09	1279.25	1272.30	1266.82	1262.48	1259.06	1250.04	1247.18	1246.27	1245.98
70,000	1414.86	1399.31	1387.17	1377.65	1370.17	1364.26	1359.60	1355.91	1346.20	1343.12	1342.13	1341.82
75,000	1515.92	1499.26	1486.25	1476.05	1468.03	1461.71	1456.71	1452.76	1442.35	1439.05	1438.00	1437.66
80,000	1616.99	1599.21	1585.34	1574.46	1565.91	1559.16	1553.83	1549.61	1538.51	1534.99	1533.87	1533.51
85,000	1718.05	1699.16	1684.42	1672.86	1663.77	1656.60	1650.94	1646.46	1634.67	1630.93	1629.73	1629.35
90,000	1819.11	1799.11	1783.50	1771.26	1761.64	1754.05	1748.05	1743.31	1730.82	1726.86	1725.60	1725.20
95,000	1920.17	1899.06	1882.59	1869.67	1859.51	1851.50	1845.17	1840.16	1826.98	1822.80	1821.47	1821.04
100,000	2021.23	1999.01	1981.67	1968.07	1957.38	1948.94	1942.28	1937.01	1923.13	1918.74	1917.33	1916.88
105,000	2122.29	2098.96	2080.75	2066.47	2055.25	2046.39	2039.40	2033.86	2019.29	2014.67	2013.20	2012.73
110,000	2223.35	2198.91	2179.83	2164.88	2153.11	2143.84	2136.51	2130.71	2115.45	2110.61	2109.06	2108.57
115,000	2324.41	2298.86	2278.92	2263.28	2250.98	2241.29	2233.62	2227.56	2211.60	2206.55	2204.93	2204.41
120,000	2425.48	2398.81	2378.00	2361.68	2348.85	2338.73	2330.74	2324.41	2307.76	2302.48	2300.80	2300.26
125,000	2526.54	2498.77	2477.08	2460.09	2446.72	2436.18	2427.85	2421.26	2403.92	2398.42	2396.66	2396.10
130,000	2627.60	2598.72	2576.17	2558.49	2544.59	2533.63	2524.96	2518.11	2500.07	2494.36	2492.53	2491.95
135,000	2728.66	2698.67	2675.25	2656.89	2642.46	2631.07	2622.08	2614.96	2596.23	2590.29	2588.40	2587.79
140,000	2829.72	2798.62	2774.33	2755.30	2740.33	2728.52	2719.19	2711.81	2692.39	2686.23	2684.26	2683.63
145,000	2930.78	2898.57	2873.42	2853.70	2838.19	2825.97	2816.31	2808.66	2788.54	2782.16	2780.13	2779.48
150,000	3031.84	2998.52	2972.50	2952.10	2936.06	2923.41	2913.42	2905.51	2884.70	2878.10	2876.00	2875.32
155,000	3132.90	3098.47	3071.58	3050.51	3033.93	3020.86	3010.53	3002.36	2980.86	2974.04	2971.86	2971.17
160,000	3233.97	3198.42	3170.67	3148.91	3131.80	3118.31	3107.65	3099.21	3077.01	3069.97	3067.73	3067.01
165,000	3335.03	3298.37	3269.75	3247.31	3229.67	3215.75	3204.76	3196.06	3173.17	3165.91	3163.59	3162.85
170,000	3436.09	3398.32	3368.83	3345.72	3327.54	3313.20	3301.87	3292.91	3269.33	3261.85	3259.46	3258.70
175,000	3537.15	3498.27	3467.92	3444.12	3425.41	3410.65	3398.99	3389.76	3365.48	3357.78	3355.33	3354.54
180,000	3638.21	3598.22	3567.00	3542.52	3523.27	3508.10	3496.10	3486.61	3461.64	3453.72	3451.19	3450.39
185,000	3739.27	3698.17	3666.08	3640.93	3621.14	3605.54	3593.22	3583.46	3557.80	3549.66	3547.06	3546.23
190,000	3840.33	3798.12	3765.17	3739.33	3719.01	3702.99	3690.33	3680.31	3653.95	3645.59	3642.93	3642.07
195,000	3941.40	3898.07	3864.25	3837.73	3816.88	3800.44	3787.44	3777.16	3750.11	3741.53	3738.79	3737.92
200,000	4042.46	3998.02	3963.33	3936.14	3914.75	3897.88	3884.56	3874.01	3846.26	3837.47	3834.66	3833.76
205,000	4143.52	4097.97	4062.42	4034.54	4012.62	3995.33	3981.67	3970.86	3942.42	3933.40	3930.53	3929.60
210,000	4244.58	4197.92	4161.50	4132.94	4110.49	4092.78	4078.79	4067.71	4038.58	4029.34	4026.39	4025.45
215,000	4345.64	4297.87	4260.58	4231.35	4208.35	4190.22	4175.90	4164.56	4134.73	4125.28	4122.26	4121.29
220,000	4446.70	4397.82	4359.66	4329.75	4306.22	4287.67	4273.01	4261.41	4230.89	4221.21	4218.12	4217.14
225,000	4547.76	4497.77	4458.75	4428.15	4404.09	4385.12	4370.13	4358.26	4327.05	4317.15	4313.99	4312.98
230,000	4648.82	4597.72	4557.83	4526.56	4501.96	4482.57	4467.24	4455.11	4423.20	4413.09	4409.86	4408.82
235,000	4749.89	4697.67	4656.91	4624.96	4599.83	4580.01	4564.35	4551.96	4519.36	4509.02	4505.72	4504.67
240,000	4850.95	4797.62	4756.00	4723.36	4697.70	4677.46	4661.47	4648.81	4615.52	4604.96	4601.59	4600.51
245,000	4952.01	4897.58	4855.08	4821.77	4795.57	4774.91	4758.58	4745.66	4711.67	4700.90	4697.46	4696.36
250,000	5053.07	4997.53	4954.16	4920.17	4893.43	4872.35	4855.70	4842.51	4807.83	4796.83	4793.32	4792.20
255,000	5154.13	5097.48	5053.25	5018.57	4991.30	4969.80	4952.81	4939.36	4903.99	4892.77	4889.19	4888.04
260,000	5255.19	5197.43	5152.33	5116.98	5089.17	5067.25	5049.92	5036.21	5000.14	4988.71	4985.05	4983.89
265,000	5356.25	5297.38	5251.41	5215.38	5187.04	5164.69	5147.04	5133.06	5096.30	5084.64	5080.92	5079.73
270,000	5457.31	5397.33	5350.50	5313.78	5284.91	5262.14	5244.15	5229.91	5192.46	5180.58	5176.79	5175.58
280,000	5659.44	5597.23	5548.66	5510.59	5480.65	5457.03	5438.38	5423.61	5384.77	5372.45	5368.52	5367.26
290,000	5861.56	5797.13	5746.83	5707.40	5676.38	5651.93	5632.61	5617.31	5577.08	5564.32	5560.25	5558.95
300,000	6063.68	5997.03	5945.00	5904.20	5872.12	5846.82	5826.83	5811.01	5769.39	5756.20	5751.99	5750.64

171

MONTHLY AMORTIZING PAYMENTS

AMOUNT OF LOAN	NUMBER OF YEARS IN TERM											
	1	2	3	4	5	6	7	8	9	10	11	12
$ 50	4.71	2.63	1.95	1.61	1.42	1.30	1.22	1.16	1.11	1.08	1.06	1.04
100	9.42	5.25	3.89	3.22	2.84	2.59	2.43	2.31	2.22	2.16	2.11	2.07
200	18.84	10.50	7.77	6.44	5.67	5.18	4.85	4.61	4.44	4.31	4.21	4.14
300	28.26	15.75	11.66	9.66	8.51	7.77	7.27	6.91	6.65	6.46	6.32	6.21
400	37.68	21.00	15.54	12.88	11.34	10.35	9.69	9.21	8.87	8.62	8.42	8.28
500	47.10	26.25	19.43	16.10	14.17	12.94	12.11	11.52	11.09	10.77	10.53	10.34
600	56.52	31.50	23.31	19.32	17.01	15.53	14.53	13.82	13.30	12.92	12.63	12.41
700	65.94	36.75	27.19	22.54	19.84	18.12	16.95	16.12	15.52	15.07	14.74	14.48
800	75.36	42.00	31.08	25.76	22.67	20.70	19.37	18.42	17.74	17.23	16.84	16.55
900	84.78	47.25	34.96	28.97	25.51	23.29	21.79	20.73	19.95	19.38	18.95	18.62
1,000	94.20	52.50	38.85	32.19	28.34	25.88	24.21	23.03	22.17	21.53	21.05	20.68
2,000	188.40	105.00	77.69	64.38	56.67	51.75	48.41	46.05	44.33	43.06	42.10	41.36
3,000	282.60	157.50	116.53	96.57	85.01	77.63	72.62	69.08	66.50	64.59	63.14	62.04
4,000	376.79	210.00	155.37	128.76	113.34	103.50	96.82	92.10	88.66	86.11	84.19	82.72
5,000	470.99	262.49	194.21	160.95	141.68	129.37	121.02	115.12	110.83	107.64	105.24	103.40
6,000	565.19	314.99	233.05	193.14	170.01	155.25	145.23	138.15	132.99	129.17	126.28	124.08
7,000	659.38	367.49	271.89	225.33	198.35	181.12	169.43	161.17	155.16	150.70	147.33	144.76
8,000	753.58	419.99	310.73	257.51	226.68	206.99	193.63	184.19	177.32	172.22	168.38	165.44
9,000	847.78	472.48	349.57	289.70	255.01	232.87	217.84	207.22	199.49	193.75	189.42	186.12
10,000	941.98	524.98	388.41	321.89	283.35	258.74	242.04	230.24	221.65	215.28	210.47	206.80
15,000	1412.96	787.47	582.61	482.83	425.02	388.11	363.06	345.36	332.48	322.92	315.70	310.20
20,000	1883.95	1049.96	776.81	643.78	566.69	517.47	484.08	460.47	443.30	430.55	420.93	413.60
25,000	2354.93	1312.44	971.01	804.72	708.36	646.84	605.10	575.59	554.13	538.19	526.17	516.99
30,000	2825.92	1574.93	1165.21	965.66	850.03	776.21	726.11	690.71	664.95	645.83	631.40	620.39
35,000	3296.90	1837.42	1359.41	1126.61	991.71	905.57	847.13	805.83	775.78	753.46	736.63	723.79
40,000	3767.89	2099.91	1553.61	1287.55	1133.38	1034.94	968.15	920.94	886.60	861.10	841.86	827.19
45,000	4238.87	2362.39	1747.81	1448.49	1275.05	1164.31	1089.17	1036.06	997.43	968.74	947.10	930.58
50,000	4709.86	2624.88	1942.01	1609.43	1416.72	1293.68	1210.19	1151.18	1108.25	1076.37	1052.33	1033.98
55,000	5180.84	2887.37	2136.21	1770.38	1558.39	1423.04	1331.21	1266.29	1219.08	1184.01	1157.56	1137.38
60,000	5651.83	3149.86	2330.41	1931.32	1700.06	1552.41	1452.22	1381.41	1329.90	1291.65	1262.79	1240.78
65,000	6122.81	3412.34	2524.61	2092.26	1841.73	1681.78	1573.24	1496.53	1440.73	1399.28	1368.02	1344.17
70,000	6593.80	3674.83	2718.82	2253.21	1983.41	1811.14	1694.26	1611.65	1551.55	1506.92	1473.26	1447.57
75,000	7064.78	3937.32	2913.02	2414.15	2125.08	1940.51	1815.28	1726.76	1662.38	1614.56	1578.49	1550.97
80,000	7535.77	4199.81	3107.22	2575.09	2266.75	2069.88	1936.30	1841.88	1773.20	1722.19	1683.72	1654.37
85,000	8006.75	4462.29	3301.42	2736.04	2408.42	2199.25	2057.32	1957.00	1884.03	1829.83	1788.95	1757.76
90,000	8477.74	4724.78	3495.62	2896.98	2550.09	2328.61	2178.33	2072.12	1994.85	1937.47	1894.19	1861.16
95,000	8948.72	4987.27	3689.82	3057.92	2691.76	2457.98	2299.35	2187.23	2105.68	2045.10	1999.42	1964.56
100,000	9419.71	5249.76	3884.02	3218.86	2833.43	2587.35	2420.37	2302.35	2216.50	2152.74	2104.65	2067.96
105,000	9890.69	5512.24	4078.22	3379.81	2975.11	2716.71	2541.39	2417.47	2327.33	2260.38	2209.88	2171.35
110,000	10361.68	5774.73	4272.42	3540.75	3116.78	2846.08	2662.41	2532.58	2438.15	2368.01	2315.11	2274.75
115,000	10832.66	6037.22	4466.62	3701.69	3258.45	2975.45	2783.43	2647.70	2548.97	2475.65	2420.35	2378.15
120,000	11303.65	6299.71	4660.82	3862.64	3400.12	3104.81	2904.44	2762.82	2659.80	2583.29	2525.58	2481.55
125,000	11774.63	6562.19	4855.02	4023.58	3541.79	3234.18	3025.46	2877.94	2770.62	2690.92	2630.81	2584.94
130,000	12245.62	6824.68	5049.22	4184.52	3683.46	3363.55	3146.48	2993.05	2881.45	2798.56	2736.04	2688.34
135,000	12716.60	7087.17	5243.42	4345.47	3825.13	3492.92	3267.50	3108.17	2992.27	2906.20	2841.28	2791.74
140,000	13187.59	7349.66	5437.63	4506.41	3966.81	3622.28	3388.52	3223.29	3103.10	3013.83	2946.51	2895.14
145,000	13658.57	7612.14	5631.83	4667.35	4108.48	3751.65	3509.54	3338.41	3213.92	3121.47	3051.74	2998.53
150,000	14129.56	7874.63	5826.03	4828.29	4250.15	3881.02	3630.55	3453.52	3324.75	3229.11	3156.97	3101.93
155,000	14600.54	8137.12	6020.23	4989.24	4391.82	4010.38	3751.57	3568.64	3435.57	3336.74	3262.20	3205.33
160,000	15071.53	8399.61	6214.43	5150.18	4533.49	4139.75	3872.59	3683.76	3546.40	3444.38	3367.44	3308.73
165,000	15542.51	8662.09	6408.63	5311.12	4675.16	4269.12	3993.61	3798.87	3657.22	3552.02	3472.67	3412.12
170,000	16013.50	8924.58	6602.83	5472.07	4816.83	4398.49	4114.63	3913.99	3768.05	3659.65	3577.90	3515.52
175,000	16484.48	9187.07	6797.03	5633.01	4958.51	4527.85	4235.65	4029.11	3878.87	3767.29	3683.13	3618.92
180,000	16955.47	9449.56	6991.23	5793.95	5100.18	4657.22	4356.66	4144.23	3989.70	3874.93	3788.37	3722.32
185,000	17426.45	9712.04	7185.43	5954.90	5241.85	4786.59	4477.68	4259.34	4100.52	3982.57	3893.60	3825.71
190,000	17897.44	9974.53	7379.63	6115.84	5383.52	4915.95	4598.70	4374.46	4211.35	4090.20	3998.83	3929.11
195,000	18368.42	10237.02	7573.83	6276.78	5525.19	5045.32	4719.72	4489.58	4322.17	4197.84	4104.06	4032.51
200,000	18839.41	10499.51	7768.03	6437.72	5666.86	5174.69	4840.74	4604.70	4433.00	4305.48	4209.30	4135.91
205,000	19310.39	10761.99	7962.23	6598.67	5808.53	5304.05	4961.76	4719.81	4543.82	4413.11	4314.53	4239.30
210,000	19781.38	11024.48	8156.44	6759.61	5950.21	5433.42	5082.77	4834.93	4654.65	4520.75	4419.76	4342.70
215,000	20252.36	11286.97	8350.64	6920.55	6091.88	5562.79	5203.79	4950.05	4765.47	4628.39	4524.99	4446.10
220,000	20723.35	11549.46	8544.84	7081.50	6233.55	5692.16	5324.81	5065.16	4876.30	4736.02	4630.22	4549.50
225,000	21194.33	11811.94	8739.04	7242.44	6375.22	5821.52	5445.83	5180.28	4987.12	4843.66	4735.46	4652.89
230,000	21665.32	12074.43	8933.24	7403.38	6516.89	5950.89	5566.85	5295.40	5097.94	4951.30	4840.69	4756.29
235,000	22136.30	12336.92	9127.44	7564.33	6658.56	6080.26	5687.87	5410.52	5208.77	5058.93	4945.92	4859.69
240,000	22607.29	12599.41	9321.64	7725.27	6800.23	6209.62	5808.88	5525.63	5319.59	5166.57	5051.15	4963.09
245,000	23078.27	12861.89	9515.84	7886.21	6941.91	6338.99	5929.90	5640.75	5430.42	5274.21	5156.39	5066.48
250,000	23549.26	13124.38	9710.04	8047.15	7083.58	6468.36	6050.92	5755.87	5541.24	5381.84	5261.62	5169.88
255,000	24020.24	13386.87	9904.24	8208.10	7225.25	6597.73	6171.94	5870.98	5652.07	5489.48	5366.85	5273.28
260,000	24491.23	13649.36	10098.44	8369.04	7366.92	6727.09	6292.96	5986.10	5762.89	5597.12	5472.08	5376.68
265,000	24962.21	13911.84	10292.64	8529.98	7508.59	6856.46	6413.98	6101.22	5873.72	5704.75	5577.31	5480.08
270,000	25433.20	14174.33	10486.84	8690.93	7650.26	6985.83	6534.99	6216.34	5984.54	5812.39	5682.55	5583.47
280,000	26375.17	14699.31	10875.25	9012.81	7933.61	7244.56	6777.03	6446.57	6206.19	6027.66	5893.01	5790.27
290,000	27317.14	15224.28	11263.65	9334.70	8216.95	7503.29	7019.07	6676.81	6427.84	6242.94	6103.48	5997.06
300,000	28259.11	15749.26	11652.05	9656.58	8500.29	7762.03	7261.10	6907.04	6649.49	6458.21	6313.94	6203.86

AMOUNT OF LOAN	NUMBER OF YEARS IN TERM											
	13	14	15	16	17	18	19	20	25	30	35	40
$ 50	1.02	1.01	1.01	1.00	0.99	0.99	0.99	0.98	0.98	0.97	0.97	0.97
100	2.04	2.02	2.01	1.99	1.98	1.97	1.97	1.96	1.95	1.94	1.94	1.94
200	4.08	4.04	4.01	3.98	3.96	3.94	3.93	3.92	3.89	3.88	3.88	3.88
300	6.12	6.06	6.01	5.97	5.94	5.91	5.89	5.88	5.84	5.82	5.82	5.82
400	8.16	8.08	8.01	7.95	7.91	7.88	7.85	7.83	7.78	7.76	7.76	7.76
500	10.20	10.09	10.01	9.94	9.89	9.85	9.82	9.79	9.72	9.70	9.70	9.69
600	12.24	12.11	12.01	11.93	11.87	11.82	11.78	11.75	11.67	11.64	11.63	11.63
700	14.28	14.13	14.01	13.92	13.84	13.79	13.74	13.70	13.61	13.58	13.57	13.57
800	16.32	16.15	16.01	15.90	15.82	15.75	15.70	15.66	15.55	15.52	15.51	15.51
900	18.36	18.17	18.01	17.89	17.80	17.72	17.66	17.62	17.50	17.46	17.45	17.44
1,000	20.40	20.18	20.01	19.88	19.77	19.69	19.63	19.58	19.44	19.40	19.39	19.38
2,000	40.80	40.36	40.02	39.75	39.54	39.38	39.25	39.15	38.88	38.79	38.77	38.76
3,000	61.20	60.54	60.03	59.63	59.31	59.07	58.87	58.72	58.31	58.19	58.15	58.14
4,000	81.59	80.72	80.04	79.50	79.08	78.75	78.49	78.29	77.75	77.58	77.53	77.51
5,000	101.99	100.90	100.04	99.38	98.85	98.44	98.11	97.86	97.19	96.98	96.91	96.89
6,000	122.39	121.07	120.05	119.25	118.62	118.13	117.74	117.43	116.62	116.37	116.29	116.27
7,000	142.78	141.25	140.06	139.12	138.39	137.81	137.36	137.00	136.06	135.77	135.67	135.64
8,000	163.18	161.43	160.07	159.00	158.16	157.50	156.98	156.57	155.50	155.16	155.05	155.02
9,000	183.58	181.61	180.07	178.87	177.93	177.19	176.60	176.14	174.93	174.55	174.44	174.40
10,000	203.98	201.79	200.08	198.75	197.70	196.87	196.22	195.71	194.37	193.95	193.82	193.77
15,000	305.96	302.68	300.12	298.12	296.54	295.31	294.33	293.56	291.55	290.92	290.72	290.66
20,000	407.95	403.57	400.16	397.49	395.39	393.74	392.44	391.42	388.73	387.89	387.63	387.54
25,000	509.93	504.46	500.19	496.86	494.24	492.18	490.55	489.27	485.92	484.86	484.53	484.43
30,000	611.92	605.35	600.23	596.23	593.08	590.61	588.66	587.12	583.10	581.84	581.44	581.31
35,000	713.90	706.24	700.27	695.60	691.93	689.05	686.77	684.98	680.28	678.81	678.34	678.20
40,000	815.89	807.13	800.31	794.97	790.78	787.48	784.88	782.83	777.46	775.78	775.25	775.08
45,000	917.87	908.02	900.34	894.34	889.62	885.92	882.99	880.68	874.64	872.75	872.16	871.97
50,000	1019.86	1008.91	1000.38	993.71	988.47	984.35	981.10	978.54	971.83	969.72	969.06	968.85
55,000	1121.84	1109.80	1100.42	1093.08	1087.32	1082.79	1079.21	1076.39	1069.01	1066.70	1065.97	1065.74
60,000	1223.83	1210.69	1200.46	1192.45	1186.16	1181.22	1177.32	1174.24	1166.19	1163.67	1162.87	1162.62
65,000	1325.81	1311.58	1300.49	1291.82	1285.01	1279.65	1275.43	1272.10	1263.37	1260.64	1259.78	1259.51
70,000	1427.80	1412.47	1400.53	1391.19	1383.86	1378.09	1373.54	1369.95	1360.56	1357.61	1356.68	1356.39
75,000	1529.78	1513.36	1500.57	1490.56	1482.70	1476.52	1471.65	1467.80	1457.74	1454.58	1453.59	1453.28
80,000	1631.77	1614.25	1600.61	1589.93	1581.55	1574.96	1569.76	1565.66	1554.92	1551.56	1550.50	1550.16
85,000	1733.75	1715.14	1700.64	1689.30	1680.40	1673.39	1667.87	1663.51	1652.10	1648.53	1647.40	1647.04
90,000	1835.74	1816.03	1800.68	1788.67	1779.24	1771.83	1765.98	1761.36	1749.28	1745.50	1744.31	1743.93
95,000	1937.72	1916.92	1900.72	1888.04	1878.09	1870.26	1864.09	1859.22	1846.47	1842.47	1841.21	1840.81
100,000	2039.71	2017.82	2000.76	1987.41	1976.94	1968.70	1962.20	1957.07	1943.65	1939.44	1938.12	1937.70
105,000	2141.69	2118.71	2100.80	2086.78	2075.78	2067.13	2060.31	2054.92	2040.83	2036.42	2035.02	2034.58
110,000	2243.68	2219.60	2200.83	2186.15	2174.63	2165.57	2158.42	2152.78	2138.01	2133.39	2131.93	2131.47
115,000	2345.66	2320.49	2300.87	2285.52	2273.48	2264.00	2256.53	2250.63	2235.20	2230.36	2228.83	2228.35
120,000	2447.65	2421.38	2400.91	2384.89	2372.32	2362.43	2354.64	2348.48	2332.38	2327.33	2325.74	2325.24
125,000	2549.63	2522.27	2500.95	2484.26	2471.17	2460.87	2452.75	2446.33	2429.56	2424.30	2422.65	2422.12
130,000	2651.62	2623.16	2600.98	2583.63	2570.02	2559.30	2550.86	2544.19	2526.74	2521.27	2519.55	2519.01
135,000	2753.60	2724.05	2701.02	2683.00	2668.86	2657.74	2648.97	2642.04	2623.92	2618.25	2616.46	2615.89
140,000	2855.59	2824.94	2801.06	2782.38	2767.71	2756.17	2747.08	2739.89	2721.11	2715.22	2713.36	2712.78
145,000	2957.58	2925.83	2901.10	2881.75	2866.56	2854.61	2845.19	2837.75	2818.29	2812.19	2810.27	2809.66
150,000	3059.56	3026.72	3001.13	2981.12	2965.40	2953.04	2943.30	2935.60	2915.47	2909.16	2907.17	2906.55
155,000	3161.55	3127.61	3101.17	3080.49	3064.25	3051.48	3041.41	3033.45	3012.65	3006.13	3004.08	3003.43
160,000	3263.53	3228.50	3201.21	3179.86	3163.10	3149.91	3139.52	3131.31	3109.83	3103.11	3100.99	3100.31
165,000	3365.52	3329.39	3301.25	3279.23	3261.94	3248.35	3237.63	3229.16	3207.02	3200.08	3197.89	3197.20
170,000	3467.50	3430.28	3401.28	3378.60	3360.79	3346.78	3335.74	3327.01	3304.20	3297.05	3294.80	3294.08
175,000	3569.49	3531.17	3501.32	3477.97	3459.64	3445.22	3433.84	3424.87	3401.38	3394.02	3391.70	3390.97
180,000	3671.47	3632.06	3601.36	3577.34	3558.48	3543.65	3531.95	3522.72	3498.56	3490.99	3488.61	3487.85
185,000	3773.46	3732.95	3701.40	3676.71	3657.33	3642.08	3630.06	3620.57	3595.75	3587.97	3585.51	3584.74
190,000	3875.44	3833.84	3801.43	3776.08	3756.18	3740.52	3728.17	3718.43	3692.93	3684.94	3682.42	3681.62
195,000	3977.43	3934.74	3901.47	3875.45	3855.02	3838.95	3826.28	3816.28	3790.11	3781.91	3779.32	3778.51
200,000	4079.41	4035.63	4001.51	3974.82	3953.87	3937.39	3924.39	3914.13	3887.29	3878.88	3876.23	3875.39
205,000	4181.40	4136.52	4101.55	4074.19	4052.72	4035.82	4022.50	4011.99	3984.47	3975.85	3973.14	3972.28
210,000	4283.38	4237.41	4201.59	4173.56	4151.56	4134.26	4120.61	4109.84	4081.66	4072.83	4070.04	4069.16
215,000	4385.37	4338.30	4301.62	4272.93	4250.41	4232.69	4218.72	4207.69	4178.84	4169.80	4166.95	4166.05
220,000	4487.35	4439.19	4401.66	4372.30	4349.26	4331.13	4316.83	4305.55	4276.02	4266.77	4263.85	4262.93
225,000	4589.34	4540.08	4501.70	4471.67	4448.10	4429.56	4414.94	4403.40	4373.20	4363.74	4360.76	4359.82
230,000	4691.32	4640.97	4601.74	4571.04	4546.95	4528.00	4513.05	4501.25	4470.39	4460.71	4457.66	4456.70
235,000	4793.31	4741.86	4701.77	4670.41	4645.80	4626.43	4611.16	4599.10	4567.57	4557.69	4554.57	4553.59
240,000	4895.29	4842.75	4801.81	4769.78	4744.64	4724.86	4709.27	4696.96	4664.75	4654.66	4651.48	4650.47
245,000	4997.28	4943.64	4901.85	4869.15	4843.49	4823.30	4807.38	4794.81	4761.93	4751.63	4748.38	4747.35
250,000	5099.26	5044.53	5001.89	4968.52	4942.34	4921.73	4905.49	4892.66	4859.11	4848.60	4845.29	4844.24
255,000	5201.25	5145.42	5101.92	5067.89	5041.18	5020.17	5003.60	4990.52	4956.30	4945.57	4942.19	4941.12
260,000	5303.23	5246.31	5201.96	5167.26	5140.03	5118.60	5101.71	5088.37	5053.48	5042.54	5039.10	5038.01
265,000	5405.22	5347.20	5302.00	5266.63	5238.88	5217.04	5199.82	5186.22	5150.66	5139.52	5136.00	5134.89
270,000	5507.20	5448.09	5402.04	5366.00	5337.72	5315.47	5297.93	5284.08	5247.84	5236.49	5232.91	5231.78
280,000	5711.18	5649.87	5602.11	5564.75	5535.42	5512.34	5494.15	5479.78	5442.21	5430.43	5426.72	5425.55
290,000	5915.15	5851.66	5802.19	5763.49	5733.11	5709.21	5690.37	5675.49	5636.57	5624.38	5620.53	5619.32
300,000	6119.12	6053.44	6002.26	5962.23	5930.80	5906.08	5886.59	5871.20	5830.94	5818.32	5814.34	5813.09

23.50%

AMOUNT OF LOAN	NUMBER OF YEARS IN TERM											
	1	2	3	4	5	6	7	8	9	10	11	12
$ 50	4.72	2.64	1.95	1.62	1.43	1.31	1.22	1.16	1.12	1.09	1.07	1.05
100	9.44	5.27	3.90	3.24	2.85	2.61	2.44	2.32	2.24	2.18	2.13	2.09
200	18.87	10.53	7.80	6.47	5.70	5.21	4.88	4.64	4.47	4.35	4.25	4.18
300	28.30	15.79	11.70	9.70	8.55	7.81	7.31	6.96	6.70	6.52	6.37	6.26
400	37.73	21.05	15.59	12.94	11.40	10.41	9.75	9.28	8.94	8.69	8.49	8.35
500	47.16	26.32	19.49	16.17	14.24	13.02	12.19	11.60	11.17	10.86	10.62	10.44
600	56.60	31.58	23.39	19.40	17.09	15.62	14.62	13.92	13.40	13.03	12.74	12.52
700	66.03	36.84	27.28	22.63	19.94	18.22	17.06	16.24	15.64	15.20	14.86	14.61
800	75.46	42.10	31.18	25.87	22.79	20.82	19.49	18.55	17.87	17.37	16.98	16.69
900	84.89	47.36	35.08	29.10	25.64	23.43	21.93	20.87	20.10	19.54	19.11	18.78
1,000	94.32	52.63	38.98	32.33	28.48	26.03	24.37	23.19	22.34	21.71	21.23	20.87
2,000	188.64	105.25	77.95	64.66	56.96	52.05	48.73	46.38	44.67	43.41	42.45	41.73
3,000	282.96	157.87	116.92	96.98	85.44	78.08	73.09	69.56	67.00	65.11	63.68	62.59
4,000	377.28	210.49	155.89	129.31	113.92	104.10	97.45	92.75	89.34	86.81	84.90	83.45
5,000	471.59	263.11	194.86	161.64	142.40	130.13	121.81	115.94	111.67	108.51	106.13	104.31
6,000	565.91	315.74	233.83	193.96	170.88	156.15	146.17	139.12	134.00	130.21	127.35	125.17
7,000	660.23	368.36	272.80	226.29	199.35	182.17	170.53	162.31	156.34	151.91	148.57	146.03
8,000	754.55	420.98	311.77	258.61	227.83	208.20	194.89	185.49	178.67	173.61	169.80	166.89
9,000	848.87	473.60	350.74	290.94	256.31	234.22	219.25	208.68	201.00	195.31	191.02	187.76
10,000	943.18	526.22	389.71	323.27	284.79	260.25	243.61	231.87	223.34	217.01	212.25	208.62
15,000	1414.77	789.33	584.57	484.90	427.18	390.37	365.41	347.80	335.00	325.51	318.37	312.92
20,000	1886.36	1052.44	779.42	646.53	569.57	520.49	487.22	463.73	446.67	434.01	424.49	417.23
25,000	2357.95	1315.55	974.28	808.16	711.97	650.61	609.02	579.66	558.33	542.52	530.61	521.53
30,000	2829.54	1578.66	1169.13	969.79	854.36	780.73	730.82	695.59	670.00	651.02	636.73	625.84
35,000	3301.13	1841.77	1363.98	1131.42	996.75	910.85	852.63	811.52	781.66	759.52	742.85	730.14
40,000	3772.72	2104.88	1558.84	1293.05	1139.14	1040.97	974.43	927.45	893.33	868.02	848.97	834.45
45,000	4244.31	2367.99	1753.69	1454.68	1281.54	1171.09	1096.23	1043.38	1004.99	976.52	955.09	938.76
50,000	4715.89	2631.10	1948.55	1616.31	1423.93	1301.21	1218.03	1159.31	1116.66	1085.03	1061.21	1043.06
55,000	5187.48	2894.21	2143.40	1777.94	1566.32	1431.33	1339.84	1275.25	1228.32	1193.53	1167.33	1147.37
60,000	5659.07	3157.32	2338.25	1939.57	1708.71	1561.45	1461.64	1391.18	1339.99	1302.03	1273.45	1251.67
65,000	6130.66	3420.43	2533.11	2101.20	1851.11	1691.57	1583.44	1507.11	1451.66	1410.53	1379.57	1355.98
70,000	6602.25	3683.54	2727.96	2262.83	1993.50	1821.69	1705.25	1623.04	1563.32	1519.04	1485.69	1460.28
75,000	7073.84	3946.65	2922.82	2424.46	2135.89	1951.82	1827.05	1738.97	1674.99	1627.54	1591.81	1564.59
80,000	7545.43	4209.75	3117.67	2586.09	2278.28	2081.94	1948.85	1854.90	1786.65	1736.04	1697.93	1668.90
85,000	8017.02	4472.86	3312.52	2747.72	2420.68	2212.06	2070.66	1970.83	1898.32	1844.54	1804.05	1773.20
90,000	8488.61	4735.97	3507.38	2909.35	2563.07	2342.18	2192.46	2086.76	2009.98	1953.04	1910.17	1877.51
95,000	8960.20	4999.08	3702.23	3070.98	2705.46	2472.30	2314.26	2202.69	2121.65	2061.55	2016.29	1981.81
100,000	9431.78	5262.19	3897.09	3232.61	2847.85	2602.42	2436.06	2318.62	2233.31	2170.05	2122.41	2086.12
105,000	9903.37	5525.30	4091.94	3394.24	2990.25	2732.54	2557.87	2434.56	2344.98	2278.55	2228.53	2190.42
110,000	10374.96	5788.41	4286.79	3555.87	3132.64	2862.66	2679.67	2550.49	2456.64	2387.05	2334.65	2294.73
115,000	10846.55	6051.52	4481.65	3717.50	3275.03	2992.78	2801.47	2666.42	2568.31	2495.55	2440.77	2399.04
120,000	11318.14	6314.63	4676.50	3879.13	3417.42	3122.90	2923.28	2782.35	2679.98	2604.06	2546.89	2503.34
125,000	11789.73	6577.74	4871.36	4040.76	3559.82	3253.02	3045.08	2898.28	2791.64	2712.56	2653.01	2607.65
130,000	12261.32	6840.85	5066.21	4202.39	3702.21	3383.14	3166.88	3014.21	2903.31	2821.06	2759.13	2711.95
135,000	12732.91	7103.96	5261.06	4364.02	3844.60	3513.26	3288.68	3130.14	3014.97	2929.56	2865.25	2816.26
140,000	13204.50	7367.07	5455.92	4525.65	3986.99	3643.38	3410.49	3246.07	3126.64	3038.07	2971.37	2920.56
145,000	13676.08	7630.18	5650.77	4687.28	4129.38	3773.50	3532.29	3362.00	3238.30	3146.57	3077.49	3024.87
150,000	14147.67	7893.29	5845.63	4848.91	4271.78	3903.63	3654.09	3477.93	3349.97	3255.07	3183.61	3129.18
155,000	14619.26	8156.40	6040.48	5010.54	4414.17	4033.75	3775.90	3593.87	3461.63	3363.57	3289.73	3233.48
160,000	15090.85	8419.50	6235.33	5172.17	4556.56	4163.87	3897.70	3709.80	3573.30	3472.07	3395.85	3337.79
165,000	15562.44	8682.61	6430.19	5333.80	4698.95	4293.99	4019.50	3825.73	3684.96	3580.58	3501.97	3442.09
170,000	16034.03	8945.72	6625.04	5495.43	4841.35	4424.11	4141.31	3941.66	3796.63	3689.08	3608.09	3546.40
175,000	16505.62	9208.83	6819.90	5657.06	4983.74	4554.23	4263.11	4057.59	3908.30	3797.58	3714.21	3650.70
180,000	16977.21	9471.94	7014.75	5818.69	5126.13	4684.35	4384.91	4173.52	4019.96	3906.08	3820.33	3755.01
185,000	17448.80	9735.05	7209.60	5980.32	5268.52	4814.47	4506.71	4289.45	4131.63	4014.58	3926.45	3859.32
190,000	17920.39	9998.16	7404.46	6141.95	5410.92	4944.59	4628.52	4405.38	4243.29	4123.00	4032.57	3963.62
195,000	18391.97	10261.27	7599.31	6303.58	5553.31	5074.71	4750.32	4521.31	4354.96	4231.59	4138.69	4067.93
200,000	18863.56	10524.38	7794.17	6465.21	5695.70	5204.83	4872.12	4637.24	4466.62	4340.09	4244.81	4172.23
205,000	19335.15	10787.49	7989.02	6626.84	5838.09	5334.95	4993.93	4753.18	4578.29	4448.59	4350.93	4276.54
210,000	19806.74	11050.60	8183.87	6788.47	5980.49	5465.07	5115.73	4869.11	4689.95	4557.10	4457.05	4380.84
215,000	20278.33	11313.71	8378.73	6950.10	6122.88	5595.19	5237.53	4985.04	4801.62	4665.60	4563.17	4485.15
220,000	20749.92	11576.82	8573.58	7111.73	6265.27	5725.31	5359.34	5100.97	4913.28	4774.10	4669.29	4589.46
225,000	21221.51	11839.93	8768.44	7273.36	6407.66	5855.44	5481.14	5216.90	5024.95	4882.60	4775.41	4693.76
230,000	21693.10	12103.04	8963.29	7434.99	6550.06	5985.56	5602.94	5332.83	5136.62	4991.10	4881.53	4798.07
235,000	22164.69	12366.14	9158.14	7596.62	6692.45	6115.68	5724.74	5448.76	5248.28	5099.61	4987.65	4902.37
240,000	22636.28	12629.25	9353.00	7758.25	6834.84	6245.80	5846.55	5564.69	5359.95	5208.11	5093.77	5006.68
245,000	23107.86	12892.36	9547.85	7919.88	6977.23	6375.92	5968.35	5680.62	5471.61	5316.61	5199.89	5110.98
250,000	23579.45	13155.47	9742.71	8081.51	7119.63	6506.04	6090.15	5796.55	5583.28	5425.11	5306.01	5215.29
255,000	24051.04	13418.58	9937.56	8243.14	7262.02	6636.16	6211.96	5912.48	5694.94	5533.62	5412.13	5319.60
260,000	24522.63	13681.69	10132.41	8404.77	7404.41	6766.28	6333.76	6028.42	5806.61	5642.12	5518.25	5423.90
265,000	24994.22	13944.80	10327.27	8566.40	7546.80	6896.40	6455.56	6144.35	5918.27	5750.62	5624.37	5528.21
270,000	25465.81	14207.91	10522.12	8728.03	7689.19	7026.52	6577.36	6260.28	6029.94	5859.12	5730.49	5632.51
280,000	26408.99	14734.13	10911.83	9051.29	7973.98	7286.76	6820.97	6492.14	6253.27	6076.13	5942.73	5841.12
290,000	27352.16	15260.35	11301.54	9374.56	8258.76	7547.00	7064.58	6724.00	6476.60	6293.13	6154.97	6049.74
300,000	28295.34	15786.57	11691.25	9697.82	8543.55	7807.25	7308.18	6955.86	6699.93	6510.13	6367.21	6258.35

AMOUNT OF LOAN	NUMBER OF YEARS IN TERM											
	13	14	15	16	17	18	19	20	25	30	35	40
$ 50	1.03	1.02	1.01	1.01	1.00	1.00	1.00	0.99	0.99	0.99	0.98	0.98
100	2.06	2.04	2.02	2.01	2.00	1.99	1.99	1.98	1.97	1.97	1.96	1.96
200	4.12	4.08	4.04	4.02	4.00	3.98	3.97	3.96	3.93	3.93	3.92	3.92
300	6.18	6.11	6.06	6.03	5.99	5.97	5.95	5.94	5.90	5.89	5.88	5.88
400	8.24	8.15	8.08	8.03	7.99	7.96	7.93	7.91	7.86	7.85	7.84	7.84
500	10.30	10.19	10.10	10.04	9.99	9.95	9.92	9.89	9.83	9.81	9.80	9.80
600	12.35	12.22	12.12	12.05	11.98	11.94	11.90	11.87	11.79	11.77	11.76	11.76
700	14.41	14.26	14.14	14.05	13.98	13.92	13.88	13.85	13.75	13.73	13.72	13.71
800	16.47	16.30	16.16	16.06	15.98	15.91	15.86	15.82	15.72	15.69	15.68	15.67
900	18.53	18.33	18.18	18.07	17.97	17.90	17.84	17.80	17.68	17.65	17.64	17.63
1,000	20.59	20.37	20.20	20.07	19.97	19.89	19.83	19.78	19.65	19.61	19.59	19.59
2,000	41.17	40.74	40.40	40.14	39.94	39.77	39.65	39.55	39.29	39.21	39.18	39.18
3,000	61.75	61.10	60.60	60.21	59.90	59.66	59.47	59.32	58.93	58.81	58.77	58.76
4,000	82.33	81.47	80.80	80.28	79.87	79.54	79.29	79.09	78.57	78.41	78.36	78.35
5,000	102.92	101.84	101.00	100.34	99.83	99.43	99.11	98.86	98.21	98.01	97.95	97.93
6,000	123.50	122.20	121.20	120.41	119.80	119.31	118.93	118.63	117.86	117.61	117.54	117.52
7,000	144.08	142.57	141.40	140.48	139.76	139.20	138.76	138.41	137.50	137.22	137.13	137.10
8,000	164.66	162.94	161.60	160.55	159.73	159.08	158.58	158.18	157.14	156.82	156.72	156.69
9,000	185.25	183.30	181.79	180.62	179.69	178.97	178.40	177.95	176.78	176.42	176.31	176.27
10,000	205.83	203.67	201.99	200.68	199.66	198.85	198.22	197.72	196.42	196.02	195.90	195.86
15,000	308.74	305.50	302.99	301.02	299.48	298.28	297.33	296.58	294.63	294.03	293.84	293.78
20,000	411.65	407.34	403.98	401.36	399.31	397.70	396.43	395.44	392.84	392.04	391.79	391.71
25,000	514.56	509.17	504.98	501.70	499.14	497.12	495.54	494.29	491.05	490.04	489.73	489.63
30,000	617.47	611.00	605.97	602.04	598.96	596.55	594.65	593.15	589.26	588.05	587.68	587.56
35,000	720.39	712.84	706.96	702.38	698.79	695.97	693.76	692.01	687.47	686.06	685.62	685.48
40,000	823.30	814.67	807.96	802.72	798.62	795.40	792.86	790.87	785.67	784.07	783.57	783.41
45,000	926.21	916.50	908.95	903.06	898.44	894.82	891.97	889.72	883.88	882.07	881.51	881.33
50,000	1029.12	1018.33	1009.95	1003.40	998.27	994.24	991.08	988.58	982.09	980.08	979.46	979.26
55,000	1132.03	1120.17	1110.94	1103.74	1098.10	1093.67	1090.18	1087.44	1080.30	1078.09	1077.40	1077.19
60,000	1234.94	1222.00	1211.94	1204.08	1197.92	1193.09	1189.29	1186.30	1178.51	1176.10	1175.35	1175.11
65,000	1337.85	1323.83	1312.93	1304.42	1297.75	1292.52	1288.40	1285.15	1276.72	1274.10	1273.29	1273.04
70,000	1440.77	1425.67	1413.92	1404.76	1397.58	1391.94	1387.51	1384.01	1374.93	1372.11	1371.24	1370.96
75,000	1543.68	1527.50	1514.92	1505.10	1497.40	1491.36	1486.61	1482.87	1473.13	1470.12	1469.18	1468.89
80,000	1646.59	1629.33	1615.91	1605.44	1597.23	1590.79	1585.72	1581.73	1571.34	1568.13	1567.13	1566.81
85,000	1749.50	1731.16	1716.91	1705.78	1697.06	1690.21	1684.83	1680.58	1669.55	1666.14	1665.07	1664.74
90,000	1852.41	1833.00	1817.90	1806.11	1796.88	1789.64	1783.93	1779.44	1767.76	1764.14	1763.02	1762.66
95,000	1955.32	1934.83	1918.90	1906.45	1896.71	1889.06	1883.04	1878.30	1865.97	1862.15	1860.96	1860.59
100,000	2058.23	2036.66	2019.89	2006.79	1996.54	1988.48	1982.15	1977.16	1964.18	1960.16	1958.91	1958.52
105,000	2161.15	2138.50	2120.88	2107.13	2096.36	2087.91	2081.26	2076.01	2062.39	2058.17	2056.85	2056.44
110,000	2264.06	2240.33	2221.88	2207.47	2196.19	2187.33	2180.36	2174.87	2160.59	2156.17	2154.80	2154.37
115,000	2366.97	2342.16	2322.87	2307.81	2296.02	2286.75	2279.47	2273.73	2258.80	2254.18	2252.74	2252.29
120,000	2469.88	2443.99	2423.87	2408.15	2395.84	2386.18	2378.58	2372.59	2357.01	2352.19	2350.69	2350.22
125,000	2572.79	2545.83	2524.86	2508.49	2495.67	2485.60	2477.68	2471.44	2455.22	2450.20	2448.63	2448.14
130,000	2675.70	2647.66	2625.85	2608.83	2595.50	2585.03	2576.79	2570.30	2553.43	2548.20	2546.58	2546.07
135,000	2778.61	2749.49	2726.85	2709.17	2695.32	2684.45	2675.90	2669.16	2651.64	2646.21	2644.52	2643.99
140,000	2881.53	2851.33	2827.84	2809.51	2795.15	2783.87	2775.01	2768.02	2749.85	2744.22	2742.47	2741.92
145,000	2984.44	2953.16	2928.84	2909.85	2894.98	2883.30	2874.11	2866.88	2848.06	2842.23	2840.41	2839.85
150,000	3087.35	3054.99	3029.83	3010.19	2994.80	2982.72	2973.22	2965.73	2946.26	2940.24	2938.36	2937.77
155,000	3190.26	3156.83	3130.83	3110.53	3094.63	3082.15	3072.33	3064.59	3044.47	3038.24	3036.30	3035.70
160,000	3293.17	3258.66	3231.82	3210.87	3194.45	3181.57	3171.43	3163.45	3142.68	3136.25	3134.25	3133.62
165,000	3396.08	3360.49	3332.81	3311.21	3294.28	3280.99	3270.54	3262.31	3240.89	3234.26	3232.19	3231.55
170,000	3498.99	3462.32	3433.81	3411.55	3394.11	3380.42	3369.65	3361.16	3339.10	3332.27	3330.14	3329.47
175,000	3601.91	3564.16	3534.80	3511.88	3493.93	3479.84	3468.76	3460.02	3437.31	3430.27	3428.08	3427.40
180,000	3704.82	3665.99	3635.80	3612.22	3593.76	3579.27	3567.86	3558.88	3535.52	3528.28	3526.03	3525.32
185,000	3807.73	3767.82	3736.79	3712.56	3693.59	3678.69	3666.97	3657.74	3633.72	3626.29	3623.97	3623.25
190,000	3910.64	3869.66	3837.79	3812.90	3793.41	3778.11	3766.08	3756.59	3731.93	3724.30	3721.92	3721.18
195,000	4013.55	3971.49	3938.78	3913.24	3893.24	3877.54	3865.18	3855.45	3830.14	3822.30	3819.86	3819.10
200,000	4116.46	4073.32	4039.77	4013.58	3993.07	3976.96	3964.29	3954.31	3928.35	3920.31	3917.81	3917.03
205,000	4219.38	4175.15	4140.77	4113.92	4092.89	4076.39	4063.40	4053.17	4026.56	4018.32	4015.75	4014.95
210,000	4322.29	4276.99	4241.76	4214.26	4192.72	4175.81	4162.51	4152.02	4124.77	4116.33	4113.70	4112.88
215,000	4425.20	4378.82	4342.76	4314.60	4292.55	4275.23	4261.61	4250.88	4222.98	4214.33	4211.64	4210.80
220,000	4528.11	4480.65	4443.75	4414.94	4392.37	4374.66	4360.72	4349.74	4321.18	4312.34	4309.59	4308.73
225,000	4631.02	4582.49	4544.74	4515.28	4492.20	4474.08	4459.83	4448.60	4419.39	4410.35	4407.53	4406.65
230,000	4733.93	4684.32	4645.74	4615.62	4592.03	4573.50	4558.93	4547.45	4517.60	4508.36	4505.48	4504.58
235,000	4836.84	4786.15	4746.73	4715.96	4691.85	4672.93	4658.04	4646.31	4615.81	4606.37	4603.42	4602.51
240,000	4939.76	4887.98	4847.73	4816.30	4791.68	4772.35	4757.15	4745.17	4714.02	4704.37	4701.37	4700.43
245,000	5042.67	4989.82	4948.72	4916.64	4891.51	4871.78	4856.26	4844.03	4812.23	4802.38	4799.31	4798.36
250,000	5145.58	5091.65	5049.72	5016.98	4991.33	4971.20	4955.36	4942.88	4910.44	4900.39	4897.26	4896.28
255,000	5248.49	5193.48	5150.71	5117.32	5091.16	5070.62	5054.47	5041.74	5008.65	4998.40	4995.20	4994.21
260,000	5351.40	5295.32	5251.70	5217.65	5190.99	5170.05	5153.58	5140.60	5106.85	5096.40	5093.15	5092.13
265,000	5454.31	5397.15	5352.70	5317.99	5290.81	5269.47	5252.68	5239.46	5205.06	5194.41	5191.09	5190.06
270,000	5557.22	5498.98	5453.69	5418.33	5390.64	5368.90	5351.79	5338.31	5303.27	5292.42	5289.04	5287.98
280,000	5763.05	5702.65	5655.68	5619.01	5590.29	5567.74	5550.01	5536.03	5499.69	5488.43	5484.93	5483.84
290,000	5968.87	5906.31	5857.67	5819.69	5789.95	5766.59	5748.22	5733.75	5696.11	5684.45	5680.82	5679.69
300,000	6174.69	6109.98	6059.66	6020.37	5989.60	5965.44	5946.43	5931.46	5892.52	5880.47	5876.71	5875.54

MONTHLY AMORTIZING PAYMENTS

AMOUNT OF LOAN	NUMBER OF YEARS IN TERM											
	1	2	3	4	5	6	7	8	9	10	11	12
$ 50	4.73	2.64	1.96	1.63	1.44	1.31	1.23	1.17	1.13	1.10	1.08	1.06
100	9.45	5.28	3.92	3.25	2.87	2.62	2.46	2.34	2.26	2.19	2.15	2.11
200	18.89	10.55	7.83	6.50	5.73	5.24	4.91	4.67	4.51	4.38	4.29	4.21
300	28.34	15.83	11.74	9.74	8.59	7.86	7.36	7.01	6.76	6.57	6.43	6.32
400	37.78	21.10	15.65	12.99	11.45	10.48	9.81	9.34	9.01	8.75	8.57	8.42
500	47.22	26.38	19.56	16.24	14.32	13.09	12.26	11.68	11.26	10.94	10.71	10.53
600	56.67	31.65	23.47	19.48	17.18	15.71	14.72	14.01	13.51	13.13	12.85	12.63
700	66.11	36.93	27.38	22.73	20.04	18.33	17.17	16.35	15.76	15.32	14.99	14.74
800	75.56	42.20	31.29	25.98	22.90	20.95	19.62	18.68	18.01	17.50	17.13	16.84
900	85.00	47.48	35.20	29.22	25.77	23.56	22.07	21.02	20.26	19.69	19.27	18.94
1,000	94.44	52.75	39.11	32.47	28.63	26.18	24.52	23.35	22.51	21.88	21.41	21.05
2,000	188.88	105.50	78.21	64.93	57.25	52.36	49.04	46.70	45.01	43.75	42.81	42.09
3,000	283.32	158.24	117.31	97.40	85.87	78.53	73.56	70.05	67.51	65.63	64.21	63.13
4,000	377.76	210.99	156.41	129.86	114.50	104.71	98.08	93.40	90.01	87.50	85.61	84.18
5,000	472.20	263.74	195.51	162.32	143.12	130.88	122.59	116.75	112.51	109.38	107.02	105.22
6,000	566.64	316.48	234.62	194.79	171.74	157.06	147.11	140.10	135.02	131.25	128.42	126.26
7,000	661.08	369.23	273.72	227.25	200.37	183.23	171.63	163.45	157.52	153.12	149.82	147.31
8,000	755.51	421.98	312.82	259.72	228.99	209.41	196.15	186.80	180.02	175.00	171.22	168.35
9,000	849.95	474.72	351.92	292.18	257.61	235.58	220.67	210.15	202.52	196.87	192.62	189.39
10,000	944.39	527.47	391.02	324.64	286.24	261.76	245.18	233.50	225.02	218.75	214.03	210.44
15,000	1416.58	791.20	586.53	486.96	429.35	392.63	367.77	350.25	337.53	328.12	321.04	315.65
20,000	1888.78	1054.93	782.04	649.28	572.47	523.51	490.36	466.99	450.04	437.49	428.05	420.87
25,000	2360.97	1318.67	977.55	811.60	715.58	654.39	612.95	583.74	562.55	546.86	535.06	526.09
30,000	2833.16	1582.40	1173.06	973.92	858.70	785.26	735.54	700.49	675.06	656.23	642.07	631.30
35,000	3305.36	1846.13	1368.56	1136.24	1001.81	916.14	858.13	817.23	787.57	765.60	749.08	736.52
40,000	3777.55	2109.86	1564.07	1298.56	1144.93	1047.02	980.72	933.98	900.07	874.97	856.09	841.74
45,000	4249.74	2373.59	1759.58	1460.88	1288.04	1177.89	1103.31	1050.73	1012.58	984.34	963.10	946.95
50,000	4721.94	2637.33	1955.09	1623.19	1431.16	1308.77	1225.90	1167.48	1125.09	1093.71	1070.11	1052.17
55,000	5194.13	2901.06	2150.60	1785.51	1574.27	1439.65	1348.49	1284.22	1237.60	1203.08	1177.12	1157.38
60,000	5666.32	3164.79	2346.11	1947.83	1717.39	1570.52	1471.08	1400.97	1350.11	1312.45	1284.13	1262.60
65,000	6138.52	3428.52	2541.62	2110.15	1860.50	1701.40	1593.67	1517.72	1462.62	1421.82	1391.14	1367.82
70,000	6610.71	3692.25	2737.12	2272.47	2003.62	1832.27	1716.26	1634.46	1575.13	1531.19	1498.15	1473.03
75,000	7082.90	3955.99	2932.63	2434.79	2146.73	1963.15	1838.85	1751.21	1687.63	1640.56	1605.16	1578.25
80,000	7555.10	4219.72	3128.14	2597.11	2289.85	2094.03	1961.44	1867.96	1800.14	1749.93	1712.17	1683.47
85,000	8027.29	4483.45	3323.65	2759.43	2432.96	2224.90	2084.03	1984.71	1912.65	1859.30	1819.18	1788.68
90,000	8499.48	4747.18	3519.16	2921.75	2576.08	2355.78	2206.62	2101.45	2025.16	1968.67	1926.19	1893.90
95,000	8971.68	5010.91	3714.67	3084.06	2719.19	2486.66	2329.21	2218.20	2137.67	2078.04	2033.20	1999.11
100,000	9443.87	5274.65	3910.18	3246.38	2862.31	2617.53	2451.80	2334.95	2250.18	2187.41	2140.22	2104.33
105,000	9916.06	5538.38	4105.68	3408.70	3005.42	2748.41	2574.39	2451.69	2362.69	2296.78	2247.23	2209.55
110,000	10388.26	5802.11	4301.19	3571.02	3148.54	2879.29	2696.98	2568.44	2475.19	2406.15	2354.24	2314.76
115,000	10860.45	6065.84	4496.70	3733.34	3291.65	3010.16	2819.57	2685.19	2587.70	2515.52	2461.25	2419.98
120,000	11332.64	6329.57	4692.21	3895.66	3434.77	3141.04	2942.16	2801.94	2700.21	2624.89	2568.26	2525.20
125,000	11804.84	6593.31	4887.72	4057.98	3577.88	3271.91	3064.75	2918.68	2812.72	2734.26	2675.27	2630.41
130,000	12277.03	6857.04	5083.23	4220.30	3721.00	3402.79	3187.34	3035.43	2925.23	2843.63	2782.28	2735.63
135,000	12749.22	7120.77	5278.74	4382.62	3864.12	3533.67	3309.93	3152.18	3037.74	2953.00	2889.29	2840.84
140,000	13221.42	7384.50	5474.24	4544.93	4007.23	3664.54	3432.52	3268.92	3150.25	3062.37	2996.30	2946.06
145,000	13693.61	7648.23	5669.75	4707.25	4150.35	3795.42	3555.11	3385.67	3262.75	3171.74	3103.31	3051.28
150,000	14165.80	7911.97	5865.26	4869.57	4293.46	3926.30	3677.70	3502.42	3375.26	3281.11	3210.32	3156.49
155,000	14638.00	8175.70	6060.77	5031.89	4436.58	4057.17	3800.29	3619.17	3487.77	3390.48	3317.33	3261.71
160,000	15110.19	8439.43	6256.28	5194.21	4579.69	4188.05	3922.88	3735.91	3600.28	3499.85	3424.34	3366.93
165,000	15582.38	8703.16	6451.79	5356.53	4722.81	4318.93	4045.47	3852.66	3712.79	3609.22	3531.35	3472.14
170,000	16054.58	8966.89	6647.30	5518.85	4865.92	4449.80	4168.06	3969.41	3825.30	3718.59	3638.36	3577.36
175,000	16526.77	9230.63	6842.80	5681.17	5009.04	4580.68	4290.65	4086.15	3937.81	3827.96	3745.37	3682.58
180,000	16998.96	9494.36	7038.31	5843.49	5152.15	4711.55	4413.24	4202.90	4050.32	3937.33	3852.38	3787.79
185,000	17471.16	9758.09	7233.82	6005.80	5295.27	4842.43	4535.83	4319.65	4162.82	4046.70	3959.39	3893.01
190,000	17943.35	10021.82	7429.33	6168.12	5438.38	4973.31	4658.42	4436.40	4275.33	4156.07	4066.40	3998.22
195,000	18415.54	10285.55	7624.84	6330.44	5581.50	5104.18	4781.01	4553.14	4387.84	4265.44	4173.42	4103.44
200,000	18887.74	10549.29	7820.35	6492.76	5724.61	5235.06	4903.60	4669.89	4500.35	4374.81	4280.43	4208.66
205,000	19359.93	10813.02	8015.86	6655.08	5867.73	5365.94	5026.19	4786.64	4612.86	4484.18	4387.44	4313.87
210,000	19832.12	11076.75	8211.36	6817.40	6010.84	5496.81	5148.78	4903.38	4725.37	4593.55	4494.45	4419.09
215,000	20304.32	11340.48	8406.87	6979.72	6153.96	5627.69	5271.37	5020.13	4837.88	4702.92	4601.46	4524.31
220,000	20776.51	11604.21	8602.38	7142.04	6297.07	5758.57	5393.96	5136.88	4950.38	4812.29	4708.47	4629.52
225,000	21248.70	11867.95	8797.89	7304.36	6440.19	5889.44	5516.55	5253.62	5062.89	4921.66	4815.48	4734.74
230,000	21720.90	12131.68	8993.40	7466.67	6583.30	6020.32	5639.14	5370.37	5175.40	5031.03	4922.49	4839.95
235,000	22193.09	12395.41	9188.91	7628.99	6726.42	6151.19	5761.73	5487.12	5287.91	5140.40	5029.50	4945.17
240,000	22665.28	12659.14	9384.42	7791.31	6869.53	6282.07	5884.32	5603.87	5400.42	5249.77	5136.51	5050.39
245,000	23137.47	12922.87	9579.92	7953.63	7012.65	6412.95	6006.91	5720.61	5512.93	5359.14	5243.52	5155.60
250,000	23609.67	13186.61	9775.43	8115.95	7155.76	6543.82	6129.50	5837.36	5625.44	5468.51	5350.53	5260.82
255,000	24081.86	13450.34	9970.94	8278.27	7298.88	6674.70	6252.09	5954.11	5737.94	5577.88	5457.54	5366.04
260,000	24554.05	13714.07	10166.45	8440.59	7442.00	6805.58	6374.68	6070.85	5850.45	5687.25	5564.55	5471.25
265,000	25026.25	13977.80	10361.96	8602.91	7585.11	6936.45	6497.27	6187.60	5962.96	5796.62	5671.56	5576.47
270,000	25498.44	14241.53	10557.47	8765.23	7728.23	7067.33	6619.86	6304.35	6075.47	5905.99	5778.57	5681.68
280,000	26442.83	14769.00	10948.48	9089.86	8014.46	7329.08	6865.04	6537.84	6300.49	6124.73	5992.59	5892.12
290,000	27387.21	15296.46	11339.50	9414.50	8300.69	7590.83	7110.22	6771.34	6525.50	6343.47	6206.62	6102.55
300,000	28331.60	15823.93	11730.52	9739.14	8586.92	7852.59	7355.40	7004.83	6750.52	6562.21	6420.64	6312.98

AMOUNT OF LOAN	NUMBER OF YEARS IN TERM											
	13	14	15	16	17	18	19	20	25	30	35	40
$ 50	1.04	1.03	1.02	1.02	1.01	1.01	1.01	1.00	1.00	1.00	0.99	0.99
100	2.08	2.06	2.04	2.03	2.02	2.01	2.01	2.00	1.99	1.99	1.98	1.98
200	4.16	4.12	4.08	4.06	4.04	4.02	4.01	4.00	3.97	3.97	3.96	3.96
300	6.24	6.17	6.12	6.08	6.05	6.03	6.01	6.00	5.96	5.95	5.94	5.94
400	8.31	8.23	8.16	8.11	8.07	8.04	8.01	7.99	7.94	7.93	7.92	7.92
500	10.39	10.28	10.20	10.14	10.09	10.05	10.02	9.99	9.93	9.91	9.90	9.90
600	12.47	12.34	12.24	12.16	12.10	12.05	12.02	11.99	11.91	11.89	11.88	11.88
700	14.54	14.39	14.28	14.19	14.12	14.06	14.02	13.99	13.90	13.87	13.86	13.86
800	16.62	16.45	16.32	16.21	16.13	16.07	16.02	15.98	15.88	15.85	15.84	15.84
900	18.70	18.50	18.36	18.24	18.15	18.08	18.02	17.98	17.87	17.83	17.82	17.82
1,000	20.77	20.56	20.40	20.27	20.17	20.09	20.03	19.98	19.85	19.81	19.80	19.80
2,000	41.54	41.12	40.79	40.53	40.33	40.17	40.05	39.95	39.70	39.62	39.60	39.59
3,000	62.31	61.67	61.18	60.79	60.49	60.25	60.07	59.92	59.55	59.43	59.40	59.38
4,000	83.08	82.23	81.57	81.05	80.65	80.34	80.09	79.90	79.39	79.24	79.19	79.18
5,000	103.85	102.78	101.96	101.32	100.81	100.42	100.11	99.87	99.24	99.05	98.99	98.97
6,000	124.61	123.34	122.35	121.58	120.97	120.50	120.13	119.84	119.09	118.86	118.79	118.76
7,000	145.38	143.89	142.74	141.84	141.14	140.59	140.15	139.81	138.94	138.67	138.58	138.56
8,000	166.15	164.45	163.13	162.10	161.30	160.67	160.17	159.79	158.78	158.48	158.38	158.35
9,000	186.92	185.00	183.52	182.36	181.46	180.75	180.20	179.76	178.63	178.28	178.18	178.14
10,000	207.69	205.56	203.91	202.63	201.62	200.83	200.22	199.73	198.48	198.09	197.97	197.94
15,000	311.53	308.34	305.86	303.94	302.43	301.25	300.32	299.60	297.71	297.14	296.96	296.90
20,000	415.37	411.12	407.82	405.25	403.24	401.66	400.43	399.46	396.95	396.18	395.94	395.87
25,000	519.21	513.89	509.77	506.56	504.05	502.08	500.54	499.32	496.18	495.22	494.93	494.84
30,000	623.05	616.67	611.72	607.87	604.85	602.49	600.64	599.19	595.42	594.27	593.91	593.80
35,000	726.89	719.45	713.68	709.18	705.66	702.91	700.75	699.05	694.66	693.31	692.90	692.77
40,000	830.73	822.23	815.63	810.49	806.47	803.32	800.85	798.91	793.89	792.36	791.88	791.74
45,000	934.57	925.00	917.58	911.80	907.28	903.74	900.96	898.78	893.13	891.40	890.87	890.70
50,000	1038.41	1027.78	1019.53	1013.11	1008.09	1004.15	1001.07	998.64	992.36	990.44	989.85	989.67
55,000	1142.25	1130.56	1121.49	1114.42	1108.90	1104.57	1101.17	1098.50	1091.60	1089.49	1088.84	1088.64
60,000	1246.09	1233.34	1223.44	1215.73	1209.70	1204.98	1201.28	1198.37	1190.83	1188.53	1187.82	1187.60
65,000	1349.93	1336.11	1325.39	1317.04	1310.51	1305.40	1301.38	1298.23	1290.07	1287.57	1286.81	1286.57
70,000	1453.77	1438.89	1427.35	1418.35	1411.32	1405.81	1401.49	1398.09	1389.31	1386.62	1385.79	1385.54
75,000	1557.61	1541.67	1529.30	1519.66	1512.13	1506.23	1501.60	1497.96	1488.54	1485.66	1484.78	1484.50
80,000	1661.45	1644.45	1631.25	1620.97	1612.94	1606.64	1601.70	1597.82	1587.78	1584.71	1583.76	1583.47
85,000	1765.29	1747.22	1733.20	1722.28	1713.75	1707.06	1701.81	1697.00	1607.01	1600.75	1602.74	1602.43
90,000	1869.13	1850.00	1835.16	1823.59	1814.55	1807.47	1801.91	1797.55	1786.25	1782.79	1781.73	1781.40
95,000	1972.97	1952.78	1937.11	1924.90	1915.36	1907.89	1902.02	1897.41	1885.49	1881.84	1880.71	1880.37
100,000	2076.81	2055.56	2039.06	2026.21	2016.17	2008.30	2002.13	1997.27	1984.72	1980.88	1979.70	1979.33
105,000	2180.65	2158.33	2141.02	2127.52	2116.98	2108.72	2102.23	2097.14	2083.96	2079.92	2078.68	2078.30
110,000	2284.49	2261.11	2242.97	2228.83	2217.79	2209.13	2202.34	2197.00	2183.19	2178.97	2177.67	2177.27
115,000	2388.33	2363.89	2344.92	2330.14	2318.60	2309.55	2302.44	2296.86	2282.43	2278.01	2276.65	2276.23
120,000	2492.17	2466.67	2446.88	2431.46	2419.40	2409.96	2402.55	2396.73	2381.66	2377.06	2375.64	2375.20
125,000	2596.01	2569.44	2548.83	2532.77	2520.21	2510.38	2502.66	2496.59	2480.90	2476.10	2474.62	2474.17
130,000	2699.85	2672.22	2650.78	2634.08	2621.02	2610.79	2602.76	2596.45	2580.14	2575.14	2573.61	2573.13
135,000	2803.69	2775.00	2752.73	2735.39	2721.83	2711.21	2702.87	2696.32	2679.37	2674.19	2672.59	2672.10
140,000	2907.53	2877.78	2854.69	2836.70	2822.64	2811.62	2802.98	2796.18	2778.61	2773.23	2771.58	2771.07
145,000	3011.37	2980.55	2956.64	2938.01	2923.45	2912.04	2903.08	2896.04	2877.84	2872.27	2870.56	2870.03
150,000	3115.21	3083.33	3058.59	3039.32	3024.25	3012.45	3003.19	2995.91	2977.08	2971.32	2969.55	2969.00
155,000	3219.05	3186.11	3160.55	3140.63	3125.06	3112.87	3103.29	3095.77	3076.32	3070.36	3068.53	3067.97
160,000	3322.89	3288.89	3262.50	3241.94	3225.87	3213.28	3203.40	3195.63	3175.55	3169.41	3167.51	3166.93
165,000	3426.73	3391.66	3364.45	3343.25	3326.68	3313.70	3303.51	3295.50	3274.79	3268.45	3266.50	3265.90
170,000	3530.57	3494.44	3466.40	3444.56	3427.49	3414.11	3403.61	3395.36	3374.02	3367.49	3365.48	3364.86
175,000	3634.41	3597.22	3568.36	3545.87	3528.29	3514.53	3503.72	3495.22	3473.26	3466.54	3464.47	3463.83
180,000	3738.25	3700.00	3670.31	3647.18	3629.10	3614.94	3603.82	3595.09	3572.49	3565.58	3563.45	3562.80
185,000	3842.09	3802.77	3772.26	3748.49	3729.91	3715.36	3703.93	3694.95	3671.73	3664.62	3662.44	3661.76
190,000	3945.93	3905.55	3874.22	3849.80	3830.72	3815.77	3804.04	3794.81	3770.97	3763.67	3761.42	3760.73
195,000	4049.77	4008.33	3976.17	3951.11	3931.53	3916.19	3904.14	3894.68	3870.20	3862.71	3860.41	3859.70
200,000	4153.61	4111.11	4078.12	4052.42	4032.34	4016.60	4004.25	3994.54	3969.44	3961.76	3959.39	3958.66
205,000	4257.45	4213.88	4180.07	4153.73	4133.14	4117.01	4104.35	4094.40	4068.67	4060.80	4058.38	4057.63
210,000	4361.29	4316.66	4282.03	4255.04	4233.95	4217.43	4204.46	4194.27	4167.91	4159.84	4157.36	4156.60
215,000	4465.13	4419.44	4383.98	4356.35	4334.76	4317.84	4304.57	4294.13	4267.14	4258.89	4256.35	4255.56
220,000	4568.97	4522.22	4485.93	4457.66	4435.57	4418.26	4404.67	4393.99	4366.38	4357.93	4355.33	4354.53
225,000	4672.81	4624.99	4587.89	4558.97	4536.38	4518.67	4504.78	4493.86	4465.62	4456.98	4454.32	4453.50
230,000	4776.65	4727.77	4689.84	4660.28	4637.19	4619.09	4604.88	4593.72	4564.85	4556.02	4553.30	4552.46
235,000	4880.49	4830.55	4791.79	4761.59	4737.99	4719.50	4704.99	4693.58	4664.09	4655.06	4652.29	4651.43
240,000	4984.33	4933.33	4893.75	4862.91	4838.80	4819.92	4805.10	4793.45	4763.32	4754.11	4751.27	4750.40
245,000	5088.17	5036.10	4995.70	4964.22	4939.61	4920.33	4905.20	4893.31	4862.56	4853.15	4850.25	4849.36
250,000	5192.01	5138.88	5097.65	5065.53	5040.42	5020.75	5005.31	4993.17	4961.80	4952.19	4949.24	4948.33
255,000	5295.85	5241.66	5199.60	5166.84	5141.23	5121.16	5105.42	5093.04	5061.03	5051.24	5048.22	5047.29
260,000	5399.69	5344.44	5301.56	5268.15	5242.04	5221.58	5205.52	5192.90	5160.27	5150.28	5147.21	5146.26
265,000	5503.53	5447.21	5403.51	5369.46	5342.84	5321.99	5305.63	5292.76	5259.50	5249.33	5246.19	5245.23
270,000	5607.37	5549.99	5505.46	5470.77	5443.65	5422.41	5405.73	5392.63	5358.74	5348.37	5345.18	5344.19
275,000	5815.05	5755.55	5709.37	5673.39	5645.27	5623.24	5605.95	5592.35	5557.21	5546.46	5543.15	5542.13
280,000	5815.05	5755.55	5709.37	5673.39	5645.27	5623.24	5605.95	5592.35	5557.21	5546.46	5543.15	5542.13
290,000	6022.73	5961.10	5913.27	5876.01	5846.89	5824.07	5806.16	5792.08	5755.68	5744.54	5741.12	5740.06
300,000	6230.41	6166.66	6117.18	6078.63	6048.50	6024.90	6006.37	5991.81	5954.15	5942.63	5939.09	5937.99

AMOUNT OF LOAN	NUMBER OF YEARS IN TERM											
	1	2	3	4	5	6	7	8	9	10	11	12
$ 50	4.73	2.65	1.97	1.64	1.44	1.32	1.24	1.18	1.14	1.11	1.08	1.07
100	9.46	5.29	3.93	3.27	2.88	2.64	2.47	2.36	2.27	2.21	2.16	2.13
200	18.92	10.58	7.85	6.53	5.76	5.27	4.94	4.71	4.54	4.41	4.32	4.25
300	28.37	15.87	11.77	9.79	8.64	7.90	7.41	7.06	6.81	6.62	6.48	6.37
400	37.83	21.15	15.70	13.05	11.51	10.54	9.88	9.41	9.07	8.82	8.64	8.50
500	47.28	26.44	19.62	16.31	14.39	13.17	12.34	11.76	11.34	11.03	10.80	10.62
600	56.74	31.73	23.54	19.57	17.27	15.80	14.81	14.11	13.61	13.23	12.95	12.74
700	66.20	37.01	27.47	22.83	20.14	18.43	17.28	16.46	15.87	15.44	15.11	14.86
800	75.65	42.30	31.39	26.09	23.02	21.07	19.75	18.82	18.14	17.64	17.27	16.99
900	85.11	47.59	35.31	29.35	25.90	23.70	22.21	21.17	20.41	19.85	19.43	19.11
1,000	94.56	52.88	39.24	32.61	28.77	26.33	24.68	23.52	22.68	22.05	21.59	21.23
2,000	189.12	105.75	78.47	65.21	57.54	52.66	49.36	47.03	45.35	44.10	43.17	42.46
3,000	283.68	158.62	117.70	97.81	86.31	78.99	74.03	70.54	68.02	66.15	64.75	63.68
4,000	378.24	211.49	156.94	130.41	115.08	105.31	98.71	94.06	90.69	88.20	86.33	84.91
5,000	472.80	264.36	196.17	163.01	143.84	131.64	123.38	117.57	113.36	110.25	107.91	106.13
6,000	567.36	317.23	235.40	195.62	172.61	157.97	148.06	141.08	136.03	132.29	129.49	127.36
7,000	661.92	370.10	274.63	228.22	201.38	184.29	172.74	164.60	158.70	154.34	151.07	148.59
8,000	756.48	422.97	313.87	260.82	230.15	210.62	197.41	188.11	181.37	176.39	172.65	169.81
9,000	851.04	475.84	353.10	293.42	258.92	236.95	222.09	211.62	204.04	198.44	194.23	191.04
10,000	945.60	528.72	392.33	326.02	287.68	263.27	246.76	235.14	226.71	220.49	215.81	212.26
15,000	1418.40	793.07	588.50	489.03	431.52	394.91	370.14	352.70	340.07	330.73	323.72	318.39
20,000	1891.20	1057.43	784.66	652.04	575.36	526.54	493.52	470.27	453.42	440.97	431.62	424.52
25,000	2363.99	1321.78	980.83	815.05	719.20	658.18	616.90	587.83	566.78	551.21	539.52	530.65
30,000	2836.79	1586.14	1176.99	978.06	863.04	789.81	740.28	705.40	680.13	661.45	647.43	636.78
35,000	3309.59	1850.49	1373.15	1141.07	1006.88	921.44	863.66	822.96	793.48	771.69	755.33	742.91
40,000	3782.39	2114.85	1569.32	1304.08	1150.72	1053.08	987.04	940.53	906.84	881.93	863.23	849.04
45,000	4255.19	2379.20	1765.48	1467.09	1294.56	1184.71	1110.42	1058.10	1020.19	992.17	971.14	955.17
50,000	4727.98	2643.56	1961.65	1630.10	1438.40	1316.35	1233.80	1175.66	1133.55	1102.41	1079.04	1061.30
55,000	5200.78	2907.92	2157.81	1793.11	1582.24	1447.98	1357.17	1293.23	1246.90	1212.65	1186.94	1167.43
60,000	5673.58	3172.27	2353.98	1956.12	1726.08	1579.61	1480.55	1410.79	1360.26	1322.89	1294.85	1273.56
65,000	6146.38	3436.63	2550.14	2119.12	1869.92	1711.25	1603.93	1528.36	1473.61	1433.13	1402.75	1379.69
70,000	6619.18	3700.98	2746.30	2282.13	2013.76	1842.88	1727.31	1645.92	1586.96	1543.37	1510.65	1485.82
75,000	7091.97	3965.34	2942.47	2445.14	2157.60	1974.52	1850.69	1763.49	1700.32	1653.61	1618.56	1591.94
80,000	7564.77	4229.69	3138.63	2608.15	2301.44	2106.15	1974.07	1881.06	1813.67	1763.85	1726.46	1698.07
85,000	8037.57	4494.05	3334.80	2771.16	2445.28	2237.79	2097.45	1998.62	1927.03	1874.09	1834.36	1804.20
90,000	8510.37	4758.40	3530.96	2934.17	2589.12	2369.42	2220.83	2116.19	2040.38	1984.33	1942.27	1910.33
95,000	8983.17	5022.76	3727.13	3097.18	2732.96	2501.05	2344.21	2233.75	2153.74	2094.57	2050.17	2016.46
100,000	9455.96	5287.11	3923.29	3260.19	2876.80	2632.69	2467.59	2351.32	2267.09	2204.81	2158.07	2122.59
105,000	9928.76	5551.47	4119.45	3423.20	3020.64	2764.32	2590.97	2468.88	2380.44	2315.06	2265.98	2228.72
110,000	10401.56	5815.83	4315.62	3586.21	3164.48	2895.96	2714.36	2586.45	2493.80	2425.30	2373.88	2334.85
115,000	10874.36	6080.18	4511.78	3749.22	3308.32	3027.59	2837.72	2704.01	2607.15	2535.54	2481.78	2440.98
120,000	11347.16	6344.54	4707.95	3912.23	3452.16	3159.22	2961.10	2821.58	2720.51	2645.78	2589.69	2547.11
125,000	11819.95	6608.89	4904.11	4075.23	3596.00	3290.86	3084.48	2939.15	2833.86	2756.02	2697.59	2653.24
130,000	12292.75	6873.25	5100.28	4238.24	3739.84	3422.49	3207.86	3056.71	2947.22	2866.26	2805.49	2759.37
135,000	12765.55	7137.60	5296.44	4401.25	3883.68	3554.13	3331.24	3174.28	3060.57	2976.50	2913.40	2865.50
140,000	13238.35	7401.96	5492.60	4564.26	4027.52	3685.76	3454.62	3291.84	3173.92	3086.74	3021.30	2971.63
145,000	13711.15	7666.31	5688.77	4727.27	4171.36	3817.40	3578.00	3409.41	3287.28	3196.98	3129.20	3077.75
150,000	14183.94	7930.67	5884.93	4890.28	4315.20	3949.03	3701.38	3526.97	3400.63	3307.22	3237.11	3183.88
155,000	14656.74	8195.03	6081.10	5053.29	4459.04	4080.66	3824.76	3644.54	3513.99	3417.46	3345.01	3290.01
160,000	15129.54	8459.38	6277.26	5216.30	4602.88	4212.30	3948.13	3762.11	3627.34	3527.70	3452.91	3396.14
165,000	15602.34	8723.74	6473.43	5379.31	4746.72	4343.93	4071.51	3879.67	3740.69	3637.94	3560.82	3502.27
170,000	16075.14	8988.09	6669.59	5542.32	4890.56	4475.57	4194.89	3997.24	3854.05	3748.18	3668.72	3608.40
175,000	16547.93	9252.45	6865.75	5705.33	5034.40	4607.20	4318.27	4114.80	3967.40	3858.42	3776.62	3714.53
180,000	17020.73	9516.80	7061.92	5868.34	5178.24	4738.83	4441.65	4232.37	4080.76	3968.66	3884.53	3820.66
185,000	17493.53	9781.16	7258.08	6031.34	5322.08	4870.47	4565.03	4349.93	4194.11	4078.90	3992.43	3926.79
190,000	17966.33	10045.51	7454.25	6194.35	5465.92	5002.10	4688.41	4467.50	4307.47	4189.14	4100.33	4032.92
195,000	18439.13	10309.87	7650.41	6357.36	5609.76	5133.74	4811.79	4585.06	4420.82	4299.38	4208.24	4139.05
200,000	18911.92	10574.22	7846.58	6520.37	5753.60	5265.37	4935.17	4702.63	4534.17	4409.62	4316.14	4245.18
205,000	19384.72	10838.58	8042.74	6683.38	5897.44	5397.01	5058.55	4820.20	4647.53	4519.86	4424.04	4351.31
210,000	19857.52	11102.94	8238.90	6846.39	6041.28	5528.64	5181.93	4937.76	4760.88	4630.11	4531.95	4457.44
215,000	20330.32	11367.29	8435.07	7009.40	6185.12	5660.27	5305.30	5055.33	4874.24	4740.35	4639.85	4563.56
220,000	20803.12	11631.65	8631.23	7172.41	6328.96	5791.91	5428.68	5172.89	4987.59	4850.59	4747.75	4669.69
225,000	21275.91	11896.00	8827.40	7335.42	6472.80	5923.54	5552.06	5290.46	5100.95	4960.83	4855.66	4775.82
230,000	21748.71	12160.36	9023.56	7498.43	6616.64	6055.18	5675.44	5408.02	5214.30	5071.07	4963.56	4881.95
235,000	22221.51	12424.71	9219.73	7661.44	6760.48	6186.81	5798.82	5525.59	5327.65	5181.31	5071.46	4988.08
240,000	22694.31	12689.07	9415.89	7824.45	6904.32	6318.44	5922.20	5643.16	5441.01	5291.55	5179.37	5094.21
245,000	23167.11	12953.42	9612.05	7987.45	7048.16	6450.08	6045.58	5760.72	5554.36	5401.79	5287.27	5200.34
250,000	23639.90	13217.78	9808.22	8150.46	7192.00	6581.71	6168.96	5878.29	5667.72	5512.03	5395.17	5306.47
255,000	24112.70	13482.13	10004.38	8313.47	7335.84	6713.35	6292.34	5995.85	5781.07	5622.27	5503.08	5412.60
260,000	24585.50	13746.49	10200.55	8476.48	7479.68	6844.98	6415.72	6113.42	5894.43	5732.51	5610.98	5518.73
265,000	25058.30	14010.85	10396.71	8639.49	7623.52	6976.62	6539.10	6230.98	6007.78	5842.75	5718.88	5624.86
270,000	25531.10	14275.20	10592.88	8802.50	7767.36	7108.25	6662.47	6348.55	6121.13	5952.99	5826.79	5730.99
280,000	26476.69	14803.91	10985.20	9128.52	8055.04	7371.52	6909.23	6583.68	6347.84	6173.47	6042.59	5943.25
290,000	27422.29	15332.62	11377.53	9454.54	8342.72	7634.79	7155.99	6818.81	6574.55	6393.95	6258.40	6155.50
300,000	28367.88	15861.33	11769.86	9780.56	8630.39	7898.05	7402.75	7053.94	6801.26	6614.43	6474.21	6367.76

AMOUNT OF LOAN	NUMBER OF YEARS IN TERM											
	13	14	15	16	17	18	19	20	25	30	35	40
$ 50	1.05	1.04	1.03	1.03	1.02	1.02	1.02	1.01	1.01	1.01	1.01	1.01
100	2.10	2.08	2.06	2.05	2.04	2.03	2.03	2.02	2.01	2.01	2.01	2.01
200	4.20	4.15	4.12	4.10	4.08	4.06	4.05	4.04	4.02	4.01	4.01	4.01
300	6.29	6.23	6.18	6.14	6.11	6.09	6.07	6.06	6.02	6.01	6.01	6.01
400	8.39	8.30	8.24	8.19	8.15	8.12	8.09	8.07	8.03	8.01	8.01	8.01
500	10.48	10.38	10.30	10.23	10.18	10.15	10.12	10.09	10.03	10.01	10.01	10.01
600	12.58	12.45	12.35	12.28	12.22	12.17	12.14	12.11	12.04	12.01	12.01	12.01
700	14.67	14.53	14.41	14.32	14.26	14.20	14.16	14.13	14.04	14.02	14.01	14.01
800	16.77	16.60	16.47	16.37	16.29	16.23	16.18	16.14	16.05	16.02	16.01	16.01
900	18.86	18.68	18.53	18.42	18.33	18.26	18.20	18.16	18.05	18.02	18.01	18.01
1,000	20.96	20.75	20.59	20.46	20.36	20.29	20.23	20.18	20.06	20.02	20.01	20.01
2,000	41.91	41.49	41.17	40.92	40.72	40.57	40.45	40.35	40.11	40.04	40.01	40.01
3,000	62.87	62.24	61.75	61.38	61.08	60.85	60.67	60.53	60.16	60.05	60.02	60.01
4,000	83.82	82.98	82.34	81.83	81.44	81.13	80.89	80.70	80.22	80.07	80.02	80.01
5,000	104.78	103.73	102.92	102.29	101.80	101.41	101.11	100.88	100.27	100.09	100.03	100.01
6,000	125.73	124.47	123.50	122.75	122.16	121.69	121.33	121.05	120.32	120.10	120.03	120.01
7,000	146.68	145.22	144.08	143.20	142.51	141.98	141.55	141.22	140.37	140.12	140.04	140.02
8,000	167.64	165.96	164.67	163.66	162.87	162.26	161.78	161.40	160.43	160.13	160.04	160.02
9,000	188.59	186.71	185.25	184.12	183.23	182.54	182.00	181.57	180.48	180.15	180.05	180.02
10,000	209.55	207.45	205.83	204.57	203.59	202.82	202.22	201.75	200.53	200.17	200.05	200.02
15,000	314.32	311.18	308.75	306.86	305.38	304.23	303.32	302.62	300.80	300.25	300.08	300.03
20,000	419.09	414.90	411.66	409.14	407.17	405.63	404.43	403.49	401.06	400.33	400.10	400.03
25,000	523.86	518.63	514.57	511.42	508.96	507.04	505.54	504.36	501.32	500.41	500.13	500.04
30,000	628.63	622.35	617.49	613.71	610.76	608.45	606.64	605.23	601.59	600.49	600.15	600.05
35,000	733.40	726.08	720.40	715.99	712.55	709.86	707.75	706.10	701.85	700.57	700.18	700.06
40,000	838.17	829.80	823.31	818.27	814.34	811.26	808.86	806.97	802.11	800.65	800.20	800.06
45,000	942.94	933.52	926.23	920.56	916.13	912.67	909.96	907.84	902.38	900.73	900.22	900.07
50,000	1047.72	1037.25	1029.14	1022.84	1017.92	1014.08	1011.07	1008.71	1002.64	1000.81	1000.25	1000.08
55,000	1152.49	1140.97	1132.06	1125.12	1119.71	1115.49	1112.18	1109.58	1102.91	1100.89	1100.27	1100.09
60,000	1257.26	1244.70	1234.97	1227.41	1221.51	1216.89	1213.28	1210.45	1203.17	1200.97	1200.30	1200.09
65,000	1362.03	1348.42	1337.88	1329.69	1323.30	1318.30	1314.39	1311.32	1303.43	1301.05	1300.32	1300.10
70,000	1466.80	1452.15	1440.80	1431.97	1425.09	1419.71	1415.50	1412.19	1403.70	1401.13	1400.35	1400.11
75,000	1571.57	1555.87	1543.71	1534.26	1526.88	1521.12	1516.60	1513.06	1503.96	1501.21	1500.37	1500.12
80,000	1676.34	1659.59	1646.62	1636.54	1628.67	1622.52	1617.71	1613.93	1604.22	1601.29	1600.40	1600.12
85,000	1781.11	1763.32	1749.54	1738.82	1730.46	1723.93	1718.81	1714.80	1704.49	1701.37	1700.42	1700.13
90,000	1885.88	1867.04	1852.45	1841.11	1832.26	1825.34	1819.92	1815.67	1804.75	1801.45	1800.44	1800.14
95,000	1990.66	1970.77	1955.36	1943.39	1934.05	1926.75	1921.03	1916.54	1905.02	1901.53	1900.47	1900.15
100,000	2095.43	2074.49	2058.28	2045.67	2035.84	2028.15	2022.13	2017.41	2005.28	2001.61	2000.49	2000.15
105,000	2200.20	2178.22	2161.19	2147.96	2137.63	2129.56	2123.24	2118.28	2105.54	2101.69	2100.52	2100.16
110,000	2304.97	2281.94	2264.11	2250.24	2239.42	2230.97	2224.35	2219.15	2205.81	2201.77	2200.54	2200.17
115,000	2409.74	2385.67	2367.02	2352.52	2341.22	2332.38	2325.45	2320.02	2306.07	2301.85	2300.57	2300.18
120,000	2514.51	2489.39	2469.93	2454.81	2443.01	2433.78	2426.56	2420.89	2406.33	2401.93	2400.59	2400.18
125,000	2619.28	2593.11	2572.85	2557.09	2544.80	2535.19	2527.67	2521.77	2506.60	2502.01	2500.62	2500.19
130,000	2724.05	2696.84	2675.76	2659.37	2646.59	2636.60	2628.77	2622.64	2606.86	2602.09	2600.64	2600.20
135,000	2828.82	2800.56	2778.67	2761.66	2748.38	2738.01	2729.88	2723.51	2707.12	2702.17	2700.66	2700.21
140,000	2933.59	2904.29	2881.59	2863.94	2850.17	2839.41	2830.99	2824.38	2807.39	2802.25	2800.69	2800.21
145,000	3038.37	3008.01	2984.50	2966.22	2951.97	2940.82	2932.09	2925.25	2907.65	2902.33	2900.71	2900.22
150,000	3143.14	3111.74	3087.42	3068.51	3053.76	3042.23	3033.20	3026.12	3007.92	3002.41	3000.74	3000.23
155,000	3247.91	3215.46	3190.33	3170.79	3155.55	3143.64	3134.31	3126.99	3108.18	3102.49	3100.76	3100.24
160,000	3352.68	3319.18	3293.24	3273.07	3257.34	3245.04	3235.41	3227.86	3208.44	3202.57	3200.79	3200.24
165,000	3457.45	3422.91	3396.16	3375.36	3359.13	3346.45	3336.52	3328.73	3308.71	3302.65	3300.81	3300.25
170,000	3562.22	3526.63	3499.07	3477.64	3460.92	3447.86	3437.62	3429.60	3408.97	3402.73	3400.84	3400.26
175,000	3666.99	3630.36	3601.98	3579.92	3562.72	3549.27	3538.73	3530.47	3509.23	3502.81	3500.86	3500.27
180,000	3771.76	3734.08	3704.90	3682.21	3664.51	3650.67	3639.84	3631.34	3609.50	3602.89	3600.88	3600.27
185,000	3876.53	3837.81	3807.81	3784.49	3766.30	3752.08	3740.94	3732.21	3709.76	3702.97	3700.91	3700.28
190,000	3981.31	3941.53	3910.72	3886.77	3868.09	3853.49	3842.05	3833.08	3810.03	3803.05	3800.93	3800.29
195,000	4086.08	4045.26	4013.64	3989.06	3969.88	3954.90	3943.16	3933.95	3910.29	3903.13	3900.96	3900.30
200,000	4190.85	4148.98	4116.55	4091.34	4071.68	4056.30	4044.26	4034.82	4010.55	4003.21	4000.98	4000.30
205,000	4295.62	4252.70	4219.47	4193.62	4173.47	4157.71	4145.37	4135.69	4110.82	4103.29	4101.01	4100.31
210,000	4400.39	4356.43	4322.38	4295.91	4275.26	4259.12	4246.48	4236.56	4211.08	4203.37	4201.03	4200.32
215,000	4505.16	4460.15	4425.29	4398.19	4377.05	4360.53	4347.58	4337.43	4311.34	4303.45	4301.06	4300.33
220,000	4609.93	4563.88	4528.21	4500.47	4478.84	4461.93	4448.69	4438.30	4411.61	4403.53	4401.08	4400.33
225,000	4714.70	4667.60	4631.12	4602.76	4580.63	4563.34	4549.80	4539.17	4511.87	4503.61	4501.10	4500.34
230,000	4819.47	4771.33	4734.03	4705.04	4682.43	4664.75	4650.90	4640.04	4612.13	4603.70	4601.13	4600.35
235,000	4924.24	4875.05	4836.95	4807.32	4784.22	4766.16	4752.01	4740.91	4712.40	4703.78	4701.15	4700.35
240,000	5029.02	4978.77	4939.86	4909.61	4886.01	4867.56	4853.12	4841.78	4812.66	4803.86	4801.18	4800.36
245,000	5133.79	5082.50	5042.78	5011.89	4987.80	4968.97	4954.22	4942.65	4912.93	4903.94	4901.20	4900.37
250,000	5238.56	5186.22	5145.69	5114.17	5089.59	5070.38	5055.33	5043.53	5013.19	5004.02	5001.23	5000.38
255,000	5343.33	5289.95	5248.60	5216.46	5191.38	5171.78	5156.43	5144.40	5113.45	5104.10	5101.25	5100.38
260,000	5448.10	5393.67	5351.52	5318.74	5293.18	5273.19	5257.54	5245.27	5213.72	5204.18	5201.28	5200.39
265,000	5552.87	5497.40	5454.43	5421.02	5394.97	5374.60	5358.65	5346.14	5313.98	5304.26	5301.30	5300.40
270,000	5657.64	5601.12	5557.34	5523.31	5496.76	5476.01	5459.75	5447.01	5414.24	5404.34	5401.32	5400.41
280,000	5867.18	5808.57	5763.17	5727.87	5700.34	5678.82	5661.97	5648.75	5614.77	5604.50	5601.37	5600.42
290,000	6076.73	6016.02	5969.00	5932.44	5903.93	5881.64	5864.18	5850.49	5815.30	5804.66	5801.42	5800.44
300,000	6286.27	6223.47	6174.83	6137.01	6107.51	6084.45	6066.39	6052.23	6015.83	6004.82	6001.47	6000.45

179

AMOUNT OF LOAN	NUMBER OF YEARS IN TERM											
	1	2	3	4	5	6	7	8	9	10	11	12
$ 50	4.74	2.65	1.97	1.64	1.45	1.33	1.25	1.19	1.15	1.12	1.09	1.08
100	9.47	5.30	3.94	3.28	2.90	2.65	2.49	2.37	2.29	2.23	2.18	2.15
200	18.94	10.60	7.88	6.55	5.79	5.30	4.97	4.74	4.57	4.45	4.36	4.29
300	28.41	15.90	11.81	9.83	8.68	7.95	7.46	7.11	6.86	6.67	6.53	6.43
400	37.88	21.20	15.75	13.10	11.57	10.60	9.94	9.48	9.14	8.89	8.71	8.57
500	47.35	26.50	19.69	16.38	14.46	13.24	12.42	11.84	11.43	11.12	10.88	10.71
600	56.81	31.80	23.62	19.65	17.35	15.89	14.91	14.21	13.71	13.34	13.06	12.85
700	66.28	37.10	27.56	22.92	20.24	18.54	17.39	16.58	15.99	15.56	15.24	14.99
800	75.75	42.40	31.50	26.20	23.14	21.19	19.87	18.95	18.28	17.78	17.41	17.13
900	85.22	47.70	35.43	29.47	26.03	23.84	22.36	21.31	20.56	20.01	19.59	19.27
1,000	94.69	53.00	39.37	32.75	28.92	26.48	24.84	23.68	22.85	22.23	21.76	21.41
2,000	189.37	106.00	78.73	65.49	57.83	52.96	49.67	47.36	45.69	44.45	43.52	42.82
3,000	284.05	158.99	118.10	98.23	86.74	79.44	74.51	71.04	68.53	66.67	65.28	64.23
4,000	378.73	211.99	157.46	130.97	115.66	105.92	99.34	94.71	91.37	88.90	87.04	85.64
5,000	473.41	264.98	196.83	163.71	144.57	132.40	124.18	118.39	114.21	111.12	108.80	107.05
6,000	568.09	317.98	236.19	196.45	173.48	158.88	149.01	142.07	137.05	133.34	130.56	128.46
7,000	662.77	370.98	275.55	229.19	202.40	185.36	173.84	165.75	159.89	155.56	152.32	149.87
8,000	757.45	423.97	314.92	261.93	231.31	211.84	198.68	189.42	182.73	177.79	174.08	171.28
9,000	852.13	476.97	354.28	294.67	260.22	238.31	223.51	213.10	205.57	200.01	195.84	192.69
10,000	946.81	529.96	393.65	327.41	289.14	264.79	248.35	236.78	228.41	222.23	217.60	214.09
15,000	1420.21	794.94	590.47	491.11	433.70	397.19	372.52	355.16	342.61	333.35	326.40	321.14
20,000	1893.62	1059.92	787.29	654.81	578.27	529.58	496.69	473.55	456.81	444.46	435.20	428.18
25,000	2367.02	1324.90	984.11	818.51	722.84	661.98	620.86	591.94	571.02	555.57	544.00	535.23
30,000	2840.42	1589.88	1180.93	982.21	867.40	794.37	745.03	710.32	685.22	666.69	652.80	642.27
35,000	3313.83	1854.86	1377.75	1145.91	1011.97	926.76	869.20	828.71	799.42	777.80	761.60	749.32
40,000	3787.23	2119.84	1574.57	1309.61	1156.54	1059.16	993.37	947.10	913.62	888.91	870.39	856.36
45,000	4260.63	2384.82	1771.40	1473.31	1301.10	1191.55	1117.54	1065.48	1027.83	1000.03	979.19	963.41
50,000	4734.04	2649.80	1968.22	1637.01	1445.67	1323.95	1241.71	1183.87	1142.03	1111.14	1087.99	1070.45
55,000	5207.44	2914.78	2165.04	1800.72	1590.23	1456.34	1365.88	1302.26	1256.23	1222.25	1196.79	1177.50
60,000	5680.84	3179.76	2361.86	1964.42	1734.80	1588.73	1490.05	1420.64	1370.43	1333.37	1305.59	1284.54
65,000	6154.25	3444.74	2558.68	2128.12	1879.37	1721.13	1614.22	1539.03	1484.64	1444.48	1414.39	1391.59
70,000	6627.65	3709.72	2755.50	2291.82	2023.93	1853.52	1738.39	1657.42	1598.84	1555.59	1523.19	1498.63
75,000	7101.05	3974.70	2952.32	2455.52	2168.50	1985.92	1862.56	1775.80	1713.04	1666.71	1631.98	1605.67
80,000	7574.45	4239.68	3149.14	2619.22	2313.07	2118.31	1986.73	1894.19	1827.24	1777.82	1740.78	1712.72
85,000	8047.86	4504.66	3345.97	2782.92	2457.63	2250.70	2110.90	2012.58	1941.44	1888.93	1849.58	1819.76
90,000	8521.26	4769.64	3542.79	2946.62	2602.20	2383.10	2235.07	2130.96	2055.65	2000.05	1958.38	1926.81
95,000	8994.66	5034.62	3739.61	3110.32	2746.76	2515.49	2359.24	2249.35	2169.85	2111.16	2067.18	2033.85
100,000	9468.07	5299.60	3936.43	3274.02	2891.33	2647.89	2483.41	2367.74	2284.05	2222.27	2175.98	2140.90
105,000	9941.47	5564.58	4133.25	3437.73	3035.90	2780.28	2607.59	2486.12	2398.25	2333.39	2284.78	2247.94
110,000	10414.87	5829.56	4330.07	3601.43	3180.46	2912.67	2731.76	2604.51	2512.46	2444.50	2393.58	2354.99
115,000	10888.28	6094.54	4526.89	3765.13	3325.03	3045.07	2855.93	2722.90	2626.66	2555.61	2502.37	2462.03
120,000	11361.68	6359.52	4723.71	3928.83	3469.60	3177.46	2980.10	2841.28	2740.86	2666.73	2611.17	2569.08
125,000	11835.08	6624.50	4920.53	4092.53	3614.16	3309.86	3104.27	2959.67	2855.06	2777.84	2719.97	2676.12
130,000	12308.49	6889.48	5117.36	4256.23	3758.73	3442.25	3228.44	3078.06	2969.27	2888.95	2828.77	2783.17
135,000	12781.89	7154.46	5314.18	4419.93	3903.29	3574.64	3352.61	3196.44	3083.47	3000.07	2937.57	2890.21
140,000	13255.29	7419.44	5511.00	4583.63	4047.86	3707.04	3476.78	3314.83	3197.67	3111.18	3046.37	2997.26
145,000	13728.70	7684.42	5707.82	4747.33	4192.43	3839.43	3600.95	3433.21	3311.87	3222.29	3155.17	3104.30
150,000	14202.10	7949.40	5904.64	4911.03	4336.99	3971.83	3725.12	3551.60	3426.07	3333.41	3263.96	3211.34
155,000	14675.50	8214.38	6101.46	5074.74	4481.56	4104.22	3849.29	3669.99	3540.28	3444.52	3372.76	3318.39
160,000	15148.90	8479.36	6298.28	5238.44	4626.13	4236.61	3973.46	3788.37	3654.48	3555.63	3481.56	3425.43
165,000	15622.31	8744.34	6495.10	5402.14	4770.69	4369.01	4097.63	3906.76	3768.68	3666.75	3590.36	3532.48
170,000	16095.71	9009.32	6691.93	5565.84	4915.26	4501.40	4221.80	4025.15	3882.88	3777.86	3699.16	3639.52
175,000	16569.11	9274.30	6888.75	5729.54	5059.83	4633.80	4345.97	4143.53	3997.09	3888.97	3807.96	3746.57
180,000	17042.52	9539.28	7085.57	5893.24	5204.39	4766.19	4470.14	4261.92	4111.29	4000.09	3916.76	3853.61
185,000	17515.92	9804.26	7282.39	6056.94	5348.96	4898.58	4594.31	4380.31	4225.49	4111.20	4025.56	3960.66
190,000	17989.32	10069.24	7479.21	6220.64	5493.52	5030.98	4718.48	4498.69	4339.69	4222.31	4134.35	4067.70
195,000	18462.73	10334.22	7676.03	6384.34	5638.09	5163.37	4842.65	4617.08	4453.90	4333.43	4243.15	4174.75
200,000	18936.13	10599.20	7872.85	6548.04	5782.66	5295.77	4966.82	4735.47	4568.10	4444.54	4351.95	4281.79
205,000	19409.53	10864.18	8069.67	6711.75	5927.22	5428.16	5091.00	4853.85	4682.30	4555.65	4460.75	4388.84
210,000	19882.94	11129.16	8266.49	6875.45	6071.79	5560.55	5215.17	4972.24	4796.50	4666.77	4569.55	4495.88
215,000	20356.34	11394.14	8463.32	7039.15	6216.36	5692.95	5339.34	5090.63	4910.70	4777.88	4678.35	4602.93
220,000	20829.74	11659.12	8660.14	7202.85	6360.92	5825.34	5463.51	5209.01	5024.91	4888.99	4787.15	4709.97
225,000	21303.15	11924.10	8856.96	7366.55	6505.49	5957.74	5587.68	5327.40	5139.11	5000.11	4895.94	4817.01
230,000	21776.55	12189.08	9053.78	7530.25	6650.05	6090.13	5711.85	5445.79	5253.31	5111.22	5004.74	4924.06
235,000	22249.95	12454.05	9250.60	7693.95	6794.62	6222.52	5836.02	5564.17	5367.51	5222.33	5113.54	5031.10
240,000	22723.35	12719.03	9447.42	7857.65	6939.19	6354.92	5960.19	5682.56	5481.72	5333.45	5222.34	5138.15
245,000	23196.76	12984.01	9644.24	8021.35	7083.75	6487.31	6084.36	5800.95	5595.92	5444.56	5331.14	5245.19
250,000	23670.16	13248.99	9841.06	8185.05	7228.32	6619.71	6208.53	5919.33	5710.12	5555.67	5439.94	5352.24
255,000	24143.56	13513.97	10037.89	8348.76	7372.89	6752.10	6332.70	6037.72	5824.32	5666.79	5548.74	5459.28
260,000	24616.97	13778.95	10234.71	8512.46	7517.45	6884.49	6456.87	6156.11	5938.53	5777.90	5657.54	5566.33
265,000	25090.37	14043.93	10431.53	8676.16	7662.02	7016.89	6581.04	6274.49	6052.73	5889.01	5766.33	5673.37
270,000	25563.77	14308.91	10628.35	8839.86	7806.58	7149.28	6705.21	6392.88	6166.93	6000.13	5875.13	5780.42
280,000	26510.58	14838.87	11021.99	9167.26	8095.72	7414.07	6953.55	6629.65	6395.33	6222.35	6092.73	5994.51
290,000	27457.39	15368.83	11415.63	9494.66	8384.85	7678.86	7201.89	6866.42	6623.74	6444.58	6310.33	6208.60
300,000	28404.19	15898.79	11809.28	9822.06	8673.98	7943.65	7450.23	7103.20	6852.14	6666.81	6527.92	6422.68

AMOUNT OF LOAN	NUMBER OF YEARS IN TERM											
	13	14	15	16	17	18	19	20	25	30	35	40
$ 50	1.06	1.05	1.04	1.04	1.03	1.03	1.03	1.02	1.02	1.02	1.02	1.02
100	2.12	2.10	2.08	2.07	2.06	2.05	2.05	2.04	2.03	2.03	2.03	2.03
200	4.23	4.19	4.16	4.14	4.12	4.10	4.09	4.08	4.06	4.05	4.05	4.05
300	6.35	6.29	6.24	6.20	6.17	6.15	6.13	6.12	6.08	6.07	6.07	6.07
400	8.46	8.38	8.32	8.27	8.23	8.20	8.17	8.16	8.11	8.09	8.09	8.09
500	10.58	10.47	10.39	10.33	10.28	10.25	10.22	10.19	10.13	10.12	10.11	10.11
600	12.69	12.57	12.47	12.40	12.34	12.29	12.26	12.23	12.16	12.14	12.13	12.13
700	14.80	14.66	14.55	14.46	14.39	14.34	14.30	14.27	14.19	14.16	14.15	14.15
800	16.92	16.75	16.63	16.53	16.45	16.39	16.34	16.31	16.21	16.18	16.17	16.17
900	19.03	18.85	18.70	18.59	18.50	18.44	18.38	18.34	18.24	18.21	18.20	18.19
1,000	21.15	20.94	20.78	20.66	20.56	20.49	20.43	20.38	20.26	20.23	20.22	20.21
2,000	42.29	41.87	41.56	41.31	41.12	40.97	40.85	40.76	40.52	40.45	40.43	40.42
3,000	63.43	62.81	62.33	61.96	61.67	61.45	61.27	61.13	60.78	60.68	60.64	60.63
4,000	84.57	83.74	83.11	82.61	82.23	81.93	81.69	81.51	81.04	80.90	80.86	80.84
5,000	105.71	104.68	103.88	103.26	102.78	102.41	102.11	101.88	101.30	101.12	101.07	101.05
6,000	126.85	125.61	124.66	123.91	123.34	122.89	122.53	122.26	121.56	121.35	121.28	121.26
7,000	147.99	146.55	145.43	144.57	143.89	143.37	142.96	142.64	141.81	141.57	141.50	141.47
8,000	169.13	167.48	166.21	165.22	164.45	163.85	163.38	163.01	162.07	161.79	161.71	161.68
9,000	190.27	188.42	186.98	185.87	185.00	184.33	183.80	183.39	182.33	182.02	181.92	181.89
10,000	211.41	209.35	207.76	206.52	205.56	204.81	204.22	203.76	202.59	202.24	202.13	202.10
15,000	317.12	314.03	311.63	309.78	308.34	307.21	306.33	305.64	303.88	303.36	303.20	303.15
20,000	422.82	418.70	415.51	413.04	411.11	409.61	408.44	407.52	405.17	404.47	404.26	404.20
25,000	528.53	523.37	519.39	516.30	513.89	512.01	510.55	509.40	506.47	505.59	505.33	505.25
30,000	634.23	628.05	623.26	619.55	616.67	614.41	612.65	611.28	607.76	606.71	606.39	606.30
35,000	739.93	732.72	727.14	722.81	719.44	716.82	714.76	713.16	709.05	707.82	707.46	707.34
40,000	845.64	837.39	831.02	820.07	822.22	819.22	810.87	815.03	810.34	808.94	808.52	808.39
45,000	951.34	942.07	934.89	929.33	925.00	921.62	918.98	916.91	911.64	910.06	909.58	909.44
50,000	1057.05	1046.74	1038.77	1032.59	1027.77	1024.02	1021.09	1018.79	1012.93	1011.17	1010.65	1010.49
55,000	1162.75	1151.41	1142.65	1135.84	1130.55	1126.42	1123.20	1120.67	1114.22	1112.29	1111.71	1111.54
60,000	1268.46	1256.09	1246.52	1239.10	1233.33	1228.82	1225.30	1222.55	1215.51	1213.41	1212.78	1212.59
65,000	1374.16	1360.76	1350.40	1342.36	1336.11	1331.23	1327.41	1324.43	1316.80	1314.53	1313.84	1313.64
70,000	1479.86	1465.43	1454.28	1445.62	1438.88	1433.63	1429.52	1426.31	1418.10	1415.64	1414.91	1414.68
75,000	1585.57	1570.11	1558.15	1548.88	1541.66	1536.03	1531.63	1528.19	1519.39	1516.76	1515.97	1515.73
80,000	1691.27	1674.78	1662.03	1652.14	1644.44	1638.43	1633.74	1630.06	1620.68	1617.88	1617.03	1616.78
85,000	1796.98	1779.45	1765.90	1755.39	1747.21	1740.83	1735.85	1731.94	1721.97	1718.99	1718.10	1717.83
90,000	1902.68	1884.13	1869.78	1858.65	1849.99	1843.23	1837.95	1833.82	1823.27	1820.11	1819.16	1818.88
95,000	2008.39	1988.80	1973.66	1961.91	1952.77	1945.64	1940.06	1935.70	1924.56	1921.23	1920.23	1919.93
100,000	2114.09	2093.47	2077.53	2065.17	2055.54	2048.04	2042.17	2037.58	2025.85	2022.34	2021.29	2020.97
105,000	2219.79	2198.15	2181.41	2168.43	2158.32	2150.44	2144.28	2139.46	2127.14	2123.46	2122.36	2122.02
110,000	2325.50	2302.82	2285.29	2271.68	2261.10	2252.84	2246.39	2241.34	2228.43	2224.58	2223.42	2223.07
115,000	2431.20	2407.49	2389.16	2374.94	2363.87	2355.24	2348.50	2343.22	2329.73	2325.70	2324.48	2324.12
120,000	2536.91	2512.17	2493.04	2478.20	2466.65	2457.64	2450.60	2445.09	2431.02	2426.81	2425.55	2425.17
125,000	2642.61	2616.84	2596.92	2581.46	2569.43	2560.04	2552.71	2546.97	2532.31	2527.93	2526.61	2526.22
130,000	2748.32	2721.51	2700.79	2684.72	2672.21	2662.45	2654.82	2648.85	2633.60	2629.05	2627.68	2627.27
135,000	2854.02	2826.19	2804.67	2787.97	2774.98	2764.85	2756.93	2750.73	2734.90	2730.16	2728.74	2728.31
140,000	2959.72	2930.86	2908.55	2891.23	2877.76	2867.25	2859.04	2852.61	2836.19	2831.28	2829.81	2829.36
145,000	3065.43	3035.53	3012.42	2994.49	2980.54	2969.65	2961.14	2954.49	2937.48	2932.40	2930.87	2930.41
150,000	3171.13	3140.21	3116.30	3097.75	3083.31	3072.05	3063.25	3056.37	3038.77	3033.51	3031.93	3031.46
155,000	3276.84	3244.88	3220.18	3201.01	3186.09	3174.45	3165.36	3158.25	3140.06	3134.63	3133.00	3132.51
160,000	3382.54	3349.55	3324.05	3304.27	3288.87	3276.86	3267.47	3260.12	3241.36	3235.75	3234.06	3233.56
165,000	3488.25	3454.23	3427.93	3407.52	3391.64	3379.26	3369.58	3362.00	3342.65	3336.87	3335.13	3334.61
170,000	3593.95	3558.90	3531.80	3510.78	3494.42	3481.66	3471.69	3463.88	3443.94	3437.98	3436.19	3435.65
175,000	3699.65	3663.57	3635.68	3614.04	3597.20	3584.06	3573.79	3565.76	3545.23	3539.10	3537.26	3536.70
180,000	3805.36	3768.25	3739.56	3717.30	3699.97	3686.46	3675.90	3667.64	3646.53	3640.22	3638.32	3637.75
185,000	3911.06	3872.92	3843.43	3820.56	3802.75	3788.86	3778.01	3769.52	3747.82	3741.33	3739.39	3738.80
190,000	4016.77	3977.59	3947.31	3923.81	3905.53	3891.27	3880.12	3871.40	3849.11	3842.45	3840.45	3839.85
195,000	4122.47	4082.27	4051.19	4027.07	4008.31	3993.67	3982.23	3973.28	3950.40	3943.57	3941.51	3940.90
200,000	4228.18	4186.94	4155.06	4130.33	4111.08	4096.07	4084.34	4075.15	4051.69	4044.68	4042.58	4041.94
205,000	4333.88	4291.61	4258.94	4233.59	4213.86	4198.47	4186.44	4177.03	4152.99	4145.80	4143.64	4142.99
210,000	4439.58	4396.29	4362.82	4336.85	4316.64	4300.87	4288.55	4278.91	4254.28	4246.92	4244.71	4244.04
215,000	4545.29	4500.96	4466.69	4440.10	4419.41	4403.27	4390.66	4380.79	4355.57	4348.03	4345.77	4345.09
220,000	4650.99	4605.63	4570.57	4543.36	4522.19	4505.67	4492.77	4482.67	4456.86	4449.15	4446.84	4446.14
225,000	4756.70	4710.31	4674.45	4646.62	4624.97	4608.08	4594.88	4584.55	4558.16	4550.27	4547.90	4547.19
230,000	4862.40	4814.98	4778.32	4749.88	4727.74	4710.48	4696.99	4686.43	4659.45	4651.39	4648.96	4648.24
235,000	4968.11	4919.65	4882.20	4853.14	4830.52	4812.88	4799.09	4788.31	4760.74	4752.50	4750.03	4749.28
240,000	5073.81	5024.33	4986.07	4956.40	4933.30	4915.28	4901.20	4890.18	4862.03	4853.62	4851.09	4850.33
245,000	5179.51	5129.00	5089.95	5059.65	5036.07	5017.68	5003.31	4992.06	4963.32	4954.74	4952.16	4951.38
250,000	5285.22	5233.67	5193.83	5162.91	5138.85	5120.08	5105.42	5093.94	5064.62	5055.85	5053.22	5052.43
255,000	5390.92	5338.35	5297.70	5266.17	5241.63	5222.49	5207.53	5195.82	5165.91	5156.97	5154.29	5153.48
260,000	5496.63	5443.02	5401.58	5369.43	5344.41	5324.89	5309.63	5297.70	5267.20	5258.09	5255.35	5254.53
265,000	5602.33	5547.69	5505.46	5472.69	5447.18	5427.29	5411.74	5399.58	5368.49	5359.20	5356.41	5355.57
270,000	5708.04	5652.37	5609.33	5575.94	5549.96	5529.69	5513.85	5501.46	5469.79	5460.32	5457.48	5456.62
280,000	5919.44	5861.71	5817.09	5782.46	5755.51	5734.49	5718.07	5705.21	5672.37	5662.56	5659.61	5658.72
290,000	6130.85	6071.06	6024.84	5988.98	5961.07	5939.30	5922.28	5908.97	5874.95	5864.79	5861.74	5860.82
300,000	6342.26	6280.41	6232.59	6195.49	6166.62	6144.10	6126.50	6112.73	6077.54	6067.02	6063.86	6062.91

24.50%

AMOUNT OF LOAN	NUMBER OF YEARS IN TERM											
	1	2	3	4	5	6	7	8	9	10	11	12
$ 50	4.75	2.66	1.98	1.65	1.46	1.34	1.25	1.20	1.16	1.12	1.10	1.08
100	9.49	5.32	3.95	3.29	2.91	2.67	2.50	2.39	2.31	2.24	2.20	2.16
200	18.97	10.63	7.90	6.58	5.82	5.33	5.00	4.77	4.61	4.48	4.39	4.32
300	28.45	15.94	11.85	9.87	8.72	7.99	7.50	7.16	6.91	6.72	6.59	6.48
400	37.93	21.25	15.80	13.16	11.63	10.66	10.00	9.54	9.21	8.96	8.78	8.64
500	47.41	26.57	19.75	16.44	14.53	13.32	12.50	11.93	11.51	11.20	10.97	10.80
600	56.89	31.88	23.70	19.73	17.44	15.99	15.00	14.31	13.81	13.44	13.17	12.96
700	66.37	37.19	27.65	23.02	20.35	18.65	17.50	16.69	16.11	15.68	15.36	15.12
800	75.85	42.50	31.60	26.31	23.25	21.31	20.00	19.08	18.41	17.92	17.56	17.28
900	85.33	47.81	35.55	29.60	26.16	23.97	22.50	21.46	20.71	20.16	19.75	19.44
1,000	94.81	53.13	39.50	32.88	29.06	26.64	25.00	23.85	23.02	22.40	21.94	21.60
2,000	189.61	106.25	79.00	65.76	58.12	53.27	49.99	47.69	46.03	44.80	43.88	43.19
3,000	284.41	159.37	118.49	98.64	87.18	79.90	74.98	71.53	69.04	67.20	65.82	64.78
4,000	379.21	212.49	157.99	131.52	116.24	106.53	99.98	95.37	92.05	89.60	87.76	86.37
5,000	474.01	265.61	197.48	164.40	145.30	133.16	124.97	119.21	115.06	111.99	109.70	107.97
6,000	568.82	318.73	236.98	197.28	174.36	159.79	149.96	143.06	138.07	134.39	131.64	129.56
7,000	663.62	371.85	276.48	230.16	203.42	186.42	174.95	166.90	161.08	156.79	153.58	151.15
8,000	758.42	424.97	315.97	263.04	232.48	213.05	199.95	190.74	184.09	179.19	175.52	172.74
9,000	853.22	478.09	355.47	295.91	261.54	239.69	224.94	214.58	207.10	201.58	197.46	194.34
10,000	948.02	531.21	394.96	328.79	290.59	266.32	249.93	238.42	230.11	223.98	219.40	215.93
15,000	1422.03	796.82	592.44	493.19	435.89	399.47	374.90	357.63	345.16	335.97	329.09	323.89
20,000	1896.04	1062.42	789.92	657.58	581.18	532.63	499.86	476.84	460.22	447.96	438.79	431.85
25,000	2370.05	1328.03	987.40	821.98	726.48	665.78	624.83	596.05	575.27	559.95	548.49	539.82
30,000	2844.06	1593.63	1184.88	986.37	871.77	798.94	749.79	715.26	690.32	671.94	658.18	647.78
35,000	3318.07	1859.24	1382.36	1150.77	1017.07	932.10	874.75	834.47	805.37	783.93	767.88	755.74
40,000	3792.07	2124.84	1579.84	1315.16	1162.36	1065.25	999.72	953.68	920.43	895.91	877.58	863.70
45,000	4266.08	2390.45	1777.32	1479.55	1307.66	1198.41	1124.68	1072.89	1035.48	1007.90	987.27	971.67
50,000	4740.09	2656.05	1974.80	1643.95	1452.95	1331.56	1249.65	1192.10	1150.53	1119.89	1096.97	1079.63
55,000	5214.10	2921.66	2172.28	1808.34	1598.25	1464.72	1374.61	1311.31	1265.59	1231.88	1206.66	1187.59
60,000	5688.11	3187.26	2369.76	1972.74	1743.54	1597.88	1499.58	1430.52	1380.64	1343.87	1316.36	1295.55
65,000	6162.12	3452.87	2567.24	2137.13	1888.83	1731.03	1624.54	1549.73	1495.69	1455.86	1426.06	1403.52
70,000	6636.13	3718.47	2764.72	2301.53	2034.13	1864.19	1749.50	1668.94	1610.74	1567.85	1535.75	1511.48
75,000	7110.14	3984.08	2962.19	2465.92	2179.42	1997.34	1874.47	1788.15	1725.80	1679.83	1645.45	1619.44
80,000	7584.14	4249.68	3159.67	2630.31	2324.72	2130.50	1999.43	1907.36	1840.85	1791.82	1755.15	1727.40
85,000	8058.15	4515.29	3357.15	2794.71	2470.01	2263.66	2124.40	2026.57	1955.90	1903.81	1864.84	1835.37
90,000	8532.16	4780.89	3554.63	2959.10	2615.31	2396.81	2249.36	2145.78	2070.96	2015.80	1974.54	1943.33
95,000	9006.17	5046.50	3752.11	3123.50	2760.60	2529.97	2374.32	2264.99	2186.01	2127.79	2084.24	2051.29
100,000	9480.18	5312.10	3949.59	3287.89	2905.90	2663.12	2499.29	2384.20	2301.06	2239.78	2193.93	2159.25
105,000	9954.19	5577.71	4147.07	3452.29	3051.19	2796.28	2624.25	2503.41	2416.11	2351.77	2303.63	2267.21
110,000	10428.20	5843.31	4344.55	3616.68	3196.49	2929.44	2749.22	2622.62	2531.17	2463.76	2413.32	2375.18
115,000	10902.20	6108.92	4542.03	3781.07	3341.78	3062.59	2874.18	2741.83	2646.22	2575.74	2523.02	2483.14
120,000	11376.21	6374.52	4739.51	3945.47	3487.07	3195.75	2999.15	2861.04	2761.27	2687.73	2632.72	2591.10
125,000	11850.22	6640.13	4936.99	4109.86	3632.37	3328.90	3124.11	2980.25	2876.33	2799.72	2742.41	2699.06
130,000	12324.23	6905.73	5134.47	4274.26	3777.66	3462.06	3249.07	3099.46	2991.38	2911.71	2852.11	2807.03
135,000	12798.24	7171.34	5331.95	4438.65	3922.96	3595.21	3374.04	3218.67	3106.43	3023.70	2961.81	2914.99
140,000	13272.25	7436.94	5529.43	4603.05	4068.25	3728.37	3499.00	3337.88	3221.48	3135.69	3071.50	3022.95
145,000	13746.26	7702.55	5726.90	4767.44	4213.55	3861.53	3623.97	3457.09	3336.54	3247.68	3181.20	3130.91
150,000	14220.27	7968.15	5924.38	4931.84	4358.84	3994.68	3748.93	3576.30	3451.59	3359.66	3290.90	3238.88
155,000	14694.27	8233.76	6121.86	5096.23	4504.14	4127.84	3873.89	3695.51	3566.64	3471.65	3400.59	3346.84
160,000	15168.28	8499.36	6319.34	5260.62	4649.43	4260.99	3998.86	3814.72	3681.70	3583.64	3510.29	3454.80
165,000	15642.29	8764.97	6516.82	5425.02	4794.73	4394.15	4123.82	3933.93	3796.75	3695.63	3619.98	3562.76
170,000	16116.30	9030.57	6714.30	5589.41	4940.02	4527.31	4248.79	4053.14	3911.80	3807.62	3729.68	3670.73
175,000	16590.31	9296.18	6911.78	5753.81	5085.32	4660.46	4373.75	4172.35	4026.85	3919.61	3839.38	3778.69
180,000	17064.32	9561.78	7109.26	5918.20	5230.61	4793.62	4498.72	4291.56	4141.91	4031.60	3949.07	3886.65
185,000	17538.33	9827.39	7306.74	6082.60	5375.90	4926.77	4623.68	4410.77	4256.96	4143.59	4058.77	3994.61
190,000	18012.33	10092.99	7504.22	6246.99	5521.20	5059.93	4748.64	4529.98	4372.01	4255.57	4168.47	4102.58
195,000	18486.34	10358.60	7701.70	6411.38	5666.49	5193.09	4873.61	4649.19	4487.06	4367.56	4278.16	4210.54
200,000	18960.35	10624.20	7899.18	6575.78	5811.79	5326.24	4998.57	4768.40	4602.12	4479.55	4387.86	4318.50
205,000	19434.36	10889.81	8096.66	6740.17	5957.08	5459.40	5123.54	4887.61	4717.17	4591.54	4497.56	4426.46
210,000	19908.37	11155.41	8294.14	6904.57	6102.38	5592.55	5248.50	5006.82	4832.22	4703.53	4607.25	4534.42
215,000	20382.38	11421.02	8491.61	7068.96	6247.67	5725.71	5373.46	5126.03	4947.28	4815.52	4716.95	4642.39
220,000	20856.39	11686.62	8689.09	7233.36	6392.97	5858.87	5498.43	5245.24	5062.33	4927.51	4826.64	4750.35
225,000	21330.40	11952.23	8886.57	7397.75	6538.26	5992.02	5623.39	5364.45	5177.38	5039.49	4936.34	4858.31
230,000	21804.40	12217.83	9084.05	7562.14	6683.56	6125.18	5748.36	5483.66	5292.43	5151.48	5046.04	4966.27
235,000	22278.41	12483.44	9281.53	7726.54	6828.85	6258.33	5873.32	5602.87	5407.49	5263.47	5155.73	5074.24
240,000	22752.42	12749.04	9479.01	7890.93	6974.14	6391.49	5998.29	5722.08	5522.54	5375.46	5265.43	5182.20
245,000	23226.43	13014.65	9676.49	8055.33	7119.44	6524.64	6123.25	5841.29	5637.59	5487.45	5375.13	5290.16
250,000	23700.44	13280.25	9873.97	8219.72	7264.73	6657.80	6248.21	5960.50	5752.65	5599.44	5484.82	5398.12
255,000	24174.45	13545.85	10071.45	8384.12	7410.03	6790.96	6373.18	6079.70	5867.70	5711.43	5594.52	5506.09
260,000	24648.46	13811.46	10268.93	8548.51	7555.32	6924.11	6498.14	6198.91	5982.75	5823.42	5704.21	5614.05
265,000	25122.46	14077.06	10466.41	8712.91	7700.62	7057.27	6623.11	6318.12	6097.80	5935.40	5813.91	5722.01
270,000	25596.47	14342.67	10663.89	8877.30	7845.91	7190.42	6748.07	6437.33	6212.86	6047.39	5923.61	5829.97
280,000	26544.49	14873.88	11058.85	9206.09	8136.50	7456.74	6998.00	6675.75	6442.96	6271.37	6143.00	6045.90
290,000	27492.51	15405.09	11453.80	9534.88	8427.09	7723.05	7247.93	6914.17	6673.07	6495.35	6362.39	6261.82
300,000	28440.53	15936.30	11848.76	9863.67	8717.68	7989.36	7497.86	7152.59	6903.17	6719.32	6581.79	6477.75

AMOUNT OF LOAN	NUMBER OF YEARS IN TERM											
	13	14	15	16	17	18	19	20	25	30	35	40
$ 50	1.07	1.06	1.05	1.05	1.04	1.04	1.04	1.03	1.03	1.03	1.03	1.03
100	2.14	2.12	2.10	2.09	2.08	2.07	2.07	2.06	2.05	2.05	2.05	2.05
200	4.27	4.23	4.20	4.17	4.16	4.14	4.13	4.12	4.10	4.09	4.09	4.09
300	6.40	6.34	6.30	6.26	6.23	6.21	6.19	6.18	6.14	6.13	6.13	6.13
400	8.54	8.45	8.39	8.34	8.31	8.28	8.25	8.24	8.19	8.18	8.17	8.17
500	10.67	10.57	10.49	10.43	10.38	10.34	10.32	10.29	10.24	10.22	10.22	10.21
600	12.80	12.68	12.59	12.51	12.46	12.41	12.38	12.35	12.28	12.26	12.26	12.26
700	14.93	14.79	14.68	14.60	14.53	14.48	14.44	14.41	14.33	14.31	14.30	14.30
800	17.07	16.90	16.78	16.68	16.61	16.55	16.50	16.47	16.38	16.35	16.34	16.34
900	19.20	19.02	18.88	18.77	18.68	18.62	18.57	18.52	18.42	18.39	18.38	18.38
1,000	21.33	21.13	20.97	20.85	20.76	20.68	20.63	20.58	20.47	20.44	20.43	20.42
2,000	42.66	42.25	41.94	41.70	41.51	41.36	41.25	41.16	40.93	40.87	40.85	40.84
3,000	63.99	63.38	62.91	62.55	62.26	62.04	61.87	61.74	61.40	61.30	61.27	61.26
4,000	85.32	84.50	83.88	83.39	83.02	82.72	82.49	82.32	81.86	81.73	81.69	81.68
5,000	106.64	105.63	104.85	104.24	103.77	103.40	103.12	102.89	102.33	102.16	102.11	102.09
6,000	127.97	126.75	125.81	125.09	124.52	124.08	123.74	123.47	122.79	122.59	122.53	122.51
7,000	149.30	147.88	146.78	145.93	145.27	144.76	144.36	144.05	143.25	143.02	142.95	142.93
8,000	170.63	169.00	167.75	166.78	166.03	165.44	164.98	164.63	163.72	163.45	163.37	163.35
9,000	191.96	190.13	188.72	187.63	186.78	186.12	185.61	185.20	184.18	183.88	183.79	183.77
10,000	213.28	211.25	209.69	208.47	207.53	206.80	206.23	205.78	204.65	204.31	204.21	204.18
15,000	319.92	316.88	314.53	312.71	311.30	310.20	309.34	308.67	306.97	306.47	306.32	306.27
20,000	426.56	422.50	419.37	416.94	415.06	413.59	412.45	411.56	409.29	408.62	408.42	408.36
25,000	533.20	528.13	524.21	521.18	518.82	516.99	515.56	514.45	511.61	510.78	510.53	510.45
30,000	639.84	633.75	629.05	625.41	622.59	620.39	618.67	617.33	613.93	612.93	612.63	612.54
35,000	746.48	739.38	733.89	729.65	726.35	723.79	721.78	720.22	716.25	715.08	714.74	714.63
40,000	853.12	845.00	838.73	833.88	830.12	827.18	824.00	823.11	818.58	817.24	816.84	816.72
45,000	959.76	950.62	943.58	938.12	933.88	930.58	928.01	926.00	920.90	919.39	918.94	918.81
50,000	1066.40	1056.25	1048.42	1042.35	1037.64	1033.98	1031.12	1028.89	1023.22	1021.55	1021.05	1020.90
55,000	1173.04	1161.87	1153.26	1146.59	1141.41	1137.37	1134.23	1131.78	1125.54	1123.70	1123.15	1122.99
60,000	1279.68	1267.50	1258.10	1250.82	1245.17	1240.77	1237.34	1234.66	1227.86	1225.85	1225.26	1225.08
65,000	1386.32	1373.12	1362.94	1355.06	1348.93	1344.17	1340.45	1337.55	1330.18	1328.01	1327.36	1327.17
70,000	1492.96	1478.75	1467.78	1459.29	1452.70	1447.57	1443.56	1440.44	1432.50	1430.16	1429.47	1429.26
75,000	1599.60	1584.37	1572.62	1563.53	1556.46	1550.96	1546.68	1543.33	1534.83	1532.32	1531.57	1531.35
80,000	1706.24	1690.00	1677.46	1667.76	1660.23	1654.36	1649.79	1646.22	1637.15	1634.47	1633.67	1633.44
85,000	1812.88	1795.62	1782.31	1772.00	1763.99	1757.76	1752.90	1749.11	1739.47	1736.62	1735.78	1735.53
90,000	1919.52	1901.24	1887.15	1876.23	1867.75	1861.16	1856.01	1851.99	1841.79	1838.78	1837.88	1837.62
95,000	2026.16	2006.87	1991.99	1980.47	1971.52	1964.55	1959.12	1954.88	1944.11	1940.93	1939.99	1939.71
100,000	2132.80	2112.49	2096.83	2084.70	2075.28	2067.95	2062.23	2057.77	2046.43	2043.09	2042.09	2041.80
105,000	2239.44	2218.12	2201.67	2188.93	2179.04	2171.35	2165.34	2160.66	2148.75	2145.24	2144.20	2143.89
110,000	2346.08	2323.74	2306.51	2293.17	2282.81	2274.74	2268.46	2263.55	2251.08	2247.39	2246.30	2245.98
115,000	2452.72	2429.37	2411.35	2307.40	2386.57	2378.14	2371.57	2366.43	2353.40	2349.55	2348.40	2348.07
120,000	2559.36	2534.99	2516.19	2501.64	2490.34	2481.54	2474.68	2469.32	2455.72	2451.70	2450.51	2450.15
125,000	2666.00	2640.62	2621.04	2605.87	2594.10	2584.94	2577.79	2572.21	2558.04	2553.86	2552.61	2552.24
130,000	2772.64	2746.24	2725.88	2710.11	2697.86	2688.33	2680.90	2675.10	2660.36	2656.01	2654.72	2654.33
135,000	2879.28	2851.86	2830.72	2814.34	2801.63	2791.73	2784.01	2777.99	2762.68	2758.16	2756.82	2756.42
140,000	2985.92	2957.49	2935.56	2918.58	2905.39	2895.13	2887.12	2880.88	2865.00	2860.32	2858.93	2858.51
145,000	3092.56	3063.11	3040.40	3022.81	3009.15	2998.52	2990.24	2983.76	2967.33	2962.47	2961.03	2960.60
150,000	3199.20	3168.74	3145.24	3127.05	3112.92	3101.92	3093.35	3086.65	3069.65	3064.63	3063.14	3062.69
155,000	3305.84	3274.36	3250.08	3231.28	3216.68	3205.32	3196.46	3189.54	3171.97	3166.78	3165.24	3164.78
160,000	3412.48	3379.99	3354.92	3335.52	3320.45	3308.72	3299.57	3292.43	3274.29	3268.93	3267.34	3266.87
165,000	3519.12	3485.61	3459.76	3439.75	3424.21	3412.11	3402.68	3395.32	3376.61	3371.09	3369.45	3368.96
170,000	3625.76	3591.24	3564.61	3543.99	3527.97	3515.51	3505.79	3498.21	3478.93	3473.24	3471.55	3471.05
175,000	3732.40	3696.86	3669.45	3648.22	3631.74	3618.91	3608.90	3601.09	3581.25	3575.40	3573.66	3573.14
180,000	3839.04	3802.48	3774.29	3752.46	3735.50	3722.31	3712.02	3703.98	3683.58	3677.55	3675.76	3675.23
185,000	3945.68	3908.11	3879.13	3856.69	3839.27	3825.70	3815.13	3806.87	3785.90	3779.70	3777.87	3777.32
190,000	4052.32	4013.73	3983.97	3960.93	3943.03	3929.10	3918.24	3909.76	3888.22	3881.86	3879.97	3879.41
195,000	4158.95	4119.36	4088.81	4065.16	4046.79	4032.50	4021.35	4012.65	3990.54	3984.01	3982.07	3981.50
200,000	4265.59	4224.98	4193.65	4169.39	4150.56	4135.89	4124.46	4115.54	4092.86	4086.17	4084.18	4083.59
205,000	4372.23	4330.61	4298.49	4273.63	4254.32	4239.29	4227.57	4218.42	4195.18	4188.32	4186.28	4185.68
210,000	4478.87	4436.23	4403.34	4377.86	4358.08	4342.69	4330.68	4321.31	4297.50	4290.47	4288.39	4287.77
215,000	4585.51	4541.86	4508.18	4482.10	4461.85	4446.09	4433.80	4424.20	4399.83	4392.63	4390.49	4389.86
220,000	4692.15	4647.48	4613.02	4586.33	4565.61	4549.48	4536.91	4527.09	4502.15	4494.78	4492.60	4491.95
225,000	4798.79	4753.10	4717.86	4690.57	4669.38	4652.88	4640.02	4629.98	4604.47	4596.94	4594.70	4594.04
230,000	4905.43	4858.73	4822.70	4794.80	4773.14	4756.28	4743.13	4732.86	4706.79	4699.09	4696.80	4696.13
235,000	5012.07	4964.35	4927.54	4899.04	4876.90	4859.67	4846.24	4835.75	4809.11	4801.24	4798.91	4798.22
240,000	5118.71	5069.98	5032.38	5003.27	4980.67	4963.07	4949.35	4938.64	4911.43	4903.40	4901.01	4900.30
245,000	5225.35	5175.60	5137.22	5107.51	5084.43	5066.47	5052.46	5041.53	5013.75	5005.55	5003.12	5002.39
250,000	5331.99	5281.23	5242.07	5211.74	5188.19	5169.87	5155.58	5144.42	5116.08	5107.71	5105.22	5104.48
255,000	5438.63	5386.85	5346.91	5315.98	5291.96	5273.26	5258.69	5247.31	5218.40	5209.86	5207.33	5206.57
260,000	5545.27	5492.48	5451.75	5420.21	5395.72	5376.66	5361.80	5350.19	5320.72	5312.01	5309.43	5308.66
265,000	5651.91	5598.10	5556.59	5524.45	5499.49	5480.06	5464.91	5453.08	5423.04	5414.17	5411.54	5410.75
270,000	5758.55	5703.72	5661.43	5628.68	5603.25	5583.46	5568.02	5555.97	5525.36	5516.32	5513.64	5512.84
280,000	5971.83	5914.97	5871.11	5837.15	5810.78	5790.25	5774.24	5761.75	5730.00	5720.63	5717.85	5717.02
290,000	6185.11	6126.22	6080.79	6045.62	6018.30	5997.04	5980.47	5967.52	5934.65	5924.94	5922.06	5921.20
300,000	6398.39	6337.47	6290.48	6254.09	6225.83	6203.84	6186.69	6173.30	6139.29	6129.25	6126.27	6125.38

24.75%   MONTHLY AMORTIZING PAYMENTS

AMOUNT OF LOAN	NUMBER OF YEARS IN TERM											
	1	2	3	4	5	6	7	8	9	10	11	12
$ 50	4.75	2.67	1.99	1.66	1.47	1.34	1.26	1.21	1.16	1.13	1.11	1.09
100	9.50	5.33	3.97	3.31	2.93	2.68	2.52	2.41	2.32	2.26	2.22	2.18
200	18.99	10.65	7.93	6.61	5.85	5.36	5.04	4.81	4.64	4.52	4.43	4.36
300	28.48	15.98	11.89	9.91	8.77	8.04	7.55	7.21	6.96	6.78	6.64	6.54
400	37.97	21.30	15.86	13.21	11.69	10.72	10.07	9.61	9.28	9.03	8.85	8.72
500	47.47	26.63	19.82	16.51	14.61	13.40	12.58	12.01	11.60	11.29	11.06	10.89
600	56.96	31.95	23.78	19.82	17.53	16.08	15.10	14.41	13.91	13.55	13.28	13.07
700	66.45	37.28	27.74	23.12	20.45	18.75	17.61	16.81	16.23	15.81	15.49	15.25
800	75.94	42.60	31.71	26.42	23.37	21.43	20.13	19.21	18.55	18.06	17.70	17.43
900	85.44	47.93	35.67	29.72	26.29	24.11	22.64	21.61	20.87	20.32	19.91	19.60
1,000	94.93	53.25	39.63	33.02	29.21	26.79	25.16	24.01	23.19	22.58	22.12	21.78
2,000	189.85	106.50	79.26	66.04	58.41	53.57	50.31	48.02	46.37	45.15	44.24	43.56
3,000	284.77	159.74	118.89	99.06	87.62	80.36	75.46	72.03	69.55	67.72	66.36	65.33
4,000	379.70	212.99	158.52	132.08	116.82	107.14	100.61	96.03	92.73	90.30	88.48	87.11
5,000	474.62	266.24	198.14	165.09	146.03	133.92	125.77	120.04	115.91	112.87	110.60	108.89
6,000	569.54	319.48	237.77	198.11	175.23	160.71	150.92	144.05	139.09	135.44	132.72	130.66
7,000	664.47	372.73	277.40	231.13	204.44	187.49	176.07	168.05	162.27	158.02	154.84	152.44
8,000	759.39	425.97	317.03	264.15	233.64	214.28	201.22	192.06	185.45	180.59	176.96	174.22
9,000	854.31	479.22	356.65	297.17	262.85	241.06	226.37	216.07	208.64	203.16	199.08	195.99
10,000	949.23	532.47	396.28	330.18	292.05	267.84	251.53	240.08	231.82	225.74	221.20	217.77
15,000	1423.85	798.70	594.42	495.27	438.08	401.76	377.29	360.11	347.72	338.60	331.79	326.65
20,000	1898.46	1064.93	792.56	660.36	584.10	535.68	503.05	480.15	463.63	451.47	442.39	435.53
25,000	2373.08	1331.16	990.70	825.45	730.13	669.60	628.81	600.18	579.53	564.34	552.99	544.42
30,000	2847.69	1597.39	1188.84	990.54	876.15	803.52	754.57	720.22	695.44	677.20	663.58	653.30
35,000	3322.31	1863.62	1386.98	1155.63	1022.18	937.44	880.33	840.25	811.34	790.07	774.18	762.18
40,000	3796.92	2129.85	1585.11	1320.72	1168.20	1071.36	1006.09	960.29	927.25	902.94	884.78	871.06
45,000	4271.54	2396.08	1783.25	1485.81	1314.23	1205.28	1131.85	1080.32	1043.16	1015.80	995.37	979.95
50,000	4746.15	2662.31	1981.39	1650.90	1460.25	1339.20	1257.61	1200.36	1159.06	1128.67	1105.97	1088.83
55,000	5220.77	2928.54	2179.53	1815.99	1606.28	1473.12	1383.37	1320.39	1274.97	1241.54	1216.57	1197.71
60,000	5695.38	3194.78	2377.67	1981.08	1752.30	1607.04	1509.13	1440.43	1390.87	1354.40	1327.16	1306.59
65,000	6170.00	3461.01	2575.81	2146.16	1898.33	1740.96	1634.89	1560.47	1506.78	1467.27	1437.76	1415.48
70,000	6644.61	3727.24	2773.95	2311.25	2044.35	1874.88	1760.65	1680.50	1622.68	1580.13	1548.35	1524.36
75,000	7119.22	3993.47	2972.08	2476.34	2190.38	2008.80	1886.41	1800.54	1738.59	1693.00	1658.95	1633.24
80,000	7593.84	4259.70	3170.22	2641.43	2336.40	2142.72	2012.17	1920.57	1854.50	1805.87	1769.55	1742.12
85,000	8068.45	4525.93	3368.36	2806.52	2482.42	2276.64	2137.93	2040.61	1970.40	1918.73	1880.14	1851.01
90,000	8543.07	4792.16	3566.50	2971.61	2628.45	2410.56	2263.69	2160.64	2086.31	2031.60	1990.74	1959.89
95,000	9017.68	5058.39	3764.64	3136.70	2774.47	2544.48	2389.45	2280.68	2202.21	2144.47	2101.34	2068.77
100,000	9492.30	5324.62	3962.78	3301.79	2920.50	2678.40	2515.21	2400.71	2318.12	2257.33	2211.93	2177.65
105,000	9966.91	5590.85	4160.92	3466.88	3066.52	2812.32	2640.97	2520.75	2434.02	2370.20	2322.53	2286.53
110,000	10441.53	5857.08	4359.05	3631.97	3212.55	2946.24	2766.73	2640.78	2549.93	2483.07	2433.13	2395.42
115,000	10916.14	6123.31	4557.19	3797.06	3358.57	3080.16	2892.49	2760.82	2665.84	2595.93	2543.72	2504.30
120,000	11390.76	6389.55	4755.33	3962.15	3504.60	3214.08	3018.25	2880.85	2781.74	2708.80	2654.32	2613.18
125,000	11865.37	6655.78	4953.47	4127.24	3650.62	3348.00	3144.01	3000.89	2897.65	2821.66	2764.92	2722.06
130,000	12339.99	6922.01	5151.61	4292.32	3796.65	3481.92	3269.77	3120.93	3013.55	2934.53	2875.51	2830.95
135,000	12814.60	7188.24	5349.75	4457.41	3942.67	3615.84	3395.53	3240.96	3129.46	3047.40	2986.11	2939.83
140,000	13289.21	7454.47	5547.89	4622.50	4088.70	3749.76	3521.29	3361.00	3245.36	3160.26	3096.70	3048.71
145,000	13763.83	7720.70	5746.02	4787.59	4234.72	3883.68	3647.05	3481.03	3361.27	3273.13	3207.30	3157.59
150,000	14238.44	7986.93	5944.16	4952.68	4380.75	4017.60	3772.81	3601.07	3477.18	3386.00	3317.90	3266.48
155,000	14713.06	8253.16	6142.30	5117.77	4526.77	4151.52	3898.57	3721.10	3593.08	3498.86	3428.49	3375.36
160,000	15187.67	8519.39	6340.44	5282.86	4672.80	4285.44	4024.33	3841.14	3708.99	3611.73	3539.09	3484.24
165,000	15662.29	8785.62	6538.58	5447.95	4818.82	4419.36	4150.09	3961.17	3824.89	3724.60	3649.69	3593.12
170,000	16136.90	9051.85	6736.72	5613.04	4964.84	4553.28	4275.85	4081.21	3940.80	3837.46	3760.28	3702.01
175,000	16611.52	9318.08	6934.86	5778.13	5110.87	4687.20	4401.61	4201.24	4056.70	3950.33	3870.88	3810.89
180,000	17086.13	9584.32	7133.00	5943.22	5256.89	4821.12	4527.37	4321.28	4172.61	4063.19	3981.48	3919.77
185,000	17560.75	9850.55	7331.13	6108.31	5402.92	4955.04	4653.13	4441.31	4288.52	4176.06	4092.07	4028.65
190,000	18035.36	10116.78	7529.27	6273.40	5548.94	5088.96	4778.89	4561.35	4404.42	4288.93	4202.67	4137.54
195,000	18509.98	10383.01	7727.41	6438.48	5694.97	5222.88	4904.65	4681.39	4520.33	4401.79	4313.26	4246.42
200,000	18984.59	10649.24	7925.55	6603.57	5840.99	5356.80	5030.41	4801.42	4636.23	4514.66	4423.86	4355.30
205,000	19459.21	10915.47	8123.69	6768.66	5987.02	5490.72	5156.17	4921.46	4752.14	4627.53	4534.46	4464.18
210,000	19933.82	11181.70	8321.83	6933.75	6133.04	5624.64	5281.93	5041.49	4868.04	4740.39	4645.05	4573.06
215,000	20408.43	11447.93	8519.97	7098.84	6279.07	5758.56	5407.69	5161.53	4983.95	4853.26	4755.65	4681.95
220,000	20883.05	11714.16	8718.10	7263.93	6425.09	5892.48	5533.45	5281.56	5099.86	4966.13	4866.25	4790.83
225,000	21357.66	11980.39	8916.24	7429.02	6571.12	6026.40	5659.21	5401.60	5215.76	5078.99	4976.84	4899.71
230,000	21832.28	12246.62	9114.38	7594.11	6717.14	6160.32	5784.97	5521.63	5331.67	5191.86	5087.44	5008.59
235,000	22306.89	12512.85	9312.52	7759.20	6863.17	6294.24	5910.73	5641.67	5447.57	5304.72	5198.04	5117.48
240,000	22781.51	12779.09	9510.66	7924.29	7009.19	6428.16	6036.49	5761.70	5563.48	5417.59	5308.63	5226.36
245,000	23256.12	13045.32	9708.80	8089.38	7155.21	6562.08	6162.25	5881.74	5679.38	5530.46	5419.23	5335.24
250,000	23730.74	13311.55	9906.94	8254.47	7301.24	6696.00	6288.01	6001.78	5795.29	5643.32	5529.83	5444.12
255,000	24205.35	13577.78	10105.07	8419.56	7447.26	6829.92	6413.77	6121.81	5911.20	5756.19	5640.42	5553.01
260,000	24679.97	13844.01	10303.21	8584.64	7593.29	6963.84	6539.53	6241.85	6027.10	5869.06	5751.02	5661.89
265,000	25154.58	14110.24	10501.35	8749.73	7739.31	7097.76	6665.29	6361.88	6143.01	5981.92	5861.61	5770.77
270,000	25629.20	14376.47	10699.49	8914.82	7885.34	7231.68	6791.05	6481.92	6258.91	6094.79	5972.21	5879.65
280,000	26578.42	14908.93	11095.77	9245.00	8177.39	7499.52	7042.57	6721.99	6490.72	6320.52	6193.40	6097.42
290,000	27527.65	15441.39	11492.04	9575.18	8469.44	7767.36	7294.09	6962.06	6722.54	6546.25	6414.60	6315.18
300,000	28476.88	15973.86	11888.32	9905.36	8761.49	8035.20	7545.61	7202.13	6954.35	6771.99	6635.79	6532.95

AMOUNT OF LOAN	NUMBER OF YEARS IN TERM											
	13	14	15	16	17	18	19	20	25	30	35	40
$ 50	1.08	1.07	1.06	1.06	1.05	1.05	1.05	1.04	1.04	1.04	1.04	1.04
100	2.16	2.14	2.12	2.11	2.10	2.09	2.09	2.08	2.07	2.07	2.07	2.07
200	4.31	4.27	4.24	4.21	4.20	4.18	4.17	4.16	4.14	4.13	4.13	4.13
300	6.46	6.40	6.35	6.32	6.29	6.27	6.25	6.24	6.21	6.20	6.19	6.19
400	8.61	8.53	8.47	8.42	8.39	8.36	8.33	8.32	8.27	8.26	8.26	8.26
500	10.76	10.66	10.59	10.53	10.48	10.44	10.42	10.39	10.34	10.32	10.32	10.32
600	12.91	12.79	12.70	12.63	12.58	12.53	12.50	12.47	12.41	12.39	12.38	12.38
700	15.07	14.93	14.82	14.73	14.67	14.62	14.58	14.55	14.47	14.45	14.45	14.44
800	17.22	17.06	16.93	16.84	16.77	16.71	16.66	16.63	16.54	16.52	16.51	16.51
900	19.37	19.19	19.05	18.94	18.86	18.80	18.75	18.71	18.61	18.58	18.57	18.57
1,000	21.52	21.32	21.17	21.05	20.96	20.88	20.83	20.78	20.68	20.64	20.63	20.63
2,000	43.04	42.64	42.33	42.09	41.91	41.76	41.65	41.56	41.35	41.28	41.26	41.26
3,000	64.55	63.95	63.49	63.13	62.86	62.64	62.47	62.34	62.02	61.92	61.89	61.88
4,000	86.07	85.27	84.65	84.18	83.81	83.52	83.30	83.12	82.69	82.56	82.52	82.51
5,000	107.58	106.58	105.81	105.22	104.76	104.40	104.12	103.90	103.36	103.20	103.15	103.14
6,000	129.10	127.90	126.97	126.26	125.71	125.28	124.94	124.68	124.03	123.83	123.78	123.76
7,000	150.61	149.21	148.14	147.30	146.66	146.16	145.77	145.46	144.70	144.47	144.41	144.39
8,000	172.13	170.53	169.30	168.35	167.61	167.04	166.59	166.24	165.37	165.11	165.04	165.01
9,000	193.64	191.84	190.46	189.39	188.56	187.91	187.41	187.02	186.04	185.75	185.67	185.64
10,000	215.16	213.16	211.62	210.43	209.51	208.79	208.24	207.80	206.71	206.39	206.29	206.27
15,000	322.74	319.74	317.43	315.64	314.26	313.19	312.35	311.70	310.06	309.58	309.44	309.40
20,000	430.31	426.32	423.24	420.86	419.01	417.58	416.47	415.60	413.41	412.77	412.58	412.53
25,000	537.89	532.89	529.04	526.07	523.77	521.98	520.58	519.50	516.76	515.96	515.73	515.66
30,000	645.47	639.47	634.85	631.28	628.52	626.37	624.70	623.40	620.11	619.15	618.87	618.79
35,000	753.05	746.05	740.66	736.50	733.27	730.77	728.82	727.30	723.46	722.34	722.02	721.92
40,000	860.62	852.63	846.47	841.71	838.02	835.16	832.93	831.20	826.81	825.54	825.16	825.05
45,000	968.20	959.20	952.28	946.92	942.78	939.55	937.05	935.10	930.17	928.73	928.31	928.18
50,000	1075.78	1065.78	1058.08	1052.14	1047.53	1043.95	1041.16	1038.99	1033.52	1031.92	1031.45	1031.31
55,000	1183.36	1172.36	1163.89	1157.35	1152.28	1148.34	1145.28	1142.89	1136.87	1135.11	1134.59	1134.44
60,000	1290.93	1278.94	1269.70	1262.56	1257.03	1252.74	1249.40	1246.79	1240.22	1238.30	1237.74	1237.57
65,000	1398.51	1385.51	1375.51	1367.78	1361.78	1357.13	1353.51	1350.69	1343.57	1341.49	1340.88	1340.70
70,000	1506.09	1492.09	1481.32	1472.99	1466.54	1461.53	1457.63	1454.59	1446.92	1444.68	1444.03	1443.84
75,000	1613.67	1598.67	1587.12	1578.20	1571.29	1565.92	1561.74	1558.49	1550.27	1547.88	1547.17	1546.97
80,000	1721.24	1705.25	1692.93	1683.42	1676.04	1670.31	1665.86	1662.39	1653.62	1651.07	1650.32	1650.10
85,000	1828.82	1811.82	1798.74	1788.63	1780.79	1774.71	1769.98	1766.29	1756.98	1754.26	1753.46	1753.23
90,000	1936.40	1918.40	1904.55	1893.84	1885.55	1879.10	1874.09	1870.19	1860.33	1857.45	1856.61	1856.36
95,000	2043.98	2024.98	2010.35	1999.05	1990.30	1983.50	1978.21	1974.09	1963.68	1960.64	1959.75	1959.49
100,000	2151.55	2131.56	2116.16	2104.27	2095.05	2087.89	2082.32	2077.98	2067.03	2063.83	2062.89	2062.62
105,000	2259.13	2238.13	2221.97	2209.48	2199.80	2192.29	2186.44	2181.88	2170.38	2167.02	2166.04	2165.75
110,000	2366.71	2344.71	2327.78	2314.69	2304.55	2296.68	2290.55	2285.78	2273.73	2270.21	2269.18	2268.88
115,000	2474.29	2451.29	2433.59	2419.91	2409.31	2401.07	2394.67	2389.68	2377.08	2373.41	2372.33	2372.01
120,000	2581.86	2557.87	2539.39	2525.12	2514.06	2505.47	2498.79	2493.58	2480.43	2476.60	2475.47	2475.14
125,000	2689.44	2664.44	2645.20	2630.33	2618.81	2609.86	2602.90	2597.48	2583.78	2579.79	2578.62	2578.27
130,000	2797.02	2771.02	2751.01	2735.55	2723.56	2714.26	2707.02	2701.38	2687.14	2682.98	2681.76	2681.40
135,000	2904.59	2877.60	2856.82	2840.76	2828.32	2818.65	2811.13	2805.28	2790.49	2786.17	2784.91	2784.53
140,000	3012.17	2984.18	2962.63	2945.97	2933.07	2923.05	2915.25	2909.18	2893.84	2889.36	2888.05	2887.67
145,000	3119.75	3090.75	3068.43	3051.19	3037.82	3027.44	3019.37	3013.08	2997.19	2992.55	2991.19	2990.80
150,000	3227.33	3197.33	3174.24	3156.40	3142.57	3131.84	3123.48	3116.97	3100.54	3095.75	3094.34	3093.93
155,000	3334.90	3303.91	3280.05	3261.61	3247.33	3236.23	3227.60	3220.87	3203.89	3198.94	3197.48	3197.06
160,000	3442.48	3410.49	3385.86	3366.83	3352.08	3340.62	3331.71	3324.77	3307.24	3302.13	3300.63	3300.19
165,000	3550.06	3517.07	3491.67	3472.04	3456.83	3445.02	3435.83	3428.67	3410.59	3405.32	3403.77	3403.32
170,000	3657.64	3623.64	3597.47	3577.25	3561.58	3549.41	3539.95	3532.57	3513.95	3508.51	3506.92	3506.45
175,000	3765.21	3730.22	3703.28	3682.46	3666.33	3653.81	3644.06	3636.47	3617.30	3611.70	3610.06	3609.58
180,000	3872.79	3836.80	3809.09	3787.68	3771.09	3758.20	3748.18	3740.37	3720.65	3714.89	3713.21	3712.71
185,000	3980.37	3943.38	3914.90	3892.89	3875.84	3862.60	3852.29	3844.27	3824.00	3818.08	3816.35	3815.84
190,000	4087.95	4049.95	4020.70	3998.10	3980.59	3966.99	3956.41	3948.17	3927.35	3921.28	3919.50	3918.97
195,000	4195.52	4156.53	4126.51	4103.32	4085.34	4071.38	4060.52	4052.06	4030.70	4024.47	4022.64	4022.10
200,000	4303.10	4263.11	4232.32	4208.53	4190.10	4175.78	4164.64	4155.96	4134.05	4127.66	4125.78	4125.23
205,000	4410.68	4369.69	4338.13	4313.74	4294.85	4280.17	4268.76	4259.86	4237.40	4230.85	4228.93	4228.36
210,000	4518.26	4476.26	4443.94	4418.96	4399.60	4384.57	4372.87	4363.76	4340.75	4334.04	4332.07	4331.50
215,000	4625.83	4582.84	4549.74	4524.17	4504.35	4488.96	4476.99	4467.66	4444.11	4437.23	4435.22	4434.63
220,000	4733.41	4689.42	4655.55	4629.38	4609.10	4593.36	4581.10	4571.56	4547.46	4540.42	4538.36	4537.76
225,000	4840.99	4796.00	4761.36	4734.60	4713.86	4697.75	4685.22	4675.46	4650.81	4643.62	4641.51	4640.89
230,000	4948.57	4902.57	4867.17	4839.81	4818.61	4802.14	4789.34	4779.36	4754.16	4746.81	4744.65	4744.02
235,000	5056.14	5009.15	4972.98	4945.02	4923.36	4906.54	4893.45	4883.26	4857.51	4850.00	4847.80	4847.15
240,000	5163.72	5115.73	5078.78	5050.24	5028.11	5010.93	4997.57	4987.16	4960.86	4953.19	4950.94	4950.28
245,000	5271.30	5222.31	5184.59	5155.45	5132.87	5115.33	5101.68	5091.05	5064.21	5056.38	5054.08	5053.41
250,000	5378.87	5328.88	5290.40	5260.66	5237.62	5219.72	5205.80	5194.95	5167.56	5159.57	5157.23	5156.54
255,000	5486.45	5435.46	5396.21	5365.88	5342.37	5324.12	5309.92	5298.85	5270.92	5262.76	5260.37	5259.67
260,000	5594.03	5542.04	5502.01	5471.09	5447.12	5428.51	5414.03	5402.75	5374.27	5365.95	5363.52	5362.80
265,000	5701.61	5648.62	5607.82	5576.30	5551.88	5532.90	5518.15	5506.65	5477.62	5469.15	5466.66	5465.93
270,000	5809.18	5755.19	5713.63	5681.51	5656.63	5637.30	5622.26	5610.55	5580.97	5572.34	5569.81	5569.06
280,000	6024.34	5968.35	5925.25	5891.94	5866.13	5846.09	5830.49	5818.35	5787.67	5778.72	5776.10	5775.33
290,000	6239.49	6181.50	6136.86	6102.37	6075.64	6054.88	6038.73	6026.15	5994.37	5985.10	5982.38	5981.59
300,000	6454.65	6394.66	6348.48	6312.79	6285.14	6263.67	6246.96	6233.94	6201.08	6191.49	6188.67	6187.85

25.00%　MONTHLY AMORTIZING PAYMENTS

AMOUNT OF LOAN	\multicolumn{12}{c}{NUMBER OF YEARS IN TERM}

AMOUNT OF LOAN	1	2	3	4	5	6	7	8	9	10	11	12
$ 50	4.76	2.67	1.99	1.66	1.47	1.35	1.27	1.21	1.17	1.14	1.12	1.10
100	9.51	5.34	3.98	3.32	2.94	2.70	2.54	2.42	2.34	2.28	2.23	2.20
200	19.01	10.68	7.96	6.64	5.88	5.39	5.07	4.84	4.68	4.55	4.46	4.40
300	28.52	16.02	11.93	9.95	8.81	8.09	7.60	7.26	7.01	6.83	6.69	6.59
400	38.02	21.35	15.91	13.27	11.75	10.78	10.13	9.67	9.35	9.10	8.92	8.79
500	47.53	26.69	19.88	16.58	14.68	13.47	12.66	12.09	11.68	11.38	11.15	10.99
600	57.03	32.03	23.86	19.90	17.62	16.17	15.19	14.51	14.02	13.65	13.38	13.18
700	66.54	37.37	27.84	23.21	20.55	18.86	17.72	16.93	16.35	15.93	15.61	15.38
800	76.04	42.70	31.81	26.53	23.49	21.55	20.25	19.34	18.69	18.20	17.84	17.57
900	85.54	48.04	35.79	29.85	26.42	24.25	22.79	21.76	21.02	20.48	20.07	19.77
1,000	95.05	53.38	39.76	33.16	29.36	26.94	25.32	24.18	23.36	22.75	22.30	21.97
2,000	190.09	106.75	79.52	66.32	58.71	53.88	50.63	48.35	46.71	45.50	44.60	43.93
3,000	285.14	160.12	119.28	99.48	88.06	80.82	75.94	72.52	70.06	68.25	66.90	65.89
4,000	380.18	213.49	159.04	132.63	117.41	107.75	101.25	96.70	93.41	91.00	89.20	87.85
5,000	475.23	266.86	198.80	165.79	146.76	134.69	126.56	120.87	116.77	113.75	111.50	109.81
6,000	570.27	320.23	238.56	198.95	176.11	161.63	151.87	145.04	140.12	136.50	133.80	131.77
7,000	665.31	373.61	278.32	232.10	205.46	188.57	177.19	169.21	163.47	159.25	156.10	153.73
8,000	760.36	426.98	318.08	265.26	234.82	215.50	202.50	193.39	186.82	182.00	178.40	175.69
9,000	855.40	480.35	357.84	298.42	264.17	242.44	227.81	217.56	210.17	204.75	200.70	197.65
10,000	950.45	533.72	397.60	331.58	293.52	269.38	253.12	241.73	233.53	227.50	223.00	219.61
15,000	1425.67	800.58	596.40	497.36	440.27	404.06	379.68	362.59	350.29	341.24	334.50	329.42
20,000	1900.89	1067.44	795.20	663.15	587.03	538.75	506.24	483.46	467.05	454.99	446.00	439.22
25,000	2376.11	1334.29	994.00	828.93	733.79	673.43	632.80	604.32	583.81	568.74	557.50	549.03
30,000	2851.33	1601.15	1192.80	994.72	880.54	808.12	759.35	725.18	700.57	682.48	669.00	658.83
35,000	3326.55	1868.01	1391.60	1160.50	1027.30	942.81	885.91	846.05	817.33	796.23	780.50	768.64
40,000	3801.77	2134.87	1590.40	1326.29	1174.06	1077.49	1012.47	966.91	934.09	909.98	892.00	878.44
45,000	4276.99	2401.72	1789.20	1492.08	1320.81	1212.18	1139.03	1087.77	1050.85	1023.72	1003.49	988.25
50,000	4752.22	2668.58	1988.00	1657.86	1467.57	1346.86	1265.59	1208.64	1167.61	1137.47	1114.99	1098.05
55,000	5227.44	2935.44	2186.80	1823.65	1614.33	1481.55	1392.14	1329.50	1284.38	1251.22	1226.49	1207.86
60,000	5702.66	3202.30	2385.59	1989.43	1761.08	1616.24	1518.70	1450.36	1401.14	1364.96	1337.99	1317.66
65,000	6177.88	3469.15	2584.39	2155.22	1907.84	1750.92	1645.26	1571.23	1517.90	1478.71	1449.49	1427.47
70,000	6653.10	3736.01	2783.19	2321.00	2054.60	1885.61	1771.82	1692.09	1634.66	1592.46	1560.99	1537.27
75,000	7128.32	4002.87	2981.99	2486.79	2201.35	2020.29	1898.38	1812.95	1751.42	1706.20	1672.49	1647.07
80,000	7603.54	4269.73	3180.79	2652.58	2348.11	2154.98	2024.94	1933.82	1868.18	1819.95	1783.99	1756.88
85,000	8078.76	4536.58	3379.59	2818.36	2494.87	2289.67	2151.49	2054.68	1984.94	1933.70	1895.48	1866.68
90,000	8553.98	4803.44	3578.39	2984.15	2641.62	2424.35	2278.05	2175.54	2101.70	2047.44	2006.98	1976.49
95,000	9029.20	5070.30	3777.19	3149.93	2788.38	2559.04	2404.61	2296.41	2218.46	2161.19	2118.48	2086.29
100,000	9504.43	5337.16	3975.99	3315.72	2935.14	2693.72	2531.17	2417.27	2335.22	2274.93	2229.98	2196.10
105,000	9979.65	5604.01	4174.79	3481.50	3081.89	2828.41	2657.73	2538.13	2451.99	2388.68	2341.48	2305.90
110,000	10454.87	5870.87	4373.59	3647.29	3228.65	2963.09	2784.28	2659.00	2568.75	2502.43	2452.98	2415.71
115,000	10930.09	6137.73	4572.38	3813.07	3375.41	3097.78	2910.84	2779.86	2685.51	2616.17	2564.48	2525.51
120,000	11405.31	6404.59	4771.18	3978.86	3522.16	3232.47	3037.40	2900.72	2802.27	2729.92	2675.98	2635.32
125,000	11880.53	6671.45	4969.98	4144.65	3668.92	3367.15	3163.96	3021.59	2919.03	2843.67	2787.48	2745.12
130,000	12355.75	6938.30	5168.78	4310.43	3815.68	3501.84	3290.52	3142.45	3035.79	2957.41	2898.97	2854.93
135,000	12830.97	7205.16	5367.58	4476.22	3962.43	3636.52	3417.08	3263.31	3152.55	3071.16	3010.47	2964.73
140,000	13306.19	7472.02	5566.38	4642.00	4109.19	3771.21	3543.63	3384.18	3269.31	3184.91	3121.97	3074.54
145,000	13781.41	7738.88	5765.18	4807.79	4255.95	3905.90	3670.19	3505.04	3386.07	3298.65	3233.47	3184.34
150,000	14256.64	8005.73	5963.98	4973.57	4402.70	4040.58	3796.75	3625.90	3502.83	3412.40	3344.97	3294.14
155,000	14731.86	8272.59	6162.78	5139.36	4549.46	4175.27	3923.31	3746.77	3619.60	3526.15	3456.47	3403.95
160,000	15207.08	8539.45	6361.58	5305.15	4696.22	4309.95	4049.87	3867.63	3736.36	3639.89	3567.97	3513.75
165,000	15682.30	8806.31	6560.38	5470.93	4842.97	4444.64	4176.42	3988.49	3853.12	3753.64	3679.47	3623.56
170,000	16157.52	9073.16	6759.18	5636.72	4989.73	4579.33	4302.98	4109.36	3969.88	3867.39	3790.96	3733.36
175,000	16632.74	9340.02	6957.97	5802.50	5136.49	4714.01	4429.54	4230.22	4086.64	3981.13	3902.46	3843.17
180,000	17107.96	9606.88	7156.77	5968.29	5283.24	4848.70	4556.10	4351.08	4203.40	4094.88	4013.96	3952.97
185,000	17583.18	9873.74	7355.57	6134.07	5430.00	4983.38	4682.66	4471.95	4320.16	4208.62	4125.46	4062.78
190,000	18058.40	10140.59	7554.37	6299.86	5576.76	5118.07	4809.22	4592.81	4436.92	4322.37	4236.96	4172.58
195,000	18533.62	10407.45	7753.17	6465.65	5723.51	5252.75	4935.77	4713.67	4553.68	4436.12	4348.46	4282.39
200,000	19008.85	10674.31	7951.97	6631.43	5870.27	5387.44	5062.33	4834.54	4670.44	4549.86	4459.96	4392.19
205,000	19484.07	10941.17	8150.77	6797.22	6017.03	5522.13	5188.89	4955.40	4787.21	4663.61	4571.46	4502.00
210,000	19959.29	11208.02	8349.57	6963.00	6163.78	5656.81	5315.45	5076.26	4903.97	4777.36	4682.96	4611.80
215,000	20434.51	11474.88	8548.37	7128.79	6310.54	5791.50	5442.01	5197.13	5020.73	4891.10	4794.45	4721.60
220,000	20909.73	11741.74	8747.17	7294.57	6457.30	5926.18	5568.56	5317.99	5137.49	5004.85	4905.95	4831.41
225,000	21384.95	12008.60	8945.97	7460.36	6604.05	6060.87	5695.12	5438.85	5254.25	5118.60	5017.45	4941.21
230,000	21860.17	12275.45	9144.76	7626.14	6750.81	6195.56	5821.68	5559.72	5371.01	5232.34	5128.95	5051.02
235,000	22335.39	12542.31	9343.56	7791.93	6897.57	6330.24	5948.24	5680.58	5487.77	5346.09	5240.45	5160.82
240,000	22810.61	12809.17	9542.36	7957.72	7044.32	6464.93	6074.80	5801.44	5604.53	5459.84	5351.95	5270.63
245,000	23285.83	13076.03	9741.16	8123.50	7191.08	6599.61	6201.36	5922.31	5721.29	5573.58	5463.45	5380.43
250,000	23761.06	13342.89	9939.96	8289.29	7337.84	6734.30	6327.91	6043.17	5838.05	5687.33	5574.95	5490.24
255,000	24236.28	13609.74	10138.76	8455.07	7484.59	6868.99	6454.47	6164.03	5954.82	5801.08	5686.44	5600.04
260,000	24711.50	13876.60	10337.56	8620.86	7631.35	7003.67	6581.03	6284.90	6071.58	5914.82	5797.94	5709.85
265,000	25186.72	14143.46	10536.36	8786.64	7778.11	7138.36	6707.59	6405.76	6188.34	6028.57	5909.44	5819.65
270,000	25661.94	14410.32	10735.16	8952.43	7924.86	7273.04	6834.15	6526.62	6305.10	6142.31	6020.94	5929.46
280,000	26612.38	14944.03	11132.76	9284.00	8218.38	7542.41	7087.26	6768.35	6538.62	6369.81	6243.94	6149.07
290,000	27562.82	15477.75	11530.35	9615.57	8511.89	7811.79	7340.38	7010.08	6772.14	6597.30	6466.94	6368.67
300,000	28513.27	16011.46	11927.95	9947.14	8805.40	8081.16	7593.50	7251.80	7005.66	6824.79	6689.93	6588.28

AMOUNT OF LOAN	NUMBER OF YEARS IN TERM											
	13	**14**	**15**	**16**	**17**	**18**	**19**	**20**	**25**	**30**	**35**	**40**
$ 50	1.09	1.08	1.07	1.07	1.06	1.06	1.06	1.05	1.05	1.05	1.05	1.05
100	2.18	2.16	2.14	2.13	2.12	2.11	2.11	2.10	2.09	2.09	2.09	2.09
200	4.35	4.31	4.28	4.25	4.23	4.22	4.21	4.20	4.18	4.17	4.17	4.17
300	6.52	6.46	6.41	6.38	6.35	6.33	6.31	6.30	6.27	6.26	6.26	6.26
400	8.69	8.61	8.55	8.50	8.46	8.44	8.41	8.40	8.36	8.34	8.34	8.34
500	10.86	10.76	10.68	10.62	10.58	10.54	10.52	10.50	10.44	10.43	10.42	10.42
600	13.03	12.91	12.82	12.75	12.69	12.65	12.62	12.59	12.53	12.51	12.51	12.51
700	15.20	15.06	14.95	14.87	14.81	14.76	14.72	14.69	14.62	14.60	14.59	14.59
800	17.37	17.21	17.09	17.00	16.92	16.87	16.82	16.79	16.71	16.68	16.67	16.67
900	19.54	19.36	19.22	19.12	19.04	18.98	18.93	18.89	18.79	18.77	18.76	18.76
1,000	21.71	21.51	21.36	21.24	21.15	21.08	21.03	20.99	20.88	20.85	20.84	20.84
2,000	43.41	43.02	42.72	42.48	42.30	42.16	42.05	41.97	41.76	41.70	41.68	41.67
3,000	65.12	64.52	64.07	63.72	63.45	63.24	63.08	62.95	62.63	62.54	62.52	62.51
4,000	86.82	86.03	85.43	84.96	84.60	84.32	84.10	83.93	83.51	83.39	83.35	83.34
5,000	108.52	107.54	106.78	106.20	105.75	105.40	105.13	104.92	104.39	104.23	104.19	104.18
6,000	130.23	129.04	128.14	127.44	126.90	126.48	126.15	125.90	125.26	125.08	125.03	125.01
7,000	151.93	150.55	149.49	148.68	148.04	147.56	147.18	146.88	146.14	145.93	145.86	145.85
8,000	173.63	172.06	170.85	169.91	169.19	168.63	168.20	167.86	167.02	166.77	166.70	166.68
9,000	195.34	193.56	192.20	191.15	190.34	189.71	189.22	188.84	187.89	187.62	187.54	187.51
10,000	217.04	215.07	213.56	212.39	211.49	210.79	210.25	209.83	208.77	208.46	208.37	208.35
15,000	325.56	322.60	320.33	318.58	317.23	316.18	315.37	314.74	313.15	312.69	312.56	312.52
20,000	434.07	430.14	427.11	424.78	422.97	421.58	420.49	419.65	417.53	416.92	416.74	416.69
25,000	542.59	537.67	533.89	530.97	528.72	526.97	525.61	524.56	521.91	521.15	520.93	520.86
30,000	651.11	645.20	640.66	637.16	634.46	632.36	630.73	629.47	626.29	625.38	625.11	625.04
35,000	759.63	752.73	747.44	743.36	740.20	737.76	735.86	734.38	730.68	729.61	729.30	729.21
40,000	868.14	860.27	854.22	849.55	845.94	843.15	840.98	839.29	835.06	833.84	833.48	833.38
45,000	976.66	967.80	960.99	955.74	951.69	948.54	946.10	944.20	939.44	938.07	937.67	937.55
50,000	1085.18	1075.33	1067.77	1061.94	1057.43	1053.93	1051.22	1049.11	1043.82	1042.29	1041.85	1041.72
55,000	1193.69	1182.87	1174.55	1168.13	1163.17	1159.33	1156.34	1154.02	1148.20	1146.52	1146.04	1145.90
60,000	1302.21	1290.40	1281.32	1274.32	1268.91	1264.72	1261.46	1258.93	1252.58	1250.75	1250.22	1250.07
65,000	1410.73	1397.93	1388.10	1380.52	1374.66	1370.11	1366.59	1363.85	1356.96	1354.98	1354.41	1354.24
70,000	1519.25	1505.46	1494.88	1486.71	1480.40	1475.51	1471.71	1468.76	1461.35	1459.21	1458.59	1458.41
75,000	1627.76	1613.00	1601.65	1592.90	1586.14	1580.90	1576.83	1573.67	1565.73	1563.44	1562.78	1562.58
80,000	1736.28	1720.53	1708.43	1699.10	1691.88	1686.29	1681.95	1678.58	1670.11	1667.67	1666.96	1666.76
85,000	1844.80	1828.06	1815.20	1805.29	1797.62	1791.68	1787.07	1783.49	1774.49	1771.90	1771.15	1770.93
90,000	1953.31	1935.59	1921.98	1911.48	1903.37	1897.08	1892.19	1888.40	1878.87	1876.13	1875.33	1875.10
95,000	2061.83	2043.13	2028.76	2017.68	2009.11	2002.47	1997.32	1993.31	1983.25	1980.35	1979.51	1979.27
100,000	2170.35	2150.66	2135.53	2123.87	2114.85	2107.86	2102.44	2098.22	2087.64	2084.58	2083.70	2083.44
105,000	2278.87	2258.19	2242.31	2230.06	2220.59	2213.26	2207.56	2203.13	2192.02	2188.81	2187.88	2187.62
110,000	2387.38	2365.73	2349.09	2336.26	2326.34	2318.65	2312.68	2308.04	2296.40	2293.04	2292.07	2291.79
115,000	2495.90	2473.26	2455.86	2442.45	2432.08	2424.04	2417.80	2412.95	2400.78	2397.27	2396.25	2395.96
120,000	2604.42	2580.79	2562.64	2548.64	2537.82	2529.43	2522.92	2517.86	2505.16	2501.50	2500.44	2500.13
125,000	2712.94	2688.32	2669.42	2654.84	2643.56	2634.83	2628.05	2622.78	2609.54	2605.73	2604.62	2604.30
130,000	2821.45	2795.86	2776.19	2761.03	2749.31	2740.22	2733.17	2727.69	2713.92	2709.96	2708.81	2708.47
135,000	2929.97	2903.39	2882.97	2867.22	2855.05	2845.61	2838.29	2832.60	2818.31	2814.19	2812.99	2812.65
140,000	3038.49	3010.92	2989.75	2973.42	2960.79	2951.01	2943.41	2937.51	2922.69	2918.42	2917.18	2916.82
145,000	3147.01	3118.46	3096.52	3079.61	3066.53	3056.40	3048.53	3042.42	3027.07	3022.64	3021.36	3020.99
150,000	3255.52	3225.99	3203.30	3185.80	3172.27	3161.79	3153.65	3147.33	3131.45	3126.87	3125.55	3125.16
155,000	3364.04	3333.52	3310.07	3292.00	3278.02	3267.18	3258.78	3252.24	3235.83	3231.10	3229.73	3229.33
160,000	3472.56	3441.05	3416.85	3398.19	3383.76	3372.58	3363.90	3357.15	3340.21	3335.33	3333.92	3333.51
165,000	3581.07	3548.59	3523.63	3504.38	3489.50	3477.97	3469.02	3462.06	3444.60	3439.56	3438.10	3437.68
170,000	3689.59	3656.12	3630.40	3610.58	3595.24	3583.36	3574.14	3566.97	3548.98	3543.79	3542.29	3541.85
175,000	3798.11	3763.65	3737.18	3716.77	3700.99	3688.76	3679.26	3671.88	3653.36	3648.02	3646.47	3646.02
180,000	3906.62	3871.18	3843.96	3822.96	3806.73	3794.15	3784.38	3776.79	3757.74	3752.25	3750.66	3750.19
185,000	4015.14	3978.72	3950.73	3929.16	3912.47	3899.54	3889.51	3881.71	3862.12	3856.48	3854.84	3854.37
190,000	4123.66	4086.25	4057.51	4035.35	4018.21	4004.93	3994.63	3986.62	3966.50	3960.70	3959.02	3958.54
195,000	4232.18	4193.78	4164.29	4141.54	4123.96	4110.33	4099.75	4091.53	4070.88	4064.93	4063.21	4062.71
200,000	4340.69	4301.32	4271.06	4247.74	4229.70	4215.72	4204.87	4196.44	4175.27	4169.16	4167.39	4166.88
205,000	4449.21	4408.85	4377.84	4353.93	4335.44	4321.11	4309.99	4301.35	4279.65	4273.39	4271.58	4271.05
210,000	4557.73	4516.38	4484.62	4460.12	4441.18	4426.51	4415.11	4406.26	4384.03	4377.62	4375.76	4375.23
215,000	4666.24	4623.91	4591.39	4566.32	4546.92	4531.90	4520.24	4511.17	4488.41	4481.85	4479.95	4479.40
220,000	4774.76	4731.45	4698.17	4672.51	4652.67	4637.29	4625.36	4616.08	4592.79	4586.08	4584.13	4583.57
225,000	4883.28	4838.98	4804.95	4778.70	4758.41	4742.68	4730.48	4720.99	4697.17	4690.31	4688.32	4687.74
230,000	4991.80	4946.51	4911.72	4884.90	4864.15	4848.08	4835.60	4825.90	4801.56	4794.54	4792.50	4791.91
235,000	5100.31	5054.05	5018.50	4991.09	4969.89	4953.47	4940.72	4930.81	4905.94	4898.76	4896.69	4896.08
240,000	5208.83	5161.58	5125.27	5097.28	5075.64	5058.86	5045.84	5035.72	5010.32	5002.99	5000.87	5000.26
245,000	5317.35	5269.11	5232.05	5203.47	5181.38	5164.26	5150.97	5140.63	5114.70	5107.22	5105.06	5104.43
250,000	5425.87	5376.64	5338.83	5309.67	5287.12	5269.65	5256.09	5245.54	5219.08	5211.45	5209.24	5208.60
255,000	5534.38	5484.18	5445.60	5415.86	5392.86	5375.04	5361.21	5350.46	5323.46	5315.68	5313.43	5312.77
260,000	5642.90	5591.71	5552.38	5522.05	5498.61	5480.43	5466.33	5455.37	5427.84	5419.91	5417.61	5416.94
265,000	5751.42	5699.24	5659.16	5628.25	5604.35	5585.83	5571.45	5560.28	5532.23	5524.14	5521.80	5521.12
270,000	5859.93	5806.77	5765.93	5734.44	5710.09	5691.22	5676.57	5665.19	5636.61	5628.37	5625.98	5625.29
280,000	6076.97	6021.84	5979.49	5946.83	5921.57	5902.01	5886.82	5875.01	5845.37	5836.83	5834.35	5833.63
290,000	6294.00	6236.91	6193.04	6159.21	6133.06	6112.79	6097.06	6084.83	6054.13	6045.28	6042.72	6041.98
300,000	6511.04	6451.97	6406.59	6371.60	6344.54	6323.58	6307.30	6294.65	6262.90	6253.74	6251.09	6250.32

25.25%

AMOUNT OF LOAN	NUMBER OF YEARS IN TERM											
	1	2	3	4	5	6	7	8	9	10	11	12
$ 50	4.76	2.68	2.00	1.67	1.48	1.36	1.28	1.22	1.18	1.15	1.13	1.11
100	9.52	5.35	3.99	3.33	2.95	2.71	2.55	2.44	2.36	2.30	2.25	2.22
200	19.04	10.70	7.98	6.66	5.90	5.42	5.10	4.87	4.71	4.59	4.50	4.43
300	28.55	16.05	11.97	9.99	8.85	8.13	7.65	7.31	7.06	6.88	6.75	6.65
400	38.07	21.40	15.96	13.32	11.80	10.84	10.19	9.74	9.41	9.18	9.00	8.86
500	47.59	26.75	19.95	16.65	14.75	13.55	12.74	12.17	11.77	11.47	11.25	11.08
600	57.10	32.10	23.94	19.98	17.70	16.26	15.29	14.61	14.12	13.76	13.49	13.29
700	66.62	37.45	27.93	23.31	20.65	18.97	17.84	17.04	16.47	16.05	15.74	15.51
800	76.14	42.80	31.92	26.64	23.60	21.68	20.38	19.48	18.82	18.35	17.99	17.72
900	85.65	48.15	35.91	29.97	26.55	24.39	22.93	21.91	21.18	20.64	20.24	19.94
1,000	95.17	53.50	39.90	33.30	29.50	27.10	25.48	24.34	23.53	22.93	22.49	22.15
2,000	190.34	107.00	79.79	66.60	59.00	54.19	50.95	48.68	47.05	45.86	44.97	44.30
3,000	285.50	160.50	119.68	99.90	88.50	81.28	76.42	73.02	70.58	68.78	67.45	66.44
4,000	380.67	213.99	159.57	133.19	118.00	108.37	101.89	97.36	94.10	91.71	89.93	88.59
5,000	475.83	267.49	199.47	166.49	147.50	135.46	127.36	121.70	117.62	114.63	112.41	110.73
6,000	571.00	320.99	239.36	199.79	176.99	162.55	152.84	146.04	141.15	137.56	134.89	132.88
7,000	666.16	374.48	279.25	233.08	206.49	189.64	178.31	170.38	164.67	160.49	157.37	155.03
8,000	761.33	427.98	319.14	266.38	235.99	216.73	203.78	194.71	188.19	183.41	179.85	177.17
9,000	856.50	481.48	359.03	299.68	265.49	243.82	229.25	219.05	211.72	206.34	202.33	199.32
10,000	951.66	534.98	398.93	332.97	294.99	270.91	254.72	243.39	235.24	229.26	224.81	221.46
15,000	1427.49	802.46	598.39	499.46	442.48	406.37	382.08	365.09	352.86	343.89	337.22	332.19
20,000	1903.32	1069.95	797.85	665.94	589.97	541.82	509.44	486.78	470.48	458.52	449.62	442.92
25,000	2379.14	1337.43	997.31	832.42	737.46	677.27	636.80	608.47	588.10	573.15	562.02	553.65
30,000	2854.97	1604.92	1196.77	998.91	884.95	812.73	764.16	730.17	705.72	687.78	674.43	664.38
35,000	3330.80	1872.40	1396.23	1165.39	1032.44	948.18	891.51	851.86	823.34	802.41	786.83	775.11
40,000	3806.63	2139.89	1595.69	1331.87	1179.93	1083.64	1018.87	973.55	940.95	917.04	899.23	885.84
45,000	4282.46	2407.37	1795.15	1498.36	1327.42	1219.09	1146.23	1095.25	1058.57	1031.67	1011.64	996.57
50,000	4758.28	2674.86	1994.61	1664.84	1474.91	1354.54	1273.59	1216.94	1176.19	1146.29	1124.04	1107.30
55,000	5234.11	2942.34	2194.07	1831.32	1622.40	1490.00	1400.95	1338.63	1293.81	1260.92	1236.44	1218.03
60,000	5709.94	3209.83	2393.54	1997.81	1769.89	1625.45	1528.31	1460.33	1411.43	1375.55	1348.85	1328.75
65,000	6185.77	3477.31	2593.00	2164.29	1917.38	1760.91	1655.67	1582.02	1529.05	1490.18	1461.25	1439.48
70,000	6661.59	3744.80	2792.46	2330.78	2064.87	1896.36	1783.02	1703.71	1646.67	1604.81	1573.65	1550.21
75,000	7137.42	4012.28	2991.92	2497.26	2212.36	2031.81	1910.38	1825.41	1764.28	1719.44	1686.06	1660.94
80,000	7613.25	4279.77	3191.38	2663.74	2359.85	2167.27	2037.74	1947.10	1881.90	1834.07	1798.46	1771.67
85,000	8089.08	4547.25	3390.84	2830.23	2507.34	2302.72	2165.10	2068.80	1999.52	1948.70	1910.86	1882.40
90,000	8564.91	4814.74	3590.30	2996.71	2654.83	2438.18	2292.46	2190.49	2117.14	2063.33	2023.27	1993.13
95,000	9040.73	5082.22	3789.76	3163.19	2802.32	2573.63	2419.82	2312.18	2234.76	2177.95	2135.67	2103.86
100,000	9516.56	5349.71	3989.22	3329.68	2949.81	2709.08	2547.17	2433.88	2352.38	2292.58	2248.08	2214.59
105,000	9992.39	5617.19	4188.68	3496.16	3097.30	2844.54	2674.53	2555.57	2470.00	2407.21	2360.48	2325.32
110,000	10468.22	5884.68	4388.14	3662.64	3244.79	2979.99	2801.89	2677.26	2587.61	2521.84	2472.88	2436.05
115,000	10944.04	6152.16	4587.60	3829.13	3392.28	3115.45	2929.25	2798.96	2705.23	2636.47	2585.29	2546.78
120,000	11419.87	6419.65	4787.07	3995.61	3539.77	3250.90	3056.61	2920.65	2822.85	2751.10	2697.69	2657.50
125,000	11895.70	6687.13	4986.53	4162.09	3687.26	3386.35	3183.97	3042.34	2940.47	2865.73	2810.09	2768.23
130,000	12371.53	6954.62	5185.99	4328.58	3834.75	3521.81	3311.33	3164.04	3058.09	2980.36	2922.50	2878.96
135,000	12847.36	7222.10	5385.45	4495.06	3982.24	3657.26	3438.68	3285.73	3175.71	3094.99	3034.90	2989.69
140,000	13323.18	7489.59	5584.91	4661.55	4129.73	3792.71	3566.04	3407.42	3293.33	3209.62	3147.30	3100.42
145,000	13799.01	7757.08	5784.37	4828.03	4277.23	3928.17	3693.40	3529.12	3410.95	3324.24	3259.71	3211.15
150,000	14274.84	8024.56	5983.83	4994.51	4424.72	4063.62	3820.76	3650.81	3528.56	3438.87	3372.11	3321.88
155,000	14750.67	8292.05	6183.29	5161.00	4572.21	4199.08	3948.12	3772.51	3646.18	3553.50	3484.51	3432.61
160,000	15226.50	8559.53	6382.75	5327.48	4719.70	4334.53	4075.48	3894.20	3763.80	3668.13	3596.92	3543.34
165,000	15702.32	8827.02	6582.21	5493.96	4867.19	4469.98	4202.84	4015.89	3881.42	3782.76	3709.32	3654.07
170,000	16178.15	9094.50	6781.67	5660.45	5014.68	4605.44	4330.19	4137.59	3999.04	3897.39	3821.72	3764.80
175,000	16653.98	9361.99	6981.13	5826.93	5162.17	4740.89	4457.55	4259.28	4116.66	4012.02	3934.13	3875.53
180,000	17129.81	9629.47	7180.60	5993.41	5309.66	4876.35	4584.91	4380.97	4234.28	4126.65	4046.53	3986.26
185,000	17605.63	9896.96	7380.06	6159.90	5457.15	5011.80	4712.27	4502.67	4351.89	4241.28	4158.94	4096.98
190,000	18081.46	10164.44	7579.52	6326.38	5604.64	5147.25	4839.63	4624.36	4469.51	4355.90	4271.34	4207.71
195,000	18557.29	10431.93	7778.98	6492.86	5752.13	5282.71	4966.99	4746.05	4587.13	4470.53	4383.74	4318.44
200,000	19033.12	10699.41	7978.44	6659.35	5899.62	5418.16	5094.34	4867.75	4704.75	4585.16	4496.15	4429.17
205,000	19508.95	10966.90	8177.90	6825.83	6047.11	5553.62	5221.70	4989.44	4822.37	4699.79	4608.55	4539.90
210,000	19984.77	11234.38	8377.36	6992.32	6194.60	5689.07	5349.06	5111.13	4939.99	4814.42	4720.95	4650.63
215,000	20460.60	11501.87	8576.82	7158.80	6342.09	5824.52	5476.42	5232.83	5057.61	4929.05	4833.36	4761.36
220,000	20936.43	11769.35	8776.28	7325.28	6489.58	5959.98	5603.78	5354.52	5175.22	5043.68	4945.76	4872.09
225,000	21412.26	12036.84	8975.74	7491.77	6637.07	6095.43	5731.14	5476.22	5292.84	5158.31	5058.16	4982.82
230,000	21888.08	12304.32	9175.20	7658.25	6784.56	6230.89	5858.50	5597.91	5410.46	5272.94	5170.57	5093.55
235,000	22363.91	12571.81	9374.66	7824.73	6932.05	6366.34	5985.85	5719.60	5528.08	5387.56	5282.97	5204.27
240,000	22839.74	12839.29	9574.13	7991.22	7079.54	6501.79	6113.21	5841.30	5645.70	5502.19	5395.37	5315.00
245,000	23315.57	13106.78	9773.59	8157.70	7227.03	6637.25	6240.57	5962.99	5763.32	5616.82	5507.78	5425.73
250,000	23791.40	13374.26	9973.05	8324.18	7374.52	6772.70	6367.93	6084.68	5880.94	5731.45	5620.18	5536.46
255,000	24267.22	13641.75	10172.51	8490.67	7522.01	6908.16	6495.29	6206.38	5998.55	5846.08	5732.58	5647.19
260,000	24743.05	13909.23	10371.97	8657.15	7669.50	7043.61	6622.65	6328.07	6116.17	5960.71	5844.99	5757.92
265,000	25218.88	14176.72	10571.43	8823.63	7816.99	7179.06	6750.01	6449.76	6233.79	6075.34	5957.39	5868.65
270,000	25694.71	14444.20	10770.89	8990.12	7964.48	7314.52	6877.36	6571.46	6351.41	6189.97	6069.80	5979.38
280,000	26646.36	14979.18	11169.81	9323.09	8259.46	7585.42	7132.08	6814.84	6586.65	6419.23	6294.60	6200.84
290,000	27598.02	15514.15	11568.73	9656.05	8554.45	7856.33	7386.80	7058.23	6821.89	6648.48	6519.41	6422.30
300,000	28549.67	16049.12	11967.66	9989.02	8849.43	8127.24	7641.51	7301.62	7057.12	6877.74	6744.22	6643.75

MONTHLY AMORTIZING PAYMENTS 25.25%

AMOUNT OF LOAN	NUMBER OF YEARS IN TERM											
	13	14	15	16	17	18	19	20	25	30	35	40
$ 50	1.10	1.09	1.08	1.08	1.07	1.07	1.07	1.06	1.06	1.06	1.06	1.06
100	2.19	2.17	2.16	2.15	2.14	2.13	2.13	2.12	2.11	2.11	2.11	2.11
200	4.38	4.34	4.31	4.29	4.27	4.26	4.25	4.24	4.22	4.22	4.21	4.21
300	6.57	6.51	6.47	6.44	6.41	6.39	6.37	6.36	6.33	6.32	6.32	6.32
400	8.76	8.68	8.62	8.58	8.54	8.52	8.50	8.48	8.44	8.43	8.42	8.42
500	10.95	10.85	10.78	10.72	10.68	10.64	10.62	10.60	10.55	10.53	10.53	10.53
600	13.14	13.02	12.93	12.87	12.81	12.77	12.74	12.72	12.65	12.64	12.63	12.63
700	15.33	15.19	15.09	15.01	14.95	14.90	14.86	14.83	14.76	14.74	14.74	14.73
800	17.52	17.36	17.24	17.15	17.08	17.03	16.99	16.95	16.87	16.85	16.84	16.84
900	19.71	19.53	19.40	19.30	19.22	19.16	19.11	19.07	18.98	18.95	18.95	18.94
1,000	21.90	21.70	21.55	21.44	21.35	21.28	21.23	21.19	21.09	21.06	21.05	21.05
2,000	43.79	43.40	43.10	42.88	42.70	42.56	42.46	42.37	42.17	42.11	42.10	42.09
3,000	65.68	65.10	64.65	64.31	64.05	63.84	63.68	63.56	63.25	63.17	63.14	63.13
4,000	87.57	86.80	86.20	85.75	85.39	85.12	84.91	84.74	84.33	84.22	84.19	84.18
5,000	109.46	108.49	107.75	107.18	106.74	106.40	106.13	105.93	105.42	105.27	105.23	105.22
6,000	131.36	130.19	129.30	128.62	128.09	127.68	127.36	127.11	126.50	126.33	126.28	126.26
7,000	153.25	151.89	150.85	150.05	149.43	148.95	148.59	148.30	147.58	147.38	147.32	147.30
8,000	175.14	173.59	172.40	171.49	170.78	170.23	169.81	169.48	168.66	168.43	168.37	168.35
9,000	197.03	195.29	193.95	192.92	192.13	191.51	191.04	190.67	189.75	189.49	189.41	189.39
10,000	218.92	216.98	215.50	214.36	213.47	212.79	212.26	211.85	210.83	210.54	210.46	210.43
15,000	328.38	325.47	323.25	321.53	320.21	319.18	318.39	317.78	316.24	315.81	315.68	315.64
20,000	437.84	433.96	430.99	428.71	426.94	425.58	424.52	423.70	421.65	421.07	420.91	420.86
25,000	547.30	542.45	538.74	535.88	533.67	531.97	530.65	529.62	527.07	526.34	526.13	526.07
30,000	656.76	650.94	646.49	643.06	640.41	638.36	636.78	635.55	632.48	631.61	631.36	631.28
35,000	766.22	759.43	754.23	750.23	747.14	744.75	742.91	741.47	737.89	736.87	736.58	736.50
40,000	875.68	867.92	861.98	857.41	853.88	851.15	849.03	847.40	843.30	842.14	841.81	841.71
45,000	985.14	976.41	969.73	964.50	900.01	957.54	955.16	953.02	940.72	947.41	947.03	946.92
50,000	1094.60	1084.90	1077.47	1071.76	1067.34	1063.93	1061.29	1059.24	1054.13	1052.67	1052.26	1052.14
55,000	1204.06	1193.39	1185.22	1178.93	1174.08	1170.33	1167.42	1165.17	1159.54	1157.94	1157.48	1157.35
60,000	1313.51	1301.88	1292.97	1286.11	1280.81	1276.72	1273.55	1271.09	1264.95	1263.21	1262.71	1262.56
65,000	1422.97	1410.37	1400.71	1393.28	1387.55	1383.11	1379.68	1377.01	1370.37	1368.47	1367.93	1367.78
70,000	1532.43	1518.86	1508.46	1500.46	1494.28	1489.50	1485.81	1482.94	1475.78	1473.74	1473.16	1472.99
75,000	1641.89	1627.35	1616.21	1607.63	1601.01	1595.90	1591.93	1588.86	1581.19	1579.01	1578.38	1578.20
80,000	1751.35	1735.84	1723.95	1714.81	1707.75	1702.29	1698.06	1694.79	1686.60	1684.27	1683.61	1683.42
85,000	1860.81	1844.33	1831.70	1821.98	1814.48	1808.68	1804.19	1800.71	1792.02	1789.54	1788.83	1788.63
90,000	1970.27	1952.82	1939.45	1929.16	1921.22	1915.08	1910.32	1906.63	1897.43	1894.81	1894.06	1893.84
95,000	2079.73	2061.31	2047.20	2036.33	2027.95	2021.47	2016.45	2012.56	2002.84	2000.07	1999.28	1999.05
100,000	2189.19	2169.80	2154.94	2143.51	2134.68	2127.86	2122.58	2118.48	2108.25	2105.34	2104.51	2104.27
105,000	2298.65	2278.29	2262.69	2250.68	2241.42	2234.25	2228.71	2224.40	2213.67	2210.61	2209.73	2209.48
110,000	2408.11	2386.78	2370.44	2357.86	2348.15	2340.65	2334.83	2330.33	2319.08	2315.87	2314.96	2314.69
115,000	2517.57	2495.27	2478.18	2465.03	2454.89	2447.04	2440.96	2436.25	2424.49	2421.14	2420.18	2419.91
120,000	2627.02	2600.76	2585.90	2572.21	2561.62	2550.43	2547.09	2542.18	2529.90	2526.41	2525.41	2525.12
125,000	2736.48	2712.25	2693.68	2679.38	2668.35	2659.83	2653.22	2648.10	2635.32	2631.67	2630.63	2630.33
130,000	2845.94	2820.74	2801.42	2786.56	2775.09	2766.22	2759.35	2754.02	2740.73	2736.94	2735.86	2735.55
135,000	2955.40	2929.23	2909.17	2893.73	2881.82	2872.61	2865.48	2859.95	2846.14	2842.21	2841.08	2840.76
140,000	3064.86	3037.72	3016.92	3000.91	2988.55	2979.00	2971.61	2965.87	2951.55	2947.47	2946.31	2945.97
145,000	3174.32	3146.21	3124.66	3108.08	3095.29	3085.40	3077.73	3071.79	3056.97	3052.74	3051.53	3051.19
150,000	3283.78	3254.70	3232.41	3215.26	3202.02	3191.79	3183.86	3177.72	3162.38	3158.01	3156.76	3156.40
155,000	3393.24	3363.19	3340.16	3322.43	3308.76	3298.18	3289.99	3283.64	3267.79	3263.27	3261.98	3261.61
160,000	3502.70	3471.68	3447.90	3429.61	3415.49	3404.57	3396.12	3389.57	3373.20	3368.54	3367.21	3366.83
165,000	3612.16	3580.17	3555.65	3536.78	3522.22	3510.97	3502.25	3495.49	3478.62	3473.81	3472.43	3472.04
170,000	3721.62	3688.66	3663.40	3643.96	3628.96	3617.36	3608.38	3601.41	3584.03	3579.07	3577.66	3577.25
175,000	3831.07	3797.15	3771.14	3751.13	3735.69	3723.75	3714.51	3707.34	3689.44	3684.34	3682.88	3682.46
180,000	3940.53	3905.64	3878.89	3858.31	3842.43	3830.15	3820.64	3813.26	3794.85	3789.61	3788.11	3787.68
185,000	4049.99	4014.13	3986.64	3965.48	3949.16	3936.54	3926.76	3919.18	3900.27	3894.88	3893.33	3892.89
190,000	4159.45	4122.62	4094.39	4072.66	4055.89	4042.93	4032.89	4025.11	4005.68	4000.14	3998.56	3998.10
195,000	4268.91	4231.11	4202.13	4179.83	4162.63	4149.32	4139.02	4131.03	4111.09	4105.41	4103.78	4103.32
200,000	4378.37	4339.60	4309.88	4287.01	4269.36	4255.72	4245.15	4236.96	4216.50	4210.68	4209.01	4208.53
205,000	4487.83	4448.09	4417.63	4394.18	4376.10	4362.11	4351.28	4342.88	4321.91	4315.94	4314.23	4313.74
210,000	4597.29	4556.58	4525.37	4501.36	4482.83	4468.50	4457.41	4448.80	4427.33	4421.21	4419.46	4418.96
215,000	4706.75	4665.07	4633.12	4608.53	4589.56	4574.90	4563.54	4554.73	4532.74	4526.48	4524.68	4524.17
220,000	4816.21	4773.56	4740.87	4715.71	4696.30	4681.29	4669.66	4660.65	4638.15	4631.74	4629.91	4629.38
225,000	4925.67	4882.05	4848.61	4822.88	4803.03	4787.68	4775.79	4766.57	4743.56	4737.01	4735.13	4734.60
230,000	5035.13	4990.54	4956.36	4930.06	4909.77	4894.07	4881.92	4872.50	4848.98	4842.28	4840.36	4839.81
235,000	5144.58	5099.03	5064.11	5037.23	5016.50	5000.47	4988.05	4978.42	4954.39	4947.54	4945.58	4945.02
240,000	5254.04	5207.52	5171.85	5144.41	5123.23	5106.86	5094.18	5084.35	5059.80	5052.81	5050.81	5050.24
245,000	5363.50	5316.01	5279.60	5251.58	5229.97	5213.25	5200.31	5190.27	5165.21	5158.08	5156.03	5155.45
250,000	5472.96	5424.50	5387.35	5358.76	5336.70	5319.65	5306.44	5296.19	5270.63	5263.34	5261.26	5260.66
255,000	5582.42	5532.99	5495.09	5465.93	5443.43	5426.04	5412.56	5402.12	5376.04	5368.61	5366.48	5365.87
260,000	5691.88	5641.48	5602.84	5573.11	5550.17	5532.43	5518.69	5508.04	5481.45	5473.88	5471.71	5471.09
265,000	5801.34	5749.97	5710.59	5680.28	5656.90	5638.82	5624.82	5613.96	5586.86	5579.14	5576.93	5576.30
270,000	5910.80	5858.46	5818.34	5787.46	5763.64	5745.22	5730.95	5719.89	5692.28	5684.41	5682.16	5681.51
280,000	6129.72	6075.44	6033.83	6001.81	5977.10	5958.00	5943.21	5931.74	5903.10	5894.94	5892.61	5891.94
290,000	6348.64	6292.42	6249.32	6216.16	6190.57	6170.79	6155.46	6143.58	6113.93	6105.48	6103.06	6102.37
300,000	6567.55	6509.40	6464.82	6430.51	6404.04	6383.57	6367.72	6355.43	6324.75	6316.01	6313.51	6312.79

25.50%　　MONTHLY AMORTIZING PAYMENTS

AMOUNT OF LOAN	NUMBER OF YEARS IN TERM											
	1	2	3	4	5	6	7	8	9	10	11	12
$ 50	4.77	2.69	2.01	1.68	1.49	1.37	1.29	1.23	1.19	1.16	1.14	1.12
100	9.53	5.37	4.01	3.35	2.97	2.73	2.57	2.46	2.37	2.32	2.27	2.24
200	19.06	10.73	8.01	6.69	5.93	5.45	5.13	4.91	4.74	4.63	4.54	4.47
300	28.59	16.09	12.01	10.04	8.90	8.18	7.69	7.36	7.11	6.94	6.80	6.70
400	38.12	21.45	16.01	13.38	11.86	10.90	10.26	9.81	9.48	9.25	9.07	8.94
500	47.65	26.82	20.02	16.72	14.83	13.63	12.82	12.26	11.85	11.56	11.34	11.17
600	57.18	32.18	24.02	20.07	17.79	16.35	15.38	14.71	14.22	13.87	13.60	13.40
700	66.71	37.54	28.02	23.41	20.76	19.08	17.95	17.16	16.59	16.18	15.87	15.64
800	76.23	42.90	32.02	26.75	23.72	21.80	20.51	19.61	18.96	18.49	18.13	17.87
900	85.76	48.27	36.03	30.10	26.69	24.53	23.07	22.06	21.33	20.80	20.40	20.10
1,000	95.29	53.63	40.03	33.44	29.65	27.25	25.64	24.51	23.70	23.11	22.67	22.34
2,000	190.58	107.25	80.05	66.88	59.30	54.49	51.27	49.02	47.40	46.21	45.33	44.67
3,000	285.87	160.87	120.08	100.31	88.94	81.74	76.90	73.52	71.09	69.31	67.99	67.00
4,000	381.15	214.50	160.10	133.75	118.59	108.98	102.53	98.03	94.79	92.42	90.65	89.33
5,000	476.44	268.12	200.13	167.19	148.23	136.23	128.17	122.53	118.48	115.52	113.32	111.66
6,000	571.73	321.74	240.15	200.62	177.88	163.47	153.80	147.04	142.18	138.62	135.98	133.99
7,000	667.01	375.36	280.18	234.06	207.52	190.72	179.43	171.54	165.88	161.72	158.64	156.32
8,000	762.30	428.99	320.20	267.50	237.17	217.96	205.06	196.05	189.57	184.83	181.30	178.65
9,000	857.59	482.61	360.23	300.93	266.81	245.21	230.69	220.55	213.27	207.93	203.96	200.99
10,000	952.88	536.23	400.25	334.37	296.46	272.45	256.33	245.06	236.96	231.03	226.63	223.32
15,000	1429.31	804.35	600.38	501.55	444.68	408.68	384.49	367.58	355.44	346.55	339.94	334.97
20,000	1905.75	1072.46	800.50	668.74	592.91	544.90	512.65	490.11	473.92	462.06	453.25	446.63
25,000	2382.18	1340.57	1000.62	835.92	741.13	681.12	640.81	612.64	592.40	577.57	566.56	558.28
30,000	2858.62	1608.69	1200.75	1003.10	889.36	817.35	768.97	735.16	710.88	693.09	679.87	669.94
35,000	3335.05	1876.80	1400.87	1170.29	1037.59	953.57	897.13	857.69	829.36	808.60	793.18	781.60
40,000	3811.49	2144.91	1600.99	1337.47	1185.81	1089.80	1025.29	980.21	947.83	924.11	906.49	893.25
45,000	4287.92	2413.03	1801.12	1504.65	1334.04	1226.02	1153.45	1102.74	1066.31	1039.63	1019.80	1004.91
50,000	4764.36	2681.14	2001.24	1671.84	1482.26	1362.24	1281.61	1225.27	1184.79	1155.14	1133.11	1116.56
55,000	5240.79	2949.25	2201.37	1839.02	1630.49	1498.47	1409.78	1347.79	1303.27	1270.66	1246.42	1228.22
60,000	5717.23	3217.37	2401.49	2006.20	1778.72	1634.69	1537.94	1470.32	1421.75	1386.17	1359.73	1339.88
65,000	6193.66	3485.48	2601.61	2173.38	1926.94	1770.92	1666.10	1592.84	1540.23	1501.68	1473.04	1451.53
70,000	6670.10	3753.60	2801.74	2340.57	2075.17	1907.14	1794.26	1715.37	1658.71	1617.20	1586.35	1563.19
75,000	7146.53	4021.71	3001.86	2507.75	2223.39	2043.36	1922.42	1837.90	1777.18	1732.71	1699.66	1674.84
80,000	7622.97	4289.82	3201.98	2674.93	2371.62	2179.59	2050.58	1960.42	1895.66	1848.22	1812.97	1786.50
85,000	8099.40	4557.94	3402.11	2842.12	2519.85	2315.81	2178.74	2082.95	2014.14	1963.74	1926.28	1898.15
90,000	8575.84	4826.05	3602.23	3009.30	2668.07	2452.04	2306.90	2205.47	2132.62	2079.25	2039.59	2009.81
95,000	9052.27	5094.16	3802.36	3176.48	2816.30	2588.26	2435.06	2328.00	2251.10	2194.77	2152.91	2121.47
100,000	9528.71	5362.28	4002.48	3343.67	2964.52	2724.48	2563.22	2450.53	2369.58	2310.28	2266.22	2233.12
105,000	10005.14	5630.39	4202.60	3510.85	3112.75	2860.71	2691.39	2573.05	2488.06	2425.79	2379.53	2344.78
110,000	10481.58	5898.50	4402.73	3678.03	3260.97	2996.93	2819.55	2695.58	2606.53	2541.31	2492.84	2456.43
115,000	10958.01	6166.62	4602.85	3845.22	3409.20	3133.16	2947.71	2818.10	2725.01	2656.82	2606.15	2568.09
120,000	11434.45	6434.73	4802.97	4012.40	3557.43	3269.38	3075.87	2940.63	2843.49	2772.33	2719.46	2679.75
125,000	11910.88	6702.84	5003.10	4179.58	3705.65	3405.60	3204.03	3063.16	2961.97	2887.85	2832.77	2791.40
130,000	12387.32	6970.96	5203.22	4346.76	3853.88	3541.83	3332.19	3185.68	3080.45	3003.36	2946.08	2903.06
135,000	12863.75	7239.07	5403.35	4513.95	4002.10	3678.05	3460.35	3308.21	3198.93	3118.88	3059.39	3014.71
140,000	13340.19	7507.19	5603.47	4681.13	4150.33	3814.28	3588.51	3430.74	3317.41	3234.39	3172.70	3126.37
145,000	13816.62	7775.30	5803.59	4848.31	4298.56	3950.50	3716.67	3553.26	3435.88	3349.90	3286.01	3238.02
150,000	14293.06	8043.41	6003.72	5015.50	4446.78	4086.72	3844.83	3675.79	3554.36	3465.42	3399.32	3349.68
155,000	14769.49	8311.53	6203.84	5182.68	4595.01	4222.95	3973.00	3798.31	3672.84	3580.93	3512.63	3461.34
160,000	15245.93	8579.64	6403.96	5349.86	4743.23	4359.17	4101.16	3920.84	3791.32	3696.44	3625.94	3572.99
165,000	15722.36	8847.75	6604.09	5517.05	4891.46	4495.40	4229.32	4043.37	3909.80	3811.96	3739.25	3684.65
170,000	16198.80	9115.87	6804.21	5684.23	5039.69	4631.62	4357.48	4165.89	4028.28	3927.47	3852.56	3796.30
175,000	16675.23	9383.98	7004.34	5851.41	5187.91	4767.84	4485.64	4288.42	4146.76	4042.99	3965.87	3907.96
180,000	17151.67	9652.09	7204.46	6018.59	5336.14	4904.07	4613.80	4410.94	4265.23	4158.50	4079.18	4019.62
185,000	17628.10	9920.21	7404.58	6185.78	5484.36	5040.29	4741.96	4533.47	4383.71	4274.01	4192.49	4131.27
190,000	18104.54	10188.32	7604.71	6352.96	5632.59	5176.52	4870.12	4656.00	4502.19	4389.53	4305.81	4242.93
195,000	18580.97	10456.43	7804.83	6520.14	5780.81	5312.74	4998.28	4778.52	4620.67	4505.04	4419.12	4354.58
200,000	19057.41	10724.55	8004.95	6687.33	5929.04	5448.96	5126.44	4901.05	4739.15	4620.55	4532.43	4466.24
205,000	19533.84	10992.66	8205.08	6854.51	6077.27	5585.19	5254.61	5023.57	4857.63	4736.07	4645.74	4577.89
210,000	20010.28	11260.78	8405.20	7021.69	6225.49	5721.41	5382.77	5146.10	4976.11	4851.58	4759.05	4689.55
215,000	20486.71	11528.89	8605.33	7188.88	6373.72	5857.64	5510.93	5268.63	5094.58	4967.09	4872.36	4801.21
220,000	20963.15	11797.00	8805.45	7356.06	6521.94	5993.86	5639.09	5391.15	5213.06	5082.61	4985.67	4912.86
225,000	21439.58	12065.12	9005.57	7523.24	6670.17	6130.08	5767.25	5513.68	5331.54	5198.12	5098.98	5024.52
230,000	21916.02	12333.23	9205.70	7690.43	6818.40	6266.31	5895.41	5636.20	5450.02	5313.64	5212.29	5136.17
235,000	22392.45	12601.34	9405.82	7857.61	6966.62	6402.53	6023.57	5758.73	5568.50	5429.15	5325.60	5247.83
240,000	22868.89	12869.46	9605.94	8024.79	7114.85	6538.76	6151.73	5881.26	5686.98	5544.66	5438.91	5359.49
245,000	23345.32	13137.57	9806.07	8191.97	7263.07	6674.98	6279.89	6003.78	5805.46	5660.18	5552.22	5471.14
250,000	23821.76	13405.68	10006.19	8359.16	7411.30	6811.20	6408.05	6126.31	5923.93	5775.69	5665.53	5582.80
255,000	24298.19	13673.80	10206.32	8526.34	7559.53	6947.43	6536.22	6248.84	6042.41	5891.20	5778.84	5694.45
260,000	24774.63	13941.91	10406.44	8693.52	7707.75	7083.65	6664.38	6371.36	6160.89	6006.72	5892.15	5806.11
265,000	25251.06	14210.02	10606.56	8860.71	7855.98	7219.88	6792.54	6493.89	6279.37	6122.23	6005.46	5917.76
270,000	25727.50	14478.14	10806.69	9027.89	8004.20	7356.10	6920.70	6616.41	6397.85	6237.75	6118.77	6029.42
280,000	26680.37	15014.37	11206.93	9362.26	8300.65	7628.55	7177.02	6861.47	6634.81	6468.77	6345.39	6252.73
290,000	27633.24	15550.59	11607.18	9696.62	8597.11	7901.00	7433.34	7106.52	6871.76	6699.80	6572.02	6476.04
300,000	28586.11	16086.82	12007.43	10030.99	8893.56	8173.44	7689.66	7351.57	7108.72	6930.83	6798.64	6699.36

AMOUNT OF LOAN	NUMBER OF YEARS IN TERM											
	13	14	15	16	17	18	19	20	25	30	35	40
$ 50	1.11	1.10	1.09	1.09	1.08	1.08	1.08	1.07	1.07	1.07	1.07	1.07
100	2.21	2.19	2.18	2.17	2.16	2.15	2.15	2.14	2.13	2.13	2.13	2.13
200	4.42	4.38	4.35	4.33	4.31	4.30	4.29	4.28	4.26	4.26	4.26	4.26
300	6.63	6.57	6.53	6.49	6.47	6.45	6.43	6.42	6.39	6.38	6.38	6.38
400	8.84	8.76	8.70	8.66	8.62	8.60	8.58	8.56	8.52	8.51	8.51	8.51
500	11.05	10.95	10.88	10.82	10.78	10.74	10.72	10.70	10.65	10.64	10.63	10.63
600	13.25	13.14	13.05	12.98	12.93	12.89	12.86	12.84	12.78	12.76	12.76	12.76
700	15.46	15.33	15.23	15.15	15.09	15.04	15.00	14.98	14.91	14.89	14.88	14.88
800	17.67	17.52	17.40	17.31	17.24	17.19	17.15	17.12	17.04	17.01	17.01	17.01
900	19.88	19.71	19.57	19.47	19.40	19.34	19.29	19.25	19.16	19.14	19.13	19.13
1,000	22.09	21.89	21.75	21.64	21.55	21.48	21.43	21.39	21.29	21.27	21.26	21.26
2,000	44.17	43.78	43.49	43.27	43.10	42.96	42.86	42.78	42.58	42.53	42.51	42.51
3,000	66.25	65.67	65.24	64.90	64.64	64.44	64.29	64.17	63.87	63.79	63.76	63.76
4,000	88.33	87.56	86.98	86.53	86.19	85.92	85.71	85.56	85.16	85.05	85.02	85.01
5,000	110.41	109.45	108.72	108.16	107.73	107.40	107.14	106.94	106.45	106.31	106.27	106.26
6,000	132.49	131.34	130.47	129.80	129.28	128.88	128.57	128.33	127.74	127.57	127.52	127.51
7,000	154.57	153.23	152.21	151.43	150.82	150.36	150.00	149.72	149.03	148.83	148.78	148.76
8,000	176.65	175.12	173.96	173.06	172.37	171.84	171.42	171.11	170.32	170.09	170.03	170.01
9,000	198.73	197.01	195.70	194.69	193.91	193.31	192.85	192.49	191.60	191.35	191.28	191.26
10,000	220.81	218.90	217.44	216.32	215.46	214.79	214.28	213.88	212.89	212.61	212.54	212.51
15,000	331.21	328.35	326.16	324.48	323.19	322.19	321.42	320.82	319.34	318.92	318.80	318.77
20,000	441.62	437.80	434.88	432.64	430.91	429.58	428.55	427.76	425.78	425.22	425.07	425.02
25,000	552.02	547.25	543.60	540.80	538.64	536.98	535.69	534.69	532.22	531.53	531.33	531.28
30,000	662.42	656.70	652.32	648.96	646.37	644.37	642.83	641.63	638.67	637.83	637.60	637.53
35,000	772.83	766.15	761.04	757.11	754.09	751.76	749.96	748.57	745.11	744.14	743.86	743.79
40,000	883.23	875.60	869.76	865.27	861.82	859.16	857.10	855.51	851.56	850.44	850.13	850.04
45,000	993.63	985.05	978.48	973.43	969.55	966.55	964.24	962.44	958.00	956.75	956.39	956.29
50,000	1104.04	1094.50	1087.20	1081.59	1077.28	1073.95	1071.37	1069.38	1064.44	1063.05	1062.66	1062.55
55,000	1214.44	1203.94	1195.91	1189.75	1185.00	1181.34	1178.51	1176.32	1170.89	1169.36	1168.93	1168.80
60,000	1324.84	1313.39	1304.63	1297.91	1292.73	1288.73	1285.65	1283.26	1277.33	1275.66	1275.19	1275.06
65,000	1435.25	1422.84	1413.35	1406.07	1400.46	1396.13	1392.78	1390.20	1383.78	1381.97	1381.46	1381.31
70,000	1545.65	1532.29	1522.07	1514.22	1508.18	1503.52	1499.92	1497.13	1490.22	1488.27	1487.72	1487.57
75,000	1656.05	1641.74	1630.79	1622.38	1615.91	1610.92	1607.06	1604.07	1596.66	1594.58	1593.99	1593.82
80,000	1766.46	1751.19	1739.51	1730.54	1723.64	1718.31	1714.19	1711.01	1703.11	1700.88	1700.25	1700.08
85,000	1876.86	1860.64	1848.23	1838.70	1831.36	1825.70	1821.33	1817.95	1800.65	1807.19	1806.52	1806.33
90,000	1987.26	1970.09	1956.95	1946.86	1939.09	1933.10	1928.47	1924.88	1915.99	1913.49	1912.78	1912.58
95,000	2097.67	2079.54	2065.67	2055.02	2046.82	2040.49	2035.60	2031.82	2022.44	2019.80	2019.05	2018.84
100,000	2208.07	2188.99	2174.39	2163.18	2154.55	2147.89	2142.74	2138.76	2128.88	2126.10	2125.32	2125.09
105,000	2318.47	2298.44	2283.11	2271.33	2262.27	2255.28	2249.88	2245.70	2235.33	2232.41	2231.58	2231.35
110,000	2428.87	2407.88	2391.82	2379.49	2370.00	2362.67	2357.01	2352.64	2341.77	2338.71	2337.85	2337.60
115,000	2539.28	2517.33	2500.54	2487.65	2477.73	2470.07	2464.15	2459.57	2448.21	2445.02	2444.11	2443.86
120,000	2649.00	2626.78	2609.26	2595.81	2585.45	2577.46	2571.29	2566.51	2554.66	2551.32	2550.38	2550.11
125,000	2760.08	2736.23	2717.98	2703.97	2693.18	2684.86	2678.43	2673.45	2661.10	2657.63	2656.64	2656.36
130,000	2870.49	2845.68	2826.70	2812.13	2800.91	2792.25	2785.56	2780.39	2767.55	2763.93	2762.91	2762.62
135,000	2980.89	2955.13	2935.42	2920.29	2908.63	2899.64	2892.70	2887.32	2873.99	2870.24	2869.17	2868.87
140,000	3091.29	3064.58	3044.14	3028.44	3016.36	3007.04	2999.84	2994.26	2980.43	2976.54	2975.44	2975.13
145,000	3201.70	3174.03	3152.86	3136.60	3124.09	3114.43	3106.97	3101.20	3086.88	3082.85	3081.71	3081.38
150,000	3312.10	3283.48	3261.58	3244.76	3231.82	3221.83	3214.11	3208.14	3193.32	3189.15	3187.97	3187.64
155,000	3422.50	3392.93	3370.30	3352.92	3339.54	3329.22	3321.25	3315.08	3299.76	3295.45	3294.24	3293.89
160,000	3532.91	3502.38	3479.02	3461.08	3447.27	3436.62	3428.38	3422.01	3406.21	3401.76	3400.50	3400.15
165,000	3643.31	3611.82	3587.73	3569.24	3555.00	3544.01	3535.52	3528.95	3512.65	3508.06	3506.77	3506.40
170,000	3753.71	3721.27	3696.45	3677.40	3662.72	3651.40	3642.66	3635.89	3619.10	3614.37	3613.03	3612.65
175,000	3864.12	3830.72	3805.17	3785.55	3770.45	3758.80	3749.79	3742.83	3725.54	3720.67	3719.30	3718.91
180,000	3974.52	3940.17	3913.89	3893.71	3878.18	3866.19	3856.93	3849.76	3831.98	3826.98	3825.56	3825.16
185,000	4084.92	4049.62	4022.61	4001.87	3985.90	3973.59	3964.07	3956.70	3938.43	3933.28	3931.83	3931.42
190,000	4195.33	4159.07	4131.33	4110.03	4093.63	4080.98	4071.20	4063.64	4044.87	4039.59	4038.09	4037.67
195,000	4305.73	4268.52	4240.05	4218.19	4201.36	4188.37	4178.34	4170.58	4151.32	4145.89	4144.36	4143.93
200,000	4416.13	4377.97	4348.77	4326.35	4309.09	4295.77	4285.48	4277.52	4257.76	4252.20	4250.63	4250.18
205,000	4526.53	4487.42	4457.49	4434.51	4416.81	4403.16	4392.61	4384.45	4364.20	4358.50	4356.89	4356.44
210,000	4636.94	4596.87	4566.21	4542.66	4524.54	4510.56	4499.75	4491.39	4470.65	4464.81	4463.16	4462.69
215,000	4747.34	4706.32	4674.92	4650.82	4632.27	4617.95	4606.89	4598.33	4577.09	4571.11	4569.42	4568.94
220,000	4857.74	4815.76	4783.64	4758.98	4739.99	4725.34	4714.02	4705.27	4683.54	4677.42	4675.69	4675.20
225,000	4968.15	4925.21	4892.36	4867.14	4847.72	4832.74	4821.16	4812.20	4789.98	4783.72	4781.95	4781.45
230,000	5078.55	5034.66	5001.08	4975.30	4955.45	4940.13	4928.30	4919.14	4896.42	4890.03	4888.22	4887.71
235,000	5188.95	5144.11	5109.80	5083.46	5063.17	5047.53	5035.43	5026.08	5002.87	4996.33	4994.48	4993.96
240,000	5299.36	5253.56	5218.52	5191.62	5170.90	5154.92	5142.57	5133.02	5109.31	5102.64	5100.75	5100.22
245,000	5409.76	5363.01	5327.24	5299.77	5278.63	5262.31	5249.71	5239.96	5215.75	5208.94	5207.02	5206.47
250,000	5520.16	5472.46	5435.96	5407.93	5386.36	5369.71	5356.85	5346.89	5322.20	5315.25	5313.28	5312.72
255,000	5630.57	5581.91	5544.68	5516.09	5494.08	5477.10	5463.98	5453.83	5428.64	5421.55	5419.55	5418.98
260,000	5740.97	5691.36	5653.40	5624.25	5601.81	5584.50	5571.12	5560.77	5535.09	5527.86	5525.81	5525.23
265,000	5851.37	5800.81	5762.12	5732.41	5709.54	5691.89	5678.26	5667.71	5641.53	5634.16	5632.08	5631.49
270,000	5961.78	5910.26	5870.83	5840.57	5817.26	5799.28	5785.39	5774.64	5747.97	5740.47	5738.34	5737.74
280,000	6182.58	6129.15	6088.27	6056.88	6032.72	6014.07	5999.67	5988.52	5960.86	5953.08	5950.87	5950.25
290,000	6403.39	6348.05	6305.71	6273.20	6248.17	6228.86	6213.94	6202.39	6173.75	6165.69	6163.41	6162.76
300,000	6624.19	6566.95	6523.15	6489.52	6463.63	6443.65	6428.21	6416.27	6386.64	6378.29	6375.94	6375.27

MONTHLY AMORTIZING PAYMENTS

AMOUNT OF LOAN	NUMBER OF YEARS IN TERM											
	1	2	3	4	5	6	7	8	9	10	11	12
$ 50	4.78	2.69	2.01	1.68	1.49	1.37	1.29	1.24	1.20	1.17	1.15	1.13
100	9.55	5.38	4.02	3.36	2.98	2.74	2.58	2.47	2.39	2.33	2.29	2.26
200	19.09	10.75	8.04	6.72	5.96	5.48	5.16	4.94	4.78	4.66	4.57	4.51
300	28.63	16.13	12.05	10.08	8.94	8.22	7.74	7.41	7.17	6.99	6.86	6.76
400	38.17	21.50	16.07	13.44	11.92	10.96	10.32	9.87	9.55	9.32	9.14	9.01
500	47.71	26.88	20.08	16.79	14.90	13.70	12.90	12.34	11.94	11.65	11.43	11.26
600	57.25	32.25	24.10	20.15	17.88	16.44	15.48	14.81	14.33	13.97	13.71	13.52
700	66.79	37.63	28.12	23.51	20.86	19.18	18.06	17.28	16.71	16.30	16.00	15.77
800	76.33	43.00	32.13	26.87	23.84	21.92	20.64	19.74	19.10	18.63	18.28	18.02
900	85.87	48.38	36.15	30.22	26.82	24.66	23.22	22.21	21.49	20.96	20.56	20.27
1,000	95.41	53.75	40.16	33.58	29.80	27.40	25.80	24.68	23.87	23.29	22.85	22.52
2,000	190.82	107.50	80.32	67.16	59.59	54.80	51.59	49.35	47.74	46.57	45.69	45.04
3,000	286.23	161.25	120.48	100.74	89.38	82.20	77.38	74.02	71.61	69.85	68.54	67.56
4,000	381.64	215.00	160.64	134.31	119.18	109.60	103.18	98.69	95.48	93.13	91.38	90.07
5,000	477.05	268.75	200.79	167.89	148.97	137.00	128.97	123.37	119.35	116.41	114.22	112.59
6,000	572.46	322.50	240.95	201.47	178.76	164.40	154.76	148.04	143.21	139.69	137.07	135.11
7,000	667.86	376.24	281.11	235.04	208.55	191.80	180.56	172.71	167.08	162.97	159.91	157.62
8,000	763.27	429.99	321.27	268.62	238.35	219.20	206.35	197.38	190.95	186.25	182.76	180.14
9,000	858.68	483.74	361.42	302.20	268.14	246.60	232.14	222.05	214.82	209.53	205.60	202.66
10,000	954.09	537.49	401.58	335.77	297.93	274.00	257.94	246.73	238.69	232.81	228.44	225.17
15,000	1431.13	806.23	602.37	503.66	446.89	410.99	386.90	370.09	358.03	349.21	342.66	337.76
20,000	1908.18	1074.98	803.16	671.54	595.86	547.99	515.87	493.45	477.37	465.61	456.88	450.34
25,000	2385.22	1343.72	1003.94	839.43	744.82	684.99	644.83	616.81	596.71	582.01	571.10	562.93
30,000	2862.26	1612.46	1204.73	1007.31	893.78	821.98	773.80	740.17	716.05	698.41	685.32	675.51
35,000	3339.30	1881.20	1405.52	1175.19	1042.75	958.98	902.76	863.53	835.39	814.81	799.54	788.10
40,000	3816.35	2149.95	1606.31	1343.08	1191.71	1095.97	1031.73	986.89	954.73	931.21	913.76	900.68
45,000	4293.39	2418.69	1807.10	1510.96	1340.67	1232.97	1160.70	1110.25	1074.07	1047.61	1027.98	1013.27
50,000	4770.43	2687.43	2007.88	1678.85	1489.64	1369.97	1289.66	1233.61	1193.41	1164.01	1142.20	1125.85
55,000	5247.47	2956.18	2208.67	1846.73	1638.60	1506.96	1418.63	1356.97	1312.75	1280.41	1256.42	1238.44
60,000	5724.52	3224.92	2409.46	2014.61	1787.56	1643.96	1547.59	1480.34	1432.10	1396.81	1370.64	1351.02
65,000	6201.56	3493.66	2610.25	2182.50	1936.53	1780.95	1676.56	1603.70	1551.44	1513.22	1484.86	1463.61
70,000	6678.60	3762.40	2811.03	2350.38	2085.49	1917.95	1805.52	1727.06	1670.78	1629.62	1599.08	1576.19
75,000	7155.64	4031.15	3011.82	2518.27	2234.45	2054.95	1934.49	1850.42	1790.12	1746.02	1713.30	1688.78
80,000	7632.69	4299.89	3212.61	2686.15	2383.42	2191.94	2063.46	1973.78	1909.46	1862.42	1827.52	1801.36
85,000	8109.73	4568.63	3413.40	2854.03	2532.38	2328.94	2192.42	2097.14	2028.80	1978.82	1941.74	1913.94
90,000	8586.77	4837.38	3614.19	3021.92	2681.34	2465.93	2321.39	2220.50	2148.14	2095.22	2055.96	2026.53
95,000	9063.82	5106.12	3814.97	3189.80	2830.31	2602.93	2450.35	2343.86	2267.48	2211.62	2170.18	2139.11
100,000	9540.86	5374.86	4015.76	3357.69	2979.27	2739.93	2579.32	2467.22	2386.82	2328.02	2284.40	2251.70
105,000	10017.90	5643.60	4216.55	3525.57	3128.23	2876.92	2708.28	2590.58	2506.16	2444.42	2398.62	2364.28
110,000	10494.94	5912.35	4417.34	3693.45	3277.20	3013.92	2837.25	2713.94	2625.50	2560.82	2512.84	2476.87
115,000	10971.99	6181.09	4618.12	3861.34	3426.16	3150.91	2966.22	2837.31	2744.85	2677.22	2627.06	2589.45
120,000	11449.03	6449.83	4818.91	4029.22	3575.12	3287.91	3095.18	2960.67	2864.19	2793.62	2741.28	2702.04
125,000	11926.07	6718.57	5019.70	4197.11	3724.09	3424.91	3224.15	3084.03	2983.53	2910.03	2855.50	2814.62
130,000	12403.11	6987.32	5220.49	4364.99	3873.05	3561.90	3353.11	3207.39	3102.87	3026.43	2969.72	2927.21
135,000	12880.16	7256.06	5421.28	4532.87	4022.01	3698.90	3482.08	3330.75	3222.21	3142.83	3083.94	3039.79
140,000	13357.20	7524.80	5622.06	4700.76	4170.98	3835.90	3611.04	3454.11	3341.55	3259.23	3198.16	3152.38
145,000	13834.24	7793.55	5822.85	4868.64	4319.94	3972.89	3740.01	3577.47	3460.89	3375.63	3312.38	3264.96
150,000	14311.28	8062.29	6023.64	5036.53	4468.90	4109.89	3868.97	3700.83	3580.23	3492.03	3426.60	3377.55
155,000	14788.33	8331.03	6224.43	5204.41	4617.86	4246.88	3997.94	3824.19	3699.57	3608.43	3540.82	3490.13
160,000	15265.37	8599.77	6425.22	5372.29	4766.83	4383.88	4126.91	3947.55	3818.91	3724.83	3655.04	3602.72
165,000	15742.41	8868.52	6626.00	5540.18	4915.79	4520.88	4255.87	4070.91	3938.25	3841.23	3769.26	3715.30
170,000	16219.46	9137.26	6826.79	5708.06	5064.75	4657.87	4384.84	4194.27	4057.59	3957.63	3883.48	3827.88
175,000	16696.50	9406.00	7027.58	5875.95	5213.72	4794.87	4513.80	4317.64	4176.94	4074.03	3997.70	3940.47
180,000	17173.54	9674.75	7228.37	6043.83	5362.68	4931.86	4642.77	4441.00	4296.28	4190.43	4111.92	4053.05
185,000	17650.58	9943.49	7429.15	6211.71	5511.64	5068.86	4771.73	4564.36	4415.62	4306.83	4226.14	4165.64
190,000	18127.63	10212.23	7629.94	6379.60	5660.61	5205.86	4900.70	4687.72	4534.96	4423.24	4340.36	4278.22
195,000	18604.67	10480.97	7830.73	6547.48	5809.57	5342.85	5029.67	4811.08	4654.30	4539.64	4454.58	4390.81
200,000	19081.71	10749.72	8031.52	6715.37	5958.53	5479.85	5158.63	4934.44	4773.64	4656.04	4568.80	4503.39
205,000	19558.75	11018.46	8232.31	6883.25	6107.50	5616.84	5287.60	5057.80	4892.98	4772.44	4683.02	4615.98
210,000	20035.80	11287.20	8433.09	7051.13	6256.46	5753.84	5416.56	5181.16	5012.32	4888.84	4797.24	4728.56
215,000	20512.84	11555.95	8633.88	7219.02	6405.42	5890.84	5545.53	5304.52	5131.66	5005.24	4911.46	4841.15
220,000	20989.88	11824.69	8834.67	7386.90	6554.39	6027.83	5674.49	5427.88	5251.00	5121.64	5025.68	4953.73
225,000	21466.92	12093.43	9035.46	7554.79	6703.35	6164.83	5803.46	5551.24	5370.34	5238.04	5139.89	5066.32
230,000	21943.97	12362.17	9236.24	7722.67	6852.31	6301.82	5932.43	5674.61	5489.69	5354.44	5254.11	5178.90
235,000	22421.01	12630.92	9437.03	7890.55	7001.28	6438.82	6061.39	5797.97	5609.03	5470.84	5368.33	5291.49
240,000	22898.05	12899.66	9637.82	8058.44	7150.24	6575.82	6190.36	5921.33	5728.37	5587.24	5482.55	5404.07
245,000	23375.09	13168.40	9838.61	8226.32	7299.20	6712.81	6319.32	6044.69	5847.71	5703.64	5596.77	5516.66
250,000	23852.14	13437.14	10039.40	8394.21	7448.17	6849.81	6448.29	6168.05	5967.05	5820.05	5710.99	5629.24
255,000	24329.18	13705.89	10240.18	8562.09	7597.13	6986.80	6577.25	6291.41	6086.39	5936.45	5825.21	5741.82
260,000	24806.22	13974.63	10440.97	8729.97	7746.09	7123.80	6706.22	6414.77	6205.73	6052.85	5939.43	5854.41
265,000	25283.27	14243.37	10641.76	8897.86	7895.06	7260.80	6835.19	6538.13	6325.07	6169.25	6053.65	5966.99
270,000	25760.31	14512.12	10842.55	9065.74	8044.02	7397.79	6964.15	6661.49	6444.41	6285.65	6167.87	6079.58
280,000	26714.39	15049.60	11244.12	9401.51	8341.95	7671.79	7222.08	6908.21	6683.09	6518.45	6396.31	6304.75
290,000	27668.48	15587.09	11645.70	9737.28	8639.87	7945.78	7480.01	7154.94	6921.78	6751.25	6624.75	6529.92
300,000	28622.56	16124.57	12047.27	10073.05	8937.80	8219.77	7737.94	7401.66	7160.46	6984.05	6853.19	6755.09

MONTHLY AMORTIZING PAYMENTS — 25.75%

AMOUNT OF LOAN	13	14	15	16	17	18	19	20	25	30	35	40
$ 50	1.12	1.11	1.10	1.10	1.09	1.09	1.09	1.08	1.08	1.08	1.08	1.08
100	2.23	2.21	2.20	2.19	2.18	2.17	2.17	2.16	2.15	2.15	2.15	2.15
200	4.46	4.42	4.39	4.37	4.35	4.34	4.33	4.32	4.30	4.30	4.30	4.30
300	6.69	6.63	6.59	6.55	6.53	6.51	6.49	6.48	6.45	6.45	6.44	6.44
400	8.91	8.84	8.78	8.74	8.70	8.68	8.66	8.64	8.60	8.59	8.59	8.59
500	11.14	11.05	10.97	10.92	10.88	10.84	10.82	10.80	10.75	10.74	10.74	10.73
600	13.37	13.25	13.17	13.10	13.05	13.01	12.98	12.96	12.90	12.89	12.88	12.88
700	15.59	15.46	15.36	15.29	15.23	15.18	15.15	15.12	15.05	15.03	15.03	15.03
800	17.82	17.67	17.56	17.47	17.40	17.35	17.31	17.28	17.20	17.18	17.17	17.17
900	20.05	19.88	19.75	19.65	19.57	19.52	19.47	19.44	19.35	19.33	19.32	19.32
1,000	22.27	22.09	21.94	21.83	21.75	21.68	21.63	21.60	21.50	21.47	21.47	21.46
2,000	44.54	44.17	43.88	43.66	43.49	43.36	43.26	43.19	43.00	42.94	42.93	42.92
3,000	66.81	66.25	65.82	65.49	65.24	65.04	64.89	64.78	64.49	64.41	64.39	64.38
4,000	89.08	88.33	87.76	87.32	86.98	86.72	86.52	86.37	85.99	85.88	85.85	85.84
5,000	111.35	110.42	109.70	109.15	108.73	108.40	108.15	107.96	107.48	107.35	107.31	107.30
6,000	133.62	132.50	131.64	130.98	130.47	130.08	129.78	129.55	128.98	128.82	128.77	128.76
7,000	155.89	154.58	153.58	152.81	152.22	151.76	151.41	151.14	150.47	150.29	150.23	150.22
8,000	178.16	176.66	175.51	174.63	173.96	173.44	173.04	172.73	171.97	171.75	171.69	171.68
9,000	200.43	198.74	197.45	196.46	195.70	195.12	194.67	194.32	193.46	193.22	193.16	193.14
10,000	222.70	220.83	219.39	218.29	217.45	216.80	216.30	215.91	214.96	214.69	214.62	214.60
15,000	334.05	331.24	329.08	327.44	326.17	325.19	324.44	323.86	322.43	322.03	321.92	321.89
20,000	445.40	441.65	438.78	436.58	434.89	433.59	432.59	431.82	429.91	429.38	429.23	429.19
25,000	556.75	552.06	548.47	545.72	543.61	541.99	540.74	539.77	537.38	536.72	536.54	536.48
30,000	668.10	662.47	658.16	654.87	652.33	650.38	648.88	647.72	644.86	644.06	643.84	643.78
35,000	779.45	772.88	767.86	764.01	761.06	758.78	757.03	755.67	752.34	751.41	751.15	751.07
40,000	890.80	883.29	877.55	873.15	869.78	867.18	865.17	863.63	859.81	858.75	858.45	858.37
45,000	1002.15	993.70	987.24	982.30	978.50	975.57	973.32	971.58	967.29	966.00	965.76	965.67
50,000	1113.50	1104.11	1096.94	1091.44	1087.22	1083.97	1081.47	1079.53	1074.76	1073.44	1073.07	1072.96
55,000	1224.85	1214.52	1206.63	1200.58	1195.94	1192.37	1189.61	1187.49	1182.24	1180.78	1180.37	1180.26
60,000	1336.20	1324.93	1316.32	1309.73	1304.66	1300.76	1297.76	1295.44	1289.71	1288.12	1287.68	1287.55
65,000	1447.54	1435.34	1426.01	1418.87	1413.39	1409.16	1405.90	1403.39	1397.19	1395.47	1394.98	1394.85
70,000	1558.89	1545.75	1535.71	1528.02	1522.11	1517.56	1514.05	1511.34	1504.67	1502.81	1502.29	1502.14
75,000	1670.24	1656.16	1645.40	1637.16	1630.83	1625.95	1622.20	1619.30	1612.14	1610.15	1609.60	1609.44
80,000	1781.59	1766.57	1755.09	1746.30	1739.55	1734.35	1730.34	1727.25	1719.62	1717.49	1716.90	1716.74
85,000	1892.94	1876.98	1864.79	1855.45	1848.27	1842.75	1838.49	1835.20	1827.09	1824.84	1824.21	1824.03
90,000	2004.29	1987.39	1974.48	1964.59	1956.99	1951.14	1946.64	1943.16	1934.57	1932.18	1931.51	1931.33
95,000	2115.64	2097.80	2084.17	2073.73	2065.71	2059.54	2054.78	2051.11	2042.05	2039.52	2030.02	2030.62
100,000	2226.99	2208.21	2193.87	2182.88	2174.44	2167.94	2162.93	2159.06	2149.52	2146.87	2146.13	2145.92
105,000	2338.34	2318.62	2303.56	2292.02	2283.16	2276.33	2271.07	2267.01	2257.00	2254.21	2253.43	2253.21
110,000	2449.69	2429.03	2413.25	2401.16	2391.88	2384.73	2379.22	2374.97	2364.47	2361.55	2360.74	2360.51
115,000	2561.04	2539.44	2522.95	2510.31	2500.60	2493.13	2487.37	2482.92	2471.95	2468.90	2468.04	2467.81
120,000	2672.39	2649.85	2632.64	2619.45	2609.32	2601.52	2595.51	2590.87	2579.42	2576.24	2576.35	2575.10
125,000	2783.74	2760.26	2742.33	2728.60	2718.04	2709.92	2703.66	2698.82	2686.90	2683.58	2682.66	2682.40
130,000	2895.08	2870.67	2852.02	2837.74	2826.77	2818.32	2811.80	2806.78	2794.38	2790.93	2789.96	2789.69
135,000	3006.43	2981.08	2961.72	2946.88	2935.49	2926.71	2919.95	2914.73	2901.85	2898.27	2897.27	2896.99
140,000	3117.78	3091.49	3071.41	3056.03	3044.21	3035.11	3028.10	3022.68	3009.33	3005.61	3004.57	3004.28
145,000	3229.13	3201.90	3181.10	3165.17	3152.93	3143.51	3136.24	3130.64	3116.80	3112.96	3111.88	3111.58
150,000	3340.48	3312.31	3290.80	3274.31	3261.65	3251.90	3244.39	3238.59	3224.28	3220.30	3219.19	3218.88
155,000	3451.83	3422.72	3400.49	3383.46	3370.37	3360.30	3352.54	3346.54	3331.75	3327.64	3326.49	3326.17
160,000	3563.18	3533.13	3510.18	3492.60	3479.09	3468.70	3460.68	3454.49	3439.23	3434.98	3433.80	3433.47
165,000	3674.53	3643.54	3619.88	3601.74	3587.82	3577.09	3568.83	3562.45	3546.71	3542.33	3541.10	3540.76
170,000	3785.88	3753.95	3729.57	3710.89	3696.54	3685.49	3676.97	3670.40	3654.18	3649.67	3648.41	3648.06
175,000	3897.23	3864.36	3839.26	3820.03	3805.26	3793.89	3785.12	3778.35	3761.66	3757.01	3755.72	3755.35
180,000	4008.58	3974.77	3948.95	3929.18	3913.98	3902.28	3893.27	3886.31	3869.13	3864.36	3863.02	3862.65
185,000	4119.93	4085.18	4058.65	4038.32	4022.70	4010.68	4001.41	3994.26	3976.61	3971.70	3970.33	3969.95
190,000	4231.28	4195.59	4168.34	4147.46	4131.42	4119.08	4109.56	4102.21	4084.09	4079.04	4077.64	4077.24
195,000	4342.62	4306.00	4278.03	4256.61	4240.15	4227.47	4217.70	4210.16	4191.56	4186.39	4184.94	4184.54
200,000	4453.97	4416.41	4387.73	4365.75	4348.87	4335.87	4325.85	4318.12	4299.04	4293.73	4292.25	4291.83
205,000	4565.32	4526.82	4497.42	4474.89	4457.59	4444.27	4434.00	4426.07	4406.51	4401.07	4399.55	4399.13
210,000	4676.67	4637.23	4607.11	4584.04	4566.31	4552.66	4542.14	4534.02	4513.99	4508.42	4506.86	4506.42
215,000	4788.02	4747.64	4716.81	4693.18	4675.03	4661.06	4650.29	4641.97	4621.46	4615.76	4614.17	4613.72
220,000	4899.37	4858.05	4826.50	4802.32	4783.75	4769.46	4758.44	4749.93	4728.94	4723.10	4721.47	4721.02
225,000	5010.72	4968.46	4936.19	4911.47	4892.47	4877.85	4866.58	4857.88	4836.42	4830.44	4828.78	4828.31
230,000	5122.07	5078.87	5045.89	5020.61	5001.20	4986.25	4974.73	4965.83	4943.89	4937.79	4936.08	4935.61
235,000	5233.42	5189.28	5155.58	5129.76	5109.92	5094.65	5082.87	5073.79	5051.37	5045.13	5043.39	5042.90
240,000	5344.77	5299.69	5265.27	5238.90	5218.64	5203.04	5191.02	5181.74	5158.84	5152.47	5150.70	5150.20
245,000	5456.12	5410.10	5374.96	5348.04	5327.36	5311.44	5299.17	5289.69	5266.32	5259.82	5258.00	5257.49
250,000	5567.47	5520.51	5484.66	5457.19	5436.08	5419.84	5407.31	5397.64	5373.79	5367.16	5365.31	5364.79
255,000	5678.82	5630.92	5594.35	5566.33	5544.80	5528.23	5515.46	5505.60	5481.27	5474.50	5472.61	5472.09
260,000	5790.16	5741.33	5704.04	5675.47	5653.53	5636.63	5623.60	5613.55	5588.75	5581.85	5579.92	5579.38
265,000	5901.51	5851.74	5813.74	5784.62	5762.25	5745.03	5731.75	5721.50	5696.22	5689.19	5687.23	5686.68
270,000	6012.86	5962.15	5923.43	5893.76	5870.97	5853.42	5839.90	5829.46	5803.70	5796.53	5794.53	5793.97
280,000	6235.56	6182.97	6142.82	6112.05	6088.41	6070.22	6056.19	6045.36	6018.65	6011.22	6009.14	6008.56
290,000	6458.26	6403.79	6362.20	6330.34	6305.86	6287.01	6272.48	6261.27	6233.60	6225.91	6223.76	6223.16
300,000	6680.96	6624.61	6581.59	6548.62	6523.30	6503.80	6488.77	6477.17	6448.55	6440.59	6438.37	6437.75

TABLE 2

PAYMENT REQUIRED TO AMORTIZE A $1,000 LOAN

Use this Table to find the payment amount required to completely pay off a $1,000 loan amount over a given loan term at a fixed rate of interest.

MONTHLY
PAYMENT REQUIRED TO AMORTIZE A $1,000.00 LOAN

TERM IN YEARS	INTEREST RATES											
	2.00%	2.25%	2.50%	2.75%	3.00%	3.25%	3.50%	3.75%	4.00%	4.25%	4.50%	4.75%
0.5	167.65	167.77	167.89	168.01	168.13	168.26	168.38	168.50	168.62	168.74	168.87	168.99
1.0	84.24	84.36	84.47	84.58	84.70	84.81	84.93	85.04	85.15	85.27	85.38	85.50
1.5	56.44	56.56	56.67	56.78	56.89	57.00	57.11	57.22	57.34	57.45	57.56	57.67
2.0	42.55	42.66	42.77	42.88	42.99	43.10	43.21	43.32	43.43	43.54	43.65	43.76
2.5	34.21	34.32	34.43	34.54	34.65	34.76	34.87	34.98	35.09	35.20	35.31	35.42
3.0	28.65	28.76	28.87	28.98	29.09	29.20	29.31	29.42	29.53	29.64	29.75	29.86
3.5	24.68	24.79	24.90	25.01	25.12	25.23	25.34	25.45	25.56	25.67	25.78	25.90
4.0	21.70	21.81	21.92	22.03	22.14	22.25	22.36	22.47	22.58	22.70	22.81	22.92
4.5	19.38	19.49	19.60	19.71	19.82	19.94	20.05	20.16	20.27	20.38	20.50	20.61
5.0	17.53	17.64	17.75	17.86	17.97	18.09	18.20	18.31	18.42	18.53	18.65	18.76
5.5	16.02	16.13	16.24	16.35	16.46	16.57	16.68	16.80	16.91	17.02	17.14	17.25
6.0	14.76	14.87	14.98	15.09	15.20	15.31	15.42	15.54	15.65	15.76	15.88	15.99
6.5	13.69	13.80	13.91	14.02	14.13	14.24	14.36	14.47	14.59	14.70	14.82	14.93
7.0	12.77	12.88	12.99	13.11	13.22	13.33	13.44	13.56	13.67	13.79	13.91	14.02
7.5	11.98	12.09	12.20	12.31	12.43	12.54	12.65	12.77	12.88	13.00	13.12	13.23
8.0	11.29	11.40	11.51	11.62	11.73	11.85	11.96	12.08	12.19	12.31	12.43	12.55
8.5	10.67	10.79	10.90	11.01	11.12	11.24	11.35	11.47	11.59	11.70	11.82	11.94
9.0	10.13	10.24	10.35	10.47	10.58	10.70	10.81	10.93	11.05	11.16	11.28	11.40
9.5	9.64	9.76	9.87	9.98	10.10	10.21	10.33	10.45	10.56	10.68	10.80	10.92
10.0	9.21	9.32	9.43	9.55	9.66	9.78	9.89	10.01	10.13	10.25	10.37	10.49
10.5	8.81	8.92	9.04	9.15	9.27	9.38	9.50	9.62	9.74	9.86	9.98	10.10
11.0	8.45	8.56	8.68	8.79	8.91	9.03	9.14	9.26	9.38	9.50	9.62	9.75
11.5	8.12	8.24	8.35	8.47	8.58	8.70	8.82	8.94	9.06	9.18	9.30	9.42
12.0	7.82	7.94	8.05	8.17	8.28	8.40	8.52	8.64	8.76	8.88	9.01	9.13
12.5	7.55	7.66	7.77	7.89	8.01	8.13	8.25	8.37	8.49	8.61	8.73	8.86
13.0	7.29	7.40	7.52	7.64	7.75	7.87	7.99	8.11	8.24	8.36	8.48	8.61
13.5	7.05	7.17	7.28	7.40	7.52	7.64	7.76	7.88	8.00	8.13	8.25	8.38
14.0	6.83	6.95	7.07	7.18	7.30	7.42	7.54	7.67	7.79	7.91	8.04	8.17
14.5	6.63	6.75	6.86	6.98	7.10	7.22	7.34	7.46	7.59	7.71	7.84	7.97
15.0	6.44	6.56	6.67	6.79	6.91	7.03	7.15	7.28	7.40	7.53	7.65	7.78
15.5	6.26	6.38	6.50	6.61	6.73	6.86	6.98	7.10	7.23	7.35	7.48	7.61
16.0	6.10	6.21	6.33	6.45	6.57	6.69	6.81	6.94	7.06	7.19	7.32	7.45
16.5	5.94	6.06	6.17	6.29	6.41	6.54	6.66	6.79	6.91	7.04	7.17	7.30
17.0	5.79	5.91	6.03	6.15	6.27	6.39	6.52	6.64	6.77	6.90	7.03	7.16
17.5	5.65	5.77	5.89	6.01	6.13	6.26	6.38	6.51	6.63	6.76	6.89	7.03
18.0	5.52	5.64	5.76	5.88	6.00	6.13	6.25	6.38	6.51	6.64	6.77	6.90
18.5	5.40	5.52	5.64	5.76	5.88	6.00	6.13	6.26	6.39	6.52	6.65	6.78
19.0	5.28	5.40	5.52	5.64	5.76	5.89	6.02	6.14	6.27	6.40	6.54	6.67
19.5	5.17	5.29	5.41	5.53	5.65	5.78	5.91	6.04	6.17	6.30	6.43	6.57
20.0	5.06	5.18	5.30	5.43	5.55	5.68	5.80	5.93	6.06	6.20	6.33	6.47
20.5	4.96	5.08	5.20	5.33	5.45	5.58	5.71	5.84	5.97	6.10	6.24	6.37
21.0	4.87	4.99	5.11	5.23	5.36	5.49	5.61	5.74	5.88	6.01	6.15	6.28
21.5	4.78	4.90	5.02	5.14	5.27	5.40	5.53	5.66	5.79	5.92	6.06	6.20
22.0	4.69	4.81	4.93	5.06	5.18	5.31	5.44	5.57	5.71	5.84	5.98	6.12
22.5	4.61	4.73	4.85	4.98	5.10	5.23	5.36	5.49	5.63	5.76	5.90	6.04
23.0	4.53	4.65	4.77	4.90	5.03	5.15	5.29	5.42	5.55	5.69	5.83	5.97
23.5	4.45	4.57	4.70	4.82	4.95	5.08	5.21	5.35	5.48	5.62	5.76	5.90
24.0	4.38	4.50	4.63	4.75	4.88	5.01	5.14	5.28	5.41	5.55	5.69	5.83
24.5	4.31	4.43	4.56	4.68	4.81	4.94	5.08	5.21	5.35	5.48	5.62	5.77
25.0	4.24	4.37	4.49	4.62	4.75	4.88	5.01	5.15	5.28	5.42	5.56	5.71
25.5	4.18	4.30	4.43	4.56	4.68	4.82	4.95	5.09	5.22	5.36	5.50	5.65
26.0	4.12	4.24	4.37	4.49	4.62	4.76	4.89	5.03	5.17	5.31	5.45	5.59
26.5	4.06	4.18	4.31	4.44	4.57	4.70	4.83	4.97	5.11	5.25	5.39	5.54
27.0	4.00	4.13	4.25	4.38	4.51	4.65	4.78	4.92	5.06	5.20	5.34	5.49
27.5	3.95	4.07	4.20	4.33	4.46	4.59	4.73	4.87	5.01	5.15	5.29	5.44
28.0	3.89	4.02	4.15	4.28	4.41	4.54	4.68	4.82	4.96	5.10	5.24	5.39
28.5	3.84	3.97	4.10	4.23	4.36	4.49	4.63	4.77	4.91	5.05	5.20	5.35
29.0	3.79	3.92	4.05	4.18	4.31	4.45	4.58	4.72	4.86	5.01	5.15	5.30
29.5	3.75	3.87	4.00	4.13	4.27	4.40	4.54	4.68	4.82	4.97	5.11	5.26
30.0	3.70	3.83	3.96	4.09	4.22	4.36	4.50	4.64	4.78	4.92	5.07	5.22
31.0	3.61	3.74	3.87	4.00	4.14	4.27	4.41	4.56	4.70	4.85	4.99	5.15
32.0	3.53	3.66	3.79	3.92	4.06	4.20	4.34	4.48	4.63	4.77	4.92	5.08
33.0	3.46	3.58	3.72	3.85	3.99	4.13	4.27	4.41	4.56	4.71	4.86	5.01
34.0	3.39	3.51	3.65	3.78	3.92	4.06	4.20	4.35	4.49	4.64	4.80	4.95
35.0	3.32	3.45	3.58	3.72	3.85	3.99	4.14	4.28	4.43	4.58	4.74	4.89
36.0	3.25	3.38	3.52	3.65	3.79	3.94	4.08	4.23	4.38	4.53	4.68	4.84
37.0	3.19	3.33	3.46	3.60	3.74	3.88	4.02	4.17	4.32	4.48	4.63	4.79
38.0	3.14	3.27	3.40	3.54	3.68	3.83	3.97	4.12	4.27	4.43	4.59	4.75
39.0	3.08	3.22	3.35	3.49	3.63	3.78	3.92	4.07	4.23	4.38	4.54	4.70
40.0	3.03	3.17	3.30	3.44	3.58	3.73	3.88	4.03	4.18	4.34	4.50	4.66

MONTHLY
PAYMENT REQUIRED TO AMORTIZE A $1,000.00 LOAN

TERM IN YEARS	INTEREST RATES											
	5.00%	5.25%	5.50%	5.75%	6.00%	6.25%	6.50%	6.75%	7.00%	7.25%	7.50%	7.75%
0.5	169.11	169.23	169.36	169.48	169.60	169.72	169.85	169.97	170.09	170.21	170.34	170.46
1.0	85.61	85.73	85.84	85.96	86.07	86.19	86.30	86.42	86.53	86.65	86.76	86.88
1.5	57.79	57.90	58.01	58.12	58.24	58.35	58.46	58.58	58.69	58.80	58.92	59.03
2.0	43.88	43.99	44.10	44.21	44.33	44.44	44.55	44.66	44.78	44.89	45.00	45.12
2.5	35.53	35.65	35.76	35.87	35.98	36.10	36.21	36.32	36.44	36.55	36.66	36.78
3.0	29.98	30.09	30.20	30.31	30.43	30.54	30.65	30.77	30.88	31.00	31.11	31.23
3.5	26.01	26.12	26.23	26.35	26.46	26.58	26.69	26.80	26.92	27.03	27.15	27.27
4.0	23.03	23.15	23.26	23.38	23.49	23.60	23.72	23.84	23.95	24.07	24.18	24.30
4.5	20.72	20.84	20.95	21.07	21.18	21.30	21.41	21.53	21.65	21.76	21.88	22.00
5.0	18.88	18.99	19.11	19.22	19.34	19.45	19.57	19.69	19.81	19.92	20.04	20.16
5.5	17.37	17.48	17.60	17.71	17.83	17.95	18.07	18.18	18.30	18.42	18.54	18.66
6.0	16.11	16.23	16.34	16.46	16.58	16.70	16.81	16.93	17.05	17.17	17.30	17.42
6.5	15.05	15.16	15.28	15.40	15.52	15.64	15.76	15.88	16.00	16.12	16.24	16.37
7.0	14.14	14.26	14.38	14.49	14.61	14.73	14.85	14.98	15.10	15.22	15.34	15.47
7.5	13.35	13.47	13.59	13.71	13.83	13.95	14.07	14.20	14.32	14.44	14.57	14.69
8.0	12.66	12.78	12.90	13.03	13.15	13.27	13.39	13.51	13.64	13.76	13.89	14.01
8.5	12.06	12.18	12.30	12.42	12.54	12.67	12.79	12.92	13.04	13.17	13.29	13.42
9.0	11.52	11.64	11.76	11.89	12.01	12.13	12.26	12.39	12.51	12.64	12.77	12.89
9.5	11.04	11.16	11.29	11.41	11.53	11.66	11.79	11.91	12.04	12.17	12.30	12.43
10.0	10.61	10.73	10.86	10.98	11.11	11.23	11.36	11.49	11.62	11.75	11.88	12.01
10.5	10.22	10.35	10.47	10.60	10.72	10.85	10.98	11.10	11.23	11.36	11.50	11.63
11.0	9.87	9.99	10.12	10.25	10.37	10.50	10.63	10.76	10.89	11.02	11.15	11.29
11.5	9.55	9.67	9.80	9.93	10.05	10.18	10.31	10.44	10.58	10.71	10.84	10.98
12.0	9.25	9.38	9.51	9.63	9.76	9.89	10.02	10.16	10.29	10.42	10.56	10.69
12.5	8.98	9.11	9.24	9.37	9.50	9.63	9.76	9.90	10.03	10.16	10.30	10.43
13.0	8.74	8.86	8.99	9.12	9.25	9.38	9.52	9.65	9.79	9.92	10.06	10.20
13.5	8.51	8.63	8.76	8.89	9.03	9.16	9.29	9.43	9.56	9.70	9.84	9.98
14.0	8.29	8.42	8.55	8.68	8.82	8.95	9.09	9.22	9.36	9.50	9.64	9.78
14.5	8.10	8.23	8.36	8.49	8.62	8.76	8.89	9.03	9.17	9.31	9.45	9.59
15.0	7.91	8.04	8.18	8.31	8.44	8.58	8.72	8.85	8.99	9.13	9.28	9.42
15.5	7.74	7.87	8.01	8.14	8.28	8.41	8.55	8.69	8.83	8.97	9.11	9.26
16.0	7.58	7.71	7.85	7.98	8.12	8.26	8.40	8.54	8.68	8.82	8.96	9.11
16.5	7.43	7.57	7.70	7.84	7.97	8.11	8.25	8.39	8.53	8.68	8.82	8.97
17.0	7.29	7.43	7.56	7.70	7.84	7.98	8.12	8.26	8.40	8.55	8.69	8.84
17.5	7.16	7.29	7.43	7.57	7.71	7.85	7.99	8.13	8.28	8.42	8.57	8.72
18.0	7.04	7.17	7.31	7.45	7.59	7.73	7.87	8.01	8.16	8.31	8.45	8.60
18.5	6.92	7.05	7.19	7.33	7.47	7.62	7.76	7.90	8.05	8.20	8.35	8.50
19.0	6.81	6.95	7.08	7.22	7.37	7.51	7.65	7.80	7.95	8.10	8.25	8.40
19.5	6.70	6.84	6.98	7.12	7.26	7.41	7.55	7.70	7.85	8.00	8.15	8.30
20.0	6.60	6.74	6.88	7.03	7.17	7.31	7.46	7.61	7.76	7.91	8.06	8.21
20.5	6.51	6.65	6.79	6.93	7.08	7.22	7.37	7.52	7.67	7.82	7.98	8.13
21.0	6.42	6.56	6.70	6.85	6.99	7.14	7.29	7.44	7.59	7.74	7.90	8.05
21.5	6.34	6.48	6.62	6.77	6.91	7.06	7.21	7.36	7.51	7.67	7.82	7.98
22.0	6.26	6.40	6.54	6.69	6.84	6.98	7.13	7.29	7.44	7.59	7.75	7.91
22.5	6.18	6.32	6.47	6.62	6.76	6.91	7.06	7.22	7.37	7.53	7.68	7.84
23.0	6.11	6.25	6.40	6.54	6.69	6.84	7.00	7.15	7.30	7.46	7.62	7.78
23.5	6.04	6.18	6.33	6.48	6.63	6.78	6.93	7.09	7.24	7.40	7.56	7.72
24.0	5.97	6.12	6.27	6.41	6.56	6.72	6.87	7.03	7.18	7.34	7.50	7.66
24.5	5.91	6.06	6.20	6.35	6.50	6.66	6.81	6.97	7.13	7.29	7.45	7.61
25.0	5.85	6.00	6.15	6.30	6.45	6.60	6.76	6.91	7.07	7.23	7.39	7.56
25.5	5.79	5.94	6.09	6.24	6.39	6.55	6.70	6.86	7.02	7.18	7.35	7.51
26.0	5.74	5.89	6.04	6.19	6.34	6.50	6.65	6.81	6.97	7.14	7.30	7.46
26.5	5.69	5.83	5.99	6.14	6.29	6.45	6.61	6.77	6.93	7.09	7.25	7.42
27.0	5.64	5.78	5.94	6.09	6.24	6.40	6.56	6.72	6.88	7.05	7.21	7.38
27.5	5.59	5.74	5.89	6.04	6.20	6.36	6.52	6.68	6.84	7.01	7.17	7.34
28.0	5.54	5.69	5.84	6.00	6.16	6.31	6.48	6.64	6.80	6.97	7.13	7.30
28.5	5.50	5.65	5.80	5.96	6.11	6.27	6.44	6.60	6.76	6.93	7.10	7.27
29.0	5.45	5.61	5.76	5.92	6.08	6.24	6.40	6.56	6.73	6.89	7.06	7.23
29.5	5.41	5.57	5.72	5.88	6.04	6.20	6.36	6.53	6.69	6.86	7.03	7.20
30.0	5.37	5.53	5.68	5.84	6.00	6.16	6.33	6.49	6.66	6.83	7.00	7.17
31.0	5.30	5.45	5.61	5.77	5.93	6.10	6.26	6.43	6.60	6.77	6.94	7.11
32.0	5.23	5.39	5.55	5.71	5.87	6.03	6.20	6.37	6.54	6.71	6.88	7.06
33.0	5.17	5.32	5.48	5.65	5.81	5.98	6.14	6.31	6.49	6.66	6.83	7.01
34.0	5.11	5.27	5.43	5.59	5.76	5.92	6.09	6.26	6.44	6.61	6.79	6.97
35.0	5.05	5.21	5.38	5.54	5.71	5.88	6.05	6.22	6.39	6.57	6.75	6.93
36.0	5.00	5.16	5.33	5.49	5.66	5.83	6.00	6.18	6.35	6.53	6.71	6.89
37.0	4.95	5.12	5.28	5.45	5.62	5.79	5.96	6.14	6.32	6.49	6.67	6.86
38.0	4.91	5.07	5.24	5.41	5.58	5.75	5.93	6.10	6.28	6.46	6.64	6.83
39.0	4.87	5.03	5.20	5.37	5.54	5.72	5.89	6.07	6.25	6.43	6.61	6.80
40.0	4.83	4.99	5.16	5.33	5.51	5.68	5.86	6.04	6.22	6.40	6.59	6.77

MONTHLY
PAYMENT REQUIRED TO AMORTIZE A $1,000.00 LOAN

TERM IN YEARS	INTEREST RATES											
	8.00%	8.25%	8.50%	8.75%	9.00%	9.25%	9.50%	9.75%	10.00%	10.25%	10.50%	10.75%
0.5	170.58	170.70	170.83	170.95	171.07	171.20	171.32	171.44	171.57	171.69	171.81	171.94
1.0	86.99	87.11	87.22	87.34	87.46	87.57	87.69	87.80	87.92	88.04	88.15	88.27
1.5	59.15	59.26	59.37	59.49	59.60	59.72	59.83	59.95	60.06	60.18	60.29	60.41
2.0	45.23	45.35	45.46	45.58	45.69	45.80	45.92	46.03	46.15	46.27	46.38	46.50
2.5	36.89	37.01	37.12	37.24	37.35	37.47	37.58	37.70	37.82	37.93	38.05	38.17
3.0	31.34	31.46	31.57	31.69	31.80	31.92	32.04	32.15	32.27	32.39	32.51	32.63
3.5	27.38	27.50	27.62	27.73	27.85	27.97	28.09	28.20	28.32	28.44	28.56	28.68
4.0	24.42	24.54	24.65	24.77	24.89	25.01	25.13	25.25	25.37	25.49	25.61	25.73
4.5	22.12	22.24	22.36	22.47	22.59	22.71	22.84	22.96	23.08	23.20	23.32	23.44
5.0	20.28	20.40	20.52	20.64	20.76	20.88	21.01	21.13	21.25	21.38	21.50	21.62
5.5	18.78	18.90	19.03	19.15	19.27	19.39	19.52	19.64	19.76	19.89	20.01	20.14
6.0	17.54	17.66	17.78	17.91	18.03	18.15	18.28	18.41	18.53	18.66	18.78	18.91
6.5	16.49	16.61	16.74	16.86	16.99	17.11	17.24	17.36	17.49	17.62	17.75	17.88
7.0	15.59	15.72	15.84	15.97	16.09	16.22	16.35	16.48	16.61	16.74	16.87	17.00
7.5	14.82	14.94	15.07	15.20	15.32	15.45	15.58	15.71	15.84	15.97	16.11	16.24
8.0	14.14	14.27	14.40	14.53	14.66	14.79	14.92	15.05	15.18	15.31	15.45	15.58
8.5	13.55	13.68	13.81	13.94	14.07	14.20	14.33	14.46	14.60	14.73	14.87	15.00
9.0	13.02	13.15	13.28	13.42	13.55	13.68	13.81	13.95	14.08	14.22	14.36	14.49
9.5	12.56	12.69	12.82	12.95	13.09	13.22	13.36	13.49	13.63	13.76	13.90	14.04
10.0	12.14	12.27	12.40	12.54	12.67	12.81	12.94	13.08	13.22	13.36	13.50	13.64
10.5	11.76	11.89	12.03	12.16	12.30	12.44	12.58	12.71	12.85	12.99	13.14	13.28
11.0	11.42	11.56	11.69	11.83	11.97	12.10	12.24	12.38	12.52	12.67	12.81	12.95
11.5	11.11	11.25	11.38	11.52	11.66	11.80	11.94	12.08	12.23	12.37	12.51	12.66
12.0	10.83	10.97	11.11	11.24	11.39	11.53	11.67	11.81	11.96	12.10	12.25	12.39
12.5	10.57	10.71	10.85	10.99	11.13	11.28	11.42	11.56	11.71	11.86	12.00	12.15
13.0	10.34	10.48	10.62	10.76	10.90	11.05	11.19	11.34	11.48	11.63	11.78	11.93
13.5	10.12	10.26	10.40	10.55	10.69	10.83	10.98	11.13	11.28	11.43	11.58	11.73
14.0	9.92	10.06	10.20	10.35	10.49	10.64	10.79	10.94	11.09	11.24	11.39	11.54
14.5	9.73	9.88	10.02	10.17	10.31	10.46	10.61	10.76	10.91	11.06	11.22	11.37
15.0	9.56	9.71	9.85	10.00	10.15	10.30	10.45	10.60	10.75	10.90	11.06	11.21
15.5	9.40	9.55	9.70	9.84	9.99	10.14	10.30	10.45	10.60	10.76	10.91	11.07
16.0	9.25	9.40	9.55	9.70	9.85	10.00	10.15	10.31	10.46	10.62	10.78	10.94
16.5	9.12	9.26	9.41	9.57	9.72	9.87	10.02	10.18	10.34	10.49	10.65	10.81
17.0	8.99	9.14	9.29	9.44	9.59	9.75	9.90	10.06	10.22	10.38	10.54	10.70
17.5	8.87	9.02	9.17	9.32	9.48	9.63	9.79	9.95	10.11	10.27	10.43	10.59
18.0	8.75	8.91	9.06	9.21	9.37	9.53	9.68	9.84	10.00	10.16	10.33	10.49
18.5	8.65	8.80	8.96	9.11	9.27	9.43	9.59	9.75	9.91	10.07	10.23	10.40
19.0	8.55	8.70	8.86	9.02	9.17	9.33	9.49	9.65	9.82	9.98	10.15	10.31
19.5	8.46	8.61	8.77	8.93	9.09	9.25	9.41	9.57	9.73	9.90	10.06	10.23
20.0	8.37	8.53	8.68	8.84	9.00	9.16	9.33	9.49	9.66	9.82	9.99	10.16
20.5	8.29	8.44	8.60	8.76	8.92	9.09	9.25	9.42	9.58	9.75	9.92	10.09
21.0	8.21	8.37	8.53	8.69	8.85	9.01	9.18	9.35	9.51	9.68	9.85	10.02
21.5	8.14	8.30	8.46	8.62	8.78	8.95	9.11	9.28	9.45	9.62	9.79	9.96
22.0	8.07	8.23	8.39	8.55	8.72	8.88	9.05	9.22	9.39	9.56	9.73	9.90
22.5	8.00	8.16	8.33	8.49	8.66	8.82	8.99	9.16	9.33	9.50	9.68	9.85
23.0	7.94	8.10	8.27	8.43	8.60	8.77	8.93	9.11	9.28	9.45	9.62	9.80
23.5	7.88	8.04	8.21	8.38	8.54	8.71	8.88	9.05	9.23	9.40	9.58	9.75
24.0	7.83	7.99	8.16	8.32	8.49	8.66	8.83	9.01	9.18	9.35	9.53	9.71
24.5	7.77	7.94	8.11	8.27	8.44	8.61	8.79	8.96	9.13	9.31	9.49	9.67
25.0	7.72	7.89	8.06	8.23	8.40	8.57	8.74	8.92	9.09	9.27	9.45	9.63
25.5	7.68	7.84	8.01	8.18	8.35	8.53	8.70	8.88	9.05	9.23	9.41	9.59
26.0	7.63	7.80	7.97	8.14	8.31	8.49	8.66	8.84	9.01	9.19	9.37	9.55
26.5	7.59	7.76	7.93	8.10	8.27	8.45	8.62	8.80	8.98	9.16	9.34	9.52
27.0	7.55	7.72	7.89	8.06	8.24	8.41	8.59	8.77	8.95	9.13	9.31	9.49
27.5	7.51	7.68	7.85	8.03	8.20	8.38	8.56	8.73	8.91	9.10	9.28	9.46
28.0	7.47	7.64	7.82	7.99	8.17	8.35	8.52	8.70	8.88	9.07	9.25	9.43
28.5	7.44	7.61	7.78	7.96	8.14	8.31	8.49	8.67	8.86	9.04	9.22	9.41
29.0	7.40	7.58	7.75	7.93	8.11	8.29	8.47	8.65	8.83	9.01	9.20	9.38
29.5	7.37	7.55	7.72	7.90	8.08	8.26	8.44	8.62	8.80	8.99	9.17	9.36
30.0	7.34	7.52	7.69	7.87	8.05	8.23	8.41	8.60	8.78	8.97	9.15	9.34
31.0	7.29	7.46	7.64	7.82	8.00	8.18	8.37	8.55	8.74	8.92	9.11	9.30
32.0	7.24	7.41	7.59	7.77	7.96	8.14	8.32	8.51	8.70	8.89	9.07	9.26
33.0	7.19	7.37	7.55	7.73	7.92	8.10	8.29	8.47	8.66	8.85	9.04	9.23
34.0	7.15	7.33	7.51	7.69	7.88	8.06	8.25	8.44	8.63	8.82	9.01	9.21
35.0	7.11	7.29	7.47	7.66	7.84	8.03	8.22	8.41	8.60	8.79	8.99	9.18
36.0	7.07	7.26	7.44	7.63	7.81	8.00	8.19	8.38	8.58	8.77	8.96	9.16
37.0	7.04	7.22	7.41	7.60	7.79	7.98	8.17	8.36	8.55	8.75	8.94	9.14
38.0	7.01	7.20	7.38	7.57	7.76	7.95	8.15	8.34	8.53	8.73	8.92	9.12
39.0	6.98	7.17	7.36	7.55	7.74	7.93	8.12	8.32	8.51	8.71	8.91	9.10
40.0	6.96	7.15	7.34	7.53	7.72	7.91	8.11	8.30	8.50	8.69	8.89	9.09

MONTHLY
PAYMENT REQUIRED TO AMORTIZE A $1,000.00 LOAN

TERM IN YEARS	11.00%	11.25%	11.50%	11.75%	12.00%	12.25%	12.50%	12.75%	13.00%	13.25%	13.50%	13.75%
					INTEREST RATES							
0.5	172.06	172.18	172.31	172.43	172.55	172.68	172.80	172.92	173.05	173.17	173.30	173.42
1.0	88.39	88.50	88.62	88.74	88.85	88.97	89.09	89.21	89.32	89.44	89.56	89.67
1.5	60.52	60.64	60.76	60.87	60.99	61.10	61.22	61.34	61.45	61.57	61.69	61.80
2.0	46.61	46.73	46.85	46.96	47.08	47.20	47.31	47.43	47.55	47.66	47.78	47.90
2.5	38.28	38.40	38.52	38.64	38.75	38.87	38.99	39.11	39.23	39.35	39.46	39.58
3.0	32.74	32.86	32.98	33.10	33.22	33.34	33.46	33.58	33.70	33.82	33.94	34.06
3.5	28.80	28.92	29.04	29.16	29.28	29.40	29.52	29.65	29.77	29.89	30.01	30.14
4.0	25.85	25.97	26.09	26.22	26.34	26.46	26.58	26.71	26.83	26.96	27.08	27.21
4.5	23.57	23.69	23.81	23.94	24.06	24.19	24.31	24.44	24.56	24.69	24.82	24.94
5.0	21.75	21.87	22.00	22.12	22.25	22.38	22.50	22.63	22.76	22.89	23.01	23.14
5.5	20.27	20.39	20.52	20.65	20.78	20.90	21.03	21.16	21.29	21.42	21.55	21.68
6.0	19.04	19.17	19.30	19.43	19.56	19.69	19.82	19.95	20.08	20.21	20.34	20.48
6.5	18.01	18.14	18.27	18.40	18.53	18.66	18.79	18.93	19.06	19.20	19.33	19.47
7.0	17.13	17.26	17.39	17.52	17.66	17.79	17.93	18.06	18.20	18.33	18.47	18.61
7.5	16.37	16.50	16.64	16.77	16.91	17.04	17.18	17.32	17.45	17.59	17.73	17.87
8.0	15.71	15.85	15.98	16.12	16.26	16.40	16.53	16.67	16.81	16.95	17.09	17.23
8.5	15.14	15.27	15.41	15.55	15.69	15.83	15.97	16.11	16.25	16.39	16.54	16.68
9.0	14.63	14.77	14.91	15.05	15.19	15.33	15.47	15.62	15.76	15.90	16.05	16.19
9.5	14.18	14.32	14.46	14.60	14.75	14.89	15.03	15.18	15.32	15.47	15.62	15.76
10.0	13.78	13.92	14.06	14.21	14.35	14.50	14.64	14.79	14.94	15.08	15.23	15.38
10.5	13.42	13.56	13.71	13.85	14.00	14.15	14.29	14.44	14.59	14.74	14.89	15.04
11.0	13.10	13.24	13.39	13.54	13.68	13.83	13.98	14.13	14.28	14.43	14.58	14.74
11.5	12.81	12.95	13.10	13.25	13.40	13.55	13.70	13.85	14.00	14.16	14.31	14.46
12.0	12.64	12.79	12.84	12.99	13.14	13.29	13.44	13.60	13.75	13.91	14.06	14.22
12.5	12.30	12.45	12.60	12.75	12.90	13.06	13.21	13.37	13.52	13.68	13.84	14.00
13.0	12.08	12.23	12.38	12.54	12.69	12.85	13.00	13.16	13.32	13.48	13.63	13.80
13.5	11.88	12.03	12.19	12.34	12.50	12.65	12.81	12.97	13.13	13.29	13.45	13.61
14.0	11.70	11.85	12.01	12.16	12.32	12.48	12.64	12.80	12.96	13.12	13.28	13.45
14.5	11.53	11.68	11.84	12.00	12.16	12.32	12.48	12.64	12.80	12.96	13.13	13.29
15.0	11.37	11.53	11.69	11.85	12.01	12.17	12.33	12.49	12.66	12.82	12.99	13.15
15.5	11.23	11.39	11.55	11.71	11.87	12.03	12.20	12.36	12.53	12.69	12.86	13.03
16.0	11.10	11.26	11.42	11.58	11.74	11.91	12.07	12.24	12.40	12.57	12.74	12.91
16.5	10.97	11.13	11.30	11.46	11.63	11.79	11.96	12.13	12.29	12.46	12.63	12.80
17.0	10.86	11.02	11.19	11.35	11.52	11.68	11.85	12.02	12.19	12.36	12.53	12.71
17.5	10.75	10.92	11.08	11.25	11.42	11.59	11.75	11.93	12.10	12.27	12.44	12.62
18.0	10.66	10.82	10.99	11.16	11.32	11.49	11.67	11.84	12.01	12.18	12.36	12.53
18.5	10.56	10.73	10.90	11.07	11.24	11.41	11.58	11.75	11.93	12.10	12.28	12.46
19.0	10.48	10.65	10.82	10.99	11.16	11.33	11.50	11.68	11.85	12.03	12.21	12.39
19.5	10.40	10.57	10.74	10.91	11.08	11.26	11.43	11.61	11.78	11.96	12.14	12.32
20.0	10.33	10.50	10.67	10.84	11.02	11.19	11.37	11.54	11.72	11.90	12.08	12.26
20.5	10.26	10.43	10.60	10.78	10.95	11.13	11.30	11.48	11.66	11.84	12.02	12.20
21.0	10.19	10.37	10.54	10.72	10.89	11.07	11.25	11.43	11.61	11.79	11.97	12.15
21.5	10.13	10.31	10.48	10.66	10.84	11.01	11.19	11.37	11.55	11.74	11.92	12.10
22.0	10.08	10.25	10.43	10.61	10.78	10.96	11.14	11.33	11.51	11.69	11.87	12.06
22.5	10.02	10.20	10.38	10.56	10.74	10.92	11.10	11.28	11.46	11.65	11.83	12.02
23.0	9.98	10.15	10.33	10.51	10.69	10.87	11.05	11.24	11.42	11.61	11.79	11.98
23.5	9.93	10.11	10.29	10.47	10.65	10.83	11.01	11.20	11.38	11.57	11.76	11.94
24.0	9.89	10.06	10.25	10.43	10.61	10.79	10.98	11.16	11.35	11.53	11.72	11.91
24.5	9.84	10.02	10.21	10.39	10.57	10.76	10.94	11.13	11.31	11.50	11.69	11.88
25.0	9.81	9.99	10.17	10.35	10.54	10.72	10.91	11.10	11.28	11.47	11.66	11.85
25.5	9.77	9.95	10.14	10.32	10.50	10.69	10.88	11.07	11.25	11.44	11.63	11.83
26.0	9.74	9.92	10.10	10.29	10.47	10.66	10.85	11.04	11.23	11.42	11.61	11.80
26.5	9.70	9.89	10.07	10.26	10.45	10.63	10.82	11.01	11.20	11.39	11.59	11.78
27.0	9.67	9.86	10.05	10.23	10.42	10.61	10.80	10.99	11.18	11.37	11.56	11.76
27.5	9.65	9.83	10.02	10.21	10.39	10.58	10.77	10.97	11.16	11.35	11.54	11.74
28.0	9.62	9.81	9.99	10.18	10.37	10.56	10.75	10.94	11.14	11.33	11.52	11.72
28.5	9.59	9.78	9.97	10.16	10.35	10.54	10.73	10.92	11.12	11.31	11.51	11.70
29.0	9.57	9.76	9.95	10.14	10.33	10.52	10.71	10.91	11.10	11.29	11.49	11.68
29.5	9.55	9.74	9.93	10.12	10.31	10.50	10.69	10.89	11.08	11.28	11.47	11.67
30.0	9.53	9.72	9.91	10.10	10.29	10.48	10.68	10.87	11.07	11.26	11.46	11.66
31.0	9.49	9.68	9.87	10.06	10.26	10.45	10.65	10.84	11.04	11.24	11.43	11.63
32.0	9.46	9.65	9.84	10.03	10.23	10.42	10.62	10.82	11.01	11.21	11.41	11.61
33.0	9.43	9.62	9.81	10.01	10.20	10.40	10.60	10.79	10.99	11.19	11.39	11.59
34.0	9.40	9.59	9.79	9.98	10.18	10.38	10.58	10.77	10.97	11.17	11.37	11.57
35.0	9.37	9.57	9.77	9.96	10.16	10.36	10.56	10.76	10.96	11.16	11.36	11.56
36.0	9.35	9.55	9.75	9.94	10.14	10.34	10.54	10.74	10.94	11.14	11.35	11.55
37.0	9.33	9.53	9.73	9.93	10.13	10.33	10.53	10.73	10.93	11.13	11.33	11.54
38.0	9.32	9.51	9.71	9.91	10.11	10.31	10.51	10.72	10.92	11.12	11.32	11.53
39.0	9.30	9.50	9.70	9.90	10.10	10.30	10.50	10.71	10.91	11.11	11.32	11.52
40.0	9.29	9.49	9.69	9.89	10.09	10.29	10.49	10.70	10.90	11.10	11.31	11.51

MONTHLY
PAYMENT REQUIRED TO AMORTIZE A $1,000.00 LOAN

TERM IN YEARS	INTEREST RATES											
	14.00%	14.25%	14.50%	14.75%	15.00%	15.25%	15.50%	15.75%	16.00%	16.25%	16.50%	16.75%
0.5	173.54	173.67	173.79	173.91	174.04	174.16	174.29	174.41	174.54	174.66	174.78	174.91
1.0	89.79	89.91	90.03	90.15	90.26	90.38	90.50	90.62	90.74	90.85	90.97	91.09
1.5	61.92	62.04	62.15	62.27	62.39	62.51	62.63	62.74	62.86	62.98	63.10	63.22
2.0	48.02	48.14	48.25	48.37	48.49	48.61	48.73	48.85	48.97	49.09	49.21	49.33
2.5	39.70	39.82	39.94	40.06	40.18	40.30	40.42	40.55	40.67	40.79	40.91	41.03
3.0	34.18	34.30	34.43	34.55	34.67	34.79	34.92	35.04	35.16	35.29	35.41	35.53
3.5	30.26	30.38	30.51	30.63	30.75	30.88	31.00	31.13	31.25	31.38	31.51	31.63
4.0	27.33	27.46	27.58	27.71	27.84	27.96	28.09	28.22	28.35	28.47	28.60	28.73
4.5	25.07	25.20	25.33	25.45	25.58	25.71	25.84	25.97	26.10	26.23	26.36	26.49
5.0	23.27	23.40	23.53	23.66	23.79	23.93	24.06	24.19	24.32	24.46	24.59	24.72
5.5	21.82	21.95	22.08	22.21	22.35	22.48	22.61	22.75	22.88	23.02	23.15	23.29
6.0	20.61	20.74	20.88	21.01	21.15	21.29	21.42	21.56	21.70	21.83	21.97	22.11
6.5	19.60	19.74	19.87	20.01	20.15	20.29	20.43	20.57	20.71	20.85	20.99	21.13
7.0	18.75	18.88	19.02	19.16	19.30	19.44	19.58	19.72	19.87	20.01	20.15	20.30
7.5	18.01	18.15	18.29	18.43	18.58	18.72	18.86	19.01	19.15	19.30	19.44	19.59
8.0	17.38	17.52	17.66	17.81	17.95	18.10	18.24	18.39	18.53	18.68	18.83	18.98
8.5	16.82	16.97	17.11	17.26	17.41	17.55	17.70	17.85	18.00	18.15	18.30	18.45
9.0	16.34	16.49	16.63	16.78	16.93	17.08	17.23	17.38	17.53	17.68	17.83	17.99
9.5	15.91	16.06	16.21	16.36	16.51	16.66	16.81	16.97	17.12	17.27	17.43	17.58
10.0	15.53	15.68	15.83	15.99	16.14	16.29	16.45	16.60	16.76	16.91	17.07	17.23
10.5	15.19	15.35	15.50	15.65	15.81	15.96	16.12	16.28	16.43	16.59	16.75	16.91
11.0	14.89	15.05	15.20	15.36	15.51	15.67	15.83	15.99	16.15	16.31	16.47	16.63
11.5	14.62	14.78	14.93	15.09	15.25	15.41	15.57	15.73	15.89	16.05	16.22	16.38
12.0	14.38	14.53	14.69	14.85	15.01	15.18	15.34	15.50	15.66	15.83	15.99	16.16
12.5	14.16	14.32	14.48	14.64	14.80	14.96	15.13	15.29	15.46	15.62	15.79	15.96
13.0	13.96	14.12	14.28	14.44	14.61	14.77	14.94	15.10	15.27	15.44	15.61	15.78
13.5	13.77	13.94	14.10	14.27	14.43	14.60	14.77	14.94	15.10	15.27	15.44	15.62
14.0	13.61	13.78	13.94	14.11	14.28	14.44	14.61	14.78	14.95	15.12	15.30	15.47
14.5	13.46	13.63	13.79	13.96	14.13	14.30	14.47	14.64	14.82	14.99	15.16	15.34
15.0	13.32	13.49	13.66	13.83	14.00	14.17	14.34	14.52	14.69	14.87	15.04	15.22
15.5	13.20	13.37	13.54	13.71	13.88	14.05	14.23	14.40	14.58	14.76	14.93	15.11
16.0	13.08	13.25	13.43	13.60	13.77	13.95	14.12	14.30	14.48	14.65	14.83	15.01
16.5	12.98	13.15	13.32	13.50	13.67	13.85	14.03	14.20	14.38	14.56	14.74	14.92
17.0	12.88	13.05	13.23	13.41	13.58	13.76	13.94	14.12	14.30	14.48	14.66	14.84
17.5	12.79	12.97	13.14	13.32	13.50	13.68	13.86	14.04	14.22	14.40	14.58	14.77
18.0	12.71	12.89	13.06	13.24	13.42	13.60	13.78	13.96	14.15	14.33	14.51	14.70
18.5	12.63	12.81	12.99	13.17	13.35	13.53	13.72	13.90	14.08	14.27	14.45	14.64
19.0	12.56	12.74	12.92	13.10	13.29	13.47	13.65	13.84	14.02	14.21	14.39	14.58
19.5	12.50	12.68	12.86	13.04	13.23	13.41	13.60	13.78	13.97	14.15	14.34	14.53
20.0	12.44	12.62	12.80	12.99	13.17	13.36	13.54	13.73	13.92	14.11	14.29	14.48
20.5	12.39	12.57	12.75	12.94	13.12	13.31	13.50	13.68	13.87	14.06	14.25	14.44
21.0	12.33	12.52	12.70	12.89	13.08	13.26	13.45	13.64	13.83	14.02	14.21	14.40
21.5	12.29	12.47	12.66	12.85	13.03	13.22	13.41	13.60	13.79	13.98	14.17	14.37
22.0	12.24	12.43	12.62	12.81	12.99	13.18	13.37	13.56	13.75	13.95	14.14	14.33
22.5	12.20	12.39	12.58	12.77	12.96	13.15	13.34	13.53	13.72	13.91	14.11	14.30
23.0	12.17	12.35	12.54	12.73	12.92	13.12	13.31	13.50	13.69	13.89	14.08	14.27
23.5	12.13	12.32	12.51	12.70	12.89	13.08	13.28	13.47	13.66	13.86	14.05	14.25
24.0	12.10	12.29	12.48	12.67	12.86	13.06	13.25	13.44	13.64	13.83	14.03	14.23
24.5	12.07	12.26	12.45	12.64	12.84	13.03	13.23	13.42	13.62	13.81	14.01	14.20
25.0	12.04	12.23	12.43	12.62	12.81	13.01	13.20	13.40	13.59	13.79	13.99	14.18
25.5	12.02	12.21	12.40	12.60	12.79	12.99	13.18	13.38	13.57	13.77	13.97	14.17
26.0	11.99	12.19	12.38	12.57	12.77	12.97	13.16	13.36	13.56	13.75	13.95	14.15
26.5	11.97	12.16	12.36	12.55	12.75	12.95	13.14	13.34	13.54	13.74	13.94	14.14
27.0	11.95	12.14	12.34	12.54	12.73	12.93	13.13	13.32	13.52	13.72	13.92	14.12
27.5	11.93	12.13	12.32	12.52	12.72	12.91	13.11	13.31	13.51	13.71	13.91	14.11
28.0	11.91	12.11	12.31	12.50	12.70	12.90	13.10	13.30	13.50	13.70	13.90	14.10
28.5	11.90	12.09	12.29	12.49	12.69	12.88	13.08	13.28	13.48	13.68	13.89	14.09
29.0	11.88	12.08	12.28	12.47	12.67	12.87	13.07	13.27	13.47	13.67	13.87	14.08
29.5	11.87	12.06	12.26	12.46	12.66	12.86	13.06	13.26	13.46	13.66	13.87	14.07
30.0	11.85	12.05	12.25	12.45	12.65	12.85	13.05	13.25	13.45	13.65	13.86	14.06
31.0	11.83	12.03	12.23	12.43	12.63	12.83	13.03	13.23	13.44	13.64	13.84	14.04
32.0	11.81	12.01	12.21	12.41	12.61	12.81	13.02	13.22	13.42	13.62	13.83	14.03
33.0	11.79	11.99	12.19	12.39	12.60	12.80	13.00	13.21	13.41	13.61	13.82	14.02
34.0	11.78	11.98	12.18	12.38	12.58	12.79	12.99	13.19	13.40	13.60	13.81	14.01
35.0	11.76	11.96	12.17	12.37	12.57	12.78	12.98	13.19	13.39	13.59	13.80	14.00
36.0	11.75	11.95	12.16	12.36	12.56	12.77	12.97	13.18	13.38	13.58	13.79	14.00
37.0	11.74	11.94	12.15	12.35	12.56	12.76	12.97	13.17	13.38	13.58	13.79	13.99
38.0	11.73	11.93	12.14	12.34	12.55	12.75	12.96	13.16	13.37	13.58	13.78	13.99
39.0	11.72	11.93	12.13	12.34	12.54	12.75	12.95	13.16	13.37	13.57	13.78	13.98
40.0	11.72	11.92	12.13	12.33	12.54	12.74	12.95	13.16	13.36	13.57	13.77	13.98

MONTHLY
PAYMENT REQUIRED TO AMORTIZE A $1,000.00 LOAN

TERM IN YEARS	INTEREST RATES 17.00%	17.25%	17.50%	17.75%	18.00%	18.25%	18.50%	18.75%	19.00%	19.25%	19.50%	19.75%
0.5	175.03	175.16	175.28	175.41	175.53	175.65	175.78	175.90	176.03	176.15	176.28	176.40
1.0	91.21	91.33	91.45	91.57	91.68	91.80	91.92	92.04	92.16	92.28	92.40	92.52
1.5	63.34	63.45	63.57	63.69	63.81	63.93	64.05	64.17	64.29	64.41	64.53	64.65
2.0	49.45	49.57	49.69	49.81	49.93	50.05	50.17	50.29	50.41	50.54	50.66	50.78
2.5	41.15	41.28	41.40	41.52	41.64	41.77	41.89	42.01	42.14	42.26	42.39	42.51
3.0	35.66	35.78	35.91	36.03	36.16	36.28	36.41	36.53	36.66	36.79	36.91	37.04
3.5	31.76	31.89	32.01	32.14	32.27	32.40	32.53	32.65	32.78	32.91	33.04	33.17
4.0	28.86	28.99	29.12	29.25	29.38	29.51	29.64	29.77	29.91	30.04	30.17	30.30
4.5	26.63	26.76	26.89	27.02	27.16	27.29	27.42	27.56	27.69	27.83	27.96	28.10
5.0	24.86	24.99	25.13	25.26	25.40	25.53	25.67	25.81	25.95	26.08	26.22	26.36
5.5	23.43	23.56	23.70	23.84	23.98	24.12	24.26	24.40	24.54	24.68	24.82	24.96
6.0	22.25	22.39	22.53	22.67	22.81	22.95	23.10	23.24	23.38	23.53	23.67	23.81
6.5	21.27	21.41	21.55	21.70	21.84	21.99	22.13	22.28	22.42	22.57	22.71	22.86
7.0	20.44	20.59	20.73	20.88	21.02	21.17	21.32	21.46	21.61	21.76	21.91	22.06
7.5	19.73	19.88	20.03	20.18	20.33	20.48	20.63	20.78	20.93	21.08	21.23	21.38
8.0	19.13	19.28	19.43	19.58	19.73	19.88	20.03	20.19	20.34	20.49	20.65	20.80
8.5	18.60	18.75	18.90	19.06	19.21	19.37	19.52	19.68	19.83	19.99	20.15	20.30
9.0	18.14	18.30	18.45	18.61	18.76	18.92	19.08	19.23	19.39	19.55	19.71	19.87
9.5	17.74	17.90	18.05	18.21	18.37	18.53	18.69	18.85	19.01	19.17	19.33	19.49
10.0	17.38	17.54	17.70	17.86	18.02	18.18	18.35	18.51	18.67	18.84	19.00	19.17
10.5	17.07	17.23	17.39	17.56	17.72	17.88	18.05	18.21	18.38	18.54	18.71	18.88
11.0	16.79	16.96	17.12	17.28	17.45	17.61	17.78	17.95	18.12	18.28	18.45	18.62
11.5	16.55	16.71	16.88	17.04	17.21	17.38	17.55	17.71	17.88	18.05	18.23	18.40
12.0	16.32	16.49	16.66	16.83	17.00	17.17	17.34	17.51	17.68	17.85	18.02	18.20
12.5	16.13	16.29	16.46	16.63	16.81	16.98	17.15	17.32	17.50	17.67	17.84	18.02
13.0	15.95	16.12	16.29	16.46	16.64	16.81	16.98	17.16	17.33	17.51	17.69	17.86
13.5	15.79	15.96	16.13	16.31	16.48	16.66	16.83	17.01	17.19	17.36	17.54	17.72
14.0	15.64	15.82	15.99	16.17	16.34	16.52	16.70	16.88	17.06	17.24	17.42	17.60
14.5	15.51	15.69	15.87	16.04	16.22	16.40	16.58	16.76	16.94	17.12	17.30	17.48
15.0	15.40	15.57	15.75	15.93	16.11	16.29	16.47	16.65	16.83	17.02	17.20	17.38
15.5	15.29	15.47	15.65	15.83	16.01	16.19	16.37	16.56	16.74	16.92	17.11	17.29
10.0	15.19	15.37	15.55	15.74	15.92	16.10	16.20	16.47	16.65	16.84	17.03	17.21
16.5	15.10	15.29	15.47	15.65	15.84	16.02	16.20	16.39	16.58	16.76	16.95	17.14
17.0	15.02	15.21	15.39	15.58	15.76	15.95	16.13	16.32	16.51	16.70	16.88	17.07
17.5	14.95	15.14	15.32	15.51	15.69	15.88	16.07	16.26	16.45	16.63	16.82	17.02
18.0	14.88	15.07	15.26	15.44	15.63	15.82	16.01	16.20	16.39	16.58	16.77	16.96
18.5	14.82	15.01	15.20	15.39	15.58	15.77	15.96	16.15	16.34	16.53	16.72	16.91
19.0	14.77	14.96	15.15	15.34	15.53	15.72	15.91	16.10	16.29	16.48	16.68	16.87
19.5	14.72	14.91	15.10	15.29	15.48	15.67	15.86	16.06	16.25	16.44	16.64	16.83
20.0	14.67	14.86	15.05	15.25	15.44	15.63	15.82	16.02	16.21	16.41	16.60	16.80
20.5	14.63	14.82	15.01	15.21	15.40	15.59	15.79	15.98	16.18	16.37	16.57	16.77
21.0	14.59	14.79	14.98	15.17	15.37	15.56	15.76	15.95	16.15	16.34	16.54	16.74
21.5	14.56	14.75	14.94	15.14	15.33	15.53	15.73	15.92	16.12	16.32	16.51	16.71
22.0	14.53	14.72	14.91	15.11	15.31	15.50	15.70	15.90	16.09	16.29	16.49	16.69
22.5	14.50	14.69	14.89	15.08	15.28	15.48	15.67	15.87	16.07	16.27	16.47	16.67
23.0	14.47	14.67	14.86	15.06	15.26	15.45	15.65	15.85	16.05	16.25	16.45	16.65
23.5	14.45	14.64	14.84	15.04	15.23	15.43	15.63	15.83	16.03	16.23	16.43	16.63
24.0	14.42	14.62	14.82	15.02	15.21	15.41	15.61	15.81	16.01	16.21	16.41	16.61
24.5	14.40	14.60	14.80	15.00	15.20	15.40	15.60	15.80	16.00	16.20	16.40	16.60
25.0	14.38	14.58	14.78	14.98	15.18	15.38	15.58	15.78	15.98	16.18	16.39	16.59
25.5	14.37	14.56	14.76	14.96	15.16	15.36	15.57	15.77	15.97	16.17	16.37	16.58
26.0	14.35	14.55	14.75	14.95	15.15	15.35	15.55	15.75	15.96	16.16	16.36	16.56
26.5	14.34	14.54	14.74	14.94	15.14	15.34	15.54	15.74	15.95	16.15	16.35	16.56
27.0	14.32	14.52	14.72	14.92	15.13	15.33	15.53	15.73	15.94	16.14	16.34	16.55
27.5	14.31	14.51	14.71	14.91	15.12	15.32	15.52	15.72	15.93	16.13	16.33	16.54
28.0	14.30	14.50	14.70	14.90	15.11	15.31	15.51	15.72	15.92	16.12	16.33	16.53
28.5	14.29	14.49	14.69	14.89	15.10	15.30	15.50	15.71	15.91	16.12	16.32	16.53
29.0	14.28	14.48	14.68	14.89	15.09	15.29	15.50	15.70	15.91	16.11	16.31	16.52
29.5	14.27	14.47	14.68	14.88	15.08	15.29	15.49	15.69	15.90	16.10	16.31	16.51
30.0	14.26	14.46	14.67	14.87	15.08	15.28	15.48	15.69	15.89	16.10	16.30	16.51
31.0	14.25	14.45	14.66	14.86	15.06	15.27	15.47	15.68	15.88	16.09	16.30	16.50
32.0	14.24	14.44	14.64	14.85	15.05	15.26	15.47	15.67	15.88	16.08	16.29	16.49
33.0	14.23	14.43	14.64	14.84	15.05	15.25	15.46	15.66	15.87	16.08	16.28	16.49
34.0	14.22	14.42	14.63	14.83	15.04	15.25	15.45	15.66	15.86	16.07	16.28	16.48
35.0	14.21	14.42	14.62	14.83	15.03	15.24	15.45	15.65	15.86	16.07	16.27	16.48
36.0	14.20	14.41	14.62	14.82	15.03	15.24	15.44	15.65	15.86	16.06	16.27	16.48
37.0	14.20	14.41	14.61	14.82	15.03	15.23	15.44	15.65	15.85	16.06	16.27	16.47
38.0	14.19	14.40	14.61	14.81	15.02	15.23	15.44	15.64	15.85	16.06	16.27	16.47
39.0	14.19	14.40	14.60	14.81	15.02	15.23	15.43	15.64	15.85	16.06	16.26	16.47
40.0	14.19	14.40	14.60	14.81	15.02	15.22	15.43	15.64	15.85	16.05	16.26	16.47

MONTHLY
PAYMENT REQUIRED TO AMORTIZE A $1,000.00 LOAN

TERM IN YEARS	INTEREST RATES											
	20.00%	20.25%	20.50%	20.75%	21.00%	21.25%	21.50%	21.75%	22.00%	22.25%	22.50%	22.75%
0.5	176.53	176.65	176.78	176.90	177.03	177.15	177.28	177.40	177.53	177.65	177.78	177.90
1.0	92.64	92.76	92.88	93.00	93.12	93.24	93.36	93.48	93.60	93.72	93.84	93.96
1.5	64.77	64.89	65.01	65.13	65.25	65.37	65.49	65.61	65.73	65.85	65.98	66.10
2.0	50.90	51.02	51.15	51.27	51.39	51.51	51.64	51.76	51.88	52.01	52.13	52.25
2.5	42.63	42.76	42.88	43.01	43.13	43.26	43.39	43.51	43.64	43.76	43.89	44.02
3.0	37.17	37.30	37.42	37.55	37.68	37.81	37.94	38.07	38.20	38.32	38.45	38.58
3.5	33.30	33.43	33.56	33.69	33.83	33.96	34.09	34.22	34.35	34.49	34.62	34.75
4.0	30.44	30.57	30.70	30.84	30.97	31.11	31.24	31.38	31.51	31.65	31.78	31.92
4.5	28.23	28.37	28.51	28.64	28.78	28.92	29.06	29.20	29.33	29.47	29.61	29.75
5.0	26.50	26.64	26.78	26.92	27.06	27.20	27.34	27.48	27.62	27.77	27.91	28.05
5.5	25.10	25.24	25.39	25.53	25.67	25.82	25.96	26.11	26.25	26.40	26.54	26.69
6.0	23.96	24.10	24.25	24.39	24.54	24.69	24.84	24.98	25.13	25.28	25.43	25.58
6.5	23.01	23.16	23.30	23.45	23.60	23.75	23.90	24.05	24.21	24.36	24.51	24.66
7.0	22.21	22.36	22.51	22.66	22.82	22.97	23.12	23.28	23.43	23.59	23.74	23.90
7.5	21.54	21.69	21.84	22.00	22.15	22.31	22.46	22.62	22.78	22.94	23.09	23.25
8.0	20.96	21.11	21.27	21.43	21.59	21.74	21.90	22.06	22.22	22.38	22.54	22.70
8.5	20.46	20.62	20.78	20.94	21.10	21.26	21.42	21.58	21.75	21.91	22.07	22.24
9.0	20.03	20.19	20.35	20.52	20.68	20.84	21.01	21.17	21.34	21.50	21.67	21.84
9.5	19.66	19.82	19.99	20.15	20.32	20.48	20.65	20.82	20.98	21.15	21.32	21.49
10.0	19.33	19.50	19.66	19.83	20.00	20.17	20.34	20.50	20.67	20.85	21.02	21.19
10.5	19.04	19.21	19.38	19.55	19.72	19.89	20.06	20.23	20.41	20.58	20.75	20.93
11.0	18.79	18.96	19.13	19.30	19.48	19.65	19.82	20.00	20.17	20.35	20.52	20.70
11.5	18.57	18.74	18.91	19.09	19.26	19.44	19.61	19.79	19.97	20.14	20.32	20.50
12.0	18.37	18.55	18.72	18.90	19.07	19.25	19.43	19.61	19.78	19.96	20.14	20.32
12.5	18.20	18.37	18.55	18.73	18.91	19.08	19.26	19.44	19.62	19.81	19.99	20.17
13.0	18.04	18.22	18.40	18.58	18.76	18.94	19.12	19.30	19.48	19.67	19.85	20.03
13.5	17.90	18.08	18.26	18.44	18.63	18.81	18.99	19.17	19.36	19.54	19.73	19.91
14.0	17.78	17.96	18.14	18.32	18.51	18.69	18.88	19.06	19.25	19.43	19.62	19.81
14.5	17.67	17.85	18.03	18.22	18.40	18.59	18.78	18.96	19.15	19.34	19.53	19.71
15.0	17.57	17.75	17.94	18.12	18.31	18.50	18.69	18.87	19.06	19.25	19.44	19.63
15.5	17.48	17.67	17.85	18.04	18.23	18.42	18.61	18.80	18.99	19.18	19.37	19.56
16.0	17.40	17.59	17.78	17.96	18.15	18.34	18.53	18.72	18.92	19.11	19.30	19.49
16.5	17.33	17.52	17.71	17.90	18.09	18.28	18.47	18.66	18.85	19.05	19.24	19.43
17.0	17.26	17.45	17.65	17.84	18.03	18.22	18.41	18.61	18.80	18.99	19.19	19.38
17.5	17.21	17.40	17.59	17.78	17.98	18.17	18.36	18.56	18.75	18.95	19.14	19.34
18.0	17.15	17.35	17.54	17.73	17.93	18.12	18.32	18.51	18.71	18.90	19.10	19.30
18.5	17.11	17.30	17.50	17.69	17.88	18.08	18.28	18.47	18.67	18.87	19.06	19.26
19.0	17.07	17.26	17.46	17.65	17.85	18.04	18.24	18.44	18.63	18.83	19.03	19.23
19.5	17.03	17.22	17.42	17.62	17.81	18.01	18.21	18.41	18.60	18.80	19.00	19.20
20.0	16.99	17.19	17.39	17.58	17.78	17.98	18.18	18.38	18.58	18.77	18.97	19.17
20.5	16.96	17.16	17.36	17.56	17.75	17.95	18.15	18.35	18.55	18.75	18.95	19.15
21.0	16.93	17.13	17.33	17.53	17.73	17.93	18.13	18.33	18.53	18.73	18.93	19.13
21.5	16.91	17.11	17.31	17.51	17.71	17.91	18.11	18.31	18.51	18.71	18.91	19.11
22.0	16.89	17.09	17.29	17.49	17.69	17.89	18.09	18.29	18.49	18.69	18.90	19.10
22.5	16.87	17.07	17.27	17.47	17.67	17.87	18.07	18.27	18.48	18.68	18.88	19.08
23.0	16.85	17.05	17.25	17.45	17.65	17.85	18.06	18.26	18.46	18.66	18.87	19.07
23.5	16.83	17.03	17.23	17.44	17.64	17.84	18.04	18.25	18.45	18.65	18.86	19.06
24.0	16.82	17.02	17.22	17.42	17.62	17.83	18.03	18.23	18.44	18.64	18.84	19.05
24.5	16.80	17.00	17.21	17.41	17.61	17.82	18.02	18.22	18.43	18.63	18.83	19.04
25.0	16.79	16.99	17.20	17.40	17.60	17.81	18.01	18.21	18.42	18.62	18.83	19.03
25.5	16.78	16.98	17.18	17.39	17.59	17.80	18.00	18.20	18.41	18.61	18.82	19.02
26.0	16.77	16.97	17.18	17.38	17.58	17.79	17.99	18.20	18.40	18.61	18.81	19.02
26.5	16.76	16.96	17.17	17.37	17.58	17.78	17.99	18.19	18.40	18.60	18.81	19.01
27.0	16.75	16.95	17.16	17.36	17.57	17.77	17.98	18.18	18.39	18.59	18.80	19.01
27.5	16.74	16.95	17.15	17.36	17.56	17.77	17.97	18.18	18.38	18.59	18.80	19.00
28.0	16.74	16.94	17.15	17.35	17.56	17.76	17.97	18.17	18.38	18.59	18.79	19.00
28.5	16.73	16.94	17.14	17.35	17.55	17.76	17.96	18.17	18.38	18.58	18.79	18.99
29.0	16.72	16.93	17.14	17.34	17.55	17.75	17.96	18.17	18.37	18.58	18.78	18.99
29.5	16.72	16.93	17.13	17.34	17.54	17.75	17.96	18.16	18.37	18.57	18.78	18.99
30.0	16.72	16.92	17.13	17.33	17.54	17.75	17.95	18.16	18.36	18.57	18.78	18.99
31.0	16.71	16.91	17.12	17.33	17.53	17.74	17.95	18.15	18.36	18.57	18.77	18.98
32.0	16.70	16.91	17.11	17.32	17.53	17.73	17.94	18.15	18.36	18.56	18.77	18.98
33.0	16.70	16.90	17.11	17.32	17.52	17.73	17.94	18.14	18.35	18.56	18.77	18.97
34.0	16.69	16.90	17.11	17.31	17.52	17.73	17.93	18.14	18.35	18.56	18.76	18.97
35.0	16.69	16.89	17.10	17.31	17.52	17.72	17.93	18.14	18.35	18.55	18.76	18.97
36.0	16.68	16.89	17.10	17.31	17.51	17.72	17.93	18.14	18.35	18.55	18.76	18.97
37.0	16.68	16.89	17.10	17.31	17.51	17.72	17.93	18.14	18.34	18.55	18.76	18.97
38.0	16.68	16.89	17.10	17.30	17.51	17.72	17.93	18.14	18.34	18.55	18.76	18.97
39.0	16.68	16.89	17.09	17.30	17.51	17.72	17.93	18.13	18.34	18.55	18.76	18.97
40.0	16.68	16.89	17.09	17.30	17.51	17.72	17.93	18.13	18.34	18.55	18.76	18.97

MONTHLY
PAYMENT REQUIRED TO AMORTIZE A $1,000.00 LOAN

TERM IN YEARS	23.00%	23.25%	23.50%	23.75%	24.00%	24.25%	24.50%	24.75%	25.00%	25.25%	25.50%	25.75%
0.5	178.03	178.15	178.28	178.41	178.53	178.66	178.78	178.91	179.03	179.16	179.28	179.41
1.0	94.08	94.20	94.32	94.44	94.56	94.69	94.81	94.93	95.05	95.17	95.29	95.41
1.5	66.22	66.34	66.46	66.58	66.71	66.83	66.95	67.07	67.20	67.32	67.44	67.57
2.0	52.38	52.50	52.63	52.75	52.88	53.00	53.13	53.25	53.38	53.50	53.63	53.75
2.5	44.14	44.27	44.40	44.53	44.65	44.78	44.91	45.04	45.17	45.30	45.43	45.56
3.0	38.71	38.85	38.98	39.11	39.24	39.37	39.50	39.63	39.76	39.90	40.03	40.16
3.5	34.89	35.02	35.15	35.29	35.42	35.56	35.69	35.83	35.96	36.10	36.24	36.37
4.0	32.06	32.19	32.33	32.47	32.61	32.75	32.88	33.02	33.16	33.30	33.44	33.58
4.5	29.89	30.03	30.17	30.32	30.46	30.60	30.74	30.88	31.03	31.17	31.31	31.46
5.0	28.20	28.34	28.48	28.63	28.77	28.92	29.06	29.21	29.36	29.50	29.65	29.80
5.5	26.84	26.98	27.13	27.28	27.43	27.57	27.72	27.87	28.02	28.17	28.32	28.48
6.0	25.73	25.88	26.03	26.18	26.33	26.48	26.64	26.79	26.94	27.10	27.25	27.40
6.5	24.81	24.97	25.12	25.28	25.43	25.59	25.74	25.90	26.05	26.21	26.37	26.53
7.0	24.05	24.21	24.37	24.52	24.68	24.84	25.00	25.16	25.32	25.48	25.64	25.80
7.5	23.41	23.57	23.73	23.89	24.05	24.21	24.37	24.54	24.70	24.86	25.03	25.19
8.0	22.87	23.03	23.19	23.35	23.52	23.68	23.85	24.01	24.18	24.34	24.51	24.68
8.5	22.40	22.57	22.73	22.90	23.06	23.23	23.40	23.57	23.74	23.90	24.07	24.24
9.0	22.00	22.17	22.34	22.51	22.68	22.85	23.02	23.19	23.36	23.53	23.70	23.87
9.5	21.66	21.83	22.00	22.17	22.34	22.51	22.69	22.86	23.03	23.21	23.38	23.56
10.0	21.36	21.53	21.71	21.88	22.05	22.23	22.40	22.58	22.75	22.93	23.11	23.29
10.5	21.10	21.28	21.45	21.63	21.80	21.98	22.16	22.34	22.51	22.69	22.87	23.05
11.0	20.87	21.05	21.23	21.41	21.59	21.76	21.94	22.12	22.30	22.49	22.67	22.85
11.5	20.68	20.86	21.04	21.22	21.40	21.58	21.76	21.94	22.12	22.31	22.49	22.67
12.0	20.50	20.68	20.87	21.05	21.23	21.41	21.60	21.78	21.97	22.15	22.34	22.52
12.5	20.35	20.53	20.72	20.90	21.09	21.27	21.46	21.64	21.83	22.02	22.20	22.39
13.0	20.22	20.40	20.59	20.77	20.96	21.15	21.33	21.52	21.71	21.90	22.09	22.27
13.5	20.10	20.29	20.47	20.66	20.85	21.04	21.22	21.41	21.60	21.79	21.98	22.17
14.0	20.00	20.18	20.37	20.56	20.75	20.94	21.13	21.32	21.51	21.70	21.89	22.09
14.5	19.90	20.09	20.28	20.47	20.66	20.85	21.05	21.24	21.43	21.62	21.82	22.01
15.0	19.82	20.01	20.20	20.40	20.59	20.78	20.97	21.17	21.36	21.55	21.75	21.94
15.5	19.75	19.94	20.13	20.33	20.52	20.71	20.91	21.10	21.30	21.49	21.69	21.89
16.0	19.69	19.88	20.07	20.27	20.46	20.66	20.85	21.05	21.24	21.44	21.64	21.83
16.5	19.63	19.82	20.02	20.21	20.41	20.61	20.80	21.00	21.20	21.39	21.59	21.79
17.0	19.58	19.77	19.97	20.17	20.36	20.56	20.76	20.96	21.15	21.35	21.55	21.75
17.5	19.53	19.73	19.93	20.12	20.32	20.52	20.72	20.92	21.12	21.32	21.51	21.71
18.0	19.49	19.69	19.89	20.09	20.29	20.49	20.68	20.88	21.08	21.28	21.48	21.68
18.5	19.46	19.66	19.86	20.06	20.25	20.45	20.65	20.85	21.05	21.26	21.46	21.66
19.0	19.43	19.63	19.83	20.03	20.23	20.43	20.63	20.83	21.03	21.23	21.43	21.63
19.5	19.40	19.60	19.80	20.00	20.20	20.40	20.60	20.81	21.01	21.21	21.41	21.61
20.0	19.38	19.58	19.78	19.98	20.18	20.38	20.58	20.78	20.99	21.19	21.39	21.60
20.5	19.35	19.55	19.76	19.96	20.16	20.36	20.56	20.77	20.97	21.17	21.38	21.58
21.0	19.33	19.54	19.74	19.94	20.14	20.34	20.55	20.75	20.95	21.16	21.36	21.57
21.5	19.32	19.52	19.72	19.92	20.13	20.33	20.53	20.74	20.94	21.14	21.35	21.55
22.0	19.30	19.50	19.71	19.91	20.11	20.32	20.52	20.72	20.93	21.13	21.34	21.54
22.5	19.29	19.49	19.69	19.90	20.10	20.30	20.51	20.71	20.92	21.12	21.33	21.53
23.0	19.27	19.48	19.68	19.89	20.09	20.29	20.50	20.70	20.91	21.11	21.32	21.52
23.5	19.26	19.47	19.67	19.88	20.08	20.29	20.49	20.70	20.90	21.11	21.31	21.52
24.0	19.25	19.46	19.66	19.87	20.07	20.28	20.48	20.69	20.89	21.10	21.30	21.51
24.5	19.24	19.45	19.65	19.86	20.06	20.27	20.48	20.68	20.89	21.09	21.30	21.51
25.0	19.24	19.44	19.65	19.85	20.06	20.26	20.47	20.68	20.88	21.09	21.29	21.50
25.5	19.23	19.43	19.64	19.85	20.05	20.26	20.46	20.67	20.88	21.08	21.29	21.50
26.0	19.22	19.43	19.63	19.84	20.05	20.25	20.46	20.67	20.87	21.08	21.29	21.49
26.5	19.22	19.42	19.63	19.84	20.04	20.25	20.45	20.66	20.87	21.07	21.28	21.49
27.0	19.21	19.42	19.62	19.83	20.04	20.24	20.45	20.66	20.86	21.07	21.28	21.49
27.5	19.21	19.41	19.62	19.83	20.03	20.24	20.45	20.65	20.86	21.07	21.28	21.48
28.0	19.20	19.41	19.62	19.82	20.03	20.24	20.44	20.65	20.86	21.07	21.27	21.48
28.5	19.20	19.41	19.61	19.82	20.03	20.23	20.44	20.65	20.86	21.06	21.27	21.48
29.0	19.20	19.40	19.61	19.82	20.03	20.23	20.44	20.65	20.85	21.06	21.27	21.48
29.5	19.19	19.40	19.61	19.82	20.02	20.23	20.44	20.64	20.85	21.06	21.27	21.48
30.0	19.19	19.40	19.61	19.81	20.02	20.23	20.44	20.64	20.85	21.06	21.27	21.47
31.0	19.19	19.40	19.60	19.81	20.02	20.23	20.43	20.64	20.85	21.06	21.26	21.47
32.0	19.18	19.39	19.60	19.81	20.01	20.22	20.43	20.64	20.84	21.05	21.26	21.47
33.0	19.18	19.39	19.60	19.81	20.01	20.22	20.43	20.64	20.84	21.05	21.26	21.47
34.0	19.18	19.39	19.60	19.80	20.01	20.22	20.43	20.63	20.84	21.05	21.26	21.47
35.0	19.18	19.39	19.59	19.80	20.01	20.22	20.43	20.63	20.84	21.05	21.26	21.47
36.0	19.18	19.38	19.59	19.80	20.01	20.22	20.42	20.63	20.84	21.05	21.26	21.47
37.0	19.18	19.38	19.59	19.80	20.01	20.22	20.42	20.63	20.84	21.05	21.26	21.47
38.0	19.17	19.38	19.59	19.80	20.01	20.22	20.42	20.63	20.84	21.05	21.26	21.46
39.0	19.17	19.38	19.59	19.80	20.01	20.22	20.42	20.63	20.84	21.05	21.26	21.46
40.0	19.17	19.38	19.59	19.80	20.01	20.21	20.42	20.63	20.84	21.05	21.26	21.46

QUARTERLY
PAYMENT REQUIRED TO AMORTIZE A $1,000.00 LOAN

TERM IN YEARS	2.00%	2.25%	2.50%	2.75%	3.00%	3.25%	3.50%	3.75%	4.00%	4.25%	4.50%	4.75%
0.5	503.76	504.23	504.70	505.17	505.64	506.11	506.58	507.05	507.52	507.99	508.46	508.93
1.0	253.14	253.53	253.92	254.32	254.71	255.10	255.50	255.89	256.29	256.68	257.08	257.47
1.5	169.60	169.97	170.34	170.70	171.07	171.44	171.81	172.18	172.55	172.92	173.30	173.67
2.0	127.83	128.19	128.55	128.90	129.26	129.62	129.98	130.34	130.70	131.06	131.42	131.78
2.5	102.78	103.12	103.47	103.83	104.18	104.53	104.88	105.23	105.59	105.94	106.30	106.65
3.0	86.07	86.42	86.76	87.11	87.46	87.80	88.15	88.50	88.85	89.21	89.56	89.91
3.5	74.14	74.48	74.83	75.17	75.52	75.86	76.21	76.56	76.91	77.26	77.61	77.96
4.0	65.19	65.54	65.88	66.22	66.56	66.91	67.25	67.60	67.95	68.30	68.65	69.00
4.5	58.24	58.58	58.92	59.26	59.60	59.95	60.29	60.64	60.99	61.34	61.69	62.04
5.0	52.67	53.01	53.35	53.69	54.04	54.38	54.73	55.07	55.42	55.77	56.12	56.47
5.5	48.12	48.46	48.80	49.14	49.48	49.83	50.17	50.52	50.87	51.22	51.57	51.92
6.0	44.33	44.66	45.00	45.35	45.69	46.03	46.38	46.73	47.08	47.43	47.78	48.14
6.5	41.12	41.46	41.80	42.14	42.48	42.83	43.17	43.52	43.87	44.23	44.58	44.94
7.0	38.37	38.71	39.05	39.39	39.73	40.08	40.43	40.78	41.13	41.48	41.84	42.19
7.5	35.98	36.32	36.66	37.01	37.35	37.70	38.05	38.40	38.75	39.11	39.46	39.82
8.0	33.90	34.24	34.58	34.93	35.27	35.62	35.97	36.32	36.68	37.03	37.39	37.75
8.5	32.06	32.40	32.74	33.09	33.44	33.78	34.14	34.49	34.84	35.20	35.56	35.92
9.0	30.43	30.77	31.11	31.46	31.80	32.15	32.51	32.86	33.22	33.58	33.94	34.30
9.5	28.97	29.31	29.65	30.00	30.35	30.70	31.05	31.41	31.77	32.13	32.49	32.86
10.0	27.65	27.99	28.34	28.69	29.04	29.39	29.74	30.10	30.46	30.82	31.19	31.56
10.5	26.46	26.80	27.15	27.50	27.85	28.20	28.56	28.92	29.28	29.65	30.01	30.38
11.0	25.38	25.72	26.07	26.42	26.77	27.13	27.49	27.85	28.21	28.58	28.94	29.32
11.5	24.39	24.74	25.09	25.44	25.79	26.15	26.51	26.87	27.23	27.60	27.97	28.35
12.0	23.49	23.84	24.18	24.54	24.89	25.25	25.61	25.97	26.34	26.71	27.08	27.46
12.5	22.66	23.00	23.35	23.71	24.06	24.42	24.78	25.15	25.52	25.89	26.26	26.64
13.0	21.89	22.24	22.59	22.94	23.30	23.66	24.02	24.39	24.76	25.13	25.51	25.89
13.5	21.18	21.53	21.88	22.24	22.59	22.96	23.32	23.69	24.06	24.44	24.82	25.20
14.0	20.52	20.87	21.22	21.58	21.94	22.30	22.67	23.04	23.41	23.79	24.17	24.55
14.5	19.91	20.26	20.61	20.97	21.33	21.70	22.06	22.44	22.81	23.19	23.57	23.96
15.0	19.34	19.69	20.04	20.40	20.76	21.13	21.50	21.87	22.25	22.63	23.01	23.40
15.5	18.80	19.15	19.51	19.87	20.23	20.60	20.97	21.35	21.73	22.11	22.49	22.89
16.0	18.30	18.65	19.01	19.37	19.74	20.10	20.48	20.85	21.24	21.62	22.01	22.40
16.5	17.83	18.18	18.54	18.90	19.27	19.64	20.01	20.39	20.78	21.16	21.55	21.95
17.0	17.39	17.74	18.10	18.46	18.83	19.20	19.58	19.96	20.34	20.73	21.12	21.52
17.5	16.97	17.33	17.69	18.05	18.42	18.79	19.17	19.55	19.94	20.33	20.72	21.12
18.0	16.58	16.93	17.30	17.66	18.03	18.41	18.78	19.17	19.56	19.95	20.34	20.74
18.5	16.21	16.56	16.92	17.29	17.66	18.04	18.42	18.80	19.19	19.59	19.99	20.39
19.0	15.85	16.21	16.57	16.94	17.32	17.69	18.07	18.46	18.85	19.25	19.65	20.05
19.5	15.52	15.88	16.24	16.61	16.99	17.36	17.75	18.14	18.53	18.93	19.33	19.74
20.0	15.20	15.56	15.93	16.30	16.67	17.05	17.44	17.83	18.22	18.62	19.03	19.44
20.5	14.90	15.26	15.63	16.00	16.38	16.76	17.14	17.54	17.93	18.34	18.74	19.15
21.0	14.61	14.98	15.34	15.72	16.09	16.48	16.87	17.26	17.66	18.06	18.47	18.88
21.5	14.34	14.70	15.07	15.45	15.83	16.21	16.60	17.00	17.40	17.80	18.21	18.63
22.0	14.08	14.44	14.81	15.19	15.57	15.96	16.35	16.74	17.15	17.55	17.97	18.38
22.5	13.83	14.20	14.57	14.94	15.32	15.71	16.11	16.50	16.91	17.32	17.73	18.15
23.0	13.59	13.96	14.33	14.71	15.09	15.48	15.88	16.28	16.68	17.09	17.51	17.93
23.5	13.36	13.73	14.10	14.48	14.87	15.26	15.66	16.06	16.46	16.88	17.30	17.72
24.0	13.15	13.51	13.89	14.27	14.66	15.05	15.45	15.85	16.26	16.67	17.09	17.52
24.5	12.94	13.31	13.68	14.06	14.45	14.84	15.24	15.65	16.06	16.48	16.90	17.33
25.0	12.74	13.11	13.48	13.87	14.26	14.65	15.05	15.46	15.87	16.29	16.71	17.14
25.5	12.54	12.92	13.29	13.68	14.07	14.46	14.87	15.27	15.69	16.11	16.54	16.97
26.0	12.36	12.73	13.11	13.50	13.89	14.29	14.69	15.10	15.52	15.94	16.37	16.80
26.5	12.18	12.56	12.93	13.32	13.71	14.11	14.52	14.93	15.35	15.77	16.20	16.64
27.0	12.01	12.39	12.77	13.15	13.55	13.95	14.36	14.77	15.19	15.62	16.05	16.49
27.5	11.85	12.22	12.60	12.99	13.39	13.79	14.20	14.61	15.04	15.46	15.90	16.34
28.0	11.69	12.06	12.45	12.84	13.23	13.64	14.05	14.46	14.89	15.32	15.75	16.20
28.5	11.53	11.91	12.30	12.69	13.09	13.49	13.90	14.32	14.75	15.18	15.62	16.06
29.0	11.39	11.77	12.15	12.54	12.94	13.35	13.76	14.18	14.61	15.04	15.48	15.93
29.5	11.24	11.62	12.01	12.40	12.81	13.21	13.63	14.05	14.48	14.91	15.36	15.80
30.0	11.11	11.49	11.88	12.27	12.67	13.08	13.50	13.92	14.35	14.79	15.23	15.68
31.0	10.85	11.23	11.62	12.02	12.42	12.83	13.25	13.68	14.11	14.55	15.00	15.45
32.0	10.60	10.99	11.38	11.78	12.19	12.60	13.02	13.45	13.89	14.33	14.79	15.24
33.0	10.37	10.76	11.15	11.56	11.97	12.38	12.81	13.24	13.68	14.13	14.58	15.05
34.0	10.16	10.55	10.94	11.35	11.76	12.18	12.61	13.05	13.49	13.94	14.40	14.86
35.0	9.95	10.34	10.74	11.15	11.57	11.99	12.42	12.86	13.31	13.76	14.22	14.69
36.0	9.76	10.16	10.56	10.97	11.39	11.81	12.25	12.69	13.14	13.60	14.06	14.53
37.0	9.58	9.98	10.38	10.79	11.21	11.64	12.08	12.53	12.98	13.44	13.91	14.39
38.0	9.41	9.81	10.22	10.63	11.05	11.49	11.93	12.37	12.83	13.30	13.77	14.25
39.0	9.25	9.65	10.06	10.48	10.90	11.34	11.78	12.23	12.69	13.16	13.63	14.12
40.0	9.10	9.50	9.91	10.33	10.76	11.20	11.64	12.10	12.56	13.03	13.51	14.00

QUARTERLY
PAYMENT REQUIRED TO AMORTIZE A $1,000.00 LOAN

TERM IN YEARS	INTEREST RATES											
	5.00%	5.25%	5.50%	5.75%	6.00%	6.25%	6.50%	6.75%	7.00%	7.25%	7.50%	7.75%
0.5	509.40	509.87	510.34	510.81	511.28	511.75	512.23	512.70	513.17	513.64	514.11	514.58
1.0	257.87	258.26	258.66	259.05	259.45	259.85	260.24	260.64	261.04	261.43	261.83	262.23
1.5	174.04	174.41	174.78	175.16	175.53	175.90	176.28	176.65	177.03	177.40	177.78	178.15
2.0	132.14	132.50	132.86	133.23	133.59	133.95	134.32	134.68	135.05	135.41	135.78	136.15
2.5	107.01	107.36	107.72	108.08	108.44	108.80	109.16	109.52	109.88	110.24	110.60	110.97
3.0	90.26	90.62	90.97	91.33	91.68	92.04	92.40	92.76	93.12	93.48	93.84	94.20
3.5	78.31	78.66	79.02	79.37	79.73	80.09	80.44	80.80	81.16	81.52	81.88	82.24
4.0	69.35	69.70	70.06	70.41	70.77	71.13	71.49	71.84	72.20	72.57	72.93	73.29
4.5	62.39	62.74	63.10	63.45	63.81	64.17	64.53	64.89	65.25	65.61	65.98	66.34
5.0	56.83	57.18	57.54	57.89	58.25	58.61	58.97	59.33	59.70	60.06	60.43	60.79
5.5	52.28	52.63	52.99	53.35	53.71	54.07	54.43	54.80	55.16	55.53	55.90	56.27
6.0	48.49	48.85	49.21	49.57	49.93	50.29	50.66	51.02	51.39	51.76	52.13	52.50
6.5	45.29	45.65	46.01	46.37	46.74	47.10	47.47	47.84	48.21	48.58	48.95	49.33
7.0	42.55	42.91	43.28	43.64	44.01	44.37	44.74	45.11	45.49	45.86	46.24	46.62
7.5	40.18	40.55	40.91	41.28	41.64	42.01	42.39	42.76	43.13	43.51	43.89	44.27
8.0	38.11	38.48	38.84	39.21	39.58	39.95	40.33	40.70	41.08	41.46	41.85	42.23
8.5	36.29	36.66	37.02	37.39	37.77	38.14	38.52	38.90	39.28	39.66	40.05	40.43
9.0	34.67	35.04	35.41	35.78	36.16	36.53	36.91	37.30	37.68	38.07	38.45	38.85
9.5	33.22	33.60	33.97	34.34	34.72	35.10	35.48	35.87	36.25	36.64	37.04	37.43
10.0	31.93	32.30	32.67	33.05	33.43	33.81	34.20	34.59	34.98	35.37	35.76	36.16
10.5	30.75	31.13	31.51	31.89	32.27	32.65	33.04	33.43	33.83	34.22	34.62	35.02
11.0	29.69	30.07	30.45	30.83	31.22	31.60	31.99	32.39	32.78	33.18	33.58	33.99
11.5	28.72	29.10	29.48	29.87	30.26	30.65	31.04	31.44	31.84	32.24	32.64	33.05
12.0	27.84	28.22	28.60	28.99	29.38	29.77	30.17	30.57	30.97	31.38	31.78	32.19
12.5	27.02	27.41	27.79	28.18	28.58	28.97	29.37	29.77	30.18	30.59	31.00	31.41
13.0	26.27	26.66	27.05	27.44	27.84	28.24	28.64	29.04	29.45	29.86	30.28	30.69
13.5	25.58	25.97	26.36	26.76	27.16	27.56	27.96	28.37	28.78	29.20	29.61	30.03
14.0	24.94	25.33	25.73	26.13	26.53	26.93	27.34	27.75	28.16	28.58	29.00	29.42
14.5	24.35	24.74	25.14	25.54	25.94	26.35	26.76	27.17	27.59	28.01	28.43	28.86
15.0	23.79	24.19	24.59	24.99	25.40	25.81	26.22	26.64	27.06	27.48	27.91	28.34
15.5	23.28	23.68	24.08	24.48	24.89	25.30	25.72	26.14	26.56	26.99	27.42	27.85
16.0	22.80	23.20	23.60	24.01	24.42	24.84	25.25	25.68	26.10	26.53	26.97	27.40
16.5	22.35	22.75	23.15	23.56	23.98	24.40	24.82	25.24	25.67	26.11	26.54	26.98
17.0	21.92	22.33	22.74	23.15	23.57	23.99	24.41	24.84	25.27	25.71	26.15	26.59
17.5	21.52	21.93	22.34	22.76	23.18	23.60	24.03	24.46	24.89	25.33	25.78	26.22
18.0	21.15	21.56	21.97	22.39	22.81	23.24	23.67	24.10	24.54	24.98	25.43	25.88
18.5	20.80	21.21	21.62	22.05	22.47	22.90	23.33	23.77	24.21	24.65	25.10	25.56
19.0	20.46	20.88	21.30	21.72	22.15	22.58	23.01	23.45	23.90	24.34	24.80	25.25
19.5	20.15	20.57	20.99	21.41	21.84	22.28	22.71	23.16	23.60	24.05	24.61	24.07
20.0	19.85	20.27	20.69	21.12	21.55	21.99	22.43	22.88	23.33	23.78	24.24	24.70
20.5	19.57	19.99	20.42	20.85	21.28	21.72	22.16	22.61	23.06	23.52	23.98	24.45
21.0	19.30	19.72	20.15	20.59	21.02	21.46	21.91	22.36	22.82	23.28	23.74	24.21
21.5	19.05	19.47	19.90	20.34	20.78	21.22	21.67	22.13	22.58	23.05	23.51	23.98
22.0	18.81	19.23	19.67	20.10	20.55	20.99	21.45	21.90	22.36	22.83	23.30	23.77
22.5	18.58	19.01	19.44	19.88	20.33	20.78	21.23	21.69	22.15	22.62	23.09	23.57
23.0	18.36	18.79	19.23	19.67	20.12	20.57	21.03	21.49	21.95	22.42	22.90	23.38
23.5	18.15	18.58	19.02	19.47	19.92	20.37	20.83	21.30	21.77	22.24	22.72	23.20
24.0	17.95	18.39	18.83	19.28	19.73	20.19	20.65	21.11	21.59	22.06	22.54	23.03
24.5	17.76	18.20	18.64	19.09	19.55	20.01	20.47	20.94	21.42	21.89	22.38	22.87
25.0	17.58	18.02	18.47	18.92	19.38	19.84	20.30	20.78	21.25	21.74	22.22	22.71
25.5	17.41	17.85	18.30	18.75	19.21	19.68	20.15	20.62	21.10	21.58	22.07	22.57
26.0	17.24	17.69	18.14	18.59	19.05	19.52	19.99	20.47	20.95	21.44	21.93	22.43
26.5	17.08	17.53	17.98	18.44	18.90	19.37	19.85	20.33	20.81	21.30	21.80	22.30
27.0	16.93	17.38	17.83	18.30	18.76	19.23	19.71	20.19	20.68	21.17	21.67	22.17
27.5	16.78	17.24	17.69	18.16	18.63	19.10	19.58	20.06	20.55	21.05	21.55	22.05
28.0	16.64	17.10	17.56	18.02	18.49	18.97	19.45	19.94	20.43	20.93	21.43	21.94
28.5	16.51	16.97	17.43	17.90	18.37	18.85	19.33	19.82	20.32	20.82	21.32	21.83
29.0	16.38	16.84	17.30	17.77	18.25	18.73	19.22	19.71	20.20	20.71	21.21	21.72
29.5	16.26	16.72	17.18	17.66	18.13	18.62	19.11	19.60	20.10	20.60	21.11	21.63
30.0	16.14	16.60	17.07	17.54	18.02	18.51	19.00	19.50	20.00	20.50	21.02	21.53
31.0	15.91	16.38	16.85	17.33	17.82	18.31	18.80	19.30	19.81	20.32	20.84	21.36
32.0	15.71	16.18	16.65	17.14	17.63	18.12	18.62	19.13	19.64	20.15	20.67	21.20
33.0	15.51	15.99	16.47	16.96	17.45	17.95	18.45	18.96	19.48	20.00	20.52	21.05
34.0	15.34	15.81	16.30	16.79	17.29	17.79	18.30	18.81	19.33	19.86	20.38	20.92
35.0	15.17	15.65	16.14	16.63	17.14	17.64	18.16	18.67	19.20	19.72	20.26	20.80
36.0	15.01	15.50	15.99	16.49	17.00	17.51	18.02	18.55	19.07	19.61	20.14	20.68
37.0	14.87	15.36	15.86	16.36	16.87	17.38	17.90	18.43	18.96	19.50	20.04	20.58
38.0	14.73	15.23	15.73	16.23	16.75	17.27	17.79	18.32	18.85	19.39	19.94	20.49
39.0	14.61	15.10	15.61	16.12	16.64	17.16	17.69	18.22	18.76	19.30	19.85	20.40
40.0	14.49	14.99	15.50	16.01	16.53	17.06	17.59	18.13	18.67	19.21	19.77	20.32

QUARTERLY
PAYMENT REQUIRED TO AMORTIZE A $1,000.00 LOAN

TERM IN YEARS	INTEREST RATES											
	8.00%	8.25%	8.50%	8.75%	9.00%	9.25%	9.50%	9.75%	10.00%	10.25%	10.50%	10.75%
0.5	515.05	515.53	516.00	516.47	516.94	517.41	517.89	518.36	518.83	519.30	519.78	520.25
1.0	262.63	263.03	263.43	263.82	264.22	264.62	265.02	265.42	265.82	266.22	266.62	267.02
1.5	178.53	178.91	179.28	179.66	180.04	180.42	180.80	181.18	181.55	181.93	182.31	182.70
2.0	136.51	136.88	137.25	137.62	137.99	138.36	138.73	139.10	139.47	139.84	140.22	140.59
2.5	111.33	111.70	112.06	112.43	112.79	113.16	113.53	113.90	114.26	114.63	115.00	115.37
3.0	94.56	94.93	95.29	95.66	96.02	96.39	96.76	97.12	97.49	97.86	98.23	98.60
3.5	82.61	82.97	83.34	83.70	84.07	84.43	84.80	85.17	85.54	85.91	86.28	86.66
4.0	73.66	74.02	74.39	74.75	75.12	75.49	75.86	76.23	76.60	76.98	77.35	77.73
4.5	66.71	67.07	67.44	67.81	68.18	68.55	68.93	69.30	69.68	70.05	70.43	70.81
5.0	61.16	61.53	61.90	62.27	62.65	63.02	63.40	63.77	64.15	64.53	64.91	65.29
5.5	56.64	57.01	57.38	57.76	58.13	58.51	58.89	59.27	59.65	60.03	60.42	60.80
6.0	52.88	53.25	53.63	54.01	54.39	54.77	55.15	55.53	55.92	56.30	56.69	57.08
6.5	49.70	50.08	50.46	50.84	51.23	51.61	52.00	52.38	52.77	53.16	53.56	53.95
7.0	46.99	47.38	47.76	48.14	48.53	48.92	49.31	49.70	50.09	50.49	50.88	51.28
7.5	44.65	45.04	45.43	45.81	46.20	46.60	46.99	47.39	47.78	48.18	48.58	48.99
8.0	42.62	43.00	43.39	43.79	44.18	44.57	44.97	45.37	45.77	46.18	46.58	46.99
8.5	40.82	41.22	41.61	42.00	42.40	42.80	43.20	43.61	44.01	44.42	44.83	45.24
9.0	39.24	39.63	40.03	40.43	40.83	41.23	41.64	42.05	42.46	42.87	43.28	43.70
9.5	37.83	38.22	38.62	39.03	39.43	39.84	40.25	40.66	41.08	41.49	41.91	42.33
10.0	36.56	36.96	37.37	37.77	38.18	38.59	39.01	39.42	39.84	40.26	40.68	41.11
10.5	35.42	35.83	36.24	36.65	37.06	37.47	37.89	38.31	38.73	39.16	39.59	40.02
11.0	34.39	34.80	35.21	35.63	36.04	36.46	36.88	37.31	37.74	38.16	38.60	39.03
11.5	33.46	33.87	34.29	34.70	35.12	35.55	35.97	36.40	36.83	37.27	37.70	38.14
12.0	32.61	33.02	33.44	33.86	34.29	34.71	35.14	35.58	36.01	36.45	36.89	37.33
12.5	31.83	32.25	32.67	33.10	33.52	33.95	34.39	34.82	35.26	35.70	36.15	36.60
13.0	31.11	31.54	31.96	32.39	32.82	33.26	33.70	34.14	34.58	35.03	35.47	35.93
13.5	30.46	30.88	31.31	31.75	32.18	32.62	33.06	33.51	33.95	34.40	34.86	35.31
14.0	29.85	30.28	30.71	31.15	31.59	32.03	32.48	32.93	33.38	33.83	34.29	34.75
14.5	29.29	29.73	30.16	30.60	31.04	31.49	31.94	32.39	32.85	33.31	33.77	34.23
15.0	28.77	29.21	29.65	30.09	30.54	30.99	31.44	31.90	32.36	32.82	33.29	33.75
15.5	28.29	28.73	29.18	29.62	30.07	30.53	30.98	31.44	31.91	32.37	32.84	33.31
16.0	27.84	28.29	28.73	29.19	29.64	30.10	30.56	31.02	31.49	31.96	32.43	32.91
16.5	27.43	27.87	28.32	28.78	29.24	29.70	30.16	30.63	31.10	31.57	32.05	32.53
17.0	27.04	27.49	27.94	28.40	28.86	29.32	29.79	30.26	30.74	31.22	31.70	32.18
17.5	26.67	27.13	27.58	28.05	28.51	28.98	29.45	29.92	30.40	30.88	31.37	31.86
18.0	26.33	26.79	27.25	27.71	28.18	28.65	29.13	29.61	30.09	30.57	31.06	31.55
18.5	26.01	26.47	26.94	27.40	27.88	28.35	28.83	29.31	29.80	30.29	30.78	31.27
19.0	25.71	26.18	26.64	27.11	27.59	28.07	28.55	29.04	29.52	30.02	30.51	31.01
19.5	25.43	25.90	26.37	26.84	27.32	27.80	28.29	28.78	29.27	29.77	30.26	30.77
20.0	25.17	25.64	26.11	26.59	27.07	27.55	28.04	28.54	29.03	29.53	30.03	30.54
20.5	24.92	25.39	25.87	26.35	26.83	27.32	27.81	28.31	28.81	29.31	29.82	30.33
21.0	24.68	25.16	25.64	26.12	26.61	27.10	27.60	28.10	28.60	29.10	29.61	30.13
21.5	24.46	24.94	25.42	25.91	26.40	26.89	27.39	27.90	28.40	28.91	29.42	29.94
22.0	24.25	24.73	25.22	25.71	26.20	26.70	27.20	27.71	28.22	28.73	29.25	29.76
22.5	24.05	24.54	25.03	25.52	26.02	26.52	27.02	27.53	28.04	28.56	29.08	29.60
23.0	23.86	24.35	24.84	25.34	25.84	26.34	26.85	27.36	27.88	28.40	28.92	29.45
23.5	23.69	24.18	24.67	25.17	25.68	26.18	26.69	27.21	27.73	28.25	28.77	29.30
24.0	23.52	24.01	24.51	25.01	25.52	26.03	26.54	27.06	27.58	28.11	28.63	29.17
24.5	23.36	23.86	24.36	24.86	25.37	25.88	26.40	26.92	27.45	27.97	28.50	29.04
25.0	23.21	23.71	24.21	24.72	25.23	25.75	26.27	26.79	27.32	27.85	28.38	28.92
25.5	23.06	23.57	24.07	24.58	25.10	25.62	26.14	26.67	27.20	27.73	28.27	28.81
26.0	22.93	23.43	23.94	24.46	24.97	25.49	26.02	26.55	27.08	27.62	28.16	28.70
26.5	22.80	23.31	23.82	24.33	24.85	25.38	25.91	26.44	26.97	27.51	28.05	28.60
27.0	22.68	23.19	23.70	24.22	24.74	25.27	25.80	26.33	26.87	27.41	27.96	28.51
27.5	22.56	23.07	23.59	24.11	24.64	25.16	25.70	26.23	26.78	27.32	27.87	28.42
28.0	22.45	22.96	23.48	24.01	24.53	25.07	25.60	26.14	26.68	27.23	27.78	28.33
28.5	22.34	22.86	23.38	23.91	24.44	24.97	25.51	26.05	26.60	27.15	27.70	28.25
29.0	22.24	22.76	23.29	23.81	24.35	24.88	25.42	25.97	26.52	27.07	27.62	28.18
29.5	22.14	22.67	23.19	23.73	24.26	24.80	25.34	25.89	26.44	26.99	27.55	28.11
30.0	22.05	22.58	23.11	23.64	24.18	24.72	25.27	25.81	26.37	26.92	27.48	28.04
31.0	21.88	22.41	22.95	23.48	24.03	24.57	25.12	25.68	26.23	26.79	27.36	27.92
32.0	21.73	22.26	22.80	23.34	23.89	24.44	24.99	25.55	26.11	26.68	27.24	27.81
33.0	21.59	22.12	22.67	23.21	23.76	24.32	24.88	25.44	26.00	26.57	27.14	27.72
34.0	21.46	22.00	22.55	23.10	23.65	24.21	24.77	25.34	25.91	26.48	27.05	27.63
35.0	21.34	21.89	22.44	22.99	23.55	24.11	24.68	25.25	25.82	26.39	26.97	27.55
36.0	21.23	21.78	22.34	22.89	23.46	24.02	24.59	25.16	25.74	26.32	26.90	27.48
37.0	21.13	21.69	22.24	22.81	23.37	23.94	24.51	25.09	25.67	26.25	26.83	27.42
38.0	21.04	21.60	22.16	22.73	23.30	23.87	24.44	25.02	25.61	26.19	26.78	27.37
39.0	20.96	21.52	22.09	22.65	23.23	23.80	24.38	24.96	25.55	26.13	26.72	27.32
40.0	20.88	21.45	22.02	22.59	23.16	23.74	24.32	24.91	25.50	26.09	26.68	27.27

QUARTERLY
PAYMENT REQUIRED TO AMORTIZE A $1,000.00 LOAN

TERM IN YEARS	11.00%	11.25%	11.50%	11.75%	12.00%	12.25%	12.50%	12.75%	13.00%	13.25%	13.50%	13.75%
						INTEREST RATES						
0.5	520.72	521.20	521.67	522.14	522.62	523.09	523.56	524.04	524.51	524.98	525.46	525.93
1.0	267.43	267.83	268.23	268.63	269.03	269.43	269.84	270.24	270.64	271.05	271.45	271.85
1.5	183.08	183.46	183.84	184.22	184.60	184.99	185.37	185.75	186.13	186.52	186.90	187.29
2.0	140.96	141.34	141.71	142.09	142.46	142.84	143.21	143.59	143.97	144.35	144.72	145.10
2.5	115.74	116.12	116.49	116.86	117.24	117.61	117.98	118.36	118.74	119.11	119.49	119.87
3.0	98.97	99.35	99.72	100.09	100.47	100.84	101.22	101.59	101.97	102.35	102.73	103.11
3.5	87.03	87.40	87.78	88.15	88.53	88.91	89.29	89.67	90.05	90.43	90.81	91.19
4.0	78.10	78.48	78.86	79.24	79.62	80.00	80.38	80.76	81.15	81.53	81.92	82.30
4.5	71.19	71.57	71.95	72.33	72.71	73.10	73.48	73.87	74.26	74.65	75.04	75.43
5.0	65.68	66.06	66.45	66.83	67.22	67.61	68.00	68.39	68.78	69.18	69.57	69.97
5.5	61.19	61.58	61.97	62.36	62.75	63.15	63.54	63.94	64.33	64.73	65.13	65.53
6.0	57.47	57.87	58.26	58.66	59.05	59.45	59.85	60.25	60.65	61.06	61.46	61.87
6.5	54.35	54.74	55.14	55.54	55.94	56.35	56.75	57.16	57.56	57.97	58.38	58.80
7.0	51.68	52.08	52.49	52.89	53.30	53.71	54.12	54.53	54.94	55.35	55.77	56.19
7.5	49.39	49.80	50.20	50.61	51.02	51.44	51.85	52.27	52.69	53.11	53.53	53.95
8.0	47.40	47.81	48.22	48.64	49.05	49.47	49.89	50.31	50.73	51.16	51.59	52.02
8.5	45.65	46.07	46.49	46.91	47.33	47.75	48.18	48.60	49.03	49.46	49.89	50.33
9.0	44.12	44.54	44.96	45.38	45.81	46.24	46.67	47.10	47.53	47.97	48.41	48.85
9.5	42.75	43.18	43.60	44.03	44.46	44.90	45.33	45.77	46.21	46.65	47.09	47.54
10.0	41.54	41.97	42.40	42.83	43.27	43.71	44.15	44.59	45.03	45.48	45.93	46.38
10.5	40.45	40.88	41.32	41.76	42.20	42.64	43.09	43.53	43.98	44.43	44.89	45.34
11.0	39.47	39.90	40.35	40.79	41.23	41.68	42.13	42.59	43.04	43.50	43.96	44.42
11.5	38.58	39.02	39.47	39.92	40.37	40.82	41.28	41.73	42.19	42.66	43.12	43.59
12.0	37.78	38.22	38.67	39.13	39.58	40.04	40.50	40.96	41.43	41.90	42.37	42.84
12.5	37.05	37.50	37.95	38.41	38.87	39.33	39.80	40.27	40.74	41.21	41.68	42.16
13.0	36.38	36.84	37.30	37.76	38.22	38.69	39.16	39.63	40.11	40.58	41.06	41.54
13.5	35.77	36.23	36.69	37.16	37.63	38.10	38.58	39.05	39.53	40.02	40.50	40.99
14.0	35.21	35.68	36.14	36.62	37.09	37.57	38.04	38.53	39.01	39.50	39.99	40.48
14.5	34.70	35.17	35.64	36.12	36.59	37.07	37.56	38.04	38.53	39.02	39.52	40.01
15.0	34.23	34.70	35.18	35.66	36.14	36.62	37.11	37.60	38.09	38.59	39.09	39.59
15.5	33.79	34.27	34.75	35.23	35.72	36.21	36.70	37.20	37.69	38.19	38.70	39.20
16.0	33.39	33.87	34.35	34.84	35.33	35.83	36.32	36.82	37.32	37.83	38.34	38.85
16.5	33.01	33.50	33.99	34.48	34.98	35.47	35.97	36.48	36.98	37.49	38.00	38.52
17.0	32.67	33.16	33.65	34.15	34.65	35.15	35.65	36.16	36.67	37.18	37.70	38.22
17.5	32.35	32.84	33.34	33.84	34.34	34.85	35.36	35.87	36.38	36.90	37.42	37.94
18.0	32.05	32.55	33.05	33.55	34.06	34.57	35.08	35.60	36.12	36.64	37.16	37.69
18.5	31.77	32.27	32.78	33.29	33.80	34.31	34.83	35.35	35.87	36.39	36.92	37.45
19.0	31.51	32.02	32.53	33.04	33.55	34.07	34.59	35.11	35.64	36.17	36.70	37.23
19.5	31.27	31.78	32.29	32.81	33.33	33.85	34.37	34.90	35.43	35.96	36.50	37.03
20.0	31.05	31.56	32.08	32.60	33.12	33.64	34.17	34.70	35.23	35.77	36.31	36.85
20.5	30.84	31.35	31.87	32.40	32.92	33.45	33.98	34.51	35.05	35.59	36.13	36.67
21.0	30.64	31.16	31.68	32.21	32.74	33.27	33.80	34.34	34.88	35.42	35.97	36.52
21.5	30.46	30.98	31.51	32.04	32.57	33.10	33.64	34.18	34.72	35.27	35.82	36.37
22.0	30.29	30.81	31.34	31.87	32.41	32.95	33.49	34.03	34.58	35.13	35.68	36.23
22.5	30.13	30.66	31.19	31.72	32.26	32.80	33.35	33.89	34.44	34.99	35.55	36.10
23.0	29.98	30.51	31.04	31.58	32.12	32.67	33.21	33.76	34.31	34.87	35.43	35.99
23.5	29.83	30.37	30.91	31.45	31.99	32.54	33.09	33.64	34.20	34.75	35.31	35.88
24.0	29.70	30.24	30.78	31.32	31.87	32.42	32.97	33.53	34.09	34.65	35.21	35.77
24.5	29.58	30.12	30.66	31.21	31.76	32.31	32.87	33.42	33.98	34.55	35.11	35.68
25.0	29.46	30.00	30.55	31.10	31.65	32.21	32.76	33.33	33.89	34.45	35.02	35.59
25.5	29.35	29.90	30.44	31.00	31.55	32.11	32.67	33.23	33.80	34.37	34.94	35.51
26.0	29.25	29.79	30.35	30.90	31.46	32.02	32.58	33.15	33.72	34.29	34.86	35.43
26.5	29.15	29.70	30.25	30.81	31.37	31.93	32.50	33.07	33.64	34.21	34.79	35.36
27.0	29.06	29.61	30.17	30.73	31.29	31.86	32.42	32.99	33.57	34.14	34.72	35.30
27.5	28.97	29.53	30.09	30.65	31.21	31.78	32.35	32.92	33.50	34.08	34.65	35.24
28.0	28.89	29.45	30.01	30.57	31.14	31.71	32.28	32.86	33.43	34.01	34.60	35.18
28.5	28.81	29.37	29.94	30.50	31.07	31.65	32.22	32.80	33.38	33.96	34.54	35.13
29.0	28.74	29.30	29.87	30.44	31.01	31.58	32.16	32.74	33.32	33.90	34.49	35.08
29.5	28.67	29.24	29.81	30.38	30.95	31.53	32.11	32.69	33.27	33.85	34.44	35.03
30.0	28.61	29.18	29.75	30.32	30.89	31.47	32.05	32.64	33.22	33.81	34.40	34.99
31.0	28.49	29.06	29.64	30.21	30.79	31.37	31.96	32.54	33.13	33.72	34.31	34.91
32.0	28.39	28.96	29.54	30.12	30.70	31.29	31.88	32.46	33.06	33.65	34.24	34.84
33.0	28.29	28.87	29.45	30.04	30.62	31.21	31.80	32.39	32.99	33.58	34.18	34.78
34.0	28.21	28.79	29.38	29.96	30.55	31.14	31.74	32.33	32.93	33.53	34.13	34.73
35.0	28.14	28.72	29.31	29.90	30.49	31.09	31.68	32.28	32.88	33.48	34.08	34.69
36.0	28.07	28.66	29.25	29.84	30.44	31.03	31.63	32.23	32.83	33.44	34.04	34.65
37.0	28.01	28.60	29.19	29.79	30.39	30.99	31.59	32.19	32.79	33.40	34.01	34.61
38.0	27.96	28.55	29.15	29.74	30.34	30.95	31.55	32.15	32.76	33.37	33.97	34.58
39.0	27.91	28.51	29.10	29.70	30.31	30.91	31.51	32.12	32.73	33.34	33.95	34.56
40.0	27.87	28.47	29.07	29.67	30.27	30.88	31.48	32.09	32.70	33.31	33.92	34.53

QUARTERLY
PAYMENT REQUIRED TO AMORTIZE A $1,000.00 LOAN

TERM IN YEARS	INTEREST RATES											
	14.00%	14.25%	14.50%	14.75%	15.00%	15.25%	15.50%	15.75%	16.00%	16.25%	16.50%	16.75%
0.5	526.41	526.88	527.35	527.83	528.30	528.78	529.25	529.73	530.20	530.68	531.15	531.63
1.0	272.26	272.66	273.06	273.47	273.87	274.28	274.68	275.09	275.50	275.90	276.31	276.71
1.5	187.67	188.06	188.44	188.83	189.22	189.60	189.99	190.38	190.77	191.16	191.54	191.93
2.0	145.48	145.86	146.24	146.62	147.00	147.39	147.77	148.15	148.53	148.92	149.30	149.68
2.5	120.25	120.63	121.01	121.39	121.77	122.15	122.53	122.91	123.30	123.68	124.06	124.45
3.0	103.49	103.87	104.25	104.63	105.02	105.40	105.79	106.17	106.56	106.94	107.33	107.72
3.5	91.58	91.96	92.35	92.73	93.12	93.51	93.89	94.28	94.67	95.07	95.46	95.85
4.0	82.69	83.08	83.47	83.86	84.25	84.64	85.04	85.43	85.82	86.22	86.62	87.02
4.5	75.82	76.22	76.61	77.01	77.40	77.80	78.20	78.60	79.00	79.40	79.80	80.21
5.0	70.37	70.76	71.16	71.57	71.97	72.37	72.77	73.18	73.59	73.99	74.40	74.81
5.5	65.94	66.34	66.75	67.15	67.56	67.97	68.38	68.79	69.20	69.62	70.03	70.45
6.0	62.28	62.69	63.10	63.51	63.92	64.34	64.76	65.17	65.59	66.01	66.43	66.86
6.5	59.21	59.63	60.04	60.46	60.88	61.30	61.72	62.15	62.57	63.00	63.43	63.86
7.0	56.61	57.03	57.45	57.87	58.30	58.73	59.16	59.59	60.02	60.45	60.89	61.32
7.5	54.38	54.80	55.23	55.66	56.09	56.53	56.96	57.40	57.84	58.27	58.72	59.16
8.0	52.45	52.88	53.31	53.75	54.19	54.63	55.07	55.51	55.95	56.40	56.85	57.30
8.5	50.76	51.20	51.64	52.08	52.53	52.97	53.42	53.87	54.32	54.77	55.23	55.68
9.0	49.29	49.73	50.18	50.63	51.08	51.53	51.98	52.44	52.89	53.35	53.81	54.27
9.5	47.99	48.44	48.89	49.34	49.80	50.25	50.71	51.17	51.64	52.10	52.57	53.04
10.0	46.83	47.29	47.74	48.20	48.66	49.13	49.59	50.06	50.53	51.00	51.47	51.95
10.5	45.80	46.26	46.73	47.19	47.66	48.13	48.60	49.07	49.55	50.02	50.50	50.98
11.0	44.88	45.35	45.82	46.29	46.76	47.23	47.71	48.19	48.67	49.15	49.64	50.12
11.5	44.06	44.53	45.00	45.48	45.95	46.43	46.92	47.40	47.89	48.38	48.87	49.36
12.0	43.31	43.79	44.27	44.75	45.23	45.72	46.20	46.69	47.19	47.68	48.18	48.67
12.5	42.64	43.12	43.60	44.09	44.58	45.07	45.56	46.06	46.56	47.05	47.56	48.06
13.0	42.03	42.52	43.01	43.50	43.99	44.49	44.98	45.48	45.99	46.49	47.00	47.51
13.5	41.48	41.97	42.46	42.96	43.46	43.96	44.46	44.97	45.47	45.98	46.50	47.01
14.0	40.97	41.47	41.97	42.47	42.97	43.48	43.99	44.50	45.01	45.52	46.04	46.56
14.5	40.51	41.01	41.52	42.02	42.53	43.04	43.56	44.07	44.59	45.11	45.63	46.15
15.0	40.09	40.60	41.11	41.62	42.13	42.65	43.16	43.68	44.21	44.73	45.26	45.79
15.5	39.71	40.22	40.73	41.25	41.77	42.29	42.81	43.33	43.86	44.39	44.92	45.45
16.0	39.36	39.87	40.39	40.91	41.43	41.96	42.48	43.01	43.54	44.08	44.61	45.15
16.5	39.04	39.55	40.08	40.60	41.13	41.65	42.19	42.72	43.25	43.79	44.33	44.87
17.0	38.74	39.26	39.79	40.32	40.85	41.38	41.91	42.45	42.99	43.53	44.08	44.62
17.5	38.47	38.99	39.52	40.06	40.59	41.13	41.67	42.21	42.75	43.30	43.84	44.39
18.0	38.21	38.75	39.28	39.82	40.35	40.89	41.44	41.98	42.53	43.08	43.63	44.18
18.5	37.98	38.52	39.06	39.60	40.14	40.68	41.23	41.78	42.33	42.88	43.44	43.99
19.0	37.77	38.31	38.85	39.39	39.94	40.49	41.04	41.59	42.14	42.70	43.26	43.82
19.5	37.57	38.11	38.66	39.21	39.76	40.31	40.86	41.42	41.97	42.53	43.10	43.66
20.0	37.39	37.94	38.48	39.03	39.59	40.14	40.70	41.26	41.82	42.38	42.95	43.51
20.5	37.22	37.77	38.32	38.88	39.43	39.99	40.55	41.11	41.68	42.24	42.81	43.38
21.0	37.07	37.62	38.17	38.73	39.29	39.85	40.41	40.98	41.55	42.11	42.69	43.26
21.5	36.92	37.48	38.03	38.59	39.16	39.72	40.29	40.85	41.43	42.00	42.57	43.15
22.0	36.79	37.35	37.91	38.47	39.03	39.60	40.17	40.74	41.31	41.89	42.47	43.04
22.5	36.66	37.22	37.79	38.35	38.92	39.49	40.06	40.64	41.21	41.79	42.37	42.95
23.0	36.55	37.11	37.68	38.25	38.82	39.39	39.96	40.54	41.12	41.70	42.28	42.86
23.5	36.44	37.01	37.58	38.15	38.72	39.30	39.87	40.45	41.03	41.62	42.20	42.78
24.0	36.34	36.91	37.48	38.06	38.63	39.21	39.79	40.37	40.95	41.54	42.12	42.71
24.5	36.25	36.82	37.40	37.97	38.55	39.13	39.71	40.30	40.88	41.47	42.06	42.65
25.0	36.16	36.74	37.32	37.89	38.47	39.06	39.64	40.23	40.81	41.40	41.99	42.58
25.5	36.08	36.66	37.24	37.82	38.40	38.99	39.57	40.16	40.75	41.34	41.93	42.53
26.0	36.01	36.59	37.17	37.75	38.34	38.92	39.51	40.10	40.69	41.29	41.88	42.48
26.5	35.94	36.52	37.11	37.69	38.28	38.87	39.46	40.05	40.64	41.24	41.83	42.43
27.0	35.88	36.46	37.05	37.63	38.22	38.81	39.40	40.00	40.59	41.19	41.79	42.38
27.5	35.82	36.40	36.99	37.58	38.17	38.76	39.36	39.95	40.55	41.15	41.74	42.34
28.0	35.76	36.35	36.94	37.53	38.12	38.72	39.31	39.91	40.51	41.11	41.71	42.31
28.5	35.71	36.30	36.89	37.48	38.08	38.67	39.27	39.87	40.47	41.07	41.67	42.27
29.0	35.66	36.25	36.85	37.44	38.04	38.63	39.23	39.83	40.43	41.03	41.64	42.24
29.5	35.62	36.21	36.81	37.40	38.00	38.60	39.20	39.80	40.40	41.00	41.61	42.21
30.0	35.58	36.17	36.77	37.36	37.96	38.56	39.16	39.77	40.37	40.97	41.58	42.19
31.0	35.50	36.10	36.70	37.30	37.90	38.50	39.11	39.71	40.32	40.92	41.53	42.14
32.0	35.44	36.04	36.64	37.24	37.84	38.45	39.06	39.66	40.27	40.88	41.49	42.10
33.0	35.38	35.98	36.59	37.19	37.80	38.41	39.01	39.62	40.23	40.84	41.45	42.07
34.0	35.33	35.94	36.54	37.15	37.76	38.37	38.98	39.59	40.20	40.81	41.42	42.04
35.0	35.29	35.90	36.50	37.11	37.72	38.33	38.95	39.56	40.17	40.78	41.40	42.01
36.0	35.25	35.86	36.47	37.08	37.69	38.31	38.92	39.53	40.15	40.76	41.38	41.99
37.0	35.22	35.83	36.44	37.05	37.67	38.28	38.90	39.51	40.13	40.74	41.36	41.98
38.0	35.19	35.81	36.42	37.03	37.64	38.26	38.88	39.49	40.11	40.73	41.34	41.96
39.0	35.17	35.78	36.40	37.01	37.63	38.24	38.86	39.48	40.09	40.71	41.33	41.95
40.0	35.15	35.76	36.38	36.99	37.61	38.23	38.84	39.46	40.08	40.70	41.32	41.94

QUARTERLY
PAYMENT REQUIRED TO AMORTIZE A $1,000.00 LOAN

TERM IN YEARS	INTEREST RATES											
	17.00%	17.25%	17.50%	17.75%	18.00%	18.25%	18.50%	18.75%	19.00%	19.25%	19.50%	19.75%
0.5	532.10	532.58	533.05	533.53	534.00	534.48	534.95	535.43	535.91	536.38	536.86	537.33
1.0	277.12	277.53	277.93	278.34	278.75	279.16	279.56	279.97	280.38	280.79	281.20	281.61
1.5	192.32	192.71	193.10	193.49	193.88	194.27	194.67	195.06	195.45	195.84	196.24	196.63
2.0	150.07	150.46	150.84	151.23	151.61	152.00	152.39	152.78	153.17	153.56	153.95	154.34
2.5	124.84	125.22	125.61	126.00	126.38	126.77	127.16	127.55	127.94	128.33	128.72	129.12
3.0	108.11	108.50	108.89	109.28	109.67	110.06	110.46	110.85	111.25	111.64	112.04	112.43
3.5	96.24	96.64	97.03	97.43	97.83	98.22	98.62	99.02	99.42	99.82	100.22	100.63
4.0	87.42	87.82	88.22	88.62	89.02	89.42	89.83	90.23	90.64	91.05	91.46	91.86
4.5	80.61	81.02	81.42	81.83	82.24	82.65	83.06	83.48	83.89	84.30	84.72	85.13
5.0	75.22	75.64	76.05	76.47	76.88	77.30	77.72	78.14	78.56	78.98	79.40	79.82
5.5	70.87	71.29	71.71	72.13	72.55	72.97	73.40	73.83	74.25	74.68	75.11	75.54
6.0	67.28	67.71	68.13	68.56	68.99	69.42	69.86	70.29	70.72	71.16	71.60	72.04
6.5	64.29	64.72	65.15	65.59	66.03	66.46	66.90	67.34	67.79	68.23	68.68	69.12
7.0	61.76	62.20	62.64	63.08	63.53	63.97	64.42	64.87	65.32	65.77	66.22	66.67
7.5	59.60	60.05	60.50	60.95	61.40	61.85	62.30	62.76	63.21	63.67	64.13	64.59
8.0	57.75	58.20	58.65	59.11	59.57	60.03	60.49	60.95	61.41	61.88	62.35	62.82
8.5	56.14	56.60	57.06	57.52	57.99	58.45	58.92	59.39	59.86	60.33	60.81	61.28
9.0	54.74	55.20	55.67	56.14	56.61	57.08	57.56	58.03	58.51	58.99	59.47	59.96
9.5	53.51	53.98	54.45	54.93	55.41	55.89	56.37	56.85	57.33	57.82	58.31	58.80
10.0	52.42	52.90	53.38	53.86	54.35	54.83	55.32	55.81	56.30	56.79	57.29	57.79
10.5	51.46	51.95	52.44	52.92	53.41	53.91	54.40	54.90	55.39	55.89	56.39	56.90
11.0	50.61	51.10	51.60	52.09	52.59	53.08	53.58	54.09	54.59	55.09	55.60	56.11
11.5	49.85	50.35	50.85	51.35	51.85	52.35	52.86	53.37	53.88	54.39	54.90	55.42
12.0	49.17	49.68	50.18	50.69	51.19	51.70	52.22	52.73	53.24	53.76	54.28	54.80
12.5	48.57	49.07	49.58	50.09	50.61	51.12	51.64	52.16	52.68	53.20	53.73	54.25
13.0	48.02	48.53	49.05	49.56	50.08	50.60	51.13	51.65	52.18	52.70	53.23	53.77
13.5	47.53	48.04	48.56	49.09	49.61	50.14	50.66	51.19	51.73	52.26	52.79	53.33
14.0	47.08	47.60	48.13	48.66	49.19	49.72	50.25	50.78	51.32	51.86	52.40	52.94
14.5	46.68	47.21	47.74	48.27	48.80	49.34	49.88	50.42	50.96	51.50	52.05	52.59
15.0	46.32	46.85	47.38	47.92	48.46	49.00	49.54	50.09	50.63	51.18	51.73	52.28
15.5	45.99	46.52	47.06	47.60	48.15	48.69	49.24	49.79	50.34	50.89	51.44	52.00
16.0	45.69	46.23	46.77	47.32	47.87	48.42	48.97	49.52	50.07	50.63	51.19	51.75
16.5	45.42	45.96	46.51	47.06	47.61	48.16	48.72	49.28	49.83	50.40	50.96	51.52
17.0	45.17	45.72	46.27	46.82	47.38	47.94	48.50	49.06	49.62	50.18	50.75	51.32
17.5	44.94	45.50	46.05	46.61	47.17	47.73	48.29	48.86	49.42	49.99	50.56	51.13
18.0	44.74	45.30	45.86	46.42	46.98	47.54	48.11	48.68	49.25	49.82	50.39	50.97
18.5	44.55	45.11	45.68	46.24	46.81	47.37	47.94	48.52	49.09	49.66	50.24	50.82
19.0	44.38	44.95	45.51	46.08	46.65	47.22	47.79	48.37	48.94	49.52	50.10	50.68
19.5	44.23	44.79	45.36	45.93	46.51	47.08	47.66	48.23	48.81	49.39	49.97	50.56
20.0	44.00	44.65	45.20	45.00	46.00	46.93	47.53	48.11	48.05	49.20	49.00	50.43
20.5	43.95	44.53	45.10	45.68	46.26	46.84	47.42	48.00	48.59	49.17	49.76	50.35
21.0	43.83	44.41	44.99	45.57	46.15	46.73	47.32	47.90	48.49	49.08	49.67	50.26
21.5	43.72	44.30	44.88	45.47	46.05	46.64	47.22	47.81	48.40	48.99	49.58	50.18
22.0	43.62	44.21	44.79	45.37	45.96	46.55	47.14	47.73	48.32	48.91	49.51	50.10
22.5	43.53	44.12	44.70	45.29	45.88	46.47	47.06	47.65	48.25	48.84	49.44	50.03
23.0	43.45	44.04	44.62	45.21	45.80	46.40	46.99	47.58	48.18	48.78	49.37	49.97
23.5	43.37	43.96	44.55	45.14	45.73	46.33	46.92	47.52	48.12	48.72	49.32	49.92
24.0	43.30	43.89	44.48	45.08	45.67	46.27	46.87	47.46	48.06	48.66	49.27	49.87
24.5	43.24	43.83	44.42	45.02	45.62	46.21	46.81	47.41	48.01	48.62	49.22	49.82
25.0	43.18	43.77	44.37	44.97	45.56	46.16	46.76	47.37	47.97	48.57	49.18	49.78
25.5	43.12	43.72	44.32	44.92	45.52	46.12	46.72	47.32	47.93	48.53	49.14	49.74
26.0	43.07	43.67	44.27	44.87	45.47	46.07	46.68	47.28	47.89	48.50	49.10	49.71
26.5	43.03	43.63	44.23	44.83	45.43	46.04	46.64	47.25	47.85	48.46	49.07	49.68
27.0	42.98	43.59	44.19	44.79	45.40	46.00	46.61	47.22	47.82	48.43	49.04	49.65
27.5	42.95	43.55	44.15	44.76	45.36	45.97	46.58	47.19	47.79	48.41	49.02	49.63
28.0	42.91	43.51	44.12	44.73	45.33	45.94	46.55	47.16	47.77	48.38	48.99	49.60
28.5	42.88	43.48	44.09	44.70	45.30	45.91	46.52	47.13	47.75	48.36	48.97	49.58
29.0	42.85	43.45	44.06	44.67	45.28	45.89	46.50	47.11	47.72	48.34	48.95	49.56
29.5	42.82	43.43	44.04	44.65	45.26	45.87	46.48	47.09	47.70	48.32	48.93	49.55
30.0	42.79	43.40	44.01	44.62	45.23	45.85	46.46	47.07	47.69	48.30	48.92	49.53
31.0	42.75	43.36	43.97	44.58	45.20	45.81	46.43	47.04	47.66	48.27	48.89	49.51
32.0	42.71	43.32	43.94	44.55	45.17	45.78	46.40	47.01	47.63	48.25	48.87	49.48
33.0	42.68	43.29	43.91	44.52	45.14	45.76	46.37	46.99	47.61	48.23	48.85	49.47
34.0	42.65	43.27	43.88	44.50	45.12	45.74	46.35	46.97	47.59	48.21	48.83	49.45
35.0	42.63	43.25	43.86	44.48	45.10	45.72	46.34	46.96	47.58	48.20	48.82	49.44
36.0	42.61	43.23	43.85	44.47	45.08	45.70	46.32	46.94	47.56	48.19	48.81	49.43
37.0	42.59	43.21	43.83	44.45	45.07	45.69	46.31	46.93	47.55	48.18	48.80	49.42
38.0	42.58	43.20	43.82	44.44	45.06	45.68	46.30	46.92	47.55	48.17	48.79	49.41
39.0	42.57	43.19	43.81	44.43	45.05	45.67	46.30	46.92	47.54	48.16	48.78	49.41
40.0	42.56	43.18	43.80	44.42	45.04	45.67	46.29	46.91	47.53	48.16	48.78	49.40

QUARTERLY
PAYMENT REQUIRED TO AMORTIZE A $1,000.00 LOAN

TERM IN YEARS	INTEREST RATES											
	20.00%	20.25%	20.50%	20.75%	21.00%	21.25%	21.50%	21.75%	22.00%	22.25%	22.50%	22.75%
0.5	537.81	538.29	538.76	539.24	539.72	540.19	540.67	541.15	541.62	542.10	542.58	543.05
1.0	282.02	282.43	282.84	283.25	283.66	284.07	284.48	284.89	285.30	285.71	286.12	286.53
1.5	197.02	197.42	197.81	198.21	198.60	199.00	199.39	199.79	200.18	200.58	200.98	201.38
2.0	154.73	155.12	155.51	155.90	156.29	156.69	157.08	157.47	157.87	158.26	158.66	159.06
2.5	129.51	129.90	130.30	130.69	131.09	131.48	131.88	132.28	132.67	133.07	133.47	133.87
3.0	112.83	113.23	113.63	114.03	114.43	114.83	115.23	115.63	116.03	116.44	116.84	117.25
3.5	101.03	101.43	101.84	102.24	102.65	103.06	103.47	103.87	104.28	104.69	105.11	105.52
4.0	92.27	92.69	93.10	93.51	93.92	94.34	94.75	95.17	95.59	96.01	96.42	96.84
4.5	85.55	85.97	86.39	86.81	87.23	87.65	88.08	88.50	88.92	89.35	89.78	90.21
5.0	80.25	80.67	81.10	81.53	81.96	82.39	82.82	83.25	83.68	84.12	84.55	84.99
5.5	75.98	76.41	76.84	77.28	77.72	78.15	78.59	79.03	79.48	79.92	80.36	80.81
6.0	72.48	72.92	73.36	73.80	74.25	74.69	75.14	75.59	76.04	76.49	76.94	77.40
6.5	69.57	70.02	70.47	70.92	71.37	71.83	72.28	72.74	73.20	73.66	74.12	74.58
7.0	67.13	67.58	68.04	68.50	68.96	69.42	69.89	70.35	70.82	71.29	71.76	72.23
7.5	65.06	65.52	65.99	66.45	66.92	67.39	67.86	68.34	68.81	69.29	69.76	70.24
8.0	63.29	63.76	64.23	64.70	65.18	65.66	66.14	66.62	67.10	67.58	68.07	68.55
8.5	61.76	62.24	62.72	63.20	63.69	64.17	64.66	65.15	65.63	66.13	66.62	67.11
9.0	60.44	60.93	61.41	61.90	62.39	62.89	63.38	63.87	64.37	64.87	65.37	65.87
9.5	59.29	59.78	60.28	60.77	61.27	61.77	62.27	62.77	63.28	63.78	64.29	64.80
10.0	58.28	58.78	59.28	59.79	60.29	60.80	61.31	61.81	62.33	62.84	63.35	63.87
10.5	57.40	57.91	58.41	58.92	59.43	59.95	60.46	60.98	61.49	62.01	62.53	63.06
11.0	56.62	57.13	57.65	58.16	58.68	59.20	59.72	60.24	60.77	61.29	61.82	62.35
11.5	55.93	56.45	56.97	57.49	58.02	58.54	59.07	59.60	60.13	60.66	61.19	61.73
12.0	55.32	55.85	56.37	56.90	57.43	57.96	58.49	59.03	59.56	60.10	60.64	61.18
12.5	54.78	55.31	55.84	56.38	56.91	57.45	57.99	58.53	59.07	59.61	60.15	60.70
13.0	54.30	54.83	55.37	55.91	56.45	56.99	57.54	58.08	58.63	59.17	59.72	60.28
13.5	53.87	54.41	54.95	55.50	56.04	56.59	57.14	57.69	58.24	58.79	59.34	59.90
14.0	53.49	54.03	54.58	55.13	55.68	56.23	56.78	57.34	57.89	58.45	59.01	59.57
14.5	53.14	53.69	54.24	54.80	55.35	55.91	56.46	57.02	57.59	58.15	58.71	59.28
15.0	52.83	53.39	53.94	54.50	55.06	55.62	56.18	56.75	57.31	57.88	58.45	59.02
15.5	52.56	53.12	53.68	54.24	54.80	55.37	55.93	56.50	57.07	57.64	58.21	58.78
16.0	52.31	52.87	53.44	54.00	54.57	55.14	55.71	56.28	56.85	57.43	58.00	58.58
16.5	52.09	52.65	53.22	53.79	54.36	54.93	55.51	56.08	56.66	57.24	57.82	58.40
17.0	51.88	52.46	53.03	53.60	54.17	54.75	55.33	55.91	56.49	57.07	57.65	58.23
17.5	51.70	52.28	52.85	53.43	54.01	54.59	55.17	55.75	56.33	56.92	57.50	58.09
18.0	51.54	52.12	52.70	53.28	53.86	54.44	55.02	55.61	56.19	56.78	57.37	57.96
18.5	51.39	51.97	52.56	53.14	53.72	54.31	54.90	55.48	56.07	56.66	57.25	57.84
19.0	51.26	51.85	52.43	53.02	53.60	54.19	54.78	55.37	55.96	56.55	57.15	57.74
19.5	51.14	51.73	52.32	52.90	53.49	54.08	54.68	55.27	55.86	56.46	57.05	57.65
20.0	51.03	51.62	52.21	52.80	53.40	53.99	54.58	55.18	55.77	56.37	56.97	57.57
20.5	50.94	51.53	52.12	52.71	53.31	53.90	54.50	55.10	55.70	56.29	56.89	57.50
21.0	50.85	51.44	52.04	52.63	53.23	53.83	54.42	55.02	55.62	56.23	56.83	57.43
21.5	50.77	51.36	51.96	52.56	53.16	53.76	54.36	54.96	55.56	56.16	56.77	57.37
22.0	50.70	51.29	51.89	52.49	53.09	53.69	54.30	54.90	55.50	56.11	56.71	57.32
22.5	50.63	51.23	51.83	52.43	53.04	53.64	54.24	54.85	55.45	56.06	56.67	57.27
23.0	50.57	51.17	51.78	52.38	52.98	53.59	54.19	54.80	55.41	56.01	56.62	57.23
23.5	50.52	51.12	51.73	52.33	52.94	53.54	54.15	54.76	55.37	55.98	56.59	57.20
24.0	50.47	51.08	51.68	52.29	52.89	53.50	54.11	54.72	55.33	55.94	56.55	57.16
24.5	50.43	51.03	51.64	52.25	52.86	53.46	54.07	54.69	55.30	55.91	56.52	57.13
25.0	50.39	51.00	51.60	52.21	52.82	53.43	54.04	54.65	55.27	55.88	56.49	57.11
25.5	50.35	50.96	51.57	52.18	52.79	53.40	54.01	54.63	55.24	55.85	56.47	57.08
26.0	50.32	50.93	51.54	52.15	52.76	53.38	53.99	54.60	55.22	55.83	56.45	57.06
26.5	50.29	50.90	51.51	52.12	52.74	53.35	53.96	54.58	55.19	55.81	56.43	57.04
27.0	50.26	50.88	51.49	52.10	52.71	53.33	53.94	54.56	55.17	55.79	56.41	57.03
27.5	50.24	50.85	51.47	52.08	52.69	53.31	53.93	54.54	55.16	55.77	56.39	57.01
28.0	50.22	50.83	51.45	52.06	52.68	53.29	53.91	54.52	55.14	55.76	56.38	57.00
28.5	50.20	50.81	51.43	52.04	52.66	53.28	53.89	54.51	55.13	55.75	56.37	56.98
29.0	50.18	50.80	51.41	52.03	52.64	53.26	53.88	54.50	55.12	55.73	56.35	56.97
29.5	50.16	50.78	51.40	52.01	52.63	53.25	53.87	54.49	55.10	55.72	56.34	56.96
30.0	50.15	50.77	51.38	52.00	52.62	53.24	53.86	54.47	55.09	55.71	56.33	56.95
31.0	50.12	50.74	51.36	51.98	52.60	53.22	53.84	54.46	55.08	55.70	56.32	56.94
32.0	50.10	50.72	51.34	51.96	52.58	53.20	53.82	54.44	55.06	55.68	56.31	56.93
33.0	50.08	50.70	51.32	51.95	52.57	53.19	53.81	54.43	55.05	55.67	56.30	56.92
34.0	50.07	50.69	51.31	51.93	52.55	53.18	53.80	54.42	55.04	55.67	56.29	56.91
35.0	50.06	50.68	51.30	51.92	52.55	53.17	53.79	54.41	55.04	55.66	56.28	56.90
36.0	50.05	50.67	51.29	51.92	52.54	53.16	53.78	54.41	55.03	55.65	56.28	56.90
37.0	50.04	50.66	51.29	51.91	52.53	53.16	53.78	54.40	55.02	55.65	56.27	56.90
38.0	50.04	50.66	51.28	51.90	52.53	53.15	53.77	54.40	55.02	55.64	56.27	56.89
39.0	50.03	50.65	51.28	51.90	52.52	53.15	53.77	54.39	55.02	55.64	56.27	56.89
40.0	50.03	50.65	51.27	51.90	52.52	53.14	53.77	54.39	55.02	55.64	56.26	56.89

QUARTERLY
PAYMENT REQUIRED TO AMORTIZE A $1,000.00 LOAN

TERM IN YEARS	23.00%	23.25%	23.50%	23.75%	24.00%	24.25%	24.50%	24.75%	25.00%	25.25%	25.50%	25.75%
					INTEREST RATES							
0.5	543.53	544.01	544.49	544.96	545.44	545.92	546.40	546.88	547.35	547.83	548.31	548.79
1.0	286.95	287.36	287.77	288.18	288.60	289.01	289.42	289.84	290.25	290.66	291.08	291.49
1.5	201.77	202.17	202.57	202.97	203.37	203.77	204.17	204.57	204.97	205.37	205.77	206.17
2.0	159.45	159.85	160.25	160.64	161.04	161.44	161.84	162.24	162.64	163.04	163.44	163.84
2.5	134.27	134.67	135.07	135.47	135.87	136.28	136.68	137.08	137.49	137.89	138.30	138.70
3.0	117.65	118.06	118.47	118.87	119.28	119.69	120.10	120.51	120.92	121.33	121.75	122.16
3.5	105.93	106.34	106.76	107.17	107.59	108.01	108.42	108.84	109.26	109.68	110.10	110.52
4.0	97.27	97.69	98.11	98.53	98.96	99.38	99.81	100.24	100.66	101.09	101.52	101.95
4.5	90.64	91.07	91.50	91.93	92.36	92.80	93.23	93.67	94.10	94.54	94.98	95.42
5.0	85.43	85.87	86.31	86.75	87.19	87.63	88.08	88.52	88.97	89.41	89.86	90.31
5.5	81.25	81.70	82.15	82.60	83.05	83.50	83.96	84.41	84.86	85.32	85.78	86.24
6.0	77.85	78.31	78.77	79.22	79.68	80.14	80.61	81.07	81.53	82.00	82.47	82.93
6.5	75.04	75.51	75.97	76.44	76.91	77.38	77.85	78.32	78.79	79.27	79.74	80.22
7.0	72.70	73.17	73.65	74.12	74.60	75.08	75.56	76.04	76.52	77.00	77.49	77.97
7.5	70.72	71.20	71.68	72.17	72.65	73.14	73.63	74.12	74.61	75.10	75.59	76.09
8.0	69.04	69.53	70.02	70.51	71.01	71.50	72.00	72.50	72.99	73.49	74.00	74.50
8.5	67.61	68.10	68.60	69.10	69.60	70.11	70.61	71.11	71.62	72.13	72.64	73.15
9.0	66.37	66.88	67.38	67.89	68.40	68.91	69.42	69.93	70.45	70.96	71.48	72.00
9.5	65.31	65.82	66.33	66.85	67.36	67.88	68.40	68.92	69.44	69.96	70.49	71.01
10.0	64.38	64.90	65.42	65.94	66.47	66.99	67.52	68.04	68.57	69.10	69.63	70.16
10.5	63.58	64.10	64.63	65.16	65.69	66.22	66.75	67.29	67.82	68.36	68.89	69.43
11.0	62.88	63.41	63.94	64.48	65.01	65.55	66.09	66.63	67.17	67.71	68.25	68.80
11.5	62.26	62.80	63.34	63.88	64.42	64.96	65.51	66.05	66.60	67.15	67.70	68.25
12.0	61.72	62.26	62.81	63.36	63.90	64.45	65.00	65.55	66.11	66.66	67.22	67.77
12.5	61.25	61.79	62.35	62.90	63.45	64.00	64.56	65.12	65.67	66.23	66.79	67.36
13.0	60.83	61.38	61.94	62.49	63.05	63.61	64.17	64.73	65.30	65.86	66.43	66.99
13.5	60.46	61.02	61.58	62.14	62.70	63.27	63.83	64.40	64.96	65.53	66.10	66.68
14.0	60.13	60.69	61.26	61.83	62.39	62.96	63.53	64.10	64.67	65.25	65.82	66.40
14.5	59.84	60.41	60.98	61.55	62.12	62.69	63.27	63.84	64.42	65.00	65.57	66.15
15.0	59.59	60.16	60.73	61.31	61.88	62.46	63.04	63.61	64.19	64.78	65.36	65.94
15.5	59.36	59.93	60.51	61.09	61.67	62.25	62.83	63.41	64.00	64.58	65.17	65.75
16.0	59.16	59.74	60.32	60.90	61.48	62.07	62.65	63.24	63.82	64.41	65.00	65.59
16.5	58.98	59.56	60.14	60.73	61.32	61.90	62.49	63.08	63.67	64.26	64.85	65.45
17.0	58.82	59.40	59.99	60.58	61.17	61.76	62.35	62.94	63.53	64.13	64.72	65.32
17.5	58.68	59.27	59.86	60.45	61.04	61.63	62.22	62.82	63.42	64.01	64.61	65.21
18.0	58.55	59.14	59.73	60.33	60.92	61.52	62.11	62.71	63.31	63.91	64.51	65.11
18.5	58.44	59.03	59.63	60.22	60.82	61.42	62.02	62.62	63.22	63.82	64.42	65.02
19.0	58.34	58.93	59.53	60.13	60.73	61.33	61.93	62.53	63.13	63.74	64.34	64.95
19.5	58.25	58.85	59.45	60.05	60.65	61.25	61.85	62.46	63.06	63.67	64.27	64.88
20.0	58.17	58.77	59.37	59.97	60.58	61.18	61.79	62.39	63.00	63.61	64.21	64.82
20.5	58.10	58.70	59.30	59.91	60.51	61.12	61.73	62.33	62.94	63.55	64.16	64.77
21.0	58.03	58.64	59.24	59.85	60.46	61.07	61.67	62.28	62.89	63.50	64.11	64.72
21.5	57.98	58.58	59.19	59.80	60.41	61.02	61.63	62.24	62.85	63.46	64.07	64.68
22.0	57.93	58.54	59.14	59.75	60.36	60.97	61.58	62.20	62.81	63.42	64.03	64.65
22.5	57.88	58.49	59.10	59.71	60.32	60.93	61.55	62.16	62.77	63.39	64.00	64.62
23.0	57.84	58.45	59.06	59.68	60.29	60.90	61.51	62.13	62.74	63.36	63.97	64.59
23.5	57.81	58.42	59.03	59.64	60.26	60.87	61.49	62.10	62.72	63.33	63.95	64.56
24.0	57.77	58.39	59.00	59.61	60.23	60.84	61.46	62.07	62.69	63.31	63.92	64.54
24.5	57.75	58.36	58.97	59.59	60.20	60.82	61.44	62.05	62.67	63.29	63.90	64.52
25.0	57.72	58.34	58.95	59.57	60.18	60.80	61.42	62.03	62.65	63.27	63.89	64.51
25.5	57.70	58.31	58.93	59.55	60.16	60.78	61.40	62.02	62.63	63.25	63.87	64.49
26.0	57.68	58.29	58.91	59.53	60.15	60.76	61.38	62.00	62.62	63.24	63.86	64.48
26.5	57.66	58.28	58.89	59.51	60.13	60.75	61.37	61.99	62.61	63.23	63.85	64.47
27.0	57.64	58.26	58.88	59.50	60.12	60.74	61.35	61.97	62.59	63.22	63.84	64.46
27.5	57.63	58.25	58.87	59.48	60.10	60.72	61.34	61.96	62.58	63.21	63.83	64.45
28.0	57.61	58.23	58.85	59.47	60.09	60.71	61.33	61.95	62.58	63.20	63.82	64.44
28.5	57.60	58.22	58.84	59.46	60.08	60.70	61.32	61.95	62.57	63.19	63.81	64.43
29.0	57.59	58.21	58.83	59.45	60.07	60.70	61.32	61.94	62.56	63.18	63.80	64.43
29.5	57.58	58.20	58.82	59.45	60.07	60.69	61.31	61.93	62.55	63.18	63.80	64.42
30.0	57.58	58.20	58.82	59.44	60.06	60.68	61.30	61.93	62.55	63.17	63.79	64.42
31.0	57.56	58.18	58.80	59.43	60.05	60.67	61.29	61.92	62.54	63.16	63.78	64.41
32.0	57.55	58.17	58.79	59.42	60.04	60.66	61.29	61.91	62.53	63.15	63.78	64.40
33.0	57.54	58.16	58.79	59.41	60.03	60.66	61.28	61.90	62.53	63.15	63.77	64.40
34.0	57.53	58.16	58.78	59.40	60.03	60.65	61.27	61.90	62.52	63.15	63.77	64.39
35.0	57.53	58.15	58.77	59.40	60.02	60.65	61.27	61.89	62.52	63.14	63.77	64.39
36.0	57.52	58.15	58.77	59.39	60.02	60.64	61.27	61.89	62.52	63.14	63.76	64.39
37.0	57.52	58.14	58.77	59.39	60.02	60.64	61.26	61.89	62.51	63.14	63.76	64.39
38.0	57.52	58.14	58.77	59.39	60.01	60.64	61.26	61.89	62.51	63.14	63.76	64.38
39.0	57.51	58.14	58.76	59.39	60.01	60.64	61.26	61.88	62.51	63.13	63.76	64.38
40.0	57.51	58.14	58.76	59.39	60.01	60.63	61.26	61.88	62.51	63.13	63.76	64.38

SEMIANNUAL
PAYMENT REQUIRED TO AMORTIZE A $1,000.00 LOAN

TERM IN YEARS	2.00%	2.25%	2.50%	2.75%	3.00%	3.25%	3.50%	3.75%	4.00%	4.25%	4.50%	4.75%
					INTEREST RATES							
0.5	1010.00	1011.25	1012.50	1013.75	1015.00	1016.25	1017.50	1018.75	1020.00	1021.25	1022.50	1023.75
1.0	507.52	508.46	509.40	510.34	511.28	512.23	513.17	514.11	515.05	516.00	516.94	517.89
1.5	340.03	340.87	341.71	342.55	343.39	344.23	345.07	345.92	346.76	347.60	348.45	349.30
2.0	256.29	257.08	257.87	258.66	259.45	260.24	261.04	261.83	262.63	263.43	264.22	265.02
2.5	206.04	206.81	207.57	208.33	209.09	209.86	210.63	211.39	212.16	212.93	213.71	214.48
3.0	172.55	173.30	174.04	174.78	175.53	176.28	177.03	177.78	178.53	179.28	180.04	180.80
3.5	148.63	149.36	150.09	150.83	151.56	152.30	153.04	153.78	154.52	155.26	156.01	156.75
4.0	130.70	131.42	132.14	132.86	133.59	134.32	135.05	135.78	136.51	137.25	137.99	138.73
4.5	116.75	117.46	118.18	118.89	119.61	120.34	121.06	121.79	122.52	123.25	123.99	124.72
5.0	105.59	106.30	107.01	107.72	108.44	109.16	109.88	110.60	111.33	112.06	112.79	113.53
5.5	96.46	97.16	97.87	98.58	99.30	100.02	100.74	101.46	102.18	102.91	103.64	104.37
6.0	88.85	89.56	90.26	90.97	91.68	92.40	93.12	93.84	94.56	95.29	96.02	96.76
6.5	82.42	83.12	83.83	84.53	85.25	85.96	86.68	87.40	88.12	88.85	89.58	90.32
7.0	76.91	77.61	78.31	79.02	79.73	80.44	81.16	81.88	82.61	83.34	84.07	84.80
7.5	72.13	72.83	73.53	74.24	74.95	75.66	76.38	77.10	77.83	78.56	79.29	80.03
8.0	67.95	68.65	69.35	70.06	70.77	71.49	72.20	72.93	73.66	74.39	75.12	75.86
8.5	64.26	64.96	65.67	66.37	67.08	67.80	68.52	69.25	69.97	70.71	71.45	72.19
9.0	60.99	61.69	62.39	63.10	63.81	64.53	65.25	65.98	66.71	67.44	68.18	68.93
9.5	58.06	58.76	59.46	60.17	60.88	61.60	62.33	63.05	63.79	64.52	65.27	66.01
10.0	55.42	56.12	56.83	57.54	58.25	58.97	59.70	60.43	61.16	61.90	62.65	63.40
10.5	53.04	53.74	54.44	55.15	55.87	56.59	57.32	58.05	58.79	59.53	60.28	61.03
11.0	50.87	51.57	52.28	52.99	53.71	54.43	55.16	55.90	56.64	57.38	58.13	58.89
11.5	48.89	49.59	50.30	51.02	51.74	52.46	53.19	53.93	54.67	55.42	56.18	56.94
12.0	47.08	47.78	48.49	49.21	49.93	50.66	51.39	52.13	52.88	53.63	54.39	55.15
12.5	45.41	46.12	46.83	47.54	48.27	49.00	49.73	50.48	51.23	51.98	52.74	53.51
13.0	43.87	44.58	45.29	46.01	46.74	47.47	48.21	48.95	49.70	50.46	51.23	52.00
13.5	42.45	43.16	43.87	44.59	45.32	46.05	46.80	47.54	48.30	49.06	49.83	50.60
14.0	41.13	41.84	42.55	43.28	44.01	44.74	45.49	46.24	46.99	47.76	48.53	49.31
14.5	39.90	40.61	41.33	42.05	42.78	43.52	44.27	45.02	45.78	46.55	47.33	48.11
15.0	38.75	39.46	40.18	40.91	41.64	42.39	43.13	43.89	44.65	45.43	46.20	46.99
15.5	37.68	38.39	39.11	39.84	40.58	41.32	42.08	42.83	43.60	44.38	45.16	45.95
16.0	36.68	37.39	38.11	38.84	39.58	40.33	41.08	41.85	42.62	43.39	44.18	44.97
16.5	35.73	36.45	37.17	37.91	38.65	39.40	40.15	40.92	41.69	42.47	43.26	44.06
17.0	34.84	35.56	36.29	37.02	37.77	38.52	39.28	40.05	40.82	41.61	42.40	43.20
17.5	34.01	34.73	35.46	36.19	36.94	37.69	38.46	39.23	40.01	40.80	41.59	42.40
18.0	33.22	33.94	34.67	35.41	36.16	36.91	37.68	38.45	39.24	40.03	40.83	41.64
18.5	32.47	33.20	33.93	34.67	35.42	36.18	36.95	37.73	38.51	39.31	40.11	40.92
19.0	31.77	32.49	33.22	33.97	34.72	35.48	36.25	37.04	37.83	38.62	39.43	40.25
19.5	31.10	31.82	32.56	33.30	34.06	34.82	35.60	36.38	37.18	37.98	38.79	39.61
20.0	30.46	31.19	31.93	32.67	33.43	34.20	34.98	35.76	36.56	37.37	38.18	39.01
20.5	29.86	30.59	31.33	32.08	32.84	33.61	34.39	35.18	35.98	36.79	37.61	38.43
21.0	29.28	30.01	30.75	31.51	32.27	33.04	33.83	34.62	35.42	36.24	37.06	37.89
21.5	28.73	29.47	30.21	30.96	31.73	32.51	33.29	34.09	34.89	35.71	36.54	37.38
22.0	28.21	28.94	29.69	30.45	31.22	31.99	32.78	33.58	34.39	35.21	36.04	36.88
22.5	27.71	28.45	29.20	29.95	30.72	31.51	32.30	33.10	33.91	34.74	35.57	36.42
23.0	27.23	27.97	28.72	29.48	30.26	31.04	31.84	32.64	33.46	34.29	35.12	35.97
23.5	26.78	27.52	28.27	29.03	29.81	30.60	31.39	32.20	33.02	33.85	34.70	35.55
24.0	26.34	27.08	27.84	28.60	29.38	30.17	30.97	31.78	32.61	33.44	34.29	35.14
24.5	25.92	26.66	27.42	28.19	28.97	29.76	30.57	31.38	32.21	33.05	33.90	34.76
25.0	25.52	26.26	27.02	27.79	28.58	29.37	30.18	31.00	31.83	32.67	33.52	34.39
25.5	25.13	25.88	26.64	27.41	28.20	29.00	29.81	30.63	31.46	32.31	33.17	34.03
26.0	24.76	25.51	26.27	27.05	27.84	28.64	29.45	30.28	31.11	31.96	32.82	33.70
26.5	24.40	25.16	25.92	26.70	27.49	28.29	29.11	29.94	30.78	31.63	32.50	33.37
27.0	24.06	24.82	25.58	26.36	27.16	27.96	28.78	29.61	30.46	31.31	32.18	33.06
27.5	23.73	24.49	25.26	26.04	26.84	27.64	28.47	29.30	30.15	31.01	31.88	32.76
28.0	23.41	24.17	24.94	25.73	26.53	27.34	28.16	29.00	29.85	30.71	31.59	32.48
28.5	23.11	23.87	24.64	25.43	26.23	27.04	27.87	28.71	29.57	30.43	31.31	32.20
29.0	22.81	23.57	24.35	25.14	25.94	26.76	27.59	28.43	29.29	30.16	31.04	31.94
29.5	22.53	23.29	24.07	24.86	25.67	26.49	27.32	28.17	29.03	29.90	30.79	31.69
30.0	22.25	23.01	23.79	24.59	25.40	26.22	27.06	27.91	28.77	29.65	30.54	31.44
31.0	21.73	22.49	23.28	24.08	24.89	25.72	26.56	27.42	28.29	29.18	30.07	30.98
32.0	21.24	22.01	22.80	23.60	24.42	25.25	26.10	26.97	27.84	28.73	29.64	30.56
33.0	20.78	21.55	22.35	23.15	23.98	24.82	25.67	26.54	27.43	28.32	29.24	30.16
34.0	20.34	21.12	21.92	22.74	23.57	24.41	25.27	26.15	27.04	27.94	28.86	29.79
35.0	19.94	20.72	21.52	22.34	23.18	24.03	24.89	25.78	26.67	27.58	28.51	29.45
36.0	19.56	20.34	21.15	21.97	22.81	23.67	24.54	25.43	26.33	27.25	28.18	29.13
37.0	19.19	19.99	20.80	21.62	22.47	23.33	24.21	25.10	26.01	26.94	27.88	28.83
38.0	18.85	19.65	20.46	21.30	22.15	23.01	23.90	24.80	25.71	26.64	27.59	28.55
39.0	18.53	19.33	20.15	20.99	21.84	22.71	23.60	24.51	25.43	26.37	27.32	28.29
40.0	18.22	19.03	19.85	20.69	21.55	22.43	23.33	24.24	25.17	26.11	27.07	28.04

SEMIANNUAL
PAYMENT REQUIRED TO AMORTIZE A $1,000.00 LOAN

TERM IN YEARS	INTEREST RATES											
	5.00%	5.25%	5.50%	5.75%	6.00%	6.25%	6.50%	6.75%	7.00%	7.25%	7.50%	7.75%
0.5	1025.00	1026.25	1027.50	1028.75	1030.00	1031.25	1032.50	1033.75	1035.00	1036.25	1037.50	1038.75
1.0	518.83	519.78	520.72	521.67	522.62	523.56	524.51	525.46	526.41	527.35	528.30	529.25
1.5	350.14	350.99	351.84	352.69	353.54	354.39	355.24	356.09	356.94	357.79	358.65	359.50
2.0	265.82	266.62	267.43	268.23	269.03	269.84	270.64	271.45	272.26	273.06	273.87	274.68
2.5	215.25	216.03	216.80	217.58	218.36	219.14	219.92	220.70	221.49	222.27	223.06	223.84
3.0	181.55	182.31	183.08	183.84	184.60	185.37	186.13	186.90	187.67	188.44	189.22	189.99
3.5	157.50	158.25	159.00	159.76	160.51	161.27	162.03	162.79	163.55	164.31	165.08	165.85
4.0	139.47	140.22	140.96	141.71	142.46	143.21	143.97	144.72	145.48	146.24	147.00	147.77
4.5	125.46	126.20	126.95	127.69	128.44	129.19	129.94	130.69	131.45	132.21	132.97	133.73
5.0	114.26	115.00	115.74	116.49	117.24	117.98	118.74	119.49	120.25	121.01	121.77	122.53
5.5	105.11	105.85	106.59	107.34	108.08	108.83	109.58	110.34	111.10	111.86	112.62	113.39
6.0	97.49	98.23	98.97	99.72	100.47	101.22	101.97	102.73	103.49	104.25	105.02	105.79
6.5	91.05	91.79	92.54	93.28	94.03	94.79	95.54	96.30	97.07	97.83	98.60	99.37
7.0	85.54	86.28	87.03	87.78	88.53	89.29	90.05	90.81	91.58	92.35	93.12	93.89
7.5	80.77	81.52	82.26	83.02	83.77	84.53	85.29	86.06	86.83	87.60	88.38	89.16
8.0	76.60	77.35	78.10	78.86	79.62	80.38	81.15	81.92	82.69	83.47	84.25	85.04
8.5	72.93	73.68	74.44	75.20	75.96	76.72	77.49	78.27	79.05	79.83	80.62	81.41
9.0	69.68	70.43	71.19	71.95	72.71	73.48	74.26	75.04	75.82	76.61	77.40	78.20
9.5	66.77	67.52	68.28	69.05	69.82	70.59	71.37	72.16	72.95	73.74	74.54	75.34
10.0	64.15	64.91	65.68	66.45	67.22	68.00	68.78	69.57	70.37	71.16	71.97	72.77
10.5	61.79	62.56	63.32	64.10	64.88	65.66	66.45	67.24	68.04	68.85	69.65	70.47
11.0	59.65	60.42	61.19	61.97	62.75	63.54	64.33	65.13	65.94	66.75	67.56	68.38
11.5	57.70	58.47	59.25	60.03	60.82	61.61	62.41	63.21	64.02	64.84	65.66	66.48
12.0	55.92	56.69	57.47	58.26	59.05	59.85	60.65	61.46	62.28	63.10	63.92	64.76
12.5	54.28	55.06	55.84	56.64	57.43	58.24	59.04	59.86	60.68	61.51	62.34	63.17
13.0	52.77	53.56	54.35	55.14	55.94	56.75	57.56	58.38	59.21	60.04	60.88	61.72
13.5	51.38	52.17	52.96	53.76	54.57	55.38	56.20	57.03	57.86	58.69	59.54	60.39
14.0	50.09	50.88	51.68	52.49	53.30	54.12	54.94	55.77	56.61	57.45	58.30	59.16
14.5	48.90	49.69	50.49	51.30	52.12	52.94	53.77	54.61	55.45	56.30	57.15	58.02
15.0	47.78	48.58	49.39	50.20	51.02	51.85	52.69	53.53	54.38	55.23	56.09	56.96
15.5	46.74	47.55	48.36	49.18	50.00	50.84	51.68	52.52	53.38	54.24	55.11	55.98
16.0	45.77	46.58	47.40	48.22	49.05	49.89	50.73	51.59	52.45	53.31	54.19	55.07
16.5	44.86	45.68	46.50	47.33	48.16	49.00	49.85	50.71	51.58	52.45	53.33	54.22
17.0	44.01	44.83	45.65	46.49	47.33	48.18	49.03	49.89	50.76	51.64	52.53	53.42
17.5	43.21	44.03	44.86	45.70	46.54	47.40	48.26	49.13	50.00	50.89	51.78	52.68
18.0	42.46	43.28	44.12	44.96	45.81	46.67	47.53	48.41	49.29	50.18	51.08	51.98
18.5	41.75	42.58	43.41	44.26	45.12	45.98	46.85	47.73	48.62	49.51	50.42	51.33
19.0	41.08	41.91	42.75	43.60	44.46	45.33	46.21	47.09	47.99	48.89	49.80	50.71
19.5	40.44	41.28	42.13	42.98	43.85	44.72	45.60	46.49	47.39	48.30	49.21	50.14
20.0	39.84	40.68	41.54	42.40	43.27	44.15	45.03	45.93	46.83	47.74	48.66	49.59
20.5	39.27	40.12	40.98	41.84	42.72	43.60	44.49	45.39	46.30	47.22	48.15	49.08
21.0	38.73	39.59	40.45	41.32	42.20	43.09	43.98	44.89	45.80	46.73	47.66	48.60
21.5	38.22	39.08	39.94	40.82	41.70	42.60	43.50	44.41	45.33	46.26	47.20	48.14
22.0	37.74	38.60	39.47	40.35	41.23	42.13	43.04	43.96	44.88	45.82	46.76	47.71
22.5	37.27	38.14	39.01	39.90	40.79	41.69	42.61	43.53	44.46	45.40	46.35	47.30
23.0	36.83	37.70	38.58	39.47	40.37	41.28	42.19	43.12	44.06	45.00	45.95	46.92
23.5	36.41	37.29	38.17	39.06	39.97	40.88	41.80	42.73	43.67	44.62	45.58	46.55
24.0	36.01	36.89	37.78	38.67	39.58	40.50	41.43	42.37	43.31	44.27	45.23	46.20
24.5	35.63	36.51	37.40	38.31	39.22	40.14	41.07	42.02	42.97	43.93	44.90	45.88
25.0	35.26	36.15	37.05	37.95	38.87	39.80	40.74	41.68	42.64	43.60	44.58	45.56
25.5	34.91	35.80	36.71	37.62	38.54	39.47	40.41	41.37	42.33	43.30	44.28	45.27
26.0	34.58	35.47	36.38	37.30	38.22	39.16	40.11	41.06	42.03	43.01	43.99	44.98
26.5	34.26	35.16	36.07	36.99	37.92	38.86	39.81	40.77	41.75	42.73	43.72	44.72
27.0	33.95	34.86	35.77	36.69	37.63	38.58	39.53	40.50	41.48	42.46	43.46	44.46
27.5	33.66	34.57	35.48	36.41	37.35	38.30	39.27	40.24	41.22	42.21	43.21	44.22
28.0	33.38	34.29	35.21	36.14	37.09	38.04	39.01	39.99	40.97	41.97	42.97	43.99
28.5	33.11	34.02	34.95	35.89	36.84	37.80	38.77	39.75	40.74	41.74	42.75	43.77
29.0	32.85	33.77	34.70	35.64	36.59	37.56	38.53	39.52	40.51	41.52	42.53	43.56
29.5	32.60	33.52	34.46	35.40	36.36	37.33	38.31	39.30	40.30	41.31	42.33	43.36
30.0	32.36	33.29	34.23	35.18	36.14	37.11	38.09	39.09	40.09	41.11	42.13	43.16
31.0	31.91	32.84	33.79	34.75	35.72	36.70	37.69	38.70	39.71	40.73	41.77	42.81
32.0	31.49	32.43	33.39	34.35	35.33	36.32	37.32	38.34	39.36	40.39	41.43	42.48
33.0	31.10	32.05	33.01	33.99	34.98	35.97	36.98	38.00	39.04	40.08	41.13	42.19
34.0	30.74	31.70	32.67	33.65	34.65	35.65	36.67	37.70	38.74	39.79	40.85	41.91
35.0	30.40	31.37	32.35	33.34	34.34	35.36	36.38	37.42	38.47	39.52	40.59	41.67
36.0	30.09	31.06	32.05	33.05	34.06	35.08	36.12	37.16	38.21	39.28	40.35	41.44
37.0	29.80	30.78	31.77	32.78	33.80	34.83	35.87	36.92	37.98	39.06	40.14	41.23
38.0	29.52	30.51	31.51	32.53	33.55	34.59	35.64	36.70	37.77	38.85	39.94	41.04
39.0	29.27	30.26	31.27	32.29	33.33	34.37	35.43	36.50	37.57	38.66	39.76	40.86
40.0	29.03	30.03	31.05	32.08	33.12	34.17	35.23	36.31	37.39	38.48	39.59	40.70

SEMIANNUAL
PAYMENT REQUIRED TO AMORTIZE A $1,000.00 LOAN

TERM IN YEARS	INTEREST RATES											
	8.00%	8.25%	8.50%	8.75%	9.00%	9.25%	9.50%	9.75%	10.00%	10.25%	10.50%	10.75%
0.5	1040.00	1041.25	1042.50	1043.75	1045.00	1046.25	1047.50	1048.75	1050.00	1051.25	1052.50	1053.75
1.0	530.20	531.15	532.10	533.05	534.00	534.95	535.91	536.86	537.81	538.76	539.72	540.67
1.5	360.35	361.21	362.06	362.92	363.78	364.64	365.49	366.35	367.21	368.07	368.94	369.80
2.0	275.50	276.31	277.12	277.93	278.75	279.56	280.38	281.20	282.02	282.84	283.66	284.48
2.5	224.63	225.42	226.21	227.00	227.80	228.59	229.39	230.18	230.98	231.78	232.58	233.38
3.0	190.77	191.54	192.32	193.10	193.88	194.67	195.45	196.24	197.02	197.81	198.60	199.39
3.5	166.61	167.39	168.16	168.93	169.71	170.48	171.26	172.04	172.82	173.61	174.39	175.18
4.0	148.53	149.30	150.07	150.84	151.61	152.39	153.17	153.95	154.73	155.51	156.29	157.08
4.5	134.50	135.27	136.03	136.81	137.58	138.36	139.13	139.91	140.70	141.48	142.27	143.05
5.0	123.30	124.06	124.84	125.61	126.38	127.16	127.94	128.72	129.51	130.30	131.09	131.88
5.5	114.15	114.92	115.70	116.47	117.25	118.03	118.82	119.60	120.39	121.19	121.98	122.78
6.0	106.56	107.33	108.11	108.89	109.67	110.46	111.25	112.04	112.83	113.63	114.43	115.23
6.5	100.15	100.93	101.71	102.49	103.28	104.07	104.86	105.66	106.46	107.26	108.07	108.88
7.0	94.67	95.46	96.24	97.03	97.83	98.62	99.42	100.22	101.03	101.84	102.65	103.47
7.5	89.95	90.73	91.53	92.32	93.12	93.92	94.73	95.53	96.35	97.16	97.98	98.80
8.0	85.82	86.62	87.42	88.22	89.02	89.83	90.64	91.46	92.27	93.10	93.92	94.75
8.5	82.20	83.00	83.81	84.61	85.42	86.24	87.06	87.88	88.70	89.53	90.37	91.21
9.0	79.00	79.80	80.61	81.42	82.24	83.06	83.89	84.72	85.55	86.39	87.23	88.08
9.5	76.14	76.95	77.77	78.59	79.41	80.24	81.07	81.91	82.75	83.60	84.44	85.30
10.0	73.59	74.40	75.22	76.05	76.88	77.72	78.56	79.40	80.25	81.10	81.96	82.82
10.5	71.29	72.11	72.94	73.77	74.61	75.45	76.29	77.15	78.00	78.86	79.73	80.60
11.0	69.20	70.03	70.87	71.71	72.55	73.40	74.25	75.11	75.98	76.84	77.72	78.59
11.5	67.31	68.15	68.99	69.84	70.69	71.54	72.40	73.27	74.14	75.02	75.90	76.78
12.0	65.59	66.43	67.28	68.13	68.99	69.86	70.72	71.60	72.48	73.36	74.25	75.14
12.5	64.02	64.87	65.72	66.58	67.44	68.31	69.19	70.07	70.96	71.85	72.75	73.65
13.0	62.57	63.43	64.29	65.15	66.03	66.90	67.79	68.68	69.57	70.47	71.37	72.28
13.5	61.24	62.11	62.97	63.85	64.72	65.61	66.50	67.40	68.30	69.20	70.12	71.03
14.0	60.02	60.89	61.76	62.64	63.53	64.42	65.32	66.22	67.13	68.04	68.96	69.89
14.5	58.88	59.76	60.64	61.53	62.42	63.32	64.22	65.13	66.05	66.97	67.90	68.83
15.0	57.84	58.72	59.60	60.50	61.40	62.30	63.21	64.13	65.06	65.99	66.92	67.86
15.5	56.86	57.75	58.64	59.54	60.45	61.36	62.28	63.21	64.14	65.07	66.02	66.97
16.0	55.95	56.85	57.75	58.65	59.57	60.49	61.41	62.35	63.29	64.23	65.18	66.14
16.5	55.11	56.01	56.92	57.83	58.75	59.68	60.61	61.55	62.50	63.45	64.41	65.37
17.0	54.32	55.23	56.14	57.06	57.99	58.92	59.86	60.81	61.76	62.72	63.69	64.66
17.5	53.58	54.50	55.41	56.34	57.28	58.22	59.16	60.12	61.08	62.04	63.02	63.99
18.0	52.89	53.81	54.74	55.67	56.61	57.56	58.51	59.47	60.44	61.41	62.39	63.38
18.5	52.24	53.17	54.10	55.04	55.99	56.94	57.90	58.87	59.84	60.83	61.81	62.81
19.0	51.64	52.57	53.51	54.45	55.41	56.37	57.33	58.31	59.29	60.28	61.27	62.27
19.5	51.07	52.00	52.95	53.90	54.86	55.83	56.80	57.78	58.77	59.76	60.76	61.77
20.0	50.53	51.47	52.42	53.38	54.35	55.32	56.30	57.29	58.28	59.28	60.29	61.31
20.5	50.02	50.97	51.93	52.89	53.87	54.85	55.83	56.83	57.83	58.83	59.85	60.87
21.0	49.55	50.50	51.46	52.44	53.41	54.40	55.39	56.39	57.40	58.41	59.43	60.46
21.5	49.09	50.06	51.03	52.00	52.99	53.98	54.98	55.98	57.00	58.02	59.05	60.08
22.0	48.67	49.64	50.61	51.60	52.59	53.58	54.59	55.60	56.62	57.65	58.68	59.72
22.5	48.27	49.24	50.22	51.21	52.21	53.21	54.22	55.24	56.27	57.30	58.34	59.38
23.0	47.89	48.87	49.85	50.85	51.85	52.86	53.88	54.90	55.93	56.97	58.02	59.07
23.5	47.53	48.51	49.50	50.50	51.51	52.53	53.55	54.58	55.62	56.66	57.71	58.77
24.0	47.19	48.18	49.17	50.18	51.19	52.22	53.24	54.28	55.32	56.37	57.43	58.49
24.5	46.86	47.86	48.86	49.87	50.89	51.92	52.95	54.00	55.04	56.10	57.16	58.23
25.0	46.56	47.56	48.57	49.58	50.61	51.64	52.68	53.73	54.78	55.84	56.91	57.99
25.5	46.26	47.27	48.28	49.31	50.34	51.38	52.42	53.47	54.53	55.60	56.67	57.75
26.0	45.99	47.00	48.02	49.05	50.08	51.13	52.18	53.23	54.30	55.37	56.45	57.54
26.5	45.72	46.74	47.77	48.80	49.84	50.89	51.94	53.01	54.08	55.16	56.24	57.33
27.0	45.47	46.50	47.53	48.56	49.61	50.66	51.73	52.79	53.87	54.95	56.04	57.14
27.5	45.24	46.26	47.30	48.34	49.39	50.45	51.52	52.59	53.67	54.76	55.85	56.95
28.0	45.01	46.04	47.08	48.13	49.19	50.25	51.32	52.40	53.49	54.58	55.68	56.78
28.5	44.79	45.83	46.88	47.93	48.99	50.06	51.13	52.22	53.31	54.41	55.51	56.62
29.0	44.59	45.63	46.68	47.74	48.80	49.88	50.96	52.05	53.14	54.24	55.35	56.46
29.5	44.39	45.44	46.49	47.56	48.63	49.71	50.79	51.88	52.98	54.09	55.20	56.32
30.0	44.21	45.26	46.32	47.38	48.46	49.54	50.63	51.73	52.83	53.94	55.06	56.18
31.0	43.86	44.92	45.99	47.06	48.15	49.24	50.34	51.44	52.56	53.68	54.80	55.93
32.0	43.54	44.61	45.69	46.77	47.87	48.97	50.07	51.19	52.31	53.44	54.57	55.71
33.0	43.25	44.33	45.42	46.51	47.61	48.72	49.83	50.96	52.09	53.22	54.36	55.51
34.0	42.99	44.08	45.17	46.27	47.38	48.50	49.62	50.75	51.88	53.03	54.17	55.33
35.0	42.75	43.84	44.94	46.05	47.17	48.29	49.42	50.56	51.70	52.85	54.01	55.17
36.0	42.53	43.63	44.74	45.86	46.98	48.11	49.25	50.39	51.54	52.70	53.86	55.02
37.0	42.33	43.44	44.55	45.68	46.81	47.94	49.09	50.24	51.39	52.56	53.72	54.90
38.0	42.14	43.26	44.38	45.51	46.65	47.79	48.94	50.10	51.26	52.43	53.60	54.78
39.0	41.97	43.10	44.23	45.36	46.51	47.66	48.81	49.97	51.14	52.32	53.49	54.68
40.0	41.82	42.95	44.08	45.23	46.38	47.53	48.69	49.86	51.03	52.21	53.40	54.58

214

SEMIANNUAL
PAYMENT REQUIRED TO AMORTIZE A $1,000.00 LOAN

TERM IN YEARS	INTEREST RATES											
	11.00%	11.25%	11.50%	11.75%	12.00%	12.25%	12.50%	12.75%	13.00%	13.25%	13.50%	13.75%
0.5	1055.00	1056.25	1057.50	1058.75	1060.00	1061.25	1062.50	1063.75	1065.00	1066.25	1067.50	1068.75
1.0	541.62	542.58	543.53	544.49	545.44	546.40	547.35	548.31	549.27	550.22	551.18	552.14
1.5	370.66	371.52	372.39	373.25	374.11	374.98	375.85	376.71	377.58	378.45	379.32	380.19
2.0	285.30	286.12	286.95	287.77	288.60	289.42	290.25	291.08	291.91	292.74	293.57	294.40
2.5	234.18	234.98	235.79	236.59	237.40	238.21	239.02	239.83	240.64	241.45	242.27	243.08
3.0	200.18	200.98	201.77	202.57	203.37	204.17	204.97	205.77	206.57	207.38	208.18	208.99
3.5	175.97	176.76	177.55	178.34	179.14	179.94	180.73	181.53	182.34	183.14	183.94	184.75
4.0	157.87	158.66	159.45	160.25	161.04	161.84	162.64	163.44	164.24	165.05	165.85	166.66
4.5	143.84	144.64	145.43	146.23	147.03	147.83	148.63	149.44	150.24	151.05	151.86	152.68
5.0	132.67	133.47	134.27	135.07	135.87	136.68	137.49	138.30	139.11	139.92	140.74	141.56
5.5	123.58	124.38	125.18	125.99	126.80	127.61	128.42	129.24	130.06	130.88	131.71	132.53
6.0	116.03	116.84	117.65	118.47	119.28	120.10	120.92	121.75	122.57	123.40	124.23	125.07
6.5	109.69	110.50	111.32	112.14	112.97	113.79	114.62	115.45	116.29	117.13	117.97	118.81
7.0	104.28	105.11	105.93	106.76	107.59	108.42	109.26	110.10	110.95	111.79	112.64	113.49
7.5	99.63	100.46	101.29	102.13	102.97	103.81	104.66	105.51	106.36	107.21	108.07	108.93
8.0	95.59	96.42	97.27	98.11	98.96	99.81	100.66	101.52	102.38	103.25	104.12	104.99
8.5	92.05	92.89	93.74	94.59	95.45	96.31	97.17	98.04	98.91	99.79	100.66	101.55
9.0	88.92	89.78	90.64	91.50	92.36	93.23	94.10	94.98	95.86	96.74	97.63	98.52
9.5	86.16	87.02	87.88	88.75	89.63	90.50	91.39	92.27	93.16	94.05	94.95	95.85
10.0	83.68	84.55	85.43	86.31	87.19	88.08	88.97	89.86	90.76	91.66	92.57	93.48
10.5	81.47	82.35	83.23	84.12	85.01	85.91	86.81	87.71	88.62	89.53	90.45	91.37
11.0	79.48	80.36	81.25	82.15	83.05	83.96	84.86	85.78	86.70	87.62	88.55	89.48
11.5	77.67	78.57	79.47	80.37	81.28	82.20	83.12	84.04	84.97	85.90	86.83	87.77
12.0	76.04	76.94	77.85	78.77	79.68	80.61	81.53	82.47	83.40	84.34	85.29	86.24
12.5	74.55	75.47	76.38	77.30	78.23	79.16	80.10	81.04	81.99	82.94	83.89	84.85
13.0	73.20	74.12	75.04	75.97	76.91	77.85	78.79	79.74	80.70	81.66	82.62	83.59
13.5	71.96	72.89	73.82	74.76	75.70	76.65	77.61	78.56	79.53	80.50	81.47	82.45
14.0	70.82	71.76	72.70	73.65	74.60	75.56	76.52	77.49	78.46	79.44	80.42	81.41
14.5	69.77	70.72	71.67	72.62	73.58	74.55	75.52	76.50	77.48	78.47	79.46	80.45
15.0	68.81	69.76	70.72	71.68	72.65	73.63	74.61	75.59	76.58	77.58	78.58	79.58
15.5	67.92	68.88	69.85	70.82	71.80	72.78	73.77	74.76	75.76	76.76	77.77	78.78
16.0	67.10	68.07	69.04	70.02	71.01	72.00	72.99	74.00	75.00	76.01	77.03	78.05
16.5	66.34	67.32	68.30	69.28	70.28	71.28	72.28	73.29	74.30	75.32	76.35	77.38
17.0	65.63	66.62	67.61	68.60	69.60	70.61	71.62	72.64	73.66	74.69	75.72	76.76
17.5	64.98	65.97	66.97	67.97	68.98	69.99	71.01	72.04	73.07	74.10	75.14	76.19
18.0	64.37	65.37	66.37	67.38	68.40	69.42	70.45	71.48	72.52	73.56	74.61	75.66
18.5	63.80	64.81	65.82	66.84	67.86	68.89	69.93	70.97	72.01	73.06	74.12	75.18
19.0	63.28	64.29	65.31	66.33	67.36	68.40	69.44	70.49	71.54	72.60	73.66	74.73
19.5	62.78	63.80	64.83	65.86	66.90	67.94	68.99	70.04	71.10	72.17	73.24	74.31
20.0	62.33	63.35	64.38	65.42	66.47	67.52	68.57	69.63	70.70	71.77	72.85	73.93
20.5	61.90	62.93	63.97	65.01	66.06	67.12	68.18	69.25	70.32	71.40	72.48	73.57
21.0	61.49	62.53	63.58	64.63	65.69	66.75	67.82	68.89	69.97	71.06	72.15	73.24
21.5	61.12	62.16	63.22	64.27	65.34	66.41	67.48	68.56	69.65	70.74	71.83	72.94
22.0	60.77	61.82	62.88	63.94	65.01	66.09	67.17	68.25	69.35	70.44	71.54	72.65
22.5	60.44	61.49	62.56	63.63	64.71	65.79	66.87	67.97	69.06	70.17	71.28	72.39
23.0	60.13	61.19	62.26	63.34	64.42	65.51	66.60	67.70	68.80	69.91	71.02	72.14
23.5	59.84	60.91	61.98	63.06	64.15	65.25	66.34	67.45	68.56	69.67	70.79	71.91
24.0	59.56	60.64	61.72	62.81	63.90	65.00	66.11	67.22	68.33	69.45	70.57	71.70
24.5	59.31	60.39	61.48	62.57	63.67	64.77	65.88	67.00	68.12	69.24	70.37	71.51
25.0	59.07	60.15	61.25	62.35	63.45	64.56	65.67	66.79	67.92	69.05	70.18	71.32
25.5	58.84	59.93	61.03	62.13	63.24	64.36	65.48	66.60	67.73	68.87	70.01	71.15
26.0	58.63	59.72	60.83	61.94	63.05	64.17	65.30	66.43	67.56	68.70	69.84	70.99
26.5	58.43	59.53	60.64	61.75	62.87	64.00	65.12	66.26	67.40	68.54	69.69	70.84
27.0	58.24	59.34	60.46	61.58	62.70	63.83	64.96	66.10	67.25	68.40	69.55	70.71
27.5	58.06	59.17	60.29	61.41	62.54	63.68	64.81	65.96	67.11	68.26	69.42	70.58
28.0	57.89	59.01	60.13	61.26	62.39	63.53	64.67	65.82	66.97	68.13	69.29	70.46
28.5	57.73	58.86	59.98	61.11	62.25	63.39	64.54	65.69	66.85	68.01	69.18	70.34
29.0	57.59	58.71	59.84	60.98	62.12	63.27	64.42	65.57	66.73	67.90	69.07	70.24
29.5	57.44	58.57	59.71	60.85	62.00	63.15	64.30	65.46	66.63	67.79	68.97	70.14
30.0	57.31	58.45	59.59	60.73	61.88	63.04	64.19	65.36	66.53	67.70	68.87	70.05
31.0	57.07	58.21	59.36	60.51	61.67	62.83	64.00	65.17	66.34	67.52	68.70	69.89
32.0	56.85	58.00	59.16	60.32	61.48	62.65	63.82	65.00	66.18	67.37	68.55	69.74
33.0	56.66	57.82	58.98	60.14	61.32	62.49	63.67	64.85	66.04	67.23	68.42	69.62
34.0	56.49	57.65	58.82	59.99	61.17	62.35	63.53	64.72	65.92	67.11	68.31	69.51
35.0	56.33	57.50	58.68	59.86	61.04	62.22	63.42	64.61	65.81	67.01	68.21	69.42
36.0	56.19	57.37	58.55	59.73	60.92	62.11	63.31	64.51	65.71	66.92	68.12	69.33
37.0	56.07	57.25	58.44	59.63	60.82	62.02	63.22	64.42	65.63	66.83	68.05	69.26
38.0	55.96	57.15	58.34	59.53	60.73	61.93	63.13	64.34	65.55	66.76	67.98	69.20
39.0	55.86	57.05	58.25	59.45	60.65	61.85	63.06	64.27	65.49	66.70	67.92	69.14
40.0	55.77	56.97	58.17	59.37	60.58	61.79	63.00	64.21	65.43	66.65	67.87	69.09

SEMIANNUAL
PAYMENT REQUIRED TO AMORTIZE A $1,000.00 LOAN

TERM IN YEARS	INTEREST RATES											
	14.00%	14.25%	14.50%	14.75%	15.00%	15.25%	15.50%	15.75%	16.00%	16.25%	16.50%	16.75%
0.5	1070.00	1071.25	1072.50	1073.75	1075.00	1076.25	1077.50	1078.75	1080.00	1081.25	1082.50	1083.75
1.0	553.10	554.06	555.01	555.97	556.93	557.89	558.85	559.81	560.77	561.74	562.70	563.66
1.5	381.06	381.93	382.80	383.67	384.54	385.42	386.29	387.16	388.04	388.91	389.79	390.67
2.0	295.23	296.07	296.90	297.74	298.57	299.41	300.25	301.09	301.93	302.77	303.61	304.45
2.5	243.90	244.71	245.53	246.35	247.17	247.99	248.81	249.64	250.46	251.29	252.11	252.94
3.0	209.80	210.61	211.42	212.24	213.05	213.87	214.68	215.50	216.32	217.14	217.96	218.79
3.5	185.56	186.37	187.18	187.99	188.81	189.62	190.44	191.26	192.08	192.90	193.72	194.55
4.0	167.47	168.28	169.10	169.91	170.73	171.55	172.37	173.20	174.02	174.85	175.67	176.50
4.5	153.49	154.31	155.13	155.95	156.77	157.60	158.42	159.25	160.08	160.92	161.75	162.59
5.0	142.38	143.21	144.03	144.86	145.69	146.52	147.36	148.20	149.03	149.88	150.72	151.56
5.5	133.36	134.19	135.03	135.86	136.70	137.54	138.39	139.23	140.08	140.93	141.78	142.64
6.0	125.91	126.75	127.59	128.43	129.28	130.13	130.99	131.84	132.70	133.56	134.42	135.29
6.5	119.66	120.50	121.36	122.21	123.07	123.93	124.79	125.66	126.53	127.40	128.27	129.15
7.0	114.35	115.21	116.07	116.93	117.80	118.67	119.55	120.42	121.30	122.18	123.07	123.96
7.5	109.80	110.67	111.54	112.41	113.29	114.17	115.06	115.94	116.83	117.73	118.62	119.52
8.0	105.86	106.74	107.62	108.51	109.40	110.29	111.18	112.08	112.98	113.89	114.79	115.70
8.5	102.43	103.32	104.21	105.11	106.01	106.91	107.81	108.72	109.63	110.55	111.47	112.39
9.0	99.42	100.32	101.22	102.12	103.03	103.95	104.86	105.78	106.71	107.63	108.56	109.50
9.5	96.76	97.67	98.58	99.50	100.42	101.34	102.27	103.20	104.13	105.07	106.01	106.96
10.0	94.40	95.32	96.24	97.17	98.10	99.03	99.97	100.91	101.86	102.81	103.76	104.72
10.5	92.29	93.22	94.16	95.09	96.03	96.98	97.93	98.88	99.84	100.80	101.76	102.73
11.0	90.41	91.35	92.29	93.24	94.19	95.15	96.11	97.07	98.04	99.01	99.98	100.96
11.5	88.72	89.67	90.62	91.58	92.54	93.51	94.48	95.45	96.43	97.41	98.39	99.38
12.0	87.19	88.15	89.12	90.08	91.06	92.03	93.01	93.99	94.98	95.98	96.97	97.97
12.5	85.82	86.78	87.76	88.73	89.72	90.70	91.69	92.69	93.68	94.69	95.69	96.70
13.0	84.57	85.54	86.53	87.51	88.50	89.50	90.50	91.50	92.51	93.52	94.54	95.56
13.5	83.43	84.42	85.41	86.41	87.41	88.41	89.42	90.44	91.45	92.48	93.50	94.53
14.0	82.40	83.39	84.39	85.40	86.41	87.42	88.44	89.47	90.49	91.53	92.56	93.60
14.5	81.45	82.46	83.47	84.48	85.50	86.53	87.55	88.59	89.62	90.66	91.71	92.76
15.0	80.59	81.61	82.62	83.65	84.68	85.71	86.75	87.79	88.83	89.88	90.94	91.99
15.5	79.80	80.82	81.85	82.88	83.92	84.96	86.01	87.06	88.11	89.17	90.23	91.30
16.0	79.08	80.11	81.15	82.19	83.23	84.28	85.33	86.39	87.46	88.52	89.59	90.67
16.5	78.41	79.45	80.50	81.55	82.60	83.66	84.72	85.79	86.86	87.93	89.01	90.09
17.0	77.80	78.85	79.90	80.96	82.02	83.09	84.16	85.23	86.31	87.39	88.48	89.57
17.5	77.24	78.29	79.35	80.42	81.49	82.56	83.64	84.72	85.81	86.90	87.99	89.09
18.0	76.72	77.78	78.85	79.92	81.00	82.08	83.17	84.26	85.35	86.45	87.55	88.66
18.5	76.24	77.31	78.39	79.47	80.55	81.64	82.73	83.83	84.93	86.03	87.14	88.26
19.0	75.80	76.88	77.96	79.05	80.14	81.23	82.33	83.44	84.54	85.66	86.77	87.89
19.5	75.39	76.48	77.56	78.66	79.76	80.86	81.96	83.08	84.19	85.31	86.43	87.56
20.0	75.01	76.11	77.20	78.30	79.41	80.51	81.63	82.74	83.87	84.99	86.12	87.25
20.5	74.66	75.76	76.86	77.97	79.08	80.20	81.32	82.44	83.57	84.70	85.83	86.97
21.0	74.34	75.44	76.55	77.67	78.78	79.90	81.03	82.16	83.29	84.43	85.57	86.71
21.5	74.04	75.15	76.27	77.38	78.51	79.63	80.77	81.90	83.04	84.18	85.33	86.48
22.0	73.76	74.88	76.00	77.12	78.25	79.38	80.52	81.66	82.81	83.95	85.11	86.26
22.5	73.50	74.63	75.75	76.88	78.02	79.15	80.30	81.44	82.59	83.75	84.90	86.06
23.0	73.26	74.39	75.52	76.66	77.80	78.94	80.09	81.24	82.39	83.55	84.71	85.88
23.5	73.04	74.17	75.31	76.45	77.60	78.75	79.90	81.05	82.21	83.38	84.54	85.71
24.0	72.84	73.97	75.11	76.26	77.41	78.56	79.72	80.88	82.05	83.21	84.38	85.56
24.5	72.64	73.79	74.93	76.08	77.24	78.40	79.56	80.72	81.89	83.06	84.24	85.41
25.0	72.46	73.61	74.76	75.92	77.08	78.24	79.41	80.58	81.75	82.92	84.10	85.28
25.5	72.30	73.45	74.61	75.77	76.93	78.10	79.27	80.44	81.62	82.80	83.98	85.16
26.0	72.14	73.30	74.46	75.62	76.79	77.96	79.14	80.31	81.49	82.68	83.86	85.05
26.5	72.00	73.16	74.32	75.49	76.66	77.84	79.02	80.20	81.38	82.57	83.76	84.95
27.0	71.87	73.03	74.20	75.37	76.55	77.72	78.91	80.09	81.28	82.47	83.66	84.86
27.5	71.74	72.91	74.08	75.26	76.44	77.62	78.80	79.99	81.18	82.38	83.57	84.77
28.0	71.63	72.80	73.97	75.15	76.33	77.52	78.71	79.90	81.09	82.29	83.49	84.69
28.5	71.52	72.69	73.87	75.05	76.24	77.43	78.62	79.82	81.01	82.21	83.41	84.62
29.0	71.42	72.60	73.78	74.96	76.15	77.35	78.54	79.74	80.94	82.14	83.34	84.55
29.5	71.32	72.50	73.69	74.88	76.07	77.27	78.46	79.66	80.87	82.07	83.28	84.49
30.0	71.23	72.42	73.61	74.80	76.00	77.19	78.39	79.60	80.80	82.01	83.22	84.43
31.0	71.08	72.27	73.46	74.66	75.86	77.06	78.27	79.48	80.69	81.90	83.11	84.33
32.0	70.94	72.14	73.34	74.54	75.74	76.95	78.16	79.38	80.59	81.81	83.02	84.24
33.0	70.82	72.02	73.23	74.43	75.64	76.86	78.07	79.29	80.51	81.73	82.95	84.17
34.0	70.72	71.92	73.13	74.34	75.56	76.77	77.99	79.21	80.43	81.66	82.88	84.11
35.0	70.62	71.84	73.05	74.26	75.48	76.70	77.92	79.15	80.37	81.60	82.83	84.06
36.0	70.55	71.76	72.98	74.20	75.42	76.64	77.87	79.09	80.32	81.55	82.78	84.01
37.0	70.48	71.70	72.92	74.14	75.36	76.59	77.82	79.04	80.27	81.51	82.74	83.97
38.0	70.42	71.64	72.86	74.09	75.31	76.54	77.77	79.00	80.24	81.47	82.70	83.94
39.0	70.36	71.59	72.81	74.04	75.27	76.50	77.74	78.97	80.20	81.44	82.68	83.91
40.0	70.32	71.55	72.77	74.00	75.24	76.47	77.70	78.94	80.17	81.41	82.65	83.89

SEMIANNUAL
PAYMENT REQUIRED TO AMORTIZE A $1,000.00 LOAN

TERM IN YEARS	17.00%	17.25%	17.50%	17.75%	18.00%	18.25%	18.50%	18.75%	19.00%	19.25%	19.50%	19.75%
					INTEREST RATES							
0.5	1085.00	1086.25	1087.50	1088.75	1090.00	1091.25	1092.50	1093.75	1095.00	1096.25	1097.50	1098.75
1.0	564.62	565.58	566.55	567.51	568.47	569.44	570.40	571.37	572.33	573.30	574.26	575.23
1.5	391.54	392.42	393.30	394.18	395.06	395.94	396.82	397.70	398.58	399.47	400.35	401.24
2.0	305.29	306.14	306.98	307.83	308.67	309.52	310.37	311.22	312.07	312.92	313.77	314.62
2.5	253.77	254.60	255.43	256.26	257.10	257.93	258.77	259.60	260.44	261.28	262.12	262.96
3.0	219.61	220.44	221.27	222.09	222.92	223.76	224.59	225.42	226.26	227.09	227.93	228.77
3.5	195.37	196.20	197.03	197.86	198.70	199.53	200.37	201.20	202.04	202.88	203.72	204.57
4.0	177.34	178.17	179.00	179.84	180.68	181.52	182.36	183.21	184.05	184.90	185.75	186.60
4.5	163.43	164.27	165.11	165.96	166.80	167.65	168.50	169.36	170.21	171.07	171.92	172.78
5.0	152.41	153.26	154.11	154.97	155.83	156.68	157.54	158.41	159.27	160.14	161.01	161.88
5.5	143.50	144.36	145.22	146.08	146.95	147.82	148.69	149.57	150.44	151.32	152.20	153.08
6.0	136.16	137.03	137.90	138.78	139.66	140.54	141.42	142.30	143.19	144.08	144.98	145.87
6.5	130.03	130.91	131.79	132.68	133.57	134.46	135.36	136.26	137.16	138.06	138.97	139.87
7.0	124.85	125.74	126.64	127.54	128.44	129.34	130.25	131.16	132.07	132.99	133.91	134.83
7.5	120.43	121.33	122.24	123.15	124.06	124.98	125.90	126.82	127.75	128.68	129.61	130.54
8.0	116.62	117.54	118.46	119.38	120.30	121.23	122.17	123.10	124.04	124.98	125.92	126.87
8.5	113.32	114.25	115.18	116.11	117.05	117.99	118.94	119.89	120.84	121.79	122.75	123.71
9.0	110.44	111.38	112.32	113.27	114.22	115.17	116.13	117.09	118.05	119.02	119.99	120.96
9.5	107.91	108.86	109.81	110.77	111.74	112.70	113.67	114.64	115.62	116.60	117.58	118.56
10.0	105.68	106.64	107.61	108.58	109.55	110.53	111.51	112.49	113.48	114.47	115.47	116.46
10.5	103.70	104.68	105.65	106.64	107.62	108.61	109.60	110.60	111.60	112.60	113.61	114.62
11.0	101.94	102.93	103.92	104.91	105.91	106.91	107.91	108.92	109.93	110.95	111.96	112.99
11.5	100.38	101.37	102.37	103.38	104.39	105.40	106.41	107.43	108.45	109.48	110.51	111.54
12.0	98.97	99.98	100.99	102.01	103.03	104.05	105.08	106.11	107.14	108.18	109.21	110.26
12.5	97.72	98.73	99.76	100.78	101.81	102.84	103.88	104.92	105.96	107.01	108.06	109.12
13.0	96.59	97.61	98.65	99.68	100.72	101.76	102.81	103.86	104.91	105.97	107.03	108.10
13.5	95.57	96.60	97.64	98.69	99.74	100.79	101.85	102.91	103.97	105.04	106.11	107.19
14.0	94.64	95.69	96.74	97.80	98.86	99.92	100.99	102.06	103.13	104.21	105.29	106.37
14.5	93.81	94.87	95.93	96.99	98.06	99.13	100.21	101.29	102.37	103.46	104.54	105.64
15.0	93.06	94.12	95.19	96.26	97.34	98.42	99.51	100.59	101.69	102.78	103.88	104.98
15.5	92.37	93.44	94.52	95.60	96.69	97.78	98.87	99.97	101.07	102.17	103.28	104.39
16.0	91.75	92.83	93.92	95.01	96.10	97.20	98.30	99.40	100.51	101.62	102.74	103.86
16.5	91.18	92.27	93.37	94.46	95.57	96.67	97.78	98.89	100.01	101.13	102.25	103.38
17.0	90.66	91.76	92.87	93.97	95.08	96.19	97.31	98.43	99.55	100.68	101.81	102.94
17.5	90.19	91.30	92.41	93.52	94.64	95.76	96.89	98.01	99.14	100.28	101.41	102.55
18.0	89.77	90.88	92.00	93.12	94.24	95.37	96.50	97.63	98.77	99.91	101.05	102.20
18.5	89.37	90.49	91.62	92.74	93.88	95.01	96.15	97.29	98.43	99.58	100.73	101.88
19.0	89.01	90.14	91.27	92.41	93.54	94.68	95.83	96.97	98.12	99.28	100.43	101.59
19.5	88.60	90.82	90.06	92.10	93.24	94.39	95.54	96.69	97.05	99.00	100.17	101.00
20.0	88.39	89.53	90.67	91.82	92.96	94.12	95.27	96.43	97.59	98.76	99.92	101.09
20.5	88.11	89.26	90.41	91.56	92.71	93.87	95.03	96.20	97.36	98.53	99.70	100.88
21.0	87.86	89.01	90.17	91.32	92.48	93.65	94.81	95.98	97.15	98.33	99.50	100.68
21.5	87.63	88.79	89.95	91.11	92.27	93.44	94.61	95.79	96.96	98.14	99.32	100.51
22.0	87.42	88.58	89.74	90.91	92.08	93.25	94.43	95.61	96.79	97.97	99.16	100.35
22.5	87.22	88.39	89.56	90.73	91.91	93.08	94.26	95.45	96.63	97.82	99.01	100.20
23.0	87.05	88.22	89.39	90.57	91.75	92.93	94.11	95.30	96.49	97.68	98.87	100.07
23.5	86.88	88.06	89.24	90.42	91.60	92.79	93.97	95.17	96.36	97.55	98.75	99.95
24.0	86.73	87.91	89.09	90.28	91.47	92.66	93.85	95.04	96.24	97.44	98.64	99.84
24.5	86.60	87.78	88.96	90.15	91.34	92.54	93.73	94.93	96.13	97.33	98.54	99.74
25.0	86.47	87.66	88.85	90.04	91.23	92.43	93.63	94.83	96.03	97.24	98.44	99.65
25.5	86.35	87.54	88.74	89.93	91.13	92.33	93.53	94.74	95.94	97.15	98.36	99.57
26.0	86.24	87.44	88.64	89.83	91.04	92.24	93.44	94.65	95.86	97.07	98.28	99.50
26.5	86.15	87.34	88.54	89.75	90.95	92.16	93.36	94.57	95.79	97.00	98.21	99.43
27.0	86.06	87.26	88.46	89.66	90.87	92.08	93.29	94.50	95.72	96.93	98.15	99.37
27.5	85.97	87.18	88.38	89.59	90.80	92.01	93.22	94.44	95.65	96.87	98.09	99.31
28.0	85.90	87.10	88.31	89.52	90.73	91.95	93.16	94.38	95.60	96.82	98.04	99.26
28.5	85.83	87.03	88.24	89.46	90.67	91.89	93.11	94.33	95.55	96.77	97.99	99.22
29.0	85.76	86.97	88.18	89.40	90.62	91.83	93.05	94.28	95.50	96.72	97.95	99.18
29.5	85.70	86.91	88.13	89.35	90.57	91.79	93.01	94.23	95.46	96.68	97.91	99.14
30.0	85.65	86.86	88.08	89.30	90.52	91.74	92.97	94.19	95.42	96.64	97.87	99.10
31.0	85.55	86.77	87.99	89.21	90.44	91.66	92.89	94.12	95.35	96.58	97.81	99.04
32.0	85.47	86.69	87.91	89.14	90.37	91.60	92.83	94.06	95.29	96.52	97.76	98.99
33.0	85.40	86.62	87.85	89.08	90.31	91.54	92.78	94.01	95.24	96.48	97.72	98.95
34.0	85.34	86.57	87.80	89.03	90.26	91.50	92.73	93.97	95.20	96.44	97.68	98.92
35.0	85.29	86.52	87.75	88.99	90.22	91.46	92.69	93.93	95.17	96.41	97.65	98.89
36.0	85.24	86.48	87.71	88.95	90.19	91.43	92.66	93.90	95.14	96.38	97.63	98.87
37.0	85.21	86.44	87.68	88.92	90.16	91.40	92.64	93.88	95.12	96.36	97.60	98.85
38.0	85.18	86.42	87.65	88.89	90.13	91.37	92.62	93.86	95.10	96.34	97.59	98.83
39.0	85.15	86.39	87.63	88.87	90.11	91.36	92.60	93.84	95.09	96.33	97.57	98.82
40.0	85.13	86.37	87.61	88.85	90.10	91.34	92.58	93.83	95.07	96.32	97.56	98.81

SEMIANNUAL
PAYMENT REQUIRED TO AMORTIZE A $1,000.00 LOAN

TERM IN YEARS	INTEREST RATES											
	20.00%	20.25%	20.50%	20.75%	21.00%	21.25%	21.50%	21.75%	22.00%	22.25%	22.50%	22.75%
0.5	1100.00	1101.25	1102.50	1103.75	1105.00	1106.25	1107.50	1108.75	1110.00	1111.25	1112.50	1113.75
1.0	576.20	577.16	578.13	579.10	580.06	581.03	582.00	582.97	583.94	584.91	585.88	586.85
1.5	402.12	403.01	403.89	404.78	405.66	406.55	407.44	408.33	409.22	410.11	411.00	411.89
2.0	315.48	316.33	317.18	318.04	318.90	319.75	320.61	321.47	322.33	323.19	324.05	324.92
2.5	263.80	264.65	265.49	266.33	267.18	268.03	268.88	269.73	270.58	271.43	272.28	273.13
3.0	229.61	230.45	231.30	232.14	232.99	233.83	234.68	235.53	236.38	237.23	238.09	238.94
3.5	205.41	206.26	207.10	207.95	208.80	209.66	210.51	211.36	212.22	213.08	213.94	214.80
4.0	187.45	188.30	189.16	190.02	190.87	191.73	192.60	193.46	194.33	195.19	196.06	196.93
4.5	173.65	174.51	175.37	176.24	177.11	177.98	178.86	179.73	180.61	181.49	182.37	183.25
5.0	162.75	163.63	164.50	165.38	166.26	167.15	168.03	168.92	169.81	170.70	171.59	172.49
5.5	153.97	154.86	155.74	156.64	157.53	158.43	159.32	160.22	161.13	162.03	162.94	163.85
6.0	146.77	147.67	148.57	149.47	150.38	151.29	152.20	153.12	154.03	154.95	155.87	156.79
6.5	140.78	141.70	142.61	143.53	144.45	145.37	146.30	147.23	148.16	149.09	150.02	150.96
7.0	135.75	136.68	137.61	138.54	139.47	140.41	141.35	142.29	143.23	144.18	145.13	146.08
7.5	131.48	132.42	133.36	134.31	135.25	136.20	137.16	138.11	139.07	140.03	140.99	141.96
8.0	127.82	128.77	129.73	130.69	131.65	132.61	133.58	134.55	135.52	136.50	137.47	138.45
8.5	124.67	125.63	126.60	127.58	128.55	129.53	130.51	131.49	132.48	133.47	134.46	135.45
9.0	121.94	122.91	123.90	124.88	125.87	126.86	127.85	128.85	129.85	130.85	131.85	132.86
9.5	119.55	120.54	121.54	122.54	123.54	124.54	125.55	126.56	127.57	128.58	129.60	130.62
10.0	117.46	118.47	119.48	120.49	121.50	122.51	123.53	124.56	125.58	126.61	127.64	128.67
10.5	115.63	116.65	117.66	118.69	119.71	120.74	121.77	122.81	123.84	124.88	125.93	126.97
11.0	114.01	115.04	116.07	117.10	118.14	119.18	120.22	121.27	122.32	123.37	124.43	125.48
11.5	112.58	113.62	114.66	115.70	116.75	117.80	118.86	119.92	120.98	122.04	123.11	124.18
12.0	111.30	112.35	113.41	114.46	115.52	116.59	117.65	118.72	119.79	120.87	121.94	123.02
12.5	110.17	111.23	112.30	113.36	114.43	115.51	116.58	117.66	118.75	119.83	120.92	122.01
13.0	109.16	110.23	111.31	112.39	113.47	114.55	115.64	116.73	117.82	118.91	120.01	121.11
13.5	108.26	109.34	110.43	111.51	112.60	113.70	114.79	115.89	116.99	118.10	119.21	120.32
14.0	107.46	108.55	109.64	110.74	111.83	112.94	114.04	115.15	116.26	117.38	118.49	119.61
14.5	106.73	107.83	108.93	110.04	111.15	112.26	113.37	114.49	115.61	116.73	117.86	118.99
15.0	106.08	107.19	108.30	109.42	110.53	111.65	112.78	113.90	115.03	116.16	117.29	118.43
15.5	105.50	106.62	107.74	108.86	109.98	111.11	112.24	113.38	114.51	115.65	116.79	117.94
16.0	104.98	106.10	107.23	108.36	109.49	110.63	111.76	112.90	114.05	115.19	116.34	117.49
16.5	104.50	105.64	106.77	107.91	109.05	110.19	111.34	112.48	113.63	114.79	115.94	117.10
17.0	104.08	105.22	106.36	107.50	108.65	109.80	110.95	112.11	113.26	114.42	115.59	116.75
17.5	103.69	104.84	105.99	107.14	108.29	109.45	110.61	111.77	112.93	114.10	115.27	116.44
18.0	103.35	104.50	105.65	106.81	107.97	109.13	110.30	111.47	112.64	113.81	114.98	116.16
18.5	103.03	104.19	105.35	106.52	107.68	108.85	110.02	111.19	112.37	113.55	114.73	115.91
19.0	102.75	103.92	105.08	106.25	107.42	108.60	109.77	110.95	112.13	113.31	114.50	115.68
19.5	102.50	103.67	104.84	106.01	107.19	108.37	109.55	110.73	111.92	113.10	114.29	115.48
20.0	102.26	103.44	104.62	105.79	106.98	108.16	109.35	110.53	111.72	112.92	114.11	115.30
20.5	102.05	103.23	104.42	105.60	106.79	107.97	109.16	110.36	111.55	112.75	113.95	115.14
21.0	101.86	103.05	104.24	105.42	106.61	107.81	109.00	110.20	111.40	112.60	113.80	115.00
21.5	101.69	102.88	104.07	105.26	106.46	107.66	108.85	110.05	111.26	112.46	113.67	114.87
22.0	101.54	102.73	103.92	105.12	106.32	107.52	108.72	109.93	111.13	112.34	113.55	114.76
22.5	101.40	102.59	103.79	104.99	106.19	107.40	108.60	109.81	111.02	112.23	113.44	114.65
23.0	101.27	102.47	103.67	104.87	106.08	107.29	108.49	109.71	110.92	112.13	113.35	114.56
23.5	101.15	102.36	103.56	104.77	105.98	107.19	108.40	109.61	110.83	112.04	113.26	114.48
24.0	101.05	102.25	103.46	104.67	105.88	107.10	108.31	109.53	110.74	111.96	113.18	114.40
24.5	100.95	102.16	103.37	104.58	105.80	107.01	108.23	109.45	110.67	111.89	113.11	114.34
25.0	100.86	102.08	103.29	104.51	105.72	106.94	108.16	109.38	110.60	111.83	113.05	114.28
25.5	100.79	102.00	103.22	104.43	105.65	106.87	108.10	109.32	110.54	111.77	113.00	114.22
26.0	100.71	101.93	103.15	104.37	105.59	106.82	108.04	109.26	110.49	111.72	112.95	114.18
26.5	100.65	101.87	103.09	104.31	105.54	106.76	107.99	109.21	110.44	111.67	112.90	114.13
27.0	100.59	101.81	103.04	104.26	105.49	106.71	107.94	109.17	110.40	111.63	112.86	114.09
27.5	100.54	101.76	102.99	104.21	105.44	106.67	107.90	109.13	110.36	111.59	112.83	114.06
28.0	100.49	101.71	102.94	104.17	105.40	106.63	107.86	109.09	110.32	111.56	112.79	114.03
28.5	100.44	101.67	102.90	104.13	105.36	106.59	107.82	109.06	110.29	111.53	112.76	114.00
29.0	100.40	101.63	102.86	104.09	105.33	106.56	107.79	109.03	110.26	111.50	112.74	113.98
29.5	100.37	101.60	102.83	104.06	105.30	106.53	107.77	109.00	110.24	111.48	112.71	113.95
30.0	100.33	101.57	102.80	104.03	105.27	106.50	107.74	108.98	110.22	111.45	112.69	113.93
31.0	100.28	101.51	102.75	103.98	105.22	106.46	107.70	108.94	110.18	111.42	112.66	113.90
32.0	100.23	101.47	102.70	103.94	105.18	106.42	107.66	108.90	110.14	111.39	112.63	113.87
33.0	100.19	101.43	102.67	103.91	105.15	106.39	107.63	108.87	110.12	111.36	112.60	113.85
34.0	100.16	101.40	102.64	103.88	105.12	106.37	107.61	108.85	110.10	111.34	112.58	113.83
35.0	100.13	101.37	102.62	103.86	105.10	106.35	107.59	108.83	110.08	111.32	112.57	113.82
36.0	100.11	101.35	102.60	103.84	105.08	106.33	107.57	108.82	110.07	111.31	112.56	113.80
37.0	100.09	101.34	102.58	103.82	105.07	106.32	107.56	108.81	110.05	111.30	112.55	113.79
38.0	100.08	101.32	102.57	103.81	105.06	106.30	107.55	108.80	110.04	111.29	112.54	113.79
39.0	100.06	101.31	102.56	103.80	105.05	106.30	107.54	108.79	110.04	111.28	112.53	113.78
40.0	100.05	101.30	102.55	103.79	105.04	106.29	107.54	108.78	110.03	111.28	112.53	113.78

SEMIANNUAL
PAYMENT REQUIRED TO AMORTIZE A $1,000.00 LOAN

TERM IN YEARS	23.00%	23.25%	23.50%	23.75%	24.00%	24.25%	24.50%	24.75%	25.00%	25.25%	25.50%	25.75%
					INTEREST RATES							
0.5	1115.00	1116.25	1117.50	1118.75	1120.00	1121.25	1122.50	1123.75	1125.00	1126.25	1127.50	1128.75
1.0	587.82	588.79	589.76	590.73	591.70	592.68	593.65	594.62	595.59	596.57	597.54	598.51
1.5	412.78	413.67	414.57	415.46	416.35	417.25	418.14	419.04	419.94	420.83	421.73	422.63
2.0	325.78	326.64	327.51	328.37	329.24	330.11	330.97	331.84	332.71	333.58	334.45	335.33
2.5	273.99	274.84	275.70	276.56	277.41	278.27	279.13	280.00	280.86	281.72	282.59	283.45
3.0	239.80	240.65	241.51	242.37	243.23	244.09	244.96	245.82	246.68	247.55	248.42	249.29
3.5	215.66	216.52	217.39	218.25	219.12	219.99	220.86	221.73	222.61	223.48	224.36	225.24
4.0	197.80	198.68	199.55	200.43	201.31	202.19	203.07	203.95	204.84	205.72	206.61	207.50
4.5	184.13	185.02	185.90	186.79	187.68	188.58	189.47	190.37	191.27	192.16	193.07	193.97
5.0	173.38	174.28	175.18	176.08	176.99	177.90	178.80	179.71	180.63	181.54	182.46	183.37
5.5	164.76	165.67	166.58	167.50	168.42	169.34	170.26	171.19	172.12	173.05	173.98	174.91
6.0	157.72	158.65	159.58	160.51	161.44	162.38	163.32	164.26	165.20	166.14	167.09	168.04
6.5	151.90	152.84	153.79	154.73	155.68	156.63	157.59	158.54	159.50	160.46	161.42	162.39
7.0	147.04	147.99	148.95	149.91	150.88	151.84	152.81	153.78	154.76	155.73	156.71	157.69
7.5	142.93	143.90	144.87	145.85	146.83	147.81	148.79	149.78	150.77	151.76	152.75	153.75
8.0	139.44	140.42	141.41	142.40	143.40	144.39	145.39	146.39	147.39	148.40	149.41	150.42
8.5	136.45	137.45	138.45	139.45	140.46	141.47	142.48	143.50	144.52	145.54	146.56	147.59
9.0	133.87	134.89	135.90	136.92	137.94	138.97	139.99	141.02	142.05	143.09	144.12	145.16
9.5	131.65	132.67	133.70	134.73	135.77	136.81	137.85	138.89	139.93	140.98	142.03	143.08
10.0	129.71	130.75	131.79	132.84	133.88	134.93	135.99	137.04	138.10	139.16	140.22	141.29
10.5	128.02	129.07	130.13	131.19	132.25	133.31	134.37	135.44	136.51	137.58	138.66	139.74
11.0	126.54	127.61	128.67	129.74	130.82	131.89	132.97	134.05	135.13	136.21	137.30	138.39
11.5	125.25	126.32	127.40	128.48	129.56	130.65	131.74	132.83	133.92	135.02	136.12	137.22
12.0	124.11	125.19	126.28	127.37	128.47	129.57	130.66	131.77	132.87	133.98	135.09	136.20
12.5	123.10	124.20	125.30	126.40	127.50	128.61	129.72	130.83	131.95	133.07	134.18	135.31
13.0	122.22	123.32	124.43	125.54	126.66	127.77	128.89	130.01	131.14	132.27	133.39	134.53
13.5	121.43	122.55	123.66	124.79	125.91	127.04	128.16	129.29	130.43	131.56	132.70	133.84
14.0	120.73	121.86	122.99	124.12	125.25	126.38	127.52	128.66	129.80	130.95	132.09	133.24
14.5	120.12	121.25	122.39	123.52	124.67	125.81	126.95	128.10	129.25	130.40	131.56	132.71
15.0	119.57	120.71	121.85	123.00	124.15	125.30	126.45	127.61	128.77	129.92	131.09	132.25
15.5	119.08	120.23	121.38	122.54	123.69	124.85	126.01	127.17	128.34	129.50	130.67	131.84
16.0	118.65	119.80	120.96	122.12	123.29	124.45	125.62	126.79	127.96	129.13	130.31	131.48
16.5	118.26	119.42	120.59	121.76	122.93	124.10	125.27	126.45	127.62	128.80	129.98	131.17
17.0	117.92	119.09	120.26	121.43	122.61	123.78	124.96	126.14	127.33	128.51	129.70	130.89
17.5	117.61	118.78	119.96	121.14	122.32	123.50	124.69	125.88	127.06	128.25	129.45	130.64
18.0	117.34	118.52	119.70	120.88	122.07	123.26	124.45	125.64	126.83	128.03	129.22	130.42
18.5	117.09	118.28	119.46	120.65	121.84	123.04	124.23	125.43	126.63	127.83	129.03	130.23
19.0	116.87	118.06	119.26	120.45	121.64	122.84	124.04	125.24	126.44	127.65	128.85	130.06
19.5	116.68	117.87	119.07	120.27	121.47	122.67	123.87	125.08	126.28	127.49	128.70	129.91
20.0	116.50	117.70	118.90	120.10	121.31	122.51	123.72	124.93	126.14	127.35	128.56	129.78
20.5	116.35	117.55	118.75	119.96	121.17	122.38	123.59	124.80	126.01	127.23	128.44	129.66
21.0	116.21	117.41	118.62	119.83	121.04	122.25	123.47	124.68	125.90	127.12	128.34	129.56
21.5	116.08	117.29	118.50	119.72	120.93	122.15	123.36	124.58	125.80	127.02	128.24	129.46
22.0	115.97	117.18	118.40	119.61	120.83	122.05	123.27	124.49	125.71	126.93	128.16	129.38
22.5	115.87	117.09	118.30	119.52	120.74	121.96	123.18	124.41	125.63	126.86	128.08	129.31
23.0	115.78	117.00	118.22	119.44	120.66	121.89	123.11	124.34	125.56	126.79	128.02	129.25
23.5	115.70	116.92	118.14	119.37	120.59	121.82	123.04	124.27	125.50	126.73	127.96	129.19
24.0	115.63	116.85	118.08	119.30	120.53	121.76	122.98	124.21	125.44	126.68	127.91	129.14
24.5	115.56	116.79	118.02	119.24	120.47	121.70	122.93	124.16	125.40	126.63	127.86	129.10
25.0	115.50	116.73	117.96	119.19	120.42	121.65	122.89	124.12	125.35	126.59	127.82	129.06
25.5	115.45	116.68	117.91	119.14	120.38	121.61	122.84	124.08	125.31	126.55	127.79	129.02
26.0	115.41	116.64	117.87	119.10	120.34	121.57	122.81	124.04	125.28	126.52	127.75	128.99
26.5	115.37	116.60	117.83	119.07	120.30	121.54	122.77	124.01	125.25	126.49	127.73	128.97
27.0	115.33	116.56	117.80	119.03	120.27	121.51	122.74	123.98	125.22	126.46	127.70	128.94
27.5	115.29	116.53	117.77	119.00	120.24	121.48	122.72	123.96	125.20	126.44	127.68	128.92
28.0	115.26	116.50	117.74	118.98	120.22	121.46	122.69	123.94	125.18	126.42	127.66	128.90
28.5	115.24	116.48	117.71	118.95	120.19	121.43	122.67	123.92	125.16	126.40	127.64	128.88
29.0	115.21	116.45	117.69	118.93	120.17	121.41	122.66	123.90	125.14	126.38	127.63	128.87
29.5	115.19	116.43	117.67	118.91	120.15	121.40	122.64	123.88	125.13	126.37	127.61	128.86
30.0	115.17	116.41	117.65	118.90	120.14	121.38	122.62	123.87	125.11	126.36	127.60	128.84
31.0	115.14	116.38	117.62	118.87	120.11	121.36	122.60	123.84	125.09	126.33	127.58	128.83
32.0	115.11	116.36	117.60	118.85	120.09	121.33	122.58	123.83	125.07	126.32	127.56	128.81
33.0	115.09	116.34	117.58	118.83	120.07	121.32	122.56	123.81	125.06	126.30	127.55	128.80
34.0	115.08	116.32	117.57	118.81	120.06	121.31	122.55	123.80	125.05	126.29	127.54	128.79
35.0	115.06	116.31	117.55	118.80	120.05	121.30	122.54	123.79	125.04	126.29	127.53	128.78
36.0	115.05	116.30	117.54	118.79	120.04	121.29	122.53	123.78	125.03	126.28	127.53	128.78
37.0	115.04	116.29	117.54	118.78	120.03	121.28	122.53	123.78	125.03	126.27	127.52	128.77
38.0	115.03	116.28	117.53	118.78	120.03	121.28	122.52	123.77	125.02	126.27	127.52	128.77
39.0	115.03	116.28	117.53	118.77	120.02	121.27	122.52	123.77	125.02	126.27	127.52	128.77
40.0	115.02	116.27	117.52	118.77	120.02	121.27	122.52	123.77	125.02	126.26	127.51	128.76

ANNUAL
PAYMENT REQUIRED TO AMORTIZE A $1,000.00 LOAN

TERM IN YEARS	\multicolumn{12}{c}{INTEREST RATES}											
	2.00%	2.25%	2.50%	2.75%	3.00%	3.25%	3.50%	3.75%	4.00%	4.25%	4.50%	4.75%
1.0	1020.00	1022.50	1025.00	1027.50	1030.00	1032.50	1035.00	1037.50	1040.00	1042.50	1045.00	1047.50
2.0	515.05	516.94	518.83	520.72	522.62	524.51	526.41	528.30	530.20	532.10	534.00	535.91
3.0	346.76	348.45	350.14	351.84	353.54	355.24	356.94	358.65	360.35	362.06	363.78	365.49
4.0	262.63	264.22	265.82	267.43	269.03	270.64	272.26	273.87	275.50	277.12	278.75	280.38
5.0	212.16	213.71	215.25	216.80	218.36	219.92	221.49	223.06	224.63	226.21	227.80	229.39
6.0	178.53	180.04	181.55	183.08	184.60	186.13	187.67	189.22	190.77	192.32	193.88	195.45
7.0	154.52	156.01	157.50	159.00	160.51	162.03	163.55	165.08	166.61	168.16	169.71	171.26
8.0	136.51	137.99	139.47	140.96	142.46	143.97	145.48	147.00	148.53	150.07	151.61	153.17
9.0	122.52	123.99	125.46	126.95	128.44	129.94	131.45	132.97	134.50	136.03	137.58	139.13
10.0	111.33	112.79	114.26	115.74	117.24	118.74	120.25	121.77	123.30	124.84	126.38	127.94
11.0	102.18	103.64	105.11	106.59	108.08	109.58	111.10	112.62	114.15	115.70	117.25	118.82
12.0	94.56	96.02	97.49	98.97	100.47	101.97	103.49	105.02	106.56	108.11	109.67	111.25
13.0	88.12	89.58	91.05	92.54	94.03	95.54	97.07	98.60	100.15	101.71	103.28	104.86
14.0	82.61	84.07	85.54	87.03	88.53	90.05	91.58	93.12	94.67	96.24	97.83	99.42
15.0	77.83	79.29	80.77	82.26	83.77	85.29	86.83	88.38	89.95	91.53	93.12	94.73
16.0	73.66	75.12	76.60	78.10	79.62	81.15	82.69	84.25	85.82	87.42	89.02	90.64
17.0	69.97	71.45	72.93	74.44	75.96	77.49	79.05	80.62	82.20	83.81	85.42	87.06
18.0	66.71	68.18	69.68	71.19	72.71	74.26	75.82	77.40	79.00	80.61	82.24	83.89
19.0	63.79	65.27	66.77	68.28	69.82	71.37	72.95	74.54	76.14	77.77	79.41	81.07
20.0	61.16	62.65	64.15	65.68	67.22	68.78	70.37	71.97	73.59	75.22	76.88	78.56
21.0	58.79	60.28	61.79	63.32	64.88	66.45	68.04	69.65	71.29	72.94	74.61	76.29
22.0	56.64	58.13	59.65	61.19	62.75	64.33	65.94	67.56	69.20	70.87	72.55	74.25
23.0	54.67	56.18	57.70	59.25	60.82	62.41	64.02	65.66	67.31	68.99	70.69	72.40
24.0	52.88	54.39	55.92	57.47	59.05	60.65	62.28	63.92	65.59	67.28	68.99	70.72
25.0	51.23	52.74	54.28	55.84	57.43	59.04	60.68	62.34	64.02	65.72	67.44	69.19
26.0	49.70	51.23	52.77	54.35	55.94	57.56	59.21	60.88	62.57	64.29	66.03	67.79
27.0	48.30	49.83	51.38	52.96	54.57	56.20	57.86	59.54	61.24	62.97	64.72	66.50
28.0	46.99	48.53	50.09	51.68	53.30	54.94	56.61	58.30	60.02	61.76	63.53	65.32
29.0	45.78	47.33	48.90	50.49	52.12	53.77	55.45	57.15	58.88	60.64	62.42	64.22
30.0	44.65	46.20	47.78	49.39	51.02	52.69	54.38	56.09	57.84	59.60	61.40	63.21
31.0	43.60	45.16	46.74	48.36	50.00	51.68	53.38	55.11	56.86	58.64	60.45	62.28
32.0	42.62	44.18	45.77	47.40	49.05	50.73	52.45	54.19	55.95	57.75	59.57	61.41
33.0	41.69	43.26	44.86	46.50	48.16	49.85	51.58	53.33	55.11	56.92	58.75	60.61
34.0	40.82	42.40	44.01	45.65	47.33	49.03	50.76	52.53	54.32	56.14	57.99	59.86
35.0	40.01	41.59	43.21	44.86	46.54	48.26	50.00	51.78	53.58	55.41	57.28	59.16
36.0	39.24	40.83	42.46	44.12	45.81	47.53	49.29	51.08	52.89	54.74	56.61	58.51
37.0	38.51	40.11	41.75	43.41	45.12	46.85	48.62	50.42	52.24	54.10	55.99	57.90
38.0	37.83	39.43	41.08	42.75	44.46	46.21	47.99	49.80	51.64	53.51	55.41	57.33
39.0	37.18	38.79	40.44	42.13	43.85	45.60	47.39	49.21	51.07	52.95	54.86	56.80
40.0	36.56	38.18	39.84	41.54	43.27	45.03	46.83	48.66	50.53	52.42	54.35	56.30
41.0	35.98	37.61	39.27	40.98	42.72	44.49	46.30	48.15	50.02	51.93	53.87	55.83
42.0	35.42	37.06	38.73	40.45	42.20	43.98	45.80	47.66	49.55	51.46	53.41	55.39
43.0	34.89	36.54	38.22	39.94	41.70	43.50	45.33	47.20	49.09	51.03	52.99	54.98
44.0	34.39	36.04	37.74	39.47	41.23	43.04	44.88	46.76	48.67	50.61	52.59	54.59
45.0	33.91	35.57	37.27	39.01	40.79	42.61	44.46	46.35	48.27	50.22	52.21	54.22
46.0	33.46	35.12	36.83	38.58	40.37	42.19	44.06	45.95	47.89	49.85	51.85	53.88
47.0	33.02	34.70	36.41	38.17	39.97	41.80	43.67	45.58	47.53	49.50	51.51	53.55
48.0	32.61	34.29	36.01	37.78	39.58	41.43	43.31	45.23	47.19	49.17	51.19	53.24
49.0	32.21	33.90	35.63	37.40	39.22	41.07	42.97	44.90	46.86	48.86	50.89	52.95
50.0	31.83	33.52	35.26	37.05	38.87	40.74	42.64	44.58	46.56	48.57	50.61	52.68

ANNUAL
PAYMENT REQUIRED TO AMORTIZE A $1,000.00 LOAN

TERM IN YEARS	INTEREST RATES											
	5.00%	5.25%	5.50%	5.75%	6.00%	6.25%	6.50%	6.75%	7.00%	7.25%	7.50%	7.75%
1.0	1050.00	1052.50	1055.00	1057.50	1060.00	1062.50	1065.00	1067.50	1070.00	1072.50	1075.00	1077.50
2.0	537.81	539.72	541.62	543.53	545.44	547.35	549.27	551.18	553.10	555.01	556.93	558.85
3.0	367.21	368.94	370.66	372.39	374.11	375.85	377.58	379.32	381.06	382.80	384.54	386.29
4.0	282.02	283.66	285.30	286.95	288.60	290.25	291.91	293.57	295.23	296.90	298.57	300.25
5.0	230.98	232.58	234.18	235.79	237.40	239.02	240.64	242.27	243.90	245.53	247.17	248.81
6.0	197.02	198.60	200.18	201.77	203.37	204.97	206.57	208.18	209.80	211.42	213.05	214.68
7.0	172.82	174.39	175.97	177.55	179.14	180.73	182.34	183.94	185.56	187.18	188.81	190.44
8.0	154.73	156.29	157.87	159.45	161.04	162.64	164.24	165.85	167.47	169.10	170.73	172.37
9.0	140.70	142.27	143.84	145.43	147.03	148.63	150.24	151.86	153.49	155.13	156.77	158.42
10.0	129.51	131.09	132.67	134.27	135.87	137.49	139.11	140.74	142.38	144.03	145.69	147.36
11.0	120.39	121.98	123.58	125.18	126.80	128.42	130.06	131.71	133.36	135.03	136.70	138.39
12.0	112.83	114.43	116.03	117.65	119.28	120.92	122.57	124.23	125.91	127.59	129.28	130.99
13.0	106.46	108.07	109.69	111.32	112.97	114.62	116.29	117.97	119.66	121.36	123.07	124.79
14.0	101.03	102.65	104.28	105.93	107.59	109.26	110.95	112.64	114.35	116.07	117.80	119.55
15.0	96.35	97.98	99.63	101.29	102.97	104.66	106.36	108.07	109.80	111.54	113.29	115.06
16.0	92.27	93.92	95.59	97.27	98.96	100.66	102.38	104.12	105.86	107.62	109.40	111.18
17.0	88.70	90.37	92.05	93.74	95.45	97.17	98.91	100.66	102.43	104.21	106.01	107.81
18.0	85.55	87.23	88.92	90.64	92.36	94.10	95.86	97.63	99.42	101.22	103.03	104.86
19.0	82.75	84.44	86.16	87.88	89.63	91.39	93.16	94.95	96.76	98.58	100.42	102.27
20.0	80.25	81.96	83.68	85.43	87.19	88.97	90.76	92.57	94.40	96.24	98.10	99.97
21.0	78.00	79.73	81.47	83.23	85.01	86.81	88.62	90.45	92.29	94.16	96.03	97.93
22.0	75.98	77.72	79.48	81.25	83.05	84.86	86.70	88.55	90.41	92.29	94.19	96.11
23.0	74.14	75.90	77.67	79.47	81.28	83.12	84.97	86.83	88.72	90.62	92.54	94.48
24.0	72.48	74.25	76.04	77.85	79.68	81.53	83.40	85.29	87.19	89.12	91.06	93.01
25.0	70.96	72.75	74.55	76.38	78.23	80.10	81.99	83.89	85.82	87.76	89.72	91.69
26.0	69.57	71.37	73.20	75.04	76.91	78.79	80.70	82.62	84.57	86.53	88.50	90.50
27.0	68.30	70.12	71.96	73.82	75.70	77.61	79.53	81.47	83.43	85.41	87.41	89.42
28.0	67.13	68.96	70.82	72.70	74.60	76.52	78.46	80.42	82.40	84.39	86.41	88.44
29.0	66.05	67.90	69.77	71.67	73.58	75.52	77.48	79.46	81.45	83.47	85.50	87.55
30.0	65.06	66.92	68.81	70.72	72.65	74.61	76.58	78.58	80.59	82.62	84.68	86.75
31.0	64.14	66.02	67.92	69.85	71.80	73.77	75.76	77.77	79.80	81.85	83.92	86.01
32.0	63.29	65.18	67.10	69.04	71.01	72.99	75.00	77.03	79.08	81.15	83.23	85.33
33.0	62.50	64.41	66.34	68.30	70.28	72.28	74.30	76.35	78.41	80.50	82.60	84.72
34.0	61.76	63.69	65.63	67.61	69.60	71.62	73.66	75.72	77.80	79.90	82.02	84.16
35.0	61.08	63.02	64.98	66.97	68.98	71.01	73.07	75.14	77.24	79.35	81.49	83.64
36.0	60.44	62.39	64.37	66.37	68.40	70.45	72.52	74.61	76.72	78.85	81.00	83.17
37.0	59.84	61.81	63.80	65.82	67.86	69.93	72.01	74.12	76.24	78.39	80.55	82.73
38.0	59.29	61.27	63.28	65.31	67.36	69.44	71.54	73.66	75.80	77.96	80.14	82.33
39.0	58.77	60.76	62.78	64.83	66.90	68.99	71.10	73.24	75.39	77.56	79.76	81.96
40.0	58.28	60.29	62.33	64.38	66.47	68.57	70.70	72.85	75.01	77.20	79.41	81.63
41.0	57.83	59.85	61.90	63.97	66.06	68.18	70.32	72.48	74.66	76.86	79.08	81.32
42.0	57.40	59.43	61.49	63.58	65.69	67.82	69.97	72.15	74.34	76.55	78.78	81.03
43.0	57.00	59.05	61.12	63.22	65.34	67.48	69.65	71.83	74.04	76.27	78.51	80.77
44.0	56.62	58.68	60.77	62.88	65.01	67.17	69.35	71.54	73.76	76.00	78.25	80.52
45.0	56.27	58.34	60.44	62.56	64.71	66.87	69.06	71.28	73.50	75.75	78.02	80.30
46.0	55.93	58.02	60.13	62.26	64.42	66.60	68.80	71.02	73.26	75.52	77.80	80.09
47.0	55.62	57.71	59.84	61.98	64.15	66.34	68.56	70.79	73.04	75.31	77.60	79.90
48.0	55.32	57.43	59.56	61.72	63.90	66.11	68.33	70.57	72.84	75.11	77.41	79.72
49.0	55.04	57.16	59.31	61.48	63.67	65.88	68.12	70.37	72.64	74.93	77.24	79.56
50.0	54.78	56.91	59.07	61.25	63.45	65.67	67.92	70.18	72.46	74.76	77.08	79.41

ANNUAL

PAYMENT REQUIRED TO AMORTIZE A $1,000.00 LOAN

TERM IN YEARS	INTEREST RATES											
	8.00%	8.25%	8.50%	8.75%	9.00%	9.25%	9.50%	9.75%	10.00%	10.25%	10.50%	10.75%
1.0	1080.00	1082.50	1085.00	1087.50	1090.00	1092.50	1095.00	1097.50	1100.00	1102.50	1105.00	1107.50
2.0	560.77	562.70	564.62	566.55	568.47	570.40	572.33	574.26	576.20	578.13	580.06	582.00
3.0	388.04	389.79	391.54	393.30	395.06	396.82	398.58	400.35	402.12	403.89	405.66	407.44
4.0	301.93	303.61	305.29	306.98	308.67	310.37	312.07	313.77	315.48	317.18	318.90	320.61
5.0	250.46	252.11	253.77	255.43	257.10	258.77	260.44	262.12	263.80	265.49	267.18	268.88
6.0	216.32	217.96	219.61	221.27	222.92	224.59	226.26	227.93	229.61	231.30	232.99	234.68
7.0	192.08	193.72	195.37	197.03	198.70	200.37	202.04	203.72	205.41	207.10	208.80	210.51
8.0	174.02	175.67	177.34	179.00	180.68	182.36	184.05	185.75	187.45	189.16	190.87	192.60
9.0	160.08	161.75	163.43	165.11	166.80	168.50	170.21	171.92	173.65	175.37	177.11	178.86
10.0	149.03	150.72	152.41	154.11	155.83	157.54	159.27	161.01	162.75	164.50	166.26	168.03
11.0	140.08	141.78	143.50	145.22	146.95	148.69	150.44	152.20	153.97	155.74	157.53	159.32
12.0	132.70	134.42	136.16	137.90	139.66	141.42	143.19	144.98	146.77	148.57	150.38	152.20
13.0	126.53	128.27	130.03	131.79	133.57	135.36	137.16	138.97	140.78	142.61	144.45	146.30
14.0	121.30	123.07	124.85	126.64	128.44	130.25	132.07	133.91	135.75	137.61	139.47	141.35
15.0	116.83	118.62	120.43	122.24	124.06	125.90	127.75	129.61	131.48	133.36	135.25	137.16
16.0	112.98	114.79	116.62	118.46	120.30	122.17	124.04	125.92	127.82	129.73	131.65	133.58
17.0	109.63	111.47	113.32	115.18	117.05	118.94	120.84	122.75	124.67	126.60	128.55	130.51
18.0	106.71	108.56	110.44	112.32	114.22	116.13	118.05	119.99	121.94	123.90	125.87	127.85
19.0	104.13	106.01	107.91	109.81	111.74	113.67	115.62	117.58	119.55	121.54	123.54	125.55
20.0	101.86	103.76	105.68	107.61	109.55	111.51	113.48	115.47	117.46	119.48	121.50	123.53
21.0	99.84	101.76	103.70	105.65	107.62	109.60	111.60	113.61	115.63	117.66	119.71	121.77
22.0	98.04	99.98	101.94	103.92	105.91	107.91	109.93	111.96	114.01	116.07	118.14	120.22
23.0	96.43	98.39	100.38	102.37	104.39	106.41	108.45	110.51	112.58	114.66	116.75	118.86
24.0	94.98	96.97	98.97	100.99	103.03	105.08	107.14	109.21	111.30	113.41	115.52	117.65
25.0	93.68	95.69	97.72	99.76	101.81	103.88	105.96	108.06	110.17	112.30	114.43	116.58
26.0	92.51	94.54	96.59	98.65	100.72	102.81	104.91	107.03	109.16	111.31	113.47	115.64
27.0	91.45	93.50	95.57	97.64	99.74	101.85	103.97	106.11	108.26	110.43	112.60	114.79
28.0	90.49	92.56	94.64	96.74	98.86	100.99	103.13	105.29	107.46	109.64	111.83	114.04
29.0	89.62	91.71	93.81	95.93	98.06	100.21	102.37	104.54	106.73	108.93	111.15	113.37
30.0	88.83	90.94	93.06	95.19	97.34	99.51	101.69	103.88	106.08	108.30	110.53	112.78
31.0	88.11	90.23	92.37	94.52	96.69	98.87	101.07	103.28	105.50	107.74	109.98	112.24
32.0	87.46	89.59	91.75	93.92	96.10	98.30	100.51	102.74	104.98	107.23	109.49	111.76
33.0	86.86	89.01	91.18	93.37	95.57	97.78	100.01	102.25	104.50	106.77	109.05	111.34
34.0	86.31	88.48	90.66	92.87	95.08	97.31	99.55	101.81	104.08	106.36	108.65	110.95
35.0	85.81	87.99	90.19	92.41	94.64	96.89	99.14	101.41	103.69	105.99	108.29	110.61
36.0	85.35	87.55	89.77	92.00	94.24	96.50	98.77	101.05	103.35	105.65	107.97	110.30
37.0	84.93	87.14	89.37	91.62	93.88	96.15	98.43	100.73	103.03	105.35	107.68	110.02
38.0	84.54	86.77	89.01	91.27	93.54	95.83	98.12	100.43	102.75	105.08	107.42	109.77
39.0	84.19	86.43	88.69	90.96	93.24	95.54	97.85	100.17	102.50	104.84	107.19	109.55
40.0	83.87	86.12	88.39	90.67	92.96	95.27	97.59	99.92	102.26	104.62	106.98	109.35
41.0	83.57	85.83	88.11	90.41	92.71	95.03	97.36	99.70	102.05	104.42	106.79	109.16
42.0	83.29	85.57	87.86	90.17	92.48	94.81	97.15	99.50	101.86	104.24	106.61	109.00
43.0	83.04	85.33	87.63	89.95	92.27	94.61	96.96	99.32	101.69	104.07	106.46	108.85
44.0	82.81	85.11	87.42	89.74	92.08	94.43	96.79	99.16	101.54	103.92	106.32	108.72
45.0	82.59	84.90	87.22	89.56	91.91	94.26	96.63	99.01	101.40	103.79	106.19	108.60
46.0	82.39	84.71	87.05	89.39	91.75	94.11	96.49	98.87	101.27	103.67	106.08	108.49
47.0	82.21	84.54	86.88	89.24	91.60	93.97	96.36	98.75	101.15	103.56	105.98	108.40
48.0	82.05	84.38	86.73	89.09	91.47	93.85	96.24	98.64	101.05	103.46	105.88	108.31
49.0	81.89	84.24	86.60	88.96	91.34	93.73	96.13	98.54	100.95	103.37	105.80	108.23
50.0	81.75	84.10	86.47	88.85	91.23	93.63	96.03	98.44	100.86	103.29	105.72	108.16

ANNUAL
PAYMENT REQUIRED TO AMORTIZE A $1,000.00 LOAN

TERM IN YEARS	INTEREST RATES											
	11.00%	11.25%	11.50%	11.75%	12.00%	12.25%	12.50%	12.75%	13.00%	13.25%	13.50%	13.75%
1.0	1110.00	1112.50	1115.00	1117.50	1120.00	1122.50	1125.00	1127.50	1130.00	1132.50	1135.00	1137.50
2.0	583.94	585.88	587.82	589.76	591.70	593.65	595.59	597.54	599.49	601.44	603.39	605.34
3.0	409.22	411.00	412.78	414.57	416.35	418.14	419.94	421.73	423.53	425.33	427.13	428.93
4.0	322.33	324.05	325.78	327.51	329.24	330.97	332.71	334.45	336.20	337.95	339.70	341.45
5.0	270.58	272.28	273.99	275.70	277.41	279.13	280.86	282.59	284.32	286.06	287.80	289.54
6.0	236.38	238.09	239.80	241.51	243.23	244.96	246.68	248.42	250.16	251.90	253.65	255.40
7.0	212.22	213.94	215.66	217.39	219.12	220.86	222.61	224.36	226.12	227.88	229.65	231.42
8.0	194.33	196.06	197.80	199.55	201.31	203.07	204.84	206.61	208.39	210.18	211.97	213.77
9.0	180.61	182.37	184.13	185.90	187.68	189.47	191.27	193.07	194.87	196.69	198.51	200.34
10.0	169.81	171.59	173.38	175.18	176.99	178.80	180.63	182.46	184.29	186.14	187.99	189.85
11.0	161.13	162.94	164.76	166.58	168.42	170.26	172.12	173.98	175.85	177.72	179.61	181.50
12.0	154.03	155.87	157.72	159.58	161.44	163.32	165.20	167.09	168.99	170.90	172.82	174.74
13.0	148.16	150.02	151.90	153.79	155.68	157.59	159.50	161.42	163.36	165.30	167.24	169.20
14.0	143.23	145.13	147.04	148.95	150.88	152.81	154.76	156.71	158.67	160.64	162.63	164.62
15.0	139.07	140.99	142.93	144.87	146.83	148.79	150.77	152.75	154.75	156.75	158.76	160.78
16.0	135.52	137.47	139.44	141.41	143.40	145.39	147.39	149.41	151.43	153.46	155.51	157.56
17.0	132.48	134.46	136.45	138.45	140.46	142.48	144.52	146.56	148.61	150.68	152.75	154.83
18.0	129.85	131.85	133.87	135.90	137.94	139.99	142.05	144.12	146.21	148.30	150.40	152.51
19.0	127.57	129.60	131.65	133.70	135.77	137.85	139.93	142.03	144.14	146.26	148.38	150.52
20.0	125.58	127.64	129.71	131.79	133.88	135.99	138.10	140.22	142.36	144.50	146.66	148.82
21.0	123.84	125.93	128.02	130.13	132.25	134.37	136.51	138.66	140.82	142.99	145.17	147.35
22.0	122.32	124.43	126.54	128.67	130.82	132.97	135.13	137.30	139.48	141.68	143.88	146.09
23.0	120.98	123.11	125.25	127.40	129.56	131.74	133.92	136.12	138.32	140.54	142.76	144.99
24.0	119.79	121.94	124.11	126.28	128.47	130.66	132.87	135.09	137.31	139.55	141.79	144.05
25.0	118.75	120.92	123.10	125.30	127.50	129.72	131.95	134.18	136.43	138.69	140.95	143.22
26.0	117.82	120.01	122.22	124.43	126.66	128.89	131.14	133.39	135.66	137.93	140.22	142.51
27.0	116.99	119.21	121.43	123.66	125.91	128.16	130.43	132.70	134.98	137.28	139.57	141.88
28.0	116.26	118.49	120.73	122.99	125.25	127.52	129.80	132.09	134.39	136.70	139.02	141.34
29.0	115.61	117.86	120.12	122.39	124.67	126.95	129.25	131.56	133.87	136.20	138.53	140.86
30.0	115.03	117.29	119.57	121.85	124.15	126.45	128.77	131.09	133.42	135.75	138.10	140.45
31.0	114.51	116.79	119.08	121.38	123.69	126.01	128.34	130.67	133.01	135.36	137.72	140.09
32.0	114.05	116.34	118.65	120.96	123.29	125.62	127.96	130.31	132.66	135.02	137.39	139.77
33.0	113.63	115.94	118.26	120.59	122.93	125.27	127.62	129.98	132.35	134.72	137.10	139.49
34.0	113.26	115.59	117.92	120.26	122.61	124.96	127.33	129.70	132.08	134.46	136.85	139.25
35.0	112.93	115.27	117.61	119.96	122.32	124.69	127.06	129.45	131.83	134.23	136.63	139.04
36.0	112.64	114.98	117.34	119.70	122.07	124.45	126.83	129.22	131.62	134.02	136.43	138.85
37.0	112.37	114.73	117.09	119.46	121.84	124.23	126.63	129.03	131.43	133.85	136.26	138.68
38.0	112.13	114.50	116.87	119.26	121.64	124.04	126.44	128.85	131.27	133.69	136.11	138.54
39.0	111.92	114.29	116.68	119.07	121.47	123.87	126.28	128.70	131.12	133.55	135.98	138.42
40.0	111.72	114.11	116.50	118.90	121.31	123.72	126.14	128.56	130.99	133.42	135.86	138.30
41.0	111.55	113.95	116.35	118.75	121.17	123.59	126.01	128.44	130.88	133.32	135.76	138.21
42.0	111.40	113.80	116.21	118.62	121.04	123.47	125.90	128.34	130.78	133.22	135.67	138.12
43.0	111.26	113.67	116.08	118.50	120.93	123.36	125.80	128.24	130.69	133.14	135.59	138.05
44.0	111.13	113.55	115.97	118.40	120.83	123.27	125.71	128.16	130.61	133.06	135.52	137.98
45.0	111.02	113.44	115.87	118.30	120.74	123.18	125.63	128.08	130.54	133.00	135.46	137.92
46.0	110.92	113.35	115.78	118.22	120.66	123.11	125.56	128.02	130.48	132.94	135.40	137.87
47.0	110.83	113.26	115.70	118.14	120.59	123.04	125.50	127.96	130.42	132.89	135.36	137.83
48.0	110.74	113.18	115.63	118.08	120.53	122.98	125.44	127.91	130.37	132.84	135.32	137.79
49.0	110.67	113.11	115.56	118.02	120.47	122.93	125.40	127.86	130.33	132.80	135.28	137.75
50.0	110.60	113.05	115.50	117.96	120.42	122.89	125.35	127.82	130.29	132.77	135.25	137.72

223

ANNUAL
PAYMENT REQUIRED TO AMORTIZE A $1,000.00 LOAN

TERM IN YEARS	INTEREST RATES											
	14.00%	14.25%	14.50%	14.75%	15.00%	15.25%	15.50%	15.75%	16.00%	16.25%	16.50%	16.75%
1.0	1140.00	1142.50	1145.00	1147.50	1150.00	1152.50	1155.00	1157.50	1160.00	1162.50	1165.00	1167.50
2.0	607.29	609.25	611.21	613.16	615.12	617.08	619.04	621.00	622.97	624.93	626.90	628.87
3.0	430.74	432.54	434.35	436.17	437.98	439.80	441.62	443.44	445.26	447.09	448.92	450.75
4.0	343.21	344.97	346.73	348.50	350.27	352.04	353.82	355.60	357.38	359.17	360.95	362.74
5.0	291.29	293.04	294.80	296.56	298.32	300.09	301.86	303.64	305.41	307.20	308.98	310.77
6.0	257.16	258.93	260.69	262.47	264.24	266.02	267.81	269.60	271.39	273.19	275.00	276.81
7.0	233.20	234.98	236.77	238.57	240.37	242.17	243.98	245.80	247.62	249.44	251.27	253.11
8.0	215.58	217.39	219.20	221.03	222.86	224.69	226.53	228.38	230.23	232.09	233.95	235.82
9.0	202.17	204.01	205.86	207.72	209.58	211.45	213.32	215.20	217.09	218.98	220.88	222.78
10.0	191.72	193.59	195.47	197.36	199.26	201.16	203.07	204.98	206.91	208.84	210.77	212.71
11.0	183.40	185.31	187.22	189.14	191.07	193.01	194.96	196.91	198.87	200.83	202.80	204.78
12.0	176.67	178.62	180.56	182.52	184.49	186.46	188.44	190.43	192.42	194.42	196.43	198.45
13.0	171.17	173.14	175.13	177.12	179.12	181.12	183.14	185.16	187.19	189.23	191.27	193.32
14.0	166.61	168.62	170.64	172.66	174.69	176.73	178.78	180.84	182.90	184.97	187.05	189.14
15.0	162.81	164.85	166.90	168.96	171.02	173.10	175.18	177.27	179.36	181.47	183.58	185.70
16.0	159.62	161.69	163.77	165.86	167.95	170.06	172.17	174.29	176.42	178.55	180.70	182.85
17.0	156.92	159.02	161.13	163.25	165.37	167.51	169.65	171.80	173.96	176.12	178.30	180.48
18.0	154.63	156.75	158.89	161.04	163.19	165.35	167.52	169.70	171.89	174.08	176.29	178.49
19.0	152.67	154.82	156.99	159.16	161.34	163.53	165.73	167.93	170.15	172.37	174.60	176.83
20.0	150.99	153.17	155.36	157.56	159.77	161.98	164.20	166.43	168.67	170.92	173.17	175.43
21.0	149.55	151.76	153.97	156.19	158.42	160.66	162.91	165.16	167.42	169.69	171.96	174.25
22.0	148.31	150.54	152.77	155.02	157.27	159.53	161.80	164.08	166.36	168.65	170.94	173.25
23.0	147.24	149.49	151.74	154.01	156.28	158.56	160.85	163.15	165.45	167.76	170.08	172.40
24.0	146.31	148.58	150.86	153.14	155.43	157.74	160.04	162.36	164.68	167.01	169.34	171.68
25.0	145.50	147.79	150.09	152.39	154.70	157.02	159.35	161.68	164.02	166.36	168.71	171.07
26.0	144.81	147.11	149.43	151.75	154.07	156.41	158.75	161.10	163.45	165.81	168.18	170.55
27.0	144.20	146.52	148.85	151.19	153.53	155.88	158.24	160.60	162.97	165.34	167.72	170.10
28.0	143.67	146.01	148.35	150.70	153.06	155.43	157.80	160.17	162.55	164.94	167.33	169.73
29.0	143.21	145.56	147.92	150.29	152.66	155.03	157.42	159.80	162.20	164.59	167.00	169.40
30.0	142.81	145.17	147.54	149.92	152.31	154.69	157.09	159.49	161.89	164.30	166.71	169.13
31.0	142.46	144.83	147.22	149.61	152.00	154.40	156.81	159.21	161.63	164.05	166.47	168.89
32.0	142.15	144.54	146.93	149.33	151.74	154.15	156.56	158.98	161.40	163.83	166.26	168.69
33.0	141.88	144.28	146.69	149.10	151.51	153.93	156.35	158.78	161.21	163.64	166.08	168.52
34.0	141.65	144.06	146.47	148.89	151.31	153.74	156.17	158.60	161.04	163.48	165.93	168.38
35.0	141.45	143.86	146.28	148.71	151.14	153.57	156.01	158.45	160.90	163.35	165.80	168.25
36.0	141.27	143.69	146.12	148.55	150.99	153.43	155.88	158.32	160.77	163.23	165.68	168.14
37.0	141.11	143.54	145.98	148.42	150.86	153.31	155.76	158.21	160.67	163.13	165.59	168.05
38.0	140.97	143.41	145.85	148.30	150.75	153.20	155.66	158.11	160.58	163.04	165.50	167.97
39.0	140.86	143.30	145.75	148.20	150.65	153.11	155.57	158.03	160.50	162.96	165.43	167.90
40.0	140.75	143.20	145.65	148.11	150.57	153.03	155.49	157.96	160.43	162.90	165.37	167.85
41.0	140.66	143.11	145.57	148.03	150.49	152.96	155.43	157.90	160.37	162.84	165.32	167.80
42.0	140.58	143.04	145.50	147.96	150.43	152.90	155.37	157.84	160.32	162.80	165.28	167.76
43.0	140.51	142.97	145.44	147.90	150.37	152.85	155.32	157.80	160.28	162.76	165.24	167.72
44.0	140.45	142.91	145.38	147.85	150.33	152.80	155.28	157.76	160.24	162.72	165.20	167.69
45.0	140.39	142.86	145.33	147.81	150.28	152.76	155.24	157.72	160.21	162.69	165.18	167.66
46.0	140.34	142.82	145.29	147.77	150.25	152.73	155.21	157.69	160.18	162.66	165.15	167.64
47.0	140.30	142.78	145.26	147.73	150.22	152.70	155.18	157.67	160.15	162.64	165.13	167.62
48.0	140.27	142.74	145.22	147.71	150.19	152.67	155.16	157.65	160.13	162.62	165.11	167.60
49.0	140.23	142.71	145.20	147.68	150.16	152.65	155.14	157.63	160.12	162.61	165.10	167.59
50.0	140.21	142.69	145.17	147.66	150.14	152.63	155.12	157.61	160.10	162.59	165.08	167.58

ANNUAL
PAYMENT REQUIRED TO AMORTIZE A $1,000.00 LOAN

TERM IN YEARS	\multicolumn{12}{c}{INTEREST RATES}											
	17.00%	17.25%	17.50%	17.75%	18.00%	18.25%	18.50%	18.75%	19.00%	19.25%	19.50%	19.75%
1.0	1170.00	1172.50	1175.00	1177.50	1180.00	1182.50	1185.00	1187.50	1190.00	1192.50	1195.00	1197.50
2.0	630.83	632.80	634.78	636.75	638.72	640.70	642.67	644.65	646.63	648.61	650.59	652.57
3.0	452.58	454.41	456.25	458.09	459.93	461.77	463.62	465.46	467.31	469.16	471.02	472.87
4.0	364.54	366.34	368.14	369.94	371.74	373.55	375.36	377.18	379.00	380.82	382.64	384.47
5.0	312.57	314.37	316.17	317.97	319.78	321.60	323.41	325.23	327.06	328.88	330.71	332.55
6.0	278.62	280.44	282.26	284.08	285.92	287.75	289.59	291.43	293.28	295.13	296.99	298.85
7.0	254.95	256.80	258.65	260.51	262.37	264.23	266.10	267.98	269.86	271.75	273.64	275.53
8.0	237.69	239.58	241.46	243.35	245.25	247.15	249.06	250.97	252.89	254.81	256.74	258.68
9.0	224.70	226.61	228.54	230.46	232.40	234.34	236.29	238.24	240.20	242.16	244.13	246.10
10.0	214.66	216.62	218.58	220.55	222.52	224.50	226.49	228.48	230.48	232.48	234.49	236.51
11.0	206.77	208.76	210.76	212.77	214.78	216.80	218.83	220.86	222.90	224.94	226.99	229.05
12.0	200.47	202.50	204.54	206.58	208.63	210.69	212.75	214.82	216.90	218.98	221.07	223.17
13.0	195.38	197.45	199.52	201.60	203.69	205.79	207.89	209.99	212.11	214.23	216.35	218.49
14.0	191.24	193.34	195.45	197.56	199.68	201.81	203.95	206.09	208.24	210.39	212.56	214.72
15.0	187.83	189.96	192.10	194.25	196.41	198.57	200.74	202.91	205.10	207.29	209.48	211.68
16.0	185.01	187.18	189.35	191.53	193.72	195.91	198.11	200.32	202.53	204.75	206.97	209.20
17.0	182.67	184.86	187.06	189.27	191.49	193.71	195.94	198.18	200.42	202.67	204.92	207.18
18.0	180.71	182.93	185.16	187.40	189.64	191.89	194.15	196.41	198.68	200.95	203.23	205.52
19.0	179.07	181.32	183.58	185.84	188.11	190.38	192.66	194.95	197.24	199.54	201.84	204.15
20.0	177.70	179.97	182.25	184.53	186.82	189.12	191.43	193.74	196.05	198.37	200.70	203.03
21.0	176.54	178.83	181.13	183.44	185.75	188.07	190.39	192.72	195.06	197.40	199.74	202.09
22.0	175.56	177.87	180.19	182.52	184.85	187.19	189.53	191.88	194.23	196.59	198.96	201.32
23.0	174.73	177.06	179.40	181.74	184.10	186.45	188.81	191.18	193.55	195.92	198.30	200.68
24.0	174.02	176.38	178.73	181.09	183.46	185.83	188.21	190.59	192.97	195.36	197.75	200.15
25.0	173.43	175.79	178.17	180.54	182.92	185.31	187.70	190.09	192.49	194.89	197.30	199.71
26.0	172.92	175.30	177.69	180.08	182.47	184.87	187.27	189.68	192.09	194.50	196.92	199.34
27.0	172.49	174.89	177.28	179.69	182.09	184.50	186.92	189.33	191.75	194.18	196.61	199.04
28.0	172.13	174.53	176.94	179.35	181.77	184.19	186.61	189.04	191.47	193.91	196.34	198.78
29.0	171.81	174.23	176.65	179.07	181.50	183.93	186.36	188.80	191.24	193.68	196.12	198.57
30.0	171.55	173.97	176.40	178.83	181.27	183.71	186.15	188.59	191.04	193.49	195.94	198.39
31.0	171.32	173.76	176.19	178.63	181.08	183.52	185.97	188.42	190.87	193.33	195.79	198.25
32.0	171.13	173.57	176.02	178.46	180.91	183.36	185.82	188.28	190.73	193.20	195.66	198.12
33.0	170.97	173.41	175.86	178.32	180.77	183.23	185.69	188.15	190.62	193.08	195.55	198.02
34.0	170.83	173.28	175.74	178.19	180.65	183.12	185.58	188.05	190.52	192.99	195.46	197.94
35.0	170.71	173.16	175.63	178.09	180.56	183.02	185.49	187.96	190.44	192.91	195.39	197.87
36.0	170.60	173.07	175.53	178.00	180.47	182.94	185.42	187.89	190.37	192.85	195.33	197.81
37.0	170.52	172.98	175.45	177.93	180.40	182.88	185.35	187.83	190.31	192.79	195.27	197.76
38.0	170.44	172.91	175.39	177.86	180.34	182.82	185.30	187.78	190.26	192.74	195.23	197.71
39.0	170.38	172.85	175.33	177.81	180.29	182.77	185.25	187.74	190.22	192.71	195.19	197.68
40.0	170.32	172.80	175.28	177.76	180.25	182.73	185.21	187.70	190.19	192.67	195.16	197.65
41.0	170.28	172.76	175.24	177.72	180.21	182.69	185.18	187.67	190.16	192.65	195.14	197.63
42.0	170.24	172.72	175.21	177.69	180.18	182.66	185.15	187.64	190.13	192.62	195.11	197.61
43.0	170.20	172.69	175.18	177.66	180.15	182.64	185.13	187.62	190.11	192.60	195.10	197.59
44.0	170.18	172.66	175.15	177.64	180.13	182.62	185.11	187.60	190.10	192.59	195.08	197.58
45.0	170.15	172.64	175.13	177.62	180.11	182.60	185.09	187.59	190.08	192.57	195.07	197.56
46.0	170.13	172.62	175.11	177.60	180.09	182.59	185.08	187.57	190.07	192.56	195.06	197.55
47.0	170.11	172.60	175.09	177.59	180.08	182.57	185.07	187.56	190.06	192.55	195.05	197.55
48.0	170.10	172.59	175.08	177.57	180.07	182.56	185.06	187.55	190.05	192.55	195.04	197.54
49.0	170.08	172.58	175.07	177.56	180.06	182.55	185.05	187.55	190.04	192.54	195.04	197.53
50.0	170.07	172.57	175.06	177.56	180.05	182.55	185.04	187.54	190.04	192.53	195.03	197.53

ANNUAL
PAYMENT REQUIRED TO AMORTIZE A $1,000.00 LOAN

TERM IN YEARS	INTEREST RATES											
	20.00%	20.25%	20.50%	20.75%	21.00%	21.25%	21.50%	21.75%	22.00%	22.25%	22.50%	22.75%
1.0	1200.00	1202.50	1205.00	1207.50	1210.00	1212.50	1215.00	1217.50	1220.00	1222.50	1225.00	1227.50
2.0	654.55	656.53	658.52	660.51	662.49	664.48	666.47	668.46	670.46	672.45	674.44	676.44
3.0	474.73	476.59	478.45	480.31	482.18	484.05	485.92	487.79	489.66	491.54	493.42	495.30
4.0	386.29	388.13	389.96	391.80	393.64	395.48	397.33	399.17	401.03	402.88	404.74	406.59
5.0	334.38	336.23	338.07	339.92	341.77	343.63	345.48	347.35	349.21	351.08	352.95	354.83
6.0	300.71	302.58	304.45	306.33	308.21	310.09	311.98	313.87	315.77	317.67	319.57	321.48
7.0	277.43	279.33	281.24	283.15	285.07	286.99	288.92	290.85	292.79	294.73	296.67	298.62
8.0	260.61	262.56	264.51	266.46	268.42	270.38	272.35	274.33	276.30	278.29	280.27	282.27
9.0	248.08	250.07	252.06	254.06	256.06	258.07	260.08	262.09	264.12	266.14	268.18	270.21
10.0	238.53	240.55	242.59	244.63	246.67	248.72	250.77	252.83	254.90	256.97	259.05	261.13
11.0	231.11	233.18	235.25	237.33	239.42	241.51	243.60	245.70	247.81	249.92	252.04	254.17
12.0	225.27	227.38	229.49	231.61	233.73	235.87	238.00	240.14	242.29	244.44	246.60	248.76
13.0	220.63	222.77	224.92	227.08	229.24	231.41	233.58	235.76	237.94	240.13	242.33	244.53
14.0	216.90	219.08	221.26	223.45	225.65	227.85	230.06	232.28	234.50	236.72	238.95	241.18
15.0	213.89	216.10	218.32	220.54	222.77	225.01	227.25	229.49	231.74	234.00	236.26	238.53
16.0	211.44	213.68	215.93	218.19	220.45	222.71	224.98	227.25	229.53	231.82	234.11	236.40
17.0	209.45	211.72	213.99	216.27	218.56	220.85	223.15	225.45	227.76	230.07	232.38	234.70
18.0	207.81	210.11	212.41	214.71	217.03	219.34	221.66	223.99	226.32	228.65	230.99	233.33
19.0	206.47	208.79	211.11	213.44	215.77	218.11	220.45	222.80	225.15	227.51	229.87	232.23
20.0	205.36	207.70	210.05	212.40	214.75	217.11	219.47	221.84	224.21	226.58	228.96	231.34
21.0	204.45	206.81	209.17	211.54	213.91	216.29	218.67	221.05	223.44	225.83	228.22	230.62
22.0	203.69	206.07	208.45	210.83	213.22	215.61	218.01	220.41	222.81	225.22	227.62	230.04
23.0	203.07	205.46	207.86	210.25	212.66	215.06	217.47	219.88	222.30	224.72	227.14	229.56
24.0	202.55	204.96	207.37	209.78	212.19	214.61	217.03	219.46	221.88	224.31	226.74	229.18
25.0	202.12	204.54	206.96	209.38	211.81	214.24	216.67	219.10	221.54	223.98	226.42	228.87
26.0	201.77	204.19	206.62	209.06	211.49	213.93	216.37	218.82	221.26	223.71	226.16	228.61
27.0	201.47	203.91	206.35	208.79	211.23	213.68	216.13	218.58	221.03	223.49	225.95	228.41
28.0	201.23	203.67	206.12	208.57	211.02	213.47	215.93	218.39	220.85	223.31	225.77	228.24
29.0	201.02	203.47	205.93	208.38	210.84	213.30	215.77	218.23	220.70	223.16	225.63	228.10
30.0	200.85	203.31	205.77	208.23	210.70	213.16	215.63	218.10	220.57	223.04	225.52	227.99
31.0	200.71	203.17	205.64	208.11	210.58	213.05	215.52	217.99	220.47	222.95	225.42	227.90
32.0	200.59	203.06	205.53	208.00	210.48	212.95	215.43	217.91	220.38	222.86	225.35	227.83
33.0	200.49	202.97	205.44	207.92	210.40	212.87	215.35	217.83	220.32	222.80	225.28	227.77
34.0	200.41	202.89	205.37	207.85	210.33	212.81	215.29	217.78	220.26	222.75	225.23	227.72
35.0	200.34	202.82	205.31	207.79	210.27	212.76	215.24	217.73	220.21	222.70	225.19	227.68
36.0	200.29	202.77	205.25	207.74	210.22	212.71	215.20	217.69	220.18	222.67	225.16	227.65
37.0	200.24	202.73	205.21	207.70	210.19	212.68	215.16	217.65	220.15	222.64	225.13	227.62
38.0	200.20	202.69	205.18	207.67	210.16	212.65	215.14	217.63	220.12	222.61	225.11	227.60
39.0	200.17	202.66	205.15	207.64	210.13	212.62	215.11	217.61	220.10	222.59	225.09	227.58
40.0	200.14	202.63	205.12	207.62	210.11	212.60	215.09	217.59	220.08	222.58	225.07	227.57
41.0	200.12	202.61	205.10	207.60	210.09	212.58	215.08	217.57	220.07	222.56	225.06	227.56
42.0	200.10	202.59	205.09	207.58	210.08	212.57	215.07	217.56	220.06	222.55	225.05	227.55
43.0	200.08	202.58	205.07	207.57	210.06	212.56	215.05	217.55	220.05	222.54	225.04	227.54
44.0	200.07	202.57	205.06	207.56	210.05	212.55	215.05	217.54	220.04	222.54	225.03	227.53
45.0	200.06	202.56	205.05	207.55	210.04	212.54	215.04	217.54	220.03	222.53	225.03	227.53
46.0	200.05	202.55	205.04	207.54	210.04	212.54	215.03	217.53	220.03	222.53	225.02	227.52
47.0	200.04	202.54	205.04	207.53	210.03	212.53	215.03	217.53	220.02	222.52	225.02	227.52
48.0	200.04	202.53	205.03	207.53	210.03	212.53	215.02	217.52	220.02	222.52	225.02	227.52
49.0	200.03	202.53	205.03	207.53	210.02	212.52	215.02	217.52	220.02	222.52	225.02	227.51
50.0	200.03	202.53	205.02	207.52	210.02	212.52	215.02	217.52	220.02	222.51	225.01	227.51

ANNUAL
PAYMENT REQUIRED TO AMORTIZE A $1,000.00 LOAN

TERM IN YEARS	23.00%	23.25%	23.50%	23.75%	24.00%	24.25%	24.50%	24.75%	25.00%	25.25%	25.50%	25.75%
					INTEREST RATES							
1.0	1230.00	1232.50	1235.00	1237.50	1240.00	1242.50	1245.00	1247.50	1250.00	1252.50	1255.00	1257.50
2.0	678.44	680.43	682.43	684.43	686.43	688.44	690.44	692.44	694.45	696.46	698.46	700.47
3.0	497.18	499.06	500.95	502.83	504.72	506.61	508.51	510.40	512.30	514.20	516.10	518.00
4.0	408.46	410.32	412.19	414.06	415.93	417.81	419.68	421.56	423.45	425.33	427.22	429.11
5.0	356.71	358.59	360.47	362.36	364.25	366.15	368.05	369.95	371.85	373.76	375.67	377.58
6.0	323.39	325.31	327.23	329.15	331.08	333.01	334.94	336.88	338.82	340.77	342.72	344.67
7.0	300.57	302.53	304.49	306.46	308.43	310.40	312.38	314.36	316.35	318.34	320.33	322.33
8.0	284.26	286.27	288.27	290.28	292.30	294.32	296.34	298.37	300.40	302.44	304.48	306.53
9.0	272.25	274.30	276.35	278.41	280.47	282.54	284.61	286.68	288.76	290.85	292.93	295.03
10.0	263.21	265.30	267.40	269.50	271.61	273.72	275.83	277.95	280.08	282.21	284.34	286.48
11.0	256.29	258.43	260.57	262.71	264.86	267.01	269.17	271.33	273.50	275.67	277.85	280.03
12.0	250.93	253.10	255.28	257.47	259.65	261.85	264.04	266.25	268.45	270.66	272.88	275.10
13.0	246.73	248.94	251.16	253.38	255.60	257.83	260.07	262.31	264.55	266.80	269.05	271.30
14.0	243.42	245.67	247.92	250.17	252.43	254.69	256.96	259.23	261.51	263.79	266.07	268.36
15.0	240.80	243.07	245.35	247.64	249.92	252.22	254.51	256.82	259.12	261.43	263.75	266.06
16.0	238.70	241.01	243.31	245.62	247.94	250.26	252.59	254.91	257.25	259.58	261.92	264.26
17.0	237.03	239.35	241.69	244.02	246.36	248.71	251.06	253.41	255.76	258.12	260.49	262.85
18.0	235.68	238.03	240.39	242.74	245.11	247.47	249.84	252.22	254.59	256.97	259.35	261.74
19.0	234.60	236.97	239.34	241.72	244.10	246.49	248.88	251.27	253.66	256.06	258.46	260.86
20.0	233.73	236.11	238.51	240.90	243.30	245.70	248.10	250.51	252.92	255.33	257.75	260.17
21.0	233.02	235.42	237.83	240.24	242.65	245.07	247.49	249.91	252.33	254.76	257.19	259.62
22.0	232.45	234.87	237.29	239.71	242.14	244.56	247.00	249.43	251.86	254.30	256.74	259.18
23.0	231.99	234.42	236.85	239.28	241.72	244.16	246.60	249.04	251.49	253.94	256.39	258.84
24.0	231.62	234.06	236.50	238.94	241.39	243.84	246.29	248.74	251.19	253.65	256.10	258.56
25.0	231.31	233.76	236.21	238.66	241.12	243.57	246.03	248.49	250.95	253.42	255.88	258.35
26.0	231.07	233.52	235.98	238.44	240.90	243.37	245.83	248.30	250.76	253.23	255.70	258.17
27.0	230.87	233.33	235.79	238.26	240.73	243.20	245.67	248.14	250.61	253.08	255.56	258.04
28.0	230.71	233.17	235.64	238.12	240.59	243.06	245.54	248.01	250.49	252.97	255.45	257.93
29.0	230.57	233.05	235.52	238.00	240.47	242.95	245.43	247.91	250.39	252.87	255.36	257.84
30.0	230.47	232.95	235.42	237.90	240.38	242.87	245.35	247.83	250.31	252.80	255.29	257.77
31.0	230.38	232.86	235.34	237.83	240.31	242.79	245.28	247.77	250.25	252.74	255.23	257.72
32.0	230.31	232.79	235.28	237.76	240.25	242.74	245.23	247.71	250.20	252.69	255.18	257.67
33.0	230.25	232.74	235.23	237.71	240.20	242.69	245.18	247.67	250.16	252.65	255.15	257.64
34.0	230.21	232.70	235.18	237.67	240.17	242.66	245.15	247.64	250.13	252.62	255.12	257.61
35.0	230.17	232.66	235.15	237.64	240.13	242.63	245.12	247.61	250.11	252.60	255.09	257.59
36.0	230.14	232.63	235.12	237.62	240.11	242.60	245.10	247.59	250.09	252.58	255.08	257.57
37.0	230.11	232.61	235.10	237.59	240.09	242.58	245.08	247.57	250.07	252.57	255.06	257.56
38.0	230.09	232.59	235.08	237.58	240.07	242.57	245.06	247.56	250.06	252.55	255.05	257.55
39.0	230.08	232.57	235.07	237.56	240.06	242.56	245.05	247.55	250.05	252.54	255.04	257.54
40.0	230.06	232.56	235.06	237.55	240.05	242.55	245.04	247.54	250.04	252.54	255.03	257.53
41.0	230.05	232.55	235.05	237.54	240.04	242.54	245.04	247.53	250.03	252.53	255.03	257.53
42.0	230.04	232.54	235.04	237.54	240.03	242.53	245.03	247.53	250.03	252.52	255.02	257.52
43.0	230.04	232.53	235.03	237.53	240.03	242.53	245.02	247.52	250.02	252.52	255.02	257.52
44.0	230.03	232.53	235.03	237.53	240.02	242.52	245.02	247.52	250.02	252.52	255.02	257.52
45.0	230.03	232.52	235.02	237.52	240.02	242.52	245.02	247.52	250.02	252.52	255.01	257.51
46.0	230.02	232.52	235.02	237.52	240.02	242.52	245.02	247.51	250.01	252.51	255.01	257.51
47.0	230.02	232.52	235.02	237.52	240.01	242.51	245.01	247.51	250.01	252.51	255.01	257.51
48.0	230.02	232.52	235.01	237.51	240.01	242.51	245.01	247.51	250.01	252.51	255.01	257.51
49.0	230.01	232.51	235.01	237.51	240.01	242.51	245.01	247.51	250.01	252.51	255.01	257.51
50.0	230.01	232.51	235.01	237.51	240.01	242.51	245.01	247.51	250.01	252.51	255.01	257.51

TABLE 3

LOAN PROGRESS CHART

Use this Table to find the fraction of an original loan amount that remains unpaid at various times during the life of the loan.

LOAN PROGRESS CHART
2.00%

AGE OF LOAN	ORIGINAL TERM IN YEARS													
	2	3	4	5	6	7	8	10	15	20	25	30	35	40
1	.5050	.6733	.7574	.8079	.8415	.8656	.8836	.9088	.9423	.9589	.9689	.9754	.9801	.9835
2	.0000	.3400	.5100	.6119	.6799	.7284	.7648	.8157	.8833	.9170	.9371	.9503	.9597	.9667
3		.0000	.2575	.4120	.5150	.5885	.6436	.7207	.8232	.8743	.9047	.9248	.9390	.9495
4			.0000	.2081	.3467	.4458	.5200	.6238	.7619	.8306	.8716	.8987	.9178	.9320
5				.0000	.1751	.3001	.3938	.5250	.6994	.7861	.8378	.8720	.8962	.9142
6					.0000	.1516	.2652	.4241	.6355	.7407	.8034	.8449	.8742	.8959
7						.0000	.1339	.3212	.5704	.6944	.7683	.8172	.8517	.8773
8							.0000	.2163	.5040	.6472	.7325	.7889	.8288	.8584
9								.1092	.4363	.5990	.6959	.7601	.8054	.8390
10								.0000	.3671	.5498	.6587	.7306	.7815	.8193
11									.2966	.4996	.6206	.7006	.7572	.7992
12									.2247	.4484	.5818	.6700	.7324	.7786
13									.1513	.3962	.5422	.6388	.7070	.7577
14									.0764	.3430	.5018	.6069	.6812	.7363
15									.0000	.2886	.4606	.5744	.6548	.7145
16										.2332	.4186	.5412	.6279	.6922
17										.1766	.3757	.5074	.6005	.6695
18										.1189	.3320	.4729	.5725	.6463
19										.0601	.2874	.4376	.5439	.6227
20										.0000	.2418	.4017	.5148	.5986
21											.1954	.3650	.4850	.5740
22											.1480	.3277	.4547	.5489
23											.0996	.2895	.4238	.5233
24											.0503	.2506	.3922	.4972
25											.0000	.2109	.3600	.4706
26												.1704	.3272	.4434
27												.1290	.2936	.4157
28												.0869	.2595	.3874
29												.0439	.2246	.3585
30												.0000	.1890	.3291
35													.0000	.1728
40														.0000

2.25%

AGE OF LOAN	ORIGINAL TERM IN YEARS													
	2	3	4	5	6	7	8	10	15	20	25	30	35	40
1	.5056	.6741	.7584	.8089	.8426	.8666	.8846	.9098	.9433	.9600	.9699	.9764	.9810	.9844
2	.0000	.3409	.5112	.6134	.6815	.7302	.7666	.8176	.8853	.9190	.9390	.9522	.9616	.9685
3		.0000	.2585	.4135	.5169	.5906	.6459	.7232	.8260	.8771	.9075	.9275	.9417	.9521
4			.0000	.2091	.3484	.4479	.5225	.6267	.7654	.8343	.8752	.9023	.9214	.9355
5				.0000	.1762	.3019	.3962	.5281	.7034	.7904	.8423	.8764	.9006	.9184
6					.0000	.1527	.2671	.4271	.6399	.7456	.8085	.8500	.8793	.9009
7						.0000	.1351	.3239	.5750	.6998	.7740	.8230	.8576	.8831
8							.0000	.2184	.5087	.6529	.7388	.7954	.8353	.8648
9								.1104	.4408	.6050	.7027	.7671	.8126	.8462
10								.0000	.3714	.5560	.6658	.7382	.7893	.8271
11									.3004	.5058	.6280	.7086	.7655	.8075
12									.2278	.4545	.5894	.6784	.7412	.7876
13									.1536	.4021	.5499	.6475	.7163	.7671
14									.0777	.3484	.5096	.6159	.6908	.7462
15									.0000	.2936	.4683	.5835	.6648	.7249
16										.2375	.4260	.5504	.6382	.7030
17										.1801	.3828	.5166	.6109	.6807
18										.1214	.3387	.4820	.5831	.6578
19										.0614	.2935	.4466	.5546	.6344
20										.0000	.2473	.4104	.5255	.6105
21											.2000	.3734	.4957	.5861
22											.1517	.3355	.4652	.5611
23											.1023	.2968	.4341	.5355
24											.0517	.2572	.4022	.5093
25											.0000	.2167	.3696	.4826
26												.1753	.3363	.4552
27												.1329	.3022	.4273
28												.0896	.2673	.3986
29												.0453	.2316	.3694
30												.0000	.1952	.3394
35													.0000	.1792
40														.0000

LOAN PROGRESS CHART
2.50%

AGE OF LOAN	ORIGINAL TERM IN YEARS													
	2	3	4	5	6	7	8	10	15	20	25	30	35	40
1	.5062	.6750	.7593	.8099	.8436	.8676	.8856	.9109	.9444	.9610	.9708	.9773	.9819	.9853
2	.0000	.3417	.5125	.6149	.6832	.7319	.7684	.8195	.8873	.9209	.9409	.9541	.9633	.9701
3		.0000	.2594	.4150	.5187	.5927	.6482	.7258	.8288	.8799	.9103	.9302	.9443	.9546
4			.0000	.2101	.3501	.4501	.5250	.6297	.7688	.8378	.8788	.9058	.9248	.9388
5				.0000	.1772	.3038	.3986	.5312	.7073	.7947	.8466	.8808	.9048	.9225
6					.0000	.1538	.2690	.4302	.6443	.7505	.8136	.8551	.8843	.9058
7						.0000	.1362	.3266	.5796	.7051	.7797	.8287	.8632	.8886
8							.0000	.2205	.5133	.6586	.7449	.8017	.8417	.8711
9								.1116	.4454	.6110	.7093	.7740	.8196	.8531
10								.0000	.3757	.5621	.6728	.7456	.7969	.8346
11									.3043	.5120	.6354	.7165	.7736	.8157
12									.2310	.4606	.5970	.6867	.7498	.7963
13									.1559	.4080	.5576	.6561	.7254	.7764
14									.0789	.3540	.5173	.6247	.7003	.7560
15									.0000	.2986	.4759	.5926	.6746	.7351
16										.2418	.4335	.5596	.6483	.7137
17										.1836	.3900	.5258	.6213	.6917
18										.1239	.3454	.4911	.5936	.6691
19										.0627	.2997	.4556	.5652	.6460
20										.0000	.2528	.4191	.5361	.6223
21											.2047	.3818	.5063	.5980
22											.1554	.3435	.4757	.5731
23											.1049	.3042	.4444	.5476
24											.0531	.2639	.4122	.5214
25											.0000	.2226	.3792	.4946
26												.1803	.3454	.4671
27												.1369	.3108	.4388
28												.0924	.2752	.4099
29												.0468	.2388	.3802
30												.0000	.2014	.3498
35													.0000	.1858
40														.0000

2.75%

AGE OF LOAN	ORIGINAL TERM IN YEARS													
	2	3	4	5	6	7	8	10	15	20	25	30	35	40
1	.5069	.6758	.7602	.8108	.8446	.8686	.8867	.9119	.9454	.9620	.9718	.9782	.9828	.9861
2	.0000	.3425	.5137	.6164	.6848	.7336	.7702	.8214	.8892	.9229	.9428	.9559	.9650	.9718
3		.0000	.2604	.4166	.5206	.5948	.6505	.7283	.8315	.8827	.9130	.9329	.9468	.9571
4			.0000	.2111	.3518	.4522	.5274	.6326	.7722	.8414	.8824	.9092	.9281	.9419
5				.0000	.1783	.3056	.4010	.5343	.7113	.7989	.8509	.8850	.9089	.9264
6					.0000	.1549	.2710	.4332	.6486	.7553	.8185	.8600	.8891	.9104
7						.0000	.1373	.3293	.5842	.7104	.7852	.8343	.8688	.8940
8							.0000	.2226	.5180	.6643	.7510	.8080	.8479	.8771
9								.1128	.4500	.6169	.7159	.7808	.8264	.8598
10								.0000	.3800	.5682	.6798	.7530	.8043	.8420
11									.3081	.5182	.6426	.7243	.7816	.8236
12									.2342	.4667	.6045	.6949	.7583	.8048
13									.1583	.4138	.5653	.6646	.7343	.7855
14									.0802	.3595	.5249	.6335	.7097	.7656
15									.0000	.3036	.4835	.6016	.6844	.7451
16										.2462	.4409	.5687	.6583	.7241
17										.1871	.3971	.5349	.6316	.7025
18										.1265	.3521	.5002	.6041	.6803
19										.0641	.3059	.4646	.5758	.6575
20										.0000	.2583	.4279	.5467	.6340
21											.2095	.3902	.5169	.6099
22											.1592	.3514	.4862	.5851
23											.1076	.3116	.4546	.5596
24											.0545	.2707	.4222	.5334
25											.0000	.2286	.3889	.5065
26												.1854	.3546	.4788
27												.1409	.3194	.4504
28												.0952	.2832	.4212
29												.0483	.2460	.3911
30												.0000	.2078	.3603
35													.0000	.1925
40														.0000

3.00%

AGE OF LOAN	ORIGINAL TERM IN YEARS													
	2	3	4	5	6	7	8	10	15	20	25	30	35	40
1	.5075	.6766	.7611	.8118	.8456	.8697	.8877	.9129	.9464	.9639	.9727	.9791	.9836	.9869
2	.0000	.3434	.5150	.6179	.6864	.7354	.7720	.8232	.8912	.9248	.9446	.9576	.9667	.9733
3		.0000	.2613	.4181	.5225	.5970	.6528	.7308	.8343	.8854	.9157	.9354	.9493	.9594
4			.0000	.2122	.3535	.4544	.5299	.6355	.7756	.8449	.8858	.9126	.9313	.9450
5				.0000	.1794	.3074	.4033	.5374	.7152	.8031	.8551	.8891	.9128	.9302
6					.0000	.1560	.2729	.4362	.6529	.7600	.8234	.8648	.8938	.9149
7						.0000	.1385	.3320	.5888	.7157	.7907	.8398	.8741	.8992
8							.0000	.2247	.5226	.6700	.7571	.8141	.8539	.8830
9								.1140	.4545	.6229	.7224	.7875	.8330	.8663
10								.0000	.3843	.5744	.6867	.7602	.8116	.8491
11									.3120	.5243	.6499	.7320	.7894	.8314
12									.2375	.4728	.6119	.7030	.7666	.8131
13									.1607	.4197	.5729	.6731	.7431	.7943
14									.0815	.3650	.5326	.6423	.7189	.7749
15									.0000	.3086	.4911	.6105	.6939	.7549
16										.2506	.4483	.5778	.6682	.7343
17										.1907	.4043	.5441	.6417	.7131
18										.1290	.3589	.5093	.6144	.6912
19										.0655	.3121	.4735	.5863	.6687
20										.0000	.2639	.4366	.5573	.6455
21											.2142	.3986	.5274	.6216
22											.1631	.3594	.4966	.5969
23											.1103	.3191	.4649	.5715
24											.0560	.2775	.4322	.5453
25											.0000	.2346	.3986	.5184
26												.1905	.3639	.4906
27												.1450	.3281	.4620
28												.0981	.2913	.4325
29												.0498	.2533	.4021
30												.0000	.2142	.3707
35													.0000	.1992
40														.0000

3.25%

AGE OF LOAN	ORIGINAL TERM IN YEARS													
	2	3	4	5	6	7	8	10	15	20	25	30	35	40
1	.5081	.6774	.7620	.8128	.8466	.8707	.8887	.9140	.9474	.9639	.9736	.9800	.9844	.9876
2	.0000	.3442	.5162	.6194	.6881	.7371	.7738	.8251	.8931	.9266	.9464	.9593	.9683	.9748
3		.0000	.2623	.4196	.5243	.5991	.6551	.7333	.8369	.8881	.9183	.9379	.9516	.9616
4			.0000	.2132	.3552	.4565	.5324	.6384	.7790	.8483	.8892	.9159	.9344	.9479
5				.0000	.1805	.3093	.4057	.5405	.7191	.8072	.8592	.8931	.9167	.9338
6					.0000	.1571	.2748	.4393	.6572	.7647	.8282	.8695	.8983	.9193
7						.0000	.1397	.3348	.5933	.7209	.7961	.8452	.8794	.9042
8							.0000	.2268	.5273	.6756	.7630	.8201	.8598	.8887
9								.1152	.4591	.6288	.7288	.7941	.8395	.8726
10								.0000	.3886	.5804	.6935	.7673	.8186	.8560
11									.3159	.5305	.6570	.7396	.7971	.8389
12									.2407	.4789	.6194	.7110	.7748	.8212
13									.1631	.4256	.5804	.6814	.7517	.8029
14									.0829	.3706	.5402	.6509	.7279	.7840
15									.0000	.3137	.4987	.6194	.7034	.7645
16										.2550	.4558	.5868	.6780	.7443
17										.1943	.4115	.5531	.6517	.7235
18										.1316	.3657	.5184	.6246	.7020
19										.0669	.3184	.4825	.5967	.6798
20										.0000	.2695	.4454	.5677	.6568
21											.2191	.4070	.5379	.6331
22											.1669	.3675	.5070	.6086
23											.1131	.3266	.4752	.5833
24											.0575	.2843	.4423	.5572
25											.0000	.2407	.4082	.5302
26												.1956	.3731	.5023
27												.1491	.3368	.4735
28												.1010	.2994	.4437
29												.0513	.2606	.4130
30												.0000	.2207	.3812
35													.0000	.2061
40														.0000

LOAN PROGRESS CHART
3.50%

AGE OF LOAN	ORIGINAL TERM IN YEARS													
	2	3	4	5	6	7	8	10	15	20	25	30	35	40
1	.5087	.6782	.7629	.8137	.8475	.8717	.8897	.9150	.9484	.9648	.9745	.9808	.9852	.9883
2	.0000	.3450	.5175	.6208	.6897	.7388	.7756	.8269	.8949	.9284	.9481	.9609	.9698	.9762
3		.0000	.2633	.4211	.5262	.6012	.6573	.7358	.8396	.8907	.9208	.9404	.9539	.9637
4			.0000	.2142	.3569	.4587	.5349	.6413	.7823	.8517	.8925	.9190	.9374	.9508
5				.0000	.1816	.3111	.4081	.5436	.7229	.8113	.8632	.8970	.9204	.9373
6					.0000	.1583	.2768	.4423	.6615	.7694	.8329	.8741	.9027	.9234
7						.0000	.1408	.3375	.5978	.7260	.8014	.8504	.8844	.9090
8							.0000	.2289	.5319	.6811	.7689	.8259	.8655	.8941
9								.1164	.4637	.6346	.7352	.8006	.8459	.8787
10								.0000	.3930	.5865	.7003	.7743	.8256	.8627
11									.3198	.5366	.6641	.7470	.8045	.8461
12									.2440	.4850	.6267	.7189	.7827	.8290
13									.1655	.4315	.5880	.6897	.7602	.8112
14									.0842	.3761	.5478	.6594	.7368	.7929
15									.0000	.3188	.5063	.6281	.7126	.7738
16										.2594	.4632	.5957	.6876	.7541
17										.1979	.4186	.5622	.6616	.7337
18										.1342	.3725	.5274	.6348	.7125
19										.0683	.3247	.4914	.6069	.6906
20										.0000	.2752	.4541	.5781	.6680
21											.2239	.4155	.5483	.6445
22											.1708	.3755	.5174	.6202
23											.1159	.3341	.4854	.5950
24											.0590	.2912	.4523	.5689
25											.0000	.2468	.4179	.5419
26												.2009	.3824	.5139
27												.1532	.3456	.4850
28												.1039	.3075	.4550
29												.0529	.2681	.4239
30												.0000	.2272	.3918
35													.0000	.2129
40														.0000

3.75%

AGE OF LOAN	ORIGINAL TERM IN YEARS													
	2	3	4	5	6	7	8	10	15	20	25	30	35	40
1	.6004	.6701	.7609	.8147	.8405	.8727	.8900	.9160	.9494	.9658	.9754	.9816	.9860	.9890
2	.0000	.3459	.5187	.6223	.6913	.7405	.7773	.8288	.8968	.9302	.9498	.9625	.9713	.9776
3		.0000	.2642	.4226	.5281	.6033	.6596	.7382	.8422	.8933	.9233	.9427	.9561	.9658
4			.0000	.2152	.3586	.4608	.5374	.6442	.7856	.8550	.8958	.9221	.9403	.9535
5				.0000	.1826	.3129	.4105	.5467	.7268	.8153	.8672	.9008	.9240	.9407
6					.0000	.1594	.2787	.4454	.6657	.7740	.8375	.8786	.9070	.9274
7						.0000	.1420	.3402	.6023	.7311	.8067	.8556	.8893	.9137
8							.0000	.2310	.5365	.6867	.7747	.8317	.8710	.8994
9								.1177	.4682	.6405	.7415	.8069	.8520	.8846
10								.0000	.3973	.5925	.7070	.7811	.8323	.8692
11									.3237	.5427	.6712	.7544	.8118	.8532
12									.2472	.4911	.6340	.7266	.7905	.8366
13									.1679	.4374	.5954	.6978	.7685	.8194
14									.0855	.3817	.5554	.6679	.7455	.8015
15									.0000	.3239	.5138	.6368	.7217	.7829
16										.2639	.4707	.6046	.6970	.7637
17										.2016	.4258	.5711	.6714	.7436
18										.1369	.3793	.5364	.6447	.7229
19										.0697	.3310	.5003	.6171	.7013
20										.0000	.2809	.4628	.5884	.6789
21											.2288	.4240	.5586	.6557
22											.1748	.3836	.5277	.6316
23											.1187	.3417	.4956	.6065
24											.0605	.2982	.4622	.5805
25											.0000	.2530	.4276	.5535
26												.2061	.3917	.5255
27												.1575	.3544	.4964
28												.1069	.3157	.4662
29												.0545	.2755	.4348
30												.0000	.2338	.4023
35													.0000	.2199
40														.0000

LOAN PROGRESS CHART
4.00%

AGE OF LOAN	ORIGINAL TERM IN YEARS													
	2	3	4	5	6	7	8	10	15	20	25	30	35	40
1	.5100	.6799	.7648	.8156	.8495	.8737	.8918	.9170	.9503	.9667	.9762	.9824	.9866	.9897
2	.0000	.3467	.5200	.6238	.6929	.7422	.7791	.8306	.8986	.9320	.9515	.9641	.9727	.9789
3		.0000	.2652	.4241	.5299	.6054	.6619	.7407	.8448	.8959	.9257	.9450	.9582	.9677
4			.0000	.2163	.3603	.4630	.5398	.6471	.7889	.8583	.8989	.9251	.9431	.9560
5				.0000	.1837	.3148	.4129	.5498	.7306	.8192	.8710	.9045	.9274	.9439
6					.0000	.1605	.2807	.4484	.6699	.7785	.8420	.8830	.9111	.9313
7						.0000	.1432	.3429	.6068	.7362	.8118	.8606	.8941	.9181
8							.0000	.2331	.5412	.6921	.7804	.8373	.8764	.9045
9								.1189	.4728	.6463	.7476	.8131	.8580	.8902
10								.0000	.4016	.5985	.7136	.7878	.8388	.8754
11									.3276	.5488	.6782	.7616	.8189	.8600
12									.2505	.4971	.6413	.7343	.7982	.8440
13									.1703	.4433	.6029	.7058	.7766	.8273
14									.0869	.3873	.5629	.6762	.7541	.8099
15									.0000	.3290	.5213	.6454	.7307	.7918
16										.2684	.4781	.6134	.7063	.7730
17										.2053	.4330	.5800	.6810	.7534
18										.1395	.3862	.5453	.6546	.7330
19										.0712	.3374	.5092	.6272	.7118
20										.0000	.2866	.4715	.5986	.6897
21											.2338	.4324	.5689	.6667
22											.1788	.3917	.5379	.6428
23											.1216	.3493	.5057	.6179
24											.0620	.3052	.4722	.5920
25											.0000	.2592	.4373	.5650
26												.2114	.4010	.5370
27												.1617	.3632	.5078
28												.1099	.3239	.4774
29												.0561	.2830	.4457
30												.0000	.2404	.4128
35													.0000	.2269
40														.0000

4.25%

AGE OF LOAN	ORIGINAL TERM IN YEARS													
	2	3	4	5	6	7	8	10	15	20	25	30	35	40
1	.5106	.6807	.7657	.8166	.8505	.8747	.8928	.9180	.9513	.9676	.9770	.9831	.9873	.9903
2	.0000	.3476	.5212	.6253	.6945	.7439	.7809	.8324	.9005	.9337	.9531	.9656	.9741	.9801
3		.0000	.2661	.4256	.5318	.6075	.6641	.7432	.8474	.8984	.9281	.9472	.9602	.9696
4			.0000	.2173	.3620	.4651	.5423	.6500	.7921	.8616	.9020	.9281	.9458	.9585
5				.0000	.1848	.3166	.4152	.5528	.7344	.8231	.8749	.9081	.9308	.9470
6					.0000	.1617	.2827	.4514	.6742	.7830	.8465	.8872	.9151	.9350
7						.0000	.1443	.3457	.6113	.7412	.8169	.8655	.8987	.9224
8							.0000	.2353	.5458	.6976	.7860	.8428	.8816	.9093
9								.1201	.4774	.6520	.7538	.8191	.8638	.8957
10								.0000	.4060	.6045	.7201	.7944	.8452	.8814
11									.3315	.5549	.6850	.7687	.8258	.8666
12									.2538	.5032	.6484	.7418	.8056	.8511
13									.1728	.4492	.6103	.7137	.7845	.8349
14									.0882	.3929	.5704	.6845	.7624	.8180
15									.0000	.3342	.5288	.6539	.7395	.8004
16										.2729	.4855	.6221	.7155	.7821
17										.2090	.4402	.5888	.6904	.7629
18										.1422	.3930	.5542	.6643	.7429
19										.0726	.3438	.5180	.6371	.7220
20										.0000	.2924	.4802	.6087	.7003
21											.2387	.4408	.5790	.6775
22											.1828	.3998	.5481	.6538
23											.1244	.3569	.5158	.6291
24											.0635	.3122	.4821	.6033
25											.0000	.2655	.4470	.5764
26												.2168	.4103	.5483
27												.1660	.3721	.5190
28												.1130	.3322	.4885
29												.0577	.2906	.4566
30												.0000	.2471	.4233
35													.0000	.2340
40														.0000

LOAN PROGRESS CHART
4.50%

AGE OF LOAN	ORIGINAL TERM IN YEARS													
	2	3	4	5	6	7	8	10	15	20	25	30	35	40
1	.5112	.6815	.7666	.8176	.8515	.8757	.8937	.9190	.9522	.9684	.9778	.9839	.9880	.9909
2	.0000	.3484	.5224	.6267	.6961	.7456	.7826	.8342	.9023	.9354	.9547	.9670	.9754	.9813
3		.0000	.2671	.4271	.5336	.6096	.6664	.7456	.8500	.9009	.9304	.9493	.9622	.9713
4			.0000	.2184	.3637	.4673	.5448	.6529	.7953	.8648	.9051	.9309	.9484	.9609
5				.0000	.1859	.3185	.4176	.5559	.7381	.8270	.8786	.9116	.9340	.9499
6					.0000	.1628	.2846	.4545	.6783	.7875	.8508	.8914	.9190	.9385
7						.0000	.1455	.3484	.6158	.7462	.8218	.8703	.9032	.9265
8							.0000	.2374	.5503	.7029	.7915	.8482	.8867	.9140
9								.1214	.4819	.6577	.7598	.8251	.8695	.9009
10								.0000	.4103	.6104	.7266	.8009	.8514	.8873
11									.3355	.5610	.6919	.7756	.8326	.8729
12									.2572	.5092	.6556	.7492	.8128	.8580
13									.1753	.4551	.6176	.7215	.7922	.8423
14									.0896	.3985	.5779	.6926	.7706	.8259
15									.0000	.3393	.5363	.6623	.7481	.8088
16										.2774	.4929	.6307	.7244	.7909
17										.2127	.4474	.5976	.6997	.7722
18										.1449	.3999	.5630	.6739	.7525
19										.0741	.3502	.5268	.6469	.7320
20										.0000	.2981	.4889	.6186	.7106
21											.2437	.4493	.5891	.6882
22											.1869	.4079	.5582	.6647
23											.1273	.3645	.5258	.6402
24											.0651	.3192	.4920	.6145
25											.0000	.2718	.4566	.5877
26												.2222	.4196	.5596
27												.1703	.3809	.5302
28												.1161	.3405	.4995
29												.0593	.2981	.4674
30												.0000	.2539	.4338
35													.0000	.2411
40														.0000

4.75%

AGE OF LOAN	ORIGINAL TERM IN YEARS													
	2	3	4	5	6	7	8	10	15	20	25	30	35	40
1	.5118	.6823	.7675	.8185	.8524	.8766	.8947	.9200	.9531	.9693	.9786	.9846	.9886	.9914
2	.0000	.3493	.5237	.6282	.6977	.7473	.7844	.8360	.9040	.9371	.9562	.9684	.9766	.9824
3		.0000	.2680	.4286	.5355	.6117	.6686	.7480	.8525	.9033	.9327	.9514	.9641	.9730
4			.0000	.2194	.3654	.4694	.5473	.6557	.7985	.8679	.9081	.9336	.9509	.9631
5				.0000	.1870	.3203	.4200	.5590	.7419	.8308	.8822	.9150	.9371	.9527
6					.0000	.1640	.2866	.4575	.6825	.7919	.8551	.8954	.9227	.9419
7						.0000	.1467	.3511	.6202	.7511	.8267	.8749	.9075	.9305
8							.0000	.2396	.5549	.7083	.7969	.8534	.8916	.9185
9								.1226	.4865	.6634	.7657	.8309	.8749	.9060
10								.0000	.4147	.6163	.7330	.8072	.8575	.8929
11									.3394	.5670	.6986	.7824	.8391	.8791
12									.2605	.5153	.6626	.7564	.8199	.8646
13									.1778	.4610	.6249	.7292	.7998	.8495
14									.0910	.4042	.5853	.7006	.7786	.8336
15									.0000	.3445	.5438	.6706	.7565	.8170
16										.2820	.5002	.6392	.7333	.7995
17										.2164	.4546	.6063	.7089	.7812
18										.1477	.4067	.5717	.6834	.7620
19										.0756	.3566	.5355	.6566	.7418
20										.0000	.3040	.4975	.6285	.7207
21											.2488	.4577	.5990	.6986
22											.1909	.4159	.5682	.6754
23											.1303	.3722	.5358	.6511
24											.0667	.3262	.5018	.6255
25											.0000	.2781	.4663	.5988
26												.2276	.4289	.5707
27												.1747	.3898	.5413
28												.1192	.3488	.5105
29												.0610	.3057	.4781
30												.0000	.2606	.4442
35													.0000	.2483
40														.0000

LOAN PROGRESS CHART
5.00%

AGE OF LOAN	ORIGINAL TERM IN YEARS													
	2	3	4	5	6	7	8	10	15	20	25	30	35	40
1	.5125	.6832	.7684	.8194	.8534	.8776	.8957	.9209	.9541	.9701	.9794	.9852	.9892	.9920
2	.0000	.3501	.5249	.6297	.6993	.7490	.7861	.8378	.9058	.9387	.9577	.9697	.9778	.9835
3		.0000	.2690	.4301	.5374	.6137	.6709	.7504	.8550	.9057	.9349	.9534	.9659	.9746
4			.0000	.2204	.3671	.4716	.5497	.6586	.8017	.8710	.9110	.9363	.9533	.9653
5				.0000	.1881	.3222	.4224	.5620	.7456	.8345	.8858	.9183	.9401	.9554
6					.0000	.1651	.2886	.4606	.6866	.7962	.8593	.8994	.9263	.9451
7						.0000	.1479	.3539	.6246	.7559	.8315	.8795	.9117	.9343
8							.0000	.2418	.5595	.7136	.8023	.8585	.8964	.9228
9								.1239	.4910	.6690	.7716	.8365	.8803	.9109
10								.0000	.4190	.6222	.7392	.8134	.8633	.8982
11									.3434	.5730	.7053	.7891	.8455	.8850
12									.2639	.5213	.6696	.7636	.8268	.8711
13									.1803	.4669	.6321	.7367	.8071	.8564
14									.0924	.4098	.5926	.7085	.7865	.8410
15									.0000	.3497	.5512	.6788	.7647	.8248
16										.2866	.5076	.6477	.7419	.8078
17										.2202	.4618	.6149	.7179	.7900
18										.1504	.4136	.5804	.6926	.7712
19										.0771	.3630	.5442	.6661	.7514
20										.0000	.3098	.5061	.6382	.7306
21											.2538	.4661	.6089	.7088
22											.1951	.4240	.5781	.6859
23											.1333	.3798	.5457	.6618
24											.0683	.3333	.5116	.6364
25											.0000	.2845	.4758	.6098
26												.2331	.4382	.5818
27												.1791	.3986	.5523
28												.1224	.3571	.5214
29												.0627	.3134	.4888
30												.0000	.2674	.4546
35													.0000	.2555
40														.0000

5.25%

AGE OF LOAN	ORIGINAL TERM IN YEARS													
	2	3	4	5	6	7	8	10	15	20	25	30	35	40
1	.5131	.6840	.7693	.8204	.8544	.8786	.8967	.9219	.9550	.9709	.9801	.9859	.9898	.9925
2	.0000	.3509	.5262	.6311	.7009	.7506	.7878	.8396	.9075	.9403	.9592	.9710	.9790	.9845
3		.0000	.2700	.4317	.5392	.6158	.6731	.7528	.8575	.9081	.9371	.9554	.9676	.9761
4			.0000	.2215	.3688	.4737	.5522	.6614	.8048	.8741	.9138	.9389	.9556	.9673
5				.0000	.1892	.3240	.4248	.5651	.7492	.8382	.8893	.9215	.9430	.9580
6					.0000	.1663	.2905	.4636	.6907	.8005	.8635	.9032	.9297	.9482
7						.0000	.1491	.3566	.6290	.7607	.8362	.8839	.9157	.9379
8							.0000	.2439	.5641	.7188	.8075	.8635	.9010	.9270
9								.1252	.4956	.6746	.7773	.8421	.8854	.9155
10								.0000	.4234	.6280	.7454	.8195	.8690	.9034
11									.3474	.5790	.7119	.7957	.8517	.8907
12									.2672	.5273	.6765	.7706	.8335	.8773
13									.1828	.4728	.6392	.7441	.8143	.8631
14									.0938	.4154	.5999	.7163	.7941	.8482
15									.0000	.3549	.5585	.6869	.7728	.8325
16										.2912	.5149	.6560	.7503	.8159
17										.2240	.4689	.6234	.7267	.7985
18										.1532	.4205	.5890	.7017	.7801
19										.0786	.3694	.5528	.6755	.7607
20										.0000	.3156	.5147	.6478	.7403
21											.2589	.4745	.6186	.7188
22											.1992	.4321	.5879	.6962
23											.1362	.3875	.5555	.6723
24											.0699	.3404	.5213	.6471
25											.0000	.2908	.4854	.6206
26												.2386	.4474	.5926
27												.1836	.4075	.5632
28												.1255	.3654	.5321
29												.0644	.3210	.4994
30												.0000	.2743	.4650
35													.0000	.2628
40														.0000

LOAN PROGRESS CHART
5.50%

AGE OF LOAN	ORIGINAL TERM IN YEARS													
	2	3	4	5	6	7	8	10	15	20	25	30	35	40
1	.5137	.6848	.7702	.8213	.8553	.8796	.8977	.9228	.9558	.9717	.9808	.9865	.9903	.9929
2	.0000	.3518	.5274	.6326	.7025	.7523	.7895	.8413	.9092	.9419	.9606	.9723	.9801	.9855
3		.0000	.2709	.4332	.5411	.6179	.6753	.7552	.8599	.9104	.9392	.9573	.9693	.9776
4			.0000	.2225	.3705	.4759	.5547	.6643	.8079	.8771	.9166	.9414	.9579	.9692
5				.0000	.1903	.3259	.4272	.5682	.7529	.8419	.8927	.9246	.9458	.9604
6					.0000	.1674	.2925	.4666	.6948	.8047	.8675	.9069	.9331	.9511
7						.0000	.1503	.3594	.6334	.7654	.8409	.8882	.9196	.9413
8							.0000	.2461	.5686	.7240	.8127	.8684	.9054	.9309
9								.1264	.5001	.6801	.7830	.8475	.8904	.9200
10								.0000	.4278	.6338	.7516	.8254	.8745	.9084
11									.3513	.5849	.7184	.8021	.8577	.8961
12									.2706	.5333	.6833	.7775	.8400	.8832
13									.1853	.4787	.6463	.7514	.8213	.8696
14									.0952	.4210	.6072	.7239	.8016	.8551
15									.0000	.3601	.5658	.6949	.7807	.8399
16										.2958	.5222	.6642	.7586	.8238
17										.2278	.4761	.6318	.7353	.8068
18										.1560	.4273	.5976	.7107	.7888
19										.0801	.3759	.5614	.6847	.7698
20										.0000	.3215	.5232	.6572	.7498
21											.2641	.4828	.6282	.7286
22											.2034	.4402	.5976	.7062
23											.1393	.3951	.5652	.6826
24											.0715	.3475	.5310	.6576
25											.0000	.2973	.4948	.6312
26												.2441	.4566	.6034
27												.1880	.4163	.5739
28												.1288	.3737	.5428
29												.0661	.3287	.5100
30												.0000	.2811	.4752
35													.0000	.2700
40														.0000

5.75%

AGE OF LOAN	ORIGINAL TERM IN YEARS													
	2	3	4	5	6	7	8	10	15	20	25	30	35	40
1	.5143	.6856	.7711	.8223	.8553	.8805	.8986	.9238	.9567	.9725	.9815	.9871	.9908	.9934
2	.0000	.3526	.5286	.6340	.7041	.7540	.7912	.8431	.9109	.9434	.9620	.9735	.9811	.9864
3		.0000	.2719	.4347	.5429	.6200	.6775	.7576	.8623	.9126	.9412	.9591	.9709	.9789
4			.0000	.2236	.3722	.4780	.5571	.6671	.8109	.8800	.9193	.9438	.9600	.9711
5				.0000	.1914	.3277	.4296	.5712	.7565	.8455	.8961	.9276	.9485	.9628
6					.0000	.1686	.2945	.4697	.6989	.8089	.8714	.9105	.9363	.9539
7						.0000	.1515	.3622	.6378	.7701	.8454	.8923	.9233	.9446
8							.0000	.2483	.5731	.7291	.8178	.8731	.9097	.9347
9								.1277	.5047	.6856	.7885	.8528	.8952	.9242
10								.0000	.4321	.6396	.7576	.8312	.8798	.9131
11									.3553	.5909	.7248	.8084	.8636	.9014
12									.2740	.5392	.6901	.7842	.8464	.8890
13									.1878	.4846	.6533	.7586	.8281	.8758
14									.0966	.4267	.6144	.7315	.8088	.8618
15									.0000	.3653	.5731	.7028	.7884	.8471
16										.3004	.5294	.6723	.7667	.8314
17										.2316	.4832	.6401	.7438	.8148
18										.1588	.4342	.6060	.7195	.7973
19										.0817	.3823	.5699	.6938	.7787
20										.0000	.3274	.5316	.6665	.7590
21											.2692	.4911	.6377	.7382
22											.2076	.4482	.6071	.7161
23											.1423	.4028	.5748	.6927
24											.0732	.3546	.5405	.6679
25											.0000	.3037	.5042	.6417
26												.2497	.4658	.6139
27												.1925	.4251	.5845
28												.1320	.3820	.5534
29												.0679	.3364	.5204
30												.0000	.2880	.4855
35													.0000	.2773
40														.0000

LOAN PROGRESS CHART
6.00%

AGE OF LOAN	ORIGINAL TERM IN YEARS													
	2	3	4	5	6	7	8	10	15	20	25	30	35	40
1	.5150	.6864	.7720	.8232	.8572	.8815	.8996	.9247	.9576	.9733	.9822	.9877	.9913	.9938
2	.0000	.3535	.5299	.6355	.7057	.7556	.7929	.8448	.9126	.9450	.9633	.9747	.9821	.9872
3		.0000	.2729	.4362	.5448	.6220	.6797	.7600	.8647	.9149	.9432	.9608	.9724	.9802
4			.0000	.2246	.3739	.4802	.5596	.6699	.8140	.8829	.9219	.9461	.9620	.9728
5				.0000	.1926	.3296	.4320	.5743	.7601	.8490	.8993	.9305	.9510	.9650
6					.0000	.1697	.2965	.4727	.7029	.8130	.8753	.9140	.9393	.9566
7						.0000	.1527	.3649	.6421	.7748	.8498	.8964	.9270	.9477
8							.0000	.2505	.5776	.7342	.8228	.8777	.9138	.9383
9								.1290	.5092	.6911	.7940	.8579	.8998	.9283
10								.0000	.4365	.6453	.7635	.8369	.8850	.9177
11									.3593	.5967	.7311	.8145	.8692	.9064
12									.2774	.5452	.6968	.7908	.8525	.8945
13									.1904	.4904	.6602	.7656	.8347	.8818
14									.0980	.4323	.6215	.7389	.8159	.8683
15									.0000	.3706	.5803	.7105	.7959	.8540
16										.3051	.5367	.6804	.7746	.8388
17										.2355	.4903	.6484	.7521	.8226
18										.1616	.4410	.6144	.7281	.8055
19										.0832	.3888	.5783	.7027	.7873
20										.0000	.3333	.5400	.6757	.7680
21											.2743	.4994	.6470	.7475
22											.2118	.4562	.6166	.7257
23											.1454	.4104	.5843	.7026
24											.0749	.3618	.5500	.6781
25											.0000	.3101	.5136	.6520
26												.2553	.4749	.6244
27												.1971	.4339	.5950
28												.1353	.3903	.5638
29												.0697	.3440	.5307
30												.0000	.2949	.4956
35													.0000	.2846
40														.0000

6.25%

AGE OF LOAN	ORIGINAL TERM IN YEARS													
	2	3	4	5	6	7	8	10	15	20	25	30	35	40
1	.5156	.6872	.7729	.8241	.8582	.8824	.9005	.9257	.9584	.9741	.9829	.9883	.9918	.9942
2	.0000	.3543	.5311	.6369	.7073	.7573	.7946	.8465	.9142	.9464	.9646	.9758	.9831	.9880
3		.0000	.2738	.4377	.5466	.6241	.6820	.7623	.8671	.9170	.9452	.9625	.9738	.9815
4			.0000	.2257	.3756	.4823	.5620	.6727	.8170	.8858	.9245	.9484	.9640	.9745
5				.0000	.1937	.3315	.4344	.5773	.7636	.8525	.9025	.9334	.9535	.9671
6					.0000	.1709	.2985	.4758	.7069	.8170	.8791	.9174	.9423	.9592
7						.0000	.1539	.3677	.6465	.7793	.8542	.9003	.9304	.9507
8							.0000	.2527	.5821	.7392	.8276	.8822	.9178	.9418
9								.1303	.5137	.6965	.7994	.8629	.9043	.9322
10								.0000	.4409	.6510	.7694	.8424	.8900	.9221
11									.3633	.6026	.7374	.8205	.8747	.9113
12									.2808	.5511	.7033	.7973	.8585	.8998
13									.1930	.4963	.6671	.7725	.8412	.8875
14									.0995	.4379	.6286	.7461	.8228	.8745
15									.0000	.3758	.5875	.7181	.8032	.8606
16										.3097	.5438	.6883	.7824	.8459
17										.2394	.4974	.6565	.7602	.8302
18										.1645	.4479	.6227	.7366	.8135
19										.0848	.3952	.5867	.7114	.7957
20										.0000	.3392	.5484	.6847	.7767
21											.2795	.5076	.6562	.7566
22											.2160	.4642	.6259	.7351
23											.1485	.4180	.5937	.7123
24											.0765	.3689	.5594	.6880
25											.0000	.3166	.5229	.6621
26												.2609	.4840	.6346
27												.2016	.4426	.6053
28												.1386	.3986	.5741
29												.0714	.3517	.5410
30												.0000	.3019	.5056
35													.0000	.2919
40														.0000

LOAN PROGRESS CHART
6.50%

AGE OF LOAN	ORIGINAL TERM IN YEARS													
	2	3	4	5	6	7	8	10	15	20	25	30	35	40
1	.5162	.6880	.7738	.8251	.8591	.8834	.9015	.9266	.9593	.9748	.9835	.9888	.9923	.9946
2	.0000	.3552	.5324	.6384	.7088	.7589	.7963	.8482	.9158	.9479	.9659	.9769	.9840	.9888
3		.0000	.2748	.4392	.5485	.6262	.6842	.7647	.8694	.9192	.9471	.9642	.9752	.9826
4			.0000	.2267	.3774	.4845	.5645	.6755	.8200	.8886	.9270	.9506	.9659	.9761
5				.0000	.1948	.3333	.4368	.5803	.7672	.8559	.9056	.9361	.9558	.9691
6					.0000	.1721	.3005	.4788	.7108	.8210	.8828	.9207	.9452	.9616
7						.0000	.1551	.3705	.6507	.7838	.8584	.9042	.9338	.9536
8							.0000	.2549	.5866	.7441	.8324	.8866	.9216	.9451
9								.1316	.5182	.7018	.8047	.8678	.9086	.9360
10								.0000	.4452	.6566	.7751	.8478	.8948	.9263
11									.3673	.6084	.7435	.8264	.8800	.9159
12									.2842	.5570	.7099	.8036	.8642	.9049
13									.1956	.5021	.6739	.7793	.8474	.8931
14									.1009	.4435	.6356	.7533	.8295	.8805
15									.0000	.3811	.5946	.7256	.8103	.8671
16										.3144	.5510	.6960	.7899	.8528
17										.2433	.5044	.6645	.7681	.8375
18										.1674	.4547	.6309	.7448	.8212
19										.0864	.4017	.5950	.7200	.8038
20										.0000	.3451	.5567	.6935	.7852
21											.2847	.5158	.6653	.7654
22											.2203	.4722	.6352	.7443
23											.1516	.4257	.6030	.7218
24											.0782	.3760	.5687	.6977
25											.0000	.3230	.5321	.6721
26												.2665	.4930	.6447
27												.2062	.4513	.6155
28												.1419	.4069	.5843
29												.0732	.3594	.5511
30												.0000	.3088	.5156
35													.0000	.2992
40														.0000

6.75%

AGE OF LOAN	ORIGINAL TERM IN YEARS													
	2	3	4	5	6	7	8	10	15	20	25	30	35	40
1	.5168	.6888	.7748	.8260	.8601	.8843	.9024	.9275	.9601	.9755	.9841	.9893	.9927	.9949
2	.0000	.3560	.5336	.6398	.7104	.7606	.7980	.8499	.9174	.9493	.9671	.9779	.9849	.9895
3		.0000	.2758	.4407	.5503	.6282	.6863	.7670	.8717	.9213	.9489	.9657	.9766	.9837
4			.0000	.2278	.3791	.4866	.5669	.6783	.8229	.8913	.9295	.9527	.9676	.9776
5				.0000	.1959	.3352	.4392	.5834	.7707	.8593	.9087	.9388	.9581	.9709
6					.0000	.1732	.3025	.4818	.7148	.8250	.8864	.9238	.9479	.9639
7						.0000	.1563	.3733	.6550	.7883	.8626	.9079	.9370	.9563
8							.0000	.2571	.5911	.7491	.8371	.8908	.9253	.9482
9								.1329	.5227	.7071	.8099	.8725	.9128	.9395
10								.0000	.4496	.6622	.7808	.8530	.8994	.9302
11									.3713	.6142	.7496	.8321	.8851	.9203
12									.2877	.5628	.7163	.8098	.8698	.9097
13									.1981	.5079	.6806	.7859	.8535	.8984
14									.1024	.4491	.6425	.7603	.8360	.8863
15									.0000	.3863	.6017	.7330	.8173	.8733
16										.3191	.5581	.7037	.7972	.8594
17										.2472	.5114	.6724	.7758	.8445
18										.1703	.4615	.6389	.7529	.8287
19										.0880	.4081	.6032	.7284	.8117
20										.0000	.3510	.5649	.7022	.7935
21											.2899	.5239	.6742	.7741
22											.2246	.4801	.6442	.7533
23											.1547	.4332	.6122	.7311
24											.0800	.3831	.5779	.7073
25											.0000	.3295	.5412	.6818
26												.2722	.5020	.6546
27												.2108	.4600	.6255
28												.1452	.4151	.5944
29												.0751	.3671	.5611
30												.0000	.3157	.5255
35													.0000	.3065
40														.0000

LOAN PROGRESS CHART
7.00%

AGE OF LOAN	\multicolumn{14}{c}{ORIGINAL TERM IN YEARS}													
	2	3	4	5	6	7	8	10	15	20	25	30	35	40
1	.5174	.6896	.7755	.8269	.8610	.8853	.9033	.9284	.9609	.9762	.9847	.9898	.9931	.9953
2	.0000	.3569	.5348	.6413	.7120	.7622	.7997	.8516	.9190	.9507	.9683	.9789	.9857	.9902
3		.0000	.2767	.4423	.5522	.6303	.6885	.7693	.8740	.9233	.9507	.9673	.9778	.9848
4			.0000	.2288	.3808	.4888	.5693	.6810	.8258	.8940	.9318	.9547	.9693	.9790
5				.0000	.1970	.3371	.4415	.5864	.7741	.8626	.9116	.9413	.9602	.9727
6					.0000	.1744	.3045	.4849	.7187	.8288	.8899	.9269	.9505	.9660
7						.0000	.1576	.3760	.6593	.7927	.8667	.9115	.9400	.9589
8							.0000	.2593	.5955	.7539	.8417	.8949	.9288	.9512
9								.1342	.5272	.7123	.8150	.8772	.9168	.9429
10								.0000	.4539	.6677	.7863	.8581	.9039	.9341
11									.3754	.6199	.7556	.8377	.8901	.9246
12									.2911	.5687	.7226	.8158	.8752	.9144
13									.2008	.5137	.6873	.7923	.8593	.9035
14									.1039	.4547	.6494	.7672	.8423	.8918
15									.0000	.3915	.6087	.7402	.8240	.8792
16										.3238	.5651	.7112	.8044	.8658
17										.2511	.5184	.6802	.7834	.8514
18										.1732	.4683	.6469	.7609	.8359
19										.0896	.4146	.6113	.7367	.8193
20										.0000	.3569	.5730	.7108	.8015
21											.2952	.5320	.6830	.7825
22											.2289	.4880	.6532	.7620
23											.1579	.4408	.6212	.7401
24											.0817	.3902	.5870	.7166
25											.0000	.3360	.5502	.6914
26												.2778	.5108	.6643
27												.2155	.4686	.6354
28												.1486	.4233	.6043
29												.0769	.3747	.5710
30												.0000	.3226	.5352
35													.0000	.3138
40														.0000

7.25%

AGE OF LOAN	\multicolumn{14}{c}{ORIGINAL TERM IN YEARS}													
	2	3	4	5	6	7	8	10	15	20	25	30	35	40
1	.5181	.6904	.7764	.8278	.8619	.8862	.9043	.9293	.9617	.9769	.9853	.9903	.9935	.9956
2	.0000	.3577	.5361	.6427	.7135	.7638	.8013	.8533	.9205	.9521	.9695	.9799	.9865	.9909
3		.0000	.2777	.4438	.5540	.6323	.6907	.7716	.8763	.9254	.9524	.9687	.9790	.9858
4			.0000	.2299	.3825	.4909	.5718	.6838	.8287	.8967	.9342	.9567	.9710	.9803
5				.0000	.1982	.3390	.4439	.5894	.7776	.8658	.9145	.9438	.9623	.9744
6					.0000	.1756	.3065	.4879	.7226	.8327	.8934	.9299	.9530	.9681
7						.0000	.1588	.3788	.6635	.7970	.8707	.9150	.9430	.9613
8							.0000	.2616	.6000	.7587	.8463	.8989	.9322	.9540
9								.1355	.5317	.7175	.8200	.8817	.9207	.9461
10								.0000	.4583	.6732	.7918	.8631	.9082	.9377
11									.3794	.6256	.7615	.8432	.8949	.9286
12									.2946	.5745	.7289	.8217	.8805	.9189
13									.2034	.5195	.6938	.7987	.8650	.9084
14									.1054	.4603	.6562	.7739	.8484	.8971
15									.0000	.3968	.6157	.7473	.8306	.8850
16										.3285	.5721	.7187	.8114	.8720
17										.2550	.5254	.6879	.7908	.8580
18										.1761	.4751	.6548	.7686	.8429
19										.0912	.4210	.6193	.7448	.8267
20										.0000	.3629	.5811	.7191	.8093
21											3004	.5400	.6916	.7906
22											2332	.4958	.6620	.7705
23											.1610	4484	.6302	.7489
24											.0834	.3973	.5959	.7257
25											.0000	.3425	.5592	.7007
26												.2835	.5196	.6739
27												.2201	.4771	.6450
28												.1520	.4315	.6140
29												.0787	.3823	.5807
30												0000	.3296	.5449
35													.0000	.3211
40														.0000

LOAN PROGRESS CHART
7.50%

AGE OF LOAN	\multicolumn{14}{c}{ORIGINAL TERM IN YEARS}
	2	3	4	5	6	7	8	10	15	20	25	30	35	40
---	---	---	---	---	---	---	---	---	---	---	---	---	---	---
1	.5187	.6913	.7773	.8287	.8629	.8871	.9052	.9302	.9625	.9776	.9858	.9908	.9939	.9959
2	.0000	.3585	.5373	.6442	.7151	.7655	.8030	.8550	.9221	.9534	.9706	.9808	.9873	.9915
3		.0000	.2787	.4453	.5558	.6344	.6929	.7739	.8785	.9273	.9541	.9701	.9802	.9867
4			.0000	.2310	.3842	.4931	.5742	.6865	.8315	.8993	.9364	.9586	.9725	.9816
5				.0000	.1993	.3409	.4463	.5924	.7810	.8690	.9173	.9462	.9643	.9760
6					.0000	.1768	.3085	.4909	.7264	.8364	.8967	.9328	.9554	.9700
7						.0000	.1600	.3816	.6677	.8013	.8746	.9183	.9458	.9636
8							.0000	.2638	.6044	.7634	.8507	.9028	.9355	.9567
9								.1368	.5362	.7226	.8249	.8860	.9244	.9492
10								.0000	.4626	.6787	.7972	.8679	.9124	.9412
11									.3834	.6313	.7673	.8485	.8995	.9325
12									.2980	.5802	.7350	.8275	.8855	.9231
13									.2060	.5252	.7003	.8049	.8705	.9131
14									.1069	.4659	.6629	.7805	.8544	.9022
15									.0000	.4020	.6226	.7543	.8370	.8905
16										.3332	.5791	.7260	.8182	.8779
17										.2590	.5323	.6955	.7979	.8643
18										.1790	.4818	.6626	.7761	.8497
19										.0929	.4274	.6272	.7526	.8339
20										.0000	.3688	.5891	.7273	.8169
21											.3056	.5479	.7000	.7986
22											.2376	.5036	.6706	.7788
23											.1642	.4559	.6390	.7575
24											.0852	.4044	.6048	.7346
25											.0000	.3489	.5680	.7099
26												.2892	.5284	.6833
27												.2248	.4856	.6546
28												.1554	.4396	.6236
29												.0806	.3900	.5903
30												.0000	.3365	.5544
35													.0000	.3284
40														.0000

7.75%

AGE OF LOAN	\multicolumn{14}{c}{ORIGINAL TERM IN YEARS}
	2	3	4	5	6	7	8	10	15	20	25	30	35	40
---	---	---	---	---	---	---	---	---	---	---	---	---	---	---
1	.5193	.6921	.7782	.8296	.8638	.8880	.9061	.9311	.9633	.9782	.9864	.9912	.9942	.9962
2	.0000	.3594	.5385	.6456	.7166	.7671	.8046	.8566	.9236	.9547	.9717	.9817	.9880	.9920
3		.0000	.2797	.4468	.5577	.6364	.6950	.7762	.8807	.9293	.9558	.9715	.9813	.9876
4			.0000	.2320	.3859	.4952	.5766	.6893	.8344	.9018	.9386	.9604	.9740	.9827
5				.0000	.2004	.3427	.4487	.5954	.7843	.8722	.9201	.9485	.9662	.9775
6					.0000	.1780	.3105	.4940	.7303	.8401	.9000	.9356	.9577	.9719
7						.0000	.1613	.3844	.6719	.8055	.8784	.9216	.9485	.9658
8							.0000	.2660	.6088	.7681	.8550	.9065	.9386	.9592
9								.1381	.5406	.7277	.8297	.8903	.9279	.9521
10								.0000	.4670	.6841	.8025	.8727	.9164	.9445
11									.3874	.6369	.7730	.8537	.9039	.9362
12									.3015	.5860	.7411	.8331	.8904	.9272
13									.2086	.5309	.7067	.8110	.8759	.9175
14									.1084	.4715	.6695	.7870	.8601	.9071
15									.0000	.4073	.6294	.7611	.8431	.8958
16										.3379	.5860	.7331	.8248	.8836
17										.2629	.5391	.7029	.8049	.8704
18										.1820	.4885	.6703	.7835	.8562
19										.0945	.4338	.6350	.7604	.8408
20										.0000	.3747	.5970	.7354	.8242
21											.3109	.5558	.7083	.8062
22											.2419	.5114	.6792	.7869
23											.1674	.4633	.6476	.7659
24											.0869	.4115	.6136	.7433
25											.0000	.3554	.5768	.7188
26												.2949	.5370	.6924
27												.2295	.4941	.6639
28												.1588	.4477	.6331
29												.0825	.3975	.5998
30												.0000	.3434	.5638
35													.0000	.3357
40														.0000

LOAN PROGRESS CHART
8.00%

AGE OF LOAN	ORIGINAL TERM IN YEARS													
	2	3	4	5	6	7	8	10	15	20	25	30	35	40
1	.5199	.6929	.7791	.8306	.8647	.8890	.9070	.9319	.9640	.9789	.9869	.9916	.9946	.9964
2	.0000	.3602	.5398	.6471	.7182	.7687	.8063	.8582	.9251	.9560	.9727	.9826	.9887	.9926
3		.0000	.2806	.4483	.5595	.6384	.6972	.7784	.8829	.9312	.9574	.9728	.9823	.9884
4			.0000	.2331	.3877	.4974	.5791	.6920	.8372	.9043	.9407	.9622	.9754	.9839
5				.0000	.2016	.3446	.4511	.5984	.7877	.8753	.9227	.9507	.9680	.9790
6					.0000	.1792	.3126	.4970	.7341	.8438	.9032	.9383	.9599	.9736
7						.0000	.1625	.3872	.6760	.8097	.8821	.9248	.9511	.9679
8							.0000	.2683	.6131	.7727	.8592	.9102	.9416	.9617
9								.1395	.5451	.7327	.8345	.8944	.9314	.9549
10								.0000	.4713	.6894	.8076	.8772	.9202	.9476
11									.3915	.6425	.7786	.8587	.9082	.9397
12									.3050	.5917	.7471	.8386	.8952	.9311
13									.2113	.5367	.7130	.8169	.8810	.9218
14									.1099	.4771	.6761	.7933	.8657	.9118
15									.0000	.4125	.6361	.7678	.8491	.9009
16										.3426	.5929	.7402	.8312	.8891
17										.2669	.5460	.7103	.8118	.8763
18										.1849	.4952	.6779	.7907	.8625
19										.0962	.4402	.6428	.7679	.8475
20										.0000	.3806	.6048	.7432	.8313
21											.3162	.5636	.7165	.8137
22											.2463	.5191	.6875	.7947
23											.1707	.4708	.6562	.7741
24											.0887	.4185	.6222	.7517
25											.0000	.3619	.5854	.7276
26												.3006	.5456	.7014
27												.2342	.5024	.6731
28												.1622	.4557	.6423
29												.0844	.4051	.6091
30												.0000	.3503	.5731
35													.0000	.3429
40														.0000

8.25%

AGE OF LOAN	ORIGINAL TERM IN YEARS													
	2	3	4	5	6	7	8	10	15	20	25	30	35	40
1	.5205	.6937	.7799	.8315	.8656	.8899	.9079	.9328	.9648	.9795	.9874	.9921	.9949	.9967
2	.0000	.3611	.5410	.6485	.7197	.7703	.8079	.8599	.9265	.9572	.9738	.9834	.9893	.9931
3		.0000	.2816	.4498	.5614	.6405	.6993	.7807	.8850	.9330	.9589	.9741	.9833	.9892
4			.0000	.2342	.3894	.4995	.5815	.6947	.8399	.9068	.9428	.9639	.9768	.9849
5				.0000	.2027	.3465	.4535	.6013	.7910	.8783	.9253	.9528	.9697	.9803
6					.0000	.1804	.3146	.5000	.7378	.8473	.9064	.9409	.9620	.9753
7						.0000	.1638	.3900	.6801	.8138	.8858	.9278	.9536	.9699
8							.0000	.2705	.6175	.7773	.8634	.9137	.9445	.9639
9								.1408	.5495	.7377	.8391	.8984	.9347	.9575
10								.0000	.4756	.6947	.8127	.8817	.9240	.9506
11									.3955	.6480	.7841	.8636	.9123	.9430
12									.3085	.5974	.7530	.8440	.8997	.9348
13									.2140	.5423	.7193	.8227	.8860	.9259
14									.1114	.4826	.6826	.7995	.8711	.9162
15									.0000	.4178	.6428	.7744	.8550	.9058
16										.3474	.5996	.7471	.8374	.8944
17										.2709	.5528	.7175	.8184	.8820
18										.1879	.5018	.6853	.7977	.8685
19										.0978	.4466	.6504	.7753	.8540
20										.0000	.3866	.6125	.7509	.8381
21											.3214	.5714	.7245	.8209
22											.2507	.5267	.6957	.8023
23											.1739	.4782	.6646	.7820
24											.0905	.4255	.6307	.7600
25											.0000	.3683	.5939	.7361
26												.3063	.5540	.7102
27												.2389	.5107	.6820
28												.1657	.4637	.6515
29												.0862	.4126	.6183
30												.0000	.3572	.5822
35													.0000	.3501
40														.0000

LOAN PROGRESS CHART
8.50%

AGE OF LOAN	ORIGINAL TERM IN YEARS													
	2	3	4	5	6	7	8	10	15	20	25	30	35	40
1	.5212	.6945	.7808	.8324	.8665	.8908	.9088	.9337	.9655	.9801	.9879	.9924	.9952	.9969
2	.0000	.3619	.5422	.6499	.7213	.7719	.8095	.8615	.9280	.9584	.9747	.9842	.9900	.9935
3		.0000	.2826	.4514	.5632	.6425	.7015	.7829	.8871	.9349	.9604	.9753	.9843	.9899
4			.0000	.2352	.3911	.5017	.5839	.6974	.8426	.9092	.9448	.9655	.9781	.9859
5				.0000	.2038	.3484	.4559	.6043	.7942	.8813	.9279	.9549	.9713	.9816
6					.0000	.1816	.3166	.5030	.7416	.8509	.9094	.9434	.9640	.9768
7						.0000	.1650	.3928	.6842	.8178	.8893	.9308	.9560	.9717
8							.0000	.2728	.6218	.7818	.8674	.9171	.9473	.9661
9								.1422	.5539	.7426	.8436	.9022	.9378	.9600
10								.0000	.4800	.6999	.8177	.8860	.9275	.9534
11									.3995	.6535	.7895	.8684	.9163	.9462
12									.3119	.6030	.7588	.8492	.9041	.9384
13									.2166	.5480	.7254	.8283	.8908	.9298
14									.1129	.4881	.6890	.8056	.8764	.9205
15									.0000	.4230	.6495	.7808	.8606	.9104
16										.3521	.6064	.7539	.8435	.8994
17										.2749	.5595	.7246	.8248	.8874
18										.1909	.5085	.6927	.8046	.8744
19										.0995	.4529	.6580	.7825	.8602
20										.0000	.3925	.6202	.7584	.8448
21											.3267	.5790	.7323	.8279
22											.2551	.5343	.7038	.8096
23											.1771	.4855	.6728	.7897
24											.0923	.4325	.6391	.7680
25											.0000	.3748	.6024	.7445
26												.3120	.5624	.7188
27												.2436	.5189	.6908
28												.1692	.4716	.6604
29												.0882	.4201	.6273
30												.0000	.3640	.5913
35													.0000	.3573
40														.0000

8.75%

AGE OF LOAN	ORIGINAL TERM IN YEARS													
	2	3	4	5	6	7	8	10	15	20	25	30	35	40
1	.5218	.6953	.7817	.8333	.8674	.8917	.9097	.9345	.9662	.9807	.9884	.9928	.9955	.9971
2	.0000	.3628	.5435	.6514	.7228	.7735	.8111	.8631	.9294	.9596	.9757	.9850	.9905	.9940
3		.0000	.2836	.4529	.5650	.6445	.7036	.7851	.8892	.9366	.9619	.9764	.9852	.9906
4			.0000	.2363	.3928	.5038	.5863	.7001	.8453	.9116	.9448	.9671	.9793	.9868
5				.0000	.2050	.3503	.4583	.6073	.7975	.8842	.9303	.9569	.9729	.9828
6					.0000	.1828	.3186	.5060	.7453	.8543	.9124	.9458	.9659	.9783
7						.0000	.1663	.3956	.6883	.8218	.8928	.9336	.9583	.9735
8							.0000	.2750	.6261	.7862	.8714	.9204	.9499	.9682
9								.1435	.5583	.7474	.8481	.9060	.9408	.9624
10								.0000	.4843	.7051	.8226	.8902	.9309	.9561
11									.4035	.6590	.7948	.8730	.9201	.9492
12									.3154	.6086	.7645	.8543	.9083	.9417
13									.2193	.5536	.7314	.8338	.8955	.9336
14									.1144	.4936	.6954	.8115	.8814	.9246
15									.0000	.4282	.6560	.7871	.8661	.9149
16										.3568	.6130	.7606	.8494	.9043
17										.2789	.5662	.7316	.8311	.8927
18										.1939	.5150	.6999	.8112	.8800
19										.1012	.4593	.6654	.7895	.8662
20										.0000	.3984	.6277	.7658	.8512
21											.3320	.5866	.7399	.8347
22											.2595	.5418	.7117	.8168
23											.1804	.4928	.6809	.7972
24											.0941	.4395	.6473	.7759
25											.0000	.3812	.6107	.7526
26												.3176	.5707	.7272
27												.2483	.5271	.6994
28												.1726	.4795	.6692
29												.0901	.4275	.6362
30												.0000	.3709	.6002
35													.0000	.3645
40														.0000

LOAN PROGRESS CHART
9.00%

AGE OF LOAN	ORIGINAL TERM IN YEARS													
	2	3	4	5	6	7	8	10	15	20	25	30	35	40
1	.5224	.6961	.7826	.8342	.8684	.8926	.9106	.9354	.9669	.9813	.9888	.9932	.9957	.9973
2	.0000	.3636	.5447	.6528	.7244	.7751	.8127	.8647	.9308	.9608	.9766	.9857	.9911	.9944
3		.0000	.2846	.4544	.5668	.6465	.7057	.7873	.8912	.9384	.9633	.9775	.9860	.9912
4			.0000	.2374	.3946	.5060	.5887	.7028	.8480	.9139	.9487	.9686	.9804	.9877
5				.0000	.2061	.3522	.4607	.6102	.8007	.8871	.9327	.9588	.9744	.9839
6					.0000	.1840	.3207	.5090	.7489	.8577	.9153	.9481	.9677	.9797
7						.0000	.1675	.3984	.6923	.8257	.8962	.9364	.9604	.9751
8							.0000	.2773	.6304	.7906	.8753	.9236	.9525	.9701
9								.1449	.5627	.7522	.8524	.9096	.9437	.9647
10								.0000	.4886	.7103	.8274	.8943	.9342	.9587
11									.4076	.6644	.8000	.8775	.9238	.9521
12									.3190	.6141	.7701	.8592	.9124	.9449
13									.2220	.5592	.7374	.8392	.8999	.9371
14									.1160	.4991	.7016	.8173	.8863	.9285
15									.0000	.4334	.6625	.7933	.8714	.9192
16										.3616	.6197	.7671	.8551	.9089
17										.2829	.5728	.7384	.8372	.8977
18										.1969	.5216	.7070	.8177	.8854
19										.1029	.4656	.6727	.7963	.8720
20										.0000	.4043	.6352	.7730	.8573
21											.3372	.5941	.7474	.8413
22											.2639	.5492	.7195	.8237
23											.1837	.5001	.6889	.8045
24											.0960	.4464	.6555	.7835
25											.0000	.3876	.6189	.7605
26												.3233	.5789	.7354
27												.2530	.5351	.7079
28												.1761	.4873	.6778
29												.0920	.4349	.6449
30												.0000	.3777	.6089
35													.0000	.3716
40														.0000

9.25%

AGE OF LOAN	ORIGINAL TERM IN YEARS													
	2	3	4	5	6	7	8	10	15	20	25	30	35	40
1	.5230	.6969	.7834	.8351	.8693	.8935	.9114	.9362	.9676	.9818	.9893	.9935	.9960	.9975
2	.0000	.3645	.5459	.6542	.7259	.7766	.8143	.8662	.9322	.9619	.9775	.9864	.9916	.9948
3		.0000	.2855	.4559	.5687	.6485	.7079	.7895	.8933	.9401	.9647	.9786	.9868	.9918
4			.0000	.2384	.3963	.5081	.5911	.7054	.8506	.9161	.9505	.9700	.9815	.9885
5				.0000	.2073	.3541	.4631	.6132	.8039	.8899	.9351	.9606	.9758	.9849
6					.0000	.1852	.3227	.5121	.7526	.8611	.9181	.9504	.9694	.9810
7						.0000	.1688	.4012	.6963	.8295	.8994	.9391	.9625	.9767
8							.0000	.2796	.6347	.7949	.8790	.9267	.9549	.9720
9								.1462	.5671	.7570	.8566	.9131	.9465	.9668
10								.0000	.4929	.7153	.8321	.8982	.9374	.9611
11									.4116	.6697	.8052	.8819	.9273	.9548
12									.3225	.6197	.7757	.8640	.9163	.9480
13									.2247	.5648	.7433	.8444	.9042	.9405
14									.1175	.5046	.7078	.8229	.8910	.9323
15									.0000	.4386	.6689	.7993	.8765	.9233
16										.3663	.6262	.7735	.8606	.9134
17										.2870	.5794	.7451	.8431	.9025
18										.2000	.5281	.7140	.8240	.8906
19										.1046	.4718	.6799	.8030	.8776
20										.0000	.4101	.6426	.7800	.8633
21											.3425	.6016	.7547	.8476
22											.2683	.5566	.7271	.8304
23											.1870	.5073	.6967	.8116
24											.0978	.4533	.6635	.7909
25											.0000	.3940	.6270	.7682
26												.3290	.5870	.7434
27												.2578	.5431	.7161
28												.1796	.4950	.6862
29												.0939	.4423	.6535
30												.0000	.3845	.6175
35													.0000	.3787
40														.0000

LOAN PROGRESS CHART
9.50%

AGE OF LOAN	ORIGINAL TERM IN YEARS													
	2	3	4	5	6	7	8	10	15	20	25	30	35	40
1	.5236	.6977	.7843	.8360	.8701	.8944	.9123	.9370	.9683	.9824	.9897	.9938	.9962	.9977
2	.0000	.3653	.5472	.6556	.7274	.7782	.8159	.8678	.9335	.9630	.9784	.9871	.9921	.9952
3		.0000	.2865	.4574	.5705	.6506	.7100	.7917	.8953	.9418	.9660	.9796	.9876	.9924
4			.0000	.2395	.3980	.5102	.5935	.7081	.8532	.9184	.9523	.9714	.9826	.9893
5				.0000	.2084	.3560	.4655	.6161	.8070	.8927	.9373	.9624	.9771	.9859
6					.0000	.1864	.3248	.5151	.7562	.8644	.9208	.9525	.9711	.9822
7						.0000	.1701	.4040	.7003	.8333	.9027	.9416	.9645	.9782
8							.0000	.2818	.6389	.7992	.8827	.9297	.9572	.9737
9								.1476	.5714	.7616	.8608	.9165	.9492	.9688
10								.0000	.4972	.7204	.8367	.9021	.9404	.9634
11									.4156	.6750	.8102	.8862	.9307	.9574
12									.3260	.6251	.7811	.8687	.9201	.9509
13									.2274	.5703	.7491	.8495	.9084	.9437
14									.1191	.5101	.7139	.8284	.8956	.9358
15									.0000	.4438	.6752	.8052	.8814	.9272
16										.3710	.6327	.7797	.8659	.9176
17										.2910	.5859	.7517	.8488	.9071
18										.2030	.5346	.7209	.8301	.8956
19										.1063	.4781	.6870	.8095	.8830
20										.0000	.4160	.6498	.7868	.8690
21											.3478	.6089	.7619	.8537
22											.2727	.5639	.7345	.8369
23											.1903	.5145	.7044	.8184
24											.0996	.4601	.6713	.7981
25											.0000	.4004	.6350	.7750
26												.3347	.5950	.7512
27												.2625	.5510	.7242
28												.1831	.5027	.6945
29												.0959	.4496	.6619
30												.0000	.3912	.6260
35													.0000	.3857
40														.0000

9.75%

AGE OF LOAN	ORIGINAL TERM IN YEARS													
	2	3	4	5	6	7	8	10	15	20	25	30	35	40
1	.5243	.6985	.7852	.8368	.8710	.8952	.9132	.9378	.9690	.9829	.9901	.9941	.9965	.9979
2	.0000	.3662	.5484	.6571	.7289	.7798	.8175	.8694	.9349	.9641	.9793	.9877	.9926	.9955
3		.0000	.2875	.4589	.5723	.6526	.7121	.7939	.8972	.9434	.9673	.9806	.9883	.9929
4			.0000	.2406	.3997	.5124	.5959	.7107	.8558	.9205	.9541	.9727	.9836	.9900
5				.0000	.2096	.3579	.4679	.6191	.8101	.8954	.9395	.9641	.9784	.9869
6					.0000	.1876	.3268	.5181	.7597	.8676	.9235	.9546	.9727	.9834
7						.0000	.1713	.4068	.7043	.8371	.9058	.9441	.9663	.9796
8							.0000	.2841	.6431	.8034	.8863	.9326	.9594	.9753
9								.1489	.5757	.7662	.8649	.9198	.9517	.9707
10								.0000	.5015	.7253	.8412	.9058	.9433	.9656
11									.4197	.6802	.8151	.8903	.9340	.9599
12									.3295	.6306	.7864	.8733	.9237	.9537
13									.2301	.5758	.7548	.8545	.9124	.9468
14									.1207	.5155	.7199	.8338	.8999	.9392
15									.0000	.4490	.6815	.8110	.8862	.9309
16										.3758	.6391	.7859	.8711	.9217
17										.2950	.5924	.7582	.8544	.9116
18										.2061	.5410	.7277	.8360	.9004
19										.1080	.4843	.6941	.8158	.8881
20										.0000	.4219	.6570	.7935	.8746
21											.3530	.6162	.7689	.8597
22											.2772	.5712	.7418	.8432
23											.1936	.5216	.7120	.8251
24											.1015	.4669	.6791	.8051
25											.0000	.4067	.6428	.7831
26												.3404	.6028	.7588
27												.2672	.5588	.7321
28												.1867	.5103	.7026
29												.0979	.4568	.6701
30												.0000	.3979	.6344
35													.0000	.3927
40														.0000

LOAN PROGRESS CHART
10.00%

AGE OF LOAN	ORIGINAL TERM IN YEARS													
	2	3	4	5	6	7	8	10	15	20	25	30	35	40
1	.5249	.6993	.7860	.8377	.8719	.8961	.9140	.9387	.9697	.9835	.9905	.9944	.9967	.9980
2	.0000	.3670	.5496	.6585	.7304	.7813	.8191	.8709	.9362	.9652	.9801	.9883	.9930	.9958
3		.0000	.2885	.4604	.5741	.6546	.7142	.7960	.8992	.9450	.9685	.9815	.9890	.9934
4			.0000	.2417	.4015	.5145	.5983	.7133	.8583	.9227	.9557	.9740	.9845	.9907
5				.0000	.2107	.3598	.4703	.6220	.8132	.8980	.9416	.9657	.9796	.9878
6					.0000	.1888	.3288	.5210	.7633	.8708	.9261	.9566	.9742	.9845
7						.0000	.1726	.4096	.7082	.8407	.9088	.9465	.9681	.9809
8							.0000	.2864	.6473	.8075	.8898	.9353	.9615	.9769
9								.1503	.5801	.7708	.8688	.9230	.9542	.9725
10								.0000	.5058	.7302	.8456	.9094	.9460	.9676
11									.4237	.6854	.8200	.8943	.9371	.9622
12									.3330	.6360	.7917	.8777	.9272	.9563
13									.2329	.5813	.7604	.8593	.9163	.9497
14									.1222	.5209	.7258	.8391	.9042	.9425
15									.0000	.4542	.6876	.8166	.8908	.9345
16										.3805	.6454	.7919	.8761	.9256
17										.2991	.5988	.7645	.8598	.9158
18										.2091	.5474	.7343	.8418	.9050
19										.1098	.4905	.7009	.8219	.8931
20										.0000	.4277	.6641	.8000	.8799
21											.3583	.6233	.7757	.8654
22											.2816	.5783	.7489	.8493
23											.1969	.5286	.7193	.8315
24											.1034	.4737	.6866	.8119
25											.0000	.4130	.6505	.7902
26												.3460	.6106	.7662
27												.2720	.5665	.7398
28												.1902	.5178	.7105
29												.0998	.4640	.6782
30												.0000	.4046	.6426
35													.0000	.3997
40														.0000

10.25%

AGE OF LOAN	ORIGINAL TERM IN YEARS													
	2	3	4	5	6	7	8	10	15	20	25	30	35	40
1	.5255	.7001	.7869	.8386	.8728	.8970	.9149	.9395	.9703	.9840	.9909	.9947	.9969	.9982
2	.0000	.3679	.5509	.6599	.7320	.7829	.8206	.8724	.9375	.9662	.9809	.9889	.9935	.9961
3		.0000	.2895	.4620	.5760	.6565	.7163	.7982	.9011	.9465	.9697	.9824	.9896	.9939
4			.0000	.2428	.4032	.5166	.6007	.7159	.8608	.9248	.9574	.9752	.9854	.9914
5				.0000	.2119	.3617	.4727	.6249	.8162	.9006	.9437	.9673	.9808	.9886
6					.0000	.1901	.3309	.5240	.7668	.8739	.9286	.9585	.9756	.9855
7						.0000	.1739	.4124	.7121	.8443	.9118	.9488	.9699	.9821
8							.0000	.2887	.6515	.8116	.8933	.9380	.9635	.9783
9								.1517	.5844	.7753	.8727	.9261	.9565	.9742
10								.0000	.5100	.7351	.8499	.9129	.9487	.9696
11									.4277	.6906	.8247	.8982	.9401	.9644
12									.3366	.6413	.7968	.8820	.9305	.9588
13									.2356	.5867	.7659	.8641	.9200	.9525
14									.1238	.5263	.7316	.8442	.9083	.9456
15									.0000	.4594	.6937	.8221	.8953	.9379
16										.3852	.6517	.7978	.8809	.9293
17										.3031	.6052	.7708	.8650	.9199
18										.2122	.5537	.7408	.8474	.9095
19										.1115	.4967	.7077	.8279	.8979
20										.0000	.4335	.6710	.8063	.8851
21											.3635	.6304	.7824	.8709
22											.2861	.5854	.7559	.8552
23											.2003	.5356	.7266	.8377
24											.1052	.4804	.6941	.8185
25											.0000	.4193	.6581	.7971
26												.3516	.6183	.7735
27												.2767	.5742	.7473
28												.1937	.5253	.7183
29												.1018	.4712	.6862
30												.0000	.4113	.6506
35													.0000	.4066
40														.0000

LOAN PROGRESS CHART
10.50%

AGE OF LOAN	\multicolumn{14}{c}{ORIGINAL TERM IN YEARS}
	2	3	4	5	6	7	8	10	15	20	25	30	35	40
1	.5261	.7008	.7877	.8395	.8737	.8978	.9157	.9403	.9710	.9845	.9913	.9950	.9971	.9983
2	.0000	.3687	.5521	.6613	.7335	.7844	.8222	.8739	.9388	.9672	.9816	.9894	.9939	.9964
3		.0000	.2905	.4635	.5778	.6585	.7183	.8003	.9030	.9481	.9709	.9833	.9903	.9943
4			.0000	.2438	.4049	.5188	.6030	.7185	.8633	.9268	.9590	.9764	.9863	.9919
5				.0000	.2130	.3636	.4750	.6278	.8192	.9032	.9457	.9688	.9818	.9894
6					.0000	.1913	.3329	.5270	.7703	.8770	.9310	.9604	.9769	.9865
7						.0000	.1752	.4152	.7159	.8479	.9147	.9510	.9715	.9833
8							.0000	.2910	.6556	.8156	.8966	.9406	.9654	.9797
9								.1531	.5886	.7797	.8765	.9290	.9587	.9758
10								.0000	.5143	.7399	.8542	.9162	.9512	.9714
11									.4317	.6957	.8294	.9020	.9429	.9665
12									.3401	.6466	.8019	.8862	.9337	.9611
13									.2384	.5921	.7713	.8686	.9235	.9551
14									.1254	.5316	.7374	.8491	.9122	.9485
15									.0000	.4645	.6997	.8275	.8996	.9411
16										.3899	.6579	.8035	.8856	.9329
17										.3072	.6115	.7768	.8701	.9238
18										.2153	.5600	.7473	.8529	.9137
19										.1133	.5028	.7144	.8337	.9025
20										.0000	.4393	.6779	.8125	.8900
21											.3688	.6374	.7889	.8762
22											.2905	.5924	.7627	.8608
23											.2036	.5425	.7337	.8438
24											.1071	.4871	.7014	.8249
25											.0000	.4256	.6656	.8038
26												.3573	.6258	.7805
27												.2814	.5817	.7546
28												.1972	.5327	.7259
29												.1038	.4783	.6940
30												.0000	.4179	.6585
35													.0000	.4134
40														.0000

10.75%

AGE OF LOAN	\multicolumn{14}{c}{ORIGINAL TERM IN YEARS}
	2	3	4	5	6	7	8	10	15	20	25	30	35	40
1	.5267	.7018	.7888	.8404	.8746	.8987	.9166	.9410	.9716	.9849	.9916	.9953	.9973	.9984
2	.0000	.3696	.5533	.6627	.7350	.7860	.8237	.8754	.9400	.9682	.9823	.9900	.9942	.9967
3		.0000	.2914	.4650	.5796	.6605	.7204	.8024	.9049	.9495	.9720	.9841	.9908	.9947
4			.0000	.2449	.4067	.5209	.6054	.7211	.8657	.9288	.9605	.9775	.9871	.9925
5				.0000	.2142	.3655	.4774	.6307	.8222	.9057	.9477	.9703	.9829	.9901
6					.0000	.1925	.3350	.5300	.7737	.8800	.9334	.9622	.9782	.9874
7						.0000	.1764	.4180	.7198	.8514	.9175	.9531	.9730	.9844
8							.0000	.2933	.6597	.8195	.8998	.9431	.9672	.9810
9								.1545	.5929	.7841	.8802	.9319	.9608	.9773
10								.0000	.5185	.7446	.8583	.9195	.9537	.9731
11									.4358	.7007	.8339	.9056	.9457	.9685
12									.3436	.6519	.8068	.8902	.9368	.9634
13									.2411	.5975	.7766	.8731	.9269	.9576
14									.1270	.5370	.7430	.8540	.9160	.9513
15									.0000	.4696	.7057	.8328	.9037	.9442
16										.3947	.6641	.8091	.8901	.9363
17										.3112	.6178	.7828	.8750	.9275
18										.2184	.5662	.7535	.8581	.9177
19										.1150	.5089	.7209	.8394	.9069
20										.0000	.4450	.6847	.8185	.8948
21											.3740	.6443	.7953	.8813
22											.2949	.5994	.7694	.8663
23											.2069	.5494	.7406	.8496
24											.1090	.4937	.7086	.8311
25											.0000	.4318	.6730	.8104
26												.3629	.6333	.7874
27												.2862	.5891	.7618
28												.2008	.5400	.7333
29												.1058	.4853	.7016
30												.0000	.4244	.6663
35													.0000	.4202
40														.0000

LOAN PROGRESS CHART
11.00%

AGE OF LOAN	2	3	4	5	6	7	8	10	15	20	25	30	35	40
1	.5273	.7024	.7894	.8412	.8754	.8996	.9174	.9418	.9722	.9854	.9920	.9955	.9974	.9985
2	.0000	.3704	.5545	.6641	.7365	.7875	.8253	.8769	.9413	.9691	.9831	.9905	.9946	.9969
3		.0000	.2924	.4665	.5814	.6625	.7225	.8045	.9067	.9510	.9731	.9849	.9914	.9951
4			.0000	.2460	.4084	.5230	.6078	.7237	.8681	.9307	.9620	.9786	.9878	.9930
5				.0000	.2154	.3674	.4798	.6336	.8251	.9081	.9495	.9716	.9839	.9908
6					.0000	.1937	.3370	.5330	.7771	.8829	.9357	.9639	.9794	.9882
7						.0000	.1777	.4208	.7236	.8548	.9203	.9552	.9745	.9854
8							.0000	.2956	.6638	.8234	.9030	.9455	.9690	.9822
9								.1559	.5971	.7884	.8838	.9347	.9628	.9787
10								.0000	.5228	.7493	.8623	.9226	.9560	.9748
11									.4398	.7057	.8384	.9092	.9483	.9704
12									.3472	.6571	.8117	.8942	.9398	.9655
13									.2439	.6028	.7819	.8774	.9302	.9600
14									.1286	.5423	.7486	.8587	.9196	.9539
15									.0000	.4747	.7115	.8379	.9077	.9471
16										.3994	.6701	.8146	.8945	.9395
17										.3153	.6239	.7887	.8797	.9311
18										.2215	.5724	.7597	.8633	.9216
19										.1168	.5149	.7274	.8449	.9111
20										.0000	.4508	.6913	.8244	.8993
21											.3792	.6511	.8015	.8862
22											.2994	.6063	.7759	.8716
23											.2103	.5562	.7474	.8553
24											.1109	.5003	.7157	.8371
25											.0000	.4380	.6802	.8167
26												.3685	.6406	.7941
27												.2909	.5965	.7688
28												.2043	.5472	.7405
29												.1078	.4923	.7090
30												.0000	.4309	.6739
35													.0000	.4270
40														.0000

11.25%

AGE OF LOAN	2	3	4	5	6	7	8	10	15	20	25	30	35	40
1	.5280	.7032	.7903	.8421	.8763	.9004	.9182	.9426	.9728	.9859	.9923	.9957	.9976	.9986
2	.0000	.3713	.5558	.6655	.7379	.7890	.8268	.8784	.9425	.9701	.9837	.9910	.9949	.9971
3		.0000	.2934	.4680	.5832	.6645	.7245	.8066	.9085	.9524	.9741	.9856	.9919	.9954
4			.0000	.2471	.4101	.5251	.6101	.7263	.8705	.9326	.9634	.9797	.9886	.9935
5				.0000	.2165	.3693	.4822	.6364	.8280	.9105	.9514	.9730	.9848	.9914
6					.0000	.1950	.3391	.5359	.7805	.8858	.9379	.9655	.9806	.9890
7						.0000	.1790	.4236	.7273	.8582	.9229	.9572	.9759	.9863
8							.0000	.2979	.6679	.8272	.9061	.9478	.9706	.9834
9								.1573	.6014	.7926	.8873	.9374	.9648	.9800
10								.0000	.5270	.7539	.8663	.9257	.9582	.9763
11									.4438	.7107	.8427	.9126	.9508	.9721
12									.3507	.6623	.8164	.8980	.9426	.9675
13									.2466	.6081	.7870	.8816	.9334	.9623
14									.1302	.5476	.7541	.8633	.9231	.9564
15									.0000	.4798	.7173	.8429	.9116	.9499
16										.4041	.6761	.8200	.8987	.9426
17										.3193	.6301	.7944	.8843	.9345
18										.2246	.5785	.7657	.8682	.9254
19										.1186	.5209	.7337	.8502	.9152
20										.0000	.4565	.6979	.8300	.9037
21											.3844	.6578	.8075	.8910
22											.3038	.6130	.7823	.8767
23											.2136	.5629	.7541	.8607
24											.1128	.5069	.7226	.8429
25											.0000	.4442	.6873	.8229
26												.3740	.6478	.8005
27												.2956	.6037	.7756
28												.2079	.5544	.7476
29												.1097	.4992	.7163
30												.0000	.4374	.6814
35													.0000	.4336
40														.0000

LOAN PROGRESS CHART
11.50%

AGE OF LOAN	ORIGINAL TERM IN YEARS													
	2	3	4	5	6	7	8	10	15	20	25	30	35	40
1	.5286	.7040	.7912	.8430	.8772	.9013	.9191	.9434	.9734	.9863	.9926	.9960	.9978	.9987
2	.0000	.3721	.5570	.6669	.7394	.7906	.8283	.8799	.9437	.9710	.9844	.9914	.9952	.9973
3		.0000	.2944	.4695	.5850	.6664	.7266	.8086	.9103	.9538	.9751	.9863	.9924	.9957
4			.0000	.2482	.4118	.5272	.6125	.7288	.8729	.9345	.9648	.9806	.9892	.9940
5				.0000	.2177	.3712	.4846	.6393	.8309	.9129	.9532	.9742	.9857	.9920
6					.0000	.1962	.3411	.5389	.7838	.8887	.9401	.9671	.9817	.9898
7						.0000	.1803	.4264	.7311	.8615	.9255	.9590	.9772	.9873
8							.0000	.3002	.6719	.8310	.9091	.9500	.9722	.9844
9								.1587	.6056	.7968	.8907	.9399	.9666	.9813
10								.0000	.5312	.7585	.8701	.9286	.9603	.9778
11									.4478	.7155	.8470	.9159	.9532	.9738
12									.3543	.6674	.8211	.9017	.9453	.9694
13									.2494	.6134	.7921	.8857	.9364	.9644
14									.1318	.5528	.7595	.8678	.9265	.9588
15									.0000	.4849	.7230	.8477	.9153	.9526
16										.4088	.6820	.8252	.9028	.9456
17										.3234	.6361	.8000	.8887	.9377
18										.2277	.5846	.7717	.8730	.9289
19										.1203	.5269	.7399	.8554	.9190
20										.0000	.4622	.7044	.8356	.9080
21											.3896	.6645	.8134	.8955
22											.3082	.6197	.7885	.8816
23											.2170	.5696	.7606	.8660
24											.1147	.5133	.7293	.8485
25											.0000	.4503	.6943	.8289
26												.3796	.6549	.8069
27												.3003	.6109	.7822
28												.2114	.5614	.7545
29												.1118	.5060	.7235
30												.0000	.4438	.6887
35													.0000	.4403
40														.0000

11.75%

AGE OF LOAN	ORIGINAL TERM IN YEARS													
	2	3	4	5	6	7	8	10	15	20	25	30	35	40
1	.5292	.7048	.7920	.8438	.8780	.9021	.9199	.9441	.9740	.9868	.9930	.9962	.9979	.9988
2	.0000	.3730	.5582	.6683	.7409	.7921	.8298	.8813	.9449	.9719	.9850	.9919	.9955	.9975
3		.0000	.2954	.4710	.5868	.6684	.7286	.8107	.9120	.9551	.9761	.9870	.9929	.9961
4			.0000	.2493	.4136	.5294	.6148	.7313	.8752	.9363	.9661	.9806	.9899	.9944
5				.0000	.2189	.3731	.4870	.6421	.8337	.9152	.9549	.9755	.9865	.9925
6					.0000	.1974	.3432	.5419	.7871	.8914	.9422	.9686	.9827	.9904
7						.0000	.1816	.4292	.7348	.8647	.9280	.9609	.9785	.9881
8							.0000	.3025	.6759	.8347	.9120	.9522	.9737	.9855
9								.1601	.6097	.8009	.8941	.9424	.9683	.9825
10								.0000	.5354	.7630	.8739	.9314	.9623	.9792
11									.4518	.7204	.8512	.9191	.9555	.9754
12									.3578	.6725	.8257	.9052	.9479	.9712
13									.2522	.6186	.7970	.8897	.9393	.9664
14									.1335	.5580	.7648	.8721	.9297	.9611
15									.0000	.4900	.7286	.8524	.9189	.9551
16										.4135	.6879	.8303	.9067	.9484
17										.3275	.6421	.8054	.8930	.9408
18										.2308	.5907	.7775	.8777	.9323
19										.1221	.5328	.7460	.8604	.9228
20										.0000	.4678	.7107	.8409	.9120
21											.3948	.6710	.8191	.8999
22											.3127	.6263	.7946	.8864
23											.2204	.5762	.7670	.8711
24											.1166	.5198	.7360	.8540
25											.0000	.4564	.7011	.8347
26												.3851	.6619	.8130
27												.3050	.6179	.7886
28												.2150	.5684	.7613
29												.1138	.5128	.7305
30												.0000	.4502	.6959
35													.0000	.4469
40														.0000

LOAN PROGRESS CHART
12.00%

AGE OF LOAN	\multicolumn{13}{c}{ORIGINAL TERM IN YEARS}
	2	3	4	5	6	7	8	10	15	20	25	30	35	40
1	.5298	.7056	.7928	.8447	.8789	.9029	.9207	.9449	.9746	.9872	.9932	.9964	.9980	.9989
2	.0000	.3738	.5594	.6697	.7424	.7936	.8313	.8827	.9460	.9727	.9856	.9923	.9958	.9977
3		.0000	.2964	.4725	.5886	.6703	.7306	.8127	.9138	.9565	.9771	.9877	.9933	.9963
4			.0000	.2504	.4153	.5315	.6172	.7339	.8775	.9381	.9674	.9825	.9905	.9948
5				.0000	.2200	.3750	.4893	.6450	.8365	.9174	.9565	.9766	.9873	.9931
6					.0000	.1987	.3453	.5448	.7904	.8942	.9443	.9700	.9837	.9911
7						.0000	.1829	.4320	.7384	.8679	.9305	.9626	.9797	.9889
8							.0000	.3048	.6799	.8383	.9149	.9542	.9751	.9864
9								.1615	.6139	.8050	.8973	.9448	.9700	.9836
10								.0000	.5395	.7675	.8776	.9342	.9642	.9804
11									.4558	.7252	.8553	.9222	.9577	.9769
12									.3613	.6775	.8302	.9087	.9504	.9729
13									.2550	.6237	.8019	.8935	.9421	.9684
14									.1351	.5632	.7700	.8764	.9328	.9633
15									.0000	.4950	.7341	.8571	.9223	.9575
16										.4181	.6936	.8353	.9105	.9511
17										.3315	.6480	.8108	.8972	.9438
18										.2339	.5966	.7832	.8822	.9356
19										.1239	.5387	.7520	.8652	.9263
20										.0000	.4735	.7169	.8462	.9159
21											.4000	.6774	.8247	.9042
22											.3171	.6329	.8005	.8909
23											.2237	.5827	.7732	.8760
24											.1185	.5261	.7425	.8592
25											.0000	.4624	.7078	.8403
26												.3906	.6688	.8190
27												.3097	.6248	.7949
28												.2185	.5753	.7678
29												.1158	.5195	.7373
30												.0000	.4565	.7029
35													.0000	.4534
40														.0000

12.25%

AGE OF LOAN	\multicolumn{13}{c}{ORIGINAL TERM IN YEARS}
	2	3	4	5	6	7	8	10	15	20	25	30	35	40
1	.5304	.7064	.7937	.8456	.8797	.9038	.9215	.9456	.9752	.9876	.9935	.9966	.9982	.9990
2	.0000	.3747	.5606	.6711	.7439	.7951	.8328	.8842	.9471	.9736	.9862	.9927	.9961	.9979
3		.0000	.2974	.4741	.5904	.6723	.7327	.8148	.9155	.9577	.9780	.9883	.9937	.9966
4			.0000	.2515	.4170	.5336	.6195	.7364	.8797	.9399	.9687	.9833	.9911	.9952
5				.0000	.2212	.3769	.4917	.6478	.8393	.9196	.9581	.9777	.9880	.9935
6					.0000	.1999	.3473	.5478	.7936	.8968	.9463	.9714	.9847	.9917
7						.0000	.1842	.4348	.7421	.8710	.9328	.9643	.9808	.9896
8							.0000	.3071	.6838	.8419	.9176	.9562	.9765	.9873
9								.1629	.6180	.8090	.9005	.9471	.9716	.9847
10								.0000	.5437	.7719	.8812	.9368	.9661	.9817
11									.4597	.7299	.8593	.9252	.9598	.9783
12									.3649	.6824	.8346	.9121	.9528	.9745
13									.2577	.6289	.8067	.8972	.9448	.9702
14									.1367	.5684	.7752	.8805	.9358	.9653
15									.0000	.5000	.7395	.8615	.9256	.9598
16										.4228	.6993	.8402	.9141	.9536
17										.3356	.6539	.8160	.9012	.9466
18										.2370	.6026	.7887	.8865	.9387
19										.1257	.5446	.7579	.8700	.9298
20										.0000	.4791	.7231	.8512	.9196
21											.4051	.6838	.8301	.9082
22											.3215	.6393	.8063	.8953
23											.2271	.5891	.7793	.8808
24											.1205	.5325	.7488	.8643
25											.0000	.4684	.7144	.8458
26												.3961	.6756	.8248
27												.3144	.6317	.8010
28												.2221	.5821	.7743
29												.1178	.5261	.7440
30												.0000	.4628	.7098
35													.0000	.4598
40														.0000

12.50%

AGE OF LOAN	ORIGINAL TERM IN YEARS													
	2	3	4	5	6	7	8	10	15	20	25	30	35	40
1	.5310	.7072	.7945	.8464	.8806	.9046	.9223	.9463	.9757	.9880	.9938	.9967	.9983	.9991
2	.0000	.3755	.5619	.6725	.7453	.7966	.8343	.8856	.9483	.9744	.9868	.9931	.9963	.9980
3		.0000	.2984	.4756	.5922	.6742	.7347	.8168	.9172	.9590	.9789	.9889	.9941	.9969
4			.0000	.2526	.4188	.5357	.6219	.7389	.8819	.9416	.9699	.9842	.9916	.9955
5				.0000	.2224	.3788	.4941	.6506	.8420	.9218	.9597	.9788	.9888	.9940
6					.0000	.2012	.3494	.5507	.7968	.8994	.9482	.9728	.9855	.9923
7						.0000	.1855	.4375	.7457	.8741	.9351	.9659	.9819	.9903
8							.0000	.3094	.6877	.8454	.9203	.9581	.9778	.9881
9								.1643	.6221	.8130	.9036	.9493	.9731	.9856
10								.0000	.5478	.7762	.8847	.9394	.9678	.9828
11									.4637	.7345	.8632	.9281	.9618	.9796
12									.3684	.6874	.8389	.9153	.9550	.9760
13									.2605	.6340	.8114	.9008	.9474	.9719
14									.1384	.5735	.7802	.8845	.9387	.9673
15									.0000	.5050	.7449	.8659	.9288	.9620
16										.4274	.7049	.8449	.9177	.9560
17										.3396	.6597	.8211	.9050	.9493
18										.2402	.6084	.7942	.8907	.9417
19										.1275	.5504	.7637	.8745	.9330
20										.0000	.4846	.7291	.8562	.9232
21											.4102	.6900	.8354	.9121
22											.3259	.6457	.8119	.8996
23											.2305	.5955	.7852	.8854
24											.1224	.5387	.7551	.8693
25											.0000	.4744	.7209	.8510
26												.4015	.6822	.8304
27												.3190	.6384	.8070
28												.2256	.5888	.7805
29												.1198	.5327	.7505
30												.0000	.4690	.7166
35													.0000	.4662
40														.0000

12.75%

AGE OF LOAN	ORIGINAL TERM IN YEARS													
	2	3	4	5	6	7	8	10	15	20	25	30	35	40
1	.5317	.7079	.7954	.8473	.8814	.9054	.9231	.9471	.9763	.9884	.9941	.9969	.9984	.9991
2	.0000	.3764	.5631	.6739	.7468	.7981	.8358	.8870	.9494	.9752	.9873	.9934	.9965	.9982
3		.0000	.2994	.4771	.5940	.6762	.7367	.8188	.9188	.9602	.9797	.9895	.9945	.9971
4			.0000	.2536	.4205	.5378	.6242	.7413	.8841	.9432	.9710	.9850	.9921	.9958
5				.0000	.2236	.3807	.4965	.6534	.8447	.9239	.9612	.9798	.9894	.9944
6					.0000	.2024	.3515	.5536	.8000	.9020	.9500	.9740	.9864	.9928
7						.0000	.1869	.4403	.7493	.8771	.9374	.9674	.9829	.9910
8							.0000	.3117	.6916	.8489	.9230	.9600	.9790	.9889
9								.1657	.6262	.8168	.9066	.9515	.9745	.9866
10								.0000	.5520	.7804	.8881	.9418	.9695	.9839
11									.4677	.7391	.8670	.9309	.9637	.9809
12									.3720	.6922	.8431	.9185	.9572	.9774
13									.2633	.6390	.8160	.9044	.9498	.9735
14									.1400	.5786	.7851	.8883	.9414	.9691
15									.0000	.5100	.7502	.8702	.9319	.9641
16										.4321	.7105	.8495	.9210	.9584
17										.3437	.6654	.8261	.9087	.9519
18										.2433	.6142	.7995	.8948	.9445
19										.1294	.5561	.7693	.8789	.9362
20										.0000	.4902	.7350	.8610	.9267
21											.4153	.6961	.8405	.9159
22											.3303	.6520	.8174	.9037
23											.2339	.6018	.7911	.8898
24											.1243	.5449	.7612	.8740
25											.0000	.4803	.7273	.8562
26												.4069	.6888	.8359
27												.3237	.6451	.8128
28												.2291	.5955	.7866
29												.1218	.5392	.7569
30												.0000	.4752	.7232
35													.0000	.4726
40														.0000

LOAN PROGRESS CHART
13.00%

AGE OF LOAN	ORIGINAL TERM IN YEARS													
	2	3	4	5	6	7	8	10	15	20	25	30	35	40
1	.5323	.7087	.7962	.8481	.8823	.9062	.9239	.9478	.9768	.9888	.9943	.9971	.9985	.9992
2	.0000	.3772	.5643	.6753	.7483	.7995	.8373	.8884	.9504	.9760	.9879	.9938	.9968	.9983
3		.0000	.3004	.4786	.5958	.6781	.7387	.8208	.9204	.9614	.9805	.9900	.9948	.9973
4			.0000	.2547	.4222	.5399	.6265	.7438	.8863	.9448	.9722	.9857	.9926	.9961
5				.0000	.2248	.3827	.4988	.6562	.8474	.9260	.9627	.9808	.9901	.9948
6					.0000	.2037	.3535	.5566	.8031	.9045	.9518	.9753	.9872	.9933
7						.0000	.1882	.4431	.7528	.8801	.9395	.9689	.9839	.9916
8							.0000	.3141	.6955	.8523	.9255	.9617	.9801	.9897
9								.1672	.6303	.8207	.9096	.9535	.9759	.9874
10								.0000	.5561	.7847	.8914	.9442	.9711	.9849
11									.4716	.7437	.8707	.9336	.9656	.9820
12									.3755	.6971	.8472	.9215	.9593	.9788
13									.2661	.6440	.8205	.9078	.9522	.9751
14									.1417	.5836	.7900	.8921	.9440	.9708
15									.0000	.5149	.7554	.8743	.9348	.9660
16										.4367	.7159	.8540	.9243	.9605
17										.3477	.6710	.8310	.9123	.9543
18										.2464	.6200	.8047	.8987	.9472
19										.1312	.5618	.7749	.8832	.9391
20										.0000	.4957	.7409	.8656	.9300
21											.4204	.7022	.8455	.9195
22											.3347	.6582	.8227	.9076
23											.2372	.6081	.7967	.8941
24											.1263	.5511	.7672	.8786
25											.0000	.4862	.7335	.8611
26												.4123	.6952	.8412
27												.3283	.6516	.8184
28												.2327	.6020	.7926
29												.1239	.5456	.7632
30												.0000	.4813	.7297
35													.0000	.4788
40														.0000

13.25%

AGE OF LOAN	ORIGINAL TERM IN YEARS													
	2	3	4	5	6	7	8	10	15	20	25	30	35	40
1	.5329	.7095	.7970	.8490	.8831	.9071	.9247	.9485	.9773	.9891	.9946	.9972	.9986	.9993
2	.0000	.3781	.5655	.6767	.7497	.8010	.8387	.8897	.9515	.9767	.9884	.9941	.9970	.9984
3		.0000	.3014	.4801	.5976	.6800	.7407	.8227	.9220	.9626	.9813	.9905	.9951	.9975
4			.0000	.2558	.4240	.5420	.6288	.7462	.8884	.9464	.9733	.9864	.9930	.9964
5				.0000	.2259	.3846	.5012	.6590	.8500	.9280	.9641	.9818	.9906	.9952
6					.0000	.2049	.3556	.5595	.8062	.9070	.9536	.9764	.9879	.9938
7						.0000	.1895	.4459	.7563	.8830	.9416	.9703	.9848	.9922
8							.0000	.3164	.6993	.8556	.9280	.9634	.9812	.9903
9								.1686	.6343	.8244	.9124	.9555	.9772	.9883
10								.0000	.5602	.7888	.8946	.9465	.9726	.9859
11									.4756	.7482	.8744	.9362	.9673	.9832
12									.3790	.7018	.8513	.9244	.9613	.9801
13									.2689	.6490	.8249	.9110	.9544	.9765
14									.1433	.5886	.7948	.8958	.9466	.9725
15									.0000	.5198	.7605	.8783	.9376	.9679
16										.4413	.7213	.8584	.9274	.9626
17										.3518	.6766	.8357	.9158	.9566
18										.2496	.6256	.8098	.9025	.9498
19										.1330	.5675	.7803	.8874	.9420
20										.0000	.5012	.7466	.8701	.9331
21											.4255	.7081	.8504	.9230
22											.3391	.6643	.8279	.9114
23											.2406	.6142	.8023	.8982
24											.1282	.5571	.7730	.8831
25											.0000	.4920	.7396	.8659
26												.4177	.7015	.8463
27												.3329	.6581	.8239
28												.2362	.6085	.7984
29												.1259	.5519	.7693
30												.0000	.4874	.7360
35													.0000	.4851
40														.0000

LOAN PROGRESS CHART
13.50%

AGE OF LOAN	ORIGINAL TERM IN YEARS

AGE OF LOAN	2	3	4	5	6	7	8	10	15	20	25	30	35	40
1	.5335	.7103	.7979	.8498	.8839	.9079	.9252	.9492	.9779	.9895	.9948	.9974	.9987	.9993
2	.0000	.3789	.5667	.6781	.7512	.8025	.8402	.8911	.9526	.9774	.9889	.9944	.9972	.9986
3		.0000	.3024	.4816	.5993	.6820	.7426	.8247	.9236	.9637	.9821	.9910	.9954	.9977
4			.0000	.2569	.4257	.5441	.6311	.7487	.8905	.9480	.9743	.9871	.9935	.9967
5				.0000	.2271	.3865	.5036	.6618	.8526	.9300	.9654	.9826	.9912	.9955
6					.0000	.2062	.3577	.5624	.8093	.9094	.9553	.9775	.9886	.9942
7						.0000	.1908	.4487	.7598	.8858	.9437	.9717	.9857	.9927
8							.0000	.3187	.7031	.8589	.9304	.9650	.9823	.9910
9								.1700	.6383	.8281	.9152	.9574	.9784	.9890
10								.0000	.5642	.7929	.8978	.9487	.9740	.9868
11									.4795	.7526	.8779	.9387	.9689	.9842
12									.3826	.7066	.8552	.9273	.9632	.9813
13									.2717	.6539	.8292	.9142	.9566	.9779
14									.1450	.5936	.7995	.8993	.9490	.9740
15									.0000	.5247	.7655	.8822	.9403	.9696
16										.4459	.7266	.8627	.9304	.9646
17										.3558	.6821	.8404	.9191	.9589
18										.2527	.6313	.8148	.9062	.9523
19										.1348	.5731	.7856	.8914	.9447
20										.0000	.5066	.7522	.8745	.9361
21											.4305	.7140	.8551	.9263
22											.3435	.6703	.8330	.9150
23											.2440	.6203	.8077	.9021
24											.1302	.5632	.7787	.8874
25											.0000	.4978	.7456	.8706
26												.4230	.7077	.8513
27												.3375	.6644	.8293
28												.2397	.6149	.8040
29												.1279	.5582	.7752
30												.0000	.4934	.7423
35													.0000	.4912
40														.0000

13.75%

AGE OF LOAN	2	3	4	5	6	7	8	10	15	20	25	30	35	40
1	.5341	.7111	.7987	.8507	.8848	.9087	.9252	.9499	.9784	.9898	.9950	.9975	.9988	.9994
2	.0000	.3798	.5679	.6794	.7526	.8039	.8416	.8925	.9536	.9782	.9893	.9947	.9974	.9987
3		.0000	.3033	.4831	.6011	.6839	.7446	.8266	.9251	.9648	.9828	.9915	.9957	.9979
4			.0000	.2580	.4274	.5462	.6334	.7511	.8926	.9495	.9753	.9878	.9939	.9969
5				.0000	.2283	.3884	.5059	.6645	.8552	.9319	.9668	.9835	.9917	.9958
6					.0000	.2075	.3597	.5653	.8123	.9117	.9569	.9786	.9893	.9946
7						.0000	.1921	.4515	.7632	.8886	.9456	.9730	.9865	.9932
8							.0000	.3211	.7069	.8621	.9327	.9666	.9833	.9916
9								.1715	.6423	.8317	.9179	.9592	.9796	.9897
10								.0000	.5683	.7969	.9009	.9508	.9754	.9876
11									.4834	.7570	.8814	.9411	.9705	.9852
12									.3861	.7112	.8591	.9300	.9650	.9824
13									.2746	.6587	.8335	.9173	.9586	.9792
14									.1466	.5986	.8041	.9027	.9513	.9755
15									.0000	.5296	.7704	.8860	.9429	.9713
16										.4505	.7318	.8669	.9333	.9665
17										.3598	.6876	.8449	.9223	.9610
18										.2559	.6368	.8197	.9097	.9546
19										.1367	.5787	.7908	.8953	.9474
20										.0000	.5120	.7577	.8787	.9390
21											.4355	.7198	.8597	.9295
22											.3479	.6762	.8379	.9185
23											.2473	.6263	.8129	.9060
24											.1321	.5691	.7843	.8916
25											.0000	.5035	.7515	.8751
26												.4283	.7138	.8561
27												.3421	.6706	.8344
28												.2433	.6212	.8096
29												.1299	.5644	.7810
30												.0000	.4994	.7483
35													.0000	.4973
40														.0000

LOAN PROGRESS CHART
14.00%

AGE OF LOAN	ORIGINAL TERM IN YEARS												
	2	3	4	5	6	7	8	10	15	20	25	30	35	40
1	.5347	.7118	.7995	.8515	.8856	.9095	.9277	.9506	.9789	.9902	.9953	.9977	.9988	.9994
2	.0000	.3807	.5691	.6808	.7541	.8054	.8430	.8938	.9546	.9789	.9898	.9950	.9975	.9988
3		.0000	.3043	.4846	.6029	.6858	.7466	.8285	.9267	.9659	.9835	.9919	.9960	.9980
4			.0000	.2591	.4292	.5483	.6357	.7535	.8946	.9509	.9763	.9884	.9942	.9971
5				.0000	.2295	.3903	.5083	.6673	.8577	.9338	.9680	.9843	.9922	.9961
6					.0000	.2087	.3618	.5682	.8153	.9140	.9585	.9796	.9899	.9950
7						.0000	.1935	.4543	.7666	.8913	.9476	.9743	.9873	.9937
8							.0000	.3234	.7106	.8653	.9350	.9681	.9842	.9922
9								.1729	.6463	.8353	.9205	.9610	.9807	.9904
10								.0000	.5723	.8009	.9039	.9528	.9767	.9884
11									.4873	.7613	.8848	.9435	.9720	.9861
12									.3897	.7158	.8628	.9327	.9667	.9835
13									.2774	.6636	.8376	.9203	.9606	.9804
14									.1483	.6035	.8086	.9061	.9535	.9769
15									.0000	.5344	.7753	.8897	.9454	.9729
16										.4551	.7370	.8709	.9361	.9683
17										.3638	.6930	.8493	.9254	.9630
18										.2590	.6423	.8245	.9132	.9569
19										.1385	.5842	.7959	.8990	.9499
20										.0000	.5173	.7631	.8828	.9418
21											.4405	.7254	.8642	.9325
22											.3522	.6821	.8427	.9219
23											.2507	.6323	.8181	.9096
24											.1341	.5750	.7897	.8956
25											.0000	.5092	.7572	.8794
26												.4336	.7198	.8608
27												.3467	.6768	.8395
28												.2468	.6274	.8149
29												.1320	.5706	.7867
30												.0000	.5053	.7543
35													.0000	.5033
40														.0000

14.25%

AGE OF LOAN	ORIGINAL TERM IN YEARS												
	2	3	4	5	6	7	8	10	15	20	25	30	35	40
1	.5354	.7126	.8004	.8523	.8864	.9102	.9277	.9513	.9794	.9905	.9955	.9978	.9989	.9995
2	.0000	.3815	.5704	.6822	.7555	.8068	.8445	.8951	.9556	.9795	.9902	.9953	.9977	.9989
3		.0000	.3053	.4861	.6047	.6877	.7485	.8304	.9282	.9669	.9842	.9923	.9963	.9982
4			.0000	.2603	.4309	.5504	.6380	.7559	.8966	.9524	.9773	.9890	.9946	.9974
5				.0000	.2307	.3922	.5106	.6700	.8602	.9356	.9693	.9851	.9927	.9964
6					.0000	.2100	.3639	.5711	.8183	.9163	.9600	.9806	.9905	.9953
7						.0000	.1948	.4571	.7700	.8940	.9494	.9755	.9880	.9941
8							.0000	.3257	.7144	.8684	.9372	.9695	.9851	.9927
9								.1744	.6502	.8388	.9231	.9627	.9818	.9910
10								.0000	.5764	.8048	.9068	.9548	.9779	.9892
11									.4912	.7656	.8881	.9457	.9735	.9870
12									.3932	.7204	.8665	.9353	.9683	.9845
13									.2802	.6683	.8417	.9232	.9625	.9816
14									.1500	.6084	.8131	.9093	.9557	.9782
15									.0000	.5392	.7801	.8933	.9478	.9744
16										.4596	.7421	.8749	.9388	.9700
17										.3679	.6983	.8536	.9284	.9649
18										.2621	.6478	.8291	.9165	.9590
19										.1403	.5897	.8009	.9027	.9522
20										.0000	.5227	.7684	.8868	.9444
21											.4455	.7310	.8685	.9355
22											.3565	.6878	.8474	.9251
23											.2541	.6381	.8231	.9132
24											.1360	.5809	.7951	.8994
25											.0000	.5149	.7628	.8836
26												.4388	.7257	.8654
27												.3512	.6828	.8444
28												.2503	.6335	.8201
29												.1340	.5766	.7922
30												.0000	.5111	.7601
35													.0000	.5093
40														.0000

LOAN PROGRESS CHART
14.50%

AGE OF LOAN	ORIGINAL TERM IN YEARS													
	2	3	4	5	6	7	8	10	15	20	25	30	35	40
1	.5360	.7134	.8012	.8532	.8872	.9110	.9285	.9519	.9798	.9908	.9957	.9979	.9990	.9995
2	.0000	.3824	.5716	.6835	.7569	.8083	.8459	.8964	.9565	.9802	.9906	.9955	.9978	.9989
3		.0000	.3063	.4876	.6064	.6896	.7505	.8323	.9296	.9679	.9849	.9927	.9965	.9983
4			.0000	.3063	.4326	.5525	.6403	.7583	.8986	.9537	.9782	.9895	.9949	.9975
5				.0000	.2614	.4326	.5525	.7583	.8986	.9537	.9782	.9895	.9949	.9975
5					.2319	.3941	.5130	.6728	.8627	.9374	.9704	.9858	.9932	.9967
6					.0000	.2113	.3660	.5740	.8212	.9185	.9615	.9815	.9911	.9957
7						.0000	.1961	.4599	.7733	.8966	.9512	.9766	.9887	.9945
8							.0000	.3281	.7180	.8714	.9393	.9709	.9859	.9932
9								.1758	.6542	.8423	.9256	.9643	.9828	.9916
10								.0000	.5804	.8087	.9097	.9567	.9791	.9899
11									.4951	.7698	.8913	.9479	.9748	.9878
12									.3967	.7249	.8701	.9377	.9699	.9854
13									.2830	.6731	.8457	.9260	.9642	.9827
14									.1517	.6132	.8174	.9124	.9577	.9795
15									.0000	.5440	.7848	.8968	.9501	.9758
16										.4641	.7470	.8787	.9414	.9716
17										.3719	.7035	.8578	.9313	.9667
18										.2653	.6532	.8337	.9197	.9610
19										.1422	.5951	.8058	.9062	.9545
20										.0000	.5279	.7736	.8906	.9470
21											.4504	.7365	.8727	.9383
22											.3609	.6935	.8519	.9282
23											.2574	.6439	.8280	.9166
24											.1380	.5866	.8003	.9032
25											.0000	.5205	.7683	.8877
26												.4440	.7314	.8698
27												.3558	.6888	.8491
28												.2538	.6395	.8252
29												.1360	.5826	.7976
30												.0000	.5169	.7658
35													.0000	.5152
40														.0000

14.75%

AGE OF LOAN	ORIGINAL TERM IN YEARS													
	2	3	4	5	6	7	8	10	15	20	25	30	35	40
1	.5366	.7142	.8020	.8540	.8880	.9118	.9292	.9526	.9803	.9911	.9959	.9980	.9991	.9996
2	.0000	.3832	.5728	.6849	.7584	.8097	.8473	.8977	.9575	.9808	.9910	.9958	.9980	.9990
3		.0000	.3073	.4891	.6082	.6915	.7524	.8342	.9311	.9689	.9855	.9931	.9967	.9984
4			.0000	.2625	.4344	.5546	.6425	.7606	.9005	.9551	.9790	.9901	.9953	.9977
5				.0000	.2331	.3961	.5153	.6755	.8651	.9391	.9716	.9865	.9936	.9969
6					.0000	.2125	.3680	.5768	.8241	.9206	.9630	.9824	.9916	.9960
7						.0000	.1975	.4626	.7766	.8992	.9530	.9777	.9894	.9949
8							.0000	.3304	.7217	.8744	.9414	.9722	.9867	.9936
9								.1773	.6580	.8457	.9280	.9659	.9837	.9922
10								.0000	.5843	.8124	.9124	.9585	.9802	.9905
11									.4990	.7739	.8945	.9500	.9761	.9886
12									.4002	.7294	.8737	.9401	.9714	.9863
13									.2858	.6778	.8496	.9287	.9660	.9837
14									.1534	.6180	.8217	.9155	.9596	.9807
15									.0000	.5488	.7894	.9002	.9523	.9772
16										.4686	.7520	.8824	.9439	.9731
17										.3759	.7086	.8619	.9341	.9684
18										.2684	.6585	.8381	.9227	.9630
19										.1440	.6004	.8106	.9096	.9567
20										.0000	.5332	.7787	.8944	.9494
21											.4553	.7418	.8768	.9410
22											.3652	.6991	.8564	.9312
23											.2608	.6496	.8327	.9199
24											.1399	.5923	.8054	.9068
25											.0000	.5260	.7737	.8916
26												.4492	.7371	.8741
27												.3603	.6946	.8537
28												.2573	.6455	.8302
29												.1381	.5885	.8029
30												.0000	.5226	.7713
35													.0000	.5210
40														.0000

15.00%

AGE OF LOAN	ORIGINAL TERM IN YEARS													
	2	3	4	5	6	7	8	10	15	20	25	30	35	40
1	.5372	.7149	.8028	.8548	.8888	.9126	.9300	.9539	.9808	.9914	.9960	.9981	.9991	.9996
2	.0000	.3841	.5740	.6863	.7598	.8111	.8487	.8990	.9584	.9814	.9914	.9960	.9981	.9991
3		.0000	.3083	.4906	.6100	.6934	.7543	.8361	.9325	.9699	.9861	.9935	.9969	.9985
4			.0000	.2636	.4361	.5567	.6448	.7630	.9024	.9564	.9799	.9906	.9956	.9979
5				.0000	.2343	.3980	.5177	.6782	.8675	.9408	.9727	.9872	.9940	.9971
6					.0000	.2138	.3701	.5797	.8270	.9227	.9643	.9833	.9921	.9963
7						.0000	.1988	.4654	.7799	.9017	.9546	.9787	.9900	.9953
8							.0000	.3327	.7253	.8773	.9434	.9735	.9875	.9941
9								.1787	.6619	.8490	.9303	.9674	.9846	.9927
10								.0000	.5883	.8162	.9151	.9602	.9812	.9911
11									.5029	.7780	.8975	.9520	.9774	.9893
12									.4037	.7338	.8771	.9424	.9728	.9871
13									.2887	.6824	.8534	.9313	.9676	.9847
14									.1551	.6227	.8259	.9184	.9615	.9818
15									.0000	.5535	.7939	.9034	.9545	.9784
16										.4731	.7568	.8861	.9463	.9746
17										.3799	.7137	.8659	.9367	.9701
18										.2716	.6638	.8425	.9257	.9648
19										.1459	.6057	.8153	.9129	.9588
20										.0000	.5384	.7837	.8980	.9517
21											.4602	.7471	.8807	.9436
22											.3695	.7046	.8607	.9341
23											.2642	.6553	.8374	.9230
24											.1419	.5980	.8104	.9103
25											.0000	.5315	.7790	.8954
26												.4543	.7426	.8782
27												.3648	.7004	.8582
28												.2608	.6513	.8350
29												.1401	.5944	.8081
30												.0000	.5283	.7768
35													.0000	.5268
40														.0000

15.25%

AGE OF LOAN	ORIGINAL TERM IN YEARS													
	2	3	4	5	6	7	8	10	15	20	25	30	35	40
1	.5378	.7157	.8037	.8556	.8896	.9134	.9307	.9539	.9812	.9917	.9962	.9982	.9992	.9996
2	.0000	.3849	.5752	.6876	.7612	.8125	.8501	.9003	.9594	.9820	.9918	.9962	.9982	.9992
3		.0000	.3093	.4922	.6117	.6952	.7562	.8379	.9339	.9708	.9867	.9938	.9971	.9987
4			.0000	.2647	.4378	.5587	.6471	.7653	.9043	.9577	.9807	.9911	.9958	.9981
5				.0000	.2355	.3999	.5200	.6809	.8699	.9425	.9738	.9878	.9943	.9974
6					.0000	.2151	.3722	.5826	.8298	.9248	.9657	.9841	.9926	.9965
7						.0000	.2002	.4682	.7832	.9042	.9563	.9798	.9906	.9956
8							.0000	.3351	.7289	.8802	.9453	.9747	.9882	.9945
9								.1802	.6657	.8523	.9326	.9688	.9855	.9932
10								.0000	.5923	.8199	.9178	.9619	.9823	.9917
11									.5067	.7821	.9005	.9539	.9785	.9900
12									.4073	.7381	.8805	.9447	.9742	.9879
13									.2915	.6870	.8571	.9338	.9692	.9856
14									.1568	.6275	.8300	.9213	.9633	.9828
15									.0000	.5582	.7983	.9066	.9565	.9797
16										.4776	.7616	.8896	.9485	.9759
17										.3838	.7188	.8698	.9393	.9716
18										.2747	.6690	.8467	.9286	.9666
19										.1477	.6110	.8199	.9160	.9608
20										.0000	.5436	.7886	.9015	.9539
21											.4651	.7523	.8846	.9460
22											.3738	.7100	.8648	.9368
23											.2675	.6608	.8419	.9261
24											.1439	.6036	.8152	.9136
25											.0000	.5370	.7842	.8991
26												.4594	.7480	.8822
27												.3692	.7060	.8626
28												.2643	.6571	.8397
29												.1421	.6002	.8131
30												.0000	.5339	.7821
35													.0000	.5325
40														.0000

LOAN PROGRESS CHART
15.50%

AGE OF LOAN	ORIGINAL TERM IN YEARS													
	2	3	4	5	6	7	8	10	15	20	25	30	35	40
1	.5384	.7165	.8045	.8564	.8904	.9141	.9314	.9546	.9817	.9920	.9964	.9983	.9992	.9996
2	.0000	.3858	.5764	.6890	.7626	.8140	.8515	.9016	.9603	.9826	.9922	.9964	.9983	.9992
3		.0000	.3103	.4937	.6135	.6971	.7581	.8398	.9353	.9717	.9872	.9942	.9973	.9988
4			.0000	.2658	.4396	.5608	.6493	.7676	.9062	.9590	.9815	.9915	.9961	.9982
5				.0000	.2367	.4018	.5224	.6835	.8722	.9441	.9748	.9885	.9947	.9975
6					.0000	.2163	.3743	.5854	.8326	.9268	.9670	.9849	.9930	.9968
7						.0000	.2015	.4709	.7864	.9066	.9579	.9807	.9911	.9959
8							.0000	.3374	.7324	.8830	.9472	.9758	.9889	.9949
9								.1817	.6695	.8555	.9348	.9702	.9863	.9937
10								.0000	.5962	.8235	.9203	.9635	.9832	.9922
11									.5106	.7861	.9034	.9558	.9796	.9906
12									.4108	.7424	.8838	.9468	.9755	.9887
13									.2943	.6915	.8608	.9363	.9707	.9864
14									.1585	.6321	.8340	.9240	.9650	.9838
15									.0000	.5629	.8027	.9097	.9584	.9808
16										.4821	.7662	.8930	.9507	.9772
17										.3878	.7237	.8736	.9418	.9731
18										.2779	.6741	.8508	.9313	.9683
19										.1496	.6162	.8244	.9191	.9626
20										.0000	.5487	.7935	.9049	.9561
21											.4699	.7574	.8883	.9484
22											.3780	.7154	.8689	.9395
23											.2709	.6663	.8463	.9290
24											.1458	.6091	.8200	.9169
25											.0000	.5423	.7892	.9027
26												.4645	.7534	.8861
27												.3737	.7116	.8668
28												.2677	.6628	.8442
29												.1442	.6059	.8180
30												.0000	.5395	.7873
35													.0000	.5381
40														.0000

15.75%

AGE OF LOAN	ORIGINAL TERM IN YEARS													
	2	3	4	5	6	7	8	10	15	20	25	30	35	40
1	.5390	.7173	.8053	.8573	.8912	.9149	.9322	.9552	.9821	.9923	.9966	.9984	.9990	.9997
2	.0000	.3866	.5776	.6903	.7640	.8154	.8528	.9028	.9611	.9832	.9925	.9966	.9985	.9993
3		.0000	.3114	.4952	.6152	.6990	.7600	.8416	.9366	.9726	.9878	.9945	.9975	.9989
4			.0000	.2669	.4413	.5629	.6516	.7700	.9080	.9602	.9822	.9920	.9963	.9983
5				.0000	.2379	.4037	.5247	.6862	.8745	.9457	.9758	.9890	.9950	.9977
6					.0000	.2176	.3763	.5882	.8353	.9288	.9682	.9856	.9935	.9970
7						.0000	.2029	.4737	.7895	.9090	.9594	.9816	.9916	.9962
8							.0000	.3398	.7360	.8858	.9490	.9770	.9895	.9952
9								.1832	.6733	.8587	.9370	.9715	.9870	.9941
10								.0000	.6001	.8270	.9228	.9651	.9841	.9928
11									.5144	.7900	.9063	.9576	.9807	.9912
12									.4143	.7467	.8870	.9489	.9767	.9894
13									.2971	.6960	.8643	.9386	.9721	.9873
14									.1602	.6368	.8379	.9267	.9666	.9848
15									.0000	.5675	.8070	.9127	.9603	.9819
16										.4865	.7709	.8964	.9528	.9785
17										.3918	.7286	.8772	.9441	.9745
18										.2810	.6792	.8549	.9340	.9699
19										.1515	.6214	.8287	.9221	.9644
20										.0000	.5538	.7982	.9082	.9581
21											.4747	.7624	.8919	.9507
22											.3823	.7206	.8729	.9420
23											.2742	.6717	.8506	.9318
24											.1478	.6145	.8246	.9200
25											.0000	.5477	.7942	.9061
26												.4695	.7586	.8899
27												.3781	.7170	.8709
28												.2712	.6684	.8487
29												.1462	.6115	.8227
30												.0000	.5450	.7924
35													.0000	.5437
40														.0000

LOAN PROGRESS CHART
16.00%

AGE OF LOAN	ORIGINAL TERM IN YEARS													
	2	3	4	5	6	7	8	10	15	20	25	30	35	40
1	.5397	.7180	.8061	.8581	.8920	.9156	.9329	.9558	.9825	.9925	.9967	.9985	.9993	.9997
2	.0000	.3875	.5788	.6917	.7654	.8168	.8542	.9041	.9620	.9837	.9928	.9968	.9986	.9994
3		.0000	.3124	.4967	.6170	.7008	.7619	.8434	.9380	.9735	.9883	.9948	.9976	.9989
4			.0000	.2680	.4430	.5650	.6538	.7722	.9098	.9614	.9830	.9924	.9966	.9985
5				.0000	.2391	.4057	.5270	.6888	.8768	.9473	.9767	.9896	.9953	.9979
6					.0000	.2189	.3784	.5911	.8380	.9307	.9694	.9863	.9939	.9972
7						.0000	.2042	.4765	.7927	.9113	.9609	.9825	.9921	.9965
8							.0000	.3421	.7395	.8885	.9508	.9780	.9901	.9955
9								.1846	.6771	.8618	.9390	.9727	.9877	.9945
10								.0000	.6040	.8305	.9252	.9666	.9850	.9932
11									.5182	.7939	.9090	.9593	.9817	.9918
12									.4178	.7509	.8901	.9509	.9779	.9900
13									.3000	.7005	.8678	.9409	.9734	.9880
14									.1619	.6414	.8418	.9293	.9682	.9857
15									.0000	.5721	.8112	.9156	.9621	.9829
16										.4909	.7754	.8996	.9549	.9797
17										.3957	.7334	.8808	.9464	.9758
18										.2841	.6842	.8588	.9365	.9714
19										.1533	.6265	.8330	.9249	.9662
20										.0000	.5588	.8028	.9113	.9600
21											.4795	.7673	.8954	.9528
22											.3865	.7258	.8767	.9444
23											.2775	.6770	.8548	.9346
24											.1498	.6199	.8291	.9230
25											.0000	.5530	.7990	.9094
26												.4745	.7637	.8935
27												.3825	.7224	.8749
28												.2746	.6739	.8530
29												.1482	.6170	.8274
30												.0000	.5504	.7973
35													.0000	.5492
40														.0000

16.25%

AGE OF LOAN	ORIGINAL TERM IN YEARS													
	2	3	4	5	6	7	8	10	15	20	25	30	35	40
1	.5403	.7188	.8069	.8589	.8928	.9164	.9336	.9565	.9829	.9928	.9968	.9986	.9994	.9997
2	.0000	.3883	.5800	.6930	.7668	.8182	.8555	.9053	.9629	.9843	.9931	.9970	.9987	.9994
3		.0000	.3134	.4982	.6187	.7027	.7638	.8452	.9393	.9743	.9888	.9950	.9978	.9990
4			.0000	.2691	.4448	.5670	.6560	.7745	.9116	.9626	.9837	.9928	.9968	.9986
5				.0000	.2403	.4076	.5294	.6915	.8790	.9488	.9777	.9901	.9956	.9980
6					.0000	.2202	.3805	.5939	.8407	.9326	.9706	.9870	.9942	.9974
7						.0000	.2056	.4792	.7958	.9135	.9623	.9833	.9926	.9967
8							.0000	.3445	.7429	.8912	.9525	.9790	.9907	.9959
9								.1861	.6808	.8649	.9411	.9740	.9884	.9948
10								.0000	.6078	.8340	.9276	.9680	.9858	.9937
11									.5220	.7977	.9117	.9610	.9827	.9923
12									.4212	.7550	.8931	.9528	.9790	.9907
13									.3028	.7049	.8713	.9431	.9747	.9887
14									.1636	.6459	.8456	.9318	.9697	.9865
15									.0000	.5767	.8153	.9184	.9638	.9839
16										.4953	.7798	.9027	.9568	.9808
17										.3997	.7381	.8843	.9486	.9771
18										.2873	.6891	.8627	.9390	.9728
19										.1552	.6315	.8372	.9277	.9678
20										.0000	.5638	.8073	.9144	.9619
21											.4842	.7722	.8988	.9549
22											.3907	.7308	.8804	.9468
23											.2809	.6823	.8589	.9372
24											.1517	.6253	.8335	.9259
25											.0000	.5582	.8038	.9126
26												.4795	.7688	.8970
27												.3869	.7276	.8787
28												.2781	.6793	.8572
29												.1502	.6225	.8319
30												.0000	.5558	.8022
35													.0000	.5547
40														.0000

LOAN PROGRESS CHART
16.50%

AGE OF LOAN	ORIGINAL TERM IN YEARS													
	2	3	4	5	6	7	8	10	15	20	25	30	35	40
1	.5409	.7196	.8077	.8597	.8936	.9171	.9343	.9571	.9833	.9930	.9970	.9987	.9994	.9997
2	.0000	.3892	.5812	.6944	.7682	.8195	.8569	.9065	.9637	.9848	.9934	.9971	.9987	.9994
3		.0000	.3144	.4997	.6205	.7045	.7657	.8469	.9406	.9751	.9893	.9953	.9979	.9991
4			.0000	.2703	.4465	.5691	.6582	.7768	.9133	.9637	.9843	.9932	.9970	.9987
5				.0000	.2415	.4095	.5317	.6941	.8812	.9503	.9785	.9906	.9959	.9982
6					.0000	.2215	.3826	.5967	.8434	.9344	.9717	.9877	.9946	.9976
7						.0000	.2069	.4820	.7988	.9158	.9637	.9841	.9930	.9969
8							.0000	.3468	.7463	.8938	.9542	.9800	.9912	.9961
9								.1876	.6845	.8679	.9430	.9751	.9891	.9952
10								.0000	.6116	.8374	.9299	.9694	.9866	.9941
11									.5258	.8014	.9144	.9626	.9836	.9928
12									.4247	.7591	.8961	.9546	.9801	.9912
13									.3056	.7092	.8746	.9453	.9760	.9894
14									.1653	.6504	.8493	.9342	.9711	.9873
15									.0000	.5812	.8194	.9212	.9654	.9848
16										.4997	.7842	.9058	.9587	.9818
17										.4036	.7428	.8877	.9507	.9783
18										.2904	.6940	.8664	.9414	.9742
19										.1571	.6365	.8413	.9303	.9694
20										.0000	.5688	.8117	.9174	.9636
21											.4889	.7769	.9021	.9569
22											.3949	.7358	.8841	.9490
23											.2842	.6875	.8628	.9397
24											.1537	.6005	.8378	.9287
25											.0000	.5634	.8084	.9157
26												.4844	.7737	.9004
27												.3912	.7328	.8825
28												.2815	.6847	.8613
29												.1523	.6279	.8363
30												.0000	.5611	.8069
35													.0000	.5601
40														.0000

16.75%

AGE OF LOAN	ORIGINAL TERM IN YEARS													
	2	3	4	5	6	7	8	10	15	20	25	30	35	40
1	.5415	.7203	.8085	.8605	.8944	.9179	.9350	.9577	.9837	.9933	.9971	.9988	.9995	.9998
2	.0000	.3901	.5824	.6957	.7696	.8209	.8582	.9077	.9645	.9853	.9937	.9973	.9988	.9995
3		.0000	.3154	.5012	.6222	.7064	.7675	.8487	.9418	.9759	.9897	.9956	.9981	.9992
4			.0000	.2714	.4482	.5711	.6605	.7790	.9150	.9648	.9850	.9935	.9972	.9988
5				.0000	.2427	.4114	.5340	.6967	.8834	.9517	.9794	.9911	.9961	.9983
6					.0000	.2228	.3847	.5995	.8460	.9362	.9728	.9883	.9949	.9978
7						.0000	.2083	.4847	.8019	.9179	.9650	.9849	.9935	.9972
8							.0000	.3492	.7497	.8963	.9558	.9809	.9917	.9964
9								.1891	.6882	.8708	.9449	.9762	.9897	.9955
10								.0000	.6155	.8407	.9321	.9707	.9873	.9945
11									.5296	.8051	.9169	.9642	.9845	.9932
12									.4282	.7631	.8990	.9564	.9811	.9918
13									.3084	.7135	.8779	.9473	.9771	.9901
14									.1670	.6549	.8529	.9365	.9725	.9880
15									.0000	.5857	.8234	.9238	.9670	.9856
16										.5040	.7885	.9088	.9604	.9828
17										.4075	.7474	.8910	.9527	.9795
18										.2935	.6988	.8701	.9437	.9755
19										.1590	.6414	.8453	.9329	.9708
20										.0000	.5737	.8161	.9202	.9653
21											.4936	.7815	.9053	.9588
22											.3991	.7408	.8876	.9511
23											.2875	.6926	.8667	.9421
24											.1557	.6357	.8420	.9314
25											.0000	.5686	.8129	.9187
26												.4892	.7785	.9038
27												.3956	.7379	.8861
28												.2849	.6899	.8653
29												.1543	.6333	.8406
30												.0000	.5664	.8116
35													.0000	.5654
40														.0000

LOAN PROGRESS CHART
17.00%

AGE OF LOAN	2	3	4	5	6	7	8	10	15	20	25	30	35	40
1	.5421	.7211	.8093	.8613	.8951	.9186	.9357	.9583	.9841	.9935	.9973	.9988	.9995	.9998
2	.0000	.3909	.5836	.6971	.7710	.8223	.8595	.9089	.9653	.9858	.9940	.9974	.9989	.9995
3		.0000	.3164	.5027	.6240	.7082	.7694	.8505	.9431	.9767	.9902	.9958	.9982	.9992
4			.0000	.2725	.4499	.5732	.6627	.7812	.9167	.9659	.9856	.9939	.9974	.9989
5				.0000	.2439	.4133	.5363	.6993	.8855	.9531	.9802	.9916	.9964	.9984
6					.0000	.2241	.3867	.6023	.8486	.9379	.9738	.9888	.9952	.9979
7						.0000	.2097	.4875	.8049	.9200	.9663	.9856	.9938	.9974
8							.0000	.3515	.7531	.8988	.9574	.9818	.9922	.9967
9								.1906	.6918	.8737	.9468	.9773	.9903	.9958
10								.0000	.6193	.8440	.9342	.9720	.9880	.9948
11									.5334	.8088	.9194	.9656	.9853	.9937
12									.4317	.7671	.9018	.9581	.9821	.9923
13									.3113	.7178	.8810	.9493	.9783	.9907
14									.1687	.6594	.8564	.9388	.9738	.9887
15									.0000	.5902	.8273	.9264	.9685	.9865
16										.5083	.7928	.9117	.9621	.9838
17										.4114	.7519	.8942	.9547	.9805
18										.2967	.7036	.8736	.9459	.9768
19										.1608	.6463	.8492	.9354	.9723
20										.0000	.5785	.8203	.9230	.9670
21											.4983	.7861	.9084	.9607
22											.4033	.7456	.8910	.9532
23											.2908	.6976	.8705	.9444
24											.1576	.6409	.8461	.9339
25											.0000	.5737	.8173	.9216
26												.4941	.7833	.9070
27												.3999	.7429	.8896
28												.2884	.6951	.8691
29												.1563	.6385	.8448
30												.0000	.5716	.8161
35													.0000	.5707
40														.0000

17.25%

AGE OF LOAN	2	3	4	5	6	7	8	10	15	20	25	30	35	40
1	.5427	.7219	.8101	.8621	.8959	.9194	.9364	.9589	.9845	.9937	.9974	.9989	.9995	.9998
2	.0000	.3918	.5848	.6984	.7723	.8236	.8609	.9101	.9661	.9863	.9943	.9976	.9990	.9996
3		.0000	.3174	.5042	.6257	.7101	.7712	.8522	.9443	.9774	.9906	.9960	.9983	.9993
4			.0000	.2736	.4517	.5752	.6649	.7835	.9184	.9669	.9862	.9942	.9975	.9990
5				.0000	.2451	.4152	.5386	.7019	.8876	.9544	.9810	.9920	.9966	.9986
6					.0000	.2254	.3888	.6051	.8511	.9397	.9749	.9894	.9955	.9981
7						.0000	.2110	.4902	.8078	.9221	.9675	.9863	.9942	.9975
8							.0000	.3539	.7564	.9013	.9589	.9827	.9927	.9969
9								.1920	.6954	.8765	.9486	.9783	.9908	.9961
10								.0000	.6230	.8472	.9363	.9732	.9886	.9952
11									.5371	.8124	.9218	.9671	.9861	.9941
12									.4351	.7710	.9046	.9598	.9830	.9928
13									.3141	.7220	.8842	.9512	.9793	.9912
14									.1705	.6637	.8599	.9410	.9750	.9894
15									.0000	.5946	.8311	.9288	.9699	.9872
16										.5126	.7969	.9144	.9638	.9846
17										.4153	.7564	.8974	.9566	.9816
18										.2998	.7083	.8771	.9480	.9779
19										.1627	.6511	.8530	.9378	.9736
20										.0000	.5834	.8245	.9257	.9685
21											.5029	.7906	.9114	.9624
22											.4074	.7503	.8943	.9552
23											.2941	.7026	.8741	.9466
24											.1596	.6459	.8501	.9364
25											.0000	.5787	.8217	.9244
26												.4989	.7879	.9100
27												.4042	.7478	.8930
28												.2918	.7002	.8729
29												.1583	.6438	.8489
30												.0000	.5767	.8205
35													.0000	.5759
40														.0000

LOAN PROGRESS CHART
17.50%

AGE OF LOAN	ORIGINAL TERM IN YEARS													
	2	3	4	5	6	7	8	10	15	20	25	30	35	40
1	.5433	.7226	.8109	.8629	.8967	.9201	.9371	.9595	.9849	.9939	.9975	.9990	.9996	.9998
2	.0000	.3926	.5860	.6997	.7737	.8250	.8622	.9113	.9669	.9867	.9945	.9977	.9990	.9996
3		.0000	.3184	.5057	.6274	.7119	.7731	.8539	.9455	.9781	.9910	.9963	.9984	.9993
4			.0000	.2747	.4534	.5773	.6671	.7857	.9200	.9679	.9868	.9945	.9977	.9990
5				.0000	.2463	.4172	.5409	.7045	.8897	.9558	.9818	.9924	.9968	.9987
6					.0000	.2267	.3909	.6079	.8536	.9413	.9758	.9899	.9958	.9982
7						.0000	.2124	.4929	.8108	.9241	.9687	.9870	.9946	.9977
8							.0000	.3562	.7597	.9037	.9603	.9835	.9931	.9971
9								.1935	.6990	.8793	.9503	.9793	.9913	.9964
10								.0000	.6268	.8504	.9384	.9743	.9893	.9955
11									.5408	.8159	.9242	.9684	.9868	.9945
12									.4386	.7749	.9073	.9614	.9839	.9932
13									.3169	.7261	.8872	.9530	.9804	.9918
14									.1722	.6681	.8633	.9431	.9762	.9900
15									.0000	.5990	.8349	.9312	.9713	.9880
16										.5169	.8010	.9172	.9654	.9855
17										.4192	.7608	.9004	.9584	.9826
18										.3029	.7129	.8805	.9500	.9791
19										.1646	.6559	.8568	.9401	.9749
20										.0000	.5881	.8285	.9283	.9700
21											.5075	.7950	.9143	.9641
22											.4115	.7550	.8976	.9571
23											.2974	.7075	.8777	.9488
24											.1616	.6509	.8540	.9388
25											.0000	.5837	.8259	.9271
26												.5036	.7924	.9130
27												.4084	.7526	.8964
28												.2951	.7052	.8765
29												.1604	.6489	.8529
30												.0000	.5818	.8248
35													.0000	.5811
40														.0000

17.75%

AGE OF LOAN	ORIGINAL TERM IN YEARS													
	2	3	4	5	6	7	8	10	15	20	25	30	35	40
1	.5439	.7234	.8117	.8637	.8974	.9208	.9377	.9601	.9852	.9941	.9976	.9990	.9996	.9998
2	.0000	.3935	.5872	.7011	.7751	.8263	.8635	.9124	.9676	.9872	.9948	.9977	.9991	.9996
3		.0000	.3194	.5071	.6292	.7137	.7749	.8556	.9466	.9788	.9914	.9965	.9985	.9994
4			.0000	.2759	.4551	.5793	.6693	.7878	.9216	.9689	.9873	.9948	.9978	.9991
5				.0000	.2476	.4191	.5433	.7070	.8917	.9571	.9825	.9928	.9970	.9988
6					.0000	.2280	.3930	.6106	.8561	.9429	.9768	.9904	.9961	.9984
7						.0000	.2138	.4957	.8136	.9261	.9699	.9876	.9949	.9979
8							.0000	.3586	.7630	.9060	.9617	.9843	.9935	.9973
9								.1950	.7026	.8820	.9520	.9802	.9918	.9966
10								.0000	.6305	.8535	.9403	.9755	.9899	.9958
11									.5445	.8194	.9265	.9697	.9875	.9948
12									.4420	.7787	.9099	.9629	.9847	.9937
13									.3198	.7302	.8902	.9548	.9813	.9923
14									.1739	.6724	.8666	.9451	.9773	.9906
15									.0000	.6034	.8385	.9336	.9726	.9886
16										.5212	.8051	.9198	.9669	.9863
17										.4230	.7651	.9034	.9601	.9835
18										.3060	.7175	.8838	.9520	.9801
19										.1665	.6606	.8604	.9423	.9761
20										.0000	.5929	.8325	.9308	.9714
21											.5120	.7993	.9171	.9657
22											.4156	.7596	.9007	.9589
23											.3007	.7123	.8811	.9508
24											.1635	.6559	.8578	.9412
25											.0000	.5886	.8300	.9297
26												.5084	.7969	.9159
27												.4127	.7573	.8996
28												.2985	.7102	.8801
29												.1624	.6539	.8568
30												.0000	.5869	.8290
35													.0000	.5861
40														.0000

261

LOAN PROGRESS CHART
18.00%

AGE OF LOAN	ORIGINAL TERM IN YEARS													
	2	3	4	5	6	7	8	10	15	20	25	30	35	40
1	.5445	.7241	.8125	.8645	.8982	.9215	.9384	.9606	.9856	.9944	.9977	.9991	.9996	.9998
2	.0000	.3943	.5884	.7024	.7778	.8277	.8648	.9136	.9684	.9876	.9950	.9980	.9992	.9997
3		.0000	.3204	.5086	.6309	.7155	.7767	.8573	.9478	.9795	.9918	.9967	.9986	.9994
4			.0000	.2770	.4568	.5814	.6714	.7900	.9232	.9699	.9879	.9951	.9980	.9992
5				.0000	.2488	.4210	.5456	.7096	.8938	.9583	.9832	.9932	.9972	.9989
6					.0000	.2293	.3951	.6134	.8586	.9445	.9777	.9909	.9963	.9985
7						.0000	.2151	.4984	.8165	.9280	.9710	.9882	.9952	.9980
8							.0000	.3609	.7662	.9083	.9631	.9850	.9939	.9975
9								.1965	.7061	.8847	.9536	.9811	.9923	.9969
10								.0000	.6342	.8565	.9423	.9765	.9904	.9961
11									.5482	.8228	.9287	.9710	.9882	.9952
12									.4455	.7825	.9125	.9644	.9855	.9941
13									.3226	.7343	.8931	.9565	.9823	.9927
14									.1757	.6767	.8699	.9471	.9784	.9912
15									.0000	.6078	.8422	.9358	.9738	.9893
16										.5254	.8090	.9224	.9683	.9870
17										.4269	.7694	.9062	.9617	.9844
18										.3091	.7220	.8870	.9539	.9811
19										.1683	.6653	.8639	.9445	.9773
20										.0000	.5976	.8364	.9332	.9727
21											.5166	.8035	.9198	.9672
22											.4197	.7641	.9037	.9606
23											.3039	.7171	.8845	.9528
24											.1655	.6608	.8615	.9434
25											.0000	.5935	.8341	.9322
26												.5131	.8012	.9187
27												.4169	.7620	.9027
28												.3019	.7151	.8835
29												.1644	.6589	.8606
30												.0000	.5918	.8331
35													.0000	.5912
40														.0000

18.25%

AGE OF LOAN	ORIGINAL TERM IN YEARS													
	2	3	4	5	6	7	8	10	15	20	25	30	35	40
1	.5452	.7249	.8133	.8652	.8989	.9222	.9391	.9612	.9860	.9945	.9978	.9991	.9996	.9999
2	.0000	.3952	.5896	.7037	.7778	.8290	.8660	.9147	.9691	.9880	.9952	.9981	.9992	.9997
3		.0000	.3214	.5101	.6326	.7173	.7785	.8590	.9489	.9802	.9921	.9968	.9987	.9995
4			.0000	.2781	.4586	.5834	.6736	.7922	.9247	.9708	.9884	.9953	.9981	.9992
5				.0000	.2500	.4229	.5479	.7121	.8957	.9596	.9839	.9935	.9974	.9989
6					.0000	.2306	.3971	.6161	.8610	.9461	.9785	.9914	.9965	.9986
7						.0000	.2165	.5011	.8193	.9299	.9721	.9888	.9955	.9982
8							.0000	.3633	.7694	.9105	.9644	.9857	.9942	.9977
9								.1980	.7096	.8873	.9552	.9820	.9927	.9971
10								.0000	.6379	.8595	.9441	.9776	.9909	.9963
11									.5519	.8262	.9309	.9722	.9888	.9955
12									.4489	.7862	.9150	.9658	.9862	.9944
13									.3254	.7383	.8959	.9582	.9831	.9932
14									.1774	.6809	.8731	.9490	.9794	.9917
15									.0000	.6121	.8457	.9380	.9750	.9899
16										.5296	.8129	.9248	.9697	.9878
17										.4307	.7736	.9090	.9633	.9852
18										.3122	.7264	.8901	.9557	.9821
19										.1702	.6699	.8674	.9465	.9784
20										.0000	.6022	.8402	.9356	.9740
21											.5211	.8076	.9224	.9687
22											.4238	.7686	.9067	.9623
23											.3072	.7217	.8878	.9547
24											.1675	.6656	.8652	.9455
25											.0000	.5983	.8380	.9346
26												.5177	.8055	.9215
27												.4211	.7666	.9057
28												.3052	.7198	.8869
29												.1664	.6639	.8642
30												.0000	.5968	.8371
35													.0000	.5961
40														.0000

LOAN PROGRESS CHART
18.50%

AGE OF LOAN	ORIGINAL TERM IN YEARS													
	2	3	4	5	6	7	8	10	15	20	25	30	35	40
1	.5458	.7257	.8141	.8660	.8997	.9229	.9397	.9618	.9863	.9947	.9979	.9992	.9997	.9999
2	.0000	.3960	.5908	.7050	.7791	.8303	.8673	.9158	.9698	.9884	.9954	.9982	.9993	.9997
3		.0000	.3224	.5116	.6343	.7191	.7803	.8606	.9500	.9808	.9925	.9970	.9988	.9995
4			.0000	.2792	.4603	.5854	.6758	.7943	.9263	.9717	.9889	.9956	.9982	.9993
5				.0000	.2512	.4248	.5501	.7146	.8977	.9607	.9846	.9939	.9976	.9990
6					.0000	.2319	.3992	.6189	.8634	.9476	.9794	.9918	.9967	.9987
7						.0000	.2179	.5038	.8221	.9318	.9732	.9894	.9958	.9983
8							.0000	.3656	.7726	.9127	.9657	.9864	.9946	.9978
9								.1995	.7130	.8899	.9567	.9828	.9932	.9973
10								.0000	.6415	.8625	.9459	.9785	.9914	.9966
11									.5556	.8295	.9330	.9734	.9894	.9958
12									.4523	.7899	.9174	.9672	.9869	.9948
13									.3282	.7423	.8987	.9598	.9840	.9936
14									.1791	.6851	.8762	.9509	.9804	.9922
15									.0000	.6163	.8492	.9401	.9761	.9905
16										.5338	.8167	.9272	.9710	.9884
17										.4345	.7777	.9118	.9648	.9860
18										.3153	.7308	.8932	.9574	.9830
19										.1721	.6745	.8708	.9485	.9795
20										.0000	.6068	.8440	.9378	.9752
21											.5255	.8117	.9250	.9701
22											.4278	.7729	.9095	.9639
23											.3105	.7263	.8910	.9565
24											.1694	.6704	.8687	.9476
25											.0000	.6031	.8419	.9369
26												.5223	.8097	.9241
27												.4252	.7710	.9087
28												.3086	.7246	.8901
29												.1684	.6687	.8678
30												.0000	.6016	.8411
35													.0000	6010
40														.0000

18.75%

AGE OF LOAN	ORIGINAL TERM IN YEARS													
	2	3	4	5	6	7	8	10	15	20	25	30	35	40
1	.5464	.7264	.8149	.8668	.9004	.9236	.9404	.9623	.9866	.9949	.9980	.9992	.9997	.9999
2	.0000	.3969	.5920	.7064	.7805	.8317	.8686	.9169	.9705	.9888	.9957	.9983	.9993	.9997
3		.0000	.3234	.5131	.6360	.7209	.7821	.8623	.9511	.9815	.9928	.9972	.9989	.9996
4			.0000	.2804	.4620	.5875	.6779	.7964	.9278	.9726	.9893	.9958	.9984	.9994
5				.0000	.2524	.4267	.5524	.7171	.8996	.9619	.9852	.9942	.9977	.9991
6					.0000	.2332	.4013	.6216	.8657	.9491	.9802	.9922	.9969	.9988
7						.0000	.2193	.5065	.8249	.9336	.9742	.9899	.9960	.9984
8							.0000	.3680	.7757	.9149	.9669	.9870	.9949	.9980
9								.2011	.7165	.8924	.9582	.9836	.9935	.9975
10								.0000	.6451	.8654	.9477	.9795	.9919	.9968
11									.5592	.8327	.9350	.9745	.9900	.9960
12									.4557	.7935	.9197	.9685	.9876	.9951
13									.3310	.7462	.9014	.9613	.9848	.9940
14									.1809	.6892	.8792	.9526	.9814	.9927
15									.0000	.6206	.8525	.9422	.9772	.9910
16										.5379	.8204	.9296	.9723	.9891
17										.4383	.7817	.9144	.9663	.9867
18										.3184	.7351	.8961	.9591	.9839
19										.1740	.6790	.8741	.9505	.9805
20										.0000	.6114	.8476	.9400	.9764
21											.5299	.8157	.9275	.9714
22											.4319	.7772	.9123	.9654
23											.3137	.7309	.8941	.9583
24											.1714	.6751	.8721	.9496
25											.0000	.6078	.8457	.9392
26												.5269	.8138	.9266
27												.4294	.7754	.9115
28												.3119	.7292	.8933
29												.1704	.6735	.8713
30												.0000	.6064	.8449
35													.0000	.6059
40														.0000

LOAN PROGRESS CHART
19.00%

AGE OF LOAN	ORIGINAL TERM IN YEARS													
	2	3	4	5	6	7	8	10	15	20	25	30	35	40
1	.5470	.7272	.8157	.8676	.9012	.9243	.9410	.9629	.9870	.9951	.9981	.9993	.9997	.9999
2	.0000	.3978	.5932	.7077	.7818	.8330	.8698	.9180	.9712	.9892	.9959	.9984	.9994	.9998
3		.0000	.3244	.5146	.6377	.7227	.7839	.8639	.9522	.9821	.9931	.9973	.9990	.9996
4			.0000	.2815	.4637	.5895	.6801	.7985	.9292	.9734	.9898	.9960	.9985	.9994
5				.0000	.2537	.4287	.5547	.7196	.9015	.9630	.9858	.9945	.9979	.9992
6					.0000	.2345	.4034	.6243	.8680	.9505	.9810	.9926	.9971	.9989
7						.0000	.2206	.5093	.8276	.9353	.9752	.9904	.9963	.9985
8							.0000	.3703	.7788	.9170	.9681	.9876	.9952	.9981
9								.2026	.7199	.8949	.9596	.9844	.9939	.9976
10								.0000	.6487	.8682	.9494	.9804	.9924	.9970
11									.5628	.8360	.9370	.9756	.9905	.9963
12									.4591	.7970	.9220	.9698	.9883	.9954
13									.3338	.7500	.9040	.9628	.9855	.9944
14									.1826	.6933	.8822	.9544	.9823	.9931
15									.0000	.6248	.8559	.9442	.9783	.9915
16										.5420	.8241	.9318	.9735	.9897
17										.4421	.7857	.9170	.9677	.9874
18										.3215	.7394	.8990	.9607	.9847
19										.1759	.6834	.8773	.9523	.9814
20										.0000	.6159	.8512	.9421	.9775
21											.5343	.8196	.9298	.9727
22											.4359	.7814	.9150	.9669
23											.3169	.7353	.8971	.9599
24											.1734	.6797	.8755	.9515
25											.0000	.6125	.8493	.9413
26												.5314	.8178	.9291
27												.4335	.7797	.9142
28												.3152	.7338	.8963
29												.1724	.6782	.8747
30												.0000	.6112	.8486
35													.0000	.6107
40														.0000

19.25%

AGE OF LOAN	ORIGINAL TERM IN YEARS													
	2	3	4	5	6	7	8	10	15	20	25	30	35	40
1	.5476	.7279	.8165	.8683	.9019	.9250	.9417	.9634	.9873	.9953	.9982	.9993	.9997	.9999
2	.0000	.3986	.5943	.7090	.7832	.8343	.8711	.9191	.9719	.9896	.9960	.9985	.9994	.9998
3		.0000	.3255	.5161	.6394	.7244	.7856	.8655	.9532	.9827	.9934	.9975	.9990	.9996
4			.0000	.2826	.4655	.5915	.6822	.8006	.9307	.9743	.9902	.9963	.9986	.9994
5				.0000	.2549	.4306	.5570	.7221	.9034	.9641	.9864	.9948	.9980	.9992
6					.0000	.2358	.4055	.6270	.8703	.9519	.9817	.9930	.9973	.9990
7						.0000	.2220	.5120	.8303	.9370	.9761	.9908	.9965	.9986
8							.0000	.3727	.7819	.9191	.9693	.9882	.9955	.9983
9								.2041	.7233	.8973	.9610	.9851	.9943	.9978
10								.0000	.6523	.8710	.9510	.9812	.9928	.9972
11									.5664	.8391	.9389	.9766	.9910	.9965
12									.4625	.8005	.9243	.9710	.9889	.9957
13									.3367	.7539	.9066	.9642	.9863	.9947
14									.1844	.6973	.8851	.9560	.9831	.9935
15									.0000	.6289	.8591	.9461	.9793	.9920
16										.5461	.8277	.9340	.9747	.9903
17										.4459	.7897	.9195	.9691	.9881
18										.3246	.7436	.9018	.9623	.9855
19										.1777	.6878	.8805	.9541	.9823
20										.0000	.6204	.8547	.9442	.9785
21											.5387	.8234	.9322	.9739
22											.4398	.7855	.9176	.9683
23											.3202	.7397	.9000	.9616
24											.1753	.6843	.8787	.9534
25											.0000	.6171	.8529	.9434
26												.5359	.8217	.9314
27												.4375	.7840	.9169
28												.3185	.7382	.8993
29												.1744	.6829	.8781
30												.0000	.6159	.8523
35													.0000	.6154
40														.0000

LOAN PROGRESS CHART
19.50%

AGE OF LOAN	ORIGINAL TERM IN YEARS													
	2	3	4	5	6	7	8	10	15	20	25	30	35	40
1	.5482	.7287	.8173	.8691	.9026	.9257	.9423	.9639	.9876	.9954	.9983	.9994	.9998	.9999
2	.0000	.3995	.5955	.7103	.7845	.8356	.8723	.9202	.9725	.9899	.9962	.9986	.9995	.9998
3		.0000	.3265	.5176	.6411	.7262	.7874	.8671	.9543	.9832	.9937	.9976	.9991	.9997
4			.0000	.2837	.4672	.5935	.6843	.8027	.9321	.9751	.9907	.9965	.9987	.9995
5				.0000	.2561	.4325	.5593	.7246	.9052	.9652	.9870	.9951	.9981	.9993
6					.0000	.2371	.4075	.6297	.8726	.9532	.9825	.9934	.9975	.9990
7						.0000	.2234	.5146	.8330	.9387	.9770	.9913	.9967	.9987
8							.0000	.3750	.7849	.9211	.9704	.9888	.9957	.9984
9								.2056	.7266	.8997	.9624	.9858	.9946	.9979
10								.0000	.6559	.8737	.9526	.9821	.9932	.9974
11									.5700	.8422	.9408	.9776	.9915	.9968
12									.4659	.8040	.9265	.9722	.9894	.9960
13									.3395	.7576	.9091	.9656	.9869	.9950
14									.1861	.7013	.8879	.9576	.9839	.9939
15									.0000	.6331	.8623	.9479	.9802	.9925
16										.5502	.8312	.9362	.9758	.9908
17										.4497	.7935	.9219	.9704	.9887
18										.3277	.7477	.9046	.9638	.9862
19										.1796	.6922	.8836	.9558	.9832
20										.0000	.6248	.8581	.9461	.9795
21											.5430	.8271	.9344	.9751
22											.4438	.7896	.9202	.9697
23											.3234	.7440	.9029	.9631
24											.1773	.6888	.8819	.9551
25											.0000	.6217	.8565	.9455
26												.5403	.8256	.9337
27												.4416	.7881	.9195
28												.3218	.7427	.9022
29												.1764	.6875	.8813
30												.0000	.6206	.8559
35													.0000	.6201
40														.0000

19.75%

AGE OF LOAN	ORIGINAL TERM IN YEARS													
	2	3	4	5	6	7	8	10	15	20	25	30	35	40
1	.5400	.7294	.8180	.8699	.9034	.9264	.9429	.9645	.9879	.9956	.9984	.9994	.9998	.9999
2	.0000	.4003	.5967	.7116	.7858	.8369	.8735	.9213	.9732	.9903	.9964	.9987	.9995	.9998
3		.0000	.3275	.5191	.6428	.7280	.7891	.8687	.9553	.9838	.9940	.9978	.9992	.9997
4			.0000	.2849	.4689	.5955	.6864	.8048	.9335	.9759	.9911	.9967	.9987	.9995
5				.0000	.2573	.4344	.5615	.7270	.9070	.9663	.9875	.9953	.9982	.9993
6					.0000	.2384	.4096	.6324	.8748	.9546	.9832	.9937	.9976	.9991
7						.0000	.2248	.5173	.8356	.9404	.9779	.9917	.9969	.9988
8							.0000	.3774	.7879	.9231	.9715	.9893	.9960	.9985
9								.2071	.7299	.9020	.9637	.9864	.9949	.9981
10								.0000	.6594	.8764	.9542	.9829	.9936	.9976
11									.5736	.8453	.9426	.9786	.9920	.9970
12									.4692	.8074	.9286	.9733	.9900	.9962
13									.3423	.7613	.9115	.9669	.9876	.9953
14									.1878	.7053	.8907	.9592	.9847	.9943
15									.0000	.6372	.8655	.9497	.9811	.9929
16										.5542	.8347	.9382	.9768	.9913
17										.4534	.7973	.9242	.9716	.9893
18										.3307	.7518	.9072	.9652	.9870
19										.1815	.6965	.8866	.9575	.9840
20										.0000	.6292	.8614	.9480	.9805
21											.5473	.8308	.9366	.9762
22											.4477	.7936	.9226	.9710
23											.3266	.7483	.9057	.9646
24											.1792	.6932	.8850	.9568
25											.0000	.6262	.8599	.9474
26												.5448	.8293	.9360
27												.4456	.7922	.9220
28												.3251	.7470	.9051
29												.1784	.6920	.8844
30												.0000	.6251	.8593
35													.0000	.6247
40														.0000

LOAN PROGRESS CHART
20.00%

AGE OF LOAN	ORIGINAL TERM IN YEARS													
	2	3	4	5	6	7	8	10	15	20	25	30	35	40
1	.5494	.7302	.8188	.8706	.9041	.9271	.9436	.9650	.9882	.9958	.9984	.9994	.9998	.9999
2	.0000	.4012	.5979	.7129	.7871	.8382	.8748	.9223	.9738	.9906	.9966	.9987	.9995	.9998
3		.0000	.3285	.5206	.6445	.7297	.7909	.8703	.9563	.9843	.9943	.9979	.9992	.9997
4			.0000	.2860	.4706	.5975	.6886	.8068	.9349	.9766	.9914	.9968	.9988	.9996
5				.0000	.2586	.4363	.5638	.7294	.9088	.9673	.9880	.9956	.9984	.9994
6					.0000	.2397	.4117	.6351	.8770	.9559	.9838	.9940	.9978	.9992
7						.0000	.2262	.5200	.8382	.9419	.9787	.9921	.9971	.9989
8							.0000	.3797	.7909	.9250	.9725	.9898	.9962	.9986
9								.2086	.7332	.9043	.9649	.9870	.9952	.9982
10								.0000	.6629	.8791	.9557	.9836	.9939	.9978
11									.5772	.8483	.9444	.9795	.9924	.9972
12									.4726	.8108	.9307	.9744	.9905	.9965
13									.3451	.7650	.9139	.9682	.9882	.9956
14									.1896	.7092	.8934	.9607	.9854	.9946
15									.0000	.6412	.8685	.9514	.9820	.9933
16										.5583	.8381	.9402	.9779	.9918
17										.4571	.8010	.9265	.9728	.9899
18										.3338	.7558	.9098	.9666	.9876
19										.1834	.7007	.8895	.9591	.9848
20										.0000	.6335	.8647	.9499	.9814
21											.5516	.8344	.9387	.9773
22											.4516	.7975	.9250	.9722
23											.3298	.7525	.9083	.9660
24											.1812	.6976	.8880	.9585
25											.0000	.6307	.8632	.9493
26												.5491	.8330	.9381
27												.4496	.7962	.9244
28												.3283	.7513	.9078
29												.1804	.6965	.8875
30												.0000	.6297	.8627
35													.0000	.6293
40														.0000

20.25%

AGE OF LOAN	ORIGINAL TERM IN YEARS													
	2	3	4	5	6	7	8	10	15	20	25	30	35	40
1	.5500	.7309	.8196	.8714	.9048	.9278	.9442	.9655	.9885	.9959	.9985	.9995	.9998	.9999
2	.0000	.4020	.5991	.7142	.7884	.8394	.8760	.9234	.9744	.9909	.9967	.9988	.9996	.9998
3		.0000	.3295	.5220	.6462	.7315	.7926	.8718	.9572	.9848	.9945	.9980	.9993	.9997
4			.0000	.2871	.4723	.5995	.6907	.8088	.9362	.9774	.9918	.9970	.9989	.9996
5				.0000	.2598	.4382	.5661	.7319	.9105	.9683	.9885	.9958	.9985	.9994
6					.0000	.2410	.4138	.6377	.8791	.9571	.9845	.9943	.9979	.9992
7						.0000	.2276	.5227	.8408	.9435	.9795	.9925	.9973	.9990
8							.0000	.3821	.7938	.9269	.9735	.9903	.9965	.9987
9								.2101	.7365	.9065	.9661	.9876	.9955	.9983
10								.0000	.6664	.8816	.9571	.9844	.9943	.9979
11									.5807	.8512	.9461	.9803	.9928	.9974
12									.4759	.8141	.9327	.9754	.9910	.9967
13									.3479	.7686	.9162	.9694	.9888	.9959
14									.1913	.7131	.8961	.9621	.9861	.9949
15									.0000	.6452	.8715	.9531	.9829	.9937
16										.5623	.8415	.9422	.9788	.9923
17										.4608	.8047	.9288	.9739	.9905
18										.3368	.7598	.9124	.9679	.9883
19										.1853	.7049	.8923	.9606	.9856
20										.0000	.6378	.8679	.9517	.9823
21											.5558	.8379	.9407	.9783
22											.4555	.8013	.9273	.9734
23											.3330	.7566	.9110	.9674
24											.1831	.7020	.8910	.9601
25											.0000	.6351	.8665	.9511
26												.5535	.8366	.9402
27												.4536	.8001	.9268
28												.3316	.7555	.9105
29												.1824	.7009	.8905
30												.0000	.6342	.8660
35													.0000	.6338
40														.0000

LOAN PROGRESS CHART
20.50%

AGE OF LOAN	ORIGINAL TERM IN YEARS													
	2	3	4	5	6	7	8	10	15	20	25	30	35	40
1	.5506	.7317	.8204	.8722	.9055	.9284	.9448	.9660	.9888	.9961	.9986	.9995	.9998	.9999
2	.0000	.4029	.6003	.7155	.7898	.8407	.8772	.9244	.9750	.9912	.9969	.9989	.9996	.9999
3		.0000	.3305	.5235	.6479	.7332	.7943	.8734	.9582	.9853	.9948	.9981	.9993	.9998
4			.0000	.2883	.4741	.6015	.6928	.8109	.9376	.9781	.9922	.9972	.9990	.9996
5				.0000	.2610	.4401	.5683	.7343	.9123	.9692	.9890	.9960	.9986	.9995
6					.0000	.2424	.4158	.6404	.8813	.9584	.9851	.9946	.9981	.9993
7						.0000	.2290	.5254	.8433	.9450	.9803	.9929	.9974	.9991
8							.0000	.3844	.7968	.9287	.9745	.9908	.9967	.9988
9								.2117	.7397	.9087	.9673	.9882	.9957	.9985
10								.0000	.6698	.8842	.9585	.9851	.9946	.9980
11									.5842	.8541	.9478	.9812	.9932	.9975
12									.4793	.8173	.9346	.9764	.9915	.9969
13									.3507	.7722	.9185	.9706	.9894	.9962
14									.1931	.7170	.8987	.9635	.9868	.9952
15									.0000	.6492	.8744	.9547	.9836	.9941
16										.5662	.8447	.9440	.9798	.9927
17										.4645	.8083	.9309	.9750	.9910
18										.3399	.7637	.9148	.9692	.9889
19										.1872	.7091	.8951	.9621	.9863
20										.0000	.6421	.8710	.9534	.9831
21											.5600	.8414	.9427	.9793
22											.4594	.8051	.9296	.9745
23											.3361	.7607	.9135	.9687
24											.1851	.7062	.8930	.9616
25											.0000	.6395	.8697	.9529
26												.5578	.8402	.9422
27												.4576	.8040	.9291
28												.3348	.7596	.9130
29												.1844	.7052	.8934
30												.0000	.6386	.8693
35													.0000	.6383
40														.0000

20.75%

AGE OF LOAN	ORIGINAL TERM IN YEARS													
	2	3	4	5	6	7	8	10	15	20	25	30	35	40
1	.5513	.7324	.8211	.8729	.9062	.9291	.9454	.9665	.9891	.9962	.9987	.9995	.9998	.9999
2	.0000	.4038	.6014	.7168	.7911	.8420	.8784	.9254	.9756	.9915	.9970	.9989	.9996	.9999
3		.0000	.3315	.5250	.6496	.7350	.7960	.8749	.9591	.9858	.9950	.9982	.9994	.9998
4			.0000	.2894	.4758	.6035	.6949	.8129	.9389	.9788	.9925	.9973	.9990	.9997
5				.0000	.2623	.4420	.5706	.7367	.9140	.9702	.9894	.9962	.9987	.9995
6					.0000	.2437	.4179	.6430	.8834	.9595	.9857	.9949	.9982	.9993
7						.0000	.2304	.5280	.8458	.9465	.9811	.9933	.9976	.9991
8							.0000	.3867	.7996	.9305	.9754	.9912	.9969	.9989
9								.2132	.7429	.9108	.9685	.9888	.9960	.9986
10								.0000	.6733	.8867	.9599	.9857	.9949	.9982
11									.5877	.8570	.9494	.9820	.9936	.9977
12									.4826	.8205	.9365	.9774	.9919	.9971
13									.3535	.7758	.9207	.9718	.9899	.9964
14									.1948	.7208	.9012	.9648	.9874	.9955
15									.0000	.6532	.8773	.9563	.9844	.9944
16										.5702	.8480	.9458	.9807	.9931
17										.4682	.8119	.9330	.9761	.9915
18										.3429	.7676	.9172	.9704	.9894
19										.1890	.7131	.8978	.9635	.9870
20										.0000	.6463	.8740	.9550	.9839
21											.5641	.8448	.9446	.9802
22											.4632	.8088	.9318	.9756
23											.3393	.7647	.9160	.9700
24											.1870	.7105	.8966	.9631
25											.0000	.6438	.8728	.9546
26												.5620	.8436	.9441
27												.4615	.8077	.9313
28												.3380	.7637	.9156
29												.1863	.7095	.8962
30												.0000	.6430	.8724
35													.0000	.6427
40														.0000

LOAN PROGRESS CHART
21.00%

AGE OF LOAN	ORIGINAL TERM IN YEARS													
	2	3	4	5	6	7	8	10	15	20	25	30	35	40
1	.5519	.7332	.8219	.8737	.9069	.9297	.9460	.9670	.9893	.9963	.9987	.9996	.9998	.9999
2	.0000	.4046	.6026	.7181	.7924	.8432	.8796	.9264	.9762	.9918	.9971	.9990	.9996	.9999
3		.0000	.3326	.5265	.6513	.7367	.7977	.8764	.9600	.9863	.9952	.9983	.9994	.9998
4			.0000	.2905	.4775	.6055	.6969	.8149	.9401	.9795	.9928	.9975	.9991	.9997
5				.0000	.2635	.4439	.5728	.7390	.9156	.9711	.9899	.9964	.9987	.9996
6					.0000	.2450	.4200	.6457	.8854	.9607	.9863	.9952	.9983	.9994
7						.0000	.2318	.5307	.8483	.9480	.9818	.9936	.9977	.9992
8							.0000	.3891	.8025	.9323	.9763	.9917	.9971	.9990
9								.2147	.7461	.9129	.9696	.9893	.9962	.9987
10								.0000	.6767	.8891	.9612	.9864	.9952	.9983
11									.5912	.8598	.9510	.9828	.9939	.9979
12									.4859	.8237	.9384	.9783	.9924	.9973
13									.3562	.7793	.9228	.9728	.9904	.9966
14									.1966	.7245	.9037	.9661	.9880	.9958
15									.0000	.6571	.8801	.9578	.9851	.9947
16										.5741	.8511	.9476	.9815	.9935
17										.4718	.8154	.9350	.9771	.9919
18										.3459	.7714	.9196	.9716	.9900
19										.1909	.7172	.9005	.9649	.9876
20										.0000	.6504	.8770	.9566	.9847
21											.5683	.8481	.9464	.9811
22											.4671	.8125	.9339	.9767
23											.3424	.7686	.9184	.9712
24											.1890	.7146	.8994	.9645
25											.0000	.6481	.8759	.9562
26												.5662	.8470	.9460
27												.4654	.8115	.9334
28												.3412	.7677	.9180
29												.1883	.7137	.8990
30												.0000	.6473	.8755
35													.0000	.6470
40														.0000

21.25%

AGE OF LOAN	ORIGINAL TERM IN YEARS													
	2	3	4	5	6	7	8	10	15	20	25	30	35	40
1	.5525	.7339	.8227	.8744	.9077	.9304	.9466	.9675	.9896	.9965	.9988	.9996	.9999	.9999
2	.0000	.4055	.6038	.7194	.7937	.8445	.8807	.9274	.9768	.9921	.9973	.9991	.9997	.9999
3		.0000	.3336	.5280	.6529	.7384	.7994	.8779	.9609	.9868	.9954	.9984	.9994	.9998
4			.0000	.2917	.4792	.6075	.6990	.8168	.9414	.9801	.9931	.9976	.9992	.9997
5				.0000	.2647	.4458	.5751	.7414	.9173	.9719	.9903	.9966	.9988	.9996
6					.0000	.2463	.4221	.6483	.8875	.9618	.9868	.9954	.9984	.9994
7						.0000	.2332	.5333	.8507	.9494	.9825	.9939	.9979	.9993
8							.0000	.3914	.8053	.9340	.9772	.9921	.9972	.9990
9								.2162	.7492	.9150	.9706	.9898	.9964	.9988
10								.0000	.6800	.8915	.9625	.9870	.9955	.9984
11									.5946	.8626	.9525	.9835	.9942	.9980
12									.4892	.8268	.9402	.9792	.9928	.9975
13									.3590	.7827	.9249	.9739	.9909	.9968
14									.1984	.7282	.9061	.9674	.9886	.9960
15									.0000	.6610	.8829	.9593	.9858	.9951
16										.5780	.8542	.9493	.9823	.9938
17										.4755	.8188	.9370	.9781	.9923
18										.3490	.7751	.9218	.9728	.9905
19										.1928	.7212	.9031	.9662	.9882
20										.0000	.6546	.8799	.9582	.9854
21											.5723	.8513	.9482	.9819
22											.4709	.8160	.9359	.9777
23											.3456	.7725	.9207	.9724
24											.1909	.7187	.9020	.9658
25											.0000	.6524	.8789	.9578
26												.5704	.8503	.9478
27												.4693	.8151	.9355
28												.3444	.7716	.9204
29												.1903	.7179	.9016
30												.0000	.6516	.8785
35													.0000	.6513
40														.0000

LOAN PROGRESS CHART
21.50%

AGE OF LOAN	ORIGINAL TERM IN YEARS

AGE OF LOAN	2	3	4	5	6	7	8	10	15	20	25	30	35	40
1	.5531	.7347	.8234	.8751	.9084	.9310	.9472	.9680	.9899	.9966	.9988	.9996	.9999	*****
2	.0000	.4063	.6050	.7206	.7949	.8457	.8819	.9284	.9773	.9924	.9974	.9991	.9997	.9999
3		.0000	.3346	.5294	.6546	.7401	.8011	.8794	.9618	.9872	.9956	.9985	.9995	.9998
4			.0000	.2928	.4809	.6095	.7011	.8188	.9426	.9808	.9934	.9977	.9992	.9997
5				.0000	.2660	.4478	.5773	.7437	.9189	.9728	.9907	.9968	.9989	.9996
6					.0000	.2476	.4241	.6509	.8895	.9630	.9874	.9957	.9985	.9995
7						.0000	.2346	.5360	.8531	.9508	.9832	.9942	.9980	.9993
8							.0000	.3938	.8081	.9357	.9780	.9925	.9974	.9991
9								.2178	.7523	.9170	.9717	.9903	.9967	.9988
10								.0000	.6834	.8939	.9638	.9876	.9957	.9985
11									.5981	.8653	.9540	.9842	.9946	.9981
12									.4925	.8299	.9419	.9801	.9931	.9976
13									.3618	.7861	.9270	.9749	.9914	.9970
14									.2001	.7319	.9085	.9686	.9892	.9963
15									.0000	.6648	.8856	.9607	.9865	.9953
16										.5818	.8572	.9510	.9831	.9942
17										.4791	.8222	.9389	.9790	.9928
18										.3520	.7788	.9240	.9738	.9910
19										.1947	.7251	.9056	.9675	.9888
20										.0000	.6586	.8828	.9596	.9861
21											.5764	.8545	.9499	.9828
22											.4746	.8196	.9379	.9786
23											.3487	.7763	.9230	.9735
24											.1929	.7220	.9040	.9671
25											.0000	.6565	.8818	.9593
26												.5746	.8536	.9496
27												.4731	.8187	.9375
28												.3476	.7755	.9227
29												.1922	.7220	.9042
30												.0000	.6558	.8815
35													.0000	.6556
40														.0000

21.75%

AGE OF LOAN	2	3	4	5	6	7	8	10	15	20	25	30	35	40
1	.5537	.7354	.8242	.8759	.9091	.9317	.9478	.9686	.9901	.9967	.9989	.9996	.9999	*****
2	.0000	.4072	.6061	.7219	.7962	.8470	.8831	.9294	.9779	.9927	.9975	.9992	.9997	.9999
3		.0000	.3356	.5309	.6563	.7418	.8028	.8809	.9627	.9876	.9958	.9986	.9995	.9998
4			.0000	.2940	.4826	.6114	.7031	.8207	.9438	.9814	.9937	.9979	.9993	.9998
5				.0000	.2672	.4497	.5795	.7461	.9204	.9736	.9911	.9970	.9990	.9997
6					.0000	.2490	.4262	.6535	.8914	.9640	.9879	.9959	.9986	.9995
7						.0000	.2360	.5386	.8555	.9521	.9838	.9945	.9981	.9994
8							.0000	.3961	.8108	.9373	.9789	.9928	.9976	.9992
9								.2193	.7554	.9190	.9727	.9907	.9968	.9989
10								.0000	.6867	.8962	.9650	.9881	.9960	.9986
11									.6015	.8679	.9555	.9849	.9949	.9983
12									.4958	.8329	.9436	.9809	.9935	.9978
13									.3646	.7894	.9290	.9759	.9918	.9972
14									.2019	.7355	.9108	.9697	.9897	.9965
15									.0000	.6686	.8882	.9621	.9871	.9956
16										.5856	.8602	.9526	.9839	.9945
17										.4827	.8255	.9408	.9799	.9931
18										.3550	.7824	.9262	.9749	.9915
19										.1965	.7290	.9080	.9687	.9894
20										.0000	.6627	.8855	.9611	.9868
21											.5804	.8576	.9516	.9835
22											.4784	.8230	.9398	.9795
23											.3518	.7801	.9252	.9746
24											.1948	.7268	.9071	.9684
25											.0000	.6607	.8846	.9607
26												.5787	.8567	.9513
27												.4769	.8222	.9395
28												.3508	.7793	.9249
29												.1942	.7260	.9068
30												.0000	.6600	.8843
35													.0000	.6598
40														.0000

LOAN PROGRESS CHART
22.00%

AGE OF LOAN	ORIGINAL TERM IN YEARS													
	2	3	4	5	6	7	8	10	15	20	25	30	35	40
1	.5543	.7362	.8250	.8766	.9097	.9323	.9484	.9690	.9904	.9968	.9989	.9996	.9999	*****
2	.0000	.4080	.6073	.7232	.7975	.8482	.8842	.9304	.9784	.9929	.9976	.9992	.9997	.9999
3		.0000	.3366	.5324	.6579	.7435	.8044	.8823	.9635	.9881	.9960	.9987	.9996	.9998
4			.0000	.2951	.4843	.6134	.7052	.8226	.9450	.9820	.9940	.9980	.9993	.9998
5				.0000	.2685	.4516	.5817	.7484	.9220	.9744	.9915	.9971	.9990	.9997
6					.0000	.2503	.4283	.6561	.8934	.9651	.9884	.9961	.9987	.9996
7						.0000	.2374	.5412	.8578	.9534	.9845	.9948	.9983	.9994
8							.0000	.3984	.8135	.9389	.9796	.9932	.9977	.9992
9								.2208	.7585	.9209	.9736	.9912	.9970	.9990
10								.0000	.6900	.8984	.9661	.9887	.9962	.9987
11									.6049	.8706	.9569	.9855	.9951	.9984
12									.4990	.8359	.9453	.9817	.9938	.9979
13									.3674	.7927	.9309	.9768	.9922	.9974
14									.2036	.7391	.9130	.9708	.9902	.9967
15									.0000	.6724	.8908	.9634	.9877	.9959
16										.5894	.8631	.9541	.9846	.9948
17										.4863	.8288	.9426	.9807	.9935
18										.3580	.7860	.9283	.9759	.9919
19										.1984	.7328	.9104	.9699	.9899
20										.0000	.6667	.8882	.9625	.9874
21											.5844	.8607	.9532	.9843
22											.4821	.8264	.9417	.9804
23											.3549	.7837	.9274	.9756
24											.1967	.7307	.9095	.9696
25											.0000	.6648	.8874	.9622
26												.5827	.8599	.9529
27												.4807	.8256	.9414
28												.3539	.7830	.9271
29												.1962	.7300	.9093
30												.0000	.6641	.8871
35													.0000	.6639
40														.0000

22.25%

AGE OF LOAN	ORIGINAL TERM IN YEARS													
	2	3	4	5	6	7	8	10	15	20	25	30	35	40
1	.5549	.7369	.8257	.8774	.9104	.9330	.9490	.9694	.9906	.9970	.9990	.9997	.9999	*****
2	.0000	.4089	.6085	.7245	.7988	.8494	.8854	.9313	.9789	.9932	.9978	.9993	.9998	.9999
3		.0000	.3376	.5339	.6596	.7452	.8061	.8838	.9644	.9885	.9962	.9987	.9996	.9999
4			.0000	.2962	.4860	.6154	.7072	.8245	.9462	.9826	.9943	.9981	.9994	.9998
5				.0000	.2697	.4535	.5840	.7507	.9235	.9752	.9918	.9973	.9991	.9997
6					.0000	.2516	.4303	.6586	.8953	.9661	.9888	.9963	.9988	.9996
7						.0000	.2388	.5438	.8601	.9547	.9851	.9951	.9984	.9995
8							.0000	.4008	.8162	.9405	.9804	.9935	.9978	.9993
9								.2224	.7615	.9228	.9746	.9916	.9972	.9991
10								.0000	.6933	.9007	.9673	.9892	.9964	.9988
11									.6083	.8731	.9582	.9862	.9954	.9985
12									.5023	.8388	.9469	.9824	.9942	.9981
13									.3701	.7960	.9328	.9777	.9926	.9975
14									.2054	.7426	.9152	.9719	.9907	.9969
15									.0000	.6761	.8933	.9647	.9883	.9961
16										.5932	.8660	.9556	.9853	.9951
17										.4898	.8320	.9443	.9815	.9939
18										.3609	.7895	.9303	.9769	.9923
19										.2003	.7366	.9128	.9711	.9904
20										.0000	.6706	.8909	.9638	.9880
21											.5884	.8637	.9548	.9850
22											.4858	.8297	.9435	.9812
23											.3580	.7874	.9294	.9766
24											.1987	.7346	.9119	.9708
25											.0000	.6688	.8901	.9635
26												.5868	.8629	.9545
27												.4845	.8290	.9432
28												.3570	.7867	.9292
29												.1981	.7339	.9117
30												.0000	.6682	.8898
35													.0000	.6680
40														.0000

LOAN PROGRESS CHART
22.50%

AGE OF LOAN	|—ORIGINAL TERM IN YEARS													
	2	3	4	5	6	7	8	10	15	20	25	30	35	40
1	.5555	.7376	.8265	.8781	.9111	.9336	.9495	.9699	.9909	.9971	.9990	.9997	.9999	*****
2	.0000	.4098	.6096	.7257	.8000	.8506	.8865	.9322	.9794	.9934	.9979	.9993	.9998	.9999
3		.0000	.3387	.5353	.6612	.7469	.8077	.8852	.9652	.9888	.9964	.9988	.9996	.9999
4			.0000	.2974	.4877	.6173	.7092	.8264	.9473	.9831	.9945	.9982	.9994	.9998
5				.0000	.2709	.4554	.5862	.7530	.9250	.9760	.9922	.9974	.9992	.9997
6					.0000	.2530	.4324	.6612	.8972	.9671	.9893	.9965	.9989	.9996
7						.0000	.2402	.5465	.8624	.9559	.9857	.9953	.9985	.9995
8							.0000	.4031	.8189	.9420	.9811	.9938	.9980	.9993
9								.2239	.7645	.9246	.9755	.9920	.9974	.9991
10								.0000	.6965	.9028	.9684	.9897	.9966	.9989
11									.6116	.8756	.9595	.9868	.9957	.9986
12									.5055	.8417	.9485	.9831	.9945	.9982
13									.3729	.7992	.9346	.9786	.9930	.9977
14									.2071	.7461	.9174	.9730	.9911	.9971
15									.0000	.6798	.8958	.9659	.9888	.9963
16										.5969	.8688	.9571	.9859	.9954
17										.4934	.8351	.9460	.9823	.9942
18										.3639	.7930	.9323	.9778	.9927
19										.2022	.7403	.9150	.9721	.9909
20										.0000	.6745	.8935	.9651	.9886
21											.5923	.8666	.9563	.9857
22											.4895	.8330	.9452	.9820
23											.3611	.7909	.9315	.9775
24											.2006	.7384	.9143	.9719
25											.0000	.6728	.8927	.9648
26												.5908	.8659	.9560
27												.4883	.8323	.9450
28												.3602	.7903	.9312
29												.2001	.7378	.9140
30												.0000	.6722	.8925
35													.0000	.6720
40														.0000

22.75%

AGE OF LOAN	|—ORIGINAL TERM IN YEARS													
	2	3	4	5	6	7	8	10	15	20	25	30	35	40
1	.5561	.7384	.8272	.8788	.9118	.9342	.9501	.9703	.9911	.9972	.9991	.9997	.9999	*****
2	.0000	.4106	.6108	.7270	.8013	.8518	.8876	.9332	.9799	.9937	.9980	.9993	.9998	.9999
3		.0000	.3397	.5368	.6629	.7486	.8093	.8866	.9660	.9892	.9965	.9989	.9996	.9999
4			.0000	.2985	.4894	.6193	.7113	.8283	.9485	.9837	.9948	.9983	.9995	.9998
5				.0000	.2722	.4573	.5884	.7553	.9265	.9767	.9925	.9976	.9992	.9997
6					.0000	.2543	.4344	.6637	.8990	.9680	.9897	.9967	.9989	.9997
7						.0000	.2416	.5491	.8646	.9571	.9862	.9955	.9985	.9995
8							.0000	.4054	.8215	.9435	.9818	.9941	.9981	.9994
9								.2255	.7675	.9264	.9763	.9923	.9975	.9992
10								.0000	.6998	.9050	.9694	.9901	.9968	.9990
11									.6150	.8781	.9608	.9873	.9959	.9987
12									.5087	.8445	.9500	.9838	.9948	.9983
13									.3756	.8024	.9364	.9795	.9933	.9978
14									.2089	.7496	.9195	.9740	.9916	.9973
15									.0000	.6835	.8982	.9671	.9893	.9965
16										.6007	.8716	.9585	.9866	.9956
17										.4969	.8382	.9477	.9831	.9945
18										.3669	.7964	.9342	.9787	.9931
19										.2040	.7440	.9172	.9732	.9913
20										.0000	.6784	.8960	.9663	.9891
21											.5962	.8695	.9577	.9863
22											.4932	.8362	.9469	.9828
23											.3641	.7944	.9334	.9784
24											.2025	.7422	.9165	.9730
25											.0000	.6767	.8953	.9661
26												.5947	.8688	.9575
27												.4920	.8355	.9467
28												.3633	.7938	.9332
29												.2020	.7416	.9163
30												.0000	.6762	.8951
35													.0000	.6760
40														.0000

23.00%

AGE OF LOAN	ORIGINAL TERM IN YEARS													
	2	3	4	5	6	7	8	10	15	20	25	30	35	40
1	.5567	.7391	.8280	.8795	.9125	.9348	.9507	.9708	.9913	.9973	.9991	.9997	.9999	*****
2	.0000	.4115	.6120	.7283	.8026	.8530	.8887	.9341	.9804	.9939	.9981	.9994	.9998	.9999
3		.0000	.3407	.5383	.6645	.7503	.8110	.8880	.9667	.9896	.9967	.9989	.9997	.9999
4			.0000	.2997	.4911	.6212	.7133	.8302	.9496	.9842	.9950	.9984	.9995	.9998
5				.0000	.2734	.4591	.5906	.7575	.9280	.9775	.9928	.9977	.9993	.9998
6					.0000	.2556	.4365	.6663	.9009	.9690	.9901	.9969	.9990	.9997
7						.0000	.2430	.5517	.8668	.9583	.9868	.9958	.9986	.9996
8							.0000	.4077	.8241	.9450	.9825	.9944	.9982	.9994
9								.2270	.7704	.9282	.9772	.9927	.9977	.9993
10								.0000	.7030	.9071	.9705	.9906	.9970	.9990
11									.6183	.8806	.9620	.9879	.9961	.9988
12									.5119	.8473	.9515	.9845	.9950	.9984
13									.3784	.8055	.9382	.9803	.9937	.9980
14									.2106	.7530	.9215	.9749	.9920	.9974
15									.0000	.6871	.9006	.9682	.9898	.9967
16										.6043	.8743	.9598	.9872	.9959
17										.5004	.8412	.9493	.9838	.9948
18										.3698	.7997	.9360	.9795	.9935
19										.2059	.7476	.9194	.9742	.9917
20										.0000	.6822	.8985	.9675	.9896
21											.6000	.8723	.9591	.9869
22											.4968	.8393	.9486	.9835
23											.3672	.7979	.9354	.9793
24											.2044	.7459	.9187	.9740
25											.0000	.6806	.8978	.9673
26												.5986	.8716	.9589
27												.4957	.8387	.9484
28												.3664	.7973	.9351
29												.2040	.7454	.9185
30												.0000	.6801	.8976
35													.0000	.6800
40														.0000

23.25%

AGE OF LOAN	ORIGINAL TERM IN YEARS													
	2	3	4	5	6	7	8	10	15	20	25	30	35	40
1	.5573	.7398	.8287	.8803	.9131	.9355	.9512	.9712	.9915	.9974	.9992	.9997	.9999	*****
2	.0000	.4123	.6131	.7295	.8038	.8542	.8898	.9350	.9809	.9941	.9981	.9994	.9998	.9999
3		.0000	.3417	.5397	.6662	.7519	.8126	.8894	.9675	.9899	.9968	.9990	.9997	.9999
4			.0000	.3008	.4929	.6232	.7153	.8320	.9506	.9847	.9952	.9985	.9995	.9998
5				.0000	.2747	.4610	.5928	.7598	.9294	.9782	.9931	.9978	.9993	.9998
6					.0000	.2569	.4386	.6688	.9027	.9699	.9905	.9970	.9991	.9997
7						.0000	.2444	.5543	.8690	.9595	.9873	.9960	.9987	.9996
8							.0000	.4101	.8266	.9464	.9832	.9947	.9983	.9995
9								.2285	.7733	.9299	.9780	.9931	.9978	.9993
10								.0000	.7061	.9091	.9715	.9910	.9972	.9991
11									.6216	.8830	.9632	.9884	.9963	.9988
12									.5151	.8500	.9529	.9851	.9953	.9985
13									.3811	.8086	.9399	.9810	.9940	.9981
14									.2124	.7564	.9235	.9759	.9924	.9976
15									.0000	.6907	.9029	.9694	.9903	.9969
16										.6080	.8769	.9612	.9877	.9961
17										.5039	.8442	.9508	.9845	.9951
18										.3728	.8030	.9379	.9804	.9938
19										.2078	.7512	.9215	.9752	.9922
20										.0000	.6860	.9009	.9687	.9901
21											.6038	.8750	.9605	.9875
22											.5004	.8424	.9502	.9843
23											.3702	.8013	.9372	.9802
24											.2063	.7496	.9209	.9750
25											.0000	.6845	.9003	.9685
26												.6025	.8744	.9603
27												.4993	.8418	.9500
28												.3694	.8008	.9370
29												.2059	.7491	.9207
30												.0000	.6840	.9001
35													.0000	.6839
40														.0000

LOAN PROGRESS CHART
23.50%

AGE OF LOAN	ORIGINAL TERM IN YEARS														
	2	3	4	5	6	7	8	10	15	20	25	30	35	40
1	.5579	.7406	.8295	.8810	.9138	.9361	.9518	.9717	.9918	.9975	.9992	.9998	.9999	*****
2	.0000	.4132	.6143	.7308	.8051	.8554	.8909	.9359	.9814	.9943	.9982	.9994	.9998	.9999
3		.0000	.3427	.5412	.6678	.7536	.8142	.8908	.9683	.9903	.9970	.9991	.9997	.9999
4			.0000	.3019	.4945	.6251	.7173	.8339	.9517	.9852	.9954	.9986	.9996	.9999
5				.0000	.2759	.4629	.5950	.7620	.9308	.9788	.9934	.9980	.9994	.9998
6					.0000	.2583	.4406	.6713	.9044	.9708	.9909	.9972	.9991	.9997
7						.0000	.2458	.5568	.8712	.9606	.9878	.9962	.9988	.9996
8							.0000	.4124	.8292	.9478	.9838	.9949	.9984	.9995
9								.2301	.7762	.9316	.9788	.9934	.9979	.9994
10								.0000	.7093	.9111	.9724	.9914	.9973	.9992
11									.6248	.8853	.9644	.9889	.9965	.9989
12									.5183	.8527	.9543	.9858	.9956	.9986
13									.3838	.8116	.9415	.9818	.9943	.9982
14									.2142	.7597	.9254	.9768	.9927	.9977
15									.0000	.6943	.9051	.9704	.9908	.9971
16										.6116	.8795	.9624	.9883	.9963
17										.5073	.8471	.9523	.9851	.9954
18										.3757	.8063	.9396	.9812	.9941
19										.2096	.7548	.9236	.9761	.9925
20										.0000	.6897	.9033	.9698	.9906
21											.6076	.8777	.9618	.9881
22											.5040	.8454	.9517	.9849
23											.3733	.8046	.9390	.9810
24											.2083	.7532	.9230	.9759
25											.0000	.6883	.9027	.9696
26												.6064	.8771	.9616
27												.5030	.8449	.9516
28												.3725	.8041	.9388
29												.2078	.7527	.9228
30												.0000	.6879	.9025
35													.0000	.6877
40														.0000

23.75%

AGE OF LOAN	ORIGINAL TERM IN YEARS														
	2	3	4	5	6	7	8	10	15	20	25	30	35	40
1	.5585	.7413	.8302	.8817	.9145	.9367	.9523	.9721	.9920	.9976	.9993	.9998	.9999	*****
2	.0000	.4140	.6155	.7320	.8063	.8566	.8920	.9368	.9818	.9945	.9983	.9995	.9998	*****
3		.0000	.3438	.5427	.6694	.7552	.8158	.8922	.9690	.9906	.9971	.9991	.9997	.9999
4			.0000	.3031	.4962	.6270	.7192	.8357	.9527	.9857	.9956	.9987	.9996	.9999
5				.0000	.2772	.4648	.5971	.7642	.9322	.9795	.9937	.9981	.9994	.9998
6					.0000	.2596	.4427	.6738	.9062	.9716	.9913	.9973	.9992	.9997
7						.0000	.2472	.5594	.8733	.9617	.9883	.9964	.9989	.9997
8							.0000	.4147	.8317	.9491	.9844	.9952	.9985	.9995
9								.2316	.7790	.9332	.9795	.9937	.9981	.9994
10								.0000	.7124	.9131	.9733	.9918	.9975	.9992
11									.6281	.8876	.9655	.9894	.9967	.9990
12									.5215	.8554	.9557	.9863	.9958	.9987
13									.3866	.8146	.9432	.9825	.9946	.9983
14									.2159	.7630	.9273	.9776	.9931	.9979
15									.0000	.6978	.9073	.9715	.9912	.9973
16										.6152	.8820	.9637	.9888	.9965
17										.5108	.8500	.9538	.9858	.9956
18										.3787	.8095	.9413	.9819	.9944
19										.2115	.7582	.9256	.9770	.9929
20										.0000	.6934	.9056	.9709	.9910
21											.6114	.8803	.9631	.9886
22											.5076	.8484	.9532	.9856
23											.3763	.8079	.9408	.9817
24											.2102	.7568	.9250	.9769
25											.0000	.6921	.9050	.9707
26												.6102	.8798	.9629
27												.5066	.8479	.9531
28												.3755	.8074	.9406
29												.2098	.7563	.9248
30												.0000	.6916	.9049
35													.0000	.6915
40														.0000

LOAN PROGRESS CHART
24.00%

AGE OF LOAN	ORIGINAL TERM IN YEARS													
	2	3	4	5	6	7	8	10	15	20	25	30	35	40
1	.5591	.7420	.8310	.8824	.9151	.9373	.9529	.9725	.9922	.9977	.9993	.9998	.9999	*****
2	.0000	.4149	.6166	.7333	.8075	.8578	.8931	.9377	.9823	.9947	.9984	.9995	.9999	*****
3		.0000	.3448	.5441	.6710	.7569	.8173	.8935	.9697	.9909	.9973	.9992	.9997	.9999
4			.0000	.3042	.4979	.6290	.7212	.8375	.9538	.9862	.9958	.9987	.9996	.9999
5				.0000	.2784	.4667	.5993	.7664	.9335	.9801	.9940	.9982	.9994	.9998
6					.0000	.2610	.4447	.6763	.9079	.9725	.9917	.9975	.9992	.9998
7						.0000	.2487	.5620	.8754	.9628	.9887	.9966	.9990	.9997
8							.0000	.4170	.8341	.9504	.9850	.9954	.9986	.9996
9								.2332	.7818	.9348	.9803	.9940	.9982	.9994
10								.0000	.7155	.9150	.9743	.9922	.9976	.9993
11									.6313	.8899	.9666	.9898	.9969	.9991
12									.5246	.8580	.9570	.9869	.9960	.9988
13									.3893	.8176	.9447	.9832	.9949	.9984
14									.2177	.7663	.9292	.9785	.9934	.9980
15									.0000	.7013	.9095	.9725	.9916	.9974
16										.6188	.8845	.9649	.9893	.9967
17										.5142	.8528	.9552	.9864	.9958
18										.3816	.8126	.9430	.9826	.9947
19										.2133	.7617	.9275	.9779	.9933
20										.0000	.6971	.9078	.9719	.9914
21											.6151	.8829	.9643	.9891
22											.5111	.8513	.9547	.9862
23											.3793	.8112	.9425	.9825
24											.2121	.7603	.9270	.9777
25											.0000	.6958	.9073	.9718
26												.6140	.8824	.9642
27												.5102	.8508	.9545
28												.3786	.8107	.9423
29												.2117	.7599	.9268
30												.0000	.6954	.9072
35													.0000	.6953
40														.0000

24.25%

AGE OF LOAN	ORIGINAL TERM IN YEARS													
	2	3	4	5	6	7	8	10	15	20	25	30	35	40
1	.5597	.7428	.8317	.8831	.9158	.9379	.9534	.9730	.9924	.9978	.9993	.9998	.9999	*****
2	.0000	.4158	.6178	.7345	.8088	.8589	.8942	.9386	.9827	.9949	.9985	.9995	.9999	*****
3		.0000	.3458	.5456	.6727	.7585	.8189	.8948	.9704	.9913	.9974	.9992	.9998	.9999
4			.0000	.3054	.4996	.6309	.7232	.8393	.9548	.9866	.9960	.9988	.9996	.9999
5				.0000	.2797	.4686	.6015	.7686	.9349	.9808	.9942	.9983	.9995	.9998
6					.0000	.2623	.4468	.6788	.9096	.9733	.9920	.9976	.9993	.9998
7						.0000	.2501	.5645	.8774	.9638	.9892	.9967	.9990	.9997
8							.0000	.4193	.8366	.9517	.9856	.9957	.9987	.9996
9								.2347	.7846	.9364	.9810	.9943	.9983	.9995
10								.0000	.7185	.9169	.9751	.9925	.9978	.9993
11									.6345	.8921	.9677	.9903	.9971	.9991
12									.5278	.8606	.9583	.9875	.9962	.9989
13									.3920	.8205	.9463	.9838	.9951	.9985
14									.2194	.7695	.9310	.9793	.9938	.9981
15									.0000	.7047	.9116	.9734	.9920	.9976
16										.6223	.8870	.9660	.9898	.9969
17										.5176	.8556	.9566	.9869	.9961
18										.3845	.8158	.9446	.9833	.9950
19										.2152	.7651	.9294	.9788	.9936
20										.0000	.7007	.9100	.9729	.9919
21											.6188	.8854	.9655	.9896
22											.5146	.8541	.9561	.9868
23											.3823	.8143	.9441	.9832
24											.2140	.7638	.9289	.9786
25											.0000	.6995	.9096	.9728
26												.6177	.8850	.9654
27												.5138	.8537	.9560
28												.3816	.8139	.9440
29												.2136	.7634	.9288
30												.0000	.6991	.9094
35													.0000	.6990
40														.0000

24.50%

AGE OF LOAN	ORIGINAL TERM IN YEARS													
	2	3	4	5	6	7	8	10	15	20	25	30	35	40
1	.5603	.7435	.8325	.8838	.9165	.9385	.9540	.9734	.9926	.9978	.9994	.9998	.9999	*****
2	.0000	.4166	.6189	.7357	.8100	.8601	.8953	.9394	.9831	.9951	.9985	.9996	.9999	*****
3		.0000	.3468	.5470	.6743	.7601	.8205	.8962	.9711	.9916	.9975	.9993	.9998	.9999
4			.0000	.3065	.5013	.6328	.7251	.8410	.9557	.9871	.9962	.9989	.9997	.9999
5				.0000	.2809	.4705	.6037	.7708	.9362	.9814	.9945	.9984	.9995	.9999
6					.0000	.2636	.4488	.6812	.9112	.9741	.9923	.9977	.9993	.9998
7						.0000	.2515	.5671	.8795	.9648	.9896	.9969	.9991	.9997
8							.0000	.4216	.8390	.9530	.9861	.9959	.9988	.9996
9								.2363	.7874	.9379	.9816	.9945	.9984	.9995
10								.0000	.7216	.9187	.9760	.9929	.9979	.9994
11									.6377	.8943	.9687	.9907	.9972	.9992
12									.5309	.8631	.9595	.9880	.9964	.9989
13									.3947	.8233	.9478	.9845	.9954	.9986
14									.2212	.7727	.9328	.9800	.9941	.9982
15									.0000	.7081	.9137	.9744	.9924	.9977
16										.6259	.8893	.9671	.9902	.9971
17										.5210	.8583	.9579	.9875	.9963
18										.3874	.8188	.9462	.9840	.9952
19										.2171	.7684	.9312	.9796	.9939
20										.0000	.7042	.9122	.9739	.9922
21											.6224	.8879	.9667	.9901
22											.5181	.8569	.9575	.9874
23											.3852	.8175	.9457	.9839
24											.2159	.7672	.9308	.9794
25											.0000	.7031	.9117	.9738
26												.6214	.8875	.9665
27												.5173	.8565	.9573
28												.3846	.8171	.9456
29												.2155	.7668	.9307
30												.0000	.7027	.9116
35													.0000	.7026
40														.0000

24.75%

AGE OF LOAN	ORIGINAL TERM IN YEARS													
	2	3	4	5	6	7	8	10	15	20	25	30	35	40
1	.5609	.7442	.8332	.8845	.9171	.9391	.9545	.9738	.9928	.9979	.9994	.9998	.9999	*****
2	.0000	.4175	.6201	.7370	.8112	.8612	.8963	.9403	.9836	.9953	.9985	.9996	.9999	*****
3		.0000	.3478	.5485	.6759	.7618	.8220	.8975	.9718	.9919	.9976	.9993	.9998	.9999
4			.0000	.3077	.5030	.6347	.7271	.8428	.9567	.9875	.9963	.9989	.9997	.9999
5				.0000	.2822	.4724	.6058	.7729	.9375	.9820	.9947	.9985	.9995	.9999
6					.0000	.2650	.4509	.6837	.9129	.9749	.9927	.9978	.9994	.9998
7						.0000	.2529	.5696	.8815	.9658	.9900	.9971	.9991	.9997
8							.0000	.4239	.8413	.9542	.9866	.9961	.9988	.9997
9								.2378	.7901	.9394	.9823	.9948	.9985	.9996
10								.0000	.7246	.9205	.9768	.9932	.9980	.9994
11									.6409	.8964	.9697	.9911	.9974	.9992
12									.5340	.8656	.9607	.9885	.9966	.9990
13									.3974	.8262	.9492	.9851	.9956	.9987
14									.2229	.7758	.9345	.9808	.9944	.9983
15									.0000	.7115	.9157	.9753	.9927	.9979
16										.6294	.8917	.9682	.9907	.9973
17										.5244	.8610	.9592	.9880	.9965
18										.3903	.8218	.9477	.9847	.9955
19										.2189	.7717	.9330	.9803	.9942
20										.0000	.7078	.9143	.9748	.9926
21											.6260	.8903	.9678	.9905
22											.5216	.8597	.9588	.9879
23											.3882	.8205	.9473	.9845
24											.2178	.7705	.9326	.9802
25											.0000	.7067	.9139	.9747
26												.6251	.8899	.9677
27												.5208	.8593	.9587
28												.3876	.8202	.9472
29												.2174	.7702	.9325
30												.0000	.7063	.9137
35													.0000	.7063
40														.0000

LOAN PROGRESS CHART
25.00%

AGE OF LOAN	ORIGINAL TERM IN YEARS													
	2	3	4	5	6	7	8	10	15	20	25	30	35	40
1	.5615	.7450	.8339	.8852	.9178	.9397	.9555	.9742	.9930	.9980	.9994	.9998	*****	*****
2	.0000	.4183	.6213	.7382	.8124	.8624	.8974	.9411	.9840	.9954	.9987	.9996	.9999	*****
3		.0000	.3489	.5499	.6775	.7634	.8236	.8988	.9724	.9921	.9977	.9993	.9998	.9999
4			.0000	.3088	.5047	.6366	.7290	.8445	.9576	.9879	.9965	.9990	.9997	.9999
5				.0000	.2834	.4743	.6080	.7751	.9387	.9825	.9950	.9985	.9996	.9999
6					.0000	.2663	.4529	.6861	.9145	.9756	.9930	.9980	.9994	.9998
7						.0000	.2543	.5722	.8834	.9668	.9904	.9972	.9992	.9998
8							.0000	.4262	.8437	.9554	.9871	.9963	.9989	.9997
9								.2394	.7928	.9409	.9829	.9951	.9986	.9996
10								.0000	.7276	.9223	.9776	.9935	.9981	.9995
11									.6441	.8985	.9707	.9915	.9975	.9993
12									.5371	.8680	.9619	.9890	.9968	.9991
13									.4001	.8290	.9506	.9857	.9958	.9988
14									.2247	.7789	.9362	.9815	.9946	.9984
15									.0000	.7149	.9177	.9761	.9931	.9980
16										.6328	.8940	.9693	.9911	.9974
17										.5277	.8636	.9605	.9885	.9967
18										.3931	.8248	.9492	.9853	.9957
19										.2208	.7750	.9348	.9811	.9945
20										.0000	.7113	.9163	.9757	.9930
21											.6296	.8927	.9689	.9910
22											.5251	.8624	.9601	.9884
23											.3912	.8236	.9488	.9851
24											.2196	.7739	.9344	.9810
25											.0000	.7102	.9159	.9756
26												.6287	.8923	.9687
27												.5243	.8620	.9600
28												.3906	.8232	.9487
29												.2193	.7735	.9343
30												.0000	.7099	.9158
35													.0000	.7098
40														.0000

25.25%

AGE OF LOAN	ORIGINAL TERM IN YEARS													
	2	3	4	5	6	7	8	10	15	20	25	30	35	40
1	.5621	.7457	.8347	.8859	.9184	.9402	.9555	.9746	.9932	.9981	.9994	.9998	*****	*****
2	.0000	.4192	.6224	.7394	.8136	.8635	.8984	.9419	.9844	.9956	.9987	.9996	.9999	*****
3		.0000	.3499	.5514	.6791	.7650	.8251	.9000	.9731	.9924	.9978	.9994	.9998	.9999
4			.0000	.3100	.5064	.6385	.7310	.8463	.9586	.9883	.9967	.9990	.9997	.9999
5				.0000	.2847	.4761	.6101	.7772	.9400	.9831	.9952	.9986	.9996	.9999
6					.0000	.2677	.4550	.6885	.9161	.9763	.9933	.9981	.9994	.9998
7						.0000	.2558	.5747	.8854	.9677	.9908	.9974	.9992	.9998
8							.0000	.4285	.8460	.9566	.9876	.9965	.9990	.9997
9								.2409	.7955	.9424	.9836	.9953	.9987	.9996
10								.0000	.7305	.9241	.9783	.9938	.9982	.9995
11									.6472	.9006	.9716	.9919	.9977	.9993
12									.5402	.8704	.9630	.9894	.9970	.9991
13									.4028	.8317	.9520	.9863	.9961	.9989
14									.2264	.7820	.9378	.9822	.9949	.9985
15									.0000	.7182	.9196	.9770	.9934	.9981
16										.6362	.8962	.9703	.9915	.9976
17										.5311	.8662	.9617	.9890	.9969
18										.3960	.8277	.9507	.9859	.9959
19										.2226	.7782	.9365	.9818	.9948
20										.0000	.7147	.9183	.9766	.9933
21											.6332	.8950	.9699	.9914
22											.5285	.8650	.9613	.9889
23											.3941	.8265	.9503	.9858
24											.2215	.7771	.9361	.9817
25											.0000	.7137	.9180	.9765
26												.6323	.8946	.9698
27												.5278	.8647	.9612
28												.3935	.8262	.9502
29												.2212	.7768	.9360
30												.0000	.7134	.9179
35													.0000	.7134
40														.0000

LOAN PROGRESS CHART
25.50%

AGE OF LOAN	\multicolumn{13}{c}{ORIGINAL TERM IN YEARS}

AGE OF LOAN	2	3	4	5	6	7	8	10	15	20	25	30	35	40
1	.5627	.7464	.8354	.8866	.9190	.9408	.9560	.9750	.9933	.9981	.9995	.9999	*****	*****
2	.0000	.4200	.6236	.7407	.8148	.8646	.8994	.9428	.9847	.9958	.9988	.9997	.9999	*****
3		.0000	.3509	.5528	.6807	.7666	.8266	.9013	.9737	.9927	.9979	.9994	.9998	*****
4			.0000	.3111	.5081	.6404	.7329	.8480	.9595	.9887	.9968	.9991	.9997	.9999
5				.0000	.2859	.4780	.6123	.7793	.9412	.9836	.9954	.9987	.9996	.9999
6					.0000	.2690	.4570	.6909	.9176	.9771	.9935	.9982	.9995	.9999
7						.0000	.2572	.5772	.8873	.9686	.9912	.9975	.9993	.9998
8							.0000	.4308	.8483	.9577	.9881	.9966	.9990	.9997
9								.2425	.7981	.9438	.9841	.9955	.9987	.9996
10								.0000	.7335	.9258	.9791	.9941	.9983	.9995
11									.6503	.9026	.9725	.9922	.9978	.9994
12									.5433	.8728	.9641	.9899	.9971	.9992
13									.4055	.8344	.9533	.9868	.9963	.9989
14									.2282	.7850	.9394	.9829	.9951	.9986
15									.0000	.7215	.9215	.9778	.9937	.9982
16										.6396	.8984	.9713	.9919	.9977
17										.5344	.8687	.9629	.9895	.9970
18										.3989	.8305	.9521	.9864	.9962
19										.2245	.7814	.9382	.9825	.9950
20										.0000	.7181	.9203	.9774	.9936
21											.6367	.8972	.9709	.9918
22											.5319	.8676	.9625	.9894
23											.3970	.8295	.9517	.9863
24											.2234	.7004	.9378	.9824
25											.0000	.7172	.9199	.9773
26												.6359	.8969	.9708
27												.5312	.8673	.9624
28												.3965	.8292	.9516
29												.2231	.7801	.9377
30												.0000	.7169	.9198
35													.0000	.7168
40														.0000

25.75%

AGE OF LOAN	2	3	4	5	6	7	8	10	15	20	25	30	35	40
1	.5004	.7471	.8361	.8873	.9197	.9414	.9565	.9754	.9935	.9982	.9995	.9999	*****	*****
2	.0000	.4209	.6247	.7419	.8160	.8658	.9005	.9436	.9851	.9959	.9989	.9997	.9999	*****
3		.0000	.3519	.5543	.6823	.7682	.8281	.9026	.9743	.9929	.9980	.9994	.9998	*****
4			.0000	.3123	.5098	.6423	.7348	.8497	.9604	.9891	.9970	.9992	.9998	.9999
5				.0000	.2872	.4799	.6144	.7814	.9424	.9841	.9956	.9988	.9997	.9999
6					.0000	.2703	.4590	.6933	.9192	.9777	.9938	.9983	.9995	.9999
7						.0000	.2586	.5797	.8892	.9695	.9915	.9976	.9993	.9998
8							.0000	.4331	.8506	.9589	.9885	.9968	.9991	.9997
9								.2440	.8007	.9451	.9847	.9957	.9988	.9997
10								.0000	.7364	.9274	.9798	.9944	.9984	.9996
11									.6534	.9046	.9734	.9926	.9979	.9994
12									.5463	.8751	.9652	.9903	.9973	.9992
13									.4082	.8371	.9546	.9873	.9965	.9990
14									.2299	.7880	.9410	.9835	.9954	.9987
15									.0000	.7247	.9233	.9786	.9940	.9983
16										.6430	.9006	.9722	.9922	.9978
17										.5376	.8712	.9640	.9899	.9972
18										.4017	.8334	.9534	.9870	.9964
19										.2263	.7845	.9398	.9832	.9953
20										.0000	.7215	.9222	.9782	.9939
21											.6402	.8995	.9719	.9921
22											.5353	.8702	.9637	.9898
23											.3999	.8323	.9531	.9869
24											.2253	.7835	.9395	.9831
25											.0000	.7206	.9219	.9781
26												.6394	.8992	.9718
27												.5346	.8699	.9636
28												.3994	.8321	.9530
29												.2250	.7833	.9394
30												.0000	.7204	.9218
35													.0000	.7203
40														.0000

TABLE 4

PRORATION

Use this Table to find either the exact number of elapsed days from January 1st to any given date, or the exact number of elapsed days from a given date to December 31st. The Table also indicates the fraction of one year (expressed as a percentage) represented by the number of elapsed days.

There are two sections to the Proration Table, one for a 360-day financial calendar, and one for an actual 365-day calendar.

PRORATIONS FROM JAN. 1st TO PRORATION DATE

DATE	JAN DAYS PAST	% OF 360	FEB DAYS PAST	% OF 360	MAR DAYS PAST	% OF 360	APR DAYS PAST	% OF 360	MAY DAYS PAST	% OF 360	JUN DAYS PAST	% OF 360	DATE
1	1	0.28	31	8.61	61	16.94	91	25.28	121	33.61	151	41.94	1
2	2	0.56	32	8.89	62	17.22	92	25.56	122	33.89	152	42.22	2
3	3	0.83	33	9.17	63	17.50	93	25.83	123	34.17	153	42.50	3
4	4	1.11	34	9.44	64	17.78	94	26.11	124	34.44	154	42.78	4
5	5	1.39	35	9.72	65	18.06	95	26.39	125	34.72	155	43.06	5
6	6	1.67	36	10.00	66	18.33	96	26.67	126	35.00	156	43.33	6
7	7	1.94	37	10.28	67	18.61	97	26.94	127	35.28	157	43.61	7
8	8	2.22	38	10.56	68	18.89	98	27.22	128	35.56	158	43.89	8
9	9	2.50	39	10.83	69	19.17	99	27.50	129	35.83	159	44.17	9
10	10	2.78	40	11.11	70	19.44	100	27.78	130	36.11	160	44.44	10
11	11	3.06	41	11.39	71	19.72	101	28.06	131	36.39	161	44.72	11
12	12	3.33	42	11.67	72	20.00	102	28.33	132	36.67	162	45.00	12
13	13	3.61	43	11.94	73	20.28	103	28.61	133	36.94	163	45.28	13
14	14	3.89	44	12.22	74	20.56	104	28.89	134	37.22	164	45.56	14
15	15	4.17	45	12.50	75	20.83	105	29.17	135	37.50	165	45.83	15
16	16	4.44	46	12.78	76	21.11	106	29.44	136	37.78	166	46.11	16
17	17	4.72	47	13.06	77	21.39	107	29.72	137	38.06	167	46.39	17
18	18	5.00	48	13.33	78	21.67	108	30.00	138	38.33	168	46.67	18
19	19	5.28	49	13.61	79	21.94	109	30.28	139	38.61	169	46.94	19
20	20	5.56	50	13.89	80	22.22	110	30.56	140	38.89	170	47.22	20
21	21	5.83	51	14.17	81	22.50	111	30.83	141	39.17	171	47.50	21
22	22	6.11	52	14.44	82	22.78	112	31.11	142	39.44	172	47.78	22
23	23	6.39	53	14.72	83	23.06	113	31.39	143	39.72	173	48.06	23
24	24	6.67	54	15.00	84	23.33	114	31.67	144	40.00	174	48.33	24
25	25	6.94	55	15.28	85	23.61	115	31.94	145	40.28	175	48.61	25
26	26	7.22	56	15.56	86	23.89	116	32.22	146	40.56	176	48.89	26
27	27	7.50	57	15.83	87	24.17	117	32.50	147	40.83	177	49.17	27
28	28	7.78	58	16.11	88	24.44	118	32.78	148	41.11	178	49.44	28
29	29	8.06	59	16.39	89	24.72	119	33.06	149	41.39	179	49.72	29
30	30	8.33	60	16.67	90	25.00	120	33.33	150	41.67	180	50.00	30
31	31												31

PRORATIONS FROM PRORATION DATE TO DEC 31st

DATE	JAN DAYS TO COME	% OF 360	FEB DAYS TO COME	% OF 360	MAR DAYS TO COME	% OF 360	APR DAYS TO COME	% OF 360	MAY DAYS TO COME	% OF 360	JUN DAYS TO COME	% OF 360	DATE
1	360	100.00	330	91.67	300	83.33	270	75.00	240	66.67	210	58.33	1
2	359	99.72	329	91.39	299	83.06	269	74.72	239	66.39	209	58.06	2
3	358	99.44	328	91.11	298	82.78	268	74.44	238	66.11	208	57.78	3
4	357	99.17	327	90.83	297	82.50	267	74.17	237	65.83	207	57.50	4
5	356	98.89	326	90.56	296	82.22	266	73.89	236	65.56	206	57.22	5
6	355	98.61	325	90.28	295	81.94	265	73.61	235	65.28	205	56.94	6
7	354	98.33	324	90.00	294	81.67	264	73.33	234	65.00	204	56.67	7
8	353	98.06	323	89.72	293	81.39	263	73.06	233	64.72	203	56.39	8
9	352	97.78	322	89.44	292	81.11	262	72.78	232	64.44	202	56.11	9
10	351	97.50	321	89.17	291	80.83	261	72.50	231	64.17	201	55.83	10
11	350	97.22	320	88.89	290	80.56	260	72.22	230	63.89	200	55.56	11
12	349	96.94	319	88.61	289	80.28	259	71.94	229	63.61	199	55.28	12
13	348	96.67	318	88.33	288	80.00	258	71.67	228	63.33	198	55.00	13
14	347	96.39	317	88.06	287	79.72	257	71.39	227	63.06	197	54.72	14
15	346	96.11	316	87.78	286	79.44	256	71.11	226	62.78	196	54.44	15
16	345	95.83	315	87.50	285	79.17	255	70.83	225	62.50	195	54.17	16
17	344	95.56	314	87.22	284	78.89	254	70.56	224	62.22	194	53.89	17
18	343	95.28	313	86.94	283	78.61	253	70.28	223	61.94	193	53.61	18
19	342	95.00	312	86.67	282	78.33	252	70.00	222	61.67	192	53.33	19
20	341	94.72	311	86.39	281	78.06	251	69.72	221	61.39	191	53.06	20
21	340	94.44	310	86.11	280	77.78	250	69.44	220	61.11	190	52.78	21
22	339	94.17	309	85.83	279	77.50	249	69.17	219	60.83	189	52.50	22
23	338	93.89	308	85.56	278	77.22	248	68.89	218	60.56	188	52.22	23
24	337	93.61	307	85.28	277	76.94	247	68.61	217	60.28	187	51.94	24
25	336	93.33	306	85.00	276	76.67	246	68.33	216	60.00	186	51.67	25
26	335	93.06	305	84.72	275	76.39	245	68.06	215	59.72	185	51.39	26
27	334	92.78	304	84.44	274	76.11	244	67.78	214	59.44	184	51.11	27
28	333	92.50	303	84.17	273	75.83	243	67.50	213	59.17	183	50.83	28
29	332	92.22	302	83.89	272	75.56	242	67.22	212	58.89	182	50.56	29
30	331	91.94	301	83.61	271	75.28	241	66.94	211	58.61	181	50.28	30
31													31

PRORATIONS FROM JAN. 1st TO PRORATION DATE

DATE	JUL DAYS PAST	JUL % OF 360	AUG DAYS PAST	AUG % OF 360	SEP DAYS PAST	SEP % OF 360	OCT DAYS PAST	OCT % OF 360	NOV DAYS PAST	NOV % OF 360	DEC DAYS PAST	DEC % OF 360	DATE
1	181	50.28	211	58.61	241	66.94	271	75.28	301	83.61	331	91.94	1
2	182	50.56	212	58.89	242	67.22	272	75.56	302	83.89	332	92.22	2
3	183	50.83	213	59.17	243	67.50	273	75.83	303	84.17	333	92.50	3
4	184	51.11	214	59.44	244	67.78	274	76.11	304	84.44	334	92.78	4
5	185	51.39	215	59.72	245	68.06	275	76.39	305	84.72	335	93.06	5
6	186	51.67	216	60.00	246	68.33	276	76.67	306	85.00	336	93.33	6
7	187	51.94	217	60.28	247	68.61	277	76.94	307	85.28	337	93.61	7
8	188	52.22	218	60.56	248	68.89	278	77.22	308	85.56	338	93.89	8
9	189	52.50	219	60.83	249	69.17	279	77.50	309	85.83	339	94.17	9
10	190	52.78	220	61.11	250	69.44	280	77.78	310	86.11	340	94.44	10
11	191	53.06	221	61.39	251	69.72	281	78.06	311	86.39	341	94.72	11
12	192	53.33	222	61.67	252	70.00	282	78.33	312	86.67	342	95.00	12
13	193	53.61	223	61.94	253	70.28	283	78.61	313	86.94	343	95.28	13
14	194	53.89	224	62.22	254	70.56	284	78.89	314	87.22	344	95.56	14
15	195	54.17	225	62.50	255	70.83	285	79.17	315	87.50	345	95.83	15
16	196	54.44	226	62.78	256	71.11	286	79.44	316	87.78	346	96.11	16
17	197	54.72	227	63.06	257	71.39	287	79.72	317	88.06	347	96.39	17
18	198	55.00	228	63.33	258	71.67	288	80.00	318	88.33	348	96.67	18
19	199	55.28	229	63.61	259	71.94	289	80.28	319	88.61	349	96.94	19
20	200	55.56	230	63.89	260	72.22	290	80.56	320	88.89	350	97.22	20
21	201	55.83	231	64.17	261	72.50	291	80.83	321	89.17	351	97.50	21
22	202	56.11	232	64.44	262	72.78	292	81.11	322	89.44	352	97.78	22
23	203	56.39	233	64.72	263	73.06	293	81.39	323	89.72	353	98.06	23
24	204	56.67	234	65.00	264	73.33	294	81.67	324	90.00	354	98.33	24
25	205	56.94	235	65.28	265	73.61	295	81.94	325	90.28	355	98.61	25
26	206	57.22	236	65.56	266	73.89	296	82.22	326	90.56	356	98.89	26
27	207	57.50	237	65.83	267	74.17	297	82.50	327	90.83	357	99.17	27
28	208	57.78	238	66.11	268	74.44	298	82.78	328	91.11	358	99.44	28
29	209	58.06	239	66.39	269	74.72	299	83.06	329	91.39	359	99.72	29
30	210	58.33	240	66.67	270	75.00	300	83.33	330	91.67	360	100.00	30
31													31

PRORATIONS FROM PRORATION DATE TO DEC 31st

DATE	JUL DAYS TO COME	JUL % OF 360	AUG DAYS TO COME	AUG % OF 360	SEP DAYS TO COME	SEP % OF 360	OCT DAYS TO COME	OCT % OF 360	NOV DAYS TO COME	NOV % OF 360	DEC DAYS TO COME	DEC % OF 360	DATE
1	180	50.00	150	41.67	120	33.33	90	25.00	60	16.67	30	8.33	1
2	179	49.72	149	41.39	119	33.06	89	24.72	59	16.39	29	8.06	2
3	178	49.44	148	41.11	118	32.78	88	24.44	58	16.11	28	7.78	3
4	177	49.17	147	40.83	117	32.50	87	24.17	57	15.83	27	7.50	4
5	176	48.89	146	40.56	116	32.22	86	23.89	56	15.56	26	7.22	5
6	175	48.61	145	40.28	115	31.94	85	23.61	55	15.28	25	6.94	6
7	174	48.33	144	40.00	114	31.67	84	23.33	54	15.00	24	6.67	7
8	173	48.06	143	39.72	113	31.39	83	23.06	53	14.72	23	6.39	8
9	172	47.78	142	39.44	112	31.11	82	22.78	52	14.44	22	6.11	9
10	171	47.50	141	39.17	111	30.83	81	22.50	51	14.17	21	5.83	10
11	170	47.22	140	38.89	110	30.56	80	22.22	50	13.89	20	5.56	11
12	169	46.94	139	38.61	109	30.28	79	21.94	49	13.61	19	5.28	12
13	168	46.67	138	38.33	108	30.00	78	21.67	48	13.33	18	5.00	13
14	167	46.39	137	38.06	107	29.72	77	21.39	47	13.06	17	4.72	14
15	166	46.11	136	37.78	106	29.44	76	21.11	46	12.78	16	4.44	15
16	165	45.83	135	37.50	105	29.17	75	20.83	45	12.50	15	4.17	16
17	164	45.56	134	37.22	104	28.89	74	20.56	44	12.22	14	3.89	17
18	163	45.28	133	36.94	103	28.61	73	20.28	43	11.94	13	3.61	18
19	162	45.00	132	36.67	102	28.33	72	20.00	42	11.67	12	3.33	19
20	161	44.72	131	36.39	101	28.06	71	19.72	41	11.39	11	3.06	20
21	160	44.44	130	36.11	100	27.78	70	19.44	40	11.11	10	2.78	21
22	159	44.17	129	35.83	99	27.50	69	19.17	39	10.83	9	2.50	22
23	158	43.89	128	35.56	98	27.22	68	18.89	38	10.56	8	2.22	23
24	157	43.61	127	35.28	97	26.94	67	18.61	37	10.28	7	1.94	24
25	156	43.33	126	35.00	96	26.67	66	18.33	36	10.00	6	1.67	25
26													26
27	155	43.06	125	34.72	95	26.39	65	18.06	35	9.72	5	1.39	27
28	154	42.78	124	34.44	94	26.11	64	17.78	34	9.44	4	1.11	28
29	153	42.50	123	34.17	93	25.83	63	17.50	33	9.17	3	0.83	29
30	152	42.22	122	33.89	92	25.56	62	17.22	32	8.89	2	0.56	30
31	151	41.94	121	33.61	91	25.28	61	16.94	31	8.61	1	0.28	31

PRORATIONS FROM JAN. 1st TO PRORATION DATE

DATE	JAN DAYS PAST	JAN % OF 365	FEB DAYS PAST	FEB % OF 365	MAR DAYS PAST	MAR % OF 365	APR DAYS PAST	APR % OF 365	MAY DAYS PAST	MAY % OF 365	JUN DAYS PAST	JUN % OF 365	DATE
1	1	0.27	32	8.77	60	16.44	91	24.93	121	33.15	152	41.64	1
2	2	0.55	33	9.04	61	16.71	92	25.21	122	33.42	153	41.92	2
3	3	0.82	34	9.32	62	16.99	93	25.48	123	33.70	154	42.19	3
4	4	1.10	35	9.59	63	17.26	94	25.75	124	33.97	155	42.47	4
5	5	1.37	36	9.86	64	17.53	95	26.03	125	34.25	156	42.74	5
6	6	1.64	37	10.14	65	17.81	96	26.30	126	34.52	157	43.01	6
7	7	1.92	38	10.41	66	18.08	97	26.58	127	34.79	158	43.29	7
8	8	2.19	39	10.68	67	18.36	98	26.85	128	35.07	159	43.56	8
9	9	2.47	40	10.96	68	18.63	99	27.12	129	35.34	160	43.84	9
10	10	2.74	41	11.23	69	18.90	100	27.40	130	35.62	161	44.11	10
11	11	3.01	42	11.51	70	19.18	101	27.67	131	35.89	162	44.38	11
12	12	3.29	43	11.78	71	19.45	102	27.95	132	36.16	163	44.66	12
13	13	3.56	44	12.05	72	19.73	103	28.22	133	36.44	164	44.93	13
14	14	3.84	45	12.33	73	20.00	104	28.49	134	36.71	165	45.21	14
15	15	4.11	46	12.60	74	20.27	105	28.77	135	36.99	166	45.48	15
16	16	4.38	47	12.88	75	20.55	106	29.04	136	37.26	167	45.75	16
17	17	4.66	48	13.15	76	20.82	107	29.32	137	37.53	168	46.03	17
18	18	4.93	49	13.42	77	21.10	108	29.59	138	37.81	169	46.30	18
19	19	5.21	50	13.70	78	21.37	109	29.86	139	38.08	170	46.58	19
20	20	5.48	51	13.97	79	21.64	110	30.14	140	38.36	171	46.85	20
21	21	5.75	52	14.25	80	21.92	111	30.41	141	38.63	172	47.12	21
22	22	6.03	53	14.52	81	22.19	112	30.68	142	38.90	173	47.40	22
23	23	6.30	54	14.79	82	22.47	113	30.96	143	39.18	174	47.67	23
24	24	6.58	55	15.07	83	22.74	114	31.23	144	39.45	175	47.95	24
25	25	6.85	56	15.34	84	23.01	115	31.51	145	39.73	176	48.22	25
26	26	7.12	57	15.62	85	23.29	116	31.78	146	40.00	177	48.49	26
27	27	7.40	58	15.89	86	23.56	117	32.05	147	40.27	178	48.77	27
28	28	7.67	59	16.16	87	23.84	118	32.33	148	40.55	179	49.04	28
29	29	7.95			88	24.11	119	32.60	149	40.82	180	49.32	29
30	30	8.22			89	24.38	120	32.88	150	41.10	181	49.59	30
31	31	8.49			90	24.66			151	41.37			31

PRORATIONS FROM PRORATION DATE TO DEC 31st

DATE	JAN DAYS TO COME	JAN % OF 365	FEB DAYS TO COME	FEB % OF 365	MAR DAYS TO COME	MAR % OF 365	APR DAYS TO COME	APR % OF 365	MAY DAYS TO COME	MAY % OF 365	JUN DAYS TO COME	JUN % OF 365	DATE
1	365	100.00	334	91.51	306	83.84	275	75.34	245	67.12	214	58.63	1
2	364	99.73	333	91.23	305	83.56	274	75.07	244	66.85	213	58.36	2
3	363	99.45	332	90.96	304	83.29	273	74.79	243	66.58	212	58.08	3
4	362	99.18	331	90.68	303	83.01	272	74.52	242	66.30	211	57.81	4
5	361	98.90	330	90.41	302	82.74	271	74.25	241	66.03	210	57.53	5
6	360	98.63	329	90.14	301	82.47	270	73.97	240	65.75	209	57.26	6
7	359	98.36	328	89.86	300	82.19	269	73.70	239	65.48	208	56.99	7
8	358	98.08	327	89.59	299	81.92	268	73.42	238	65.21	207	56.71	8
9	357	97.81	326	89.32	298	81.64	267	73.15	237	64.93	206	56.44	9
10	356	97.53	325	89.04	297	81.37	266	72.88	236	64.66	205	56.16	10
11	355	97.26	324	88.77	296	81.10	265	72.60	235	64.38	204	55.89	11
12	354	96.99	323	88.49	295	80.82	264	72.33	234	64.11	203	55.62	12
13	353	96.71	322	88.22	294	80.55	263	72.05	233	63.84	202	55.34	13
14	352	96.44	321	87.95	293	80.27	262	71.78	232	63.56	201	55.07	14
15	351	96.16	320	87.67	292	80.00	261	71.51	231	63.29	200	54.79	15
16	350	95.89	319	87.40	291	79.73	260	71.23	230	63.01	199	54.52	16
17	349	95.62	318	87.12	290	79.45	259	70.96	229	62.74	198	54.25	17
18	348	95.34	317	86.85	289	79.18	258	70.68	228	62.47	197	53.97	18
19	347	95.07	316	86.58	288	78.90	257	70.41	227	62.19	196	53.70	19
20	346	94.79	315	86.30	287	78.63	256	70.14	226	61.92	195	53.42	20
21	345	94.52	314	86.03	286	78.36	255	69.86	225	61.64	194	53.15	21
22	344	94.25	313	85.75	285	78.08	254	69.59	224	61.37	193	52.88	22
23	343	93.97	312	85.48	284	77.81	253	69.32	223	61.10	192	52.60	23
24	342	93.70	311	85.21	283	77.53	252	69.04	222	60.82	191	52.33	24
25	341	93.42	310	84.93	282	77.26	251	68.77	221	60.55	190	52.05	25
26	340	93.15	309	84.66	281	76.99	250	68.49	220	60.27	189	51.78	26
27	339	92.88	308	84.38	280	76.71	249	68.22	219	60.00	188	51.51	27
28	338	92.60	307	84.11	279	76.44	248	67.95	218	59.73	187	51.23	28
29	337	92.33			278	76.16	247	67.67	217	59.45	186	50.96	29
30	336	92.05			277	75.89	246	67.40	216	59.18	185	50.68	30
31	335	91.78			276	75.62			215	58.90			31

PRORATIONS FROM JAN. 1st TO PRORATION DATE

DATE	JUL DAYS PAST	% OF 365	AUG DAYS PAST	% OF 365	SEP DAYS PAST	% OF 365	OCT DAYS PAST	% OF 365	NOV DAYS PAST	% OF 365	DEC DAYS PAST	% OF 365	DATE
1	182	49.86	213	58.36	244	66.85	274	75.07	305	83.56	335	91.78	1
2	183	50.14	214	58.63	245	67.12	275	75.34	306	83.84	336	92.05	2
3	184	50.41	215	58.90	246	67.40	276	75.62	307	84.11	337	92.33	3
4	185	50.68	216	59.18	247	67.67	277	75.89	308	84.38	338	92.60	4
5	186	50.96	217	59.45	248	67.95	278	76.16	309	84.66	339	92.88	5
6	187	51.23	218	59.73	249	68.22	279	76.44	310	84.93	340	93.15	6
7	188	51.51	219	60.00	250	68.49	280	76.71	311	85.21	341	93.42	7
8	189	51.78	220	60.27	251	68.77	281	76.99	312	85.48	342	93.70	8
9	190	52.05	221	60.55	252	69.04	282	77.26	313	85.75	343	93.97	9
10	191	52.33	222	60.82	253	69.32	283	77.53	314	86.03	344	94.25	10
11	192	52.60	223	61.10	254	69.59	284	77.81	315	86.30	345	94.52	11
12	193	52.88	224	61.37	255	69.86	285	78.08	316	86.58	346	94.79	12
13	194	53.15	225	61.64	256	70.14	286	78.36	317	86.85	347	95.07	13
14	195	53.42	226	61.92	257	70.41	287	78.63	318	87.12	348	95.34	14
15	196	53.70	227	62.19	258	70.68	288	78.90	319	87.40	349	95.62	15
16	197	53.97	228	62.47	259	70.96	289	79.18	320	87.67	350	95.89	16
17	198	54.25	229	62.74	260	71.23	290	79.45	321	87.95	351	96.16	17
18	199	54.52	230	63.01	261	71.51	291	79.73	322	88.22	352	96.44	18
19	200	54.79	231	63.29	262	71.78	292	80.00	323	88.49	353	96.71	19
20	201	55.07	232	63.56	263	72.05	293	80.27	324	88.77	354	96.99	20
21	202	55.34	233	63.84	264	72.33	294	80.55	325	89.04	355	97.26	21
22	203	55.62	234	64.11	265	72.60	295	80.82	326	89.32	356	97.53	22
23	204	55.89	235	64.38	266	72.88	296	81.10	327	89.59	357	97.81	23
24	205	56.16	236	64.66	267	73.15	297	81.37	328	89.86	358	98.08	24
25	206	56.44	237	64.93	268	73.42	298	81.64	329	90.14	359	98.36	25
26	207	56.71	238	65.21	269	73.70	299	81.92	330	90.41	360	98.63	26
27	208	56.99	239	65.48	270	73.97	300	82.19	331	90.68	361	98.90	27
28	209	57.26	240	65.75	271	74.25	301	82.47	332	90.96	362	99.18	28
29	210	57.53	241	66.03	272	74.52	302	82.74	333	91.23	363	99.45	29
30	211	57.81	242	66.30	273	74.79	303	83.01	334	91.51	364	99.73	30
31	212	58.08	243	66.58			304	83.29			365	100.00	31

PRORATIONS FROM PRORATION DATE TO DEC 31st

DATE	JUL DAYS TO COME	% OF 365	AUG DAYS TO COME	% OF 365	SEP DAYS TO COME	% OF 365	OCT DAYS TO COME	% OF 365	NOV DAYS TO COME	% OF 365	DEC DAYS TO COME	% OF 365	DATE
1	184	50.41	153	41.92	122	33.42	92	25.21	61	16.71	31	8.49	1
2	183	50.14	152	41.64	121	33.15	91	24.93	60	16.44	30	8.22	2
3	182	49.86	151	41.37	120	32.88	90	24.66	59	16.16	29	7.95	3
4	181	49.59	150	41.10	119	32.60	89	24.38	58	15.89	28	7.67	4
5	180	49.32	149	40.82	118	32.33	88	24.11	57	15.62	27	7.40	5
6	179	49.04	148	40.55	117	32.05	87	23.84	56	15.34	26	7.12	6
7	178	48.77	147	40.27	116	31.78	86	23.56	55	15.07	25	6.85	7
8	177	48.49	146	40.00	115	31.51	85	23.29	54	14.79	24	6.58	8
9	176	48.22	145	39.73	114	31.23	84	23.01	53	14.52	23	6.30	9
10	175	47.95	144	39.45	113	30.96	83	22.74	52	14.25	22	6.03	10
11	174	47.67	143	39.18	112	30.68	82	22.47	51	13.97	21	5.75	11
12	173	47.40	142	38.90	111	30.41	81	22.19	50	13.70	20	5.48	12
13	172	47.12	141	38.63	110	30.14	80	21.92	49	13.42	19	5.21	13
14	171	46.85	140	38.36	109	29.86	79	21.64	48	13.15	18	4.93	14
15	170	46.58	139	38.08	108	29.59	78	21.37	47	12.88	17	4.66	15
16	169	46.30	138	37.81	107	29.32	77	21.10	46	12.60	16	4.38	16
17	168	46.03	137	37.53	106	29.04	76	20.82	45	12.33	15	4.11	17
18	167	45.75	136	37.26	105	28.77	75	20.55	44	12.05	14	3.84	18
19	166	45.48	135	36.99	104	28.49	74	20.27	43	11.78	13	3.56	19
20	165	45.21	134	36.71	103	28.22	73	20.00	42	11.51	12	3.29	20
21	164	44.93	133	36.44	102	27.95	72	19.73	41	11.23	11	3.01	21
22	163	44.66	132	36.16	101	27.67	71	19.45	40	10.96	10	2.74	22
23	162	44.38	131	35.89	100	27.40	70	19.18	39	10.68	9	2.47	23
24	161	44.11	130	35.62	99	27.12	69	18.90	38	10.41	8	2.19	24
25	160	43.84	129	35.34	98	26.85	68	18.63	37	10.14	7	1.92	25
26													26
27	159	43.56	128	35.07	97	26.58	67	18.36	36	9.86	6	1.64	27
28	158	43.29	127	34.79	96	26.30	66	18.08	35	9.59	5	1.37	28
29	157	43.01	126	34.52	95	26.03	65	17.81	34	9.32	4	1.10	29
30	156	42.74	125	34.25	94	25.75	64	17.53	33	9.04	3	0.82	30
31	155	42.47	124	33.97	93	25.48	63	17.26	32	8.77	2	0.55	31
	154	42.19	123	33.70			62	16.99			1	0.27	

                                    Interest   Points   Payment
                                                                           1050.41
                                    5.5   at 2.5 = 4625 $ 1021.66
$ 185000   5.25   4.7   8695 $ 102.58
                                    6.0   No points $ 1109.17
                                    6.5   1165.50

$ 1109   Payment
$ 300   Escrow
$ 150   water + Electric
_____
$ 1559   Total Expences   185000
                                          + 37000 20%
   100 + Maybe pmi ? $ 222000
_____
   1700

$ 2000   Rent Roll
- 1700   Expences
_____
$ 300   profit

    4 56000